FAMILY HISTORY MONTHLY

The UK's fastest-growing magazine for the family historian

EVERY ISSUE CONTAINS:

- Research tips and advice
- Lots of sources
- Forthcoming events
- A surname and its origin
- Family history and archive news
- Latest computer information
- Free listings on our contact pages
- A Competition

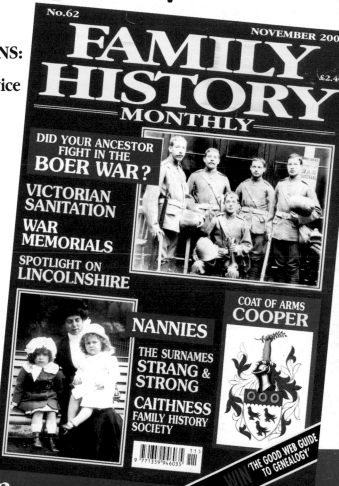

No.62
NOVEMBER 2000

FAMILY HISTORY MONTHLY

£2.40

DID YOUR ANCESTOR FIGHT IN THE **BOER WAR?**

VICTORIAN SANITATION

WAR MEMORIALS

SPOTLIGHT ON **LINCOLNSHIRE**

NANNIES

THE SURNAMES **STRANG & STRONG**

CAITHNESS FAMILY HISTORY SOCIETY

COAT OF ARMS **COOPER**

WIN 'THE GOOD WEB GUIDE TO GENEALOGY'

9 771359 946035

Available from W.H. Smith's and all leading newsagents.

FAMILY HISTORY MONTHLY

The UK's fastest-growing family history magazine is essential reading for anybody tracing their family tree. Every issue contains fascinating articles on different aspects of genealogy – all fully illustrated to help bring the subjects to life. And we tell you where to go to find out more. In addition, we include in-depth news from archives around the country, authoritative reviews and a complete list of meetings and other events. *Family History Monthly's* computer pages also keep readers up-to-date with the latest developments in software, as well as suggesting the best web sites to visit.

Family History Monthly **is an essential accompaniment to researching your family tree.**

TO SUBSCRIBE – Annual subscription (12 copies) costs £30.

Ring Janice Mayne on (020) 8579 1082 or complete the order form below and return it to *Family History Monthly.*

– – – – – – – – · ORDER FORM – – – – – – – – ·

I wish to pay a total of £.................., being the cost of a subscription for 1 year.

METHODS OF PAYMENT: All payments to be made payable to **'PARKER MEAD LTD'.** Due to high bank charges, the following are the only methods of payment we can accept: You may pay by crossed cheques, postal orders or credit cards. **WE CAN ACCEPT THE FOLLOWING CREDIT CARDS**

VISA DELTA SWITCH JCB DELTA

I authorise you to debit my account with the total amount of £...................

Card No

Issue No *(Switch card only)*

Expiry date of card

Name...

Address ....

....

.... Postcode ....

Day Tel. No .... Signature...

SEND THIS ORDER FORM WITH YOUR PAYMENT TO:

**THE MAGAZINE EDITOR, FAMILY HISTORY MONTHLY,
43-45 ST. MARY'S ROAD, EALING, LONDON W5 5RQ, UK
or e-mail: fhm@parkermead.co.uk**

The
Genealogical Services Directory

Family
and
Local History
Handbook

Edited & Co~~~

by

Robert Blatchford

Contents

7 Feature Articles

7	Family & Local History	Alan Crosby
8	Starting Out - A Beginners Guide to Family History	Doreen Hopwood
11	There's a whole world out there	Carolynn Boucher
14	Catholics in England and Wales - What to read	Michael Gandy
19	Newspapers for Family & Local Historians	Simon Fowler
22	Criminal Ancestors - 17th to 19th Century Criminals	Colin Chapman
26	Chapman County Codes	
28	Parish Registers	Pauline Litton
33	Ag labs, fwks & other anachronisms	Kate Thompson
36	The Coroners Courts	Doreen Hopwood
40	Parliamentary Papers	Simon Fowler
44	Apprenticeship and the new Poor Law	Kate Thompson
48	Man of Kent or Kentish Man ?	Veronica Craig-Mair
51	Drawing Up Your Family Tree	Marie Lynskey
53	Identifying the Unknown	Audrey Linkman
56	Plastic - that will do nicely !	Colin Parkinson
58	.... on the use and abuse of books	Sue Callaghan
60	Clothing the Past	Jayne Shrimpton
62	The Horwoods and the Pecks	Jill Groves
66	Post Office Heritage	Andrew Perry
70	York Minster Archives - a hidden treasure ?	Louise Hampson
74	Lloyd's Register of Shipping	Barbara Jones & Emma Taaffe
78	Local Register Offices & Family History	Doreen Hopwood
82	*The Jewish Victorian* and the Victorian Jews	Doreen Berger
85	Serendipity	Cecil R Himphery-Smith
86	Places of Belonging	Gabriel Alington
90	Indexing Public Records	Stuart Tamblin
92	The Public Record Office	
94	The Family Records Centre	
95	The Professional Genealogist	Cecil R Himphery-Smith
96	Voices from the Past	Anne Batchelor
100	Do I really need a Computer ?	David Tippey
106	Registry of Shipping & Seamen	Neil Staples
111	Special Collections in the Society of Genealogists	Sue Gibbons
115	Ancestral Occupations; A guide to literature	Stuart A Raymond
120	The National Library of Wales	Eirionedd A Baskerville
122	A Walk on the Dark Side	Eirionedd A Baskerville
127	General Register Office for Scotland & Scots Origins	
130	Digital Imaging of the 1891 Census for Scotland	Bruno Longmore
132	The National Archives of Scotland	David Brown
134	National Library of Scotland	Janice McFarlane
136	Family History in Ayrshire	Jim Steel
138	The Genealogy of Archives	Iain Flett
141	The Public Record Office of Northern Ireland	Anne McVeigh
144	National Library of Ireland	Colette O'Flaherty
146	National Archives of Ireland	Aideen M Ireland
148	The Church of Ireland - Genealogy and Family History	
150	Dublin Archives	
151	Irish Genealogical Project	Kathleen Neill
153	Irish Genealogy in Review	Jim Ryan
154	Census Returns in Canada	Sherry Irvine & Dave Obee
157	New Zealand treasures await	Elizabeth K Parkes

161 Local History

162	The Grateful Thanks of Our Descendants		
	Peter Christie		
165	Abiding Strength	Alan Crosby	
166	Late 20th Century Ritual Structure		
	Alan Crosby		
167	Babes and Sucklings	Alan Crosby	
168	Phoenix Revisited	Alan Crosby	
169	Not So Empty Landscapes	Alan Crosby	
170	All in a Norfolk Name	Alan Crosby	
171	Regional Perspectives	Alan Crosby	

172	The History of Our Own Times
	Alan Crosby
174	The Faversham Society
	Arthur Percival
177	Pembroke Dock - a 19th Century New Town
	Basil H J Hughes
180	Local History Societies - Listings
192	Victoria County History
	Dr Jane Batchelor
195	Port Sunlight Village

196 Military History

196	Imperial War Museum
	-Department of Printed Books
199	Commonwealth War Graves Commission
201	Civilian Roll of Honour
202	National Inventory of War Memorials
203	The National Army Museum
	Julian Humphreys
205	Imperial War Museum - North
	Ann Carter
206	Register of Men Fallen at Gallipoli
	1915 - 1916
207	White, Red & Blue or in Search of Heroes
	Fred Feather
211	Military & Reginmental Museum
	- Listings

216 Family History Societies

216	The Romany & Traveller
	Family History Society
218	Doncaster & District
	Family History Society
219	Weston Super Mare
	Family History Society
220	Montgomeryshire Genealogical Society
221	Central Scotland
	Family History Society
222	Family History Societies
	- Advertising & Listings

268 Record Offices and Archives

268	The Record office for Leicestershire,	
	Leicester & Rutland	Pat Grundy
270	Lancashire Record Office	Bruce Jackson
272	Central Index of Decrees Absolute	
273	The Land Registry	Ken Young
276	Certificate Services - Southport	
	Carol M Clarke	
278	Probate Records	The Probate Service
281	Probate Records in the Borthwick Institute	
	Professor D M Smith	
282	Record Offices & Archives - Listings	

253 Registrars of Births Marriages & Deaths

253	England
261	Wales
263	Scotland

343 Libraries

343	Libraries & Genealogical Research
	Stuart A Raymond
346	Libraries - Listings

308 Heritage Sites & Museums

308	English Heritage
311	CADW Welsh Heritage
312	Historic Scotland
313	Royal Armouries Nicholas Boole
315	Museums - Listings

364 Ancestral Research

	Professional Researchers, Research & Support Services
401	State Library of New South Wales, Australia
403	The United States Library of Congress
404	The National Archives United States of America
405	The Church of Jesus Christ of Latter Day Saints
406	Family History Centres

409 Family History Fairs, Events Diary & Index

4

Editorial

The phenomenal growth in family history over the past twelve months has been engendered by the internet and television. BBC television's *"Bloodties"* and *"Meet the Ancestors"* series together with Channel 4's *"Extraordinary Ancestors"* and all the other history programmes have further stimulated interest in the fascinating subjects of family and local history.

We have seen an increased demand for each of our four editions. The 2000 edition had to be reprinted five months after publication and that sold out very quickly. The advance orders for this edition are exceptional.

This our fifth edition has to be our *best* yet. We have reorganised the layout and improved readability in most areas.

We are constantly surprised by the critical acclaim we receive for each edition. This time we have been able to gather together leading family and local historians to provide you with articles on many interesting subjects. We have included over 80 new articles on topics as diverse as Parish Registers, Newspapers, Parliamentary Papers, Catholic Ancestry, Criminal Ancestors, Occupations, Jewish Ancestors, Coroners Courts as well as many others on family and local history. The Local History section has been expanded to emphasise the importance of its links with family history and vice versa.

Our extensive listings have been updated and increased of which there are now over 5000 addresses.

Suggestions from our readers are always welcome and where possible we implement them in future editions.

Welcome to both our new and regular readers and we hope that you enjoy this edition as much as previous ones

Robert Blatchford
The Genealogical Services Directory

*tracing the birth parents
of adopted persons
in England and Wales*

federation of
FAMILY
HISTORY
SOCIETIES

*research services:
a code of practice
for family historians*

federation of
FAMILY
HISTORY
SOCIETIES

*the strays clearing
house and the
national strays index*

federation of
FAMILY
HISTORY
SOCIETIES

*in search of your
soldier ancestors*

federation of
FAMILY
HISTORY
SOCIETIES

*you and your record office:
a code of practice for family historians
using county record offices*

federation of
FAMILY
HISTORY
SOCIETIES

*new to family history:
can we help?*

federation of
FAMILY
HISTORY
SOCIETIES

Family History and Local History
– You can't have one without the other
Alan Crosby discusses the connection ....

I often give talks in this subject to organisations involved in both areas of research and I find that almost without exception people are excited by the challenge and the opportunities which linking these two themes can offer. It is in some ways obvious that the two subjects do go together, and are inextricably entwined. We cannot understand local communities - their origins, development and character - without giving the fullest possible attention to the people who made up those communities. After all, the farms and the fields, the streets and the houses, the industries and the churches, are all the product of untold human endeavour over the centuries.

If we ignore the people we ignore the reason why, and that is absurd. Yet, at the same time, we cannot really understand the lives of individuals and the stories of families unless we consider their world, the environment they lived in and the lifestyles they enjoyed (or, maybe, didn't enjoy but rather suffered!).

How often, in researching your family history, have you wondered about what it was like for the people whose names, dates and brief historical record you have uncovered? What sort of housing did they live in, what clothes did they wear, what were their working conditions, what was the landscape which they knew from day to day and how did they fit into local society? Have you asked yourself why they moved from one place to another, what they felt about their fellow-citizens, how greater and lesser events

> **Local History can answer many such questions. It can set the lives of your forebears....**

impinged upon them, and what rituals and customs they encountered in birth, marriage and death. What sort of education was available to them - if any - and how did they tackle the burdens and oppressions of poverty, early and sudden death, natural disaster, illness and ill-health. What lightened their lives and what did they look forward to?

Local history can answer many such questions. It can set the lives of your forebears firmly in their proper context, helping to explain why they did what they did and what they met along life's path. All over the British Isles local history is a 'growth industry'. There are many hundreds of societies which are devoted to furthering the cause of local history - undertaking research, using original sources; holding lecture meetings and field visits; publishing the fruits of research and writing; campaigning for the extraordinarily rich heritage which is the legacy of the past and seeking to ensure its conservation and enhancement for future generations.

Local history is endlessly diverse, full of rewards and unexpected surprises, and something which is available and accessible to everybody. The British Association for Local History helps to further the cause of this fascinating and valuable subject. BALH promotes the study of, and interest in, our local heritage and history.

All those who are interested in the history of the family will find that the study of local history can provide a much clearer and deeper understanding of where we came from and how it was in the past.

Starting Out
A Beginners Guide to Family History
Doreen Hopwood guides you through the early stages

Every family has its own, unique history, and our ancestors have helped to make us what we are today. For those of you about to embark on the ancestral trail, here are some basic guidelines to help you to proceed effectively and efficiently.

Until recently, it was the families of the rich and famous (or infamous!) whose histories were researched, but the same investigative techniques must be applied whatever the status of the family in order to produce a family tree. Patience and perseverance are two 'musts' for the prospective family historian, along with a 'sense of the past'. As research takes you back in time, be prepared for surprises -and maybe the odd shock! We need to step back into the contemporary world of our forebears to understand their daily lives and you'll soon find yourselves delving into local and social history to find out more. What did a puddler do for a living? Court Heneage in Aston Manor may sound like a very grand address, but was a set of back to back houses in Victorian Birmingham!

Success with research may also depend on the survival of records, whether your family moved frequently, their status and even the popularity of the surname being studied. Perhaps you have an unusual surname and want to find out more - but be aware that in the nineteenth century many of our ancestors were illiterate and you may well encounter changes in spelling as they were written down as they sounded. On the plus side, however, names like Jones aren't prone to this problem!

Whilst this directory contains information about all of the major repositories in the United Kingdom - the Public Record Office, the Family Records Centre, county record offices and libraries - these are NOT the places to start your research. Your first steps should be to talk to members of your family and gather together as much information as you can. In addition to 'official' documents such as birth, death and marriage certificates, wills etc, the following may provide valuable information to aid research:

A family bible is a great find, as it usually records dates of events as they happened. Memorial cards, obituaries and grave papers. School reports, apprenticeship papers, graduation certificates, occupational pensions. Military service records, medals or other awards. Society/club membership cards or trade union subscription cards. Diaries, scrapbooks, letters, newspaper cuttings, old address or birthday books.

Photograph albums are particularly helpful as 'memory joggers' when talking to older members of the family, and if possible, make a recording of any interviews. Whilst there are certain questions you need to ask, take care not to be too demanding - several short interviews may be more productive than one long one. This is also a good time to ensure that you have recorded on your own photos 'who, when and where'. Future generations will thank you for it!

Don't discount the family myth or legend - every family has at least one. They are usually firmly based on the truth, but like Chinese whispers, they tend to become embellished or distorted as they are passed on from generation to generation. Set out to verify the information with documentary evidence and share your findings with other family members. You may find out that someone is already researching your family's history, or is interested in joining in with you. This is an excellent way of sharing the workload and the costs. There are numerous books about genealogical research available, and you may be able to borrow some of these from your library. Monthly family history magazines usually contain a 'Readers Interests' section in which people submit details of the surname, period, and area of their research, and you may find a possible entry for your family. If you do respond to any of these, please remember to enclose a stamped address envelope or international reply coupon.

Joining your local family history society will bring you into contact with individuals with the same interest - see the addresses of members of the Federation of Family History Societies in this directory. As well as regular meetings, you'll receive newsletters containing details of their publications and a 'members interest' section. As you progress with your research, you may also want to join the society covering the area where your ancestors lived.

Attend a family history class. There is a whole range available, ranging from one-off workshops to academic courses leading to formal qualifications. Your local Education Authority will be able to advise you of locally run courses and look out for information at libraries and family history journals.

In this electronic age, more and more information is becoming available through the Internet. This is a great way of finding out about resources held in the area you are interested in and there are some excellent genealogical websites. However, don't expect to be able to compile your family tree solely from the world wide web. Whilst there are many indexes and resources accessible in this way, you will need to carry out research in numerous repositories - and this is part of the fun of family history. Nothing is more rewarding than seeing a 150 year old signature of one of your ancestors in a parish register, or visiting the church where family events were celebrated!

YOU are the most important person in your family tree, because you must always work from the known back to the unknown, generation by generation - yourself, parents, grandparents, great grandparents and so on. Never try to come forwards with your research - you may end up with an impressive family tree, but not necessarily your own.

For most of us the first major national source we encounter is the General Register Office (GRO) Index, which includes every birth, death and marriage registered in England and Wales since the introduction of civil registration on 1 July 1837. Scotland and Ireland have their own registration systems which commenced in 1855 and 1864 respectively. The index has separate volumes for birth, death and marriage and until 1984, when it became an annual cumulative index, it is split into four quarters: March events registered in January, February and March; June events registered in April, May and June; September events registered in July, August and September; December events registered in October, November and December

Each index is arranged alphabetically by surname, then by forename(s) and shows the district where the event was registered, the volume and page number. As a period of up to 42 days is allowed between the birth and its registration, check the quarter following the birth.

Your birth certificate shows your parents names and mothers maiden name THEN Your parents marriage certificate shows the names of both grandfathers THEN Your parents birth certificates show your grandparents names and grandmothers maiden name THEN Your grandparents marriage certificates show the names of both greatgrandfathers and so on.

The General Register Office Index is now available in many libraries and other repositories. The Office of National Statistics (ONS) at Smedley Hydro, Trafalgar Road, Birkdale, Southport, Merseyside, PR8 2HH can provide details of local holdings. Once you have traced the entry you require, the full copy certificate can be purchased by post from the above address, from the register office at which the event was registered or by personal visit to the Family Records Centre at Myddleton Place, Myddleton Street, London EC1R 1UW. In the latter case, the certificate can either be collected a few days later or posted to you.

Before the establishment of civil registration, it was the responsibility of the Church to record baptisms, marriages and burials, and in order to utilise the church registers, you will need to know the parish where the events took place. A census - a count of the population - has been taken every 10 years since 1801 with the exception of 1941. The census of 1841 is the earliest to contain information about individuals and as there is a 100 year closure on public access to the census enumerators' books, the most recent that is currently available (for England and Wales) is the 1891 census -until 2 January 2002 when the 1901 census is due to be released. More recent returns for Scotland and Ireland are already available.

Census returns contain lists of all inhabited buildings, showing the names, ages, occupations, marital status, birth places and relationship to the head of household of everyone resident on the night the census was taken - but with less detail on the 1841 return. It is usually necessary to know an address or at least a street to 'find' a household as the returns are arranged by enumeration district, but there is a surname index to the 1881 census of the whole of England and Wales. Many local family history societies have produced indices for their own locality in respect of other returns. The census enumerators books for the whole of England and Wales are available at the Family Records Centre, whilst county record offices and main libraries usually hold copies covering their locality.

The Church of Jesus Christ of Latter Day Saints (the Mormon Church) has produced the International Genealogical Index (IGI) which is a worldwide resource and regularly expanded in its on-line form as FamilySearch on the Internet. Much of the information has been taken from original parish registers and complemented by family histories submitted by Church members. In its microfiche format, it is arranged by country then region/county and within these, alphabetically by surname, then forename and chronologically by event. For England and Wales, the majority of entries cover baptisms and marriages in the Established Church and may go back to the introduction of parish registers in the mid sixteenth century. The IGI can be found at major libraries, county record offices and at Church of Jesus Christ of Latter Day Saints Family History Centres. Their addresses can be found in telephone directories. Once an entry has been found on the IGI/FamilySearch always obtain a copy of the entry from the relevant repository as this will, in most cases, provide additional information, including the signatures of the bride groom and witnesses at marriages. Whilst some churches still hold their parish registers, the majority will be found in the Diocesan Record Office - which is often based at the County Record Office. As well as registers of baptism, marriage and burial, the 'Parish Chest' contains numerous other records relating to the Church, its officers and its parishioners. You may find that one of your ancestors was a prominent member of the church and appears as a Churchwarden or other parish

official. Alternatively, an ancestor may have hit hard times and appear in the Overseers of the Poor's accounts as being in receipt of parish relief.

More and more 'finding aids' and indexes are being produced for family history and by the time that this directory is published, the National Burials Index should be available to complement the published books of monumental inscriptions transcribed from (legible) gravestones in church burial grounds. You can 'browse' the catalogue of the Public Record Office (PRO) on-line prior to paying a visit and so organise your time effectively. The series of information leaflets is also available on the Internet at http:www.pro.gov.uk and these cover a wide range of topics for family history.

Since 1858 it has been the responsibility of the Government to administer wills and grant probates. The national, annual indexes (Index of Wills and Letters of Administration) can be found in major libraries and other record offices and the extracts include sufficient information to enable a full copy will to be purchased. They are arranged in alphabetical order by surname, then forename, and appear in the index covering the year in which the probate was granted - which may be several years after the date of death. Don't assume that only the rich or gentry left wills - a glance at the above indexes shows how many 'ordinary' people made wills -and whilst the monetary value may be negligible, the amount of genealogical information can be enormous.

Do keep an open mind as you carry out research -whilst official documents provide evidence of names, dates, occupations and addresses, there are many other sources that will help to put your ancestors in their contemporary setting. Maps and photographs of the area in which the family lived will show how much (or how little) it has changed over time, whilst local newspapers give an account of what was going on. National and global events - such as the world wars of the twentieth century - affected our families and the demise of a local industry/employer might have instigated migration or a complete change of occupation for family members.

You may have thought that your family was 'Brummie born and bred' but as you progress back in time, you will probably find that your ancestors came from all over the British Isles - and maybe beyond. The search will take you far afield in geographical terms as well as in time, adding to the fascination that is family history.

There's a whole world out there...
Carolynn Boucher
enthuses about family history

In recent years more available leisure time and various newspaper articles and television programmes have lead to a phenomenal growth in the interest in family history. Genealogy, once only for aristocrats and the landed gentry, has consequently become one of this country's fastest growing hobbies and is now for everyone, even if they spring from the humblest of origins.

The main research rules are to work from the known to the unknown and to always check one's sources. The direction people take on tracing their family history will reflect the individual's personal interest or family traditions and stories. Whilst some choose to follow their paternal line, others will follow their maternal line - perhaps a more certain line of descent! An interesting career for great-uncle Silas or Auntie Jane may focus on that person's life and times and help to "put flesh on the bones".

Like most hobbies there's a whole world out there waiting to support you. Courses are run by local authorities and organisations within the family history world for the beginner, intermediate or advanced student. These may even lead to examinations and qualifications if desired. There are at least three monthly magazines available through high street newsagents or direct from the publishers to introduce you to research and help expand your knowledge.

Over the past quarter of a century family history societies have mushroomed covering every county in the U.K. Societies overseas deal with their own records and also have links with Britain. Their regular meetings and journals offer mutual help, informative talks and articles and enjoyment. Many new friendships have been made in this way and previously unknown family members contacted. Some families arrange "gatherings" with members travelling across continents to attend. For those people who like socialising nearer home with like-minded folk there are family history conferences, weekend courses and groups recording churchyards - not as morbid as it sounds, it can be great fun!

Genealogy fairs both large and small, take place in London, Birmingham and York and other venues around the country and throughout the year. Thousands of people are attracted by the "help desks", stalls selling books, memorabilia, postcards; software, microfiche and film readers, societies showing the advantages of membership and representatives from Record Offices as well as other interested organisations, in fact everything to assist you in your researches.

Documents of former times are usually written in a hand (or language) which is not immediately understandable today. Courses and books to help learn these new skills exist and practice makes perfect. At first it is like deciphering a code but having "cracked" it the satisfaction gained from being able to read the original document is enormous. However, if this is not for you there are experts who can undertake document transcriptions and translations for you.

Through the centuries mankind has followed numerous occupations to provide for themselves and their families. Some of these have died out whilst others have appeared and many occupations have required some sort of documentation usually for wage or tax purposes. Military records and regimental museums, hospitals and ecclesiastical records and the treasure trove of records in the county and public record offices help us to discover the way of life and conditions of some of our ancestors. Many people have become expert in researching a particular occupation or profession, identifying medals, uniforms and dating costumes from photographs and are prepared to share their expertise.

Although many records have been lost over the years, millions still exist and throughout the world people are indexing records which interest them at home or in record offices, sometimes alone, sometimes in groups. Parish records, baptism, marriages, burials registers, censuses, wills, criminal records, school records, monumental inscriptions, family photographs, bible inscriptions even occupational records for woad people and brushmakers ; people everywhere seem to be indexing information useful to other family historians and making it available free or for a small fee.

Family history hasn't let technology pass it by either. In towns and villages people are using computers with CD-ROMs and the various genealogy packages now available. The internet, too, has thousands of genealogy web-sites. Genealogy has fast become one of the most popular reasons for "surfing the net". Increasingly information from records is being put on line from record offices, other organisations and individuals to make this hobby more available.

Spending one's holiday following some family history research is not unusual and holiday accommodation is advertised for this purpose. If you live too far from the record office or area in which your ancestors lived - no problem there are professional researchers around the country and abroad willing to do the work for you and even a professional association, many folk conduct their research by post. The British have always travelled and lived abroad and the population of these islands is made up of many races, a large proportion of whom have inter-married. It is an unusual family who do not have someone who originally came from overseas or who died abroad. There are many British cemeteries abroad, both military and civil and firms who organise trips to visit them.

This hobby has such a variety of aspects that everyone should find something which interests them . This Directory lists many sources for the researcher so however you wish to pursue your hobby of family history this book should help you - so welcome to the world of family history and good hunting!

The Institute
of Heraldic and
Genealogical Studies

The Institute of Heraldic and Genealogical Studies is a charitable educational trust that was established in Canterbury, Kent in 1961 to promote the study of the history and structure of the family. To fulfil this aim a series of day, residential, evening and correspondence courses are run throughout the year for the benefit of family historians and genealogists. The courses range from those suitable for complete beginners to the subject, to those aimed at individuals wishing to pursue genealogical research as an income earning profession.

The day and residential courses offered in 2001 are—

Advanced Genealogy	Residential Course	**16-18 March**
Heraldry	Day School	**7 April**
The Professional Approach	Day School	**12 May**
Paleography	Day School	**16 June**
Tracing Your Family History	Residential Course	**23-27 July**
Tracing Your Family History	Residential Course	**6-10 August**
Wills and Probate	Day School	**15 September**
Library Sources and Pedigrees	Day School	**13 October**
The Parish and the Manor	Residential Course	**16-18 November**

Accommodation for the residential courses is provided at one of the historic hotels in the delightful medieval city of Canterbury, close to the Institute's comprehensive library.

The Institute also runs a pair of linked evening courses that encompass the whole of its syllabus required for qualification in genealogical research. These two courses, Introducing Genealogy (28 weeks) and Practical Genealogy (30 weeks) are both held each year in central London at the London School of Economics. One of the courses is also offered at Canterbury. These lead to graded assessments and examinations for certificates and diploma.

Introducing Genealogy	28 week evening course at the LSE	**24 September**
Practical Genealogy	30 week evening course at the LSE	**24 September**
Practical Genealogy	30 week evening course at IHGS	**27 September**

For those students not able to study in Canterbury or London, the Institute runs a very popular correspondence course that is accredited by the Open and Distance Learning Quality Council. This is composed of a series of 24 in-depth assignments, each requiring written answers to questions on the particular topic. Individual tutorial guidance is given. The course is also open to students from abroad with an interest in British genealogical research and takes two or three years to complete, studying on a part-time basis.

Full details of all the courses can be obtained from the Registrar on receipt of a large SAE.
Please send your enquiry to IHGS, 79-82 Northgate, Canterbury, Kent, CT1 1BA
Tel 01227 768664 Fax 01227 765617 registrar@ihgs.ac.uk www.ihgs.ac.uk

Catholics in England and Wales: What to read
Michael Gandy's guide to research ....

Background
Roman Catholic religious practice was illegal in various degrees between 1559 and 1829. However, in some parts of the country substantial numbers survived. There were large pockets in Lancashire, Northumberland, Durham, Staffordshire, Worcestershire, the Yorkshire Moors, Breconshire and the border of Herefordshire and Monmouthshire. There were also many Catholics in London, though some were visitors or foreigners from Catholic countries. Elsewhere particular gentry families were able to provide protection in their immediate area.

In the 19th century Irish immigrants began to arrive in very large numbers and all the northern and Midland industrial cities had large numbers of Irish Catholics By 1851 the population of England and Wales was nominally about 8% Catholic.

In the late 16th and 17th centuries state records tend to call Catholics 'recusants' or 'papists'. Many Catholics appear in Quarter Sessions records because of their refusal to attend Anglican services; the ones with property may appear in the Pipe Rolls (1581-1591; abstracts published by the Catholic Record Society (Vol 71, 1986) or the Recusant Rolls (1592-1691). The first four recusant rolls (1592-1596) have been published by CRS; the original records are in the PRO. There is a great deal about Catholics in State Papers Domestic, ecclesiastical court records and Bishops' Visitations. Most Catholics were Royalists during the Civil War and Jacobites after the abdication of James II, so they also appear in the records relating to those groups.

Social history reading
There are a number of excellent histories of English Catholics since the 16th century. The following may be available in second-hand bookshops or through your library system (most of them are out of print):

Aveling, J.C.H.	The Handle and the Axe. (1976).
Beck, G.A.	The English Catholics 1850-1950. (1950)
Bennett,	Canon Father Nugent of Liverpool. (1949; reprinted 1993).
Bossy, J.	The English Catholic Community 1570-1850. (1975)
Caraman, P.	The Other Face: Catholic Life under Elizabeth I. (1960)
Caraman, P.	The Years of Siege: Catholic Life from James I to Cromwell. (1966)
Duffy, E.	The Stripping of the Altars: Traditonal Religion in England 1400-1580. (1992).
Guilday, P.	The English Catholic Refugees on the continent 1558-1795. (1914)
Gwynn, D.	The Second Spring 1818-1852.
Gwynn, D.	A Hundred Years of Catholic Emancipation 1829-1929. (1929)
Havran, M.J.	The Catholics in Caroline England. (1962)
Hibbert, C.	King Mob. (1959)
Hodgetts, M.	Secret Hiding Places. (1989)
Kenyon, J.	The Popish Plot. (1972)
Leys, M.D.R.	Catholics in England 1559-1829: A Social History. (1961)
Loomie, A.J.	The Spanish Elizabethans. (1963)
Magee, B.	The English Recusants. (1938)
Mathew, D.	Catholicism in England 1535-1935. (1936)
Norman, E.	Roman Catholicism in England from the Elizabethan Settlement to the Second Vatican Council. (1986)
Watkin, E.I.	Roman Catholicism in England from the Reformation to 1950. (1957)

Of these Norman is the most modern but Leys is probably the best on the lives of ordinary Catholics over the whole of our period. Magee has a great many interesting statistics and lists all the Catholic nobility and gentry of the 17th century, information not brought together anywhere else. Caraman's two books are compilations and Hodgetts investigates the reality of 'priest-holes' which are almost as common as smugglers' caves!. Kenyon is about the Titus Oates Plot of 1678-1681 and Hibbert covers the Gordon Riots of 1780. Gwynn's Second Spring is about that extraordinary group of Anglicans from the late 1820s onwards who talked themselves into being Catholics, often without having actually met any. Bennett's biography of Father Nugent is the best guide to Catholic attempts at 'social work' in the mid 19th century. The achievements were extraordinary considering the size of the problems they faced.

Beck's The English Catholics 1850-1950 is a

compendium of articles and, at over six hundred pages, the best guide to the English Catholic world of our grandparents. The following are some of the articles it contains:

Hughes, P.	The English Catholics in 1850
Albion, G.	The Restoration of the Hierarchy
Sweeney, M.V.	Diocesan Organisation and Administration
Wheeler, G.	The Archdiocese of Westminster
Hughes, P.	The Bishops of the Century
Mathew, D.	Old Catholics and Converts
Johnson, J.T.	Cardinal Newman
Gwynn, D.	The Irish Immigration
Evennett, H.O.	Catholics and the Universities
Battersby, W.J.	Secondary Education for Boys
Battersby, W.J.	Educational Work of the Religious Orders of Women
Beales, A.C.F.	The Struggle for the Schools
Gwynn, D.	Growth of the Catholic Community
Cruise, E.	Development of the Religious Orders
Dwyer, J.J.	The Catholic Press
Hutton, E.	Catholic English Literature
Bennett, J.	The Care of the Poor

Most of these authors were the well-known experts of their day and, for the most part, their work has not been superceded.

There are a number of good histories of the Irish in England, particularly at local level but most of them have very little to say about the religious aspect - and nothing at all about records for family history!

Tracing a family
For a straightforward account of how to trace your Catholic ancestors see Michael Gandy, Basic Facts about Tracing Your Catholic Ancestry in England (Federation of Family History Societies, 1998) For researchers such as One-Namers who do not know of any Catholic barnches but would like to check out the possibility) see Michael Gandy, Catholics in your One Name Study. The Journal of One-Name Studies (Guild of One-Name Studies) Vol 3 No 11 (July 1990) pp327-331.

Non-Catholic records
For a full description of the non-Catholic records see J.Anthony Williams, Sources for Recusant History (1559-1791) in English Official Archives. Recusant History Vol 16 No 4 (CRS, Oct 1983) and D.J.Steel, Sources for Roman Catholic Family History. National Index of Parish Registers Vol 3 (SoG, 1974, reprinted 1986).

Mission Registers
Catholics did not establish a parish system in England and Wales until the First World War and early chapels are usually known as missions. They were often hired rooms and, in the mid-19th century, it was often thought more important to raise money for a school than a church. Once a mission was established there are usually baptism, confirmation and marriage registers but there may not be any burial registers as most Catholics were buried in Anglican churchyards until 1853 and borough cemeteries thereafter. Full details of known Catholic registers are given in Michael Gandy, Catholic Missions and Registers 1700-1880 (6 vols inc Scotland, 1994) which lists all missions including those for which no registers are known. This should be used in combination with Michael Gandy, Catholic Parishes in England, Wales and Scotland: An Atlas (1994). A simple summary of the historical background of every mission functioning in 1907 is given in Bernard W. Kelly, Historical Notes on English Catholic Missions. (Kegan Paul, Trench, Trubner and Co, 1907. Reprinted Michael Gandy 1995). There are also some detailed diocesan histories (eg Brentwood, Middlesbrough, Nottingham, Salford, Shrewsbury) and many hundreds of individual mission histories. They are vital for the late 19th and 20th centuries but, if they cover earlier centuries their authors have usually researched them from the classic works referred to later in this article.

For confirmations see also Bishop Leyburn's Confirmation Register of 1687 (North West Catholic History Society, 1997: an index is available from Catholic FHS) and the Midlands District Confirmation Register 1768-1815 (Catholic FHS, 1999). Catholic FHS intends to publish the London District Confirmation Register 1826-1844, early in 2001. This covers all the southeastern counties and the Channel Islands as well as London itself.

Monumental Inscriptions
There were no specifically Catholic graveyards until the 19th century except for Windleshaw Chantry and the Harkirk, both in Lancashire, and Winchester in Hampshire. Catholics were buried in Anglican churchyards often with no indication of their Catholicity. See in particular F.T.Cansick. A Collection of Curious and Interesting Epitaphs...Saint Pancras, Middlesex. (J.Russell Smith, 1869) as a high proportion of middle and upper class Catholics who died in London were buried there.

Wills and Estates
Catholic wills appear in the usual sources but in the 18th century they were supposed to be enrolled in the Close Rolls. For a simple list see Wills Enrolled in the Close Rolls. The Genealogist (NS) Vol 1 p267 and Vol 2 pp59-60, 279-282. See also J.O.Payne, Records of the English Catholics of 1715 (Burns and Oates, 1889, republished 1970) which includes abstracts of over 400 wills and administrations relating to known Catholics of the 18th century

and G.Anstruther, Abstracts of Wills (mostly of priests and their relations). London Recusant Vol 3 No 2 (May 1973) - London Recusant (NS) No 1 (1980) passim. For some years Mrs Christine Ackers has been abstracting the wills of known Catholics in Lancashire (up-to-date print-outs at SoG).

At the same time Catholics were also obliged to enrol the details of their estates. See E.E.Estcourt and J.O.Payne, The English Catholic Nonjurors of 1715 (Burns and Oates, 1885). The original, very detailed records are in the PRO (Class E 174); those for Lancashire have been published by the Record Society of Lancashire and Cheshire (Vols 98, 108, 117).

Biography and Family History

Catholics appear in all the standard sources and many histories of the older missions are, in practice, histories of the gentry families which protected them. The prime Catholic work is Joseph Gillow, A Bibliographical Dictionary of the English Catholics (Burns and Oates, 5 vols, 1887-1902, republished c1968). This enormous work is concerned with Catholics who wrote so that many people of social importance are not included. See also Rev. John Kirk, Biographies of English Catholics in the 18th Century (Burns and Oates, 1909. Reprinted 1969). For the background see Mark Bence-Jones, The Catholic Families (Constable, 1992) which deals with the great aristocratic families of the 19th century. For the 19th century see also W.Gordon-Gorman, Converts to Rome: a list of over 3000 Protestants who have become Roman Catholics since the commencement of the 19th century (W.Swan Sonnenschein and Co. 1884). Arranged by occupation; later, expanded editions to 1910 were arranged alphabetically).. For the 20th century see The Catholic Who's Who (34th edition, 1941; 35th edition 1952). Includes Catholics of standing in Great Britain and the British Empire.

The Clergy and Religious

During the 17th and 18th centuries all clergy and religious, male and female, were trained abroad and there were about 40 institutions specifically for English Catholics, many of them also providing an education for English Catholic children. For a general history see Peter Guilday, The English Catholic Refugees on the Continent 1558-1795 (Longmans, Green and Co. 1914). Most of these institutions returned to England in the 1790s and quite a few still survive today. The records of many of them have been published by the Catholic Record Society. The following general works should be consulted first.

Male: The following handlists are as complete as the present stage of research allows:
D.A.Bellenger, English and Welsh Priests 1558-1800 (Downside Abbey, 1984); Charles Fitzgerald-

Lombard, English and Welsh Priests 1801-1914 (Downside Abbey, 1993).

For biographies of individuals:
Godfrey Anstruther OP, The Seminary Priests: A Dictionary of the Secular Clergy of England and Wales 1558-1850 (Mayhew-McCrimmon, 4 vols to1800 (Vol 5 not published), 1969- 1977).
Dom Henry Norbert Birt, Obit Book of the English Benedictines 1600-1912. (Edinburgh, 1913. Republished, Gregg International, 1970).
B.Zimmerman, Carmel in England: A History of the English Mission of the Discalced Carmelites 1615-1849 (Burns and Oates, 1899).
Walter Gumbley OP, Obituary Notices of the English Dominicans from 1555 to 1952   (Blackfriars Publications, 1955).
Fr Thaddeus OFM The Franciscans in England 1600-1850 (1898).
Henry Foley SJ, Records of the English Province of the Society of Jesus (Burns and Oates, 8 vols, 1877-1883)

There are many other histories of these Orders but the above all give full details of individuals. By 1900 there were nearly 50 religious orders of men working in England and Wales. For a general history of each see Francesca M.Steele, Monasteries and Religious House of Great Britain and Ireland (R. and T. Washbourne, 1903). There are some biographical dictionaries of priests in th modern dioceses which were set up in 1850, eg, Found Worthy: A Biographical Dictionary of the Secular Clergy of the Archdiocese of Liverpool (Deceased) since 1850, Brian Plumb (1986) and To Preserve their Memory: Shrewsbury Diocesan Priests (Deceased) 1850-1995, E.M.Abbott (1996)

Female: The records of many of the recusant convents (including detailed biographies of the nuns and their families) have been published by CRS. In the 19th century a great many new Orders began to work in England and by 1900 there were about 90 - far too many to list here. The best general surveys are: Dom Basil Whelan OSB, Historic English Convents of Today (Burns Oates and Washbourne, 1936) and Francesca M. Steele, The Convents of Great Britain (Sands and Co, 1902). There are no published lists of 19th century nuns but the Catholic Family History Society has an index of about 14,000 which it hopes to publish eventually.

Martyrs and Prisoners

Short biographies of all the canonised and beatified martyrs will be found in The Martyrs of England and Wales 1535-1680. (Catholic Truth Society, 1985). The classic biography of most of them is in Richard Challoner, Memoirs of Missionary Priests (Burns Oates and Washbourne, 1924). Some martyrs have been written up frequently and in great detail but very little is known about others and the family backgrounds of many - especially the converts - remains to be researched.

There are no central lists of prisoners though many local lists, especially those of the London prisons, have been published by CRS. A great deal of information has been published in local sources (Quarter Sessions, Bishops' Visitations, Presentments by Churchwardens, Family and Estate Papers) which are beyond the scope of this article. There is a lot of mythology about priests' hiding places. For a serious expert account see Michael Hodgetts, Secret Hiding Places. (Veritas Publications, 1989)

Civil War
Catholics were closely involved in the Civil War and almost all took the Royalist side. See in particular P.R.Newman, Roman Catholic Royalists: Papist Commanders under Charles I and Charles II. Recusant History Vol 15 No 6 (Oct 1981) pp396-405. Catholic sympathies are noted in P.R.Newman, Royalist Officers in England and Wales, 1642-1660 and in the Calendar of the Proceedings of the Committee for Compounding with Delinquents 1643-1660 (HMSO, 5 vols) though both are concerned with Royalists rather than Catholics.

Jacobites
Jacobites too were not necessarily Catholics. See in particular C.E.Lart, Jacobite extracts from the Parish Registers of St-Germain-en-Laye, 1689-1720 (2 vols, The St Catherine Press Ltd, 1910-1912) and The Records of the Forfeited Estates Commission (HMSO, 1965) (includes rentals, leases, wills and estate papers). The records of the Forfeited Estates Commission are in the PRO.

Education
There were a number of local schools run by Catholic teachers but these were illegal throughout the penal period and most education took place abroad. Many schools lists have been published by CRS. Otherwise see A.C.F.Beales, Education under Penalty: English Catholic Education from the Reformation to the Fall of James II (The Athlone Press, 1963). The appendix lists 35 boys' schools on the continent (including Irish and Scots) of which the most important were Douai, Rome, Valladolid, Seville, St Omer, Dieulouard, Madrid, Lisbon and Bornhem. The records of most of these have been published by CRS. In the 1790s the surviving colleges returned to England and are represented by St Edmund's College, Ware, Ushaw, Downside, Stonyhurst and Ampleforth. They joined Sedgley Park and the Bar Convent, York, which had both been functioning in England for many years. All the above have published lists of students. For 19th century developments see W.J.Battersby, Secondary Education for Boys; W.J.Battersby, Educational Work of the Religious Orders of Women and H.O.Evenett, Catholics and the Universities in G.A.Beck, ed,

The English Catholics 1850-1950 (Burns Oates, 1950).

There is no national account of the work done for the 19th century urban Catholic poor but for an excellent account of work done in Liverpool see Canon Bennett, Father Nugent of Liverpool. (1949. Reprinted Nugent Care Society 1993).

Journals and Periodicals
For the 19th century press see John R. Fletcher, Early Catholic Periodicals in England.. Dublin Review Vol 198 No 397 (Apl 1936) pp284-310 and J.J.Dwyer, The Catholic Press in G.A.Beck, ed, The English Catholics 1850-1950 (Burns Oates, 1950)

Other Material
This article has only referred to the most important printed material. A number of long-established Catholic local history journals have produced hundreds of articles and a great deal of material has appeared elsewhere.
This material is analysed with explanations in four books by Michael Gandy (1996):
Catholic family history: a bibliography of general sources £8.00+ 80p p& p
Catholic family history: a bibliography of local sources £8.00 + 80p p& p
Catholic family history: a bibliography for Scotland £3.00 + 60p p&p
Catholic family history: a bibliography for Wales £3.00 + 60p p&p
Kelly's Historical Notes on English Catholic Missions costs £12.00 + £1.80 p&p. All are available from SoG and Family Tree Magazine, together with the volumes of Catholic Missions and Registers 1700-1880 (£6.00 each + 80p p&p)

Catholic Family History Society
This Society covers all aspects of Catholic ancestry (including Irish) in England, Scotland Wales (but not Ireland).
Secretary: Mrs Judith Goggin, 45 Gates Green Road, West Wickham, Kent BR4 9DE. A full list of articles published in Catholic Ancestor, the Society's journal, is available on receipt of an A5 stamped addressed envelope.

Newspapers
for family and local historians
Simon Fowler
on the news of the day....

Newspapers can be a vital source for family and local historians but are often forgotten about because they are surprising difficult to use. This article hopes to encourage readers to turn the pages of history as it was made.

There's an old newspaper adage about nothing being as dead as yesterday's news. From our point of view it is yesterday's news that we are interested in, for newspapers can tell us a great deal about our ancestors and the world that they lived in. It's a dull ancestor who did not appear in their lifetimes at least once in a local newspaper. And it's a dull local historian who can't find something of interest in a newspaper for his or her study of the nineteenth or twentieth century community.

National
The earliest newspapers appeared in the late seventeenth century. One of the first was the London Gazette, now the Government's official journal, which began life as the Oxford Gazette in 1666. The idea spread rapidly during the eighteenth century, when several papers which remain household names today first appeared, particularly The Times (1785) and The Observer (1791). Newspapers spread out from London to the provinces, so by 1800 most large cities or towns had a paper of some sort.

Early newspapers were different in many ways to the papers we read today. They were far smaller, rarely more than four pages long, with much less news which indeed was usually copied from other sources, particularly papers published in London. News travelled at the pace of the stagecoach or the sailing ship. The Norfolk diarist Parson James Woodforde heard of the fall of the Bastille on 24 July 1789, ten days after the storming of the prison. He noted in his diary 'Very great rebellion in France by the papers.'

These early newspapers shared with their modern day descendants advertising and a love of the trivial. Advertising normally appeared on the front and back pages, and might in colonial newspapers include details of runaway slaves, whereas adverts in British newspapers were usually more prosaic for patent medicines, beer and agricultural equipment. It was not unusual for servants, such as governesses, to advertise their availability for employment. The first issue of the Manchester Guardian, published on 5 May 1821, was not untypical in carrying advertisements for property, clothing and umbrellas for sale. There was also an illustrated announcement for 'Eagland's Improved Trusses for Ruptures' and a description of a missing man 'supposed by his friends to be drowned or murdered.'

Papers were full of stories about strange occurrences, whether natural phenomena or human. Court cases, then as now, were popular. The Observer for 5 January 1800, managed to combine both 'A poulterer at Hounslow named Clifford father by three wives to 35 children, on Thursday gave evidence against T.Allard who he stated fired at him before it was light.'

Newspapers in the way that we know them however really develop in the middle years of the nineteenth century. This is for three reasons. Firstly there was an increasingly literary population with a thirst for news, secondly new steam driven printing presses could print many more newspapers far more cheaply, and lastly the government abolished stamp duties on newspapers in 1855 thus considerably reducing their price. In 1800 The Observer cost sixpence an issue, a century later it was two pence. The numbers of newspapers soared, as well as their readership. The first national paper to take advantage of these new conditions was the Daily Telegraph, started in 1855, with the slogan: 'the largest, best, and cheapest newspaper in the world'. The Telegraph, The Times and most other newspapers catered for an affluent middle class audience which had time to read long reports of parliamentary debates and company annual general meetings.

The first mass newspaper, however was the Daily Mail (1896), quickly followed by the Daily Express (1900) and the Daily Mirror (1904). These new papers pioneered the use of photographs and pithily written human interest stories. They were instant successes, even if critics sniffed that the Mail was 'written by office boys for office boys.'

By the First World War the most popular newspapers were selling close to a million copies every day, while The Times sold less than a hundred thousand. Even so The Times had influence considerably greater than its circulation suggested for it was generally agreed that 'all who were concerned with public affairs must read it'. Perhaps it is little wonder that The Times could devote no more than a paragraph to the great disaster at the Ibrox stadium in Glasgow which saw eighty people lose their lives after an Scotland-England soccer game in April 1908.

Between the wars saw the rise of the Daily Express particularly amongst the middle classes, and the Daily Mirror for the workers. Newspapers attempted to boost their sales by almost any means possible, often by offering free insurance to readers, which was very much like the bingo wars of more recent times. The 'insurance wars' were more of a 'sickness' bingo, and to get a two pound payout you had to get shingles, chicken pox, sunstroke, mumps, scarlet fever, diphtheria, whooping cough, measles or scurvy. But to get the £25,000 jackpot as a reader of the Daily Mail or the Daily Express, required both the reader and his wife being killed in a railway accident.

After the Second World War saw the rise of the tabloid press, particularly with the seemingly irresistible rise of The Sun. Newspapers had increasingly to compete with television as a source of news and entertainment. They had to reflect their readers interests and views, and as a result have expanded considerably in size, and with new sections on cooking, gardening, and personal finance. Although newspaper circulation has as a whole declined, Britain still has the highest daily readership in the world, and newspapers remain very influential, which is why politicians spend a considerable amount of time seeking their support.

Local

Local or provincial newspapers have long been important in towns and cities, as well as in rural areas. Their growth was slower than their national cousins, but by the end of the eighteenth century most large towns or cities had a newspaper which was published at least weekly and sometimes more often. The articles they contained were in many ways not dissimilar to the national press, indeed they were sometimes lifted straight from the London papers, but the advertising remained resolutely local.
Many local papers grew up after stamp duty was abolished in 1855, which meant that for the first time ordinary people could afford newspapers. Most towns had one if not more local paper. In Richmond, for example the Richmond and Twickenham Times was founded in 1872 and its long time rival the Richmond Herald began in

1884. To modern eyes these papers can often be only differentiated by the political party they supported at elections or the side they supported in local scandals.

The heyday of the local newspaper was the period between 1880 and about 1970 when most events were covered in surprising detail. Verbatim accounts of court cases and council meetings, for example, are very common. Because of the expensive technology needed to reproduce them photographs only came in very slowly and it was not until after the First World War that they became common. Again advertisements, normally on the front and back pages, were an important source of income to papers and of course have delighted generations of readers since. Would you perhaps be interested in purchasing 'Rodine' the 'Rapid Rat Remover' as sold by Henry Tinker, Chemist of Pendleton?

Whereabouts
By far the largest collection of newspapers in Britain, local as well as national, is at the **British Library Newspaper Library** Colindale Ave, London NW9 5HE Tel: 020-7412 7353 Email: newspaper@bl.uk
The Library also holds many newspapers from around the world. More details can be found on their website
http://minos.bl.uk/collections/newspaper/

Most local record offices and local study libraries will have newspapers, usually on microfilm, for their locality. Large reference libraries may also have sets of national newspapers, particularly The Times, on microfilm. Manchester Central Reference Library, for example, has runs for some of the national newspapers as well as the Manchester Guardian and local papers for the Greater Manchester area. At the Public Record Office (PRO) there is a set of The Times, which can be found in the Microfilm Reading Room. The PRO has few other newspapers, although there is a collection of colonial newspapers sent to the Colonial Office in London between the 1820s and 1840s.

It can however sometimes still be difficult to identify which local papers served which area. If you have access to the Internet, the MagNet service can help you find magazines, journals and newspapers throughout the United Kingdom. **www.earl.org.uk/magnet/**

The best published list of newspapers and their locations is Jeremy Gibson, Local Newspapers, 1750-1920 originally published by the Federation of Family History Societies in 1987 and now sadly out of print. The Society of Genealogist (SoG)'s Library has copies and local family history societies should also have copies in their libraries. Other useful introductions are Colin R. Chapman, An Introduction to

... Using Newspapers and Periodicals (Federation of Family History Societies, 1996) and Michael Murphy, Newspapers and Local History (British Association for Local History, 1991).

How to use newspapers
Newspapers can be a very valuable source for both family and local history. On the other hand their shear bulk can present problems to the researcher, for there is so much information to sift through before you might find what you are looking for. With the exception of The Times there are very few detailed indexes to newspapers commonly available, although it is worth enquiring at the local record office or local studies library to see whether one is available for your area or period. Indexes to articles over the past four or five years are often available on the websites of national newspapers.

Palmer's index, or, after 1906, the Official Index to The Times is available either on CD-ROM or in book form. These indexes include many references to individuals, not just the great and good, but the accused in court cases, sports personalities, and obituaries, in addition to the great events of the time. Unfortunately adverts are not indexed. Copies of the CD-ROM for 1785 to 1905 are in the SoG Library as well as at the PRO. I have yet to come across a library that has the recently published CD-ROM for the period between 1906 and1980. Many libraries have copies of the books, which were published quarterly.

Newspapers tend to have similar layouts. This was especially true during the nineteenth century. The first and last couple of pages tended to be advertisements, while the news and editorial columns were in the middle. It was only with the arrival of the Daily Mail that news stories began to appear on the front page. The Times only abandoned the practise in the mid-1960s. Letters to the editor were often squeezed in where there was room, rather than kept together as they are today. Headlines were small, but often sensational. Early headlines in the Daily Telegraph included 'A Child Devoured by Pigs',

'Extraordinary Discovery of Man-Woman in Birmingham' and 'Shocking Occurrence: Five Men Smothered in a Gin Vat'. They were for stories which might go for a column or two of tiny print with few if any illustrations to break up the text. With the small print it can be difficult to read long stories, especially if your microfilm reader is worn out, as many machines at local record offices often are.

Pitfalls
1. It is easy to get sidetracked; there are always much more interesting stories to read;
2. Allow plenty of time to find what you want. Microfilm readers in particular can strain the eyes, so you may find you can only spend an hour or so going through the papers before you need a rest.

3. It may not be easy to find the right article, because there is just so much material to go through in each issue. During the nineteenth century especially obviously significant material usually received the same coverage as the ephemeral, so don't expect to find important stories near the front of a newspaper as would happen today.

4. Newspapers often have an obvious editorial bias and can, and do, make mistakes. My experience over many years is that if journalists can get it wrong they will, so do not trust what you read. Local historians who are researching a subject based largely on newspaper sources should be particularly aware of bias not just in editorials but throughout the paper. Frustratingly long running stories can often be dropped, presumably for reasons of space, before any conclusion is reached.

Conclusion
Newspapers can be an important source for local and family historians. They can be frustratingly difficult to use at times, but provided you know the approximate date of an event - say a funeral or the opening of a railway station - they can give considerable amounts of information that might not be available elsewhere.

Criminal Ancestors
17th to 19th Century Criminals & Records
Colin R Chapman discusses your criminal ancestors

If your ancestors fell foul of the law in any way, that could be good news for you as a family historian, though perhaps not for your ancestors; in any case, their names and maybe other details, are likely to be noted somewhere in an official record and possibly in also a report of the event, say in a newspaper or journal. Even an ancestor accused of departing from the accepted behaviour of the time, but later found innocent, can also be obligingly documented. For us, looking through past records, those ancestors who led respectable lives without upsetting their neighbours are, sadly, unlikely to be extensively documented individually. Of course, ancestors who were pillars of society, or local or national heroes are also good news, but there are not so many of them. In any case, a horrific crime and brutal punishments seem to add a bit of sparkle to a family chronicle.

We must not forget that not all who were brought to account, apprehended by a manorial or parish constable, hauled before a magistrate, presented at an ecclesiastical or temporal court, or thrown into the village lock-up or town goal awaiting trial, were necessarily criminals or even only suspected of being involved in crimes. Misdemeanors less serious than crimes were committed, perhaps by an ancestor or two, but these ancestors and their antics are equally likely to have been noted somewhere, and so such events are also useful in compiling pictures of our families and their lives years ago.

Who were the Criminals?
It will be useful at this point to understand who were described as criminals in the past, so that we can applaud, condemn, or justify our ancestors' actions.

A Criminal was (and still is) a person who committed a crime and could be a Principal, or an Accessory. A crime was an act committed (or omitted) in violation of a public law, either forbidding or commanding it. In other words, a crime was a wrong of a public nature.

Wrongs of a Private Nature
There was a long list of other offences defined as wrongs of a private nature; whilst these may have been objectionable or amounted to grave misconduct, being of a private nature they were not crimes - and those participating in such activities were, accordingly, not criminals. Some typical examples of wrongs of a private nature were assault and battery, slander, libel (these latter two were regarded as civil injuries), malicious prosecution, false imprisonment, abduction and adultery (whilst adultery was seen as a civil injury by the temporal courts, the ecclesiastical courts treated adultery as a serious criminal injury, and awarded appropriate punishment). Other private wrongs were distress for rent, debt, trespass, nuisance, waste and disturbance (of franchises, commons, ways, tenure or patronage).

If you discover that any of your ancestors were found guilty of one, or even several, of the above wrongs of a private nature, you may wish to keep the facts to yourself or broadcast them widely. But you cannot claim the individuals as criminals, for their offences were not defined as crimes in the 17th and 18th Centuries, at least.

Categories of Crimes
In contrast to private wrongs, there were five important groups of offences that most certainly were regarded as crimes, some of which could attract harsh punishments, including death. Let us look briefly at some of the crimes in each group:

Crimes Injurious to God and Religion
Within this group were Apostacy (the total renunciation of Christianity), Heresy (denial of the essential doctrines of Christianity), Nonconformity, Blasphemy, Cursing and Swearing, Witchcraft (this included Conjuration, Enchantment and Sorcery), Simony (the corrupt presentation to an ecclesiastical benefice for gift or reward), Sabbath Breaking, Lewdness and having bastard children. Sunday shopping and trading were definitely off, years ago, and those who participated were sure criminals.

Crimes Transgressing the Law of Nations
Within this group were Violating Safe Conduct, Infringing Ambassadors' Rights and Piracy, which need no elaboration. However, it is worth noting that certain acts of piracy were overlooked from time to time, especially when the spoils were taken from vessels belonging to an enemy, even if not military targets, and those spoils shared with persons in authority. Pirates were then regarded as privateers and, off the record, often as heroes.

Crimes Affecting the Power of the State
Within this group were High Treason, almost

always punishable by death, and Felonies against the Royal Prerogative, normally punished by the forfeiture of goods and lands.

High Treason could be against the sovereign's person, levying war against the sovereign in the realm, adhering to the sovereign's enemies within the realm (or aiding them elsewhere), violating the Queen (or the King's eldest unmarried daughter, or the wife of the King's eldest son), counterfeiting the Royal Great or Privy Seal or money, or staying judges in the execution of their offices. Apparently, to violate (or "deflower", to quote the term used in 18th Century documents) the King's youngest unmarried daughter or the wife of one of his younger sons was not High Treason; though doubtless if any of your ancestors were found guilty of such actions they would have been otherwise reprimanded.

Felonies against the Royal Prerogative included offences relating to the coin, offences against the Privy Council, serving foreign states, embezzling royal stores, desertion, seducing soldiers or sailors (which meant encouraging them to desert or otherwise be disloyal to the Crown - it did not mean enticing them immorally) and negative and positive misprisions. Concealing a treason or felony was a typical negative misprision. Examples of positive misprisions, usually regarded as high misdemeanors, included maladministration of public offices, embezzling public money, speaking or writing against the King's person and government, drinking to the pious memory of a traitor, refusing or neglecting to take oaths, and maliciously striking someone in the King's Palace or in Westminster Hall whereby blood is drawn. It is difficult for us today, in an era of free speech, to appreciate that public criticism of the Government or the Royal Family was formerly a crime in Britain.

Crimes Infringing the Rights of the Public
Within this group were Offences against Public Justice, against Public Peace, against Public Trade and against the Health and Police of the Community.

Among the offences against public justice were crimes such as embezzling or vacating records, abuses by gaolers, obstructing arrest, escaping from custody, rescuing a person from custody, returning from transportation, taking reward for stolen goods, receiving stolen goods, conspiracy, willful and corrupt perjury (such as false swearing), bribery, embracery (influencing a jury corruptly) and extortion.

Offences against public peace included rioting,

organising seditious meetings, unlawful hunting, sending threatening letters, destroying locks, sluices, turnpike gates, tollhouses and weighing machines, taking part in an affray (this involved two or more persons fighting in a public place; when such behaviour took place in private it was termed an assault). Routs and unlawful assemblies, forcible entries, riding armed and uttering false prophecies were also considered as offences against public peace. Again, it is difficult for us to imagine that publishing "Your Stars" in the past, as many magazines and tabloid newspapers do nowadays, was defined as a criminal offence only two centuries ago.

The category of offences against public trade included owling (transferring wool or sheep out of the kingdom), smuggling, fraudulent bankruptcy, usury (loaning money intending to make an excessive profit), cheating, monopoly, forestalling, regrating, engrossing and seducing artificers and manufacturers (persuading them to settle overseas). The laws against forestalling, regrating and engrossing, which were designed to protect the small trader, the equivalent of a small corner shopkeeper, were repealed in 1844.

Offences against the health and police of the community involved violating restrictions for plague victims and quarantine arrangements for ships, selling unwholesome provisions, participating in or arranging clandestine marriages, bigamy, vagrancy, common nuisances and, without an appropriate licence, participating in betting and lotteries and involvement with keeping, hunting and shooting game.

Crimes Derogating from the Rights and Duties of Individuals
Crimes within this group included homicide, suicide, manslaughter, murder, petit treason (a servant killing his master, a wife killing her husband or an ecclesiastic killing a superior), mayhem (violently depriving another person of a limb such that they were rendered unable to

defend themselves or annoy an adversary), forcible abduction and marriage, rape, actions contrary to nature with man or beast, kidnapping (the forcible abduction of a man, woman or child), arson, burglary (breaking and entering premises at night with the intention of committing a robbery, murder, rape or any other felony), larceny (stealing and removing property worth more than one shilling), malicious mischief and forgery.

Procedures Against Alleged Offenders

Following an accusation of an alleged offence, a person might be arrested for that alleged offence in one of four ways: by warrant, by an official without a warrant, by any individual without a warrant, or by hue and cry.

A range of courts was available at which a decision was made as to the guilt of the alleged offender and, if found guilty, the punishment deemed appropriate at that time. The court chosen depended largely on the circumstances of the accusation and the officials or individuals making the accusation and possible subsequent arrest. For example, a churchwarden could present a parishioner before a church court for an alleged adultery - an ecclesiastical crime. A manorial constable or headborough could take a tenant to a manorial court for failing to scour a ditch or for keeping an abnoxious privy - both offences under the laws of the manorial system. A parish constable could bring a local drunkard, accused of being disorderly and failing to keep the peace, to the petty sessions where magistrates (Justices of the Peace), without a jury, would decide whether to commit the offender to the stocks or impose a financial fine. Borough sessions were similar courts at which borough magistrates dealt with matters concerning only that borough.

Serious offenders were held in the local gaol before being brought before county magistrates presiding over a jury at one of the three-monthly sittings of the county quarter sessions. Very serious offences and crimes were heard at annual or twice-yearly assizes presided over by a judge from London. England and Wales were divided into circuits covering three or four counties and the assize judges travelled "on circuit" from county town to county town spending a few days in each, hearing cases of alleged crimes and pronouncing judgements on those found guilty. Some cases heard at an assize had been referred to this superior court from a quarter sessions court because of the severity or complexity of the alleged crime.

Persons serving in the armed forces who transgressed the conditions of their service were taken before a military court (a court martial). The procedures in these courts are beyond the scope of this article, but for completeness, the whereabouts of the records of these courts are identified below.

Original Criminal and Related Records

Records of alleged offenders presented before the ecclesiastical courts are among diocesan or archdiocesan records, now mostly held in county record offices; however, records for the north of England are in the Borthwick Institute in York and for the Welsh church courts are in the National Library of Wales.

Records of alleged offences heard under the manorial system (which in some parts of the country lasted from Saxon times to the 20th Century) were written on manor court rolls deposited in a variety of locations: county archives, museums and the Public Record Office (PRO). A local archivist can advise on the whereabouts of material for the immediate area.

Records of alleged offences brought before petty, borough and quarter sessions are in county or equivalent record offices. Some of this material is well indexed with names of all alleged offenders, victims and witnesses in comprehensive indexes at the relevant archives; in other cases only the alleged offenders appear in the indexes and in some cases there are no indexes at all. In the latter situations, to find your hapless ancestor, you will have to browse through all the court or minute books, usually kept in date order.

Records of alleged offenders in the military services brought before a court martial are at the PRO in the appropriate series: for the navy, in the ADM1 series until 1890 and in ADM156 from 1890 to 1957. Alphabetical and chronological indexes from 1803 to 1856 and from 1812 to 1855, respectively, appear in the ADM13 series; ADM194 has other naval court martial records. Persons executed at Execution Dock are in the High Court of Admiralty (HCA55) series of PRO records. For alleged offences of soldiers and of those connected with the army from 1666 to 1986, you will have to consult the proceedings and charge books in the WO series of records; WO71 contains proceedings, registers are in WO 86 to 92, with some indexes in WO93. Most recent records are closed to researchers.

Records of the assize court hearings, and of arrangements made during the assizes, and even officials' expenses claims, are in the PRO in the ASSI series, arranged under circuits - the Midland Circuit, the South-Eastern Circuit, and so on. Assize records include agenda and minute books, indictments and, in a few cases, separate depositions. Be aware that counties did not remain in the same circuit throughout the period we are considering, but the relevant PRO catalogues state when changes took place. Some assize records are comprehensively indexed, others less so, and some are missing altogether. Requests from county sheriffs between 1715 and 1832 for payments relating to hanging, whipping, the pillory, and so on, are in the Exchequer (E370/35 to 51) series. Expenses incurred by county justices for keeping prisoners in gaol between 1738 and 1822 (though not a continuous series of records), but arranged by county and with the names of many criminals, are in Treasury papers in the T90/146 to170 series. There are also Treasury Warrants from 1676 to 1839, in the T53/1 to 68 series, comprising payments to county sheriffs for apprehending and convicting criminals; each volume has an index at the back. Lists of persons tried at assizes (and also at quarter sessions), with their names, ages, occupations, the charge, the verdict and the sentence, are in the Home Office, HO140 series.

In the PRO, also in the HO series, are various records from 1782 to 1909 of persons charged with indictable offences, or held in goals awaiting trial, or in floating prisons where convicted prisoners were held on disused ships (convict hulks) before being transported to America (until 1776 and to Australia from 1787). For some of the convicts, details are given of their ages, convictions, sentences, health and behaviour. The names of a few criminals are in papers in the HO series relating only to them, such as petitions from the criminals or their relatives (1819 to 1854), others may be found mixed with matters relating to general policy. The Privy Council series of records also contains (in PC1/67 to 92) some correspondence from convicts and their families in monthly bundles between 1818 and 1844. Some documents of the Prison Commission, in the PCOM series, also in the PRO, include registers of prisoners and habitual criminals (from 1770 to 1916; a few of these contain photographs of the offenders - was your ancestor one of those?) and licences for male and female prisoners to be at large (from 1853 to 1887).

Reports of Alleged Crimes and Other Offences
Newspapers, almost from their inception in the early 18th Century, carried newsworthy items that would assist increased sales. Alleged offenders and details of court hearings, verdicts passed on the guilty and punishments imposed, traditionally made "good reading". Major trials and serious crimes often merited enterprising local printers preparing special posters or handbills to broadcast the outcome of a heart-rending trial or to advertise an impending execution, which always drew huge crowds. Most county towns had their popular sites for the gallows where audiences would gather to enjoy these morbid spectacles. Gibbeting was abolished in 1834 but the last public execution in England

was on 26 May 1868 at the Old Bailey. At subsequent private executions, well into the 20th Century, crowds still gathered outside prison walls all over the country, hoping to hear some sound of the final moments of the life of a convicted criminal. Many newspaper accounts contain colourful details of a court hearing and include notes of the gasps or applause from those in the public gallery, customarily criticized by the judge. Or you may read of the mood of the crowd surrounding the gallows and the last words of the criminal about to be executed. The British Library Newspaper Library at Colindale in north London has an excellent collection of local and newspapers, whilst some county archives hold copies of local publications. The Gentleman's Magazine, published monthly from 1731 and indexed every six months, usually made reference to major crimes or offences by prominent persons from all over the country. Many large reference libraries hold copies of this publication.

In Conclusion
Criminals, or those believed to be guilty of crimes or even of lesser offences, are often well documented in local or national records and in reports of their alleged (and proven) offences. Many criminal records portray the events themselves and the persons involved including notes on their appearances, ages, homes and families. In family history research where such details are eagerly sought you may, therefore, be hoping that one or more of your ancestors was a criminal. The information given above should aid your hunt for those ancestors and, after all, whether you hate or love them you cannot be blamed for what they did!

County & Country Codes
(Pre 1974 counties)

England	ENG	Wales	WLS	Ireland (Eire)	IRL	Canada	CAN
All Counties	ALL	Anglesey AGY		Antrim	ANT	Alberta	ALB
Bedfordshire	BDF	Brecknockshire	BRE	Armagh	ARM	British Columbia	BC
Berkshire	BRK	Caernarvonshire	CAE	Carlow	CAR	Manitoba	MAN
Buckinghamshire	BKM	Cardiganshire	CGN	Cavan	CAV	New Brunswick	NB
Cambridgeshire	CAM	Carmarthenshire	CMN	Clare	CLA	Newfoundland	NFD
Cheshire	CHS	Denbighshire	DEN	Cork	COR	North West Terr	NWT
Cornwall	CON	Flintshire	FLN	Donegal	DON	Nova Scotia	NS
Cumberland	CUL	Glamorgan	GLA	Down	DOW	Ontario	ONT
Derbyshire	DBY	Merionethshire	MER	Dublin	DUB	Prince Edward Is	PEI
Devonshire	DEV	Monmouthshire	MON	Fermanagh	FER	Quebec	QUE
Dorsetshire	DOR	Montgomershire	MGY	Galway	GAL	Saskatchewan	SAS
Durham	DUR	Pembrokeshire	PEM	Kerry	KER	Yukon Territory	YUK
Essex	ESS	Radnorshire	RAD	Kildare	KID		
Gloucestershire	GLS			Kilkenny	KIK	Austria	OES
Hampshire	HAM	**Scotland**	**SCT**	Leitrim	LEI	Belarus	BRS
Herefordshire	HEF	Aberdeenshire	ABD	Leix(Queens)	LEX	Belgium	BEL
Hertfordshire	HRT	Angus	ANS	Limerick	LIM	Croatia	CRO
Huntingdonshire	HUN	Argyllshire	ARL	Londonderry	LDY	Czechoslovakia	CS
Isle of Wight	IOW	Ayrshire	AYR	Longford	LOG	Czech Republic	CZR
Kent	KEN	Banffshire	BAN	Louth	LOU	Denmark	DEN
Lancashire	LAN	Berwickshire	BEW	Mayo	MAY	Estonia	EST
Leicestershire	LEI	Bute	BUT	Meath	MEA	Finland	FIN
Lincolnshire	LIN	Caithness-shire	CAI	Monaghan	MOG	France	FRA
London (city)	LND	Clackmannanshire	CLK	Offaly(Kings)	OFF	Germany (1991)	BRD
Middlesex	MDX	Dumfriesshire	DFS	Roscommon	ROS	German Old Emp	GER
Norfolk	NFK	Dunbartonshire	DNB	Sligo	SLI	Greece	GR
Northamptonshire	NTH	East Lothian	ELN	Tipperary	TIP	Hungary	HU
Northumberland	NBL	Fifeshire	FIF	Tyrone	TYR	Italy	ITL
Nottinghamshire	NTT	Forfarshire	ANS	Waterford	WAT	Latvia	LAT
Oxfordshire	OXF	Invernessshire	INV	Westmeath	WES	Liechtenstein	LIE
Rutland	RUT	Kincardineshire	KCD	Wexford	WEX	Lithuania	LIT
Shropshire	SAL	Kinrossshire	KRS	Wicklow	WIC	Luxembourg	LUX
Somerset	SOM	Kirkcudbrightshire	KKD			Netherlands	NL
Staffordshire	STS	Lanarkshire	LKS	**Channel Islands**	**CHI**	New Zealand	NZ
Suffolk	SFK	Midlothian	MLN	Alderney	ALD	Norway	NOR
Surrey	SRY	Moray	MOR	Guernsey	GSY	Poland	POL
Sussex	SSX	Nairnshire	NAI	Jersey	JSY	Romania	RO
Warwickshire	WAR	Orkney Isles	OKI	Sark	SRK	Russia	RUS
Westmorland	WES	Peebleshire	PEE	**Isle of Man**	**IOM**	Slovakia	SLK
Wiltshire	WIL	Perthshire	PER			Slovinia	SLO
Worcestershire	WOR	Reffrewshire	RFW	**Australia**	**AUS**	Spain (Espagne)	ESP
Yorkshire	YKS	Ross & cromarty	ROC	Capital Territory	ACT	Sweden	SWE
YKS E Riding	ERY	Roxburghshire	ROX	New South Wales	NSW	Switzerland	CH
YKS N Riding	NRY	Selkirkshire	SEL	Northern Territory	NT	Ukraine	UKR
YKS W Riding	WRY	Shetland Isles	SHI	Queensland	QLD	United Kingdom	UK
		Stirlingshire	STI	South Australia	SA	United States	USA
		Sutherland	SUT	Tasmania	TAS	USSR	SU
		West Lothian	WLN	Victoria	VIC	Yugoslavia	YU
		Wigtownshire	WIG	Western Australia	WA		
						Papua New Guinea	PNG
						Rep South Africa	RSA

These codes are used to avoid confusion in the use of abbreviations for countries and counties.
Created by Dr Colin Chapman they are universally recognised and should always be used.

Lochin Publishing
6 Holywell Road, Dursley GL11 5RS England

Parish Registers

Pauline M. Litton BA FSG(Assoc)
Vice President
Federation of Family History Societies

York, All Saints' Church, Pavement

What are Parish Registers?

Parish registers are records kept by the established church of each country within the British Isles. They give details of baptisms/christenings, marriages and burials and occasionally of births and deaths. The established church in England, Wales, the Channel Islands and the Isle of Man has, since 1534, normally been the Anglican Church (Church of England). In Ireland, until its disestablishment in 1869, it was the (Anglican) Church of Ireland; in Scotland, it is the Presbyterian Church. The Episcopal (Anglican) Church of Scotland and the Roman Catholic Church in all U.K. countries were also parish-based so their records may be referred to as 'parish registers'.

When do parish registers begin?

In England and Wales the first injunction ordering the keeping of parish registers was issued in 1538 and several hundred registers survive (principally in England) which contain entries from the 1500s. In Scotland the keeping of registers (for baptisms and marriages) was introduced in 1551 but there are fewer than 20 registers with entries before 1600 and the majority begin in the 18th century. In Ireland there are no pre-1600 registers (the first requirement to keep them was in 1634); most Church of Ireland registers begin in the late 18th century and many Roman Catholic ones not until the 19th century. A few parishes in England have a full set of registers from 1538 to the present day but many books, especially the early ones, have not survived. If the register you need has been lost, you may (in England and Wales only) locate the missing information in the Bishops' Transcripts (copies of the register which were normally sent annually to the diocesan registry between 1597 and the mid-19th century). Parish Registers continue to the present day and their format has changed little since 1813 (1837 for marriages).

Where shall I find parish registers?

In each part of the British Isles, apart from England, there is one repository which holds the majority of original registers (or transcripts or microform copies of them) for that country from their earliest date until at least the mid-19th century (after which they may still be held at the church); they should also know the whereabouts of any which have not been deposited. An increasing number of records are available in microform, with copies available in several places, so it always pays to check, before making a special journey, whether there is a microfilm or microfiche copy in a repository convenient to you.

In England, registers may be held in a County Record or Archive Office, a Diocesan Record Office or may still be at the church. In Wales they may be at the National Library of Wales (Aberystwyth), a County Record Office or at the church. It is essential to check before visiting any record repository that they do hold the particular documents, or film or fiche copies, that you need. Many counties underwent substantial boundary changes in 1974 and again in the 1990s. The majority of books and maps used by family historians are based on the 'historic' pre-1974 counties but, since that date, a substantial volume of records has been transferred to new 'administrative' counties. Original Parish Registerss for historic Yorkshire, for example, are now scattered between 16 record offices in five counties.

Old Parish Registers (pre-1855) for Scotland are mostly at New Register House in Edinburgh with a few elsewhere. Entries from these registers are the most accessible for family historians to search as they available world-wide on microfilm, are largely computerised and indexed and are also available on the Internet (fees payable).

Ireland causes particular problems because most early Church of Ireland registers were destroyed in 1922; books on tracing your Irish ancestors will explain what records survive and suggest alternative sources which may fill some of the gaps. Surviving Church of Ireland registers, or copies, may be in Dublin in the National Archives, National Library, or Representative Church Body Library or in the Public Record Office of Northern Ireland in Belfast. Roman Catholic registers are generally still held at the church with copies in the National Library in Dublin.

Original registers for the Channel Islands are still held in the parishes with many indexes and microfilms held by family history societies and libraries on Jersey and Guernsey. Registers for the Isle of Man are held at the General Registry with copies both here and at the Manx National Heritage Library (both in Douglas).

Many parish registers have been transcribed, some have been printed and indexed, and the local record office, library or family history society should be able to tell you the location of original registers, microform copies and printed works for their area. Most registers have been microfilmed or microfiched and generally you will not see the original documents.

The country articles in Section 2 of this book give more details of various repositories and their holdings and include addresses and web sites.

What information is contained in parish registers?
This can vary between countries, dioceses, parishes and even from year to year. Do not expect uniformity or consistency. In England, Wales and the islands you should, theoretically, be able to find baptism, marriage and burial entries for most of your ancestors at least from the 17th century. Broadly speaking, parish registers in Scotland and Ireland frequently start at a later date, survive less often, and contain less information than those elsewhere in the British Isles. Many of the statutes concerning parish registers (including Hardwicke's Marriage Act), passed by the English parliament at Westminster, either did not apply to, or were never enforced in, Scotland and Ireland. The islands in general followed England's lead but not to the letter and there are some variations in their registers.

Parish Registers 1538-1812
The 1538 injunction said that every Church in England and Wales was to "keep one Book or Register wherein [the incumbent] shall write the day and year of every Wedding, Christening and Burial" together with the names of those married, baptised or buried. The book was to be kept in a chest with two (later three) locks - the key to one to be held by the minister and to the other(s) by the churchwardens - and entries were to be made each Sunday by the minister in the presence of the churchwardens, after which the book was to be locked away again. This was intended to ensure that no one person had the opportunity to forge or alter entries. Parish Registers were accepted as legal documents and were often the only written evidence available, especially in inheritance cases, to verify the existence of a marriage or the legitimacy of a child.

The parish was responsible for providing, and paying for, its own Register book. Early ones were commonly of paper, which was cheaper than parchment but more easily damaged. Some parishes could not, or would not, provide the necessary funds and, in some cases, no register was purchased before the 17th century. In 1598 an Act ordered that the Registers should be copied into parchment books, which would be much stronger (and more expensive). Unfortunately, the Act was badly worded. Entries from the old Registers were to be copied 'but especially since the first year of Her Majesty's reign'. Elizabeth I had come to the throne in 1558 so this gave an excuse, to those who begrudged spending extra time and money, to copy only from 1558, which is why many Registers begin with that year.

Individual ministers and parish clerks were left free

to devise a format for their registers so some include separate records of baptisms, marriages and burials in columns on the same page, others use different parts of the same book (often with marriages in the middle), and many run all three types of event together in a chronological sequence. As parchment was expensive some ministers used minute writing and others would fill in any small gaps with events which happened several years later than most of those on the page. Try to make sure that records are present for every year. Particularly when looking at registers in microform it is all too easy to overlook a note scribbled at the bottom of a page which says 'for baptisms in 1664 turn back 9 pages' where you may find a few written into a small space in the middle of the burials for 1623. Early registers in particular often contained the minimum amount of information required by law but, as was usually the case, much depended on the individual responsible for writing up events.

A gap occurs in many Parish Registers and associated records during the period of the Civil War and Interregnum (1643-1660). They were often not kept properly in these years and the details in, and completeness of, the registers (if any) vary considerably with the area. Neither bishops' transcripts nor marriage licences were maintained for much of this period. In 1733, entries in Latin in English parish registers (the only country in the British Isles where the practice had been widespread) were stopped but Latin continued to be used in Roman Catholic registers.

After 1754, almost all Anglican parishes maintained a separate marriage register. This gave many incumbents the opportunity to amend the format of their existing parish register, often writing baptism entries in the front of the book and turning it upside down to enter burials at the back, rather than the haphazard system many clergymen had used previously. Some incumbents began to include extra information in their registers, in addition to the names which were all they were duty bound to include for baptisms and burials. Where, and for how long, this happened depended very much on individual clergymen or parish clerks, and sometimes on bishops or archbishops who instructed their clergy to record certain facts. Be grateful if you find your ancestors in a parish register which gives more than the basic facts, but don't assume that this bonus will continue indefinitely or that it will occur in a neighbouring parish.

Baptism Registers
The 1538 injunction specified only that the name of the person being baptised must be recorded and some 16th century baptism registers give only the name of the child, with no parentage mentioned. By the late 18th century many registers give Christian names for both parents, and some add the father's occupation or place of residence, but others, as late as 1812, include the name of the father but not the mother. In Scotland the mother's maiden name is often included in the entry, as is the

Market Place, Richmond, North Yorkshire

From about the beginning of the 18th century in England and Wales (the starting date varying from diocese to diocese) entries began to record whether the marriage was by banns or licence. Details of banns were rarely retained before 1754 (except during the period 1653-1659 and in Scotland where a few earlier ones survive) but, if a marriage was by licence, you should enquire whether the marriage bonds and allegations survive as these often provide much more information about the couple. (Licences, issued to the couple to hand to the minister marrying them rarely survive but the source documentation often does.)

date of birth.

In 1783 a Stamp Duty of threepence (just over 1p in decimal currency) was imposed on all entries recorded in parish registers (including Scotland). Some people avoided the tax by claiming to be paupers (because they were exempt from it), others by not having their children baptised. The Act was repealed in 1794 and it is worth looking after this date for several children in a family being baptised on the same day. Many clergymen were sympathetic to those trying to escape paying the duty and, particularly in Scotland, some ministers helped their parishioners by performing the relevant ceremony but not entering it in the register, thus avoiding the payment of tax but meaning that some baptisms are not recorded in the register.

Particularly in the north of England between 1770 and 1812 you may be fortunate enough to find an ancestor (or a sibling) in a Dade Register, named after William Dade, the Yorkshire clergyman who devised their format. A true Dade Register will include, at a baptism, the date of birth together with details of a child's position in the family and the names of its parents, grandparents (and occasionally some great grandparents). The Archbishop of York tried to extend Dade's scheme throughout the Diocese of York, with varying degrees of success. Full Dade registers covering the entire period are rare but many parishes maintained them for a few years and others did include some extra details.

Most true Dade registers occur in Yorkshire but similar registers are found in Nottinghamshire and parts of Lancashire, which were controlled from York; clergymen in the Dioceses of Durham, Norwich and Salisbury were at various times instructed to include extra (although not as much) information in their registers; some Welsh nonconformist Registers used a format very similar to Dade; and occasional parishes in Cheshire, Devon, Essex and Surrey also adopted the Dade format.

Marriage Registers

Until the early 1700s the majority of marriage entries just included the names of the couple (some parishes gave even less information with William Johnson married his wife being not uncommon).

Lord Hardwicke's Act 'for the better preventing of Clandestine [Secret] Marriages' took effect on 25 March 1754 in England and Wales (it never applied in Scotland or Ireland, to marriages overseas or to marriages involving Jews or Quakers). Its main provisions were that all marriages must be preceded by either the publication of banns in church on three successive Sundays or the obtaining of a licence; written parental consent was necessary for those marrying by licence under the age of 21 (until 1929 the legal age at which a marriage could take place with parental consent was 12 for girls and 14 for boys); marriages and banns were to be recorded in proper Books of Vellum, or good and durable Paper, with ruled and numbered pages (to avoid fraudulent entries being added later or pages being torn out); and the minister, the couple and two witnesses were to sign the register (or make their marks).

Marriage registers, contrary to popular belief, did not have to be printed as long as they followed the "Form of Register" shown in the Act and entries included the names of the couple, their parishes of residence, whether they married by banns or licence, who married them and the names (or marks) of two witnesses. Note that there is no mention of marital status for either of the couple, or of occupation for the groom, so legally there was no requirement to enter this information. Many parishes included marital status for the bride and either occupation or marital status for the groom, but rarely both.

Hardwicke's Act also said that from 1754, in Anglican Churches, a record of the banns (if called) should be made but it omitted to specify how they were to be recorded. Some parishes purchased a separate Banns Book for this purpose; others included the banns as part of the marriage entry. Always ask whether the banns book has survived (many have not). Where bride and groom came from different parishes, the banns were read in both so you may find details of an intended marriage in another parish or county which might otherwise be hard to trace. Banns and marriage licences are both evidence of an intention to marry but neither is a guarantee that the marriage took place. The marriage entry should always be located to confirm that the event did happen.

Burial Registers

As with baptisms, the 1538 injunction required only the name of the person being buried to be registered. Once again, the information given depended largely on the individual imcumbent. In some parishes, through to 1812, little information was given apart from the name (and even that might be entered as Widow Smith or Old Mother Brown); in others, from the 1600s, relationships, ages, occupations and causes of death were included at various times and for varying periods. Dade burial registers may include details of parents and grandparents of the deceased; there are examples where the person being buried is aged 80+ and these details are given, giving an information span of well over a century.

Hawkshead Parish Church, Cumberland
(now Cumbria)

In 1678 an Act, intended to help the wool trade, was passed. This stipulated that no one (apart from plague victims) should be buried wearing anything but wool and that coffins should be lined with woollen cloth. It remained in force until 1814 but in most areas was ignored long before this. A sworn statement had to be made within eight days of the funeral that the Act had been obeyed and a penalty of £5 was payable if it had not. Many parishes did not mention this Act in their registers; others added 'affidavit sworn', or an abbreviation or badly spelt attempt of the words, after the entry; a few kept separate registers to record burials in woollen. If a family preferred to bury the corpse in silk or flax (linen) they could pay the fine and do so and the register may either record the fact or note that no affidavit was brought.

There are few burial registers in Scotland or for the Roman Catholic Church in Ireland. Where there are burial registers in Scotland entries often include a woman's maiden name.

1813-present day

George Rose's Act of 1812 (effective 1813 except in Scotland and Ireland) stated that each parish should purchase from the King's Printer separate books of paper or parchment for baptisms, marriages and burials (the first time that individual books and printed forms had been required for each event) and that these should be written up and signed in the case of marriages at the time and for baptisms and burials within seven days.

The format of baptism and burial registers has remained unaltered in England, Wales and the islands since this date. That of marriage registers was changed in 1837 to bring them in line with civil registration certificates introduced in July that year but has remained unaltered since . Printed register books were not introduced in Scotland and Ireland until much later.

Baptism entries were to contain: date of baptism; child's Christian name; parents' Christian names and surname; abode [place of residence]; quality [social status], trade or profession; and by whom the ceremony was performed. In the Channel Islands dates of birth and baptism were included and column headings were given in French and English - in that order.

Marriage entries (1813-1837) were to include: name and parish of residence of groom and bride; where married; whether by banns or licence; whether with consent of parents or guardians [necessary for those under 21]; when married; by whom married; together with the signature of the minister, and signatures or marks of the parties married and two witnesses.

Burial entries were to give: name; abode; when buried; age; and by whom the ceremony was performed.

This information was the minimum required by law. It provided for more detail than had been compulsory before this date but less than had been customary in some areas. An occasional clergyman maintained the high level of information included in Dade registers. Others inserted the date of birth or the mother's maiden name at a baptism (always common practice in Scotland but not elsewhere); or the date of death or marital status at a burial (for a married woman, the name of her husband was often included; for a child at least the father's name) but most recorded only what was legally required.

Bibliography

National Index of Parish Registers series (Society of Genealogists: 1967 to date) especially Vol. 1 (General Articles); Vol. XII (Scotland and Vol. XIII (Wales)

History of Parish Registers JS Burn (London 1862)

Basic Facts About Using:

Baptism Records for Family Historians Pauline M. Litton (FFHS: 1996)

Marriage Records for Family Historians Pauline M. Litton (FFHS: 1996)

Death & Burial Records for Family Historians Lilian Gibbens (FFHS: 2nd ed.1999)

Parish Registers : Pauline M. Litton - June 2000

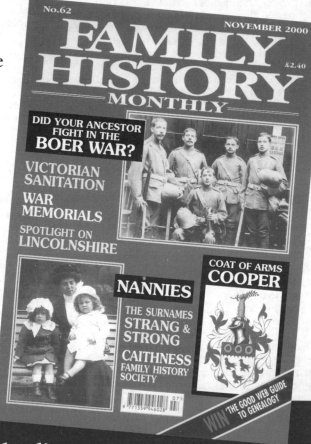

Ag labs, fwks and other anachronisms
Kate Thompson
looks at strange occupations

Occupations that were once common-place have disappeared over the last few decades as we have seen the nature of work change. Heavy industrial trades have largely gone, together with their associated occupations. The saggar maker's bottom knocker - of which more later - is now merely an anachronism beloved of quiz-setters.

The occupations found in the census returns sometimes puzzle researchers, especially as they are often abbreviated. The books on the census published by the Public Record Office refer to the more common of these although they cannot hope to cover all the examples. In rural areas the most common occupation was that of an agricultural labourer, invariably abbreviated to 'Ag lab'. Others include 'FS' for female servant, 'MS' for male servant, 'Ind' for someone of independent means, 'Ann' for a person in receipt of an annuity and 'J' for journeyman, ie someone paid by the day.

Family historians working in the east midlands will frequently find the abbreviation 'Fwk'. It is short for framework knitter, a trade which employed thousands of men and women in the region, working with wool (mainly in Leicestershire), cotton (Nottinghamshire) and silk (Derbyshire). Hand knitting began in Britain during the 15th century when the woollen industry was rapidly expanding, and was often undertaken in rural areas to supplement the family's income. The Rev William Lee, the curate of Calverton, Nottinghamshire, invented the stocking frame in 1589, allegedly because a young woman he was courting seemed more interested in her knitting than in him! He took his machine to London and tried to interest the queen in his invention but failed because the fabric was not as fine as that produced by the royal hand knitters. In addition the government was unwilling to issue a patent that could threaten hand knitters at a time when there was severe under-employment in the country at large. Lee then took his machines to France where he was equally unsuccessful and died there; however, his frames were subsequently used to establish a French silk knitting industry.

Lee's brother James brought the stocking frame back to London and made improvements to it which enabled a finer fabric to be produced. Its use spread slowly and there were less than 100 frames in use by the outbreak of the civil war. A Company of Framework Knitters was formed in London and incorporated by charter in 1657 and 1663. The trade could now be regulated with master framework knitters taking on apprentices, but attempts to impose restrictions on the trade led to it moving to the east midlands where the frame had begun life; by 1782 nearly 90% of the 20,000 stocking frames in use in Britain were in the region.

During the 18th century improvements were made to the stocking frame, which enabled a wider range of goods to be produced, but by about 1800 it had reached the limits of its versatility. The next stage in the process would be the application of power, as was happening in the spinning and weaving industries in other parts of the country, but the internal organisation of framework knitting together with an abundance of cheap labour and changes in fashion kept powered machines out of the hosiery trade for another 50 years.

Framework knitting was essentially home-based and often involved a man, his wife and children in various stages of the process. Although there were women framework knitters, it was hard manual work and was usually done by men; women worked as seamers and older children as winders. It was not an easy life and the framework knitter was a cog in a bigger wheel, paid on piece work - that is, he was paid for the goods he produced and was dependent on a master hosier for his wages. The master hosiers often had to use the services of a middleman such as a putter out (who acted as an intermediary between a knitter and the hosier, paying the knitter the prices given by the hosier after deducting something for himself), an undertaker (who contracted with a hosier to make a certain quantity of yarn for a given price) or a bag hosier who obtained yarn from a number of warehouses and marketed the goods himself). Few knitters owned their own frames but rented them from master hosiers or others. Frame rent could represent a significant percentage of a knitter's outgoings and had to be paid whether he had enough work or not.

In the early part of the 19th century the trade became depressed, with too many operatives and not enough work for them all. Framework knitters could not afford to apprentice their children to other trades, which merely added to the problem. There were other difficulties connected with the organisation of the industry and 'as poor as a stockinger' became a common saying. One of the best sources for this period is the 1845 government report on the plight of the framework knitters which contains some fascinating testimony of those involved in the trade.

Mechanisation began in the 1850s and 60s and by the end of the century hosiery factories developed extensively. This brought about a change in the hosiery industry as women could operate the machines, freeing men for other work such as boot and shoe making (notably in Leicestershire) and engineering.

In the heyday of framework knitting successful operatives began by having a frame in their house, then built an extension to house it and in some cases had a special workshop in the garden. There are two small museums where framework knitting can be studied - at Ruddington in Nottinghamshire and Wigston Magna in Leicestershire. Both put on demonstrations of knitting from time to time, as does the industrial museum at Snibston (Coalville, Leicestershire). There are several cottages in the east mid-lands which can be identified as former framework knit-ters' residences; like weavers' cottages in Yorkshire and Lancashire they can often be recognised by their long rows of windows which allowed the maximum amount of light.
Anyone interested in finding out more is recom-mended to consult Marilyn Palmer's Shire Album, Framework Knitting (1984, reprinted 1986) or her collaboration with Peter Neaverson, Industrial Landscapes of the East Midlands (Phillimore, 1992).

Other trades connected with hosiery included the frame-smiths (who built the frames) and sinker makers (who made the small metal plates, hanging vertically between the needles, which made and transferred the loops of thread).

In other parts of the country similar textile trades used terms unfamiliar today. Handloom weavers did weaving on a hand loom, usually in their own houses, and suffered in a similar way to framework knitters when mechanised looms became common; they disappeared altogether in the 1830s and 40s. A doubler laid (doubled) threads of fibre together before they were twisted to form a usable yarn and a throwster twisted the strands together. The beamer wound warp onto a roller before putting it onto a loom and the fettler cleaned the machines in woollen mills. A comber (also known as a kempster), as the name suggests, combed wool and a fuller was responsible for shrinking, beating and pressing cloth; pieces of cloth were churned around in a soapy liquid which had the effect of felting the fibres together, producing a stronger and warmer cloth. A lace runner embroidered patterns onto lace.

The manufacture of other articles of cloth-ing and associated trades generated their own terms, some of which are still used today but will no doubt be unfamiliar to many readers. In boot and shoe making a clicker cuts out the uppers for shoes from pieces of leather (or, these days, other materials) and a closer assembles the com-ponents for the finished shoe. The term cordwainer, which became synonymous with shoemaker, originally denoted some-one who worked with leather from Cordoba in Spain. Elastic web manufacture was a small, but important, trade in Leicestershire in the 19th century, being used to produce the material for elastic-sided boots, the webbing on gloves, and corsets among other things; the operatives were known as weavers. The occupations of a stay maker and peruke maker are easy to work out.

In Hertfordshire and Bedfordshire straw plaiting was used rather like framework knitting to supplement the family income; the operatives plaited wheat straw into patterned 'twist' for making straw hats, bonnets and other articles of apparel. The trade flourished from the 17th century to the first world war and was entirely a cottage industry carried on by women and children; in its heyday during the Napoleonic wars - when blockade and high import duties excluded foreign (especially Italian) plait - straw plaiting wives could earn appreciably more than their husbands. When Queen Victoria passed through Hitchin in 1851 on her way to Balmoral the station was decorated with straw plait! Like many industries before and since, the demise of straw plaiting came about because of cheaper foreign imports allied to a change in fashion.

Agriculture and its associated trades also had their particu-lar terms. A fellmonger removed hair and wool from hides and a lorimer (or loriner) made bits for horses' har-ness and other small iron ware. As well as the familiar tanner, a whittawer turned hide into white leather using alum and salt to retain the natural colour; the term came to mean a saddler or harness-maker. An oil cake maker pro-duced the cattle food - still used today - from rape or simi-lar seeds. The wainwright built or repaired wagons.

Domestic life gives us the terms (licensed) victualler, who supplied provisions, bodger - a maker of wooden chair legs and spars - and verge maker, who made the spindles used in clocks and watches. As well as the tiler, the shin-gler used wooden instead of slate tiles in roof construc-tion. The better off might have a scullion, a male servant who did menial work, as well as the more familiar domestics.

And so to the saggar maker's bottom knocker, a term which comes from the pottery industry. The saggar maker made fireclay containers - saggars - used for firing pottery and the bottom knocker was his assistant who tapped the bottom of the pots to check if they were sound. The bottom maker moulded the bottoms for the saggars.

The extractive industries give us a good crop of obsolete occupations, especially since coal and tin mining and similar occupations now play a very small role compared with the past. The hewer dug at the coal face and the putter filled trucks with hewn coal. Bal maidens were female mine workers employed on the surface and the term is also found in the clay and pottery industries. One of the least salubrious occupations was that of drawer, undertaken by women and children, the latter sometimes as young as six. They pulled the full baskets or wagons of coal: they wore a canvas belt to which a chain was attached which passed between their legs and hooked up to a sledge which was pulled to the surface. Graphic evidence on conditions can be found in a number of sources and especially in an 1833 government report; in 1842 it became illegal for girls and women, and boys under 10 years of age, to work underground. The banksman was in charge of the cages at the pit head.

Iron making is another industry which was enormously important in the past. The problem of converting cast to wrought iron was solved in the 1780s by a method known as 'puddling', one of the most arduous trades in early industry. The puddler heated cast iron in a reverbatory furnace and the molten metal was continuously stirred to allow the hot air to circulate through it; the carbon of the cast iron was oxidised and pure wrought iron left. It was a skilled as well as a hot and dirty job. The term was also used for someone who worked clay into a puddle to make things, such as canal walls, watertight. Transport gives us a number of unfamiliar terms although navvy is still used; originally it denoted a 'navigator', ie someone who worked on constructing the canals or railways. Similarly, a fireman stoked boilers, most commonly in railway engines, rather than put out fires. An apronman was a mechanic and an auger maker made augers, used for boring holes in wood.

In the professions terms from the past are still in use today, although the nature of their work may have changed. Even here, however, there are terms which are associated with a particular line of work which no longer exists: the system of poor relief in the 19th century, for example, gave us relieving officer and workhouse master as well as other occupations which are applicable to different organisations - medical officer, clerk, and so on.

This is just a small selection of terms for trades and occupations which either no longer exist or which have changed their nature beyond recognition. There are many more which could have been included. So where do you go for information on an occupation which is unfamiliar? Large dictionaries, such as the Oxford series, will cover some former occupations but they tend to concentrate on those with a longer time-span; 'modern' industries, such

as steel-making, pottery, and so on tend not to be included. Books on social and industrial history may help, especially those on particular industries. A 'new' tool, the internet, is an excellent source as in so many areas of life these days. While doing the research for this article I discovered two useful web sites: **http://cpcug.org/user/jlacombe/terms.html** and **www.rmhh.org.uk/occup.htm** The latter is the web site of the Hall family and must represent the tip of a very large iceberg. Try typing in an occupation term and see what comes up! The Open University has produced a Dictionary of Occupational Terms on CD-Rom, which costs £12.95 including postage and packing; further details can be found at **http://socsci.open.ac.uk/SocSci/da301/occs.html** where you can also try your hand at a quiz to see how many obsolete terms you can identify.

Occupations (such as cooper, farmer, smith) form one of the four main sources for family names in Britain so the reasons for wanting to know the derivation of an unusual term may extend beyond an interest in an ancestor's occupation. Occupations which became surnames will of course only include those in use when the use of family names to distinguish people became common, from about the 13th century; you won't, for example, find someone called Framework-knitter.

Because the nature of work is constantly changing, new terms are being coined all the time, or new meanings ascribed to existing words. The ICT industry is particularly rich (or poor, depending on your point of view!) giving us words such as word processor operator, programmer, web editor (or web master), software engineer, and so on. Similarly modern business and government has devised terms such as personal assistant, consultant, executive, auditor, social worker, etc. Developments in medicine introduces occupations which did not exist before the 20th century - radiographer, occupational therapist or paediatrician for example, together with practitioners of alternative medicine, such as aromatherapists, reflexologists or acupuncturists. Our descendents will not find it any easier than we have, trying to work out just what their ancestors did!

The Coroners Courts
Doreen Hopwood
explains this ancient inquiry

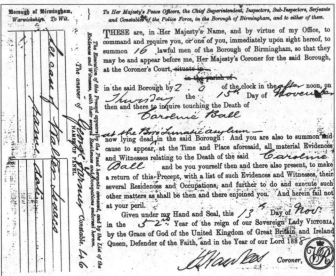

Since 1194, it has been the responsibility of the coroner to hold inquests on bodies of persons whose deaths were deemed to be sudden, unnatural or suspicious. Although survival of these records can be (at best) patchy and (at worst) virtually nil, they contain a wealth of information about our ancestors and the society in which they lived. The records of individual inquests are closed to public inspection for 75 years after the date of the inquest, but it is often possible to find a report about the case in a local, or even national, newspaper, provided that the date of death and/or inquest is known. In England and Wales, civil registration certificates of death show the verdict of the inquest in the 'cause of death' column and the coroner's name appears as the informant with the date and place of the inquest.

The medieval coroner was a person of high social standing, such as a knight, and also acted as Keeper of Crown Pleas and collected revenue associated with these for the Crown. Whilst the status of the coroner remained high, during Tudor times, his function and authority were reduced so that his sole responsibility became the holding of inquests on dead bodies.

Most surviving coroner's records are deposited in County Record Offices - often with the Quarter Sessions records - but some are held at the Public Record Office at Kew. Generally these relate to coroner's inquests which were handed to the assize justices and are for specific areas, like the Palatinates of Chester and Lancaster. Inquests held on prisoners who died in the Kings Bench Prison and the Millbank Penitentiary cover the mid-18th - 19th centuries and can be informative, especially concerning previous occupations (most of the prisoners in the Kings Bench Prison were debtors).

The inquest verdicts, which were in Latin until 1733, give the cause of death and the surviving depositions (the statements given by witnesses) contain fuller information.

The translated inquest of Simon Longe reads as follows:

8 Mar 1558. Petworth. Nicholas Lewkenor, county coroner. Jurors: William Ford, Robert Ford, Thomas Smythe, John Porborn, Richard Ford, Jervis Gobyll, John Shoccher, Robert Woodcott, Richard Gobyll, Thomas Hull, John Vennyll, Richard Lawrens, William Bishipe. About 2 p.m. on 7 Mar. Simon Longe was taken ill at Petworth and suddenly and unexpectedly died of his illness.

England and Wales were divided into circuits in 1558 and surviving 16th century inquests indicate that most were quickly and efficiently despatched to the Kings Bench by the coroners. It appears that the practice of handing in inquests had generally ceased in most circuits by about 1750, but there are exceptions. Although these records are numerous, they are not indexed at the PRO so can be difficult to locate, being filed with local indictment of crimes.

Generally speaking, the earlier the coroner's record, the less informative it will be for the family historian, but as well as giving the verdict of the inquest, the names of the jurors are listed. This could consist of between 12 and 23 "good and lawful" men summoned within one or two days of the discovery of a body and the number was reduced to between 7 and 11 in 1926. There were many debates as to whether or not local men made the most suitable jurors, and Judge William Blackstone in the 1760s recognised the problems which could arise

'A jury coming from the neighbourhood is in some respects a great advantage, but is often liable to strong expectations ... where one of the parties is popular and the other a stranger or obnoxious ... to summon a jury, labouring under local prejudices, is laying a snare for their consciences'.

In 1761, Edward Umfreville, Coroner for Middlesex suggested that in order to make a sound judgement, jurors should be 'of Sufficient Understanding and Competency of Estate, and at least Suspitious'.

Inquests could only be held upon view of the whole body - super visum corporis - and whilst this was deemed to be an unpleasant task for the jurors, the custom continued until the end of the nineteenth century. One of the Birmingham coroners found that, contrary to his expectations, jurors sometimes had to be persuaded to leave the place where the body was found. He had to resort to "such an expedient as suggesting a fever in order to effect a clearance - a stratagem which is instantaneously effectual".

It was not until 1860 that coroners became salaried individuals and all payments came from local rates. No legal or medical qualification was required until the passing of the 1926 Coroner's Act, and as recently as 1892 only a sixth of all coroners were doctors. The only prerequisite was that the appointed person was a landowner. Until 1887 coroners were elected by freeholders and then appointed by the local authority. Fees and payments varied from place to place, but from 1487 a coroner could receive a fee of 13s.4d per inquest resulting from homicide. Under the 1752 Act, fees were not to exceed £1.00 per inquest in gaols and £1.00 per inquest outside gaols plus 9d per mile for the journey from home to the body provided that the place where the body was found contributed to the county rate.

The coroner's bill (or voucher) often included the name of the deceased, the date and place of inquest, cause of death and verdict. One Wiltshire coroner's bill of 1775 reads:

'Alexander Applegarth, swallowed over three pints of distilled spirits called brandy and rum, instantly killed himself'

The cause of death in this case was fairly obvious, but not all verdicts were so cut and dried.

There was no legislative provision for the payment of medical witnesses testifying at inquests prior to 1836, so coroners were often discouraged from calling for medical evidence. Doctors who were selected by coroners to conduct an autopsy and give expert medical evidence after 1836 received a flat fee of one guinea (£1.05p) - however long the inquest lasted - plus one guinea for the autopsy. These fees remained fixed until the 1926 Coroners Act. The system was extended to incorporate boroughs in the The Municipal Corporations Act of 1835 and empowered magistrates to question (and sometimes refuse!) coroner's fees and expenses. Petty rivalry between coroners and magistrates continued throughout the 19th century, and coroners were careful not to antagonise the local authorities who controlled the purse strings by holding unnecessary inquests. Under the 1887 Act, coroners were obliged to conduct these where there was 'reasonable cause' to suspect that the subject had suffered 'either a violent or unnatural death, or had died a sudden death of which the cause is unknown'. This could be loosely interpreted and sometimes led to further tragedies as in the case of the seven-year-old son of Sarah Freeman who died in 1843 in Somerset of stomach pains after eating bread and butter. No inquest was held, despite the suspicions of the local doctor. She went on to kill her husband, brother and mother before being brought to trial and hanged in 1845.

Whenever a person was killed or died in the street his/her body was taken to the nearest public house

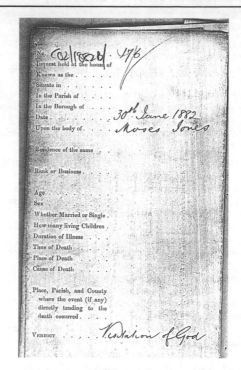

and, until after the inquest, it lay in some outbuilding - to the pain and mortification of relatives who wished to see the remains. By the late 19th century, most towns and cities had erected public mortuaries in different districts to alleviate this problem - and the health hazard of dead bodies remaining in overcrowded courts. It was also safer for the jurors who were obliged to see the body. An article in The Owl on 1st November 1899 commended this improvement '... so that jurymen can view them without risking their necks by ascending rickety stairs'. Until the 1870s, when a single jury was summoned for a day, separate juries could be appointed for individual inquests, therefore involving up to 100 persons for a days inquests. By the 1880s this reduced the annual number of jurors in Birmingham to 2,000 from 12,000 - to the relief of the ratepayers and court officials alike.

In the 19th century the majority of inquests were held in public houses. A Birmingham publican or innkeeper in 1845 was paid 'for the use of a room for a dead body until the inquest is held' a sum not exceeding 7s.6d, while he received the sum of 3s.6d per day for the use of a room for an inquest or inquests. The sheer volume of people coming and going from the makeshift courtrooms must have caused some congestion, although the licensed victualler may have enjoyed an increased profit!

Municipal mortuaries started being built after the Sanitary Act of 1866, but the use of public houses as inquest venues was not abolished until the 1910 Licensing Act. This was welcomed by the bereaved relatives who would no longer be exposed to the painful ordeal of an inquest in a beery and often ribald atmosphere.

The deodand was the object, which, by its movement, was deemed to be the cause of death. By ancient custom it could be given to the next of kin of the deceased, the parish or the manor. Alternatively, this could take the form of its monetary value but the practice died out by the mid 19th century because, by that time, people were being killed by the movement of heavy (and expensive!) machinery.

Deaths are usually reported to the coroner by either a doctor, registrar or the police in the form of a Notice to Coroner. If the coroner decides that an inquest is required, he instructs the police to summon the jurors and ensure that the witnesses appear at the Coroner's Court. The depositions, as in the case of Moses Jones, who died during punishment on the treadwheel at a Birmingham Prison in 1882, are usually retained with the inquest papers. As well as the witnesses' accounts of the circumstances surrounding the death, they may contain a character reference and quite detailed biographical information. The Inquisition shows the verdict of the court and includes the signatures of the jurors. The date is given as the year of the reign of the monarch, so the year of 1882 is written as 'the forty sixth year of the reign of our Sovereign Lady Victoria'.

Coroners could also be alerted by concerned individuals. In the case of Private White, in 1846, it was the vicar of Heston in Middlesex who intervened by refusing to bury the body without an inquest. White, aged 27, had been flogged under military law, but as the inquest progressed, it soon became evident that it was not simply an enquiry into the death of a young soldier, but that the whole system of corporal punishment in the army was on trial. Despite an active campaign, the use of the 'cat' was not finally abolished until 1881.

The entry in the regimental muster book reads under 'Reduction in strength':

Place of birth:	Camberwell
Trade when enlisted:	Hosier
Place and date on which became non-effective:	
	Hounslow 11 July 1846
How became non-effective:	Died

The cause of death on the original death certificate was given as a complaint of the liver, but was amended on 8th September 1846 as being due to '150 whip lashes'. The trial was eagerly followed by the public in newspapers and was the subject of many handbills.

When the post of Coroner became vacant in Birmingham in 1875, a treatise given by Thomas Gutteridge, surgeon, stressed the importance of appointing a qualified medical practitioner to the post:

'In the earliest times the coroner no more than the Leech could determine the with precision the influences that combined to stop life ... Anatomy has become paramount in the scientific analysis and surer than ordinary ocular observation and vocal testimony as to the infliction of injury and its consequences through which the individual perished'.

The lack of medical training on the part of the coroner is particularly evident in the early days of civil registration, where the verdict as to the cause of death is given as 'Visitation of God'. This term (or syncope) was often used to describe a sudden death where there were no suspicious circumstances. In 1846 Elizabeth Ayres, aged 45 years, was deemed to have died due to 'apoplexy brought on by passion' and the Coroner duly informed the registrar who recorded the verdict on the death certificate. Unfortunately the coroner's records have not survived, so what form the 'passion' took will never be known! Of the 1416 inquests held in the Borough of Birmingham between 1839 and 1844, no less than 562 showed a verdict of 'Visitation of God'.

Coroners often held office for many years, and Birmingham's first coroner, John Birt Davies, served from 1838 to 1875. Although having no political power, coroners - and their office - were highly respected.

It is important that the coroner's inquest and modern post mortem (medical examination) are not confused with the Inquisition Post Mortem. The latter is concerned in establishing the identity of the rightful heir of a deceased person, not the cause of death.

Coroners are also concerned about health and safety in workplaces, and any death due to an industrial disease also has to be reported to the coroner. Where an accident occurred (such as a colliery disaster or factory explosion), it is probable that much additional information can be obtained from local newspapers. The numbers of deaths due to house fires was reduced during the coronership of Henry Hawkes in Birmingham in the late 1800s because he consistently charged parents with neglect where children were burned to death. There was also an associated rise in the sale of fireguards.

Birmingham Daily Post
AND JOURNAL

THURSDAY, MARCH 5, 1914.

BRISTOL ROAD MOTOR SMASH.

RESUMED INQUEST.

JURY FIND THAT SPEED WAS EXCESSIVE.

The Birmingham City Coroner (Mr. I. Bradley) yesterday afternoon resumed the inquest on the body of Ernest Charles Bottle (26), dentist, of 131, Christchurch Road, Boscombe, who was killed in a motor smash in Bristol Road, Birmingham, on February 22. Mr. Bottle, whose skull was fractured, was a passenger in a motor-car owned and driven by Mr. Denham, of Alcester Lanes End, which collided with a taxi-cab at the corner of Belgrave Road and Bristol Road on Sunday week. Mr. A. Ward (instructed by Thwaite and Co.) appeared for Mr. Denham, Mr. A. J. Hatwell for deceased's family, Mr. Povey Harper for McKeever, the driver of the taxi-cab, and Mr. Urry (P. Baker and Co.) for McKeever's employers.

William Lloyd, 24, Horse Fair, said he was standing at the corner by St. Catherine's Church, in Bristol Street, when Mr. Denham's car passed. He estimated the speed at between forty and fifty miles an hour, and commented upon it to his friends.

accounts and the verdict of the coroner was instrumental in increasing road safety.

Occupational deaths were investigated, often leading to improvements in working conditions, although tragedies still happened - like the bell manufacturer who was killed by a fall of bells at the parish church, and the acrobat who gambolled off the stage into the orchestra pit.

Occasionally there are miscellaneous documents included in the coroner's records, such as the notes made by Isaac Bradley in Birmingham during the First World War. These record the deaths of over a hundred soldiers who died in the University Hospital from wounds and include home addresses for Australian, Irish and Belgian soldiers as well as an account of the circumstances of their wounding (where known).

Sadly, the survival of coroner's records is not consistent, but Jeremy Gibson's "Coroner's Records" is a comprehensive guide, county by county, to those which are known to have been deposited in record offices, libraries and other repositories. Once records are 15 years old, they can be weeded or sampled by the coroner - or he/she may decide to retain all papers - either at the coroner's office or place them in a relevant repository. However, certain classes of record have to be kept, and these include the indexed 'Registers of Deaths Reported', matters relating to treasure trove and cases of unique historical interest. For all of us family historians with an ancestor who was the subject of an inquest, we would hope that the case falls within the last category.

As well as giving details of individuals, the surviving coroners' records can give us an insight into the general conditions of the area in which our ancestors lived. The witnesses gave their statements under oath, so a true picture of circumstances surrounding a particular event is painted. Although the records themselves have a closure period of 75 years, under certain circumstances, and at the discretion of the coroner, they may be made available to members of the family.

During the Second World War, it was fairly unusual to find that a coroner's inquest had been held. Death certificates often simply show the cause of death as 'due to war operations'. Similarly, because of censorship, it is unlikely to find a report in the local newspapers.

Of all public officials it was the coroner who received the deepest insight into human tragedy, from tiny babies to the elderly. Few could have been as harrowing as the tragic demise of Stephen Potts, in 1851, who died at the age of ten weeks. The cause of death was given as 'accidental suffocation through compression against his mother's left breast when carried in arms and sucking in a snowstorm'. The large numbers of babies who suffocated in bed with parents or siblings is a sad testimony to the appalling overcrowded and unhealthy conditions in the back-to-back houses of Victorian cities. This is generally referred to as "overlaying" and was also the centre of much controversy as parents were accused of intentionally suffocating their offspring in this way.

As the amount of traffic increased on the roads, so did the number of road accidents and the collision in which Ernest Bottle died in 1914 made the headlines in the local press - as shown in the cutting. The inquest papers themselves consist of numerous witness

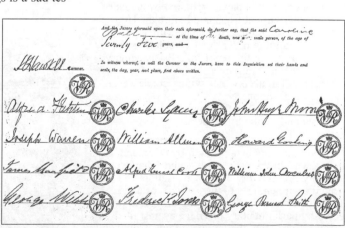

Parliamentary Papers
for Local and Family Historians
Simon Fowler suggests politics can help.....

Introduction
Over the years both family and local historians
have fought shy of using British Parliamentary
Papers, leaving them largely to academics. This is
a pity because they can contain material impossible
to find elsewhere and illuminate the lives of individuals and communities in a unique way. In addition they are remarkably well indexed and are so
easy to use.

Over the years these publications have had a variety of names, but in general they contain much of
the information needed by Parliament to conduct
its business. Collectively they are generally
known as Parliamentary Papers, although techni-
cally they are Sessional Papers, because they were
traditionally presented to Parliament by order. The
Victorians however generally knew them as Blue
Books, because they were bound in blue paper.
The tradition is continued today for 'white papers'
outlining government proposals for policy, and
'green papers' consultative documents published
by the government are still often to be found in
white or green covers.

Both the House of Lords and the House of
Commons have the right to call for papers to be
published. In practise however the sessional
papers produced for each house are virtually identical, and most researchers just use the papers produced for the Commons as the most important of
the houses of Parliament.

Parliamentary papers can be broken down into the
following categories:
* Returns made in response to an order made by
    the House;
* Command papers presented by command of
    the Sovereign;
* Act papers, that is papers required by an act of
    Parliament to be laid before the House;
* Papers presented in accordance with a
    standing order or to a resolution of the
    House to the report of a Parliamentary
    select committee;
* Papers laid in accordance with secondary
    legislation;
* Petitions laid before the House;
* Private and public bill papers.

Also included are the Command Papers which
are government papers printed 'by command' of
the Crown. In the eighteenth century they were
normally presented by Privy Counsellors and
printed as appendices to the Journals of the
House of Commons. After 1833 they were protected by parliamentary privilege against libel
action. From 1921 the number of new Command

Papers was radically reduced as an economy measure, but treaties, White Papers, and reports of
Royal Commissions and other major committees of
enquiry continued to be published as Command
Papers.

Contents
The first Parliamentary Papers date from the seventeenth century. Some of the earliest surviving
records concern petitions made to Parliament for
redress of grievances. In February 1641, for example, the Company of Weavers petitioned the
Commons complained of certain imposts granted
in 1638 by the King to Thomas Bushell and
Thomas Carlton. In the same month Richard
Cowdrey of Basingstoke, husbandman, petitioned
the Commons against Richard Bagnall who took
the petitioners' only barn and yard to make saltpe-
tre. There is rather less material for the eighteenth
century. Even so some interesting material can be
found, such as the extensive collections of papers
known as the Papists' Returns of 1705-6, 1767 and
1781 which list every individual Roman Catholic.
Age, occupation and residence for the people listed
are often included. Many of the seventeenth and
eighteenth century Parliamentary Papers, including the Papists' Returns, were not published and
can only be seen at the Parliamentary Archives

(formerly the House of Lords Record Office) in manuscript form. Details are given below. Fortunately by the end of the eighteenth century an increasing proportion of papers were being printed and published.

The Victorians

The heyday of the Parliamentary Paper was undoubtedly the Victorian period reflecting a contemporary obsession with facts and statistics. An obsession which of course was mocked in Charles Dickens's Hard Times. Vast numbers of papers were published each year on almost every subject under the sun. In part this was the result of the increasing complexity and extent of Victorian government.

New departments and offices which were set up, such as the Public Record Office, the Registrar of Friendly Societies, and the Poor Law Commissioners, were usually obliged to submit an annual report to Parliament which often included voluminous appendices on all aspects of the department's work. The PRO's annual report, for example, included a detailed description of the classes of records listed each year. Indeed these lists were so comprehensive that for some records they are still the main finding aid. The Poor Law Commission, and its successors, often gave details of cases relating to individual paupers particularly if some new precedent was being made.

These new departments were established as the result of recommendations made by Royal Commissions or Parliamentary select committees. These bodies would make prepare a report for Parliament, which were often accompanied by voluminous books of evidence and transcripts of interviews with witnesses.

Two of the most famous of these commissions were the royal commissions on the poor law that sat between 1832 and 1834 and 1906 and 1909. The earlier commission recommended the establishment of a nationwide network of workhouses. But its appendices vividly show the state of the poor law across England and Wales, even down to individual pauper families.

At St Lawrence, Reading, the commissioners came across the Benn family and their children Francis, John, Charles and Mary who was married to John Parker. The local poor law commissioner 'asked the governor [of the workhouse] how this last and most widely spread branch arose? - that he said was our overseer's doing. I warned him against it but he would do it. Benn's daughter became pregnant by a weaver named Parker and the overseer made him marry her and see what the parish has got by it - eight more mouths to feed already and eight more backs to find clothes for.'

In another part of the appendices can be found a list of poor of the village of Thurgarton, Nottinghamshire. The list included Robert Barker who had had eleven children, seven living. The rent of his cottage and garden was 21 shillings a year. He had £25 11 shillings and sixpence in a savings book. His wages were 10 shillings a week which increased to 12 shillings during the harvest. Living at home was a grown up daughter 'almost an idiot.' Where else could you find such information?

Incidentally the commissioners seem to have had a keen interest in the beer available at workhouses. At St Lawrence Reading one of the commissioners, Edwin Chadwick, tasted the local brew and found it 'excellent.'

Sixty years later the other great royal commission on the poor law gathered voluminous evidence about the state of welfare for the poor at the beginning of the twentieth century. They were particularly concerned about the abuse of the many small local charities that existed in many places. An unnamed clergyman in York told the commissioners that: 'In my own parish there were 'great rows' unless every one got a share of the endowed charities. He added 'I think there is a general feeling among the clergy that the less they have to do with the Christmas doles the better. My churchwarden often has a window broken, and one of my clerical brethren has his bell-handle pulled off. I live outside the parish luckily.'

The enquiring nature of the Victorians also meant that the records of the select committees also offer a fascinating insight into the society of the period. Select committees were, and indeed still are, groups of MPs or peers set up to investigate issues of the day. During the 1850s several such committees, for example, investigated the scandal of the emigration ships taking emigrants to new lives in America. Witnesses described the over crowded conditions on board. One such was Lt Hutchinson RN, the harbour master of Kingstown near Dublin, who told MPs 'I should recommend that the berthing of passengers below should be fitted up in quite a decent manner. I think it is most indecent to have four persons sleeping in a compartment of six feet by six feet; they have not more than their coffins.'

Another popular subject was crime, especially in

the early years of the nineteenth century which experienced a crime wave. A London policeman told a committee on the police in 1816 about 'the easy mode servant girls have of turning any thing they can bring away into money. There is scarcely what is called a chandler's shop in any part of the Metropolis... but buys old bottles or linen, or anything that a servant girl, when she goes there to purchase things, can take with her... This species of domestic robbery... is increasing still greatly. Servants have become vile in the extreme; servant girls in particular; they are infamous.'

Various Parliamentary committees also exposed the administrative chaos of the Crimean War. After the war in 1856 Florence Nightingale told one such committee: 'By an oversight, no candles were included among the stores brought to the Crimea. Lamps and wicks were brought but not oil. These omissions were not supplied until after possession had been taken of Balaklava, and the purveyor had an opportunity of purchasing candles and oil from the shipping and the dealers in the town. It appears to us that the hospital accommodation in the field for the sick and wounded has been very inadequate. Bell tents, as well as from the materials of which they are made as from their shape and size are peculiarly ill-adapted for hospital purposes.'

Of course Parliamentary Papers continue to be published. Indeed the number published now is probably greater than ever before, but curiously they seem less informative, certainly less vivid, than their predecessors of a century or so ago.

Location and use

It can be hard to track down sets of Parliamentary Papers. Many university libraries will have sets as should the largest reference libraries. The Parliamentary Archives, of course, has a complete set including those papers which it was decided for one reason or another not to publish. For many people however the most accessible set is the one to be found on microfiche in the Microfilm Reading Room at the PRO in Kew. The PRO also has a set of original Parliamentary Papers up to 1801 in class ZHC 1. More about the PRO's holdings can be found in a leaflet Parliamentary Papers (Domestic Records Information 7) available from the PRO or downloadable from the PRO website.

The Society of Genealogists however has very little, reflecting the lack of interest traditionally shown by family historians in this material. However, it does have lists of paupers who had been in workhouses for more than five years published in 1865; lists of Royal Naval invalids and pensioners in 1866 and 1868, a list of Trinity House petitioners of 1836, and lastly a list of Polish refugees who received grants from the British government between 1837 and 1841.

Fortunately Parliamentary Papers are well indexed, so it shouldn't be difficult to see whether there is anything on your subject. The index, between 1801 and 1997, has been published on CD-ROM, a copy of which is held in the PRO library. Otherwise it is necessary to use the published General Indexes which were published in three volumes for the periods 1801-1851, 1852-1899, and 1900-1949. There is also a similar index for the eighteenth century.

Whether you use the CD-ROM or the General Indexes you will need to grasp the reference system. Each parliamentary paper is assigned a unique reference which describes the Parliamentary Session (ie 1914) with the volume the paper can be found in always given in lower case Roman numerals (i.e. lxix) followed by the page number where the paper can be found in the volume (i.e. 598). Thus the 'Statement for each Month of the Year 1914 of the Number of Paupers Relieved in England and Wales' is Parliamentary Paper 1914.lxix.598. It is very easy to confuse your Roman numerals and on occasion volumes have not been paginated. But in general it is a simple system which works well.

In addition Command papers have their own numbering system.
* Between 1833 and 1869 - unprefixed numbers 1-4222
* 1869-1899   - C.1-9250
* 1900-1918   - Cd. 1-9239
* 1919-1956   - Cmd. 1-9889
* 1956-1986   - Cmnd. 1-9927
* 1986   - Cm. 1-

Pitfalls

Parliamentary papers are a complete hotchpotch.

This is their joy and their greatest downfall. All too often a promising series of statistics, such as lists of paupers, are published only for a year or two and then abandoned as the MP who called for the original papers to be kept looses interest or leaves the House. In other cases what seems to be promising material turns out to be deeply disappointing, while conversely what seems almost ephemeral turns out to be crock of gold.

These papers can also be maddeningly inconsistent, with similar subjects or enquiries covered in completely different ways. And at times, for a layman, they can be difficult to follow.

Researchers too should be wary that these papers are political documents that may have been doctored to suit particular interests and should not necessarily be taken at face value. Witnesses used the forum of a select committee to advocate one particular view or exaggerate a problem in order to make a point.

But for all that Parliamentary Papers are a wonderful source, particularly for nineteenth century social history. They may appear daunting but with a bit of practise their riches are open to almost anyone. Local historians will find them of most use, but family historians, particularly those who are interested in the lives lead by his or her ancestors, can also find them a fascinating source.

Further reading
The PRO leaflet mentioned above offers a good (if slightly dated) introduction. The only detailed guide is Maurice Bond, The Records of Parliament: a Guide for Genealogists and Local Historians (Phillimore, 1964) which is long out of print. In the last year or so The Stationery Office has reprinted a selection of the more generally interesting investigations in a new series of 'Uncovered Editions', such as the ones on the Siege at Mafeking and Ladysmith in 1899-1900 to the House of Lords debate on UFOs in 1979. For more information see the rather confusing Stationery Office website - www.the-stationery-office.co.uk - Many bookshops sell these editions as well.

The major source for all aspects of Parliamentary History is the Parliamentary Archives, whose address is:
House of Lords, London SW1A 0PW
(020)- 7219 3074 (Telephone)
(020)- 7219 2570 (Fax)
hlro@parliament.uk (e-mail)
http://www.parliament.uk/archives

The Archives is open to the general public, but potential visitors should make an appointment in advance and have a pretty good idea of what he or she is looking for.

Simon Fowler is the Editor of Family History Monthly and worked for many years at The Public Record Office. Prior to becoming editor of Family History Monthly he was at the Society of Genealogists.

Apprenticeship
and the new poor law

Kate Thompson

Most family historians will associate the system of pauper apprenticeship with the old poor law and may not be aware that the system continued after 1834, despite attempts by central authority to stop the practice. It was felt, no doubt with some justification, that the children put out as apprentices were subject to serious abuse, and cases of cruelty and neglect were fairly common. When total abolition proved impossible, legislation was passed in 1844 and 1851 designed to restrict the term of apprenticeship and thus avoid the worst abuses. The 1844 Act abolished compulsory apprenticeship and prescribed the duties of masters and the terms and conditions of the indentures. No child under the age of nine or who could not read and write his own name was to be bound; no premium was to be paid unless the apprentice was maimed, deformed or suffering from permanent infirmity; no one over fourteen was to be bound without his consent and no one under sixteen without his father's consent (if still alive); no term of apprenticeship was to exceed eight years. The 1851 Act provided for the prosecution of cases of neglect or ill-treatment, and for a register of all those under sixteen to be kept; the apprentices were to be visited at least twice a year by the relieving officer or other nominated member of staff. In practice many of these regulations were ignored, especially the one on premiums.

The Leicester Poor Law Union, among others, felt that the regulations introduced in 1844 were too restrictive and persuaded the Poor Law Commissioners to amend some of them. The guardians seem to have tried to ensure that their apprentices were well taught and treated kindly, and they used a system of inter-union co-operation for weeding out unsuitable employers. They also demonstrated a sensible attitude towards the town's economy by resolving not to bind a boy to a framework knitter 'as generally speaking the object of the Master is only to obtain the premium; and the Trade is so over-handed already that it is only Apprenticing a boy to learn pauperism under another name'.[1]

Leicester shared a common problem with its apprentices: there were cases of boys absconding and masters who ill-treated their charges. A committee of three guardians was appointed to visit the apprentices as laid down in 1851, and the relieving officers also paid them regular visits. An apprenticeship register survives from November 1844 and contains entries up to 1927.[2] It records the name of the apprentice, date of the apprenticeship, sex, age, parents' names (if alive), residence, parish, name of master, his trade and residence, the term

of the apprenticeship and the premium paid. There are 476 entries covering the period of the volume and the information contained can be analysed in a number of different ways by local historians, as well as being used by family historians seeking information on particular individuals. However, it is not indexed by surname so, unless the date of apprenticeship is known, it could be a frustrating task to find relevant information on a named individual.

The pattern of apprenticeship

476 entries over 43 years gives an average of about eleven apprenticeships a year but of course the pattern varied considerably. The greatest activity occurred in the first ten years and the maximum number of boys (34) were apprenticed in 1849. Towards the end of the period numbers dropped significantly to the extent that no cases at all were recorded in some years. The economy of the town improved considerably after about 1850 and the reduction in pauper apprentices no doubt owes as much to this fact as to a changing attitude towards the system.

Figures for the number of children in the workhouse are not available for exactly the same period as covered by the apprenticeship register, but the surviving records show that in 1848 to 1853 there was an average of 56 children aged seven to fifteen in the workhouse, made up of 34 boys and 22 girls and representing 18% of the inmates. In the period 1853-1871 the ages recorded are for nine to sixteen year olds, children more eligible for apprenticeship than the slightly younger group. The average had risen to 72 (43 boys, 29 girls) but they represented only 14% of the workhouse population. There was a much higher number of children in the schools (156: 88 boys and 68 girls) and undergoing industrial training (40: 26 boys, 14 girls), indicating the board of guardians' belief in the value of education for pauper children. The only discernible change in the period 1853 to 1871 is that the number of children given industrial training rose from 19 in the mid 1850s to 47 in the 1860s.

Only one of the 476 cases involved a girl and this was a particularly interesting one, so much so that Sidney and Beatrice Webb in their monumental work on the new poor law, refer to it[3]; it is described in more detail later in this article. 252 (53%) of the children were orphans and a further 56 (12%) had been deserted by their parents, so that these two categories, as might be expected, made up the majority of cases. The parents of two boys were transported, four were in the asylum and one in gaol.

The age of the apprentices and length of service
The 'traditional' view that boys were universally apprenticed at the age of 14 for seven years has been successfully challenged by local studies of the subject, although most apprenticeships conformed roughly to that pattern. The Leicester records indicate that the pattern was quite varied: the youngest boys were 11 although there were only two of them, and the eldest (only one) was 18. The other figures are:
Age 12 - 22, Age13 - 135,Age 14 - 154, Age 15 - 117, Age 16 - 37, Age 17 - 4
The vast majority, therefore, fell in the 13 to 15 age range, accounting for 406, or 85% of the total; the ages for four boys was not recorded.

Seven years was the most common term, accounting for 175 boys or 37% of the total, but there was a range between two and nine years; there was a discernible trend towards shorter terms at the end of the period covered by the register. Curiously, six year terms were not as popular as those for five or seven. Terms were sometimes for less than whole years so in the following table they have been given to the nearest whole figure:

Two years	1
Three years	8
Four years	36
Five years	124
Six years	79
Seven years	178
Eight years	45
Nine years	1

The terms of four boys were similarly unrecorded.

Occupational pattern
Nationally the most popular trade for apprentices was shoemaking, followed by tailoring; in Norfolk, for example, 80% of boys apprenticed between 1834 and 1863 were assigned to shoemakers.[4] A slightly less striking pattern was found in Leicester, where after about 1850 shoemaking became an important trade. 95 boys were appren-

ticed to cordwainers and 47 to boot and shoe makers, giving a total of 142 or 30% of the total; a further 122 (26%) were apprenticed to tailors so that over half of all apprenticeships were to these two trades. Thereafter the figures dropped substantially: the next most common occupation for apprentices was that of blacksmith (41 boys, 9%) and only two other trades made double figures: bakers and confectioners (25 boys) and barbers and hairdressers (10 boys). Appendix 1 lists all the trades to which boys were apprenticed, together with the numbers involved. Unusual apprenticeships were to fishermen (considering how far Leicester is from the coast) and to an attorney; other masters reflected the town's principle trades, such as framesmith, sinker maker and last maker.

Place of apprenticeship
Not surprisingly most boys were apprenticed to men in the town of Leicester, accounting for 318 (67%) but this was more evident at the beginning of the period than at the end. Most of the remainder went to villages within the county and only 23 (5%) travelled outside Leicestershire; of these, all but the four boys who were apprenticed to fishermen in Grimsby went to neighbouring counties but not, somewhat surprisingly, to Rutland. The maximum number apprenticed to any one place outside Leicester was nine (to Earl Shilton). Appendix 2 gives details of all the places to which boys were sent.

The case of Catherine Roberts
The most unusual apprenticeship and the only one involving a girl, was that of Catherine Roberts, who was deaf and dumb. When her term at the London Deaf and Dumb Asylum ended at Christmas 1854 the board went to considerable trouble to find someone to take her as an apprentice. Eventually a Miss Mary Weston of Kibworth Harcourt, a milliner and dressmaker, agreed to do so on condition that she did not have to provide medical attendance and at a considerably increased premium of £40, made up of four half-yearly instalments of £8, and £8 worth of clothing. The Poor Law Board was very reluctant to agree but eventually issued a special order. At first Roberts appeared to do well but in March 1857 came the first sign of trouble when her mother wanted to take her away from Kibworth. The clerk to the guardians wrote to the girl at some length, pointing out all that the board had done for her - in return for which they wanted her to try to maintain her respectability, which she could never do if she lis-

apprenticeship could not be established as it would have given the girls a settlement in Mayfield. The board apparently went ahead with the plan without the approval of the Poor Law Commissioners who were opposed to it. The arrangement continued until about 1859 and girls were sent from time to time to Mayfield and also to the neighbouring Hanging Bridge Mill, owned by a Mr Cooper. The board appeared to think the scheme a success, telling the Ashby de la Zouch union in 1853: 'All the Girls we have sent have turned out exceeding well, and they were treated in the kindest manner and provided for most comfortably'.[7] The Clerk to the Board also sometimes wrote to the girls themselves and on one occasion there is a hint that all was not well when he urged them: 'Be good girls don't be inclined to grumble at trifles, and [if] ever you feel uncomfortable or discontented think also, how much worse off you might be, - God bless You all'.[8]

Conclusion

There is considerable evidence in the records of the Leicester Poor Law Union to show that the guardians took greater care than others in the welfare of the children put out to apprentice; the Bangor and Beaumaris Union for example took little care to see that its apprentices were treated humanely by their masters until shamed into doing so in the 1860s by the school inspector.[9] Moreover the Leicester board was anxious that the apprentices should not bear any obvious marks of pauperism; on one occasion it said: 'We wish to give the boys a start in the world without it appearing either by their dress or otherwise that [they] had been paupers'.[10] The apprenticeship register, while not unique, covers a long time span and the large number of entries makes it possible to draw several conclusions on the pattern of pauper apprenticeship in the town. No doubt further work of a social, demographic or genealogical nature could be undertaken and for family historians there is a wealth of personal detail on the apprentices and the men to whom they were bound.

tened to the 'temptings' of her mother: 'Were you to yield to her wishes the result would possibly be, that you would be deprived of your Clothing bit by bit, to provide her with intoxicating drink, and again find your way back to the Workhouse and remain a pauper to the end of your days'.[5] The following February Miss Weston complained about Roberts' behaviour. In his reply the clerk expressed his anger that after all the trouble and expense the board had taken in the case 'all should be thrown away and that she should prefer the vagabond life of her mother, to decency and order'. He added, in an interesting comment on contemporary thought: 'it is enough to make us believe that there is something so inherently bad in the nature of these poor, ignorant creatures, that no care and attention will eradicate it, and that the raising either them or their children in the social scale is altogether lost labour'.[6] There are no further references to Roberts beyond an instruction to the clerk to go to Kibworth so the eventual outcome is unknown.

Mayfield Mills

There is a further interesting case which was not strictly concerned with apprenticeship but which involved a number of female paupers who, as already indicated, did not figure in the statistics. In late 1844 the Leicester board of guardians received an offer from a Mr Chambers, the owner of a cotton mill at Mayfield just outside Ashbourne on the Derbyshire/Staffordshire border. He was looking for girls to train as doublers (as the name suggests they doubled thread for spinning) and would provide them with food, lodging and clothing for three years. The guardians were anxious to accept the offer and after enquiry were satisfied with Chambers' character; however a formal

Appendix 1: occupational pattern

[NB some linking of occupations has been made]

tailor/draper	122
wheelwright/coachbuilder	5
cordwainer	95
machinist; sinker-maker; boot/shoe maker	47
stone mason; fisherman	4
blacksmith, etc	41
rope maker; engineer/mechanic	3
baker/confectioner	25
watch/clock maker; bricklayer; barber/hairdresser	10
ironmonger; last maker; fancy carpenter, joiner, etc	9
hosier; basket maker; brush painter & decorator; builder	8
maker; chairmaker/upholsterer	2
nail/screw/needle maker; saddler; attorney; plasterer; cooper; silk wood turner	7

dyer; milliner/dressmaker	1
tinman/brazier; framesmith; butcher; coal miner; grocer; plumber/glazier; cabinet maker	6

Appendix 2: place of apprenticeship

Leicester	318
Earl Shilton	9
Coalville	8
Ibstock	7
Anstey; Burbage; Countesthorpe	5
Aylestone; Desford; Frolesworth; Market Bosworth	4
Belgrave; Hinckley; Oadby; Sapcote; Shepshed; Stoney Stanton; Whitwick; Wigston	3
Barwell; Carlton; Dunton Bassett; Gilmorton; Market Harborough; Mountsorrel; Nailstone: Newbold Verdon; Sileby; Thurmaston; Whetstone	2
Arnesby; Billesdon; Broughton Astley; Congerstone; Evington; Fleckney; Gaddesby; Glenfield; Great Dalby; Halstead; Higham on the Hill; Houghton on the Hill; Hugglescote; Kibworth Harcourt; Kilby; Kirby Muxloe; Knossington; Leire; Lubenham; Markfield; Medbourne; Melton Mowbray; Narborough; North Kilworth; Primethorpe; Quorn; Ratby; Ravenstone; Shackerstone; Snarestone; Somerby; Stretton Parva; Syston; Thurlaston	1
Bedworth (Warwickshire)	6
Grimsby (Lincolnshire)	4
Long Eaton (Derbyshire); Nuneaton, Rugby (Warwickshire);	2
Repton, Woodville (Derbyshire); Castle Bytham, Wisbech (Lincolnshire); Kettering, Welford, Weston by Welland (Northamptonshire)	1

References
1 Leicestershire Record Office (LRO), records of the Leicester Poor Law Union, 26D68/239, no 2073, 8 December 1845
2 LRO, 26D68/1181
3 S & B Webb, *English Poor Law Policy* (1963), p 113n
4 N Longmate, *The Workhouse* (1974), p 188
5 LRO, 26D68/249, no 153, 26 March 1857
6 *Ibid*, no 272, 12 September 1857; 26D68/250, no 44, 3 February 1858
7 LRO, 26D68/246, no 107, 20 January 1853
8 LRO, 26D68/247, no 86, 18 April 1854
9 H G Williams, 'The education of workhouse children in the Bangor and Beaumaris Union 1846-80', *Gwynedd Archives Service Bulletin*, no 2, 1975
10 LRO, 26D68/247, no 196, 24 August 1854

Man of Kent or Kentish Man?

Veronica Craig-Mair B.A. M.A.

The River Medway forms a natural boundary between East and West Kent, and traditionally those born south of the river (East Kent) are Men of Kent and those born north (West Kent) are Kentish Men. Although sometimes derided as "a distinction without a difference", the distinction between Men of Kent and Kentish Men can make a considerable difference when searching for ancestors in the county.

There is debate over some of the issues described in the following brief history, but it is widely accepted that the name of the county, Kent, derives from the Celtic tribe inhabiting the region two thousand years ago. In De Bello Gallico Julius Caesar, writing of his invasion of Britain in 55/54BC said: 'Ex his hominibus longe sunt humanissime qui Cantium incolunt', that is 'of all these people by far the most civilised are those who inhabit Kent'. A reputation those with Kentish origins still maintain.

Towards the end of Roman rule in Britain, Germanic tribes were initially invited to settle in return for their assistance in defending the country against marauding Saxons. Under their leaders Hengist and Horsa these first incomers, arguably Jutes, were granted lands in the south and east of the county. After the defeat of the British king Vortigern at the Battle of Aylesford in 455, more Germanic peoples arrived, probably from Frisia, who settled north of the river Medway. It seems then that there may have been a cultural distinction between the two parts of Kent from this period.

There are references in the Anglo-Saxon Chronicle to both Men of Kent and Kentish Men, indicating that a distinction may well have been recognised during the Saxon period, and certainly East and West Kent were sometimes ruled by different kings. When King Alfred the Great divided the country into counties in 892, East and West Kent were united and, as the only old kingdom to retain its boundaries, Kent can rightly claim to be the oldest county.

Despite Duke William's successful invasion in 1066, Kent claims never to have been conquered. According to Thomas Spot, a chronicler of St Augustine's Abbey in Canterbury, Stigande, the Archbishop of Canterbury and Egelsine, the Abbot of St Augustines, incited the men of Kent to take a stand against the Normans invaders. A meeting was arranged with the king at Swanscombe, where each Man gathered a green bough which he held over his head. At first King William was amused, thinking it was a wood miraculously moving towards him, but he was then confronted by their spokesman offering an ultimatum from the Commons of Kent: Peace if they were allowed to keep their 'ancient liberties', otherwise war. William wisely agreed to their demands. War was avoided and Kent's motto, Invicta, still proclaims the fact that the county was never conquered.

Amongst the ancient liberties demanded by the Commons of Kent was their system of inheritance called Gavelkind. As in most parts of England at the time, Norman inheritance was by primogeniture, i.e. by right the eldest son inherited all his father's estate. In contrast, under Gavelkind the estate was divided equally between all sons, or daughters if there were no sons, with the youngest inheriting the hearth. In the days when life expectancy was short, and men could expect to die before their children reached adulthood, this was an extremely practical and wise law, since it meant that children too young to fend for themselves were not made homeless and that widows, too, were given protection.

Primogeniture encouraged estates to be passed on intact, but through Gavelkind the division of an estate between offspring led to holdings decreasing in size over time until eventually they could become too small to support a family. To avoid this many families co-operated as a kin group, with childless men arranging for their land to go back into the family land pool on their death. There was also a very active land market, as families bought, sold and exchanged quite small plots of land in an attempt to build up a holding large enough to be viable. Gavelkind was not removed from the Statute books until 1926, and as a result land records and deeds can be a particularly fruitful source of genealogical information.

Just as Gavelkind land could be sold, it could also be bequeathed and with time greater numbers of men chose to leave their main estates to the eldest son. Here wills are a wonderful source of information but, beware... Prior to 1858 wills were proved in church courts, of which there were a number in Kent, with both Canterbury and Rochester having Consistory and Archdeaconry courts, as well as the exempt deanery of Shoreham and the Peculiar of Cliffe. Unfortunately there is no comprehensive index to the wills proved in all these courts.

Over the centuries kings and their subjects had bequeathed land to the Church for political and pious reasons, with the Church being the second largest landholder after the king. This was particularly the case in Kent where, by the time of the Domesday survey, the Church held some 50% and Odo, Bishop of Bayeux another 30% of the land in Kent. Perhaps surprisingly, this has advantages for the genealogist. The Church was a careful record keeper, and had both the scribes to make the records and the facilities in which to store them. In particular the monks of Christ Church and of St Augustine's Abbey kept a close eye on the tithes and rents due to them, and in these are listed many ordinary men and women. Through these accounts, although it may not be possible to establish a firm pedigree, it is sometimes possible to show that a family was resident in a specific part of Kent way back to the fourteenth or even thirteenth centuries.

On arrival in 597 St Augustine created the first English diocese at Canterbury, but when Pope Gregory's strategy for the conversion of the English did not go to plan, Rochester diocese was established in 604. There are some who consider the distinction between Men of Kent and Kentish Men to be based on these dioceses, and to have ecclesiastical rather than lay origins. The weakness of this argument lies in the fact that although Rochester diocese covers all of West Kent, because Rochester Cathedral is on the south bank of the river a chunk of East Kent land had to be granted to the new diocese. As it is possible to be born south of the river but in Rochester diocese, it is not the diocese in which a man is born which affects his status, although the ecclesiastical division can have an impact on research for family historians.

When it comes to tracing ancestors, Kentish Men have advantages in that West Kent parishes are quite well covered by the IGI, and also by the excellent series of transcripts of parish registers up to 1813 on microfiche, published by the Kent Family History Society. At present East Kent is very poorly represented on the IGI, and coverage by the KFHS microfiche transcripts is also very patchy. However, whilst they may not be so well indexed, Men of Kent are better served by diocesan records than Kentish Men. In general the survival rate of parish registers is better in Canterbury than Rochester diocese, and the Archbishop's Transcripts are more complete than the Rochester diocese Bishop's Transcripts. For the Archdeaconry of Canterbury there are also Archdeacon's Transcripts, which means the parishes within this area are well served indeed.

Besides the long established families, Kent's geographical situation as the point nearest the continental mainland has made it the entry point for waves of migrants over the centuries, especially those fleeing religious or political persecution. Some families established themselves firmly in the county, such as the Huguenot community in Canterbury. Others moved on quite quickly, but often left a trace of their passage in the records. And, of course, as well as immigrants, Kent was also the last stopping place for many emigrants before departure. American descendants of some of the passengers on the Mayflower can trace their line through the registers of Sandwich parish where a group of non-conformists gathered and continued to produce offspring whilst they awaited the financing of their migration to be completed. As well as migrants, the Kent coast is famously the departure point for armies in times of conflict, with men from all over the country stationed in barracks in Kent, meeting local lasses, fathering children, and even dying on home soil both before and after their service on the battlefield.

Although other counties may have claim to a longer coastline, the number and importance of Kent's ports has led to many traders and sailors leaving a fleeting mark in the records. But, besides those just 'passing through', Kent's ports also pulled in men in search of work, especially in the Medway area. In the 16th century places like Chatham and Gillingham were small villages, unable to supply the labour required in the rapidly developing Royal Dockyards at Chatham. From a village of a few hundred people in 1600, by 1700 Chatham had become a town with a population of over 5,000. Some had come willingly, but many others were conscripted, chiefly from ports such as Portsmouth and Weymouth. Some, such as shipwrights, were pressed for their skills, but there was such a great demand for labour generally that the conscripts included the young and the unskilled, from inland as well as along the coast.

Of course the movement of workers has not been all one way. London has long been a magnet for those looking for opportunities and, being on Kent's doorstep, has always drawn in Kent folk. Following local government boundary changes, first Greenwich and Lewisham in 1889, then Bromley and Bexley in 1965, became London boroughs and the Capital took over the administration, if not the hearts, of some Kentish Men. Those trying to trace their ancestors in this part of Kent have particular problems.

For many counties the County Record Office is also the home of the diocesan archives, with civil and ecclesiastical records conveniently held in the same repository, but this is far from being the case in Kent. The Kent Archives Service has been working on their collection policy, but it is beyond the scope of this article to attempt even to précis the resultant document. Where county-wide collections cannot be split, e.g. Quarter Session records, they are held at the Centre for Kentish Studies at Maidstone, but otherwise documents are collected according to the relevant Diocese, Archdeaconry or Local Government Administrative District. A list of the main Kentish repositories can be found at the end of this article, and the warning to phone before a visit, to ensure the documents you wish to consult are available, is particularly vital in Kent. The staff are always pleased to check, and can often suggest alternative documentary sources to save you travelling to numerous locations.

I acknowledge that, in using the masculine form throughout I could be accused of political incorrectness, but there is no such 'distinction' for females. Joan Plantagenet (1328-1385), the daughter of Edmund, Earl of Kent, married Edward, the Black Prince in 1361 and was described by Froissart in his Chronicle as "the most beautiful woman in all the realm of England, and the most loving". She was in return loved by all the people. It is after Joan that all Kent females, from East or West of the county, are known as Fair Maids of Kent.

The main Kent Archives and their phone numbers:
Centre for Kentish Studies - 01622 694363
Canterbury Cathedral Archives - 01227 865330
East Kent Archives Centre - 01304 829306
Medway Archives & Local Studies Centre - 01634 732714
Bromley Public Library, Archives Sect- (020) 8460 9955
Bexley Local Studies & Archives Centre - 01322 562574

Veronica Craig-Mair B.A. M.A.
After a first career in librarianship, a family move to Canterbury provided Veronica with the opportunity to read History at the University of Kent at Canterbury. She then built on a long-standing interest in family history by studying for her genealogical qualifications at the Institute of Heraldic and Genealogical Studies, and now works as a genealogist specialising in Kent families and local history.

Founded **AGRA** *1968*
Incorporated *1998*

The Association of
Genealogists & Record Agents

was founded in **1968** to promote high standards and professional conduct amongst family historians providing a research service to the public. Membership is open to those with recognised qualifications or inspection of case work by AGRA's Board of Assessors. Successful applicants must agree to abide by a Code of Practice.

An annual publication is produced listing members, their addresses and areas of expertise. This can be purchased from **The Society of Genealogists, Guildhall Library** or **The Secretaries, AGRA, 29 Badgers Close, Horsham, West Sussex RH12 5RU.** Please send £2.50 or 6 IRCS.

Web site: www.agra.org

Family History

F H i

Indexes
(from sources at the Public Record Office)

Stuart Tamblin
14 Copper Leaf Close
Moulton
NORTHAMPTON
NN3 7HS

01604-495106
fhindexes@genfair.com
www.genfair.com/fhindexes/

Prices valid to 31/12/01.
Cheques please to S Tamblin.

Criminal Register Indexes (1805-16)
on fiche or disk (ASCII text)

Cheshire; Middlesex; Sussex; Wiltshire; Herefordshire/Worcs; Wales/Monmouth; Oxon/Berkshire; Bucks/Herts; Northants/Leics/Rutland; Beds/Cambs/Hunts; Cumb' d/Westm' d/N' berland/Durham;
- **£4.69 each volume inland; £5.53 airmail**

Som/Dorset; Glos; Hants; Salop/Staffs; Warks
- **£5.69 each volume inland; £6.53 airmail**

Devon/Cornwall; Derbys/Notts/Lincs; Essex
- **£6.69 each volume inland; £7.53 airmail**

Norfolk/Suffolk; Surrey; Kent; Yorkshire
- **£7.69 each volume inland; £8.53 airmail**

Lancashire - **£13.69 inland; £14.53 airmail**

Later periods available for some counties

Criminal Lunatics, 1799-1843
- **£3.69 inland, £4.53 airmail**

Send large SAE for latest details.

Drawing Up Your Family History

Marie Lynskey

Do you have files of family history papers, the culmination of many years research, with the whole history of a family sitting on shelves unseen? Have you often thought of having a chart of your ancestors drawn up to hang on the wall as a culmination of your efforts? The task is one you can tackle yourself with a little guidance from this article and 'Family Trees- A Manual for their Design, Layout & Display'.

Not everybody has the artistic ability to produce neat or attractive hand written lettering but much can be achieved by the most unartistic with the use of good technical drawing instruments. If all else fails you can turn to lettering stencils which are available in many sizes down to letters 2mm high which produce extremely accurate, neat lettering. Rotring U.K. can give you the name of your nearest supplier of their pens and stencils. If you feel able to tackle hand written lettering, acquire good equipment. Firstly, choose an ink which will not fade, the best type is Chinese ink available in bottles from Falkiner Fine Papers. Most fountain pen inks will fade dramatically after a few years exposure to sunlight. You will need a pen with a good sharp nib, calligraphy pens such as 'William Mitchell' are the best for this sort of work. Whatever writing technique you use the best way to ensure straight, even lettering is to write between pencilled guidelines which are removed when the text is complete. It is not necessary to take a crash course in calligraphy provided you are prepared to put a little care and effort into your work. Simple but legible lettering suitable for family trees can be written with a Rotring technical drawing pen. Writing with a calligraphy pen demands a little more expertise but the lettering produced with a nib that can make thick and thin strokes can be very attractive. Stencilled lettering can be created using a Rotring stencil which matches the technical drawing pens. Care must be taken to line up the letters correctly. You will also need good quality paper and paint.

There are various ways of laying out a family tree but the most popular and the easiest to read is the familiar drop-line pedigree. The framework which connects together people on the chart revolves around the use of the = sign to denote a marriage. From each marriage sign descends a line connecting to a row of offspring and the whole chart is built up with a network of marriages and connecting lines. When drawing up your chart be prepared to re-arrange the information several times before you arrive at the best layout. Many people start with a large sheet of paper and write the first few generations beautifully only to find as they get further down the page that the information becomes smaller and smaller to fit into the rapidly diminishing space. You should have a complete draughted rough copy before you start on the final

piece then you will be sure of producing a good clear chart.

Begin the layout by making sure that the generations are correctly aligned across the page. This will make the chart much easier to read and will show up relationships between family members at a glance. Sometimes when relatives in different generations marry this arrangement is spoilt slightly but most problems of this kind can be resolved with careful planning. The main aim is to make sure that each person on the chart is clearly recognisable and that all parts fit together in the most straight-forward manner. Take a large sheet of paper and draw a faint line down the centre. Mark the required number of generations at equal points down the centre line, allow 5-6cm per generation, this can be altered later if less or more space is needed. Working with the widest generation, space the names evenly to either side of the central line. Join together the family groups then work through the generations above and below, fitting families together until the whole chart is plotted. At this stage just jot down the names or initials in pencil.

When this loosely plotted draught is complete write all the lettering in the chosen manner then position it on the draught. I write all the text on separate paper then cut out each name and stick it to the chart with masking tape on the reverse, if you spoil a name you can write it again. This is good practise for writing on the proper chart and you will gain confidence in using your pen. It looks better to write the names larger than the rest of the biographical details and most charts benefit from a large title at the top. The advantages of writing all the lettering in rough first are (a) to make sure all the information will fit (b) to see exactly how much space each word occupies so that you can neatly centralise all the information on the final copy and (c) if the layout is poor you can alter the spacing. Draw in all the connecting lines to make sure that you have left them plenty of room. Any parts of the chart which do not look right can now be altered. If you have unbalanced areas with hardly any text and other areas where all the names are squashed up, re-arrange them to improve the spacing. If you use masking tape to stick the lettering to the draught it will easily peal off for repositioning. If you have too little space for all the biographical details then you will be able to see where extra room is needed. Alternatively if the amount of space allowed was too great it can be reduced on the final copy.

When all the text is written and alterations have been made as required you are ready to start on the actual piece. Paper for family trees should be very durable to make it last for future generations. Good quality papers in large sheets are available from Falkiner Fine

Papers. Fabriano paper, an acid free conservation grade paper with a good surface for lettering, is one of the best for this type of work. Some art shops sell good papers in large sheets. A paper on which the ink will not spread and with a smooth surface so that the pen does not catch on loose fibres is needed. Ordinary cartridge paper is fine for practise lettering but does not last well. Whatever you choose test it before starting to make sure that you can produce sharp well defined letters. You will also need a ruling pen to make long straight connecting lines. The chart will look clearer with the lines in another colour to the text. Use Designers Gouache, a water based paint available in tubes from most art shops. It is mixed with water to the consistency of thin cream then applied to the ruling pen with a paint brush. The pen is then drawn along the edge of a rule to give a perfectly straight line.

Cut your paper to the size required and mark out the writing lines and connecting lines in pencil. Take great care when ruling the guidelines as small discrepancies make a big difference to the lettering size. Write the lettering working through the text from top left to bottom right so that you are never writing over wet letters. It is a good idea to keep a guard sheet underneath your hands as you write. Hands always transmit grease to the paper and this can spoil it so that the ink will not take properly, it is therefore sensible to allow your hands to touch the paper as little as possible. When all the lettering is finished rule in the connecting lines. Rule all the horizontals first then when the paint is dry turn the page round and add the vertical lines. Rub out the writing lines with a soft rubber taking care not to smudge the ink or paint. If you make mistakes when writing do not dispair, if your paper is of a good quality errors can be removed. Use a pencil typewriter rubber to carefully remove the incorrect lettering. Rub very gently, checking that you are not spoiling the paper, then brush away the paper and rubber dust. Where the paper surface has become rough from rubbing smooth it flat again with a smooth hard object, such as the back of a teaspoon, taking care not to mark the paper. When the surface is smooth again write the correct letters but be careful that the ink does not spread into any loose fibres. It is worth experimenting at removing letters on a scrap piece of the chosen paper. Proof read the finished text carefully as errors can creep in unnoticed. When complete the chart is ready for framing. High street framers offer a wide range of attractive and inexpensive frames made to measure. Choose plain glass rather than non-reflective which tends to mar the clarity of the lettering.

There are many other ways of laying out a family tree such as left to right format, narrative style, circular and semi-circular formats or as a book with a simple binding. Pictures and illustrations can also be added. All these and many more items are explained in detail in 'Family Trees - A Manual'.

My new books are entitled "An Introduction to Calligraphy" and "An Introduction to Illuminated Letters". The Calligraphy one was published October 2000 and the Illumination book April 2001. Full details on my website as soon as possible. They are both in full colour and fully illustrated throughout and are fantastic value at £11.99 each.

Identifying the Unknown:

Family Photographs and their Interpretation

Audrey Linkman
interprets the picture .....

family photographs. Indeed those unfortunates (like me) who missed out on this blessing can consider themselves hard done by! The reason is that portrait photographs circulated in the mass market in the nineteenth century. It is important to remember that the pattern of commercial development in portrait photography differs in detail in every country, but the pattern for Britain was broadly as follows. The first commercial portrait studio opened in Regent Street, London in March 1841 selling daguerreotypes. For a variety of reasons the daguerreotype in Britain remained a luxury article with sales restricted largely to the genteel classes. By 1853 a new product hit the market in the shape of the wet collodion positive, known at the time as the glass positive. This used glass as the medium for the negative which was subsequently converted into a positive and placed in cases and frames similar to those used for daguerreotypes. The collodion process was easier and cheaper than its predecessor. More studios opened on the highstreet, where increasing competition lowered prices. The decade of the 1850s which had opened with the luxury daguerreotype, closed with the cheap glass positive which could be had for as little as sixpence – cases twopence extra!

1860 brought another innovation in the shape of the card-mounted paper print, the so-called carte de visite. Cartes were intended for insertion in the purpose designed photo album which came onto the market at the same time. Card portraits were produced to a standard size and retailed in quantity - half a dozen, a dozen, twenty, even a hundred. The early years of the 1860s saw massive sales. In 1866 the cabinet portrait made its debut, another card-mounted portrait for the album but larger in size than the carte de visite. Together, the carte and cabinet form the backbone of the Victorian family album because they remained the major articles of commerce in various guises until the second decade of the twentieth century. It is this extended lifespan of fifty years or so which makes the dating of card formats so difficult. [1]

Another problem for the family historian is the apparent similarity of studio portraits which gives rise to the feeling that once you have seen one you have seen them all. Added to that is our perception of the studio as an unreal setting which can never satisfy our desire to see aspects of life as it was actually lived in the past. This means that in a very real sense we stop looking at them and cease

Many family historians have inherited family photographs from the nineteenth century. It is not unusual for you to be unable to identify the sitters. Few Victorians troubled to write names on the backs of portraits. Why should they? After all the family knew its own members. It is only three or four generations down the line that this information no longer has currency. Most of you, too, will be unable to date your early portraits, which adds to the difficulties of trying to assign identities. In addition, most of you will probably not even have asked yourselves about the possible event or occasion that triggered the trip to the studio. Within the average Victorian family, however, there was usually some very sound reason why hard-earned money should be spent on a luxury item like a photograph.

Our ancestors usually visited the studio photographer to celebrate some special occasion that reflected well on the family. Studio portraits commemorate rites of passage such as breeching, engagement, marriage, etc., or record career success or achievement in some field of endeavour. Sometimes the occasion is obvious when special dress or accessories advertise the event. Christening robes for example are easy to identify because we still observe the custom today. Sometimes the occasion is more obscure. *Armed with an approximate date and a likely occasion, the family historian can begin to assign possible identifications to unidentified portraits.*

I mentioned above that many people have inherited

to register precisely what we are looking at. And it is perfectly true that commercial photography in the nineteenth century followed set patterns. Both photographers and sitters the length and breadth of the country knew what was required and set about doing it

So let us now explore those similarities and the reasons behind them. It is certainly no accident that portraiture emerged as the major commercial application of photography in the early years and retained its dominance throughout most of the nineteenth century. This happened because the camera was able to mechanise a well established and buoyant trade in the sale of hand-crafted likenesses. Demand from all sectors of society was satisfied by a variety of different products, silhouettes for those in modest circumstances, miniatures in watercolours for the comfortable and portraits in oils for the rich. Since the camera could produce likenesses more accurately, quickly and cheaply than the other available processes it quickly routed competition and established itself as the market leader.

However, in appropriating this established industry photographers came up against a set of theories and practices about the portrait which had been refined by artists over many years. The currency of these ideas was such that photographers probably had little option but to take them on aboard and force the camera to conform to the dictates of a rhetoric devised for painted portraiture. One fundamental principle of this alien rhetoric was the need to idealise the sitter. Though the camera had the potential to show things as they were, portrait photographers of the nineteenth century believed it was their moral duty to reveal the beauties and hide the defects of their sitters. Every element of the portrait - expression, pose, background and lighting - was orchestrated towards this end.

Facial expression was important because it was thought to reveal the innermost soul of the sitter. The Victorians did not interpret the smile as we perceive it today. For us the smile indicates cheerfulness, poise, confidence, success and warmth. To the Victorians, its appearance in a portrait indicated a person who did not take themselves seriously and could not therefore expect others to do so. Smiles almost equated with featherbrained and represented a person who lacked gravity or dignity. Smiles were considered acceptable for children and actresses. The choice of expression was not determined by the length of exposure.[2]

Though Victorian photographers continually stressed the need to achieve a natural pose they had in mind the elegant bearing that distinguished people of 'good breeding' who occupied the privileged upper strata of Victorian society. Small wonder then that many of our ancestors, consciously aping the body language of their 'superiors', appear constrained, formal and even uncomfortable in their photographs. Pose was also used to hide or

blur facial blemish or physical deformities as this was thought to present the sitter to advantage.

The choice of background and accessories in studio portraiture were obviously influenced by painterly precedent. Drapery, pedestal, urn and balustrade were all stolen from the portrait painter's standard repertoire. The photographer's backdrop depicting the well furnished interior or gracious parkland conferred anonymity but also implied an elegance of lifestyle to which few sitters ever experienced. The usual accessories that litter the studios were all intended to confer credit by association. The book, for example, one of the most commonplace accessories, implied education at a period when that was neither universal nor free.

And, finally in their use of lighting (natural daylight for the most part) photographers obeyed the laws of idealisation. They used lighting to hide or shadow physical imperfections, to soften and smooth wrinkles and to highlight those features considered attractive to prevailing tastes. And if all else failed photographers resorted to the gentle art of retouching the negative in order to remove freckles and warts, reduce the number of chins or slice a judicious inch off an errant waistline.

Conformity to these rules in a sphere of mass production brought tremendous similarity in treatment and style. But this very sameness can be made to work to our advantage as it allows us to detect exceptions and deviations. These in turn require explanations which can shed new light on the sitter and the portrait. And perhaps the best way of illustrating what can be achieved through careful analysis is to look in detail at one example. The photograph on the next page of Mary Hannah Blackwell and James Sharples

However unexceptional it may appear to us today, the pose of this couple is unusual in one outstanding particular viz. in the positioning of their hands. In nineteenth century photographic portraiture physical contact between adults was formulaic, totally devoid of any feeling of sensation, excitement or emotion. A couple can be photographed standing together arm in arm as they could be seen in public. More usually, however, one person is seated with the other standing at their side. The hand of the partner who stands rests casually and impersonally on the shoulder of the other. This form of physical contact between sitters implies connection or family relationship. For the act of touching, however, to hint at any sort of genuine feeling or physical intimacy is most unusual. In this delightful portrait touch actually conveys feeling. His fingers cover hers and both hands rest on her thigh (though quilted skirt, woollen jacket and excessive quantities of undergarment intervene between flesh and flesh). This firm clasp does manage to convey some sense of earnestness on his part.

The disregard of conventional practice in this portrait has occurred precisely where we should

Mary Hannah Blackwell and James Sharples
Photographer Unknown   Wet Collodion Positive. c1877
Courtesy of the Documentary Photography Archive, Manchester. Ref: 1007/1

mer portrait at the seaside

No ring is displayed which suggests that at this stage the couple was not married. No respectable woman, however, would agree to be photographed with a man to whom she was not related unless she wished to publicise the message implicit within this photograph that both parties had reached an understanding and intended to marry. Such a photograph served a similar purpose for less privileged couples as the formal studio engagement portrait for the more affluent. Through the good offices of a kind researcher [thank you, Helen] we know that the couple married in 1877 which provides a good approximate date for the portrait. Mary would then have been aged about twenty two, and her suitor twenty seven.

Mary worked as a cotton weaver; James was a plate layer on the railway. This outdoor occupation may account for James' ruddy complexion. Throughout the nineteenth century the tonal translation of colour in black and white photography was incorrect. Colours at the red, yellow, orange end of the spectrum translated darker; whereas blues, lilacs etc. translated whiter. James' face appears dark, particularly on his cheeks and nose, which suggests that those areas were redder than the rest. His hat would have covered his forehead.

While James appears earnest but slightly uncomfortable Mary projects a composure which suggests a degree of contentment at future prospects. After marriage James and Mary Hannah lived in Hawk Green, Marple where he worked on the railway. They had eight children of whom one died in early childhood and two were killed in France during World War One.

Hopefully this lovely picture of Mary and James serves to reveal how studio portraits hold clues and pointers which can shed light on the sitters. Through a careful 'reading' of the image many early photographs can be made to yield their secrets.

[1] AUDREY LINKMAN, The Expert Guide to Dating Victorian Family Photographs, Manchester GMCRO, (2000) offers one useful guide to dating card formats.

[2] These arguments are stated in full in AUDREY LINKMAN, The Victorians: Photographic Portraits, Tauris Parke, London (1993) which is about the Victorian Family Album

© 2000 Audrey Linkman

expect to find it - in front of the camera of the itinerant photographer. Itinerants operated al fresco studios in the suburban street at any time, on the sands in the summer, in the fairground during highdays and holidays, and in public parks and local beauty spots on Sundays. These speculative operators were held in contempt by the proprietors of respectable highstreet businesses. Among their many faults they were accused of paying scant regard to posing by allowing each customer to "have his own way entirely" as long as "he pays his sixpence in advance". This photograph is a glass positive (the crack in this example sadly reveals its inherent fragility). Elbowed out of the highstreet studio by the arrival of the carte de visite, glass positives found sanctuary among itinerant operators because they could be finished 'while-you-wait' - i.e. within five minutes or so. They were therefore suitable for sale at the seaside or fairground where customers might only spend a day or afternoon. The cheap framing of this example confirms its lowly, itinerant origins. Mary's quilted skirt implies cold weather which may in turn suggest a fairground studio rather than a sum-

Plastic - that will do nicely!

Colin Parkinson

This article complements the two articles in last year's Directory, "Caring for your Family Records" and "The Conservation and Restoration of Family Documents". It looks at the types of plastic pockets now popularly used for storing certificates, photographs and memorabilia; what will protect the family historians treasures and what can damage them. It will touch upon how best to ensure these genealogical valuables are preserved and yet still making them accessible.

The views in this article are my own based on talking to manufacturers, seeking advice over the years from more learned sources and studying relevant literature. I do not pretend to be an academic expert on the subject but happy to pass on my experiences from the lessons learnt during the past 12 years in supplying certificate binders and safe polypockets. This article is not aimed at the scientifically minded but some technical references are made by way of comparison. The objective is to give general guidance as to which materials are suitable and which should be avoided.

When I talk to family historians it appears that many still store such important documents, for example GRO certificates (Birth, Marriage & Death certificates) folded up, in a brown envelope, in a shoe box and out of sight. Any folded document that is regularly opened and refolded will eventually tear along the fold line. The importance of certificates to family historians is such that it is essential that certificates are properly stored and nicely presented. Photos and memorabilia, to make any sense, need to be properly sorted and organised. Purpose made binders, albums and plastic pockets make this possible. The cost of certificates should encourage us to protect them rather than be left folded in an inappropriate sized pocket. They look better when flat, even with any fold lines; how much better would they be without those fold lines! Maybe there is a case for GRO certificates to be sent out unfolded?

Many family historians are uncertain what plastic pockets are available and which plastic pockets are safe. They may have heard the terms "acid free" and "inert" but are unclear what these mean.

Many old documents, perhaps an ancestor's original birth certificate, will continue to deteriorate unless properly protected. Large documents, newspapers, indentures, family trees for example can be stored and displayed in large sized plastic pockets, A2 & A3 pockets are available.

But what is a plastic?

This scientific bit is best avoided by those prone to headaches. "Plastic" really refers to the way a material melts and flows. A more correct term is polymer. The word polymer arrives from the Greek "poly" meaning many, and "meros", units or parts. A polymer is a group of many units, the combination of many monomers (one unit) creates a polymer. The different combinations of monomers results in different polymers, with different properties. Polymers are formed commercially through chemical reaction under pressure and heat.

Other ingredients are needed to control how the polymer is formed and to produce the proper molecular length and desired properties. This chemical process is called "polymerisation".

Best practice regarding archival storage is covered in the UK by British Standard 5454:1977 and 1989, "The Storage & Exhibition of Archival Documents". This is written by representatives from, amongst others, the British Museum, the Royal Society and the Public Record Office. BS 5454 recommends the main polymers, or plastics, suitable for archival storage which are Polyethylene (or Polythene - ICI's trade name) and Polyethylene terephthalate (commonly known as Polyester). These materials are naturally soft, stable and safe.

Polyethylene is a plastic polymer of ethylene with many uses including for containers, electrical insulation and packaging. When produced thick enough for pockets to store certificates and photographs it can appear to be unclear. It doesn't have the best transparency amongst the available plastics. Poor quality polyethylene pockets can be "gritty", with tiny pieces of damaging grit or dirt trapped within the polymer, these are easily seen. Polyethylene is relatively cheap.

Polyester is a synthetic polymer in which the structural units are linked by ester groups. Its main virtue is that it is crystal clear with glass-like clarity. Polyester is generally recognised by museums and archivists as the premier storage material and is probably the most thoroughly tested polymer for archival purposes. Polyester can be prone to develop static, easily cleared by an anti-static brush or cloth. Polyester has a peculiar phenomenon such that when the two surfaces of a polyester pocket are touching this can create a visual effect, a trick of light, similar to oil pooling on water. This is quite natural and harmless and will disappear when the surfaces are separated, such as when the pocket is filled with a certificate or an item of memorabilia. Polyester is relatively expensive.

Another plastic that is readily available is Polypropylene. It is closely related to polyethylene, in genealogical terms a sibling rather than a distant cousin! Polyprop, as it is sometimes shortened to, generally has greater strength and better clarity than polyethylene. Polypropylene is, in my opinion, a good all round pocket. It is clearer than polyethylene and less expensive than polyester. Plastic pockets found in High Street shops are likely to be made from polypropylene because of their cheapness and acceptable clarity. Some polypropylene products have an orange peel finish, a mottling effect, which will reduce its clarity.

PVC (polyvinyl chloride, popularly called vinyl) is not naturally soft, stable and safe and must be avoided for archival storage. PVC is naturally hard and in that state is ideal for plastics used in the building trade, e.g. gutters and drainpipes. In order to make PVC flexible for pockets etc. plasticisers have to be added. Plasticisers are not completely stable and very slowly harden and crack. Those of us who have used PVC pockets for storing certificates for several years will know that, in time, they will lift off or dissolve the print, particularly the photocopy print section of a modern copied certificate. Similarly, photographs will stick to a PVC pocket, making their removal impossible without destroying the surface of the photo. PVC pockets are not recommended for long term storage purposes, and anyone still using them is advised to change them for a safer alternative. In hindsight it is a disappointment that PVC pockets were around for so long but their use should continue to decline as users become aware of the damage PVC can cause and that safer alternatives are available.

Any storage material which contains acid is harmful and when buying look for products that are marked "acid-free", "inert" or "copy safe". Inert means the material does not have any active properties. The three plastics mentioned, polyethylene, polypropylene and polyester, are all inert. If they are not clearly marked, how can you tell one from the other? Other than with an experienced eye there is no easy or practical test, particularly if you are standing in your local stationery shop. As a simple guide a sample of polyethylene or polypropylene will float, polyester doesn't, but take care as PVC also sinks. When a pack of PVC pockets are opened there is a distinct plastic smell. Polypropylene tends to be clearer and stronger than polyethylene, when the latter is pulled it stretches and stays stretched. If, when buying there is any doubt then ask, if still uncertain it is best to avoid the material.

A relatively new product which can have archival uses

are Tyvek envelopes (Tyvek is a trade name of Du Pont). They are not transparent but are white and look similar to paper. However, it is made from spun polypropylene, it is very difficult to tear, can be written on and is safe for storing documents. As an envelope it is ideal for posting documents. Tyvek envelopes come in a variety of sizes and are readily available.

Learning the lessons of using safe plastic pockets is important to the genealogist. But do not overlook mounting card, mounts or other materials used within the pocket as these should also be safe. Card and mounts should therefore be acid free or they can react against the stored item.

Many original certificates and photographs are irreplaceable. A safe protection and storage system is critical to ensure their survival. The cost of current certificates is such that genealogists are wise to invest in an appropriate and safe storage system. The displaying of photographs and memorabilia in an organised manner is both satisfying and essential in the recording of your family history to be cherished by yourself and future generations.

British Standards 5454 is available from HMSO and all good Reference Sections of Libraries.
Thanks to John Dalton B Sc., LRIC for technical guidance.

Colin & Sue Parkinson have been supplying specialised certificate binders since 1988 when they felt there was no appropriate sized binder and polypockets for the genealogist. They introduced the 151/2 x 9 ins (39.8 x 23.4 cms) pocket format for certificate storage and now supply a variety of genealogical storage products.

... on the use and abuse of books

Sue Callaghan - Bookbinder

Despite the relentless march of the electronic age books and documents in their original form are here to stay. Fortunately the two technologies can exist happily side by side and I think that they will do so for many years to come.

Digital recording and microfilming are of course forms of conservation. The original documents are permanently recorded whilst at the same time being made available to a large number of researchers without the risk of damage by excessive handling. As a keen amateur family historian and an avid book collector I think it is amazing that material, that until recently has only been available at a limited level, has suddenly arrived on our computer screens in our own homes. I am in awe of the massive amount of information that is now available on microfiche or CD - and thankfully it keeps coming.

Computers are here to stay, but so are books.
Every researcher, by virtue of the very nature of their quest, will certainly amass copious quantities of documents, books, ephemera and miscellaneous loose papers. Whether these are inherited, purchased or otherwise acquired it is our duty to preserve and care for them for future generations to enjoy and learn from. It has been said that 'one never owns a book, but is just its custodian during ones lifetime'. A statement worth a bit of thought, I think.

The printed book has been abused and ravaged in many ways since its first appearance in 1456. Flood and fire damage, insect infestation and other acts of God have all contributed to the lament of the book. However, as a professional bookbinder for the last 23 years I have concluded that Man has the edge in the 'damage to books' department. We have destroyed countless individual books and documents and even whole collections over the centuries, either by wilful or ignorant abuse.

Apart from large-scale destruction of collections during war years and deliberate book burnings by fanatics, we have destroyed many more rare and irreplaceable volumes by our own ignorance. I have seen eighteenth century books repaired with black electrician's tape or the dreaded self adhesive cellulose tape (which I think is a marvellous invention, but not for repairing books). My own Grandfather's speciality was to repair book covers with surgical sticking plaster, which is a bit of a nightmare because I inherited a lot of them. Rusty pins, safety pins or paper clips are often embedded into pages and heat stains from hot mugs of tea on fine nineteenth century bindings. Pressed flowers are a favourite and whole roses, thorns n'all that have been carefully pressed between the pages of large family Bibles.

Just six weeks before writing this article I was asked to restore a rare nineteenth century fishing book that had suffered a frenzied knife attack. With every slash of the blade the cuts went through about 10 pages and then the next 10 pages were attacked and so on. The customer found it hard to believe that anyone could mistreat a book in this way and indeed so did I.

Now I am not suggesting that everybody who owns a book deliberately damages it in some way. However I do suggest that knowing a few do's and don'ts of library care might prevent inadvertent mistreatment and help to prolong the life of those treasured tomes that are so carefully collected.

The rules apply to both antiquarian and modern books and also to documents, maps and ephemera, where applicable. Even a modest collection will benefit from a bit of TLC.

As your collection grows there will be a temptation to cram just one more book onto that already over crowded shelf. Resist the temptation as this will cause the books to become misshapen and they will inevitably be damaged when they are prised off the shelf by hooking a finger into the headcap at the top of the spine. Remove books by grasping them around the spine, having first pushed the books on either side back a little way until the required book can be withdrawn. If they are allowed to lean at an angle, it will eventually cause the hinges to break and the boards will separate from the book. Use felt covered bookends to support the books in an upright position. Very large volumes should be stored on their sides if possible so as not to allow the weight of the paper to pull the binding out of shape and therefore cause damage to the stitching and joints.

Shelves should be constructed of smooth material with no rough edges or sharp protrusions. Keep shelves well away from radiators, as the heat will dry out the bindings and make them brittle. Avoid putting shelves where the books would be in direct sunlight. The harmful ultra violet rays will quickly fade the colours of both cloth and leather covers.

Damp conditions should also be avoided because this will enable moulds and fungi to thrive. These are difficult to eradicate and are very destructive. Cellars and basements are therefore not good places to keep books.

Ideally the 'library' should be located in a room that has good ventilation and is not kept too warm. The books and shelves should be dusted regularly and inspected carefully for signs of moisture damage or insect infestation. Wood boring beetles, silverfish and moths are the most common, harmful insects found in and around books. The damage varies with the insect. Some signs to lookout for are pages and covers which have holes in them as a result of beetle larvae eating their way out of the book (bookworms). Silverfish graze the surface of the pages and cause a 'lace' effect. A telltale pile of dust falling from inside the spine might be seen if a book is tapped gently. On closer inspection eggs, larvae or the insects themselves might be seen. If an infestation is suspected the books should be isolated and expert help sought.

Don't ever use staples, pins or paper clips to attach things to the pages and don't use books to press flowers. If the boards have become detached, use soft cotton or linen tapes, instead of rubber bands, to tie them up until they are properly repaired. Unless you have expert knowledge it is best not to try repairs yourself, but if you do make an attempt never do anything that cannot be undone. I'm sure that I speak for every bookbinder in the world when I beg you not to use self adhesive cellulose tape to make any repairs on old or new books or documents. It leaves an irreversible stain long after the adhesive has worn off. There are non-yellowing archival tapes available and these should be used if you feel that this kind of repair is necessary to repair dust jackets etc.

Finally after all this nagging don't forget to enjoy your books and the knowledge contained within them. Apparently Charles Dickens once said 'There are books of which the backs and covers are by far the best parts', but I haven't come across many of those in the course of tracking down my ancestors.

Census Returns

A Census has been taken every 10 years since 1801 except in 1941 during the Second World War.
The census returns for 1801, 1811, 1821, 1831 were not preserved. However there are some areas where returns for these years have been found. The first census that is useful to researchers is the one taken in 1841.
The Census returns were taken on:

1841	7th June 1841	1851	30th March 1851	1861	7th April 1861
1871	2nd April 1871	1881	3rd April 1881	1891	5th April 1891

These census returns can be consulted. They were subject to public closure for 100 years because of the sensitive personal information they contained. At the present time the 1901 census is subject to that closure until 2nd January 2002.

Clothing the Past: Dating and Analysing the Dress worn by our ancestors in old family photographs

Jayne Shrimpton looks at past fashions....

Most family historians find themselves confronted at some stage with the problem of undocumented photographs, portraits of ancestors without a name, date or location. How satisfying it would be to discover more about these enigmatic figures from the past who gaze at us with fixed expressions, encased in their strange, formal garments. It is in fact their very appearance which may hold the key to their origins, for the details of dress worn in a photograph (or portrait in other media) are primary historical evidence which can indicate a likely date for that image. The accurate dating of a photograph, in turn, often assists with identification of its subject(s), thereby supplying vital missing links in the visual history of a family. In addition, it provides that picture with a valuable historical context and offers the basis for further research. As I shall explain later, dress - that is, clothing, accessories, hairstyles - also tells a fascinating story of its own.

Dating dress and identifying photographs

Photography as we know it is now over 150 years old and, given the enormous number of both professional and amateur photographs which have survived the passage of time, some of us are fortunate enough to possess photographic portraits which span many years of family history. Whilst fashions seen in photographs taken during the past 40 or 50 years or so perhaps seem familiar, few people feel confident about judging the styles of dress worn in pictures from more distant periods. In some early photographs the details of dress may be indistinct, or else the types of clothing seen in different photographs may appear superficially similar, but in reality be decades apart in origin. Contrary to what we may assume, fashions in the past changed regularly as they do today, especially in the case of women, and even when particular styles seem to have dominated fashion for a long time, there could be subtle changes, slight shifts in detail - for example the shape of a sleeve, the length of a hem, the form of a hat. To the trained eye, such features of dress are not simply 'Victorian' or 'Edwardian' but are recognisably typical of a more specific time period, and therefore constitute a valuable tool in the dating of an undocumented photograph.

In my experience it is usually possible to date dress to within five years or, in certain cases, within a given decade. It is not realistic to attempt dating an image to an exact year on the basis of dress alone, for whereas its earliest possible date can be determined by knowledge of when a particular style first appeared, its latest possible date is less certain as there are various reasons why clothing may have continued to be worn beyond its fashionable date: for

Fig 1

example, older people tend to be more modest in their dress and often wear outmoded garments in a photograph, or those of more conservative taste may have been slower to adopt (and to relinquish) the latest fashions. Dating dress to within about five or - where this is not possible - ten years, rather, offers a reliable circa date for a photograph which is also significant in a genealogical context. Often, knowledge of approximately when a photograph was taken can lead to the positive identification of its subject(s), perhaps by narrowing down the possibilities where the names of likely contenders are known. At the very least, it can place him/her/them firmly within a particular generation, like the photograph in Fig.1. This photograph dates palpably from the end of the 1860s or beginning of the 1870s, judging from the complex hairstyle, the type of silhouette and particular forms of elaborate detailing on the clothing worn by this fashionable young lady. She has always been supposed to represent the great-grandmother of the owner of the photograph, but it is now clear, from her appearance, that she hails from the previous generation of relatives.

Understanding dress in historical photographs

In some cases, the dress worn in old photographs, besides aiding identification of the wearer, is significant in its own right, revealing something of the age, status, tastes, perhaps occupation of the wearer. In the days before amateur photography became popular, people might commission a professional photograph to comemmorate an important event in their lives and for this they wore their best, most fashionable clothing, often garments suited specifically to the occasion. Just as today we sometimes employ a professional photographer to take wedding photographs, so did the young couple portrayed in Fig.2. The owner of the photograph had always believed that this photograph depicted his grandparents at the time of their marriage in 1904: this supposition is supported by the evidence of costume, which in style dates from this time period and is suitably formal and elaborate in its detail to have been worn for such an event, coupled with the pose of the couple, which prominently displays the lady's wedding ring. Other occasions which might entail a visit to the photographer included the 'breeching' of male children at around the age of five, so that many old photographs survive of little boys wearing their first pair of long, 'grown-up' trousers or breeches. In further images, the recent death of a loved one may be indicated by the subject's (or subjects') self-conscious adoption and display of the distinctive mourning dress which was prescribed by Victorian and Edwardian etiquette and which played such an important social role in the lives of our forbears. In some old family photographs the dress simply looks beautiful or intriguing and suggests an avenue for further research.

Sources of information about historical dress: researching from books and photographs or seeking professional assistance

If you possess family photographs which you wish to date and/or research for yourself, you might try your local library or bookshop for costume books containing dated fashion images with which to compare the styles of dress in your own pictures. B.T. Batsford publishers (sadly no longer in existence) have produced many reputable costume books over the years although these and other costume books have tended to go out of print quickly and can be difficult to find. Look out for the Fashion in Photographs series covering the years 1860-1940 in 4 volumes, published jointly by Batsford and the National Portrait Gallery between 1991 and 1993, the Visual History of Costume series, again published by Batsford (1980s) and earlier books on the chronology of fashion by century, written by C. Willett and P. Cunnington, (published by Faber). Several costume books, besides containing many illustrations, offer a more analytical view of nineteenth and twentieth century clothing, for example, Nineteenth Century Fashion by Penelope Byrde (Batsford 1992), History of 20th Century Fashion by Elizabeth Ewing (Batsford 1st edition 1974 and subsequent editions) and Through the Looking Glass: A History of Dress from 1860 to the Present Day by Elizabeth Wilson and Lou Taylor (BBC Books 1989). As well as costume books, try local history books and works on historical photography for useful images showing details of dress. A very informative general work is The Victorians: Photographic Portraits by Audrey Linkman (Tauris Parke Books 1993), which is based largely on the collection of photographs housed in the Documentary Photography Archive in Manchester. This is a reminder that there are also many important photographic collections to be found in large libraries throughout the country, in museums such as the Museum of London, and of course, the National Portrait Gallery, London, which maintains a large Archive of portrait images, including a separate Photographs section. Such collections are often open to private researchers, by appointment.

Being aware that not all family historians can afford the time to scour such sources and that few are

Fig. 2

either trained in the evolution of fashion or experienced in interpreting historical clothing, I offer a professional service dating and, if required, analysing the dress which appears in old family photographs. As I have mentioned earlier, provided that the details of dress are fairly clear, I aim to date dress to within a decade, for instance '1850's', or, where evidence permits, closer, to within about five years - perhaps 'late 1880s' or 'c.1900-1905'. An extended report includes a circa date and a detailed discussion of the clothing in your photograph, within a historical context, as appropriate.

An understanding of why our ancestors looked the way they did can help to bring their images alive and draws us closer to our past.

Jayne Shrimpton studied for her MA in the History of Dress at the Courtauld Institute of Art (London University). Following this, she worked for seven years in the Archive of the National Portrait Gallery whilst researching towards a PhD thesis. She has published articles, lectured widely and contributed to exhibitions within the field of dress and textile history. She now specialises in dating and analysing the clothing worn in historical photographs and portraits in other media, including paintings, drawings, prints and silhouettes.

www.photographdating.freeserve.co.uk
Jayneshrimpton@photographdating.freeserve.co.uk

The Horwoods and The Pecks

Jill Groves looks at two Families involved in the
Straw-plaiting Industry in Bedfordshire and Hertfordshire

I became interested in the straw plaiting industry of Bedfordshire and Hertfordshire when I began to research my ancestors on my late mother's side of the family. I found that most of the women of the family in the nineteenth century, whether married or not, were engaged in either the straw-plaiting industry or the straw hat industry. Straw-plait went to make straw hats, and which part of the industry they were employed in depended on where they lived. My great-great-great grandmother Hannah Horwood, her daughters and her granddaughters (daughters of her son Thomas), living in the north Hertfordshire village of Great Offley, were straw plaiters. Her granddaughters, Elizabeth and Eleanor Horwood, daughters of her youngest son James, living in the burgeoning town of Luton, took that straw plait and sewed it into hats and fancy goods.

The straw plait area covered south Bedfordshire, north Hertfordshire, Buckingshamshire, Essex and Suffolk. The alternative method of employment for women and children in north Bedfordshire was lace-making. [1]

Most of the plait in Bedfordshire and north Hertfordshire was destined for the hat and bonnet trade centred on Dunstable and Luton, often via the straw plait markets. [2]

Type of Straw Used and Method of Straw Plaiting
The type of straw used was wheat. The part of the straw used was that between the last joint in the stem and the base of the ear. The wheat straw to be used for plaiting had to be specially cut, not just thrashed with the rest. The great rival to English straw was Tuscan straw, from what grown specially for the purpose of making plait. The Tuscan straw was much finer, so in order to compete English straws were split. This was done by hand at first, which was time-consuming. Then a simple machine was invented, possibly by more than one person, which split the straw into four equal parts. Some say that it was invented by Thomas Simmons, a blacksmith's apprentice from Chalfont St. Peter's in the late 1780s. Others that it was invented by French prisoners of war at Yaxley barracks near Stilton and copied in iron by a Dunstable blacksmith at the turn of the nineteenth century. [3]

The type of plaiting done was learnt at an early age in plaiting schools, usually by both boys and girls from the age of five, although children as young as three were known to have been sent to plaiting school. However, normally boys went on to be agricultural labourers, whilst girls continued plaiting, whether married or not, having children or not, for most of the rest of their lives.

A woman could plait as much as 30 yards of plait a day. If she didn't work Sundays, this meant that she would have 150 yards of straw plait to send to the nearest market in Luton on a Monday. [4] In theory in the mid-1840s the adult females of the Horwood fam-

ily, including those married but still living in the parish of Offley, could have produced enough plait to fill a cart going to market every week. [5]

To produce this much straw plait meant working at it constantly even 'whilst walking, with a stock of straw lodged under the arm. Indeed it was reported in the 1860s that it was rare in straw plaiting areas to see a girl out of doors who was not working away at her plait.' [6]

Straw plaiting was hard work. It mainly took place between January and May, although some continued until harvest when the women abandoned the plaiting to work out in the fields. Winter plait was sold for lower prices than spring and summer plait. [7]

When Hannah Horwood began learning to plait as a young girl at the end of the eighteenth century the prices paid were very good. [8] She might have earned a shilling a day even as a young girl. When Hannah married James in 1814 she would have been earning 18s a week, double what her young husband could have earned as an agricultural labourer.

Mary Prudden of Barton-in-the-Clay would have been earning slightly less than this when she married my 3xgreat grandfather Samuel Peck in 1820. Earnings from straw plaiting dipped after the end of the Napoleonic Wars but still women like Hannah Horwood and Mary Peck could earn as much as their agricultural labourer husbands, if not more. As the children came along they were sent to plaiting school when they were about five. So Ann Horwood would have attended such a 'school' before she and the rest of her family moved five miles eastwards to the north Hertfordshire village of Offley in 1821/22.

Straw plait schools were places where children were sent to learn how to plait straw and to make as much plait as their parents said they should. The masters, or more often mistresses, were paid 3d a week by parents for each child to teach plaiting. The 'schools' were usually in small cottages. Thirty or forty children could be packed into a small cottage kitchen, so much so that even in winter such a place could be hot and smelly. The heat was necessary in winter to keep the children's little fingers supple. George Culley, collecting information in Bedfordshire in 1867 for the Royal Commission into the Employment of Women, Young Persons and Children in Agriculture, commented in his report:

'A return of the number of children attending such schools in the central and south-eastern divisions of Bucks was kindly given to me by the chief constable, from which it appears that there were 1,457 children, of whom 658 were under 8 years of age, in attendance at 102 plait schools in those districts, and there can be no doubt that if the straw plaiting trade had not been in an unusually depressed state at the time the return was made a very much larger number of children, especially of the younger ones, would have been found in attendance. I visited several plait schools about the time this return was being collected, and in three of these where I asked the question the teachers confessed to having from 30 to 40 per cent more children when "plait was good". From these returns it will be see that the hours of work most common in schools at the time the returns were made were six or seven hours, which, howeverm, are length-ened to nine or ten when "plait is good", or the extra three or four hours considered necessary to make out a fair day's plaiting are worked out at home. Some of the schools I visited, even with the reduced number of learn-ers, were very close and offensive, and the accounts I received of their state in times when plait "went well" were enough to justify the very strong feeling exisiting in the plait district that some legislative interference is nec-essary, if only to protect children from the physical injury sustained by working in close heated rooms, Warmth appears to be so necessary to insure [ensure] sufficient suppleness of the fingers, that in cold weather every breath of air is carefully excluded from the little cottage kitchen where 30 or 40 children are packed together as closely as they can sit. Although there is a general pretence of teaching the children to read, the teachers themselves are often unable to do that which they profess to teach the children to do, and the reading is reduced to the repetition of a few verses of the Bible which they all know by heart. In some plait schools there is not even this pretence, and the result is that a great many children (girls especially) are growing up without any education..."[9]

Hannah Horwood's granddaughter, Jane Horwood, daughter of her second son Thomas, with her sisters Sarah, Esther, Emily and Anne Elizabeth, came into straw plaiting in the 1850s and 1860s. They would have known plait schools like those described above. Jane would have been earning 7s 6d a week and her younger sisters 3s to 4s a week in the 1860s. Jane never married and continued straw plaiting into the 1890s and probably well into the twentieth century to keep her elderly father Thomas after the death of her mother. Meanwhile straw plaiting in the area declined as most of the Luton straw hat makers imported Japanese and Tuscan plait. However, there was a niche in the American market for straw hats for what was called 'English brilliant' plait.[10] As a skilled worker, Jane would have supplied this market, possi-bly until the First World War. A year after her father's death in 1915, Jane would have been able to retire aged seventy, just three years before her own death in 1919.[11] Some of Hannah Horwood's Goodge great-grandchildren in Offley, the grandchildren of her old-est daughter, Ann, ranging from Anne junior aged five to the veteran Ellen aged fourteen, learnt to straw plait in the 1870s and 1880s, although they possibly also went to proper school. In Barton-in-the Clay Mary Peck was still plaiting straw at the age of eighty-one.[12]

Sewing straw hats
In the mid-1850s Hannah Horwood junior, aged twenty-four, the fifth daughter of James and Hannah, moved to Luton with her youngest brother James, then aged twenty, my 2xgreat grandfather. They prob-ably moved with their elder sister Elizabeth Roberts, her husband James and their family. James Roberts was a shoemaker and there was more work for him and for his young brother-in-law/apprentice, James Horwood. A short time later Hannah met and married in Luton Frederick Godfrey from Pegsden, Hertfordshire. Two years later, in 1858, James met and married Mary Ann Woodbridge, a straw plaiter from Amersham.[13] In the same year my other 2xgreat grandfather Albert Peck, third son of Samuel Peck, moved from Barton-in-the-Clay with his young wife Susannah and first child, Emily, to Luton. Albert, being the son of a bricklayer, helped to build some of the new houses being constructed. Finally, Samuel Horwood, the third brother, moved to Luton with his first wife Esther and nine children. They didn't care for Luton itself and quickly moved out to the nearby village of Stopsley, probably where there was more work for Samuel as an agricultural labourer.[14]

Why was Luton so attractive in the late 1850s? Well, the railway had arrived by then, which gave a boost to the straw hat industry, since these could now be carried in great quantities to be sold in London and elsewhere. The railway meant that Luton was a good centre for other businesses, so there was a great deal of building going on, albeit small-scale, unregulated mainly without amenities. There was work in Luton for both the men and the women in a family. However, the living conditions may have been worse than even the overcrowded family cottage in Offley. James moved into Spring Place, with his new wife and baby daughters Louisa and Elizabeth, and made boots and shoes for Luton people in a tiny workshop in his tiny terraced house. Spring Place, built eighteen years before, was already a slum.

'Ill-ventilated, shoddily constructed, no facilities for lighting or sanitation: districts such as Spring Place,… soon became bywords for squalor and its associated problems.'[15]

James continued making shoes. Some time between 1864 and 1881 he moved his family from the tiny house and workshop in Spring Place round the corner into New Street, which was the same age as Spring Place and not much better. Albert Peck also continued in Luton as a bricklayer, with his eldest son Albert as his apprentice. They were living in Davis Fields, not far from James Horwood. Just as the hat trade was booming in Luton, so the building trade was also booming. In fact, even when the hat trade had slumped there was still a boom in the building trade.[16]

By 1881 Samuel had moved back to Luton and was working as a labourer in one of the new dye works. He, his second wife, Elizabeth, and his two youngest children lived only five minutes' walk away from James and his family. Samuel Horwood, junior, like his father, was an agricultural labourer in the village of Round Green, just north of Luton, where he lived with his wife, Emily, their two young children and Emily's father, David Young. One of Samuel senior's daughters, Alice, had moved out of the family home and was boarding in a house in Dudley Street and working as a straw hat sewer. The 1881 census shows Joseph Horwood, Samuel's eldest son, also living in Luton with his family and making a living as a straw hat maker.[17]

In 1881 James Horwood had five of his nine children working, four of them in the straw hat industry. Only Horace William, my great-grandfather, was working in another industry, as a stone mason. Priscilla Peck, my great-grandmother and second eldest daughter of Albert, was noted as not working, but she claimed to be working in the straw hat trade well before her marriage to Horace William (which took place only two years later).

In the family of James Horwood's nephew Joseph, those old enough to work, which included Joseph, his wife and his eldest child Louisa, worked in the straw hat industry. Those of Samuel Horwood's family still living in the same house, three out of four of them worked, directly or indirectly, in the straw hat industry.

At this time the straw hat industry was still a cottage industry, despite the many advances made in machinery made in the 1860s and 1870s with the introduction of blocking machines and machines capable of sewing straw hats. Many houses in Luton were specially adapted with two large rooms at the back. In the ground floor room the men blocked the hats, stiffened them and packed them. Upstairs the women sat by windows sewing the hats. James's wife Mary Ann and her daughters Elizabeth and Eleanor were probably still working in this way in 1881, with her sons Charles and Fred probably blocking and packing the hats for them.

As well as making the hats, members of the family were also hat and plait dealers and small manufacturers. Frederick Godfrey, who had married Hannah Horwood in the 1850s, was a straw hat dealer with his own small factory, known as a plait shop, at 3 Albert Road, Luton. He did so well that by the 1870s he had bought four houses in Liverpool Road, Luton to rent out.[18] Back in Offley James's youngest sister Sarah and her husband William Claridge were plait and general dealers, operating out of Claypit Cottages, Offley.[19]

However, by the end of the 1880s the whole process had moved into factories.[20] This was boom time for the hat industry in Luton. However, it was still not enough to keep younger members of the Horwood and Peck families in the town, or even in the trade. Samuel's youngest son, Walter, became a blacksmith/farrier serving in the Bedfordshire Regiment from 1886 to 1901. Between 1886 and 1888 he served in India. In 1895 he was serving near Exeter when he met and married his wife Mary Haydon.[21]

Horace William Horwood, the son of James, became a stonemason. He and his wife Priscilla (née Peck), and their young family moved to Battersea in the mid-1890s, to the recently built model homes in the Shaftesbury Park estate, and to work on the renovation of Marble Arch. As I write this article a hundred years later, at least one of Horace William's and Priscilla's grandchildren is still living very close to where they moved.

Straw plaiting and straw hat making were hard work for the women, but I am grateful to that industry because it enabled my family, and probably many others, to make enough money not only for a relatively comfortable living when times were good but also, especially in straw hat making, enabled the children of James and Samuel Horwood and Albert Peck to go to school, perhaps even before the 1870 Education Act. There were a number of chapels, Sunday Schools and other schools close to where James and Samuel lived. Horace William, the stonemason, and his cousin Walter, the farrier, would have needed to be literate to some degree. Because of their opportunities they went forward into the skilled upper working class. Their children became managers and moved into the middle classes.

In 1905 another industry, destined to shape Luton in the twentieth century, arrived - the Vauxhall and West Hydraulic Engineering Co., which became Vauxhall Motors two years later. Perhaps after his time in the army, Walter moved into the embryo car industry when it arrived in Luton in the early 1900s. As a blacksmith, he would have had just the skills the industry needed then.[22]

Notes

1. Agrarian History quoted in Population, economy and family structure in Hertfordshire in 1851. Volume 1: The Berkhamsted region, p.35.
2. Population, economy and family structure in Hertfordshire in 1851. Volume 1: The Berkhamsted region, p.36.
3. Victoria County History of Bedfordshire, Vol.II, pp.119-20.
4. Tracing Ancestors in Bedfordshire, p.28. There were also straw plait markets in Leighton Buzzard and Potton in Bedfordshire, Baldock, Hemel Hempstead, Royston, St. Albans, and Tring in Hertfordshire.
5. The adult females of the Horwood family in 1845 included Hannah Horwood, her daughters Ann Goodge and Elizabeth Roberts, her daughters-in-law Mary and Elizabeth Horwood.
6. Population, economy and family structure in Hertfordshire in 1851. Volume 1: The Berkhamsted region, pp.36-37.
7. Population, economy and family structure in Hertfordshire in 1851. Volume 1: The Berkhamsted region, p.37.
8. Hannah was born Hannah Cobb in the village of Totternhoe in 1793, the daughter of Thomas and Sarah Cobb (née Durrant).
9. Royal Commission into the Employment of Women, Young Persons and Children in Agriculture, Information collected in 1867 by George Culley, reprinted in The Bedfordshire Farm Worker in the Nineteenth Century, p.25.
10. Population, economy and family structure in Hertfordshire in 1851. Volume 1: The Berkhamsted region, p.37; Victoria County History of Bedfordshire, Vol.II, pp.119-20.
11. Parish of Offley, Herts, 1891 Census; Offley Parish Burial Register.
12. Information from 1881 Census CD-ROM published by the LDS
13. Information from Mrs Janet Horwood; the 1881 Census CD-ROM; marriage certificate of James and Mary Ann Horwood.
14. 1881 Census CD-ROM
15. IGI for Bedfordshire; 1881 Census CD-ROM; Strawopolis: Luton Transformed 1840-1876 by Stephen Bunker, Bedfordshire Historical Record Society.
16. 1881 Census CD-ROM: Strawopolis: Luton Transformed 1840-1876. Spring Place and New Street were demolished in the 1930s, along with Davis Fields and other parts of the 'New Town Street' area. According to Dr Bunker, Spring Place and New Street were by no means the worst slums in Luton.
17. 1881 Census CD-ROM; information from Mrs Helen Belcher. Esther Horwood (née Rule) died on 4th March, 1868, leaving Samuel with several children on his hands. He married shortly afterwards to Elizabeth Lane of Luton, a woman then in her late thirties. The older children moved out or married shortly after that. By 1881 Samuel and Elizabeth only had Arthur and Walter living with them.
18. 1881 Census CD-ROM; information from Dr Stephen Bunker.
19. 1881 Census CD-ROM.
20. 1881 Census CD-ROM; Old Ordnance Map of Luton, 1922, reprinted by Alan Godfrey Ltd with commentary.
21. Information from Mrs Janet Horwood.
22. Old Ordnance Map of Luton, 1922.

This article first published in
Open History, the magazine of the
Open University History Society

Post Office Heritage
Andrew Perry
Research Assistant

The Bath to London Mail Coach
The man at the right hand side is passing up a bag of mail which is picked up without the coach having to stop
©Crown Copyright

What is Post Office Heritage?
For over a century, the Post Office has been gathering together its heritage and making it available to the public. Our collections span over 360 years of postal service and reflect the variety of operations and services The Post Office has provided over the years. Through the activities of The Post Office, great improvements in communications, literacy, commerce, transport and technology occurred, all of which can be traced through our records. The Post Office has been one of the largest employers in the country, and of particular interest to family historians are our records of appointments and pensions and gratuities, which are detailed below. I have also highlighted other sources which we have for individual grades. Our records are organised into various POST Classes according to type of information.

Establishment and Early Development
Many people believe that the Post Office began in 1840 with Rowland Hill and the introduction of the penny post. However, it actually goes back a lot further than that. Prior to 1635, the Royal Posts carried letters for the King and his Court. A few private letters were allowed, but most merchants either made their own arrangements or used commercial carriers. However, in 1635 Charles 1, in an effort to raise money, issued a proclamation from his court at Bagshot. This formally opened his Royal posts to the general public, and set the foundations for the Post Office we know today. Routes were quickly established radiating out from London, with the mail being carried by mounted post-boys. They had their own area, riding between posts to deliver the mail to the Postmaster. He would then hand it on to the next post-boy, like a relay race. This was a slow process, but there were severe penalties for delaying the mail. The service did not improve greatly until Ralph Allen, Postmaster of Bath, was appointed to run it in 1720. He established an elaborate network of cross posts connecting not only the major towns but developing manufacturing centres as well. By his death in 1764, England had daily post along all the principal post roads.

Appointment, Pension & Gratuities Register
In 1831, a centralised register detailing every established Post Office employee throughout the country was started. Although the original appointment papers have not survived, there are bound volumes which provide details of a person's name, date of appointment, grade and place of work. These volumes can be found in POST 58 and are arranged in years under surnames. Details of pensions and gratuities can be found in POST 1. Until the introduction

of the 1859 Superannuation Act, not everyone was eligible for a pension. The early records are mainly for senior or clerical grades, with the few issued to other grades often being for hardship cases. From 1860 onwards, applications for pensions and gratuities were entered onto a standard form and sent to the Treasury. The form includes details of the applicant's name, rank, date of birth, years of service, wages, reason for application, appointments held, absences, and their general conduct. In November 1940, the Treasury delegated the power to grant pensions to the Post Office, and so only exceptional cases resulted in a form to the Treasury. However, there are one line entries to confirm when an award was paid to an individual. These continue until 1959 when control was transferred to Chesterfield.

Postmasters and Subpostmasters
One of the earliest employees of the Post Office were Postmasters, originally known as Deputies as they ran the local postal service as deputies to the Post Master General. Until circa 1800, most were innkeepers, and as well as handling the mail, they were responsible for providing horses for the post-boys. After this period, they tended to be people who had a business in a location suitable for the distribution of mail and for callers to the Post Office. By 1850, there were purpose built Crown Post Offices staffed by Postmasters working solely on postal business. Details of early appointments and running of offices can be found in POST 1. For the period 1672-1692 POST 94, Roger Whitley's letter books, includes letters from Whitley, the Deputy Postmaster General, to Postmasters about local services and details of their salaries. POST 2 and 3 are Monthly and Annual Cash Books 1677-1850. These list all Postmasters, the town where they worked, and various financial details. POST 9 is a collection of various account books including payments to and from Postmasters. In POST 58 are separate volumes of appointments, vacancies, and bonds of Postmasters. POST 59 establishment books are lists of senior staff produced peri-

odically from 1742, and they include names of Postmasters. A list of principal officers was produced annually from 1857, with names, offices, appointment dates and salaries of Postmasters appearing from 1893. Dates of birth were added in 1920.

There are fewer records on Subpostmasters and Subpostmistresses because most were not actually employed by the Post Office. Like today, they had a main business like a sweet shop or a general store, and the Post Office was a little side line to help stimulate their main income. Early Subpostmasters were known as letter receivers and were mostly shopkeepers to whom a letter could be taken for onward despatch. Lists of London receivers from 1798 can be found in POST 7 and also POST 9. Some appointment records can be found in separate volumes in POST 58. Details of Postmasters and Subpostmasters and how they were running their offices can be found in POST 35, 38 and 42 - the Postmaster General's 'Report' series and 'Minute' series of records 1792-1973, listed under the name of the town or village they were working in. A separate run of POST 36 Irish minutes were added in 1831, and POST 37 Scottish minutes from 1842.

Packet Boat Agents & Captains
Regular despatches of mail to and from the continent were already in place before 1635. A packet station was established at Harwich in 1660 to carry mail to Holland, with a station started at Falmouth in 1689 for mail to Spain and Portugal, and by 1700 packet boats to France and Flanders were sailing from Dover. Packet Agents were appointed at the stations to see that the service was running properly, and details of their salaries and reports can be found in POST 4. Payments to Packet Captains for hire of their ships can be found in POST 2 and 3, and details of Captains, their ships and their crew can be found in POST 1 and Post 43. Appointment details for both Agents and Captains can be found in POST 58, as well as in the POST 59 establishment books.

There are a number of interesting accounts of the packets being attacked by French Privateers. A notable incident occurred in 1794 between the packet Antelope and French Privateer Atalanta. The French succeeded in casting grappling irons, and two boarding parties prepared to raid the Antelope. Her Captain, Edward Curtis, ordered the two bow guns to fire on the first party, which killed or disabled all of the raiders. The other borders were shot or thrust back into the sea with handpikes. At this point, the Captain was killed and the responsibility of command passed to the boatswain, John Pasco. Officially, Captains of packet ships were forbidden to engage ships of larger force, and so Pasco should have made off to safety with the mails. However his blood was stirred, and he continued bombarding the Privateer for another half an hour until she surrendered. On arriving home, John Pasco and his crew were hailed as heroes and substantially rewarded.

Letter Carriers/Postmen & Postwomen
It was not until 1883 that the title Postman formally replaced the original title Letter Carrier. The introduction of the parcel post service that same year meant that the men were now carrying more than just letters. London's General Post Letter Carriers were the first to be issued with a uniform in 1793. One of

1900 Postman using a Penny farthing bicycle
©Crown Copyright

the reasons for the issue was to be able to spot men loitering in pubs when they should have been working. Although large numbers of women were employed on clerical duties and as telephonists, there were few established Postwomen. It was not until 1916, when large numbers of women were temporarily employed to replace the men away fighting, that they received their first uniform. For London Letter Carriers, names and some appointment dates from 1742 can be found in POST 59, as well as appointment details for 1810-1824 contained in POST 58. Annual lists can be found in POST 7 from 1843-1856. Details of Letter Carriers outside of London can be found in the report and minute series of POST 35, 36, 37, 38 and 42. However, it tends to be when they had done something outstanding, either good or bad.

Clerks
Details of clerks in London, Edinburgh and Dublin can be found in POST 59 from 1742. They also appear in the annual List of principal officers from 1857 including details of their appointments and salaries. There are three separate volumes of appointments in POST 58 from 1856-1859, and details of salaries in POST 7. Anthony Trollope was a junior clerk in the Secretary's Office in 1834. He wrote many of his novels whilst working for the Post Office, and one of his recommendations when he was a Post Office Surveyor in the Channel Islands was the establishment of roadside pillar boxes. The first was erected on St. Hellier, Jersey in 1852, and they were introduced on mainland Britain the following year. They were painted dark green until changed to the familiar red in 1874.

c1912 Woodbridge Post Office & Staff
© Crown Copyright

January 1838 in the form of a converted horse box. The speed and reliability of the railways saw the last London-based mail coach leave for Norwich in January 1846. Mail coaches survived on services between some provincial towns until the 1850s. Long distance horse-drawn coaches were re-introduced in 1887 to carry parcels.

Telegraph Messengers
The monopoly of running the telegraph service was handed to the Post Office in 1870, and uniforms had to be supplied to the new grade of Telegraph Messenger. Boys as young as 13 were employed to deliver the messages, but few appear in the general run of appointments as anyone below the age of 16 was not normally recorded. However, there are two separate volumes of appointments for Messengers in POST 58 from 1871-1882. They were taken on at an early age to educate and train them to Post Office standards, with the aim for them to progress further in the Post Office. Messengers who passed an exam at the age of 16 had the chance to progress to the rank of Junior Postman, Sorting Clerk, or a job on the engineering side.

One of the most peculiar things a Messenger has been asked to deliver must surely be two suffragettes. On 23 February 1909, in an attempt to see Prime Minister Asquith, the women posted themselves as express letters from the East Strand Post Office to 10 Downing Street. Only the Messenger boy was allowed into No.10, but Mr Asquith's butler refused to accept the letters and both ladies were returned to the Post Office as dead letters.

Expansion of Services
The Post Office Savings Bank was introduced in 1861 offering savings facilities for ordinary wage earners. At that time there were few banks outside major towns, but now there were 700 Post Offices providing saving facilities. Within two years this had risen to 2,500 offices, and by the mid-1880s there were 31/2 million accounts with deposits of nearly £50 million. In 1881, the Post Office began operating its own telephone exchanges and also introduced postal orders. The Post Office took over the National Telephone Company in 1912 to offer a unified telephone system throughout most of Britain. Although the working papers on telecommunications have now been transferred to B T Archives, we still hold details of staff as they were Post Office employees at the time.

Experiments in motorised transportation began in 1897 with motor vans driven by steam, electricity, and oil. A small Daimler oil van produced the best results of the three vehicles tested, and trials continued until results became reliable enough in 1902 for motor services under contract to operate for carrying parcels. The Post Office brought its own fleet of vehicles in 1919. That same year, the world's first public overseas airmail service began between London and Paris. The service rapidly extended to other countries, and by 1937, the Empire Air Mail Scheme was introduced to carry mail throughout the

Mail Guards
Mail coaches were introduced in 1784 to speed the mail and provide a secure alternative to the unarmed post-boys, who were often robbed. The only Post Office employee aboard the coach was the Mail Guard. He was heavily armed, carrying two pistols and a blunderbuss, and wore a uniform consisting of a black hat with a gold band and a scarlet coat with blue lapels and gold braid. He had a timepiece which was regulated in London to keep pace with the changes in local time, and he recorded the coach's arrival and departure times at each stage of the journey on a time bill. As the coach travelled through towns or villages where it was not due to stop, the guard would throw out the bags of letters to the Letter Receiver or Postmaster. At the same time, the guard would snatch from him the outgoing bags of mail. Guards were expected to not only keep the mail safe, but to ensure that it got to its destination at all costs. A separate volume of Mail Guards' appointments can be found in POST 58. It not only gives the date of appointment but also his place of birth and former trade. Details of Guards can also be found in incidents recorded in the report and minute series of POST 35, 36, 37, 38, and 42, as well as mail coach reports in POST 10 from 1835.

There is only one recorded incident of a highwayman attempting to rob a mail coach. It occurred in 1786 when, on the approach to London, a coach was challenged, but the highwayman was shot dead on the spot by the Mail Guard and no one ever tried it again. Another form of attack occurred on Salisbury Plain in October 1816 when the Exeter to London coach was set upon by a lioness which had escaped from a travelling zoo. One horse was badly mauled and the passengers had to run for shelter at a nearby inn. The lioness's owners eventually recovered her form underneath a granary. The demise of the mail coaches was brought about by the development of the railways. Letters were first carried by rail in 1830 on the newly opened Liverpool and Manchester railway. The travelling post office, a means of sorting the mail whilst on board moving trains, made its first journey on 20

Barnett Head Post Office
Taken during 1914-1918 War and shows the uniform
worn by Postwomen
Copied from a photograph loaned by
MAG Scarisbrook, Assistant Post Master Barnett GPO Neg P6020
© Crown Copyright

ing background information on major subjects. Other collections include all the stamps of Great Britain and their artwork from the Penny Black onwards, postal history, pillar boxes, vehicles and social mail.

How to access our records
Anyone interested in finding details of ancestors or in any aspect of Post Office history are welcome to visit us. Unfortunately, we are only a small unit and so are unable to conduct research on behalf of individuals. Our public search room is open Monday to Friday 9am - 4.15pm except Bank Holidays, and has photocopying facilities, microfilm readers, power points for portable computers and a rest area with a drinks machine. Trained staff are on hand to provide any assistance and to show people how to use the records. No appointment is necessary to visit the Public Search Room, though you must book in advance to consult philatelic material, and proof of identity will be required before entry. The records are classed as public records, therefore not only published but most unpublished material over 30 years old may be examined. Temporarily, access to the artefacts collections is not possible.

We are located in central London at the back of Mount Pleasant Sorting Office, just a few minutes away from the Family Records Centre in Myddelton Street. We have information sheets available on how to trace postal workers through our records and on postal history. We also have a brochure which includes details of our holdings and a map showing our location. General enquiries should be directed to Post Office Heritage, Freeling House, Phoenix Place, London, WC1X 0DL, telephone: 020 7239 2570, fax: 020 7239 2576.

Empire at a standard rate per half ounce.

The Second World War saw many services suspended, and postal charges were increased to provide funds for the hard-pressed Treasury. Many Post Office workers were called up, and in addition 75,000 joined the Post Office's own Home Guard Units. Women were taken on again to cover the short falls, often working long shifts. However, they did win the right to be able to wear trousers. The Post Office also had its own Air Raid Wardens, Bomb Disposal Squad, Fire Brigade, First Aid Detachments, and Rescue Parties. To aid the movement of traffic in darkened streets, the plinths of pillar boxes were painted white. Also, to enable Air Raid Wardens to detect the presence of gas, the tops of boxes were painted with a yellowish green detector paint.

Additional Material
POST 92 and 115 feature publications produced for and by Post Office staff, as well as Union and Civil Service publications. We also have a considerable collection of visual images and artefacts. The images include photographs, paintings, posters, and original artwork. These can add detail to an ancestor's life with the Post Office by showing the pay, working conditions, and uniforms that were worn. We have a small reference library featuring books on Post Office history, a local history collection, and a portfolio collection featur-

1933 Loading Air Mail from a
Royal Mail Van at Croydon Airport
© Crown Copyright

York Minster Archives
~ a hidden treasure?

Louise Hampson M.A.
Archivist - Dean & Chapter of York

Fig.1 The Minster Library and Archives
showing the new Alcuin Wing
© The Dean & Chapter of York

Many people reading this will have no idea that York Minster not only maintains its own archive facility for the study of records dating back to the mediaeval period, but that facility is open to the public four and a half days a week: this is understandable in part, as many of you will have had no occasion to need our records, and there are hundreds of repositories in the country. However, many people resident in and native to York are in the same position, and many more will find that we have the answers to their questions in our records, but will not have realized we were here to ask. This is a position I hope this article will go some way to remedying, but also, perhaps, explain how this situation can have arisen, and what we are doing about it.

The Minster's archive holdings are primarily the records of the Dean and Chapter generated in the course of their business of governing the Minster and its properties. They span over nine hundred years, and are still accruing as the modern records of the Minster are regularly transferred for safe keeping. In addition, there are collections of records from allied bodies, such as the Vicars Choral, who sang the services in the Minster on behalf of the canons who did not wish to undertake that part of their duties for themselves. As they were not a monastic order, they survived the Reformation and continued until 1936, when they were finally dissolved. Most of their records of historic interest are from the mediaeval period and give a marvellous insight into 'ordinary' York - more about this later! Lastly, there are the collections which are here almost by chance, often deposited here because of historical accident, lack of other facility at the time, or because the breadth of content made it impossible to locate in one or another specific local authority record office. We are usefully outside the geographical system from that point of view, but reasonably centrally accessible given the size of Yorkshire. Nowadays, however, we focus very much on material which is directly related to the Minster or existing collections, and do not seek to acquire material which more properly belongs in one of the other local repositories.

So how has this great treasure house of records gone comparatively unnoticed for so long?

Well, although we are quite heavily used by academics and overseas researchers, our family history holdings are not of the most obvious categories - we do not hold parish records, for example - so one of the largest groups of users will have little cause to search us out. The lack of local knowledge is, however, I suspect, down to geography. We are situated in the converted and extended chapel of the mediaeval archbishops' palace, in the park behind the Minster. Pleasantly concealed by trees, and behind iron railings, our presence has not been widely advertised or promoted, and the aspect of the building itself has not encouraged the casual enquirer. With the opening of the new Alcuin Wing in 1998, however, this has all changed and we are now much more visible both physically and metaphorically (fig. 1). The new facilities for the storage and consultation of the Minster Archives are now open and in use.

As a source for both family history and local history, the archive holdings here at the Minster have enormous potential. As well as very detailed records for long periods, sometimes covering the mediaeval period through to the modern day, about who was employed by the Dean and Chapter, there are also many property records which help to place people in a locality, and track their movements and their economic lives. I referred earlier to the Vicars Choral archives, and their records are a prime example. People left small pieces of property to the Vicars in return for them remembering and praying for their souls after death. This was a less expensive option than establishing a chantry, where a priest was specifically employed to sing masses, as the Vicars could include the names of many on the anniversary of their death when reciting their 'bede roll' or list of the deceased to be remembered. These small properties were often tenements or shops in the narrow streets of York, and would be let out by the Vicars to gen-

erate income through rent.
They would be let to tradesmen,
craftsmen, the ordinary people
of York, and their names and
trades recorded as part of the
information recited in the deeds.
The names and details of many
people, particularly for the
mediaeval period, who would
otherwise leave little or no trace
in the written records of history
are preserved in these records,
but they also give an extraordinarily vivid picture of the economic life of York at that period. Some of the most rare
items are those which record
transactions with the thriving
Jewish community of York after
the Clifford's Tower massacre
of 1190 and before the mass
expulsion of 1289. Researchers
are often surprised that these
dealing included transactions

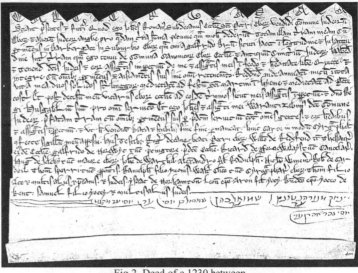

Fig 2. Deed of c.1230 between
Sub Dean John Romanus and the Jewish community of York.
(YMA ref. VC3/Vi/22) © Dean & Chapter of York

with the Dean and Chapter, hinting at a much
more tolerant and cordial relationship than the
larger political histories would have us believe.
One of the most noted of the items is a tiny deed
(some 6" x 4") of c.1230 between John
Romanus the Sub-Dean of York and the leaders
of the Jewish community of York for the provision of a plot of land just outside the walls to be
used as a burial ground them (fig. 2). It is witnessed by Jewish leaders from all over the country, which gives some idea of the significance of
this event to the community at that time. It is in
the Vicars' collection because of the subsequent
history of the tenure of the land after the 1289
expulsion, and this (ironically) helped to ensure
its survival in this rather obscure collection.

The mediaeval will volumes for the Peculiar
Court of the Dean and Chapter are also stored
with us, as are many of the accompanying
inventories. These give family history details of
course, but often also give glimpses into the
lives and households of York people, some of
which are most intriguing. Why does a draper
(confusingly called Lokesmith) feel the need to
keep a bow and arrows, a sword and gun in his
bedroom? Why does a priest have no books in
his house at all? What on earth is a 'trynylin' -
no, it's not 'crinoline'! All these and many
other clues to the lives of people past are contained in the records here.

So far the records mentioned have been largely
from the mediaeval period. Whilst these are fascinating, and often very useful to genealogists
who have 'lost' the vital link in their trees, it
would be wrong to give the impression that the
collections are solely for that period. One of the

most heavily used collections is the Hailstone
Collection, an invaluable resource for the history of Yorkshire. Edward Hailstone was a
wealthy West Riding solicitor in the nineteenth
century who was passionately interested in the
history of Yorkshire. His father, Samuel, had
collected political material from the late eighteenth and early nineteenth centuries, and passed
both his collection and his interest on to his son,
but Edward's interests were much broader and
his collection reflects this. He was particularly
interested in folk history and customs, and was
very concerned that the rapid industrialisation of
his native West Riding was destroying traditional skills and regional attributes. We have a
splendid photograph of him (fig. 3) dressed in a
check suit with knickerbockers made from a
hand dyed and hand woven cloth. What the
photograph does not show, but we know from
other sources, is that the suit was yellow and
green! Hailstone collected perhaps more widely
than wisely - some items he bought at auctions
are not in fact Yorkshire-related at all - but it is
this very catholic taste which now gives the collection its breadth and interest. Many very rare
ephemeral items survive in his collection where
another more 'discerning' collector may have
disposed of them, or not collected them at all. A
good example of this is the Ballads and
Broadsheets collection, which is now fully catalogued onto a database. These flimsy sheets of
political propaganda, popular songs, theatre
posters, and lurid accounts of contemporary
events were avidly collected by Hailstone and
now form a wonderful source of information on
local politics, attitudes to slavery, reform, religion and all manner of subjects. Some of the
early to mid nineteenth century songs,

Fig 3. Edward Hailstone
sporting his yellow and green suit
© Dean & Chapter of York

archivist's primary duty is to preserve the records in their care, but the next most important issue is how best to make them safely available to researchers. Whilst there is little merit in keeping items in such a way that they are perfectly preserved but never used, equally we must ensure that our use of them does not unduly prejudice their survival for future generations. This means the employment of techniques and practices such as the appropriate use of gloves, careful handling, and restrictions on indiscriminate copying which will be familiar to anyone who uses a record office.

Prior to the new facilities here being completed, it was increasingly difficult to provide suitable storage or search facilities for the records. Many were having to be stored in unsuitable out-stores, and research facilities were cramped and cold. With the completion of the Alcuin Wing we now have a storage facility which enables us to bring all the archival collections together in ideal environmental conditions for document life (nothing is forever!), without the need for air conditioning. There is a light, airy searchroom for the consultation of archive material, which is supervised constantly when material is in use. A p.c. has been moved into the searchroom as a first step towards a future goal of having the archive catalogues available digitally, eventually to be available 'on-line' to researchers all over the world.

We can now address issues long ignored: for example, the reuniting of some Dean and Chapter items, so that collections are once again complete and coherent. It is, of course, important that the present spare capacity in the strongroom is not filled up indiscriminately, but we are now able to offer a home to the very important Evelyn Collection of photographs, in the charge of the YAYAS, as described above. The move here, on deposit, will make the collection more readily available to researchers, and mean that it will be stored in good environmental conditions. The York Glaziers Trust also wish to store their glass archive in the new facility, which will help to ensure the stability and safety of this precious resource for future use in the care and maintenance of that glory of the Minster, its stained and painted windows.

The new conservation facilities, together with the (currently) spacious storage area mean we can now begin to tackle some of the problems in the collections: the parchment and vellum of the manuscript collections; the cataloguing and sifting of the modern material which flows into the Archives from every Minster department, apparently in ever-increasing amounts. We can now work more efficiently and effectively on cataloguing some of the collections which have only been partially accessible in the past; for exam-

for example, are in a style which attempts to reproduce the speech of black southern state Americans: whether satirically or innocently is unclear, but they are a very colourful example of popular culture at that time. Others, clearly satirical, are versions of popular songs whose words have been adapted to lampoon political figures or situations. Some of the allusions are now quite difficult to understand, but clearly had great resonance in their own day.

Other records collected by Hailstone include property and estate records, prints, drawings and maps. It is a very disparate collection, with an amazing range of material: some mid-twelfth century charters for land grants to Rievaulx Abbey contain some of the earliest written reference to iron workings on that site, whilst some drawings of large estates from the eighteenth and nineteenth centuries show ambitious house and garden plans for work that was never carried out.

A large photographic collection, including the Evelyn Collection on deposit from the York Archaeological and Yorkshire Architectural Society (YAYAS), covers many aspects of the Minster, York and Yorkshire. Many of these are only in glass negative format, and we are in the final throes of securing funding for the last stage of a project to digitise these images, so that they can be made more widely available. An

ple, a new classification scheme for the Hailstone Collection which will bring together material long separated by historical accident, or never catalogued in the first place. The database described above is just the start of a process which will open up this collection to a wider readership, and make it possible to use it in ways which are presently impossible, or very time-consuming to undertake. We can begin to address the very real problems of storage and future accessibility of information created and retained solely in a digital format: the potential threat of the Millennium Bug was merely a drop in the archival ocean when one has to consider how to ensure that our records are as available in 3000 AD as the York Gospels (an Anglo-Saxon Gospel book written c.1000AD) are to us (fig.4)

Fig 4. The Opening of the Gospel of St. Matthew from the York Gospels c. 1000AD (YMA ref. AddMSS 1) © Dean & Chapter of York

The development of new technologies, and the pace of change mean the world of archives is changing forever, and with it the historical record we are leaving for our descendants. As well as a greatly increased public expectation for access to collections and the information they contain, fuelled by the apparently limitless information available on the Internet, there are philosophical challenges to face about how records are preserved, and what aspects of them, beyond the basic information they contain, can and should be preserved? As an example, the earliest surviving building accounts of the Minster date from 1360, and are hand written on parchment rolls. These consist of sheets (or membranes) of parchment sewn end to end to form a long continuous sheet, which was then rolled for storage. The number of membranes was dictated by the amount of information to be recorded, so they were an economical use of expensive materials, and once rolled they were very compact to store. The very name of the records series, The Fabric Rolls, ('fabric' here referring to the building) is a description of their form. The physical form of these documents is as much a part of their history as the detailed accounts they contain, and the change to book form after the Civil War reflects the change from the old order to the new just as much as any official document, and far more forcibly. The storage of digital data is unlikely to include preservation of original form: machines and programmes become obsolete, and data has to be transferred to new media to continue to be accessible. One alternative, trying to maintain old machines and software, is impractical in the long term. Another, that of printing out items for

long-term preservation, is tempting as a short-term expedient, but in the long term ultimately misguided, as this is not preserving the way that information was really created or used: it is, in a sense, falsifying the historical record. The loss of the creation of earlier versions and drafts as people increasingly rely on word processors is an issue for the literary, political and musical worlds especially. There were two or three earlier drafts of this article, complete with typing errors, but these (perhaps mercifully!) disappeared at the stroke of a key.

It is right that we should be looking outwards and forwards, seeking new ways of working, and expanding our readership as widely as possible. Everybody in our records is someone's relative, even at several removes, and every property deed is potentially the missing piece in someone's complex jigsaw. It would be a great pity if someone never found that piece because they did not know that the collections here were another place to look. As resources cannot always keep pace with the demands placed upon them, it is essential that we maximise what we have and ensure that these new facilities are put to the best use possible. The world of archives is all about trying to second-guess the future and accurately recover the past. We are now able to do so in an environment which allows us to address these matters, safe in the knowledge that the material is stable and protected, but available to all who wish to contribute to that process. The Minster Archives has and contains a long history, and I have barely begun to touch on its treasures: it is my hope that it and the records have a long future, and that the years to come will bring new users and uses.

Lloyd's Register of Shipping

Barbara Jones & Emma Taaffe
Information Services

Manchester Ship Canal

Not to be confused with the insurance market Lloyd's of London, Lloyd's Register (LR) is an independent classification society, which has been engaged for some 240 years in the survey of ships and in the development of Rules and Regulations for the Classification of Ships. For more than 80 years, Lloyd's Register has been the preferred certifying authority for industrial inspection, offshore projects and, latterly, quality management systems. LR has been involved in projects ranging from the Hibernia Platform off Newfoundland through to the Rio Niteroi Bridge, Brazil. This is in addition to our traditional classification work.

A brief history ...
Though two completely separate organisations, both Lloyd's Register and Lloyd's of London owe their name and foundation to the seventeenth century Coffee House of Edward Lloyd. Like many other coffee houses within the City of London in this period, Lloyd's Coffee house was a centre of business intelligence. Those with an interest could read the newspapers and letters from ports, and listen to the buzz of gossip - political, social and commercial - brought in from the outside world. It was unusual for businessmen to own their own offices in London at the time and consequently many chose to transact their business within the walls of the coffee houses. Because of its proximity to the London Docks, Lloyd's was frequented by merchants, marine underwriters and others with interests in the shipping world.

The Register Society & *Lloyd's Register of Ships*
In 1760 the Register Society was founded by customers of the Lloyd's Coffee House, by then owned by Thomas Jemson. Located in the Coffee House itself, this world's first classification society would later become known as Lloyd's Register of Shipping.

The Register Society's income came from subscriptions to their publication the Lloyd's Register of Ships, payment of which could be "made at the bar". Surveyors were employed from the earliest days to report on the condition of the vessels recorded in the Register. The first Register, the 1764-65-66 volume, discloses that surveyors were based at fifteen ports: London, Liverpool, Hull, Leith, Poole, Cowes, Topsham, Whitehaven, Exeter, Lynn, Teignmouth, Weymouth, Yarmouth, Portsmouth and Starcross.

The Lloyd's Register of Ships was originally intended to provide both underwriters and merchants with a way of identifying the condition of the ships that they insured and chartered. Early editions of the Register show the ownership, master, tonnage, date and place of build and number of guns of a ship. Until the mid 1870s only those vessels inspected by surveyors of Lloyd's Register were listed in the Register. The condition of the hull and equipment - or 'class' - of a vessel was first indicated by a system of letters. The condition of the hull was characterised by the vowels A, E, I, O and U, in descending order of merit. The state of the 'Outfit', i.e. the masts and rigging, &c, was indicated by the letters G, M and B - or Good, Middling and Bad. This system was modified a number of times and, by 1775, the state of the Outfit was indicated by the numbers 1, 2 and 3 in descending order of merit. The 1775/76 Register was the first to show class in this way and hence the first Register to feature the now famous classification symbol 'A1', which represented a ship of first class condition. From 1870, the Lloyd's Register of Ships became more comprehensive, aiming to list all sea-going, merchant ships of 100 gross tons and above, regardless of class and nationality.

The Society began to change its classification rules at the end of the 18th century, causing disputes among the Committee and the subscribers to the Register. The majority of the Register Society members were underwriters. It is probable that the Society's surveyors were employed on an ad-hoc basis and that they were either master mariners or received their training in the Royal Naval dockyards. Little consistency existed between the reports and standards of individual surveyors as there were no rules or guidelines published at that time. A surveyors recommendation for class was based upon his knowledge and experience, together with best local practice. The number of years that a vessel could hold the highest class, was limited by its place of build, regardless of how well it was maintained. Ships constructed on the River Thames could remain within the highest class for longer than those built elsewhere. This procedure caused a rift within the Society and the rivalry between shipowners and underwriters culminated in 1799 with the production of a separate Register by the shipowners. The shipowners' register was entitled The New Register Book of Shipping, but became popularly known as the 'Red Book', while the underwriters' register became known as the 'Green Book'. The mounting antagonism of the shipowners towards the underwriters' classification system was expressed eloquently by strong-minded Yorkshire shipowner John Marshall. In 1823, Marshall supplied the drive and precedents for an alternative ethical system of ship classification, the Register Society Committee, however, did not adopt it. The underwriters and shipowners continued to dispute classification prerogatives and procedure for many years, and the conflict between the Red and Green Books gathered momentum until they had competed to the point of insolvency.

During the summer of 1833 a Sub-Committee was set up to confer with the Committees of the Red and the Green Registers. On 14th August a meeting, attended by five representatives of the Red Book, six of the Green and five delegates from the Corporation of Lloyd's, concluded thus:

1st.   *That it is not practicable to carry on two Register Books as at present circumstanced.*

2nd.   *That in the opinion of this meeting it is desirable that an union of the Committees of the two Registers take place for the purpose of establising one good and efficient Register.*

On October 24th, 1833 a draft of the new constitution was produced for the approval of the Joint Committee. Ironically, the new constitution adopted John Marshall's recommendations. Included was the requirement that surveyors would be recruited as exclusive officers to the Society with the following clause on the classification of ships:

... the characters to be assigned shall be, as nearly as circumstances will permit, a correct indication of the real and intrinsic quality of the ship; and that the same shall no longer be regulated, as heretofore, by the incorrect standard of the port of building nor on the decision of the Surveyors; but will henceforward be in all cases finally affixed by the Committee, after due inspection of the Reports of the Surveyors and the documents which may be submitted to them.

The provisional committee dissolved on the anniversary of Trafalgar, October 21st, 1834, and handed over to the permanent committee of Lloyd's Register of British and Foreign Shipping. The adoption of the Lloyd's name may seem a little surprising. It was certainly not relished by some of the shipowners, who felt that they had suffered a good deal at the hands of the underwriters, and still others who thought the name would suggest a predominance of underwriting interests. The choice was made on the basis that the Corporation of Lloyd's had put up a loan of £1,000 to the Society, without which the Society would not have been able to continue. In addition, the Lloyd's name had already earned prestige in international regard and this would prove advantageous to Lloyd's Register. 80 years later the name was changed to Lloyd's Register of Shipping.

Records and Research at Lloyd's Register ...
Lloyd's Register has maintained a library, which is

Lloyd's Register Machinery Certificate issued to a steamer
Sir Francis Drake
This was one of the earliest certificates issued by Lloyds Register

open to the general public, since the early 1900s. The resources available to researchers include a complete set of the Lloyd's Register of Ships dating from 1764 to the present day. Other Lloyd's Register publications, such as the Lloyd's Register of Yachts and Casualty Returns, and a number of relevant reference books are also available.

Lloyd's Register of Ships 1764 - to date
The Register, published for the years 1764-66, 1768-71 and then annually since 1775, records the details of merchant vessels of the world. Since the 1870's Lloyd's Register has tried to include all merchant vessels over 100 gross tons, which are self-propelled and sea-going. Vessels are listed alphabetically by their current name and their entries provide the following details:

Place of Build   Rig (for sailing vessels)   Classification
Shipbuilder (since 1860s)   Ex names (where known)
Survey Dates   Date of Build
Official Number (since 1872)   Navigational Aid
Call Sign (since 1874)   Cargo Facilities
Destined Voyage (1764 to 1873)   Speed (since 1966)
Manager   Port of Registry and Flag
Dimensions (since 1863)   Machinery (if any)
Owner
Master/Captains name:1764-1921 (Steamers)

Starting construction of Barnsley Dock, Hull

1764-1947 (Sailing vessels)

List of Shipowners 1876 to date
The List of Shipowners was first published in 1876 and in its early years was bound with the Lloyd's Register of Ships. It is organised alphabetically by name of shipowner and gives the owner's address and brief details of their fleet. It has existed as an annual publication since 1955.

List of Shipbuilders and Existing Ships 1886 to date
This annual list of shipbuilders was first published in 1886 and included only British shipbuilders only. From 1887 the volume was expanded to include the details of shipbuilders worldwide. The publication lists shipbuilders' addresses and brief details of the ships built by them and still extant in each year. Originally published with the Register, the List of Shipbuilders and Existing Ships was subsequently published within the Appendix to the Register from 1890, and most recently within the Maritime Guide from 1984.

Subsidiary Sections of the Register 1884 to date
Published annually, these include details of world-wide dry docks, wet docks and floating docks (since 1884); telegraphic addresses of shipping companies (since 1886); and Lloyd's Register committees, staff and offices (since 1834). Originally published with the Register, the List of Shipbuilders and Existing Ships was subsequently published within the Appendix to the Register from 1890, and most recently within the Maritime Guide from 1984.

Lloyd's Register Rules and Regulations for the Classification of Ships
Lloyd's Register have published Rules and Regulations for the Classification of Ships, to which all Lloyd's Register classed ships must conform, since 1834. Between 1834 and 1870 the Rules were bound within the Lloyd's Register of Ships. Since 1870 they have been published separately. This is a closed collection and application to view must be made in writing to the Rules Production Department at the Fenchurch Street address.

Lloyd's Register of Yachts 1878 to 1980
An annual register, which lists British and foreign yachts classed by Lloyd's Register, yachts belonging to subscribers of Lloyd's Register publications and certain other yachts above a specified size. It is not a comprehensive source. The Register of Yachts is organised alphabetically by name of yacht and contains the following details:

Owners	Builder
Designer	
Date of Build	Yacht Type and Material
Tonnage	Principal
Dimensions	
Sail Area	Engines
Port of Registry	Home Port
LR classification (if inspected)	

Subsidiary sections of this Register include details of yacht owners, yacht builders, sailing clubs, owners' private burgees and yacht club burgees. The Register of Yachts ceased publication in 1980, to be replaced by the Lloyd's Register of Classed Yachts, which includes details of only those yachts surveyed by LR.

Lloyd's Register of American Yachts 1903 - 1977
North American Yacht Yacht Register 1978 - 1979

Statistical Tables 1878 to date (latterly *World Fleet Statistics*)
The Statistical Tables provide analyses of the world's merchant fleets by number and by tonnage. They are published annually like the Lloyd's Register of Ships and reflect the information contained therein. Prior to 1886, the Statistical Tables only covered new ships classed by Lloyd's Register according to material, sail/steam and where built, together with numbers of ships disclassed and never classed by Lloyd's Register.

Between 1886 and 1914 tables include those showing fleets of the world by flag and country of build; new ships classed LR and total LR classed fleet; and ships added from the British flag register. Since 1919 additional tables have been added to include analyses by ship type, size and age, propulsion, dimensions, ships launched and completed, time series, shiptypes, tankers, motorships and ships totally lost and broken up.

Merchant Shipbuilding Returns 1887 to date
Published quarterly and annually, these are statistical returns of ocean-going merchant ships over 100 gross tons, which are on order, under construction, launched or completed, worldwide.

Early Returns comprise quarterly analyses of ships built in the UK only, according to material, propulsion, place of build and port of registry. Figures for foreign shipbuilding were introduced in 1889 (2nd quarter) and the first annual summary appears in 1892. Some early returns include figures for warships under construction in the UK (prior to 1914). Over the years tables have been added to include analyses by country of build, ship type, tonnage and registration.

Casualty Returns July 1890 to date (now *World Casualty Statistics*)
Not pertaining to lives lost at sea, as one might expect, but to total losses of ocean-going merchant ships over 100 gross tons. The Returns were pub-

lished quarterly and annually and recorded losses according to flag and cause of loss. A separate section gives brief details of ships by name in the following loss categories: foundered, missing, burnt, collision, lost, wrecked and broken up.

Early *Quarterly Returns* give figures for steam and sailing vessels by flag and cause of loss, and for total tonnage owned in each country. Details of the ships cover tonnage, flag, description (i.e. 'iron paddle steamer' or 'wood brig'), voyage, cargo, and date, circumstances and place of loss. Later editions also show the year of build (since 1928) and ship type (since 1939).

Early *Annual Summaries*, published since 1891, give total number of losses for the year for steam and sailing vessels, by flag and cause of loss. Later issues also included analyses by size, principal type and age (since 1967) and world maps showing approximate positions of ships foundered, burnt, wrecked and lost by collision during that year (since 1970). Details of ships not already included in the quarterly returns were also given. The Returns have been published annually, rather than quarterly, since 1984.

Wreck Books 1940 - 1977
Reports of Classed Vessels lost, 1892 - 1940
A manuscript source for information on losses of all causes including shipwreck, war losses and demolitions, from which the Casualty Returns were compiled. Between 1940 and 1945 a system of posted reference codes links the posted editions of Lloyd's Register of Ships to the Wreck Books, wherever a ship was lost by whatever cause. The Information Services library holds the single set of Wreck Books. In addition the Information Services library holds an incomplete set of Reports of losses of LR classed vessels, 1892-1940.

Underwriters' Registry for Iron Vessels, Liverpool
1862 - 1884
These annual registers contain details of ships classed by the Underwriters Registry for Iron Vessels, Liverpool, which was established in 1862. They also list details of other iron steamers and sailing ships above 75 tons 'gathered from official sources'. Particulars include master, tonnage, dimensions, owner, build, date of build, rig or machinery, survey dates and class details. Brief details are also given, where known, on vessels totally lost. In 1884, this Register was amalgamated with Lloyd's Register.

British Corporation Register 1893 - 1947 (incomplete

collection)
The first far reaching change for LR, post 1945, was amalgamation with the British Corporation in 1949, which opened a new chapter in classification history. The previous professional rivalry between the two organisations did not affect the amicable pooling of their joint resources, and the amalgamation was effected without loss of goodwill from the shipping community, which realised that the combined technical services could only be of lasting benefit. The Information Services library holds a number of the British Corporation Register of Ships.

The Information Services library holds a number of reference works covering naval architecture, shipwreck, sailing vessels, maritime history from the earliest times to date, shipping company histories, as well as a number of periodicals. We also hold a selection of Lloyd's of London's publications including Lloyd's War Losses, for the First and Second World Wars; Lloyd's Weekly Casualty Returns (1953-1990, 1998 to date); and bound facsimile copies of Lloyd's List (1741-1826).

The Information Services library is open to the public from Monday through Friday during the hours 09:30 - 12:00 and 13:00 - 16:30. Please note that we close at weekends and for public holidays. Prior notice is appreciated. Please contact Information Services, Lloyd's Register of Shipping, 77 Fenchurch Street, London EC3M 4BS. Telephone: (020) 7423 2475 or (020) 7423 2531.

We also run a research service, providing both historical and current information to enquirers. Charges are available on application.

Local Register Offices & Family History
Doreen Hopwood

REGISTER OF BIRTHS,

Pursuant to the Births and Deaths Registration Acts, 1836 to 1874.

Superintendent Registrar's District of *Aston*

Registrar's Sub-District of *Aston Manor*

County of *Warwick*

Nº 50

LONDON:
PRINTED BY AUTHORITY OF THE REGISTRAR-GENERAL.
1899.

P. & B., Ltd.—1000 Bks.—8.99.

To most of us, the local register office is the place we go to register a birth or a death, to attend a civil marriage ceremony - or possibly for our own wedding! Since the establishment of civil registration in England and Wales on 1 July 1837, the registration service has been responsible for the registration of births, deaths and marriages, arranging and conducting marriage ceremonies and issuing certified copies of register entries. The original registers remain in the custody of the superintendent registrar of the register office at which the registration took place, and he/she should be able to supply certified certificates, provided that sufficient information is given to enable the correct entry to be identified.

The wider availability of the General Register Office Index of Births, Deaths and Marriages (GRO) at main libraries, some county record offices and Latter Day Saints family history centres means that we can do the searches without having to visit the Family Records Centre in London. The index is also still known as the St Catherine's House Index named after its former repository on Kingsway. The Office of National Statistics (ONS) at Smedley Hydro can advise you about local holdings of the GRO Index, but coverage varies considerably. Some centres may have only a limited number of years, whilst others hold the complete range from 1837 to 1996 (the most recent years available at the time of writing). Format may also vary. The indexes were first produced on microfilm, but are now on microfiche and may become available on CD-Rom. Once you have found the entry you require, application can be made to the superintendent registrar at the registration district shown. There are several publications currently available listing addresses of register offices throughout the country, such as District Register Offices in England and Wales by the East Yorkshire Family History Society, and addresses can also be found in the relevant telephone directory under "Registration of Births, Deaths and Marriage". However, if you ask for the number from "Directory Enquiries", ensure that you say register office not registry, or you will probably be given the Probate Registry Office number! The Internet is another source of information, and the Family History Society of Cheshire maintains a complete list of current Register Office addresses, which can be found at

http://www.users.zetnet.co.uk.

You may find that the registration district shown in the GRO Index no longer exists, but it should not be too difficult to determine its successor either by reference to St Catherine's House Districts by Ray Wiggins or using a gazetteer to find the nearest main town and contacting the superintendent registrar. Information can also be found on the World Wide Web at http://www.genuki.org.uk and many register offices have their own website. Birmingham Register Office holds all Birmingham registers from 1837, plus most of the former Aston Registration District, and some of the registers from the disestablished Kings Norton and West Bromwich Districts - consisting of some 17,000 registers containing about six million entries. However, some of the former Greater London districts have been changed several times so, in these cases, it may be easier to obtain the certificate through the GRO postal service (from Smedley Hydro), by visiting the Family Record Centre or by using an agent to purchase it where the GRO reference is known. Local registrars have do not have access to the GRO Index and can only supply certified copies of entries from their own registers. Certificates relating to still births and adoption - from 1927 when registration of these commenced - can only be obtained from the GRO as these registers are maintained centrally.

There are definite advantages in applying for certificates from the local register office, but do help the superintendent registrar to help you. The GRO reference number shown in the index (ie 6d 123) is given when the national index is compiled so it   does not correspond to the local reference, and is of no relevance to the registrar. Every registration district is divided into sub-districts, each having its own series of registers so, whilst an entry appearing in the GRO Index as Aston 6d 456, locally, its reference reads Der 100/234, meaning that it was registered as entry number 234 in Volume 100 of the sub-district of Deritend in the Aston Registration District. Application does not need to be made on a standard form, such as the one shown here, but do give as much relevant information as you can. This will ensure that the correct entry is found and that you don't receive an unwanted certificate. Information can only be supplied in the form of a certified certificate, so if you ask the superintendent registrar to issue the birth certificate of Emily Underwood whose registration has been found at that office in the December Quarter of 1881, without any additional information, that is the one that you will get. However, if you tell the registrar that you only want the certificate if the name of Emily's father is shown to be Edward Underwood (taken from her marriage certificate), then your fee will be returned if this does not tally. By clarifying what you don't want, as well as what you do, you won't end up purchasing certificates you don't need.

The reason why most family historians apply for full copy birth certificates is to establish the maiden name of the mother, but if you know her forename(s) - possibly from a baptism/census entry - or the father's occupation, give this information to the registrar, along with the year, quarter and district of registration. The local knowledge held by registrars can also be of great benefit - especially concerning how surnames may have been spelt in their area in the days when many of our ancestors were illiterate, so couldn't tell whether or not the registrar had entered their names correctly. Even on 20th century certificates the name of a hospital or institution at which an event took place is not necessarily shown - to protect those in asylums or workhouses - so the address would mean nothing to GRO staff. On the other hand, local registrars can immediately recognise the relevant sub-district for hospitals and institutions at their office. The superintendent registrar at Birmingham regularly receives requests for births at Sorrento or Hollywood and issues the certificates. This does not mean that the geographical scope of Birmingham has become global - one was a maternity hospital, and the other is a suburb! Events must be registered at the place where they occur, irrespective of the place of residence of the person(s) concerned. If someone dies whilst away on holiday or in a hospital elsewhere, the registration will be held by the office covered by the place of death, even though the person is taken back "home" for burial.

The pre-1865 GRO Death Indexes are the least helpful as far as identifying whether or not the correct entry has been discovered, and here, the local register office can really "come up trumps". As the age of the deceased is not given in the index, the entry you have found in the name of Jane Prescott could relate to a day old baby or to

an octogenarian. Therefore, when applying to the local register office, give as much information as you can. In addition to the details from the GRO Index tell the superintendent the name of the spouse, (or if a child, the parent's names), the age of the deceased, place of death, home address, occupation and, if known the date of burial. Dates of birth and maiden names of married women are only helpful from 1969 when the format of the certificates changed and incorporate this information.

Whilst there is no guarantee that the entry you have found in the GRO Indexes of Birth or Death is the one you are looking for, it is easier to be sure that the correct marriage entry has been traced. By cross-referencing entries in the names of both the bride and the groom, you know that you have the right one. When applying for a marriage certificate from a local register office, try to provide additional information, such as the ages of both parties, marital status and the place of marriage. If the latter is not known, it may not be possible to obtain the certificate from the local register office because the marriage registers are kept in separate sequences for each church/place of marriage. Birmingham Register Office holds registers for over 400 churches as well as those covering ceremonies at the Register Office itself and other approved premises, but because all of these registers are on a computerised index, it is possible to supply a full copy certificate when only the names of the bride and groom, and the year and quarter of the marriage are known. The computerised index also has a facility to search for similar sounding names, which can be extremely helpful for unusual surnames or those

ALPHABETICAL LIST OF CHRISTIAN NAMES.

Office and the other either remains at the church or is deposited at the Diocesan Record Office. Therefore, many Anglican registers , and non-conformist ones after 1898 when appointed person status became possible, are generally freely available at County Record Offices and the details can be transcribed. Prior to 1898 the civil part of the ceremony had to be performed by a registrar at non conformist and Roman Catholic marriages. For obvious reasons, certificates for civil marriages at Register Offices can only be supplied by the relevant registrar. The two church register entries and the marriage certificate given to the newly-weds should be identical, but this is not always so. Recently I saw all three entries relating to the same marriage but the groom's age was different on each one and he was described as a bachelor on two and a widower on the third - a clerical error in the truest sense!

prone to mis-spelling. Sometimes the name of one of the parties may not be found on the GRO Index, and if you are fairly certain that the event took place at that particular district, do write to the superintendent registrar to see if the entry relates to the couple you are seeking.

Transcription errors can occur between the local register office and the GRO - as with all indexing - so persevere! A few years ago I was searching for the marriage of a couple who I was confident had married in Birmingham within a specific period. Having found three entries in the groom's name of Michael Power, but no matching entry for his bride, (H)annah/Honora Whelan - despite trying every conceivable spelling of her surname - I contacted the superintendent registrar who promptly issued the certificate. The couple were Irish and Honora's surname had obviously posed a problem for the "Brummie" registrar who spelt it phonetically - as Quelan!

Not all register offices have computerised indexes, and superintendents will generally check only the marriage registers for the parish church and the Register Office if you have no other information. He/she will then advise you to obtain the certificate from the GRO and refund your fee. Under certain circumstances it is only possible to obtain a full copy marriage certificate from the appointed person at the place where the marriage occured, but if this is the case, the superintendent registrar will advise you how to apply. There are two marriage registers completed in respect of all church ceremonies and both remain at the church until they are full. As these can contain 500 entries, some small churches - especially in rural areas where the population has declined - are still using the register which started on 1 July 1837. Each appointed person must send a quarterly return of all marriages performed at his/her venue to the relevant superintendent registrar, and when the registers are full, one is sent to the Register

Do your "homework" before applying to the local register office - the superintendent registrars will do their best to help you, but don't expect them to compile your family tree. There is no linkage or cross-referencing between family events in official records, but if the GRO entry that you have found does not match your requirements exactly, the registrar may contact you to see if you have any other information to verify that it is the entry you want. He/she cannot divulge any details from the register - other than in the form of a copy certificate - but may discuss discrepancies. The Registrar General has set a search limit of a maximum of five years for any application which is usually taken to be the year that you specify plus two years either side. This search can only be carried out once - if the entry is not found, you cannot ask for a further one. Where there is no computerised index, this is a time-consuming task for the register office staff, involving the examination of a large number of sub-district indexes - which, contrary to popular belief, are rarely in "copperplate" handwriting! The entries are arranged within initial of surname, but, as this page from the All Saints sub-district index shows, they are not alphabetical within surname, because events happen chronologically not alphabetically!

Certificates cannot be issued until payment has been made - currently £6.50 for a full copy birth, death or marriage certificate or £5.00 for the short version birth certificate - so your application must be accompanied by a cheque or postal order (sterling only). It is advisable to contact the register office before sending payment as some only accept cheques or POs made payable to the local council, although for the majority "The Superintendent Registrar" is acceptable. Some register offices also have a facility for payment by credit card and application by fax. If applying for more than one certificate it is advisable to either send separate cheques or one endorsed "not to exceed ..." because if you send one payment for six certificates and they cannot all be traced, the superintendent registrar will not be able to issue any of them as there is no facility for sending part refunds. Your cheque will be returned and you will be advised to re-apply for the certificates which have been found. This obviously creates a delay on your part - and more work for the registrar.

A stamped self-addressed envelope should be enclosed with your application for the return of the certificate(s), and include your daytime telephone number in case the registrar needs to contact you. Applications can also be made in person - Monday to Friday only - but do check the opening hours before making your visit as some smaller offices are only open at for part of the week. It may be possible to have the certificate issued whilst you wait, or it may be posted to you within the next day or so. Do not expect to see the actual registers - there is no public access to these.

However, if you are looking for entries in very common names, such as John Smith, you will probably find several entries in the same registration district within each quarter. Under these circumstances, you may find the General Search facility offered by local register offices useful. It would also be helpful where you know that events you are seeking all occurred in the same district or if carrying out a specific name survey. A General Search allows you (or your representative) to search the indexes for a maximum of six consecutive hours and currently costs £18.00. Within this fee, six references, taken from the indexes, will be checked, free of charge, unless a certificate is issued for one of these references, in which case a further reference will be checked in its place. The superintendent registrar will be able to advise you of the necessary arrangements, which are usually only by prior appointment. The standard fees apply to certificates issued.

Sometimes the forename(s) of a child had not been chosen by the date of registration - within 42 days of the birth - and these appear as "male" and "female" at the end of the entries for that particular surname. These often refer to infants who died soon after birth, so a corresponding death entry may appear, but if the birth registration you are looking for cannot be found and

there is a male/female entry you think may be relevant, make an application to the local register office. Forenames can be added up to 12 months after the date of registration, either on the verification of the minister who baptised the child, or by a certificate of naming. The register will be amended accordingly, and the Registrar General informed. I recently obtained a birth certificate locally for a "male" who turned out to be the seventh child and was later named Septimus!. The late nineteenth century registers include a page of suggested boys and girls names and this reflects the change in the popularity of names over the last hundred years.

Each register of birth and death (prior to 1969) contains five entries per page and the Registrar General set out detailed instructions for their completion at the beginning of each register. Marriage registers contain two entries per page. All certificates issued are certified as a true copy of the entry, but you can only get a copy of the original register entry from the local register office - everything else is, in fact, a copy of a copy. All copy certificates are checked before being issued, but errors can sometimes occur despite this. Not all (former!) superintendent registrars had clear handwriting and occupations can be open to misinterpretation - such as lawyer/sawyer or carrier and currier. If you feel that you have received a certificate containing a transcription error, return it to the superintendent registrar who will replace it if necessary

The benefits of obtaining certificates from local register offices rather than the GRO greatly outweigh the pitfalls - the service is generally quicker, copies are made from the original entries, certificates are cheaper than through the GRO postal application system and the local knowledge of superintendent registrars works to the applicants advantage. However, do help them to help you - they can only work on the information that you send.

EXAMPLES showing how MARRIAGES solemnized in the presence of a REGISTRAR should be registered.

The Jewish Victorian & The Victorian Jews

Doreen Berger

examines jewish newspapers

The Victorian age began at six in the morning of June 20, in the year 1837, when Alexandrina Victoria, known as Victoria, was told that her uncle, William, had passed away and she herself was Queen of England.

A fascinating story is told of Sir Moses Montefiore(1795-1885), doyen of the Jewish community and Baronet in England. In the year 1816, Edward, Duke of Kent had been forced to live abroad in consequence of the unsettled state of his finance. The Duke was visited by the then Mr. Moses Montefiore, in order to arrange some business affairs. Mr. Montefiore took the opportunity of calling the Duke's attention to the expected change in the occupancy of the English throne and advising him to return to his native country. The Duke, however, was unwell and postponed his departure. Mr. Montefiore then urgently impressed on the Duchess that no-one could be heir to the throne unless they were actually born in England, and she owed it to heself and her coming child to go to England. The death of King George IV was imminently expected and the Royal Dukes were childless. Thus it was that on the 24th May, 1819 the longed-for heir to the throne of England was born in her native country. True or not, this story was published in the Jewish Chronicle on 24th January, 1879.

The Jews have always been a trading people and after the Norman invasion of Britain in 1066, Jewish merchants had followed. In this country they found a safe haven for many years, until the community was brought to an end in 1290 in the time of Edward the Confessor. From new beginnings in 1656, when official permission was given to a group of Spanish-Portuguese Jewish merchants, refugees from the Inquisition, to live and worship openly, the community had matured and thrived. Since the time of the re-admission, Jewish immigration has continued - sometimes in large numbers, as at times of persecution and war, and sometimes in very small numbers, by individuals and small groups, both to better themselves financially and to find safety and shelter.

The Jewish community in England was well settled by the time Queen Victoria ascended the throne. It is thought that by 1840 the number of Jews living in Great Britain was probably between thirty and forty thousand, with more than twenty thousand of them domiciled in London. From 1841 to 1871 the Jewish population remained nearly constant at about two per cent of the population. In the year 1871 the number of Jewish marriages, according to the Registrar of Births, Deaths and Marriages, had risen to 396. Of these, 267 were registered in London, 227 being solemnised in the City of London itself. By 1878, the Jewish population in England had been computed unofficially at 68,300 souls.

The following joke is to be found within the pages of the Jewish World, a popular newspaper of the time. A young couple went to a clergy-man to get married. By an innocent mistake he began to read from his prayer-book as follows:- "Man that is born of woman is full of trouble, and hath but a short time to live." The astonished bridegroom suddenly exclaimed, "Sir, you mistake; we came to be married." - "Well," replied the clergyman, "if you insist I will marry you; but believe me, my friend, you had better be buried."

Intermarriage between Jew and non-Jew did take place, and today it sometimes happens that people seeking their roots find, to their surprise, their antecedents include a Jewish ancestor, who possibly had not remained within the Jewish community. Many young people had ventured far afield to seek their fortunes. The diamond fields of South Africa and the gold fields of California were popular destinations to the adventurous and sometimes the lone prospector, away from the influence of family and friends, did not marry within the Jewish fold. Missionaries were active in the nineteenth century. Conversions of Jewish people did take place, particularly among the poor and lonely in a foreign land, and sometimes individuals preferred not to identify themselves as being of the Jewish faith, when starting a new life in their country of choice.

Some of the problems of Anglo-Jewish genealogy are unique to that community. The person looking for a Jewish ancestor cannot look at parish records, as the births, marriages and deaths of Jews would not appear in these registers, and there is simply no equivalent for Jewish genealogists. Some, although not all, of the synagogue records were filmed by The Church of the Latter Day Saints, and we, as genealogists, owe them a debt of gratitude for this undertaking, particularly where they copied entries before the civil registration of 1837.

One of the difficulties during the Victorian period is the fact that there was not a great deal of variety in either first name or surname. It was not uncommon to find the same first names handed down in all branches of a large family, often being the name of a deceased family member. Thus, there are to be found many individuals with both the same first names and same surnames in each generation, possibly, although not necessarily, related to each other.

Another problem for those seeking their Jewish roots is relationships. It was not unusual for first cousins to marry and, in any case, many of the Anglo-Jewish community married amongst their near relatives, or favoured families. Many of these were arranged marriages. Sorting out family relationships can be extremely difficult. People sometimes "anglicised" their names, as they established themselves in this country, and this can present us with problems.

Another thorny problem is the "irregular" marriages that occurred among the immigrant, but not native born, Jewish population. In these cases a religious marriage occurred, which was perfectly legal in Jewish law, but one that was not under the auspices of an established synagogue, where a marriage secretary was able to provide a civil marriage certificate complying with the laws of the land. No trace of these marriages will be found in the indexes of The Family Record Centre, but they undoubtedly took place.

"The Jewish Victorian: Genealogical Information from the Jewish Newspapers 1871-80", helps to sort out many of these problems. This important reference book contains just under 600 pages of the births, marriages and deaths of the Jewish community. It is arranged in the form of an alphabetical index. If your ancestor's name appeared in the Jewish newspapers of the period, whether because of a family celebration, obituary, inquest, award, prize, charitable donation or involvement in a legal matter, if your family entered their thanks for letters and visits on the loss of a relative, or if there was just a snippet of information about them, expect to find the details in this volume.

Under each individual's details are listed their family genealogy, cross referenced, including their spouse's close relations. Thus, you can turn from family to family, sorting out the intricacies of their relationships, vitally important during this period where Jewish families are involved. In fact, there are more than 20,000 entries and thousands of pedigrees listed of both rich and poor.

Besides the births, marriages and deaths of the community, there are some fascinating, long forgotten joys and tragedies within the pages of The Jewish Victorian. To name but a few, you can read the account of the assassination attempt on Sir George Jessel, first Jewish Master of the Rolls, the adventures of Sir Moses Montefiore, as he travelled, now in his nineties, to Russia and the Holyland, the reaction of both the church and the Jewish community on the marriage of Hannah Rothschild, heiress of Mentmore to Lord Rosebery, aspiring politician, the accident that befell Mrs. Hyams, when she fell down a disused well, the problem of the pension of James Joseph Sylvester, renowned mathematician, the fate of the foundling, Samuel Fountain, the career of the child prodigy, Sophia Flora Heilbron, the execution of Isaac Marks for murder, the deaths of three of the brothers Rothschild, and many references to people who had started new lives in the Americas and the then Colonies. You can read of women dying in childbirth, second and third marriages, forgotten murder mysteries, court proceedings, heroism and academic success. Some of the news items in this reference book, from contemporary accounts of the time, are of importance to English as well as Jewish history.

The story of how The Jewish Victorian Genealogical Information from the Jewish Newspapers 1871-80, a vital genealogical resource, came about makes a fascinating tale. When I first came into my future husband's family, I was regaled by my mother-in-law with the family stories, one of which was the missing money, and the famous will, which seemed to obsess all parts of her family. When my husband's great grandfather, a self made man, had died in 1898, she told me there had been a will which had left money and jewellery in trust for his children and minor children. Two of his sons-in-laws had been executors and when my husband's grandmother came to be married, it was discovered most of the money had gone, including her portion, allegedly mishandled by the executors. My mother-in-law very much wanted a copy of this will, the original being with two maiden cousins, whose father, it was alleged, had been one of those who had mishandled the money. Intrigued and determined, I eventually set to work to find the will and my success in finding it started me on a new career. I was now a genealogical detective. I became so involved in this hobby, and so obsessed by the entries the family had put in the Jewish newspapers, that I found I had amassed a large collection of records.

While helping a friend with genealogical work for a biography he was working on, the suggestion was made that I should make a card index of my records. Computers at this time had not come into their own. Being frustrated by the fact that every time I found a family marriage I had another maternal family to research, I decided to index all the births, marriages and deaths from the Jewish newspapers, concentrating on the eighteen seventies. This was a period when the number of family entries were increasing in the Jewish newspapers and seemed to me to be a middle period from an historic point of view. In addition, well knowing the difficulties with relationships in Anglo-Jewish genealogy, I decided to cross reference the genealogies. At the same time, and because so many of Anglo-Jewry married among the same families, I made the decision to include the in-laws in the cross referencing as well.

By the time The Jewish Genealogical Society of Great Britain held their inaugural meeting, I had a very large card index indeed. It was at that meeting, in the middle of 1992, I decided to try and have my work published to benefit as many people as possible. Yes, I know it is a few years ago now, but what are a few years to a dedicated genealogist? It was about this time that I found two more Jewish newspapers, previously unknown to me, from this period and so, of course, these had to be indexed. The happy day came when I could set my pen down, but somehow I was not satisfied. I decided the reason that I was not satisfied was that I had not included the obituaries. While working on the obituaries, I felt I ought to include the many interesting news items I found on individuals, realising their importance. In fact, it is often inside small news items that one finds genealogical gems. At last the day came that I felt I had finished. All I had to do was to get my work published. What could be easier.

Needless to say, it was not that easy. I had to find a publisher and then to become computer literate. I also felt no one else could possibly proof read this important work, so again I made more work for myself. However, as you may have gathered, we genealogists never give up. The Jewish Victorian has now been published and The Jewish Genealogical Society of Great Britain is now thriving. This Society has over six hundred members, mostly in England, but many overseas. It publishes a quarterly journal and a regular newsletter, as well as meeting on a monthly basis and holding regular activities. Special interest groups are held and there is a growing library. The Jewish Genealogical Society is a secular society and is open to anyone with an interest in Jewish genealogy, whatever their religion.. London will be the venue and The Society will be the hosts at the Twenty First Annual International Conference on Jewish Genealogy to be held between 8th and 13th July, 2001. Details of this interesting Conference can be viewed on www.jewishgen.org/london2001. The Society can be contacted at PO Box 13288, London N3 3WD and their website can be seen at www.ort.org/jgsgb.

The Jewish Victorian and Victorian Jews are complimentary to each other and this reference book, besides being a vital genealogical resource, is an important social history of Victorian England.

Doreen Berger is a founder member of the Jewish Genealogical Society of Great Britain. She writes regular articles on stories from the Jewish newspapers of the past and is is a contributor to the New Dictionary of National Biography to be published by Oxford University Press. She has given many talks on Anglo-Jewish genealogy and featured on the Jewish radio station 'Spectrum Radio'. Her report on the Jewish Cemetery at Ball's Pond Road was instrumental in enabling English Heritage to declare the cemetery a site of local historic interest and enable Islington Council to refuse planning permission for the site to be built on and the occupants re-interred.

The Jewish Victorian Genealogical Information from the Jewish Newspapers 1871-80 transcribed and edited by Doreen Berger ISBN 1 899536 38 8 at £34.95, postage UK £4.50, overseas surface mail £6 per copy, ISBN 1899536388. The next volume in this series will cover the eighteen sixties.
Published by Robert Boyd Publications 260 Colwell Drive, Witney, Oxfordshire, OX8 7LW, Telephone: 01993 201182   Fax: 01993 201183

Serendipity

Cecil R. Humphery-Smith FSA, FSG, FHS.

Principal of The Institute of Heraldic and Genealogical Studies

A well-known genealogist discovered a fascinating entry in an East Anglian parish register that has provided not a few family tree makers with the very answer to the problem of their long-standing lost ancestor's birth: "Last week, or perhaps the week before, I baptised a child, the names of whose parents I have failed to recall." It might do for some, but the word serendipity was invented by Horace Walpole in his fairy tale The Three Princes of Serendip, a place in Sri Lanka (Ceylon). It is the faculty of making happy and unexpected discoveries by accident.

My first experience was certainly accidental. I was going to visit a friend one dark winter evening in the 1950's. Relived on a house boat moored at D'Oyley Carte Island on the River Thames. I parked my cycle (no security chains needed in those days) by the old school at Addlestone, Surrey and began to walk through the graveyard path by the church to the river bank where his skiff would be tied up. Tripping over a curb stone, my torch fell out of my hand. Hearing me, my friend came to the rescue with his torch and it alighted on the headstone of the grave. It was to the memory of a missing great-great-great grandfather who was headmaster of the school when he died aged 82 in the 1842. I had previously found him as master of the village school at Shepperton in Middlesex where many of the family settled and where my grandmother had taken me to visit his grand daughter when I was a boy. The monumental inscription informed me that he had been born in Chichester, Sussex.

With the relatively common south country name of Strudwick, I would have been hard put to search so many parish registers of Surrey, Sussex and Middlesex to prove an ancestral ascent, but for such a chance encounter. Nevertheless, while the accident might not have occurred had I exercised more care the result could have been anticipated if my research planning had been less like that of a butterfly in search of more attractive pollen. The incident was illustrated in the late Gerald Hamilton-Edward's classic, In Search of Ancestry.

Troubled by trying to identify a fifteenth century craftsman, I dreamt of my problem from time to time and one night woke up with a number in my head. Unable to sleep until it had been erased, I wrote it down. I knew not what it signified and for several years transferred it with other notes from one diary to the next. One day, while waiting for a manuscript to arrive at my seat in the old and much mourned round room of the PRO when it was in Chancery Lane, London, I was browsing through those excellent books on the open shelves, many of them the index-

ing projects of fire watchers during the Second World War. There was my number. Obviously, unless one accepts something claire voyant, I must have seen this listing at some time before and subconsciously stored it in the expectation of returning to investigate further. I did investigate and found the answer I required.

During a lecture to a group in Folkestone many years ago, I explained the pattern of descent of the family Bible through the female lines, mentioning the entries in my paternal great grandmother's Bible which had descended to me. A lady in the audience identified one of the names as borne by the previous owner of her car. Telephoning him led to a profitable contact with previously unknown cousins in Australia who had a mass of family history to exchange.

After the Land reforms of the 1920's, sadly, many land tenure deeds and manorial documents were thrown out by stewards and solicitors. In the build up of salvage before the Second World War many thousands of these documents were saved from destruction but collected for subsequent marketing by booksellers and dealers. Tragically, hundreds were made into fashionable lampshades! Tracing a Kentish family over a period of many years, I was missing essential evidence to prove the distinction between one and another of the same name in the same area of parishes. One very hot summer evening, having lectured at Wye, I treated myself to a cool cider on my way home. Leaning against the bar waiting for it to be poured out, I started to read the panels on a lampshade in the pub... and the problem was solved by a deed of lease and release which described the abutments of lands.

More recently, a lady wrote to me that she had seen my name on The Atlas and Index published by Phillimore and that her husband had come across some documents about a family of Humphrey Smith. In reply I informed her of the spelling of our family used consistently since the 1730's. It has been part of the surname since a marriage in 1815. On re-examining the bundle of documents, she was able to send me missing evidence from the estate of my late father's great uncle, a London solicitor, Leslie Humphery Smith.

Serendipity is certainly the kindest spirit to assist family historians but, like all aids to research, it does need to be cultivated. Keep your eyes open, and consider circumstances in which such chances of such good luck may arise and pursue them. If any on needs help, I shall gladly advise. One never knows, you, too, may be as fortunate.

e-mail: principal@ihgs.ac.uk

Places of Belonging

Gabriel Alington
reveals a connection between two mansions

Two manor houses, both large and imposing, evidently places of importance; yet they are less than a mile apart. Where are these 'mansions'? Who are their owners? Are they occupied?

Their setting is rarely beautiful for, surrounded by parkland, they stand on the south bank of the river Usk, within the northern boundary of the Brecon Beacons National Park. The magnificent beacons, snow-capped in winter, tower above them, the Usk flows past, rushing after rain, meandering in drought.

And why the proximity of two such properties? In fact it is understandable for their owners are from the same family - they are second cousins - descended from forbears who have owned these manors with their estates for many centuries; in the case of Abercamlais, the westerly house, since about 1572, and the other, Penpont, since about 1660. What's more the land, with much of the surrounding area, was granted to the family long before, as far back as the 11th century.

The story begins soon after the Conquest when the Norman baron, Bernard de Neufmarche, was created the Lord of Brecon. With him from Normandy came a young knight, Sir Thomas de Boulougne, who, in due course, was rewarded for his loyal service, with the ownership of land, an area which included 'Talgarth and Wernfawr' as well as much of the upper Usk valley.

In time some of the younger de Boulougnes moved away from the region and settled in England where, eventually the name lost its French flavour, becoming anglicised to plain Bullen. Nor did the descendants who remained in Wales manage to hang on to the French version of their name, for they had to comply with Welsh custom of the time; that of adding the Christian name of the father, preceded by 'ap', to the name of the child. For example a son of William would be Thomas ap William, whose son in turn might be Owen ap Thomas with grandsons, Thomas and William ap Owen. Eventually Henry VIII ordered that surnames should be fixed, that the current name should be permanent. As at that point this happened to be William, so it has remained.

Records dating back to the 15th century reveal a branch of the Bullen family living in Norfolk. It was one of their decendants, Thomas Bullen, Earl of Ormonde and Wiltshire, who, in 1527 became Ambassador in France to Henry VIII. While in France he appears to have adopted a more French sounding version of his name, becoming known as Boleyn.

It was Thomas Boleyn's second daughter, Anne, who married the King and gave birth to a daughter, Elizabeth, the future queen.

Another direct descendant of Sir Thomas de Boulougne was Thomas Williams, who was the Vicar of Llanspyddid in the upper Usk valley during the latter part of the 16th century. In 1571 Vicar Gwyn as he was known - the name came from the white surplice he always wore in church ('gwyn' means white in Welsh), unheard of before in the area - moved into a house on the bank of the Usk at the point where it meets the Camlais brook. Its name was Abercamlais. Vicar Gwyn must have been proud of his royal connection, for when he died in 1613, his link with Queen Elizabeth, albeit remote, was engraved on his tombstone in Llanspyddid churchyard.

Abercamlais, which from that time became the Williams family home, was inherited by Vicar Gwyn's eldest grandson, Thomas, who like his father, Daniel also went into the church. The second son, John, with his wife Margaret, nee Penry,.(thereafter the first son of succeeding generations was almost always named Penry) moved into a nearby farmhouse called Abercamlais Isaf. Having built an adjoining stone house to the east of the old farmhouse, they renamed the property Penpont.

It was the fourth son, Richard, who lived at Aberbran, another nearby property, medieval in origin, who introduced the name Garnons to the family. In 1800 Richard's great, great grandson, Robert, married Annabella Garnons of Trelewch, near Hereford. In 1828 their grandson was christened Garnons. Like the name Penry, Garnons was repeated in future generations resulting in the Abercamlais branch of the family becoming known as Garnons Williams.

Remarkably from 1571, when Vicar Gwyn moved to Abercamlais, till 1935 all but one owner of the house went into the church.
Many of these prelates attained high office, almost all attended Oxford University and with considerable distinction. What's more, without exception, they were strong personalities, respected squires, including the one non-cleric, Thomas Williams, who in the late 17th century became High Sheriff

of the area.

Naturally those of such status required a residence of suitable size and style. For Vicar Gwyn, when he first moved to Abercamlais in 1571 the house must have seemed, if not ideal, at least substantial and convenient, if perhaps a bit damp with the river so near. The Elizabethan Abercamlais was, in fact, far smaller and less imposing, more a farmhouse than the squire's manor house it later became. The change took place from 1710, when the Reverend Thomas, having married an heiress, could afford major alterations. The house was enlarged in size and height; the main entrance was moved from the east side to the south, with a fashionable Georgian front entirely transforming its appearance. Since then little has changed. A porch was added in 1866 and in 1910 dormer windows were built. The latter must have been greatly welcomed by the servants whose attic bedrooms had previously been devoid of daylight and fresh air.

Certain interior furnishing, the oak wall cupboards in the kitchen, for instance, date from the 17th century. The hall and dining room are both panelled in dark oak and there is a handsome boxwood staircase. The drawing room ceiling and mantlepiece, installed at Abercamlais about 1820, are thought to have come from Fonthill Abbey in Wiltshire.

In 1861 Garnons Williams, The Vicar of Brecon as well as of Penpont, moved into Abercamlais. True Victorians, Garnons and his wife, Catherine, produced ten children, only one of whom died in infancy. Abercamlais was scarcely large enough to house them all, so a conservatory was built on the south side of the house. This turned out to be the first of a series of additions for, before long, Catherine learned that she had been left a substantial legacy. She decided to spend the then enormous sum of £100 on the house. A larder was built on to the north side, then a scullery, and, on the site of an old courtyard, a coachman's room and servants' hall.

The gardens at Abercamlais, which include a large walled garden, were laid out in the late 18th century. Both are on north side of the Usk and can be reached either via the 16th century stone bridge built by Vicar Gwyn, which is just wide enough for a farm wagon, or, since about 1850, across an iron suspension footbridge, narrow and somewhat precarious.

A great convenience to the owners of both Abercamlais and Penpont was the railway line built in the 19th century, which ran from Brecon to Neath. Trains would trundle regularly along the north bank of the Usk stopping when requested at the halt belonging to each of the manor houses. The service went on until 1962 when the line was closed, sadly for it must have been a beautiful ride through the farming land, the extensive estates owned by Abercamlais and Penpont, as well as the countryside beyond.

And since as long ago as about 1720 Abercamlais has been able to boast of another convenience, an extremely useful and, in its day and amazingly modern one. In the ground floor of the stone dovecote beside the house, is a privy. The handsome octagonal building with its graceful weathervane, spans the Camlais brook which flows into the Usk and was designed so that while the doves nested in the upper story, the lower part, which has holes bored in the wooden floor, could be used as a natural water closet. It is divided in two one part for the gentlemen of the house, the other for male servants. Presumably such out door arrangements were deemed immodest as well as too rugged for females.

Penpont also has its dovecote, but one away from running water, one strictly for doves. It stands in a paddock behind the house, a square building of rendered brick set on four legs, basic and sturdy, but atop the stone-tiled roof is a charming hexagonal cupola with holes in its base to allow the doves to fly in and out.

It is not only the dovecotes of Penpont and Abercamlais that are different. The two houses vary in appearance. Abercamlais is a four-story 'squarsonage', (a squire's-parsonage), a substantial country manor. Penpont has a more elegant air, it is Regency in style.

When, about 1660, Daniel Williams rebuilt the small medieval farmhouse, Abercamlais Sais, he did so on an ambitious scale. While the finished house, built of stone, foursquare with a hipped roof and dormer windows, was typical of Breconshire at that time, few could boast a decorated facade nor the richness of dark oak panelling and a wide, central staircase. It was the building of the four-arched stone bridge across the Usk which prompted Daniel Willaims to rename the house Penpont (bridge-end). Records show that before long the Abercamlais bridge was widened to match that of their cousins downstream.

Daniel Williams not only laid out formal gardens on both sides of the Usk with several walled enclosures to the north, he planted rare trees, one being the oldest larch in Wales. He also built nearby, for his second wife, Sybil, though, in fact, she never lived there, a charming round-ended dower house. It stands close to Penpont church, which then was a small medieval chapel, Capel Betwys. (the word 'betwys' probably stems from

the early English 'bed-hus', a prayer house.)

It was during the 19th century that the chapel was rebuilt. Some alterations were made in May, 1835, then thirty years later a major restructuring was carried out. The then owner and vicar of Penpont was Herbert Williams, who had taken over the living from his brother, Garnons, the Vicar of Brecon. The brothers knew the architect, Sir George Gilbert Scott, who, at their request, agreed to rebuild the chapel. The result is a delightfully rounded church, larger and considerably more spacious; the high box pews were replaced by light, open ones and an organ chamber added on the south side of the chancel. The building was rounded at both the east and west ends and given an unusual round tower. The cost was a steep £1000. Apart from re-roofing and redecoration the present church is as Scott created it.

The 19th century also saw an alteration in the appearance of the house. This was carried out by a Penry Williams who must have moved into Penpont as a very young man. In 1804 he married Maria Yeates but, as is shown in a painting of the house dated 1802, he had already raised the height of the house, making the dormer floor a full story. He had also improved the stables and granary around the stable yard, as well as restyling the gardens. More ambitious alterations came two decades later when to the designs of a Cheltenham architect, Henry Underwood, the front of the house was refaced with Bath stone, a colonnade with 22 Doric columns was added and the two front rooms were remodelled and lengthened. Underwood also designed a south-facing conservatory, gracefully domed, with insets of coloured glass, a most elegant addition, at, probably, a daunting price for its construction was delayed until 1865.

For the next 130 years succeeding generations of Williams continued

caring for all those who worked for them, supervising the farms, planting trees and hedges, generally practising good husbandry as well as supporting the neighbourhood. Then in 1991 the pattern was broken; the continuity of the linked estates was about to end - or so it seemed.

And the reason? In 1932 the Penpont estate had gone to John Murray, the nephew of the eldest of five sisters, whose only brother, Penry, had died young. John Murray, as devoted a landlord as his predeccessors, married Josephine Hooker. They had no children and when John died in 1968, his widow lived on, increasingly reclusive, for 22 years. By the time she died, aged 103, the house appeared a time-warp, unchanged for decades and sadly neglected. Josephine Murray left almost the entire contents to a Hooker relation. The estate went to John Murray's widowed niece, Anne Gethin-Jones, who had at that time been caught up in the Lloyds crisis. The house was in dire need of costly repairs and for a time it seemed the place would have to be sold. Then Anne Gethin-Jones's second daughter and husband moved in and set about the task of reclaiming it. A Herculean task. Grants were applied for; some came good, enough - just, backed up by funds raised by offering bed and breakfast, the hosting of weddings and charity events, the sale of trees and plants...

It has taken eight years of extremely hard work but with the help of friends and the support of the local community, Penpont has been saved. Not only the house, now a home again, with a warm and welcoming atmosphere, but the outside buildings, gardens and grounds. Trees have been planted, a new bridge built across the Penpont brook from a single oak, an echo of the past when the oak beams supporting Big Ben at Westminster came from Penpont oak. The latest project to the south of the house is a maze in the image of a Green Man's head, to celebrate not only the Millennium but also the achieving of a task, which must have often seemed impossible.

So the pattern has fallen into place again. The two estates, Abercamlais and Penpont, owned by one family for centuries, are secure, indeed it seems they are flourishing. Perhaps the secret, in each case, has been that the owner has loved the place; it has been, and is, where they belong.

Indexing Public Records
Stuart Tamblin

What are the Public Records?
I live in an area where it seems that most family historians are too frightened to do their research anywhere other than at the local library or county record office. They sometimes ask advice about a certain topic and the answer I give may be 'Try Class such-and-such'. When they ask where? and the answer is, at the PRO, they sometimes switch off and appear not to be interested in that topic any more. *Are you one of these people or do you want to know more?*

When you start genealogy in England and Wales, you firstly go back beyond word of mouth by looking at civil registration and censuses, thence to parish registers. All of these primary sources can be found in county record offices or at the Family Records Centre in London. Copies and limited indexes may be found all over the country with the more progressive family history societies and local archives. The county record offices hold the records of local government and are often the official repositories for their dioceses - hence the holdings of parish registers. However, an arguably more interesting and valuable series of documents is to be found at the PRO where we find the records of central government and the Law Courts.

Under the Public Record Office Act of 1838 and later Public Records Acts, these documents dating from the Domesday Book were brought together in one central place - Chancery Lane. By the 1970's, space was lacking and the second site, at Kew, was opened, mainly to house the 'modern' records. The records of central government cover not just the cabinet and the London headquarters of the departments of government as some may assume. They are far more wide-ranging and cover everything world-wide that was organised at its highest level centrally rather than locally.

Thus, we find documents from the Home Office covering prisoners throughout the Empire but especially in England and Wales; from the War Office, Admiralty and Air Ministry which relate to every serviceman and woman; from several departments covering the Law and so touching the most humble plaintiff and defendant as well as the most exalted; from the nine hundred railway companies and even from the dear old Inland Revenue. If you think that only two things in life are certain - death and taxes - even you must have an ancestor represented in the vast holdings of the Public Record Office!

How I came to use the Public Records.
In 1989, I was trying to find the baptism of my great great grandmother, Susannah Mayes, which should have been about 1825. She was married in Leicestershire but the registers at the County Record Office for the main parishes of interest did not have her baptism. An alphabetical blanket search, starting with the parishes of the Borough of Leicester, soon showed her though - on the first page of "All Saints". In the 'new style' (post 1812) baptismal register, it was obvious from the tabulated entries that Susannah,s mother was single but what was more interesting was that her abode was given as 'Town Gaol'.

The next visit was to the library to have a look at the contemporary newspapers. In one weekly edition these clearly showed Hannah Mayes ready to stand trial and in the next was news of her conviction. Because of the severity of her offence (stealing a sovereign), she was sentenced to transportation to the colonies and there the story seemed to end.

After looking at the contemporary newspapers, however, it appeared to be necessary to have a look at official documentation in order to gain further information. I went to the Public Record Office at Kew and was soon looking at the Home Office Criminal Registers (Class HO 27). As a result of the sentence of transportation, it was logical to look through the microfilms of the censuses and musters for New South Wales for the second quarter of the nineteenth century. Hannah did not appear in these, although some relations from Northamptonshire did. As I eventually realised that I was not Australian anyway (!) I had to research the Home Office documents in more detail.

A deeper look at the Criminal Registers.
From 1791, the Home Office had been compiling lists of criminals in Middlesex and PRO Class HO 26 carries the titles 'Newgate Prisoners' and 'Middlesex Criminal Registers.' From 1805, the series was expanded to cover all counties in England and Wales with amended, shortened information. It seems that there were two intentions held by the Home Secretary and his staff. Firstly, a few pages show tallies kept of males and females so there must have been some statistical analysis. Secondly, a few entries are annotated, a spurious sentence, or the like - showing that an eye was being kept on sentencing trends and adhesion to the 'rules' necessitated by the various statutes in force. Middlesex continues separately until 1850 but the new series is in the custody of the PRO as HO 27. These books are arranged in annual editions and cover every county in England and Wales alphabetically from 1805 to 1892. Within each county listing, the various court sittings are shown and all persons charged with indictable offences are given. In columns are recorded: Name, Alias, Offence and Sentence or Acquittal.

Indexing begins.
Reading through the registers, you can see all manner of human nature and social situation and I quickly realised the importance of these records. Taking the six counties which accounted for most of my ancestors, I started in March 1994 to copy all the details and store them on a database. As HO 27 is brief in detail and essentially to be treated (by the family historian) as a finding aid, it was relatively easy to create fields in the database which closely mimic the tabular contents of the original registers and which have space for any of the likely entries. In the years towards the close of HO

27, the format changes and there may have to be some flexibility if all details are still to be included. For the majority of the registers a clerk in the Home Office evidently compiled his records from returns sent from the provinces. He not only copied errors made by the local clerks but surely made a few himself! At the end of the series, the local returns are merely pasted into the Criminal Registers - lessening the faults but giving plenty of opportunity for non-standard renderings.

The database grew to just less than three thousand records by the time the six counties were complete for 1805-1816. I chose this initial time-span because each annual register is held in just one volume. From 1817, there are two volumes per annum (arranged alphabetically by county) and later still, there are three volumes per annum. These records were printed off in a very rudimentary way and there were many abbreviations in this first draft, involving frequently looking back to a key in the introduction.

The problem of abbreviations was overcome when I changed the printed format to allow longer entries, although with many fewer records per page. The tedium (and possible inaccuracy) of repeated typing was also obviated when I used Windows Recorder (TM) to standardise many of the entries found in the Criminal Registers. This means that my indexes are not transcripts in the literal sense but they do convey the full and precise meaning of every record.

Looking at a few adjoining counties, I had earlier determined that most others were too large to consider indexing. However, I now carried straight on with seventeen more counties. It was time to publish the indexes in some format and I investigated the prices of photocopying and printing but soon realised that to have microfiches made was much more realistic. This would have the advantages of keeping the selling price down without reducing availability to keen family historians and of presenting fewer problems with storage and postage. The indexes were well received and research into the other counties and certain later periods continued for some time. Finally, the whole of England and Wales was copied and indexed in twenty-four volumes for the initial twelve-year period. Certain large counties warrant their own volumes but most are presented in an index covering neighbouring counties as well. Later indexes and supplements bring the total of indexesavailable to thirty-four.

Other indexes and formats - the early years
At the same time as my criminal research, I was interested in military matters and had been a joint author of PRO Readers, Guide number 19: 'Army Service Records of the First World War'. Whilst writing the original case studies for this, I had started another database to help me record and review the various documents in which I could find mention of the persons involved. Listing each person by surname and forename, there were standard fields to record which service (Army, Navy etc) and unit they were in, along with information about the document - date and reference number. After a while of slowly adding individuals, I went through the many photocopies I had with names from medal rolls, service records and the like and input all the names, not just those relevant to the military careers of my own family members.
In this way, this database (eventually known as 'PRONames') also became about three thousand

entries strong. Printed out when it reached seven thousand, it was shown to members of the Friends of the Public Record Office and a copy was lodged in their room at Kew. I was asked what was going to be done with the information and it was not much longer before it had grown to thirteen thousand entries and was ready to be published. This time, the index appeared not only on microfiche but also on floppy disk (same data, same price) at the same time.

At the SoG Fair in Westminster in 1997, copies were selling like hot cakes and many hundreds of people soon had copies. They bought for various reasons. It was a new idea - publishing on disk. I've found my uncle. What have you got on the Army?

As a result of my main areas of interest, the PRONames series is biased towards military and criminal documents but there is quite a variety nonetheless and you could find just about anything from the PRO in there. The original PRONames was renamed PRONames 97 in the following year, so that PRONames 98 could follow and hopefully more indexes in subsequent years. When an annual series could not be guaranteed, PRONames 97 became PRONames 1 and it was joined by PRONames 2 and, in 1999, by PRONames 3.

FHi up to date
What is just as significant, though, is that the buoyant sales of these disks prompted publication of disk copies of the Criminal Register Indexes in parallel to the fiches. Renewed copyright permission was sought from the PRO for the new media as the original registers remain in Crown Copyright and future plans are to put many of the indexes onto compact disk and to make them compatible with Apple Macs as well as IBM compatible PCs.The product range has widened and 'stand-alone' indexes to interesting and topical subjects have also been published. 'Criminal Lunatics' lists people who were patients at the famous Bethlem Hospital with many lengthy case studies (eg the arsonist of York Minster) as well as many from around the country in register format. 'Courts Martial and Executions' covers the topical First World War period as well as troubles in Ireland up to 1921. There are plans to add to these data in a new publication encompassing all three armed services during the century up to 1979.

'Cornwall Railway' is a list of all staff in employment when this company was taken over by the Great Western in 1889. Job titles are given with wages/salaries, as well as some dates of birth and all locations. 'The Jutland Roll of Honour' was a labour of love due to having three close relations present and numbers almost seven thousand men found in the official Admiralty Registers of Killed and Wounded.

Soon to be published at the time of writing are an index to burials in Everton, Low Hill, Cemetery from 1825 and an enlarged series of 'Prisoners Pardoned' to cover 1782 to 1805. I hope you enjoy whichever is most relevant to your research.

The author has been researching records at the Public Record Office at Kew, Surrey relating to his family for over a decade. Having spent five years before that at county record offices, he has now spent more than double that with the Public Records.

The Public Record Office
John Wood
Reader Information Services Department

The Public Record Office is the national archives of England Wales and the United Kingdom. The PRO, as it is popularly known amongst its users, is based at Kew in south west London. It houses one of the most definitive archive collections in the world representing the events and people of the past millennium. The records stored on 167 km of shelving at Kew were created in the course of government and dispensing of justice. Although the PRO is recognised as a major international research institution in fact around 80% of the visitors use the records for family history or local history research. This is not surprising when you delve into the records, for although the government wouldn't have a file solely dedicated to you, your ancestors or your community it will come as no shock to find that somewhere in the mountain of paper there is something to fill out your search. After all nearly 65,000 visitors a year are using the facilities to do just that. From the ex serviceman looking for the missing details in the exploits of his unit or ship during the second world war, the woman searching for details of exactly when their cousin sailed away to America or to the classroom researching the coming of the Railway to their town, all are visiting the PRO as the definitive source of such information.

Starting your research?
Although ultimately your research trail should lead you to the PRO or it's sister organisation, the Family Records Centre, for those new to family or local history research the PRO is not usually the best place to start. This is because the records held here were not formed with the future researcher in mind - the government kept records for the purpose of administering the country - not histories of individuals or communities. It is always best to try local sources before research in any record office. A good starting point is your local library. They often stock books dedicated to local history as well as a range of books designed to help beginners get started in family history research. They also may have access to back editions of local newspapers and these can be invaluable to researchers. Other overlooked sources are local studies centres and the resources of the local family history society, many of which feature in this publication. There are also monthly magazines dedicated to family history and local history research that are available from any good news outlet. Last but not least word

of mouth is often a good starting point, older members of the community or relatives are particularly useful in that regard.

Why the PRO ?
After the initial groundwork has been done the question arises of where to go next?. The modern answer is often the Internet. The PRO's website is geared up to the needs of family and local historians. Not only does the website on http://www.pro.gov.uk/ allow you access to nearly two hundred the 'easy search' information leaflets providing practical information on how to research individual topics but the PRO has also made its catalogue available on the website. The website also has links to other sites of interest to the research community. For areas of popular research the first stop on the PRO website are the research information leaflets. They run through the diverse range of the material available at the PRO from subjects as varied as Apprenticeships, Coastguards, Soldiers discharge papers, Immigration, and Railway staff records through to Shipwrecks, Bankruptcy and Court records. These leaflets, also available onsite at Kew, are easily downloaded. Once read they give pointers into which areas of the PRO catalogue to browse either over the website or in the reading rooms. Although you cannot access the original documents on the website the online catalogue allows you to make a 'keyword' search so that you can readily see the range of files available before you make a visit to Kew. There is a full 'help' facility on the catalogue browser.

There is also the PRO telephone information line on **020 8392 5200**, staffed during Office hours, to provide general research information on the material available. Once you have discovered the wealth of material that is available then all that remains is for you to make arrangements for your visit.

Opening hours
The PRO is open 6 days a week generally throughout the year but the Office does close on bank and public holiday weekends as well as the annual stocktaking week - usually in December. The daily opening times vary slightly between 9 and 10 am. The Office closes at 5pm each day except Tuesdays and Thursdays when it is open until 7pm. You can write in for a general opening times leaflet if your library or family or local history society

doesn't have one. Before setting off check the website or telephone the information line for up to date information. As well as confirming the opening times the information line is also a good source for travel tips to make your journey to the Office easier.

All roads lead to Kew
The PRO is easy to get to by either public transport or by road. The Office is 200 yards level walk from Kew Gardens station which is served by both the District underground line as well as the Silverlink Metro rail service. Kew Bridge station is only half a mile away. Local bus services run nearby. As the PRO is situate next to the A406 South Circular road, one of the main London road arteries, road access to all the main London motorways is good. Free parking is available on site. Many family history and local history groups run regular coach trips to the PRO. They are always booked in advance. They are a useful way of sharing the cost of travel as well as sharing those all important research tips. Details of the nearest Society to you are found elsewhere in this book. There is limited parking for coaches and they need to be booked well in advance. To request a coach party booking simply telephone the information line or email coach-bookings@pro.gov.uk

What can I expect?
Admission to the PRO is free and, other than for coach parties and large groups, no advance booking is required. You will need to obtain a readers ticket on arrival. To do so you will need to bring means of identification such as a passport, driving licence or national identification card. If you are unsure whether you have the right means of identification then the information line will put you right beforehand. Once registered you will usually be given a short induction and tour by staff to help you familiarise with the research trail in the PRO. Features of the induction are practical instruction on how to use the document ordering system and how to use the self service system in the microfilm reading room. The PRO has a policy of microfilming heavily used records, often those most popular with family history researchers. These are all available in the microfilm reading room. In the other reading rooms there are always staff on hand to help you make the most of your research and to advise on the different avenues that you can follow. Please remember that for the preservation of the files and documents there are strict rules as to what you can take into the reading rooms. For example, pencils, note books and laptop computers are allowed, but pens, erasers and foodstuffs are strictly out of bounds. Access for the disabled is good with a lift to all floors. There are a wide range of facilities on site. There is an extensive range of document copying facilities. The ground floor shop is a goldmine of useful books and other publications with many titles dedicated to family

history or local history topics. The shop also has a mail order service, details on the website. The restaurant is a focal point for friends and strangers to meet up and pass on research tips - as well as having lunch. The PRO gardens and the lakes make for a pleasant interlude.

Into the new Millennium
In late spring the new Museum and Visitor centre will open on the ground floor. This will feature live document displays as well as graphic representations displaying key events form the nations history. Although at the time of going to press the displays are not finalised it is expected that the Magna Carta, Guy Fawkes confession, Shakespeare's will, the abdication of Edward VIII and Nelson's logbook from the Victory will all make an appearance at some stage in unique collection. The PRO is also a participant in the River Thames based 'String of Pearls' series of events to be staged throughout 2000. With open days, exhibitions and guest lectures throughout the year there is something for everyone. Full details of all the events can be obtained form the PRO website or by telephoning the events team on 020 8392 5323.

World War 1 experience
World War 1 was a defining point in history. The PRO has a wealth of original material that together with the census records and births marriages and deaths indexes available at the Family Records Centre form a valuable source for family and community historians. Throughout the year a series of exhibitions, workshops and talks both onsite and around the country will focus on the ongoing programme of releasing the surviving service records of the period and matching them to records with a local significance that together make the World War 1 experience.

Outreach
The PRO has an extensive outreach programme. Members of staff regularly present talks, lectures and workshops throughout the country dedicated to aspects of Family or Local history. The Office attends major family history fairs across the country where staff are on hand to provide practical advice. Details of the appearance schedule can be found on the website and are covered in the monthly family history magazines.

Essential contacts and information
The Public Record Office
Kew, Richmond, Surrey
TW9 4DU, United Kingdom
website: http://www.pro.gov.uk/
Information Line: (02) 8392 5200
Fax: 020 8392 5286
Email: enquiry@pro.gov.uk
Events: 020 8392 5323
Bookshop: 020 8392 5266
Coach Party bookings: (020) 8392 5200
Email: coach-bookings@pro.gov.uk

Family Records Centre

John Wood Reader Information Services, PRO
A service provided by The Public Record Office &
The Office for National Statistics

The
Family Records
Centre

Main Holdings
• Indexes of births marriages and deaths for
England and Wales since 1837
• Indexes of legal adoptions in England and
Wales since 1927
• Indexes of births, marriages and deaths of
some British citizens abroad since1796,
including deaths in the two World Wars
•Census returns for England and Wales 1841- 1891
• Prerogative Court of Canterbury wills and
administrations 1383 - 1858
• Death Duty Registers 1796 -1858 & indexes
1796 - 1903
• Many non-conformist registers 1567 - 1858
Other Resources at the Centre
FamilySearch
CD-ROMs compiled by the Church of Jesus Christ of
Latter Day Saints (LDS) containing:
• International Genealogical Index (IGI) for
Britain, Ireland and other countries (IGI
for Britain and Ireland is also available
at the FRC on microfiche)
• Ancestral Search (family trees donated by
researchers)
• Scottish Church Records from the late1500's to
mainly 1854 but some as late as 1900
• USA Social Security Death Index and Military
Index
No fee is charged to use the above but there is a time
limit of one hour per customer to use the CD-ROM
version
1881 Census Index
CD-ROMs containing an index of surnames from the
1881 Census covering England, Wales, Scotland, Isle
of Man and the Channel Islands (Also available at the
FRC on microfiche but not including Scotland) No
fee is charged to use the above but there is a time
limit of one hour per customer to use the CD-ROM
version

Public Record Office (PRO) Catalogue
On-line link to the PRO catalogue at Kew
Scottish Link
On-line link to the General Register Office in
Edinburgh. The link comprises:
• Indexes to statutory registers of births,
marriages & deaths in Scotland since
1855
•Scottish parish registers from 1553 to 1854
• Index to divorces in Scotland since 1984

Booking is essential. There is a maximum time limit
of two hours searching per customer per day and a fee
of £4 per half hour is charged. For further information
& booking telephone (020) 7533 6438
Northern Ireland Birth Index
• Computerised index of births recorded in Northern
Ireland from 1922 to 1993
There is no charge to use this facility
Electoral Registers
The latest version available of Electoral Registers for
England and Wales, Scotland and Northern Ireland.

Archive versions are not available. A charge is made
for business customers but not for personal enquirers
Copying Facilities
Copies of certified certificates of births, marriages
and deaths relating to entries in the indexes for
England and Wales can be ordered and collected or
posted to you after four working days . There is a
charge of £6.50 per certificate. A next day priority
service is available at the charge of £22.50

Pages from the census for England and Wales 1841 to
1891, and PCC wills and administrations can be
copied for a small charge at the time of visiting the
FRC, either on a self service basis or by asking staff
to carry out the work at a slightly increased charge.
Rechargeable copy cards may be purchased if customers intend to do a large amount of copying over
time.
A photocopier is also available for use by customers.
Refreshment Area
A refreshment area is provided on the lower ground
floor with vending machines dispensing sandwiches,
rolls, crisps, confectionery etc as well as hot and cold
drinks.
A place to eat is provided for customers who have
brought their own food.
There are a large number of outlets in the vicinity of
the FRC which provide drinks, snacks and meals
Directions to the FRC
There is a map at Angel underground station on the
main concourse which features the FRC. There is a
similar map at Farringdon station.
Bus routes 19, 38 and 341 run very close to the FRC:
visitors should ask for Tysoe Street or Finsbury Town
Hall
There are commercial car parks in Bowling Green
Lane and Skinner Street as well as a limited number
of parking meters in the surrounding streets
Groups Visiting the FRC
We welcome visits from family history societies and
other organisations but we do need to know in
advance when you are coming. Please arrange your
visit by telephoning 020 8392 5300. Coach drivers
should be asked to drop passengers in Rosebery
Avenue
Disabled Users
There is reserved parking at the FRC for visitors with
disabilities but spaces must be booked in advance of
your visit. Please telephone (020) 7533 6460
Opening Hours
FRC opening times are as follows:

Monday, Wednesday and Friday	0900 - 1700
Tuesday	1000 - 1900
Thursday	1000 - 1900
Saturday	0930 - 1700

We are closed on Sundays and Bank & Public
Holidays as well as the Saturdays at Christmas and
Easter

For further information about
The Family Records Centre
Telephone (020) 8392 5300
Internet http://www.pro.gov.uk

The Professional Genealogist

Cecil R. Humphery-Smith FSA, FSG, FHS.

Principal of The Institute of Heraldic and Genealogical Studies

Those endowed with common sense do not engage a barrack room lawyer to defend an action in a court of law, nor a first aider to carry out major surgery, however enthusiastic they may be. When one has a hurt, one might go into the pharmacy to have it "put right"; in uncertainty, you go off to the doctor or hospital. That takes time and the prescription costs money. If an operation is required, time off work is loss of earning capacity to someone and fees have to be paid by yourself or an insurance scheme which gets its funding from somewhere. Never the less, whatever the cost, you will have more confidence in the professional service, whether you have a cure or not, that with some "quack" pretending to know all about medial problems.

While this analogy is weak and there is nothing derogatory intended against the amateur or the part timer earning pin money, there is a similar distinction between the quality and reliability of their work and that of the properly trained genealogical researcher. Not unnaturally, since the latter probably has the subject as the sole source of income, there will be a difference in costs and expenditure.

The amateur will carry out his given task methodically and scrupulously but often with a preconceived notion as to what he wants to achieve. If he lives a distance from the source of his information, and has not had previous experience with the sources, he may perhaps find difficulty in gaining access, not be able to read them accurately and still not have his answer. he may send his request to a local researcher who advertises but he has no means of determining the competence or what may be expected or what costs may be incurred.

One who engages a properly qualified professional genealogist should expect the genealogist to do the thinking for him without prejudice or bias towards one conclusion or another. Results should be analysed and researches scheduled on the most economical basis. The professional will have means of determining the competence of a strategically placed team of record searchers using documentation with which he is familiar and to which he can point them, just as would the surgeon with his theatre staff. He will call upon a vast experience of his own and that acquired from those who have been his teachers and mentors.

The Institute of Heraldic and Genealogical Studies is the only fully accredited body offering qualifications for those wishing to enter the genealogical profession. Some may be able to gain admittance to examinations on the basis of long standing experience or apprenticeship with professionals whose competence is acknowledged. Those who have been trained full time up to Diploma level at the Institute have been put through four or more years of vigorous courses of instruction and practical experience. Much more is demanded of Licentiates and Fellows. They have the highest standards of practice instilled into them in order that they may retain the reputation and integrity of the profession. The Association of Genealogists and Record Agents which helps to protect the profession accepts, as full members, those who have made the grade with the Institute. The Institute has a permanent member of AGRA as an assessor on its Examinations Board.

Those who have completed courses at or through The Institute are eligible to engage in the sort of work which is paramount in the Institute's research programme, studying the pedigrees of those families with propensities to inherited diseases on behalf of medical research teams. In this work speculations and mistakes cannot be made. It requires more qualified researchers. It requires funding and the support of the whole world of family history.

e-mail: principal@ihgs.ac.uk:

Voices from the past ....

Anne Batchelor - *the Miss Marple of family history* -

and the fascination of diaries and letters

Portrait from the Attic

When asked why we spend so much time on family history research, most of us would say, " -because the people we research are our own flesh and blood - part of our family without whom we would not exist." Have I got news for you, dear reader!

I have just made the amazing discovery that uncovering the story of people who have no connection at all with my family can be just as absorbing, rivetting, satisfying and touching. Perhaps it is that nosey-parker within all of us which responds to the fun of reading other people's messages on the backs of postcards at Family History Fairs.

I remember chuckling over the message from "John" to "Mother" which read, "Dear Mother, I have nothing to say, so I'll say nowt. Your loving son John." Obviously she had said to him, "Send me a card then I'll know that you we arrived safely." And what about, "Dear Sis, Just heard that Uncle Edgar has died. All I can say is good riddance! Lily." Wonderful stuff!

Through the written word we can often discover the real person. My mother still has a bundle of brown and crumbling letters, sent to her in 1944 by her young brother, Will, fighting with the Royal Fusiliers in Italy. I only remember meeting him once, when I was five or six but on reading his letters I found a real person was being revealed - a gentle, humorous man with a great affection for his sister. "Yes, my dear," he wrote "I do remember kissing you goodnight on the landing, and when this is over we shall soon be together again and kissing goodnight." Three days later he was killed by a landmine.

Similarly, in the letters and diaries 1 have accumulated over the past year from car-boot sales, antique fairs and such like, I have found real people coming out of the mists of time and revealing themselves to me.

In an antique shop in Woburn I found a family journal, dated 1898, in which Winifred Cowing recorded her marriage to Edward Herbert Jukes, the births of her three children, Hazel, Kathleen and Trevor, and even complete conversations she had with them when they were tiny.

HAZEL, aged $2^1/_2$, took her doll's temperature.
ME: What is it, Hazel?
HAZEL: 5 + 20 to 2!

TREVOR (aged 5) Oh Mummy, poor Kathleen is being snowballed. Oh, poor thing!
ME Don't waste your pity on her. She likes it.
TREVOR I can't waste my pity. I've always more pity.

Pity isn't a thing you can run out of - like eggs.

In her journal Winifred recorded the minutiae of her family life -their dog, Mickey Ridd and his sad death, the family holidays in Pulborough and Filey, the visits to the theatre - "Macbeth at the Lyceum - Forbes Robertson and Mrs. Patrick Campbell!" In her household accounts she even listed the daily duties of her cook and housemaid, and often mentioned " tea at Winyatts." This, I discovered, was her mother's house at Barnet, which she later inherited and where I, many years after that, also took tea when I visited it to further my research of this charming and talented family.

I wrote to my Woburn antique shop and asked what else they had belonging to the Cowing and Jukes families. I was able to buy a sketch book belonging to Winifred's sister, May, in which I found a small sketch of EHJ - Winifred's husband, Herbert!
I was also able to buy a large book of poems written by the children containing

Cardony mill Valley
July 6 . 99

Grandma + mother.

Winifred the journal writer (Left) with her Mother from Mary Cowing's sketchbook

home-made birthday cards sent by the two little girls and their brother to each other as they grew up. Great stuff! Trevor wrote a wonderful poem dedicated to " - a white grub, found inside a new bar of Caley's chocolate," while Kathleen wrote a fine limerick -"To the lady who had influenza "Quinine!" said the Doc who attends her.

But the taste was so bad She found out that he had By mistake sent her lavatory cleanser!"

These were their own voices through which Hazel, Kathleen and Trevor became real people to me, and which drove me on to find out what became of them. Miss Marple rides again!

This proved to be a real challenge, as none of them had married and had descendants who could tell me all about them. But you know me - I can't resist this kind of mystery! As they were born in 1901, 1902 and 1911, it seemed likely that only Trevor, the baby of the family, might still be around.

A number of friends, pitying me because 1 don't have (and won't have) a computer, searched for Trevor on the Internet for me. They sent me pages and pages of paper about Jukes people (blitzing the rainforests again!) but no Edward Herbert Trevor Jukes. Eventually I found him myself - without a computer!

I made a cardboard badge out of a cornflake packet and a safety pin. "EDWARD HERBERT TREVOR JUKES, aged 85" it said, "DO YOU KNOW HIM?" I wore it pinned to my bosom at the Family History Fair in London, where it was spotted by Rosemary Roome at one of the stalls. She mentioned it to a friend who put me in touch with the Barnet Society. Sadly I found that he had died only two years ago, but that contact led to the uncovering of his story and that of his two caring and talented sisters.

I feel a real affection for the three of them as I look at their photographs - yes, I even tracked down pictures of them! In Trevor's will he mentioned the name and address of his god-daughter. She sent me a photograph of him at her christening. Through Kathleen's will I found an old lady who told me that Kathleen had her own school in Bexhill, Sussex, A letter to a Bexhill newspaper found me two of Kathleen's pupils from the 1950s, who both sent me school photographs and their affectionate memories of " our Miss Jukes."

As for Hazel, when I visited "Winyatts" I found some old neighbours who gave me a photograph of the elderly Hazel with their daughter. I think I even have a picture of Winifred, for a framed photograph was found in the attic at Winyatts, overlooked by the house-clearance people after Trevor's death. I feel sure that the face looking back at me is Winifred. All of this exciting and satisfying research, all this fun, came about because I heard Winifred's voice through the writing in her journal.

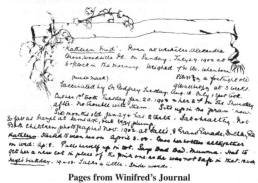

Pages from Winifred's Journal

Diaries, too, can make the past become real, and reveal the thoughts and feelings of individuals long gone. At an antique fair at Harrogate I picked up a small, leather-bound diary. The writer, Augustus Frederick Manley, had kept a holiday and climbing diary. I opened it and read, " Today I reached the summit of the Matterhorn!" The year was 1894.

Avidly I read the crabbed writing of this obviously wealthy man as he boringly describes the hotels, the weather and the food. However, when he writes, in the second half of his diary, the account of his climbing exploits between 1885 and 1894, the narrative comes to life. He climbs the Jungfrau, the Eiger and the Matterhorn, naming as his guides the same men used by Edward Whymper only a few years earlier when he made the first ascent of the Matterhorn.

Augustus has some narrow escapes -" I got into a crevasse going up but the rope was a good one and kept tight by the guides before and behind me, so I soon got out all right."

When he reaches the summit of the Matterhorn he forgets his English reserve and, at last, describes his feelings -"The view was most magnificent - all the peaks of the Alps perfectly clear. I shall never-forget it!"

Of course, I had to know more about this man, didn't I ? With help from the Staffordshire Record Office and the Lichfield Mercury I discovered that he died at the early age of forty-one, not on an ice-clad mountain but in the grounds of Manley Hall when out alone shooting pigeons!

The inquest reveals that Augustus had a habit of thumping his gun on the ground after use. His gun that fateful day had a very light trigger " - which needed only 31/2lb of pressure to fire rather than the usual 7lb." My poor Augustus was killed by a shot under the chin. I felt so sad when I read that. I had become quite fond of him and his meticulously boring account of his Grand Tour. How tragic that he should die in this way rather than on his beloved mountains.

Of course I could not leave the story there, so I decided to see how far back I could take his story - but where to begin? When in doubt, go back to the beginning. So I reread the diary and noticed that Augustus had visited Oxford on his way home from the Alps and "-saw my old Oxford coach. "

Frustratingly the Leeds Family History library was closed for months for refurbishment, and I knew they had a copy of Alumni Oxoniensis which would tell me about Augustus and his years at Oxford. Never one to be foiled by such a minor setback as a closed library, I decided to write one of my famous grovelling letters to Oxford Library, explaining my problem.

They were very understanding and sent, by return post, a page from Alumni Oxoniensis which gave details of his time at Oxford and also said, "See Eton School List" So I did! The Eton archivist wrote that " Manley does not seem to have had a particularly distinguished career here. He won no school prizes and appears in no school teams, so I am afraid there is little I can give you in the way of further information." Pity!

On the other hand, Alumni Oxoniensis listed eleven other Manleys, four of them his ancestors, including his 3xgt.grandfather, John Manley of London and Newton, Cheshire, and his great-grandfather, Isaac George Manley, who it said - sailed with Captain Cook on his first voyage around the world. Well I never! It also told me that my Manleys were armigers (they had a right to arms.)

ENGAGEMENTS.

Dinner. Time. Evening. Time.

Page from Augustus Frederick Manley's Diary

In Burkes General Armory I found a description of arms for Manley of Co. Chester, "derived from one of the companions in arms of the conqueror whose name appears in the Battell Abbey Roll." The arms include a black hand. Imagine my surprise when, one evening, I saw the last few minutes of a B.B.C. Meet the Ancestors programme about a Manley family who had originated in Cheshire and had a black hand on their coat of arms!

Of course I wrote to the R.B.C. that very night. They tell me a full Manley tree was researched for the programme and have offered to pass on any letter I might like to write to the family. I sent one immediately (first class mail!) and am biting my nails as I await their reply. Watch this space.

From a collectors' shop in Scarborough came another diary. The year is 1901 and the writer a Mrs.S. A.Brown. She writes on the first page,
"I would have liked to have kept a diary for a full year, but Arthur did not give me this until the year was several months old. Must try to do better next year. "
What a pity.
By following the clues she gives me,(Lansdowne Street, Bourne Chapel,Walker Street, "Arthur working at Cottingham today-") I identified her home town as Hull She had a husband, Arthur, a six-year-old son, Eddie, and a small three-year-old she calls "Baby". Her diary tells me of her chapel-centred life. A typical week goes thus -
Sunday - Chapel, both services
Monday - Washing
Tuesday - very busy ironing all day
Wednesday - Cleaning. Chapel Sewing Meeting at night
Thursday - Cleaning. Christian Endeavour at night
Friday - To the shops. Baked fifty buns for Chapel Sale
Saturday - Family went for a walk.

She works very hard in those days before vacuum cleaners, washing machines and microwave ovens, and often confesses in her diary to being very tired. She is a typical housewife, but the fact that she records her life, however ordinary, makes her special. As she speaks to me through the pages of her diary, I long to see her photograph, to put a face to the name. Perhaps one day I shall find one of her descendants and get the whole story. Meanwhile I wonder - did she continue her diary-writing? Did she "do better" in 1902, as she promised? Yesterday my postie brought me another small piece of her story. Little Eddie's birth certificate arrived, telling me her name. Now she is no longer Mrs. S.A.Brown. She is Sarah Abigail. We are on first name terms at last!

My latest diary was from a jumble sale, but disappointingly it was only from 1957. Then 1 realised that although the Fifties seem to me to be just yesterday, they were in fact half a century ago! This diary was an account of a holiday in Denmark taken by two lady doctors from Scotland, Elizabeth Laird and Elinor Johnston. A third lady, Jean Mann, was to have gone with them but had to cancel at the last minute, so Elizabeth kept a complete day by day account of the holiday for Jean - complete with photographs of the two doctors on their travels and of the rather dishy young men they met on the ferry! In the diary are luggage labels, ferry tickets, (Newcastle to Esbjerg), maps, brochures, paper serviettes, menus, an opera programme, guide books to museums, newspaper cuttings -even a gastronomic dictionary to help you order your meal. "Okse steg" is obviously beef steak, but would you know that "Rodgrod med flode" is fruit jelly with cream, or "Hummer " is lobster ?

As the diary gave me Dr. Elizabeth's home address, I decided, almost fifty years later, to write to "The Occupier" of her house in Portobello, Midlothian, asking for any news of her. Amazingly I had a phone call from the present occupier, telling me that my Dr. Elizabeth had married the

Dr Elizabeth and friends on the ferry

local doctor, and they ran a combined practice for many years until their deaths.

Having got to know her through the closely written pages of her diary and seen her face on the holiday photographs, I was so pleased to hear that she had gone on to have a happy and fulfilled life.

I can't finish without mentioning a very recent and very special message from the past. My late father was never one for writing very much, but after his death I found half a page that he had written in his photograph album. In it he describes his forty-two years as a delivery driver for Schweppes. His first vehicle had solid tyres, gate change gears and paraffin lamps. Imagine having to get out and light your lamps when it was growing dark!

He describes how he drove all over Yorkshire, and finishes with these words - "And if I had my time again, I would do it all the same." There speaks a contented man. I was so moved to read those words. You see, the very recent past, too, has its magic!

Now for your homework. Before this year is over I want you to write down the story of your life so far, or start a diary, or write an account of your children and the things they do and say. Don't imagine that your life is too ordinary to be of interest to anyone. Remember, fifty years from now your ordinary life will be history! Think how wonderful it would be if you could read your 4xgt.grandfather's diary. So, for the sake of future generations of family historians, get writing - now!

Anne Batchelor's first two books are being reprinted
A Batchelor's Delight -Details from Anne
My Gallant Hussar -Details from Anne
My Name is Frances - £8.95 plus £1 postage
Available from 34 Barncroft Heights, Leeds LS14 1HP

Do I really need a computer?
What exactly will it do for me?
David Tippey discusses computers......

Courtesy of Apple Computers

Researching family history is not a new hobby, although since the advent of computers and the Internet it seems to have rocketed from relative obscurity, into such prominence that large corporations are now viewing genealogists as sources of potential wealth. It's rise in popularity started in the 19th century, but the information and help available to todays researcher is far greater in scope and more readily accessible than our ancestors enjoyed. This hopefully makes the task a little easier and the fruit of our labours more accurate, although this latter point may sometimes be debatable.

The greatest rise in the numbers of researchers has been during the last quarter of the 20th century and since the advent of the affordable home computer there seems to be no end to the number of budding family historians. Family history programs sit on the high street shelves alongside CD encyclopaedia and games programs and the specialist magazines are full of writers like myself, extolling the virtues of the latest program, upgrade or data CD, so the newcomer could be forgiven for thinking that the computer is an absolutely essential piece of equipment. The lure of the computer is that it will do the work for you, in reality it only enables to to do the job better. I will state unequivocally that it's not a fundamental requirement for family history research; but it certainly does make life easier and I don't think I would have had the discipline and organisation to have carried out my researches without one.

Your typical researcher?
We are all individuals of course, but we family historians used to fall very loosely into only two categories; experienced or novice. There is a blurred middle ground between the two extremes, but the arrival of the home computer has split both groups in two, and each category now also includes those using and those not using computers.

Although you will probably fall between these extremes, you we can all find a lot in common with some aspects of the following four groups of mythical researchers.

The Paper workers
Experienced Family Historian eschewing computers and quite happy keeping track of everything with card indexes, notebooks and very large pieces of paper. They are often not totally techno-phobic, because they have mastered the fiche reader and photo-copier and may well have persuaded a friend to "just do a quick chart on the computer" or

"check out this URL for me" or even used the library computer! However they have somehow convinced themselves that they don't need a computer at home or can't cope with learning to use one.

Novice Researcher, whose pile of cards and bits of paper filed in folders and carrier bags, is starting to get out of hand. They haven't decided yet whether to tidy up the paper system or invest the money on a computer. They at least have an advantage by not starting their research expecting the computer to work miracles, and are likely to view it as a means to organising their ever increasing chaos.

The Techno researchers
Seasoned Researcher embracing the new technology as an additional and very useful tool for their research; enhancing the storing, searching and presentation of data and easing communication. They can be spotted at the archives with their laptops, PDAs and hand scanners, but despite the gadgetry they do understand fully how to carry out the research by traditional methods, and use the computer to maximise the results of their efforts and to present them in a clear, professional manner)

New Family History Program Owner, at present a dabbler, who was possibly looking for something they could do on the new family PC. The hype surrounding computers and the Internet leads them to expect almost instant results and they are still under the delusion that you can do all your research sitting at your PC.

Pitfalls for the unwary novice
This last group is rapidly growing and they represent a significant part of the recent upsurge of interest in Family History. This new interest is fuelled by the large number of home computers currently being bought and the readily available commercial genealogy software. Many will be "bitten by the bug" and go on to become seasoned researchers, but they won't all prosper. Unfortunately when a family history program is bought on the High Street, it is probably with the expectation that by using the pile of CDs supplied in the fancy packaging and with access to the Internet, all the tools and information necessary for research will be available. Old hands know this

isn't the case, there are many research avenues to be followed and the actual data available on CD and the Internet is as yet, a mere drop in the ocean. These users start with the benefits the computer brings in terms of storing and presenting their research, but lacking basic research knowledge, as too few of the programs offer any in depth advice, particularly for British research.

So naive to the basic elements of research, because software manufacturers don't include enough guidance on research techniques, they try to do everything via computer, using CDs and the Web. They are in great danger of being shot down in "flames" when they discover mailing lists and show their eagerness and ignorance of the subject by expecting everyone else to carry out their research.

No matter where you fit, it's my view that all researchers would benefit from owning a computer, but many have yet to grasp the extent of the computer's abilities, learning it's strengths and shortfalls, enabling them to use it to it's potential. This article is principally addressed to those not using computers, but if there is one thing all family researchers quickly learn, it's that you can never know everything.

Computers don't do research but...
The computer it is far better at doing some tasks than we will ever be and it can perform complex search and sort routines, checking thousands of entries in seconds not missing a single one; quickly draw family charts and redraw them again in a different form almost instantly; scan text into editable documents; copy and retouch valuable old photographs and documents and many other tasks. The computer isn't a panacea, at the end of the day it can't perform your research for you, although it can open up the way to new research possibilities by giving you access to new sources. It's your brain and not the machine's which will solve the complex problems of relationships and possibilities involved in family history research. Together you can create reports, books, letters, research lists and bibliographies, your computer filing all the material away for easy retrieval and further work. In reality it's a research assistant which will help you get the maximum out of your own hard work.

This is the point where the New Family History Program Owner can run into problems. They may have mastered the computer basics, but a family history program is just like a word processor or spreadsheet software, it doesn't do anything by itself. The hype associated with the programs and the vast bundles of CDs containing "important Data and Indexes" that accompany them in their glossy boxes, all helps to add weight to the myth that you can trace your family history without leaving your computer, but the reality is that it's purely a tool and all the hard work is still down to you.

Some programs do try to explain basic research principles, but the information tends to be US oriented which can be even more bewildering to the novice At this point the Internet beckons because we all know that with all the information out there, the vital piece you need is only a search engine away. It's true, all you have to do is log onto the Internet to trace your ancestors back to William the Conqueror, or so it seems at times, and some people are busily importing and merging GEDCOM files into their genealogy databases to create "their family history", without doing any basic research or even checking the sources of the "facts" they are avidly collecting. The consequence of this is that amongst all the well researched and carefully checked family history material, there is also a lot of "Junk Genealogy" on the Web, caveat emptor. This is not an entirely new phenomenon, as anyone who has carefully checked some of the Victorian pedigrees will know, their sole reason for creating family trees seems to have been to include someone famous or titled in their pedigree, but with the aid of computers, the scale of the problem will escalate in the future. The computer hasn't brought instant results to family history research, but it is leading in the right direction as important projects like the 1881 Census Index show. All the records we would like, are not available on-line and won't be for a long time, if ever, and although you can capture some useful data via the internet or from the plethora of data CDs currently flooding the market, most of the facts you seek will still have to be found the "old fashioned way" in libraries and archives. Computers do have other uses, besides searching the Web or CD for that elusive piece of information.

The Investment
Having said what the computer can't or won't do, then why do you need one? The simple answer to that is, it will enhance your researching experience by aiding you to sort and place the data you have collected, presenting it in a clear and professional manner so that it's of use to others and allowing you to communicate effectively with other researchers throughout the World. Of course if you don't already own or have access to a computer all these benefits do come with a price tag. Beware the horror stories of them being obsolete before you worked out how to connect the bits together, it doesn't matter. If it is capable of doing everything you want now, it will still be doing the same jobs in 5 years time. This article was keyed on my veteran 6 year old machine and my now "middle aged" 2 year old will do just about everything that the latest models will, but a bit slower, rather like me.

Before you can reap all the benefits that software and the Web offer, you need the hardware, and the good new is that because home computers have been around for quite a while now and technology marches ever on, prices are dropping all the time. The argument that they are too expensive no longer holds true, but if you genuinely can't afford to buy even a secondhand one, they are available for use in public libraries, colleges and Internet cafes, so there is no need to miss out on many of the benefits. Most family history applications and utilities do not require the latest or fastest technology, so the cheapest of the new computer packages at around £500 or less will do. If you're on a tight budget, virtually any secondhand machine capable of running Windows 95, can be pressed into service. If you would like the ease of use that the Macintosh offers, then try and get a PowerMac, as it will run the latest versions of software and open up other possibilities by using Windows PC programs and data packages via a Windows emulator program. Pre PowerMac models can run older versions of Reunion, the one major family history program on the platform, plus a wide variety of standard packages. The one I'm using right now can do everything I need, as long as I am happy without the latest software versions and a similar machine could be bought as a complete package for less than £150.

A printer is an essential additional item to the basic computer package and a modem and scanner will greatly enhance it's usefulness. Once again these have dropped dramatically in price in the last couple of years.

Once you have the hardware?
A computer without software is like a TV without an aerial, totally useless, so you will need to build up a suitable collection of programs to perform all the tasks you require. This needn't be too expensive, although the old adage of "you get what you pay for" often applies. For every "industry standard" package there are dozens of lesser programs which will satisfy many users and it is always worth looking at the better shareware programs and watching the computer magazine cover disks for old versions of those industry standards.

Family history program
I don't think it really matters which word processor, spreadsheet or graphics package you use, you are unlikely to use all the features anyway, so as long as they offer the ones you do want, they don't have to be the market leaders. However I think the choice of family history program is much more important as this is the key piece of software, right at the heart of your research efforts. You will still need some other programs to support your efforts, but the choice of a good genealogy program is essential. It is possible to work without one, using other standard programs, but for flexibility and ease of use it's sensible for most family historians to centre their research about this main program. The basic genealogy software package takes the form of a linked database holding details of individuals and the major events in their lives, with the ability to create pedigree charts and print reports. The most basic of programs will usually do this much, but it's the usability and the other features such as good searching, sorting and tagging facilities for records, easy correction of incorrectly linked individuals and merging of duplicates, which makes a good program. The latest versions of commercial software packages are generally very capable, but it pays to try demonstration ver-

sions of likely packages before making a decision.

The choice is wide, but my all round favourite on the Windows platform is Generations, which used to be Reunion for Windows and so is closely related to the Macintosh Reunion program. I don't just favour this program because I principally use the Mac platform, as I can run both Mac & Windows family history programs on my machines and can choose which I consider the best from the many I have tried. I like Generations / Reunion for it's flexibility, you can customise the program and it's output in many ways, and it offers a great many features demanded by the advanced researcher, whilst remaining easy to use. The program's interface is a very clear, with a no gimmick family card view showing the parents with all their data, both sets of grandparents and all the children in one view. This interface is easily customisable and you can select which facts are on view and which are hidden, plus include photographs, highlight major lines and show the status of children. The other main feature of these two packages are the fully customisable charts and the fact that reports are created with your own word processing program and are fully editable, giving you complete control over the presentation of your research.

Database and spreadsheets
The family history program is very good for storing all your linked individuals and events, and for presenting that data in pedigree charts or in printed reports, but when you accumulate lots of as yet unlinked data you may be better off putting it into a standard database or spreadsheet program. You will probably have these on your machine anyway, as they tend to get bundled along with a word processor in the basic package. These programs are very good at storing and sorting unrelated events, so are good for keeping all your unattached "Smiths" or whoever you've collected from the IGI, 1818 Census Index, GRO indexes or parish records. The computer is in it's element when searching and sorting large amounts of data, it's untiring and won't overlook anything, no matter what time of the day or night, so you can safely throw all your oddments into the database to be searched out and retrieved when you need them. I prefer the use of a database for my stray data, as it is fairly easy to jumble up your information by incorrectly sorting in a spreadsheet, with potentially disastrous results. You don't have to create your own database if you don't want to, databases have been specially created for researchers; an excellent example is Custodian, with it's many pre-formatted forms covering just about any type of British data. A slightly different sort of event database is offered by BIRDIE, which has the very useful additional mapping function, where you can display the distribution of selected entries from your database on a map. If you really want, you can also use spreadsheets or drawing packages to create pedigree charts, although I think that a good family history program with customisable charts is a much better route.

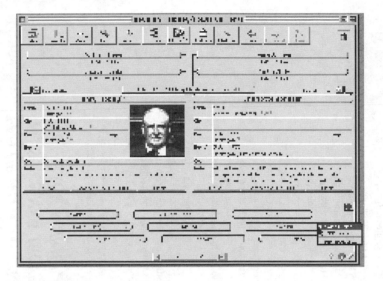

Word processors

That most fundamental of programs, which started out as an electronic typewriter, resides on virtually every computer. Modern heavyweight programs like Microsoft Word offer features which blur the old definitions of what you can do with a word processor, but no matter what program you use, this is a piece of software which is useful for a wide variety of relatively straightforward organisational tasks. Besides using it for your general correspondence it can be used to create a wide variety of To Do lists, bibliographies, research diaries, reports and of course the text of your best selling family history.

Graphics and OCR software

Affordable scanners are a recent phenomenon, my first B&W scanner cost £600, but you can buy a good colour scanner for just over a tenth of that now. With the crash in prices, scanning and manipulating photographs and documents became tasks that anyone could aspire to. You can copy precious old photographs and use the images to enhance family trees and reports and with modern digital cameras you can add stills or video directly to many family history programs too. Graphics software ranges widely from cheap shareware to the industry standard, Photoshop, but an adequate package for most family history will probably come bundled with the scanner. The other piece of software often packaged with scanners is the OCR program, which converts scanned printed text from books and documents, into fully editable text files which can then be added to your notes and reports. This can be a very useful feature and is often overlooked.

Internet programs

With the addition of a modem, a suitable web browser and email software, you have access to the largest virtual reference library in the World and the ability to communicate almost instantly, with other researchers around the globe. The software is free and access via most Internet Service providers should cost no more than the local phone call rate, but you can elect to pay a fixed monthly sum for totally free access with many ISPs. One extra piece of software is essential for computers connected to the Internet; an anti-virus program to protect your computer against malicious attacks which can seriously disrupt your computer and damage your data.

Having said that you can't do your research at the keyboard, it is becoming possible to locate or find data via the Internet which you may not have found by conventional means. The data itself may not be directly accessible, but knowing it is available allows you to pursue it by other means. The amount of British data available on the World Wide Web is still small but growing significantly, with large scale volunteer projects like the Free BMD index and Immigrant Ships Transcribers Guild alongside FamilySearch.com and the plethora of GEDCOM, Surname Interest and other genealogy sites.

As I wrote earlier, computers don't do research, people do that, and one of the greatest resources available via the Internet is the easy communication with other like minded individuals and access to their knowledge. Mailing lists, especially the regional ones, have got to be one of the most useful resources and contributors go to great lengths to help each other, in the knowledge that their assistance will be reciprocated when it's needed. I can highly recommend subscribing to any relevant lists, as you will learn as much about your hobby via other's questions and answers, as you do from your own.

Half of all the British family history researchers are currently using computers to aide them in their research, some estimates put the figures even higher. That number will continue to rise as more existing researchers recognise the real benefits of using a computer, and more new computer owners become interested in their family history. The writing is on the wall for file cards, folders and rolls of wallpaper and even if it takes several weeks to move all your data from a manual system, the immediate benefits and flexibility the computer brings will make the effort very worthwhile.

David Tippey is a Freelance writer &
Computer Editor for Family History Monthly

A Review of The New Generation Version 8~UK Software
Mike Portlock of Back to Roots
assesses this major family tree program

Generations Family Tree has been a firm favourite with family historians for a great many years. Version 8 UK has certainly lived up to its reputation and will thrill both the experienced and confirmed users as well as those new to family history software.

Generations Grande Suite UK Version 8 is the first edition of a major family tree program to contain UK research material, something that all Family Historians have been waiting patiently for a very long time . The speed and functionality of this program have been greatly improved whilst still keeping and enhancing such features as "Easy Tree", "Easy Chart", Internet Research Centre" and the valuable name databases in the Heritage Quest Research Centre.

Generations has always had a reputation for its first class charting capabilities where it is possible to move boxes, branches or entire generations, add photos and captions anywhere in the charts or group pages etc., change line types, colours and boxes, also add shadows.

It is a straight forward process to add notes and medical records and create lists of addresses.

Key features include:

• A new Multimedia Tutorial
• Photo importing allowing photos to be placed into the Family Tree
• A new Easy Chart which helps make your family history spring into life
• A new collection of internet tools
• A new internet detective allowing immediate access to Cyndi Howells' list
• Free access through Heritage Quest to one billion names

The complete package comes with 20 CD's

Griffiths Valuation of Ireland – a useful tool to those searching for Irish Ancestors. This CD is a scanned image from a film, although it is readable.

UK Deeds database – giving a telephone number to call if you find a copy of a deed referring to your family. This CD contains a scattering of Scottish deeds, some Welsh, a few from Ireland, the rest mainly English. As this list is constantly changing, it is probably best to ring and check anyway.

Index to UK Wills – a list of wills between 1400's and 1800's – this gives names and places but no reference to actually be able to pick up a will although if you are successful it would be as well to check at the Family Records Centre in London and get a copy of the Will.

The Magna Carta of Baronial Pedigrees – containing historical biographical and genealogical information on the ancestors and descendants of the 25 Surety Barons.

Index to Scottish Surnames – taken from the book Surnames of Scotland, their Origins, Meanings and Histories. Reads as a book on line.

British Isles Maps 1856-1920 – contains 208 maps many of which are in colour and shows counties in great detail and principal cities. Very useful to help bring your family history to life.

European Maps 1856-1920 – again many in colour.

WW1 and WW2 POW listings – these are American.

Generations Grande Suite Version 8 UK also contains two books in addition to the Generations Guide – *'Netting Your Ancestors'* by Cyndi Howells and *Tracing Your British Ancestors.*

Through the program – you also have access to 200 million names.

To sum up – Generations is one of the easiest, yet powerful and very comprehensive of packages available, containing a wealth of UK research material. It is quick and very professional. A *'must have'* for family historians.

Generations also have a Version 8 UK called the starter pack, which has many of the facilities of Grande Suite minus most of the CD's for those who do not require research materials.

System requirements (minimum)

Windows 95 or 98
Pentium 100 of higher (Preferred Pentium 166 or higher)
16 MB RAM (Preferred 24 MB RAM)
4 x CD ROM Drive (Preferred 24 x CD ROM Drive)
100 MB Free Hard Drive Space
SVGA 800 x 600 @ 16 Bit high colour
Window compatible mouse and printer
For Internet Options 14.4 BPS Modem (Preferred 33.6 BPS Modem) 32 Bit Internet Service Provider

MacOS
Macintosh PowerMac
System 8.6 or higher with PC Emulator - and Connectix VirtualPC™

Registry of Shipping & Seamen
Neil Staples
Records Officer

Maritime and Coastguard Agency

This is a guide to the library of seaman and ships records held at the Registry of Shipping and Seamen. It also identifies records transferred to other locations. If you wish to obtain copies of any records held at RSS you should submit a written application to the Records Officer at the above address. The application should include as many details as you are able to provide together with the requisite fee. Further details on fees are shown against each category of record below If you require information from records now held by other record offices you should contact them directly for details on how to make your application. Addresses and contact details for all organisations mentioned in this guide are given on the final pages. The information we give on these offices is accurate at the time of printing but we advise you to check with the organisation concerned before making personal applications.

1. Merchant Navy Seaman's Sea Service Records 1992 - 2000 Sea Service Records

This office is able to provide details of a merchant seaman's service for the above years. This information is taken from the ships official logbooks and crew agreements on which the seaman sailed. There is a charge of £11.00 per logbook to extract this information, the details of which are then included on a Certificate of Sea Service in respect of the seaman. Further charges are made for additional information and these are listed below.

1973 to 1991 Sea Service Records

This office is not able to supply information concerning the sea service details of individual Merchant Seamen from 1973 to 1999. After 1973 the Registrar General was not required by legislation to keep these records.

1941 to 1972 Fifth Register of Merchant Seaman's Service.

Records of individual Merchant Seamen's sea service details are held in alphabetical surname order. These details include the following information: Name of seaman, Date of birth, Discharge book number, Rank. Details of the ships on which he served, these include: Name of ship and official number, date of engagement (Joining ship), Date of discharge (Leaving ship). Details shown in these records are similar to those contained in an individual seaman's discharge book and are thus confidential to the seaman himself or, if deceased, his next of kin. If you wish to obtain details of a family member you must provide documentary evidence that you are related to the seaman concerned. If you are trying to obtain details of a seaman's service a fee of **£11. 00** is charged for an **initial** search in our records. If no records are held this fee is not refundable. MSF 5323

Having paid the fee you would then be advised whether or not we have a record and will be given details of the seaman. This may be a photocopy of the hand-written sea service held in our records. The sea-

man's details as outlined above can be obtained on a Certificate of Sea Service. There is a fee for this document that is based on the following: £6.60 for the seaman's first voyage and £1.10 for each subsequent voyage. A Certificate of Sea Service for a seaman who had sailed on four ships would therefore cost £9.90.

Cheques or postal orders should be made payable to the Maritime and Coastguard Agency (MCA). If writing from abroad please ensure that any cheque is made out in sterling and may be drawn at an UK bank.

1941 is the earliest date which the Registry of Shipping and Seamen hold records of seaman. Records prior to this date have now been transferred to the **Public Record Office, Kew, Richmond, Surrey, TW9 4DU**.

1913 to 1940 Fourth Register of Merchant Seaman's service.

These records are available at the Public Record Office and are held in classifications **BT 364 Register of Seaman, Combined Numerical Index (CR1, CR2 and CR 10)**. Microfiche of these three index series are held in the following classes: **BT 348: Register of Seamen, Central Index, Numerical Series (CR 2), BT 349: Register of Seamen, Central Index, Alphabetical Series (CR 1) and BT 350: Register of Seamen, Special Index, Alphabetical Series (CR 10).**

The original records for the above named classifications are now held at : **Southampton Archives, Southampton City Council, South Block Civic Centre, Southampton, S014 7LY.** This office is open Tuesdays to Fridays 9.30am to 4.30pm, with one late evening opening each month. There is no charge for a personal visit. Alternatively enquiries for information from the records may be made by post, e-mail or fax but there will be a charge for this.

* 1857 - 1918 for gaps between these records see section later on in leaflet concerning certificates of competency and service

1854 - 1856 Third Register of Merchant Seaman's service.

This register of Merchant Seamen service was opened in 1854. This was arranged in alphabetical order and contained the following details of seaman: age, place of birth, details of voyage, including name of ship and port of departure. In 1856 it was considered that the obligation to maintain a register of seaman was satisfied by the crew list and the register was closed. The records of this are held at the Public Record Office in the following classification **BT 116: Register of Seamen: Series 111.**

1845 - 1854 Second Register of Merchant Seaman's Service.

The Merchant Shipping Act 1844 stipulated that every British seaman should have a register ticket. The details given when applying for a ticket were: Name, Date and place of birth, Date and capacity of first going to sea, Capacity since: any Royal Navy ship served in, and capacity; Present employment at sea, home address. These records are held at the Public Record Office under the following classifications: **BT 113: Registers of Seaman's Tickets.** (1845-1853). In Certificate number order. **BT 114: Alphabetical Index to registers of Seamanís Tickets.** **BT 115: Alphabetical Register of Masters tickets.**

1835 to 1844 First Register of Merchant Seaman's service.

The registration of seamen was introduced by the Merchant Shipping Act 1835. These records are held at the Public Records Office under the following classifications: **BT 120: Register of Seamen Series 1.** (1835-1836). These records are arranged alphabetically. **BT 112: Register of Seamen: Series 11.** (1835-1844). **BT 119 Alphabetical Index to Seamen.** This index provides the registration number of the seaman.

2. Log Books and Crew Agreements

Logbooks are the records of a period of time in the life of a vessel, these usually are in existence for a one year to eighteen month period.

The logbook is divided up into two sections, the **tabular** section and the narrative section. The **tabular** section contains the information concerning "Notice of Freeboard" this is a record of all the ports the vessel docked at, and other information. This form is used for tax purposes. Births and deaths are also recorded in the tabular section along with other more routine information. The **narrative** section of the logbook contains written entries concerning various events that occur on each voyage: Disciplinary matters, illness amongst the crew and accidents.

Fees for photocopies of logbooks.

There is a charge of £11 to extract a logbook from our records and also additional photocopying charges. Please note blank pages with no information on are not photocopied

Crew Agreements

This document is a legal agreement between the crew of a vessel and the owners. It lists all the crew by name, includes their signatures and the last ship on which they sailed. When requesting a copy of a logbook the attached crew agreement would also be photocopied.

Log Books and Crew Agreements 1991 - 1999

These records are held at the Registry of Shipping and Seamen in their entirety. A certificate of sea service for individual seaman who sailed on ships from this period may be obtained from these records

Log Books and Crew Agreements 1977 - 1990

A 10% sample of all log books for the above period 1977 to 1990 are held at the Public Record Office, in classification **BT 99: Agreements and Crew Lists, Series 11**. The 10% between 1981 - 1989 are held at RSS awaiting transfer to the Public Record Office.

Log Books and Crew Agreements 1951 to 1976

A 10% sample of all logbooks from the above period are held at the Public Record Office, in classification **BT 99 Agreements and Crew Lists, Series 11**. 80% of the records are now held at the **Maritime History Archive, Memorial University of Newfoundland, St. John's, Newfoundland, Canada, A1C 5S7.**
Canada Tel: 709 737 8428 Fax: 709 737 3123
Website: http://www.mun.ca/mha/
E-Mail: mha@morgan.ucs.mun.ca

The remaining 10% of these logbooks and crew agreements are kept at the **National Maritime Museum, Greenwich, London, SE10 9NF**. This last address keeps the years ending in "5", i.e. 1955, 1965, 1975.

Log Books and Crew Agreements 1947 to 1948

The Public Record Office holds all surviving logbooks and crew agreements for 1947 and 1948. These include both Merchant and Fishing vessels

Ships Logbooks and Crew Agreements 1939 to 1946. & 1950

Log books and crew agreements for the above period are held at the RSS. These are held at this office by special permission of the Public Record Office to help with the issue of medals.

These are held in order of the ship's official number. It is therefore advisable to find out the official number of the ship in that you are interested before contacting this office. We would also require the name of the ship.

NB. Log books and crew agreements for the year 1949 are currently unavailable, they are in the process of being prepared for the Public Record Office.

Allied Crew List 1939 - 1945

The following documents concerning allied vessels are held at this office, in alphabetical order of ship's name: Return of British members of the crew of a foreign Ship that has been requisitioned or chartered by, or on behalf of H M Government.

Account of changes in the crew of a foreign-going ship.

Agreement and list of the crew of a foreign-going ship. Some Official Logbooks of these vessels are also held. The records also include those records of the British crew of allied vessels who were lost at sea.

An additional record was also kept of the British seamen who served on **Dutch** and **Norwegian** ships. These are held in alphabetical ship order.

Ships log books and Crew Lists 1861 to 1938

10% of logbooks and crew agreements for the above period are held at the Public Record Office in classification **BT 99. Agreements and Crew Lists, Series 11.** 80% of the records are held at the **Maritime History Archive, Canada.**

The remaining logbooks are held at the National Maritime Museum, Greenwich. They hold the years where the last digit ends in "5", from 1861 onwards: i.e. 1865, 1875, 1885 etc.

Log books and crew agreements not included in the above for the years 1861 to 1913 have been retained by some local records office. If you wish to obtain a list of where these records are held please write in to the Registry of Shipping and this will be supplied.

Ships Log Books and Crew Lists 1835-1860

From 1835 onwards the masters of foreign going British ships over 80 tons were required to carry on board a written agreement with every seaman employed. These agreements contained the following: wage rate, The capacity he served in, and the nature of

the voyage.These records are held at the Public Record Office under the following classification: **BT 98. Agreement and Crew Lists: Series 1.** Records prior to 1854 are arranged by the port of registry numbers, later records are arranged in official number order. From 1852 onwards the official logbook of the vessel was kept with the agreement and crew list.

Ships Log Books and Crew Lists 1747 - 1851
From 1747 onwards masters or owners of merchant ships were obliged to keep muster rolls of each voyage. These contained: names of the seamen employed on the ship, their home address, when they joined ship and the last ship on which they sailed. This system continued to be compiled until 1851. These records are held at the Public Record Office in **BT 98: Agreements and Crew Lists: Series 1.**

Special Ships 1861 onwards
A selection was made of logbooks and crew agreements from famous ships, for example the SS Titanic and Great Britain. These records are held at the Public Record Office in category **BT 100. Agreements and Crew Lists Series 111.** A 10% sample of similar records for fishing vessels of less than 80 tons, can be found at the Public Record Office in category **BT 144. Agreements and Crew Lists Series 1V** for the period 1884 - 1919. Later records of fishing vessel are included in BT 99 (as above)

World War 1 Log Books and Crew Agreements
Log books and crew agreements for 1914-1918 are held at the Public Record Office in classification **BT 165. Agreements and Crew Lists.**

Log Books - entries of Births & Deaths at Sea
Log books containing information concerning births and deaths at sea were segregated. These log books for the years 1902 - 1938 are held at the Public Record Office in classification **BT 165. Ship's Official Log Books.**

Copyright
If you are planning to include a reproduction of a logbook or crew agreement or any part of these documents in a publication, you have to obtain written permission from this office to do so. You should acknowledge the Registry of Shipping and Seamen and include our full address. This should appear on the same page as the reproduced document.

3. Deaths at Sea. Merchant Seamen & Passengers
The registers of deaths at sea are public documents and are open to inspection by the public. The various registers concerning deaths at sea contain the following information regarding Merchant Seamen and passengers: Name of person, Rank/Occupation,age/date of birth, address, date of death, place of death (This is often given in Lat. and Long.), cause of death: name,

official number and port of registry of the ship.

Registers of Births and Deaths at Sea. 1965 to present day.
These records are held at the Registry of Shipping and Seamen. A search may be made in these registers for the fee of £11.

Registers of Births, Marriages and Deaths at Sea Death Registers: 1891 to 1964
These records are held at the Public Record Office under category **BT 334: Registers and indexes of Births, Deaths and Marriages at Sea.** These records contain the death registers of those passengers and crew who died on the SS Titanic and SS Lusitania.

Registers of Births, Marriages and Deaths at Sea 1851 to 1890
From 1854 registers were compiled from ships official logbooks of births, marriages and deaths of passengers at sea. All these are recorded from 1854-1883, births and deaths only from 1883 -1887 and deaths only from 1888 onwards. These records are held at the Public Record Office in category **BT 158. Registers of Births, Marriages and Deaths of Passenger at Sea.** Masters were also required from 1874 to report births and deaths of UK subjects and foreign subjects to the Registrar General of Shipping and Seamen. These records are held at the Public Record Office in category **BT 160: Registers of Births of British Nationals at Sea** and **BT 159: Registers of deaths at sea of British Nationals.**

From 1851 onwards Masters of UK ships were required to surrender to the Board of Trade the wages and effects of any seaman who died during a voyage. These records included the following information concerning the seaman: name, date and place of joining the ship, date and cause of death, name, official number (after 1854) and port of ship: name of master, date and place of payment of wages, the amount of wages and date of receipt by Board of Trade.

These records are held at the Public Record Office in category **BT 153: Registers of Wages and Effects of Deceased Seamen (1852 to 1881).** To access these records you have to consult the following categories **BT 154: Indexes to Seamen's Names and Indexes to Ship's Names (1853 - 1889)** These provide the relevant numbers of the pages in the register.

Monthly Lists of Dead Seaman 1886 - 1889
Monthly lists of dead seamen were compiled giving: name, age, rating, nationality and birthplace, home address and cause of death. Lists for 1886 - 1889 are at the Public Record office in category **BT 156: Monthly Lists of Deaths of Seamen.** There are also nine manuscript registers of half yearly lists of deaths 1882-1888 classified by cause in category **BT 157 Registers of Seaman's Death Classified by Cause.**

Deaths at Sea - Returns of Death
When a death at sea occurs on an UK vessel the master is required to complete a Return of Death. This return includes the following information: name, official number and port of registry of ship, date and place of death, name, age, rank/occupation, address and cause of death of deceased.

The reverse of the form includes an extract of the ship's logbook that gives an account of the events that led to the death at sea. Please note however, that the log book extract is not always included. The return of death forms the basis of the death registration (See above).

The earliest surviving returns of death, date from1914 to 1919 are now held at the **National Maritime Museum, Greenwich.** No returns exist between 1920-1938, Returns from 1939 to 1964 are also held at the National Maritime Museum. Returns from 1965 to the present day are held at the Registry of Shipping. Please note that there are also some gaps in these records.

Inquiries into Deaths at Sea, Papers and Reports
Inquiry reports concerning deaths at sea, conducted under the provisions of the Merchant Shipping Acts are held at the Public Record Office in classification: **BT 341. Inquiries into Deaths at Sea, Papers and Reports.** These documents contain statements, log book entries, medical reports and other relevant information regarding the particular death at sea. These cover the years 1939 to 1946 and the year 1964. The Returns of Death which originally accompanied these papers are now held at the National Maritime Museum (See above). These records are organised in year order and in alphabetical order of ship name. They correspond to the Registers of death held in BT 334

Casualties and Deaths Lists (C & D)
When a vessel was lost at sea, the ship's official log-book would have been lost with the vessel. In these circumstances the owners of the vessel would submit a copy of the crew list to the Registrar General of Shipping and Seamen. These lists would be used for the registration of the deaths of the crew members. Casualties and deaths lists (C & D) for the years 1920-1938 are held at the National Maritime Museum, Greenwich. **Casualties and deaths on fishing vessel's (List D)** for the years 1920-1938 have also been transferred to that office. These records are organised by the official number of the ship. The official numbers of ships can be obtained from the extensive collection of Lloyds registers held at the National Maritime Museum. Many lists C & D are included in the 1939 - 1950 logbooks and crew agreements held at the Registry of Shipping.

Graves of Seamen/Memorials
The Registry of Shipping and Seamen holds no records of the last resting place of seamen. Those who were lost/buried at sea and have no known grave are commemorated on the Tower Hill Memorial, London, and are also included in the Tower Hill Memorial Registers for both World Wars.

For information concerning the Tower Hill Memorial, you may wish to contact the following address: **The Commonwealth War Graves Commission, 2 Marlow Road, Maidenhead, Berkshire, SL6 7DX.**

Merchant seamen who are buried in various graves and war cemeteries around the world are included on index cards that have been transferred to the Commonwealth War Graves Commission. These cards also record those seamen included on the Halifax Memorial.

Rolls of Honour, Wars of 1914 - 1918 & 1939 - 1945
These records are held at The Public Record Office in their classification BT 339. These include the Rolls of Honour of the Merchant Navy and Fishing Fleets, Ships list and Seaman list, The Albert Medal register, Nominal lists and Runnymede Memorial.

4. Daily Casualty Registers. War of 1939-1945
These records comprise of 7 volumes of the daily casu-

alties to Merchant Shipping between 8th June 1940 to 15th September 1945. These are held at the Public Record office in their classification BT 347.

5. Registers of Certificates of Competency & Service Masters and Mates
From 1845 masters and mates of foreign going vessels took voluntary examinations of competency. These exams became compulsory in 1850, and from 1854 masters and mates of home trade vessels were also required to take these examinations. The certificates were entered into registers arranged in numerical order and provide: name of seaman: place and date of birth, register ticket, if any, rank examined for, or served in, and date of issue of certificate. Some additional information concerning the seamen may also be included in this record i.e. Deaths, injuries, previous ships etc. Seamen judged by the examiners to have sufficient experience as a master or mate, and also men retiring from the Royal Navy were eligible, without formal examination, for certificates of service. Those without sufficient service, or wishing to progress in the ranks were granted certificates of competency on passing examinations. These registers are arranged in 6 classes, which are held at the Public Record Office, Kew.
A. Certificates of Competency: Masters and Mates Foreign Trade. BT 122. (1845 - 1900). Held in Numerical order of certificate number.
B. Certificates of Service: Masters and Mates: Foreign Trade. BT 124. (1850 - 1888). Held in Numerical Order of Certificate number.
C. Certificates of Competency: Masters and Mates: Home Trade: BT 125. 1855 -1921. Held in Numerical order of Certificate number.
D. Registers of certificates of Competency: Masters and Mates of Steamships: Foreign Trade. BT 123. (1881 - 1906) Held in certificate number order.
E Registers of Certificates of Service: Masters and Mates: Home Trade BT 126. (1855 - 1888). Held in certificate number order.
F. Alphabetical Register of Masters. BT 115. 1845 - 1854.
The means of reference to these series are the indexes to the registers **BT 127: Index to the Registers** that give the date and place of birth and the certificate number.

Registers of Passes and Renewals of Master' & Mates' Certificates 1917 to 1968
These are held at the Public Record Office in classification **BT 317.** These registers include details of individual seamen passing certificate of competency examinations and also the replacement of lost certificates. These records are in numerical order of certificate number.

Registers of Changes of Masters 1893 to 1948
These records are held at the Public Record Office in their classification BT 336. The registers contain lists of those masters who were in command of vessels registered in the United Kingdom. The registers are arranged in numerical order by the official number of the individual ship. Each entry contains the name of the vessel: the port where the master joined the vessel with relevant date and also the name and seaman's number of the master.

Engineers
Examinations of competence were extended to engineers in 1862. The registers of certificates are held at the Public Record Office in the following classifications: **BT 139: Certificates of Competency: Engineers. (1863 - 1921)** and **BT 142: Certificates of Service: Engineers. (1862 - 1921).** The means of ref-

erence to these records are the indexes to registers in BT 141: Certificates of Competency: Engineers. This index is arranged alphabetically by surname, and gives date and place of birth and the certificate number **BT 143 Registers of Certificates of Competency and Service, Miscellaneous. (1845 -1849)**

Fishing Boats
The Merchant Shipping (Fishing Boats) Act 1883 extended the examination system to the skippers and mates of fishing vessels. The registers of certificates are held at the Public Record Office in the following classifications **BT 129. Certificates of Competency: Skippers and Mates of Fishing Boats.** (1880 - 1921) and **BT 130: Certificates of Service: Skippers and Mates of Fishing Boats.** The means of reference to these records are **BT 138. Indexes to Registers of Competency and Service: Skippers and Mates of Fishing Boats.** These records are held in alphabetical order according to the seaman's surname.

6. Merchant Seamen Prisoner of War Records 1939 to 1945.
These records are held at the Public Record Office, in their following classification **BT 373.** These are organised by the name of ship from which the seamen were captured. The information is held in pouches in alphabetical order. These records contain the names of those men captured from merchant ships and where they were held in captivity. These records also include additional information supplied by the Red Cross and also information regarding the deaths of POWís.

7. Precedent Books, Establishment Papers etc.
This section can be regarded as a miscellaneous section contain a number of different types of records, these include policy files, precedent books and black books. These are books that deal with disciplinary conduct. These records are held at the Public Record Office in classification **BT 167.**
Marine Safety Agency (Now the Maritime and Coastguard Agency): **Business Plans.** These date from 1994 to 1998. These are held at the Public Record Office in classification **MT 173.**

8. Apprentices
These records are held at the Public Record Office the following classifications **Index of Apprentices BT 150 (1824 -1953), BT 151 Apprentices Indentures (1845 - 1962) and BT 152. Apprentices Indentures for Fishing (1895 to 1935)** In accordance with the Merchant Seamen's act 1823 Masters of British merchant ships were required to carry a given number of indentured apprentices. In London they were registered with the Registrar General of Seamen, in other ports customs officers were required to submit quarterly list to the Registrar General. These papers consist of indexes of all apprentices whose indentures were registered (BT 150), together with specimens taken at five-yearly intervals of the copy indentures (BT 151 and 152).

9. Royal Naval Reserve: Rating Records of Service
These are held at Public Record Office in their classification **BT 377.** This series contains microfiche copies of service record cards of Royal Naval Reserve rating, mainly covering men who served during the First World War. The filmed cards are arranged in service number order. Indexes to service numbers are included in the class.

10. Passenger Lists 1878 - 1960
(Information provided by Guildhall Library, Aldermanbury, London EC2P 2EJ)
Passenger lists for the period before 1890 have not survived in England, with the exception of a few relating to vessels in the United Kingdom between 1878 and 1888. These, and the surviving lists for the period between 1890 and 1960, are held at the **Public Record Office.** The classifications you would require at that address are as follow:

BT 26. Inwards Passenger Lists 1878 to 1960.
The information given in these lists include the age, occupation, address in the United Kingdom and the date of entering the country of passengers entering the United Kingdom by sea from ports outside Europe and the Mediterranean. They are arranged under the names of the ports of arrival. The registers containing this information are held in classification **BT 32. Registers of Passenger Lists 1906 to 1951**. Prior to 1920 they are under the different ports, the names of ships and the month of arrival and departure: after 1920 the date of arrival or departure is recorded. Before 1908 the registers relate only to the ports of Southampton, Bristol and Weymouth.

BT 27. Outward Passenger Lists. 1890 to 1960
Lists, similar to BT 26, of passengers leaving the United Kingdom. They are arranged under the names of the ports of departure. For registers see BT 32 (as above).

There have been several resources published specifically aimed at helping family historians locate passenger lists outside the UK. Copies of these are now held at **The Guildhall Library, Aldermanbury, London, EC2P 2EJ.** These include
Filby, P.W.: **Passengers and immigration lists index (and annual supplements)**, that cover North America. It can be found in the Reference Collection at R 325/2 and lists individuals by surname and shows where the passenger list can be found;
The Morton Allan Directory of European Steamship arrivals ... 1890 - 1930 at the ports of New York, Philadelphia, Boston & Baltimore, Closed Access LB 286, is also useful.
British Immigration to Victoria - assisted immigrants 1839 - 1891 (microfiche 3)
Index of New South Wales Convict Indents (microfiches 29)
Immigration Index to assisted immigrants arriving Sydney 1844 - 96, Closed Access 387/5, and Hughes, 1A:
9 assorted list to Port Phillip, c 1839 - 51, Closed Access 387/5, cover Australia.
Guildhall Library holds a number of shipping indexes that were compiled for the popular immigration ports in Australia and New Zealand. These include:
Shipping arrivals & departures, Victorian ports, 1798-1855 (2 vols.),
Shipping arrivals & departures, Sydney, 1788-1844 (3 vols.),
Shipping arrivals & departures, Tasmania, 1803-1843, (2 vols.) and **Shipping to New Zealand 1839-1889** (known as the Comber Index), all Closed Access 387/2.
Some other books held by the Library also provided potentially useful information, such as **Dictionary of Western Australians. 1829 - 1914**, Closed Access 325/941 and British settlers in Natal 1824 - 1857. Closed access 325/684

The Registry of Shipping and Seamen
P.O. Box 165 Cardiff CF14 5FU
Tel: (029) 2076 8227 Fax: (029) 2074 7877
Email: RSS@mcga.gov.uk
Website :http://www.mcagency.org.uk

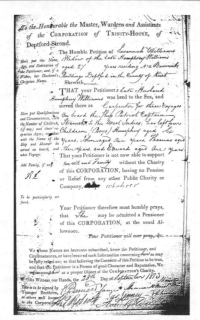

Special Collections in the Library of the Society of Genealogists

Sue Gibbons

The Society of Genealogists was founded in 1911 to promote the study of genealogy. This it does by lobbying government and other institutions to allow greater access to records, by its active support of the Federation of Family History Societies, by running lectures and events on genealogical and historical subjects, by publishing material of interest to family historians and, last but not least, by the provision of the largest genealogical library in Britain. The library is located a short walk from the Barbican underground station and the Family Records Centre at 14 Charterhouse Buildings, Goswell Road, London EC1M 7BA. It is open from 10am to 6pm Tuesday to Saturday with late nights till 8pm on Wednesday and Thursday and can be used by non-members on payment of search fees starting at £3 for one hour.

Apart from register copies, tombstone inscriptions, civil registration, marriage, census and will indexes, the library is rich in special, sometimes unique, collections of material which are of great value in family history research. The brief article which follows gives just a small taste of some of these. Those who are unable to visit the library and who have Internet access should log onto the Society's website at www.sog.org.uk to find out what can be done from home. In particular some of the Society's largest indexes will be going on-line towards the end of 2000 and further information about this can be found on the Origins website at www.origins.net

General Sources

Bernau Index

Charles Bernau was one of the principal founder members of the SoG and when he died in 1961 was the last surviving signatory of the original Articles of Association of 50 years before. In about 1913 in his mid thirties, he became a professional genealogical researcher. During the course of his work he became aware of the vast amount of genealogical information hidden in the then unindexed records of the Court of Chancery. Between 1914 and 1929, he, and a team of helpers began to compile a card index to this and other material which is mainly at the PRO. By the end, they had references to some 4? million individuals between roughly 1350 and 1800, but with the emphasis on the 18th century. The source material for the index is detailed in Hilary Sharp's "How to use the Bernau index".

Coleman's catalogues & index

James Coleman was an heraldic and genealogical bookseller and publisher in London in the second half of the 19th century. As a second hand dealer he sold marriage settlements, wills, rent rolls, peerage claims, private and local Acts of Parliament, appeal cases, pedigrees, deeds, autograph letters, maps and so on as well as new and second hand books on heraldry, topography and biography. His catalogues give brief details of the items for sale and the names of the people involved.

We have bound copies of these catalogues from 1859-1911. A card index of nearly 50,000 names was compiled in 1936, giving the volume and catalogue number for the item where that person was mentioned.

Document collections

The Document Collection, which is divided into 3 sections, began life with the Society itself in the offices of George Tudor Sherwood in the Strand. It was Sherwood who, from 1911 until his death in 1958, was responsible for the collection and its organisation.

The **surname section** of the Document Collection contains a mass of miscellaneous genealogical information on families from Britain and the English speaking world arranged in A-Z order of surname. The documents themselves include pedigrees, wills, birth, marriage and death certificates, letters, extracts from parish registers and so on.

Large collections on particular families or from a specific source such as Bernau's correspondence dealing with work done for clients, form a separate A-Z sequence known as the **Special Document Collections.**

Documents relating to several people or families in a particular place, such as deeds, monumental inscriptions, census returns etc. are filed alphabetically by county and place (or country if overseas) in the **Topographical Document Collection.**

Great card index

In September 1910, before the SoG was founded, George Sherwood published an article entitled "Proposals for a Society of Genealogists". It suggested a reference library be created in central London to house amongst other things "A great consolidated index in one alphabet, on slips, on the card index system." Before the end of 1911, 12-13,000 cards had been received and the proposal was made that every time an index was created, the cards left after it had been typed up should be sorted into the Great Card Index. By 1912 the number of slips received had risen to 500,000 and by 1931 it was almost three million.

The major sources used in its compilation are parish registers, marriage licences notably those of the Bishop of London 1700-1780, wills and admons, MIs especially

"*Memorials of the Dead in Ireland*", obituaries, Chancery records, subscription lists, deeds and so on.

The geographical spread is primarily Britain but it includes references from all over the English speaking world from the Norman Conquest to the 19th century. It is especially rich in material relating to the 18th century.

Holworthy Collection

Richard Holworthy was a founder member of the Society of Genealogists and his bequest consists of two separate collections: two boxes of abstracts of wills arranged in alphabetical order of testator and five boxes of notes on armorial families also in A-Z order. The armorial collection, although it bears his name, was not the work of Holworthy but of his friend and brother-in-law Frederick Arthur Jewers. Jewers was a noted heraldist and fellow of the Society of Antiquaries.

Jewers' heraldic notes were the research for a projected "General armory". This was never completed although selections of this work appeared in parts in The Genealogist, New Series, vols. 13-29 (1897-1913).

Whitmore collection

Major John Beach Whitmore was the author of the Genealogical Guide which continued Marshall's work and joint author of the London Visitation Pedigrees. He served on the Council of the Harleian Society and was a Fellow both of the SoG and the Society of Antiquaries. The major part of his collection consists of 61 files of notes and pedigrees on miscellaneous families including eight from Shropshire where Whitmore's own antecedents came from and four on the Worsley family.

There are also a number of bound manuscript volumes on the London/Middlesex shelves dealing with will abstracts, aldermen, pedigrees, parishes and an index to the MIs and burials in Lyson's Environs of London.

Training and Occupational Sources
Apprenticeship collections

An Act of Parliament in Queen Anne's reign ruled that from May 1st 1710 a tax was to be paid on all apprenticeship indentures excepting those where the fee was less than one shilling or those arranged by parish or public charities. It was abolished in 1804 but the last tardy payments continued to trickle in until January 1811. The Society has indexed the names of the apprentices and their masters from 1710-1774.

Up to about 1750, the name, occupation and place of origin of the father, guardian or widowed mother of the apprentice is usually given. The name, occupation and place of work of the master is given throughout the series. There are well over a million names of masters and apprentices in the original registers.

The Society also holds a collection of original apprenticeship indentures covering the periods 1641-1749 and 1775-1888.

Civil Service Evidences of Age

Between 1855 and 1939 candidates for Civil Service examinations and applicants for certain jobs had to provide proof of their age to the Civil Service Commission: a birth certificate for the post-civil registration period or something like a certified extract from a baptismal register for the period before this or in countries of origin which did not have civil registration of births. The period covered is therefore people born from the early 19th to the early 20th centuries. The geographical spread is extremely wide - there are many births in Ireland, the Channel Islands, Malta and Gibralta and others for British people born all over the world especially in India - everything from Russian baptismal certificates to Indian horoscopes drawn up at the child's birth!

Since the collection is still being worked on, access to it must be severely restricted for a while but it is hoped that the indexing will be completed before the end of 2000.

Trinity House Petitions
(Merchant seamen and their families)

The Corporation of Trinity House at Deptford was, amongst other things, a charitable body for the relief of distressed mariners and their widows and orphans. As an example of this last function in 1815, it supported 144 almspeople at Deptford and Mile End and over 7000 out-pensioners and it is this function which is the source of the Trinity House Petitions. The surviving petitions run from 1787 to 1854 and are thought to be complete.

Another set of documents, apparently not connected to the Petitions, consisting of christening and marriage certificates, petitions etc. seem to relate to pension and almshouse applications between 1790 & 1890 with most falling into the period 1830-80.

The petitions or application forms give certain standard information including: name, age, address, occupation or husband's name if a widow; date of mariner's going to sea and length of service; dates and names of vessels served on and rank held on each; date, cause and circumstances of death or leaving the service; names and ages of dependants; statement of financial circumstances.

The collection may include details of men who served for part of their lives in the Royal as well as the Merchant Navy and cover the important Napoleonic wars period.

Fawcett Index *(Clergy and North Country)*

The Fawcett index is described as being of clergy and north country families and contains entries from the 12th to the early 20th centuries.

Three types of source were used in it's compilation:-

> *General works* such as Musgrave's Obituary, the Gentleman's and London Magazines.
> *Various fasti and clergy lists* eg Le Neve, the Churchman's Almanac, Stubb's Episcopal Successions, Who's Who in Methodism. Fawcett also used the Australian Handbook between the 1870s and 1890s to pick up British clergy appointed to positions in Australia.
> *Histories of Durham, Yorkshire, Cumberland and Westmorland* etc, for instance, Surtees' and Hutchinson's histries of Durham, Yorkshire Notes and Queries, Whellan's Cumberland and Westmorland.

County and Country Sources
Snell Collection *(Berkshire)*

Frederick Snell died in November 1914, leaving over 50 manuscript volumes of research, abstracts and indexes to the Society of Genealogists.

The collection broadly falls into 3 sections:-

> 1. His *general genealogical collection* comprising mainly MIs and register extracts from London/Middlesex, the

Home Counties and Oxfordshire; indexes of names in Archdeaconry of Berkshire wills 1480-1710 and notes on Snell and other families.
2. Abstracts of Berkshire wills in the Prerogative Court of Canterbury 1391 1738.
3. A calendar of Chancery Depositions before 1714 worked up partly from Snell's notes by Charles Bernau.

Rogers Bequest (Cornwall)
John Percival Rogers was a solicitor, town clerk at Helston and a Fellow of the Society of Genealogists. At his death in 1966 he bequeathed a large collection of manuscript and printed books on Cornwall to the Society. Of the manuscript volumes seven contained pedigrees of Cornish families and it is these which are generally known as the Rogers Collection. An index of the families included was published in the Genealogists' Magazine.

Glencross Collection (Primarily Cornwall, some Devon)
This collection was compiled by Reginald Glencross, a Founder Fellow of the Society and a professional genealogist. The files of loose papers were incorporated into the Document Collection and consisted of pedigrees, abstracts from wills and parish registers and other documents.

The card index bearing his name contains references to most, but not all, of the loose papers filed into the Document Collection. The index is more than a guide to the files, however, as it includes additional references and notes on material which was not abstracted such as Cornish wills and admons in the PCC.

The Glencross Collection is usually described as being for Cornwall. Certainly that and Devon were Glencross's main interest. However, a brief examination of the index also shows references to other areas:- Marriage licences from Chester and Taunton, wills, not only from Exeter, but also Hampshire, Surrey, London and Chester and many Lancashire references.

CamplingCollection (East Anglia)
Arthur Campling was descended from the Camplings of Haynford, Norfolk and maintained a lifelong interest in the heraldry and genealogy of families from that and neighbouring counties. He was Hon. Librarian of the Norfolk and Norwich Archaeological Society and worked for many years at the College of Arms. He co-edited and annotated the **1664 visitation of Norfolk** (Harleian Society vols. 85 and 86).

The largest part of his collection is a series of 5,200 files on nearly 2000 surnames and consists mainly of pedigrees of East Anglian families. The sources used were: Heralds' visitations, collections at the College of Arms, Norfolk Record Society and the Norfolk and Norwich Archaeological Society, wills, marriage licences, original grants of arms at the British Museum and the Society of Antiquaries, Norwich City Archives, British Museum Additional MSs etc.

In 1939 and 1947 the Harleian Society also published as volumes 91 and 97, Campling's **East Anglian Pedigrees**. This was only a selection from his collection. In addition to the sources mentioned above, Campling had access to information at the College of Arms which was gathered by the heralds during their visitations but which did not become part of the official record of the armigerous families of the county. So, for instance, sixteen Norfolk & Suffolk men whom the Heralds summoned at their visitations in 1664-66, disclaimed any right to arms. It was these families and those whose pedigrees had not appeared in print or been recorded in the visitations which Campling included in these East Anglian pedigrees.

Another part of the Campling collection is his extracts of Norfolk and Suffolk marriage licences. Most of the entries are from Norwich Consistory Court but also included are others from the Archdeaconries of Norfolk, Suffolk and Sudbury, Faculty Office, Vicar General and Bishop of London. The extracts have not been precisely dated but certainly range from 1549 to 1799.

Whitehead Collection (East Anglia)
This is a large varied collection compiled by L Haydon Whitehead and is mainly, but not exclusively, East Anglian material. 14 drawers in the index of small cards are concerned with East Anglian individuals. Others in the same cabinet are descriptions of churchyards, stonemasons, PCC wills mainly for Suffolk but also for Cambridgeshire, Hertfordshire, Norwich and Hitchin testators. The largest number of drawers (15) are monumental inscriptions mainly for Essex, Cambridgeshire, Derbyshire and Hertfordshire, but including other English counties from Bedfordshire to Yorkshire.

There is a second card index of large cards which seems to be data on his own East Anglian families as several of the most commonly occuring surnames are matched by roll pedigrees which were also part of this bequest. There were in addition a large number of loose papers and wills which were listed and then dispersed into the document collection and some MS notebooks.

Finally there are Hearth Tax returns for Essex 1662; birth, marriage and death cuttings from fairly modern issues of the Daily Telegraph and most importantly a huge number of typed and MS transcripts of East Anglian parish registers, BTs and register bills, chiefly for Cambridgeshire, Essex and Suffolk.

Dwelly Index (West country families)
Edward Dwelly was a Fellow of the SoG and of the Society of Antiquaries of Scotland. He was also a genealogist and record searcher and as such compiled, over many years, a card index of references useful to his work. By his death in 1939 there were something like half a million slips. The period covered by the index is from the 11th to 20th centuries but it is fullest for the 17th century.

The Dwelly index is always described as containing west country families but like many other collections at the Society this description is inadequate and conceals its relevance beyond the stated coverage. It also contains material from elsewhere in the country such as:- Norwich testators before 1637; MIs from many parishes such as Herne in Kent; strays found in Manchester Cathedral marriage registers 1573-1750; Nottinghamshire Baptist registers; foreigners naturalised in the American colonies c. 1747-61. There are also entries culled from a wide range of more general sources: Harleian and Additional MSS at the British Museum and other MS sources; Chancery proceedings before 1714 and Exchequer Deponents c. 1547-1726; pedigrees from the Plea Rolls published in the

Genealogist; persons mentioned in PCC and other wills etc.

Macleod Papers *(Scotland)*
In 1949 the Society purchased its only large MS collection dealing with Scottish families - the Macleod papers. This work was compiled between 1880 & 1940 by two highly respected professional record searchers: the Revd. Walter Macleod of Edinburgh and his son John. The collection consists of notes compiled for their case reports but also includes other general genealogical material. (For instance, amongst the 7 bound volumes which are part of the collection, there are 3 volumes of Edinburgh Commissariat testaments).

Carey's Irish Lists
Captain Cary became a life member of the Society in 1913 but it was not until 1948 that he began making his collection of Irish lists. Most of the families in which he had a personal interest were of English or French origin, settled in Ireland. Soon he had made extracts from all the printed books available to him and turned to manuscript sources. Eventually there were 7 volumes containing over 1,800 pages of closely typed lists. The contents of the volumes include JPs and magistrates, militia, volunteer and yeomanry officers, coroners, notaries public, high sheriffs, mayors, clergy, householders and landowners, bailiffs, church wardens, apprentices etc. He also made extracts from registers and newspapers (especially marriage and obituary notices). The period covered is principally 17th to 19th centuries.

Percy-Smith or India Index
H Kendal Percy-Smith was a career soldier who was posted to India in 1919. His abiding interest in the Honourable East India Company and its employees dates from this period. About 1933 he began to compile a card index of births, marriages and deaths of British people in India. In 1949 he was preparing an index to marriages registered in the India Office Records from 1698-1900, covering Bengal, Madras, Bombay, Burma, St Helena, Singapore, Penang, Bencoolen and Macao. These were presumably added to the already existing index. It is likely that another index compiled by H E Stapleton of Europeans in Dacca, Bengal was also amalgamated with Percy-Smith's index.

This index consists of 4 main types of information: data on military officers, military medical staff, civil servants and births, marriages and deaths culled from a variety of sources. The main period of coverage for the index is 1790-1857 but also contains references to dates outside these years.

Smith Collection *(West Indies)*
In 1913 the Society was given 43 volumes of pedigrees and lists compiled by Mrs Vernona Smith which mainly relate to people living in the West Indies.

Principal sources used appear to be: inhabitants lists of various Barbados parishes 1676-80; notes, will abstracts, Colonial Papers, Close Rolls and Chancery Proceedings relating to families in Grenada, Antigua, Jamaica, Nevis, St. Kitts, Carolina and Virginia; christenings from several St. Kitts parishes 1721-30; references to West Indian people from the Gentleman's Magazine. However, volumes 10 & 18 also include a lot of material relating to families in Warwickshire (mainly Birmingham), Worcestershire and Shropshire, volume 16 contains French and Flemish families in London and Southampton and there are extended visitation pedigrees

relating to people from all over England. A film copy of her abstracts of Jamaican wills 1625-1792 is also held. The original is at the British Library.

Jewish Collections
Colyer Fergusson Collection
Sir Thomas Colyer-Fergusson was a council member of the Jewish Historical Society and a vice-president of the Society of Genealogists. His collection consists of 10 boxes of pedigrees and 11 of newspaper cuttings:-

Pedigrees
The sources used for these were extracts from PCC wills, the Gentleman's Magazine, synagogue registers, gravestone inscriptions, newspaper entries and so on.

Newspaper cuttings
These cover subjects of Jewish interest as well as articles on individuals. They are taken mostly from the Jewish Chronicle, but also from the Jewish World, the Jewish Guardian, the Sphere, the Crown, the Sketch etc. They chiefly consist of obituaries and death notices, but there are also appointments, biographical articles, genealogies, interviews, bequests and legal notices, births, engagements and marriages.

Hyamson collection
Albert Montefiore Hyamson was a civil servant and Director of Immigration in Palestine. On his return from Palestine he increased his labours on behalf of the Jewish Historical Society, of which, by the time of his death, he had been a member for 55 or more years. He was its President from 1945-1947. The main part of the Hyamson collection is arranged in family bundles and is preceded by a contents list and surname index. There is also a small subject section covering areas such as bankrupts, congregations in Canterbury, Exeter and Falmouth, obituaries etc.

Mordy collection
Isobel Mordy's interest in her mother's Jewish genealogy only really took off in 1965 with her retirement as a Childrens' Welfare Officer in Bournemouth. From then until her death in 1993, she compiled a large card index of information on a huge number of Jewish individuals and families.

In 1984 Miss Mordy allowed the Mormons to film her card index but she continued working on it and any material which she added between the 1984 filming and her death in 1993 has not been assessed for quantity or filmed.

The collection consists of four sections:-

1. *Data cards* for data derived from original sources such as census returns, wills, birth, marriage and death certificates, naturalsation and denization papers, changes of name etc.; information extracted from printed sources such as birth, marriage and death notices published in the Jewish Chronicle 1844-1863 and some after that period, abstracts from newspapers; data derived from other collections or from family members or hearsay.

2. A *locality index* to the data cards.

3. A collection of *"compiled pedigrees"*, which are cards giving details of individuals and their families.

4. An *index* to every name in the compiled pedigrees.

Ancestral Occupations:
a guide to the literature
Stuart A. Raymond

In 1891, James A'Court and Mary Ann Hill were inmates of Wincanton Union Workhouse when the census enumerator came to record their presence. Under the heading 'occupation' he wrote 'none'. These were the only two inmates for whom nothing could be said. Occupations arc given for all the other 145 inmates and staff of the workhouse, despite the fact that the inmates had no work. An extraordinary range of occupations are recorded; in addition to the ubiquitous 'labourers', 'servants' and 'scholars' (i.e. schoolchildren), there was a watchmaker, an army pensioner, a hair seat weaver, a gamekeeper, a printer, a toll collector, a retired policeman, a coach painter, etc. etc.

Some of these occupations may provide clues to finding further information on the people mentioned. In order to follow these clues, we need to know where to look. There are numerous books and journal articles to guide you - basic introductions to sources for particular occupations, descriptions of occupational archives, biographical dictionaries, trade directories, lists of the members of professional and trade organizations, bibliographies, etc., etc. If you need to identify works on particular occupations, then you should consult my *Occupational sources for Genealogists* 2nd ed., F.F.H.S., 1996, *Londoners Occupations: a genealogical guide* 2nd ed., F.F.H.S., forthcoming, *Yorkshire occupations: a genealogical guide* F.F.H.S., 2000, and the county volumes in my *British Genealogical Library Guides* series.

Two occupations in particular are likely to be of interest to all genealogists, since many of our ancestors had some experience of them. In recent centuries, increasing numbers of our ancestors went to school, and all were liable to be called up to serve the Crown in the armed forces. The records of both occupations are extensive; army records are mainly to be found in the Public Record Office, but educational sources must be sought in numerous different record offices throughout the county. The best introduction to educational records is Colin Chapman's *The Growth of British Education and its Records.* 2nd ed. Lochin Publishing, 1992. This volume includes details of the various types of record available - admission registers, school log books, minute books, etc., - as well as what the author describes as 'pupil-based school records', e.g. school reports, prizes, exercise books. For London, Cliff Webb's *An Index of London Schools and their records.* Society of Genealogists, 1999 gives extensive list of surviving school records. School admission registers are a particularly valuable sourcc for genealogists; many public and grammar school registers have been published, and their editors have frequently added biographical information to entries for particular individuals. A detailed listing of published school registers is provided by P.M.Jacob's *Registers of the Universities, Colleges and Schools of Great Britian and Ireland: a list.* Athlone Press, 1964. More up to date listings are given in my own county bibliographies.

The most extensive registers are probably those of the universities of Oxford and Cambridge; these are widely available in public and academic libraries, and should be consulted by every genealogist. For Cambridge, extensive details are provided in the ten volumes of J. & J.A.Venn's *Alumni Cantabrigienses.* Cambridge University Press, 1922-54; Oxford students are listed in the 8 volumes of Joseph Foster's *Alumni Oxonienses.* James Parker & Co., 1888-91.

School and university was followed, for many of our ancestors, by service in the armed forces. In recent years, an extensive literature on sources for soldier ancestors has arisen; it is not possible here to do more than indicate a few of the most useful books. M.J. & C.T.Watts' *My ancestor was in the British Army.* Society of Genealogists, 1995 is a good introductory guide, as is Simon Fowler's *Army Records for Family Historians.* P.R.O. Publications, 1992. More specialised - but nevertheless of importance for most of us - is Norman Holding's World War I army ancestry. 3rd ed. F.F.H.S., 1997, and its companion volume, *More sources of World War I Army Ancestry.* 3rd ed.F.F.H.S.1998.

In addition to the many guides written specifically for genealogists there are also innumerable histories of particular regiments and units. These frequently contain honour rolls, lists of officers and men, and other lists of names. The most useful regimental histories for genealogists are listed in my county bibliographies; for a full listing, consult A.S.White's *A Bibliography of Regimental Histories of the British Army.* Society for Army Historical Research, 1965.

Introductory guides to naval and airforce records are also available, although not in such profusion as those for soldiers. N.A.M. Rodger's *Naval Records for Genealogists.* H.M.S.O., 1988 is the standard guide to seamen; for the air force, consult Simon Fowler's *R.A.F. Records in the P.R.O.* P.R.O.Publications, 1994, or Eunice Wilson's *The Records of the Royal Air Force: how to find the few.* F.F.H.S., 1991.

A number of other occupations also have introductory guides for genealogists. Criminals (if one can call that an occupation?) are well served by David Hawkings' extensive *Criminal Ancestors: a guide to historical criminal records.* Sutton Publishing, 1992. If you want to find out more about merchant seamen, you should consult C.T.Watt's *My ancestor was a Merchant Seaman: how can I find out more about him?* Society of Genealogists, 1991. Sources for apprentices are listed in L. Gibbens' *My ancestor was an*

Apprentice. Society of Genealogists, 1997. A number of occupational guides for genealogists are in fact lists of archives rather than discussions of the various sources; in this category falls David Hawkings *Railway ancestors: a guide to the staff records of the railway companies of England and Wales, 1822-1947.* Alan Sutton, 1995. Tom Richards *Was your Grandfather a Railwayman?* 2nd ed. F.F.H.S., 1989; Jeremy Gibson's *Victuallers Licences: Records for Family and Local Historians.* F.F.H.S. 1994, L. Bridgeman & C. Emsley, *Guide to the Archives of the Police Forces of England and Wales.* Police History Society, 1991, and David Loverseed's *Gas works Ancestors.* D.C.S., 1994.

At a broader level, business and trade union archives may yield much information of an occupational character. Personnel records, membership lists, shareholders registers etc. all have their genealogical uses. E.D. Probert's *Company and Business Records for family historians* F.F.H.S., 1994 is a basic guide to business archives, which may be supplemented by J. Orbell's *A guide to tracing the history of a business.* Gower, 1987. For trade union records, consult J. Bennett's *Trade Union and related records.* 4th ed. University of Warwick, 1987.

The archives of trade organizations may also be useful. The obvious example are the records of London livery companies, for which see C.R.H. Cooper's *The Archives of the City of London Livery Companies and related organizations.* Guildhall Library, 1985. Numerous works on these companies are listed in my *Londoners Occupations.* Livery company histories usually provide lists of officers, and sometimes provide extensive biographical information. Full listings of their apprentices are currently being edited by Cliff Webb and published by the Society of Genealogists.

Biographical dictionaries are another important source of information. H.M. Colvin's *A Biographical Dictionary of British Architects 1600-1840.* Rev. ed. John Murray, 1978 is a standard work in its field, as is Geoffrey Beard and Gilbert Christopher's *Dictionary of English Furniture Makers, 1660-1840.* Furniture History Society, 1986. Notes on 1,482 missionaries are to be found in James Sibree's *London Missionary Society: a register of missionaries, deputatins, etc., from 1796 to 1923.* London Missionary Society, 1923, and sculptors are treated in Rupert Gunnis's *Dictionary of British sculptors 1660-1851.* New ed. Murrays, 1968. Some biographical dictionaries are contemporary rather than historical; for librarians in 1954, R.L. Collinson's *Who's who in librarianship.* Bowes & Bowes, 1954 should be consulted; brief biographies of mine owners and managers in 1908 are included in *Who's who in mining and metallurgy.* Mining Journal, 1908; electrical tradesmen are listed in the *Electrical who's who.* Electrical Review Publications, 1950.

There are also innumerable lists of the members of particular occupations - some are lists of members of professional organizations, others may be required by act of Parliament. *The Medical Register,* begun in 1859, is probably the best known of the latter, but there is also the General Nursing Council's *Register of Nurses,* dating from 1922, and the *Register of Veterinary Surgeons,* which has been published annually since 1884, and irregularly before that. Most professional organizations publish lists of their members; for example, the *Library Association Year Book* (in which my own name appears!) has been issued annual-

ly since 1891, the Institute of Chartered Accountants has published its *List of Members* regularly since 1896; *The Law List* was begun under that title in 1841, succeeding a number of older lists of the legal profession.

Trade directories are another source of occupational lists. In the present context I am referring to publications such as *The Electricians Directory.* 2 vols. James Gray, 1883-4, the *Directory of Health practitioners, professional naturopaths, osteopaths, chiropractors, botano-therapists, biochemists, psychotherapists, etc.* 1935, and Marchant & Co's *Metropolitan and provincial engineers, iron & metal trades directory* for 1857. General trade directories are also useful in identifying particular occupations; they are listed in J.E.Norton's *Guide to the national and provincial directories of England and Wales, excluding London, before 1856.* Royal Historical Society, 1950, which is continued by G. Shaw & A. Tipper's *British Directories.* Leicester University Press, 1988, for the period 1850-1950.

Many lists of office-holders in church and state are also available. John Le Neve's *Fasti Ecclesiae Anglicanae,* listing English and Welsh diocesan dignitaries, was re-compiled in the 1960's in 3 series of volumes covering 1066-1300, 1300-1541, and 1541-1857. Numerous lists of parochial clergy are also available; for example the *Fasti Parochialis* series for the Diocese of York published by the Yorkshire Archaeological Society in its record series; A.J.Willis's *Winchester Ordinations 1660-1829.* 2 vols. The author, 1964-5; George Hennesy's *Novum repertorium ecclesiasticum parochiale Londinense, or, London Diocesan clergy succession from the earliest times to the year 1898.* Swan Sonnenschein, 1898. The best-known source for identifying clergy is probably *Crockford's Clerical Directory,* published annually since 1856, although its diocesan equivalents should not be overlooked.

A variety of civil service lists are available; the most useful is probably the *British Imperial Calendar and Civil Service List,* which began in 1809 and became the *Civil Service Yearbook* from 1974. An invaluable series of historical lists by J.C.Sainty is available in his *Office-holders in modern Britain* series begun in 1972; this series includes titles such as *Treasury officials 1660-1870,* and *Officials of the Board of Trade, 1660-1870.*

This article has merely skimmed the surface of the material that is available, and many specific occupations deserve an entire article to themselves. Sources for the clergy, for lawyers, for medical workers, could all be treated at length; I have not even mentioned the book trades, artists, East India men, or nonconformist clergy, all of which are the subjects of extensive literature. Hopefully, however, I have whetted your appetite to find out more.

Stuart Raymond is the author of the British Genealogical library guides series, which includes Occupational sources for genealogists 2nd ed. £5.50, Londoners occupations: a genealogical guide 2nd ed. forthcoming; Yorkshire occupations £5.20, and county bibliographies for many English counties. Those currently available include Cheshire (2 vols.) £17.25; Dorset £6.60; Essex (2 vols.) £13.60; Hampshire £9.00; Kent (3 vols.) £19.50; Lancashire (3 vols.) £17.60; Lincolnshire £8.10; London & Middlesex (2 vols) £14.00; Norfolk £6.60 and Yorkshire (6 vols.) £39.00. Prices include p&p.

P.O.Box 35, Exeter, EX1 3YZ;
Email: stuart@samjraymond.softnet.co.uk

Open a new page on your United Kingdom research with Ancestry.com.℠

- **Instant access to over 600 million online records.**

- **Quick search results.** Ancestry.com will never send you to another site for information. Our records are stored directly on our site for fast and easy researching.

- **Build an Online Family Tree.** Add to and collaborate on your family history directly on the site.

- **Free genealogy newsletter.** Stay up-to-date with feature articles, the latest news, expert tips, and much more.

- **Access over 125,000 genealogy message boards.** Browse and participate in research on surnames, geographic regions, and time periods.

- **The Great Migration Begins. New Site Exclusive.** Comprehensive biographical information on over 1,000 New England settlers from 1620-1633; published by NEHGS. Also available on CD-ROM.

- **Access to over 2,500 databases.** Ancestry.com adds new databases every business day. Your subscription includes full access to these UK genealogical sources:

Ancestry.com.

Member Login | Free Membership | MyAccount

The No. 1 Source for Family History Online

⌂ Home 🔍 Search ✐ Learn 🔗 Share ▤ Record 🛒 Shop ?

Today @ Ancestry | Thinking of Joining? | Top Things to Do | Partner with Us

Home > Primo Magazine

October 13, 2000

Genealogy Research in the United Kingdom

Learn the ins and outs of beginning your family history research at Ancestry.com. Gather insight about your roots in the United Kingdom by searching our databases, browsing our online library, visiting our map center, subscribing to our magazine, or purchasing reference tools that will aid in your research.

About Ancestry.com

Ancestry.com is the premier resource for family history online. The site offers thousands of fully searchable databases containing information on hundreds of millions of individuals. New databases are being added to the site each business day. By the end of 2000, the company expects to have more than one billion searchable records on the site. Ancestry.com offers quick search results, access to over 100,000 genealogy message boards, an online library, a free genealogy newsletter, Online Family Tree, Images Online, and much more.

Discover the top things to do at Ancestry.com

See for yourself why more than 215,000 people subscribe to

Maps of the UK
- British Isles
  - Central Britain, 1715-45
  - Dublin, 1610
  - England & Wales, 1660-1892
  - Ireland, 1641-1892
  - Scotland, 1641-1892
  - Western England, 1685-88
  - Western Ireland, 1691

UK Databases
Get the Complete List of UK Databases

Research Help
The Census in Great Britain, Part 1: How It Began

Letter to the Editor: Scottish Links - A reader submits his personal Web sites containing Scottish genealogy

Scottish Links and Resources - A list of Scottish links and research

UK Databases Sampler

Early U.K. & U.S. Directories & Lists — 1680-1830.

A massive collection of biographical records from national, town, and trade directories of the UK and USA, including all known book subscription lists; all birth, marriage, death, promotion, court martial, and bankruptcy notices from a number of regular journals; and all extant society membership lists from the period. The database will be distributed in five installments, which together provide information on over 5 million individual names. Each installment lists roughly 1 million names. Two installments have been issued to date and the entire project will be completed before 2001.

England Topographical Dictionary

Contains over 30,000 historical and statistical descriptions of English towns and land.

Persons of Quality Original Lists

Emigrants from Great Britain to the United States 1600-1700.

Irish Records Index, 1500-1920

Name index to some Irish records contained in the Family History Library, Salt Lake City.

Irish Times (Dublin), Obituaries, 1999

Vital records from Irish counties including records from roughly 1600-1874.

Leuchars, Scotland Parish Census, 1841

Collection of parish census records from Leuchars, Fife County, Scotland in 1841.

. . .and many more. Visit us online today.

Ancestry.com℠

Part of MyFamily.com, Inc.

Ancestry.com Library Resources on the United Kingdom

Can You Find Your British Ancestors?

British resources at the Family History Library are easily accessible from the Library and at your own computer–thanks to FamilySearch.org and the extensive British microfilm project of the 1940s.

Manuscripts and Monuments in England

The Royal Commission on Historical Manuscripts has a number of responsibilities related to fostering the preservation and use of historical records. Most important for family historians is its responsibility to identify, locate, and record the particulars of manuscripts and archival collections.

November in England

For the fifth time in ten years the author has made a research trip to England in November. Here are her findings and recommendations.

Tips for Finding Your Immigrant Ancestors, Part 1

Between the year 1607 and the 1920s, it is estimated that over 30 million people immigrated to America. While finding the origins of your immigrant ancestors can be one of the most difficult aspects of family history research, it can also be one of the most rewarding. In this first installment of a two-part series, Kip Sperry will discuss how to get started on the trail of immigrant ancestors.

---

of the index including its organization, and gives examples of where and how it can enhance your British research.

Results of Fire and Famine: Census Records in Ireland 1813-1911 – The Irish census struggled with setbacks in its early years.

Destination Dublin - Find out where to do research in this ancient and history-rich Irish city.

Irish Place Names and Family Names - Learn about researching Irish Place Names and Family Names. Excerpted from the Introduction to "Irish Records: Sources for Family and Local History," by James G. Ryan, Ph.D.

Irish Genealogy Links and Addresses - Peruse these Irish research resources.

In the Store

- Your Scottish Ancestry
- Wales & Your Welsh Ancestry Video
- Your English Ancestry
- A New Genealogical Atlas of Ireland
- The Oxford Guide to Heraldry
- They Came in Ships

Connect Your Family

Keep your Italian family connected. Set up your free MyFamily.com site today!

For a complete listing of Ancestry.com resources for genealogical research in the United Kingdom, please visit **www.ancestry.com/home/celebrate/UK.htm**

For your FREE 2-week trial subscription, go to **www.ancestry.com/freetrial** and enter access code **G11GJ.**

© 2000 MyFamily.com, Inc. All Rights Reserved.

SUB1000GDSUK

Llyfrgell Genedlaethol Cymru
The National Library of Wales

Eirionedd A. Baskerville
Head of Readers' Services - Department of Manuscripts and Records

An interest in family history is part of the Welsh psyche. According to the Laws of Hywel Dda, it was necessary to know one's relatives to the ninth remove, and Giraldus Cambrensis on his crusading tour of Wales in 1188 noted that the humblest person was able to recite from memory his family tree, going back six or seven generations.

The National Library of Wales is the premier centre for family history research in Wales, holding as it does abundant records covering the whole of Wales. Its three main Departments all have something different to offer. The Department of Printed Books holds electoral lists, newspapers and directories, while the Department of Pictures and Maps has plans, sale catalogues, and tithe maps and schedules. However, the most important Department from the point of view of genealogical research is the Department of Manuscripts and Records, which holds a whole range of useful resources.

The Department has microform copies of the returns for the whole of Wales for each of the ten-yearly censuses 1841-91, and microfiche copies of the index to the 1881 census for the English counties as well as those for Wales. In addition, some of the returns have been transcribed and indexed by enthusiastic individuals and societies who have kindly made them available to the Library's users.

Civil registration of births, marriages and deaths was introduced in England and Wales on 1 July 1837, and microfiche copies of the General Register Office's indexes of the registration records from 1837 to 1992 are available for searching free of charge at the National Library. The Library does not issue certificates, but a search of the indexes can be undertaken for a fee.

Before the introduction of civil registration, the `rites of passage' were noted in parish registers, following the order of 5 September 1538 that a register of every baptism, marriage and burial in every parish should be kept. However, the earliest surviving registers for most Welsh parishes do not commence until after 1660, although starting dates vary greatly. Parish registers held at the National Library are available on microfilm to readers. The Library also holds transcript copies of some parish registers, which have been kindly donated by the compilers. In addition, the 1988 edition of the International Genealogical Index, while far from complete, can prove a useful starting point for tracing the parish in which a baptism or marriage was registered.

Although the ravages of weather and rodents, inept vicars and disrespectful parishioners have resulted in the disappearance of many original parish registers, the bishops transcripts (annual returns submitted by Anglican parish clergy to the bishops containing copies of all the entries recorded in their parish registers during the preceding twelve months), often come to the rescue of the family historian. Transcripts were ordered to be sent annually from 1597 onwards, but there are no transcripts before 1661 in the records of the Church inhales deposited in the Library. Even after this date there are many gaps in the returns, only a few transcripts before 1723 being extant for parishes in the diocese of Llandaff, and hardly any for the eighteenth century for parishes in the archdeaconries of Cardigan and St David's.

The transcripts cease at dates varying from parish to parish during the middle of the nineteenth century, although there are a few examples from the early twentieth century from some parishes. Transcripts of marriage entries normally cease with the introduction of civil registration in 1837. The transcripts held by the Library are listed in schedules available in the Department of Manuscripts and Records. At present the original transcripts are available to readers, but the task of preparing microfiche copies is underway.

Marriage bonds and allegations are the next most important class of Anglican Church record of use to the genealogist. These documents were executed in order to obtain a licence to marry without having banns called publicly in Church on three Sundays before the solemnisation of the marriage. Generally speaking, these records cover the eighteenth and nineteenth centuries and the first three decades of the twentieth century. The amount and nature of the information varies with the type of document, and are particularly valuable when the approximate date of a marriage is known but not its venue. The pre-1837 bonds and allegations in the Library have been indexed and may be searched on computer in the Department's Catalogue room. Also available for the diocese of St David's are registers of marriage licences, mainly for the nineteenth century.

Another class of records of paramount interest to the genealogist is wills and administrations, and those which before the introduction of Civil Probate on 11 January 1858 were proved in the Welsh ecclesiastical courts, have been deposited in the Library. Roughly speaking, the covering dates of the surviving probate records of each of the consistory courts are: Bangor, 1635-1858; Brecon, 1543-1858; Chester (Welsh Wills), 1557-1858; Hawarden, 1554-1858; Llandaff, 1568-1857; St Asaph, 1565-1857; St David's, 1556-1858. These wills have also been indexed and may be searched on computer.

For the period after 1858 the Library has custody of register copy wills from five registries, covering all but one (Montgomeryshire) of the Welsh counties, and a full microfiche set of the annual index of all wills and administrations granted in England and Wales (the Calendar of Grants), from 1858 to 1972.

Despite the fact that they are much less comprehensive than the records of the Anglican Church in Wales, Nonconformist records are an important source of information for genealogists. Many registers of dissenting congregations were deposited with the Registrar-General after the Civil Registration Act of 1836, and the Library has microfilm copies of these. A few registers of that period which never found their way to London and some other later registers are now deposited at the Library.

Other nonconformist records of genealogical value at the Library include manuscript lists of members and contribution books of individual chapels, printed annual reports, usually including lists of members and their contributions, which have been produced by many chapels since about 1880, and denominational periodicals, which often contain notices of births, marriages and deaths.

Records of the Court of Great Sessions of Wales, the most important legal and administrative body between the Act of Union and its abolition in 1830, may also prove useful for genealogical purposes. Occasionally challenge pedigrees were filed in connection with certain actions, and other documents of considerable value are depositions, which often state the age of the deponent, jury lists and coroners' inquests.

Whereas the official Quarter Sessions records for the county of Cardigan, held by the Library comprise little more than the order books from 1739, there are also some related materials among the archives of landed estates or solicitors' firms, for example a few sessional rolls and land tax records 1780-1839 from Cardiganshire, some land tax records (the most useful class of records for the genealogist) for Montgomeryshire and Breconshire, order books 1647-75 and rolls, 1643-99 for Denbighshire, and sessions records from Montgomeryshire.

Local government at a level between county and parish was practically non-existent before the formation of Poor Law Unions under the the the Poor Law Amendment Act 1834 Most Poor Law Union records are now deposited at the appropriate county record office, but there are some records at the Library, mainly from Montgomeryshire. Civil parish records are also mainly held by the appropriate county record office, although the Library holds vestry books and other parochial records for many parishes for which parish registers have been deposited.

The manorial records held by the Library are mainly to be found with the estate records and listed with them They are most comprehensive for Montgomeryshire (mainly the Powis Castle and Wynnstay estate records),

with substantial holdings for Glamorgan and Monmouthshire also (mainly the Badminton, Bute and Tredegar estate records). It should be noted that in many parts of Wales the manorial system never really took root.

The Library has recently prepared a manorial database for Wales in conjunction with HMC available to readers on the Internet http://www2.hmc.gov.uk/Welsh_Manorial_Documents_Register.htm.
Most of the estate records and personal papers held by the Department of Manuscripts and Records are detailed in typescript schedules. The estate records contain title deeds, rentals, account books, correspondence, etc. Rentals may prove particularly useful in indicating a death or change of residence when a name disappears from a series of rentals.

The Department holds many manuscript pedigrees. These vary from descents of nobility, compiled in the later Middle Ages and copied time and again with additions by later genealogists, to charts which are the work of amateurs of modern times who have given copies of their compilations to the Library. For searchers particularly interested in the pedigrees of gentry families there are several important printed works available.

There is a general card index to most of the typescript schedules of the collections in the Department of Manuscripts and Records, and probably the most useful for the family historian are the sections devoted to wills, marriage settlements, inquisitions post mortem, and pedigrees. The index to the general collections of manuscripts (NLW MSS) may also be of use to genealogists. In addition, a basic inventory of the contents of the Library's Annual Report up to 1996 is available on-line in the Catalogue room.

For further information on sources for family history research at the National Library of Wales, it is worth consulting the Department of Manuscripts and Records' pages at the Library's web site at: http://www.llgc.org.uk/

A Walk on the dark side:
The Records of the Court of Great Sessions
Eirionedd A. Baskerville

The Court of Great Sessions was established by the Second Act of Union in 1543 and remained in existence until 1830. It was to sit twice a year, each session was to last for six days, and it was directed to hear all pleas 'in as large and ample a manner' as the courts of Kings Bench and Common Pleas. For legal purposes the Act divided Wales into four circuits, with three counties to each circuit, namely:

Chester, for the counties of Denbigh, Flint and Montgomery
North Wales, for the counties of Anglesey, Caernarfon and Merioneth
Brecon, for the counties of Brecon, Glamorgan and Radnor, and
Carmarthen, for the counties of Cardigan, Carmarthen and Pembroke

There was no room for Monmouthshire in this new scheme and it was, therefore, assigned to the Oxford assize circuit. The records of this circuit are in the Public Record Office.

With some notable exceptions, there is little of value in the records for the genealogist, but for social and legal historian they contain a vast amount of untapped information.

In searching for a case, whether it is one you think came before the court or one that you know came before the court but you do not know the date, you should always begin with the volumes compiled by the clerks of the court and which are now used as indexes. The Court of Great Sessions spent most of its time hearing civil actions, the majority of actions being simple cases of debt, and the main record of this aspect of its work is the plea roll, a formal record of the pleas of litigants. They do, however, contain minor actions involving land such as trespass, and ejectment, breaches of contract, slander and a small number of actions arising from physical assaults where the aggrieved party sued for damages. The judgements of the court are also enrolled on the plea rolls. Indexes to the plea rolls have yet to be compiled but the dockets, in the form of a roll or a book, can be used as such. These docket rolls or books contain a record of all civil actions including those that did not reach issue, each entry giving the name of the parties, the nature of the action, and what

Miniature Portrait of King Henry VIII
at the head of the first Plea Roll for the new County of Brecon.
10th July 1542 Great Sessions 4/17/1
Reproduced with the Permission of
Llyfrgell Genedlaethol Cymru   The National Library of Wales
© The National Library of Wales 2001

stage the action had reached by the end of the session, and it is possible to follow through to conclusion those actions which were continued from session to session.

Other records compiled by the clerks of the Court include order books, containing the formal orders of the court, and minute books which comprise the clerk's notes of what was happening at the time in court and were later formally copied on to the order books. Documents entirely unrelated to civil actions were also enrolled on the early plea rolls; for example, a small number of deeds and sometimes indictments against criminals, but both deeds and indictments had virtually disappeared from the plea rolls by about 1600. In some circuits the order books contain formal orders to punish convicted offenders, including executions and, after 1718, transportations. The minute books also contain details of verdicts and sentences, but the information about crimes and criminals given in these volumes is very uneven.

The responsibility for keeping the records of the civil side of the Court belonged to the chief clerk of the court, the Prothonotary, and one type of document filed with the prothonotary papers which can be said to be of a genealogical nature is the challenge pedigree. This was drawn up by the plaintiff to prove that he (or his wife) was related within the 4th degree of consanguinity to the sheriff (or his wife), who was responsible for selecting juries, in order to request the court to appoint one of the coroners instead of the sheriff to empanel the jury. The plaintiff could also challenge one or both of the coroners after he had successfully challenged the sheriff. If his challenge to the coroner(s) was successful the court would appoint independent electors to choose a jury. Why did the plaintiff declare his relationship to the sheriff ? It was a pre-emptive move on the part of the plaintiff since, if he did not declare his relationship, the defendant could challenge the jury array and, if successful, the jury would be quashed and the plaintiff would have to re-commence the procedure from issue. The pedigrees, drawn up in the familiar family tree fashion, are enrolled as part of the pleadings, and a rough count suggests that a minimum of 800 challenge pedigrees are filed on the pre-1700 prothonotary files.

However promising a source the pedigrees might appear for family historians, their usefulness in a genealogical context is diminished by a number of factors:
* they have all but disappeared from the files by c. 1700
* many of the pedigrees virtually duplicate each other because, when a plaintiff challenged the sheriffs and both coroners, he drew up three pedigrees, each containing almost identical information, which means that there are less individual pedigrees than might at first appear
* since the sheriffs and coroners belonged to the upper ranks of Welsh society, the pedigrees are almost exclusively limited to Welsh gentry families
* they are not indexed, which means that it is impossible to know which challenge pedigrees exist short of trawling through the papers themselves.

The pedigrees are available in more convenient form elsewhere, both in manuscript and print, but since challenge pedigrees were compiled for a legal purpose it can be argued that they are more reliable than contemporary pedigree books which contain errors and which were drawn up to satisfy the pretensions of the gentry.

The main record of the criminal side of the court is the Gaol Files. Only the most serious offences (thefts and assaults) came before the court of Great Sessions; minor offences were heard by the court of Quarter Sessions. Normally the Gaol File will contain a calendar (list) of prisoners waiting to stand trial, including the names of the prisoners, the nature of their offences, who committed the prisoner to gaol and, quite often,

the Clerk of the Crown will have added the verdict and, where appropriate, the sentence. The calendar, in effect, serves as an index to the file. Later calendars also include lists of prisoners serving terms of imprisonment in the county goal or the House of Correction to which they had been sentenced by the Great Sessions or the Quarter Sessions. These later calendars give the prisoner's name, the offence, the sentence, and when and at which court the case was tried, but not the names of those awaiting trial who had been released on bail. After c. 1800 they include the prisoner's age, ability to read/write and behaviour.

The formal written charge against a prisoner was the indictment which contained the name, occupation and residence of the accused; the date, place and nature of the offence and, where appropriate, the name of the victim. Sometimes a clerk of the court will have noted the prisoner's plea, the verdict and, where applicable, the sentence handed down by the judge. Indictments have been extensively used by historians of crime to postulate crime rates, which can then be related to such factors as economic oppressions or booms, war and peace, and to study topics such as the seasonability of crime, whether crimes were committed by outsiders, and the status of offenders. Unfortunately, indictments are often seriously flawed - they ascribe the residence of a prisoner to the parish where the offence took place, the occupation of the accused is often given as 'labourer' or 'yeoman', irrespective of whether he was perhaps a miner, an ironworker, a weaver or a tailor, and the date when the offence took place may be incorrect, especially when the crime had occurred some years, or even a few months, prior to the apprehension of the suspect.

Some of the errors can be eliminated by using examinations (where they exist) and recognizances, which are also kept on the Gaol Files.. The most interesting documents in the files are the written examinations or depositions of witnesses made by victims of crimes and their witnesses and examinations of the accused (oral testimony before the court was not recorded). Ironically, it is this type of document which, more often than not, has been destroyed; there was no legal obligation to preserve them because they were not, strictly speaking, records of the court. They were taken before justices of the peace in the early stages of a prosecution, sometimes well before the actual trial took place. However, they are far more important than mere tools to check the accuracy or otherwise of indictments. They provide circumstantial evidence, incidental information and cameos of everyday life virtually unmatched by any other type of historical document. Thus we discover that the best time for arranging an ambush in the late sixteenth century was when the victim was on the way home from Church, and the preferred place for hiding stolen goods was the dunghill! Taken to an extreme this is where, in 1735, Margaret Thomas Prees of Glasgwm, co. Radnor, hid the body of her bastard male child; the child's bones were found some months after the birth and she was charged with infanticide.

Reference to historical occurrences are found in Great Sessions 4/1002/4, where Jane Griffith, St Asaph, on a charge of infanticide, claimed that she had 'never perceived the said child alive within her since she had heard the beat of a drum on the king's birthday', and in Great Sessions 4/826/6 we find eyewitness accounts of the last attempted invasion on British soil. Samuel Griffiths of Brawdy, Pembrokeshire, was accused of treason - aiding and abetting the French army, numbering 1400 soldiers, under the command of an American, General Tate, in their invasion of the kingdom. On the examination of Thomas John on the same charge 'some of the French...observed a great many more than 300 [soldiers] he the said Thomas John replied that half were women with red flannels'. In an almost monoglot Welsh society anyone who spoke English was viewed with suspicion by some in authority. This is reflected in a letter, dated 15 June 1773, from John Price of Talgarth, Breconshire, to the Rev. John Jones (D. T. M. Jones Collection). The writer states "We have shocking accounts in the weekly papers of a desperate gang of thieves in Devonshire and I have great reason to suspect their having crossed the channel for yesterday at Hay fair there were several strangers part of some notorious gang...I think that we who are on the confines of England should follow the example of the Carmarthenshire gent[ry] and ask every Englishman that comes among us his business".

One of the most fascinating cases which appears on the Goal files is that relating to the murder of Joseph Rogers, churchwarden of the parish of Chirk, in 1736. David Whitley, yeoman, was accused of beating the deceased on the left side of the head near the temple with an 'oaken stick' following an affray. Among the written depositions are those of Robert Rogers, the Vicar of Chirk, and William Speed of the City of Chester, surgeon. The Vicar states that, having examined Joseph Rogers, he and a Dr Weaver decided that Rogers had a fractured skull which they believed needed trepanning - a procedure which involves cutting out small pieces of bone, especially from the skull, with a surgical instrument in the form of a crown-saw. William Speed

was sent for from Chester; he found a perforation through the dura mater and much contusion. Unfortunately, Joseph Rogers died the next day. David Whitely pleaded not guilty to the charge of murder, but the jury's verdict was 'Guilty of manslaughter' and he was sentenced to be burnt in the hand. Here, then, we find, in north-east Wales in 1736, the survival of an ancient medical procedure, known to Neolithic man, his achievement being all the more incredible when we consider the most rudimentary instruments at his disposal, and that his patients usually survived!

Recognizances were bonds to ensure the presence of both prosecutor and witnesses, and those accused who had been released on bail, at the next sessions of the court. They are factually more reliable than indictments because the court needed to have the correct names and addresses in order to levy the sums of money forfeited if the prosecutor, witness or bailed person failed to appear.

Cases of sudden or unexplained deaths had to be investigated by the coroner, and many coroner's inquests were also filed on the Goal file. They include examples of murder, manslaughter, infanticide, suicide, but mainly unexplained death and accidental death. The latter include traffic accidents; accidents in the home; accidents to children at play and to adults and children at work; accidents on farms; accidents in Anglesey copper mines, Flintshire and Cardiganshire lead mines, Caernarfonshire slate quarries and Glamorgan coal mines, and shipping disasters.

Order and minute books can be used as rough indexes to the Gaol Files, but the Crown Books and 'Black Books' are far more convenient for this purpose. Unfortunately, Crown Books are only to be found for Flintshire for the years 1542-63, 1667-1708 and 1757-90, while the 'Black Books' cover only the Brecon circuit and only from 1726 until 1830. From 1726 to 1751 the 'Black Books' are basically a list of the contents of the gaol files, noting the presence of the writ of summons and return, the number of justices' recognizances on the file, the grand jury list and the calendar of prisoners, when it was on the file. Coroners' inquests are also listed, giving the name of the body viewed and briefly, the cause of death. Thus we find, in the Glamorgan session in 1750, that Christian Lewis was said to have suffocated in a boghouse, David Morgan perished with cold on Hirwaun, and John Miller was suffocated by the 'Damp' (poisonous gas) in a coalpit. There are also a great number of cases of the inhabitants of parishes being presented for not repairing the high roads in their parishes. These entries serve as indexes to the inquests on the gaol files, although they do not appear in the Black Books between 1733 and 1736. Both classes contain names of prisoners and note the offence and, sometimes, the verdict and sentence.

Calendar rolls should also be used as indexes to the Gaol Files, but these are restricted to the counties of Radnor, 1555-69, Glamorgan, 1555-1601, Cardigan, 1542-1602, and Pembroke, 1542-1674. To aid researchers, an index of cases entered on the Gaol Files, 1730-1830, has been compiled and should be available on the web pages of the Department of Manuscripts and Records in the near future. Searches can be made under the following headings: name of accused, parish of offence, parish of accused, status and offence, the latter listing offences from A for 'abandoning a child' through to W for 'worrying animals'.

To judge from the number of cases brought before the Court, the equity side, which dealt with disputes over marriage settlements, oral agreements, wills, mortgages, and trusts, was the least important aspect of its work, but these could reveal details of interest to family or local historians. The overwhelming majority of equity cases were heard either at the Court of the Council of Wales and the Marches sitting at Ludlow or before the Court of Chancery in London. The equity records of the Court of

Great Sessions do not begin until 1689, the year the Council of Wales and the Marches was finally abolished, but those of the Chester circuit do not begin until 1730. Bill Books serve as indexes to pleadings on the equity side of the Court, giving the names of both the complainants and the defendants, and the date of filing all the pleadings.

If I have whetted your appetite for learning more about the records of the Court of Great Sessions I must also sound a word of warning. There is no easy route through the records; all records prior to 1733 are in Latin, except for written testimony in criminal cases, records of the court during the Commonwealth period and all records of the equity side of the court. The handwriting can cause problems, especially in the earlier records and, apart from those contained in Murray Chapman's volume, Criminal Proceedings in the Montgomeryshire Court of Great Sessions. Transcripts of Commonwealth Gaol Files 1650-1660 (1996, Powysland Club/National Library of Wales) no transcripts are available. Prospective researchers should be prepared to exhibit a great deal of patience and perseverence; good eyesight is also a prerequisite!

General Register Office for Scotland

Registration of births, deaths and marriages in Scotland

Registration of baptisms and proclamations of marriage was first enacted in Scotland by a Council of the Scottish clergy in 1551. The earliest recorded event - a baptism of 27 December 1553 - can be found in the register of baptisms and banns for Errol in Perthshire. Following the Reformation registration of births, deaths and marriages became the responsibility of the ministers and session clerks of the Church of Scotland. Standards of record-keeping varied greatly from parish to parish, however, and even from year to year. This together with evidence of the deterioration and loss of register volumes through neglect led to calls for the introduction of a compulsory and comprehensive civil registration system for Scotland. This came into being on 1 January 1855 with the establishment of the General Register Office for Scotland headed by the Registrar General and the setting up of 1027 registration districts. In 2000 registration districts number 331.

Records in the custody of the Registrar General

The main series of vital events records of interest to genealogists are held by the Registrar General at New Register House in Edinburgh. They are as follows:

Old parish registers (1553-1854): the 3500 surviving register volumes (the OPRs) compiled by the Church of Scotland session clerks were transferred to the custody of the Registrar General after 1855. They record the births and baptisms; proclamations of banns and marriages; and deaths and burials in some 900 Scottish parishes. They are far from complete, however, and most entries contain relatively little information. Microfilm copies of these records are available world-wide and there are computerised and microfiche indexes to baptisms and marriages. A project to index the death and burial entries got under way in 1997 and is still ongoing.

Register of neglected entries (1801-1854): this register was compiled by the Registrar General and consists of births, deaths and marriages proved to have occurred in Scotland between 1801 and 1854 but which had not been recorded in the OPRs. These entries are included in the all-Scotland computerised indexes.

Statutory registers of births, deaths and marriages (from 1855): these registers are compiled by district registrars. They are despatched by the district examiners to New Register House at the end of each calendar year ready for the creation of all-Scotland computerised indexes. Microfiche copies of the register pages are available in the New Register House search rooms.

Adopted children register (from 1930): persons adopted under orders made by the Scottish courts. The earliest entry is for a birth in October 1909.

Register of divorces (from 1984): records the names of the parties, the date and place of marriage, the date and place of divorce and details of any order made by the court regarding financial provision or custody of children. Prior to May 1984 a divorce would be recorded in the RCE (formerly the Register of Corrected Entries, now the Register of Corrections Etc), and a cross-reference would be added to the marriage entry.

Births, deaths and marriages occurring outside Scotland (The Minor Records): these relate to persons who are or were usually resident in Scotland.

Marine Register of Births & Deaths (from 1855)
Air Register (from 1848)
Service Records (from 1881)
War Registers (from 1899) for the Boer War (1899-1902) and the two World Wars

Consular returns (from 1914)
High Commissioners' returns (from 1964)
Foreign Marriages (from 1947)
Register of births, deaths & marriages in foreign countries (1860-1965)
Census records (from 1841): these are the enumerators' transcript books of the decennial census of the population of Scotland. They record the name, age, marital state, occupation and birthplace of every member of a household present on census night. Census records are closed for 100 years and only the schedules for the 1841 to 1891 Censuses are open to the public. The 1901 Census records will be opened to the public in January 2002.

(To discover more details about the history of the records held by the GROS, buy a copy of our new publication "Jock Tamson's Bairns: a history of the records of the General Register Office for Scotland" by Cecil Sinclair, ISBN 1 874451 591, 52 pages, cost GBP6.99 (USD10.50). See http://www.gro-scotland.gov.uk for details of how to order.)

Searching at New Register House

New Register House was opened in 1861 as a purpose-built repository for Scotland's civil registration records. Today it provides 100 search places and is open to the public from 09:00 to 16:30, Monday to Friday. Access to the indexes requires payment of a statutory fee but this also allows self-service access to microform copies of all the open records. The fee can be for a day, a week, four weeks, a quarter or a year. There are discount arrangements and a limited number of seats can be booked in advance. There is also provision for group evening visits.

Indexes to the statutory records (including overseas events), OPR baptism and marriage entries, and the 1881 and 1891 Census records are available on computer. There is self-service access to the statutory register pages on microfiche and the OPR and Census records on roll microfilm. It is also possible to order official extracts of any entry.

Since July 2000, the GROS has made available a single-step linked imaging search facility. This allows customers to search the indexes of the 1891 Census returns, and the statutory registers of births, deaths and marriages for the year 1891, which have been linked to digital images of the record pages. Currently, this facility remains available only for on-site users based in New Register House, but we do intend to place these linked images on the Internet in due course.

Online Access to the New Register House Indexes

The all-Scotland computerised indexes can also be accessed from local registration offices which have links to the New Register House system. Some local registration offices provide search room facilities with access to microfiche copies of the statutory registers for their area The Family Records Centre in London has also been provided with online access (- the "Scotlink"); while the indexes to records over 100 years old for births and marriages, and over 75 years old for deaths, have been made available for searching over the Internet on the pay-per-view website 'Scots Origins'.

To find out more see the GROS website at
http://www.gro-scotland.gov.uk.
Pay-per-view search website is
http://www.origins.net/

The Scots Origins Internet Service
General Register Office for Scotland

Scots Origins is the GROS's fully searchable pay-per-view database of historical indexes on the World Wide Web, and has been running since 6 April 1998. It is maintained on behalf of the department by OMS Services Ltd and provides access to the indexes of birth and marriage records over 100 years, and death records over 75 years old. To avoid raising concerns about browsing among records relating to living persons, indexes to birth and marriage entries less than 100 years old and deaths less than 75 years, are not available on the Internet.

The Indexes
Origins provides access to indexes of Scottish birth and marriage records from 1553 to 1899 and death records from 1855 to 1899. As yet, there is no all-Scotland index to the pre-1855 death and burial entries. All-Scotland indexes to the 1891 census returns are available and indexes for the 1881 census returns will become available in the latter part of 2000, at which point there will be access to some 30 million index entries. An additional year of historical index data is added to the database at the beginning of each year, so 1900 birth and marriage data, and 1925 death data will become available in 2001.

Searching
New users can look at a demonstration version and refer to a detailed online guide to searching the indexes before they actually log on. They are then invited to register with the database and give name, postal address and credit-card details over a secure link to the Origins server. The complex security software has the approval of one of Britain's largest retail banks, the National Westminster, and authorisation is in real-time taking approximately 10 seconds. Card details are not stored and are transferred via an encrypted channel. Following authorisation by the bank that issued the card the server debits the card account with the GBP6 fee and gives the user a credit worth 30 pages to be viewed within a 24 hour period (allowing a customer to log off and on the Internet as required via a designated user code and password).

Those familiar with the New Register House system will find that Origins is slightly different in several respects. Searches can be made across the database, that is, for OPR, statutory and census indexes; for a given year plus or minus up to five years; for all or just one type of event; on more than one name; and narrowed down to a particular district name. Tables of registration district and parish names are available online with links to UK maps. A Soundex option can be used to search for similar-sounding names an important point as the spelling of names can vary considerably (Mac changing to Mc and so on) particularly in the OPRs.

The search form is easy to use being similar to those of web search-engines with check-boxes and blank data-entry fields. Search terms can be in upper or lower case and can include the standard wild-card characters '*' and '?'. The results of a search are initially displayed as an on-screen summary of the number of 'hits' found on the database and the number of pages (comprising a minimum of one and a maximum of 15 entries) it would take to display them all. It is then possible either to download the pages or to refine the search.

Once downloaded a page can be stored as a file on the user's computer (for viewing off-line or printing at a later date) or it can be consulted again gratis on the Origins database as often as required during the same session. The hits are displayed in a colour-coded table - there is an explanatory key at the bottom of the screen - with columns for event, sex, age, date (in the statutory index this is the year, but in the OPR index the date in full), surname, first name, parents' or spouse's name (depending on event type) and the district or parish. A miscellaneous column gives the parents or spouse and OPR microfilm frame number where appropriate. Microfilm copies of the OPR and open census records can be consulted at libraries and family history centres run by the Genealogical Society of Utah world-wide.

Ordering extracts
Alongside each index entry is a button which can be selected to order the full register extract direct from the database. There is a charge of GBP10 per document which includes postage. Online helptext provides full details of what is contained in the different types of register extract backed up by images of sample pages from the statutory, OPR and census records. Orders are processed by staff at GROS in Edinburgh who send out the paper documents by ordinary post, aiming at a response within 15 working days.

Future developments
Looking further ahead it is likely that developments in scanning and Internet technology will allow access not just to indexes text, but to images of the actual records themselves - a huge task for the department but a logical extension to the policy of providing wider access to the historical records in its care. The first steps in this have already been taken with the availability since July 2000 of a single-step linked imaging search facility for the indexes of the 1891 Census returns, and the statutory registers of births, deaths and marriages for the year 1891. These have been linked to digital images of the record pages. Currently, this searching facility is available only to on-site users based in New Register House, but we do intend to place these linked images on the Internet in due course.

SCOTS ORIGINS
can be accessed at http://www.origins.net.

Digital Imaging of the 1891 Census for Scotland

Bruno Longmore Departmental Record Officer General Register Office for Scotland

On 6th July 2000, the Registrar General for Scotland, Mr John Randall, launched two new products which will be of particular interest to family and local historians. The historical records to which these products relate are held by the General Register Office for Scotland (GROS) in New Register House, Edinburgh and reflect a very exciting future particularly for family history research.

The first product represents old-style technology, in the form of a new book written by Cecil Sinclair, author of the best-selling 'Tracing Your Scottish Ancestors', which describes the main categories of records held in the GROS. The second, represents an entirely new service, the computerised digital images of the 1891 Scottish Census records and the use of cutting-edge new information technology to make our records more easily accessible.

Jock Tamson's Bairns

The historical records which are held in New Register House form an important part of Scotland's cultural heritage - just as important as buildings or artefacts. The records described in this new book fall into three main groups: the statutory registers of births, deaths and marriages, accumulated since January 1855 when civil registration commenced in Scotland; the old parochial registers (OPRs), records which were kept by the established church, the Church of Scotland, which preceded the statutory registers and which in some cases date back to the 16th Century; and the open census records for Scotland, which date from the 19th Century.

A key feature of the records held by the GROS is their universality, their inclusiveness. We do not just hold records of famous people, for example the marriage banns of Mary Queen of Scots, or the birth and death entries of Robert Louis Stevenson, but everyone who was born, married or died in Scotland appears (or should appear) in our records.

The title of the new book "Jock Tamson's Bairns" was therefore felt to be appropriate. The popular 19th century Scots expression "we're a' Jock Tamson's bairns" epitomises common humanity, and that we are all united by common sentiments or interests. There can be no more uniting factors than those of birth, death and marriage.

The book was written for the interested layman, not for experts, and brings history to life using actual examples to illustrate the general themes. It is not another guide to tracing family trees, more a fascinating review of Scotland's social and cultural history.

1891 Census Images

The second product specifically involved the open Census records for Scotland, one of the main sets of records held in New Register House, and particularly the returns for the 1891 Census.

In Scotland, unlike other countries, the census records were retained by the originating department - the GROS - which remains responsible for conducting the modern decennial census of the Scottish population. Like English & Welsh census records, Scottish returns take the form of enumerators' transcript books, which were prepared by census enumerators after collection of the census schedules from individual householders. The books were not indexed at time of enumeration, and the original paper records for the 1891 census - when Scotland's population was just over 4 million - have remained in New Register House since it was collected on the evening of 5/6 April 1891.

The original paper records were converted to microfilm during the 1950's and 1960's, and this has been the recognised method of viewing these returns for many years. During the early 1990's, the GROS undertook a large-scale indexing project to create a computerised index of all the individual named entries held within the 1891 census transcript records. Since completion, the index has been made available to customers who visit New Register House and local search centres based in Scottish registration offices, and to those who use the 'Scotlink' search facility at the Family Records Centre in London. It has also been placed on the GROS pay-per-view search site on the Internet, 'Scots Origins' (http://www.origins.net.)

The important next step was to consider the capture of electronic images of the record pages themselves, and link these to the individual computerised index entries. This was a brave step using new state-of-the-art technology, as yet untried in this field by equivalent record holding institutions anywhere else in the world.

During 1999 therefore, the GROS undertook a pilot project with a private contractor to test this new technology. It was decided to use the 1891 Scottish census returns for this pilot and to link the 4 million individual index entries with 250,000 pages held in the census books. This was done by scanning each page, using 35mm archive quality microfilms rather than the original paper registers, and capturing them as electronic images. Individual page entries were then linked to every named index entry. The introductory pages, including the street indexes (i.e. pages without people's names) were also digitised and indexed separately.

The new 1891 computerised images can now be viewed as part of our normal public service to those visitors who come to New Register House. Users at workstations can view the whole page and zoom into selected areas. A quality (.tif) image has been used for viewing purposes, and the image files are stored in an industry-standard format which can be made readily available using standard products in a Windows 95/NT environment and can be viewed by a standard Internet browser. This will permit, at some future date, the images to be made available online on the Internet.

Digitising our records in this way, so that they can be

viewed electronically, is at the heart of our strategy for improving the accessibility to all of our historical records. The GROS holds over 6.5 kilometres of paper records in New Register House and a computerised index of more than 60 million individual names. If we can find the resources for the investment required, we should like to digitise all of our main sets of historical records, so that within a few years our customers would be able to access these through the computer screens, either at New Register House or on the Internet. This would do away with the present method of looking at these records only through viewing microfilm or by buying paper copies or certificates.

There is no doubt that the demand for both historical census and other registration records is world-wide, and is growing. The 1891 Census digitisation project has taught us a great deal about the technologies involved, and the costs of undertaking such enterprises. It will also influence the way in which the GROS handles the release of the 1901 Scottish census returns, which like the returns for England and Wales, are due for release by January 2002. Imaging the 1901 Scottish census returns will happen, but only after we have fully considered the results of the pilot project.

One thing is certain however, the 1901 Scottish census returns will also be available in a conventional 35mm microfilm format, as we feel that genealogists will still want us to produce the record in this traditional medium. We are therefore currently filming the 1901 Scottish returns on 35mm archive film, though as yet these films remain unavailable for public purchase.

Future Developments

In April 1998 we launched our Internet searching site for genealogists - "Scots Origins" - a pioneering Government e-commerce initiative. Since then demand for paper extracts from our registers has more than doubled over these 2 years, and currently over half of the paper documents we sell are now ordered through the Internet. We intend to develop the services offered through this website in the years to come. (http://www.origins.net.)

Genealogy is big business and we recognise that Scotland has special opportunities. It is estimated that there are 25 million people of Scottish origin (the Scottish diaspora) in different parts of the world.

Genealogical tourism is a growing phenomenon and has recently been identified as one of the markets to which the Scottish tourism industry should give closer attention.

From our experience, we feel that better access to our historical records, including access to them on the Internet, can only further stimulate this tourism potential for Scotland. People in America or Canada may well do some of their research before they venture abroad, but they will still want to come and visit the places where their ancestors lived. Moreover, genealogical tourism is not an area where we are in competition with other countries, or where different parts of Scotland compete with each other, as the genealogical tourist is inevitably drawn to the specific location of their ancestral origin.

The 1891 Census imaging project is only one part of our drive to use this new technology to improve our business, to modernise our systems, and to meet the needs of our customers in a more efficient and effective way. Throughout Scotland, 200 local registration offices are now computerised, and 97% of all births, deaths and marriages that occur in Scotland are registered using a computer rather than by the local Registrar hand-writing out the details. This is an incredible transformation from the position, only 10 years ago, when the first computerised system was introduced into the registration service in Scotland. By modernising and joining-up Government, we will provide a better service for the public and all our users.

The National Archives of Scotland
David Brown - Head of Reader Services

The National Archives of Scotland (NAS) holds one of the most varied collections of records in Britain. Occupying some 60 kilometres of shelving, the records date from the 12th century to the present day. They include the formal records of pre- and post-Union government, the law courts, the public registers of deeds and sasines (land transfers), the records of the Church of Scotland as well as those of some other denominations, estate papers of landed families, a large collection of maps and plans, the Scottish railway archives, and the records of a variety of businesses, charitable institutions and public bodies.

Two books, both by Cecil Sinclair, give much fuller information about these and other records. They are: Tracing Your Scottish Ancestors. A Guide to Ancestry Research in the Scottish Record Office (Stationery Office, 1997, price £9.99) and T racing Scottish Local History (Stationery Office, 1994, £7.95). Both enable family historians to assess likely sources of information before they visit us, so as to make the best use of their time in our search rooms.

Before visiting the NAS, it is advisable to start investigating Scottish ancestry in the records held by the General Register Office for Scotland (GROS). Hopefully these should provide a skeleton tree, to be fleshed out from the records held by us. As most readers of this Directory will know, the GROS is located at New Register House, Edinburgh EH1 3YT. This is next door to our main building, HM General Register House. Both are at the east end of Princes Street. The GROS holds old parish registers of the Church of Scotland (up to 1854), statutory registers of births, marriages and deaths (from 1855) and census returns (from 1841 - open up to 1891).

For family historians, the most popular NAS records are the registers of wills and testaments, dating from the 16th century to 1984. Testaments from 1985 are held by the Edinburgh Commissary Office, 27 Chambers Street, Edinburgh EH2 1 LB. To search for a testament in NAS you need to have an idea of the date of death and - for wills recorded before 1 876 - a place of residence. There are good indexes for the years to 1823, arranged by locality. From 1876 to 1959 there is a detailed annual index covering all Scotland. Indexes for other periods are currently less satisfactory. NAS has just embarked as a partner in a major project, the Scottish Archive Network. Financed principally by the Heritage Lottery Fund, partly by NAS itself and partly by the Genealogical Society of Utah, one object of the Network is to generate digital images of all the testaments for the years before 1876 and produce a union index for them. Each image will be linked electronically to its index entry, enabling readers to gain almost instant access to any testament. The index will also be freely available on the Internet. The imaging process will take some time, and the original testaments are being progressively withdrawn from public access between now and the end of 2001. They will be replaced by substitutes, either microfilms or digitally generated photocopies. Consequently readers intending to visit are advised to contact us to confirm whether particular records are available.

Perhaps the second most popular class of records is the Register of Sasines, beginning in 1617 and recording the transfer of lands and houses, together with transactions in which land was used to secure loans. Sasines contain infor-

mation or clues about the individuals and families involved in these transactions, although they do not mention tenants. There are good indexes for the years after 1781, but before that the indexes are less straightforward and searching may have to be done using minute books. The Royal burghs kept a separate series of their own for urban property transactions.

The Retours (or Services of Heirs) deal with the inheritance of land. Although they deal only with landowners, a small proportion of the population, they can be a valuable resource. They run from 1530 until modem times, although they are of declining importance after 1868. When a vassal of the Crown died, his heir had to prove his right to inherit his ancestor's lands by obtaining an inquest by jury which delivered a return ('retour') to Chancery. The procedure could similarly be used by people who were not Crown vassals in order to provide evidence of their right to inherit land. Until 1847 the record was kept in Latin and the published indexes for the years before 1700 (the Inquisitionum ad Capellam Regis Retornatarum A hhreviatio) are also in Latin. Retours are very stylised documents, however, and a researcher will need only a minimum of instruction to understand their contents. The indexes from 1700 are in English.

The church records held by NAS are often consulted by family historians who have been unsuccessful in tracing an ancestor in the Old Parish Registers held by the GROS. These records, although catalogued, are not indexed. In consequence the most profitable searches tend to be those where a family has an association with a particular denomination and parish. The largest bodies of these records are those for the kirk sessions of the Church of Scotland (minute books, communion rolls, etc) and those for the other presbyterian churches which broke away from the Church of Scotland in the years after 1733, and which subsequently reunited with it. The collection is large, but not complete. Another group of church records meriting special mention is that of the Roman Catholic Church. These consist of bound sets of photocopies of Scottish Catholic parish registers, particularly of baptisms and marriages. The earliest of these dates from the 18th century, but in most parishes they do not start until the 19th century. They are not indexed.

The NAS operates two search rooms in Edinburgh. One, the Historical Search Room at General Register House, Princes Street, EH1 3YY, is used mainly by family historians. The other, at West Register House, Charlotte Square, may hold relevant material and is the principal store both for judicial records and for our plans collection. Please telephone well before any visit, to check which search room is most appropriate for your work and to ask about any arrangements for consulting out-housed records. You should also make sure that your visit does not coincide with public holidays. The NAS has its annual stocktaking in November and the Historical Search Room is closed for the first two full weeks in that month, the West Search Room for the third. We respond to every written or e-mailed enquiry but the pressure of correspondence is considerable and we cannot undertake research for enquirers.

Enquiries:
Telephone: 0131 535 1334
E-mail:
Website: www.nas.gov.uk

National Library of Scotland

Janice McFarlane
Head of Reference Services

National
Library of
Scotland

The National Library of Scotland is Scotland's largest library, serving both as a general research library of international importance, and as the world's leading repository for the printed and manuscript record of Scotland's history and culture.

As a legal deposit library, with the right to claim a copy of all UK and Irish publications, the National Library receives about 320,000 items each year and now holds around 7 million printed and new media items and around 120,000 volumes of manuscripts; it has about 1.6 million maps; it receives some 25,000 periodicals and annual publications; and every week an average of 6,000 printed items alone are added to its stock.

These collections include a wide range of material which can be of use to family historians of all levels of experience and expertise.

Beginners can find books and journals explaining how to carry out research themselves, as well as directories of genealogical services providers; those only interested in a broader picture of their family or clan can consult published histories; while those researching their family tree can search for information on specific individuals.

Although census records and registers of births, deaths and marriages in Scotland are held by the General Register Office for Scotland the National Library can provide access to the International Genealogical Index and Old Parish Registers (OPR) via FamilySearch on CD-ROM and microfiche indices. The publications of numerous family and local history societies include indices to local census records while monumental inscriptions record information inscribed on gravestones erected in local cemeteries across Scotland before 1855.

Publications produced by the various Scottish Historical Clubs and Societies, mainly founded in the 19th century, include a wide range, but rather ad hoc selection, of genealogical information taken from church and town records, including some details of local tax payers (List of pollable persons within the shire of Aberdeen 1696. Spalding Club 39, 1844) and records of marriages (Parish of Holyroodhouse or Canongate: register of marriages, 1564-1800. Scottish Record Society, 1915). Published copies of state papers, the originals of which are held in the National Archives of Scotland or the Public Record Office, can provide information on individuals who came in to contact with the national authorities.

Directories cover a wide range of useful topics. Although the Library's holdings are not comprehen-

sive they do contain collections of trade and street directories covering many parts of Scotland from the late-18th century onwards, although the bulk of the collection concentrates on Glasgow and Edinburgh.

Professional directories and biographical dictionaries list members of the medical and legal professions as well as the clergy of many Scottish and UK churches. For instance the multi-volume Fastii Ecclesiae Scoticanae lists ministers of the Church of Scotland from the Reformation to 1975.

Army (from 1714), Navy (from 1806) and Air Force (from 1919) Lists together with militia listings and biographical dictionaries listing those awarded medals in specific conflicts can help family historians track the military history of their ancestors.

The Library also holds matriculation and graduation rolls which can provide details of students who attended Scotland's older universities as well as graduates from Oxford and Cambridge.

Scotland's long history of emigration is reflected in biographical dictionaries covering emigrants to various parts of the globe (Whyte, Donald: Dictionary of Scottish emigrants to Canada before Confederation. Toronto, 1986) while other publications give basic details taken from emigrant passenger lists. The passenger and immigrant lists index lists immigrants arriving in the US and Canada from the mid-16th to the mid-20th century.

The National Library's collection of Scottish electoral registers and valuation rolls is largely complete from 1946 onwards. Prior to that date coverage is very sporadic and mainly covers Edinburgh.

Newspapers can provide useful information for the family historian. While the National Library's collection of Scottish newspapers is not complete it still has a wide range of titles going back to the 18th century. Collections of the main Scottish and UK national daily and weekly press are maintained, while the Library's policy is to also collect Scottish regional, evening, community and free newspapers. A selection of major morning dailies published in the North of England are also held. However it is important to note that few newspapers have been indexed and tracking information can be difficult if researchers are unsure about the date of any incident they may be trying to track down.

Biographies, autobiographies and biographical dictionaries cover an enormous range of individuals. While chiefly concentrating on 'people of note' there has been a growth in the publication of diaries and autobiographies covering a wider range of the social spectrum.

Local and social history can also provide useful information about the way our ancestors lived. The publications of local history societies can help to broaden the picture given of parish life in more famous publications such as the multi-volume Statistical account of Scotland produced in the 1790s and the New statistical account of Scotland of the 1840s.

While the National Library's collections are very extensive they do not cover the whole of the printed output of UK and international publishers. However the Library's holdings do contain numerous bibliographies allowing researchers to identify titles of works which may be held by other libraries. One such publication, Joan Ferguson's Scottish family histories, was published by the National Library in 1986. It lists published and manuscript family histories held by the National Library and other Scottish libraries and can prove to be a valuable starting point for the family historian.

The Library's collections of books, pamphlets, journals and newspapers can provide a wealth of information, but they are not the only sources of use to the family historian.

The Library's Map Library is one of the largest in the world and its collection of approximately 1.6 million maps includes about 1 million of various parts of the United Kingdom, including a full set of modern and historic Ordnance Survey maps of all scales. It also holds a strong collection of gazetteers which can help identify locations which do not appear on modern maps.

The manuscript collections cover a wide range of topics which can be extremely useful to some family historians. Experience has shown the collections most frequently used by genealogists to be those covering family and estate papers, including those of the Sutherland estates, and world mission records of the Church of Scotland.

An online index to the named manuscript collections is available through the Library's website. (URL: http://www.nls.uk). The website also provides access to our online catalogue which covers the bulk of our collections of printed books and serials. However it is important to realise that large parts of our collections (including the majority of our manuscript and map collections) are still only accessible via catalogues which have to be consulted in our reading rooms.

An additional resource, also accessible via our website, is the Bibliography of Scotland (BOS). This covers books, periodicals and major articles of Scottish interest published all over the world since 1976. Included in the broader Scottish Bibliographies Online the BOS indexes a range of publications of value to the family historian including the journals Scottish Genealogist, Family History and Genealogist's Magazine.

Access to the National Library of Scotland's collections is available, free of charge, to anyone requiring to consult them. However applicants should have made full use of collections available through their local libraries before visiting the National Library and they may be redirected to alternative resources if appropriate. All applicants must provide evidence of identity, such as a passport or driving licence, before a ticket will be issued and will be asked to provide name and address details.

The collections are only available for consultation in the Library's reading rooms. They cannot be taken home. While some family history material is shelved in the General Reading Room the bulk of the collections are housed in areas inaccessible to readers. Those wishing to consult items have to identify required material using the catalogues provided. Requested items are then delivered to the appropriate reading room. Delivery can take between 20-90 minutes dependent on the storage location and volume of demand.

The Library has 5 public reading rooms, differentiated by format and subject coverage. Family historians make use of 4 of these areas. The Map Library is based in our Causewayside Building, 33 Salisbury Place, Edinburgh EH9 1SL. The General Reading Room is the one most frequently used by genealogists and, together with the Microform and Rare Books & Manuscript reading rooms, is located in our main building at George IV Bridge, Edinburgh EH1 1EW.

Opening hours vary and full details are provided on our website. The General Reading Room and Rare Books & Manuscripts Reading Room have the longest opening hours:
Monday, Tuesday, Thursday, Friday: 09.30-20.30
Wednesday: 10.00-20.30
Saturday: 09.30-13.00

The Microform Reading Room closes 30 minutes before the General Reading Room and the Map Library, although open on Saturday mornings, closes at 17.00 Monday-Friday.

Although Library staff will deal with straightforward enquiries relating to our family history resources they will not carry out detailed genealogical research. Enquirers are encouraged to consult our website for fuller details of our services and resources.

Contact details: address for general enquiries to Reference Services, National Library of Scotland, George IV Bridge, Edinburgh EH1 1EW
Telephone: 0131 226 4531
e-mail: enquiries@nls.uk
web: http://www.nls.uk.

Specific enquiries about our map or manuscript collections should be addressed to the appropriate department.

Family History in Ayrshire

Jim Steel BA guides us in one Scottish County

Ayrshire is the only County in Scotland to have four independent Family History Societies within its boundaries. The two eldest societies in Ayrshire are based in Troon and Largs. These societies, the Troon & District FHS, c/o M.E.R.C., Troon Library, South Beach, Troon, Ayrshire, and the Largs and North Ayrshire FHS, c/o Largs Library, Largs, North Ayrshire were joined about three years ago by the East Ayrshire FHS, c/o The Dick Institute, Elmbank Ave., Kilmarnock, East Ayrshire, which was followed a short time later by the Alloway and South Ayrshire FHS, c/o Alloway Library, Doonholm Road, Alloway, South Ayrshire.

Local and family history has been alive and vibrant in Ayrshire for many years and all societies are members of the Ayrshire Federation of Historical Societies. The four family history societies are of course all members of the Scottish Association of Family History Societies (SAFHS) and indeed the Largs and North Ayrshire Society will be host to the Annual SAFHS Conference 2001.

Recently, the Four Societies as they are known, have been coming together in many ways, sharing research problems, visiting each others meetings and having joint discussion meetings on a regular basis. Usually if someone asks which particular society they should join, they are advised to contact whichever society covers the area where the bulk of their research is based. Apart from this each society will assist the others with any of their respective members problems. It is hoped to develop in this manner, each society preserving its own identity and working within its own boundaries in archival and research work.

An attempt was made to start a family history society on the beautiful Island of Arran. Situated off the coast of Ayrshire Arran is a 50 minute trip on the ferry from Ardrossan. It has high mountains, and is often referred to as being a Scotland in Miniature. The family history society did not succeed but there are some records (and much personal knowledge) of family history and material to be found at the excellent museum situated at the Arran Heritage Museum, Brodick, Arran, a short bus trip from the pier at Brodick.

With the formation of the three council areas in Ayrshire, and to satisfy legal requirements, the Ayrshire Archives Centre, Craigie Estate, Ayr, KA8 0SS, financed by the three separate authorities was opened two years ago. Staffed by two permanent Archivists, with support staff, the centre is open on Tuesday, Wednesday and Thursday of each week. Amongst their ever growing material you can access the original of the Poor Law Records for many of the local parishes also such records as Voters Rolls, Cess Rolls, and some Records of the Church of Scotland. There is a wealth of smaller items like the Symington Church Treasurers Book, a number of gifted collections such as the Donald Family Papers, Maps, Burgh Records etc. Branches of the Archives Centre can be found at The Baird Institute, 3 Lugar Street, Cumnock, East Ayrshire and the Ardrossan Library, 39-41 Princess Street, Ardrossan, North Ayrshire.

The Poor Law records of the county (1825-1930) have recently been filmed by the Mormon Church and will be available on order at any of the Mormon Family History Centres world-wide.

East Ayrshire Family History Society's logo is a Coal Pit's winding gantry (known as a whorl) and two stacks of hay (known as stooks) illustrating the area's connections with mining and farming. The society covers a large part of the County and, although based in Kilmarnock, it reaches far-flung members by holding a monthly Workshop, also open to non-members at Cumnock in the southern part of the county. The society has embraced modern technology in its use of computers, both for holding a number of databases, in its archival work and with its Email address and a web page that has links to other such pages. Recently a chat room for the use of distant members has been included on the Web Page. Thanks to a Lottery Grant the society is able to travel about the area, giving talks to a wide variety of public life, using an electronic projector, linked to its lap-top computer.

With an increasing membership the society has both a reference and lending library. Its Members Interests database is available free of charge to members and a copy can be found on its Web Page. The main project being done by members is the indexing of the 1861 Ayrshire Census. This is being done in three parts, the first being East Ayrshire area, which is due to be published on fiche during winter of 2000. A member of the society has indexed the Poor Applications for Ardrossan, one of the main ports of Irish Immigration during the 19th century and the Poor Register of Kilmarnock. Work is ongoing with indexing of the Parishes of New Cumnock, Maybole and Beith.

Also being prepared is a Family History book containing details of various holdings in the County of interest to family historians. Amongst many items of interest to family historians will be indexes of all place names taken from 1790, 1856 and present day maps of the County, lists of photographers showing dates and places of business, the location and details of various record centres, and the records that they hold, all existing Monumental Inscriptions, location of cemeteries and dates of first burial, Old Parish Records, Burial Records, Registrars details etc. It is anticipated that this book will be presented in loose-leaf style to facilitate an update every two years in the shape of inserts as record centres add to their collections.

In Ayrshire Family History is well and truly alive. The only problem is that it does not have a suitable home. The ideal, would be to amalgamate the joint interests of family and local history and have a Heritage Centre based somewhere in the County, each type of history interacting with the other. In fact this would no doubt be the ideal for any County area of the United Kingdom!

Jim Steel was a Council Member for the Glasgow & West of Scotland Family History Society for three years and was the their research coordinator. He was coordinator for the 1881 Indexing project of the Renfrewshire Census and followed this up with the 1851 census of Ayrshire. His special interest is in the poor Law and he has indexed a number of poor Law Applications and Registers of the County of Ayrshire. He was a founder member of the International Police association - Genealogy Group and the East Ayrshire Family History Society being its first Chairman - he is now Secretary of the Society. He has recently published the Index to the Kilmarnock Poor Register 1845 - 1900 and is now completing another on family history holdings in the County of Ayrshire.

The Genealogy of Archives

Iain Flett Dundee City Archives

Family historians and local historians are familiar with using archives in their search for genealogy; the swathe cut by the last Local Government Reorganisation in 1996[1] means that archivists already are having to use the skills of genealogists to work out the labyrinthine trail of the survival and location of official fonds, or original records.

Broadly speaking, Scottish local government until the major reorganisation of 1975[2] consisted of a rich collection of burghs, many originating from the 12th century, all with their own heritage and records, all proudly guarded by their Town Clerks, and of a range of shires or counties, which were well documented after the eighteenth century. In 1975 the alien concept of 'regionalisation' was imposed on the country, riding roughshod over a practical evolution of 800 years of administration, when even the four major cities were reduced to district council (housing, libraries and parks) status.

The only authorities to escape with all-purpose responsibility, with associated heritage and record keeping were the Island Authorities of Orkney, Shetland and the Western Isles. In theory this would logically have been followed by a blanket imposition of regional archive centres, possibly on the French model, but thankfully, as it turned out, the record keeping provisions of the 1973 Act were left so permissive and elastic as to allow local arrangements. Thus the City of Dundee District Council looked after the records of Tayside Regional Council, and Strathclyde Regional Council looked after the records of the City of Glasgow District Council, while within Aberdeen there co-existed, with some duplication, the separate repositories of Grampian Regional Council and of the City of Aberdeen District Council.

The reorganisation of 1996 returned all-purpose responsibility to the four Cities of Edinburgh, Glasgow, Edinburgh and Dundee, and gave all-purpose status to recognisable, if not historically accurate, county areas. Most important of all, in record-keeping terms, the Act not only gave local government offices in Scotland the legitimacy that England and Wales had enjoyed since 1974[3], but in fact gave the Keeper of the Records of Scotland powers to lay down standards of record keeping, record collection, and access that will now statutorily have to be developed by every single local government authority in Scotland.

If only this structure is allowed to exist for more than 21 years, then there is real hope of a comprehensive and integrated local record service, with integrated finding aids and a common high standard of service, but ironically the imminent arrival of another tier of government, in the form of the revitalised Scottish Parliament, very probably heralds yet another reorganisation.

For the time being it may therefore be useful to provide a quick Cook's (or more appropriately, Macbrayne's) tour by former Regional and Islands Authorities, to summarise current provision, and gaps being filled.[4] The regional councils have now all been disbanded, together with their geographical postal descriptions, but for the purpose of this exercise they can provide a rough guide to archival births, deaths, marriages, divorces and adoptions. The established archival theory of transmission would prefer that archives should be at the sharp record creating end, such as the old Town Clerk's Department, now known by a plethora of 'Yes-Minister-speak' such as those of Corporate Affairs, Executive or Administration.

However, in practice many archives can be found in museums or libraries services, who now face the unaccustomed additional heavy statutory burden of records management. Records Management is the complete genealogy of record keeping from the cradle to the grave, which brings an awesome responsibility of dealing with tonnes and tonnes of traditional records and megabytes of electronic information. If you are intending to use their services, please assume that advance booking will be necessary for all offices.

Family historians unused to Scottish records should bear in mind that a different and separate administrative and church history has led to different and separate record series. The established church in Scotland is the Presbyterian Church of Scotland, which means that other churches, including the Scottish Episcopal Church are not established. Civil registration began in Scotland in 1855, and amid great debate about the legality of this action at the time, the Registrar General collected together all the Church of Scotland (but not including the Free Church) registers of baptisms, marriages and funerals up to that date. These Old Parochial Records (known as the OPR's) are held centrally in New Register House, Edinburgh, although microfilms of the baptisms and marriages are widely available throughout libraries, archives and family history societies in Scotland.

A good internet guide to family history sources and locations has been written by Vivienne S Dunstan [5]. The Historical Search Room, Scottish Record Office, HM General Register House, Edinburgh EH1 3YY, will be pleased to help locate any records of non-established churches that are known to be in the care of local government repositories and the Scottish Record Office. The Scottish Record Office, unlike the Public Record Office in Kew, has centrally collected a wide range of church records, including the non-OPR elements of the Church of Scotland, and has copied series such as some Roman Catholic church records. Records held in the Scottish Record Office are available for inspection free of charge, whereas records in New Register House are liable to production charges. Dundee City Archives and Dumfries & Galloway Archives both have flourishing Friends organisations, which are proving invaluable in enriching the collections through voluntary work. Such voluntary labour (directed so as not to weaken the establishment of professional archive posts), and application to external funding such as Lottery and the EEC, will hopefully strengthen the Scottish local archives network into becoming an enviable resource in European terms.

SHETLAND ISLANDS COUNCIL
Shetland Archives, 44 King Harald Street, Lerwick ZE1 0EQ. Continuation of previous service.
ORKNEY ISLANDS COUNCIL
Orkney Archives, The Orkney Library, Laing Street, Kirkwall KW15 1NW. Continuation of previous service.
WESTERN ISLES COUNCIL
Western Isles Council, Council Offices, Sandwick Road, Stornoway HS1 2BW -developing an archive service.
HIGHLAND REGIONAL COUNCIL
Highland Council Archive, The Library, Farraline Park, Inverness IV1 1NH. Continuation of previous service, with future planned expansion to deal with records management.
North Highland Archive, Wick Library, Sinclair Terrace, Wick KW1 5AB. Built with EEC assistance, this successful area office may herald a pragmatic strategy of dealing with local heritage in a vast rural sparsely populated area
GRAMPIAN REGIONAL COUNCIL
Aberdeenshire Council Archives. Broadly the records inherited from Grampian Regional Council. At the moment being managed by Aberdeen City Archives. Aberdeen City Archives, Town House, Broad Street, Aberdeen AB10 1AQ. Continuation of City of Aberdeen District Council, who are now also managing Aberdeenshire Archives.
Moray Council Archives, Grant Lodge, Cooper Park, Elgin IV30 1HS. Former Moray
District Archives at Forres are being restructured, but records can be produced by prior appointment.
CENTRAL REGIONAL COUNCIL
Stirling Council Archives Services, Unit 6, Burghmuir Industrial Estate, Stirling FK7 7PY. Continuation of Central Regional Council Archives Department, but Falkirk and Clackmannan records have mostly been transferred to appropriate authorities.
Falkirk Council Archives, Falkirk Museum, Callendar House, Callendar Park, Falkirk FK1 1YR. Continuation of Falkirk District Archives, with appropriate transfers from Stirling Archives.
Clackmannanshire Council Archives, 26-28 Drysdale Street, Alloa FK10 1JL. New service set up with transfers from Stirling Archives.
TAYSIDE REGIONAL COUNCIL
Dundee City Archives, 21 City Square, Dundee DD1 3BY. Continuation of City of Dundee District Council Archive Centre, which managed the records of Tayside Regional Council, but Perth & Kinross and Angus/Forfarshire records have been transferred to appropriate authorities. First local government Friends organisation in Scotland, followed by Dumfries & Galloway.
Angus Archives, Montrose Library, 214 High Street, Montrose DD10 8PH. Continuation of Angus District Archives, with transfers from Dundee City Archives.
Perth & Kinross Council Archive, A.K.BELL Library, 2-8 York Place, Perth PH2 8EP. Continuation of Perth & Kinross District Council Archives, with transfers from Dundee City Archives.
FIFE REGIONAL COUNCIL
Fife Council, Fife House, North Street, Glenrothes KY7 5LT is developing an archive service. Consultant's report being considered. Alison Baillie, Team Leader, General Services, can locate records within the Council.
STRATHCLYDE REGIONAL COUNCIL
Glasgow City Archives, Mitchell Library, North Street, Glasgow G3 7DN. Continuation of Strathclyde Regional Archives and its predecessor Glasgow City Archives Office, but many records are being transferred to appropriate offices.
Argyll & Bute Council Archives, Manse Brae, Lochgilphead PA31 8QU. Continuation of Argyll & Bute District Archives, with transfers from Glasgow City Archives.
West Dunbartonshire Council, Council Offices, Garshake Road, Dumbarton G82 3PU is developing an archive service.
East Dunbartonshire Council, Tom Johnston House, Civic Way, Kirkintilloch G66 4TJ, is developing an archive service.
Inverclyde Council, Municipal Buildings, Greenock PA15 1LY, is developing an archive service.
Renfrewshire Council, The Robertson Centre, 16 Glasgow Road, Paisley PA1 3QG, is developing an archive service.
East Renfrewshire Council, Council Offices, Eastwood Park, Rouken Glen Road, Glasgow G46 6UG is developing an archive service.
North Lanarkshire Archive, 10 Kelvin Road, Lenziemill, Cumbernauld G67 2BA.
Includes geographical area of historical Dunbartonshire and Stirlingshire, and inherited records of Cumbernauld New Town.
South Lanarkshire Archives and Information Management Service, Records Management Unit, 30 Hawbank Road, College Milton, East Kilbride G74 5EX.

Includes geographical area of historical Lanarkshire proper, and inherited records of East Kilbride Development Corporation, local district councils and burghs.

Ayrshire Archives is a joint service being developed between North Ayrshire Council, East Ayrshire Council and South Ayrshire Council, whereby the Archivist has intellectual control over the various sites in the area. North Ayrshire Council inherited the records management centre of Irvine Development Corporation, and is developing its historical collections.

East Ayrshire Council is developing a modern record centre at Kilmarnock. South Ayrshire is providing the headquarters of the service at Ayrshire Archives Centre, Craigie Estate, Ayr KA8 0SS, in a newly adapted building, which vies with Falkirk in being near to excellent catering facilities.

LOTHIAN REGIONAL COUNCIL

City of Edinburgh Council Archives, City Chambers, High Street, Edinburgh EH1 1YJ, is a continuation of the City of Edinburgh District Council Archives, who have inherited the records of Lothian Regional Council.

West Lothian Council Archives, Rutherford Square, Bellsquarry, Livingston EH54 9BU has inherited the modern records of Livingston New Town, and is now collecting historical material.

Midlothian Council Archives, Library Headquarters, 2 Clerk Street, Loanhead EH20 9DR, inherited the modern records of Midlothian District Council, & co-operates with the Local Studies section in preserving historical records.

East Lothian Council, Council Buildings, Haddington EH41 3HA, is developing an archive service.

DUMFRIES AND GALLOWAY REGION

Dumfries and Galloway Archive Centre, 33 Burns Street, Dumfries DG1 2PS, is a continuation of the Dumfries Archive Centre, which has merged with Dumfries and Galloway Libraries to provide a council-wide service and is exploring Heritage Lottery funding for an archive centre in Sanquhar. At the moment has the only Friends organisation in Scotland apart from Dundee City.

BORDERS REGION

Scottish Borders Archive and Local History Centre, St Mary's Mill, Selkirk TD7 5EW, is a continuation of the former Borders service. Can locate records in dispersed centres.

[1] The Local Government etc. (Scotland) Act 1994 c.39

[2] The Local Government (Scotland) Act 1973 c.65

[3] The Local Government Act 1972

[4] For those of you with access to a computer linked to the Internet, or to a public library with Internet facilities, the following sites will give you more up to date and detailed information; the Historical Manuscripts Commission list all Scottish sites with manuscripts on <http://www.hmc.gov.uk/nra/locresult.asp?lctry=Scotland> and archivists themselves run an information site on <http://www.archivesinfo.net/uksites. html>. Both sites have useful links to related topics on history and genealogy.

[5] <http://www-theory.dcs.st-and.ac.uk/~mnd/genuki/intro.html>

This article by Iain Flett is based on an earlier version which appeared in *Scottish Archives* (Volume 4 1998) published by The Scottish Records Association.

The Scottish Records Association

The Scottish Records Association was founded in 1977
to be an organisation concerned with the preservation and use of Scotland's historical records.
It provides a forum for users, owners and archivists and other custodians of records
to discuss all relevant topics. We hold an annual conference on a historical theme;
the most recent have covered the records of crime, politics, education, banking and tourism.
Our annual journal *Scottish Archives* contains articles of general and particular interest,
while our *Datasheets* provide summary information on the holdings of
many local and special record repositories,
of use to family and local historians.
The SRA does not conduct family searches.

Subscriptions and Details from
The Secretary
Scottish Records Association
National Archives of Scotland
HM General Register House
Edinburgh EH1 3YY

The Public Record Office of Northern Ireland
Anne McVeigh

The Public Record Office of Northern Ireland has had an incredibly busy year. Apart from dealing with the usual number of personal callers from far and wide (running at just over 18,000 visitors per year), and answering written queries, including a huge increase in e-mails, we have been busy on other fronts.

Public Talks
Back in March 2000, we offered a new service to the public. Called 'PRONI made Easy', visitors were invited behind the scenes to see what it was like from the staff's point of view. They were shown round the stores, where our 53 kilometres of records are kept, and into the Conservation section, where they saw at first hand the work involved in making damaged records fit for public use again. Back in the Exhibition Hall, a PowerPoint presentation was used to give visitors a brief overview of the history of the Record Office, the categories of records held and the wide range of subjects covered. The rationale for running the service was to help our readers appreciate exactly what was involved in the daily work of a record office.

We knew, from comments made by our readers, that some of our rules and regulations appeared arbitrary and illogical. And it is true that too often what goes on behind the scenes does appear mysterious and incomprehensible. For instance: we often get complaints about the length of time taken to produce documents. We can deliver 90% of documents within 30 minutes, although most arrive within 20 minutes. For most people, accustomed to a library service, this seems an unnecessarily long wait. Yet, take people 'backstage', show them the huge scale of the stores, and they immediately understand why it appears to take so long for documents to arrive. Knowing that there is a good reason for the delay, our readers no longer complain - instead they use the waiting time more productively.

Another seemingly pointless rule - that pens may not be used in the Reading Room - becomes perfectly understandable when one sees at first hand how much damage can be caused to an unique document by pens, and the amount of time and effort that needs to be expended by our Conservation staff to repair that damage. The Conservation Section is one of the most fascinating aspects of the tour - we have to literally drag the visitors away!

If you would like to take part in one of the

'PRONI made Easy' tours, our contact number is at the end of this article. Other talks available (tour not included) are: Tracing your Family Tree at PRONI, which outlines most of the sources available together with the advantages and problems associated with each source: and Sources for Local History at PRONI, which explains the sources and provides a worked example of how to use them. In addition to the above-mentioned talks, held in PRONI, our staff can visit outside institutions, by appointment, to talk to interested groups.

PRONI Outreach Centres
We realise that it is not easy for everyone who is interested in our records to travel to Belfast. We have, therefore, decided that if they can't come to us, we can - to a degree - go to them! Our pilot outreach centre was in Blacklion, Co, Cavan, where it proved very successful. Indeed, so successful that we have been asked to open other centres throughout Northern Ireland. In partnership with Derry City Council's Heritage and Museum

Present at the opening of the PRONI Outreach Centre, Harbour Museum, Londonderry, were: the Lord Mayor of Derry, Cathal Crumley, the Minister for the Department of Culture, Arts and Leisure, Mr Michael McGimpsey, MLA, and the Nobel Peace Prize-winner, John Hume, MP, MLA

Service, we officially opened the new outreach centre in Londonderry on the 25 June, 2000.

The Outreach Centre allows those living some distance from PRONI to carry out some basic research before making the trip to Belfast. Researchers can then be certain that PRONI does hold the records in which they are interested, and ensure that the best use is made of the time spent in Belfast. The Foyle Outreach Centre, located in the Harbour Museum, Harbour Square, Londonderry, has computerised databases of most of the records available at the Public Record

Office, Balmoral Avenue, Belfast, as well as an off-line copy of the PRONI web-site. Visitors to the Harbour Museum can use the computers to find information about PRONI and its records, and to obtain the relevant PRONI reference numbers of the documents they would like to consult at PRONI. There is also a small but useful reference library of PRONI publications and guidebooks to which visitors can refer. The Centre will be of benefit to anyone interested in research but particularly to the family or local historian.

New Centres

By the time this article goes to print, the Outreach Centres in Morrow's Shop Museum, Bridge Street, Ballymena, and the St Patrick's Trian Centre, Armagh, will have received their official launch, both due in October, 2000. Again, both centres will contain computerised databases, the off-line PRONI web-site, catalogues relevant to their area, information leaflets and guides.

New Book Launched

On Tuesday, 27 June, 2000 (co-incidentally, the same day that he received an honorary doctorate from The Queen's University of Belfast) Jonathan Bardon's latest opus, A guide to local history sources in PRONI (Blackstaff Press, Belfast, 2000) was officially launched by Michael McGimpsey, MLA, at the Interpoint Centre in Belfast. The book, designed to aid those using PRONI to trace the history of their local area, is competitively priced at £9.99 and is available at all good bookshops.

Each chapter deals with a different source, for example, there are sections on Local Government records, Ordnance Survey maps, Church records and Valuation books, to name but a few. Mr McGimpsey claimed it would be invaluable to those whose experience of research methods was limited as it was user-friendly, accessible and written in an informative but easy to read style.

Act of Union Bicentenary Project

At the request of Mr McGimpsey PRONI is taking the lead in organising the events for commemorating the passing of the Act of Union. The Act of Union, that united Ireland and Great Britain into one political entity, came into force on the 1st January, 1801. Among the projects under way to commemorate this historic event is a new multimedia exhibition that will include a touring component; a souvenir publication, and a public lecture by an eminent historian.

Naturally, PRONI is thrilled to be involved in so exciting and prestigious a venture and has assigned some of its most talented and experienced personnel to the project. Dr Lammey has previously been involved with a number of exhibitions, including 'France and Northern Ireland,' which marked the bicentenary of the French Revolution; 'Northern Ireland and New Zealand 1840-1940,' a sesquicentenary display reflecting Northern Ireland - New Zealand links; 'The Williamite War and its Aftermath,' commemorating the tercentenary of the

Battle of the Boyne in 1690; 'The Belfast Blitz, 1941', and the 'Tale of two Churches' exhibition. The two Churches, May Street Presbyterian Church and St Malachy's Roman Catholic Church, opened up their archives to us and, supplemented by items already in our possession, we held the exhibition first in the atrium of Clarence Court, the Department of the Environment headquarters in Adelaide Street, before moving to May Street, then St Malachy's; from there it went to the Ulster Bank in Donegall Square East, and negotiations are currently under way to show it at the Waterfront Hall.

The new exhibition on the Bicentenary of the Act of Union, to be launched in March, 2001, will involve many of the museums, libraries and heritage centres in Northern Ireland, as well as the Royal Irish Academy, Dublin, and the Public Record Office, Kew. It is hoped to involve as wide a cross section of the population of these islands as possible, not forgetting the school children. A 'Schools Study Day' will be held in April, and a special teachers' pack is being produced.

Assisting with the background research and organisation of the events is David Huddleston who, alongside his colleague, Stephen Scarth, has been responsible for evaluating, assessing, and listing a considerable number of the collections in PRONI's holding.

New Collections

Among the private collections processed during 1999-2000, and now available to the public, are three collections of emigrant letters. These are (i) the papers of the affluent Pinkerton family of Ballycastle, Co. Antrim (D/4212), who emigrated to Wangaratta, Australia, (ii) those of the more humble Weir family of Edenclaw, Co. Fermanagh (D/4231), who migrated to Michigan and California, America, and (iii) the letters of the Davison family of Glenarm, Co. Antrim, and Castleblayney, Co. Monaghan, 1841-43 (D/4221). These documents include letters from William and Thomas Davison in New York, their sister Anne Jane Davison of Laragh, Castleblayney, Co. Monaghan, and father Alexander Davison in Glenarm, relating tales of working in America, marriage, family gossip, life and death.

A major policy drive to acquire the papers of 20th century politicians has continued to be extremely productive. As a consequence, leading figures in Northern Ireland's political history have donated their records to PRONI. These include the constituency papers of Seamus Mallon of Markethill, Co. Armagh, Deputy First Minister of the Northern Ireland Assembly and Deputy Leader of the Social Democratic and Labour Party (D/4219). The Mallon archive is particularly welcome because it augments the recently catalogued SDLP papers (D/3072).

Collections relating to leading figures of the Ulster Unionist Party include those of Sir George Anthony Clark, former president of the Ulster Unionist Council and head of the Orange Order

(D/4234) and Senator Robert Armstrong (D/4242). Other Unionist deposits include those of Ulster Popular Unionist Party leader, James Kilfedder, and those of Betty Holland, of the Democratic Unionist Party. One other political collection that deserves special mention is the Major Robert Stephens archive (D/4251). Stephens was secretary to the Governors of Northern Ireland, c.1935-80, and his papers comprise six volumes, 21 photographs and several newspaper cuttings documenting the period of his service as private secretary to Lord Wakehurst, Lord Erskine of Rerrick and the recently deceased Lord Grey of Naunton. The papers are unique in providing a personal insight into the official duties of the Governor of Northern Ireland prior to the Troubles.

Accessions of estate papers included four Armar Corry estate rentals (D/4233) relating to the Lowry-Corry family estate in Cos Antrim, Down and Fermanagh, 1886-1928. One of their many Belfast properties was the Theatre Royal in Castle Lane. C.100 volumes of estate rentals relating to the Needham estate in Newry and Mourne were added to the Kilmorey papers (D/2638), while the rentals of the Dundalk estate of the Earl of Roden were microfilmed by PRONI (see MIC/681).

Collections of sporting associations include the now defunct St. Mary's Cricket Club (D/4248), based at Glenbank, Ballysillan, North Belfast; and the 9th Belfast Old Boys Association Lawn Tennis Club (D/4226), 1926-83.

In the arena of the arts, PRONI acquired two disparate archives relating to the forerunners of the Ulster Museum, Stranmillis Road, Belfast. The first are the papers of the Belfast Natural History Society (D/4223) containing membership lists, reports, addresses and appeals relating to the establishment of the museum, 1821-59. The second contains records of the Belfast City Museum and Art Gallery (D/4228), comprising financial records, publications, architectural plans and correspondence, 1888-1965. There is also a series of diaries written by Charles Elcock, curator of the museum.

Literature and architecture are also represented by the Anne Crone archive (D/4230) and the Brumwell Thomas archive (D/4225). The papers of Anne Crone, the Dublin-born author of Bridie Steen (New York, 1948); This Pleasant Lea (1951) and My Heart and I (1955), include two school jotters containing youthful stories and more mature critiques of English literature, respectively. The Brumwell Thomas archive contains reports, correspondence and plans relating to the work of Sir Brumwell Thomas, the architect of the Belfast City Hall and Garden of Remembrance.

In the field of education, PRONI acquired the research papers and correspondence of the educationalist, writer and broadcaster, Professor H. Rex Cathcart of Coleraine, Co. Londonderry (D/4235), c.1950-90. Cathcart was Professor of the Department of Further Professional Studies in Education at The Queen's University, Belfast,

(QUB). Among his many publications are: The Most Contrary Region: A history of the BBC, 1924-84 (Blackstaff Press) and William III and Ireland (Irish History Series), and his television credits included producing the UTV series, 'Ulster Landscapes'. Further lecture notes were added to the existing David Johnson archive (D/4217). Mr Johnson was a former Head of the Department of Economic and Social History at QUB.

The substantial amount of business archives held in PRONI was augmented with the acquisition of papers of the construction firm, John Graham (Dromore) Ltd, Co. Down (D/4224), 1904-1968, which included seven volumes of letter books and haulage journals relating to building contracts; a letterbook of the Dromore Electric Light and Power Company Ltd., 1931-1939, and a register of shareholders of the Antrim Gaslight Company, 1854-1899, listing the names, addresses and shareholders (D/4239). Additional trade union records were received relating to the National Union of Tailors and Garment Workers (D/1050/17).

We also acquired a disparate collection of Mid-Ulster Orange Order memorabilia (D/4246), including minute books of the Loyal Orange Lodges, 338, 375 and 1620, correspondence, membership certificates and District Chapter Returns, c.1854-1918.

One final small but choice collection is a series of eight letters (D/3994/5) from the Ulster Banking Company, Belfast, to Messrs Perkins, Bacon & Petch, London solicitors, relating to alterations to Ulster banknotes, 1836-38.

And Finally ...
PRONI preserve the records of all the public bodies of Northern Ireland, as well as those of churches, business firms, sporting associations and private individuals. This year we have put a tremendous amount of effort into making PRONI more 'user-friendly', whether through providing talks, mounting exhibitions, adding to our collections, producing books and guides and, of course, opening our new Outreach Centres. We hope this short article goes some way towards whetting your appetite. If so, and you haven't already visited us, then think about coming to one of our introductory talks, or taking advantage of some of the other services we provide.

If you are interested in attending one of PRONI's talks or would like further information, then contact

Reader Services,
66 Balmoral Avenue
Belfast BT9 6NY
Tel: (028) 90 255902
Fax: (028) 90 255999
E:mail: Reader Services
Web: http://proni.nics.gov.uk

National Library of Ireland
Colette O'Flaherty

The National Library of Ireland derives its origins from the Library of the Royal Dublin Society, founded in 1731. In 1877 a substantial portion of the Royal Dublin Society library was purchased by the State and the new National Library of Ireland was established.

Situated in Kildare Street, Dublin, the Library aims to collect, preserve and make accessible materials on or relating to Ireland, whether published in Ireland or abroad, together with a supporting reference collection. The Library's current collection of some six million items constitutes probably the most outstanding collection of Irish documentary material in the world, an invaluable representation of Irish history and heritage. Books, serial publications, newspapers, manuscripts, maps, photographs, official publications, prints, drawings and ephemera make up the bulk of the collections.

The National Library has long been one of the key centres for family history research in Ireland. In recognition of this the Library's Genealogy Service - an expert service staffed by a panel of professional genealogists, together with experienced Library staff - is designed with the specific needs of family history researchers in mind. The Service, which is freely available to all visitors to the Library, offers the opportunity to consult with expert researchers who will advise on specific records and research procedure. Visitors to the Genealogy Service are offered expert advice on their research together with access to reference material and finding aids. Information leaflets, including a series on family history research in the Library, are readily available.

While the Genealogy Service is of particular value to first-time researchers, the Library also encourages more experienced family history researchers to continue to use the facilities for next-step advice from the genealogists and Library staff there.

The records most used by family history researchers in the National Library fall under the following headings:

(a) Parish Records
For most family history researchers parish registers are the earliest direct source of family information, providing clear evidence of links between one generation and another (via baptismal registers) and one family and another (via marriage registers). They are particularly important for any information they provide for the period before the commencement of civil or State registration of all births, marriages and deaths in 1864.

The National Library holds microfilm copies of almost all Roman Catholic parish registers up to circa 1880. Most of the registers begin in the period 1810-1830 but some - particularly in counties along the western seaboard - begin somewhat later. In a number of counties in the province of Leinster registers begin in the 1780-1790s, while in the cities the start dates may be as early as 1760. In the case of three dioceses - Kerry, Limerick and Cashel and Emly - formal writ-ten permission to consult registers must be obtained in advance from the relevant diocese. Contact addresses and telephone numbers for these dioceses are listed in National Library Family History leaflet no. 2 (Parish registers), a copy of which may be obtained from the Library.

The Library's parish register microfilming programme is ongoing, with gaps in the collection being steadily reduced. A comprehensive listing, by diocese, of the Library's holdings may be consulted in the Genealogy Service and in the main Reading Room.

(b) 19th Century Valuation Records
The Library holds copies of Griffith's Valuation (on microfiche) and of the Tithe Applotment Books (on microfilm). A CD-ROM index to Griffith's Valuation is also available for consultation.

The county by county Index of Surnames, a listing of the surnames recorded in Griffith's Valuation and the Tithe Books, continues to be a much-used source. The Index of Surnames acts as a valuable aid to pinpointing relevant parishes and parish records, and to understanding the distribution of particular surnames in parishes throughout the country.

(c) Trade and Social Directories
The National Library has extensive holdings of Dublin, provincial and countrywide trade and social directories. The first of the Dublin directories dates from 1751. Dublin directories, which steadily expanded in scope over the years, continue in publication up to the present time. While the earliest of the provincial directories - Ferrar's Directory of Limerick - dates from 1769, the nineteenth century saw the widespread publication of such directories. The nineteenth-century also saw the publication of countrywide directories such as Pigot's Commercial Directory of Ireland (1820 and 1824) and Slater's Directories (1846, 1856, 1870, 1881 and 1894), all of which may be consulted in the Library.

(d) Newspapers
The National Library has the largest newspaper collection in Ireland, with complete files of many local as well as national newspapers. In newspapers, the bulk of information relevant to genealogical research occurs in the form of advertisements and biographical notices (of birth, death or marriage). As there are few indexes available, relevant family information can be difficult to locate. As with the trade and social directories, newspaper information tends to be exclusive of the majority of the population: most births, marriages

and deaths went unannounced and daily life continued without advertisement or report. Nonetheless, while direct family information may not be available, newspapers are rich in context and provide a sense of the community and times in which particular ancestors lived.

A comprehensive listing of Irish newspapers, including the National Library's holdings, may be found in the publication NEWSPLAN - Report of the NEWSPLAN Project in Ireland (Revised edition, 1998. Edited by Sara Smyth). The Report includes a town and county index of places of publication, subdivided chronologically. The updated NEWSPLAN database may be consulted on the National Library of Ireland website.

(e) Manuscripts Records
The main components of the Library's manuscripts collections are Gaelic manuscripts, landed estates archives, maps, political material and literary papers. Of these, it is the archives of the former landed estates that are of particular interest to family history researchers. Among the more notable of these archives held by the Library are Castletown (Co. Laois), Clements (Cos. Leitrim and Donegal), Clonbrock (Co. Galway), Coolattin (Co. Wicklow), De Vesci (Co. Laois), Doneraile (Co. Cork), Headford (Co. Meath), Inchiquin (Co. Clare), Lismore (Co. Waterford), Monteagle (Co. Limerick), O'Hara (Co. Sligo), Ormond (Cos. Tipperary and Kilkenny), Powerscourt (Co. Wicklow), Prior-Wandesforde (Co. Kilkenny), Sarsfield (Co. Cork) and Wicklow (Co. Wicklow). Estate archives contain the records of the administration of estates by landlords and their agents, and generally include leases, rentals, accounts, correspondence and maps, mostly dating from the eighteenth and nineteenth centuries.

Also of interest to family history researchers in the Department of Manuscripts are a number of collections of wills and will abstracts.

Information on Department of Manuscripts catalogues and guides is readily available from the National Library. For those intent on searching for relevant estate material, the expert advice from the Library's Genealogy Service will be of assistance in pinpointing who the relevant landowner might have been.

(f) Maps
The Library's map collections comprise some 150,000 maps and include cartographic materials ranging from a 12th century coloured sketch map of Europe to the most recent Ordnance Survey maps. Special collections include the Down Survey maps (18th century copies of 17th century originals), 18th century estate maps - including the collection of surveyors Brownrigg, Longfield and Murray, maps commissioned by the County Grand Juries (late 18th - 19th century) and Ordnance Survey maps (1830s onwards).

Both printed and manuscript maps are listed in a card catalogue. Manuscripts maps are also listed in the various manuscripts catalogues.

(g) Other Sources
Other sources regularly consulted by family history researchers in the National Library include many printed family histories, often compiled and published for private circulation by individuals who have researched their own family history. It should also be noted that publications of local history societies from around the country often contain valuable transcripts of local sources, including gravestone inscriptions, freeholders lists, etc. Other relevant material in the Library's collections include the annual printed Army Lists, Navy Lists, Royal Irish Constabulary (RIC) publications including the annual RIC Directories, the 1796 Spinning Wheel Premium Entitlement List (microfiche) and various other records of trades and professions, as well as a comprehensive series of Registers of Electors. Also, as research progresses, the appendices to nineteenth-century Parliamentary reports may prove useful.

The Library's photographic collections - held at the National Photographic Archive in Meeting House Square, Dublin 2 - may also be of interest. Collections acquired from various commercial photographic studios such as Poole (Waterford and surrounding counties) and Wynne (Castlebar) include studio portraits and an unparalleled collection of topographical images of Ireland.

There are comprehensive finding aids to Library collections available in the Library Reading Rooms. Regularly updated information leaflets - with information on various Library collections and services - are readily available.

Exhibitions and publications: Exhibitions are held in both the main Library building and in the National Photographic Archive. The Library publishes a wide range of materials including books and guides, reports, booklets, document facsimile folders, CD-ROMS, calendars and postcards. These are available in the Library shop.

Admission to the National Library of Ireland: For Genealogy (microfilms) and Newspaper research, passes - which may be obtained in the main Library building - are required. Other readers must apply for a Readers Ticket (for which proof of identity and two passport photos are necessary). To view manuscripts, a supplementary Manuscripts Readers Ticket, issued by the Duty Librarian, is required.

The Readers Ticket Office is open during the following hours:
Mon-Wed 1000-1230, 1400-1700;
Thu-Fri 1000-1230, 1400-1630; Sat 1000-1230).

Library Opening Hours:
Main Reading Room/ Microform Reading Room
Mon-Wed 1000-2100
Thu-Fri 1000-1700 Sat 1000-1300
Manuscripts Reading Room
Mon-Wed 1000-2030
Thu-Fri 1000-1630 Sat 1000-1230

National Photographic Archive Reading Room
Mon-Fri 1000-1700

Contact details:
National Library of Ireland, Kildare Street, Dublin 2
Tel: +353-1-6030 200
Fax: +353-1-6766 690
Email: info@nli.ie
Internet: http://www.nli.ie/

National Archives of Ireland

Aideen M Ireland National Archives of Ireland

The National Archives comprises the holdings of the former Public Record Office of Ireland and of the State Paper Office. The combined holdings date from medieval times to the present day.

The holdings comprise the records of the former Chief Secretary's Office in Dublin Castle, including papers relating to the Rebellion of 1798, the Fenian movement of the 1860s, and crimes and convictions throughout the nineteenth century. The Transportation Records are of particular importance to Australians whose ancestors were transported from Ireland to Australia as convicts in the period 1788 to 1868. Microfilms and a computerised index of the most important records relating to transportation have been deposited in the Australian National Library in Canberra and copies of the microfilms are available at state libraries throughout Australia. Record collections include those relating to the employment of Resident magistrates and other local government officials. There are also excellent prison records.

The national Archives collections also comprise the records of the former Public Record Office of Ireland. This office suffered in 1922 during the Civil War and many of the records were destroyed. However, in many cases there are copies, transcripts, précis and indexes of this material. Many other records of genealogical and historical interest have been acquired since 1922.

Among other records which are available in the National Archives are the census returns of 1901 and 1911 (and nineteenth century census returns for the decades 1821 - 1851, if extant), which list all persons living in Ireland on the nights on which the census were compiled. There are also some eighteenth century census collections.

For the nineteenth century Griffith's Primary Valuation of Ireland of 1846 - 1863 lists all immediate house and land occupiers except those living in tenements. This is a return of the head of the family only. The Tithe Applotment Books of 1823 - 1837 list all those holding over one acre of (agricultural) land who were obliged to pay a tithe for the maintenance of the local Church of Ireland clergyman. This also is a return of the head of the family only. The Tithe Applotment Books are least satisfactory for urban areas. The census returns and the records of the Primary Valuation and of the Tithe Applotment are available in microform and there are comprehensive finding aids.

Wills, grants of probate, grants of administration, and schedules of assets survive for the twentieth century and are available for consultation if older than twenty years. Many of the records also survive for the nineteenth century and earlier - either in copy or precis form. Much of the testamentary material has been abstracted by professional genealogists in the period before 1922 or by the Commissioners for Charitable Donations and Bequests and is available for research. Some Inland Revenue returns of wills, grants of probate and grants of administration survive for the first half of the nineteenth century. The testamentary collection is a particularly rich and important source for genealogists. There are comprehensive finding aids to all these testamentary collections.

Records for the Church of Ireland survive in original, copy or extract form. The records in local custody have, in many instances, been copied on microfilm and are also available for research. There is a comprehensive finding-aid to all known surviving records.

Many other collections will also be of interest to the genealogist. These include the records of the National School system up to modern times (especially regarding the employment of National School teachers), admission registers to workhouses (where they survive), estate collections (including leases and tenants' agreements), Voters' registers (where they survive) and the records of local administration in Ireland throughout the nineteenth century.

The National Archives is open to the public, Monday to Friday from 10.00 a.m. to 5.00 p.m. Documents are not produced after 4.30 p.m. However, the reading room does not close over lunchtime. The office is closed for periods at Christmas and Easter and on Public Holidays. Staff are always available in the reading room to give advice and help researchers. There are comprehensive finding aids in the Reading Room and printed leaflets, which are updated regularly, are available to assist the researcher.

Bishop Street is easily accessible on foot from both St Stephen's Green and St Patrick's Cathedral.
From O'Connell Street via Trinity College - O'Connell Street O'Connell Bridge, Westmorland Street College Green (passing the Front Gate of Trinity College on your left, Grafton Street, St Stephen's Green West, Cuffe Street Kevin Street Lower, Bride Street Bishop Street (West end).
From the Four Courts via St Patrick's Cathedral - Inns Quay, O'Donovan Rossa Bridge, Winetavern Street (passing under the arch of Christ Church),Nicholas Street, Patrick Street (passing St Patrick's Cathedral on your left) Kevin Street Upper, Bishop Street (West end).
From the National Library and Genealogical Office - Kildare Street, St Stephen's Green North, St Stephen's Green West, Cuffe Street, Kevin Street Lower, Bride Street, Bishop Street (West end).
From the General Register Office - Either Lombard Street East, Pearse Street, College Street and get the number 83 or 155 bus. - Or, Lombard Street East, Westland Row, Lincoln Place, Leinster Street, Kildare Street and continue walking as from the National Library.

The best bus routes from the City Centre to Bishop Street are the number 83 to Kimmage and the number 155 to Greenhills Get of at the stop on Redmond's Hill cross the road at the next traffic lights, walk along Kevin Street Lower, turn right onto Bride Street and almost immediately again onto Bishop Street and cross the street . The National Archives is the building in front of you as you cross Bishop Street.

The Church Of Ireland -
Genealogy and Family History

The archives of the Church of Ireland, and particularly parochial registers of baptisms, marriages, and burials, are a primary source for genealogists and family historians. Although many registers were destroyed in the past, especially in the fire in the Public Record Office of Ireland in 1922, many others have survived in a number of custodies and are available to researchers.

Survival of Parish Registers
Almost half of the surviving registers were destroyed in 1922 and others have been lost at earlier periods. However, much of the lost information survives in transcripts and abstracts. The most recent published listing of parish registers is Noel Reid (ed) A table of Church of Ireland parochial records and copies (Irish Family History Society, Naas, 1994). In addition useful genealogical information may be had from other parish records especially vestry minute books, churchwardens' account books and cess applotment books.

Location of Parish Records
The Representative Church Body Library is the Church of Ireland's principal repository for its archives and manuscripts, and holds records from some 600 parishes in the Republic of Ireland. Records from a small number of parishes in the Republic are in the National Archives, and the remainder are in the custody of local clergy.

In Northern Ireland most parish registers are available in copy form in the Public Record Office of Northern Ireland (PRONI), while original parish records are either in the custody of the local clergy or in PRONI.

Names and addresses of local clergy may be had from the Church of Ireland Directory, published annually, which is available from the Religious Education Resource Centre, Holy Trinity Church, Church Avenue, Rathmines, Dublin 6 and the APCK Bookcentres at 61 Donegal Street, Belfast, BT1 2QH and St Ann's Church, Dawson Street, Dublin 2.

Access to Parish Records
Access to records in the RCB Library, National Archives and PRONI is straightforward but it is mutually beneficial if potential researchers contact the repository in advance to check on opening hours and conditions of admittance.
However, repositories will not usually undertake genealogical research on behalf of enquirers.

Records in the custody of local clergy may be more difficult to see and the following procedure is recommended:
1. Write to the clergyman detailing the information which you need and ask if he will perform a

Christ Church, Kilbrogan, Bandon, Cork, Ireland
now Bandon Heritage Centre
© Robert Blatchford 1994

search. If the clergyman agrees to perform a search there will be a fee of £5 per hour and it would be prudent to offer some payment in advance.

2. Clergy are not required to conduct searches on behalf of researchers, but they are required to make the registers available to researchers or their agents: this is a statutory requirement under the terms of the Constitution of the Church of Ireland, and relevant national archives and public records legislation in the Republic of Ireland and Northern Ireland.

If you are making the search yourself you should write to the clergyman to make an appointment and confirm that appointment by telephone before travelling. However, many clergy work alone and occasionally pastoral emergencies may cause the last minute cancellation of your appointment. The clergy are required to supervise your search and there is a fee of £5 per hour for this activity.

Reprography
Certified copies of entries in parish registers can be issued by local clergy or by the certifying officers in the repositories. Certified copies of entries of all baptisms and burials and marriages before 1845 cost £5 each. The cost of copies from civil marriage registers from 1845 is set by the respective governments and varies from time to time. Photocopying of parish records is forbidden on all occasions. Photography from parish records may only be undertaken with the written permission of the owner of the copyright. Further information on copyright matters may be had from the RCB Library.

Preparing for Searches
Most Church of Ireland parish registers do not have indexes and there is no single comprehen-

sive index to all their contents. In general, in order to prosecute a successful search in parish registers you need a name, a date and a place name. However, there are a number of ongoing projects to index genealogical material on a county basis and some of these projects have included Church of Ireland records: details may be had from the Irish Family History Society.

The following publications and agencies can help with your preparations:
* Donal Begley (ed) Irish genealogy. A record finder (Heraldic Artists, Dublin, 1981)
* John Grenham Tracing your Irish ancestors (Gill & Macmillan, Dublin, 1992)
* Maire Mac Conghail & Paul Gorry Tracing Irish ancestors (Harper Collins, Glasgow, 1997)
* Brian Mitchell A new genealogical atlas of Ireland (Genealogical Publishing Co, Baltimore, 1988)
* Raymond Refaussé Handlist of Church of Ireland parish registers in the Representative Church Body Library (copies of this list, which is updated regularly, are available from the RCB Library at IR£2.50 including postage)
* Association of Professional Genealogists, c/o Genealogical Office, 2 Kildare Street, Dublin 2
* Irish Family History Society, PO Box 36, Naas, Co Kildare
* Irish Genealogical Research Society, The Irish Club, 82 Eaton Square, London SW1W 9AL
* National Archives, Bishop Street, Dublin 8
* Public Records Office of Northern Ireland, 66 Balmoral Avenue, Belfast, BT9 6NY
* Ulster Historical Foundation, Balmoral Buildings, 12 College Square East, Belfast, BT1 6DD

It may be helpful to visit the Directory of Irish Websites at http://doras.eircom.net/ and search for sites using the keyword "genealogy".

Other Genealogical Sources in the RCB Library
Apart from Church of Ireland archives, the RCB Library holds a number of collections with obvious attraction to genealogists. Among the more important are the biographical succession lists of Church of Ireland clergy, compiled by J B Leslie; collections of copy wills; extracts from the destroyed 1766 religious census; and collections of pedigrees.

New Book on Church of Ireland Records
One of the more remarkable of phenomena in Irish historiography in recent years has been the upsurge in interest in local history. Often this is spontaneous and arises from the curiosity of people who have moved to a new locality, but increasingly it is structured either through local historical societies or in schools, colleges and universities.

Central to most local historical endeavours in Ireland is the Church, which is the only institution to have survived from the earliest times to the present day. Its longevity combined with its sustained presence in almost every corner of the country suggests that it is, or has been, the most profound influence on the development of Irish society.

The Church of Ireland as the lineal descendant, legally at least, of the Church in Ireland follow-

St Peter's Church, Ballymodan, Bandon, Cork, Ireland
©Robert Blatchford 1994

ing the Reformation, and, subsequently as the established Church until the late nineteenth century, has inherited responsibility for many of the sources which are fundamental to Irish local history. Records of parishes, dioceses and cathedrals, church buildings and graveyards, memorials in stone, glass and silver contain much valuable information not only about local Church of Ireland people but also the wider communities in which they lived and worked.

In order to make such resources better known a new series of guides entitled "Maynooth Research Guides for Irish Local History" is being developed under the general editorship of Dr Mary Anne Lyons from the history department of St Patrick's College, Drumcondra. The first guide in this series Church of Ireland Records, which has been written by the Librarian and Archivist of the Church of Ireland, Dr Raymond Refaussé, has just appeared.

Church of Ireland Records offers an introduction to the archives and manuscripts of the Church of Ireland and to the administrative structures which produced these records. Access to the records, both intellectually and physically, is discussed, as are problems of interpretation. Church of Ireland Records is published by Irish Academic Press at IR£9.95 and is available through bookshops.

The staff of the RCB Library will be glad to offer advice on all queries concerning Church of Ireland archives and manuscripts and related printed and reference works. It should be stressed, however, that they will not undertake genealogical research on behalf of readers.

If you have any queries, please contact the RCB Library library@ireland.anglican.org - in the first instance.

Dublin Archives

Dublin City Archives comprise the historic records of the municipal government of Dublin from the twelfth century to the present. The City Archives contain a significant number of medieval documents, including two important bound manuscripts written on vellum: the White Book of Dublin (also known as the 'Liber Albus' and the Chain Book of Dublin. The City Archives also include a series of Assembly Rolls, written on parchment, which record the minutes of the Dublin City Assembly (a forerunner of today's City Council) from 1447 to 1841. The Assembly Rolls, together with the White Book and Chain Book, were transcribed and translated by Sir John T. and Lady Gilbert and published as Calendar of Ancient Records of Dublin (19 vols, Dublin, 1889-1944).

In addition to these published materials, the Dublin City Archives contain a wealth of records which have not been published and are available for research. These records include City Council and committee minutes, account books, correspondence, reports, court records, charity petitions, title deeds, maps and plans, photographs and drawings, all of which document the development of Dublin over eight centuries. The Archives hold the magnificent series of 102 charters granted to the city by successive English monarchs. The earliest was issued by King Henry II in 1171/2, giving the men of Bristol the right to live in the city of Dublin. Later charters contain grants to Dublin of rights, privileges and property, and taken together they form the basis of municipal law in Ireland.

The Ancient Freedom of the City of Dublin
The Dublin City Archives holds lists of citizens who received the Freedom of Dublin between 1468 and 1918. It is possible to trace several generations of old Dublin families through these lists, which are a useful source for genealogical research. The ancient Freedom of Dublin was instituted at the time of the Norman Invasion in the late 12th century, Holders of the Freedom were known as "Free Citizens" and were entitled to significant trading privileges and the right to vote in municipal and parliamentary elections . Admission to the Freedom of Dublin was granted by the Dublin City Assembly at the great feasts of Christmas, Easter, Midsummer and Michaelmas. In order to qualify for the Freedom, it was usually necessary to have been born within the city boundaries, or "franchises", and to be a member of one of the Trade Guilds of Dublin. Members of "the Irish Nation" were excluded, but in practice many people with Irish surnames succeeded in obtaining the Freedom. Under the Penal Laws, Roman Catholics were excluded from the Freedom of Dublin from 1691 until 1793.
There were six main categories of admission:
1. Admission by Service was granted to those who completed an apprenticeship in one of the Trade Guilds of Dublin.
2. Admission by Birth was granted to sons, and sometimes daughters, of Free Citizens. Several generations of one family could hold the Freedom of Dublin.
3. Admission by Marriage was granted to sons-in-law of Free Citizens.
4. Admission by Fine was confined to prosperous professional men who were required to pay a substantial sum of money into the city treasury. Sometimes the Fine consisted of the presentation of a pair of gloves to the Lady Mayoress.
5. Admission by Grace Especial also known as Special Grace was the equivalent of the modern Honorary Freedom, and was reserved for dignitaries and for craftsmen who were not in a trade guild.
6. Admission by an Act of Parliament to "Encourage Protestant Strangers to Settle in Ireland" was granted to French Huguenots and Quakers from England.

Lists of those admitted to the ancient Freedom of Dublin survive for the period 1225-1250, 1468-1512 and 1575-1918. These lists may be consulted at Dublin Corporation Archives, City Hall, Dublin 2. A computerised index to the lists is being prepared by the Dublin Heritage Group. The lists are of interest to students of social and economic history and are also important for genealogical research.

Honorary Freedom of the City of Dublin
The Honorary Freedom of Dublin was instituted under the Municipal Privileges Act, 1876 and is presently conferred under the provisions of the Local Government Act 1991. The founder of the Home Rule Party, Isaac Butt, was the first person to receive the Honorary Freedom of Dublin. Other illustrious recipients include Charles Stewart Parnell, George Bernard Shaw, John Count McCormack and John Fitzgerald Kennedy, President of the United States of America. In recent years, it has been conferred on Pope John Paul II;Mother Teresa of Calcutta; the world champion cyclist Stephen Roche; and the former President of Ireland, Dr. Patrick Hillery. Nelson Mandela received the Freedom in 1988, whilst still a political prisoner. It has also been conferred on Jack Charlton, manager of the Republic of Ireland football team; & Bill Clinton, President U.S.A.

Wide Streets Commission
The Wide Streets Commission was established in 1757 to develop wide and convenient streets through the city of Dublin. Among its other achievements, the Commission built Parliament St., Westmoreland St. and D'Olier St. as well as Carlisle Bridge (now O'Connell Bridge). The minute books, maps, title deeds and architecttral drawings produced for the Commission before it was abolished in 1849 are all held in the Dublin City Archives. These important records tell the story of the lay-out and development of much of Georgian Dublin.

Mansion House Fund for Relief of Distress
Ireland was beset by harvest failure during the 1870's and in 1880 famine threatened the country. To prevent this, the Mansion House Fund was set up to collect money from Irish emigrants all over the world. The records of the Fund are held in the Dublin City Archives and are important for local history because they contain reports from 800 local committees which distributed relief in every county in Ireland. Records of other relief committees are also available for inspection.

Records of Urban District Councils
The areas of Rathmines and Rathgar and of Pembroke

each had their own local government until 1930, and their records are preserved in the Dublin City Archives, describing the development of these suburbs from the mid 19th century. The records of the Howth Urban District Council are also available, from 1318 to 1940.

Dublin City Archives are housed in the City Assembly House (beside the Powerscourt Town House Centre) where a Reading Room is provided for members of the public who wish to consult the Archives. An advance appointment is essential. Some records, because of their antiquity or fragile condition, may be withdrawn for conservation treatment

and may not always be available for research.The City Archives are for reference and research and may not be borrowed; access to the storage area is not permitted. The Archivist will be pleased to answer any queries relating to the records. Photocopying, photography and microfilm services are provided as appropriate. The Archivist can advise on costs and conditions of copyright.
Dublin City Archives, City Assembly House, 58 South William Street, Dublin 2.
Tel: (01) 677 5877 Fax: (01) 677 954 Opening Hours: Monday-Friday, 10.00- 13.00; 14.15- 17.00

Irish Genealogical Project

Kathleen Neill AUGRA (Hon. Life Mem.) & IGCO (RG)

Genealogy in Ireland has changed in the last few years. This is a brief guide to available sources. Compulsory civil registration of births, deaths and Roman Catholic marriages did not begin in Ireland until 1864 (non Catholic marriages had been registered by law since 1845). Prior to these dates all such events were voluntarily recorded in local parish church records (the condition and accuracy of which depended entirely upon the interest of the clergyman in office at the time). As very few of these parish records were indexed, this meant that if you wanted to find vital records for an individual you needed to know where their family lived, and worshipped, at the time of his/her birth and you needed to know the name of the town, village or parish. Even the name of the county alone was not normally sufficient as it covered a large administrative area - the equivalent of a State in the USA Many people did not have that information and found that their attempts to trace their family was halted before it began.

The Irish Genealogical Project, sponsored by the International Fund for Ireland and by other central and local government departments in the north and south of Ireland is to make genealogical information in Ireland more readily available. Computer indexing centres have been, and are being, set up throughout the country and some of the established independent genealogists and genealogical organisations have received grant aid to enable them to computer index their holdings. The index will guide the inquirer to the relevant centre or Genealogical Organisation. The index will contain the person's name, date, type of record (i.e. baptismal record, birth certificate, marriage record, obituary notice, gravestone inscription, etc.), county of origin and the name of the Centre or Genealogical Organisation.

When fully developed, the Irish Genealogical Project will prove to be the most important development ever in Irish genealogy. Irish Genealogy Limited, is to oversee the development of the project and its standards. The Company is a partnership between Centres,some government bodies, tourist boards, training agencies, record repositories and The Association of Professional Genealogists in Ireland (APGI), c/o 2 Kildare Street, Dublin 2, Irish Republic, and Association of Ulster Genealogists and Record Agents (AUGRA), c/o Glen Cottage, Glenmachan Road, Belfast BT4 2NP. Irish Genealogy Limited, ESB Complex, Parnell Avenue, Harold's Cross, Dublin 12, Irish Republic. It should be remembered that some computer indexing had started before the project was started. The indexing started with Roman Catholic Church records, then the church registers of other denominations. It will take between three and seven years to complete the project.

A list of the Centres and their progress is as follows:

Co.Antrim /	Ulster Historical Foundation, 12 College Square East, Belfast BT1 6DA,
Co Down	Has completed the Catholic parishes of Belfast.
Co.Armagh	Armagh Records Centre, Ara Coeli, Armagh BT61 7QY, Northern Ireland.
	Has computerised the Catholic records for the Diocese of Armagh which also includes
parts	
	of Co.'s Tyrone, Louth & Down. These records can be accessed through: Armagh Ancestry, 42 English Street, Armagh, Co. Armagh.
Co.Carlow	No Centre has yet been designated
Co.Cavan	Cavan Heritage & Genealogy Centre, c/o Cavan County Library, Cavan, Ireland. Almost all County Catholic Church Records & Griffith's Valuation & Tithes.
Co.Clare	The Clare Genealogy Centre, Corofin. Co. Clare, Irish Republic. Complete indexing of all county church records as well as some other major sources.
Co.Cork	Mallow Heritage Centre, 27-28 Bank Place, Mallow, Co. Cork, Irish
North	Republic. Complete indexing of most of the Catholic records for north Cork and substantial proportion of the Church of Ireland records for that county.
Co.Donegal	Donegal Genealogical Committee, Letterkenny, Co. Donegal; Ramelton Heritage Project, The Old Meeting House, Ramelton, Co. Donegal. Indexed almost all the county Presbyterian Church records and the Catholic

	records for the Inishowen peninsula as well as most of the rest of the county.
Co.Down	see Antrim and Armagh.
Co.Dublin North	The Fingall Heritage Centre, The Carnegie Library, Swords, Co. Dublin, Irish Republic. Centre has indexed a substantial number of the Catholic records.
Dublin City	Dublin Heritage Group, Clondalkin Library, Clondalkin, Co. Dublin, Irish Republic. Indexed church records for west Dublin & some Dublin city records.
Co.Dublin South	Dun Laoghaire Heritage Centre, Moran Park House, Dun Laoghaire, Co.Dublin Complete Index - Dun Laoghaire Catholic church records, work continues other parishes.
Co.Fermanagh Co.Tyrone	Irish World, 26 Market Square, Dungannon, Co. Tyrone, Northern Ireland. Computerising Griffith's Valuation, Tithe Books and gravestone inscriptions in Co.Tyrone. Gravestone inscriptions for more than 300 graveyards (N.I.)
Co.Galway East	Woodford Heritage Centre, Main Street, Woodford, Co. Galway, Irish Republic. Over 50 of the Catholic records for Co. Galway - indexed and some of the Church of Ireland for Galway East.
Co.Galway West	Co. Galway Family History Society, 34 Upper Abbeygate Street, Galway, Co. Galway. The Society has indexed over 50 of the Catholic records for west Galway.
Co.Kerry	No centre designated as yet.
Co.Kildare	Kildare Genealogical Committee, County Library, Newbridge, Co. Kildare. Have indexed around half the Catholic records for the county.
Co.Kilkenny	Kilkenny Archaeological Society, Rothe House, Kilkenny, Co. Kilkenny. Over 50 of the county Catholic church records indexed and a some Church of Ireland records and a large number of gravestone inscriptions for the county.
Co.Laois / Co.Offaly	Family History Research Centre, Charleville Road, Tullamore, Co. Offaly Have completed over 75 of all county church records. This centre also holds a large number of other sources and is very active in local history.
Co.Leitrim	Leitrim Heritage Centre, County Library, Ballinamore, Co. Leitrim. This centre has completed all the church records for the county as well as Griffith's Valuation, Tithe Books and other sources.
Co.Limerick	Limerick Archives, The Granary, Michael Street, Limerick. All church records for the county are now indexed along with a wide range of other sources.
Co.Longford	Longford Genealogical Centre, c/o VEC, Battery Road, Longford. Has indexed over 50 of the Catholic church records for the county on cards.
Co.Louth	see Meath.
Co.Londonderry	Inner City Trust, Genealogy Centre, 8 Bishop Street, Londonderry BT48 6PW, N Ireland. Complete indexing of well over half the Catholic church records, Griffith's Valuation, Tithe Books, emigration records, the 1831 census,a number of Presbyterian church records for the county as well as emigration records for the port of Londonderry.
Co.Mayo Mayo North	North Family History Research Centre, The Boreen, Crossmolina, Co. Mayo. Completed indexing of virtually all the church records for the county.
Co.Mayo South	Family History Centre, Town Hall, Ballinarobe, Co. Mayo,. Completed almost all Catholic and Church of Ireland records for the county this centre also has a large collection of indexed school rolls.
Co.Meath / Co Louth	Meath Heritage Centre, Trim, Co. Meath. Has completed most of the surviving Church of Ireland records & around 50 of the Catholic records for Co. Meath and some for Co. Louth.
Co.Monaghan	Monaghan Ancestral Research centre, 6 Tully, Monaghan. Around 50 of the total church records for the county and a wide variety of other sources have now been indexed
Co.Offaly	see Laois.
Co.Roscommon	Roscommon Heritage & Genealogical Centre, Strokestown, Co. Roscommon. Has virtually completed the indexing of the Catholic church records and a large proportion of those of the Church of Ireland for the county.
Co.Sligo	Sligo Heritage & Genealogical Centre, Stephen's Street, Sligo, Co. Sligo. Complete indexing of all church records and almost all gravestone inscriptions for the county.
Co.Tipperary North	Nenagh District Heritage Society, Governor's House, Nenagh, Co. Tipperary. More than 50 of the Catholic and Church of Ireland records completed.
Co.Tipperary South	Boru Boru Heritage Centre, Cashel, Co. Tipperary. Access to the Catholic Church records for the Diocese is limited by the Bishop.Holds a wide range of other indexed sources, including civil records.
Co.Tyrone	see Fermanagh.
Co.Waterford	Waterford Heritage Survey Ltd, St. John's College, Waterford, Co.Waterford, Indexed almost all of the parishes in the Diocese of Waterford and Lismore.
Co.Westmeath	Dun ni Si Heritage Centre, Moate, Co. Westmeath. Have completed some Catholic and Church of Ireland records. The centre is in its early stages.
Co.Wexford	Tagoat Community Council, Tagoat, Rosslare, Co. Wexford, Irish Republic. Has completed more than 50 of the Catholic records for the county.
Co.Wicklow	Wicklow Heritage Centre, Court House, Wicklow, Co. Wicklow,. Almost all the Catholic church records for the county indexed.

Irish Genealogy in Review
Jim Ryan looks at developments in 1999

At Government level, a report on the services available for Family history in the state was published by the Heritage Council. The report's brief was to describe the current situation regarding genealogical records; to evaluate the effectiveness of the existing State services; and to make recommendations as to improving the effectiveness, access and protection of records and archives. The report consulted very widely with the public and all relevant state and private organisations. Its major recommendation is the establishment of an 'Irish Family History Research Centre' (IFHC). The IFHC will 'function as a self-service research facility using copies of original material'. The IFHC should also develop relevant educational programmes, and continually assess, and provide, the types of information required by researchers. The report is available from the Heritage Council (See http://www.heritagecouncil.ie) This report is a recommendation only and there is no indication that it will be taken up by the Government. The concept of a central facility would appear to be contrary in many respects to the Government policy of distributing the genealogy research function to locally-based heritage centres.

The development of these centres, which were set up to index records in Irish counties and make them available to researchers for a fee, is part of the Irish Genealogical Project which is managed by Irish Genealogy Ltd. (www.irishgenealogy.ie). This company has recently appointed a new CEO – Eamonn Rossi, and will shortly present a new Business plan to its funding organisations. During 1999 two Heritage Centres, in Kerry and in Derry, closed, mainly due to staff shortages, but both are expected to re-open shortly. A significant Irish Genealogy Ltd project is the 'Central Signposting Index' that will assist those researchers who do not know from which part of Ireland their ancestors came. When completed, this facility will refer such enquiries to the appropriate local heritage centre. In the current phase of the project over 1 million records from Northern counties have been indexed. The index will eventually cover all counties and will not be available for enquiries until all records have been indexed.

Another significant development was the decision of Dun Laoghaire Genealogical Society to change its name to the Genealogical Society of Ireland. Dun Laoghaire is a harbour town just south of Dublin and the local society has been the most active in the country for many years. The change in name and status reflects the fact that the society's members have interests in many different parts of Ireland, and has published material from several different counties. The new GSI has an active publishing programme including a journal; an excellent newsletter – 'The Genie Gazette- (which is available electronically); and a series of family history publications (the 'Irish Genealogical Sources' series). The new GSI website can be viewed at http://welcome.to/GenealogyIreland and e-mail contact is GenSocIreland@iol.ie.

Flyleaf Press, a major publisher of Irish Genealogical materials, launched a new website www.flyleaf.ie and Dublin office, and is contactable by phone and fax at 353 1 283169

The on-going saga regarding the eventual location of Civil Birth, Marriage and Death records continued. These records are curently being computerised and it is expected that this will be completed in mid 2002. At that stage athe original records will be moved from Dublin to Roscommon, as part of the Government's long-time policy of decentralisation of state offices. The concern to family historians is clearly to ensure continuing and convenient access to the records for researchers. Roscommon is some 90 miles from Dublin where most of the other archives are located, and where most professional researchers are based. The Genealogical Society of Ireland and the Council of Irish Genealogical Organisations (CIGO) have been lobbying the Arts & Heritage Minister to place microfilm copies of records (over 70 years old) in the National Library. The Minister, Sile Devalera has recently described this proposal as 'interesting' and stated that it is 'receiving consideration'.

The Valuation Office was the subject of criticism during 1999 for increasing its fee for access to their records to £8. While this fee may be acceptable to legal offices and commercial clients, the Genealogical organisations have been protesting at the high cost to individual researchers. At the moment the fee remains at £8. The Valuation office (www.valoff.ie) is located in central Dublin and houses land records including the Griffith's Valuation papers.

The National Archives continues to make new material available. New accessions, and materials becoming available on-line, are detailed on the excellent website – (www.nationalarchives.ie) It is also expected that the NAI will withdraw the original 1901 and 1911 Census returns to prevent further damage from excessive handling. Instead microfilms will be made available on a self-service basis. These microfilms will also be made available for purchase. The NAI has also introduced a new readers' ticket system. The plastic credit-card-sized tickets carry a photograph and bar-code and may be issued for a period of as little as one day or for periods of up to 3 years.

In the National Library, the Genealogy Service, established in 1998, continues to make a key contribution to overall service provision in the Library, with user numbers continuing to rise. The Service is freely available to all personal callers to the Library, offering them the opportunity to discuss their family history research with a professional genealogist or experienced staff member. Relevant finding aids are available on open access and a series of specially devised information panels may be consulted. During 1999 the service greeted their 10,000th visitor, despite the fact that it has not been publicised or promoted in any way. In all, the Genealogy Service assisted 10,100 persons in 1999, the busiest month being July (1,256) and the slowest January and December (350 approximately). American visitors (40%) constituted the largest single group, 22% were Irish residents and significant numbers also come from the UK (12%), Australia (8%) and Canada (4%). The service does not conduct specific research for individuals, but does make available a list of professional researchers.

The National Library is also adding to its collection of microfilmed Catholic records. The registers of several major Dublin parishes had, for one reason or another, been filmed before. During 1999, the Library filmed the records of the following Dublin parishes: Balbriggan (1770-1901); Ballybrack (1860-1908); Blackrock (1854-1900); Cabinteely (1863-1910); Dalkey (1861-1910); Donny-brook (1871-1905); Dundrum (1854-1901); Glasthule (1865-1902); Haddington Road (1798-1905); Harrington Street (1865-1901); Sandyford and Glencullen (1823-1905). Microfilms of registers of registers from the Catholic dioceses of Kerry and Limerick are still not available to individual researchers without the prior consent in each case of the bishop, although this consent is usually given by fax and without delay.

The National Library also began work in 1999 on the development of a new Library website (www.nli.ie) assisted by a special grant from the Department of Arts, Heritage, Gaeltacht and the Islands. This website will include catalogue records, (including those already converted from the card catalogue), as well as the Newsplan database of Irish newspapers. It will also include selected images from the Library's photographs, prints and drawings collections.

Census Returns in Canada

Sherry Irvine BA, CGRS, FSA(Scot) & Dave Obee

Census records are one of the most valuable sources of genealogical information, and it pays to be aware of what each country offers in the way of surviving census documents. In Canada, as in other countries, the availability of census records depended on what was happening politically. The first census in the new Dominion of Canada, formed in 1867 from the provinces of Ontario, Quebec, New Brunswick and Nova Scotia, was in 1871.

There were earlier nominal census returns but they were taken under the authority of the colonial government. Their content is not uniform, they were not taken everywhere, and many parts have been lost. This article surveys census returns from the union of Upper and Lower Canada in February, 1841, up to and including the 1901 census.

The first census to include nearly all of present-day Canada was taken in 1881. It did not include Newfoundland as that province did not join Confederation until 1949. Newfoundland's census history is quite different and will be treated separately. Census records can be used to track a family's movements through the generations. They can provide clues as to where a family came from, and how prosperous the family was. They enable researchers to put people into family groups. Used in conjunction with other public records, it is possible that census records will enable the researcher to paint a detailed picture of a long-dead ancestor.

These records are not only of interest to the descendants. Many families in the British Isles saw one or two sons or daughters leave for Canada in the latter years of the 19th century, or early in the 20th. The census records that are available can be a guide to where the people went, and what they did. Armed with that knowledge, today's researcher can use other resources to track down descendants of those immigrants - people who are possibly third or fourth cousins. Census records may also be used by people whose research has hit a dead end. A check for census information on siblings may open up new paths to the past.

Content of the Records

For many places in present-day Ontario and Quebec, head of household enumerations from 1842 have survived. Although these enumerations were less informative than the ones that followed, it is worthwhile determining whether this record exists for the area of a search. The numbers of males and females within the household in various age ranges is given, the occupation of the head of the household is listed, there is an indication whether anyone is not at home at the time as well as the number of years the person named has been in the country. Except for some New Brunswick

records, this last fact does not appear again on a census until 1901.

In 1851 and 1861 all persons in a household are named, and for each there is given the following information: Occupation Place of birth (usually only the colony, for example New Brunswick, or the country) Religion Age (Note - the 1851 census was actually taken in early 1852 and the question was for 'age next birthday') The census also says whether people were part of a family or not - the fun part is trying to figure out which family.

The 1871 census was the first under the authority of the new Canadian government. Information on it was expanded to include: Sex Age Country or province of birth Religion Origin Occupation Marital status Whether married within the previous 12 months Whether any infirmities.

The 1881 census form contains much the same information as in 1871, but quality of the filming is generally poor. In 1891, additional information was required. It included the relationship of each individual to the head of the household, and the birthplace for each individual's mother and father. There is also information on the construction of the home, the number of floors and the number of rooms.

It is a bonus if an elderly family member survived to 1901 to be recorded. The information requested was: Sex Colour Relationship to the head of the household Marital status Month, date and year of birth Age last birthday Country or place of birth Year of immigration to Canada Year of naturalization Racial origin Nationality Religion Profession or occupation (and several questions about employment) Months at schoolWhether can read or write Whether can speak English or French Mother tongue.

Two of these nuggets of information - date of birth and year of immigration - are especially helpful in tracking down more details about a family, and the lives of its members. There are some additional details worth noting. There were incomplete head-of-household enumerations in Ontario in 1848 and 1850. There are no surviving returns for the City of Toronto in 1851. Returns from that census generally still exist for only one township or area - for instance, only lots one through five of Downie Township, and only one division of London Township still survive. This problem is common across Ontario.

There were several head-of-family enumerations in Manitoba in the 1830s and 1840s, with a nominal census in 1870. There is no 1871 return from Prince Edward Island as it didn't join Confederation until 1873. There were, however, head-of-household enumerations in 1841 and 1861. British Columbia did not join Confederaton until 1871 thus its first census came 10 years later, in 1881.

The Prairie provinces can be misleading. Until 1905, the provinces of Alberta and Saskatchewan did not exist, but there were districts with those names in the old Northwest Territories. The districts covered much, but not all, of the populated areas of today's two provinces. Researchers must, therefore, look under the Territories when tracing an ancestor who lived in either of those two provinces. Similarly, Manitoba was expanded several times, taking land from the Territories.

Locating the Records
Within Canada, most large libraries and provincial archives have copies of the census returns on microfilm. Some of these collections are complete for the country, while others are regional. There is a complete set in the National Archives of Canada in Ottawa. Where films are not available, they can be ordered in from the National Archives on inter-library loan. When selecting or ordering a film it is necessary to quote the correct National Archives reference. To determine the correct number, consult one of these guides:
* Catalogue of Census Returns
        on Microfilm 1666 - 1891,
        Ottawa, National Archives of Canada, 1987
*Catalogue of Census Returns
        on Microfilm 1901, Ottawa,
        National Archives of Canada, 1993
The catalogues list the names of villages, towns, cities, townships and counties alphabetically within each province or territory. These refer directly to the appropriate film numbers - so it is necessary to know the name of the place to look for. A community may not be under the same heading for each census, and some small places can change from one county to another, or from a district of one name to a county of another. If the correct geographical heading is not clear from the catalogue, then maps and gazetteers should be consulted. This is especially important when dealing with rural areas.

For researchers outside Canada, census films may be ordered through the Family History Centers of the Church of Jesus Christ of Latter-day Saints. The LDS filming of the 1871 census returns does not include all the schedules, only the first one - Nominal Return of the Living. This means that the 1871 agricultural census is not available.

Searching for Ancestors

Begin by visiting the Web site of the National Archives of Canada (www.archives.ca) where you will find advice on genealogical research and an index to the 1871 census of Ontario. This is a head of household index, but also includes individuals in households where the surname differs from that of the head of the household. This census index is an important one, because it took place just before a sizeable migration to Western Canada began. Many people in the western four provinces have connections back to Ontario in the 1870s.

Printed versions of this census are also available, on a county-by-county basis. They include maps and extra information that is helpful in locating ancestors and areas. Many other census indexes have been compiled, and cover many areas of Canada - although there are still many crucial gaps in the work. Indexes cover Manitoba, parts of Ontario and most of British Columbia in 1881. Census indexes have also been done for most of Saskatchewan and Alberta in 1891. They are available for both large areas and small localities. The 1901 census of Alberta is another one which has been indexed. Many local societies have active indexing projects. For example, the club in Campbell River, B.C. is indexing its area from the 1901 census. Ontario has many active indexing projects. The London branch of the Ontario Genealogical Society has been indexing the 1861 census for Middlesex County and the project is almost complete. The Perth County branch is indexing 1851 through 1901, for husbands, wives and strays. Most other branches are working on their own indexing projects.

A number of returns for Ontario and Manitoba in 1901 are appearing on the subscription website, www.ancestry.com. One drawback is that this is a databse, so depending on the form it takes, the user may or may not be able to sort out who the strays are living with. Census indexing is always going on, so everyone busy with Canadian research should check with the appropriate regional society home page for the latest developments. Go through the Canadian GenWeb project site to do this, through www.rootsweb.com.

If you don't find an index, you will have to check one of the volumes of the Catalogue of Census Returns on Microfilm to verify the place under which your part of the country appears, and to find film reel numbers. Most of the published indexes include helpful guides to finding areas and further information.

Tips and Traps
Remember that names changed as the country grew. Fort Garry became Winnipeg; Bytown became Ottawa; Berlin became Kitchener. Be sure to look for the name of the community as it was known at the time of the census. Check maps carefully, especially if an area underwent considerable growth. Many areas of Canada saw a huge influx of new residents in a short period of time. What may have been an enumeration district in one year may not have existed in the previous census. In fact, some places are so situated that they appear on two, three or four films, before finally being consolidated.

In 1851, 1861 and 1871, an agricultural census was done in conjunction with the regular one. Use it to help you find people. These tabulations give information on land under cultivation. If you know an ancestor was farming and roughly where, finding the agricultural entry in 1851 and 1861 can lead you to the correct township and the correct place on the film - without reading every name. The 1871 census has no names on the agricultural schedule. The researchers needs the page and line number from the nominal census to determine which line of the agricultural census to consult. Of course, the agricultural census can also provide information about how the ancestors lived, and how they were doing financially in comparison with their neighbours. Information includes lot and concession number of the farm, acreage under cultivation, acreage in each crop, and cash value of implements and stock.

Land records are included in the 1901 census films. They were filmed separately from the nominal returns, but will help researchers learn more about their ancestors. Using these records, for example, it is possible to learn the precise address where a person lived. In the census returns from Quebec, it is more common for women to be listed using their maiden names. It is very helpful to find the maiden name of a wife or mother. Watch for mortality schedules, which survive for 1861 and 1871. They record the names of the people who died in the previous 12 months, with information as to cause of death. Note that the LDS filming for 1871 does not include these schedules.

Not all cities were enumerated the same way. For large centres such as Toronto, it was by wards. A map of city wards will certainly speed the process of searching. Good sources of much-needed addresses are local directories, photo albums, letters, and gazetteers. Rural areas in Ontario are found by searching by county - and the county names are often similar to the ones still in use. In Western Canada, however, researching is more difficult, because names for regions within each district were usually quite different from what they are today. Names used for local areas are sometimes names that are not found on modern maps.

Always retain some skepticism. You will need it when you become highly frustrated because the entry you're looking for simply isn't there! This may be a missing record, but it may also be that you are tired and should repeat the search; or, that you are actually working from incorrect information. Be prepared to shift your sights and look outside the originally set boundaries of time and place.

Newfoundland

When it comes to the census, this province's Johnny-come-lately appearance in Confederation is a distinct advantage to genealogists. The census returns which predate 1949 - the year Newfoundland joined Canada - are not subject to the same restrictions that limit availability to 20th century census records for the rest of Canada. That means returns collected in the 1920s and 1930s are already open for genealogical research.

Sherry Irvine and Dave Obee are partners in Interlink Bookshop and Genealogical Services Victoria, B.C. Canada.
Books and maps from Europe —
http://www.GenealogyUnlimited.com
British Isles, Canada, United States —
http://www.InterlinkBookshop.com
4687 Falaise Drive, Victoria, B.C. V8Y 1B4 Canada
Phone (250) 658-3989
Fax (anytime) (250) 658-3947

New Zealand treasures await...

Elizabeth K. Parkes GrinzDipFH(Prof.)

A former British colony, the south sea isles of New Zealand contain material of value not only to descendants of people who emigrated there, but of possible value to those not descended from immigrants too. This article attempts to describe just some of those records and the positioning of family happenings against historical events. The majority of my comments are largely about the European population in New Zealand rather than the indigenous Maori population.

It is arguable whether the settling of New Zealand by Europeans was done in an orderly fashion but it is indisputable that New Zealand contains rich, varied and accessible records. The great majority of European settlers to New Zealand went to better themselves. Land, work and freedom from rigid class systems were powerful enticement. It is tempting to believe that because a record is available for one end of the country it will be available for the other. This is not necessarily so and it is important that all comments in this article be viewed with that proviso in mind.

Earliest Records

Records begin from when the first missionaries began their work in the Bay of Islands in 1814. The first settlers arrived in the 1830s and the type of record available widens. In addition to possible personal records kept by individuals, e.g. family bibles, diaries, journals, letters, newspaper cuttings and etc., passenger records come into play, as do baptisms, marriages and burials. In 1848 births and deaths began to be officially recorded. Until 1842 New Zealand was under the New South Wales government and wills of New Zealanders may be found there. Coroners' Inquests are available from 1845 onwards up to fifty years ago.

Mobile Populations

The mistake if often made of thinking the population of the 19th century was static. Many family historians have discovered this is not so. Even "problem" forebears can be investigated. A person might have left any point in Europe, Scandinavia or even Russia and travelled, for instance, to London, lived there for a while and departed for New Zealand leaving behind a wife and children to commence a new life. The records mentioned in this article not only have the potential to identify such a person but to provide additional information about them.

Where the fate of a seafaring relative is unknown, it could be that he ended his days in New Zealand. If the name and approximate year of a voyage of a British registered ship is known during the period searches can be made for the ship's papers. Depending on time period these papers include crew agreements in which seamen's ages and places of origin are likely to be shown. These are held at Public Record Office, Kew and Maritime

Museum, Memorial University of Newfoundland, Canada. Records differ depending on time period and not all records survive.

The discovery of gold in 1856 what is now called Golden Bay saw the first rush of goldminers to New Zealand followed by greater goldrushes to other places soon after. This influx of mostly men was from Australia, Europe and California. The goldrushes are an historical event against which to investigate the possible movements of otherwise unaccounted for relatives. The same applies to the land wars which occurred in the 1860s and 1870s and involved British troops. Copies of their records are available in New Zealand but persons in Britain may best access them at the Public Record Office, Kew.

Immediately before and after the two world wars saw huge influxes of immigrants from Europe including Britain, to New Zealand. The Armed Forces files of New Zealand service personnel are available.

By and large, passenger lists from 1911 onwards are not indexed so these would not be the first record to attempt to access to prove a relative's presence in New Zealand after this time. Directories, electoral rolls, marriages and deaths are better options.

Births, Deaths and Marriages

Post-1875 births contain parents' ages, places of birth, date and place of marriage and the mother's maiden surname. The Adult Adoption Information Act 1985 permits only adoptees and their natural parents access to adoption records and pre-adoption birth registrations. Post-1875 deaths contain, among other things, parents' names including mother's maiden surname, when and where buried, place of birth and length of residence in New Zealand, place of marriage, age at marriage and spouse's name including females' maiden surnames, and sex and number of living issue. From 1880 onwards marriages contain, among other things, the parties' ages and places of birth, usual residence, present residence, parents' names including mothers' maiden surnames, and fathers' occupations. From 1857 notices of intention to marry will contain the name and relationship of the person providing permission for a minor to marry. Not available in the marriage document, this is an additional detail available only in Notices. And in the case of a pre 1880 marriage when parents' names are not in marriage registrations, this is particularly valuable and can provide that vital clue for identifying the family in their place of overseas origin.

Naturalisation

From 1843 'aliens' could apply for naturalisation. The contents of naturalisation papers varies but almost always provide place of origin and age or date of birth; sometimes their original name and their Anglicised name. Naturalisation papers are very useful for finding out about non-UK ancestors.

Land Records
The dream of owning their own land came true for many settlers. Land Information offices throughout New Zealand are the main repositories for land records. Strange as it may seem to Kiwis today, until the passing of the Land Transfer (Compulsory Registration of Titles) Act 1924 it was not compulsory for land documents to be registered. Nevertheless most were registered and are searchable. Hand-written copies or photocopies may be obtained depending on the format of the original documentation. Land documents help paint a fuller picture of forebears' lives. The changing values of land may be seen. A landowner's will registered over land in the form a Transmission may be the only surviving copy of that person's will.

Photographs
Nothing quite matches seeing one's ancestors' features for the first time. Enterprising settlers included photographers. As towns sprang up, so did photography businesses. A directory is available which describes and locates extant collections and indicates the subject of each collection and whether or not prints are available. The Nelson Provincial Museum, Nelson holds the largest collection of historic photographs in the southern hemisphere. Numbering 1.2 million mostly portrait negatives taken in Nelson city and environs, the collection dates from 1856 to circa 1980. Prints are obtainable.

Clearly, photograph collections are of interest to persons whose ancestors were in New Zealand but family historians living outside New Zealand whose g.g.grandparents emigrated together with some of their children should also be interested. A person living in the UK or elsewhere and descended from one of the children who did not emigrate, could have a photograph of their g.g.grandparents in New Zealand just waiting to be discovered. Photographs of businesses, street scenes, public events and panoramic views are also common and a family's environment as it was when they were alive, may be seen.

Probate Files
No restrictions exist to accessing probate files throughout New Zealand. Copies may be obtained not only of the will in a probate file but of the accompanying affidavits as well for no additional fee. Containing less information but nevertheless potentially useful, are letters of administration where a person died intestate.

Schools
One thing of importance to New Zealand settlers was the setting up of a free education system for all. Prior to 1852 education was largely left to the churches or to private enterprise. In 1852 the provincial governments took control.
School records of most use to family historians are admissions registers. While the extent of their details varies, the child's birthdate, parent's name and address, and the child's previous school (if any) and subsequent destination (another school, work, home or etc.) are usually recorded.

Electoral Rolls
Having one of the first women in the world to vote in your family is something to celebrate especially when considering that it is usually more difficult to find out about women than men. In 1893 New Zealand became the first country to grant universal suffrage to women. While many women entered their occupation as 'domestic duties' or similar, a surprising number gave occupations indicating their involvement in business. Electoral rolls are available from 1858 up to the present day.

Directories
Personal, business and postal directories abound. Many are all-New Zealand-inclusive and are therefore useful finding aids. The first directories were published in 1842. Personal and trade directories faded in the late 1950s with the proliferation of telephone directories.

Censuses
The greatest disappointment in New Zealand records is the lack of censuses as successive governments have failed to preserve census records. Yet a few censuses have survived! If you are lucky enough to have relatives in New Plymouth, Auckland or Nelson in the 1840s you may be able to find information about them not available elsewhere. Those three places all have censuses taken in 1845 but Nelson has a census taken in 1849 and this is by far the most valuable. It contains details of all persons in households (but the name of only the head of each household), births deaths and marriages that have occurred in each household, educational standard of each person, occupation of householder, family's religious denomination, country of origin, number of persons employed on site, structure of buildings, kinds and numbers of animals, types and acreage of crops, and sometimes comments about the state of the roads and bridges (usually the dire need of!) and the need or otherwise of schools.

Some censuses of portions of the Maori population have survived and these are especially valuable because, generally, there are fewer records for the Maori population than for the New Zealand European population.

Conclusion
A pot pourri of possibilities awaits anyone with New Zealand connections. Preserving its comparatively short European history is of vital importance to many New Zealanders and copying and indexing original records is on-going. Few restrictions exist to accessing records and its possible to build full and colourful pictures of New Zealand ancestors and their historical environment.

Elizabeth Parkes is a full-time
qualified professional genealogist who searches for
people's ancestry and for missing living people.
She says her slogan "I find people ~ dead or alive" very
neatly sums up what she does.

BACK TO ROOTS 16 Arrowsmith Drive, Stonehouse, GL10 2QR
Computer Programs and Software FREEPHONE: 0800 2985894

Family Tree Maker Upgrade V 8	£20.00
Family Tree Maker Data CDs	
1851 Census Extract	£29.00
Griffiths Valuation	£47.00
Irish Immigrants 1803-1871	£39.00
Irish Records 1500s-1800s	£29.00
Irish Census	£19.00
Complete Book of Emigrants	£24.00
Passenger and Immigration	
Lists 1500-1900s	£39.00
Immigrants to the New World	
1600s-1800s	£24.00
Generations Grande Suite V 8 (UK)	£49.95
Generations Starter Kit V8 (UK)	£38.00
Generations Deluxe Version	£16.00
Family Origins V 8	£29.00
Family Origins Upgrade V 8	£19.00
Ultimate Family Tree Deluxe (UK)	£21.00
Ultimate Family Tree Basic (UK)	£12.00
Comptons Family Tree	£8.00
Europress Family Tree	£8.00
Easy Family Tree	£16.00
LDS Companion	£16.50
Genmap (Historical Mapping system)	£24.95
Birdie 32	£18.99
Wizard	£9.95
Value of the Pound	£6.95
Date Calculator	£6.95
Data CDs	
Pigots 1834 Northumberland & Durham	£20.00
Pigots 1830 Buckinghamshire	£20.00
1902 Street & Trade Dir for Scarborough,	
Filey & surrounding villages	£11.99

Yorkshire

Kelly s Post Office Dir for East Riding	£11.99
Kelly s 1897 Residents Dir - East Riding	£11.99
Kelly s Street & Trade Dir of York,	
Including York Inns with photos	£11.99
Baines 1822 Trade Dir for West Riding	£11.99
Kelly s 1872 Dir of North & East Riding	£11.99
Kelly s 1897 Street & Trade Dir of	
North Yorkshire	£11.99
White s 1822 Trade Dir for East Riding	£11.99
White s 1822 Trade Dir for York	£11.99
White s 1822 Trade Dir for North Riding	£11.99
Slaters 1848 Trade Dir- Northumberland	£11.99
Pigot s 1822 Trade Dir- Northumberland	£11.99
Pigot s 1834 Trade Dir for Cumberland	£11.99
Pigot s 1834 Trade Dir for Durham &	
surrounding villages	£11.99
Kelly s 1897 Trade Dir for Hull &	
surrounding villages	£11.99
Newcastle & Gateshead 13th & 14th	
Century Journal	£11.99
Pigot s 1828-9 Trade Dir for Cheshire	£11.99
Pigot s N Wales 1828-9 - S Wales 1830	£11.99
Staffordshire 1828-9 Trade Dir	£11.99
Slater s 1848 Trade Dir for Lancashire	£11.99
Slater s 1848 Trade Dir for Liverpool	£11.99
Slater s 1848 Trade Dir for Manchester	£11.99

Sheffield Town Centre 1822	£11.99
Leeds 1853 Street Directory	£11.99
Slater s 1855-9 Trade Dir — Shropshire	£11.99
Edinburgh & Leith 1848 Trade Dir	£11.99
Principal Cities 1822 Trade Directory	£11.99
Kelly s 1919 Trade Dir of Cornwall	£11.99
Pigot s 1830 Trade Dir of Devonshire	£11.99
Pigot s 1933-34 for Essex	£11.99
Slater s 1851 Trade Dir for Wiltshire	£11.99
Slater s 1851 Trade Dir for Somerset	£11.99
Pigot s 1828-9 for Worcestershire	£11.99
Slater s 1852-3 Trade Dir of Bristol	£11.99
Pigot s 1839 Trade Dir for Middlesex	£11.99
Kent 1832-3-4 Trade Directory	£11.99
Cambridge 1830 Trade Directory	£11.99
Norfolk 1830 Trade Directory	£11.99
Suffolk 1840 Trade Directory	£11.99
Sussex 1832-3-4 Trade Directory	£11.99
Surrey 1840 Trade Directory	£11.99
London 1865 Trade Dir Part 1 A-L	£11.99
London 1865 Trade Dir Part 2 L-Z	£11.99
London 1865 Commerical Dir Part 1 A-K	£11.99
London 1865 Commerical Dir Part 2 L-Z	£11.99

Criminal Registers 1805-1816 on disk

Somerset & Dorset	£4.99
Devon & Cornwall	£5.99
Wiltshire	£3.99
Gloucestershire & Bristol	£4.99
Wales & Monmouthshire	£3.99
Oxfordshire & Berkshire	£3.99
Northamptonshire, Leicestershire &	
Rutland	£3.99
Buckinghamshire & Herefordshire	£3.99
Bedfordshire, Cambridgeshire &	
Huntingdonshire	£3.99
Cumberland, Westmorland,	
Northumberland & Durham	£3.99
Middlesex	£3.99
Hampshire	£4.99
Derbyshire, Nottinghamshire &	
Lincolnshire	£5.99
Cheshire	£3.99
Shropshire & Staffordshire	£4.99
Herefordshire & Worcestershire	£3.99
Warwickshire	£4.99
Norfolk & Suffolk	£6.99
Essex	£5.99
Surrey	£6.99
Kent	£6.99
Sussex	£3.99
Lancashire	£12.99
Yorkshire	£6.99

Criminal Registers 1817-1828 on disk

Cornwall	£3.99
Dorset	£3.99
Bedfordshire	£3.99
Devon	£8.99
Bristol	£3.99
Leicestershire	£4.99

The grateful thanks of our descendants

Peter Christie

As Reviews Editor for *The Local Historian* I receive a constant flow of books and magazines. Although my postman might not agree I cannot think of a better position to hold. Every day brings new surprises as to what sources local and family historians are exploring in their quest for material. The 'classic' sources feature heavily of course – those concerning the working of the Poor Law, parish registers and court records all appear regularly as do census based studies.

A few months ago I was sent a new book with the intriguing title *Investigating the Twentieth Century. Sources for Local Historians*. Written by Evelyn Lord (published by Tempus Publishing and in the BALH catalogue) it attempts to steer researchers through the labyrinth of 'modern' records that were created last century (it still seems odd to write that!) Needless to say it cannot cover everything and its gaps made me start considering not just what had been overlooked but, on a more practical basis, what should we be preserving ourselves? I think I can safely assume that many reading this will be users of record offices – yet how many of us ask how the archives we use actually got there? True a large proportion were produced at the behest of the State – an entity which now orders their preservation. Many, however, have been put into care by people who wanted, for whatever reason, to see such material preserved for posterity. So what should we be putting aside now for the benefit of later generations of researchers?

The question is of interest if only because so many of the records we use in our studies are not being created today, or if they are, are not being kept. Obvious examples spring to mind – letters replaced by e-mails, faxes (very short lived) and telephones, social services' records shredded wholesale in the name of privacy. Given this then what items might go into our personal archives?

First and foremost must be diaries – think how thrilled we would be to find an ancestor's diary. Not everyone keeps a daily record however but even appointment diaries would make fascinating reading a hundred years from now. If you are one of those people who still writes letters what better to add to the diaries? I don't get letters you might say – but recently the 'Christmas letter' has become popular with many. Packed with family details they arrive in ever greater numbers at Christmas to tell us about what far distant relatives have been doing over the preceding year – a treasure trove for future researchers.

Another obvious personal record worth saving are photographs – yet how many of us actually inscribe place/date/names on the back of them? Is anything more frustrating than clearing up a dead relative's estate and finding family photographs without knowing who the people are or when the pictures were taken?

Similarly many people keep newspaper cuttings where they or their family members are mentioned – exam results, weddings, obituaries – and all should be dated and the source noted. Again many people keep copies of important newspapers. In the past 'Royalty' issues were widely preserved (ask any secondhand bookseller if you don't believe me) but of late more interesting issues are being put away. How many people kept the first papers of the twenty-first century – and have you carefully saved the paper(s) that appeared on the birth day of a child related to you – after all why pay pounds to buy such copies in 18 years time?

If you are a really dedicated historian you might like to consider compiling files of cuttings on specific topics. I have come across collections on many subjects including archaeological finds, obituaries, news of local societies and even crime in the

PHONE : 227   **THE RECTORY**
                 WINTERTON,
                         GT YARMOUTH

1954

Flegg Pigeon Shooting.

Dear Sportsman,
     Please be in the Woods every
Wednesday and Saturday as from
February 2nd., until the end of April
--help the nations's food supply by
killing all you can.
     A very Happy New Year to you.
     Yours very sincerely,
          GEO. WATERS BECK.

area. Such cuttings, neatly mounted in scrap albums, quickly become a fascinating documents in their own right – indeed some nineteenth century collections annotated by their compilers have actually been published in the last few years – a sure indication of their value to historians.

One of the major sources used by both local and family historians is the nineteenth century directory – yet how many of us can afford to buy these now extremely pricey volumes? Every year, however, we casually discard their modern equivalents when we throw out our old Yellow Pages. I realise that not may of us have the room to keep such hefty tomes but just consider how ecstatic we would be to discover a cache of Victorian directories hoarded by an ancestor.

If you think that suggestion bizarre how many people keep election leaflets? Anyone who has tried to research local politics (as opposed to national) will know just how sparse is the survival of such ephemeral items. Indeed many record offices have no holdings at all, yet the importance of these leaflets to future historians is obvious. Additionally, of course, you can use them to check up on what your elected councillors promised to do if elected!

One of the three oddest collections I have come across was that of pictorial paper bags issued by shops in one town. Many businesses do not now use such items but the collection I saw had been collected surprisingly quickly yet contained many examples from shops that only lasted a very short time.

A second unusual accumulation consists of posters for local musical and theatrical events. These have been saved for some time by a business man I know who regularly displays them in the windows of his shop before putting them aside. As he says such things are generally thrown away yet provide a wonderful archive for illustrating the cultural life of a community.

The third apparently eccentric collection was that of estate agents' details of houses for sale in one village. Extending over some 20 years each contained a photograph of the property along with a wealth of detail about the houses – a wonderful resource for a lucky village historian in the future.

So will these collections really be of use to future researchers? I believe that undoubtedly they will and to prove my point I will just refer to a collection that I inherited some years ago. A relative of mine was the printer in a small Norfolk village who, as most printers do, kept a specimen of everything he ever printed. On his death I collected this enormous accumulation which covers the period 1920 – 1955 and provides an all-encompassing snapshot into the community over those years.

So next time you are about to throw something away stop for a moment and think 'would I like to have found a Victorian/Edwardian/Georgian version of this to help my researches?' If the answer is yes do consider preserving it – we can all be archivists of the present and look forward to receiving the grateful thanks of local and family historians in the future – including our own descendants.

THE LOCAL HISTORIAN
Journal of the British Association for Local History

Volume 29, appeared in February, May, August and December 1999, containing some 16 articles. Once again, there was a considerable range in period, from the Anglo-Saxon (a study of sources for English beekeeping) to the almost contemporary (open-air schools in Birmingham, 1911-1970). Our contributors were representative of the wide variety of people who have an interest in local history, from the full-time teachers of the subject in further and higher education, to those who work as free-lance researchers and writers; from retired professionals who have developed an interest in local history, to people who work in related fields, such as archivists and librarians. The geographical spread of contributions was restricted to the British Isles this year, although an article on the effects of the First World War on Scottish tourism did allow the author to mention the overseas destinations of Scottish travellers, and there was an Irish dimension in the discussion of the Irish in two London boroughs in 1851.

The nineteenth century still exercises a strong influence over the choice of research topics for local history, and this is reflected in two articles discussing aspects of enclosure (in Yorkshire and in Buckinghamshire), two making use of census material (the Irish in Hammersmith and Fulham, 1851; kinship ties in Sheffield, 1841–91), and another analysing retailing patterns (using Wolverhampton as a case study, and ranging in period from 1800 to 1950).

One very pleasing feature of the year was the use made of hitherto unrecognised forms of 'documentary' evidence. Scraps of clothing accompanying registration papers for foundlings led to a breakthrough in costume and textile history (infant fashion in the eighteenth century). An exploration and recording of those mysterious marks on the outside of letters, rather than the content of the letters themselves, gave an insight into postal routes and postal practice in Berkshire in the eighteenth century.

On a more traditional note, the potential of friendly society records for research was fully revealed, and we were challenged to think about the very nature and methodology of local history in an article which will probably continue to stir up debate well into the next year. The third Phillimore Lecture, published in November's issue, gave a masterly exposition of the current state of research and thinking into the patterns of trade and the role of towns in medieval England. We reviewed 27 books in some depth, and in his annual Round-up, the Reviews Editor surveyed some of the many publications issued to commemorate the 80th anniversary of the First World War.

www.thelocalhistorian.org
or details from BALH PO BOX 1576 SALISBURY SP2 8SY

Abiding Strength

Of the controversies which have generated debate in local history in the last 50 years, the most persistent is the relationship between the amateur and the professional. The renaming of the *The Amateur Historian* as *The Local Historian* in the mid-1960s reflected the fact that many who were amateur, in that they were retired or were employed in other work so that local history was their 'leisure pursuit', were professional in their impressive skills in research, analysis and writing. By that time, 'amateur', like 'antiquary' a hundred years before, was fast becoming a term of abuse or disdain. In the first chapter of *Researching and Writing Local History: a practical guide for local historians* (BALH 1999 – buy it if you haven't already done so) David Dymond usefully summarises some of these issues, as they have been debated over the last thirty years.

These debates have been conducted almost exclusively by professional regional and local historians. For the great majority of those who work in local history the issues are unknown or are regarded as irrelevant or tedious. Most amateur local historians undertake their work for pleasure, not for remuneration, and if they work in a way which offends the academic judgements of certain professionals, they are rightly unconcerned as long as they achieve satisfaction from doing the work in their way. But many who have contributed to the debate seem to imply that the professional should not only encourage and inform the amateur but should also seek to impose an orthodoxy of method and approach, an intellectually-approved way of doing local history research. Amateurs, they hint, cannot be trusted to do the work in the 'right' way and so should be discouraged from embarking upon such tasks until they have received the correct wisdom.

A quick look at the occupations of those who have written articles in *The*

Local Historian in the last couple of years reveals a high proportion of 'academics' (just over 50% of all authors, though quite a few of these worked not in history but in associated disciplines). The occupations of the other 50% demonstrate the broadness of the church which is local history. One contributor was proud to call himself an 'amateur local historian' and we also had, among others, two archivists, an economist, a couple of civil servants, several administrators of charities and 'interest' groups, a freelance social services project director, a management consultant, a retired tropical entomologist and a consultant physician specialising in endocrinology. This broad range of backgrounds characterises our subject and represents one of its greatest strengths. Local history is one of the comparatively few areas in which non-professionals can compete on roughly equal terms with those who hold paid or salaried posts in the field.

> This broad range of backgrounds characterises our subject and represents one of its greatest strengths.

Some are apprehensive about or downright condemnatory of this very fact – the ubiquitous presence of 'non-professionals' is, after all, one of the justifications for the low status which local history has in the eyes of a significant number of mainstream historians. We must have academic debate but nobody should seek to impose his or her views on others and if local historians choose not to go along with the debate, so be it. Everybody else is free to accept or reject their methods and findings – and that, of course, is equally true of the work of professional historians. The presence of 'amateurs' is not a weakness but an abiding strength.

Late 20th Century Ritual Structure

Alan Crosby looks at redevelopment

'Why they built it there I simply cannot imagine', he admitted. 'It is not in a central location, it clearly had poor accessibility and, of course, we don't yet know what the purpose of the structure was, though we believe that it may have had ritual significance. One theory is that its alignment was in some way connected with astronomical patterns, but the whole site seems only to have been used for a short period and we can't as yet see any obvious motive for what must, by any criterion, have been a massive construction project.' The reporters gazed across the vast excavation site, the immense ring of post-holes, the evidence – easily visible with the eye of faith – of internal structures and, beyond, the winding course of the river which had eroded away the eastern side of the great circle.

> We've tried to date it but the demolition job seems to have been unusually effective

' One of the remarkable features', he went on, 'is that we have so little evidence of wear and tear. It is as though this massive building, erected hastily and then demolished only a few years later, had scarcely been used at all. The entrance areas show few signs of erosion, of the sort we'd expect if, say, they had been used by millions of people passing through in a short space of time, and so another theory is that the structure was some form of temple used by only a very few, perhaps just for one spectacular event. We've tried to date it but the demolition job seems to have been unusually effective, and all we can say is that by about the second decade of the 21st century the site was covered with an extremely closely-packed settlement of small houses, some open space, what seem to have been retail facilities or warehouses (perhaps connected with wharves on the nearby frontage) and a massive area of flat and featureless asphalt, marked out into small rectangular spaces with white paint'.

We've found very little datable material, but we were very excited to find a thick layer of wrappings or other discarded components made of polystyrene, a contemporary material which, though intrinsically unsophisticated and incapable of development as an advanced medium for artistic expression, does from our point of view have the merit of being well-nigh indestructible. What excited us particularly was that many of these items bore a maker's mark, a bright red double arch or 'M' symbol on a yellow background. Now we've found similar marks in archaeological sites all across the world, and here perhaps have convincing evidence of the global nature of the cult, or religion, for which the temple (if indeed it was a temple) was constructed. In the late 20th century this particular cult, associated with ritual consumption of particular foodstuffs, spread very widely indeed, and here – given the quantity of refuse found in a particular layer, and with the certainty that the structure was only in use for maybe three years, perhaps we can begin to construct a possible interpretation. Maybe – our conclusions are only tentative as yet – maybe a relatively small number of carefully-chosen individuals, perhaps even those from a priestly caste, came to this dome-shaped building, consumed very large quantities of this ritual food, threw away the containers and other vessels in which the food and drink was brought, and then dispersed once more.

They may have celebrated some event of fundamental importance, but one which was essentially ephemeral and irrelevant to the great majority of the population who, no doubt, carried on their daily lives unaffected by the upheavals or changing procedures of those higher up the social scale, in positions of authority or influence.' But perhaps', he concluded, ' we shall never know. And in any case, the new spaceport project will soon destroy all the physical evidence'.

Babes and Sucklings

My children suffer acutely because, as a historian with a dislike of theme parks amounting to a phobia, I inflict instructive holiday visits upon them with a vicious and merciless fanaticism. Sometimes they express vociferous objection which can be ended only by large-scale bribery in the form of unsuitable fast food or teeth-rotting confectionery, but often they are pleasingly tolerant. Castles and monastic sites, earthworks and Roman forts, all seem to appeal. Functioning churches and cathedrals, and National Trust houses do not. If there is an opportunity to roll down a high grassy bank, infiltrate the muddy recesses of a monastic latrine, or peer through an arrow hole at the top of a vertiginous tower, that's fine. Gazing at valuable Chinese porcelain or identifying the portrait of the 12th Earl is much less enticing. I confess to sometimes feeling the same myself, as my eyes glaze over in yet another State Bedroom or I try to remember what biscuitware is. We all have our strengths and weaknesses.

There is a lack of chronological perspective. Not long after my daughter started school she drew a highly-imaginative portrait of Henry VIII (as a proud parent I felt that she could teach that Holbein a thing or two) and she asked when the king had lived. We discussed the point, I naively referring to the numbers of years ago, and eventually concluded, correctly if imprecisely, that he had flourished sometime between Jesus and Grandma. The English language can cause problems. We visited the Bishops Palace at St David's when Anna was four. 'What is this place?', she asked. 'It's a ruined Bishop's Palace.' 'You could fit a lot of ruined bishops in here', she concluded. Maybe, with the clarity and accuracy of childhood, she was aware of the state of the Anglican Church?

It is the reality of history which most stimulates the imagination and guards against that evil spirit which wails, 'I'm bored, can't we go somewhere interesting now?'. Hadrian's Wall with marching soldiers (let's pretend to be ...) or Mount Grace Priory (this is how the monks lived ...) or the Weald and Downland Museum (isn't it smoky in here ...) have all been very successful. So have Roman forts with bathhouses, churches with squints and spiral staircases, and almost anything with a Viking connection. In country houses they love kitchens and bathrooms (ideally with a hideous hip bath or primitive shower contraption), delighting in looking at the servants' quarters while bored silly by the grand rooms. Museums are often OK – stuffed animals and grinning skulls are always popular even if deeply unfashionable – and anything with machinery (working waterwheels, agricultural implements, steam engines) likewise.

> **It is the reality of history which most stimulates the imagination**

The reconstruction of the miners' lodgings at the Kilhope Lead Mining Museum in County Durham, complete with stuffed rats, real peat fire, and models of men sleeping three to a bed, was very well received, as was the underground trip down the mine itself. But the most enjoyable bit of that visit was getting soaked to the skin in icy water as they pretended to be small Victorian boys working the ore sieves. Ask them to do any physical work at home (tidying bedroom, for example) and they slump exhausted in front of the video at the mere thought. Ask them, on a cold August day high in the Pennines, to fill wheelbarrows with shovelfuls of earth and rock, then rinse and sort the material in troughs of muddy icy water, and pick over the debris by hand, and you can't tear them away. History, they grudgingly agree, can be alright – but audience participation seems an essential ingredient for the magic recipe.

Phoenix Revisited

Three years ago I wrote about the devastation of central Manchester after the IRA bomb of June 1996. The implementation of reconstruction plans is now well advanced and a dramatically re-orientated and re-conceived townscape is appearing. New squares and impressive modern architecture are combined with the rehabilitation of fine Victorian buildings which survived the 1940 blitz and the 1960s planners. One of the most unusual elements is the 16th century timber-framed buildings of the Old Wellington Inn, Manchester's oldest vernacular building, which have been moved 200 yards to a new location beside the cathedral. That the same buildings were re-located 35 years ago, when a concrete shipping precinct was built, adds to the strangeness of their history. May they now remain undisturbed in their new home!

Manchester 1855

The new centre will be judged as one of Britain's most significant examples of late 20th century urban design, its principles reflecting accurately the public concerns of our time. Manchester may thus be added to the catalogue of visionary grand strategies for town planning which includes, among others, Wren's unfulfilled plan for post-Fire London; the magnificent Edinburgh New Town of the late 18th century, the rebuilding of Plymouth and Coventry in the 1950s and the post-war new towns such as Stevenage and Milton Keynes.

In Manchester's case, if the project is an overall success and subsequent stages are completed, historians may seek to identify reasons for the effectiveness of the strategy and design. Analysis so far focuses on the pragmatic and innovative approach of the city council, the willingness of central government to contribute financially, and the desire of the private sector to be fully involved (including its acceptance that substantial remodelling of property boundaries and street lines was required). Perhaps the salutary lesson of the failure of Wren's plan for London, when the entrenched vested interests and the great financial implications proved too much of a deterrent, was noted?

But in Manchester, as in other convincing designs of the last 200 years, vision was also required. The intangible but vital feeling that here was an opportunity to make things better and to improve the quality of the city centre was a powerful driving force behind the speed and efficiency of reconstruction, serving to unite the different agencies behind a single (though far from simple) goal. It is ironic that in conjuring up a vision of a better Manchester and implementing it in physical form, those who designed the new centre deliberately chose as a major theme the reversal of the earlier large-scale but piecemeal re-developments – for a main aim of those changes, thirty to forty years ago, was also to make things better and to improve the quality of the city centre. The earlier vision proved horribly flawed. Let us hope that today's replacement will be more durable and better appreciated.

> The new centre will be judged as one of Britain's most significant examples of late 20th century urban design

We might wonder whether, if the devastation had been not in Manchester but in Mansfield or Merthyr Tydfil, the same degree of government and private initiative would have been forthcoming. But that is a cynical view. To me, the rebuilding of central Manchester is a fascinating process to watch on the ground, and equally interesting is to see the social and environmental principles of the late 1900s translated into reality. But time itself will be watching to see whether they, and the buildings, squares and streets stand its rigorous test.

Not so empty landscapes

Glossop Dale, Derbyshire

On holiday in France this spring I found myself in some evocative places, beautiful and disturbing, where once there had been human occupation and today virtually nothing remains. I have encountered the same feelings in, for example, Scottish valleys emptied by the clearances, but never before have I felt the sense of loss and departure so strongly because here the departure was so recent. We drove across the Causse de Gramat, a waterless limestone plateau in the nowhere land between the Auvergne and Perigord, 25 miles of emptiness which only 50 years ago was full.

The area has been depopulated by agricultural change, the drift to the towns, and the sheer hardship of eking a living from its thin poor soils. Mile after mile of drystone walls line the roads, identical to those of Derbyshire and the Yorkshire Dales except that these are swathed in fragrant blankets of honeysuckle and clematis. Behind them are abandoned fields where the bare rock pokes through the surface, an old agricultural landscape of broken stone cottages and tiny tracks which now lead to nothing in particular.

The fields are being invaded by thickets of silver birches, hazel, rose and gorse. The grassland, never ploughed or doused in herbicides, supports a glorious assemblage of flowers, among them the vivid purples and shocking pinks of countless orchids. Before long, all will have vanished beneath the encroaching woodland which already conceals much of the landscape. A few small fields remain in use, grazed by flocks of thin sheep, and there are a couple of remote and half-forgotten villages, but everywhere else Nature is reclaiming her own in a riotously effective fashion. Like many of the marginal areas of rural France this is a haunted landscape, full of ghosts of people who were tied to the land and toiled on its stony acres, and the recollections of those who, much more recently, left behind their native pays and went to urban agglomerations new.

We stayed in a house on the side of a magnificent wooded gorge. Behind it an overgrown footpath climbed steeply between jagged rocks, through oak and gorse scrub, before plunging into a darkly oppressive wood and ending abruptly at the foot of a waterfall rushing noisily through the gloom. The path had been cut into the hillside, with narrow slots in the rock to give an even gradient. Up its long and difficult slope – maybe only half a century ago – the inhabitants of the house, peasants who tended their cattle on the high pastures, had toiled to fetch their water, dipping pails into the pool by the fall.

> I found the wood a worrying place, for there was that disquieting feeling of not being entirely alone.

I found the wood a worrying place, for there was that disquieting feeling of not being entirely alone. And climbing the path made me realise, with startling clarity, how harsh had been the daily lot of these people. How many of them, over the generations, had struggled up that slope? Which of them had so painstakingly hacked a way through the rock? How often had the pails of women and children dipped in that dark pool by the waterfall? And do their descendants, in flats in Bordeaux or suburbs of Clermont Ferrand, know or care about the achievement of their ancestor? I hope that they do and that I, as a local historian, never forget or become blasé about the scale of the human endeavour which has produced so much of what I see, study, analyse and narrate.

All in a Norfolk name

Every now and then the newspapers highlight the odd names given to an unfortunate child by its fond and eventually-to-be-detested parents, who, under the influence of new parenthood, burden the infant with absurd or unimaginably embarrassing appellations. A minor pleasure of historical research is to note that this cruelty is not a recent phenomenon. There are those who believe that almost everybody in the past bore sensible names, such as John, William, Mary and Elizabeth, and indeed a lot did, but tell that tale to the shades of Cardinal Wolsey Armes who was born in Kings Lynn in 1802, or his exact contemporary from Great Yarmouth, Marmarice Caromania Barcham, and they might give you another view. Norfolk parish and other records are unusually rich in such eccentricities (some of my dearest friends are of and around Norfolk, and I lived there for five very happy years, so this is not going to be a racist slur upon the county such as that which last year enlivened the columns of the *Eastern Evening News* and the *Eastern Daily Press* – the bishop had made disparaging remarks upon the mental acuity and agility of the people of his adopted county). No, the names which I lovingly collected over the years when I researched in the Norfolk Record Office emphasised the glorious individuality of the county and its people.

There was much evidence of a deep religious faith, as exemplified by Christian Church, Christian Beans, Christian Wasp, Christian Salter, Christian Bear ('gladly the cross-eyed bear?') and the spectacular marriage in 1795 at All Saints, Norwich, of George Christian and Christian Wright. Think about it. There was the adoration of Yuletide as a festival: Christmas Breeze, Christmas Bush, Christmas Eve Steward (who came before Christmas Knight and Christmas Day) and – maybe one those many breakaway sects which proliferated in the 18th century – Christian Freaks. There was an irresistible cleverness about Mr and Mrs Boatwright calling their child

Noah (Thrigby, 1753), and a juicy story was probably made known to the world when Fanny by Desire Parker was christened at Great Ryburgh in 1769. No writer of fiction could, or perhaps should, have made up the marriage of John Bream Fish and Mary Scales at Attleborough in 1789, and no restaurateur ought to miss putting Lemon Herring (Swanton Morley, 1716) on the menu, or its alternative Christian Plaice (Hockering, 1676).

> Can't you just picture Jolly Punchard, Hunting Jolly and Jolly Bloss

Can't you just picture Jolly Punchard, Hunting Jolly and Jolly Bloss, don't you sympathise with Rivett Anguish and feel compassion for poor Colville Lumpkin. Midsummer Calf must have felt a trifle silly – fine for a young girl, not so appropriate for an elderly woman. Those of us who have too much work to do know all about February Backlog and we might have employed Brighten Silver, who was probably useful around the house, perhaps cleaning up Grime Liddelow using a lot of Washwhite Fellow (the new super soap powder?) with plenty of Time and Patience [all one name] Fowler on her side. But someone as respectable as she clearly was would have nothing to do with that rather doubtful woman down the street, Bosom Body [actually it was a he, not a she!] or with Freelove Smith, and would prefer instead Virtue Love, especially if she was carefully wrapped in a Modesty Towel (Gunthorpe, 1726). In the croft Lettuce [sic] Got would be grazing quietly, but elsewhere the rural tranquillity was disturbed by some very alarming characters – Neptune Blood and Baal l'Estrange were indulging in strange rites. It all makes Brooklyn Beckham seem very unremarkable (and all the names are entirely genuine!).

Regional Perspectives

Among those who theorise about the nature and purpose of local history are many who urge that a regional perspective should be taken. It is crucial, they insist, that we do not confine our researches to the often arbitrary boundaries which have been imposed for administrative convenience in the past 150 years but instead look at communities (I make no attempt here to define or interpret that word) in their context, whether that be geographical, social or economic or (ideally perhaps) all three. Recently this whole question – and its lack of real answers – has been thrown into sharper relief as a result of the moves towards the creation of administrative regions and institutions within England, and the imminence of devolved government in Scotland and Wales.

Although since 1707 Scotland has not had a separate legislative body, it has retained a clearly distinct set of institutions – such as its legal and educational systems – and its national identity and borders are unquestioned. In Wales the national territory is also reasonably clear (allowing for the frequently anomalous position of Monmouthshire) but the institutions are not comparable to those of Scotland. In 1707, on the union with England, Scotland was a fully-fledged nation but, in 1536, Wales was not so. The establishment of Welsh institutions has therefore been a much more recent development and one which has been largely an external process, granted or imposed from London.

In the English regions the establishment of regional assemblies is becoming a possibility rather than an improbability. The suggestion generally put forward is that assemblies, and hence defined political regions, should be established if there is support among the electorate of the rele-

Nothing to do with local history? Far from it.

vant areas. Piecemeal and voluntary devolution is the favoured approach. I live in North-West England, an area which, with the North-East and Yorkshire, is often considered one of the regions where an assembly might be established and there is certainly a growing interest in this possibility among local authorities, business interests and other groups within the old counties of Cheshire, Lancashire, Westmoreland and Cumberland. From the perspective of Preston, which aspires to be the future capital city of North West England (sorry, Manchester; bad luck, Liverpool!) the region is already being created.

In all sorts of ways the changes which may now be in progress have important implications for our work. Regional Cultural Consortia have now been set up as agencies which will deal with many aspects of government and lottery funding for the arts and cultural activities, including museums, archives and libraries, and these may one day be assimilated within the work of regional assemblies. Regional approaches to a wide range of projects such as film and sound archives, newspapers conservation, the creation of bibliographic resources and the investigation of archaeological and landscape issues are now commonplace, as (on a more down to earth level) are regional local history fairs. But even more important, perhaps, is that we should all recognise that there are regional dimensions to the history of our locality. Family historians recognise regional patterns in the movement of our forbears and we should allow that what happened beyond the parish boundary was not irrelevant, either to those places in the past or to our researches in the present and future.

The History of Our Own Times

For many people the word 'history' implies a past which is much more distant than yesterday or the day before, and most parents experience a slight shock on finding that their own childhoods are being studied in history lessons. As local historians, though, we should recognise that recent events and themes are extremely relevant to our work. Indeed, some have suggested that local history should be taught backwards from the present, partly to counter the tendency for modern times to receive little attention. When I was at school, history stopped in 1945 (rather daring that, since it was only twenty odd years earlier). However, the *real* end of history was considered by some members of staff to be 1914, as exemplified by the 'English history from the Congress of Vienna to the outbreak of the First World War' syllabus. Being schoolboys, we were convinced that for certain incredibly ancient teachers that *was* contemporary. It is disconcerting to realise that they were actually a little older then than I am now.

For many undergraduates today, 20th century history is much the most relevant and most exciting part of their course. Modules on American policy in Vietnam, women in Nazi Germany, and other near-contemporary subjects (well, they seem so to me) pack the lecture theatres, while medieval and early modern themes are apparently perceived as unexciting and irrelevant. I suspect that in local history, for a variety of reasons, such a chronological narrowness will never become a problem, but it is very satisfying to note how articles on twentieth century topics are increasingly found in the pages of, for example, *The Local Historian*. The last hundred years have seen, in every community, changes which are among the most concentrated and the most profound in all history. When we review the hallmarks of the century which is ending - global warfare, motor transport, electricity, new communications media, the planning system, the welfare state, home ownership, universal education and universal

suffrage, the changing roles of local and national government, environmental devastation and environmental awareness, the 'decline of religion', mass leisure, 'heritage' and conservation, to name some of many – it is obvious that to stop our researches and our analyses in 1914, or to pretend that somehow the last hundred years can be relegated to a mere footnote in a historical narrative, is increasingly untenable.

Thus, some of the most fascinating and important work in local history today is about our own times or those just gone, and challenging new sources are available for such work – photographs, film, and the output of oral historians, for example. We should not shy away from considering as history subjects and events with which we have a personal familiarity, and we should also start to investigate the apparently mundane aspects of our lives from a historical perspective. Supermarkets, office employment, car showrooms, trips to Majorca, European elections, the internet, SATS tests for schoolchildren ... they are all history too, so maybe articles on such subjects will soon appear in *The Local Historian*. I've now reached the age when items from my childhood appear in museums (1950s formica-topped tables, early Tupperware, very small black and white televisions) so I ought to be putting fingers to keyboard myself. Or perhaps calling in an oral history interviewer to recount my memories of pens, filing paper and index cards from the days, oh, way back in the early 1980s, when local history was still a traditional folk craft.

articles on twentieth century topics are increasingly found in the pages of, for example, *The Local Historian*

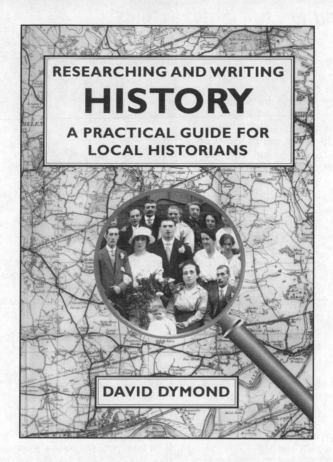

This book is essential reading for anybody who has written, is writing or might one day write local history. The earlier version of the book, Writing Local History, was first published in 1981 and became an instant classic. Now it has been totally rewritten, extended and updated so that local historians in the early 21st century, will have an even better reference book to help them produce work of the highest quality. David Dymond has spent most of a lifetime as a professional local historian, and he writes from that personal knowledge and experience. The contents of the book include an assessment of the present state of local history; the challenge of writing; choosing a subject; the search for sources; transcribing; analysing and assembling evidence; interpreting the evidence; writing techniques; the final draft; and numerous appendices which illustrate sample styles of local historians, show how to present information, and demonstrate good and bad practice in writing. It is, in short, an invaluable, stimulating and often entertaining exposition of how we should approach our subject.

180 pages   £12.00 (£10.00 for members)
from BALH (P) PO BOX 1576 SALISBURY SP2 8SY

Forging ahead in Faversham

Arthur Percival

reviews the work of the Faversham Society

Fleur de Lis, Faversham

Faversham has quite a few famous, and infamous, sons and daughters. At least in the town itself perhaps the best-known is Thomas Arden, who was murdered here at the instigation of his wife, Alice, in February 1551.

Just another eternal triangle? Not quite. Alice was the daughter of the builder of the Mary Rose; and her step-father was Sir Edward North (later Lord North), a Privy Councillor and Chancellor of the Court of Augmentations, which master-minded the sale of the monastic property confiscated by Henry VIII. Thomas was a whizz-kid parvenu, who was close to Sir Edward and had made his pile dealing in such property. He was business-obsessed, with little time for Alice, and she had sought affection elsewhere.

Because the leading players were close to the centre of the national stage, the crime hit the headlines, to be immortalised, first in Holinshed s Chronicles and then, in 1592, in a play, Arden of Feversham, which has stayed in the repertory ever since. The author is unknown but Shakespeare, or Marlowe, or both, may have had a hand in it. It marks a milestone in English drama because effectively it is the first piece to be based not on mythology or national history but on recent real-life events. It can also be seen as the first comedy-drama, with the droll antics of Thomas s assassins counterpointing the passion and plotting of Alice and her lover. A case can even be made for regarding it as the English stage s first thriller, since the Mayor, when called to the scene of the crime, applies sound Holmesian technique to work out who the culprits are.

Remarkably, perhaps, the scene of the crime still survives, in the shape of Arden s House, in Abbey Street, with a garden large enough for the play to be performed in it every few years (most recently, in August and September 2000). Perhaps nowhere else in the United Kingdom can a Shakespearian-era drama be played against the backcloth of the building in which the main events portrayed in it actually took place.

Originally built in about 1475, probably as the guest-house of Faversham Abbey, the building served as a farmhouse - Abbey Gate Farm - for centuries after Arden s murder. It continued to dominate Abbey Street, whose other properties, for centuries, too, were occupied mainly by sea-captains, merchants and others whose interests were bound up with the tidal Creek onto which it backed.

Then, in the 19th century, Faversham began to expand in a big way. Abbey Gate Farm lost some of its land and its farmhouse became an ordinary home. The Creek was busier than ever before and on the strength of its new prosperity the owners of old-fashioned timber-framed houses in Abbey Street were able to trade up to new homes with all mod. cons

By the 1950s Abbey Street was in a bad way, or so it seemed. Its old houses were let to rent-controlled tenants whose landlords could not afford maintenance costs. With their crumbling plasterwork and neglected paintwork, they looked life-expired. They lacked essential modern amenities. It had a reputation, probably undeserved, as a red-light district and, significantly, no-one ever photographed it. The sanitary inspector ruled that the properties were unfit and suggested that they should be replaced by council houses. The owner of Arden s House tried to sell it, but, even at £950, could find no buyer. He applied to demolish it, and the County Council saw no reason to object. Then a miracle or two. The Daily Telegraph carried a story that Arden s was going begging, and a sympathetic purchaser came forward. A new Town Clerk arrived, realised the importance and potential of the rest of the Street, and persuaded the Borough Council to buy the properties under slum clearance powers but then, instead of knocking them down, sell them to buyers who with the aid of improvement grants would restore them. He also persuaded the Historic Buildings Council (English Heritage, we would say today) to offer help, and so Britain s first town scheme was launched. This was one where the group value of buildings, as opposed to their individual merit, made them eligible for grant. The County Council pitched in, too, with a pioneering scheme to narrow the carriageway, so that the houses suffered less traffic disturbance.

So, by the early 1960s, Abbey Street was on course to be revived as one of the finest medieval streets in Britain. But what of the rest of

Faversham s town centre, also chock-full of fine medieval and Georgian buildings - around 400 altogether? This was the era of central area redevelopment , when town vied with town, city with city, to see how it could modernise its shopping areas by wholesale reconstruction. This craze was to ruin many of Britain s historic towns, and its legacy still disfigures most of them. Was Abbey Street to be kept as a kind of stage-set showpiece while the rest of the historic town succombed to a tide of nonentity?

One small, but particularly vacuous, piece of redevelopment was enough to convince local people that this was the wrong route. When the Faversham Society was formed, basically as an environmental watchdog, in 1962, it won immediate support and has contined to command it ever since. In a small-ish town of about 18,000 people it has 800 members.

From the start, the Society realised that past, present and future are inextricably intertwined, if only because you cannot plan properly for the future without understanding the past and the present. This sounds like a truism, and it is, but it is amazing how in the past developers, planners and engineers were either ignorant of the principle or closed their eyes to it.

There was no local history society in the town, so the Society decided to fulfil this function as well. This strengthened it immeasurably. It meant its environmental work was based - as far as possible - on sound understanding of the past: equally it meant that the role of its historians was not to wallow in unhealthy nostalgia but to enhance that understanding and sharpen its vision.

Its mettle was soon put to the test at two critical Public Inquiries in the late 1960s. At the first it successfully marshalled opposition to opportunist plans to create a marina on a remote site on the south bank of The Swale, the channel which divides the Kentish mainland from the Isle of Sheppey. The ace up the developers sleeve, they thought, was that this was a brownfield site which until recently had formed part of a huge high explosives factory. Huge explosives factory, yes, but recently, no. The Society was able to show that the use had ceased at the end of World War I and that the site had reverted to nature and was an important haunt of wildlife. It has since been recognised as of international importance for its birdlife and is now a nature reserve.

On this occasion the Society had allies. At the second Inquiry, it was on its own, with the might of the County and Borough Councils ranged against it. They wanted to endow the town with the kind of ring road which was fashionable at the time and was to wreak so much environmental havoc in other historic towns. The Society undertook a full

Arden House, Faversham

traffic survey, which the authorities had failed to do. This revealed that their plans were based on intuition rather than proper research, and on the basis of its own findings the Society put forward proposals which were cheaper and far less damaging. At the Inquiry, against all the odds, David defeated Goliath, though it took another 20 years for the Society s proposals to be brought to fruition.

In Faversham they had made gunpowder as well as high explosives. Indeed the town may have been the cradle of the UK explosives industry; and for a time it was certainly its main centre, with six factories in operation in the early 20th century. The last three closed in 1934, and much of their plant and many of their staff transferred to Ardeer in Ayrshire. The rest of the machinery, considered life-expired, had to be de-contaminated - an industry euphemism for destroyed , since there can be nasty accidents if traces of explosives are left in process buildings.

One 18th-century water-powered powder mill was reprieved because it had been fitted with an auxiliary drive to pump water from a well to irrigate nearby gardens. It was soon abandoned, however, and by the early 1960s was derelict. It was then, when interest in industrial archaeology was just starting, that the Faversham Society discovered it mouldering away beside its millstream in a thicket of bamboo. The surrounding factory area was due to be redeveloped for housing and the mill was destined for the scrapyard.

The Society managed to secure a stay of execution while it sought to raise money for purchase and restoration. It got little support from the Government or experts, one of whom told it it was wasting its time as there was an older powder mill at Waltham Abbey in a far better state of preservation . However it pressed on. Local people were generous, the money was raised, and by 1969 restoration was complete. It later emerged that the Waltham Abbey mill had been destroyed in the 1940s and that the Faversham mill was the oldest of its kind in the world. It has since served as the prototype for working replicas at the former Royal

Gunpowder Factory at Ballincollig, Co Cork, and Launceston, Tasmania.

The Society is proud of having pioneered active interest in the monuments of the national explosives industry. An exhaustive survey has recently been undertaken by the Royal Commission on Historical Monuments and the Waltham Abbey site itself is to be restored as a tourist attraction at a cost of £9m. In Faversham the Society is currently involved in a similar, but much less costly, restoration scheme for the second oldest of the local factories, the Oare Works, begun by Huguenot immigrants soon after the Revocation of the Edict of Nantes in 1685. A descendant of the Huguenot proprietor has recently been in touch with the Society as a result of a genealogical enquiry - but that is another story!

Faversham had no museum when the Society started; so, in the absence of any initiative on the part of the authorities, it decided to start collecting for one. Its efforts were successful, and within three years of its formation it was able to mount a small permanent display at the Maison Dieu, Ospringe, a 13th-century building on the town s outskirts. The space soon proved inadequate, so the Society sought permanent premises of its own. A local brewery offered it the Fleur de Lis, a main-street 16th-century pub which had recently been de-licensed. The Society had no money to buy it, but secured a loan from the Borough Council, and then raised the purchase price by running a charity shop on the premises.

More money was need to give the building a 400-year-service and fit it out. This, too, was raised, and the Fleur de Lis Heritage Centre, first of its kind in the south of the UK, opened in 1977. Run entirely by voluntary effort, and including a networked Tourist Information Centre since 1978, it is now overcrowded. With the aid of a £473,000 Heritage Lottery Fund grant, not to mention many generous contributions from trusts, companies, members and friends, it is due to expand into adjacent premises, already acquired by the Society, in 2001.

From the start the Society saw it as important to promote pride and interest in the area by means of publications of various kinds. In 1964 it began publication of the Faversham Papers - studies of aspects of the area s past, printed in-house by volunteers. How many might there be eventually? we wondered at the time. 10, perhaps, or - pushing it a bit - 20? So far in fact over 75 have appeared and more are in the pipeline. The Society makes a point of keeping almost all of them permanently in print, and some of the earliest Papers have now sold well over 5,000 copies. One or two of the topics are not local. At the authors request we have published the history of a family (Nash) based on a village about 15 miles away (1997); a study of Blackpowder Manufacture in Cumbria (1995); and Traveller s Joy (1999), a practical manual for local history and civic societies interested in making the most of their areas visitor appeal. All the Papers are priced very reasonably, at under a fiver, but still make a useful profit. This is all-important since for most of its activities the Society receives no revenue funding from the authorities.

The Society has also published a range of over 100 local-interest picture postcards, and issues attrac-

tive souvenirs - a range of 23 local-interest illustrated china thimbles, for example. Its finest publication to date must be Thomas Arden in Faversham: The Man behind the Myth (1996), by its member Patrica Hyde. Running to over 600 pages, lavishly illustrated, and with a proper cloth binding, this is the first full account of the victim of the 1551 crime, and in its appendices contains a wealth of information for local and family historians alike.

Hundreds of family history enquiries now arrive at the Society s Fleur de Lis HQ every year. If our volunteers hear an American, Canadian, Aussie or Kiwi accent, it is probably someone who has come specially to see if the Society can help trace their local ancestors. Other enquirers get in touch by letter, fax or email. In every case we do our best to help - we have built up a vast, but random and uncomputerised, information base which means there are few enquirers we cannot assist.

The service is free of charge - though we hope, if we are honest, that, since we are a charity run by voluntary effort and always need hard cash, people will make a donation in return. Sadly, not all do, and there are even some who do not have the courtesy to thank us for the information we have sent, often after two or three hours research. Compensating for these, to an extent, are those who value our work. Specially cheering, for example, was a recent letter from an enquirer with an uncommon surname, who told us that through the information and contacts we had supplied he had increased his worldwide family, within a matter of weeks, from a dozen to over 600!

Family history and local history run hand-in-hand, or such is our conviction. Of course there are those family historians whose only obsession appears to be tracing their descent back as far as they can go. There may be a degree of satisfaction in this, but - thankfully - more and more family historians are wanting to flesh out their ancestry, to put their forebears in context, to find out how and where they lived, what they did, and what their relationship was with contemporary events and trends. This brings them alive in a way that no mere family tree can ever do. It can also be very useful to historians of the locality in which they lived and worked. May the links between family and local historians grow and prosper!

The Faversham Society is at the Fleur de Lis Heritage Centre, 13 Preston Street, Faversham, Kent ME13 8NS (tel. 01795 534542, fax 01795 533261, email faversham@btinternet.org). The Centre is within three minutes drive of the M2 and three minutes walk of the mainline railway station (trains from London (Victoria) every 30 minutes).

The Faversham Society also manages the Maison Dieu, Ospringe; the Chart Gunpowder Mills; and the ruins of Stone Church, the only church in the UK to incorporate a heathen Roman shrine. It always welcomes as members those in sympathy with its aims and ideals. To learn more about Faversham, why not visit the town website at **http://www.faversham.org**

Military Road 1905

Pembroke Dock
~ a Nineteenth Century New Town

Basil H J Hughes BA(Hons)

The town of Pembroke Dock or Pater as it was then known, was specifically built to house the workers at the new Admiralty ship building yard. The town was essentially an Admiralty rather than a naval town. The Commissioners of the Navy Board and, after 1832, the Lords Commissioners of the Admiralty, influenced most aspects of public and private life outside the Dockyard walls.

When Vice Admiral of the Blue, Lord Horatio Nelson, sailed up the Milford Haven Waterway in the summer of 1802, the area now occupied by the town a green field site. Nelson would have seen the Government battery at Pater Point, the old mansion of Paterchurch, a few farms and cottages and the home of the Meyrick family at Llanion. Within 12 years, however, all was to be transformed. After the negotiations by the Admiralty to buy the land at nearby Milford - where warships were already being built for His Majesty s Navy - broke down. A new site was selected and the move saw the birth of Pembroke Dock, Over the next 108 years, over 250 ships were to be built for the Navy - from sixth rates of 1816 to an oilier of 1922.

What was the cost?

Mr. John Narbeth of Pembroke recording in his diary
In the year of the Lord 1 January 1813 began the enclosing of the new Dockyard, Pater, and the fitting up of workshops for the men and sheds for all sorts of materials; there was a temporary dock dug out to take in a 74old gun ship for a storehouse, and the upperdeck for offices for the Builder and Storekeeper; the yard enclosed with wooden palings.

By 1st January 1814 the whole of the of the workmen were able to come there to commence their shipbuilding with Mr. Roberts as their builder, and not so much as one house on the spot, only Paterchurch farm, so poor old Pembroke was well filled with both officers and men for a few years .

On the 14th day of May 1814, Mr.. Lowless and myself left poor old Pembroke to commence its rival, so on that day was the first shaving cut and first window frame made by John Narbeth, and by September 25th 1814, was the first four houses ready. Mr.S. Thomas the foreman of Shipwrights wife came to take possession, and we drank to the success of the first house in Pater. Mr. Thomas, foreman of Shipwrights; Mr. Stephens, foreman of Blacksmiths; Mr. Clun, issuer of stores; and Mr. Honeydear, public house were the first four inhabitants of the new town, Michaelmas Day 1814. After that we built a public house for Mr. Phillips on the corner of Middle St.

Interesting that two out of the five first houses built in the town were Public houses

1815 February 22 Cresswell Quay
Extract from a letter from Hugh Wilson to J Harcourt Powell, Esq.
Great exertions are making to build houses adjoining the yard. There are now near one hundred building and engaged to build on Mr. Meyrick s property .

By 1816 the new Yard was expanding rapidly and more men were required. There was an immigration of large numbers of skilled tradesmen and their families, from the other Royal Dockyards necessitating a massive house building programme. Houses were erected as fast as possible many with the aid of the dockyard workers who worked on them after a day s work in the yard, but even so some were occupied before they were completed and many were of very poor standard. The founding fathers of Pater were thus largely, but not exclusively, new men and constituted the most radically distinct influx into South Pembrokeshire since the arrival of the Flemings in the twelfth century.

The town planned by the Admiralty and laid out on a chessboard pattern was originally known as Pater. By 1817 the framework for the town was set down outside the east wall of the dockyard in a grid-iron arrangement of streets, some quite spacious, running north-south and east-west. The Admiralty Board and the Meyricks granted leases to an army of small builders who gradually lined the new thoroughfares with houses, sometimes in piecemeal fashion. The roads were muddy tracks and many of the workers had to find accommodation in the outlying villages and travel to work by boat. Such was the situation that the Navy Board actually help fund an improved road from Pembroke.

In 1818 Bethany Chapel was erected with a cemetery on the west side. It was the first place of worship to be erected .in the new town and was lighted inside by tallow candles that smoked needing deacons to go round, during the singing of the hymn before the sermon, with a pair of snuffers to lop of the burnt wick.

A description of the town in 1834 reads
Pembroke Dock, sometimes likewise called PATER, or PATERCHURCH, is situated on the southern shore of Milford Haven, about two miles from the old town. It consists of several streets of neat and well-built houses, and is partially paved, but not lighted: there are numerous good shops for the supply of the population, several of which are branches from the larger establishments in the borough. A handsome enclosed market place was erected here about five years ago; but it has hitherto been but scantily supplied, and

Military Road 2000

most of the inhabitants frequent the market at Pembroke.

Was that really a true Picture?

As families poured in, attracted by the growing industry, the town became the scene of an increasing housing shortage. Terraced houses were built in large numbers the population increasing from about six in 1814 to 14000 by 1860. Some of these houses were very small. It is said of some that you could stoke the fire and open the front door at same time. Wages were 19s per week for tradesmen and 10s for laborers and the men were paid out by their ganger at his favorite Public house.

The main water supply, a stream, which started on the hill just below the Bethany Chapel, was purchased by the Admiralty to provide a fresh water supply for the Dockyard. Unfortunately they soon found the cemetery at Bethany Chapel contaminated it and burials were stopped. The houses of the town obtained water from large casks in the gardens, which held the rainwater from the roofs and from shallow wells. The problem with these was that all the houses had a privy and a pigsty in the back garden and many were built on the slopes of the town so the wells at the lower end of the town, where the poorer people lived, became contaminated. The only other sources of water were springs in the surrounding area, which necessitated carrying buckets a considerable distance. At one time the town practically suffered from a water famine, and whenever there was a spell of dry weather it was very scarce.

It wasn t until 1898 that a water supply was brought into the town with taps placed at convenient places throughout the principal parts of the town.

The main fuel burned was culm, a mixture of anthracite dust and mud and it was a common practice for heaps of this mixture to be left in the street overnight for kneading and making into balls the next day. There were no streetlights so it is easy to imagine the condition some workers arrived home in after spending a few hours at one the many public houses. The condition of the streets was such that the ladies had to wear pattens to keep their feet out of the mud .

The housing conditions of the poor at the time were notoriously bad, some families lived in single room cellars or in lodging houses facing streets fouled by open sewers - not paved and in the rain seas of mud - in the hot sun stinking: Some of these cellars were very damp and chest complaints were common. Because of the overcrowding it was common for several sick people to be crowded into one room. Infectious diseases spread rapidly and were a source of concern to the Dockyard Authorities as it affected

the attendance of their work force. Lodgings were so hard to come by that the bed of a diseased would be occupied by the next night. In 1832 there was cholera outbreak so bad that alarm was raised amongst the Dockyard Authorities

Action was taken to temporarily alleviate some of the worst housing conditions. On investigation they found hunger, nakedness, bare earthen floors and unfurnished houses with unwhited walls and over-crowding. Funds were raised and a soup kitchen started in the Dockyard for the workers. Shortly afterwards the Admiralty budget became tighter and an order was implemented that money outlayed in paying for coffins, by the Dockyard, for workers Discharged Dead was to be recovered from their families. The dreaded letters DD in red ink denoted the Royal Navy abbreviation for Discharged Dead , the final epitaph of many of the workmen.

William Williams aged forty-five, Labourer No 1899, from Bush Street, had been greasing cogs in a machine in No 2 Fitters Shop on the morning of 21 May 1900 when he was caught in the machinery. He was taken to the Surgery with a fractured skull and his right hand amputated all except his thumb . William Williams received his DD in red ink the following day. His widow received £193 14s.11d. in compensation from the Admiralty.

The cost of coffins was a major outlay against which Dockyard workers had to make prudent provision. The Royal Dockyard Interment Society formed in about 1870 to do away with collections in the Dockyard collected weekly two pence subscriptions as an insurance against funeral costs.

Cholera again struck in 1853 so severe that Lord Palmeston wrote a letter on the subject.
 One of those laws connects health with the absence of those gaseous exhalations which proceed from overcrowded human beings, or from decomposing substances, whether animal or vegetable and the same laws render sickness the almost inevitable consequence of exposure to those noxious influences

There was an outbreak of Smallpox in 1857. Eight people died in Pembroke Dock, the first being Mrs Evans of Queen St. An investigation was carried out by Medical and Senior Officers from the Dockyard into the causes of the outbreak and the conclusion was reached that all those who died had acquired second hand clothing from a street hawker who had originated in Swansea and travelled to Pembroke Dock to sell his infected stock.

Cholera struck again in August 1866 spreading throughout the Pennar area, but is alleged not out of the area because the people of Pennar sealed themselves off. The first person to die was a man named Peter Morris. The victims had to be buried within twelve hours and such was the rapid spread of the infection that on 29th August 1866 as well as Peter Morris, also buried were Emma Jones, Margaret Griffiths and I.Day. On the 2nd September Thomas Charles Powell , Seth John Stephens, and George Jenkins were buried. The next day only one, William Wilcox, and Ann Preese on the 5th, but by the sixth of September the death toll had again risen, Maria Morgan, Anne Stephens, and John Ormond. The Ormond family was again bereaved with Elizabeth

Ormond being buried the next day. The 8th of September was the worst day with five victims being buried, like all the others by the Curate of Pembroke Dock, Rev. George Edward McHugh. They were Michael Birmingham, Mary Williams, George Davies, Elizabeth Price and Mary May. This was the peak but there was to be still more bereaved families as on the 10th September Ann Jones, Stephen Morgan, and Jane Preese were buried.

The Jones family suffered more losses with Ann Jones being buried on the 14th, John Jones on the 15th, Mary Ann Jones and Fanny Jones, twin sisters, on the 16th and Mary Ann Jones as well as Elizabeth Vaulk on the 17th. The last two of the victims to be buried were Thomas Mabe and Mary Griffiths on the 19th September. A year later scarlet fever raged, it struck again in 1909. Typhoid was present in 1879/80 with over twenty people being affected but fortunately all recovered and the Curate of the time records in the Church Magazine that the problem with the health in Pennar was, that, although these diseases were preventable and that warnings had been given both after the 1853 and the 1866 outbreak,   We would again call attention to the water supply, which is generally admitted to be the viaticum of typhoid fever, and which we hear is in a worse state than ever .

The Council attitude was that This supply is believed to be adequate to the wants of the community (remarks made by members of the Town Council at a meeting to discuss the sufficiency of the water supply of Pembroke and Pembroke Dock) but it is fairly open to doubt whether it would be found equal to the demands of exceptional dry seasons, which may reasonably be expected, and for which it should be the object of the Town Council to provide

In 1892 smallpox was present, many children, and parents who could, went away, others were re-vaccinated. With the turn of the century came measles and influenza, the latter was exceptionally severe in 1915

and 1919 when the Baptismal Register for St Patrick s Church records young babies being baptised by the Nurse. Then in the 1920 s after the closure of the Dockyard the area was hit with a diphtheria epidemic - The old offices of the Shipbuilding Company by Jacob s Pill being used as an isolation Hospital. After that time these scourges seem to have been less violent, probably because of better health care and an improved water supply.

The Dockyard closed in 1926. Pembroke Dock is now almost entirely a town of unemployed and pensioners , commented the Telegraph Almanac in 1927. The direct consequence of State policy was thus to destroy a town and between 1921 and 1931 some 3,500 people, a quarter of the town s inhabitants, migrated and over half of the insured population of the borough were unemployed.

Today almost nothing remains of those former glories. The building slips have almost all disappeared beneath new developments. A few surviving Dockyard offices, priceless examples of the stonemason s art, are slowly crumbling. The old Dockyard Chapel has been stripped of its memorial window to the lost Atalanta, its oak pews were taken away by the Royal Air Force and its famous bell, captured from the Spaniards, gone without trace.

Basil Hughes is a retired shipwright who worked for the Admiralty at the small maintenance base that was all that remained of the Admiralty Dock Yard at Pembroke Dock. In the early 1970's he became very interested in local history and found that very little research had been done. Much of his research was carried out in the local Record Office and whatever research he did, no matter how scrappy, has either put it into print or deposited a copy at the local record office.

Pembrokeshire Local History Books

More Names in the History of Pembrokeshire Hearth Tax 1670 (£10) ISBN 1- 898687-06- 4
Haverfordwest 1539-1660 (£4) ISBN 1-898687- 07- 2
Some Names in the History of South Pembrokeshire (£7.50) ISBN 1-898687-09-9
More names in the History of South Pembrokeshire - Land Tax Castlemartin Hundred 1791 / 2
(£10) ISBN 1-898687-10-2
Baptisms at St Patrick's Church Pennar Pembroke Dock 1895 to 1934(£3) ISBN 1-898687-11-0
Jottings and Historical Records with Index on the History of South Pembrokeshire Vol. 1 1066-1389
(£10) ISBN-1 898687-00-5
Jottings & Historical Records with Index on the History of South Pembrokeshire
Vol. 2 Manorial Accounts 1324 – 1333 (£10) ISBN 1 898687 02 1
Jottings and Historical Records with Index on the History of South Pembrokeshire Vol. 3 1389 - 1535
(£10) ISBN 1- 898687- 08- 0
Jottings and Historical Records with Index on the History of South Pembrokeshire -
Monkton Parish pre 1900 (£7.50) ISBN 1-898687-05-6
Jottings on the History of Pennar, Pembroke Dock (£5) ISBN 1-898687-4-8
Jottings on the History of South Pembrokeshire - St Daniel's Church (Pembroke) (£3) ISBN 1-898687-01-3
Jottings on the History of South Pembrokeshire - Llanstadwell Parish pre 1900 (£5) ISBN 1-898687-03- X

All A4 Paperback book and obtainable from the Author.
BASIL H J HUGHES BA (HON.)
37 Owen St, Pennar, Pembroke Dock
Pembrokeshire SA72 6SL
Tel(UK) 01646681391
Email – BasHughes@AOL.COM
Post and Packing – UK 50p

History Societies & Organisations

British Isles National Organisations & Specialist Subject Societies

Anglo-Zulu War Historical Society
Woodbury House, Woodchurch Road, Tenterden, Kent,
TN30 7AE Tel: 01580-764189 Fax: 01580-766648
Web: www.web-marketing.co.uk/anglozuluwar
Association of Local History Tutors
47 Ramsbury Drive, Earley, Reading, Berkshire, RG6 7RT
Tel: 0118-926-4729
Baptist Historical Society
60 Strathmore Avenue, Hitchin SG5 1ST Tel: 01462-431816
& Tel: 01462-442548 Email: slcopson@dial.pipex.com
Black & Asian Studies Association
28 Russell Square, London, WC1B 5DS Tel: 020-7862-8844
Email: marikas@sas.ac.uk
Brewery History Society
Manor Side East, Mill Lane, Byfleet, West Byfleet, Surrey,
KT14 7RS Email: jsechiari@rmcbp.co.uk
British Archaeological Association
Burlington House, Piccadilly, London, W1V 0HS
British Association for Local History
PO Box 1576, Salisbury, SP2 8SY Tel: 01722-332158
Fax: 01722-413242 Web: www.balh.co.uk
British Association of Paper Historians
2 Manor Way, Kidlington, Oxfordshire, OX5 2BD
Web: www.Gaph.freeserve.co.uk
British Brick Society
9 Bailey Close, High Wycombe, Buckinghamshire, HP13
6QA Tel: 01494-520299 Fax: 01344-890129
Email: brick@brick.org.uk
British Empire & Commonwealth Museum
Clock Tower Yard, Temple Meads, Bristol, BS1 6QH
Tel: 0117-925-4980 Fax: 0117-925-4983
Email: staff@empiremuseum.co.uk
Web: www.empiremuseum.co.uk
British Records Association
40 Northampton Road, London, EC1R 0HB
Tel: 020-7833-0428 Fax: 020-7833-0416
Email: archives@charity.ufree.com
British Records Society
Stone Barn Farm, Sutherland Road, Longsdon ST9 9QD
Tel: 01782-385446 & 01538-385024
Email: britishrecordsociety@hotmail.co
Email: carolyn@cs.keele.ac.uk
Web: www.members.tripod.co.uk/carolyn_busfield
British Society for Sports History
Dept of Sports & Science, John Moore s University, Byrom
Street, Liverpool, Merseyside, L3 3AF
Colne Smack Preservation Society
76 New Street, Brightlingsea CO7 0DD Tel: 01206-304768
Web: www.colne-smack-preservation.rest.org.uk
Costume Society South of England Branch
Borough House, 101 The Borough, Downton, Salisbury,
Wiltshire, SP5 3ZX Tel: 01725-511649
Email: user@boroughhouse.in2home.co.uk
Council for British Archaeology
Bowes Morrell House, 111 Walmgate, York YO1 9WA
Tel: 01904-671417 Fax: 01904-671384
Email: info@britarch.ac.uk Web: www.britarch.ac.uk/cba
Current Archaeology
9 Nassington Road, London, NW3 2TX Tel: 020-7435-7517
Fax: 020-7916-2405 Email: editor@archaeology.co.uk
Web: www.archaeology.co.uk
Family & Community Historical Research Society
56 South Way, Lewes, East Sussex, BN7 1LY
Field Studies Council
Head Offices, Preston Montford, Shrewsbury, SY4 1HW
Tel: 01743-852100 Fax: 01743-852101 Email: fsc.headof-
fice@ukonline.co.uk Web: www.field-studies-council.org
Friends of War Memorials
4 Lower Belgrave Street, London, SW1 W 0LA
Tel: 020-7259-0403 Fax: 020-7259-0296
Email: enquiries@war-memorials.com
Web: www.war-memorials.com

Garden History Society
77 Cowcross Street, London, EC1M 6EJ Tel: 020-7608-2409
Fax: 020-7490-2974
Email: gardenhistorysociety@compuserve.com
Web: www.gardenhistorysociety.org
Heraldry Society
PO Box 32, Maidenhead SL6 3FD Tel: 0118-932-0210
Fax: 0118-932-0210 Email: heraldry-society@cwcom.net
The Historical Association
59A Kennington Park Road, London, SE11 4JH
Tel: 020-7735-3901 Fax: 020-7582-4989
Email: enquiry@history.org.uk Web: www.history.org.uk
Historical Medical Equipment Society
14 The Avenue, Cliftonville, Northampton NN1 5 BT
Labour Heritage
13 Grovewood, Sandycombe Road, Kew, Richmond, Surrey,
TW9 3NF Email: sfowler@sfowler.force9.co.uk
Legion of Frontiersmen of Commonwealth
4 Edwards Road, Belvedere, Kent, DA17 5AL
Lighthouse Society of Great Britain
Gravesend Cottage, Gravesend, Torpoint, Cornwall, PL11
2LX Email: k.trethewey@btinternet.com
Web: www.lsgb.co.uk
Local Population Studies Society
78 Harlow Terrace, Harrogate, North Yorkshire, HG2 0PN
Tel: 01423-560429 Fax: 01423-560429
Email: sir_david_cooke@compuserve.com
London & North Western Railway Society
34 Falmouth Close, Nuneaton, Warwickshire, CV11 6GB
Tel: 02476-381090 Fax: 02476-373577
Email: nuneatonian@compuserve.com
Mercia Cinema Society
5 Arcadia Avenue, Chester le Street, Co Durham, DH3 3UH
Midland Railway Society
4 Canal Road, Yapton, West Sussex, BN18 0HA
Tel: 01243-553401 Email: BeeFitch@aol.com
Museum of the Royal Pharmaceutical Society
1 Lambeth High Street, London, SE1 7JN
Tel: 020-7735-9141-ext-354 Fax: 020-7793-0232
Email: museum@rpsgb.org.uk Web: www.rpsgb.org.uk
Museums Association
42 Clerkenwell Close, London, EC1R 0PA
Tel: 020-7250-1789 Fax: 020-7250-1929
North East Labour History Society
Department of Historical & Critical Studies, University of
Northumbria, Newcastle upon Tyne, NE1 8ST
Tel: 0191-227-3193 Fax: 0191-227-4630
Email: joan.hugman@unn.ac.uk
North Eastern Police History Society
Brinkburn Cottage, 28 Brinkburn Street, High Barnes,
Sunderland SR4 7RG Tel: 0191-565-7215
Email: harry.wynne@virgin.net
Web: freespace.virgin.net/carol.almond/index.htm
North West Sound Archive
Old Steward s Office, Clitheroe Castle, Clitheroe, Lancashire,
BB7 1AZ Tel: 01200-427897 Fax: 01200-427897
Web: www.nw-soundarchive.co.uk
Open University History Society
111 Coleshill Road, Chapel End, Nuneaton, Warwickshire,
CV10 0PG Tel: 024-7639-7668
Oral History Society
British Library National Sound Archive, 96 Euston Road,
London, NW1 2DB Tel: 020-7412-7405, or 020-7412-7440
Fax: 020-7412-7441 Email: rob.perks@bl.uk
Web: www.essex.ac.uk/sociology/oralhis.htm
Police History Society
37 Greenhill Road, Timperley, Altrincham, Cheshire, WA15
7BG Tel: 0161-980-2188 Email: alanhayhurst@cs.com
Postal History Society
60 Tachbrook Street, London, SW1V 2NA
Tel: 020-7821-6399

Prehistoric Society
Inst of Archaeology, 31-34 Gordon Square, London WC1H0PY
Railway & Canal Historical Society
c/o The National Waterways Museum, Llanthony Warehouse, Gloucester Docks, Gloucester, GL1 2EH
Richard III Society
20 Rowington Road, Norwich, NR1 3RR
Royal Archaeological Institute
c/o English Heritage, 23 Savile Row, London, W1X 1AB
Royal Photographic Society Historical Group
PO Box 28, Borehamwood, Hertfordshire, WD6 4SY
Royal Society of Chemistry Library & Information Centre
Burlington House, Piccadilly, London, W1V 0BN
Tel: 0207-437-8656 Fax: 0207-287-9798
Email: library@rsc.org Web: www.rsc.org
Social History of Learning Disability Research Group
School of Health & Social Welfare, Open University, Milton Keynes, Bedfordshire, MK7 6AA
Society For Genealogy & History of The Family
136 Lennard Road, Beckenham, BR3 1QT
Society for Name Studies in Britain & Ireland
22 Peel Park Avenue, Clitheroe, Lancashire, BB7 1ET
Tel: 01200-423771 Fax: 01200-423771
Society of Antiquaries
Burlington House, Piccadilly, London, W1J 0BE
Tel: 020-7479-7080 Fax: 020-7287-6967
Email: admin@sal.org.uk Web: www.sal.org.uk
Society of Brushmakers Descendants
13 Ashworth Place, Church Langley, Essex, CM17 9PU
Tel: 01279-629392 Email: s.b.d@lineone.net
Web: www.brushmakers.com
Society of Genealogy & History of The Family
136 Lennard Road, Beckenham, BR3 1QT
Tennyson Society
Central Library, Free School Lane, Lincoln, Lincolnshire, LN2 1EZ Tel: 01522-552862 Fax: 01522-552858
Email: linnet@lincolnshire.gov.uk
Thoresby Society
23 Clarendon Road, Leeds, LS2 9NZ
United Reformed Church History Society
Westminster College, Madingley Road, Cambridge, Cambridgeshire, CB3 0AA Tel: 01223-741300
Victorian Society
1 Priory Gardens, Bedford Park, London, W4 1TT
Tel: 020-8994-1019 Fax: 020-8995-4895
Email: admin@victorian-society.org.uk
Web: www.victorian-society.org.uk
Voluntary Action History Society
National Centre for Volunteering, Regents Wharf, 8 All Saints Street, London, N1 9RL Tel: 020-7520-8900
Fax: 020-7520-8910 Web: www.instvolres.aol.com
Volunteer Corps of Frontiersmen
Archangels Rest, 26 Dark Lane, Witney OX8 5LE
War Research Society
27 Courtway Avenue, Maypole, Birmingham, B14 4PP
Tel: 0121-430-5348 Fax: 0121-436-7401
Email: battletour@aol.com Web: www.battlefieldtours.co.uk
Wesley Historical Society
34 Spiceland Road, Northfield, Birmingham B31 1NJ
Email: 106364.3456@compuserve.com
No records held - advice only given
West of England Costume Society
4 Church Lane, Long Ashton, Nr Bristol, BS41 9LV
Tel: 01275-543564 Fax: 01275-543564

London & Greater London

Acton History Group
30 Highlands Avenue, London, W3 6EU, Tel: 020-8992-8698
Birkbeck College
Malet Street, London, WC1E 7HU, Tel: 020-7631-6633
Fax: 020-7631-6688 Email: info@bbk.ac.uk
Web: www.bbk.ac.uk
Brentford & Chiswick Local History Society
25 Hartington Road, London, W4 3TL
Brixton Society
82 Mayall Road, London, SE24 0PJ, Tel: 020-7207-0347
Fax: 020-7207-0347 Email: apiperbrix@aol.com

Bromley Borough Local History Society
1 South Drive, Orpington, Kent, BR6 9NG
Centre for Metropolitan History
Institute of Historical Research, Senate House, Malet Street, London, WC1E 7HU, Tel: 020-7862-8790
Fax: 020-7862-8793 Email: o-myhill@sas.ac.uk
Web: www.history.ac.uk/cmh/cmh.main.html
Croydon Local Studies Forum
Flat 2, 30 Howard Road, South Norwood, London, SE25 5BY, Tel: 020-8654-6454
Croydon Local Studies Forum
208 Turnpike Lane, London, CR0 5NZ
East London History Society
13 Three Crowns Road, Colchester, Essex, CO4 5AD
Fulham & Hammersmith Historical Society
Flat 12, 43 Peterborough Road, Fulham, London, SW6 3BT, Tel: 020-7731-0363 Fax: 020-7731-0363
Email: fhhs@ukonline.co.uk
Web: http://web.ukonline.co.uk/fhhs
Fulham & Hammersmith History Society
85 Rannoch Road, Hammersmith, London, W6 9SX
Hendon & District Archaeological Society
13 Reynolds Close, London, NW11 7EA, Tel: 020-8458-1352
Fax: 020-8731-9882 Email: denis@netmatters.co.uk
Hornsey Historical Society
The Old Schoolhouse, 136 Tottenham Lane, London, N8 7EL, Tel: 020-8348-8429 Web: www.hornseyhistorical.org.uk
House Mill
Three Mills Island, Three Mill Lane, Bromley by Bow, London, E3 3DU, Tel: 020-8980-4626
London & Middlesex Archaeological Society
Placements Office, University of North London, 62-66 Highbury Grove, London, N5 2AD
London Record Society
c/o Institute of Historical Research, Senate House, Malet Street, London, WC1E 7HU, Tel: 020-7862-8798
Email: creaton@sas.ac.uk
Web: www.ihr.sas.ac.uk/ihr/associnstits/lrsmnu.html
Middle Thames Archaeological & Historical Society
1 Saffron Close, Datchet, Slough, SL3 9DU,
Tel: 01753-543636
Mill Hill Historical Society
41 Victoria Road, Mill Hill, London, NW7 4SA,
Tel: 020-8959-7126
Newham History Society
52 Eastbourne Road, East Ham, London, E6 6AT,
Tel: 020-8471-1171
Paddington Waterways & Maida Vale Society
19a Randolph Road, Maida Vale, London, W9 1AN
The Peckham Society
178 Peckham Rye, London, SE22 9QA
Walthamstow Historical Society
173 Brettenham Road, Walthamstow, London, E17 5AX,
Tel: 0208-523-2399 Fax: 0208-523-2399
Wandsworth Historical Society
7 Coalecroft Road, London, SW15 6LW, Tel: 020-8788-0015

England — Regional Organisations

Council for British Archaeology - East Midlands
c/o Dept of Archaeology, University Park, Nottingham, NG7 2RD Tel: 0115-951-4841 Fax: 0115-951-4812
Council for British Archaeology - Mid Anglia
34 Kingfisher Close, Wheathamstead AL4 8JJ
Tel: 01582-629433 Fax: 01582-629433
Email: derek.hills@virgin.net
Council for British Archaeology - North West
39 Stalbridge Avenue, Liverpool, L18 1HA
Tel: 0151-280-2669, or 0151-706-7811 Fax: 0151-709-6206
Email: carolynek@career.u-net.com
Council for British Archaeology - South East
47 Durrington Gardens, The Causeway, Goring, Worthing, Sussex BN12 6BX, Tel: 01903-504510
Council for British Archaeology — South West
52 Sylvan Road, Pennsylvania, Exeter, EX4 6EY,
Tel: 01392-432184 Email: keithsgardner@compuserve.com

Council for British Archaeology - West Midlands
c/o Rowleys House Museum, Barker Street, Shrewsbury,
SY1 1QH, Tel: 01743-361196 Fax: 01743-358411

Bedfordshire

Ampthill & Dist Archaeological and Local History Society
14 Glebe Avenue, Flitwick, Bedford, MK45 1HS,
Tel: 01525-712778 Email: petwood@waitrose.com
Web: www.museums.bedfordshire.gov.uk/localgroups/ampthill2/html
Ampthill & District Preservation
Seventh House, 43 Park Hill, Ampthill MK45 2LP
Bedfordshire Archaeological & Local History Society
7 Lely Close, Bedford, MK41 7LS, Tel: 01234 365095
Web: www.museums.bedfordshire.gov.uk/localgroves
Bedfordshire Historical Record Society
50 Shefford Road, Meppershall SG17 5LL, Tel: 01462-813363
Bedfordshire Local History
14 Glebe Avenue, Flitwick, Bedfordshire, MK45 1HS
Bedfordshire Local History Association
29 George Street, Maulden, Bedford, MK45 2DF
Tel: 01525-633029
Biggleswade History Society
6 Pine Close, Biggleswade, Bedfordshire, SG18 0EF
Caddington Local History Group
98 Mancroft Road, Caddington, Nr. Luton LUL 4EN
Carlton & Chellington Historical
3 High Street, Carlton, Bedfordshire, MK43 7JX
Dunstable Historic & Heritage Studies
184 West Street, Dunstable LU6 1 NX, Tel: 01582-609018
Harlington Heritage Trust
2 Shepherds Close, Harlington, Nr Dunstable LU5 6NR
Luton & District Historical Society
22 Homerton Road, Luton LU3 2UL, Tel: 01582-584367
Shuttleworth Veteran Aeroplane Society
PO Box 42, Old Warden Aerodrome, Biggleswade,
Bedfordshire, SG18 9UZ, Tel: 01767-627398
Email: svas@oldwarden.fsnet.co.uk
Toddington Historical Society
17 Alma Farm Road, Toddington, Dunstable LU5 6BG,
Tel: 01525-873825 Email: dgwhitfield@netscape.co.uk

Berkshire

Berkshire Archaeological Society
30 Salcombe Drive, Earley, Berkshire, RG6 2HU
Berkshire Aviation Trust - Film & Video Archives
6 Richmond Road, Caversham Heights, Reading RG4 7PP,
Tel: 0118-947-3924
Berkshire Industrial Archaeological Group
5 Harefield Close, Winnersh, Wokingham RG11 5NP
Berkshire Local History Association
37 Heron Island, Caversham, Reading, RG4 8DQ,
Tel: 0118-947-7345 Fax: 0118-947-7345
Email: heronisland@netscapeonline.co.uk
Berkshire Record Society
c/o Berkshire Record Office, 9 Coley Avenue, Reading, RG1
6AF Tel: 0118-901-5130 Fax: 0118-901-5131
Bracknell & District Historical Society
16 Harcourt Road, East Hampstead, Bracknell RG12 7JD
Chiltern Heraldry Group
Magpie Cottage, Pondwood Lane, Pondwood Lane,
Shottesbrooke, Berkshire, SL6 3SS
Cox Green Local History Group
29 Bissley Drive, Maidenhead, SL6 3UX, Tel: 01628-823890
Goring & Streatley Local History Society
45 Springhill Road, Goring On Thames, Reading, Berkshire,
RG8 OBY, Tel: 01491-872625
Hungerford Historical Association
11 Regent Close, Hungerford, Berkshire, RG17 0LF
Newbury District Field Club
Glenwood, 30 Monkswood Close, Newbury RG14 6NS,
Tel: 01635-43554
Wargrave Local History Society
6 East View Close, Wargrave, Berkshire, RG10 8BJ,
Tel: 0118-9403121 Email: history@wargrave.net
Web: www.wargrave.net/history

Birmingham (see also Midlands - West Midlands

Alvechurch Historical Society
Bearhill House, Alvechurch, Birmingham, B48 7JX
Barr & Ashton Local History Society
17 Booths Farm Road, Great Barr, Birmingham, 642 2NJ
Birmingham & District Local History Association
112 Brandwood Road, Kings Heath, Birmingham, B14 6BX,
Tel: 0121-444-7470
Birmingham Canal Navigation s Society
37 Chestnut Close, Handsacre, Rugeley, Staffs WS15 4TH
Quinton Local History Society
15 Worlds End Avenue, Quinton, Birmingham, B32 1JF,
Tel: 0121-422-1792 Fax: 0121-422-1792
Email: qlhs@bjtaylor.fsnet.co.uk Web: www.qlhs.co.uk
Small Heath Local History Society
381 St Benedicts Road, Small Heath, Birmingham, B10 9ND

Bristol

Alveston Local History Society
The Bodyce, 1 Greenhill Down, Alveston, Bristol, BS35 3PA
Avon Local History Association
5 Parry s Grove, Bristol, BS9 1TT, Tel: 0117-9684979
Fax: 0117-9684979
Bristol & Avon Archaeological Society
3 Priory Avenue, Westbury-on-Trym, Bristol, BS9 4DA,
Tel: 0117-9620161 (evenings only)
Bristol & Gloucestershire Archaeological Society
22 Beaumont Road, Gloucester, Gloucestershire, GL2 0EJ,
Tel: 01452-302610 Web: www.ihr.sas.ac.uk/ihr/bg/
Bristol Records Society
c/o Department of Historical Studies, University of Bristol,
13-15 Woodland Road, Bristol, BS8 1TB
Congresbury History Group
Venusmead, 36 Venus St, Congresbury, Bristol, BS49 5EZ,
Tel: 01934-834780 Email: rogerhards-venusmead@breathemail.net
Downend Local History Society
141 Overndale Road, Downend, Bristol, B516 2RN
Keynsham & Saltford Local History Society
33 Martock Road, Keynsham, Bristol, B53 1XA
Whitchurch Local History Society
62 Nailsea Park, Nailsea, Bristol, B519 1BB
Yatton Local History Society
27 Henley Park, Yatton, Bristol, BS49 4JH Tel: 01934-832575

Buckinghamshire

Buckinghamshire Archaeological Society - Archives
Buckinghamshire County Museum, Church Street, Aylesbury,
HP20 2QP, Tel: 01296-331441-Ext 217(Wed only)
Buckinghamshire Record Society
County Record Office, County Hall, Aylesbury HP20 1UU
Tel: 01296-303013 Fax: 01296-382274
Chesham Society
54 Church Street, Chesham, Buckinghamshire, HP5 IHY
Chess Valley Archealogical & Historical Society
16 Chapmans Crescent, Chesham HP5 2QU
Pitstone Local History Society
Vicarage Road, Pitstone, Nr Ivinghoe Tel: 01582-605464
Princes Risborough Area Heritage Society
Martin s Close, 11 Wycombe Road, Princes Risborough
HP27 OEE, Tel: 01844-343004 Fax: 01844-273142
Email: sandymac@risboro35.freeserve.co.uk

Cambidgeshire

Upwood & Raveley History Group
The Old Post Office, 71-73 High Street, Upwood,
Huntingdon, Cambridgeshire, PE17 1QE
Cambridge Antiquarian Society
PO Box 376, Cambridge, CB4 6HT
Cambridgeshire Archaeology Society
Castle Court, Shire Hall, Cambridge, CB3 0AP
Cambridgeshire Local History Society
1A Archers Close, Swaffham Bulbeck, Cambridge, CB5 0NG
Cambridgeshire Records Society
5 Bateman Street, Cambridge, CB2 1NB, Tel: 01223-364706
Email: francesca@bateman5.demon.co.uk

The Hemingfords Local History Society
12 Hemingford Road, St Ives, Cambridgeshire, PE17 4HF
March & District Museum
March & District Museum Society, High Street, March,
Cambridgeshire, PE15 9JJ, Tel: 01354-655300
Oundle Historical Society
13 Lime Avenue, Oundle, Peterborough PE8 4PT
Sawston Village History Society
21 Westmoor Avenue, Sawston, Cambridge, CB2 4BU

Cheshire

Altrincham History Society
10 Willoughby Close, Sale, Cheshire, M33 6PJ
Ashton & Sale History Society
Tralawney House, 78 School Road, Sale M33 7XB
Tel: 0161-969-2795
Cheshire Heraldry Society
24 Malvern Close, Congleton, Cheshire, CW12 4PD
Cheshire Local History Association
Cheshire Record Office, Duke Street, Chester CH1 1RL,
Tel: 01244-602559 Fax: 01244-603812
Email: recordoffice@cheshire.gov.uk
Chester Archaeological Society
Grosvenor Museum, 27 Grosvenor Street, Chester, CH1 2DD,
Tel: 01244-402028 Fax: 01244-347522
Email: p.carrington@chestercc.gov.uk
Web: www.morpork.u-net.com
Chester Archaeological Society
Ochor House, Porch Lane, Hope Mountain, Cacgwrlc L12 9LS
Christleton Local History Group
25 Croft Close, Rowton CH3 7QQ, Tel: 01244-332410
Congleton History Society
45 Harvey Road, Congleton, Cheshire, CWI2 2DH
Email: awill0909@aol.com
County Palatine of Chester Local History Committee
Department of History, University College Chester, Cheveney
Road, Chester, Cheshire, CH1 4BJ
Lymm Local History Society
2 Statham Drive, Lymm, Cheshire, WA13 9NW
Macclesfield Historical Society
42 Tytherington Drive, Macclesfield, Cheshire, SK10 2HJ
Tel: 01625-420250
Poynton Local History Society
33 Beech Crescent, Poynton, Stockport, Cheshire, SK12 1AW
Stockport Historical Society
59 Malmesbury Road, Cheadle Hulme, Stockport, Cheshire,
SK8 7QL Tel: 0161-439-7202
Weaverham History Society
Ashdown, Sandy Lane, Weaverham, Northwich CW8 3PX
Tel: 01606-852252
Wilmslow Historical Society
4 Campden Way, Handforth, Wilmslow SK9 3JA
Tel: 01625-529381

Cleveland

Cleveland & Teesside Local History Society
150 Oxford Road, Linthorpe, Middlesbrough TS5 5EL

Cornwall

Bodmin Local History Group
1 Lanhydrock View, Bodmin, Cornwall, PL31 1BG
Cornwall Association of Local Historians
St Margaret s Cottage, St Margaret s Lane, Polgooth, St
Austell, Cornwall, PL26 7AX
Email: backhouse.dodds@btinternet.com
Cornwall Family History Society
5 Victoria Square, Truro, Cornwall, TR1 2RS
Tel: 01872-264044 Email: secretary@cornwallfhs.com
Web: www.cornwallfhs.com
Fal Family History Group
4 Downside Close, Treloggan, Newquay, Cornwall, TR7 2TD
Royal Institution of Cornwall
The Courtney Library, Royal Cornwall Museum, River Street,
Truro, TR1 2SJ Tel: 01872-272205 Fax: 01872-240514
Email: RIC@royal-cornwall-museum.greeserve.co.uk
Web: www.cornwall-online.co.uk/ric

County Durham

Architectural & Arch Soc of Durham & Northumberland
Brancepeth Castle, Brancepeth, Durham DH7 8DF
Tel: 0191-378-3383
Derwentdale Local History Society
36 Roger Street, Blackhill, Consett, Co Durham, DH8 5SX
Durham County Local History Society
3 Briardene, Margery Lane, Durham, Co Durham, DH1 4QU
Tel: 0191-3861500
Durham Victoria County History Trust
Redesdale, The Oval, North Crescent, Durham, County
Durham, DH11 4NE Tel: 0191-384-8305
The Victoria History of the Counties of England c/o Institute
of Historical Research, University of London
Lanchester Local History Society
11 St Margaret s Drive, Tanfield Village, Stanley, Co Durham,
DH9 9QW Tel: 01207-236634
Monkwearmouth Local History Group
75 Escallond Dr, Dalton Heights, Seaham, SR7 8JZ
North-East England History Institute (NEEHI)
Dept of History University of Durham, 43 North Bailey,
Durham, DH1 3EX Tel: 0191-374-2004 Fax: 0191-374-4754
Email: S.F.Ketelaar@durham.ac.uk
Web: www.chic.tees.ac.uk/neehi/
Teesdale Heritage Group
26 Wesley Terrace, Middleton in Teesdale DL12 0SW
Tel: 01833-641104
Tow Law History Society
27 Attleee Estate, Tow Law DL13 4LG Tel: 01388-730056
Email: RonaldStorey@storey42.freeserve.co.uk
Wheatley Hill History Club
Broadmeadows, Durham Road, Wheatley Hill DH6 3LJ
Tel: 01429-820813 or 0370-985577 Email: wheathistory@onet.co.uk
Web: www.members.home.net/wheathill/HISTORY/index.ht

Cumbria

Appleby-In-Westmorland Society
67 Glebe Road, Appleby-In-Westmorland, CA16 6EU
Cartmel & District Local History Society
1 Barton House, Kents Bank Rd, Grange-Over-Sands LA11 7HD
Cartmel Peninsula Local History Society
Fairfield, Cartmel, Grange/Sands, Cumbria, LA11 6PY
Tel: 015395-36503
Cumberland & Westmoreland Antiquarian & Arch Soc
2 High Tenterfell, Kendal, Cumbria, LA9 4PG
Tel: 01539-773542 Fax: 01539-773538
Email: info@cwaas.org.uk Web: www.cwaas.org.uk
Cumbria Industrial History Society
Coomara, Carleton, Carlisle CA4 0BU Tel: 01228-537379
Fax: 01228-596986 Email: gbcooksvec@netscapeonline.co.uk
Cumbria Local History Federation
Sidegarth, Staveley, Kendal, Cumbria, LA8 9NN
Tel: 01539-821854 Email: joescott@clara.net
Friends of Cumbria Archives
Redbourn House, 52 Main street, St Bees CA27 0AD
Sedbergh & District History Society
c/o 27a Main Street, Sedbergh LA10 5AD Tel: 015396-20504
Email: history@sedberghcomoff.force9.co.uk
Staveley & District History Society
1 Oakland, Windermere, WA23 1AR

Derbyshire

Allestree Local Studies Group
30 Kingsley Road, Allestree, Derby, DE22 2JH
Arkwright Society
Cromford Mill, Mill Lane, Cromford, Derbyshire, DE4 3RQ
Tel: 01629-823256 Fax: 01629-823256
Email: info@cromfordmill.co.uk
Web: www.cromfordmill.co.uk
Chesterfield & District Local History Society
Melbourne House, 130 Station Road, Bimington, Chesterfield,
Derbyshire, S43 1LU Tel: 01246-229085
Derby & District Local History Forum
230 Woodbridge Close, Chellaston, Derby DE73 1QW

Derbyshire Archaeological Society
2 Watermeadows, Swarkestone, Derbyshire, DE73 1JA
Tel: 01332-704148 Email: barbarafoster@talk21.com
Web: www.coc.nottingham.ac.uk/~aczsjm/das.html
Derbyshire Local History Societies Network
Derbyshire Record Office, Libraries & Heritage Dept, County
Hall, Matlock, Derbyshire, DE4 3AG
Tel: 01629-580000-ext-35201 Fax: 01629-57611
Derbyshire Record Society
57 New Road, Wingerworth, Chesterfield S42 6UJ
Holymoorside & District History Society
12 Brook Close, Holymoorside, Chesterfield S42 7HB
Tel: 01246-566799
Ilkeston & District Local History Society
c/o 28 Kensington, Ilkeston, Derbys, DE7 5NZ
New Mills Local History Society
High Point, Cote Lane, Hayfield, High Peak SK23
Tel: 01663-742814 Fax: 01663-742814
Old Dronfield Society
2 Gosforth Close, Dronfield, Derbyshire, S18 INT

Devon

Devon & Cornwall Record Society
7 The Close, Exeter, Devon, EX1 1EZ
Web: www.gendex.com/users/branscombe/genuki/devon.htm
Devon History Society
c/o 82 Hawkins Avenue, Torquay TQ2 6ES Tel: 01803-613336
Modbury Local History Society
Cawte Cottage, Brounston Street, Modbury PL21 ORH
Moretonhampstead History Society
School House, Moreton, Hampstead, Devon, TQ13 8NX
Newton Tracey & District
Home Park, Lovacott Newton, Tracey, Barnstaple, EX31 3PY
Ogwell History Society
East Ogwell, Newton Abbott, South Devon, TQI2 6AR
Old Plymouth Society
625 Budshead Road, Whiteleigh, Plymouth, PL5 4DW
Tavistock & District Local History Society
18 Heather Close, Tavistock PL19 9QS Tel: 01822-615211
Thorverton & District History Society
Ferndale, Thorverton, Exeter, Devon, EX5 5NG
Tel: 01392-860932 Fax: 01392-860932
Yelverton & District Local History Society
4 The Coach House, Grenofen, Tavistock, Devon, PL19 9ES

Dorset

Bournemouth Local Studies Group
6 Sunningdale, Fairway Drive, Christchurch, Dorset, BH23
1JY Tel: 01202-485903 Email: mbhall@tinyonline.co.uk
Dorchester Association For Research into Local History
68 Maiden Castle Road, Dorchester, Dorset, DT1 2ES
Dorset Natural History & Archaeological Society
Dorset County Museum, High West Street, Dorchester,
Dorset, DT1 1XA Tel: 01305-202735 Fax: 01305-217180
Dorset Record Society
Dorset County Museum, High West Street, Dorchester,
Dorset, DT1 1XA Tel: 01305-262735
William Barnes Society
Pippins, Winterborne Zelston, Blandford Forum DT11 9EU
(Dorset Dialect Poet)

Dorset - West Dorset

Bridport History Society
c/o 22 Fox Close, Bradpole, Bridport, West Dorset, DT6 3JF
Tel: 01308-456876

Essex

Barking & District Historical Society
11 Coulson Close, Dagenham, Essex, RM8 1TY
Tel: 020-8590-9694 Email: pgibbs9@tesco.net
Barking Historical Society
11 Coulson Close, Dagenham, RM8 1TY Tel: 0208-590-9648
Email: pgibbs9@tesco.net
Billericay Archaeological & Historical Society
24 Belgrave Road, Billericay CM12 1TX Tel: 01277 658989

Brentwood & District Historical Society
51 Hartswood Road, Brentwood CM14 5AG
Tel: 01277-221637
Burnham & District Local History & Archaeological Soc
The Museum, The Quay, Burnham On Crouch CM0 8AS
Colchester Archaeological Group
172 Lexden Road, Colchester CO3 4BZ Tel: 01206 575081
Dunmow & District Historical/Literary Society
18 The Poplars, Great Dunmow, Essex, CM6 2JA
Essex Archaeological & Historical Congress
Birds Hill House, 59 Wroths Park, Loughton IG10 1SH
Tel: 020-8508-5582 Email: 1001104.1041@compuserve.com
Essex Architectural Research Society
4 Nelmes Way, Hornchurch, Essex, RM11 2QZ
Tel: 01708-473646 Email: kpolrm11@aol.com
Essex Society for Archaeology & History
2 Landview Gardens, Ongar, Essex, CM5 9EQ
Tel: 01277-363106 Email: leaches@breathemail.net
Friends of Historic Essex
11 Milligans Chase, Galleywood, Chelmsford, CM2 8QD
Tel: 01245-244611 Fax: 01245-244655
Email: geraldine.willden@essex.gov.uk
Friends of The Hospital Chapel
174 Aldborough Road, Seven Kings, Ilford, Essex, IG3 8HF
Tel: 020-8590-9972 Fax: 020-8590-0366
Halstead & District Local History Society
Y Magnolia, 3 Monklands Court, Halstead, Essex, C09 LAB
Ingatestone & Fryerning Historical & Arch Society
36 Pine Close, Ingatestone CM4 9EG Tel: 01277-354001
Loughton & District Historical Society
97 Staples Road, Loughton IG10 1HR Tel: 020-8508-0776
Maldon Society
15 Regency Court, Heybridge, Maldon, Essex, CM9 4EJ
Nazeing History Workshop
16 Shooters Drive, Nazeing EN9 2QD Tel: 01992-893264
Romford & District Historical
5 Rosemary Avenue, Romford, Essex, RM1 4HB
Tel: 01708-730150 Fax: 01708-730150
Thurrock Local History Society
13 Rosedale Road, Thurrock Grays, Essex, RM17 6AD
Waltham Abbey Historical Society
28 Hanover Court, Quaker Lane, Waltham Abbey EN9 1HR
Tel: 01992-716830
Wanstead Historical Society
28 Howard Road, Ilford, Essex, IG1 2EX
West London Local History Society
316 Brook Road, South Brentford, TW8 0NN
Witham History Group
35 The Avenue, Witham CM8 2DN Tel: 01376-512566

Gloucestershire

Campden & District Historical & Archaeological Society
14 Pear Tree Close, Chipping Campden GL55 6DB
Charlton Kings Local History Society
19 Lyefield Road, Charlton Kings, Cheltenham,
Gloucestershire, GL53 8EZ Tel: 01242-524258
Cheltenham Local History Society
39 Tivoli Road, Cheltenham, Gloucestershire, GL50 2TD
Cirencester Archaeological & Historical Society
Corinium Museum, Park Street, Cirencester GL7 2BX
Forest of Dean Local History Society
120 Farmers Close, Witney, Oxfordshire, OX8 6NR
Tel: 01993-773927 Email: i.pope@brookes.ac.uk
Web: www.users.waitrose.com/~iapope/LHSopening.html
Friends of Gloucestershire Archives
17 Estcourt Road, Gloucester, GL1 3LU Tel: 01452-528930
Gloucestershire County Local History Committee
Gloucestershire RCC, Community House, 15 College Green,
Gloucester, Gloucestershire, GL1 2LZ Tel: 01452-309783
Fax: 01452-528493 Email: grcc@grcc.ndirect.co.uk
Leckhampton Local History Society
15 Arden Road, Leckhampton, Cheltenham, GL53 OHG
Web: www.geocities.com/llhsgl53
Moreton-In-Marsh & District Local History Society
Chapel Place, Loughborough, GL56 0QR Tel: 01451-830531

Newent Local History Society
Arron, Ross Road, Newent GL18 1BE Tel: 01531-821398
Painswick Local History Society
Canton House, New Street, Painswick, Gloucestershire, GL6
6XH Tel: 01452-812419 Fax: 01452-812419
Stroud Civic Society
Blakeford House, Broad St, Kings Stanley, Stonehouse GL10 3PN
Stroud Local History Society
Coombe House, 213 Slad Road, Stroud GL5 1RJ
Swindon Village Society
3 Swindon Hall, Swindon Village, Cheltenham, GL51 9QR
Tel: 01242-521723
Tewkesbury Historical Society
7 Moulder Road, Tewkesbury GL20 8EB Tel: 01684-292633

Gloucestershire -South Gloucestershire

Frenchay Tuckett Society & Local History Museum
247 Frenchay Park Road, Frenchay BS16 1LG
Tel: 0117-9569324 Email: raybulmer@compuserve.com
Web: www.ourworld.compuserve.com/homepages/raybulmer
Marshfield & District Local History Society
Garth Cottage, Weir Lane, Chippenham, Wiltshire, SN14 8NB
Tel: 01225-891829

Hampshire

Aldershot Historical & Archaeological Society
10 Brockenhurst R d, Aldershot GU11 3HH Tel: 01252 26589
Andover HIstory & Archaeology Society
140 Weyhill Road, Andover SP10 3BG Tel: 01264-324926
Basingstoke Archaeological & Historical Society
16 Scotney Road, Basingstoke, Hampshire, RG21 2SR
Tel: 01256 322090 Email: jtherring@aol.com
Bishops Waltham Museum Trust
8 Folly Field, Bishop s Waltham, Southampton, SO32 1EB
Tel: 01489-894970
Bitterne Local History Society
Heritage Centre, 225 Peartree Avenue, Bitterne, Southampton
Tel: 023-8044-4837 Fax: 023-8044-4837
Email: sheaf@sheafrs.freeserve.co.uk
Web: www.bitterne2.freeserve.co.uk
Botley & Curdridge Local History Society
38 Bryony Gardens, Horton Heath, Eastleigh, SO50 7PT
Fareham Local History Group
Wood End Lodge, Wood End, Wickham, Fareham PO17 6JZ
Fleet & Crookham Local History Group
5 Rosedene Gardens, Fleet, Hampshire, GU13 8NQ
Fordingbridge Historical Society
26 Lyster Road, Manor Park, Fordingbridge SP6 1QY
Tel: 01425-655417
Hampshire FC & A Society (Local History Section)
c/o Hampshire County Record Office, Sussex Street,
Winchester, Hampshire, SO23 8TH
Hampshire Field Club & Archaeological Society
PO Box 136, Hedge End, Hampshire, SO32 3WD
Web: www.fieldclub.hants.org.uk/
Havant Museum
56 East Street, Havant, Hampshire, P09 1BS
Tel: 023-9245-1155 Fax: 023-9249-8707
Email: musmcp@hants.gov.uk
Web: www.hants.gov.uk/museums
Lymington & District Historical Society
Larks Lees, Coxhill Boldre, Nr Lymington,SO41 8PS
Milford on Sea Historical Records Society
New House, New Road, Keyhaven, Lymington, S041 0TN
Milford-on-Sea Historical Record
New House, New Road, Keyhaven, Lymington S041 OTN
Newchurch Parish History Society
1 Mount Pleasant, Newport Road, Sandown, P036 OLS
North East Hampshire Historical & Archaeological Soc
36 High View Road, Farnborough, Hampshire, GU14 7PT
Tel: 01252-543023 Email: nehh@netscape.net
Web: www.hants.org/nehhas
Somborne & District Society
Forge House, Winchester Road, Kings Somborne,
Stockbridge, Hampshire, S020 6NY Tel: 01794-388742

Southampton Local History Forum
Specials Collections Library, Civic Centre, Southampton
SO14 7LW
Stubbington & Hill Head History
34 Anker Lane, Stubbington, Fareham PO14 3HE
Tel: 01329-664554
West End Local History Society
20 Orchards Way, West End, Southampton, S030 3FB
Tel: 023-8057-5244
Winchester Historical Association
66 St Cross Road, Winchester, SO23 9PS

Herefordshire

Eardisland Oral History Group
Eardisland, Leominster, Herefordshire, HR
Ewyas Harold & District Wea
C/O Hillside, Ewyas Harold, Hereford HR2 0HA
Kington History Society
Kington Library, 64 Bridge Street, Kington HR5 3BD
Tel: 01544-230427
Leominster Historical Society
Fircroft, Hereford Rd, Leominster HR6 8JU Tel: 01568-612874
Weobley & District Local History Society
Weobley Museum, Back Lane, Weobley HR4 8SG
Tel: 01544-340292

Hertfordshire

Abbots Langley Local History Society
80 Abbots Road, Abbots Langley, Hertfordshire, WD5 0BH
Codicote Local History Society
34 Harkness Way, Hitchin SG4 0QL Tel: 01462-622953
East Herts Archaeological Society
1 Marsh Lane, Stanstead Abbots, Ware SG12 8HH
Tel: 01920-870664
Harpenden & District Local History Society
The History Centre, 19 Arden Grove, Harpenden AL5 4SJ
Hertford & Ware Local History Society
10 Hawthorn Close, Hertford, SG14 2DT
Hertfordshire Archaeological Trust
The Seed Warehouse, Maidenhead Yard, The Wash, Hertford,
SG14 1PX Tel: 01992-558-170 Fax: 01992-553359
Hertfordshire Association for Local History
Lamb Cottage, Whitwell, nr Hitchin SG4 8JP Tel: 01438-871207
Hertfordshire Association for Local History
c/o 64 Marshalls Drive, St Albans, Hertfordshire, AL1 4RF
Tel: 01727-856250 Fax: 01727-856250
Email: ClareEllis@compuserve.com
Hertfordshire Record Society
119 Winton Drive, Croxley Green, Rickmansworth WD3 3QS
Tel: 01923-248581 Email: info@hrsociety.org.uk
Hitchin Historical Society
c/o Hitchin Museum, Hitchin, Hertfordshire, SG5 1EQ
Kings Langley Local History & Museum Society
c/o Kings Langley Library, The Nap, Kings Langley WD48ET
Tel: 01923-263205 & 01923-26410
Email: frankdavies4@hotmail.com &
alan@penwardens.freeserve.co.uk
London Colney Local History Society
51a St Annes Road, London Colney, Nr. St. Albans AL2 1PD
North Mymms Local History Society
89 Peplins Way, Brookmans Park, Hatfield AL9 7UT
Potters Bar & District Historical Society
23 Osborne Road, Potters Bar, Hertfordshire, EN6 IR2
Rickmansworth Historical Society
20 West Way, Rickmansworth, Hertfordshire, WD3 2EN
Tel: 01923-774998 Email: geoff@gmsaul.freeserve.co.uk
Royston & District Local History Society
8 Chilcourt, Royston SG8 9DD Tel: 01763-242677
South West Hertfordshire Archaeological & Historical Soc
29 Horseshoe Lane, Garston, Watford, WD2 6LN
St. Albans & Herts Architectural & Archaeological Society
24 Rose Walk, St Albans AL4 9AF Tel: 01727-853204
Welwyn & District Local History Society
9 York Way, Welwyn AL6 9LB Tel: 01438-716415

Welwyn Archaeological Society
The Old Rectory, 23 Mill Lane, Welwyn AL6 9EU
Tel: 01438-715300 Fax: 01438-715300

Hull

Hull Central Library Family & Local History Club
Hull Central Library, Albion Street, Kingston upon Hull, HU1
3TF Tel: 01482-616828 Fax: 01482-616827
Email: gareth.watkins@hullcc.gov.uk
Web: www.hullcc.gov.uk/genealogy/

Huntingdonshire

Huntingdonshire Local History Society
2 Croftfield Road, Godmanchester, Cambs PE18 8ED

Isle of Wight

Isle of Wight Natural History & Archaeological Society
Salisbury Gardens, Dudley Rd, Ventnor, Isle of Wight PO38 1EJ
Roots Family & Parish History
San Fernando, Burnt House Lane, Alverstone, Sandown, Isle
Of Wight, PO36 0HB, British Isles, Tel: 01-983-403060
Email: peters.sanfernando@tesco.net

Kent

Ashford Archaeological & Historical Society
9 Wainwright Place, Newtown, Ashford, TN24 0PF
Tel: 01233 631017
Canterbury Archaeology Society
Dane Court, Adisham, Canterbury, CT3 3LA
Council for Kentish Archaeology
3 Westholme, Orpington, Kent, BR6 0AN
Crayford Manor House Historical & Archaeological Soc
17 Swanton Road, Erith, Kent, DA8 1LP Tel: 01322-433480
Faversham Society
Fleur de Lis Heritage Centre & Museum
13 Preston Street, Faversham, Kent, ME13 8NS
Tel: 01795-534542 Fax: 01795-533261
Email: faversham@btinternet.com Web: www.faversham.org
Fawkham & District Historical Society
6 Nuthatch, New Barn, Longfield, Kent, DA3 7NS
Gravesend Historical Society
58 Vicarage Lane, Chalk, Gravesend, Kent, DA12 4TE
Tel: 01474-363998
Kent Archaeological Society
Three Elms, Woodlands Lane, Shorne, Gravesend DA12 3HH
Tel: 01474-822280 Email: ai_moffat@compuserve.com
Web: www.outworld.compuserve.com/homepages/ai.moffat
Kent History Federation
48 Beverley Avenue, Sidcup, Kent, DA15 8HE
Maidenhead Archeological & Historical Society
7c Lambourne Drive, Maidenhead, Kent, SL6 3HG
Maidstone Area Archaeological Group
14 The Quarter, Cranbrook Road, Staplehurst, TN12 0EP
Maidstone Historical Society
37 Bower Mount Rd, Maidstone ME16 8AX Tel: 01622 676472
Romney Marsh Research Trust
11 Caledon Terrace, Canterbury CT1 3JJ Tel: 012227-472490
Email: s.m.sweetinburgh.ac.uk Web: www.ukc.ac/mts/rmrt
Sandwich Local History Society
Clover Rise, 14 Stone Cross Lees, Sandwich, Kent, CT13
OBZ Tel: 01304-613476 Email: frankandrews@freenet.co.uk
Tonbridge Historical Society
8 Woodview Cresent, Hildenborough, Tonbridge, TN11 9HD
Tel: 01732-838698 Fax: 01732-838522
Email: s.broomfield@dial.pipex.com
Tonbridge History Society
8 Woodview Crescent, Hildenborough, Tonbridge, Kent,
TN11 9HD Tel: 01732-838698
Wealden Buildings Study Group
64 Pilgrims Way, East Otford, Sevenoaks, Kent, TN14 5QW

Lancashire

Aspull & Haigh Historical Society
3 Pennington Close, Aspull, Wigan, Lancashire, WN2 2SP

Blackburn Civic Society
20 Tower Road, Blackburn, Lancashire, BB2 5LE
Burnley Historical Society
66 Langdale Road, Blackburn BB2 5DW Tel: 01254-201162
Chadderton Historical Society
18 Moreton Street, Chadderton, Lancashire, OL9 0LP
Tel: 0161-652-3930 Web: www.chadderton-hs.freeuk.com
Ewecross History Society
Gruskholme, Bentham, Lancaster LA27AX Tel: 015242-61420
Fleetwood & District Historical
54 The Esplanade, Fleetwood, Lancashire, FY7 6QE
Garstang Historical & Archealogical Society
7 Rivermead Cabus, Garstang PR3 1SS Tel: 01995-604913
Lancashire & Cheshire Antiquarian Society
59 Malmesbury Road, Cheadle Hulme, Cheshire, SK8 7QL
Lancashire Family History/Heraldry Society
66 Glenluce Drive, Farringdon Park, Preston PRI 5TD
Lancashire History
4 Cork Road, Lancaster, Lancashire, LA1 4AJ
Lancashire Local History Federation
101 Todmorden Road, Littleborough OL15 9EB
Tel: 01706-379949 Email: secretary@lancashirehistory.co.uk
Web: www.lancashirehistory.co.uk
Lancashire Parish Register Society
188 Greenwood Crescent, Houghton Green, Warrington,
Cheshire, WA2 0EG Email: tobrien@freeuk.com
Web: www.genuki:org.uk/big/eng/LAN/lprs
Leyland Historical Society
172 Stanifield Lane, Farington; Leyland, Preston PR5 2QT
Littleborough Historical & Archaeological Society
8 Springfield Avenue, Littleborough LA15 9JR Tel: 01706 377685
Mourholme Local History Society
173a Main Street, Warton, Carnforth, Lancashire, LA5 9QF
Nelson Local History Society
5 Langholme Street, Nelson BB9 0RW Tel: 01282-699475
Saddleworth Historical Society
7 Slackcote, Delph, Oldham, OL3 5TW Tel: 01457-874530

Leicestershire

Desford & District Local History Group
Lindridge House, Lindridge Lane, Desford LE9 9FD
East Leake & District Local History
35 Sycamore Road, East Leake, Loughborough, LE12 6PP
Glenfield & Western Archaeological & Historical Group
50 Chadwell Road, Leicester, LE3 6LF Tel: 1162873220
Leicestershire Archaeological & Historical Society
The Guildhall, Leicester, LE1 5PQ Tel: 0116 2703031
Web: www.le.ac.uk/archaeology/lahs/lahs.html
Leicestershire Local History Council
c/o Leicestershire Record Office, Long St, Wigston Magna LE18 2AH
Vaughan Archaeological & Historical Society
c/o Vaughan College, St Nicholas Circle, Leicester, LE1 4LB

Lincolnshire

Alford Civic Trust/Manor House Museum Alford
Manor House Museum, West Street, Alford, Lincolnshire,
LN13 9DJ Tel: 01507-463073
Lincoln Record Society
Lincoln Cathedral Library, TheCathedral, Lincoln, LN2 1PS
Society for Lincolnshire History & Archaeology
Jews Court, Steep Hill, Lincoln, Lincolnshire, LN2 1LS
Tel: 01522-521337 Fax: 01522-521337
South Holland Family & Local History Group
54 Wygate Road, Spalding, Lincolnshire, PE11 1NT
Stamford Historical Society
14 Castle Rise, Belmesthorpe, Stamford, PE9 4JL
Tel: 01780 64213

London - see Page 185

Manchester

Denton Local History Society
94 Edward Street, Denton, Manchester, M34 3BR

Stretford Local History Society
26 Sandy Lane, Stretford, Manchester, M32 9DA
Tel: 0161-283-9434 Email: mjdawson@cwcom.net
Web: www.maurice.mcmail.com

Merseyside

Birkdale & Ainsdale Historical Research Society
20 Blundell Drive, Birkdale, Southport, PR8 4RG
Historic Society of Lancashire & Cheshire
East Wing Flat, Arley Hall, Northwich, Cheshire, CW9 6NA
Tel: 01565-777231 Fax: 01565-777465
Maghull & Lydiate Local History Society
15 Brendale Avenue, Maghull, Liverpool, L31 7AX
Merseyside Archaeological Society
20 Osborne Rd, Formby, Liverpool L37 6AR Tel: 01704 871802

Middlesex

Borough of Twickenham Local History Society
258 Hanworth Road, Hounslow, Middlesex, TW3 3TY
British Deaf History Society
288 Bedfont Lane, Feltham, Middlesex, TW14 9NU
Edmonton Hundred Historical Society
7 Park Crescent, Enfield EN2 6HT Tel: 020-8367-2211
Hounslow & District History Society
16 Orchard Avenue, Heston, TW5 0DU Tel: 020-8570-4264
Middlesex Heraldry Society
4 Croftwell, Harpeden, Hertfordshire, AL5 1JG
Northwood & Eastcote Local History Society
7 The Greenway, Ickenham, Uxbridge, Ruislip UBLO 8LS
Pinner Local History Society
8 The Dell, Pinner, Middlesex, HA5 3EW Tel: 0208-866-1918
Email: mwg@pinnerLhs.freeserveco.uk
Web: www.pinnerLhs.freeserve.co.uk/index.html
Ruislip Northwood & Eastcote Local History Society
7 The Greenway, Ickenham, Uxbridge UB10 8LS
Sunbury & Shepperton Local
95 Gaston Way, Shepperton, Middlesex, TW17 8ET

Midlands - West Midlands

Aldridge Local History Society
45 Erdington Road, Walsall, West Midlands, WS9 8UU
Association of Friends of Waterloo Committee
2 Coburn Drive, Four Oaks, Sutton Coldfield B75 5NT
Tel: 0121-308-4103 Email: jwhite02@globalnet.co.uk
Birmingham War Research Society
43 Norfolk Place, Kings Norton, Birmingham B30 3LB
Tel: 0121-459-9008 Fax: 0121-459-8128
Black Country Local History Consortium
Black Country Living Museum, Tipton Road, Dudley, West
Midlands, DY1 4SQ Tel: 0121-557-9643
Black Country Society
PO Box 71, Kingswinford, West Midlands, DY6 9YN
Romsley & Hunnington History Society
Port Erin, Green Lane, Chapmans Hill, Romsley, Halesowen,
West Midlands, B62 0HB Tel: 01562-710295
Email: ejhumphreys@compuserve.com
Smethwick Local Hist Society
47 Talbot Road, Smethwick, Warley B66 4DX
Smethwick Local History Society
94 Victoria Court, Messenger Road, Smethwick, B66 3DY

Norfolk

Blakeney Area Historical Society
Hillside, Morston Road, Blakeney NR25 7BG
Tel: 01263-740589
Federation of Norfolk Hist & Arch Organisations
14 Beck Lane, Horsham St Faith, Norwich NR10 3LD
Feltwell (Historical & Archaeological) Society
16 High Street, Feltwell, Thetford IP26 Tel: 01842 828448
Email: petefeltwell@tinyworld.co.uk Museum-The Beck,
Feltwell - limited opening
Narborough Local History Society
101 Westfields, Narborough, Kings Lynn, Norfolk, PE32 ISY
Norfolk & Norwich Archaeological Society
30 Brettingham Avenue, Cringleford, Norwich NR4 6XG
Tel: 01603 455913

Norfolk Archaeological & Historical Research Group
50 Cotman Road, Norwich, NR1 4AH Tel: 01603 435470
Norfolk Heraldry Society
22 Cintra Road, Norwich, NR1 4AE Tel: 01603-436149

Northamptonshire

Bozeat Historical & Archaeological Society
44 Mile Street, Bozeat, NN9 7NB Tel: 01933 663647
Brackley & District Historical Society
32 Church Lane, Evenley, Brackley NNL3 5SG
Brackley & District History Society
32 Church Lane, Evenley, Brackley NN13 5SG Tel: 01280-703508
Higham Chichele Society
3 Bramley Close, Rushden, Northamptonshire, NN10 6RL
Houghtons & Brafield Local History Society
C/O 5 Lodge Road, Little Houghton, NN7 1AE
Northamptonshire Association for Local History
12 Frog Lane, Upper Boddington, Daventry NN11 6DJ
Northamptonshire Record Society
Wootton Park Hall, Northampton NN4 8BQ Tel: 01604-762297
Rushden & District History Society
25 Byron Crescent, Rushden, Northamptonshire, NN10 6BL
Email: rdhs.rushden@virgin.net
Web: www.freespace.virgin.net/bob.safford/rdhs/home.htm
Weedon Bec History Society
35 Oak Street, Weedon, Northampton, NN7 4RR
Houghtons & Brafield History
5 Lodge Road, Little Houghton, Northamptonshire, NN7 IAE
Northamptonshire Association for Local History*
Clack Mills, Lodge Road, Little Houghton, Northamptonshire,
NN7 1AE
West Haddon Local History Group
Bramley House, 12 Guilsborough Rd, West Haddon NN6 7AD

Northumberland

Association of Northumberland Local History Societies*
c/o Centre for Continuing Education, King George VI
Building, Newcastle upon Tyne University, Newcastle upon
Tyne, NEl 7RU
Felton & Swarland Local History Society
23 Benlaw Grove, Felton, Morpeth NE65 9NG Tel: 01670-787476
Hexham Local History Society
Dilstone, Burswell Villas, Hexham NE46 3LD Tel: 01434-603216
Morpeth Antiquarian Society
14 Southgate Wood, Morpeth, Northumberland, NE61 2EN
Morpeth Nothumbrian Gathering
Westgate House, Dogger Bank, Morpeth NE61 1RF
Prudhoe & District Local History Society
Prudhoe Community Enterprise Office, 82 Front Street,
Prudhoe, Northumberland, NR42 5PU
Stannington Local History Society
Glencar House, 1 Moor Ln, Stannnington, Morpeth NE61 6EA
War Memorials Survey - NE Bilsdale, Ulgham, Morpeth,
Northumberland, NE61 3AR Tel: 01670-790465
Email: gjb@bilsdale.freeserve.com

Nottinghamshire

Beeston & District Local History Society
16 Cumberland Ave, Beeston NG9 4DH Tel: 0115-9223008
Keyworth & District Local History Society
Innisfree, Thelda Avenue, Keyworth, Nottingham NG12 5HU
Tel: 0115-9372908 Fax: 0115-9372908
Nottingham Historical & Archaeological Society
48 Banks Road, Toton, Beaston NG9 6HA Tel: 0115 9734284
Nottinghamshire Local History Association
128 Sandhill Street, Worksop, Nottinghamshire, S80 1SY
Tel: 01909-488878, or 07773-887803
Numismatic Society of Nottinghamshire
Nottinghamshire Tel: 0115-925-7674
Retford & District Historical & Archaeological Society
Cambridge House, 36 Alma Road, Retford DN22 6LW
Tel: 01777-701902 Fax: 01777-707784
Email: joan@j.a+esewell.demon.co.uk
Ruddington Local History Society
36 Brook View Drive, Keyworth, Nottingham, NG12 5JN

Thoroton Society of Nottinghamshire
59 Briar Gate, Long Eaton, Nottingham NG10 4BQ
Tel: 0115-972-6590 Email: thoroton@keithgoodman.com
Web: www.cthulu.demon.co.uk/thoroton.htm

Oxfordshire

Abingdon Area Archaeological & Historical Society
17 Fitzharrys Road, Abingdon OX14 1EL Tel: 01235-531566
Ashbury Local History Society
Claremont, Ashbury, Swindon, Wiltshire, SN6 8LN
Banbury History Society
c/o Banbury Museum, 8 Horsefair, Banbury, OX16 OAA
Blewbury Local History Group
Spring Cottage, Church Rd, Blewbury, Didcot OX11 9PY
Tel: 01235-850427 Email: audrey@blewbury427.freeserve.co.uk
Chinnor Historical & Archealogical Society
7 Cherry Tree Road, Chinnor, Oxfordshire, 0X9 4QY
Cumnor History Society
4 Kenilworth Road, Cumnor, Nr Oxford OX2 9QP
Faringdon Archaeological & Historical Society
1 Orchard Hill, Faringdon, Oxfordshire, SN7 7EH
Email: fdahs@bigfoot.com
Longworth Local History Society
10 Bellamy Close, Southmoor, Oxfordshire, OX13 5AB
Oxfordshire Architectural & Historical Society
c/o Centre for Oxfordshire Studies, Westgate, Oxford,
Oxfordshire, OX1 1DJ Web: www.demon.co.uk/adodd/oahs
Oxfordshire Local History Association
12 Meadow View, Witney OX8 6TY Tel: 01993-778345
Oxfordshire Local History Society
3 The Square, Aynho, Nr Banbury, Oxfordshire, 0X17 3BL
Oxfordshire Record Society
Bodelian Library, Oxford, Oxfordshire, OX1 3BG
Wallingford Historical & Archaeological Society
Wallingford Museum Flint House, 52a High Street,
Wallingford, Oxfordshire, OX1O 0DB Tel: 01491 837720
Wychwoods Local History Society
Littlecott, Honeydale Farm, Shipton-Under-Wychwood,
Chipping Norton, Oxfordshire, OX7 6BJ

Plymouth

Wembury Amenity Society
5 Cross Park Road, Wembury, Plymouth, PL9 OEU

Rutland

Rutland Local History & Record Society
c/o Rutland County Museum, Catmos Street, Oakham,
Rutland, LE15 6HW Tel: 01572-723654 Fax: 01572-757576

Shropshire

Cleobury Mortimer Historical Society
24 High St, Cleobury Mortimer, Kidderminster, DY14 8BY
Tel: 01299-270110 Fax: 01299-270110
Email: history@mbaldwin.free-online.co.uk
Shropshire Archaeological & Historical Society
Lower Wallop Farm, Westbury, Shrewsbury SY5 9RT
Tel: 0743 891215 Fax: 01743 891705
Email: walloparch@farming.co.uk
Whitchurch History & Archaeology Group
The Field House, Wirswall, Whitchurch SY13 4LA
Tel: 01948 662623

Somerset

Axbridge Archaeological & Local History Society
King John s Hunting Lodge, The Square, Axbridge, Somerset,
BS26 2AR Tel: 01934 732012
Bathford Society
36 Bathford Hill, Bathford, Somerset, BA1 7SL
Castle Cary & District Museum and Preservation Society
1 Fir Tree Cottages, Lower Ansford, Castle Carey BA7 7YY
Oakhill & Ashwick Local History Society
Bramley Farm, Bath Road, Oakhill, Somerset, BA3 5AF
Tel: 01749-840241 Fax: 01749-841195
Somerset Archaeological & Natural History Society
Taunton Castle, Taunton, Somerset, TA1 4AD
Tel: 01823-272429 Fax: 01823-272429

Somerset Record Society
Somerset Studies Library, Paul Street, Taunton, Somerset,
TA1 3XZ Tel: 01823-340300 Fax: 01823-340301
South East Somerset Archaeological & Historical Society
Abbascombe Barn, Lilly Lane, Templecombe BA8 OHN
Tel: 01963 371163
South Petherton Local History
Crossbow, Hele Lane, South Petherton, Somerset, TA13 5DY
South Petherton Local History Group
Cobbetts Droveway, South Petherton TA13 5DA
Tel: 01460-240252
Yeovil Archaeological & Local History Society
Plantagenet Chase, Yeovil, Somerset Tel: 01935 78258

Somerset - North Somerset

Nailsea & District Local History Society
13 Fosse Lane, Nailsea, North Somerset, BS48 2AR

Staffordshire

Berkswich Local History Group
1 Greenfield Road, Stafford, Staffordshire, ST17 OPU
Landor Society
38 Fortescue Lane, Rugeley WS15 2AE Tel: 01889-582709
Lawton Heritage Society
9 Woodgate Avenue, Church Lawton, Stoke on Trent, ST7
3EF Tel: 01270-878386 Email: dmcall12280@aol.com
Ridware History Society
Priory Farm, Blithbury, Nr. Rugeley WSI5 3JA Tel: 01889-504269
Stafford Historical & Civic Society
86 Bodmin Avenue, Weeping Cross, Stafford, Staffordshire,
ST17 0EQ Tel: 01785-612194 Email: esj@supanet.com
Staffordshire Archaeological & Historical Society
6 Lawson Close, Aldridge, Walsall W59 0RX Tel: 01922-452230
Staffordshire Local Studies Forum
PO Box 23, First Office, Stafford ST17 4AY Tel: 01785 278353

Suffolk

Brett Valley History Society
17 Manor Road, Bildeston, Ipswich, Suffolk, IP7 7BG
Elmswell Parish Council Village Recorder
Hill Court, Church Road, Elmswell, Suffolk, P30 9DY
Essex Archealogical & Historical Congress
Lowe Hill House, Stratford St Mary, Suffolk, C07 6JX
Framlingham & Dist Local History & Preservation Soc
43 College Road, Framlingham, Suffolk
Lowestoft Archaeological & Local History Society
1 Cranfield Close, Pakefield, Lowestoft NR33 7EL
Tel: 01502-586143
Suffolk Institute of Archaeology & History
Roots, Church Lane, Playford, Ipswich, IP6 9DS
Tel: 01473-624556
Suffolk Local History Council
Suffolk Community Resource Centre, 2 Wharfdale Road,
Ipswich, Suffolk, IP1 4LG

Surrey

Addlestone History Society
53 Liberty Lane, Addlestone, Weybridge, Surrey, KT15 1NQ
Beddington Carshalton and Wallington Arch Society
57 Brambledown Road, Wallington, Surrey, SM6 0TF
Tel: 020-8647-8540
Bourne Society
54 Whyteleafe Road, Caterham, Surrey, CR3 5EF
Carshalton Society
43 Denmark Road, Carshalton, Surrey, SM5 2JE
Croydon Natural History & Scientific Society Ltd
96A Brighton Road, South Croydon, Surrey, CR2 6AD
Tel: 020-8668-6909 Web: www.croydon.gov.uk/cnhss/
Domestic Buildings Research Group (Surrey)
Meadow Cottage, Brook Hill, Albury, Guildford GUS 9DJ
Farnham & District Museum Society
Tanyard House, 13a Bridge Square, Farnham GU9 7QR
Friends of the Public Record Office
The Public Record Office, Ruskin Avenue, Kew, Richmond,
Surrey, TW9 4DU Tel: 020-8876-3444 Ext 2226
Email: friends-pro@pro.gov.uk
Web: www.pro.gov.uk/friends/default.htm

Guildford Archaeology Group
6 St Omer Road, Guildford, GU1 2DB Tel: 01483 532201
History of Thursley Society
50 Wyke Lane, Ash, Aldershot, Hampshire, GU12 6EA
Email: norman.ratcliffe@ntlworld.com
Web: www.home.clara.net/old.norm/thursley
Leatherhead District Local History Society
Leatherhead Museum, 64 Church Street, Leatherhead, Surrey,
KT22 8DP Tel: 01372-386348
Nonsuch Antiquarian Society
17 Seymour Avenue, Ewell, Epsom, Surrey, KT17 2RP
Tel: 020-8393-0531
Richmond Local History Society
9 Bridge Road, St Margarets, Twickenham, TWI IRE
Send & Ripley History Society
St Georges Farm House, Ripley, Surrey, GU23 6AF
Tel: 01483-222107 Fax: 01483-222107
Email: slatford@johnone.freeserve.co.uk
Shere Gomshall & Peaslake Local History Society
Twiga Lodge, Wonham Way, Gomshall, Guildford, GU5 9NZ
Tel: 01483-202112 Email: twiga@gomshall.freeserve.co.uk
Surrey Archaeological Society
Castle Arch, Guildford, Surrey, GU1 3SX Tel: 01483-532454
Fax: 01483-532454 Email: surreyarch@compuserve.com
Web: www.ourworld.compuserve.com/homepages/surreyarch
Surrey Local History Council
Guildford Institute, University of Surrey, Ward Street,
Guildford, Surrey, GU1 4LH
Surrey Record Society
Surrey History Centre, 130 Goldsworth Road, Woking,
Surrey, GU21 1ND
Walton & Weybridge Local History Society
67 York Gardens, Walton-on-Thames, Surrey, KT12 3EN
Walton On The Hill and District Local History Society
5 Russell Close, Walton On The Hill, Tadworth, Surrey,
KT2O 7QH Tel: 01737-812013

Sussex

Forest Row History Group
32 Freshfield Bank, Forest Row, Sussex, RH18 5HG
Lewes Archaeological Group
Rosemary Cottage, High Street, Barcombe, near Lewes, BN8
5DM Tel: 01273 400878
Sussex Archaeological Society
Barbican House, 169 High Street, Lewes, East Sussex, BN7
1YE Tel: 01273-405738 Email: library@sussexpost.co.uk
Web: www.sussexpost.co.uk
Sussex History Forum
Barbican House, 169 High Street, Lewes, East Sussex, BN7
1YE Tel: 01273-405736 Fax: 01273-486990
Email: research@sussexpast.co.uk
Web: www.sussexpast.co.uk
Sussex History Study Group
Colstock, 43 High Street, Ditchling, BN5 8SY
Sussex Past
Anne of Cleves House, 52 Southover High Street, Lewes,
BN7 1JA Tel: 01273-405738 Fax: 01273-486990
Email: library@sussexpast.co.uk Web: www.sussexpast.co.uk
Sussex Record Society
West Sussex Record Office, County Hall, Chichester, West
Sussex, PO19 1RN Tel: 01243-75600 Fax: 01243-533959
Email: peter.wilkinson@westsussex.gov.uk

Sussex - East Sussex

Blackboys & District Historical Society
6 Palehouse Common, Framfield, Nr Uckfield, East Sussex,
TN22 5QY
Brighton & Hove Archaeological Society
115 Braeside Avenue, Patcham, Brighton BN1 8SQ
Eastbourne Natural History & Archaeological Society
11 Brown Jack Avenue, Polegate BN26 5HN Tel: 01323 486014
Forest Row Local History Group
32 Freshfield Bank, Forest Row, East Sussex, RH18 HG
Friends of East Sussex Record Office
The Maltings, Castle Precincts, Lewes, East Sussex, BN7
1YT Tel: 01273-482349 Fax: 01273-482341
Web: www.esrole.freeserve.co.uk

Maresfield Parish Historical
Hockridge House, London Road, Maresfield, East Sussex,
TN22 2EH Tel: 01825-765386
Peacehaven & Telscombe Historical Society
2 The Compts, Peacehaven, East Sussex, BN1O 75Q
Tel: 01273-588874 Fax: 01273-589881
Email: sbernard@mcafeemail.com
Uckfield & District Preservation Society
8 Cambridge Way, Uckfield, East Sussex, TN22 2AD
Warbleton & District History Group
Hillside Cottage, Bodle Street Green, Hailsham, East Sussex,
BN27 4RG Tel: 01323-832339

Sussex - West Sussex

Angmering Society
Holly Lodge, Rectory Lane, Angmering BNI6 4JU
Tel: 01903-775811
Beeding & Bramber Local History Society
23 Primrose Court, Goring Road, Steyning, West Sussex,
BN44 3FY Tel: 01904-81-6480
Billingshurst Local History
27 Carpenters, Billingshurst, West Sussex, RH14 9RA
Bolney Local History Society
Challoners, Jeremy s Lane, Bolney, Haywards RH17 5QE
Chichester Local History Society
20 Cavendish Street, Chichester, West Sussex, P019 3BS
Horsham Museum Society
Horsham Museum, 9 The Causeway, Horsham, West Sussex,
RH12 1HE Tel: 01403-254959
Mid Sussex Local History Group
Woodborough, Stockport Road, Balcombe, Sussex, RH17
6LH Tel: 01444-811275 Email: marks@marksm.fsnet.co.uk
Steyning Society
30 St Cuthmans Road, Steyning, West Sussex, BN44 3RN
West Sussex Archives Society
c/o West Sussex Record Office, County Hall, Orchard Street,
Chichester, PO19 1RN Tel: 01243-753600/753617, or
01243-533911 Fax: 01243-533959
Email: records.office@westsussex.gov.uk
Web: www.westsussex.gov.uk/cs/ro/rohome.htm
Wivelsfield Historical Society
Middlefield Cottage, Fox Hill, Haywards Heath RH16 4QY

Tyne & Wear

Association of Northumberland Local History Societies
Centre for Lifelong Learning, King George VI Building,
University of Newcastle upon Tyne, Newcastle upon Tyne,
NE1 7RU Tel: 0191-222-7458 & 0191-222-5680
Cullercoats Local History Society
35 St Georges Road, Cullercoats, North Shields, Tyne and
Wear, NE3O 3JZ Tel: 0191-252-7042
Northumbria Historic Churches Trust
The Vicarage, South Hylton, Sunderland SR4 0QB
Society of Antiquaries of Newcastle upon Tyne
Black Gate, Castle Garth, Newcastle upon Tyne, NE1 1RQ
Tel: 0191-261-5390, or 0771-216-0431

Warwickshire

Alcester & District Local History Society
43 Seymour Road, Alcester, Warwickshire, B49 6JY
Dugdale Society
The Shakespeare Centre, Stratford-on-Avon CV37 6QW
Kineton & District Local History Group
The Glebe House, Lighthorne Road, Kineton, Warwickshire,
CV35 0JL Tel: 01926-640298 Fax: 01926-640298
Email: p.holdsworth@virgin.net
Shakespeare Birthplace Trust - Records Office
Henley Street, Stratford Upon Avon CV37 6QW
Tel: 01789-201816, or 01789-204016 Fax: 01789-296083
Email: records@shakespeare.org.uk
Web: www.shakespeare.org.uk
Warwickshire Local History Society
9 Willes Terrace, Leamington Spa, Warwickshire, CV31 1DL

Watford

Watford & District Industrial History Society
79 Kingswood Road, Garston, Watford, WD2 6EF

Wiltshire

Marshfield & District Local
150 High Street, Marshfield, Chippenham SN14 8LU
Mid Thorngate Society
Yewcroft, Stoney Batter, West Tytherley, Salisbury, SP5 ILD
Redlynch & District Local History Society
Hawkstone, Church Hill, Redlynch, Salisbury, SP5 2PL
Email: pat.mill@btinternet.com
Salisbury Civic Society
4 Chestnut Close, Laverstock, Salisbury, Wiltshire, SP1 1SL
Swindon Society
4 Lakeside, Swindon, Wiltshire, SN3 1QE Tel: 01793-521910
Trowbridge Civic Society
43 Victoria Road, Trowbridge, Wiltshire, BA14 7LD
Wiltshire Archaelogical & Natural History Society
41 Long Street, Devizes SN1O INS Tel: 01380-727369
Fax: 01380-722150 Email: wanhs@wiltshireheritage.org.uk
Wiltshire Archaeological & Natural History Society
Wiltshire Heritage Library, 41 Long Street, Devizes, Wiltshire,
SN10 5JH Tel: 01380-727369 Fax: 01380-722150
Wiltshire Local History Forum
Tanglewood, Laverstock Park, Salisbury SP1 1QJ
Tel: 01722-328922
Wiltshire Record Society
County Record Office, Libraries HQ, Trowbridge, Wiltshire,
BA14 8BS Tel: 01225-713136

Worcestershire

Bewdley Historical Research Group
8 Ironside Close, Bewdley, Worcestershire, DY12 2HX
Tel: 01299-403582 Email: arp@handbag.com
Droitwich History & Archaeology Society
45 Moreland Rd, Droitwich Spa WR9 8RN
Tel: 01905-773420
Feckenham Forest History Society
Lower Grinsty Farm House, Callow Hill, Redditch, B97 5PJ
Tel: 01527-542063 Fax: 01527-542063
Kidderminster & District Archaeology & History Society
178 Birmingham Road, Kidderminster DY10 2SJ
Kidderminster & District Local History Society
39 Cardinal Drive, Kidderminster, Worcestershire, DY10 4RZ
Email: bob.millward@virgin.net
Kidderminster Field Club
C/O 7 Holmwood Avenue, Kidderminster DYL 1 6DA
Pershore Heritage & History Society
6 Abbey Croft, Pershore, Worcestershire, WR10 1JQ
Wolverley & Cockley Historical Society
18120 Caunsall Road, Cookley, Nr Kidderminster
Wolverley & Coekley Historical
18/20 Caunsall Road, Cookley, Kidderminster DY11 5YB
Worcester Archaeological Service
Woodbury Hall, University College Worcester, Henwick
Grove, Worcester WR2 6AJ Tel: 01905-855455
Fax: 01905-29054 Email: archaeology@worcestershire.gov.uk
Web: www.worcestershire.gov.uk/archaeology
Worcestershire Archaeological Society
The Greyfriars, Friar St Worcester, WR1 2LZ Tel: 01905-23571
Worcestershire Local History Forum
45 Moreland Road, Droitwich WR9 8RN Tel: 01905-773420
Worcestershire Nd. Archealogical & Local History Society
19 Grayling Close, Broomhall, Worcestershire, WR5 3HY

Yorkshire

Yorkshire Archaeological Society
Claremont, 23 Clarendon Road, Leeds LS2 9NZ
Tel: 0113-245-6342, or 0113-245-7910 Fax: 0113-244-1979
Email: j.heron@sheffield.ac.uk Web: www.yas.org.uk
Yorkshire Archaeological Soc - Local History Study Section
Email: blong@historydb.force9.co.uk
Yorkshire Heraldry Society
35 Holmes Carr Road, West Bessacarr, Doncaster, South
Yorkshire, DN4 7HJ Tel: 01302-539993

Yorkshire - East Yorkshire

Boothferry Family & Local History Group
17 Airmyn Avenue, Goole, DN14 6PF

East Riding Archaeological Society
455 Chanterland Avenue, Hull, HU5 4AY Tel: 01482 445232
East Yorkshire Local History Society
13 Oaktree Drive, Molescroft, Beverley, HU17 7BB

Yorkshire - North Yorkshire

Northallerton & District Historical Society
17 Thistle Close, Romanby Park, Northallerton DL7 8FF
Poppleton History Society
Russett House, The Green, Upper Poppleton, York YO26 6DR
Tel: 01904-798868 Fax: 01904-613330
Email: susan.major@virgin.net
Web: www.onwards.to/poppleton-history
Ripon Prison & Police Museum
Ripon Museum Trust (Contact address), St Marygate, Ripon
HG4 1LX Tel: 01765-690799 24hr answering
Tel: 01765-690799 Email: ralph.lindley@which.net
Museum located at Allhallowgate, Ripon
Scarborough Archaeological & Historical Society
10 Westbourne Park, Scarborough, YO12 4AT
Tel: 01723-354237 Email: archaeology@scarborough.co.uk
Snape Local History Group
Garthland, Snape, Bedale, North Yorkshire, DL8 2TF
Tel: 01677-470769 Email: debbie.fiona@ukgateway.net
Stokesley & District Local History Study Group
21 Cleveland Avenue, Stokesley, North Yorkshire, TS9 5EZ
Upper Wharfdale Museum Society & Folk Museum
The Square, Grassington, North Yorkshire, BD23 5AU
Upper Wharfedale Field Society (Local History Section)
Brookfield, Hebden nr Grassington, Skipton, North Yorkshire,
BD23 5DX Tel: 01756-752012

Yorkshire - South Yorkshire

Bentley with Arksey Heritage Society
45 Finkle Street, Bentley, Doncaster DN5 0RP
Doncaster Group of the Yorkshire Archaeological Society
Merrylees, 1b Ellers Road, Doncaster, DN4 7BE Tel: 01302
531581 Email: acruse@globalnet.co.uk
Greneside & District Local History Group
50 St Michael s Road, Ecclesfield, Sheffield, S35 9YN
South Yorkshire Archaeology Unit & Museum Bld
Ellin Street, Sheffield Tel: 0114 2734230

Yorkshire - West Yorkshire

Halifax Antiquarian Society
7 Hyde Park Gardens, Haugh Shaw Road, Savile Park,
Halifax, West Yorkshire, HX1 3AH Tel: 01422-250780
Kippax & District History Society
8 Hall Park Croft, Kippax , Leeds LS5 7OF
Lowertown Old Burial Ground Trust
16 South Close, Guisley, Leeds, West Yorkshire, LS20 8TD
Olicana Historical Society
54 Kings Road, Ilkley, West Yorkshire, LS29 9AT
Tel: 01943-609206
Ossett & District Historical Society
29 Prospect Road, Ossett, West Yorkshire Tel: Ossett 279449
Wetherby & District Historical Society
27 Marston Way, Wetherby, West Yorkshire, LS22 6XZ

Yorkshire - York

Archaeological Resource Centre - York
St.Saviour Church, St Saviourgate, York, YO1 8NN
Tel: 01904-654324
Email: enquiries.arc.yat@yorkarch.demon.co.uk
Web: www.jorvik-viking-centre.co.uk

WALES

Abergele Field Club and Historical Society
Rhyd y Felin, 47 Bryn Twr, Abergele LL22 8DD
Tel: 01745-832497
Abertillery & Dist Museum Society
5 Harcourt Terrace, Glandwr Street, Abertillery NP3 1TS
Abertillery & District Museum
5 Harcourt Terrace, Glandwr Street, Abertillery NP3 ITS

Carmarthenshire Antiquarian Society

Ty Picton, Llansteffan, Carmarthenshire, SA33 5JG
Tel: 01267-241727
Ceredigion Antiquarian Society
Henllys, Lon Tyllwyd, Llanfarian, Aberystwyth, Ceredigion SY23 4UH
Clwyd-Powys Archaeological Trust
7A Church Street, Welshpool, Powys, SY21 7DL
Tel: 01938-553670 Fax: 01938-552179
Email: trust@cpat.org.uk Web: www.cpat.org.uk
Cymdeithas Hanes Beddgelert
Creua, Llanfrothen, Penrhyndeudraeth, Gwynedd, LL48 6SH,
Tel: 01766-770534
Denbighshire Historical Society
1 Green Park, Erddig, Wrexham, LL13 7YE
Flintshire History Society
69 Pen-y-Maes Avenue, Rhyl, Denbighshire, LL18 4ED,
Tel: 01745-332220
Friends of The Clwyd Archives
16 Bryntirion Avenue, Rhyl, LL18 3NP Tel: 01745-342168
Glamorgan History Society
7 Gifford Close, Two Locks, Cwmbran, NP44 7NX
Tel: 07967-139256 Email: rosemary_hewlett@yahoo.co.uk
Gwendraeth Valley Hist Society
19 Grugos Ave, Pontyberem, Llanelli, Carms SA14 5AF,
Gwent Local History Council
8 Pentonville, Newport, Gwent, NP9 5XH Tel: 01633-213229
Fax: 01633-221812 Email: byron.grubb@gavowales.org.uk
Kenfig Society
6 Locks Lane, Porthcawl, CF36 3HY Tel: 01656-782351
Email: terry.robbins@virgin.net
Web: http://freespace.virgin.net/terry.robbins/
Llantrisant & District Local History Society
Cerrig Llwyd, Lisvane Road, Lisvane, Cardiff, CF14 0SG,
Tel: 029-207-56151 Email: BDavies203@aol.com
Merioneth Historical & Record Society - Cymdeithas Hanes a Clofrodion Sir Feirionnydd
Archifdy Meirion Cae Penarlag, Dolgellau, Gwynedd, LL40 2YB Tel: 01341-424444 Fax: 01341-424505
Merthyr Tydfil Historical Society
c/o Ronamar, Ashlea Drive, Twynyrodyn, Merthyr Tydfil, Mid Glamorgan, CF47 0NY Tel: 01685-385871
Newport Local History Society
72 Risca Road, Newport, South Wales, NP20 4JA
Pentyrch & District Local History Society
34 Castell Coch View, Tongwynlais, Cardiff, CF15 7LA,
Pontypool Local History Society
24 Longhouse Grove, Henllys, Cwmbran, Gwent, NP44 6HQ,
Tel: 01633-865662
Radnorshire Society
Pool House, Discoed, Presteigne, Powys, LD8 2NWEmail: sadie@cole.kc3ltd.co.uk
Ruthin Local History Group
27 Tan y Bryn, Llanbdr DC, Ruthin, Denbighsire, LL15 1HH,
Tel: 01824-702632 Fax: 01824-702632
Email: gwynnemorris@btinternet.com
South Wales Record Society
12 The Green, Radyr, Cardiff, CF15 8BR
Wrexham Maelor Historical Society
37 Park Avenue, Wrexham, LL12 7AL

ISLE OF MAN

Isle of Man Natural History & Antiquarian Society
Ballacrye Stream Cottage, Ballaugh, Isle of Man, IM7 5EB,
Tel: 01624-897306
Isle of Man Natural History & Local History Society
Argan Peveril Avenue, Peel, Isle Of Man, MS

ISLE OF WIGHT

St Helens Historical Society
Gloddaeth, Westfield Road, St. Helens, Ryde Isle Of Wight,
PO33 LUZ

CHANNEL ISLANDS - JERSEY

Societe Jersiase
7 Pier Road, St Helier, Jersey, JE2 4XW
Email: societe@siciete-jersiaise.org
Web: www.societe-jersiaise.org

SCOTLAND

Abertay Historical Society
27 Pitcairn Road, Downfield, Dundee, DD3 9EE
Tel: 01382-858701
Ayrshire Federation of Historical Societies
11 Chalmers Road, Ayr, KA7 2RQ
Bridge of Weir History Society
41 Houston Road, Bridge Of Weir, Renfrewshire, PA11 3QR
Cawdor Heritage Group
Wester Barevan, Cawdor, Nairn, IV12 5XU
Email: 106637,3442 (compuserve)
Dunning Parish History Society
May Cottage, Newtown-Of-Pitcairns, Dunning, Perth, PH2 0SL
Friends of Dundee City Archives
c/o Archive & Record Office, 21 City Square, Dundee, DD1 3BY, Scotland, Tel: 01382-434494 Fax: 01382-434666
Email: richard.cullen@dundeecity.gov.uk
Web: www.dundeecity.gov.uk/dcchtml/sservices/archives.html
Linlithgow Union Canal Society
Manse Road Basin, Linlithgow, West Lothian, EH49 6AJ,
Tel: 01506-671215 (Answering unit) Email: lucs@linnet.co.uk
Web: www.linet.co.uk/lucs
Monklands Heritage Society
141 Cromarty Road, Cairnhill, Airdrie, ML6 9RZ
Paisley Philosophical Institution
388 Glasgow Road, Paisley, Renfrewshire, PAL 3BG
Renfrewshire Local History Forum
388 Glasgow Road, Paisley, Renfrewshire, PA1 3BG,
Scotland, Tel: 0141-883-8685 Web: www.rlhfas.org.uk
Scottish Local History Forum
45 High Street, Linlithgow, West Lothian, EH49 7ED
Tel: 01506-844649 Fax: 0131-260-6610
Email: chantal.hamill@dial.pipex.com
Scottish Museums Council
County House, 20/22 Torphichen Street, Edinburgh, EH3 8JB,
Scotland, Tel: 0131-229-7465 Fax: 0131-229-2728
Email: inform@scottishmuseums.org.uk
Web: www.scottishmuseums.org.uk
Scottish Records Association
National Archives of Scotland, HM General Register House,
Edinburgh, EH1 3YY
Society of Antiquaries of Scotland
Royal Museum of Scotland, Chambers Street, Edinburgh, EH1 1JF Tel: 0131-247-4115 or 0131-247-4133
Fax: 0131-247-4163

NORTHERN IRELAND

Federation of Ulster Local Studies
18 May Street, Belfast, BT1 4NL Tel: 028-9023-5254
Presbyterian Historical Society of Ireland
Church House, Fisherwick Place, Belfast, BT1 6DW
Tel: (028)-9032-2284
Ulster American Folk
Mellon Road, Castletown, Omagh, Co Tyrone, BT78 8QY,

IRELAND

Federation of Local History Societies
Rothe House, Kilkenny, Ireland
Mayo North Family Heritage Centre
Enniscoe, Castlehill, Ballina, County Mayo, Ireland,
Tel: 353-96-31809 Fax: 353-96-31885 Email: normayo@iol.ie
South Mayo Family Research Centre
Main Street, Ballinrobe, County Mayo, Ireland,
Tel: 353-92-41214 Email: soumayo@iol.ie
Web: www.mayo.irish-roots.net/

$\mathcal{V}ictoria$ $\mathcal{C}ounty$ $\mathcal{H}istory$
- not just about Victorians
Dr Jane Batchelor

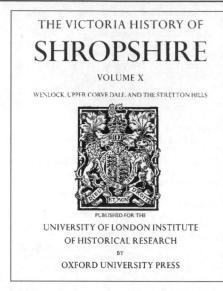

THE VICTORIA HISTORY OF

SHROPSHIRE
VOLUME X
WENLOCK, UPPER CORVE DALE, AND THE STRETTON HILLS

PUBLISHED FOR THE
UNIVERSITY OF LONDON INSTITUTE
OF HISTORICAL RESEARCH
BY
OXFORD UNIVERSITY PRESS

The name Victoria History of the Counties of England, often shortened to the Victoria County History and even the VCH, deserves some explanation as its meaning may not be clear to the general reader searching for help with family and British local history. The Victoria County History is a charitable research project which produces a series of books on local history, but, contrary to what the reader might expect, the Victoria County History is not Victorian County History. The history does relate to Queen Victoria in that it was started in 1899 and dedicated to her and is, arguably, Victorian in its ambition, for the history was begun with the idea of writing a history of all the counties in England from prehistory to present. For each county there is or is planed a set of volumes covering its complete history. In each county published volumes are divided into "general volumes" covering topics of countrywide relevance such as agriculture and religion, and "topographical volumes" which focus in more detail on particular places.

A history of all the English counties
The Victoria County History aims to give an account of each city, town and village in England, which is why it continues to be important to us today. For, if Victoria County History is a national history, it is also history on a small local scale, a scale relevant to all of us in our everyday lives, and concerns the houses we live in and the places we call our own. This article aims to cast a bit more light on what the Victoria County History actually is, where it can be found, and why it is useful not only to the experienced researcher but to everyone with an interest in history.

Victoria County History: A Century of Progress
Since 1933 the Victoria County History has been managed by the Institute of Historical Research (London University), a centre of excellence for historical research with a well-stocked library at its heart. Since 1947 local sponsorship has greatly assisted the progress of the project. Sums of money provided by local authorities, universities and other bodies support the compilation of a

history so comprehensive that work on it still continues today.

The progress of each county may be easily seen by reading our general leaflet, which lists the full range of volumes available (see next section, "How to obtain Victoria County History volumes"). Sadly, we cannot guarantee to carry out research in every county we would like to. So, whilst the reader researching Hampshire may be delighted to see that all volumes are complete, readers interested in Yorkshire will notice that there is unfortunately no volume on Yorkshire West Riding at present. Nevertheless, the progress of the VCH continues to be impressive. Fourteen county sets have been completed, for a further thirteen all general volumes have been published, and nearly every county has at least one volume to its credit.

How to obtain Victoria County History Volumes
Victoria County History volumes are easily obtainable. Those in print (and most are) can be ordered from any good bookseller. Volumes published in the last two years may be ordered directly from the publisher Oxford University Press (tel no: 01865 556767). Older volumes and reprints may be ordered from the distributors Dawson UK Ltd (tel no: 01303 850440). Local libraries usually have a copy of a volume relating to their area, or can order it for the reader through inter-library loan; larger libraries generally hold the full set. Libraries, booksellers and individuals who wish to know more about published volumes may wish to obtain a copy of our general leaflet; this may be obtained either by calling in person at the Institute of Historical Research, or by contacting us at the address below:

Victoria County History
Institute of Historical Research
Senate House, Malet St, London
WC1E 7HU
Telephone: 020 7862 8770 Fax:
020 7862 8749
Email: ihrvch@sas.ac.uk
Website:
http://www.history.ac.uk/vch

Professor Pugh
General editor of the Victoria County History 949 - 977

The Victoria County History itself
also sells a small stock of volumes,
some at reduced prices, which can
be obtained by contacting us as
above. Moreover, readers may purchase volumes from our stand at
the Society of Genealogists'
History Fair, which we currently attend every
other year.

Using the Victoria County History
1. The General Introduction and Supplement: a
helpful guide
The mass of information in Victoria County
History volumes can be quite confusing,
especially for those new to research. An
excellent place to begin, if you are not sure
where to start, is with the General
Introduction and Supplement volumes.

The General Introduction starts by explaining
more about the Victoria County History.
Following on from this there is a list of volumes, where the contents of each book are
listed by subject and by page. At the back of
the volume is a subject and place index to
guide the reader. For example, here is the
subject entry for information about bleaching
and dyeing:
Bleaching and dyeing, Notts ii: Bleaching,
Dyeing and Calico Printing, Surr. ii ; Bleaching,
Finishing and Dyeing, Lancs ii (p. 241).

Notice that three counties, Nottingham,
Surrey, and Lancashire, are listed as specialising in printing and dyeing; also, the different kinds of bleaching and dyeing processes
are specified, so that readers can pick out the
example which interests them. Another example is the entry for Elwes family (p.243): Cary-
Elwes Family, see Genealogy, Elwes
Here the cross-reference directs the reader to
Genealogy; turning to the entry for
Genealogy on pp. 250 - 1 there is a long list
of families, including the Elwes family, with
places with which they are associated:

*..Elwes...formerly of Throcking in Hertfordshire,
now of Great Billing...*

The reader now has the names of some places to
begin searching for a particular family.
Confusion between place-names is avoided by
listing the volumes in which individual places
can be found, for example distinguishing
between Whitwell in Hampshire and Whitwell
in Rutland (p. 272).

Published later than the General Introduction,
the Supplement traces the progress of the
Victoria County History between 1970 - 1990,
listing later volumes and their contents. For references to some post-1990 volumes it is best to
consult the VCH website (see (3) below).

2.Using Individual Volumes
Once readers have located the place, subject,
family, or area of specialist interest they wish to
know about they can turn to the individual volumes themselves. Many volumes have an introduction, giving an overview of the areas which
they cover. All except the earliest volumes have
a place and subject index at the back, covering a
wide variety of topics; for example the recently
published Middlesex XI volume's index men-
tions John Bacheler, fishmonger of London (p.
265), Bethnal Green (p.267), cowkeeping and
dairies (p.273), St Paul's Cathedral (p.282) and
the White Hart Brewery (p.296). Even this small
example shows how each volume represents a
rounded view of each locality.

All references in volumes are fully footnoted.
This is invaluable for the researcher, who can go
directly from the VCH volume to the archive
armed with accurate references. For instance,
looking in Gloucester V at the footnote of the
passing of an estate to John Greyndour, (died
1415/16), we are told not only that his will is in
the Public Record Office, but that it includes
mention of his son Rob. Greyndour and (half)

brother Thomas Huntley (p.210, footnote 28).

3. The World Wide Web
VCH web address: http://www.history.ac.uk/vch

The Victoria County History is for everyone, and since it is for everyone, the staff are always interested to hear people's views and comments. As befits a local history, local people are involved in fund-raising, and in writing the histories researchers will often consult those who have lived in areas a long time. Having said this, as the website for the Victoria County History of Wiltshire points out *"Researching and writing a parish history is a time-consuming project"*, and it is not really practicable for staff to spend long hours answering the public's research queries when there is so much research and writing to be done on the books themselves.

Nevertheless, staff do appreciate that it is not easy researching local and family history, and do their best to make as much information available to the public as possible. One means of doing this is through the Victoria County History website **http://www.history.ac.uk/vch**

This website is the central Victoria County History website, and gives news and information about us, together with a list of central staff; equally usefully, it provides links to the county Victoria County History websites, of which there are a growing number, and which can be most informative. For example, the Essex website provides a list of current Essex parishes available, whilst the Wiltshire website explains the detailed processes by which researchers carry out their work. Names and contact numbers for the various county editors can also be found on the websites. In particular, it is hoped that a website listing all the parishes may be established within the next year. Future plans, described below, aim to identify and test a strategy by which the whole of the Victoria County History's output can be made easily accessible on the world wide web in a rapidly searchable form.

Local History on a National Scale
Victoria County History and the Fitch Lecture
Every year the Victoria County History has a conference, when representatives from the different counties come to hear of its progress, and talk about how the History may move forward and realise its full research potential. In June 2000 for the first time the Victoria County History conference was followed by the Fitch Lecture, held at the Institute of Historical Research.

This new free lecture about local history has been established with generous support from the Marc Fitch Fund in recognition of the Victoria County History's importance in the field of local history, and is open to all who are interested. This year's lecture by Professor Christopher Dyer (University of Birmingham) was entitled "Small Places with Large Consequences: The Importance of Small Towns in England, 1000 - 1550". In his lecture Professor Dyer focused on the value of small towns in all their variety. Small towns, he emphasised, were important places, each one representing a microcosm of national life; indeed, during a period when much of England was composed of small towns, he suggested, it could be argued that they represented the very fabric of the country.

The lecture was followed by a reception with wine during which local historians, academics and members of the general had a chance to mingle and discuss their ideas. It is intended to hold this new and important public lecture every year, so that all aspects of the exciting subject of local history can be explored. Future lectures and other VCH events will be advertised on the VCH's website.

Research and Development:
New research for a New Century
The fact that the Victoria County History is a project of national importance is reflected in the £179,500 grant it has recently be awarded by the Heritage Lottery Fund. The money is to be used to fund a year-long pilot study to review the Victoria County History's working methods and to investigate ways in which its accessibility to the general public may be increased. Extra staff have been employed in Oxfordshire and County Durham, where local interest has helped the revival of the County Durham Victoria County History.

This grant represents a welcome and necessary catalyst for the successful completion of the Victoria County History.

Victoria County History: the future
Finally, a word about us and our future. The Victoria County History has indeed been very successful in securing funding for its work on local history, but we are a charity, and, like all charities, rely heavily on donations to support our research. It is not always easy for us to tell everyone who might be interested who we are, and what we do. There are many ways in which you can help us, not all of which cost money. You can tell your friends, booksellers and

librarians about our work; you can write to your local councillor or MP to express your support. If you think our work is of value, if you would like us to work on a specific county, please write and tell us so: the more support we have, the better chance we have of securing funding from research organisations, local bodies and interested parties.

A charitable trust, the Victoria County History Trust, has been set up especially to support the research and writing of the Victoria County History, c/o The Institute of Historical Research. Donations and endowments of any amount are welcome, whether for the work of the Victoria County History in general or for a particular county, place or purpose. With your help, we can make sure that the large consequences of local history are made clear.

Useful Addresses
For Victoria County History volumes published in the last two years
Oxford University Press
Walton St
Oxford OX2 6DP
Telephone: 01865 556767
Website: http://www.oup.ac.uk

For older volumes
Dawson UK Ltd
Cannon House, Folkestone
Kent CT19 5EE
Telephone: 01303 850440
Email: bid@dawson.co.uk

Port Sunlight Village

reproduced by kind permission of

The Port Sunlight Village Trust

In 1887 William Hesketh Lever, a successful soap manufacturer, began looking for a new site for his factory as his business had outgrown its original premises on the banks of the River Mersey in Warrington. He needed land on which to build his new works and have space for future expansion. The site also needed to be near to a river for importing raw materials, and a railway line for transporting the finished products. The marshy, uninspiring ground that he discovered was eventually to be transformed into the village of Port Sunlight, which was named after his famous Sunlight Soap.

Port Sunlight is a garden village which was founded in 1888 by Lever to house his soap factory workers. In line with his ideas on prosperity-sharing, the building, maintenance and upkeep of the village was subsidised with a portion of the profits from Lever Brothers Limited. With his own money, Lever financed the church, technical institute and the Lady Lever Art Gallery. Lever took great pleasure in helping to plan this picturesque garden village and he employed nearly thirty different architects to create its unique style.

The well-being of the Port Sunlight community was very important to Lever. He introduced

many schemes for welfare, education and the entertainment of his workers. A cottage hospital was built in 1907 which continued until the introduction of the National Health Service in 1948. Lever also encouraged games, recreations and any organisations which promoted art, literature, science or music. Many clubs and societies flourished in the village, such as The Royal British Legion, The Boys Brigade, Port Sunlight Players (the amateur dramatics group) and many sports clubs.

The history of the village and its community is explored in Port Sunlight Heritage Centre, where you will find a scale model of the village and of a Victorian Port Sunlight house, a video of early film footage, copies of the original plans for the buildings and displays of period advertising and soap packaging.

Port Sunlight is now a designated Conservation Area, still within its original boundaries. Residency is no longer restricted to Unilever employees and the village and the Heritage Centre are now managed by The Port Sunlight Village Trust. Today houses can be bought on the open market, although the Trust remains responsible for the environment and landscape in Port Sunlight.

Family History in the Department of Printed Books ~ Imperial War Museum

The Imperial War Museum was formed in 1917 to record the part played by the British and Imperial Forces in the First World War. It was officially opened by King George V at Crystal Palace in 1920, but moved to its present home at Lambeth Road in South London, the former Bethlem Mental Hospital (commonly known as Bedlam) in 1936. When the second major war of the century began in 1939 the Museum's remit was extended to include this, and was later extended again to include all post-1945 conflict.

The Museum has also grown in size and now has several outstations; Duxford, a former Royal Air Force station near Cambridge; HMS Belfast, a Second World War cruiser anchored next to Tower Bridge on the Thames; Churchill's Cabinet War Rooms beneath Whitehall; and the projected Imperial War Museum North, a progressively-designed gallery scheduled to open in the Manchester area in 2002. None of these outstations have reference facilities open to the public, but each has a unique insight and experience to offer the interested visitor. The main Museum building in London however, remains the focal point for archival access and can be a real treasure trove for the family historian.

From the beginning the Museum was keen to include all aspects of warfare, not just the experiences of the fighting man at the front. In an age of total war the whole of society has been involved. From the Museum's earliest days a Women's Work Subcommittee was established to record the experiences of women in the First World War - whether in the services, working in a medical capacity or in munitions factories, driving ambulances and buses, or pounding the beat in the police force. Rationing and air raids, conscription and conscientious objection, evacuation and internment, are all well covered at the Imperial War Museum.

There are seven different reference departments - Art, Documents, Exhibits and Firearms, Film and Video, Photographs, Printed Books and Sound - within the Museum. Of these, the Department of Printed Books (the reference library) is the most usual starting point for those pursuing their family history. Well over 100,000 books, as well as periodicals, maps and ephemeral collections are held here. It is important to note, however, that individual service records and official documentation collated by the War Office, Admiralty and Air Ministry are not held by the Imperial War Museum.

The family historian will need to be in possession of some basic facts before he or she can take advantage of our collections. If details of service are unknown then this information needs to be obtained from elsewhere - usually the Public Record Office or the Ministry of Defence. The Department of Printed Books does, however, hold a large collection of printed and published materials, which can help flesh out the bare facts surrounding an individual's career. Once details of the relevant battalion, ship or squadron are known we can advise on available published sources. For those genealogists at the beginning of their enquiries, we are happy to provide more detailed guidance on the probable availability and location of official documentation. We have recently produced a series of new guides called Tracing your family history, which provide full details about where records can be found and how to interpret them, as well as information about the structure and organisation of the various branches of the Armed Forces. These have been written in response to the questions we most frequently get asked, and we believe that they will be extremely helpful for people researching relatives who served in the Armed Forces in the twentieth century. There are separate books for the Army, Royal Navy, Royal Air Force and Merchant Navy, each available directly from the address below for the price of £5.50.

To put the Museum's collections in context, visitors should be aware that we only cover the period from 1914 onwards. For information on British units and campaigns before this date it would be more appropriate to contact the National Army Museum at Chelsea, the National Maritime Museum at Greenwich, or the Royal Naval Museum at Portsmouth. Details of pre-1914 service are held at the Public Record Office, Kew.

Sadly, it is usually the case that if an individual died in service then you are likely to find out more about him than if he survived. If the serviceman died but details of his unit are unknown, the best initial source is generally the Commonwealth War Graves Commission based at Maidenhead. The Commission has created a database, entitled Debt of Honour, from the huge collection of original ledgers covering fatalities in both world wars, including civilian deaths in the Second World War, and this can now be accessed from their website (http://www.cwgc.org) or via the link from our own website. This database makes the search by name easier than it has ever been. A set of cemetery and memorial registers for both wars is available for consultation in the Imperial War Museum reading room. These contain useful information about the history of a site, including a map and details of how to access the sites. They may also provide further clues, for example, details of medical facilities in the locality, where relatives who died of wounds or disease may have been treated. These registers are often studied by those seeking to record all the men from one particular unit who died, or by people researching the names on a war memorial.

A digitised source that has made searching for Army unit information much simpler is the CD-ROM version of Soldiers Died in the Great War, 1914-19. The original eighty-volume work was published by HMSO in 1921, and reprinted in association with the Imperial War Museum in 1989. However, being arranged by regiment and then alphabetically within each battalion, it was essential to know the individual's regiment before full use could be made of the publication. The information supplied is quite brief but helpful in confirming details of the individual's unit and date of death. The entry includes the regimental number and rank, place of birth and enlistment (and often includes a place of residence), rough cause of death (such as killed in action, died of wounds, or died of natural causes) and theatre of death. If the soldier was awarded any gallantry medals these

will also be indicated as will a former regiment and regimental number. There is also a companion volume called Officers Died in the Great War, although this is less detailed. Copies of both the original volumes and the commercially produced CD-ROM are available for consultation in the reading room. A more recently published reference work by S D and J B Jarvis, the multi-volume Cross of Sacrifice, is also readily accessible to our readers. These are very useful as they provide brief details combined with a reference to the Commonwealth War Graves Commission register so that details can be cross-referred. The different volumes cover Army officers, as well as members of the Royal Air Force, Royal Navy and Merchant Navy.

One potentially useful unpublished source held by Printed Books is a copy of the War Office roll of honour for members of the British Army, listed by regiment, who died during the Second World War. The Public Record Office also has a copy. A multi-volume published version of this is currently being commercially produced by Promenade Publications.

Many individual rolls of honour were produced after both world wars, and these can be extremely useful to the family historian. The Department of Printed Books has an extensive collection covering schools, colleges, professional bodies, churches, companies, societies and other organisations. There are more of these for the First World War than the Second, but it is always worth checking. Local histories of towns and villages often include personal details. Interest in local war memorials has been partially stimulated by the work of the National Inventory of War Memorials, which is based at the Museum. It should be noted that the NIWM does not record individual names inscribed on the memorial on their database, but much information is kept in supplementary files. We are always grateful to be notified about any new publications arising from this growth in local interest, or to be put in contact with local history enthusiasts who have have knowledge of war memorials that have been moved or destroyed.

For the relative tracing events surrounding a death on active service, an extremely useful source is the British official history. The Department of Printed Books has reprinted all the First World War volumes, covering war on land, sea and air, and a selection

from the Second World War, in an attempt to make this valuable source more widely available. A full list of our publications can be seen on the Museum website or a copy of our catalogue can be requested from the telephone number at the end of this article. The First World War official histories contain particularly useful sketch maps, which can then be supplemented by more detailed trench maps. Generally, if the date of death or service details are known, it is possible to build a very detailed picture of how and where the serviceman died - sometimes to the very trench - from the available published unit histories for individual divisions, regiments, ships and squadrons.

Basic information on officers can usually be supplied by the Army, Navy and Air Force Lists. The Department also has a good collection of material relating to the Commonwealth. For example, there is a complete run of the Indian Army List from 1914 to 1947. For the First World War we also hold nominal rolls for most of the original Canadian Expeditionary Force as well as a microfiche nominal roll of the Australian Imperial Force. In addition to complete sets of all the official history volumes produced by the different nationalities, there are large numbers of unit histories relating to both our allies and our opponents, including an excellent collection of First World War German regimental histories, and an extensive number of titles on the American Forces.

A little known strength of the Department of Printed Books' collection is the quantity and quality of the large numbers of service and prisoner of war periodicals among its holdings. Regimental journals can be very informative, giving a valuable taste of service life - especially in the inter-war and post-war years. Coverage may include sports days, births, marriages, deaths, exercises and trooping abroad. Old Comrades Associations also produce newsletters and magazines, although sadly, these are dwindling. Traditionally, these have been a very good way of establishing contacts with possible informants or of tapping very specific expertise.

These publications are complemented by material held in some of the other collecting archives. The Department of Printed Books shares the reading room with the Department of Documents, making it easy to consult both departments' holdings on the same day. The latter's unique collection of unpublished diaries, letters and memoirs is essentially of a personal nature and may contain references unavailable elsewhere. There are a number of items such as the Changi Internment Camp Register and the Milag Nord Register (a Second World War prison camp for captured merchant seamen in Germany) which list names and provide additional details. If you are able to locate a collection written by an individual who served in the same unit as your relative, this can prove extremely helpful for background information. This may also be true of the personal accounts recorded by the Sound Archive and the contemporary miles of film stored by the Film and Video Archive. At the very least they will provide a more human personal context to your research.

The Photograph Archive may be able to produce an official unit photograph from their collection of six million prints. However, the Archive does not contain pictures of every single serviceman, and it is probably very unlikely that you will be able to positively identify your relative. Portraits of named individuals tend to be those of higher rank or those who have won the highest awards for gallantry. Even so, these pictures do form a visual record which may prove useful, and to find a picture of a ship on which a relative served, or a hospital where they worked, can be very rewarding. Please note that neither staff in the Photograph Archive nor Printed Books are able to identify photographs sent in by researchers. We do have a large collection of reference books on badges, uniforms, buttons and medals and we are happy to recommend titles that may be of assistance.

This summary of our collection and its fellow departments will, we hope, encourage you to make an appointment to use them. The military side has, necessarily, been stressed. However, we are also proud of the social, economic and political content of the library, and of our coverage of other conflicts that the public may not expect, from the Spanish Civil War to Vietnam and Kosovo. We have probably the largest public collection of war literature and poetry in the United Kingdom, a good collection of local history sources and a fine and unusual collection of ephemeral items. All of this material is available for public consultation by prior appointment.

Books in the Tracing Your Family History series can be obtained directly from the telephone number below at a cost of £5.50 each (including postage and packing)
Tracing Your Family History: Army (98 pages) (ISBN 1-901623-35-1)
Tracing Your Family History: Royal Navy (72 pages) (ISBN 1-901623-36-X)
Tracing Your Family History: Royal Air Force (76 pages) (ISBN 1-901623-40-8)
Tracing Your Family History: Merchant Navy (85 pages) (ISBN 1-901623-37-8)

Department of Printed Books, Imperial War Museum, Lambeth Road, London SE1 6HZ
Opening hours: Monday to Saturday from 10am-5pm (appointment necessary)
Tel: 020 7416 5342 (general enquiries & appointments)
Tel:020 7416 5346 (requests for catalogue and Tracing Your Family History books)
Fax: 020 7416 5246
Email: books@iwm.org.uk
Museum website: http://www.iwm.org.uk

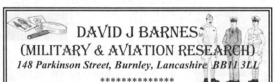

The Commonwealth War Graves Commission

Peter Francis

Commonwealth War Graves Commission

The Commonwealth War Graves Commission, was established by Royal Charter of 21 May 1917, the provisions of which were amended and extended by a Supplemental Charter of 8 June 1964. Its duties are to mark and maintain the graves of the forces of the Commonwealth who died during two world wars, to build and maintain memorials to the dead whose graves are unknown, and to keep records and registers. The cost is shared by the partner governments - those of Australia, Canada, India, New Zealand, South Africa and the United Kingdom - in proportions based upon the numbers of their graves.

The Commission is responsible for 1.7 million commemorations, with war graves at over 23,000 locations and in some 150 countries. The work is founded upon the principles that each of the dead should be commemorated individually by name either on the headstone on the grave or by an inscription on a memorial; that each of the headstones and memorials should be permanent; that the headstones should be uniform; and that no distinction should be made on account of military or civil rank, race or creed.

Today, the Commission's major concern is the maintenance of those graves, cemeteries and memorials, to the highest standards, in the face of exposure to the elements and the passage of time - to ensure that "Their Name Liveth For Evermore". In addition to the day to day horticultural and structural maintenance of the cemeteries and memorials, an enquiry service is on offer to the public, whereby the commemorative details for any Commonwealth casualty who died during either of the two world wars can be provided. Commemorative information for Commonwealth civilians who died as a result of enemy action during the Second World War is also available on a Roll of Honour numbering over 66,400 names.

Originally, casualty data was stored on card indexes in over 3,000 drawers. After the First World War, details were compiled into some 1,500 cemetery registers. All enquiries were handled by a wholly manual process until 1995. The work was carried out, as it had been for decades, by dedicated, knowledgeable staff, using large ledgers. The ledgers are organised by country, name of cemetery and alphabetically by surname. To overcome the challenge of an enquirer only knowing a casualty's surname and not the place of burial, there are large volumes of alphabetical lists, cross-referenced by code numbers to the appropriate cemetery register. In late autumn 1995 the Commission's vast resource of information was computerised, allowing for a more efficient service to be offered to the public. The information for each entry was broken down into searchable 'fields' - For example, Surname, Age, Regiment, Cemetery Name, Date of Death e.t.c.

Not only do the computerised records allow for better access to the casualty details and place of commemoration, it also allows the operator to trace single casualties more quickly, from less information, and offer services like casualty-listing reports. This has become increasingly important as the value of the database for educational purposes is recognised and enquiries become more complex. Some of the most popular criteria for casualty listings include a same surname search, a regimental search and a home town search. It is even possible to trace, for example, how many Captains were killed on the first day of the Battle of the Somme.

In line with this public access policy, the Commission took the initiative to use the Internet to further promote access to the records. In November 1998, to coincide with the eightieth anniversary of the Armistice that brought to an end the First World War, the Debt of Honour Register was launched. The Register, a search by surname database, is available to the public via the Commission's web site at www.cwgc.org. The database provides known details of the casualty as well as the name of the cemetery or memorial, directions on how to find it and the exact plot, row, grave or memorial panel reference to enable the enquirer to locate the place of burial or commemoration should they make a pilgrimage to the cemetery or memorial. A second page on the web site prints the casualty details in the form of a commemorative certificate for the enquirer.

The launch of the Debt of Honour Register on the Internet has been an incredible success - the site averages 500,000 hits a week. The Register has widened public knowledge and interest in commemoration, reunited families with the records of their long-fallen loved ones, assisted the historian, researcher and the student and most importantly, proved a highly effective way of keeping the names of those the Commission commemorates alive in the hearts and minds of a new generation. Enhancements to the site since it was launched have reduced down time and increased the accessibility of the site still further. The Commission anticipates further enhancements to the site in the near future.

In 1926, the Commission's founder, Fabian Ware, said the cemeteries and memorials built and maintained by the Commonwealth War Graves Commission, 'will bear a message to future generations as long as the stone of which they are constructed endures.' With the launch of the Debt of Honour Register, names once kept alive only in stone are now readily available to be carried in the hearts and minds of a new generation. As we move further away from the two world wars the

Commission will ensure the stone, the gardens, the records, the memory and the message endure - that 'Their Name Liveth for Evermore".

Further Information
The Commission welcomes enquiries from the public. We request that you supply the Commission's enquiries department with as much information as possible. This will enhance the chances of a positive trace.

A full list of the Commission's services and publications on offer to the public is available from:

The Records & Enquiries Section
The Commonwealth War Graves Commission
2 Marlow Road
Maidenhead
Berkshire
SL6 7DX
United Kingdom
Tel: 01628 634221
Fax: 01628 771208
E-mail: casualty.enq@cwgc.org
Web Site: www.cwgc.org

The Commonwealth War Graves Commission
Civilian Roll of Honour
Peter Francis
Commonwealth War Graves Commission

In 1938, the Imperial, now Commonwealth, War Graves Commission unveiled the Australian Memorial at Villers-Bretonneux. It was the last of the Great War memorials to be completed from the war that was to end all wars and yet within a year the Second World War had started and the Commission was called upon to prepare for a new harvest of death. This second catastrophe of the twentieth century was a very different conflict to the one that had taken place only twenty or so years previously. The war was one of quick movement - the German Blitzkrieg sweeping all before it and forcing the Commission to temporarily relinquish control of the cemeteries and memorials in occupied Europe.

With the conquest of mainland Europe complete, Hitler's forces concentrated their efforts on the invasion of the United Kingdom. In order to invade, Germany had first to achieve total air superiority and so began the Battle of Britain and the large-scale bombing of airfields, factories and later in an attempt to smash the morale of the British people, cities. Distinctions between soldiers and non-combatants were non-existent. The phrase Total War was coined to represent the fact that civilian populations as well as front line troops were now considered targets.

On 7 September 1940 the first major air raid on a British city was carried out by the Luftwaffe. The Commission's founder, Fabian Ware, witnessed first hand the deaths of women, children, firemen and air-raid wardens. This new and horrifying war was impacting on communities like never before. Surely, he reasoned, each casualty deserved a fitting commemoration? Soon London itself was a target of the Blitz. Ware decided to act and wrote to the Prime Minister, Winston Churchill, on 18 September, urging the commemoration of those civilians killed by enemy action. In his words, "The deliberate slaughter of civilians was creating a new category of normal war casualties. Theirs should be counted an equal sacrifice".

Churchill, who had so successfully argued for the Commission's principle of equality of treatment for the war dead while Chairman of the Commission during the parliamentary debates on commemoration of

the early 1920s, had no objection. In fact, he believed that civilian deaths might well outnumber military casualties - fortunately, he was not proved correct.

In January 1941, the Commission began to keep records of all civilian deaths caused by enemy action and its Royal Charters were adjusted to give it the necessary powers to do so. The biggest single obstacle to this task was obtaining the names and addresses of those killed. The information provided by the authorities, like the Registrar General, was not always complete and often did not include the addresses of next of kin. In February 1941, to encourage a greater flow of information and further publicise the commemoration of civilians, Ware decided to make a tour of the hard-hit areas. During his tour he enlisted the help of mayors and local authorities and the information provided to the Commission greatly improved. In November 1941, he made a further appeal on national radio and in the press for help and the records began to take shape - the Commission already had over 18,000 individuals recorded.

However, Ware was not satisfied with the mere recording of names at the Commission's headquarters. As the Commission would have no responsibility for the graves of civilians, Ware suggested to the Dean of Westminster in January 1942 that the names should be inscribed on a Roll of Honour which might be placed in the Warrior's Chapel of the Abbey. "The symbolic significance of ...the admission of these civilian dead to the adjacency and companionship with the Unknown Soldier would...give a right inspiration." The Dean readily agreed.

In December 1942 the first typed lists, leather bound in three volumes, were deposited for safekeeping at Westminster. The volumes were not put on display until after the war because it was believed that if the extent of civilian casualties were known, it might damage the morale of the nation. It was not until 1956 that the completed volumes of the Civilian Roll of Honour were handed to the Dean of Westminster by the Duke of Gloucester. Today, there are six volumes with over 66,000 names recorded. In a fitting tribute to those commemorated, the books are still on display to the public at the Abbey. A new page of the

Civilian Roll of Honour is turned every day and so unfolds 66,000 tragic stories - the sudden death of a pensioner aged one hundred or of an infant a few hours old, of 163 people killed in an instant when a V2 rocket fell on Woolworth's at New Cross, and of the 1,500 dead of Malta.

What information does the Civilian Roll of Honour have? The casualty details available include the person's name, age, date of death, last known address and the particulars of the next of kin. The entries are structured along the lines of the old Borough system and then alphabetically by surname. Just one moving example reads: Betty Francis, Civilian War Dead. Died 9 April 1941, Aged 2. Daughter of Emily and the late Tom Francis of Clevedon Road, Balasall Heath. County Borough of Birmingham. The civilian records, like the military records, are still updated to this day. Amendments made on the computerised sys-tem are later added to the leather bound volumes at the Abbey twice a year by a member of the Commissionís records department. In this way, that 'equal sacrifice' is preserved for future generations.

For the family historian, all of this information is available from the Commission's enquiries department in Maidenhead and the Debt of Honour Register at www.cwgc.org The Civilian Roll of Honour is a highly moving tribute not only to the many innocents who had their lives brutally cut short by war but to the bravery of services like the Fire Brigade and Ambulance crews who risked their lives to save others. The Commonwealth War Graves Commission keeps faith with them all, ensuring that
Their Name Liveth For Evermore.

The National Inventory of War Memorials

Based at and administered by the Imperial War Museum, this national survey was initiated in 1989 with the aim of surveying all of Britain's estimated 54,000 war memorials. Although full time office staff are employed to organise field work and collate the information as it arrives, all the field work itself is carried out by enthu-siastic volunteers from a wide variety of backgrounds. We would welcome the assistance of further volunteers if they felt able to lend us their time, energy and expertise.

The work would involve liaising with existing NIWM fieldworkers and, in some cases, local Co-ordinators. We encourage volunteers to have their names added to our list of field workers, as we have found this to be the most effective means of taking full advantage of people's valuable time and minimising the risk of duplication.

The survey is nearing completion, with just under two years remaining of the current National Heritage Memorial Fund grant, but a recent audit of the collection has identified the following areas of England and Wales which urgently require additional field work in order to ensure their completion. In particular, local Co-ordinators are still required for Northern Wales and Cornwall. In Scotland a comprehensive survey under the guidance of an independent Co-ordinator is nearing completion. In Northern Ireland a comprehensive survey has been initiated by the Western Front Association. Details of Co-ordinators are given below:

England
Tyne and Wear
Janet Brown, Bilsdale, Ulgham, Northumberland
Tel:01670 790465
North-West England
(Greater Manchester and Lancashire)
Stephen Lowe 130 Gawsworth Rd, Macclesfield,
Cheshire SK11 8UQ Tel:(01625) 424 921
The Midlands (West Midlands and Warwickshire)
Gillian Ellis 42 Tyndale Crescent, Great Barr,
Birmingham B43 7NP
The South East
(Kent, Essex and East/West Sussex)
Paul Rason 1 South Drive, Orpington, Kent BR6 9NG
Tel: 01689 855 061

Lincolnshire
John Chester, 8 Laburnam Grove, Spalding
Lincolnshire PE11 2LX
Gloucestershire
Mrs P Utechin The Lodge, Headington House, Old
Headington, Oxford OX3 9HU
Greater London
Co-ordinator: Hilary Wheeler 17 Bath House, Bath
Terrace, London SE1 6PU
Hertfordshire
Roger Bardell 1 Nathans Close, Welwyn
Herts AL6 9QB
Cornwall
Co-ordinator: To be confirmed

Most other English counties have broadly been very well surveyed. However, we do have a list of around forty administra-tive districts which require work to bring them up to the standard of the rest of their counties. So, if you would like to help but are not based in any of the above areas please contact us anyway, as you may find that you can still help.

Wales
Northern Wales
Co-ordinator: To be confirmed
Southern Wales
David Hughes 23 St Teilos Way, Caerphilly
South Wales CF83 1FA

Scotland
Tony Martin Birch Grove, Harviestoun Rd, Dollar,
Clackmannanshire FK14 7PT
Northern Ireland
Jim Heyburn 56 Orpen Rd, Finaghy
Belfast BT10 0BQ

If you feel you could help in any way or would just like to find out more details, we would really like to hear from you. Please contact either the Project Co-ordinator, Nick Hewitt, or one of the Project Assistants, Jane Armer and Lorraine Knight, at:
The National Inventory of War Memorials
Imperial War Museum
Lambeth Road, London SE1 6HZ
Tel: (0171) 416 5353/5281 Fax: (0171) 416 5379 E-mail: memorials@iwm.org.uk

NATIONAL
ARMY
MUSEUM
CHELSEA

The National Army Museum

Julian Humphreys Senior Information Officer

In the 1950s a few enthusiastic individuals began to plan the creation of a museum which would do justice to the long history of the British Army and also tell the story of the Indian Army and those colonial units which have served with the British Army overseas and which form part of the history of the British Empire.

By 1960 the National Army Museum had been established by Royal Charter and set up in a former riding school at the Royal Military Academy, Sandhurst. The site soon proved inadequate to house the enormous amount of material acquired so an appeal was launched to provide a specially designed building in central London. Thanks largely to the initiative of Field Marshal Sir Gerald Templer the Museum moved in 1970 to its present purpose-built site next door to Wren's Royal Hospital in Chelsea.

The Museum is now home to some of Britain's finest military treasures. As well as chronicling the campaigns and battles fought by the British over the last 500 years, the Museum's Galleries offer a remarkable insight into the lives of Britain's soldiers through the ages. The colourful displays include weapons, paintings, equipment, models, medals and items from one of the world's largest collections of military uniform. The recent opening of a new Gallery on the Modern Army enables visitors to trace the story of the British soldier right up to the present day while regular Special Exhibitions take a detailed look at aspects of Army history.

Exhibits on display in the Museum include twenty Victoria Crosses, a fifty square metre model of the Battle of Waterloo with over 70,000 tiny model soldiers, a lamp used by Florence Nightingale and even the skeleton of Napoleon's horse! The exhibits are supported by large reconstructions linked to audio-visual displays illustrating military life in war and peace at home and abroad. A visit to the Museum Galleries is particularly useful if you have ancestors who served in the Army and you want to find out more about what life was like for them and about the campaigns in which they served. Admission to the Museum is free of charge.

Enquiries
The National Army Museum is not a repository for official records and so it does not hold material which relates to the personal details of special officers or the service and personal details of other ranks. Museum staff will endeavour to answer specific questions relating to our collections which are held by five separate departments: Archives, Photographs, Film and Sound; Fine and Decorative Art; Printed Books; Uniform, Badges and Medals; Weapons, Equipment and Vehicles. The Museum's website at www.national-army-museum.ac.uk includes an introduction to the history of the Army, information about the Museum's galleries details about our collections and news about current and forthcoming Special Exhibitions and events. Enquiries can be sent by e-mail to info@national-army-museum.ac.uk. Please remember to include a postal address on all e-mail enquiries to allow for the prompt despatch of material where appropriate. Enquirers should also bear in mind that the Museum receives a large number of enquiries, so it may not be possible to respond to e-mails immediately. All enquiries, in whatever form, are dealt with by the Departments in the order of their receipt.

Reading Room
The Reading Room is open to holders of Readers' Tickets which are available to anyone aged 18 and above. Application forms are available from the Department of Printed Books. These need to be completed with a reference and returned to the Department in advance of your first visit. The Reading Room is open from Tuesday to Saturday inclusive from 10am to 4.30pm (except for the Saturdays of Bank Holiday weekends and the last two

A Napoleonic Recruiting Sergeant recreated at a recent Special Events Weekend at The National Army Museum

full weeks of October when we are closed for stocktaking).

Like its Galleries, the Museum's Reading Room facilities are likely to be helpful to those wishing to carry out research of a general nature into aspects of the history of the British Army, the Indian Army and its antecedents. The collections available to researchers visiting the Reading Room are books and periodicals, prints and drawings, archives and historic photographs. Copy photographs of other material, such as oil paintings are also available for consultation. The Reading Room facilities include microfilm/microfiche equipment and a photocopying service.

Books and periodicals

The Department of Printed Books contains about 40,000 books and over 200 current historical and regimental journals are taken. Reference works, such as Army Lists and current periodicals are available on open shelves in the Reading Room. Other material, such as regimental and campaign histories, military biographies and drill books are available on request, either in advance or from 10am to 12noon, and from 2pm to 4.15pm.

Prints and drawings

These include the Crookshank Collection of contemporary battle prints (to 1868) transferred from the British Museum, and the Ogilby Boxed Collection, a pictorial archive compiled by the Army Museums Ogilby Trust. The majority of the prints and drawings illustrate campaigns and uniforms. Prints and drawings are available from the Print Room by request in the Reading Room from 10am to 12noon, 2pm to 4.15pm, Monday to Friday and on Saturdays by advance ordering.

Archives

The archives contain collections of private, regimental and business papers. The main strengths of the collections date from the period 1800 to 1920 and include the papers of the 1st Marquess of Anglesey (Napoleonic Wars), Lord Raglan (Crimea), Lord Chelmsford (Zulu War), Lord Roberts (Boer War), Lord Rawlinson (First World War) and the United Service Club. Details of the Museum's holdings may be obtained from the National Register of Archives.

Historic Photographs

The collection numbers about 500,000 images. There is material of historic importance dating back to the 1840s and the collection is also particularly strong in Indian Army and pre-1914 images.

Photograph orders

Copy photographs and transparencies of items in the collections can be supplied, provided that copyright of the image is held by the Museum. Please note that, under current EU legislation, copyright remains with the artist or photographer of a work for 70 years after their death and that, in these cases, the Museum cannot supply any reproductions, for any reason. For more information about ordering copy photographs, please contact the Museum's Photographic Department by e-mail to photo@national-army-museum.ac.uk , by telephone on extension 2225 or by fax on 020 7823 6573.

Group visits

We welcome visits from groups and societies and can offer pre-booked parties free illustrated talks on a variety of subjects. These sessions usually make use of slides, music and a wide selection of original and replica artefacts for the group to handle. Visitors might try on Civil War armour, see the items Florence Nightingale or Mary Seacole would have used, or examine First World War uniforms, weapons and equipment. Sessions are available on weekdays throughout the opening hours of the Museum while Special Events weekends are frequently organised. Popular themes include Army wives, the First World War and Army food. Subject to availability, coach parking may be booked through the Education Department. To discuss a group visit, make a booking or for further information on any of our services please contact the Education Department on extension 2228.

Facilities for visitors with Special Needs

We encourage visits from groups and individuals with special needs and pride ourselves on our flexibility. All galleries are accessible to visitors in wheelchairs via ramps, lifts and chair lifts. A toilet for wheelchair users is available. Guide dogs are welcome. A leaflet detailing services for special needs schools is available on request.

The National Army Museum
Royal Hospital Road
Chelsea
London SW3 4HT
Tel: 020 7730 0717
Fax: 020 7823 6573
e-mail: info@national-army-museum.ac.uk
website: www.national-army-museum.ac.uk

Opening hours:
Daily, 10.00am to 5.30pm
(except 1 Jan, Good Friday, Early May Public Holiday, 24-26 December)
Nearest Tube Station: Sloane Square
Admission free

The Imperial War Museum
– North
Ann Carter
Imperial War Museum

In 2002 the Imperial War Museum will open a major new branch in Trafford, Greater Manchester. The new Imperial War Museum-North will be housed in a remarkable building designed by renowned architect Daniel Libeskind and will contain exhibition galleries, an education suite for schools, colleges and other groups, a Microgallery, a shop and café. It will be the first branch of the Museum to open since 1984 and the only one outside the south east of England.

Why create a new branch?
The Imperial War Museum has been working for over a decade to establish a branch in the north of England to make its collections, exhibitions and education service more widely available. All four of its current sites - the headquarters building in Lambeth, the Cabinet War Rooms, Churchill's wartime headquarters in Whitehall, HMS Belfast, a battle cruiser moored in the Pool of London close to Tower Bridge and Duxford Airfield in Cambridgeshire - are based in the south east of England. An initial seventy-one sites were put forward by thirty-six local authorities in the north of England for the new Museum. Two sites were eventually short-listed, Trafford in Greater Manchester and Birkenhead on the Wirral. Trafford was eventually chosen because the site offered a superb location, not only because it is close to other arts and leisure facilities such as the Lowry and Manchester United's Old Trafford Ground, but also because it is in easy reach of some 15.5 million people. It also offered excellent and supportive partners, Trafford Metropolitan Borough Council and Peel Holdings plc. Building work began in January 2000 and the new Museum is now rapidly taking shape.

Who is it for?
The Imperial War Museum-North is being designed to appeal to the wide range of people who live and work in or visit the north of Britain. Over 300,000 people are expected to visit the museum in its first year, 50,000 of them from schools and colleges in the region. The Museum team is working closely with local schools, community groups and businesses to encourage participation in and contributions to the exhibitions and events programme. An on-site Visitor Centre, located just off Trafford Wharf Road in Trafford, will be open to visitors from autumn 2000.

What will it be like?
The Building Architect, Daniel Libeskind, has designed an extraordinary building to reflect how conflict has affected the world.

"Conflict has been a constant factor of the 20th century as the world has repeatedly fragmented into warring factions. I have imagined the globe broken into fragments and taken the pieces to form the building – three shards – together they represent the conflict on land, in the air and on water." He has also designed an intriguing landscape based on the twenty-four time zones of the world to further emphasise the global nature of war.

Visitors will enter the museum through the Air Shard, which rises 55 metres into the air. From a viewing platform visitors will be able to look out across Manchester, itself an example of an industrial city which has been affected by conflict both in the past and more recently with the IRA bomb. The Air Shard will contain some suspended objects and other exhibits at ground level.

From the Air Shard visitors will move into the Earth Shard which contains the main exhibition gallery. The structure of this part of the building is shaped to reflect the curvature of the Earth's surface. When visitors enter the main exhibition gallery they will feel as if they are on top of the world and both the floor and ceiling will curve gently away. The gallery will be monumental - at its highest point it will be 12 metres high. The Earth Shard will also house the temporary exhibition gallery, an education suite, a microgallery, a shop, cloakroom and ticketing facilities.

Register of Men
Fallen at Gallipoli 1915-16

Gallipoli, April 1915 - January 1916:
Before dawn on the morning of April 25, 1915, a combined force of British, Australian, New Zealand, Indian and French forces carried out an amphibious assault on the Gallipoli Peninsula. The goal of the assault was to secure the Dardanelles, the strait, which separates European Turkey from Asian Turkey and connects the Aegean Sea to the Sea of Marmara. The success of this operation would have forced the surrender of Turkey, allowing the British to better assist Russia in its fight against Germany in the east. Two assaults earlier in the year - one by sea and the other by a small force of Royal Marines - had failed to achieve any success. They had, however, alerted the Turks to the aims of the British and allowed them to prepare an almost impenetrable defence.

The assault took place in two sectors located 12 miles apart. British and French troops landed at Helles to the north, and Australian and New Zealand troops (along with the Ceylon Planters Rifles and units of the Royal Marines) landed to the south. The invaders called this southern sector Anzac, after the Australian-New Zealand Army Corps (ANZAC) to which many of the troops belonged. Elements of the all-Jewish Zion Mule Corps also landed in both sectors.

The assault failed to achieve nearly all of its objectives, and what was supposed to have been a quick victory against the Turkish defenders turned into a long and costly land and sea campaign. The failure of several major assaults against the Turks between April and July 1915 resulted in landings in a new sector in August. The opening of the Suvla sector, which bordered Anzac immediately to the north, coincided with a major effort by the Australians and New Zealanders (along with Indians and British troops which had been secretly landed in the area) to break out of their sector and thus link up with the troops at Suvla. This in turn coincided with a major diversionary assault in the Helles sector (the Battle of Krithia Vineyard).

Like the earlier battles, those of August were costly yet unsuccessful. From then on the campaign devolved into a campaign of trench warfare, the monotony occasionally broken by small raids against the enemy. In September 1915 the Newfoundland Regiment, the final Dominion to send troops to Gallipoli, landed and began suffering casualties.

By the time the last troops were evacuated from Gallipoli on the night of January 8/9, 1916, 34,000 British and Dominion troops, and several thousand French and French colonial troops, had lost their lives. Nobody will ever know how many men died as a result of their Gallipoli service after they left the Peninsula, but the number must be considerable. The shame of it all is that the men who sent them to their deaths did so knowing that they had virtually no chance of success.

About the Register
For the past 10 years I have been working diligently to commemorate each of the 34,000 British and Dominion servicemen who died at Gallipoli. I am also including those men who died as a result of wounds and illness sustained at Gallipoli after they left the Peninsula, those who died in Turkish prisoner of war camps and two nurses of the Canadian Army Medical Corps who died while treating casualties at Mudros on the Greek island of Lemnos.

My goal is to include as much information as I possibly can about each person. I am also trying to locate photographs of each man and first hand accounts of their deaths. I am trying to include the following details about each person:

Name; Date and place of birth; Service number and Service Unit and or Regiment; Date and place of enlistment; Names of parents (to include mothers maiden name, father's occupation and address in 1915); Name of spouse (to include maiden name, date and place of marriage and address in 1915); Names and birth dates of children; Education; Occupation; Date and place of death: Circumstances of death: Place of burial; Location of photograph (even if I cannot reproduce it)
Personal details and anecdotes (physical description, personality, interests, aspirations and interesting experiences)

Using a variety of sources I am trying to put together as complete a picture of each person as is possible. These include regimental histories, casualty rolls, printed rolls of honour and commemorative books, cemetery registers, unit and personal diaries, letters, and newspaper reports and obituaries.

Additionally, I am relying on the help of genealogists all over the world for information about family members. As a genealogist myself, the value of the information which only people like us think to preserve about our families is quite clear to me. While the main intention is to commemorate the people who fell at - and as a result of - Gallipoli my secondary goal is to create an educational tool, which will be useful for the novice. Too often historians make the mistake of assuming that their audience knows just as much about their subject as they do, an assumption which is all too often incorrect.

Thus, in an effort to make my register useful and understandable to everyone, an introductory section will be included which will briefly explain life on the Gallipoli Peninsula, diet (poor diet resulted in the deaths of hundreds of men due to dysentery), the evacuation and treatment of casualties, burials, etc. A glossary will also be added which will explain the location and naming of the major and minor geographical features at Gallipoli including, where possible, the colourfully named trenches.

Over the last four years I have proven 12 Gallipoli deaths and 2 burials to the Commonwealth War Graves Commission (at the time of writing, I am building a case for 9 more deaths). I have also corrected numerous errors in the records of the Commission, resulting in changes to cemetery and memorial registers, memorials and gravestones. As a result, the Commission has requested a completed copy of my register so that it might update and correct it's records.

I would like to personally appeal to everyone with ancestors who died at Gallipoli; people with diaries, letters and photographs in their possession; and anyone with an interest in local men who died at Gallipoli for help. Without your help, this register can never hope to be the memorial it is intended to be.

Gallipoli Campaign 1915 - 1916 Biographical Index
Patrick Gariépy, 3966 Robin Avenue, Eugene, Oregon
97402,U.S.A.
e-mail: patrick@efn.org

His Majesty's Royal Cornwall Regiment of Militia, whereof
William Eliot is Colonel.

THESE are to certify, That the Bearer hereof, *William Woon*
Sergeant - in the aforesaid
Regiment, born in the *Parish* of *Roach*

White, Red & Blue
or in Search of Heroes
Fred Feather
Chairman of the Essex Society for Family History

We have oft been told that the important part of a journey is not arrival, but the people you meet on the way. It was easy to half-heartedly listen to my motherís stories of Arctic explorers, relatives who went over Niagara Falls in a barrel and others whose heads bore the marks from when the lion had shut its jaws. I never asked questions. Then suddenly it was too late, for the stories had ended. Only the name Woon remained. A trip to Canada set my wife to reading everything about that country that the library supplied and this had its reward in Leslie Neatby's book *'The Search for Franklin'* (confirmed by another book: 'The White Ribbon'). There it was in black and white: 'Awarded the Arctic Medal - John Woon, Sergeant-Royal Marines, *H.M.S.Investigator.*' This was the precursor to a quarter century of research. I set out looking for one hero but discovered so much more. It will be clearer if I put it in the order in which it happened rather than the order in which we found it.

The Woon family, from the time of Good Queen Bess, was prominent in St.Enoder, Cornwall, with Christian names such as Melchisadeck and Zenobia. After troubles like the Civil War and the Monmouth Rebellion they moved nearer to Bodmin and Cornish *Protestation Returns* and *Hearth Taxes* locate them in Roche. My line probably started with Bartholomew Woon born circa 1690, his son William, then his grandson, churchwarden William, then his great-grandson William, born in 1762.

The Militia
William Woon joined the Cornwall Militia (muster lists at the Public Record Office) which was compulsory for those unsuccessful in the ballot. Often, militia was armed peasantry, reluctantly flourishing billhooks and used to fill in gaps when regular regiments were abroad, for they could not, by law, serve outside the kingdom. Men of worth were soon recognised in such a setting and he swiftly became sergeant. During the French Revolution disorder threatened to spread to Ireland and there was severe rioting in Bristol, to which the Militia were sent. Their posting there was a success and it ended as they marched back to Cornwall to the 'Huzzahs' of the Bristolians. Sergeant William Woon used the opportunity to marry, in Holy Cross or Temple (now ruined by bombing). On 25th August 1797 a child called William Woon was born in Bristol, where the name is rare (army discharge certificate at P.R.O.). The Napoleonic Wars continued and the Cornwall Militia renamed Royal Cornwall Militia. They were embodied into the army, the troops uniformed and the Grenadier Company issued with bearskin caps (documents in the National Army Museum library

and'Tradition' magazine). The regimental flag bore the 15 gold bezants on a black ground, heraldry still used in Cornwall and impressed upon fine biscuits purveyed by the estates of the present Duke of Cornwall (Prince of Wales). To prevent men running away home for the harvest they were deployed away from Cornwall. They were at Plymouth, on Barham Down near Canterbury (officer's diary in the N.A.M.), on Dartmoor, where French prisoners were building the prison. In 1810 the regiment was at the huge prisoner of war camp at Norman Cross near Peterborough.

Father and Son?
What does an amateur genealogist accept as a connection? Two men of the age of a father and son with the same unusual name, serving in the same company of an obscure regiment? Not me, I am afraid, it is only a very strong possibility. Two males joined the Royal Cornwall Militia in 1807, one was called John Woon and the other was but ten. He was posted to the same company as Sergeant Woon and it is not a huge stretch of the imagination that they were father and son. One married in Bristol in 1794, the other was born there in 1797. Army documents confirm the child's age. They were not together for long. Sergeant Woon's pension record (P.R.O.) reports his discharge after 28 years service. He made his was back to Cornwall to became a Chelsea 'Out' Pensioner. In the 1841 census he was living near Bodmin at Indian Queens and he died in 1846. In 1810 Private William Woon, was just 13. When he became 16 he was attested as a full soldier and made a drummer boy, later a bugler. He married in 1817 at Bodmin, where the bugles of the Royal Cornwall Militia were reported upon as the regiment paraded for major fires, executions at Bodmin Jail, and various events recorded in the local newspaper. (parish records at Bodmin and 'The West Briton') His children had the date of birth and day recorded in a family bible (in family possession). They were Elizabeth (Wednesday 6th January 1818), William Coleman (Monday 17th April 1820), Mary Ann (Thursday 28th March 1822), then John the hero of our story, (Monday 10th October 1825). The parish register of Saint Petroc, Bodmin, records his baptism in December 1825.

The Hero (*Part 1*)
At the time John was born his father was promoted corporal and family finances improved. The next baby was Ellenora Violetta (Saturday 10th February 1828). As a sideline could we discuss a contemporary aspect of the outbreak of Italian names in the south-west and Plymouth? One plausible explanation was the Battle of

Maida in 1806, the only battle fought in Italy in our history to that date. One Devon based infantry regiment had one third of its 700 strength killed by the French. According to their muster lists (P.R.O.) these losses were immediately made up by enlisting Neapolitan soldiers (there was no Italian state at the time) and when they came home, the newly-made, Italian-speaking, English soldiers had an important influence on life in Devon and Cornwall. When Napoleon died the threat of war was gone and the militia regiments were reduced to cadres, which had the effect that corporal William Woon was demoted to being a bugler. Perhaps the family were grateful that he was still on the regimental muster. Their wages dropped but the babies kept coming: Edwin (Sunday 25th July 1830), my great-grandmother Jane (Monday 25th March 1833), Emily (Thursday 18th June 1835), Thomas (Thursday 12th April 1838) and Henry (Saturday 26th September 1840). Then, as peace became even more secure, the Royal Cornwall Militia disembodied from the regular army. William, father of a large family was out of work and they soon moved from Bodmin in Cornwall to Plymouth in Devon, where he became a foreman in His Majest'ís gunwharf. In the 1841 census the family was almost complete, except for the elder daughter Elizabeth, and the eldest son William Coleman Woon, who had become a 'Dissenting Minister.' The childrenís baptisms show a change in religion from Church of England to Wesleyan. We recently traced William Coleman Woon's gravestone to Kingswood in Gloucestershire, where he was Congregational Minister. His mother Mary Anne nee Coleman died on 17th February 1842. His father lived on and was found in most census returns until his death in 1879 at Plymouth. John Woon was then a 15 year old labourer. Royal Marine history and documents give many clues about his life and times (P.R.O. and the Royal Marines Museum, Southsea). On 28th June 1844, when nearly 20, John became a private in the 16th company of the Woolwich Division of the Royal Marines. His first voyage was upon the freight ship Resistance, between April and June 1848, by which time he had been promoted corporal in 12th company of the Woolwich Division and upon his return he was made sergeant in the 16th company at Woolwich on 31st August 1848. Promotion was followed by his great adventure, the expedition on H.M.S.Investigator from 23rd December 1849 to 17th October 1854. This epic Arctic voyage was in search of a lost expedition of Sir John Franklin (chronicled extensively in the newspapers and Illustrated London News). The 24 year old sergeant was featured for bravery and resourcefulness, as one of the crew marooned in Arctic ice for several years. His story can be read in many contemporary works ('Heroes of Britain' by Edwin Hodder, 'The Discovery of the North-West Passage' by McClure, 'Knights of the Frozen Sea' and Mierching's 'Frozen Ships'). The Investigator's company had been the first to find the north-west passage around Canada and returned home to substantial financial awards. Captain McClure had Woon promoted colour sergeant on 17th February 1854 and his new wealth meant that he could afford a bride. He married Sarah Blaxell on November 25th 1854 at Saint Mary Castel on Guernsey (Parish Records). He was to sign for the pure white ribbon of the Arctic Medal on 7th April 1757 (P.R.O. ADM 171/9).

The Hero *(Part 2)*

At the time of the Crimean War the Royal Marines were divided into two forces: the 'Red Marines' or Royal Marine Light Infantry and the 'Blue Marines' or Royal Marine Artillery. The period 1854 to 1857 was a particularly busy time for the armed services, with the Crimean War, the Indian Mutiny and then the 2nd China War. A unit of Royal Marine Light Infantry was told off for the latter and embarked on 12th August 1857 upon the Brazilian Steamship Companyís troopship *Imperatriz*, for ultimate transfer to wooden walled battleship *H.M.S.Calcutta*. Woon, colour sergeant of 32nd company, was Acting Sergeant-Major for the battalion formed from Woolwich and Chatham Divisions. His adventures in China, particularly in 1857 at Canton, are outlined in newspapers, periodicals and books (Clowes in Volume 7 of 'History of the Royal Navy'î and Colonel Cyril Field R.M.L.I in volume 2 of 'Britain's Sea Soldiers -1924'). The action was one in which British troops were severely repulsed whilst storming a Chinese fortress. His bravery was remarked upon and Clowes reported that there was a move to give him the newly instituted Victoria Cross. This was not done as we had lost the battle. His actions included the incident where a neutral American sailor, who helped our wounded, coined the phrase '*blood is thicker than water.*' For China, Woon initially received the *red and gold ribbon* and 2nd China War Medal (Canton 1857 clasp), signed for on 5th April 1862 (P.R.O/ADM 171/30). The loss of the proposed Victoria Cross was somewhat ameliorated by the alternative award of the naval version of the Meritorious Service Medal, which carried an annual stipend of £10 (as did the Victoria Cross). This *navy blue ribbon* and medal completed his medal cluster. The citation, dated 7th November 1859: 'Vice W.Healey, promoted Q.M. - Arctic Expedition 1849-1854 *H.M.S.Investigato*r and Mentioned in Dispatches for conspicuous gallantry at Pei Ho forts on 25th June 1857'. He remained in China until the 6th March 1860 and, soon after his return, on 5th November 1861 became a full Woolwich Division sergeant major. Queen Victoria was anxious that her forces should have more officers who had risen from the ranks and John Woon was commissioned on 13th September 1867 and posted to Chatham as Quartermaster. This signal honour meant that he had to give up the £10 for Meritorious Service to Sergeant Thomas Smithson, but he was allowed to continue to wear the medal and ribbon. After two years at Chatham he was posted to Deal upon the disbandment of the Woolwich Division. He died on parade at Deal on 8th March 1877. The '*Deal Telegram*' reported his death and huge military funeral which included the band of the 24th Foot. That regiment was to feature in southern Africa two years later and was commemorated in the film '*Zulu*'. The tombstone of John, his wife Sarah and baby Rupert stand against the wall of the garden of rest in the former North Barracks at Deal.

An outbreak of Heroism

His children were orphaned when Sarah died in 1882; they were John Blaxell (1856), Frances Sarah (1857) William Henry (1861), Florence Roseland (1863), Frank Maxwell (1866), Albert Allen (1868), Ernest Walter (1871),

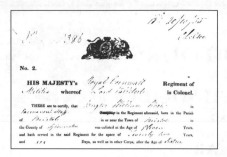

Martha Grace Louise (1874) and Rupert Stewart (1877). They survived in boarding schools and on charity. Miss Fanny Woon received a small sum as organist in a Deal church.

John Blaxell Woon was commissioned into the Royal Marine Artillery in 1873 and served on *H.M.S.Agincourt* as gunnery officer for 6 years.(Military almanacs) He then transferred to the Indian Staff Corps and rose through the ranks to the command of his own regiment, 20th Punjab Infantry at Peshawar. His fighting qualities in the Khyber Pass were commented upon (Winston Churchill's 'Frontiers and Wars'). As a colonel or brigadier he was sent to help with the relief of the Siege of Peking in 1900, then commanded brigades and divisions. By 1911 he was Lieutenant General Sir John Blaxell Woon K.C.B. His grandson, John Watson, told me that the old man, who died in 1938 as a full General, told him that he loaned a horse to King George V at the Delhi Durbar. How in that snobbish age did a Knight of the Order of the Bath explain that his grandfather was an 11 year old drummer boy?. ('Who was Who' and 'Whitaker's Almanack' 1938)

William Henry Woon went to South Africa. His 1909 book, written under the pseudonym of *'A Colonial Officer'*, covers the period of the Boer War and many other cataclysmic events.('Twenty five years soldiering in South Africa'). He rose from private in the Cape Mounted Rifles, which had both a police function but became a cavalry unit in war, to the rank of captain, and later served with Steinackerís Horse. He was severely wounded and was nursed by a sister in England. Frank Maxwell Woon went to America. All that is known of him is that he was an attorney in Virginia and died whilst proceeding as a volunteer to the Spanish American War. Enquiries are still being made with the National Archives in Washington. Ernest Walter Woon joined the Cape Police, later South Africa Police and rose to the rank of Inspector.(South African Defence Ministry Service Records). Serving as an infantryman he became lieutenant-colonel in the South African infantry and is mentioned in the German East African campaigns during the Great War. He was awarded both the Distinguished Service Order and the Military Cross. He married, became secretary of the Pretoria Country Club and died childless in 1943. His impressive medal cluster has just been identified amongst Sir John's effects. Albert Allen Woon also went to South Africa, joined the Natal Mounted Police and at some stage met his brother William. He served both in the Transvaal and the Orange River and, as a lieutenant, was wounded at the siege of Ladysmith. He died from

the effects of that wound in February 1902. His horse 'Squib' was led in his funeral procession carrying his reversed spurred boots.(contemporary unidentified magazine) Research into the lives of John Woon's daughters is harder but is still being pursued.

So, how many heroes can one family take? It is perhaps fortunate that I was a private in the Army Catering Corps. Perhaps that makes me a hero for surviving that much vilification!! Wait - there is more...

A fourth medal has been traced to the Glenbow Museum in Calgary, Alberta. This is the only example of what the experts have called the Arctic Gallantry Medal, it is engraved John Woon, Colour Sergeant R.M. and was purchased in a sale in 1950. It is round, unlike the six sided Arctic Medals of the time, but has the white ribbon. It bears the Queen's portrait so it cannot be a private issue. It does not show in the cluster on his photograph but adds a further intrigue to his story. Then.....

THE CONGRESSIONAL MEDAL OF HONOUR
The American Victoria Cross

WOON John - Born England - Bosun's Mate at the Battle of Grand Gulf, 29th April 1863, on board U.S.S.Pittsburgh. 'Woon showed courage and devotion to duty during these bitter engagements.'
(United States of America - Navy Department - 'Medal of Honour 1861-1949')

Now, where can I find out if he had that weekend off?

NAPOLEONIC WARS
1ST or GRENADIER FOOT GUARDS & OTHER REGIMENTS

Researching Army Ancestors 1793 -1815

Indexes to 'Regimental Service Returns 1806' Public Record Office Reference W025/871-1120. These are a general muster of regiments at this date. On going indexing project published in volumes in book or fiche of around 3,500 to 4,500 names. Volumes 1 to 6 published, covering 1st to 14th Regiments of Foot & Life Guards, Horse Guards, 1st to 3rd Dragoon Guards. (July 2000)

Indexes 'Army of Reserve 1803' reference Public Record Office E182. Published by counties, those sending to the same Regiment or reserve battalion grouped together. On going project published in volumes in book or fiche. Published to date, Volume 1 covering Berkshire, Dorset, Gloucestershire, Hampshire, Isle of Wight & Wiltshire, Volume 2 Herefordshire, Monmouth & Wales. (July 2000)

'Do I Have Army Ancestors?'
A brief guide to starting points for researching this period.

Two books on the lives and deaths of ordinary soldiers in the 1st Foot Guards from 1803 - 1823, including biographies on several hundred men.
John COLLETT and a Company of Foot Guards (Book one 1803-1813)
John COLLETT and a Company of Foot Guards (Book two 1813- 1823)
Details on over 12,000 men who served in this regiment from 1793 -1823 held on a data base information available on request.

Details of all the above from:
Barbara CHAMBERS
39, Chatterton, Letchworth Garden City, Hertfordshire, SG6 2JY UK
e-mail BJCham2809@aol.com
web <http://members.aol.com/BJCham2O9/homepage.html>

BATTLEFIELD TOURS
with
THE WAR RESEARCH SOCIETY
2001 TOURS

1st WORLD WAR

ITALIAN CAMPAIGN

ASSIAGO   PIAVE   ISONZO   CAPORETTO

MONS   SOMME   YPRES   MARNE   AISNE

MAMETZ WOOD / TANKS IN THE GT. WAR / FRONT LINE

1st JULY WAR WALKS

POETS TOUR   AIR ACES TOUR   VC's TOUR

PLUGSTREET/SALIENT POINTS   ARMISTICE IN YPRES

2nd WORLD WAR

ST.NAZAIRE   NORMANDY   POLAND   GREAT ESCAPES

DAMBUSTERS RAID   DIEPPE / BRUNEVAL   COLDITZ CASTLE

ARNHEM   NIJMEGEN   BERLIN   BELSEN   V2 ROCKET SITES

MONTE CASSINO   ANZIO   SALERNO   EAGLE'S NEST

WATERLOO -   RE ENACTMENT TOUR

SOUTH AFRICA
ZULU AND BOER WAR TOUR

EDINBURGH MILITARY TATTOO

SCOTTISH SPECTACULAR

LOCH LOMOND / LOCH NESS /INVERNESS/ CULLODEN

For full details please send an A5 S.A.E. to:-

Ian C. ALEXANDER
27 Courtway Avenue,
Birmingham B14 4PP
Tele: 0121 430 5348   Fax: 0121 436 7401
Email: battletour@aol.com
Website: www.battlefieldtours.co.uk

Military Museums

England

Bedfordshire
Bedford Museum Bedfordshire Yeomanry
Castle Lane, Bedford, MK40 3XD Tel: 01234
353323 Fax: 01234 273401
Bedfordshire and Hertfordshire Regimental Museum
Luton Museum, Wardown Park, Luton, LU2 7HA
Tel: 01582 546719

Berkshire
Commonwealth War Graves Commission
2 Marlow Road, Maidenhead, SL6 7DX Tel:
01628-634221 Fax: 01628-771208
R.E.M.E. Museum of Technology
Isaac Newton Road, Arborfield, Reading, RG2
9NJ Tel: 0118-976-3567 Fax: 0118-976-3672
Email: reme-museum@gtnet.gov.uk
WWW:
http://www.eldred.demon.co.uk/reme-museum/index.htm
Royal Berkshire Yeomanry Cavalry Museum
T A Centre, Bolton Road, Windsor, SL4 3JG Tel:
01753-860600
The Household Cavalry Museum
Combermere Barracks, Windsor Tel: 01753
755112 Fax: 01753 755112

Buckinghamshire
Royal Army Education Corps Museum, HQ
Beaconsfield Station, Wilton Park, Beaconsfield,
HP9 2RP Tel: 01494 683232

Cambridgeshire
Cambridgeshire Regimental Collection, Ely
Museum, The Old Goal, Market Street, Ely, CB7
4LS Tel: 01353-666655

Cheshire
South Lancashire Regiment Prince of Wales Volunteers Museum
Peninsula Barracks, Warrington

Cornwall
Duke of Cornwall's Light Infantry Museum
The Keep, Bodmin, PL31 1EG Tel: 01206-72610

County Durham
Durham Light Infantry Museum
Aykley Heads, Durham, DH1 5TU Tel: 0191-384-
2214 Fax: 0191-386-1770 Email:
dli@durham.gov.uk

Cumbria
Border Regiment & Kings Own Royal Border Regt Museum
Queen Mary's Tower, The Castle, Carlisle, CA3
8UR Tel: 01228-532774 Fax: 01228-521275
Email: rhq@kingsownborder.demon.co.uk

Derbyshire
Regimental Museum of the 9th/12th Royal Lancers, Derby City Museum and Art Gallery,
The Strand, Derby, DE1 1BS Tel: 01332 716656
Fax: 01332 716670
Email: akelsall@derbymuseum.co.uk
WWW: www.derby.gov.uk/museums

Devon
Museum of Barnstaple & North Devon incorporating Royal Devon Yeomanry Museum
The Square, Barnstaple, EX32 8LN Tel: 01271
346 747 Fax: 01271 346407

Dorset
Royal Signals Museum
Blandford Camp, Nr Blandford Forum, DT11
8RH Tel: 01258-482248
Tel: 01258-482267 Fax: 01258-482084
WWW: www.royalsignalsarmy.org.uk/museum/
Tank Museum
Bovington, BH20 6JG Tel: 01929 405096
Fax: 01929 405360
Email: admin@tankmuseum.co.uk
WWW: www.tankmuseum.co.uk
The Keep Military Museum
The Keep, Bridport Road, Dorchester, DT1 1RN
Tel: 01305 264066 Fax: 01305 250373
Email: keep.museum@talk21.com
WWW: www.keepmilitarymuseum.orguk

Essex
Essex Regiment Museum
Oaklands Park, Moulsham Street, Chelmsford,
CM2 9AQ Tel: 01245 615101 Fax: 01245 611250
Email: pompadour@chelsfordbc.gov.uk,
http://www.chelmsfordbc.gov.uk

Gloucestershire
Soldiers of Gloucestershire Museum
Gloucester Docks, Commercial Road, Gloucester,
GL1 2EH Tel: 01452 522682 Fax: 01452 311116

Hampshire
Aldershot Military Museum
Queens Avenue, Aldershot, GU11 2LG Tel:
01252-314598 Fax: 01252-34294
Email: musim@hants.gov.uk
Army Medical Services Museum
Keogh Barracks, Ash Vale, nr Aldershot, GU12
5RQ Tel: 01252 340212 Fax: 01252 340332
Email: museum@keogh72.freeserve.co.uk
Army Physical Training Corps Museum
ASPT, Fox Line, Queen's Avenue, Aldershot,
GU11 2LB Tel: 01252 347168 Fax: 01252 340785
Museum of Army Flying, Middle Wallop,
Stockbridge, SO20 8DY Tel: 01980 674421
Fax: 01264 781694
Email: daa@flying-museum.org.uk
WWW: www.flying-museum.org.uk

Queen Alexandra's Royal Army Nursing Corps Museum
RHQ Army Medical, Keogh Barracks, Ash Vale, Aldershot, GU12 5RQ

Royal Marines Museum
Eastney, Southsea, PO4 9PX Tel: (023) 92 819385-Exts-224 Fax: (023) 92 838420
Email: matthewlittle@royalmarinesmuseum.co.uk
WWW: www.royalmarinesmuseum.co.uk

Royal Naval Museum
H M Naval Base (PP66), Portsmouth, PO1 3NH
Tel: (023) 92723795 Fax: (023) 92727575

Royal Navy Submarine Museum
Haslar Jetty Road, Gosport, PO12 2AS
Tel: (023) 92510354

The Gurkha Museum
Peninsula Barracks, Romsey Road, Winchester, SO23 8TS Tel: 01962 842832 Fax: 01962 877597

The King's Royal Hussars Museum (10th Royal Hussars PWO 11th Hussars PAO and Royal Hussars PWO)
Peninsula Barracks, Winchester, SO23 8TS
Tel: 01962 828540 Fax: 01962 828538
Email: beresford@krhmuseum.freeserve.co.uk
WWW:
www.hants.gov.uk/leisure/museum/royalhus/index.html

The Light Infantry Museum
Peninsula Barracks, Romsey Road, Winchester, SO23 8TS Tel: 01962 868550

The Royal Green Jackets Museum (Oxford and Bucks Light Infantry King's Royal Rifle Corps and The Rifle Brigade)
Peninsula Barracks, Romsey Road, Winchester SO23 8TS Tel: 01962 828549
Fax: 01962 828500

Royal Hampshire Regimental Museum
Serle's House, Southgate Street, Winchester, SO23 9EG Tel: 01962 863658

Hertfordshire
Hertford Museum (Hertford Regiment), 18 Bull Plain, Hertford, SG14 1DT
Tel: 01992 582686 Fax: 01992 534797

Kent
Buffs Regimental Museum
The Royal Museum & Art Gallery, 18 High Street, Canterbury, CT1 2RA Tel: 01227-452747 Fax: 01227-455047

Princess of Wales and Queen's Regiment Museum
Inner Bailey, Dover Castle, Dover, CT16 1HU Tel: 01304-240121

Princess of Wales's Royal Regt & Queen's Regt Museum
Howe Barracks, Canterbury, CT1 1JY Tel: 01227-818056 Fax: 01227-818057

Royal Engineers Library
Brompton Barracks, Chatham, ME4 4UG Tel: 01634-822416 Fax: 01634-822419

Royal Engineers Museum
Prince Arthur Road, Gillingham, ME4 4UG
Tel: 01634 406397 Fax: 01634 82237
Email: remuseum.rhgre@gtnet.gov.uk
WWW: http://www.army.mod.uk/armymuseums

The Queen's Own Royal West Kent Regiment Museum
Maidstone Museum and Art Gallery, St. Faith's Street, Maidstone, ME14 1LH Tel: 01622 754497
Fax: 01622 602193

Lancashire
King's Own Royal Regimental Museum
The City Museum, Market Square, Lancaster, LA1 1HT Tel: 01524 64637 Fax: 01524 841692
Email: kingsownmuseum@iname.com

Museum of Lancashire (Queen's Lancashire Regiment Duke of Lancaster's Own Yeomanry Lancashire Hussars 14th/20th King's Hussars)
Stanley Street, Preston, PR1 4YP
Tel: 01772 264075

Museum of the Manchesters
Ashton Town Hall, Market Place, Ashton-u-Lyne, OL6 6DL, Tel:0161 342 3078/3710 or 343 1978

Museum of the Queen's Lancashire Regiment (East South and Loyal North LancashireRegiments)
Fulwood Barracks, Preston, PR2 8AA Tel: 01772 260362 Fax: 01772 260583
Email: rhqqlr@aol.com

The Fusiliers Museum Lancashire, Bury, BL8 2PL Tel: 0161 764 2208

South Lancashire Regiment Prince of Wales Volunteers Museum
Peninsula Barracks, Warrington

Leicestershire
Royal Leicestershire Regiment Museum
Newark Museum, 53 New Walk, Leicester, LE1 7AE Tel: 0116 2470403, , Postal enquiries: Newarke Houses Museum, The Newarke, Leicester LE2 7BY

Lincolnshire
The Queen's Royal Lancers Regimental Museum (16th/5th and 17th/21st Lancers)
Belvoir Castle, nr Grantham , NG32 1PD Tel: 0115 957 3295 Fax: 0115 957 3195

London
Guards Museum
Birdcage Walk, London, SW1E 6HQ
Tel: (020) 7414 3271/3428
Fax: (020) 7414 3429

Imperial War Museum
Lambeth Road, London, SE1 6HZ
Tel: (020) 7416-5000 Tel: (020) 7416 5348
Fax: (020) 7416 5374 (020) 7416 5246
Email: books@iwm.org.uk
WWW: www.iwm.org.uk

National Army Museum
Royal Hospital Road, London, SW3 4HT
Tel: (020) 7730-0717 Fax: (020) 7823-657
 Email: info@national-army-museum.ac.uk
WWW: http://www.national-army-museum.ac.uk
National Maritime Museum
Romney Road, Greenwich, London, SE10 9NF
Tel: (020) 8858-4422 Fax: (020) 8312-6632
WWW: http://www.nmm.ac.uk
Royal Air Force Museum
Grahame Park Way, Hendon, London, NW9 5LL
Tel: (020) 8205-2266 Fax: (020) 8200 1751
Email: info@refmuseum.org.uk
WWW: http://www.rafmuseum.org.uk
Royal Artillery Regimental Museum
Old Royal Military Academy, Red Lion Lane,
Woolwich, London, SE18 4DN
Tel: (020) 8781 5628 ext 3128
The Royal Regiment of Fusiliers
H M Tower of London, London, EC3N 4AB
Tel: (020) 7488 5610

Merseyside
King's Regiment Collection
Museum of Liverpool Life, Pier Head, Liverpool,
L3 1PZ Tel: 0151-478-4062 Fax: 0151-478-4090

Norfolk
Royal Norfolk Regimental Museum
Shirehall, Market Avenue, Norwich, NR1 3JQ Tel:
01603 493649 Fax: 01603 765651

Northamptonshire
**Abington Museum and Museum of The
Northamptonshire Regiment**
Abington Park Museum, Abington, NN1 5LW Tel:
01604 635412

Northumberland
Fusiliers Museum of Northumberland
The Abbot's Tower, Alnwick Castle, Alnwick,
NE66 1NG Tel: 01665-602151 Fax: 01665-
603320 Email: fusmusnorthld@btinternet.com
King's Own Scottish Borderers Museum
The Barracks, Berwick upon Tweed, TD15 1DG
Tel: 01289-307426

Nottinghamshire
Sherwood Foresters Museum and Archives
RHQ WFR, Foresters House, Chetwynd Barracks,
Chilwell, Nottingham, NG9 5HA
Tel: 0115-946-5415 Fax: 0115-946-5712
**Sherwood Foresters (Notts and Derbys.
Regtiment) Museum**
The Castle, Nottingham, NG1 6EL Tel: 0115 946
5415 Fax: 0115 946 9853
Address for enquiries: RHQ WFR, Foresters
House, Chetwynd Barracks, Chilwell, Nottingham
NG9 5HA

Oxfordshire
**Oxfordshire and Buckinghamshire Light
Infantry Regimental Museum**
Slade Park, Headington, Oxford, OX3 7JL
Tel: 01865 780128

Shropshire
**Shropshire Regimental Museum (King's
Shropshire Light Infantry, Shropshire Yeomanry)**
The Castle, Shrewsbury, SY1 2AT
Tel: 01743-358516 Tel: 01743-262292

Somerset
Fleet Air Arm Museum
Box D61, RNAS Yeovilton, Nr Ilchester, BA22
8HT Tel: 01935-840565 Fax: 01935-840181
**Somerset Military Museum (Somerset Light
Infantry Yeomanry)Militia and Volunteers
County Museum**
The Castle, Taunton, TA1 4AA Tel: 01823 333434
Fax: 01823 351639

Staffordshire
Museum of The Staffordshire Regiment
Whittington Barracks, Lichfield, WS14 9PY
 Tel: 0121 311 3240 Tel: 01422 354823
Tel: 0121 311 3229 Fax: 0121 311 3205
Museum of the Staffordshire Yeomanry
The Ancient High House, Greengate Street,
Stafford, ST16 2HS
Tel: 01785 40204 (Tourist Info. Office)

Suffolk
Suffolk Regiment Museum
Suffolk Record Office, 77 Raingate Street, Bury St
Edmunds, IP33 2AR Tel: 01284-352352
Fax: 01284-352355
Email: bury.ro@libhev.suffolkcc.gov.uk

Surrey
**Queen's Royal Surrey Regiment Museum
(Queen's Royal Surrey, East Surrey & Queen's Royal
Surrey Regiments)**
Clandon Park, West Clandon, Guildford, GU4
7RQ Tel: 01483 223419 Fax: 01483 224636
Email: queenssurreys@caree4free.net
WWW: www.surrey-on;line.co.uk/queenssurreys
Regimental Museum Royal Logistical Corps
Deepcut, Camberley, GU16 6RW
Tel: 01252-340871-&-01252-340984

Sussex
Royal Military Police Museum
Roussillon Barracks, Chichester, PO19 4BN
Tel: 01243 534225 Fax: 01243 534288
Email: museum@rhqrmp.freeserve.co.uk
WWW: www.rhqrmp.freeserve.co.uk
**Sussex Combined Services Museum
(Royal Sussex Regt & Queen's Royal Irish Hussars)**
Redoubt Fortress, Royal Parade, Eastbourne,
BN22 7AQ Tel: 01323 410300

Tyne & Wear
A Soldier's Life 15th/19th The King's Royal Hussars
Northumberland Hussars & Light Dragoons
Discovery Museum, Blandford Square, Newcastle-upon-Tyne, NE1 4JA Tel: 0191 232 6789
Fax: 0191 230 2614
Email: ralph.thompson@tyne-wear-museums.org.uk

Warwickshire
Regimental Museum of The Queen's Own Hussars (3rd King's Own and 7th Queen's Own Hussars)
The Lord Leycester Hospital, High Street, Warwick, CV34 4EW, Tel:01926 492035
Royal Warwickshire Regimental Museum
St. John's House, Warwick , CV34 4NF, Tel:01926 491653
Warwickshire Yeomanry Museum
The Court House, Jury Street, Warwick, CV34 4EW Tel: 01926 492212 Fax: 01926 494837

Wiltshire
Duke of Edinburgh's Royal Regiment (Berks & Wilts) Museum
The Wardrobe, 58 The Close, Salisbury, SP1 2EX Tel: 01722-414536
Royal Army Chaplains Department Museum
Netheravon House, Salisbury Road, Netheravon, SP4 9SY Tel: 01980-604911 Fax: 01980-604908

Worcestershire
The Worcestershire Regiment Museum
Worcester City Museum & Art Gallery, Foregate Street, Worcester, WR1 1DT Tel: 01905-25371 Museum Tel: 01905 354359 Office Fax: 01905-616979 Museum 01905 353871 Office Email: rhq_wfr@lineone.net Postal Address: The Curator, The Worcestershire Regimental Museum Trust, RHQ WFR, Norton Barracks, Worcester WR5 2PA
Worcestershire Regiment Archives (Worcester and Sherwood Forester's Regiment)
RHQ WFR Norton Barracks, Worcester, WRS 2PA Tel: 01905-354359

Yorkshire
East Yorkshire
Museum of Army Transport
Flemingate, Beverley, HU17 0N Tel: 01482-860445

North Yorkshire
Eden Camp Museum
Malton, YO17 6RT Tel: 01653-697777
Fax: 01653-698243
Email: admin@edencamp.co.uk
WWW: http://www.edencamp.co.uk
Green Howards Regimental Museum
Trinity Church Square, Richmond, DL10 4QN Tel: 01748-822133 Fax: 01748-826561
Royal Dragoon Guards Military Museum (4th/7th Dragoons & 5th Inniskilling Dragoons)
3A Tower Street, York, YO1 9S Tel: 01904-662790

Yorkshire Air Museum
Halifax Way, Elvington, York, YO41 5AU
Tel: 01904-608595

South Yorkshire
King's Own Yorkshire Light Infantry Regimental Museum
Doncaster Museum & Art Gallery, Chequer Road, Doncaster, DN1 2AE Tel: 01302 734293
Email: museum@doncaster.gov.uk
WWW: www.doncaster.gov.uk
Regimental Museum 13th/18th Royal Hussars and The Light Dragoons
Cannon Hall, Cawthorne, Barnsley, S75 4AT Tel: 01226 790270
York and Lancaster Regimental Museum
Library and Arts Centre, Walker Place, Rotherham, S65 1JH Tel: 01709 823635
Email: guy.kilminster@rotherham.gov.uk
WWW: www.rotherham.gov.uk

West Yorkshire
Duke of Wellington's Regimental Museum
Bankfield Museum, Akroyd Park, Boothtown Road, Halifax, HX3 6HG Tel: 01422 354823
Fax: 01422 249020

Wales
The Royal Welch Fusiliers Regimental Museum
The Queen's Tower, The Castle, Caernarfon, LL55 2AY Tel: 01286-673362 Fax: 01286-677042

Cardiff
1st The Queen's Dragoon Guards Regimental Museum
Cardiff Castle, Cardiff, CF1 2RB Tel: (029) 2022 2253 Tel: (029) 2078 1232 Fax: (029) 2078 1384
Email: morris602.hhq@netscapeonline.co.uk
WWW: www.QdDG.org.uk

Monmouthshire
Monmouthshire Royal Engineers (Militia)
Castle and Regimental Museum, The Castle, Monmouth, NP5 3BS Tel: 01600-712935
Nelson Museum & Local History Centre
Priory St, Monmouth, NP5 3XA
Tel: 01600 713519 Fax: 01600 775001
Email: nelsonmuseum@monmouthshire.gov.uk

Powys
South Wales Borderers & Monmouthshire Regimental Museum of the Royal Regt of Wales (24th/41st Foot)
The Barracks, Brecon, LD3 7EB Tel: 01874-613310 Fax: 01874-613275
Email: rrw@ukonline.co.uk
WWW: http://www.ukonline.co.uk/rrw/index.htm

Scotland
Museum of The Royal Highland Fusiliers (Royal Scots Fusiliers & Highland Light Infantry)
518 Sauchiehall Street, Glasgow, G2 3LW Tel: 0141 332 0961 Fax: 0141 332 5439

Royal Scots Regimental Museum
The Castle, Edinburgh, EH1 2YT Tel: 0131-310-5014 Fax: 0131-310-5019

Aberdeenshire
Gordon Highlanders Museum
St Lukes, Viewfield Road, Aberdeen, AB15 7XH
Tel: 01224 311200 Fax: 01224 319323
Email: museum@gordonhighlanders.com
WWW: www,gordonhighlanders.com

Ayrshire
Ayrshire Yeomanry Museum
Rozelle House, Monument Road, Alloway by Ayr, KA7 4NQ Tel: 01292 445400
(Museum Tel: 01292 264091

Invernesshire
Queen's Own Highlanders (Seaforths & Camerons) Regimental Museum Archives
Fort George, Ardersier, Inverness, IV1 2TD
Tel: 01463-224380

Lanarkshire
The Cameronians (Scottish Rifles) Museum
c/o Low Parks Museum, 129 Muir Street, Hamilton, ML3 6BJ Tel: 01698 45571
Tel: 01698 328232 Fax: 01698 328232

Perthshire
Regimental Museum & Archives of Black Watch
Balhousie Castle, Hay Street, Perth, PH1 5HS
Tel: 0131-3108530 Tel: 01738 621281 ext 8530
Fax: 01738-643245
Email: bwarchivist@btclick.com

Scottish Horse Regimental Museum
The Cross, Dunkeld, PH8 0AN

Stirlingshire
Regimental Museum Argyll and Sutherland Highlanders
Stirling Castle, Stirling, FK8 1EH
Tel: 01786 475165 Fax: 01786 446038

Northern Ireland

Royal Irish Fusiliers Museum
Sovereign's House, Mall East, Armagh, BT61 9DL
Tel: (028) 3752 2911 Fax: (028) 3752 2911
Royal Ulster Rifles Regimental Museum
RHQ Royal Irish Rifles, 5 Waring Street, Belfast, BT1 2EW Tel: (028) 90232086

Co Fermanagh
Royal Inniskilling Fusiliers Regimental Museum
The Castle, Enniskillen, BT74 7BB
Tel: (028) 66323142 Fax: (028) 66320359

Belgium

In Flanders Fields Museum
Lakenhallen, Grote Markt 34, Ieper, B-8900
Tel: 00-32-(0)-57-22-85-84
Fax: 00-32-(0)-57-22-85-89
WWW: www.inflandersfields.be

The Romany and Traveller Family History Society

"Gypsy ancestors? I don't suppose you can find out much about them, can you?" It's a typical reaction when members of our Society strike up conversations with other researchers at Record Offices or family history meetings.

But the short answer is: yes you can! Which is how there comes to be a Romany and Traveller Family History Society (R&TFHS).

The Society was launched in 1994 at the instigation of Janet Keet-Black and Alan McGowan by a group of half a dozen or so keen family historians with British Gypsy/Traveller ancestors. Janet and Alan and members of that founding group are still actively involved in the running of the Society - and our membership has expanded dramatically both in numbers and geographically. We're now also members of the Federation of Family History Societies.

You'll now find over 300 R&TFHS members around the world, mostly in English-speaking countries and many of who are researching their roots among the Gypsy families of England, Scotland and Wales. But the term 'Traveller' in our Society's name is there to show that we also welcome people whose ancestors were nomadic but not necessarily of the kaulo rat: the 'black blood' of the Romany people.

For example, we have a good number of members whose families were 'fairground folk' - travelling showmen. Some are interested in circus people or travelling actors. There were naturally close economic links and often family ties between all these groups in the past because they were frequently travelling the same road and attending the same fairs, feasts and markets. (We also sometimes get approached by people whose ancestors were bargees. We can't claim to be specialists in this but there were some Romany Gypsies who made their livelihood as 'water Gypsies', travelling the canals.)

Meetings
Unlike family history societies that are county-based, our Society has no natural geographical focal point and our membership is spread far and wide. For this reason we don't attempt to hold regular local meetings but instead make sure that as many members as possible get the chance to attend our annual conferences/AGMs. We do this by holding them in a different county every year. In our six-year history, these meetings have been held in Hampshire, Sussex, the old county of Flintshire in

North Wales, Oxfordshire, Lincolnshire and Kent. Wherever we go, we make sure that our conferences include the chance to hear specialist speakers on Gypsy/Traveller subjects - ranging from traditional travelling patterns, occupations and fairground history to portraits of specific families. We also cover more general family history sources that are particularly relevant to Gypsy family history: from the Poor Law to Army records.

Experience over the years has shown that what members really enjoy and enthuse about most at these events is the chance to 'network' with other members. This is a particularly important and potentially fruitful aspect of the day when you consider that our Gypsy/Traveller ancestors for the most part lived and worked as a relatively 'closed community'. Families would travel together and intermarry with each other. This means that our members always stand a very good chance of finding themselves face to face with 'cousins' at our meetings or with descendants of families that the records show lived side by side with our own ancestors.

Our annual conference takes place in May - and for the past two years it's been complemented by a more informal meeting in the Autumn. These popular 'Open Days' give people the chance to drop in and meet the Committee and old friends, have a chat, swop notes and experiences and use the Society's growing library of books, microfiche and microfilms. These meetings too are held in a different location each year but generally in what the old Travellers would call a 'south country' location. This is because a big proportion of our British members live in southern England! To date we've met in Hook, Hampshire, and Uckfield, Sussex.

Publishing
Like most family history societies we publish a journal four times a year. This is distributed to members as part of their membership fee. Called 'Romany Routes' and under the expert editorship of Janet Keet-Black, this always features a wide variety of articles on many subjects: from items on specific families to social history, occupations, interesting finds in historical documents, family photographs, illustrations, book reviews and useful Websites plus members' interests.

The Society also pursues a very active book publishing programme. We see it as part of our collective mission to gather in and broadcast as much information as we can about our Gypsy/Traveller

forebears. This has resulted in the publication of a wide variety of titles over the years. These range from books recording the memories of older members of Traveller families to a research guide, extracts from census returns, transcriptions of documents with a Gypsy/Traveller interest and works on specific family names. The Society is also working on a series of reprints of important books from the past on Gypsy life and culture in order to put some of these rare texts within easier reach of the pockets of modern-day readers. (Classic Gypsy books are becoming increasingly hard to find and therefore increasingly expensive to buy!)

You can see our full range of current titles on our Website - or write with a stamped addressed envelope (or two International Reply Coupons) for a publication list to: R&TFHS Publications, 6 St James Walk, South Chailey, E. Sussex BN8 4BU, UK.

The Robert Dawson Romany Collection
In 1998 the Society received from one of its members the very generous donation of a large collection of Gypsy books, manuscript notebooks, documents, recordings, crafts and ephemera. This had been collected over many years by Bob Dawson, one of Britain's greatest modern-day Gypsy experts. To ensure that the Collection could be made available to the widest possible audience - both Society members and other researchers - it was deposited on permanent loan at the Rural History Centre, University of Reading, in February 2000 and has been named 'The Robert Dawson Romany Collection' in honour of its donor. The Rural History Centre's library and museum form a unique resource of national and international importance relating to the history of English rural society, agriculture, the landscape and the environment. So it's a fitting home for a Collection that records and celebrates the important contribution Gypsies have made to the rural economy of Britain

for 500 years. Researchers are welcome to visit The Robert Dawson Romany Collection by appointment.

Membership
Membership of the Romany and Traveller Family History Society costs £8.00 a year for British members. You can get full details and a membership form from our Website (address below) or by sending a stamped addressed envelope (or two International Reply Coupons) to: The Membership Secretary, R&TFHS, 27 Conyers Close, Hersham, Surrey KT12 4NG, UK.

Researchers overseas can also join our Society through our stand on the GenFair site at: www.genfair.com

Please pass it on!
Even if you don't have Gypsy/Traveller blood yourself, please do keep us in mind when you're working your way through records and come across references that could be useful to us. Your contributions will be welcomed at either of the addresses above.

As a clue to what to look out for: before 1700 you're likely to see Gypsies referred to as 'Egyptians' - which is what the word 'Gypsy' comes from. After 1700 or so, they could be referred to by one of many spellings of Gypsy - Gipsy, Gypsey, Gipsey - or as 'Travellers', 'Vagrants', 'Vagabonds', 'Sojourners', 'Itinerants', 'Travelling through', 'Strangers' etc - and naturally often of 'no fixed abode'.

Visit our Website
You can find details about Society membership, publications and much of interest about Gypsy/Traveller family history on our Website at: http://website.lineone.net/~rtfhs
It also includes links to other useful sites for those with Gypsy/Traveller ancestry.

Doncaster & District Family History Society
(Registered Charity 516226)

Doncaster & District FHS celebrated its 20th anniversary in January 2000. The Society was originally known as the Doncaster Society for Family History, but later changed its name to better describe the area which we now cover. This includes the Archdeaconry and Metropolitan Borough of Doncaster, reaching Norton to the north, Tickhill and Bawtry to the south, Adlingfleet to the east and Wombwell to the west.

Many members are actively involved with work on local records, particularly those which are in danger of being lost through damage or regular usage. Even those with little time to spare take part in some way in the many various projects - including the transcription of Memorial Inscriptions in churches, churchyards and cemeteries, and then checking and rechecking the results prior to final indexing and publication. Projects completed so far include: the Doncaster Health Authority Death Registers Index; Marriage Index - an alphabetical list of the names of brides and grooms who married between 1800 and 1837; Census Returns for 1851; MIs for 66 churches and churchyards within our area, also burial entries taken from the commencement of the parish registers to at least 1900. In addition, published in A5 booklet form, are the 'Freemen of Doncaster', 'Non Conformist Churches and Chapels of Thorne' and the 'Settlement Indexes1692 - 1846'. All societies rely heavily on volunteers, without whom they would not function. It is to this 'dedicated army' that the D & DFHS are indebted, they give up their time to ensure that the Society functions to a high standard in all its aspects.

Doncaster & District FHS hold monthly meetings, where members can share experiences, sort out problems, exchange information, borrow journals of other societies and enjoy the guest speakers whose topics cover a wide range of Family History topics. Due to the popularity of our hobby we have recently moved to a new venue for our meetings, these are now held at the Danum Hotel, High St, Doncaster. There is a Search Service available for the 1891 and 1871 census. Beginners and Intermediate courses are held regularly and an evening is spent each week learning to read old documents such as wills and inventories. Our journal, The Doncaster Ancestor, published quarterly, is distributed free to all members.

Our newest venture is the opening of the Glenville Research Room, which is situated in the grounds of the Residential School for the Deaf. Housed there are the GRO indexes 1837 – 1950; the 1881 census and the International Genealogical Index (IGI) for the whole country; Boyd's Marriage Indexes for Yorkshire, Lancashire, Somerset and Northumberland; copies of Doncaster Hyde Park, Mexborough, and Conisbrough Cemetery Registers; the 1871 and 1891 census covering most of our area; seven fiche readers and much, much more. The research room will continue to

improve its facilities by the ever-increasing number of records, transcriptions and publications that will be available to both members and visitors. Opening times are Monday, Tuesday and Friday 10.00am to 4.00pm and Wednesday evening 7.00pm to 9.00pm.

Our annual Family History Day is held on the last Saturday in October at the Residential School for the Deaf, Doncaster. Each year, there are three excellent speakers, together with a help and advice table, four computers with our large databases and a selection of CDs. These are manned by volunteers offering their expertise. A separate room situated nearby is also set aside for research purposes together with our large library of fiche and four readers. Fiche and booklets are on sale and many other groups and societies, both local ones and those outside the county, are present.

Overseas membership has an important part to play in the Society's recent thinking, this side of the membership has increased over the past few years, and more access to the Society's facilities can be found on its web site. Computers have enabled the sharing of information to be more effective for the hobby we all love and information can be transferred using e-mail, which has greatly enhanced the friendliness of members from all over the world. Ordering of publications has also been simplified by use of e-mail and a secure finance method.

Tracing ancestors has been proven to be a fascinating and addictive hobby. Genealogy in its simplest form constructs the Family Tree, which contains the names and the dates - Family History adds the detail. These discoveries - noting where the families lived, their occupations and activities, what they ate and what they wore, their sorrows and joys - can bring the past vividly to life, and we gain a greater insight into the day-to-day existence of our forbears. It is rather like detective work, unravelling clues, and finding skeletons in cupboards! The main problem always is – how and where to make a start. This is where all Family History Societies come to the aid of those just starting out on their Ancestral Hunt, by offering beginners guidance and expert advice.

Doncaster & District FHS is always pleased to welcome both old and new members. Annual subscription rates due January 1st are: Individual £8.00; Family £11.00; Senior £6.50; Overseas £10.00.

Our web page is www.doncasterfhs.freeserve.co.uk . Publications and membership can be ordered and paid for via www.GENfair.com or by contacting the Secretary Mrs J. Staniforth, 125 The Grove, Wheatley Hills, Doncaster, South Yorkshire, DN2 5SN.

DDFHS is a Member of the Federation of Family History Societies.

Weston Super Mare Family History Society

The Society, which was founded in 1984 by a few dedicated Family History class students, exists to help members to help themselves and with this in mind publishes a magazine on a regular basis. There are ten meetings a year two of which are set aside to enable members to discuss and exchange views on family history particularly in regard to their own research. In conjunction with other societies, visits are arranged to London repositories, and members endeavour to help those from other areas on a reciprocal basis. All this with a view to encouraging and stimulating interests in family history generally.

The area covered by the society is Weston-super-Mare and the surrounding parishes including Worle, Uphill, Lympsham, Hutton, Yatton, Congresbury, Hewish, Cleeve, Clevedon, Nailsea etc which is basically what would have been old North Somerset.

There was talk initially about us becoming a branch of one of the two neighbouring Societies. In the end we decided to stay independent but work alongside both Somerset & Dorset FHS and Bristol & Avon.

From a hardcore of 30 people we now have a membership of over 160. As we grew in size we moved around Weston in various halls and at present we meet on the last Tuesday of the month (excluding August and December) at Crossroads Carers Centre in Graham Road, Weston-super-Mare. At these meetings members share experiences, help to solve problems or at least put a new angle on things, listen to guest speakers, beginners' night and quizzes in fun, to find out 'how much you know about family history and related topics'.

A request from Somerset & Dorset FHS came asking our members to complete memorial inscriptions from a few of the Parishes missing from their own records, such as Chew Magna, Berrow and Brean. We have since added to these and have also printed the Parish Records from 1813 - 1837 for Uphill, Hutton and St John's the Parish Church of Weston.

The first and third Saturdays of every month we are at Weston Library between 2 - 4pm helping with research enquiries. This enables us to encourage the tracing of the family and help to put 'flesh on the bones', finding out what life was like for our forebears. Often the 'skeletons' in the family are those you can find out more about, you may find a description of them in old newspapers, Prison records or those unfortunates who end up in the Workhouse. The most common questions are "How do I get started?" and the one we all dread, "I want you to find my grandfather" Do you know his name? No! To this person we would suggest they do some further research and come back when they do know his name and possibly armed with a birth or marriage certificate with some further details. And other reason by a few people for coming into the Library on these Saturdays is "I've got half an hour I'll do my family history!"

Weston Library facilities includes the IGI, Local 1841 - 1891 census, Parish Records, Ordnance survey maps, extensive records of local families and a treasury of local knowledge available in the Local Studies Room.

On the first Thursday of each month we have an 'Ask the Archivist' session; Julie Mansfield, a professional Archivist brings requested documents and fiche up from Somerset Archive and Record Service in Taunton, to view in the Library. This enables people who would sometimes find it difficult to get to Taunton to carry on their family or house history.

We have our own library available at meetings and a complete list is available from the librarian. We have members who have extensive knowledge on Uphill, Axbridge Workhouse and Waterloo Soldiers Databases amongst other things.

In 1996 we started indexing Weston Cemetery, taking the monumental Inscriptions from the head and kerb stones, then checking them with the Burial Registers at the Crematorium to fill in the missing details from those without headstones. This work has been an immense task and with the help of many of our members is now being printed. We were surprised at how many 'strays' we found and how much of a holiday/retirement town it was, with many burials coming from people who spent a lifetime elsewhere.

Once a year we have 'The Harry Galloway Memorial Lecture. Harry had a keen interest in Family History and spent over 25 years in the local library service investing a lot of time in creating and preserving Genealogical records in Bristol (Central Library on College Green) and in Weston and the surrounding districts. He jointly formed Harry Galloway Publishing with Adrian Webb and together produced nearly 40 new titles and also reprints of out of print books to aid further research.

We have a biennial Open day in July at a venue in the town attended by other Family History and Local History Societies get together for the sale of research material and to answer questions about their areas. In 1997 the South West Area Group (SWAG) of Family History Societies take over the Winter Gardens for a huge fair attended by a thousand people. This was successfully repeated in 1999 and this years SWAG fair will take place on July 7th 2001, open between 10 - 4.

We are a friendly supportive group who welcomes new members, Ordinary membership in £7.00 per year, with Family membership £9.00 and overseas membership £10.00. The magazine is free to paid up members.

Have you caught the bug? Do you want help in this locality? Contact us by email on kes.jack@virgin.net or by visiting our website on http://members.aol.com/WSMFHS/index.html or by mail to 55 Osborne Road, Weston-super-Mare, North Somerset, BS23 3EJ

Montgomershire Genealogical Society
Cymdejthas Achyddol Maldwyn
Stephen Jones Society Secretary

Montgomeryshire Genealogical Society was founded in 1994 to provide a forum for people with family history interests in the historical county of Montgomeryshire, North Wales, and its borders. The society now has 500 members.

Montgomeryshire was created in 1536 as a result of the Act of Union of England and Wales and was based largely on the medieval Welsh princedom of Powys Wenwynwyn. The county was the only one in Wales which extended all the way from the English border to the Irish sea. Referred to in Welsh by the name "Powys Paradwys Cymru" or "Powys Paradise of Wales", the county has always been noted for its natural beauty and in particular its gentle, rolling landscape - "Mwynder Maldwyn" or the "Mildness of Montgomeryshire". In 1974, Montgomeryshire was subsumed within the modern county of Powys, which incorporated the three earlier counties of Montgomery, Brecon and Radnor, and bore little resemblance to the medieval princedom of the same name.

It is important for outsiders to understand that Montgomeryshire, like many other parts of the "Celtic fringe", has been heavily influenced by emigration. For much of the 19th century, Montgomeryshire had over 60,000 inhabitants. Between the 1830s and the 1860s, America was a particular haven for Montgomeryshire emigrants, but the descendants of Montgomeryshire people are to be found all over the world, in Australia, New Zealand, Canada, South Africa, Patagonia and elsewhere. Emigration, inspired by economic hardship and the thirst for religious freedom, reduced the population of the county from an all time high of 70,000 in 1841 to just 43,000 at the time of the 1971 census. It has since recovered somewhat and currently stands at approximately 47,000.

From the point of view of the family historian, the main result of a declining population has been that the large amount of genealogical source material is not matched by the number of skilled hands willing and able to undertake transcription and research work. It may be noted that before the Montgomeryshire GS published some of the registers of Mochdre parish in 1999, the last large scale publication of any of the county's parish registers, by its historical society the Powysland Club, was as long ago as 1915-1920. Even now, the registers of almost all of the 60-plus parishes in the county remain unpublished.

The society has made important inroads into the backlog of untranscribed material. The main priority for family historians is of course memorial inscriptions in burial grounds, which even in country areas are subject to the constant twin threats of vandalism (both private and public!) and physical decay. Most of the burial grounds in Montgomeryshire, which include many belonging to the Nonconformists, have now been transcribed and are steadily being published by the society.

Despite the great effort which this work involves, we have also managed to undertake other transcribing projects. We have published a transcript and index of the 1841 census for the whole county and members have access to a computerised transcript of the 1891 censuses, also for the whole county.

There is also a long term programme of parish register transcription. The periods covered thus far include all marriages for 1813 to 1837, most baptisms 1813-1837 and a large number of marriages and baptisms from the period 1754-1837.

Like other family history societies, we have a regular social programme and we publish a society journal three times annually (the "Record" - chosen because it means the same in English and Welsh!) which is distributed free to members. Talks are held on a variety of family history related subjects, mostly in Newtown, and we have a popular summer outing and Christmas lunch. We are always pleased to advise members on their family history problems.

The society is a member of the Federation of Family History Societies and the Association of Family History Societies of Wales, and we are regularly to be seen at Society of Genealogists' and other fairs. We hold two annual open events of our own, an Open and Research Day in March, and a summer Open Morning, which invariably coincides with the issue of new publications.

New members are always welcome. Our annual subscription rates are: Individual (in UK or EU) £5.00; Family (two members at same address, in UK or EU) £6.00; Overseas (outside UK and EU) £10. Subscriptions are due on January 1st. Website: http://home.freeuk.net/montgensoc

---

**Montgomeryshire
Genealogical Society**

founded 1994 for everybody interested in family history
in the historical county of Montgomeryshire and its borders
* meetings, outings and excursions
* members' interests
* journal three times annually
* access to a growing library
Vast number of Montgomeryshire records on computer
including -
* 1841 and 1891 censuses (whole county)
* marriages 1813-1837 (whole county)
* memorial inscriptions for most county parish churchyards
Annual subscription:
£5 (individual)
£6 (family) or £10 (overseas).

For an application form please write to:
Miss P. G. Egerton
Cedewain, Llanllwchhaiarn Newtown, Powys, SYI6 2AS
or
Mr D. Peate
20 Henley Road, Little Neston, South Wirral
Cheshire, L64 OSG

Email: montgensoc@freeuk.com

Website: http://freeuk.net/montgensoc

Central Scotland
Family History Society

The Society was formed in 1990, its area delineated by the boundaries of Central Regional Council (now no longer in existence). The area includes Stirlingshire, Clackmannanshire, parts of West Perthshire and a small part of West Lothian, to give the areas their old county names. The area is made up of 40 parishes, stretching from Killin in the north-west to Baldernock in the south and eastwards as far as Muckhart and Carriden.

The history and landscape of the area are diverse. There are proposed National Park areas, rich agricultural landscapes, mountains and hills forming the backdrop to such man-made marvels as Stirling Castle and the Wallace Monument. The industrial scene is now mainly confined to the Falkirk/Grangemouth area with its vast petrochemical works but in times gone by local people worked in agriculture, spinning and weaving (many coming over from Ireland), mining, slate quarrying, brewing, pistol manufacture (in Doune), the famous Carron ironworks (which produced canon used in many major battles) and in shipping, when the upper reaches of the River Forth were still navigable. Falkirk was the venue for huge cattle markets, stock being driven from all over the highlands and islands of Scotland. The castle was always an important garrison and soldiers from many parts of the country have been stationed there. The area has always been at the crossroads between the north and south of Scotland and people from all over the country have settled here. In common with all other parts of Scotland, many thousands have also left the area to seek a better life in the New World.

The aim of the Society is to cater for members who either wish to pursue further their existing knowledge, or to provide support for those wishing to begin their research. A campaign is under way to attract more new members and also to encourage existing members to use their skills to help develop the Society's activities.

The Society members currently meets from October to April, on the third Wednesday of the month, in the Smith Art Gallery & Museum, Stirling. Guest speakers are invited from all parts of Scotland (and occasionally from further afield) to cover topics ranging from general family history research and local interest subjects to how best to conserve documents and artefacts. Members also take centre stage to talk about "Favourite Forebears" where they give a brief insight into the life of one of their ancestors. This has proved to be such a hit that it now appears on the syllabus every year. Meetings are very friendly and relaxed and always finish off with coffee and a chance for everyone to socialise and share information. A social evening and dinner is held in December each year at which several members display and talk about an item relating to their family history.

Realising that many people would love to find out about family history but don't know where to start, the Society has run a number of successful workshops for beginners. There are also visits two or three times a year to New Register House in Edinburgh to allow access to civil registration records and OPRs for the whole of Scotland. Sometimes a visit to somewhere such as the National Library of Scotland's Map Library is included in these outings to Edinburgh. Part of the fun of these trips is the train journey, especially the homeward leg when everyone is keen to

share details of the interesting bits of information found, not to mention confessions about family scandals discovered!

Although still fairly small, the Society attracts members both locally and from across the UK, as well as many overseas countries - Scots emigrated to all parts of the world and many of their descendants are now keen to trace their Scottish roots. Understandably many members are unable to attend the monthly meetings but a summary of talks appears in the bi-annual newsletter. The newsletter also offers members the opportunity to exchange family information, contribute news and views, give details of interests and queries as well as containing articles of general interest to family historians. In an attempt to help keep both new and old members up-to-date, the Society periodically issues a list of members interests on a fiche which is sent out with the newsletter.

Members are still busy on the transcription of the some of the 1851 census returns for the area and as each parish is completed the index is published. Another group is involved with the National Burial Index. Some parishes have no surviving burial records, one has only 20 entries whilst another has over 3000. In common with other parts of the country, the legibility of some of these records means that this is no easy task to undertake. The fact that in some parishes many of the inhabitants were at one time Gaelic speakers adds to the complexities of deciphering the old records.

All of the Society's publications are made available at the bookstall that operates at each meeting and also at various family history fairs and conferences. Details of what is available can be found on our web site. Other items of interest are also made available on the bookstall, a service which is much appreciated by members as local bookshops do not usually carry such specialised material.

The Society doesn't yet have its own premises but its aim is to open its own research centre in the future and methods of funding such a venture are being investigated. In the meantime some of the Society's holdings are kept on open access in the Stirling Council Archives at Burghmuir Industrial Estate. Thanks to the support of Stirling Council Library Service some items are also kept in Bridge of Allan Library. It's here that you'll find a microfiche reader belonging to the Society and filmed copies of the OPRs for our area, as well as some censuses.

The Society is always keen to welcome new members both at home and abroad. Annual subscription rates are UK: Individual £7.50; Retired, Student, Unwaged £5; Institution, Society or Company £7.50 and Family £10. All Overseas: £10. Membership enquiries should be sent to the Colin Bendall, CSFHS Membership Records, 19 Mosshouse, Stirling, FK7 9HE. General enquiries should be sent to the Secretary, CSFHS, 4 Fir Lane, Larbert, Stirlingshire, FK5 3LW.

Further information is available on the Society's web site - www.dgnscrn.demon.co.uk/CSFHS - this web site was set up and is maintained by one of our members in USA, which just goes to show that people can help the Society no matter where they live!

Sheffield and District Family History Society

The Flowing Stream

The Society meets on the 3rd Monday of the month
(except August and December) 7.00 p.m. for 7.30 p.m.

We cover the Metropolitan District of Sheffield
including
Bradfield, Stocksbridge, Ecclesall, Dore, Norton,
Mosborough, Attercliffe, Darnall, Ecclesfield.
This covers the ancient townships of Sheffield, Ecclesall Bierlow,
Brightside Bierlow, Nether Hallam and Upper Hallam.

Society Publications: on microfiche and computer disk
1861 census index for Sheffield and Rotherham Metropolitan districts
Burial transcriptions and indexes for over 250,000 burials in the Sheffield area

Other publications:
FFHS, Local History materials and maps. All publications available by post or via http://www.genfair.com

Quarterly journal *The Flowing Stream*

Name Search & Print-out service for the 1861 census, Burial transcriptions and World War One soldiers' index

Annual Membership: £8 individual membership UK & surface mail; £10 joint membership or airmail.
For Membership details please contact: Mrs P.A. Heath, 4 Norton Park Road, Sheffield S8 8GQ (enclosing an sae please)

For all other details including publications information, please contact the Hon Secretary,
Mrs J. Pitchforth, 10 Hallam Grange Road, Sheffield S10 4BJ (enclosing an sae please)

Email: sdfhs@harbottle.demon.co.uk
Web page: http://mtx.net.au/~exy/sheffield_fhs.html

WAKEFIELD & DISTRICT
FAMILY HISTORY SOCIETY

We cover the parishes of : Ackworth, Badsworth, Castleford, Crofton, Darrington, Featherstone, Ferry Fryston, Hemsworth, Horbury, Knottingley, Normanton, Ossett, Pontefract, Sandal Magna, South Kirkby, Wakefield, Warmfield, West Bretton, Woolley, Wragby, and parts of the parishes of Dewsbury, Felkirk, Royston & Thornhill.

Meetings are on the first Saturday of each month except August, from 10.00 am at St. John's Parish Hall, Wentworth Street, Wakefield: speakers, bookstall, library, fiche reader, quarterly journal.

Publications include the 1851 Census Index in 40 volumes, 1813-1837 marriage indexes in 28 volumes, Bishop's Transcripts series.

CONTACT : Mrs. D. Shackleton, 18 Rosedale Avenue, Sandal, Wakefield, WF2 6EP
email : Dorothy@harland57.freeserve.co.uk

website : http://homepage.virgin.net/wakefield.fhs

ELVET LOCAL & FAMILY HISTORY GROUPS
COURSES IN FAMILY & LOCAL HISTORY
Institute of Heraldic & Genealogical Studies Accredited
also
FRIENDLY RESEARCH SERVICE

Based in Durham City
with access to Durham based Archives & Record Offices
Vast archival resources linked to National Records:
monastic; estate records; mining; bibliographical; etc.

For details send s.a.e.

Margot Johnson, MA, FLA
37 Hallgarth Street, Durham DH1 3AT
Tel/Fax: 0191 386 4098

Pontefract & District Family History Society

Meet Third Thursday
in each Month (except August) 7.30.p.m.
Micklegate Methodist Church, Pontefract

Membership Secretary
Mrs M Walters, 1 Coltsfoot Close, Carlton Glen, Pontefract WF8 2RY

Doncaster & District
Family History Society

The Society meets on the 3rd Thursday of each month (except August)
7.00 pm for 7.30 pm
Danum Hotel, High Street, Doncaster

PUBLICATIONS - A5 Books

Burial Indexes – taken from *commencement* of parish registers to at least 1900 for many of the parishes within the Archdeaconry of Doncaster

1851 Census Index and Marriage Indexes – for all parishes covered by the Society

MICROFICHE

Cemetery Registers – for Bentley with Arksey, Conisbrough, Mexborough (New), Mexborough (Old) and Doncaster Hyde Park

Monumental Inscriptions – All churches and churchyards within the Archdeaconry of Doncaster, and Doncaster Hyde Park

1891 Census – A complete transcription of most parishes covered by the Society

Doncaster Health Authority Death Registers – for deaths in Doncaster from 1875 to 1928

Name Search and Printout Service on various records covering Doncaster and District:

1851 Census Master Index, 1881 Census Index, 1891 Census (full transcription), 1871 Census (for Doncaster only), Surname Index on MIs in all the churches and churchyards in the Archdeaconry of Doncaster, Bawtry and Doncaster Cemetery MIs, and Vital Records Index for the British Isles.

We now have a dedicated Research Room
The Glenville Research Room at the Doncaster College for the Deaf is open on
Monday, Tuesday and Friday 10 am to 4 pm
and bookings only on Wednesday 7 pm to 9 pm

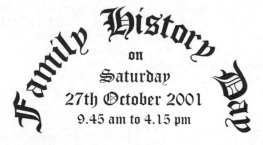

Family History Day
on
Saturday
27th October 2001
9.45 am to 4.15 pm

at Yorkshire Residential School for the Deaf, Leger Way, Doncaster
With Guest Speakers

Society resources and various databases available during early morning, coffee breaks and lunch time

Ample free parking   -   Disabled facilities   -   Optional lunch

Send SAE for further details and leaflets for any of the above to:

Mrs June Staniforth, 125 The Grove, Wheatley Hills, Doncaster, DN2 5SN.
Tel: 01302 367257

Website: http://www.doncasterfhs.freeserve.co.uk

The South West Group of Family History Societies
Cooperation in the South West of England and South Wales

In 1984/85 it was considered by the Executive Committee of the Federation of Family History Societies that there was a need to create a link at regional level, with each member of the Executive Committee developing contact with their neighbouring Family History Societies. Richard Moore agreed to act in this capacity for South Central England. The area was originally defined as the seven or eight societies located west of London and as far as Bristol.

At first a casual connection began, with Richard attending a number of committee meetings as a visitor in Oxford, Reading and Bristol. However, before this process could be expanded, Richard was elected Chairman of the Council of the Federation and as a result, all activities in this time were suspended for the duration of his time in office.

So it was not until 1988 that the first annual meeting of Chief Officers of the various Family History Societies was held, with an all day meeting in Swindon. The primary purpose of this meeting was to permit invited officers to get to know each other and more importantly, compare the ways in which each society operated and how they were expanding.

Topics discussed included the creation of branches, i.e. the way in which Bristol and Avon FHS had encouraged its branches in Gloucester, Swindon and Calne to evolve and form their own separate county societies in Gloucestershire and Wiltshire and how the various office holders were organising their tasks

This pattern was followed in the next few years with the constituent Family History Societies taking a turn in the hosting of the meetings. At a later stage it was agreed, after a successful meeting hosted by the Somerset and Dorset FHS to use the Village Hall at Ruishton, near Taunton as the Groups regular meeting place. This was due to its central location and easy access just off the M5 motorway, but still with the various Family History Societies acting as host in turn.

By this time Cornwall, Glamorgan, Gwent and Weston-super-Mare had joined the Group. Which together with the societies of Bristol and Avon, Devon, Dorset, Hampshire, Gloucestershire, Isle of Wight, Somerset and Dorset and Wiltshire has resulted in a strongly knit, but voluntary grouping which we trust has been of benefit to the societies and their members. Some societies have elected to send the same representative in order to maintain continuity, while others have chosen to vary their committee members to encourage them to learn more about their neighbouring societies and to appreciate their problems and benefits.

A future development of the Group, was the Group's unanimous agreement to organise and to initially fund a biennial Family History Fair. The first Fair was Held in 1997 at the Winter Gardens, Weston-super-Mare and the third fair will be held this year in July 2001.

Family History & Genealogical Societies

All Family History & Genealogical Societies have been circulated to confirm the information is correct and up to date. Some Societies have not responded (January 2001)

National & Regional Organisations

Ancestral Rescue Club
Briar Rose House, 109 Furness, Glascote, Tamworth, Staffordshire, B77 2QH Tel: 01827-65322
Email: ancestral@rescue-fsnet.co.uk
Web: www.rootsweb.com/~engarc/index.html
British Association for Local History
PO Box 1576, Salisbury, SP2 8SY Tel: 01722-332158
Fax: 01722-413242 Web: www.balh.co.uk
East Anglian Group of Family History Societies
2 Burleigh Road, St Ives, Hungtingdon, Cambridgeshire, PE17 6DF Email: 114040.3430@compuserve.com
Federation of Family History Societies
PO Box 8684, Shirley, Solihull, B90 4JU
Tel: 07041-492032 Fax: 07041-492032
Email: info@ffhs.org.uk Web: www.ffhs.org.uk
Federation of Family History Societies
PO Box 8684, Shirley, Solihull, B90 4JU
Tel: 07041-492032 Fax: 07041-492032
Email: info@ffhs.org.uk Web: www.ffhs.org.uk
Institute of Heraldic & Genealogical Studies
79 - 82 Northgate, Canterbury, Kent, CT1 1BAGSD
Tel: 01227-768664 Fax: 01227-765617
Email: ihgs@ihgs.ac.uk Web: www.ihgs.ac.uk
North East Group of Family History Societies
11 Colins Street, Great Horton, Bradford, BD7 4HF
North West Group of FHS Family History Fairs
North West Group of Family History Societies, 4 Lawrence Avenue, Simonstone, Burnley, Lancashire, BB12 7HX
Tel: 01282-771999 Email: ed@gull66.freeserve.co.uk
South West Group of Family History Societies
55 Osborne Road, Weston Super Mare, Somerset, BS23 3EJ
Tel: 01934-627053
Society of Genealogists - Library
14 Charterhouse Buildings, Goswell Road, London, EC1M 7BA Tel: 020-7251-8799, 020-7250-0291
Fax: 020-7250-1800 Email: librarg@sog.org.uk - Sales at sales@sog.org.uk Web: www.sog.org.uk

London & Greater London

East of London Family History Society
18a Canewdon Gardens, Wickford, Essex, SS11 7BJ
London & North Middlesex Family History Society
7 Mount Pleasant Road, New Malden, Surrrey, KT3 3JZ
Tel: 020-8949-6765
London Branch of the Welsh Family History Societies
25 Broomfield Road, Sevenoaks, Kent, TN13 3EL
Tel: 01732-453964 Email: rd9@le.ac.uk,
North West Kent Family History Society
6 Windermere Road, Bexleyheath, Kent, DA7 6PW
Web: www.users.ox.ac.uk/~malcolm/nwkfhs
Waltham Forest Family History Society
1 Gelsthorpe Road, Romford, Essex, RM5 2NB
Westminster & Central Middlesex Family History Society
2 West Avenue, Pinner, Middlesex, HA5 5BY
Tel: 020-8866-7017 Fax: 020-8866-7018
Email: rookledge@compuserve.com

England by Counties

AVON

Bristol & Avon Family History Society
784 Muller Road, Eastville, Bristol, BS5 6XA
Email: aubrilov1@tinyonline.co.uk

BEDFORDSHIRE

Bedfordshire Family History Society
PO Box 214, Bedford, Bedfordshire, MK42 9RX
Email: bfhs@bfhs.org.uk Web: www.bfhs.org.uk
East Anglian Group of Family History Societies
2 Burleigh Road, St Ives, Hungtingdon, Cambridgeshire, PE17 6DF Email: 114040.3430@compuserve.com

BERKSHIRE

Berkshire Family History Society
5 Wren Close, Burghfield Common, Berkshire, RG7 3PF
Tel: 0118-983-6523 Email: john.gurnett@btinternet.com
Web: www.berksfhs.org.uk

BIRMINGHAM

Birmingham & Midland Society for Genealogy & Heraldry
2 Castle Croft, Oldbury, West Midlands, B68 9BQ
Tel: 0121-429-9712
Email: birmingham@terrymorter.fsnet.co.uk
Web: www.bmsgh.org

BRISTOL

Bristol & Avon Family History Society
784 Muller Road, Eastville, Bristol, BS5 6XA
Email: aubrilov1@tinyonline.co.uk

BUCKINGHAMSHIRE

Buckinghamshire Family History Society
PO Box 403, Aylesbury, Buckinghamshire, HP21 7GU
Tel: 01494-712258 Fax: 01296-484783
Email: society@bucksfhs.org.uk
Web: www.bucksfhs.org.uk
Hillingdon Family History Society
20 Moreland Drive, Gerrards Cross, Buckinghamshire, SL9 8BB Tel: 01753-885602 Email: gillmay@dial.pipex.com
Web: http//www.dspace.dial.pipex.com/town/terrace/xmq42/

CAMBRIDGESHIRE

Cambridge University H&GS
c/o Crossfield House, Dale R, Stanton, Bury St Edmunds, Suffolk, IP31 2DY Web: www.cam.ac.uk/societies/cuhags/
Cambridgeshire Family History Society
1 Ascham Lane, Whittlesford, Cambridgeshire, CB2 4NT
Tel: 01223-832680
East Anglian Group of Family History Societies
2 Burleigh Road, St Ives, Hungtingdon, Cambridgeshire, PE17 6DF Email: 114040.3430@compuserve.com
Peterborough & District Family History Society
33 Farleigh Fields, Orton Wistow, Peterborough, PE2 6YB

CHESHIRE

Family History Society of Cheshire
Mayfield, 101 Irby Road, Heswall, Wirral, CH61 6UZ
Email: h2@massey48.freeserve.co.uk
North Cheshire Family History Society
2 Denham Drive, Bramhall, Stockport, Cheshire, SK7 2AT
Tel: 0161-439-9270,
Web: www.genuki.org.uk/big/eng/chs/NorthChsFHS
South Cheshire Family History Society
PO Box 1990, Crewe, Cheshire, CW2 6FF

CLEVELAND

Cleveland, North Yorkshire & South Durham Family History Society
1 Oxgang Close, Redcar, Cleveland, TS10 4ND
Tel: 01642-486615

CORNWALL

Cornish Forefathers Society
Credville, Quakers Road, Perranwell, Truro TR3 7PJ
Cornwall Family History Society
5 Victoria Square, Truro, Cornwall, TR1 2RS
Tel: 01872-264044 Email: secretary@cornwallfhs.com
Web: www.cornwallfhs.com
Fal World-wide Family History Group
57 Huntersfield, South Tehidy, Camborne TR14 0HW
Tel: 01209-711557 Fax: 01209-711557

COUNTY DURHAM

Cleveland, North Yorkshire & South Durham F.H.S.
1 Oxgang Close, Redcar TS10 4ND Tel: 01642-486615
Elvet Local & Family History Groups
37 Hallgarth Street, Durham, Durham, DH1 3AT
Tel: 0191-386-4098 Fax: 0191-386-4098
Email: Turnstone-Ventures@durham-city.freeserve.co.uk
Newton Aycliffe Family History Society
25 Anne Swyft Road, Newton Aycliffe, County Durham,
DL5 5HD Tel: 01325-315538
Northumberland & Durham Family History Society
2nd Floor, Bolbec Hall, Westgate Rd, Newcastle-on-Tyne
NE1 1SE Tel: 0191-261-2159,
Web: www.geocities.com/athens/6549/

COVENTRY

Coventry Family History Society
61 Drayton Crescent, Eastern Green, Coventry,
Warwickshire, CV5 7EL Tel: 024-7646-4256
Email: enquiries@covfhs.demon.co.uk

CUMBRIA

Cumbria Family History Society
Ulpha, 32 Granada Road, Denton, Manchester, M34 2LJ
Web: www.genuki.org.uk/big/eng/CUL/cumbfhs
/membership.html
Furness Family History Society
64 Cowlarns Road, Hawcoat, Barrow-in-Furness LA14 4HJ
Tel: 01229-830942 Email: julia.fairburn@virgin.net,

DERBYSHIRE

Chesterfield & District Family History Society
Mayfield House, 376 Worksop Road, Mastin Moor,
Chesterfield, Derbyshire, S43 3DJ Tel: 01246-471983
Email: cadfhs@chesterfield24.fsnet.co.uk
Derbyshire Ancestral Research Group
86 High Street, Loscoe, Heanor, Derbyshire, DE75 7LF
Tel: 01773-604916

Derbyshire Family History Society
Bridge Chapel House, St Mary's Bridge, Sowter Road,
Derby, DE1 3AT Tel: 01332-608101,
Web: www.dfhs.org.uk

DEVON

Devon Family History Society
8 King Henry's Road, Exeter, Devon, EX2 6AL
Tel: 01392-275917

DORSET

Dorset Family History Society
45 Chetnole Close, Canford Heath, Poole, Dorset, BH17
8BD Tel: 01202-699011
Email: shirley@dfhs.freeserve.co.uk
Web: www.dfhs.freeserve.co.uk/index.htm
Somerset & Dorset Family History Society
Unit 10, Kent House, Wood Street, Taunton, Somerset
TA1 1UW Tel: 01823-327466 Fax: 01823-327466
Email: sdfhs@lds.co.uk
Web: www.lds.co.uk/ajbrown/s&dfhs/

ESSEX

Essex Society for Family History
Research Centre, c/o Essex Record Office, Wharf Road,
Chelmsford CM2 6YT Tel: 01245-244670 Secretary:
"Windyridge", 32 Parsons Heath, Colchester CO4 3HX
Web: www.genuki.org.uk/big/eng/ESS/efhs
Waltham Forest Family History Society
1 Gelsthorpe Road, Romford, Essex, RM5 2NB

GLOUCESTERSHIRE

Gloucestershire Family History Society
Rowan House, 14 Alexandra Road, Gloucester, GL1 3DR
Web: www.cix.co.uk/~rd/genuki/gfhs.htm

GLOUCESTERSHIRE -SOUTH GLOUCESTERSHIRE

Frenchay Tuckett Society & Local History Museum
247 Frenchay Park Road, Frenchay, South Gloucestershire,
BS16 1LG Tel: 0117-9569324
Email: raybulmer@compuserve.com
Web: www.ourworld.compuserve.com/homepages/raybulmer
Sodbury Vale Family History Group
36 Westcourt Drive, Oldland Common, Bristol, BS30 9RU
Tel: 01179-324133 Email: sladekf@netlineuk.net,

HAMPSHIRE

Hampshire Genealogical Society
22 Portobello Grove, Portchester, Fareham, Hampshire,
PO16 8HU Email: hampshire@genfair.com
Web: www.hantsgensoc.demon.co.uk

HEREFORDSHIRE

Herefordshire Family History Society
6 Birch Meadow, Gosmore Road, Clehonger, Hereford,
HR2 9RH Tel: 01981-250974
Email: prosser_brian@hotmail.com
Web: www.freespace.virgin.net/bruce.donaldson

HERTFORDSHIRE

East Anglian Group of Family History Societies
2 Burleigh Road, St Ives, Hungtingdon, Cambridgeshire,
PE17 6DF Email: 114040.3430@compuserve.com
Hertfordshire Family & Population History Society
2 Mayfair Close, St Albans, Hertfordshire, AL4 9TN
Email: hfphs@btinternet.com
Web: www.btinternet.com/~hfphs/index.htm

Letchworth & District Family History Group
84 Kings Hedges, Hitchin, Hertfordshire, SG5 2QE
Royston & District Family History Society
60 Heathfield, Royston, Hertfordshire, SG8 5BN
Tel: 01763-241762
Welwyn & District Local History Society
9 York Way, Welwyn, Hertfordshire, AL6 9LB
Tel: 01438-716415

HUNTINGDONSHIRE

Huntingdonshire Family History Society
16 Kidmans Close, Hilton, Huntingdon PE18 9QB
Tel: 01480-830199 Email: ghb@brkr.freeserve.co.uk
Web: www.genuki.org.uk/big/eng/HUN/HFHS

KENT

Folkestone & District Family History Society
41 Reachfields, Hythe, Kent, CT21 6LS Tel: 01303-264561
Email: jennifer.killick@virgin.net
Web: www.freespace.virgin.net/jennifer.kilick/folkestone&districtfhs
Kent Family History Society
Two Ways, Salisbury Road, St Margaret's Bay CT15 6DP
Email: dickbarton@aol.com
Web: www.canterhill.co.uk/kfhs
North West Kent Family History Society
6 Windermere Road, Bexleyheath, Kent, DA7 6PW
Web: www.users.ox.ac.uk/~malcolm/nwkfhs
Tunbridge Wells Family History Society
The Old Cottage, Langton Road, Langton Green, Tunbridge
Wells, Kent, TN3 0BA Tel: 01892-521495
Email: s.oxenbury@virgin.net
Web: www.kcckal.demon.co.uk
Woolwich & District Family History Society
132 Belvedere Road, Bexleyheath, Kent, DA7 4PF

LANCASHIRE

Bolton & District Family History Society
A branch of Manchester & Lancashire Family History
Society, 205 Crompton Way, Bolton, Lancashire, BL2 2RU
Lancashire Family History & Historical Society
15 Christ Church Street, Accrington, Lancashire, BB5 2LZ
Tel: 01254-398579
Email: jhunt@christchurch92.freeserve.co.uk
Web: www.lfhhs.mcmail.com/
Lancaster Family History Group
94 Croston Road, Garstang, Preston, Lancashire, PR3 1HR
Web: www.fhgroup.freeserve.co.uk
Liverpool & S.W. Lancashire Family History Society
8 Paltridge Way, Pensby, Wirral, CH61 5YG
Web: www.lswlfhs.freeserve.co.uk
Manchester & Lancashire Family History Society
Clayton House, 59 Piccadilly, Manchester, M1 2AQ
Tel: 0161-236-9750 Fax: 0161-237-3512
Email: office@mlfhs.demon.co.uk
Web: www.mlfhs.demon.co.uk
North Meols Family History Society
108 High Park Road, Southport, Lancashire, PR9 7BY
Tel: 020-7228244
Oldham & District Branch (Manchester & Lancashire FHS)
Clayton House, 59 Piccadilly, Manchester, M1 2QA
Tel: 0161-236-9750 Fax: 0161-237-3512
Email: office@mlfhs.demon.co.uk
Web: www.mlfhs.demon.co.uk
Ormskirk & District Family History Society
c/o Ormskirk College, Hants Lane, Ormskirk, Lancashire,
L39 1ND Tel: 01695-578604
Email: petert@skelmersdale.co.uk
Web: www.odfhs.freeserve.co.uk

Wigan Family History Society
464 Warrington Road, Goose Green, Wigan, Lancashire,
WN3 6QF

LANCASHIRE (NORTH)

Cumbria Family History Society
Ulpha, 32 Granada Road, Denton, Manchester, M34 2LJ
Web: www.genuki.org.uk/big/eng/CUL/cumbfhs/member-
ship.html

LEICESTERSHIRE

Leicester & Rutland Family History Society
11 Faldo Close, Rushey Mead, Leicester LE4 7TS

LINCOLNSHIRE

Lincolnshire Family History Society
135 Balderton Gate, Newark NG24 1RY Tel: 01636-671192,
Web: www.genuki.org.uk/big/eng/LIN/ifhs
South Holland Family & Local History Group
54 Wygate Road, Spalding, Lincolnshire, PE11 1NT

LIVERPOOL AND MERSEYSIDE

Liverpool & S.W. Lancashire Family History Society
8 Paltridge Way, Pensby, Wirral, CH61 5YG
Web: www.lswlfhs.freeserve.co.uk

MANCHESTER

Manchester & Lancashire Family History Society
Clayton House, 59 Piccadilly, Manchester, M1 2AQ
Tel: 0161-236-9750 Fax: 0161-237-3512
Email: office@mlfhs.demon.co.uk
Web: www.mlfhs.demon.co.uk

MIDDLESEX

Hillingdon Family History Society
20 Moreland Drive, Gerrards Cross, Buckinghamshire, SL9
8BB Tel: 01753-885602 Email: gillmay@dial.pipex.com
Web: http//www.dspace.dial.pipex.com/town/terrace/xmq42/
London & North Middlesex Family History Society
7 Mount Pleasant Road, New Malden, Surrrey, KT3 3JZ
Tel: 020-8949-6765
West Middlesex Family History Society
10 West Way, Hounslow, Middlesex, TW5 0JF
**Westminster & Central Middlesex Family History
Society**
2 West Avenue, Pinner, Middlesex, HA5 5BY
Tel: 020-8866-7017 Fax: 020-8866-7018
Email: rookledge@compuserve.com

MIDLANDS - WEST MIDLANDS

Black Country Local History Consortium
Black Country Living Museum, Tipton Road, Dudley, West
Midlands, DY1 4SQ Tel: 0121-557-9643

NORFOLK

Mid-Norfolk Family History Society
Codgers Cottage, 6 Hale Road, Bradenham, Thetford,
Norfolk, IP25 7RA
Email: melanie.donnelly@codgerscottage.fsnet.co.uk
Web: www.uea.ac.uk/~s300/genuki/nfk/organisations/midnfhs
Norfolk Family History Society
Headquarters and Library, Kirby Hall, 70 St Giles Street,
Norwich, Norfolk, NR2 1LS Tel: 01603-763718
Email: nfhs@paston.co.uk
Web: www.uea.ac.uk/~S300/genuki/nfk/organisation/nfhs

NORTHAMPTONSHIRE

Northamptonshire Family History Society
The Old Bakehouse, Achurch, Nr Oundle, Peterborough,
Cambridgeshire, PE8 5SL
Email: northamptonshire_fhs@tesco.net
Web: www.crazydiamondcorp.demon.co.uk/nfhs/

NORTHUMBERLAND

Northumberland & Durham Family History Society
2nd Floor, Bolbec Hall, Westgate Road,
Newcastle-on-Tyne, Tyne and Wear, NE1 1SE
Tel: 0191-261-2159,
Web: www.geocities.com/athens/6549/

NOTTINGHAMSHIRE

Mansfield & District Family History Society
15 Cranmer Grove, Mansfield, Nottinghamshire, NG19 7JR
Email: flinthambe@aol.com
Nottinghamshire Family History Society
39 Brooklands Drive, Gedling, Nottingham,
Nottinghamshire, NG4 3GU Email: tracy.dodds@tesco.net
Web: www.nottsfhs.org.uk

OXFORDSHIRE

Oxfordshire Family History Society
19 Mavor Close, Woodstock, Oxford, Oxfordshire, OX20
1YL Tel: 01993-812258
Email: julie@kennedy91.fsnet.co.uk

RUTLAND

Leicester & Rutland Family History Society
11 Faldo Close, Rushey Mead, Leicester, Leicestershire,
LE4 7TS

SHROPSHIRE

Cleobury Mortimer Historical Society
24 High Street, Cleobury Mortimer, Kidderminster
DY14 8BY Tel: 01299-270110 Fax: 01299-270110
Email: history@mbaldwin.free-online.co.uk
Shropshire Family History Society
Redhillside, Ludlow Road, Church Stretton, Shropshire,
SY6 6AD Tel: 01694-722949 Email: secretary@sfhs.org.uk,

SOMERSET

Burnham & Highbridge FHS - Disbanded April 1998
1 Greenwood Close, West Huntspill, Somerset, TA9 3SF
Somerset & Dorset Family History Society
Unit 10, Kent House, Wood Street, Taunton TA1 1UW
Tel: 01823-327466 Fax: 01823-327466
Email: sdfhs@lds.co.uk
Web: www.lds.co.uk/ajbrown/s&dfhs/
Weston-Super-Mare Family History Society
55 Osbourne Road, Weston Super Mare BS23 3EJ
Tel: 01934-627053 Email: kes.jack@virgin.co.uk

STAFFORDSHIRE

Ancestral Rescue Club
Briar Rose House, 109 Furness, Glascote, Tamworth,
Staffordshire, B77 2QH Tel: 01827-65322 Email: ances-
tral@rescue-fsnet.co.uk Web: www.roots
Web.com/~engarc/index.html
Audley & District Family History Society
20 Hillside Avenue, Endon, Stoke on Trent, Staffordshire,
ST9 9HH

**Birmingham & Midland Society for Genealogy &
Heraldry** 2 Castle Croft, Oldbury B68 9BQ
Tel: 0121-429-9712 Web: www.bmsgh.org
Email: birmingham@terrymorter.fsnet.co.uk

SUFFOLK

Felixstowe Family History Society
Drenagh, 7 Victoria Road, Felixstowe, Suffolk, IP11 7PT
Tel: 01394-275631 Fax: 01394-275631,
Web: www.midcs.ac.uk/genuki/big/eng/SFK/ffhs
Suffolk Family History Society
123 Cedarcroft Road, Ipswich, Suffolk, IP1 6BP
Tel: 01473-748677 Fax: 01473-744854
Email: barfield@cedarcroft.fsnet.com
Web: www.genuki.org.uk/big/eng/SFK/sfhs/sfhs.htm

SURREY

East Surrey Family History Society
27 Burley Close, London, SW16 4QQ
Email: stephenturner1@compuserve.com
Web: scorpio.gold.ac.uk/genuki/sry/esfhs
West Surrey Family History Society
Deer Dell, Botany Hill, Sands, Farnham, Surrey, GU10 1LZ
Web: www.surrey Web.org.uk/wsfhs/index.html

SUSSEX

Sussex Family History Group
54 Shirley Drive, Hove, Sussex, BN3 6UF
Tel: 01273-556382 Email: tonyh@sfhg.org.uk
Web: www.sfhg.org.uk

SUSSEX - EAST SUSSEX

**Family Roots Family History Society (Eastbourne &
District)**
6 Winchester Way, Willingdon, Eastbourne, East Sussex,
BN22 0JP Tel: 01323-504412 Email: goward@mistral.co.uk
Hastings & Rother Family History Society
Flat 22 The Cloisters, St Johns Road, St Leonards on Sea,
East Sussex, TN37 6JT Tel: 01424-422139

TYNE & WEAR

Northumberland & Durham Family History Society
2nd Floor, Bolbec Hall, Westgate Road,
Newcastle-on-Tyne, Tyne and Wear, NE1 1SE
Tel: 0191-261-2159,
Web: www.geocities.com/athens/6549/

WARWICKSHIRE

**Birmingham & Midland Society for Genealogy &
Heraldry** 2 Castle Croft, Oldbury B68 9BQ
Tel: 0121-429-9712 Email: birmingham@terrymorter.fsnet.co.uk
Web: www.bmsgh.org
Coventry Family History Society
61 Drayton Crescent, Eastern Green, Coventry,
Warwickshire, CV5 7EL Tel: 024-7646-4256
Email: enquiries@covfhs.demon.co.uk
Nuneaton & North Warwickshire Family History Society
6 Windmill Road, Atherstone, Warwickshire, CV9 1HP
Web: www.nnwfhs.org.uk
Rugby Family History Group
17 St Mary's Close, Southam, Leamington Spa,
Warwickshire, CV33 0EW Tel: 01926-817667
Email: durnomitchell@Jamesdurno.swinternet.co.uk
Warwickshire Family History Society
7 Mersey Road, Bulkington, Warwickshire, CV12 9QB
Email: n.wetton.@virgin.net,

WESTMORLAND

Cumbria Family History Society
Ulpha, 32 Granada Road, Denton, Manchester, M34 2LJ
Web: www.genuki.org.uk/big/eng/CUL/cumbfhs
/membership.html

WILTSHIRE

Wiltshire Family History Society
10 Castle Lane, Devizes, Wiltshire, SN10 1HU
Email: wfhs@devizes39.freeserve.co.uk

WORCESTERSHIRE

Bewdley Historical Research Group
8 Ironside Close, Bewdley, Worcestershire, DY12 2HX
Tel: 01299-403582 Email: arp@handbag.com
**Birmingham & Midland Society for Genealogy &
Heraldry** 2 Castle Croft, Oldbury B68 9BQ
Tel: 0121-429-9712 Email: birmingham@terrymorter.fsnet.co.uk
Web: www.bmsgh.org
Malvern Family History Group
22 Jasmine Road, Malvern Wells WR14 4XD

YORKSHIRE

Yorkshire Archaeological Society - Family History Sect
Claremont, 23 Clarendon Road, Leeds, LS2 9NZ
Web: www.users.globalnet.co.uk/~gdl/yasfhs.htm
**Yorkshire Consortium of Family History Societies -
London Group**
20 Avon Close, Watford, Herts, WD2 6DN Tel: 01923-672691
Yorkshire Heraldry Society
35 Holmes Carr Road, West Bessacarr, Doncaster, South
Yorkshire, DN4 7HJ Tel: 01302-539993

YORKSHIRE - EAST YORKSHIRE

Boothferry Family & Local History Group
17 Airmyn Avenue, Goole, DN14 6PF
East Yorkshire Family History Society
12 Carlton Drive, Aldbrough, East Yorkshire, HU11 4SF
Web: www.astrogen.freeserve.co.uk/eyfhs.html

YORKSHIRE - North Yorkshire & City of York

City of York & District Family History Society
4 Orchard Close, Dringhouses, York, YO24 2NX
Email: secretary@yorkfamilyhistory.org.uk
Web: www.yorkfamilyhistory.org.uk
Cleveland, North Yorkshire & South Durham FHS
1 Oxgang Close, Redcar, Cleveland, TS10 4ND
Tel: 01642-486615
**Ripon Historical Society & Ripon
Harrogate & District Family History Group**
18 Aspin Drive, Knaresborough, North Yorkshire, HG5
8HH Tel: 01423-863728 Email: gdl@globalnet.co.uk
Web: www.users.globalnet.co.uk/~gdl/index.htm
Wharfedale Family History Group
47 Hall Park Ave, Horsforth, Leeds LS18 5LR Tel: 0113-258-6697
Email: wfhg@yorksgen.org.uk Web: www.yorksgen.org.uk

YORKSHIRE - SOUTH YORKSHIRE

Barnsley Family History Society
58A High Street, Royston, Barnsley, South Yorkshire, S71
4RN Email: kath@barnsleyfhs.freeserve.co.uk
Web: www.barnsleyfhs.freeserve.co.uk
Doncaster & District Family History Society
Marton House, 125 The Grove, Wheatley Hills, Doncaster,
DN2 5SN Tel: 01302-367257 Email: tonyjunes@aol.com
Web: www.doncasterfhs.freeserve.co.uk

Isle of Axholme Family History Society
11 Barnet Green, Hatfield, Doncaster DN7 4HL
Tel: 01302-350849
Rotherham Family History Society
12 Hall Grove, Moorgate, Rotherham S60 2BS
Sheffield & District Family History Society
10 Hallam Grange Road, Sheffield S10 4BJ
Email: sdfhs@harbottle.demon.co.uk
Web: mtx.net.au/~exy/sheffield_fhs.html

YORKSHIRE - WEST YORKSHIRE

Bradford Family History Society
2 Leaventhorpe Grove, Thornton, Bradford, West Yorkshire,
BD13 3BN Email: Dflax@aol.com
Web: www.genuki.org.uk/big/eng/YKS/bfhs/
Calderdale Family History Society inc Halifax & Dist
61 Gleanings Avenue, Norton Tower, Halifax, West
Yorkshire, HX2 0NU Tel: 01422-360756
Huddersfield & District Family History Society
292 Thornhills Lane, Clifton, Brighouse, West Yorkshire,
HD6 4JQ Email: Alan_Starkey@compuserve.com
Web: www.hdfhs.demon.co.uk
Keighley & District Family History Society
2 The Hallows, Shann Park, Keighley, West Yorkshire,
BD20 6HY Tel: 01535-672144
Morley & District Family History Group
26 Wynyard Drive, Morley, Leeds, LS27 9NA
Pontefract & District Family History Society
6 Vickers Avenue, South Elmsall, Pontefract, West
Yorkshire, WF9 2LN Web: www.genfair.com
Wakefield Family History Society
11 Waterton Close, Walton, Wakefield, WF2 6JT
Tel: 01924-258163
Email: howgate@close66.freeserve.co.uk
Web: www.homepage.virgin.net/wakefield.fhs
Wharfedale Family History Group
47 Hall Park Avenue, Horsforth, Leeds, West Yorkshire,
LS18 5LR Tel: 0113-258-6697
Email: wfhg@yorksgen.org.uk Web: www.yorksgen.org.uk

ISLE OF WIGHT
Isle of Wight Family History Society
Westwards, Hulverstone, Newport, Isle of Wight, PO30
4EH Tel: 01983-740421 Email: dina@clara.net
Web: www.dina.clara.net
Roots Family & Parish History
San Fernando, Burnt House Lane, Alverstone, Sandown, Isle
Of Wight, PO36 0HB Tel: 01-983-403060
Email: peters.sanfernando@tesco.net,

ISLE OF MAN
Isle of Man Family History Society
3 Minorca Hill, Laxey, Isle of Man, IM4 7DN
Tel: 01624-862088

CHANNEL ISLANDS
GUERNSEY
Family History Section of La Societe Guernesiaise
PO Box 314, Candie, St Peter Port, Guernsey, GY1 3TG,
Channel Islands,
JERSEY
Channel Islands Family History Society
PO Box 507, St Helier, Jersey, JE4 5TN, Channel Islands,

WALES

Cardiganshire Family History Society
PO Box 37, Aberystwyth, Cardiganshire, SY23 2WL, Wales,
Tel: 01974-298884, Web: www.heaton.celtic.co.uk/cgnfhs
Clwyd Family History Society
The Laurels, Dolydd Road, Cefn Mawr, Wrexham, LL14
3NH, Wales, Tel: 01978-822218
Dyfed Family History Society
38 Brynmelyn Avenue, Llanelli, Carmarthenshire, SA15
3RT, Wales, Tel: 01554-774545
Email: john.h.james@nationwideisp.net
Web: www.westwales.co.uk/dfhs/dfhs.htm
Glamorgan Family History Society
7 Phillip Street, Robertstown, Aberdare, CF44 8ET, Wales,
Tel: 01685-877086, 0771-2202329
Web: www.hometown.aol.com/gfhsoc
Gwent Family History Society
11 Rosser Street, Wainfelin, Pontypool, Gwent, NP4 6EA,
Wales, Email: secretary@gwent.org.uk
Web: welcome.to/gwent.fhs
Gwynedd Family History Society
36 Y Wern, Y Felinheli, Gwynedd, LL56 4TX, Wales,
Tel: 01248-670267 Email: gwynedd.roots@tesco.net
Web: www.gwynedd.fsbusiness.co.uk
London Branch of the Welsh Family History Societies
25 Broomfield Road, Sevenoaks, Kent, TN13 3EL
Tel: 01732-453964 Email: rd9@le.ac.uk,
Montgomeryshire Genealogical Society
1Moreton Road, South Croydon, Surrey, CR2 7DN
Email: montgensoc@freeuk.com
Web: http://home.freeuk.net/montgensoc
Powys Family History Society
Oaker's Lodge, The Vineyards, Winforton, Herefordshire,
HR3 6EA Tel: 01544-327103 Fax: 01544-327103
Email: 114241.2276@compuserve.com
Web: ourworld.compuserve.com/homepages
/michaelmacsorley/powys1.htm and also via Genuki

SCOTLAND

Scottish Genealogy Society
15 Victoria Terrace, Edinburgh, EH1 2JL
Tel: 0131-220-3677 Fax: 0131-220-3677
Email: scotgensoc@sol.co.uk
Web: www.scotsgenealogy.com
Scottish Association of Family History Societies
51/3 Mortonhall Road, Edinburgh, EH9 2HN
Tel: 0131-667-0437 Fax: 0131-667-0437
Email: scots@safhs.org.uk,
Aberdeen & North East Scotland Family History Society
164 King Street, Aberdeen, AB24 5BD Tel: 01224-646323
Fax: 01224-639096 Email: enquiries@anesfhs.org.uk
Web: www.anesfhs.org.uk/
Alloway & Southern Ayrshire Family History Society
c/o Alloway Public Library, Doonholm Road, Alloway, Ayr,
Ayrshire, KA7 4QQ
Borders Family History Society
Pentennen, 15 Edinburgh Rd, Greenlaw, Berwickshire,
TD10 6XF
Central Scotland Family History Society
4 Fir Lane, Larbert, Stirlingshire, FK5 3LW
Web: www.dgnscrn.demon.co.uk/CSFHS

Dumfries & Galloway Family History Society
Family History Research Centre, 9 Glasgow Street,
Dumfries, DG2 9AF, Scotland, Tel: 01387-248093,
Web: www.nevisuk.net/dgfhs
East Ayrshire Family History Society
c/o Dick Institute, Elmbank Avenue, Kilmarnock, East
Ayrshire, KA1 3BU
Email: eastayrfhs@crosshoose.freeserve.co.uk
Web: www.home.clara.net/tshaw/eastayrfhs.htm
Fife Family History Society
GlenMoriston, Duric Street, Leven, Fife, KY8 4HF,
Email: fife@ffhsoc.freeserve.co.uk Web: www.wk
Web4.cableinet.co.uk/donmanson/ffhs.html
Glasgow & West of Scotland Family History Society
Unit 5, 22 Mansfield Street, Glasgow, G11 5QP, Scotland,
Tel: 0141-339-8303 Fax: 0141-339-8303,
Web: www.gwsfhs.org.uk
Highland Family History Society
c/o Reference Room, Inverness Public Library, Farraline
Park, Inverness, IV1 1NH, Scotland,
Lanarkshire Family History Society
c/o Ref Department, Hamilton Central Library, 98 Cadzow
Street, Hamilton, Lanarkshire, ML3 6HQ, Scotland,
Largs & North Ayrshire Family History Society
12 Kelvin Gardens, Largs, Ayrshire, KA30 8SX, Scotland,
Tel: 01475-674057,
Web: www.freeyellow.com/members7/lnafhs/index.html
Lothians Family History Society
c/o Lasswade High School Centre, Eskdale Drive,
Bonnyrigg, Midlothian, EH19 2LA Tel: 0131-660-1933
Fax: 0131-663-6634
Email: anne_agnew@online.rednet.co.uk
Orkney Family History Society
Leckmelm, Annfield Crescent, Kirkwall, Orkney, KW15
1NS Tel: 01856-873917
Renfrewshire Family History Society
c/o Museum & Art Galleries, High Street, Paisley,
Renfrewshire, PA1 2BA
Web: www.geocities.com/renfrewshirefhs
Shetland Family History Society
6 Hillhead, Lerwick, Shetland, ZE1 0EJ, Scotland,
Email: shetland@zetnet.co.uk
Tay Valley Family History Society
Family History Research Centre, 179 - 181 Princes Street,
Dundee, DD4 6DQ, Scotland, Tel: 01382-461845
Fax: 01382-455532 Email: tayvalleyfhs@sol.co.uk
Web: www.sol.co.uk/t/tayvalleyfhs/
Troon & District Family History Society
c/o M.E.R.C., Troon Public Library, South Beach, Troon,
Ayrshire, KA10 6EF

NORTHERN IRELAND

Irish Heritage Association
A.204 Portview, 310 Newtownards Road, Belfast, BT4
1HE, Northern Ireland, Tel: 028-9045-5325
North of Ireland Family History Society
c/o Graduate School of Education, 69 University Street,
Belfast, BT7 1HL Email: R.Sibbett@tesco.net
Web: www.nifhs.org
Ulster Historical Foundation
Balmoral Buildings, 12 College Square East, Belfast, BT1
6DD Tel: 02890-332288 Fax: 02890-239885
Email: enquiry@uhf.org.uk Web: www.uhf.org.uk also
www.ancestry.ireland.com

REPUBLIC OF IRELAND

Council of Irish Genealogical Organisations
186 Ashcroft, Raheny, Dublin 5, Ireland
Genealogical Society of Ireland
11 Desmond Avenue, Dun Laoghaire, Co Dublin
Tel: 353-1284-2711 Email: gensocireland@iol.ie
Web: www.welcome.to/genealogyireland
Irish Family History Society
PO Box 36, Naas, Co KildareEmail: ifhs@eircom.net
Web: www.homepage.eircom.net/~ifhs
Ballinteer Family History Society
29 The View, Woodpark, Ballinteer, Dundrum, Dublin, 16,
Tel: 01-298-8082 Email: ryanc@iol.ie
Cork Genealogical Society
c/o 4 Evergreen Villas, Evergreen Road, Cork City, Ireland,
Tel: 086-8198359 Email: micaconl@eircom.net
Web: www.homepage.eircom.net/~adcoleman

Irish Genealogical Research Society
c/o 82 Eaton Square, London, SW1W 9AJ
Raheny Heritage Society
4 Thorndale Drive, Artane, Dublin, 5, Ireland,
Tel: 01-831-9028
Wexford Family History Society
24 Parklands, Wexford, Ireland, Tel: 053-42273
Email: murphyh@tinet.ie
Wicklow County Genealogical Society
1 Summerhill, Wicklow Town, Co Wicklow, Ireland

SPECIALIST FAMILY HISTORY SOCIETIES

Anglo-French Family History Society
31 Collingwood Walk, Andover, Hampshire, SP10 IPU
Anglo-German Family History Society
20 Skylark Rise, Plymouth, Devon, PL6 7SN
Tel: 01752-696978 Fax: 01752-696978
Email: petertowey@compuserve.com
Anglo-Scottish Family History Society
A specialist group of Manchester & Lancashire Family
History Society, Clayton House, 59 Piccadilly, Manchester,
M1 2AQ Tel: 0161-236-9750 Fax: 0161-237-3512
Email: mlfhs.demon.co.uk, Web: www.mlfhs.demon.co.uk
Australian Society of the Lace Makers of Calais Inc
PO Box 946, Batemans Bay, New South Wales, 2536,
Tel: 0244-718168, 0244-723421
Email: carolynb@acr.net.au
British Ancestors in India Society
2 South Farm Avenue, Harthill, Sheffield, S26 7WY
Tel: 01909-774416 Fax: 01909-774416
Email: editorial@indiaman.com, Web: www.indiaman.com
British Association for Cemeteries in Southern Asia
76 1/2 Chartfield Avenue, London, SW15 6HQ
Tel: 020-8788-6953
Catholic Family History Society
45 Gates Green Road, West Wickham, Kent, BR4 9DE
Clans of Ireland Ltd
Grange Clare, Kilmeague, Naas, Co Kildare, Ireland,
Tel: 028-6632-2353 Email: coolavin@indigo.ie,
Web: www.irishclans.com
Descendants of Convicts Group
PO Box 12224, A'Beckett Street, Melbourne 3000, Victoria,
Australia
Families in British India Society
81 Rosewood Avenue, Elm Park, Hornchurch RM12 5LD
Genealogical Society of Utah (UK)
185 Penns Lane, Sutton Coldfield, West Midlands, B76 1JU
Tel: 0121-384-2028 Fax: 0121-382-5948
Heraldry Society
PO Box 32, Maidenhead, Berkshire, SL6 3FD
Tel: 0118-932-0210 Fax: 0118-932-0210
Email: heraldry-society@cwcom.net
Historical Medical Equipment Society
14 The Avenue, Cliftonville, Northampton,
Northamptonshire, NN1 5 BT
Hugenot & Walloon Research Association
Malmaison, Church St, Great Bedwyn, Wiltshire, SN8 3PE

International Genealogy Fellowship of Rotarians
10 Fox Tail Lane, Brookfield, CT, 6804, USA
**International Police Association - British Section -
Genealogy Group**
Thornholm, Church Lane, South Muskham, Newark,
Nottinghamshire, NG23 6EQ Tel: 01636-676997
International Society for British Genealogy & FH
PO Box 3115, Salt Lake City, Utah, 84110-3115 USA
Tel: 801-272-2178, Web: www.homestart.com/isbgfh/
Irish Ancestry Group - Manchester & Lancashire FHS
Clayton House, 59 Piccadilly, Manchester, M1 2AQ
Tel: 0161-236-9750 Fax: 0161-237-3512
Email: mlfhs.demon.co.uk, Web: www.mlfhs.demon.co.uk
Irish Genealogical Research Society
c/o 82 Eaton Square, London, SW1W 9AJ
Jewish Genealogical Society of Great Britain
Finchley Synagogue, Kinloss Gardens, London, N3 3DU
Tel: 01923-825147 Fax: 01923-820323,
Web: www.ort.org/JGSGB
Lancashire Parish Register Society
188 Greenwood Crescent, Houghton Green, Warrington,
Cheshire, WA2 0EG Email: tobrien@freeuk.com,
Web: www.genuki:org.uk/big/eng/LAN/lprs
Lighthouse Society of Great Britain
Gravesend Cottage, Gravesend, Torpoint, Cornwall
PL11 2LX Email: k.trethewey@btinternet.com
Web: www.lsgb.co.uk
Liverpool & S.W. Lancashire Family History Society
8 Paltridge Way, Pensby, Wirral, CH61 5YG
Web: www.lswlfhs.freeserve.co.uk
Local Population Studies Society
78 Harlow Terrace, Harrogate, North Yorkshire, HG2 0PN
Tel: 01423-560429 Fax: 01423-560429
Email: sir_david_cooke@compuserve.com
London & North Western Railway Society
34 Falmouth Close, Nuneaton, Warwickshire, CV11 6GB
Tel: 02476-381090 Fax: 02476-373577
Email: nuneatonian@compuserve.com
North East England Family History Club
5 Tree Court, Doxford Park, Sunderland, Tyne and Wear,
SR3 2HR Tel: 0191-522-8344
Open University (DA3OI)
Open University, Walton Hall, Milton Keynes, MK7 6AA
Police History Society
37 Greenhill Road, Timperley, Altrincham, Cheshire, WA15
7BG Tel: 0161-980-2188 Email: alanhayhurst@cs.com

Polish Genealogical Society of America
984 N. Milwaukee Ave, Chicago, IL, 60622, USA
Port Genealogical Society of Victoria Inc
PO Box 1070, Warrambool, Victoria, 3280, Australia
Email: joyceaustin@start.co.au
Quaker Family History Society
32 Ashburnham Road, Ampthill, Bedfordshire, MK45 2RH
Email: info@qfhs.co.uk, Web: www.qfhs.co.uk
Railway Ancestors Family History Society
Lundy, 31 Tennyson Road, Eastleigh, Hampshire, SO50 9FS
Tel: 02380-497465, 02380-900923 Fax: 02380-497465
Email: jim@railwayancestors.demon.co.uk
Web: www.railwayancestors.demon.co.uk
Rolls Royce Family History Society
25 Gisburn Road, Barnoldswick, Colne, Lancashire, BB8
5HB Tel: 01282-815778 Email: kranson560@aol.com
Romany & Traveller Family History Society
6 St James Walk, South Chailey, East Sussex, BN8 4BU
Web: www.website.lineone.net/~rtfhs.html

Scottish Association of Family History Societies
51/3 Mortonhall Road, Edinburgh, EH9 2HN, Scotland,
Tel: 0131-667-0437 Fax: 0131-667-0437
Email: scots@safhs.org.uk,
Scottish Interest Group NZ Society of Genealogists Inc.
P O Box 8164, Symonds Street, Auckland, 1003, New
Zealand,
Society for Name Studies in Britain & Ireland
22 Peel Park Avenue, Clitheroe, Lancashire, BB7 1ET
Tel: 01200-423771 Fax: 01200-423771,
Society of Brushmakers Descendants FHS
13 Ashworth Place, Church Langley, Essex, CM17 9PU
Tel: 01279-629392 Email: s.b.d@lineone.net
Web: www.brushmakers.com
Tennyson Society
Central Library, Free School Lane, Lincoln, Lincolnshire,
LN2 1EZ Tel: 01522-552862 Fax: 01522-552858
Email: linnet@lincolnshire.gov.uk,

ONE NAME SOCIETIES

Guild of One Name Studies
14 Charterhouse Buildings, Goswell Road, London, EC1M
7BA Tel: 01293-411136 Email: guild@one-name.org
Web: www.one-name.org

Alabaster Society
No 1 Manor Farm Cottages, Bradenham, Thetford, Norfolk,
IP25 7QE Tel: 01362-821243
Email: Laraine_Hake@compuserve.com
Web: ourworld.compuserve.com/homepages/Laraine_Hake
Alderson Family History Society
13 Spring Grove, Harrogate HG1 2HS Tel: 01423-565871
Allsop Family Group
86 High Street, Loscoe, Heanor, Derbyshire, DE75 7LF
Armstrong Clan Association
7 Riverside Park, Canonbie, Dumfriesshire, DG14 0UY
Scotland Tel: 013873-71876 Fax: 013873-71876
Email: ted.armclan@kencomp.net
Beresford Family Society
2 Malatia, 78 St Augustines Avenue, Sth Croydon CR2 6JH
Tel: 020-8686-3507 Fax: 020-8681-3740
Email: beresford@atlas.co.uk
Web: www.beresfordfamilysociety.freeserve.co.uk
Blanchard Family History Society
Mill Farm, Church St, Bainton, East Yorkshire,YO25 9NJ
Bliss Family History Society
Spellowgrove Farm, Station Road, Clenchwarton, Kings
Lynn, Norfolk, PE34 4DH Tel: 01553-772953
Email: bliss@one-name.org
Web: www.members.aol.com/keithbliss/fhs/main.htm
Braund Society
12 Ranelagh Road, Lake, Sandown, Isle of Wight, PO36
8NX Email: braundsociety@fewiow.freeserve.co.uk
Brooking Family History Society
37 Church Mead, Keymer, Hassocks, West Sussex, BN6
8BW Tel: 01273-842560 Email: bob@brooking.fsnet.co.uk
Bunting Society
'Firgrove', Horseshoe Lane, Ash Vale, Surrey, GU12 5LL
Tel: 01252-325644 Fax: 01252-325644
Email: firgrove@compuserve.com
Web: www..homepage.virgin.net/teebee.axemeister/Bunting
Society.htm
Burntwood Family History Group
10 Squirrels' Hollow, Burntwood, Staffordshire, WS7 8YS
Tel: 01543-672946 Email: manlaw@freeuk.com
Caraher Family History Society
142 Rexford Street, Sistersville, VA 26175, USA

Society for Name Studies in Britain & Ireland
22 Peel Park Avenue, Clitheroe Lancashire BB7 1ET
Tel: 01200 423771 Fax: 01200 423771

Cave Society
45 Wisbech Road, Thorney, Peterborough, PE6 0SA
Clan Davidson Association
Aisling, 67 Shore Rd, Kircubbin, Newtownards, Co Down,
BT22 2RP Tel: (028) 427-38402 Email: RCDavison@msn.com
Web: www.phdavison.com/clandavidson
Clan Gregor Society
2 Braehead, Alloa, Clackmannanshire, FK10 2EW
Tel: 01259-212076 Fax: 01259-720274
Email: clangregor@sol.co.uk
Web: www.clangregor.com/macgregor
Cobbing Family History Society
89a Petherton Road, London, N5 2QT Tel: 020-7226-2657
Cory Society
2 Pankhurst Close, Bexhill on Sea, East Sussex, TN39 5DL
Courtenay Society
Powderham Castle, Kenton, Exeter, Devon, EX6 8JQ
Tel: 01626-891554, 01626-891367 Fax: 01626-890729
Email: courtenay@courtsoc.demon.co.uk
Dalton Genealogical Society
11 Jordan Close, Leavesden, Watford WD2 7AF
Tel: 01923-661139 Email: pam-lynam@lineone.net
East Family History Society
64 Bearsdown Road, Eggbuckland, Plymouth, PL6 5TR
Tel: 01752-771157
Family History Society of Martin
PO Box 9, Rosanna, Victoria, 3084, Australia
Family History Society of Martin (UK)
5 Otlinge Road, St Mary Cray, Orpington, Kent, BR5 3SH
Tel: 01689-816114
Goddard Association of Europe
2 Lowergate Rd, Huncoat, Accrington BB5 6LN
Tel: 01254-235135
Web: www.eese.qut.edu.au/~goddard/gae01.htm
**Hamley, Hambly & Hamlyn Family History Society
(International)**
59 Eylewood Road, West Norwood, London, SE27 9LZ
Tel: 020-8670-0683 Fax: 020-8670-0683
Email: hamley@one-name.org
Web: www.freespace.virgin.net/ham.famis/

Hards Family Society
Venusmead, 36 Venus St, Congresbury, Bristol, BS49 5EZ
Tel: 01934-834780 Email: rogerhards-venusmead@
breathemail.net Web: www.hards.freewire.co.uk

Haskell Family History Society
73 Oakley Close, Holbury, Southampton SO45 2PJ

Holdich Family History Society
19 Park Crescent, Elstree, Hertfordshire, WD6 3PT
Tel: 020-8953-7105 Email: apogee@tesco.net

International Relf Society
Chatsworth House, Sutton Road, Somerton TA11 6QL
Tel: 01458-274015
Email: chris.relf@bucklebury.demon.co.uk

Krans-Buckland Family Association
P0 Box 1025, North Highlands, California, 95660-1025,
United States of America Tel: (916)-332-4359
Email: jkbfa@worldnet.att.net

Leather Family History Society
134 Holbeck, Great Hollands, Bracknell, Berkshire, RG12
8XG Tel: 01344-425092 Email: s.leather@ic.ac.uk

Lin(d)field One Name Group
Southview, Maplehurst, Horsham, West Sussex, RH13 6QY
Tel: 01403-864389 Email: lindfield@one-name.org
Web: www.lindfield.force9.co.uk/long

Mackman Family History Society
Chawton Cottage, 22a Long Ridge Lane, Nether Poppleton,
YorkYO26 6LX Tel: +44-(0)1904-781752
Email: mackman@one-name.org

Mayhew Ancestory Research
28 Windmill Road, West Croydon, Surrey, CR0 2XN

Metcalfe Society
29 Farriers Close, Bramley RG26 5AX Tel: 01256-883633
Fax: 01256-883633 Email: diane.howarth@virgin.net
Web: www.metcalfe.org.uk

Morbey Family History Group
23 Cowper Crescent, Bengeo, Hertford, Hertfordshire, SG14
3DZ

Morgan Society of & Wales
11 Arden Drive, Dorridge, Solihull, West Midlands, B93
8LP Tel: 01564-774020 Fax: 01564-774020
Email: morgansociety@tesconet
Web: www.freepages.genealogy.rootsweb.com/~morgansociety

Moxon Family Research Trust
1 Pinetree Close, Cowes, PO31 8DX Tel: 01983-296921
Email: john@j.c.moxon.freeserve.co.uk
Web: www.moxon.org.uk

Moxon Society
59 Grantham Road, Sleaford., Lincolnshire, NG34 7NG
Tel: 01529-304426

Offley Family Society (incl Offler & Offiler families)
2 The Green, Codicote, Hitchin, Hertfordshire, SG4 8UR
Tel: 01438-820006

Orton Family History Society
25a Longwood Avenue, Bingley, West Yorkshire, BD16 2RX
Email: derek@beckd.freeserve.co.uk
Web: www.redflag.co.uk/ortonfhs.htm

Palgrave Society
Crossfield House, Dale Road, Stanton, Bury St Edmunds,
Suffolk, IP31 2DY Tel: 01359-251050 Fax: 01359-251050
Email: DerekPalgrave@btinternet.com
Web: www.ffhs.org.uk/members/palgrave.htm

Penty Family Name Society
Kymbelin, 30 Lych Way, Horsell Village, Surrey, GU21
4QG Tel: 01483—764904
Email: PENTYTREE@AOL.COM

Percy-Piercy Family History Society
32 Ravensdale Avenue, North Finchley, London, N12 9HT

Pomerology
The Keep, 3 Stokehouse Street, Poundbury, Dorchester,
Dorset, DT1 3GP Tel: 01305-257570 Fax: 01305-257912
Email: pomerology@compuserve.com

Rose Family Society
62 Olive Street, Grimsby, Ontario, L3M 2C4, Canada
Tel: **-905-945-3352 Email: gordrose@vaxxine.com

Sermon Surman Family History Society
24 Monks Walk, Bridge Street, Evesham, Worcestershire,
WR11 4SL Tel: 01386-49967 Fax: 01386-48242
Email: design@johnsermon.demon.co.uk
Web: www.johnsermon.demon.co.uk

Silverthorne Family Association
1 Cambridge Close, Lawn, Swindon, Wiltshire, SN3 1JQ

Society of Cornishes
216 Outland Road, Plymouth, Devon, PL2 3PE
Tel: 01752-773518 Fax: 01752-773518
Email: cornish@one-name.org

Sole Society
49 Kennel Ride, North Ascot, Berkshire, SL5 7NJ
Tel: 01344-883700 Email: info@sole.org.uk
Web: www.solesociety.freeserve.co.uk/sole.htm

Spencer Society
1303 Azalea Lane, Dekalb, Illinois, 60115, United States of
America

Stockdill Family History Society
6 First Avenue, Garston, Watford, Hertfordshire, WD2 6PZ
Tel: 01923-675292 Fax: 01923-675292
Email: roystock@compuserve.com Web: ourworld.com-
puserve.com/homepages/roystock

Stockton Society
The Leas, 28 North Road, Builth Wells, Powys, LD2 3BU,
Wales Tel: 01982-551667 Email: cestrienne@aol.com

Swinnerton Society
30 Coleridge Walk, London, NW11 6AT
Tel: 020-8458-3443 Email: roger.swynnerton@whichnet

Talbot Research Organisation
142 Albemarle Avenue, Elson, Gosport., Hampshire, PO12
4HY Tel: 023-925-89785
Web: www.kiamara.demon.co.uk/index.html

Toseland Clan Society
40 Moresdale Lane, Seacroft, Leeds, West Yorkshire, LS14
5SY Fax: 0113-225-9954

Watkins Family History Society
PO Box 1698, Douglas, Georgia, 31534-1698, United States
of America Tel: 912-383-0839 Email: buzzwatk@aol.com
Web: www.iinet.net.au/~davwat/wfhs/

Witheridge Family History Society
6 Nore Close, Gillingham., Kent, ME7 3DG

FAMILY HISTORY SOCIETIES
AUSTRALASIA & SOUTHERN AFRICA

AUSTRALIA

Society of Australian Genealogists
Richmond Villa, 120 Kent Street, Observatory Hill, Sydney
2000 Tel: 61-02-92473953 Fax: 61-02-92414872
Email: socgenes@ozemail.com.au

NEW SOUTH WALES

1788-1820 Pioneer Association
PO Box 57, Croydon, New South Wales, 2132
Tel: (02)-9797-8107
Australian Society of the Lace Makers of Calais Inc
PO Box 946, Batemans Bay, New South Wales, 2536
Tel: 0244-718168, 0244-723421
Email: carolynb@acr.net.au
Bega Valley Genealogical Society Inc
PO Box 19, Pambula, New South Wales, 2549
Berrima District Historical & Family History Society Inc
PO Box 851, Bowral, New South Wales, 2576
Blayney Shire Local & Family History Society Group Inc
c/o The Library, 48 Adelaide Street, Blayney, New South
Wales, 2799 Email: blayney.library@cww.octec.org.au
Botany Bay Family History Society Inc
PO Box 1006, Sutherland, New South Wales, 2232
Broken Hill Family History Group
PO Box 779, 75 Pell Street, Broken Hill, New South Wales,
2880 Tel: 08-80-881321
Burwood Drummoyne & District Family History Group
c/o Burwood Central Library, 4 Marmaduke Street,
Burwood, New South Wales, 2134
Cape Banks Family History Society
PO Box 67, Maroubra, New South Wales, NSW 2035
Email: hazelb@compassnet.com.au
Web: www.ozemail.com.au/mhazelb/capebank
Capital Territory Historical & Genealogical Society of Canberra
GPO Box 585, Canberra, ACT 2601
Casino & District Family History Group Inc
PO Box 586, Casino, New South Wales, 2470
Email: hughsie@nor.com
Coffs Harbour District Family History Society Inc
PO Box 2057, Coffs Harbour, New South Wales, 2450
Cowra FHG Inc
PO Box 495, Cowra, New South Wales, 2794
Deniliquin Family History Group Inc
PO Box 144, Multi Arts Hall, Cressy Street, Deniliquin,
New South Wales, 2710 Tel: (03)-5881-3980
Fax: (03)-5881-1270
Family History Society - Singleton Inc
PO Box 422, Singleton, New South Wales, 2330
Fellowship of First Fleeters
First Fleet House, 105 Cathedral Street, Woolloomooloo,
New South Wales, 2000 Tel: (02)-9360-3988
Forbes Family History Group Inc
PO Box 574, Forbes, New South Wales, 2871
Tel: 0411-095311-(mobile)
Goulburn District Family History Society Inc
PO Box 611, Goulburn, New South Wales, 2580
Griffith Genealogical & Historical Society Inc
PO Box 270, Griffith, New South Wales, 2680
Gwydir Family History Society Inc
PO Box EM61, East Moree, New South Wales, 2400
Tel: (02)-67549235-(President)
Hastings Valley Family History Group Inc
PO Box 1359, Port Macquarie, New South Wales, 2444
Hawkesbury FHG
C/o Hawkesbury City Council Library, Dight Street,
Windsor, New South Wales, 2756
Hill End Family History Group
Sarnia, Hill End, New South Wales, 2850
Hornsbury Kuring-Gai FHS Inc
PO Box 680, Hornsby, New South Wales, 2077

Inverell District FHG Inc
PO Box 367, Inverell, New South Wales, 2360
Leeton Family History Society
PO Box 475, Centre Point, Pine Avenue, Leeton, New South
Wales, 2705 Tel: 02-6955-7199, 02-6953-2301
Little Forest Family History Research Group
PO Box 87, 192 Little Forest Road, Milton, New South
Wales, 2538 Tel: 02-4455-4780, 02-4456-4223
Email: cathyd@shoalhaven.net.au
Web: www.shoalhaven.net.au/~cathyd/groups.html
Liverpool & District Family History Society
PO Box 830, Liverpool, New South Wales, 2170
Manning Wallamba FHS
c/o Greater Taree City Library, Pulteney Street, Taree, New
South Wales, 2430
Milton Ulladulla Genealogical Society Inc
PO Box 619, Ulladulla, New South Wales, 2539
Tel: 02-4455-4206
Nepean Family History Society
PO Box 81, Emu Plains, New South Wales, 2750
Tel: (02)-47-353-798 Email: istack@penrithcity.nsw.gov.au
Web: www.penrithcity.nsw.gov.au/nfhs/nfhshome.htm
New South Wales Association of Family History Societies
PO Box 48, Waratah, New South Wales, 2298
Newcastle Family History Society
PO Box 189, Adamstown, New South Wales, 2289
Orange Family History Society
PO Box 930, Orange, New South Wales, 2800
Port Stephens-Tilligerry & Districts FHS
PO Box 32, Tanilba Bay, New South Wales, 2319
Richmond River Historical Society Inc
PO Box 467, 165 Molesworth Street, Lismore, New South
Wales, 2480 Tel: 02-6621-9993
Richmond-Tweed Family History Society
PO Box 817, Ballina, New South Wales, 2478
Email: warmer@nor.com.au
Ryde District Historical Society Inc
770 Victoria Road, Ryde, New South Wales, 2112
Tel: (02)-9807-7137
Scone & Upper Hunter Historical Society Inc
PO Box 339, Kingdon Street, Upper Hunter, Scone, New
South Wales, 2337 Tel: 02-654-51218
Shoalhaven Family History Society Inc
PO Box 591, Nowra, New South Wales, 2541
Tel: 02-44221253 Fax: 02-44212462
Email: jmoorley@shoal.net.au
Snowy Mountains Family History Group
PO Box 153, Cooma, New South Wales, 2630
Wagga Wagga & District Family History Society Inc
PO Box 307, Wagga Wagga, New South Wales, 2650
Wingham FHG
PO Box 72, Wingham, New South Wales, 2429
Young & District FHG Inc
PO Box 586, Young, New South Wales, 2594
Blue Mountains Family History Society
PO Box 97, Springwood, NSW, NSW 2777
Fax: 02-4751-2746
Dubbo & District Family History Society Inc
PO Box 868, Dubbo, NSW, 2830 Tel: 068-818635
Illawara Family History Group
The Secretary, PO Box 1652, South Coast Mail Centre,
Wollongong, NSW, 2521 Tel: (02)-42622212
Web: www.magna.com.au/~vivienne/ifhg.htm
Lithgow & District Family History Society
PO Box 516, Lithgow, NSW, 2790

NORTHERN TERRITORY

Genealogical Society of the Northern Territory
PO Box 37212, Winnellie, Northern Territory, 0821
Tel: 08-898-17363

QUEENSLAND

Queensland Family History Society
PO Box 171, Indooroonilly, Brisbane, Oueensland, 4O68
Beaudesert Branch
Genealogical Soc of Queensland Inc
PO Box 664, Beaudesert, Queensland, 4285
Bundaberg Genealocical association Inc
PO Box 103, Bundaberg, Queensland, 4670
Burdekin Contact Group Family Hist Assn of N Qld Inc
PO Box 393, Home Hill, Queensland, 4806
Caboolture FH Research Group Inc
PO Box 837, Caboolture, Queensland, 4510
Cairns & District Family History Society Inc
PO Box 5069, Cairns, Queensland, 4870 Tel: 07-40537113
Central Queensland Family History Asociation
PO Box 6000, Rockhampton Mail Centre, Queensland, 4702
Charters Towers & Dalrymple F H Association Inc
PO Box 783, 54 Towers Street, Charters Towers,
Queensland, 4820 Tel: 07-4787-2124
Cooroy Noosa Genealogical & Historical Research Group Inc
PO Box 792, Cooroy, Queensland, 4563
Email: wefielder@bigpond.com.au
Dalby FHS inc
PO Box 962, Dalby, Queensland, 4405
Darling Downs Family History Society
PO Box 2229, Toowoomba, Queensland, 4350
Genealogical Society of Queensland Inc
PO Box 8423, Woolloongabba, Queensland, 4102
Gladstone Branch G.S.Q.
PO Box 1778, Gladstone, Queensland, 4680
Gold Coast & albert Genealogical Society
PO Box 2763, Southport, Queensland, 4215
Gold Coast Family History Research Group
PO Box 1126, Southport, Gold Coast, Queensland, 4215
Goondiwindi & District Family History Society
PO Box 190, Goondiwindi, Queensland, 4390
Tel: 0746712156 Fax: 0746713019
Email: pez@bigpond.com
Gympie Ancestral Research Society Inc
PO Box 767, Gympie, Queensland, 4570
Ipswich Genealogical Society Inc.
PO Box 323, 1st Floor, Ipswich Campus Tafe, cnr.
Limestone & Ellenborough Streets, Ipswich, Queensland,
4305 Tel: (07)-3201-8770
Kingaroy Family History Centre
PO Box 629, James Street, Kingaroy, Queensland, 4610
Mackay Branch Genealogical Society of Queensland Inc
PO Box 882, Mackay, Queensland, 4740
Tel: (07)-49426266
Maryborough District Family History Society
PO Box 408, Maryborough, Queensland, 4650
Mount Isa Family History Society Inc
PO Box 1832, Mount Isa, Queensland, 4825
Email: krp8@+opend.com.au
North Brisbane Branch - Genealogical Soc of Queensland Inc
PO Box 353, Chermside South, Queensland, 4032
Queensland FHS Inc
PO Box 171, Indooroophilly, Queensland, 4068
Rockhampton Genealogical Society of Queensland Inc
PO Box 992, Rockhampton, Queensland, 4700
Roma & District Local & Family History Society
PO Box 877, Roma, Queensland, 4455
South Burnett Genealogical & Family History Society
PO Box 598, Kingaroy, Queensland, 4610
Southern Suburbs Branch - G.S.Q. Inc
PO Box 844, Mount Gravatt, Queensland, 4122
Sunshine Coast Historical & Genealogical Resource Centre Inc
PO Box 1051, Nambour, Queensland, 4560
Toowoomba Family History Centre
c/o South Town Post Office, South Street, Toowoomba,
Queensland, 4350 Tel: 0746-355895
Townsville - Fam Hist Assoc of North Queensland Inc
PO Box 6120, Townsville M.C., Queensland, 4810
Whitsunday Branch - Genealogical Soc of Queensland Inc
PO Box 15, Prosperpine, Queensland, 4800

SOUTH AUSTRALIA

South Australian Genealogical & Heraldic Society
GPO Box 592, Adelaide 5001, South Australia
Tel: (08)-8272-4222 Fax: (08)-8272-4910
Email: saghs@dove.net.au Web: dove.net.au/~saghs
South East FHG Inc
PO Box 758, Millicent, South Australia, 5280
Southern Eyre Peninsula FHG
26 Cranston Street, Port Lincoln, South Australia, 5606
Whyalla FHG
PO Box 2190, Whyalla Norrie, South Australia, 5608
**Yorke Peninsula Family History Group - 1st Branch
SAGHS**
PO Box 260, Kadina, South Australia, 5554

TASMANIA

Genealogical Society of Tasmania
PO Box 60, Prospect, Tasmania, 7250

VICTORIA

Ararat Genealogical Society inc
PO Box 361, Ararat, Victoria, 3377
Australian Institute of Genealogical Studies
PO Box 339, Blackburn, Victoria, 3130
Email: aigs@alphalink.com.all
Web: www.alphalink.com.au/~aigs/index.htm
Benalla & District Family History Group Inc
PO Box 268, St Andrews Church Hall, Church Street,
Benalla, Victoria, 3672 Tel: (03)-57-644258
Bendigo Regional Genealogical Society Inc
PO Box 1049, Bendigo, Victoria, 3552
Cobram Genealogical Group
PO Box 75, Cobram, Victoria, 3643
East Gippsland Family History Group Inc
PO Box 1104, Bairnsdale, Victoria, 3875
Echuca/Moama Family History Group Inc
PO Box 707, Echuca, Victoria, 3564
Emerald Genealogy Group
62 Monbulk Road, Emerald, Victoria, 3782
Euroa Genealogical Group
43 Anderson Street, Euroa, Victoria, 3666
First Fleet Fellowship Victoria Inc
Cnr Phayer & Barnet Streets, South Melbourne, Victoria, 3205
Geelong Family History Group Inc
PO Box 1187, Geelong, Victoria, 3220
Email: flw@deakin.edu.au
Web: www.home.vicnet.net.au/wgfamhist/index.htm
Genealogical Society of Victoria
Ancestor House, 179 Queen Street, Melbourne, Victoria,
3000 Tel: +61-3-9670-7033 Fax: +61-3-9670-4490
Email: gsv@alphalink.com.au
Web: www.alphalink.com.au/~gsv/
Genealogical Society of Victoria
Ancestor House, 179 Queen Street, Melbourne, Victoria,
3000 Tel: +61-3-9670-7033 Fax: +61-3-9670-4490
Email: gsv@alphalink.com.au
Web: www.alphalink.com.au/~gsv/
Hamilton Family & Local History Group
PO Box 816, Hamilton, Victoria, 3300 Tel: 61-3-55-724933
Fax: 61-3-55-724933 Email: ham19.@mail.vicnet.net.au
Web: www.freenet.com.au/hamilton
Italian Historical Society
185 Faraday Street, Carlton, Victoria, 3053
Kerang & District Family History Group
PO Box 325, Kerang, Victoria, 3579
Mid Gippsland Family History Society Inc
PO Box 767, Morwell, Victoria, 3840
Mildura & District Genealogical Society Inc
PO Box 2895, Mildura, Victoria, 3502
Narre Warren & District Family History Group
PO Box 149, Narre Warren, Victoria, 3805
Web: www.ozemail.com.au/~narre/fam-hist.html
Nathalia Genealogical Group Inc
R.M.B. 1003, Picola, Victoria, 3639

Port Genealogical Society of Victoria Inc
PO Box 1070, Warrambool, Victoria, 3280
Email: joyceaustin@start.co.au
Sale & District Family History Group Inc
PO Box 773, Sale, Victoria, 3850
Stawell Biarri Group for Genealogy Inc
PO Box 417, Stawell, Victoria, 3380
Swam Hill Genealogical & Historical Society Inc
PO Box 1232, Swan Hill, Victoria, 3585
Toora & District Family History Group Inc
PO Box 41, Toora, Victoria, 3962
Wangaratta Genealogical Soc Inc
PO Box 683, Wangaratta, Victoria, 3676
West Gippsland Genealogical Society Inc
PO Box 225, Old Shire Hall, Queen Street, Warragul,
Victoria, 3820 Tel: 03-56252743 Email: watts@dcsi.net.au
Web: www.vicnet.net.au/~wggs/
Wimmera Association for Genealogy
PO Box 880, Horsham, Victoria, 3402
Wodonga FHS Inc
PO Box 289, Wodonga, Victoria, 3689
Yarram Genealogical Group Inc
PO Box 42, 161 Commercial Road, Yarram, Victoria, 3971

WESTERN AUSTRALIA

**Australasian Federation of Family History Organisations
(AFFHO)**
c/o 6/48 May Street, Bayswater, Western Australia, 6053
Geraldton FHS
PO Box 2502, Geralton 6531, Western Australia
Web: www.com.au/gol/genealogy/gfhs/gfhsmain.htm
Goldfields Branch
West Australian Genealogical Society Inc
PO Box 1462, Kalgoorlie, Western Australia, 6430
Melville Family History Centre
PO Box 108 (Rear of Church of Jesus Christ Latter Day
Saints, 308 Preston Point Road, Attadale, Melville, Western
Australia, 6156
Western Australia Genealogical Society Inc
6/48 May Street, Bayswater, Western Australia 6053
Tel: 08-9271-4311 Fax: 08-9271-4311
Email: wags@cleo.murdoch.edu.au
Web: www.cleo.murdoch.edu.au/~wags

NEW ZEALAND

Bishopdale Branch NZ Society of Genealogists Inc.
c/o 19a Resolution Place, Christchurch, 8005 Tel: 03 351 0625
Cromwell Family History Group
3 Porcell Court, Cromwell, 9191
Fairlie Genealogy Group
c/o 38 Gray Street, Fairlie, 8771
General Research Institute of New Zealand
PO Box 12531, Thorndon, Wellington, 6038
Hawkes Bay Branch NZ Society of Genealogists Inc.
P O Box 7375, Taradale, Hawkes Bay
Kapiti Branch NZ Society of Genealogists Inc.
P O Box 6, Paraparaumu, Kapiti Coast, 6450
Mercury Bay Branch NZ Society of Genealogists Inc.
31 Catherine Crescent, Whitianga, 2856 Tel: 0 7 866 2355
Morrinsville Branch NZ Society of Genealogists Inc.
1 David St., Morrinsville, 2251
N.Z. Fencible Society
P O Box 8415, Symonds Street, Auckland, 1003
New Zealand Family History Society
P O Box13,301, Armagh, Christchurch Tel: 03 352 4506
Email: ranz@xtra.co.nz
New Zealand Family History Society Inc
PO Box 13301, Armagh, Christchurch
Email: ranz@extra.co.nz
New Zealand Society of Genealogists Inc
PO Box 8795, Symonds Street, AUCKLAND, 1035
Tel: 09-525—0625 Fax: 09-525-0620
Northern Wairoa Branch NZ Society of Genealogists Inc.
60 Gordon Street, Dargaville, 300

NZ Society of Genealogists Inc. - Alexandra Branch
21 Gregg Street, Alexandra, 9181
Palmerston North Genealogy Group
P O Box 1992, Palmerston North, 5301
Panmure Branch NZ Society of Genealogists Inc.
29 Mirrabooka Ave, Howick, Auckland, 1705
Papakura Branch NZ Society of Genealogists Inc.
P O Box 993, Papakura, Auckland
Polish Genealogical Society of New Zealand
Box 88, Urenui, Taranaki Tel: 06 754 4551
Email: pgs.newzealand@clear.net.nz
Rotorua Branch NZ Society of Genealogists Inc.
17 Sophia Street, Rotorua, 3201 Tel: 0 7 347 9122
Scottish Interest Group NZ Society of Genealogists Inc.
P O Box 8164, Symonds Street, Auckland, 1003
South Canterbury Branch NZ Society of Genealogists Inc.
9 Burnett Street, Timaru, 8601
Tairua Branch NZ Society of Genealogists Inc.
c/o 10 Pepe Road, Tairua, 2853
Te Awamutu Branch NZ Society of Genealogists Inc.
Hairini, RD1, Te Awamutu, 2400
Te Puke Branch NZ Society of Genealogists Inc.
20 Valley Road, Te Puke, 3071
Waimate Branch NZ Society of Genealogists Inc.
4 Saul Shrives Place, Waimate, 8791
Wairarapa Branch NZ Society of Genealogists Inc.
34 Rugby Street, Masterton, 5901
Whakatane Branch NZ Society of Genealogists Inc.
P O Box 203, Whakatane, 3080
Whangamata Genealogy Group
116 Hetherington Road, Whangamata, 3062
Whangarei Branch NZ Society of Genealogists Inc.
P O Box 758, Whangarei, 115 Tel: 09 434 6508

South Africa

Genealogical Institute of South Africa
115 Banheok Road, Stellenbosch, Western Cape, South
Africa Tel: 021-887-5070
Email: GISA@RENET.SUN.AC.ZA
Genealogical Society of South Africa
Suite 143, Postnet X2600, Houghton, 2041, South Africa
Human Sciences Research Council
Genealogy Information, HSRC Library & Information
Service, Private Bag X41, Pretoria 0001, South Africa
Tel: (012)-302-2636 Fax: (012)-302-2933
Email: ig@legii.hsrc.ac.za
West Rand Family History Society
The Secretary, PO Box 760, Florida 1710, South Africa

Zimbabwe

Heraldry & Genealogy Society of Zimbabwe
Harare Branch, 8 Renfrew Road, Eastlea, Harare, Zimbabwe

NORTH AMERICA
CANADA

ALBERTA

Alberta Family Histories Society
PO Box 30270, Station B, Calgary, Alberta, T2M 4P1
Alberta Genealogical Society (Edmonton Branch)
Room 116, Prince of Wales Armouries, 10440-108 Avenue,
Edmonton, Alberta, T5H 3Z9 Tel: (403)-424-4429
Fax: (403)-423-8980 Email: agsedm@compusmart.ab.ca
Web: www.compusmart.ab.ca/abgensoc/branches.html
Alberta Genealogical Society Drayton Valley Branch
PO Box 6358, Drayton Valley, Alberta, T7A 1R8
Tel: 403-542-2787 Fax: 403-542-2787
Email: c_or_c@telusplanet.net
Alberta Genealogical Society Fort McMurray Branch
PO Box 6253, Fort McMurray, Alberta, T9H 4W1
Alberta Gene Soc Grande Prairie & District Branch
PO Box 1257, Grande Prairie, Alberta, T8V 4Z1

Alberta Gen Society Medicine Hat & District Branch
PO Box 971, Medicine Hat, Alberta, T1A 7G8
Alberta Gen Society Red Deer & District Branch
PO Box 922, Red Deer, Alberta, T4N 5H3
Email: evwes@telusplanet.net
Brooks & District Branch Alberta Genealogical Society
PO Box 1538, Brooks, Alberta, T1R 1C4
Ukrainian Genealogical & Historical Society of Canada
R.R.2, Cochrane, Alberta, T0L 0W0 Tel: (403)-932-6811
Fax: (403)-932-6811

BRITISH COLUMBIA

British Columbia Genealogical Society
PO Box 88054, Lansdowne Mall, Richmond V6X 3T6
Campbell River Genealogy Club
PO Box 884, Campbell River, British Columbia, V9W 6Y4
Email: rcase@connected.bc.ca
Web: www.connected.bc.ca/~genealogy/
Comox Valley Family History Research Group
c/o Courtenay & District Museum & Archives, 360 Cliffe
Street, Courtenay, British Columbia, V9N 2H9
Kamloops Genealogical Society
Box 1162, Kamloops, British Columbia, V2C 6H3
Kelowna & District Genealogical Society
PO Box 501, Station A, Kelowna, British Columbia, V1Y
7P1 Tel: 1-250-763-7159 Fax: 1-250-763-7159
Email: doug.ablett@bc.sympatico.ca
Nanaimo FHS
PO Box 1027, Nanaimo, British Columbia, V9R 5Z2
Port Alberni Genealogy Club
Site 322, Comp. 6, R.R.3, Port Alberni V9Y 7L7
Powell River Genealogy Club
PO Box 446, Powell River, British Columbia, V8A 5C2
Prince George Genealogical Society
PO Box 1056, Prince George, British Columbia, V2L 4V2
Revelstoke Genealogy Group
PO Box 2613, Revelstoke, British Columbia, V0E 2S0
Shuswap Lake Genealogical Society
R.R.1, Site 4, Com 4, Sorrento, British Columbia, V0E 2W0
South Okanagan Genealogical Society
c/o Museum, 785 Main Street, Penticton V2A 5E3
Vernon & District FHS
PO Box 1447, Vernon, British Columbia, V1T 6N7
Victoria Genealogical Society
PO Box 45031, Mayfair Place, Victoria V8Z 7G9

MANITOBA

Canadian Federation of Gen & Family History Societies
227 Parkville Bay, Winnipeg, Manitoba, R2M 2J6
Web: www.geocities.com/athens/troy/2274/index.html
East European Genealogical Society
PO Box 2536, Winnipeg, Manitoba, R3C 4A7
La Societe Historique de Saint Boniface
220 Ave de la Cathedral, Saint Boniface, Manitoba, R2H 0H7
Manitoba Genealogical Society
Unit A, 1045 St James Street, Winnipeg, Manitoba, R3H 1BI
South West Branch of Manitoba Genealogical Society
53 Almond Crescent, Brandon, Manitoba, R7B 1A2
Tel: 204-728-2857 Fax: 204-725-1719
Email: mla@access.tkm.mb.ca
Winnipeg Branch of Manitoba Genealogical Society
PO Box 1244, Winnipeg, Manitoba, R3C 2Y4

NEW BRUNSWICK

Centre d'Etudes Acadiennes
Universite de Moncton, Moncton, New Brunswick, E1A 3E9
New Brunswick Genealogical Society
PO Box 3235, Station B, Fredericton E3A 5G9

NEWFOUNDLAND & LABRADOR

Newfoundland & Labrador Genealogical Society
Colonial Building, Military Road, St John's A1C 2C9

NOVA SCOTIA

Archelaus Smith Historical Society
PO Box 291, Clarks Harbour, Nova Scotia, B0W 1P0
Email: timkins@atcon.com
Cape Breton Genealogical Society
PO Box 53, Sydney, Nova Scotia, B1P 6G9
Genealogical Association of Nova Scotia
PO Box 641, Station Central, Halifax, Nova Scotia, B3J 2T3
Queens County Historical Society
PO Box 1078, Liverpool, Nova Scotia, B0T 1K0
Shelburne County Genealogical Society
PO Box 248 Town Hall, 168 Water St, Shelburne B0T 1W0

ONTARIO

British Isles Family History Society of Greater Ottowa
Box 38026, Ottawa, Ontario, K2C 1N0
Bruce & Grey Branch - Ontario Genealogical Society
PO Box 66, Owen Sound, Ontario, N4K 5P1
Bruce County Genealogical Society
PO Box 1083, Port Elgin, Ontario, N0H 2C0
Elgin County Branch Ontario Genealogical Society
PO Box 20060, St Thomas, Ontario, N5P 4H4
Essex County Branch Ontario Genealogical Society
PO Box 2, Station A, Windsor, Ontario, N9A 6J5
Halton-Peel Branch Ontario Genealogical Society
PO Box 70030, 2441 Lakeshore Road West, Oakville,
Ontario, L6L 6M9 Email: jwatt@ica.net
Web: www.hhpl.on.c9/sigs/ogshp/ogshp.htm
Hamilton Branch Ontario Genealogical Society
PO Box 904, LCD 1, Hamilton, Ontario, L8N 3P6
Huron County Branch Ontario Genealogical Society
PO Box 469, Goderich, Ontario, N7A 4C7
Jewish Genealogical Society of Canada
PO Box 446, Station A, Willowdale, Ontario, M2N 5T1
Email: henry_wellisch@tvo.org
Kawartha Branch Ontario Genealogical Society
PO Box 861, Peterborough, Ontario, K9J 7AZ
Kent County Branch Ontario Genealogical Society
PO Box 964, Chatham, Ontario, N7M 5L3
Kingston Branch Ontario Genealogical Society
PO Box 1394, Kingston, Ontario, K7L 5C6
Lambton County Branch Ontario Genealogical Society
PO Box 2857, Sarnia, Ontario, N7T 7W1
Lanark County Genealogical Society
PO Box 512, Perth, Ontario, K7H 3K4
Email: gjbyron@magma.ca
Web: www.globalgenealogy.com/LCGs
Marilyn Adams Genealogical Research Centre
PO Box 35, Ameliasburgh, Ontario, K0K 1A0
Tel: 613-967-6291
Niagara Peninsula Branch Ontario Genealogical Society
PO Box 2224, St Catharines, Ontario, L2R 7R8
Nipissing District Branch Ontario Genealogical Society
PO Box 93, North Bay, Ontario, P1B 8G8
Norfolk County Branch Ontario Genealogical Society
PO Box 145, Delhi, Ontario, N4B 2W9
Email: oxford.net/~mihaley/ogsnb/main.htm
Nor-West Genealogy & History Society
PO Box 35, Vermilion Bay, Ontario, P0V 2V0
Tel: 807-227-5293
Norwich & District Historical Society
c/o Archives, R.R. #3, Norwich, Ontario, N0J 1P0
Tel: (519)-863-3638
Ontario Genealogical Society
Suite 102, 40 Orchard View Boulevard, Toronto, Ontario,
M4R 1B9 Web: www.ogs.on.ca
Ontario Genealogical Society (Toronto Branch)
Box 513, Station Z, Toronto, Ontario, M4P 2GP
Ottawa Branch Ontario Genealogical Society
PO Box 8346, Ottawa, Ontario, K1G 3H8
Perth County Branch Ontario Genealogical Society
PO Box 9, Stratford, Ontario, N5A 6S8 Tel: 519-273-0399
Simcoe County Branch Ontario Genealogical Society
PO Box 892, Barrie, Ontario, L4M 4Y6

Sioux Lookout Genealogical Club
PO Box 1561, Sioux Lookout, Ontario, P8T 1C3
Societe Franco-Ontarienne DHistoire et de Genealogie
C.P.720, succursale B, Ottawa, Ontario, K1P 5P8
Stormont Dundas & Glengarry Genealogical Society
PO Box 1522, Cornwall, Ontario, K6H 5V5
Sudbury District Branch Ontario Genealogical Society
c/o Sudbury Public Library, 74 MacKenzie Street, Sudbury,
Ontario, P3C 4X8 Tel: (705)-674-9991 Fax: (705)-670-6574
Email: fredie@isys.ca
Thunder Bay District Branch Ontario Genealogical Soc
PO Box 10373, Thunder Bay, Ontario, P7B 6T8
Upper Ottawa Genealogical Group
PO Box 972, Pembroke, Ontario, K8A 7M5
Waterdown East Flamborough Heritage Society
PO Box 1044, Waterdown, Ontario, L0R 2H0
Tel: 905-689-4074
Waterloo-Wellington Branch Ontario Genealogical Soc
153 Frederick Street, Ste 102, Kitchener, Ontario, N2H 2M2
Email: lestrome@library.uwaterloo.ca
Web: www.dos.iwaterloo.ca/~marj/genealogy/ww.html
West Elgin Genealogical & Historical Society
22552 Talbot Line, R.R.#3, Rodney, Ontario, N0L 2C0
Whitby - Oshawa Branch Ontario Genealogical Society
PO Box 174, Whitby, Ontario, L1N 5S1

QUEBEC

Brome County Historical Society
PO Box 690, 130 Lakeside, Knowlton, Quebec, J0E 1V0
Tel: 450-243-6782
Federation Quebecoise des Societies de Genealogie
C.P. 9454, Sainte Foy, Quebec, G1V 4B8
Les Patriotes Inc
105 Prince, Sorel, Quebec, J3P 4J9
Missisquoi Historical Society
PO Box 186, Stanbridge East, Quebec, J0J 2H0
Tel: (450)-248-3153 Fax: (450)-248-0420
Email: sochm@globetrotter.com
Quebec Family History Society
PO Box 1026, Postal Station, Pointe Claire, Quebec,
H9S 4H9
Societ de Genealogie de la Maurice et des Bois Francs
C.P. 901, Trois Rivieres, Quebec, G9A 5K2
**Societe de Conservation du Patrimoine de St Fracois de
la Riviere du Sud**
C P 306, 534 Boul St Francois Ouest, St Francois, Quebec,
G0R 3A0
Societe de Genealogie de Drummondville
545 des Ecoles, Drummondville, Quebec, J2B 8P3
Societe de Genealogie de Quebec
C.P. 9066, Sainte Foy, Quebec, G1V 4A8
Societe de Genealogie des Laurentides
C.P. 131, 185 Rue Du Palais, St Jerome, Quebec, J7Z 5T7
Tel: (450)-438-8158
Web: www.societe-genalogie-laurentides.gc.ca
Societe de Genealogie et d'Histoire de Chetford Mines
671 boul. Smith Sud, Thetford Mines, Quebec, G6G 1N1
Societe d'Histoire d'Amos
222 1ere Avenue Est, Amos, Quebec, J9T 1H3
Societe d'Histoire et d'Archeologie des Monts
C.P. 1192, 675 Chemin du Roy, Sainte Anne des Monts,
Quebec, G0E 2G0
Societe d'Histoire et de Genealogie de Matane
145 Soucy, Matane, Quebec, G4W 2E1
Societe d'Histoire et de Genealogie de Riviere du Loup
300 rue St Pierre, Riviere du Loup, Quebec, G5R 3V3
Tel: (418)-867-4245 Email: shgrd@icrdl.net
Web: www.icrdl.net/shgrdl/index.html
Societe d'Histoire et de Genealogie de Verdun
198 chemin de lAnce, Vaudreuil, Quebec, J7V 8P3
Societe d'histoire et de genealogie du Centre-du-Quebec
34-A, rue Laurier est, Victoriaville, Quebec, G6P 6P7
Tel: (819)-357-4029 Fax: (819)-357-9668
Email: geneatique@netscape.net
Web: www.geneatique.qc.ca

Societe d'Histoire et de Genealogie Maria Chapdeleine
1024 Place des Copains, C.P. 201, Dolbeau, Quebec, G8L 3N5
**Societe d'Histoire et Genealogie de Salaberry de Valley
Field**
75 rue St Jean Baptiste, Valleyfield, Quebec, J6T 1Z6
Societe Genealogie d'Argenteuil
378 Principale, Lachute, Quebec, J8H 1Y2
Societe Genealogique Canadienne-Francaise
Case Postale 335, Place d Armes, Montreal, Quebec, H2Y 2H1
Societie de Genealogie de L'Outaouaid Inc
C.P. 2025, Succ. B , Hull, Quebec, J8X 3Z2

SASKATCHEWAN

Battleford's Branch Saskatchewan Genealogical Society
8925 Gregory Drive, North Battleford, Saskatchewan, S9A 2W6
**Central Butte Branch Saskatchewan Genealogical
Society**
P.O. Box 224, Central Butte, Saskatchewan, S0H 0T0
Grasslands Branch Saskatchewan Genealogical Society
P.O. Box 272, Mankota, Saskatchewan, S0H 2W0
Tel: 306-264-5149
Grenfell Branch Saskatchewan Genealogical Society
P.O. Box 61, Grenfell, Saskatchewan, S0G 2B0
Tel: (306)-697-3176
Moose Jaw Branch Saskatchewan Genealogical Society
1037 Henry Street, Moose Jaw, Saskatchewan, S6H 3H3
Pangman Branch Saskatchewan Genealogical Society
P.O. Box 23, Pangman, Saskatchewan, S0C 2C0
Radville Branch Saskatchewan Genealogical Society
P.O. Box 27, Radville, Saskatchewan, S0C 2G0
Regina Branch Saskatchewan Genealogical Society
95 Hammond Road, Regina, Saskatchewan, S4R 3C8
Saskatchewan Genealogical Society
1870 Lorne Street, Regina, Saskatchewan, S4P 3E1
South East Branch Saskatchewan Genealogical Society
P.O. Box 460, Carnduff, Saskatchewan, S0C 0S0
West Central Branch Saskatchewan Genealogical Society
P.O. Box 1147, Eston, Saskatchewan, S0L 1A0
Yorkton Branch Saskatchewan Genealogical Society
28 Dalewood Crescent, Yorkton, Saskatchewan, S3N 2P7

YUKON

Dawson City Museum & Historical Society
P.O. Box 303, Dawson City, Yukon, Y0B 1G0
Tel: 867-993-5291 Fax: 867-993-5839
Email: dcmuseum@yknet.yk.ca

SOME MAJOR FAMILY HISTORY SOCIETIES OF THE UNITED STATES OF AMERICA

ALASKA

Alaska Genealogical Society
7030 Dickerson Drive, Anchorage, Alaska, 99504
Anchorage Genealogical Society
PO Box 212265, Anchorage, Alaska, 99521-2265
Tel: 907-337-6377
Fairbanks Genealogical Society
PO Box 60534, Fairbanks, Alaska, 99706-0534
Tel: 907-479-2895
Genealogical Society of South East Alaska
PO Box 6313, Ketchikan, Alaska, 99901

ARIZONA

Apache Genealogy Society
PO Box 1084, Sierra Vista public Library, Sierra Vista,
Arizona, 85636-1084 Tel: 602-458-7770
Arizona Society of Genealogists
6565 East Grant Road, Tucson, Arizona, 85715
Arizona State Genealogical Society
PO Box 42075, Tucson, Arizona, 85733-2075
Family History Society of Arizona
PO Box 310, Glendale, Arizona, 85311

Genealogical Society of Arizona
PO Box 27237, Tempe, Arizona, 85282
Mohave County Genealogy Society
400 West Beale Street, Kingman, Arizona, 864014
Tel: 602-458-7770
Northern Arizona Genealogical Society
PO Box 695, Prescott, Arizona, 86302

ARKANSAS

Arkansas Genealogical Society
PO Box 908, Hot Springs, Arkansas, 71902-0908
North East Arkansas Genealogical Association
PO Box 936, 314 Vine Street, Newport, Arkansas, 72112
North West Arkansas Genealogical Association
PO Box 796, Rogers, Arkansas, 72757
Sevier County Genealogical Society
717 Maple Street, De Queen, Arkansas, 71832

CALIFORNIA

British Isles Family History Society
134, 2531 Sawtelle Boulevade, Los Angeles, California,
90064-3163
British Isles Family History Society - USA
2531 Sawtelle Boulevard, #134, Los Angeles, California,
CA 90064-3163 Email: dotom2@aol.com
Web: www.rootsweb.com/~bifhsusa
California Genealogical Society
Suite 200, Latham Office Building, 1611 Telegraph Avenue,
Oakland, California, 94612-2152 Tel: 510-663-1358
Email: calgensoc@aol.com Web: www.calgensoc.com
California State Genealogical Alliance
4808 East Garland Street, Anaheim, California, 92807-1005
Tel: 714-777-0483
Croatian Genealogical Society
2527 San Carlos Ave, San Carlos, CA, 94070, USA
Professional Genealogists of California
5048 J Parkway, Sacramento, California, 95823
Santa Barbara County Genealogical Society
PO Box 1303, Goleta, Santa Barbara, California, CA
93116-1303 Tel: 1-805-884-9909
Web: www.compuology.com/sbarbara

COLORADO

**Association of Professional Genealogists - Denver
Colorado**
PO Box 40393, Denver, Colorado, 80204-393
Colorado Genealogical Society
PO Box 9218, Denver, Colorado, 80209-0218
Colorado Council of Genealogical Societies
PO Box 24379, Denver, Colorado, 80224-0379

CONNECTICUT

Connecticut Society of Genealogists Inc
PO Box 435, Glastonbury, Connecticut, 06033-0435
Tel: 203-569-0002
International Genealogy Fellowship of Rotarians
10 Fox Tail Lane, Brookfield, CT, 6804, USA

FLORIDA

Florida Genealogical Society
PO Box 18624, Tampa, Florida, 33679-8624
Florida Society for Genealogical Research
8461 54th Street North, Pinellas Park, Florida, 33565
Florida State Genealogical Society
PO Box 10249, Tallahassee, Florida, 32302-2249
Email: rootsweb.com/~flsgs/

GEORGIA

Georgia Genealogical Society
PO Box 54575, Atlanta, Georgia, 30308-0575
Tel: 404-475-4404
Email: http://www.state.ga.us/SOS/Archives/

HAWAII

Sandwich Islands Genealogical Society
Hawii State Library, 478 South King Street, Honolulu,
Hawaii, 96813

IDAHO

Idaho Genealogical Society Inc
204, 4620 Overland Road, Boise, Idaho, 83705-2867
Tel: 208-384-0542

ILLINOIS

Polish Genealogical Society of America
984 N. Milwaukee Ave, Chicago, IL, 60622, USA
Illinois State Genealogical Society
PO Box 10195, Springfield, Illinois, 62791-0195
Tel: 217-789-1968

INDIANA

Indiana Genealogical Society Inc
PO Box 10507, Fort Wayne, Indiana, 46852-0507
Tel: 219-269-1782 Fax: 219-396-2136
Email: alock@kconline.com Web: www.indgensoc.org

IOWA

Iowa Genealogical Society
PO Box 7735, 6000 Douglas, Des Moines, Iowa,
50322-7735 Tel: 515-276-0287 Email: igs@digiserve.com
Web: www.digiserve.com/igs/igs.htm

KANSAS

Jefferson County Genealogical Society
Box 174, Oskalobsa, Kansas, 66066
Kansas Council of Genealogical Societies Inc
PO Box 3858, Topeka, Kansas, 66604-6858
Tel: 913-774-4411
Kansas Genealogical Society Inc
PO Box 103, 2601 Central, Dodge City, Kansas, 67801-0103
Tel: 316-225-1951

KENTUCKY

Kentucky Genealogical Society Inc
PO Box 153, Frankfort, Kentucky, 40602
Tel: 502-875-4452

LOUISIANA

Louisiana Genealogical & Historical Society
PO Box 3454, Baton Rouge, Louisiana, 70821

MAINE

Maine Genealogical Society
PO Box 221, Farmington, Maine, 04938-0221

MARYLAND

Maryland Genealogical Society
201 West Monument Street, Baltimore, Maryland, 21201
Tel: 410-685-3750

MASSACHUSETTS

Massachusetts Genealogical Council
PO Box 5393, Cochituate, Massachusetts, 1778
Massachusetts Society of Genealogists Inc
PO Box 215, Ashland, Massachusetts, 01721-0215
New England Historic Genealogical Society
99 -101 Newbury Street, Boston, Massachusetts, 02116
Tel: 617-536-5740 Fax: 617-536-7307 Email: member-
ship@nehgs.org Web: www.nehgs.org

MICHIGAN

Michigan Genealogical Council
PO Box 80953, Lansing, Michigan, 48908-0953

MINNESOTA

Czechoslovak Genealogical Society International
PO Box 16225, St Paul, MN, 55116-0225, USA
Dakota County Genealogical Society
PO Box 74, 347 12th Avenue North, South St Paul,
Minnesota, 55075 Tel: (651)-451-6260, (651)-455-3626
Fax: (651)-455-2897 Email: valbu@worldnet.att.net
Irish Genealogical Society International
PO Box 16585, St Paul, Minnesota, 55116-0585
Tel: (612)-574-1436 Fax: (612)-574-0316
Email: blmkerry@pclink.com
Web: www.rootsweb.com/~irish
Minnesota Genealogical Society
5768 Olson Memorial Highway, Golden Valley, Minnesota,
55422 Tel: 612-595-9347

MISSISSIPPI

Historical & Genealogical Association of Mississippi
618 Avalon Road, Jackson, Mississippi, 39206
Tel: 601-362-3079
Mississippi Genealogical Society
PO Box 5301, Jackson, Mississippi, 39296-5301

MISSOURI

Missouri State Genealogical Association
PO Box 833, Columbia, Missouri, 65205-0803

MONTANA

Big Horn County Genealogical Society
PO Box 51, Hardin, Montana, 59034
Montana State Genealogical Society
PO Box 555, Chester, Montana, 59522

NEBRASKA

Nebraska State Genealogical Society
PO Box 5608, Lincoln, Nebraska, 68505-0608

NEVADA

Carson City Genealogical Society
1509 Sharon Drive, Carson City, Nevada, 89701
Tel: 702-687-4810
Nevada State Genealogical Society
PO Box 20666, Reno, Nevada, 89515

NEW HAMPSHIRE

New Hampshire Society of Genealogists
PO Box 633, Exeter, New Hampshire, 03833-0633
Tel: 603-432-8137

NEW JERSEY

Genealogical Society of New Jersey
PO Box 1291, New Brunswick, New Jersey, 8903
Tel: 201-356-6920
**Genealogy Club of the Library of the New Jersey
Historical Society**
230 Broadway, Newark, New Jersey, 7104
Tel: 201-483-3939

NEW MEXICO

New Mexico Genealogical Society
PO Box 8283, Alberquerque, New Mexico, 87198-8283
Tel: 505-256-3217

NEW YORK

Irish Family History Forum
PO Box 67, Plainview, New York, 11803-0067
Email: ifhf@ifhff.org Web: www.ifhff.org
New York Genealogical & Biographical Society
122 East 58th Street, New York, New York, 10022-1939
Tel: 212-755-8532 Fax: 212-754-4218
Email: nygbs@sprynet.com Web: www.nygbs

NORTH CAROLINA

North Carolina Genealogical Society
PO Box 1492, Raleigh, North Carolina, 27602

OHIO

Ohio Genealogical Society
713 South Main Street, Mansfield, Ohio, 44907-1644
Tel: 419-756-7294 Fax: 419-756-8601
Email: ogs@ogs.org Web: www.ogs.org/

OKLAHOMA

Genealogical Institute of Oklahoma
3813 Cashion Place, Oklahoma City, Oklahoma, 73112
Federation of Oklahoma Genealogical Societies
PO Box 26151, Oklahoma City, Oklahoma, 73126
Oklahoma Genealogical Society
PO Box 12986, Oklahoma City, Oklahoma, 73157-2986
Web: www.rootsweb.com/~okgs/fftt.htm

OREGON

Genealogical Forum of Oregon Inc
Room 812, 1410 S W Morrison Street, Portland, Oregon,
97205 Tel: 503-227-2398
Genealogical Heritage Council of Oregon Inc
PO Box 628, Ashland, Oregon, 97520-0021
Oregon Genealogical Society
PO Box 10306, Ashland, Oregon, 97440-2306
Tel: 503-746-7924

PENNSYLVANIA

Bucks County Genealogical Society
PO Box 1092, Doylestown, Pennsylvania, 18901
Tel: (215)-230-9410 Email: bucksgenpa.@erols.com
Genealogical Society of Pennsylvania
1300 Locust Street, Philadelphia, Pennsylvania, 19107-5699

RHODE ISLAND

Rhode Island Genealogical Society
13 Countryside Drive, Cumberland, Rhode Island,
02864-2601

SOUTH CAROLINA

South Carolina Genealogical Society
PO Box 16355, Greenville, South Carolina, 29606

SOUTH DAKOTA

South Dakota Genealogical Society
Rt 2 Box 10, Burke, South Dakota, 57523
Tel: 605-835-9364

TENNESSEE

Tennessee Genealogical Society
PO Box 111249, Memphis, Tennessee, 38111-1249
Tel: 901-327-3273

TEXAS

Amarillo Genealogical Society
PO Box 2171, 413 East Fourth Street, Amarillo, Texas,
79189-2171 Tel: 806-378-3054
Federation of Genealogical Societies
PO Box 830220, Richardson, Texas, 22207-2399
Tel: 972-907-9727
Texas State Genealogical Society
2507 Tannehill, Houston, Texas, 77008-3052
Tel: 713-864-6862

UTAH

Utah Genealogical Association
PO Box 1144, Salt Lake City, Utah, 84110-1144

VERMONT

Genealogical Society of Vermont
PO Box 422, Main Street, Pittsford, Vermont, 5763
Tel: 802-483-2900

VIRGINIA

Genealogical Research Institute of Virginia
PO Box 29178, Richmond, Virginia, 23242-0178
National Genealogical Society
4527 17th Street North, Arlington, Virginia, 22207-2399
Tel: (703)-525-0050, (800)-473-0060 Fax: (703)-525-0052
Email: membership@ngsgenealogy.org
Web: www.ngsgenealogy.org
Virginia Genealogical Society
Suite 115, 5001 West Broad Street, Richmond, Virginia,
23230-3023 Tel: 804-285-8954 Web: www.vgs.org
West Virginia Genealogical Society Inc
PO Box 249, 5236 A Elk River Road North, Elk District, Elk
View, Kanawha County, West Virginia, 25071
Tel: 1-304-965-1179

WASHINGTON

National Society Daughters of the American Revolution
1776 D Street NW, Washington, DC, 20006-5392
Washington State Genealogical Society
PO Box 1422, Olympia, Washington, 98507
Tel: 206-352-0595
**Association of Professional Genealogists - Washington
DC**
3421 M Street N W Suite 236, Washington, DC, 20007-3552

WISCONSIN

Wisconsin Genealogical Council Inc
Rt 3 Box 253, Black River Falls, Wisconsin, 54615-9405
Tel: 608-378-4388
Wisconsin State Genealogical Society
PO Box 5106, Madison, Wisconsin, 53705-0106
Tel: 608-325-2609

WYOMING

Cheyenne Genealogical Society
Laramie County Library Service - Ge, 2800 Central Avenue,
Cheyenne, Wyoming, 82001 Tel: 307-634-3561

FAMILY HISTORY SOCIETIES
EUROPE

AUSTRIA

Heraldisch-Genealogische Gesellschaft 'Adler'
Universitatsstrasse 6, Wien, A-1096, Austria

BELGIUM

Cercle de Genealogie Juive de Belgique
74 Avenue Stalingrad, Bruxelles, B-1000, Belgium Tel: 32 0
2 512 19 63 Fax: 32 0 513 48 59
Email: mjb<d.dratwa@mjb-jmb.org>
Federation des Associations de Famille
Bruyeres Marion 10, Biez, B-1390, Belgium
Federation Genealogique et Heraldique de Belgique
Avenue Parmentier 117, Bruxelles, B-1150, Belgium
Office Genealogique et Heraldique de Belgique
Avenue C Thielemans 93, Brussels, B-1150, Belgium

CROATIA

Croatian Genealogical Society
2527 San Carlos Ave, San Carlos, CA, 94070, USA

CZECHOSLOVAKIA

Czechoslovak Genealogical Society International
PO Box 16225, St Paul, MN, 55116-0225, USA

DENMARK

Danish Soc. for Local History
Colbjornsensvej 8, Naerum, DK-2850, Denmark
Sammenslutningen af Slaegtshistoriske Foreninger
Klostermarker 13, Aalborg, DK-9000, Denmark
Email: ulla@silkeborg.bib.dk
Society for Danish Genealogy & Biography
Grysgardsvej 2, Copenhagen NV, DK-2400, Denmark
Web: www.genealogi.dk

ESTONIA

Estonia Genealogical Society
Sopruse puiestec 214-88, Tallin, EE-0034, Estland

FINLAND

Genealogiska Samfundet i Finland
Fredsgatan 15 B, Helsingfors, SF-00170, Finland
Helsingfors Slaktforskare R.F.
Dragonvagen 10, Helsingfors, FIN-00330, Finland

FRANCE

Amicale des Familles d'alliance Canadiennne-Francaise
BP10, Les Ormes, 86220, France
Amities Genealogiques Bordelaises
2 rue Paul Bert, Bordeaux, Aquitaine, 33000, France Tel: 05
5644 8199 Fax: 05 5644 8199
Assoc. Genealogique et Historique des Yvelines Nord
Hotel de Ville, Meulan, 78250, France
Association Catalane de Genealogie
BP 1024, Perpignan Cedex, Languedoc Rousillon, 66101,
Association de la Bourgeoisie Ancienne Francaise
74 Avenue Kleber, Paris, 75116, France
Association Genealogique de la Charente
Archives Departementales, 24 avenue Gambetta,
Angouleme, Poitou Charentes, 16000, France
Association Genealogique de l'Anjou
75 rue Bressigny, Angers, Pays de la Loire, 49100, France
Association Genealogique de l'Oise
BP 626, Compiegne Cedex, Picardie, 60206, France
Association Genealogique des Bouches-du-Rhone
BP 22, Marseilles Cedex, Provence Alpes Cote d'Azur, 1,
Association Genealogique des Hautes Alpes
Archives Departementales, route de Rambaud, Gap,
Provence Alpes Cote d'Azur, 5000, France
Association Genealogique du Pas de Calais
BP 471, Arras Cedex, Nord-Pas de Calais, 62028, France
Fax: 03 2107 8239
Association Genealogique du Pays de Bray
BP 62, Serqueux, Normandie, 76440 Fax: 02 3509 8756
Association Genealogique du Var
BP 1022, Toulon Cedex, Provence Alpes Cote d'Azur,
83051, France
Association Genealogique Flandre-Hainaut
BP493, Valenciennes Cedex, Nord-Pas de Calais, 59321,
**Association Recherches Genealogiques Historique
d'Auvergne**
Maison des Consuls, Place Poly, Clermont Ferrand,
Auvergne, 63100, France
Bibliotheque Genealogique
3 Rue de Turbigo, Paris, 75001, France Tel: 01 4233 5821
Brive-Genealogie
Maison des Associations, 11 place J M Dauaier, Brive,
Limousin, 19100, France
Centre de Recherches Genealogiques Flandre-Artois
BP 76, Bailleul, Nord-Pas de Calais, 59270, France
Centre d'Entraide Genealogique de France
3 Rue de Turbigo, Paris, 75001, France Tel: 33 4041 9909
Fax: 33 4041 9963 Email: cegf@usa.net
Web: www.mygale.org/04cabrigol/cegf/
Centre Departemental d'Histoire des Familles
5 place Saint Leger, Guebwiller, Alsace, 68500, France
Email: cdhf@telmat-net.fr Web: web.telemat-net-fr~cdhf
Centre Entraide Genealogique Franche Comte
35 rue du Polygone, Besancon, Franche Comte, 25000

Centre Genealogique de la Marne
BP 20, Chalons-en-Champagne, Champagne Ardennes, 51005
Centre Genealogique de Savoie
BP1727, Chambery Cedex, Rhone Alpes, 73017, France
Centre Genealogique de Touraine
BP 5951, Tours Cedex, Centre, 37059, France
Centre Genealogique des Cotes d'Armor
3bis rue Bel Orient, Saint Brieuc, Bretagne, 22000, France
Fax: 02 9662 8900
Centre Genealogique des Landes
Societe de Borda, 27 rue de Cazarde, Dax, Aquitaine, 40100,
Centre Genealogique des Pyrenees Atlantique
BP 1115, Pau Cedex, Aquitaine, 64011, France
Centre Genealogique du Perche
9 rue Ville Close, Bellame, Normandie, 61130, France
Tel: 02 3383 3789
Centre Genealogique du Sud Ouest
Hotel des Societes Savantes, 1 Place Bardineau, Bordeaux,
Aquitaine, 33000, France
Centre Genealogique et Heraldique des Ardennes
Hotel de Ville, Charleville Mezieres, Champagne Ardennes, 8000
Centre Genealogique Protestant
54 rue des Saints-Peres, Paris, 75007, France
Cercle de Genealogie du Calvados
Archives Departementales, 61 route de Lion-sur-Mer, Caen,
Normandie, 14000, France
Cercle de Genealogie et d'Heraldique de Seine et Marne
BP 113, Melun Cedex, 77002, France
Cercle de Genealogie Juive (Jewish)
14 rue St Lazare, Paris, 75009, France Tel: 01 4023 0490
Fax: 01 4023 0490 Email: cgjgeniefr@aol.com
Cercle d'Etudes Genealogiques et Heraldique d'Ile-de-France
46 Route de Croissy, Le Vesinet, 78110, France
Cercle d'Histoire et Genealogique du Perigord
2 rue Roletrou, Perigueux, Aquitaine, 24000, France
Cercle Genealogique Bull
rue Jean Jaures, BP 53, Les-Clayes-sous-Bois, 78340,
Cercle Genealogique d'Alsace
Archives du Bas-Rhin, 5 rue Fischart, Strasbourg, Alsace, 67000
Cercle Genealogique d'Aunis et Saintonge
c/o Mr Provost, 10 ave de Metz, La Rochelle, Poitou
Charentes, 17000, France
Cercle Genealogique de la Manche
BP 410, Cherbourg Cedex, Normandie, 50104, France
Cercle Genealogique de la Meurthe et Moselle
4 rue Emile Gentil, Briey, Lorraine, 54150, France
Cercle Genealogique de la Region de Belfort
c/o F Werlen, 4 ave Charles de Gaulle, Valdoie, Franche
Comte, 90300, France
Cercle Genealogique de l'Eure
Archives Departementales, 2 rue de Verdun, Evreux Cedex,
Normandie, 27025, France
Cercle Genealogique de Saintonge
8 rue Mauny, Saintes, Poitou Charentes, 17100, France
Cercle Genealogique de Vaucluse
Ecole Sixte Isnard, 31 ter Avenue de la Trillade, Avignon,
Provence Alpes Cote d'Azur, 84000, France
Cercle Genealogique des Deux-Sevres
26 rue de la Blauderie, Niort, Poitou Charentes, 79000,
Cercle Genealogique des P.T.T.
BP33, Paris Cedex 15, 75721, France
Cercle Genealogique d'Ille-et-Vilaine
6 rue Frederic Mistral, Rennes, Bretagne, 35200, France
Tel: 02 9953 6363
Cercle Genealogique du C.E. de la Caisse d'Epargne Ile de France-Paris
19 rue du Louvre, Paris, 75001, France
Cercle Genealogique du Finistere
Salle Municipale, rue du Commandant Tissot, Brest,
Bretagne, 29000, France Fax: 02 9843 0176
Email: cgf@eurobretagne.fr
Web: www.karolus.org/membres/cgf.htm
Cercle Genealogique du Haut-Berry
place Martin Luther King, Bourges, Centre, 18000, France
Fax: 02 4821 0483 Email: cgh-b@wanadoo.fr

Cercle Genealogique du Languedoc
18 rue de la Tannerie, Toulouse, Languedoc Rousillon,
31400, France Tel: 05 6226 1530
Cercle Genealogique du Loir-et-Cher
11 rue du Bourg Neuf, Blois, Centre, 41000 Tel: 02 5456 0711
Cercle Genealogique d'Yvetot et du Pays de Caux
Pavillion des Fetes, Yvetot, Normandie, 76190, France
Cercle Genealogique et Historique du Lot et Garonne
13 rue Etienne Marcel, Villeneuve sur Lot, Aquitaine, 47340
Cercle Genealogique Poitevin
22bis rue Arsene Orillard, Poitiiers, Poitou Charentes, 86000
Cercle Genealogique Rouen Seine-Maritime
Archives Departementales, Cours Clemenceau, Normandie,
76101, France
Cercle Genealogique Saone-et-Loire
115 rue des Cordiers, Macon, Bourgogne, 71000, France
Cercle Genealogique Vendeen
Bat.H, 307bis, Cite de la Vigne aux Roses, La
Roche-sur-Yon, Pays de la Loire, 85000, France
Cercle Genealogique Versailles et Yvelines
Archives Departementales, 1 avenue de Paris, Versailles,
78000, France Tel: 01 3952 7239 Fax: 01 3952 7239
Cercle Genologique du Rouergue
Archives Departementales, 25 av Victor Hugo, Rodez,
Midi-Pyrenees, 12000, France
Club Genealogique Air France
CE Air France Roissy Exploitation, BP 10201, Roissy CDG
Cedex, 95703, France Fax: 01 4864 3220
Club Genealogique Group IBM France
CE IBM St Jean de Braye-Ste Marie, 50-56 ave Pierre
Curie, St Jean de Braye Cedex, 45807, France
Confederation Internationale de Genealogie et d'Heraldique
Maison de la Genealogie, 3 rue Turbigo, Paris, F - 75001,
Etudes Genealogique Drome-Ardeche
14 rue de la Manutention, Valence, Rhone Alpes, 26000,
Federation Francaise de Genealogie
3 Rue de Turbigo, Paris, 75001, France Tel: 01 4013 0088
Fax: 01 4013 0089 Web: www.karolus.org
France-Louisuane/Franco-Americanie
Commission Retrouvailles, Centre CommercialeGatie, 80
avenue du Maine, Paris, Overseas, 75014 Fax: 01 4047 8321
Web: www.noconnet.com:80/forms/cajunews.htm
Genealogie Algerie Maroc Tunisie
Maison Marechal Alphonse, Juin 28 Av. de Tubingen, Aix en
Provence, 13090, France
Genealogie Entraide Recherche en Cote d'Or
97 rue d'Estienne d'Orves, Clarmart, Bourgogne, 92140,
Genealogie et Histoire de la Caraibe
Pavillion 23, 12 avenue Charles de Gaulle, Le Pecq,
Overseas, 78230, France Email: ghcaraibe@aol.com
Web: //members.aol.com/ghcaraibe
Groupement Genealogique de la Region dy Nord
BP 62, Wambrechies, Nord-Pas de Calais, 59118, France
Groupement Genealogique du Havre et de Seine Maritime
BP 80, Le Havre Cedex, Normandie, 76050 Tel: 02 3522 7633
Institut Francophone de Genealogie et d'Histoire
5 rue de l'Aimable Nanette, le Gabut, La Rochelle,
Overseas, 17000 Tel: 05 4641 9032 Fax: 05 4641 9032
Institut Genealogique de Bourgogne
237 rue Vendome, BP 7076, Lyon, Bourgogne, 69301,
Loiret Genealogique
BP 9, Orleans Cedex, Centre, 45016, France
Salon Genealogique de Vichy et du Centre
48 Boulevard de Sichon, Vichy, Auvergne, 3200, France
Web: www.genea.com
Section Genealogique de l'Assoc. Artistique-Banque de France
2 rue Chabanais, Paris, 75002, France
Societe Genealogique du Bas-Berry
Maison des Associations, 30 Espace Mendez France,
Chateauroux, Centre, 36000, France
Societe Genealogique du Lyonnais
7 rue Major Martin, Lyon, Rhone Alpes, 69001, France

GERMANY

Arbeirkreis fur Familienforschung e.V
Muhlentorturm, Muhlentortplatz 2, Lubeck,
Schleswig-Holstein, D - 23552, Germany
Bayerischer Landesverein fur Familienkunde
Ludwigstrasse 14/1, Munchen, Bayern, D - 80539, Germany
Tel: 089 28638 398 Email: blf@rusch.m.shuttle.de
Web: www.genealogy.com/gene/reg/BAY/BLF-d.html
Deutsche Zentalstelle fur Genealogie
Schongaver str. 1, Leipzig, D - 04329, Germany
Dusseldorfer Verein fur Familienkunde e.V
Krummenweger Strasse 26, Ratingen, Nordrhein Westfalen,
D - 40885, Germany
**Herold - Verein fur Genealogie Heraldik und Reiwandte
Wissen-Scahaften**
Archiv Str. 12-14, Berlin, D -14195, Germany
Niedersachsischer Gesellschaft fur Familienkunde e.V
Stadtarchiv, Am Bokemahle 14 - 16, Hannover,
Niedersachsen, D - 30171, Germany
Oldenburgische Gesellschaft fur Familienkunde
Lerigauweg 14, Oldenurg, Niedersachsen, D - 26131,
Germany
**Verein fur Familien-U. Wappenkunde in Wurttemberg
und Baden**
Postfach 105441, Stuttgart, Baden-Wuerttemberg, D -
70047, Germany
**Westdeutsche Gesellschaft fur Familienkunde e.V Sitz
Koln**
Unter Gottes Gnaden 34, Koln-Widdersdorf, Nordrhein
Westfalen, D - 50859, Germany Tel: 49 221 50 48 88
Zentralstelle fur Personnen und Familiengeschichte
Birkenweg 13, Friedrichsdorf, D - 61381, Germany

GREECE

Heraldic-Genealogical Society of Greece
56 3rd Septemvriou Str., Athens, GR - 10433, Greece

HOLLAND

Centraal Bureau voor Genealogie
P O Box 11755, The Hague, NL - 2502 AT, Netherlands
Tel: 070 315 0500 Fax: 070 347 8394 Web: www.cbg.nl

HUNGARY

Historical Society of Hungary
University of Eoetveos Lorand, Pesti Barnabas utca 1,
Budapest, H - 1052, Hungary Tel: 267 0966

ICELAND

The Genealogical Society
P O Box 829, Reykjavick, 121, Iceland Fax: 354 1 679840

ITALY

Ancetres Italien
3 Rue de Turbigo, Paris, 75001, France Tel: 01 4664 2722
Web: //members.aol.com/geneaita/

NETHERLANDS

Centraal Bureau voor Genealogie
P O Box 11755, The Hague, NL - 2502 AT, Netherlands
Tel: 070 315 0500 Fax: 070 347 8394 Web: www.cbg.nl
Central Bureau Voor Genealogie
PO Box 11755, 2502, The Hague, Netherland
**Koninklijk Nederlandsch Genootschap voor Geslacht-en
Wapen-Kunde**
P O Box 85630, Den Haag, 2508 CH, Netherlands
**Koninklijk Nederlandsch Genootschap voor Geslacht-en
Wapen-Kunde**
P O Box 85630, Den Haag, 2508 CH, Netherlands
Nederlandse Genealogische Vereniging
Postbus 976, Amsterdam, NL - 1000 AZ, Netherlands
Email: info@ngu.nl Web: www.ngu.nl

Nederlandse Genealogische Vereniging
Postbus 976, Amsterdam, NL - 1000 AZ, Netherlands
Email: info@ngu.nl Web: www.ngu.nl
Stichting 'Genealogisch Centrum Zeeland'
Wijnaardstraat, Goes, 4416DA Tel: 0113 232 895
Stichting 'Genealogisch Centrum Zeeland'
Wijnaardstraat, Goes, 4416DA Tel: 0113 232 895
The Caledonian Society
Zuiderweg 50, Noordwolde, NL 8391 KH Tel: 0561 431580
The Caledonian Society
Zuiderweg 50, Noordwolde, NL 8391 KH Tel: 0561 431580

NORWAY

Norsk Slektshistorik Forening
Sentrum Postboks 59, Oslo, N - 0101, Norway Tel: 2242
2204 Fax: 2242 2204

POLAND

Polish Genealogical Society of America
984 N. Milwaukee Ave, Chicago, IL, 60622, USA
Polish Genealogical Society of New Zealand
Box 88, Urenui, Taranaki, New Zealand Tel: 06 754 4551
Email: pgs.newzealand@clear.net.nz

SLOVAKIA

Slovak GHS At Matica Slovenska
Novomeskeho, 32, 036 52 Martin, Slovakia

SPAIN

Asociacion de Diplomados en Genealogia y Nobilaria
Alcala 20, 2 Piso, Madrid, 28014, Spain Tel: 34 522 3822
Fax: 34 532 6674
Asociacion de Hidalgos a Fuerto de Espana
Aniceto Marinas 114, Madrid, 28008, Spain
Cercle Genealogic del Valles
Roca 29, 5 2, Sabadell, Barcelona, 8208, Spain
Circulo de Estudios Genealogicos Familiares
Prado 21, Ateneo de Madrid, Madrid, 28014, Spain
Instituto Aragones de Investigaciones Historiograficas
Madre Sacremento 33, 1', Zaragoza, 50004, Spain
**Instituto de Estudios Heraldicos y Genealogicos de
Extremadura**
Lucio Cornelio Balbo 6, Caceres, 1004, Spain
Real Academia Matritense de Heraldica y Genealogia
Quintana 28, Madrid, 28008, Spain
**Sociedad Toledana de Estudios Heraldicos y
Genealogicos**
Apartado de Correos No. 373, Toledo, Spain
**Societat Catalona de Genealogia Heraldica Sigillografia
Vexillologia**
P O Box 2830, Barcelona, 8080, Spain
**Societat Valenciana de Genealogia Heraldica Sigillografia
Vexillologia**
Les Tendes 22, Oliva, 46780, Spain

SWEDEN

Sveriges Slaktforskarforbund
Box 30222, Stockholm, 104 25, Sweden Tel: 08 695 0890
Fax: 08 695 0824 Email: genealog@genealogi.se

SWITZERLAND

Genealogical & Heraldry Association of Zurich
Dammbodenstrasse 1, Volketswil, CH-8604, Switzerland
Swiss Genealogical Society
Eggstr 46, Oberengstringen, CH 8102, Switzerland
Web: www.eye.ch/swissgen/SGFF.html
Swiss Society for Jewish Genealogy
P O Box 876, Zurich, CH-8021, Switzerland
Zentralstelle fur Genealogie
Vogelaustrasse 34, CH-8953, Switzerland
Fax: 44 1 742 20 84 Email: aicher@eyekon.ch

Registrars of Births, Marriages & Deaths
England, Wales and Scotland

All Registrars have been circulated to confirm the information is correct and up to date. Some did not reply (January 2001)

Following is a list of Superintendent Registrars of Births, Marriages and Deaths in alphabetical order by County. We have also included details of Registration Sub Districts. **Note:** Many of the Registration Officers listed here share Office accommodation with other parties. When using the addresses given they should be prefixed "Superintendent Registrar, Register Office ...."

We offer the following advice to help readers and Superintendent Registrars
The volume and page number references which are found on the microfiche and film indexes of the General Register Office must only be used when applying for certificates from the GRO. These reference numbers are not a reference to the filing system used at local register offices and do not assist Superintendent Registrars in any way to find the entry. The General Register Office hold the records for the whole of England and Wales and therefore have their own filing system, whereas the majority of register offices are still manually searching handwritten index books which is extremely time consuming. Most offices only became computerised in the early 1990s and do not hold records before this date on computer and will never have the staff for time to backlog 150 years of records. Finally, many offices are only part time, some just open a few hours per week. Unlike the larger offices they do not have receptionists or staff employed specifically to assist people researching their family history, and have to devote the majority of their time to providing certificates urgently required for passport applications, marriage bookings and pension applications.

Once the applicant has carried out their research fully using all the records and data widely available to them at no cost, they can apply to their local office with sufficient information for the Registrar to trace the entry within minutes instead of hours.

England

Bath & North East Somerset
12 Charlotte St, Bath, BA1 2NF Tel: 01225-312032 Fax: 01225-334812
Bath & North East Somerset (Norton Radstock SD)
The Library, 119 High St, Midsomer Norton, Bath BA3 2DA Tel: 01761-41876

Bedfordshire
Ampthill Court House, Woburn St, Ampthill, MK45 2HX Tel: 01525-403430 Fax: 01525-841984
Email: denmanm@csd.bedfordshire.gov.uk
Bedford Pilgrim House, 20 Brickhill Drive, MK41 7PZ Tel: 01234-354554 Fax: 01234 270215
Biggleswade 142 London Rd, Biggleswade, SG18 8EL Tel: 01767-312511 Fax: 01767-315033
Dunstable Grove House, 76 High Street North, Dunstable, LU6 1NF Tel: 01582-660191 Fax: 01582-471004
Leighton Buzzard Bossard House, West St, Leighton Buzzard, LU7 7DA Tel: 01525-851486 Fax: 01525-381483

Luton
Luton 6 George Street West, Luton, LU1 2BJ Tel: 01582-722603 Fax: 01582-429522

Berkshire
Windsor & Maidenhead Town Hall, St Ives Rd, Maidenhead, SL6 1RF Tel: 01628-796101 Fax: 01628-796625
(Ascot SD) Bridge House, 18 Brockenhurst Rd, Ascot SL5 9DL Tel: 01344-628135 Fax: 01344-628135
(Maidenhead SD) Town Hall, St Ives Rd, Maidenhead, SL6 1RF Tel: 01628-796181
(Windsor SD) York House, Sheet St, Windsor, SL4 1DD Tel: 01628-683652 Fax: 01682-683629
Wokingham (Wokingham SD) Council Offices, Shute End, Wokingham, RG40 1BN Tel: 0118-978-2514 Fax: 0118-978-2813
Bracknell Forest, Easthampstead House, Town Square, Bracknell, RG12 1AQ Tel: 01344-352027 Fax: 01344-352010
Kingsclere & Whitchurch Council Offices, Swan St, Kingsclere, Nr Newbury, RG15 8PM Tel: 01635-298714
Newbury, Peake House, 112 Newtown Rd, Newbury RG14 7EB Tel: 01635-48133 Fax: 01635-524694
Slough 'Revelstoke House', 1-5 Chalvey Park, Slough SL1 2HX Tel: 01753-520485 Fax: 01753-787605

Bournemouth
Bournemouth The Register Office,159 Old Christchurch Rd, Bourncmouth, BH1 1JS
Tel: 01202-551668 Fax: 01202-789456

City of Bristol
Quakers Friars, Bristol, BS1 3AR Tel: 0117-929-2461 Fax: 0117-925-8861

Buckinghamshire
Aylesbury Vale County Ofices, Walton St, Aylesbury, HP20 1XF Tel: 01296-382581 Tel: 01296-395000 Fax: 01296-382675
Chiltern & South Bucks Transferred to Chiltern Hills RD wef November 1998
Chiltern Hills Wycombe Area Offices, Easton St, High Wycombe, HP11 1NH Tel: 01494-475209 Fax: 01494-475040

Cambridgeshire
Cambridge Castle Lodge, Shire Hall, Castle Hill, Cambridge, CB3 0AP Tel: 01223-717021 Fax: 01223-717888
Ely Old School House, 74 Market St, Ely, CB7 4LS Tel: 01353-663824
Fenland The Old Vicarage, Church Terrace, Wisbech, PE13 1BW Tel: 01945-463128
Huntingdon Wykeham House, Market Hill, Huntingdon, PE18 6NR Tel: 01480-425822 Fax: 01480-375725
Peterborough, The Lawns, 33 Thorpe Rd, Peterborough, PE3 6AB Tel: 01733-566323 Fax: 01733-566049

Cheshire
Cheshire East Park Green, Macclesfield, SK11 6TW Tel: 01625-423463 Fax: 01625-619225
Cheshire Vale Royal Transferred to Cheshire Central wef April 1998
Chester West Goldsmith House, Goss St, Chester CH1 2BG Tel: 01244-602668 Fax: 01244-602934
Halton Heath Rd, Runcorn, WA7 5TN Tel: 01928-576797 Fax: 01928-573616
Cheshire Central Delamere House, Chester Street Crewe CW1 2LL Tel: 01270-505106 Fax: 01270 505107
Warrington Museum St, Warrington, WA1 1JX Tel: 01925-442762 Fax: 01925-442739

Stockport MD
Greenhale House, Piccadilly, Stockport, SK1 3DY Tel: 0161-474-3399 Fax: 0161-474-3390

Tameside MD
Town Hall, King St, Dukinfield, SK16 4LA
Tel: 0161-330-1177 Fax: 0161 342 2625

Trafford MD
Trafford Town Hall, tatton Rd, Sale, M33 1ZF
Tel: 0161-912-3025 Fax: 0161 912 3031

Cleveland
Middlesbrough Corporation Rd, Middlesbrough, TS1 2DA
Tel: 01642-262078 Fax: 01642 262091
Redcar & Cleveland Westgate, Guisborough, TS14 6AP
Tel: 01287-632564 Fax: 01287 630768
Stockton-on-Tees Nightingale House, Balaclava St,
Stockton-on-Tees, TS18 2AL Tel: 01642-393156
Fax: 01642-393159

Cornwall
Bodmin Lyndhurst, 66 Nicholas St, Bodmin, PL31 1AG
Tel: 01208-73677 Fax: 01208-73677
Camborne-Redruth Roskear, Camborne, TR14 8DN
Tel: 01209-612924 Fax: 01209-612924
Falmouth Berkeley House, 12-14 Berkeley Vale,
Falmouth, TR11 3PH Tel: 01326-312606
Fax: 01326-312606
Kerrier The Willows, Church St, Helston, TR13 8NJ
Tel: 01326-562848 Fax: 01326-562848
Launceston 'Hendra', Dunheved Rd, Launceston
PL15 9JG Tel: 01566-777464 Fax: 01566-777464
Liskeard, 'Graylands', Dean St, Liskeard, PL14 4AH
Tel: 01579-343442 Fax: 01579-343442
Penzance St. John's Hall, Penzance, TR18 2QR
Tel: 01736-330093 Fax: 01736-330067
St. Austell 12 Carlyon Rd, St. Austell, PL25 4LD
Tel: 01726-68974 Fax: 01726-67048
St. Germans Plougastel Drive, St Germans, Saltash, PL12
6DL Tel: 01752-842624 Fax: 01752-848556
Stratton The Parkhouse Centre, Ergue Gaberic Way, Bude,
EX23 8LD Tel: 01288-353209 Fax: 01288-353209
Truro The Leats, Truro, TR1 3AH Tel: 01872-72842
Fax: 01872-261625

Darlington
Central House, Gladstone St, DL3 6JX Tel: 01325-346600
Fax: 01325-346605

County Durham
Durham Central 40 Old Elvet, Durham, DH1 3HN
Tel: 0191-3864077
Durham Eastern Acre Rigg, York Rd, Peterlee, SR8 2DP
Tel: 0191-5866147 Fax: 0191-51846007
Durham Northern 7 Thorneyholme Terrace, Stanley
DH9 0BJ Tel: 01207-235849 Fax: 01207-235334
(Chester le Street SD) Civic Centre, Chester le St
DH3 3UT Tel: 0191-388-3240
(Consett SD) 39 Medomsley Rd, Consett, DH8 5HE
Tel: 01207-502797
(Stanley SD) 7 Thorneyholme Terrace, Stanley, DH9 0BJ
Tel: 01207-235849
Durham South Western 30 Galgate, Barnard Castle,
DL12 8BH Tel: 01833-637997
Durham Western, Cockton House, Waddington St, Bishop
Auckland, DL14 6HG Tel: 01388-607277
Fax: 01388-603404
(Bishop Auckland SD) Cockton House, Waddington St,
Bishop Auckland, DL14 6HG Tel: 01388-603404
(Crook SD) The Community Health Clinic, Hope St,
Crook, DL15 9HU Tel: 01388-767630
(Weardale SD) The Health Centre, Dales St, Stanhope,
Bishop Auckland, DL13 2XD Tel: 01388-527074
Hartlepool
Raby Rd, Hartlepool, TS24 8AF Tel: 01429-236369
Fax: 01429-236373 Email: registrar@hartlepool.gov.uk

Coventry MD
Cheylesmore Manor House, Manor House Drive, CV1 2ND
Tel: 01203-833137 Fax: 01203-833110

Cumbria
Cockermouth 67 Wood St, Maryport, CA15 6LD
Tel: 01900-325960
(Maryport SD) 67 Wood St, Maryport, CA15 6LD
Tel: 01900-812637
(Workington SD) Hill Park, Ramsay Brow, Workington,
CA14 4AR Tel: 01900-325160
Kendal County Offices, Kendal, LA9 4RQ
Tel: 01539-773567
(Kirkby Lonsdale SD) 15 Market Square, Kirkby
Lonsdale, Carnforth, LA6 2AN Tel: 01542-71222
(Lakes SD) Windermere Library, Ellerthwaite, Windermere,
LA23 2AJ Tel: 015394-62420
Penrith Friargate, Penrith, CA11 7XR Tel: 01768-242120
Fax: 01768-242122
(Alston SD) Alston Register Office Townhead, Alston
CA9 3SL Tel: 01434-381784 Fax: 01434-381784
(Appleby SD) Shire Hall, The Sands, Appleby in
Westmorland, CA16 6XN Tel: 017683-52976
Barrow-in-Furness 74 Abbey Rd, Barrow-in-Furness,
LA14 5UB Tel: 01229-894511 Fax: 01229-894513
Carlisle 23 Portland Square, Carlisle, CA1 1PE
Tel: 01228-607432 Fax: 01228-607434
Millom The Millom Council Centre, St Georges Rd,
Millom, LA14 4DD Tel: 01229-772357 Fax: 01229-773412
Ulverston Town Hall, Queen St, Ulverston, LA12 7AR
Tel: 01229-894170 Fax: 01229-894172
Whitehaven 75 Lowther St, Whitehaven, CA28 7RB
Tel: 01946-693554
Wigton Council Offices, South End, Wigton, CA7 9QD
Tel: 016973-42155 Fax: 016973-49967

Derbyshire
Amber Valley Market Place, Ripley, DE5 3BT
Tel: 01773-841380 Fax: 01773-841382
Ashbourne Town Hall, Market Place, Ashbourne, DE6 1ES
Tel: 01335-300575 Fax: 01335-345252
Bakewell Town Hall, Bakewell, DE45 1BW
Tel: 0162-981-2261
(Matlock SD) Firs Parade, Matlock, DE4 3AS
Tel: 01629-582870
Chesterfield New Beetwell St, Chesterfield, S40 1QJ
Tel: 01246-234754 Fax: 01246-274493
Derby 9 Traffic St, Derby, DE1 2NL Tel: 01332-363609
Fax: 01332-368310
Erewash 87 Lord Haddon Rd, Ilkeston, DE7 8AX Tel:
0115-932-1014 Fax: 0115-932-6450
High Peak, Council Offices, Hayfield Rd, Chapel-en-le-Frith,
High Peak, SK23 0QJ Tel: 01663-750473
(Buxton SD) The Registrar's Office, Hardwick Square
West, Buxton, SK17 6PX Tel: 01298-25075
(Chapel en le Frith SD) The Town Hall
Chapel en le Frith, SK23 0HB Tel: 01298-813559
Glossop SD) 46-50 High Street West, Glossop, SK13 8BH
Tel: 01457-852425
South Derbyshire Traffic St, Derby, DE1 2NL
Tel: 01332-363618 Fax: 01332-368310
(Sub-district) The Registrars Office, Civic Way,
Swadlincote, DE11 0AB Tel: 01283-21397
Fax: 01283-213976

Devon
East Devon Dowell St, Honiton, EX14 8LZ
Tel: 01404-42531 Fax: 01404-41475
Exeter, 1 Lower Summerlands, Heavitree Rd, Exeter, EX1
2LL Tel: 01392-270941 Fax: 01392-499540
Holsworthy 8 Fore St, Holsworthy, EX22 6ED
Tel: 01409-253262

Mid Devon The Great House, 1 St Peter St, Tiverton, EX16 6NY Tel: 01884-255255 Fax: 01884-255255
North Devon Civic Centre, Barnstaple, EX31 1ED
Tel: 01271-388456
Okehampton, Transferred to West Devon wef July 1997
Plymouth
Lockyer St, Plymouth, PL1 2QD Tel: 01752-268331
Fax: 01752-256046
South Hams, Follaton House, Plymouth Rd, Totnes, TQ9 5NE Tel: 01803-861234 Fax: 01803-868965
Teignbridge 15 Devon Square, Newton Abbot, TQ12 2HR
Tel: 01626-353642 Fax: 01626-353636
Torbay Oldway Mansion, Paignton, TQ3 2TU
Tel: 01803-207130 Fax: 01803-525388
Torridge Council Offices, Windmill Lane, Northam, Bideford, EX39 1BY Tel: 01237-474978 Fax: 01237-473385
West Devon Town Council Offices, Drake Rd, Tavistock, PL19 8AJ Tel: 01822-612137 Fax: 01822-618935

Dorset
East Dorset, King George V Pavillion, Peter Grant Way, Ferndown, BH22 9EN Tel: 01202-892325 Fax:
North Dorset Salisbury Rd, Blandford Forum, DT11 7LN
Tel: 01258-484096 Fax: 01258-484095
Poole Civic Centre Annexe, Park Rd, Poole, BH15 2RN
Tel: 01202-633744 Fax: 01202 633725
South Dorset, The Guildhall, St Edmund St, Weymouth, DT4 8AS Tel: 01305-760899 Fax: 01305-772611
West Dorset 32 South St, Bridport, DT6 3NQ
Tel: 01308-456047

East Yorkshire
Beverley 34 Lairgate, Beverley, HU17 8ES Tel: 01482-864205 Fax: 01482-679155
(Withernsea SD) The Court House, Railway Crescent, Withernsea, HU19 2HF Tel: 01964-612344
Fax: 01964-612344
(Beverley B SD) The Council Offices, Market Green, Cottingham, HU16 5QG Tel: 01482-883510
Fax: 01482-883510
Beverley (Hornsea SD) The Court House, off Railway St, Hornsea, HU18 1PS Tel: 01964-534111 Fax: 01964-534111
Bridlington, Town Hall, Quay Rd, Bridlington, YO16 4LP
Tel: 01262-422662 Fax: 01262-422664
(Driffield SD) 51 Manorfield Rd, Driffield, YO25 5JE
Tel: 01377-254051 Fax: 01377-254051
Pocklington Burnby Hall, Pocklington, YO4 2QQ
Tel: 01759-303614 Fax: 01759-306722
Goole Council Offices, Church St, Goole, DN14 5BG
Tel: 01405-722371 Fax: 01405- 722379

East Sussex
Eastbourne, Town Hall, Grove Rd, Eastbourne, BN21 4UG
Tel: 01323-410000 Fax: 01323-431386
Hastings & Rother
Bohemia Rd, Hastings, TN34 1EX Tel: 01424-721722
Fax: 01424-465296
Brighton & Hove
Royal York Buildings, Old Steine, Brighton, BN1 1NH
Tel: 01273-292016 Fax: 01273-292019
Hove Transferred to Brighton & Hove RD wef November 1998
Lewes, Southover Grange, Southover Rd, Lewes, BN7 1TP
Tel: 01273-475916 Fax: 01273-488073
Uckfield Beaconwood, Beacon Rd, Crowborough
TN6 1AR Tel: 01892-653803 Fax: 01892-669884

Essex
Brentwood 1 Seven Arches Rd, Brentwood, CM14 4JG
Tel: 01277-233565 Fax: 01277-262712
(Basildon SD) Burghstead Lodge, 143 High St, Billericay, CM12 9AB Tel: 01277-623939 Fax: 01277-636162

Castle Point & Rochford, Civic Centre, Victoria Avenue, Southend-on-Sea, SS2 6ER Tel: 01702-343728
(Sub-district) District Council Offices, Hockley Rd, Rayleigh, SS6 8EB Tel: 01268-776362 Fax: 01268-776362

Barking & Dagenham
Barking & Dagenham Arden House, 198 Longbridge Rd, Barking, IG11 8SY Tel: (020)-8270-4742
Fax: (020)-8270-4745
Braintree, John Ray House, Bocking End, Braintree CM7 9RW Tel: 01376-323463 Fax: 01376-342423
Chelmsford 17 Market Rd, Chelmsford, CM1 1GF
Tel: 01245-430701 Fax: 01245-430707
Colchester Stanwell House, Stanwell St, Colchester CO2 7DL Tel: 01206-572926 Fax: 01206-540626
Epping Forest St Johns Rd, Epping, CM16 5DN
Tel: 01992-572789 Fax: 01992-571236
Harlow Watergarden Ofices, College Square, The High, Harlow, CM20 1AG Tel: 01279-427674 Fax: 01279-444594
Havering LB
'Langtons', Billet Lane, Hornchurch, RM11 1XL
Tel: 01708-773403 Fax: 01708-444180
Redbridge LB
Queen Victoria House, 794 Cranbrook Rd, Barkingside, Ilford, IG6 1JS Tel: (020)-8478-9497 Fax: 0181 478 9483
Southend-on-Sea Civic Centre, Victoria Avenue, Southend-on-Sea, SS2 6ER Tel: 01702-343728 Fax: 01702-612610
Thurrock 2 Quarry Hill, Grays, RM17 5BT
Tel: 01375-375245 Fax: 01375-392649
Uttlesford, Council Offices, London Rd, Saffron Walden, CB11 4ER Tel: 01799-510319 Fax: 01799-510332

Gloucestershire
Cheltenham St. Georges Rd, Cheltenham, GL50 3EW
Tel: 01242-532455 Fax: 01242-254600
Cirencester Old Memorial Hospital, Sheep St, Cirencester, GL7 1QW Tel: 01285-650455 Fax: 01285-640253
Forest of Dean Belle Vue Centre, 6 Belle Vue Rd, Cinderford, GL14 2AB Tel: 01594-822113
Fax: 01594-826352
Gloucester, Maitland House, Spa Rd, Gloucester, GL1 1UY
Tel: 01452-425275 Fax: 01452-385385
North Cotswold, North Cotswold Register Office, High St, Moreton-in-Marsh, GL56 0AZ Tel: 01608-651230
Fax: 01608-651226
Stroud Parliament St, Stroud, GL5 1DY Tel: 01453-766049
Fax: 01453-752961

Hampshire
Winchester (Eastleigh SD) 101 Leigh Rd, Eastleigh, SO50 9Dr Tel: 01703-612058 Fax: 01703-612058
Alton 4 Queens Rd, Alton, GU34 1HU Tel: 01420-85410
Andover, Wessex Chambers, South St, Andover, SP10 2BN
Tel: 01264-352513 Fax: 01264-366849
Basingstoke 60 New Rd, Basingstoke, RG21 7PW
Tel: 01256-350745 Fax: 01256-350745
New Forest, Hillcroft, New St, Lymington, SO41 9B
Tel: 01590-673425 Fax: 01590-688509
(Lymington SD) Public Offices, 65 Christchurch Rd, Ringwood, BH24 1DH
(New Forest SD) Totton Health Centre, Testwood Lane, Totton, Southampton, SO4 3AP Tel: 01703-863168
Fax: 01703-863168
North-East Hampshire 30 Grosvenor Rd, Aldershot GU11 3EB Tel: 01252-322066 Fax: 01252-338004
Petersfield, The Old College, College St, Petersfield GU31 4AG Tel: 01730-265372 Fax: 01730-265396
Ringwood & Fordingbridge Public Office, Ringwood, BH24 1DJ Tel: 01425-470150 Fax: 01425-471732
Romsey, Hayter House, Hayter Gardens, Romsey, SO51 7QU Tel: 01794-513846 Fax: 01794-830491
South-East Hampshire 4-8 Osborn Road South, Fareham, PO16 7DG Tel: 01329-280493 Fax: 01329-823184

(Fareham SD) 4 - 8 Osborn Road South, Fareham
PO16 7DG Tel: 01329-280493
(Gosport SD) 3 Thorngate Way, Gosport, PO12 1DX
Tel: (023)-92580629 Fax: (023)-92580629
(Havant SD) Fernglen, Town Hall Rd, Havant, PO9 1AN
Tel: (023)-92482533 Fax: (023)-92482533
Winchester Station Hill, Winchester, SO23 8TJ
Tel: 01962-869608 Tel: 01962-869594 Fax: 01962-851912

Southampton
Southampton 6A Bugle St, Southampton, SO14 2LX
Tel: 01703-631422 Fax: 01703-633431

Herefordshire
Bromyard, Council Offices, 1 Rowberry St, Bromyard,
Hereford, HR7 4DU Tel: 01885-482730
Hereford, County Offices, Bath St, Hereford, HR1 2HQ
Tel: 01432-350461 Fax: 01432-363264
Kington Market Hall St, Kingston, HR5 3DP
Tel: 01544-230156 Fax: 01544-231385
Ledbury Town Council Offices, Church St, Ledbury
HR8 1DH Tel: 01531-632306
Leominster The Old Priory, Leominster, HR6 8EQ
Tel: 01568-610131
Ross, The Old Chapel, Cantilupe Rd, Ross on Wye
HR9 7AN Tel: 01989-562795 Fax: 01989 564869

Hertfordshire
Barnet 29 Wood St, Barnet, EN5 4B
 Tel: (020)-8731-1100 Fax: (020)-8731-1111
Bishops Stortford 2 Hockerill St, Bishops Stortford
CM23 2DL Tel: 01279-652273 Fax: 01279-461492
Email: gill.wenzer@hertscc.gov.uk
Broxbourne, Borough Offices, Churchgate, Cheshunt
EN8 9XQ Tel: 01992-623107
Dacorum, The Bury, Queensway, Hemel Hemstead
HP1 1HR Tel: 01442-228600 Fax: 01442-243974
Hatfield 19b St Albans Road East, Hatfield, AL10 0NG
Tel: 01707-283920
Hertford & Ware, County Hall, Pegs Lane, Hertford,
SG13 8DE Tel: 0192-555590
Hitchen & Stevenage Danesgate, Stevenage, SG1 1WW
Tel: 01438-316579 Fax: 01438-357197
St Albans, Hertfordshire House, Civic Close, St. Albans,
AL1 3JZ Tel: 01727-816806 Fax: 01727-816804
Watford 36 Clarendon Rd, Watford, WD1 1JP
Tel: 01923-231302 Fax: 01923 246852

Hull
Kingston-upon-Hull
Municipal Offices, 181-191 George St, Hull, HU1 3B
 Tel: 01482-615400 Fax: 01482 615411

Isle of Wight
County Hall, High St, PO30 1UD Tel: 01983-823230
Tel: 01983-823233 Fax: 01983-823227

Kent
Ashford with Shepway, Elwick House, Elwick Rd,
Ashford, TN23 1NR Tel: 01233-62466 Fax: 01233-642962
Bexley LB
Bexley, Manor House, The Green, Sidcup, DA14 6BW
Tel: (020)-8303-7777 Ext 32 Fax: (020)-8308-4967
Canterbury with Swale Wellington House, 4 StStephen's
Rd, Canterbury, CT2 7RD Tel: 01227-470480
Fax: 01227-780176
Chatham Ingleside, 114 Maidstone Rd, Chatham, ME4 6DJ
Tel: 01634-844073 Fax: 01634-840165
Gravesend 132 Windmill St, Gravesend, DA12 1BE
Tel: 01474-333451 Fax: 01474-564428
Maidstone The Archbishop's Palace, Palace Gardens, Mill
St, Maidstone, ME15 6YE Tel: 01622-752891
Fax: 01622 663690

Thanet with Dover, Aberdeen House, 68 Ellington Rd,
Ramsgate, CT11 9ST Tel: 01843-591417
Tunbridge Wells, Divisional County Offices, 39 Grove Hill
Rd, Tunbridge Wells, TN1 1SL Tel: 01892-527332 Fax:
01892 528518

Lancashire
Blackburn with Darwen
(Darwen & Turton SD) Town Hall, Croft St, Darwen
BB3 2RN Tel: 01254-702443
Garstang, Fleetwood & Fylde South King St, Blackpool,
FY1 4AX Tel: 01253-477177 Fax: 01253-477170
(Fleetwood SD) Fleetwood Central Library, North Albert
St, Fleetwood, FY7 6AJ Tel: 01253-874580
(Fylde SD) The Library, Clifton St, Lytham, FY8 5ED
Tel: 01253-737530
Hyndburn & Rossendale The Mechanics Institute, Willow
St, Accrington, BB5 1LP Tel: 01254-871360
Fax: 01254 239391
(Rossendale SD) 1 Grange St, Rawtenstall, Rossendale,
BB4 7RT Tel: 01706-215496
Blackburn Jubilee St, Blackburn, BB1 1EP
Tel: 01254-57602 Tel: 01254 587524 Fax: 01254 587538
Blackpool & Fylde South King St, Blackpool, FY1 4AX
Tel: 01253-477177 Fax: 01253-477176
Bolton MD
Bolton Mere Hall, Merehall St, Bolton, BL1 2Q
Tel: 01204-525165 Fax: 01204-525125
Burnley & Pendle 12 Nicholas St, Burnley, BB11 2AQ
Tel: 01282-36116 Fax: 01282 412221
Bury MD
Bury, Town Hall, Manchester Rd, Bury, BL9 OSW
Tel: 0161-253-6027 Fax: 0161-253-6028
Chorley 16 St. George's St, Chorley, PR7 2AA
Tel: 012572-63143 Fax: 01257-263808
Lancaster 4 Queen St, Lancaster, LA1 1RS
Tel: 01524-65673 Fax: 01524-842285
(Garstang SD) Croston Villas, High St, Garstang, PR3 1EA
Tel: 01995-603330
(Preesall SD) The Over Wyre Medical Centre, Pilling Lane,
Preesall, FY6 0FA Tel: 01253-810722
Oldham MD
Oldham, Metropolitan House, Hobson St, Oldham
OL1 1PY Tel: 0161-678-0137 Fax: 0161 911 3729
Preston & South Ribble Guildhall Offices, Guildhall St,
Preston, PR1 3PR Tel: 01772-823739 Fax: 01772 263809
Ribble Valley Off Pimlico Rd, Clitheroe, BB7 2BW Tel:
01200-425786 Fax: 01200-425786
Rochdale MD
Rochdale, Town Hall, The Esplanade, Rochdale
OL16 1AB Tel: 01706-864779 Fax: 01706-864786
Calderdale MD
Todmorden, Municipal Offices, Rise Lane, Todmorden,
OL14 7AB Tel: 01706-814811
West Lancashire, Greetby Buildings, Derby St, Ormskirk,
L39 2BS Tel: 01695-576009 Fax: 01695 585819
Wigan MD
Wigan & Leigh, New Town Hall, Library St, Wigan
WN1 1NN Tel: 01942-705000 Fax: 01942-705013

Leicestershire
Coalville 41 Ravenstone Rd, Coalville, LE67 3NB
Tel: 01530-832007 Fax: 01530-815802
Hinckley, The Chestnuts, 25 Mount Rd, Hinckley, LE10
1AD Tel: 01455-637259 Fax: 01455-612817
Leicester 5 Pocklington's Walk, Leicester, LE1 6BQ
Tel: 0116-253-6326 Fax: 0116 253 3008
Loughborough 202 Ashby Rd, Loughborough, LE11 3AG
Tel: 01509-611954
Market Harborough 42 Coventry Rd, Market Harborough,
LE16 9BZ Tel: 01858-431124 Fax: 01858-432955

Melton Mowbray, County Council Area Offices, Leicester Rd, Melton Mowbray, LE13 0DG Tel: 01664-482267 Fax: 01664-481910

Rutland
Catmore, Oakham, Rutland, E15 6JU Tel: 01572-756547

Lincolnshire
East Elloe 25 West St, Long Sutton, PE12 9BN Tel: 01406-363874 Fax: 01406 365325
(Holbeach SD) 33 Boston Rd, Holbeach, Spalding, PE12 7LR Tel: 01406-423166 Fax: 01406-422812
(Long Sutton SD) 25 West St, Long Sutton, PE12 9BN Tel: 01406-363874
Boston County Hall, Boston, PE21 6LX Tel: 01205-310010 Fax: 01205-356690
Bourne, Saxonhurst, 35 West St, Bourne, PE10 9NE Tel: 01778-422269 Fax: 01778-421081
Caistor Council Offices, Caistor, LN7 6LX Tel: 01472-851153 Fax: 01472-852678
Gainsborough 156 Trinity St, Gainsborough, DN21 1JP Tel: 01427-612312 Fax: 01427-678185
Grantham, The Priory, Market Place, Grantham, NG31 6LJ Tel: 01476-561061 Fax: 01476 562235
Horncastle, Holmeleigh, Foundry St, Horncastle, LN9 6AQ Tel: 01507-522576 Fax: 01507 524849
Lincoln 4 Lindum Rd, Lincoln, LN2 1NN Tel: 01522-552501/2 Fax: 01522-589524
Louth, Louth Town Hall, Eastgate, Louth, LN11 9NH Tel: 01507-603529 Fax: 01507-608346
Sleaford, PO Box 2, Council Offices, Eastgate, Sleaford, NG34 7EB Tel: 01529-414144-Ext.-2520 Fax: 01529 413728
Spalding, Sessions House, Sheep Market, Spalding, PE11 1BB Tel: 01775-769064 Fax: 01775-714392
Spilsby, Offord House, Church St, Spilsby, PE23 5EF Tel: 01790-752550 Fax: 01790-752162
(Skegness SD) 30 Roman Bank, Skegness, PE25 2SG
Stamford 2 St Mary's Hill, Stamford, PE9 2DR Tel: 01780-756004 Fax: 01780 752659

London

Bromley LB
Room S101, Bromley Civic Centre, Stockwell Close, Bromley, BR1 3UH Tel: (020)-8313-4666 Fax: (020)-8313-4699
Camden LB
Camden Register Office, Camden Town Hall, Judd St, WC1H 9JE Tel: (020)-7314-1900 Fax: (020)-7860-5792
City of London
Finsbury Town Hall, Roseberry Avenue, EC1R 4QT Tel: (020)-7833-3210 Fax: (020)-7477-3744
City of Westminster LB
Westminster Council House, Marylebone Rd, NW1 5PT Tel: (020)-7641-1161/2/3 Fax: (020)-7641-1246
Croydon LB
Mint Walk, Croydon, CR0 1EA Tel: (020)-8760-5617 Fax: (020)-8760-5633
Ealing LB
Ealing Town Hall, New Broadway, Ealing, W5 2BY Tel: (020)-8758-8946 Fax: (020)-8758-8722
Greenwich LB
Town Hall, Wellington St, SE18 6PW Tel: (020)-8854-8888 Fax: (020)-8317-5747
Hackney LB
Town Hall, Mare St, E8 1EA Tel: (020)-8356-3376 Fax: (020)-8356-3552
Hammersmith & Fulham LB
Fulham Register Office, Old Town Hall, 553/561 Fulham Rd, London, SW6 1ET Tel: (020)-8576-521 Fax: (020)-8576-5072

Hammersmith & Fulham LB
Nigel Playfair Ave, London, W6 9JYTel: (020)-8748-3020 Tel: (020)-8576-5032 Fax: (020)-8748-6619
Haringey LB
Civic Centre, High Rd, Haringey, N22 4LE Tel: (020)-8528-0186 Fax: (020)-8862-2912
Islington LB
Finsbury Town Hall, Roseberry Ave, EC1R 4QT Tel: (020)-7837-4941 & (020) 8 527 6350 Fax: 0171 527 6355
Kensington & Chelsea LB
The Kensington & Chelsea Register Office, Chelsea Old Town Hall, Kings Rd, London, SW3 5EE Tel: (020)-7361-4100 Fax: (020)-7361-4054
Lambeth MB
357-361 Brixton Rd, London, SW9 7DA Tel: (020)-7926-9420 Fax: 0171 926 9426
Lewisham LB
368 Lewisham High St, London, SE13 6LQ Tel: (020)-8690-2128 Fax: 0181 314 1078
Newham LB
Passmore Edwards Building, 207 Plashet Grove, East Ham, London, E6 1BT Tel: (020)-8471 5128 Fax: 0181 557 8973
Southwark LB
34 Peckham Rd, London, SE5 8QA Tel: (020)-7525-7669 Fax: 0171 525 7652
Tower Hamlets LB
Bromley Public Hall, Bow Rd, E3 3AA Tel: (020)-8980-8025 Fax: 0181 981 9931
Waltham Forest LB
106 Grove Rd, Walthamstow, E17 9B Tel: (020)-8520-8617 Fax: 0181 509 1388
Wandsworth LB
The Town Hall, Wandsworth High St, SW18 2PU Tel: (020)-8871-6120 Fax: 0181 871 8100

Manchester
Manchester MD
Cumberland House, Spinningfield, Off Deansgate, M60 3RG Tel: 0161-234-7878 Fax: 0161-234-7888 Email: register-office@manchester.gov.uk
Salford MD
'Kingslea', Barton Rd, Swinton, M27 5WH Tel: 0161-793-0077 Fax: 0161-794-4797

Merseyside
Knowsley MD
District Council Offices, High St, Prescot, L34 3LH Tel: 0151-443-5210 Fax: 0151-443-5216
Liverpool MD
7 Brougham Terrace, West Derby Rd, Liverpool, L6 1AF Tel: 0151-225-4977 Fax: 0151-225-4944
Sefton MD
Sefton North, Town Hall, Corporation St, Southport PR8 1DA Tel: 01704-533133 Fax: 0151-934-2014
Sefton South, Crosby Town Hall, Great Georges Rd, Waterloo, Liverpool, L22 1RB Tel: 0151-934 3045 Fax: 0151 934 3044
St Helens MD
St. Helens Central St, St Helens, WA10 1UJ Tel: 01744-23524 Tel: 01744-732012 Fax: 01744 23524
Wirral MD
Wallasey Town Hall, Wallasey, L44 8ED Tel: 0151-691-8505
Wirral, Town Hall, Mortimer St, Birkenhead, L41 5EU Tel: 0151-666-3953 Fax: 0151-666-3955

Middlesex
Brent LB
Brent Town Hall, Forty Lane, Wembley, HA9 9EZ Tel: (020)-8937-1010 Fax: (020)-8937-1021 Email: "name"@brent.gov.uk

Enfield LB
Public Offices, Gentlemen's Row, Enfield, EN2 6PS
Tel: (020)-8367-5757 Fax: (020)-8379-8562
Harrow LB
The Civic Centre, Station Rd, Harrow, HA1 2UX
Tel: (020)-8424-1618 Fax: (020)-8424-1414
Hendon
182 Burnt Oak, Broadway, Edgware, HA8 0AU
Tel: (020)-8952-0876 Tel: (020)-8952-0024 Fax: (020)-8381-2346, Transferred to Barnet wef April 1999
Hillingdon LB
Hillingdon Civic Centre, Uxbridge, UB8 1UW
Tel: 01895-250418 Fax: 01895-250678
Hounslow LB
88 Lampton Rd, Hounslow, TW3 4DW
Tel: (020)-8862-5022 Fax: (020)-8577-8798

Milton Keynes
Bracknell House, Aylesbury St, Bletchley, MK2 2BE
Tel: 01908-372101 Fax: 01908 645103

Norfolk
North Walsham 18 Kings Arms St, North Walsham
NR28 9JX Tel: 01692-403075 Tel: Fax: 01692-406220
(Erpingham SD) Council Offices, North Lodge Park, Overstrand Rd, Cromer, NR27 0AH Tel: 01263-513078
(Smallburgh SD) 18 Kings Arms St, North Walsham, NR28 9JX Tel: 01692-403075
Depwade, Council Offices, 11-12 Market Hill, Diss
IP22 3JX Tel: 01379-643915 Fax: 01379 643915
Downham 15 Paradise Rd, Downham Market, PE38 9HS
Tel: 01366-388080 Fax: 01366 387105
East Dereham, 59 High St, Dereham, NR19 1DZ
Tel: 01362-698021 Fax: 01362 698021
Fakenham 37 Market Place, Fakenham, NR21 9DN
Tel: 01328-855910 Fax: 01328-855910
Great Yarmouth 'Ferryside', High Rd, Southtown, Great Yarmouth, NR31 0PH Tel: 01493-662313
Fax: 01493-602107
King's Lynn St Margaret's House, St Margaret's Place, King's Lynn, PE30 5DW Tel: 01553-669251
Fax: 01553 669251
Norwich, Churchaman House, 71 Bethel St, Norwich, NR2 1NR Tel: 01603-767600 Fax: 01603 632677
Wayland, Kings House, Kings St, Thetford, IP24 2AP
Tel: 01847-754115 Tel: Fax: 01847-765996

North East Lincolnshire
Town Hall Square, Grimsby, DN31 1HX Tel: 01472-324860
Tel: Fax: 01472-324867

North Lincolnshire
92 Oswald Rd, Scunthorpe, DN15 7PA Tel: 01724-843915
Tel: Fax: 01724 872668

North Somerset
North Somerset 41 The Boulevard, Weston-super-Mare, BS23 1PG Tel: 01934-627552 Fax: 01934-412014
(Clevedon SD) 37a Old Church Rd, Clevedon, BS21 6NN
(Weston Super Mare SD) 41 The Boulevard
Weston Super Mare, BS23 1PG

North Yorkshire
North Yorkshire Registration Service Bilton House, 31 Park Parade, Harrogate, HG1 5AG Tel: 01423-506949
Fax: 01423-502105
(Malton Out Station) Ryedale House, Malton, YO17 0HH
Tel: 01653-692285
(Northallerton Out Station) County Hall, Northallerton, DL7 8XE Tel: 01609-780780
(Pickering Out Station) 38 The Mount, Potter Hill, Pickering, YO18 8AE Tel: 01751 476708
(Richmond Out Station) 12 Queens Rd, Richmond, DL10 4AJ Tel: 01748-823008

(Scarborough Out Station) 14 Dean Rd, Scarborough, YO12 7SN Tel: 01723-360309
(Selby Out Station) The Annexe, Brook Lodge, Union Lane, Selby, YO8 0AL Tel: 01757-706590
(Settle Out Station) Council Offices, Castle Hill, Settle, BD24 9EU Tel: 01729-823624
(Skipton Out Station) Area Offices, Water St, Skipton, BD23 1PB Tel: 01756 793005
(Whitby Out Station) 'Eskholme', Upgang Lane, Whitby, YO21 3DR Tel: 01947-602731 Fax: 01947-602731

Northamptonshire
Brackley, Brackley Lodge, High St, Brackley, NN13 5BD
Tel: 01280-702949
Corby Civic Centre, Corby, NN17 1QB Tel: 01536-203141
Daventry, Council Offices, Lodge Rd, Daventry, NN11 5AF Tel: 01327-302209 Fax: 01327-300011
Kettering 75 London Rd, Kettering, NN15 7PQ
Tel: 01536-514792 Fax: 01536 411359
Northampton, The Guildhall, St Giles Square, Northampton, NN1 1DE Tel: 01604-233500
Fax: 01604 238507
Towcester, Brackley Road Towcester Tel: 01327-350774
Wellinborough, Council Offices, Swanspool, Wellingborough, NN8 1BP Tel: 01933-442553

Northumberland
Northumberland Central 94 Newgate St, Morpeth
NE61 1BU Tel: 01670-513232
(Blyth Valley SD) 107a Waterloo Rd, Blyth, NE24 1AD
Tel: 01670-352450
(Morpeth SD) 94 Newgate St, Morpeth, NE61 1BU
Tel: 01670 513232
(Wansbeck SD) Post Office Chambers, Station Rd, Ashington, NE63 8RJ Tel: 01670-812243
Northumberland North First 49-51 Bridge St, Berwick upon Tweed, TD15 1ES Tel: 01289-306479
(Belford SD) Linhope, 29 King St, Seahouses, NE68 7XW
Tel: 01665-721676
(Berwick SD) 49-51 Bridge St, Berwick on Tweed
TD15 1ES Tel: 01289-307373
(Wooler SD) 33 Glendale Rd, Wooler, NE71 6DN
Tel: 01668-281656
Northumberland North Second 6 Market Place, Alnwick, NE66 1HP Tel: 01665-602363 Fax: 01665 510079
(Alnwick SD) 6 Market Place, Alnwick, NE66 1HP
(Rothbury SD) Court House, Front St, Rothbury, NE65 2TZ
(Warkworth SD) 73 Queen St, Amble, Morpeth
NE65 0DA Tel: 01665-710744/5
Northumberland West, Abbey Gate House, Market St, Hexham, NE46 3LX Tel: 01434-602355 Tel: 01434 602605
Fax: 01434 604957
(Bellingham SD) Sutherland House, 3 St Cuthbert's Terrace, Bellingham, Hexham, NE48 2JR
Tel: 01434-220321
(Haltwhistle SD) Haltwhistle Library, Westgate, Haltwhistle, NE49 0AX Tel: 01434-0AX
(Hexham SD) Abbey Gate House, Market St, Hexham, NE46 3LX Tel: 01434-602355 Tel: 01434-602605
(Prudhoe SD) Prudhoe Fire Station, Front St, Prudhoe, NE42 5DQ Tel: 01661-832248

Nottinghamshire
Basford Highbury Rd, Bulwell, NG6 9DA
Tel: 0115-927-1294 Fax: 0115 977 1845
(Beeston & Stapleford SD) Register Office, Marvin Rd, off Station Rd, Beeston, NG9 2AP Tel: 0115-925-5530
Carlton Sub-district) County Council Offices, Carlton Square, Carlton, NG4 3BP Tel: 0115-961-9663
(Eastwood SD) Eastwood Health Clinic, Nottingham Rd, Eastwood, NG16 3GL Tel: 01773-712449
Newark, County Offices, Balderton Gate, Newark, NG24 1UW Tel: 01636-705455 Fax: 01636 705455

Southwell SD) North Muskham Prebend, Church St, Southwell, NG25 0HG Tel: 01636-814200
East Retford, Notts County Council Offices, Chancery Lane, Retford, DN22 6DG Tel: 01777-708631 Fax: 01777 860667
Mansfield, Notts CC Offices, St John St, Mansfield, NG18 1QH Tel: 01623-476564 Fax: 01623 636284
Nottingham 50 Shakespeare St, Nottingham, NG1 4F Tel: 0115-947-5665 Fax: 0115-941-5773
Rushcliffe, The Hall, Bridgford Rd, West Bridgford, NG2 6AQ Tel: 0115-981-5307 Fax: 0115-969-6189
Worksop, Queens Buildings, Potter St, Worksop, S80 2AH Tel: 01909-535534 Fax: 01909 501067

Oxfordshire
Abingdon, Roysse Court, Bridge St, Abingdon, OX14 3HU Tel: 01235-520156
Banbury, Bodicote House, Bodicote, Near Banbury, OX15 4AA Tel: 01295-263268 Fax: 01295-263268
Bullingdon Littleworth Rd, Wheatley, OX33 1NR Tel: 01865-874702
Henley, Easby House, Northfield End, Henley-on-Thames, RG9 2JW Tel: 01491-573047 Fax: 01491 573047
Oxford Tidmarsh Lane, Oxford, OX1 1NS Tel: 01865-815167 Fax: 01865 815632
Ploughley, Waverley House, Queen's Avenue, Bicester, OX6 8PY Tel: 01869-252917
Wallingford 197 The Broadway, Didcot, OX11 8RU Tel: 01235-818706
Wantage, The Civic Centre, Portway, Wantage, OX12 9BX Tel: 012357-65796
West Oxfordshire Welch Way, Witney, OX8 7HH Tel: 01993-703062

Peterborough
Cundle & Thrapston 17 Mill Rd, Cundle, PE8 4BW Tel: 01832-273413

Portsmouth
Milldam House, Burnaby Rd, PO1 3AF Tel: 01705-829041 Fax: 01705 831996

Reading
Reading & Wokingham Yeomanry House, 131 Castle Hill, RG1 7TA Tel: 0118-957-1213 Fax: 0118-951-0212

Shropshire
Ludlow Stone House, Corve St, Ludlow, SY8 1DG Tel: 01584-874941 Fax: 01584-872971
(Craven Arms SD) The Library, School Rd, Craven Arms, SY7 9PE Tel: 01588-673455
(Ludlow SD) The Red Cross Centre, The Smithfield, Lower Galdeford, Ludlow, SY8 1SB Tel: 01584-874422
North Shropshire, Edinburgh House, New St, Wem, Shrewsbury, SY4 5DB Tel: 01939-238418
(Market Drayton SD) Health Centre, Cheshire St, Market Drayton, TF9 3AA Tel:
North Shropshire (Whitchurch SD) 29 St Mary's St, Whitchurch, SY13 1RA Tel: 01948-663402
(Wem SD) Edinburgh House, New St, Wem, Shrewsbury, SY4 5DB Tel: 01939-238418 Fax:
Bridgnorth 12 West Castle St, Bridgnorth, WV16 4AB Tel: 01746-762589 Fax: 01746 764270
Clun, The Pines, Colebatch Rd, Bishop's Castle, SY9 5JZ Tel: 01588-638588
Oswestry Holbache Rd, Oswestry Tel: 01691-652086
Shrewsbury The Shirehall, Abbey Foregate, Shrewsbury, SY2 6LY Tel: 01743-259921 Fax: 01743 252922
Wrekin, The Beeches, 29 Vineyard Rd, Wellinton, Telford, TF1 1HB Tel: 01952-248292

Somerset
Mendip 19b Commercial Rd, Shepton Mallet, BA4 5BU Tel: 01749-343928 Fax: 01749 343928

(Frome SD) West Hill House, West End, Frome BA11 3AD Tel: 01373-462887
(Shepton Mallet SD) 19 Commercial Rd, Shepton Mallet, BA4 5BU Tel: 01749-342268
(Wells SD) Town Hall, Market Place, Wells, BA5 2RB Tel: 01749-675355
Yeovil, Maltravers House, Petters Way, Yeovil, BA20 1SP Tel: 01935-422230 Fax: 01935-413993
(Chard SD) Holyrood Lace Mill, Holyrood St, Chard, TA20 2YA Tel: 01460-63139 Fax: 01460-260402
(Wincanton SD) Council Offices, Churchfield, Wincanton, BA9 9AG Tel: 01963-435008 Fax: 01963-34182
Sedgemoor, Morgan House, Mount St, Bridgewater TA6 3ER Tel: 01278-422527
Taunton, Flook House, Belvedere Rd, Taunton, TA1 1BT Tel: 01823-282251 Fax: 01823 351173
West Somerset, 2 Long St, Williton, Taunton, TA4 4QN Tel: 01984-633116

South Gloucestershire
Poole Court, Poole Court Drive, Yate, BS37 5PY Tel: 01454-863140 Fax: 01454-863145

South Yorkshire
Doncaster MD
Elmfield Park, South Parade, Doncaster, DN1 2EB Tel: 01302-364922 Fax: 01302-364922
Mexborough SD) Council Offices, Main St, Mexborough, S64 9LU Tel: 01302-735705
Barnsley, Barnsley, Town Hall, Church St, Barnsley S70 2TA Tel: 01226-773085 Tel: 01226 773080
Rotherham MD
Rotherham, Bailey House, Rawmarsh Rd, Rotherham S60 1TX Tel: 01709-382121
Sheffield MD
Sheffield Surrey Place, Sheffield, S1 1YA Tel: 0114-203-9423 Fax: 0114-203-9424

Southampton
Hampshire, Droxford, Bank House, Bank St, Bishop's Waltham, SO32 1GP Tel: 01489-894044 Fax: 01489-892219

Staffordshire
South Staffordshire, Civic Centre, Gravel Hill, Wombourne, Wolverhampton, WV5 9HA Tel: 01902-895829 Fax: 01902-326779
(Seisdon SD) Civic Centre, Gravel Hill, Wombourne, Wolverhampton, WV5 9HA Tel: 01902-895829 Fax: 01902-326779
(Penkridge SD) Haling Dene Centre, Cannock Rd, Penkridge, ST19 5DT Tel: 01785-715260 Fax: 01785-715260
Cannock Chase 5 Victoria St, Cannock, WS11 1AG Tel: 01543-503255 Fax: 01543-468306
(Rugeley SD) Council Offices, Anson St, Rugeley, WS15 2BH Tel: 01889-585322
East Staffordshire, Rangemore House, 22 Rangemore St, Burton-upon-Trent, DE14 2ED Tel: 01283-538701 Fax: 01283 547338
(Burton on Trent SD) Rangemore House, 22 Rangemore St, Burton on Trent, DE14 2ED Tel: 01283-538701 Fax: 01283-547338
(Uttoxeter SD) 63 High St, Uttoxeter, ST14 7JD Tel: 01889-562168 Fax: 01889-569935
Lichfield (Tamworth SD) 26 Albert Rd, Tamworth, B79 7JS Tel: 01827-62295 Fax: 01827-62295
Newcastle-under-Lyme 20 Sidmouth Avenue, The Brampton, Newcastle-under-Lyme, ST5 0QN Tel: 01782-297581 Fax: 01782-297582
(Kidsgrove SD) The Town Hall, Liverpool Rd, Kidsgrove, ST7 4EH
Stafford, Eastgate House, 79 Eastgate St, Stafford, ST16 2NG Tel: 01785-277880 Fax: 01785 277884

(Stone SD) 15 Station Rd, Stone, ST15 8JR Tel: 01785-812087 Fax: 01785-286123
Staffordshire Moorlands High St, Leek, ST13 5EA
Tel: 01538-373166 Fax: 01538-386985
(Biddulph SD) Biddulph Library Annexe, Tunstall Rd,
Biddulph, ST8 6HH Tel: 01782-512619
(Cheadle & Alton SD) Council Offices, Leek Rd, Cheadle,
ST10 1JF Tel: 01538-752435 Fax: 01538-752435
Leek & Cheddleton SD) High St, Leek, ST13 5EA
Tel: 01538-373191
Lichfield, The Old Library Buildings, Bird St, Lichfield,
WS13 6PN Tel: 01543-510771 Fax: 01543-510773
Stoke-on-Trent Town Hall, Albion St, Hanley, Stoke on
Trent, ST1 1QQ Tel: 01782-295640 Fax: 01782-295648

Suffolk
Bury St. Edmunds St. Margarets, Shire Hall, Bury
StEdmunds, IP33 1RX Tel: 01284-352373
Fax: 01284 352376
Deben Council Offices, Melton Hill, Woodbridge, IP12
1AU Tel: 01394-444331 Tel: 01394-444682
Fax: 01394-383171
Gipping & Hartismere, Milton House, Milton Road South,
Stowmarket, IP14 1EZ Tel: 01449-612060
Fax: 01449-775103
Ipswich, St Peters House, 16 Grimwade St, Ipswich
IP4 1LP Tel: 01473-583050 Fax: 01473-584331
Sudbury 14 Cornard Rd, Sudbury, CO10 6XA
Tel: 01787-372904
Waveney, St Margarets House, Gordon Rd, Lowestoft,
NR32 1JQ Tel: 01502-405325 Fax: 01502-508170

Surrey
Kingston-upon-Thames LB
35 Coombe Rd, Kingston upon Thames, KT2 7BA
Tel: (020)-8546-7993 Fax: 0181 287 2888
Merton LB
Merton, Morden Cottage, Morden Hall Rd, Morden
SM4 5JA Tel: (020)-8540-5011 Fax: (020)-8543-2906
Mid Surrey, Ashley House, Ashley Rd, Epsom, KT18 5AB
Tel: 01372-721747 Fax: 01372-747308
North Surrey, 'Rylston', 81 Oatlands Drive, Weybridge,
KT13 9LN Tel: 01932-254360 Fax: 01932 227139
Richmond Upon Thames LB
Richmond upon Thames 1 Spring Terrace, Richmond,
TW9 1LW Tel: (020)-8940-2853 Fax: (020)-8940-8226
South-East Surrey 44 Reigate Hill, Reigate, RH2 9NG
Tel: 01737-243359 Fax: 01737 223163

Sutton LB
Sutton, Russettings, 25 Worcester Rd, Sutton, SM2 6PR
Tel: (020)-8770-6790 Fax: (020)-8770-6772
West Surrey, Artington House, Portsmouth Rd, Guildford,
GU2 5DZ Tel: 01483-562841 Fax: 01483-573232
Wokingham Yeomanry House, 131 Castle Hill, Reading,
RG1 7TA Tel: 0118-957-1213 Fax: 0118-951-0212

Tyne & Wear
Gateshead MD
Gateshead Civic Centre, Regent St, Gateshead, NE8 1HH
Tel: 0191-477-1011 Fax: 0191-477-9978
South Tyneside, Jarrow Suffolk St, Jarrow, NE32 5BJ
Tel: 0191-489 7595 Fax: 0191 428 0931
Newcastle-upon-Tyne MD
Newcastle-upon-Tyne Civic Centre, Barras Bridge,
Newcastle-upon-Tyne, NE1 8PS Tel: 0191-232-8520
 Fax: 0191 211 4970

North Tyneside MD
North Tyneside, Maritime Chambers, Howard St, North
Shields, NE30 1LZ Tel: 0191-2006164
South Tyneside MD
South Shields 18 Barrington St, South Shields, NE33 1AH
Tel: 0191-455-3915 Fax: 0191-427-7564

Sunderland MD
Town Hall & Civic Centre, PO Box 108, Sunderland
SR2 7DN Tel: 0191-553-1760 Fax: 0191 553 1769

Warwickshire
Mid Warwickshire, Pageant House, 2 Jury St, Warwick,
CV34 4EW Tel: 01926-494269 Fax: 01926 496287
(Leamington Spa SD) 1 Euston Square, Leamington Spa,
CV32 4NE Tel: 01962-428807 Fax: 01962-339923
(Southam SD) The Grange, Coventry Rd, Southam
CV33 0ED Tel: 01926-812636
South Warwickshire 7 Rother St, Stratford-on-Avon,
CV37 6LU Tel: 01789-293711 Fax: 01789 261423
(Alcester SD) The Court House, Priory Rd, Alcester
B49 5DZ Tel: 01789-765441
(Shipston on Stour SD) Clark House, West St
Shipston on Stour, CV36 4HD Tel: 01608-662839
Stratford on Avon SD) Register Office, 7 Rother St,
Stratford on Avon, CV37 6LU Tel: 01789-293397
Fax: 01789-261423
North Warwickshire
Warwick House, Ratcliffe St, Atherstone, CV9 1JP
 Tel: 01827-713241 Fax: 01827 720467
Nuneaton & Bedworth Riversley Park, Coton Rd,
Nuneaton, CV11 5HA Tel: 01203-348948
Fax: 01203-350988
Rugby 5 Bloxam Place, Rugby, CV21 3DS
Tel: 01788-571233 Fax: 01788-542024

West Midlands
Birmingham MD
Birmingham 300 Broad St, Birmingham, B1 2DE
Tel: 0121-235-3421 Fax: 0121-303-1396
Dudley MD
Dudley, Priory Hall, Priory Park, Dudley, DY1 4EU
 Tel: 01384-815373 Fax: 01384-815339
Sandwell MD
Sandwell, Highfields, High St, Sandwell, B70 8RJ
Tel: 0121-569-2480 Fax: 0121-569-2473
Solihull MD
Solihull North The Library, Stephenson Drive, Chelmsley
Wood, Birmingham, B37 5TA Tel: 0121-788-4376
Fax: 0121 788 4379
Solihull South Homer Rd, Solihull, B9 3QZ
Tel: 0121-704-6100 Fax: 0121 704 6123
Dudley MD
Stourbridge, Crown Centre, Crown Lane, Stourbridge,
DY8 1YA Tel: 01384-815384 Fax: 01384-815397
Walsall MD
Walsall Hatherton Rd, Walsall, WS1 1TN
Tel: 01922-652260
Wolverhampton Civic Centre, St Peters Square,
Wolverhampton, WV1 1RU Tel: 01902-554989
Fax: 01902-554987

West Sussex
Crawley, Town Hall, The Boulevard, Crawley, RH10 1UZ
Tel: 01293-438341 Fax: 01293-526454
(Sub-district) County Buildings, Northgate Avenue,
Crawley, RH10 1XB Tel: 01293-514545
Fax: 01293-553832
Chichester, Greyfriars, 61 North St, Chichester, PO19 1NB
Tel: 01243-782307 Fax: 01243-773671
(Bognor SD) Health Centre, West St, Bognor Regis
PO21 1UT Tel: 01243-823453 Fax: 01243-823453
(Midhurst SD) Capron House, North St, Midhurst
 GU29 9XX Tel: 01730-813245 Fax: 01730-813245
Worthing, County Buildings, 15 Mill Rd, Worthing
 BN11 4JY Tel: 01903-708250 Fax: 01903-708263
(Chanctonbury SD) 26 West St, Storrington, RH20 4EE
Tel: 01903-744275
(Shoreham by the Sea SD) Shoreham Health Centre, Pond
Rd, Shoreham by the Sea, BN4 5US Tel: 01273-440550

Registrars of Births Marriages & Deaths

(Littlehampton SD) County Buildings, East St, Littlehampton, BN17 6AP Tel: 01903-715460 Fax: 01903-715460
Haywards Heath, West Sussex County Council Offices, Oaklands Rd, Haywards Heath, RH16 1SU Tel: 01444-452157 Fax: 01444-410128
Horsham, Town Hall, Market Square, Horsham RH12 1EU Tel: 01403-265368 Fax: 01403-2170778

West Yorkshire
Bradford MD
Bradford 22 Manor Row, Bradford, BD1 4QR Tel: 01274-752151 Fax: 01274-305139
Keighley, Town Hall, Bow St, Keighley, BD21 3PA Tel: 01535-618060
Kirklees MD
Dewsbury Wellington St, Dewsbury, WF13 1LY Tel: 01924-324880 Fax: 01924 324882
Huddersfield, Civic Centre, 11 High St, Huddersfield HD1 2PL Tel: 01484-221030
Leeds MD
Leeds, Belgrave House, Belgrave St, Leeds, LS2 8DQ Tel: 0113-247-6711 Fax: 0113-247-4192
Calderdale MD
Halifax 4 Carlton St, Halifax, HX1 2AH Tel: 01422-353993 Fax: 01422-252370
Wakefield MD
Pontefract Town Hall, Pontefract, WF8 1PG Tel: 01977-722670 Fax: 01977-722676
Wakefield 71 Northgate, Wakefield, WF1 3BS Tel: 01924-361635 Fax: 01924-371859

Wiltshire
Chippenham 10-11 Market Place, Chippenham, SN15 3HF Tel: 01249-654361 Fax: 01249-658850
Devizes & Marlborough, The Beeches, Bath Rd, Devizes, SN10 2AL Tel: 01380-722162 Fax: 01380-728933
Marlborough 1 The Green, Marlborough, SN8 1AL Tel: 01672-512483
Salisbury, The Laburnums, 50 Bedwin St, Salisbury SP1 3UW Tel: 01722-335340 Fax: 01722 326806
Trowbridge, East wing Block, County Hall, Trowbridge, BA14 8JQ Tel: 01225-713000 Fax: 01225 713097
Warminster 3 The Avenue, Warminster, BA12 9AB Tel: 01985-213435 Fax: 01985 217688
Thamesdown, Swindon, 1st Floor Aspen House, Temple St, Swindon, SN1 1SQ Tel: 01793-521734 Fax: 01793 433887

Worcestershire
Bromsgrove School Drive, Bromsgrove, B60 1AY Tel: 01527-578759 Fax: 01527-578750
Droitwich, Council Offices, Ombersley St, Droitwich WR9 8QX Tel: 01905-772280 Fax: 01905-776841
Evesham, County Offices, Swan Lane, Evesham WR11 4TZ Tel: 01386-443945 Fax: 01386-448745
Kidderminster Council Offices, Bewdley Rd, Kidderminster, DY11 6RL Tel: 01562-829100 Fax: 01562-60192
Malvern, Hatherton Lodge, Avenue Rd, Malvern WR14 3AG Tel: 01684-573000 Fax: 01684-892378
Pershore, Civic Centre, Queen Elizabeth Drive, Pershore, WR10 1PT Tel: 01386-565610 Fax: 01386-553656
Redditch 29 Easmore Rd, Redditch, B98 8ER Tel: 01527-60647
Tenbury, Council Buildings, Teme St, Tenbury Wells Tel: 01584-810588
Worcester 29-30 Foregate St, Worcester, WR1 1DS Tel: 01905-765350 Fax: 01905-765355

York
56 Bootham, York, YO30 7DA Tel: 01904-654477 Fax: 01904-638090

Isles of Scilly
Isles of Scilly Town Hall, St Marys, TR21 0LW Tel: 01720 422537 Fax: 01720-422202

Wales

Anglesey
Ynys Môn, Shire Hall, Glanhwfa Rd, Llangefni LL77 7TW Tel: 01248-725264

Cardiff
Cardiff 48 Park Place, Cardiff, CF1 3LU Tel: 01222-871690 Fax: 01222-871689

Caerphilly
Bargoed SD) Register Office, Hanbury Square, Bargoed, CF8 8QQ Tel: 01443-875560 Fax: 01443-822535
(Islwyn SD) Council Offices, Pontllanfraith, Blackwood, NP2 2YW Tel: 01495-226622 Ext 5188
Caerphilly, The Council Offices, Ystrad Fawr, Ystrad Mynach, CF82 7SF Tel: 01443-863478 Fax: 01443-863385

Ceredigion
Cardiganshire Central 21 High St, Lampeter, SA48 7BG Tel: 01570-422558 Fax: 01570-422558
Cardiganshire North, Swyddfar Sir, Marine Terrace, Aberystwyth, SY33 2DE Tel: 01970-633580
Cardiganshire South, Glyncoed Chambers, Priory St, Cardigan SA43 1BX Tel: 01239-612684 Fax: 01239-612684

Carmarthenshire
St Peters St, Carmarthen, SA31 1LN Tel: 01267-230875 Fax: 01267-221974
Llanelli
County Council Offices, Swansea Rd, Llanelli, SA15 3DJ Tel: 01554-774088 Fax: 01554-749424

Comwy
Conwy CB Public Protection Department Civic Offices, Colwyn Bay, LL29 8AR Tel: 01492 575183 Fax: 01492 575204

Colwyn
New Clinic & Offices, 67 Market St, Abergele, LL22 7BP Tel: 01745-823976 Fax: 01745-823976
(Sub-district) Bod Alaw, Rivieres Avenue, Colwyn Bay, LL29 7DP Tel: 01492-530430
Aberconwy, Muriau Buildings, Rose Hill St, Aberconwy, LL32 8LD Tel: 01492-592407 Fax: 01492-2315

Denbighshire
Denbighshire North, Morfa Hall, Church St, Rhyl, LL18 3AA Tel: 01745-353428 Fax: 01745-361424
Denbighshire South Station Rd, Ruthin, LL15 1BS Tel: 01824-703782 Fax: 01824-704399

Flintshire
Flintshire East, The Old Rectory, Rectory Lane, Hawarden, CH5 3NN Tel: 01244-531512 Fax: 01244-534628
Flintshire West Park Lane, Holywell, CH8 7UR Tel: 01352-711813 Fax: 01352-713292

Glamorgan
Vale of Glamorgan, Vale of Glamorgan 2-6 Holton Rd, Barry, CF63 4HD Tel: 01446-700809 Fax: 01446 746861

Gwent
Blaenau Gwent
Blaenau Gwent, The Grove, Church St, Tredegar, NP2 3DS Tel: 01495-722305
(Abertilley SD) Council Offices, Mitre St, Abertilley, NP3 1AE Tel: 01495-216082
(Ebbw Vale & Tredegar SD) The Grove, Church St, Tredegar, NP2 3DS Tel: 01495-72269

Newport
8 Gold Tops, Newport, NP9 4PH Tel: 01633-265547
Fax: 01633 220913
Torfaen
Hanbury Rd, Pontypool, NP4 6YG Tel: 01495-762937
Fax: 01495 769049

Gwynedd
Ardudwy, Bryn Marian, Church St, Blaenau Ffestiniog,
LL41 3HD Tel: 01766-830217
Bangor
Town Hall, Bangor, LL57 2RE Tel: 01248-362418
Caernarfon
Swyddfa Arfon, Pennrallt, Caernarfon, LL55 1BN
Tel: 01286-682661
De Meirionndd
Bridge St, Dolgellau, LL40 1AU Tel: 01341-424341
Dwyfor
35 High St, Pwllheli, LL53 5RT Tel: 01758-612546
Fax: 01758-701373
Penllyn
5 Plasey St, Bala, LL23 7SW Tel: 01678-520428
Fax: 01678-520474

Merthyr Tydfil
Oldway House, Castle St, CF47 8BJ Tel: 01685-723318
Fax: 01685 721849

Mid Glamorgan
see **Rhondda Cynon Taff**

Rhondda Cynon Taff
Pontypridd Court House St, Pontypridd, CF37 1JS
Tel: 01443-486869 Fax: 01443 406587
Cynon Valley SD) The Annexe, Rock Grounds, Aberdare,
CF44 7AE Tel: 01685-871008
(Rhondda No1 SD) De Winton Field,Tonypandy,CF40 2NJ
(Rhondda No 2 SD) Crown Buildings, 69 High St,
Ferndale, Rhondda, CF43 4RR Tel: 01443-730369
(Taff Ely SD) Courthouse St, Pontypridd, CF37 1LJ
Tel: 01443-486870 Fax: 01443-406587

Bridgend
Bridgend, County Borough Offices, Sunnyside, Bridgend,
CF31 4AR Tel: 01656-642391 Fax: 01656-642391

Neath Port Talbot
119 London Rd, Neath, Neath Port Talbot, SA11 1HL
Tel: 01639-643696 Fax: 01639 760023

Monmouthshire
Monmouth, Coed Glas, Firs Rd, Abergavenny, NP7 5LE
Tel: 01873 735435 Fax: 01837 735841
(Abergavenny SD) 26a Monk St, Abergavenny, NP7 5NP
Tel: 01873-735435
(Chepstow SD) High Trees, Steep St, Chepstow, NP6 6RL

Pembrokeshire
Haverfordwest Tower Hill, Haverfordwest, SA61 1SS
Tel: 01437-762579 Fax: 01437 763543
(Fishguard & Cemaes SD) Town Hall, Fishguard
SA65 9HE Tel: 01348-872875 Fax: 01348-872875
(Haverfordwest & Milford Haven SD) Tower Hill,
Haverfordwest, SA61 1SS Tel: 01437-762579
South Pembroke East Back, Pembroke, SA71 4HL
Tel: 01646-682432 Fax: 01646 621433

Powys
Mid Powys, Powys County Hall, Llandrindod Wells
LD1 5LG Tel: 01597-826386 Fax: 01597-826220
(Builth SD) The Strand hall, Strand St, Builth Wells
LD2 3AA Tel: 01982-552134
(Radnorshire West SD) Register Office, Powys County
Hall, Llandrindod Wells, LD1 5LG Tel: 01597-826382
Newtown Room 4 Council Offices, The Park, Newtown,
SY16 2NZ Tel: 01686-627862

(Llanidloes SD) Town Hall, Llanidloes, SY18 6BN
Tel: 01686-412353
Welshpool & Llanfyllllin
Neuadd Maldwyn, Severn Rd, Welshpool, SY21 7AS
Tel: 01938-552828-ext-228 Fax: 01938 551233
(Llanfyllin SD) Old County School, Llanfyllin, SY22 5AA
Tel: 01691-648794
Brecknock, Neuadd Brycheiniog, Cambrian Way, Brecon,
LD3 7HR Tel: 01874-624334 Fax: 01874 625781
Hay, The Borough Council Offices, Broad St, Hay-on-Wye,
HR3 5BX Tel: 01479-821371 Fax: 01479 821540
Machynlleth 11 Penrallt St, Machynlleth, SY20 8AG
Tel: 01654-702335 Fax: 01654-703742
Radnorshire East 2 Station Rd, Knighton, LD7 1DU
Tel: 01547-528332

Swansea
Swansea The Swansea Register Office, County Hall,
Swansea, SA1 3SN Tel: 01792-636188 Fax: 01792-636909

Ystradgynlais
County Council Offices, Trawsffordd, Ystradgynlais
SA9 1BS Tel: 01639-843104

Wrexham
Wrexham 2 Grosvenor Rd, Wrexham, LL11 1DL
Tel: 01978-265786 Fax: 01978-262061

Northern Ireland
General Register Office of Northern Ireland Oxford
House, 49 - 55 Chichester St, Belfast, BT1 4HL
Tel: 028 90 252033 Fax: 028 90 252044
Email: stanley.campbell@dfpni.gov.uk

Superintendent Registars Scotland

ABERCHIRDER 91 Main Street, Aberchirder, AB54 5TB
Tel: 01466-780735

ABERDEEN St Nicholas House Upperkirkgate, Aberdeen,
AB10 1EY Tel: 01224-522616, Fax: 01224-522616

ABERFELDY, DULL & WEEM Municipal Buildings
Crieff Road, Aberfeldy, PH15 2BJ Tel: 01887-820773

ABERFOYLE + MENTHEITH 4 Montrose Road,
Aberfoyle, FK8 3UL Tel: 01877-382311

ABERLOUR 46 High Street, Aberlour, AB38 9QD
Tel: 01340-871635

ABOYNE District Council Offices Bellwood Road,
Aboyne, AB34 5HQ Tel: 01339-886109, Fax: 01339-86798

AIRDRIE Area Registration Office 37 Alexander Street,
Airdrie, ML6 0BA Tel: 01236-763322

AIRTH 100 South Green Drive Airth Falkirk, FK8 8JR
Tel: 01324-831538

ALFORD Council Office School Road, Alford, AB33 8PY
Tel: 01975-652421, Fax: 01975-563286

ALLOA Marshill House, Marshill Alloa, FK10 1 AD
Tel: 01259-123850

ANNAN Moat House Bruce Street, Annan, DG12 5DE
Tel: 01461-204914

APPLECROSS Coire-ringeal Applecross, Kyle Ross-shire
IV54 8LU Tel: 01520-744248

ARBROATH Academy Lane, Arbroath, DD11 1EJ
Tel: 01241-873752

ARDGOUR 9 Clovullin Ardgour by Fort William, PH33
7AB Tel: 01855-841261

ARROCHAR 1 Cobbler View, Arrochar, G83 1 AD
Tel: 01301-702289

ASSYNT Post Office House, Lochinvar by Lairg, IV27 4JY
Tel: 01571-844201

AUCHINLECK 154 Main Street Auchlinleck Cummock,
KA18 2AS Tel: 01290-420582

AUCHTERARDER 187 High Street, Auchterarder
PH3 1AF Tel: 01764-663581

AUCHTERDERRAN 145 Station Road, Cardenden,
KY5 0BN Tel: 01592-414800

AUCHTERMUCHTY Town House High Street,
Auchtermuchty, KY14 7AP Tel: 01337-828329
Fax: 01337-821166

AVIEMORE Tremayne Dalfaber Road, Aviemore
PH22 1PU Tel: 01479-810694

AYR Sandgate House 43 Sandgate, Ayr, KY7 1JW
Tel: 01292-284988, Fax: 01292-885643

BAILLIESTON Council Office 89 Main Street,
Baillieston, G69 6AB Tel: 0141-771-1901

BALLACHULISH 5 Wades Rood Kinlochleven, Argyll,
PA4O 4QX Tel: 01855-831350

BALLATER An Creagan S Queens Road., Ballater
AB35 5RJ Tel: 01339-755535

BANCHORY Aberdeenshire Council The Square High
Street Banchory, AB3 1 Tel: 01330-822878

BANFF Seafield House 37 Castle Street, Banff, AB4S DQ
Tel: 01261-812001

BARRA Council Offices, Castlebay Dana, HS9 5XD
Tel: 01871-810431

BARRHEAD Council Office 13 Lowndes Street, Barrhead,
078 2QX Tel: 0141-8813551/2, Fax: 0141-5773553

BATHGATE 76 Mid Street, Bathgate, EH48 1QD
Tel: 01506-653162

BEAULY 7 Viewfield Avenue, Beauly, 1V4 7BW
Tel: 01463-782264

BELLSHILL 20/22 Motherwelt Road, Bellshill, ML4 1RB
Tel: 01698-747145

BENBECULA Council Offices Balivanich Benbecula
South Uist, HS7 5LA Tel: 01870-602425

BIGGAR 4 Ross Square, Biggar, MLI2 EAT
Tel: 01899-220997

BIRSAY Sandveien Dounby, Orkney, KW15 2118
Tel: 01856-771226

BISHOPDRIOGS Council Office 1 Balmuildy Road,
Bishopbriggs, G64 2RR Tel: 0141-772-1154/5

BLACK ISLE (NORTH) Operating from Dingwall
Tel: 01349-863113, Fax: 01349-866164

BLACK ISLE (SOUTH) Black Isles Centre, Service Point
Office Deans Road, Fortrose, IV10 8TJ
Tel: 01381-620797/8, Fax: 01381-621085

BLAIR ATHOLL Lauchope The Terrace, Blair Atholl,
PH15 5SZ Tel: 01796-481242

BLAIRGOWRIE Council Buildings 46 Leslie Street,
Blairgowrie, PH10 6AW Tel: 01250-872051
Fax: 01250-876029

BO'NESS + CARRIDEN 12 Corbiehail, Bo'ness
EH51 0AP Tel: 01506-778990

BOISDALE Post Office Hse Daliburgh, South Uist
PA81 5SS Tel: 01878-700300

BONAR + KINCARDINE Post Office Bonar Bridge,
Ardgay, IV24 3EA Tel: 01863-766219

BONNYBRIDGE Operating from Denny
Tel: 01324-504280

BRAEMAR Piedmont 9 Auchendryne Square, Eraemar,
AB35 5YS Tel: 01339-741501

BRECHIN 32 Panmure Street, Brechin, DD9 6AP
Tel: 01356-622107

BRESSAY No 2 Roadside Bressay, Lerwick Shetland
ZE2 9BL Tel: 01595-820356

BROADEORD Fairwinds, Broadford Skye 1V49 9AB
Tel: 01471-822270

BUCKIE 1 West Church Street, Buckie, AB56 1UN
Tel: 01542-832691

BUCKNAVEN Council Office 96 Wellesley Road,
Buckhaven, KY8 1HT Tel: 01592-414444
Fax: 01592-414490

BUCKSBURN Nea Office 23 Inverurie Rd., Bucksburn,
AB2 9LJ Tel: 01224-712866

BURRA ISLES Roadside Hannavoe, Lerwick Shetland
ZEZ 9LA Tel: 01595-859201

CALLANDER 1 South Church Street, Callander
FKI7 B2N Tel: 01877-330166

CAMBUSLANG Council Office 6 Glasgow Rd,
Cambuslang, G72 7BW Tel: 0141-641-8178

CAMPBELTOWN Council Office Witchburn Road,
Campbeltown, PA28 6313 Tel: 01586-555253

CARLO WAY The Registry, Carloway Lewis PA86 9AU
Tel: 01851-643264

CARLUKE 25 High Street., Carluke, MLB 4A3
Tel: 01555-772273

CARNOCH Bridgend, Strathconon Muir Of Ord 1V6 7QQ
Tel: 01997-477254

CARNOUSTIE Council Chambers, Carnoustie
DDV 6AP Tel: 01241-853335/6

CASTLE DOUGLAS District Council 5 Street Andrew
Street, Castle Douglas, D07 1DE Tel: 01557-330291

CASTLETON Dalkeith House 13 Douglas Square,
Newcastleton, TD9 OQD Tel: 01387-375835

CATRINE 9 Co-operative Aye, Catrine, KA5 6SG
Tel: 01290-551638

CHIRNSIDE White House, Chirnside Duns, TD11 3XL
Tel: 01890-818339

CHRYSTON Lindsaybeg Road Muirhead Glasgow
G69 9HW Tel: 0141-779-1714

CLYNE Gower Lane, Brora, KW9 6NT Tel: 01408-621233

COALBURN 'Pretoria 200 Coalburn Road, Coolburi,
ML11 0LT Tel: 01555-820664

COATBRIDGE 183 Main Street, Coatbridge, ML5 3HH
Tel: 01236-422133

COIGACH The Stores, Achilibuie Ullapool, IV26 2Y0
Tel: 01854-622256

COLDSTREAM Operating from Duns
Tel: 01361-882600

COLL 9 Carnan Road, Isle Of Coll PA78 6TA
Tel: 01879-230329

COLONSAY & ORONSAY Scalasaig Farm, Colonsay,
PA6 1 7YW Tel: 01951-200357

COUPAR-ANGUS Union Bank Buildings, Coupar- Angus,
PH13 9AJ Tel: 01828-628395

COWDENBEATH 320 High Street, Cowdenbeath
KY4 9QX Tel: 01383-313131

CRAWFORD 76 Carlisle Road Crawford Biggar
ML12 6TW Tel: 01864-502633

CRIEFF 14 Comrie Street, Crieff, PH7 4AZ
Tel: 01764-655151

CUMBERNAULD Fleming House Tryst Road,
Cumbernauld, G67 1JW Tel: 01236-616390
Fax: 01236-616386

CUMBRAE 49 Stuart Street, Millport, KMS GAG
Tel: 01475-53074112, Fax: 01475-530891

CUPAR County Buildings St Catherine Street, Cupar
KYl5 4TA Tel: 01334-412200, Fax: 01334-412110

CURRIE 133 Lanark Road West, Currie, EH14 5NY
Tel: 0131-449-5318

DALBEATTIE Town Hall Buildings Water Street,
Dalbeattie, DG5 '41X Tel: 01557-330291-Ext323

DALKEITH 2-4 Buccieuch Street, Dalkeith, EH22 IHA
Tel: 0131-660-7570/1

DALMELLINGTON Area Office 1 New Street,
Dalmellington, KA6 7QX Tel: 01292-550229
Fax: 01292-550229

DALRY 42 Main Street Daly, Castle Douglas, DG7 3UW
Tel: 01644-430310

DARVEL Operating from Galston. Tel: 01563-820218

DELTING Soibakkan, Mossbank Shetland ZE2 9R13
Tel: 01806-242209

DENNY Carronbank House Carronbank Crescent, Denny,
PK4 2DE Tel: 01324-504280

DING WALL Council Offices Ferry Road, Dingwall
IV15 Tel: 01349-863113, Fax: 01349-866164

DORNOCH Cathedral Square, Dornoch, 1V25 3SW
Tel: 01862-810202, Fax: 01862-810166

DOUGLAS Post Office Ayr Road, Douglas, ML1 I OPU
Tel: 01555-851227

DUFFTOWN Brentwood Villa Albert Place, Dufftown,
AB55 4AY Tel: 01340-820663

DUMBARTON 18 College Way, Dumbarton, G82 1LJ
Tel: 01389-767515

DUMFRIES Municipal Chambers Buccleuch Street,
Dumfries, DO 1 2AD Tel: 01387-260000
Fax: 01387-269605

DUNBAR Town House 79/85 High Street, Dunbar, EH42
IER Tel: 01368-863434, Fax: 01368-865728

DUNBLANE Municipal Buildings, Dunblane, FK15 OAG
Tel: 01786-822214, Fax: 01786-822214

DUNDEE 89 Commercial Street, Dundee, DD1 2AO
Tel: 01382-435222/3, Fax: 01382-435224

DUNFERMLINE 34 Viewfield Terrace, Dunfermline,
KY12 7HZ Tel: 01383-3-12121

DUNKELD Buchanans Bridge Street, Dunkeld, P118 OAR
Tel: 01350-727268

DUNOON Council Offices Hill Street, Dunoon, PA23 7AP
Tel: 01369-704374, Fax: 01369-705948

DUNROSSNESS Wiltrow, Dunrossness Shetland 2E2 930
Tel: 01950-460792

DUNS 8 Newtown Street, Duns, TD11 3AS
Tel: 01361-882600

DUNVEGAN Tigh-na- Bruaich, Dunvegan Isle Of Skye
IV55 8WA Tel: 01470-521296

DURNESS Mid Villa Durine, Durness by Lairg, 1W7 4PN
Tel: 01971-511340

EALKIRK Old Burgh Buildings Newmarket Street,
Falkirk, FK1 lIE Tel: 01324-506580, Fax: 01324-506581

EAST CALDER East Calder Library 200 Main Street, East
Calder, EH53 0EJ Tel: 01506-884680, Fax: 01506-883944

EAST KILBRIDE Civic Centre Cornwall Street East
Kilbride Glasgow, G74 1AF Tel: 01355-220841

EAST NEUK Municipal Office Ladywalk, Anstruther,
KYID 3EY Tel: 01333-31227R

EASTWOOD + MEARNS Council Offices Easiwood Park
Roukenglen Rd Giffnock, G46 7JS Tel: 0141-638-7588

EDAY + PHARAY Redbanks, Eday Orkney, KW1 2AA
Tel: 01857-622239

EDINBURGH 2 India Buildings Victoria Street,
Edinburgh, EH1 2EX Tel: 0131-220-0349
Fax: 0131-220-0351

EDINBURGH (L) 30 Ferry Road, Edinburgh, EH6 4AE
Tel: 0131-554-8452

ELGIN 240 High Street, Elgin, IV30 1BA
Tel: 01343-541202, Fax: 01343-541202

ELLON Area Office Schoolhill Road, Ellon, AB41 9AN
Tel: 01358-720295

ERASERBURGH 14 Saltoun Square, Fraserburgh
AB43 5DB Tel: 01346-513281

EYEMOUTH Community Centre Albert Road, Eyemoulh,
TD14 5DE Tel: 01890-750690

FAIR ISLE Field, Fair Isle Shetland ZE2 9JU
Tel: 01595-760224

FETLAR Lower Toft Funzie, Fetlar Shetland 7E2 9DJ
Tel: 01957-733273

FIRTH & STENNESS Langbigging, Stenness Orkney
KWI6 3LB Tel: 01856-850320

FLOTTA Post Office, Flotta Kirkwall Orkney KWI6 3NP
Tel: 01856-701252

FORFAR The Cross, Forfar, DD8 1BX Tel: 01307-464973

FORRES Forres House High Street, Fortes, 1V36 0BU
Tel: 01309-672792

FORT AUGUSTUS Cich Collage, Fort Augustus
PH32 4DH Tel: 01320-366245

FORT WILLIAM Tweeddale Buildings High Street, Fort
William, PH33 EEU Tel: 01397-704583,Fax: 01397-702757

FORTH 4 Cloglands, Forth, ML11 8ED Tel: 01535-811631

FOULA Magdala Foula, Shetland 7E2 9PN
Tel: 01595-753236

GAIRLOCH (NORTH) 12 Bualnaluib, Aultbea, IV22 2JH
Tel: 01445-731320

GAIRLOCH (SOUTH) District Office Poolewe,
Achnasheen Ross-shire IV22 2JU Tel: 01445-781243
Fax: 01445-781315

GALASHIELS Library Buildings Lawyers Brac,
Galashiels, TU1 3JQ Tel: 01896-752822

GALSTON 11 Cross Streel, Galston, KA4 8AA
Tel: 02563-820218

GIGHA The Post Office, Gigha, PA4 17AA
Tel: 01583-505251

GIRTHON & ANWOTH Bleachfield Birtwhistle Street,
Gatehouse Of Fleet, DG7 2JJ Tel: 01557-814046

GIRVAN 22 Dalrymple Street, Girvan, KA26 9AE
Tel: 01465-712894, Fax: 01465-715576

GLASGOW 1 Martha Street, Glasgow, G1 1JJ
Tel: 0141-287-7677, Fax: 0141-225-7666

GLASGOW (PC) 22 Park Circus, Glasgow, G3 6BE
Tel: 0141-287-8350, Fax: 0141-225-8357

GLENELG Taobl Na Mara, Gleneig Kyle Ross-shire
IV40 8JT Fax: 01599-522310

GLENROTHES Albany House Albany Gate Kingdom
Centre, Glenrothes, KY7 5NX Tel: 01592-414141-Ext-4900

GOLSPIE Murrayfield Main Street, Golspie, KW10 6TG
Tel: 01408-633150

GORDON Operating from Kelso, , Tel: 01573-225659

GRANGEMOUTH Municipal Chambers Bo'ness Road,
Grangemouth, FK3 3AY Tel: 01324-504499

GRANTOWN-ON-SPEY Council Offices The Square,
Grangetown On Spey, PH26 3HP Tel: 01479-872539

GREENOCK 40 West Stewart St., Greenock, PA15 1YA
Tel: 01475-720084, Fax: 01415-781647

GRETNA Central Avenue, Orcina, DG16 5AQ
Tel: 01461-337648, Fax: 01461-338459
HADDINGTON 25 Court Street, Haddington, EH41 3HA
Tel: 01620-827308/368
HAMILTON 21 Beckford Street, Hamilton, ML3 0BT
Tel: 01698-454211
HARRAY New Breckan, Harray Orkney KW17 2JR
Tel: 01856-771233
HARRIS Council Offices, Tarbert Harris HS3 3DJ
Tel: 01859-502367, Fax: 01859-502283
HAWICK Council Offices 12 High Street, Hawick, TD9
9EF Tel: 01450-364710, Fax: 01450-364720
HELENSBURGH Council Offices 25 West King Street,
Helensburgh, G84 8UW Tel: 01436-673909
HELMSDALE 12 Dunrobin Street, Helmsdale, KW8 6LA
Tel: 01431-821751
HOLM & PAPLAY The Register Office, Netherbreck
Holm Orkney KW17 2RX Tel: 01856-382130
HOY Laundry House Melsetter, Longhope Orkney
KW16 3NZ Tel: 01856-791337
HUNTLY 25 Gordon Street, Huntly, AB54 5AN
Tel: 01466-794488
INSCH Marbert George Street, lnsch, AB52 6JL
Tel: 01464-820964
INVERARAY Municipal Office, Inveraray, PA32 8UZ
Tel: 01499-302124
INVERBERVIB Area Office Church Street, Inverbervie,
DD10 0RU Tel: 01561-361255, Fax: 01561-362802
INVERESK Brunton Hall Ladywell Way, Musselburgh,
EH21 6AF Tel: 0131-665-3711
INVERKEITHING 6 Fleriot Street, Inverkeithing,
KY11 1ND Tel: 01383-411742
INVERNESS Farraline Park, Inverness, IV1 1NH
Tel: 01463-239798
INVERURIE Gordon House Blackhall Road, Inverurie,
AB51 3WA Tel: 01467-620981, Fax: 01467-628012
IRVINE 106-108 Bridgegate Hse, Irvine, KA12 8BD
Tel: 01294-279333, Fax: 01294-312879
ISLAY Council Office Jamieson Street Bowmore Islay,
PA43 7HL Tel: 01496-810332
ISLE OF BUTE Council Office Mount Pleasant Road,
Rothesay, PA20 9HH Tel: 01700-50331/551
JEDBURGH Library Building Castlegate, Jedburgh,
TD8 6AS Tel: 01835-863670
JOHNSTONE 16-18 Mc Dowall Street, Johnstone,
PA5 8QL Tel: 01505-320012, Fax: 01505-382130
JURA Forestry Cottage Craighouse, Jura, PA60 7AY
Tel: 01496-820326
KEITH Area Office Mid Street, Keith, AE55 5DY
Tel: 01542-882166-Ext-39, Fax: 01542-882014
KELSO Rose Lane, Kelso, TD5 7AP Tel: 01573-225659
KELTY Kelly Local Services Sanjana Court 51 Main Street
Kelty, KY4 0AA Tel: 01383-839999
KENMORE The Old Schoolhouse, Acharn by Aberfeldy,
PH15 2HS Tel: 01887-830307 Fax: Same-as-tel-no
KENNOWAY Sandybrae Community Centre, Kennoway
Fife, KY8 5JW Tel: 01333-351721
KILBIRNIE, BEITH & DALRY 19 School Wynd,
Kilbirnie, KA25 7AY Tel: 01505-682416
Fax: 01505-684334
KILBRANDON + KILCHATTAN Cnoc Groin
Isle Of Seil by Oban PA34 4RF Tel: 01852-300380
KILFINICHEN & KILVICKEON The Anchorage,
Fionnphori Isle Of Mull PA66 6BL Tel: 01681-700241
KILLIN Ardlun 17 Monemore, Killin, FK21 8XD
Tel: 01567-820618
KILMARNOCK Civic Centre John Dickie Street,
Kilnianiock, KA1 1HW Tel: 01563-576695/6
KILSYTH Health Centre Burngreen Park, Kilsyth
G65 0HU Tel: 01236-822151
KILWINNING 32 Howgale, Kilwinning Ayrshire
KAI3 6EJ Tel: 01294-55226112

KINGUSSIE Town Hall Spey Street, Kingussie, PH21 1EH
Tel: 01540-661867
KINLOCHBERVIE 114 Inshegra, Rhiconich Lairg,
IV27 4RH Tel: 01971-521388
KINLOCHLUICHART The Old Manse, Garve Ross-shire
IV23 2PX Tel: 01997-414201
KINROSS 40 High Street, Kinross, KY13 7AN
Tel: 01577-862405
KIRKCALDY 7 East Fergus Place, Kirkcaldy, KY1 1XT
Tel: 0I592-412121, Fax: 01592-412123
KIRKCONNEL Nith Buildings Greystone Avenue
Kelloholm Kirkconnel, DG4 6RX Tel: 01659-67206,
Fax: 01659-66052
KIRKCUDBRIGHT District Council Offices,
Kirkcudbrigbt, DG6 4JG Tel: 01557-330291-Ext-234
KIRKINTILLOCH Council Office 21 Southbank Road,
Kirkintilloch, G66 1NH Tel: 0141-776-2109
KIRKLISTON 19 Station Road, Kirkliston, EH29 9BB
Tel: 0131-333-3210
KIRKMABRECK The Bogxie Creetowm, Newton
Stewart, DG8 73W Tel: 01671-820266
KIRKTON (FARR) 47 Crask, Bettyhill by Thurso,
KW14 7SZ Tel: 01641-521335
KIRKWALL Council Offices School Place, Kirkwall
Orkney KW15 1NY Tel: 01856-873535-Ext-2109
KIRRIEMUIR CouncilChambers, Kirriemuir, DD8 8BJ
Tel: 01575-572845
KNOYDART Knoydari Estate Office, Inverie Knoydart by
Mallaig, PH41 4PL Tel: 01681-462331, Fax: 01687-462243
LAIRG 4 Lochside, Lairg Sutherland IV27 4EG
Tel: 01549-402424
LAMLASH District Council Office, LamLash
Isle Of Arran KA27 8LB Tel: 01770-600338,
Fax: 01770-600028
LANARK 25 Hope Streel, Lanark, ML11 7NN
Tel: 01555-664679
LANGHOLM Town Hall, Langholm, DG13 0JQ
Tel: 01387-380255
LARBERT 318 Main Street, Lathed, FK5 3BE
Tel: 01324-503580
LARGS Macturn 24 Greenock Road, Largs,
KA30 8NE Tel: 01475-674521, Fax: 01475-689227
LARKHALL Council Office 55 Victoria Street, Larkhall,
ML9 2BN Tel: 01698-882454/5
LATHERON Post Office, Latheron, KW5 6DG
Tel: 01593-741201
LAUDER Session House Old Causeway East High St
Lauder, TD2 6FX Tel: 01578-722795
LAURENCEKIRK Royal Bank Buildings, Laurencekirk,
AB30 1AF Tel: 01561-377245, Fax: 01561-378020
LEADHILLS Violet Bank 30 Station Road, Leadhills,
ML12 6XS Tel: 01659-74260
LENNOXTOWN Council Office 132 Main Street,
Lennoxtown, 065 7DA Tel: 01360-311362
LERWICK County Buildings, Lerwick Shetland ZE1 OHD
Tel: 01595-693535-Ext-368
LESMAHAGOW 40/42 Abbeygreen, Lesmahagow, ML11
0DE Tel: 01555-893314
LEVEN 12 Station Road, Leven, KYS 4NH
Tel: 01333-592538
LINLITHGOW 29 The Vennel, Linlithgow, EH49 7EX
Tel: 01506-775373, Fax: 01506-775374
LISMORE Bachuil, Lismore Oban PA34 5UL
Tel: 01631-760256
LIVINGSTON Lammermuir House Owen Sq, Almondvale
S. Livingston, EH54 6PW Tel: 01506-414218,
Fax: 01506-462575
LOCH DUICH Aird View Dornie, Kyle Of Lochalsh,
IV40 8EZ Tel: 01599-555201
LOCHALSH Hamilton House Plock Road, Kyle
IV40 8BL Tel: 01599-534270

LOCHCARRON Curaig Lochcarron, Strathcarron IV54 8YD Tel: 01520-722390
LOCHGELLY Lochgelly Local Office Town House Hall Street Lochgelly, KY5 911 Tel: 01592-782614
LOCHGILPHEAD Dairiada House Lochnell Street, Lochgilphead, PA31 8ST Tel: 01546-604511
LOCHGOILHEAD The Register Office, Creiganiver Lochgoilhead, PA14 8AJ Tel: 01301-703222
LOCHHROOM Locality Office 29 Market Street, Ullapool, 1V26 2XE Tel: 01854-612426, Fax: 01854-612717
LOCHORE The Register Office, Rosewell Lochore by Lochgelly, KY5 SDA Tel: 01592-860237
LOCHRANZA Operating from LarnlashTel: 01770-600338 Tel: 01770-600028
LOCKERBIE Town Hall High Street, Lockerbie DG11 2ES Tel: 01576-204267/8
LOGIERAIT Operating from Pitlochry Tel: 01796-472409
LONGFORGAN 8 Norval Place Longforgan Dundee DD2 5ER Tel: 01382-360283
LUNNASTING Vidlin Farm, Vidlin Shetland, 7E2 9QB Tel: 01806-577204
MALLAIG Golden Sands Morar, Mallaig Inverness-shire PH40 4PA Tel: 01687-462383
MAUCHLINE 2 The Cross, Mauchline Ayrshire KA5 5DA Tel: 01290-550231, Fax: 01290-551991
MAUD County Offices, Maud Aberdeenshire AB4 SND Tel: 01771-613667
MAYBOLE Council Office 64 High Street, Maybole KAI9 713Z Tel: 01655-882124
MELROSE Public Library \larket Square, Meirose T06 9PN Tel: 01896-823114
MEY Operating from Thurso Tel: 01847-892786 Fax: 01847-894611
MID + SOUTH YELL Schoolhouse, Ulsia Yell, ZE2 98D Tel: 01957-722260
MILNATHORT Rowallan' 21 Church Street, Milnathort, KY13 7XE Tel: 01577-862536
MOCHRUM Granite House 85 Main Street, Fort William, DG8 9HR Tel: 01988-700265
MOFFAT Town Hall High Street., Moffat, DG10 9HF Tel: 01683-220536
MONTROSE 51 John Street, Montrose Angus DD10 8LZ Tel: 01674-672351
MORVERN Dungrianach, Morvern by Oban PA34 5XW Tel: 01961-421662
MOTHER WELL & WISHAW Civic Centre Windmillhill Street, Motherwell, ML1 1TW Tel: 01698-302222
MUCKHART + GLENDEVON Operating from Alloa Tel: 01259-723850
MUIRKIRK 33 Main Street, Muirkirk, KA18 39R Tel: 01290-661227
NAIRN The Court House, Nairn, IV12 4AU Tel: 01667-458510
NESTING Laxfirth Brettabister, Lerwick Shetland ZE2 9PR Tel: 01595-694737
NETHYBRIDGE Operating from Grantown-on-Spey Tel: 01479-872539
NEW ABBEY 1 Ingleston View New Abbey Dumfries, DG2 8BZ Tel: 01387-850343
NEW CUMNOCK Town Hall The Castle, New Cumnock, KA18 4AN Tel: / Fax: 01290-338214
NEW KILPATRICK Council Office 38 Roman Road, Bearsden, G61 2SH Tel: 0141-942-2352/3
NEW MI LN S Operating from Galston Tel: 01563-820218/9
NEWBURGH Tayside Institute High Street, Newburgh, KY4 6DA Tel: 01337-840917
NEWPORT-ON-TAY Blyth Hall Blyth Street, Newport On Tay, DD6 8BJ Tel: 01382-542839

NEWTON STEWART AREA The Old Town HaIl 79 Victoria Street, Newton Stewart, DG8 6NL Tel: 01671-404187
NORTH BER WICK 2 Quality Street, North Berwick, EH39 4HW Tel: 01620-893957
NORTH RONALDSAY Waterhouse, North Ronaldsay Orkney KW17 2BE Tel: 01857-633263
NORTH UIST Fairview' Lochmaddy, North Uist HS6 5AW Tel: 01876-500239
NORTH YELL Breckon, Cullivoe Yell, ZE2 9D Tel: 01957-744244
NORTHMAVEN Uradell, Eshaness Shetland ZEZ 9RS Tel: 01806-503362
OBAN Council Office Albany Street, Oban, PA34 4AR Tel: 01631-562137
OLD CUMNOCK Council Office Millbank 14 Lugar Street., Cummock, KA18 1AB Tel: 01290-420666 Fax: 01290-426164
OLD KILPATRICK 57 Kilbowie Road, Clydebank G81 1BL Tel: 0141-952-1330
OLD MELORUM Gordon Cottage Urquhart Road, Oldmeldrum, AB51 0EX Tel: 01651-873028 Fax: 01651-872060
ORPHIR The Bu, Orphir Kirkwall, KW17 2RD Tel: 01856-811319
PAISLEY Registration Ornce Cotton Street, Paisley PA1 1BU Tel: 0141-889-1030
PAPA STOUR North House Papa Stout, Lerwick Shetland ZE2 9PW Tel: 01595-873238
PAPA WESTRAY Backaskaill, Papa Westray Kirkwall, KW17 2BU Tel: 01857-644221
PEEBLES Chambers Institute High Street., Peebles, EH45 8AF Tel: 01721-720123
PENICUIK & GLENCORSE 33 High Street, Penicuik, EH26 8HS Tel: 01963-672281
PERTH Rose Terrace, Perth, PH1 5HA Tel: 01738-632486, Fax: 01738-444133
PERTH Rose Terrace, Perth, PH1 5HA Tel: 01738-632486, Fax: 01738-444133
PETERCULTER Lilydale 102 North Deeside Road, Peterculter, AB1 0QB Tel: 01224-732648/9
PETERHEAD County Offices 88 King Street, Peterhead, AB42 6UH Tel: 01779-472761/2, Fax: 01779-476435
PITLOCHRY District Area Office 21 Atholl Road, Pitlochry, PH16 5BX Tel: 01796-472409
POLMONT + MUIRAVONSIDE Council Offices Redding Road Brightons Falkirk, FK2 0HG Tel: 01324-712745
PORT GLASGOW Scarlow Street., Port Glasgow PA14 5EY Tel: 01475-742140
PORTREE Registrars Office King's House The Green Portree, IV51 9BS Tel: 01478-613277, Fax: 01478-613277
PORTSOY 2 Main Street, Portsoy Banffshire AB45 2RT Tel: 01261-843843
PRESTONPANS Aldhammer House High Street, Prestonpans, EH32 9SE Tel: 01875-810232
PRESTWICK 2 The Cross, Prestwick, KA9 1AJ Tel: 01292-671666
QUEENSFERRY Council Office 53 High Street, South Queensferry, EH30 9HN Tel: 0131-331-1590
RAASAY Operating from Portee, , Tel: 01478-613217 Fax: 01478-613277
RANNOCH + FOSS Bridgend Cottages, Kinloch-rannoch Pitlochry, PH16 5PX Tel: 01882-632359
RATHO Operating from India Buildings, Ratho Tel: 0131-220-0349, Fax: 0131-2200351
RENFREW Town Hall, Renfrew, PA4 8PF Tel: 0141-886-3589
ROSNEATH Willowburn Clynder by Helensburgh, G84 0QQ Tel: 01436-831212, Fax: 01436-831212
ROSSKEEN Invergordon Service Point 62 High St, Invergordon, IV18 0DH Tel: 01349-853139

ROUSAY + EGILSAY Braehead Rousay, Kirkwall KW17 2PT Tel: 01856-821222

RUTHERGLEN Town Hall Buildings King Street, Rutherglen, G73 1BD Tel: 0141-647-1072

SALTCOATS 45 ARoadrossan Road, Saltcoats, KA21 5BS Tel: 01294-463312/604868

SANDAY 2 Lettan, Sanday Kirkwall KWI7 2BP Tel: 01857-600280

SANDNESS 13 Melby, Sandness Shetland ZE2 9PL Tel: 01595-870257

SANDSTING + AITHSTING Modesty, West Burrafirth Aithsting ZE2 9NT Tel: 01595-809428

SANDWICK Yeldabreck, Sandwick Stromness KWI6 3LP Tel: 01856-841596

SANDWICK+CUNNINGSBUR Pytaslee Leebitton, Sandwick Shetland ZE2 9HP Tel: 01950-431367

SANQUHAR Council Offices 100 High Street, Sanquhar, DG4 6DZ Tel: 01659-50347

SAUCHEN Fresta Cottage 6 Main Street, Sauchen AB51 7JP Tel: 01330-833254

SCOURIE 12 Park Terrace, Scourie by Lairg IV27 4TD Tel: 01971-502425

SELKIRK Municipal Buildings High Street, Selkirk TD7 4JX Tel: 01750-23104

SHAPINSAY Girnigoe, Shapinsay Orkney KWI7 2EB Tel: 01856-711256

SHIELDAIG The Register Office, Baramore Shieldaig Strathcarron IV54 8XN Tel: 01520-755296

SHOTTS Council Ornee 106 Station Road, Shells ML7 8BH Tel: 01501-823349

SKENE & ECHT 25 Glebe Land Kirkion Of Skene, Westhill Aberdeenshire AB32 6XX Tel: 01224-743371

SLAMANNAN Operating from Falkirk Tel: 01324-506580

SMALL ISLES Kildonan House, Isle Of Eigg PH42 4RL Tel: 01687-482446

SOUTH COWAL Copeswood Auchenlochan High Rd, Tighnabruaich, PA21 2BE Tel: 01700-811601

SOUTH LOCHS 7 Kershader, South Lochs Isle Of Lewis PA86 9QA Tel: 01851-880339

SOUTH RONALDSAY West Cara Grimness South Ronaldsay, KWI7 2TH Tel: 01856-831509

ST ANDREWS Area Office St Man's Place, St Andrews, KY16 9UY Tel: 01334-412525

STIRLING Municipal Buildings Corn Exchange Road, Stirling, FK8 2HU Tel: 01786-432343

STONEHAVEN Viewrnount Arduthie Road, Stonehaven, AB39 2DQ Tel: 01569-762001-EXT:-8360

STORNOWAY Town Hall 2 Cromwell Street, Stornoway, HS1 2BW Tel: 01851-709438

STRACHUR Memorial Hall, Strachur Argyll PA27 8DG Tel: 01369-8603I6

STRANRAER AREA 23 Lewis Street, Stranraer DG9 7AB Tel: 01776-702151-Ext-254

STRATHAVEN R Bank Of Scot Blds 36 Common Green, Strathaven, ML10 6AF Tel: 01357-520316

STRATHDON Old Engine House Candacraie Nursery Garden, Strathdon, AB36 8XT Tel: 01975-651226

STRATHENDRICK District Office 32 Buchanan St., Balfron, G63 0TR Tel: 01360-440315

STRATHY Hillside Portskerra Melvich Thurso, KWI4 7YL Tel: 01641-531231

STROMNESS 5 Whitehouse Lane, Stromness Orkney KW16 3EY Tel: 01856-850854

STRONSAY Strynie Stronsay Kirkwall, KWI7 2AR Tel: 01857-616239

STRQNTIAN Easgadail Longrigg Road, Strontian Acharacle Argyll PH36 4HY Tel: 01967-402037

TAIN Operating from Rosskeen Tel: 01862-853139

TARBAT The Bungalow Chaplehill Portmahomack Portmathom Tain, IV20 1XJ Tel: 01862-871328

TARBERT Argyll House School Road, Tarbert, PA29 6UJ Tel: 01880-820374

TARRADALE Service Point Office Seaforth Road, Muir Of Ord, IV6 7TA Tel: 01463-870201

TARVES Post Office Udny, Ellon Aberdeenshire AB4 I 0PQ Tel: 01651-842253

TAYINLOAN Bridge House, Tayinloan Tarbert, PA29 6XG Tel: 01583-441239

TAYPORT Burgh Chambers, Tayport, DD6 9JY Tel: 01382-552544

THORNHILL 15 Dalgarnock Road, Thornhill Dumfriesshire DG3 4JW Tel: 01848-330108

THURSO District Office Davidson's Lane, Thurso KW14 7AF Tel: 01847-892786, Fax: 01847-894611

TINGWALL 20 Meadowfield Road Scalloway Lerwick Shetland ZEI 0UT Tel: 01595-880732

TOBERMORY Council Offices Breadalbane Street, Tobennory, PA75 6PX Tel: 01688-302051

TOMINTOUL Jubilee Cottage 51 Main Street, Tomintoul, AB37 9HA Tel: 01807-580207

TONGUE The Kyle Centre, Tongue Lairg, IV27 4XB Tel: 01847-601330

TORPHINS Willowbank, Kincardine O' NeilI, AB34 5AX Tel: 01339-884308

TRANENT 8 Civic Square, Tranent, EH33 1LH Tel: 01875-610278

TROON Municipal Buildings 8 South Beach, Troon, KA10 6EF Tel: 01292-313555, Fax: 01292-318009

TURRIFF Towie House Manse Road, Turiff, AB53 7AY Tel: 01888-562427, Fax: 01888-568559

TYREE The Register Office, Crossapol Isle Of Tyree PA77 6UP Tel: 01879-220349

UIG(LEWIS) 10 VaItos Uig Lewis, PA86 9HR Tel: 01851-672213

UIG(SKYE)(INVERNESS) 3 Ellishadder Staffin Portree, IV51 9JE Tel: 01410-562303

UNST New Noose, Ballsound Unst, ZE2 9DX Tel: 01957-711348

UPHALL 99 East Main Street, Broxburn, EH52 5JA Tel: 01506-775500, Fax: 01506-775505

VALE OF LEVEN 77 Bank Street, Alexandria, G83 0LE, Fax: 01389-752413

WALLS Victoria Cottage, Walls Lerwick Shetland ZE2 9PD Tel: 01595-809384

WANLOCKHEAD Operating from Sanquhar Tel: 01659-74287

WEST CALDER 1 East End, West Calder, EH55 8AB Tel: 01506-871763

WEST FIFE The Health Centre Chapel St High Valleyfield, Dunferrnline, KY12 8SJ Tel: 01383-880682

WEST KILBRIDE Kirktonhall 1 Glen Road, West Kilbride, KA23 9BL Tel: / Fax: 01294-823569

WEST LINTON Council Office, West Linton, EH46 7ED Tel: 01968-660267

WESTERN ARDNAMURCHAN Post Office, Kilchoan Acharacle, PH36 4LL Tel: 01972-510209

WESTRAY Myrtle Cottage, Pierowall Westray Orkney KW1 2DH Tel: 01857-677278

WHALSAY Conamore Brough, Whalsay Shetland ZE2 9AL Tel: 01806-566544

WHALSAY-SKERRIES Fairview, East Isle Skerries Lerwick ZE2 9AS Tel: 01806-515224

WHITBURN 5 East Main Street, Whitburn, EH47 0RA Tel: 01501-678000, Fax: 01506-678026

WHITENESS & WEISDALE Vista, Whiteness Shetland ZE2 9LJ Tel: 01595-830332

WHITHORN AREA 75 George Street, Whithom DG8 8NU Tel: 01988-500458

WICK Town Hall Bridge Street, Wick, KW1 4AN Tel: 01955-605713

WIGTOWN AREA Council Sub-office County Buildings, Wigtown, DG8 9HR Tel: 01988-402624

The Record Office for Leicestershire, Leicester & Rutland

Pat Grundy - Researcher

The Record Office for Leicestershire, Leicester and Rutland is supported by the three authorities named in its title. Almost eight years ago we moved into our present building which is a converted Victorian school in Wigston Magna, four miles south of Leicester on the A5199 with easy access from the M1.

Previously the record office was housed in a large detached house in Leicester with four outstores around the city. Now everything is together under one roof and when we moved, we were joined by the Leicestershire Local Studies Collection which had previously been a part of the main reference library in Leicester.

Situated virtually in the middle of Leicestershire, we provide a one-stop service for research in Leicestershire and Rutland. We hold archive material for Leicester, Leicestershire and Rutland including parish records, census returns, poor law, quarter sessions and a vast amount of other material filling five miles of shelving in our purpose built repository. We also have records of the archdeaconry of Leicester with wills dating back to 1496. Because Rutland belongs to the Diocese of Peterborough, the archdeaconry records for Rutland are held at Northamptonshire Record Office, including wills, marriage bonds and allegations and tithe maps.

The amalgamation with the Leicestershire Collection has provided the record office with a more extensive library, electoral registers, trade directories and an excellent newspaper and periodical collection. The Leicestershire Collection also includes film, video and music collections.

We have a team of three conservators who have the task of protecting and repairing this diverse collection of material. Their expertise and careful restoration has made available documents which would otherwise be too fragile and delicate for production.

The record office is open five and a half days a week from 9.15 each morning Monday to Saturday. Closing time is 5 p.m. on Monday, Tuesday and Thursday, 7.30 p.m. on Wednesday, 4.45 p.m. on Friday and 12.15 p.m. on Saturday.

There is no essential booking system although it is possible for people travelling a distance to book film & fiche readers. We do not close for lunch and we have all the usual facilities including disabled access.

A member of the County Archive Research Network, this is a particularly busy office. In the first six months of this year we have had over seven thousand visitors, we have received almost seven thousand telephone calls and over five hundred postal enquiries. These figures do not include requests for photocopies and printouts.

Most of the most regularly used documents such as parish registers, census, wills and quarter sessions are in microform. Since the move to Wigston Magna, it has been possible for searchers to make printouts using two self-service machines in the first searchroom. The second searchroom is for the production of documents from the strongrooms. Documents are produced on demand except when circumstances, usually pressure of demand, necessitate a cessation

for a short time. In the first six months of this year over eleven thousand original documents have been produced in the second searchroom. Depending on the condition of the document, photocopies can be made but there is no self-service with the photocopier.

Although the largest group of visitors are family historians, there are always people in the searchrooms working on a wide variety of research. Every television programme about the history of houses brings a large number of people into the office to research their own houses. European legislation concerning farm land has brought in harassed and bemused farmers looking for maps of their property. Every academic year produces a stream of young people involved in local history projects as part of their course work. Then there are people involved in post graduate research and authors researching books on a wide variety of topics. As the millennium approached, many local history groups and societies were keen to publish histories of their local areas and their members were to be found carrying out their research in our searchrooms.

Many visitors to the Record Office have interesting family stories to tell. One family came accompanied by a television crew (by prior arrangement) because their research had led them to **Joseph Meyrick** who was known as the Elephant Man. They were filmed looking at an Admission and Discharge register of Leicester Union Workhouse for a programme that was shown in the QED series on BBC2. Most people would like to discover that they had an ancestor who was famous or notorious but most of us have to make do with ordinary folk like ourselves.

As well as producing documents and generally helping people in the searchrooms, staff have other responsibilities such as cataloguing and indexing, arranging talks and evening visits to the record office, arranging exhibitions to held here and around the county. Also included in those 'other responsibilities' are the sale of microfiche of parish registers and of prints from photographs in the photographic collections which include the extensive collections of local photographers S.W.A. Newton (building of the Great Central Railway c.1895-1899) and George M. Henton (topographical views of Leicestershire, Rutland, The Thames Valley, Ireland etc.).

A significant proportion of our enquiries are from abroad and the very busy searchroom staff do not have time to do more than answer short and specific or general enquiries. For this reason we have a research service. The Research Service costs £18 per hour with half-hour personal consultations for £9 by appointment. The Research Service deals with enquiries from abroad, from within the United Kingdom and several from Leicestershire and Rutland from people who simply do not have time or are unable to make a personal visit. The largest proportion of the enquiries involve Family History but there are also other requests which cover a wide variety of subjects including house history, business history, and all aspects of local history research. Requests are received from people who are studying and involved in writing theses and dissertations, from authors and from academics involved in research projects. Requests are also received for transcriptions which are currently done at the research rate of £18 per hour.

For sometime it has been possible to accept payment by visa or mastercard which is especially useful for people living abroad. In some parts of Australia and America it is particularly difficult and expensive to arrange payment in sterling. This facility is especially useful now that we have an E-mail address and people are able to E-mail their requests with their card details.

In addition to carrying out research for people who are unable, for whatever reason, to make a personal visit, the Researcher provides a personal consultation for half an hour. People can, of course, book a longer time if they wish. This provides more in-depth help for people who have a problem with their research or just require some extra help. People who travel a long way to spend a day in the search-room often find that the extra help that can be provided in this way is particular beneficial.

Another off-shoot of the Research Service is a series of Workshops for Beginners : An Introduction to Family History, The Next Step (further steps in family history) and How to trace the history of your house. These are all short, two hour sessions which currently cost £5 and are designed to give people some basic knowledge.

The Record Office for Leicestershire, Leicester & Rutland
Long Street, Wigston Magna, Leicestershire
LE18 2AH.
Tel : (0116) 257 1080
Fax : (0116) 257 1120
E-mail : recordoffice@leics.gov.uk
Web site : we have a page on the website of the
Leicestershire & Rutland Family History Society :
http://www.freepages.genealogy.rootsweb.com/~leicsrut

Lancashire Record Office - 60 Years On

Bruce Jackson County Archivist

When first asked by the editors to produce an article on some aspect of the work or holdings of Lancashire Record Office for this year s Directory, needless to say, I agreed to do so. It was only as the deadline approached, and I recalled my undertaking, that I thought I had better decide on what I would write!

Inspiration of a sort was not far away. The year 2000 is the 60th anniversary of the establishment of Lancashire Record Office in a form which would be recognisable by modern searchers, and I thought it might be useful to look at how record offices generally, but Lancashire in particular, have changed over the years. However, I do not aim to produce an administrative history, but rather look at how things have changed for the user of documents.

60 years is a comparatively short span of time (particularly to an archivist!) and some of the individuals who used the Record Office in its year of opening were still active (as searchers) in the year 2000! We were pleased to welcome several of them as guests at an Open Day on 13 February 2000, attended by 886 interested people. In the course of these 60 years our searchroom use has changed dramatically - compared to 67 who use the Lancashire searchroom in the first year it was open, our daily average number in 1999/2000 was 66.86! But I do not want to look simply at this astonishing change in the levels of use, but also at what has changed for the users, and attempt to explain why it cannot be like it was , and why from the viewpoint of most searchers most aspects have changed beyond recognition.

Firstly, in 1940, there were still many areas of the United Kingdom where there were no Record Offices. When I first started working as an archivist in 1975 there were large areas of Scotland where services either were just developing, or still did not exist. In England, Northumberland was only established in the late 1950s, and Durham and the joint Carlisle, Cumberland and Westmoreland service in the early 1960s. Today few areas have no service, although in both Ireland and some parts of Scotland services are only a few years old. While there are great variations in standards and level of provision (generally due to financial constraints) there will generally be somewhere that records of value can be preserved and made available, and some professional guidance to ensure their subsequent survival.

While some records could be consulted by interested individuals before there were local record offices, the process was rarely simple. For records of a business or family, some form of personal introduction was often required, while access to the records of local government itself was a difficult matter. Even a source that now seems essential to most searchers - the records of churches - was far from easy to consult. As recently as the 1970s, many parish records were still in the hands of the incumbents, who had to

be tracked down in person, and in some cases paid a fee before the registers could be consulted. The present day situation, where most registers are on self-service access on microfilm, frequently in libraries as well as the record offices which house the originals, represents a huge improvement in accessibility. I know some users feel cheated when only allowed to consult film copies, but it cannot be overstressed that this is necessitated by the reality that the originals would already have deteriorated beyond saving they had continued to be produced. The ability to duplicate films and make them available at multiple access points must also not be overlooked as a real benefit to users.

Today s searchers may not also appreciate how much simpler life (and research) is when so many sources are gathered in one place. In Lancashire for example, we hold records for over 400 Anglican parishes, in addition to Roman Catholic, Methodists, Baptists and other non-conformist churches including Quakers. For a genealogist starting with very basic information, the task has been immeasurably simplified by bringing so much together under one roof! While it has to be said that Record Offices owe most of their expanding userbase to genealogy, it also has to be accepted that without the development of the local authority archive network genealogy would not have become the mass phenomenon it now is!

In addition the second part of the 20th century witnessed a huge extension in both the range and nature of records held. Few, if any, business records were available for public study until record offices started large scale collection in the 1960s, and while these are mainly of interest to other groups of users than genealogists, they can still be vital on occasion. Records of courts, hospitals and other official bodies are now increasingly accessible, and the role of record offices will become of increasing importance in making these available to us all as citizens as Freedom of Information legislation becomes effective. This may result in some groups of more recent records becoming available for research, although the effects of Data Protection legislation may well counterbalance this - only time will tell.

All this is greatly removed from the limited range of records housed in the early years, which in many counties focused on quarter sessions material, and in most city archives centred on the ancient records of the borough. In time this came to be supplemented by the records of landed families and their estates, and the collections of solicitors practices. The records of local administrations, such as Guardians of the Poor, or civil and religious parishes, were increasingly transferred in the 1950s and 1960s, and by the early 1970s the range of records available was approximating to those available today. The quantity held is now massive - Lancashire houses about 8 miles of records compare to 1 mile held in

1950.

Facilities for users have also changed. Few offices now close over lunch hours, and many have some evening or weekend opening. Many now have public refreshment rooms, although as yet none provides full catering facilities, unless it shares premises with a museum. As victims of their own success, many offices still suffer from overcrowding, but this is not new. When Lancashire moved to new premises in the Sessions House in Preston in 1960, the County Archivist proudly ruled over a searchroom measuring 800 square feet, with one microfilm viewer. By contrast, the present searchroom is about 2000 square feet with 34 microfilm readers, and our searchroom is relatively less overcrowded than it was prior to the relocations of the office in both 1960 and 1975. While I could not deny that a great deal has been lost in terms of the amount of time which can be devoted to the needs of individual searchers (I can recall in the early 1980s being berated by an irate searcher that we did not give him cups of tea as happened in the neighbouring County Record Office), this must be set against the rise in the number of searchers dealt with.

In 1996 I calculated that if I had the same staff/visitor ratio that existed in Lancashire in 1950, I would have had a staff of 90, 40 of whom would have been archivists. Instead, I had a staff of 25 including 8 archivists. This figure included the staff of the North West Sound Archives at Clitheroe, and also staff administering the Records Management operation for the County Council s own records, neither of which functions were carried out in 1950. Of necessity this has meant that users cannot be given the degree of individual attention which had previously been possible, and also that many visitors to record offices will not receive advice from an archivist, but rather deal with one of the non-professional staff.

Of course the users themselves have changed in 60 years. There were few genealogists until the 1960s, and these few were often professionals working on other people s trees for legal reasons. There were exceptions, but often these were people seeking to prove a connection to gentry or nobility. The development of the widespread interest dates form the 1960s but did not really take off until the 1970s or even 1980s. The interest now is to trace ancestors whoever they might be, regardless of status, and this means that most users are looking to use a narrower range of types of records - such as census and civil registration and church records. This concentration on a narrower range of types has made it easier for Record Offices to cope than would otherwise have been the case. For example, census and many parish registers will be used on fiche, and on a self-service basis. Many users quickly come to understand the sources they are using, and need consult the searchroom staff fairly infrequently. The contrast with the amount of guidance time required by, for example, many undergraduate or postgraduate history students, is significant. The problems we encounter with such students is repeated when we have to deal with some local historians and many genealogists who have to turn to more unusual record sources. Many of these problems are a reflection of the changing educational priorities of society generally, as well as of the much wider user base consulting the records.

Perhaps the most striking example is in decline in the number of searchers who can read Latin, which at one time was taught to most grammar or secondary school pupils. Now few searchers under 40 have any knowledge (although many do learn enough to carry on their research), and so record office staff now find themselves increasingly asked what a document says . The amount of time any of us can give to this is very limited, and I am sure this often seems to searchers (especially those not familiar with record offices) as being deliberately unhelpful. Very similar problems arise in reading some of the earlier difficult handwriting. A high proportion of our searchers of 60 years ago (solicitors and academics) would be familiar with these hands, but now few even of these groups, let alone the general user public, have the skills to read these older scripts. While many determined individuals will master the basic skills required, I am sure that many others are discouraged from future use by the difficulty, especially as staff do not have the time to provide detailed assistance. It is easy to forget how fast the knowledge base is changing. There is now a generation with no knowledge of pounds, shillings and pence, (let alone roods, poles, perches, chains, links) which can mean a staff member easily overlooking something that requires explanation.

I was recently asked by a college lecturer to explain to his undergraduate students what a file is, as many of his students knew only of computer files! Added to this is the widespread idea that everything will be on computer by now , with the resultant expectation that record offices will be able to provide precise information tailored to the very specialist requirements of the user, who will simply collect the extracted information, miraculously translated and transcribed as required. I know that most users know this is not the way it is in the real world, but readers may be surprised how often enquiries make this assumption. Similarly there are many remote enquiries which assume that we will be able to make a vast range of records available digitally overnight.

So where does this leave us 60 years on? More records survive and are accessible than ever before, but more users are frustrated because they feel they are being denied access. Records may be unlisted, or closed by statute, or be so physically fragile that they cannot be produced, but it is difficult to explain such niceties to a frustrated searcher when time is in ever shortening supply. What is obvious is that many users find it difficult to accept that many records have been lost through historical accident or carelessness before the Record Office ever had a chance to ensure their survival, rather than as a result of some arcane bureaucratic plan. Public levels of expectation have reached a level few services can satisfy, both in terms of the facilities provided and the records which have survived and can be made available. One fact certainly has not changed in 60 years - if the record has not survived than it cannot be made available for future users.

The Central Index of Decrees Absolute

The Central Index is a record of all decrees absolute granted by Courts in England and Wales since 1858. It is kept and controlled by the Principal Registry of the Family Division and anyone is entitled to apply for a search to be carried out, and to receive a certificate of the result and any decree absolute traced.

People may wish to apply for a search of the Central Index for a number of reasons, the most common of which are:-
¥To obtain a copy of their decree absolute, if they have lost the original
¥To find out whether they have been divorced, following a long separation from their spouse
¥To find out whether a friend or relative has been divorced to help trace a family tree or other historical reasons

To apply for a search complete a Form D440 and send it to the address below. Form D440 can be obtained from the above address or you can attend in person at the office. Staff can only search a three year period whilst you wait, if the years to be searched are prior to 1981. In such cases, the result of the remainder of the period requested to be searched, will be sent to you within 10 working days.

There is a fee of £20.00 to pay for each ten year period or part thereof searched. For example, if you wish a thirteen year period to be searched (ie 1958 to 1970 inclusive), the fee would be £40.00. The fee can be paid by cash, cheque or postal order. Cheques and postal orders should be made payable to HM Paymaster General or HMPG . Cash should not be sent through the post. You may be exempt from paying a fee if you are receiving Income Support or Family Credit. You will need to fill in a form entitled Application for Fees Exemption and supply the Court with a copy of your benefit book, if you wish to apply for exemption. The Form Application for Fees Exemption is available from the above address. The questions on Form D440 are straightforward and you should try to answer as many as you can. The court requires the full names of both parties to the marriage, ensure that the names are spelt correctly. Incorrect spelling may result in an unsuccessful search! Once completed the form should be sent to the Principal Registry together with the fee or the Form Application for Fees Exemption and a copy of any benefit book, if appropriate.
If all is in order, a certificate of the result of the search will be sent within 10 working days. If there is anything wrong with the application, it will be returned with a letter giving reasons for its return. In the case of a successful search where the divorce proceedings are found to have taken place in the Principal Registry of the Family Division, you will also receive with your certificate a sealed or sealed and certified copy of the decree absolute. If the divorce took place other than at this Court, you will be notified of the name of the court and the case number, and we will write to that court, on your behalf, to instruct them to send you a copy of the

decree absolute. A sealed and certified copy will only be supplied if you state in your application that the decree absolute is required in connection with matters outside of England and Wales. If there is no trace of a decree having been granted, you will be issued with a no trace certificate.

The Principal Registry does not keep any documents in relation to cases issued in other Courts, it simply holds a record of any decrees absolute granted by them. If, therefore, you require a copy of a decree absolute and already know the case number and name of the court which granted the decree, you should write direct to that court for a copy thereof and for any other information you may require.

General Information
If you are submitting your documents by post please address them to:

Principal Registry of the Family Division
First Avenue House, 42 - 49 High Holborn
London, WC1V 6NP
Tel: (020) 7936 6000 (Switchboard)
Opening Hours:
10.00.a.m. to 4.3Opm Monday to Friday

The offices are closed on public and certain other holidays. The main entrance to the building is on High Holborn.

Land Registry

The Land Registry
The Open Register
A Guide to Information and how to obtain it.
Ken Young Head of Information

Since 3 December 1990 the register of title in England and Wales has been open for inspection by the Public. The object of registering title to land is to create and maintain a register of land owners whose title is guaranteed by the State and thus simplifying the sale (transfer) and mortgage of such land. Anybody can now obtain information which is held on the register of a registered title. Prior to December 1990 only registered owners and persons with the owner s consent could inspect the register.

A registered title is the legal evidence of title to land which has been registered at HM Land Registry. When a title is registered the register provides an up-to-date official record of the legal ownership and certain other matters relating to the property or piece of land in question.

How do I find out if land is registered? The Registry holds a series of large scale Ordnance Survey maps covering the whole of England and Wales on which is shown the extent of land in every registered title. These maps are called Index Maps and each single map is called a Section . Index Maps will indicate whether or not a particular piece of land is registered and, if it is, the registered title number and whether the registration is of freehold or leasehold land.

An application for an official search (inspection) of the Index Map should preferably be made by post and must be on Land Registry Form 96. In some instances, for example when information is required in respect of land sited on a rural area, it may be necessary for you to supply a plan to enable its precise whereabouts on the Index Map to be established. Further details of this service may be obtained from HM Land Registry Practice Leaflet No. 15. Alternatively, a copy of an Index Map Section may be obtained on application in Land Registry Form 96B. The title numbers of all registered properties falling within the area covered by the Section would be shown on the copy Index Map supplied. Further information concerning this service is provided in HM Land Registry Explanatory Leaflet No. 16.

The Property Register identifies the geographical location and extent of the registered property by means of a short verbal description (usually the address) and a reference to an official plan which is prepared for each title. it may also give particulars of any rights that benefit the land, for example, a right of way over adjoining land. In the case of a leasehold title, it gives brief details of the lease. The official title plan is based on the large scale maps of the Ordnance Survey. Further information regarding boundaries in land registration is provided in HM Land Registry Explanatory Leaflet No. 18.

The Proprietorship Register specifies the quality of the title. It also gives the name and address of the legal owner and shows whether there are any restrictions on their power to sell, mortgage or otherwise deal with the land. Where the Land Registry is entirely satisfied about the ownership of the property absolute title will have been given. In some cases, however, a more limited class of title will have been given.

The charges register contains identifying particulars of registered mortgages and notice of other financial burdens secured on the property (but does not disclose details of the amounts of money involved). It also gives notice of other rights and interests to which the property is subject such as leases, rights of way or covenants restricting the use of the property.

How can I inspect the register? The best and most convenient method of obtaining information from the register is to apply by post on Land Registry Form 109 for a copy of the register entries and/or a copy of the title plan, as required. One form is required for each registered title inspected. If you think the property is probably registered but do not know the title number you may, should you wish, dispense with applying for an official search of the Index Map in Form 96 (in the manner described in paragraph 5 above) and instead complete Form 109 applying for a copy of the register and/or title plan but leaving the title number box blank. A fee to cover the cost of the additional work for the Registry in checking the Index Map on your behalf may be payable. The fee will be refunded if the title proves to be unregistered. If application is made in this manner please write in capitals at the head of the Form 109 PLEASE SUPPLY THE TITLE NUMBER .

Can I inspect copies of documents referred to on the register?
Yes; once you have received a copy of the register you may, if you wish, apply by post on Land Registry Form 110 specifying which documents you require. Copies of such documents will be forwarded to you. See below regarding the fee payable. Please note that copies of documents not actually referred to on the register are not generally open to inspection. Also copies of Leases or Charges (mortgages) referred to on the register of title are not generally open to inspection.

Can I make a personal inspection of the register, title plan or copies of documents referred to on the register? Yes; a personal inspection can be made by completing a Land Registry Form 111 when you visit a Land Registry office. One form is required for each registered title inspected It is requested that at least four days notice of intention to make a personal inspection be given to the registry office concerned. Without such notice — which may be provided by telephone — there is a risk that the register, title plan or documents might not be available when you arrive. If you do not know the title number you may, if you wish, dispense with applying for an official search of the Index Map in Land Registry Form 96 (in the manner described above) and instead complete Land Registry Form 111 leaving the title number box blank. A fee to cover the cost of the additional work for the Registry in checking the Index Map on your behalf may be payable. Visits to registry offices may be made between the hours of 9am and 4.30pm, Mondays to Fridays only. Alternatively, a postal application is strongly recommended.

Where do I apply?

You should send your application to the district land registry serving the area in which the property the subject of your enquiry is situated. If in doubt you should telephone your nearest Land Registry office and ask them to advise you. A personal inspection can be made at any district land registry or at the Registry s headquarters office. The four days notice of intention to make such a search as mentioned above should be given at the office where you intend to made the search.

Is there a simpler way that I can obtain the name and address of the owner of a property? If a property is registered and can be identified by a single postal address, (for example, 23, Coniston Drive, Kerwick) and you only want to know the name and address of the registered owner, you may apply by post on Land Registry form 313.

This service although covering all registered properties in England and Wales, is currently only available from The Customer Information Centre, Room 105, The Harrow District Land Registry, Lyon House, Lyon Road, Harrow, Middx, HA1 2EU, to which office Land Registry forms 313 should be addressed.

If the land does not have a single postal address, (for example, land lying to the west of Augustine Way, Kerwick) or information other than details of the registered owner is wanted, then application should be made for an office copy or a personal inspection of the register as set out above.

What fees are payable?

a) Postal search of the Index Map
> (1) Where any part of the land to which the search relates is registered, and until further notice, the Chief Land Registrar has exercised his discretion and has waived this fee where a result of search discloses up to and including 10 registered titles.Where more than 10 registered titles are disclosed, the application for search will be charged only for the excess over 10 titles.E.g.15 registered titles disclosed will attract a fee of 5 x £4 = £20.
> (2) Where no part of the land to which the search relates is registered until further notice, the Chief Land Registrar has exercised his discretion and has waived this fee.

(b) Copy of the register or any part thereof
> – per copy £4

(c) Copy of the title plan – per copy £4

(d) Copy of any or all of the documents referred to in the register - per copy or set £4

(e) Personal inspection of the register or any part thereof – per title £4

(f) Personal inspection of the title plan – per title £4

(g) Personal inspection of any or all of the documents referred to in the register –per title £4

(h) The supply of a copy of an Index Map Section –

per copy £40

(h) Where the applicant does not know the title number and endorses the application form "Please supply title number" a £4 fee will be payable if more than 10 registered titles are disclosed.

(j) The supply of the name and address of the registered proprietor of land identified by its postal address– per application £4

These fees may change from time to time
The appropriate fee payable must accompany the relevant application form. Fees should be paid by cheque or postal order drawn in favour of HM LAND REGISTRY. Bank notes or coins should not be sent through the post. Credit cards cannot be used.

What documents are not held by the registry and cannot therefore be inspected?
Amongst documents that are not held by the Land Registry Re:-
(a) Title deeds dated prior to the date of first registration of the property other than those referred to on the register as filed. [When a property is first registered with the Land Registry the title deeds existing at that time are lodged at the Registry. After registration has been completed such deeds are returned to the person applying for registration or their solicitors.]
(b) Copies of deeds not referred to on the register
(c) Court Orders
(d) Birth, Marriage or Death Certificates
(e) Grants of Probate or Letters of Administration

N.B. Items (c), (d) and (e) are documents of public record and copies can be obtained from the appropriate court officials, the Registrar of Births, Deaths and Marriages or the Probate Registry.

What information relating to land cannot be obtained from the registry?
There are many matters which relate to land and property for which the Land Registry is not responsible and does not hold records. Amongst such matters are:
(a) Individual land or property values
(b) Matters relating to planning permission, compusory purchase, land redevelopment, road charges, public health charges, building lines or tree conservations. (Such matters should be recorded as local land charges by the local authority.)
(c) Unregistered titles
(d) Tenancy agreements
(e) Land held under a Lease for a term of 21 years or less
(f) Land or property outside England and Wales
(g) Matters relating to the Community Charge/Council Tax/Rating assessment

Copies of all Land Registry forms and other leaflets may be obtained by writing to any District Land Registry
or from

HM Land Registry
Lincoln's Inn Fields, London WC2A 3PH
Tel: (020) 7917 8888

Areas Served by
The District Land Registries for England & Wales

HM Land Registry
HM Land Registry, Lincoln s Inn Fields, London, WC2A 3PH

England

Birkenhead District Land Registry
Rosebrae Court, Woodside Ferry Approach, Birkenhead,
Merseyside, L41 6DU Tel: 0151 473 1110
Tel: 0151 473 1106 Enquiries Fax: 0151 473 0366
Cheshire; London Boroughs of Kensington, Chelsea,
Hammersmith, Fulham

Birkenhead District Land Registry
Old Market House, Hamilton Street, Birkenhead,
Merseyside, L41 5FL Tel: 0151 473 1110
Tel: 0151 473 1106 Enquiries, Fax: 0151 473 0251
Merseyside; Staffordshire; Stoke on Trent

Coventry District Land Registry
Leigh Court, Torrington Ave, Tile Hill, Coventry, CV4 9XZ,
Tel: 01203 860860 Tel: 01203 860864
Enquiries Fax: 01203 860021
West Midlands

Croydon District Land Registry
Sunley House, Bedford Park, Croydon, CR9 3LE
Tel: 0181 781 9100 Tel: 0181 781 9103 Enquiries
Fax: 0181 781 9110
London Boroughs of Croydon, Sutton, Bromley, Bexley

Durham (Boldon House) District Land Registry
Boldon House, Wheatlands Way, Pity Me, Durham, County
Durham, DH1 5GJ, Tel: 0191 301 2345 Fax: 0191 301 2300
Cumbria; Surrey

Durham (Southfield House) District Land Registry
Southfield House, Southfield Way, Durham, County
Durham, England Tel: 0191 301 3500 Tel: 0191 301 0020
Darlington; Durham; Hartlepool; Middlesbrough;
Northumberland; Redcar & Cleveland; Stockton on Tees
Tyne & Wear

Gloucester District Land Registry
Twyver House, Bruton Way, Gloucester, Gloucestershire,
GL1 1DQ Tel: 01452 511111 Fax: 01452 510050
Berkshire; Bristol; Gloucestershire; Oxfordshire; South
Gloucestershire; Warwickshire

Harrow District Land Registry
Lyon House, Lyon Road, Harrow, Middlesex, HA1 2EU
Tel: (020) 8235 1181 Fax: (020) 8862 0176
London Boroughs of Barnet, Brent, Camden, Islington, City
of London; City of Westminster; Harrow, Inner & Middle
Temples

Kingston Upon Hull District Land Registry
Earle House, Portland Street, Hull, HU2 8JN
Tel: 01482 223244 Fax: 01482 224278
East Riding of York; Kingston Upon Hull; Lincolnshire
Norfolk; N E Lincolnshire; North Lincolnshire; Suffolk

Leicester District Land Registry
Westbridge Place, Leicester, Leicestershire, LE3 5DR
Tel: 0116 265 4000, Tel: 0116 265 4001 Enquiries
Fax: 0116 265 4008
Buckinghamshire; Leicester; Leicestershire; Milton Keynes,
Rutland

Lytham District Land Registry
Birkenhead House, East Beach, Lytham St Annes FY8 5AB
Tel: 01253 849 849 Tel: 01253 840012 Enquiries
Fax: 01253 840001 (Manchester, Salford, Stockport,
Tameside & Trafford)
Fax: 01253 840002 (Bolton, Bury, Oldham, Rochdale &
Wigan) Fax: 01253 840013 (Lancashire)
Greater Manchester; Lancashire

Nottingham District Land Registry
Chalfont Drive, Nottingham, Nottinghamshire, NG8 3RN
Tel: 0115 935 1166 Fax: 0115 936 0036 for
Nottinghamshire, Derby; Derbyshire, Nottinghamshire;
South Yorkshire West Yorkshire

Peterborough District Land Registry
Touthill Close, City Road, Peterborough, PE1 1XN
Tel: 01733 288288 Fax: 01733 280022
Bedfordshire; Cambridgeshire; Essex; Luton;
Northamptonshire

Plymouth District Land Registry
Plumer House, Tailyour Road, Crownhill, Plymouth, Devon,
PL6 5HY, Tel: 01752 636000, Tel: 01752 636123 Enquiries,
Fax: 01752 636161
Bath; North Somerset; Cornwall; Isles of Scilly; North
Somerset; Somerset

Portsmouth District Land Registry
St Andrews Court, St Michael s Road, Portsmouth,
Hampshire, PO1 2JH, Tel: 01705 768888
Tel: 01705 768880 Enquiries, Fax: 01705 768768
Brighton & Hove; East Sussex; Isle of Wight; West Sussex

Stevenage District Land Registry
Brickdale House, Swingate, Stevenage, Hertfordshire, SG1
1XG, Tel: 01438 788888, Tel: 01438 788889 Enquiries
Fax: 01438 780107
Hertfordshire
London Boroughs of Barking & Dagenham, Enfield,
Hackney, Haringey, Havering, Newham, Redbridge, Tower
Hamlets, Waltham Forest

Swansea District Land Registry
Ty Bryn Glas, High Street, Swansea, SA1 1PW
Tel: 01792 458877 Fax: 01792 473236
London Boroughs of Ealing, Hillingdon, Hounslow

Telford District Land Registry
Parkside Court, Hall Park Way, Telford TF3 4LR
Tel: 01952 290355 Fax. 01952 290356
Hereford; Worcester; Shropshire, Greenwich Kingston upon
Thames London Boroughs of Lambeth, Lewsiham, Merton,
Richmond upon Thames, Southwark, Wandsworth

Tunbridge Wells District Land Registry
Curtis House, Forest Road, Tunbridge Wells TN2 5AQ
Tel: 01892 510015 Fax: 01892 510032 Kent

Weymouth District Land Registry
Melcombe Court, 1 Cumberland Drive, Weymouth, Dorset,
DT4 9TT, Tel: 01305 363636 Fax: 01305 363646
Hampshire Poole; Portsmouth; Southampton; Swindon
Wiltshire; Dorset

York District Land Registry
James House, James Street, York, YO1 3YZ
Tel: 01904 450000 Fax: 01904 450086
North Yorkshire; York

Wales

District Land Registry for Wales
Ty Cwm Tawe, Phoenix Way, Llansamlet, Swansea
SA7 9FQ, Tel: 01792 355000, Tel: 01792 355095 Enquiries
Fax: 01792 355055

Certificate Services - Southport

Carol M Clarke - Operations Manager

Whilst many people will be familiar with the Family Records Centre in Islington, considerably less are aware of the parent department in Southport that plays a vital role for Family Historians.

Certificate Services is part of the General Register Office (GRO) and is based in Southport, Merseyside. Here are held microfilm tapes containing copies of all births, marriages and deaths registered in England and Wales since 1st July 1837. Producing certificates for applications made at the FRC is not our sole responsibility. Requests for certificates can also be made by post, telephone, fax and e-mail direct to Certificate Services, Southport.

When certificates are applied for in person from the Family Records Centre, all application forms complete with the GRO Index reference number that has been obtained from the paper indexes in the FRC, are transported to Southport overnight. The race then begins to produce all certificates and have them ready for either transfer back to the FRC for collection, or to be posted out on the fifth working day.

When applications are received from the FRC, each is quoting the relevant GRO Index reference number obtained from the indexes - however,

Smedley Hydro, Southport
Reproduced with the permission of Martin Perry, Southport Civic Society

the FRC is not the only place from where to obtain the GRO Index reference. Microfiche copies of the indexes are also held at over 100 locations, such as libraries, County Record Offices and other institutions in various parts of the UK and abroad. To find out the nearest one to you, telephone 0151 471 4816.

Visiting one of the libraries or other institutions that hold copies of the GRO indexes on microfiche allows you to conduct your own research. Once you have identified which certificate is required, make a note of the GRO Reference number relating to the entry and this will then ensure you receive a cheaper, quicker service when you apply to Southport for the copy certificate.

If you wish to apply for a copy of a birth, marriage or death certificate and you have obtained the GRO Index reference, then you can apply direct to Southport and the certificate will be supplied to you within 10 working days of receipt. The cost of this service, where the reference is quoted is £8.00.

If however, you do not wish to conduct your own research, then staff in Certificate Services can carry out the search on your behalf. For the cost of £11.00 a 3 year search will be undertaken to try to locate the GRO Index reference number of the certificate you require. Once the application has been received, we aim to despatch your certificate within 2 - 4 weeks.

To assist us in our search, you will need to supply as much information as possible about the person on the certificate that you are trying to obtain. For example, for a birth - full name, date of birth (or approximate), place of birth, and if known both parents names, including mothers maiden name.

For a marriage, you will need to supply the names of both the bride and groom, date of marriage (approximately), place of marriage, and if known, names of both the fathers. For a death, a full name, approximate date of death, place of death will be required, and if the subject was female, their marital status. The occupation of the deceased will also assist staff to identify that the correct entry has been found.

Unfortunately, there is no facility for the public to call in person at Southport, however, we are accessible in other ways!

Our telephone service is manned from 8.00am - 6.00pm Monday to Thursday, 8.00am - 5.00pm on a Friday and 10.00am - 4.00pm on a Saturday. Our telephone number is 0151 471 4816, or you can write to us at

The General Register Office
PO Box 2
Southport
Merseyside
PR8 2JD

Alternatively, you can take a look at our website -
www.statistics.gov.uk
E-mail : certificate.services@ons.go.uk

If you have access to a fax machine and wish to send us your application, our fax number is 01704 550013.

The staff in Certificate Services are waiting to deal with your application!

Probate Records

Reading the Will

Information from Probate records can provide vital pieces of the genealogical puzzle. Although often not as useful as records of births, marriages and deaths, which can evidence crucial links to previous generations, they can provide evidence of relatedness within generations, and often contain fascinating insights into the financial affairs of people in times past.

Probate is a process whereby some person or persons, usually the executor(s) of a Will if there was one, or one or more of the next-of-kin if there was no Will, are appointed in law to administer the estate of someone who has died. This is usually only necessary if the deceased person left fairly substantial assets, so don t expect to find any Probate record relating to the estate of a person who had little or no estate of their own. The Probate concept of estate refers just to assets held in the sole name of the person who has died, and so Probate isn t necessary for the release of assets held jointly with another person. When an application for Probate is made, any Will that the deceased person left must be submitted to the Probate Registry. The Will, if judged to be valid, is thereafter kept on file, and it is normally possible for anyone to obtain a copy of it. There are exceptions, however, such as the Wills of members of the Royal family. The important point is that Wills are available from the Probate Registries only as a by-product of the Probate process: if Probate wasn t needed, then the Probate Registries have no record of the estate at all.

You should bear in mind that the Probate record, if any, will be dated some time after the date of death of the person concerned, so start searching from the year of death, or the year in which you think the person died. You should normally expect to find the Probate record within the first year or two after the date of death, and, if you have not found it within three, you can usually assume that Probate wasn t necessary. However, in a very small number of cases, Probate is granted many years after the person in question died. Take a tip from the professionals: if you don t find a probate record within the first few years, the next most likely time to search is the year in which their heir(s) died. This is because unadministered estate is most likely to come to light at that time. How far you want to go with the search will probably depend on how crucial the person in question is to your research, but there is as yet no shortcut: you will have to search the index for each year separately.

Control of Probate record-keeping passed from the Church to the state in 1858, at which point the records were unified into one Calendar index. These indexes, which summarise all Probate grants for England and Wales during a given year, act as a table of contents for the vast store of records held by the Probate Registries. If the subject of your research died before 1858, it will be more difficult to trace their Will. However, if they were very wealthy or owned a lot of land, consult the indexes of the Prerogative Court of Canterbury (PCC) first, and then those of the lesser ecclesiastical courts of the region in which they lived. PCC records are held by the Family Records Centre in London (Tel: (020) 8392 5300), but records of the lesser ecclesiastical Probate courts are highly dispersed. Try the local authority archives, such as public libraries and County Record Offices of the appropriate region, and also any local historical research institutes. Major ecclesiastical centres are also likely to have their own archives.

The table below lists the Calendar indexes held by the various Probate Registries in England and Wales. You can usually call in to consult the indexes, but check with the Registry concerned first, especially if you intend to travel any distance. Probate grants for each year are listed alphabetically by surname. The crucial parts of the Probate record are the Grant type, which is usually Probate , Administration or Administration with Will , the issuing Registry, and the grant issue date. They are normally written in sequence towards the end of the index entry, but the older books give the grant date first and highlight the issuing Registry in the text of the entry. The grant type can be inferred from the text, but note that the indexes prior to 1871 listed the Administration grants in a separate part of the book from the Probate and Administration with Will grants, so be sure to search in both places for years prior to this. In addition, there may be a handwritten number next to entries for Wills proved in the Principal Probate Registry (London) between 1858 and 1930. This is the Folio number, which is used by the Probate Registries when obtaining copies of the Will. Always make a note of this if applicable.

If the grant type is Administration , this tells you that the person in question did not leave a valid Will. However, the Probate Registries can still supply a copy of the grant, which is the document naming the person appointed in law as the administrator of the estate. This can provide genealogical information, especially in older grants where the relationship of the applicant to the deceased was stated. It also gives the value of the estate, although in most cases this is stated as not exceeding a certain figure rather than quoting an exact amount. In fact, the Probate record contains very little information about the estate at all, and no information about its composition. Don t expect to find inventories on file for records after 1858, although they sometimes form part of the Probate record prior to this.

In many cases you can save a lot of time and money by making the search yourself, but there is a postal service by which a search is made on your behalf for a period of four years. There is a fee of £5 for this, but this includes copies of the Will and/or grant if a record is found. It also gives you the benefit of the experience of Probate staff, for instance in knowing when to search and judging under which name the record is likely to be listed. If you want the Probate Registry to conduct a search for a period longer than the standard four years, there is an additional fee of £3 for each 4-year period after the first four. Thus, an 8-year search will cost £8, a 12-year search £11, and so on.

If you want to make a postal search, contact
The Postal Searches and Copies Department, The Probate Registry, Duncombe Place, York YO1 7EA UK Tel: +44 (1904) 624210   Fax: +44 (1904) 671782.

Applications for searches must be made in writing, and give the full name, last known address and date of death of the person concerned. A search can normally be made using less detail, but if the date of death is not known, you must state the year from which you want the search to be made, or give some other evidence that might indicate when the person died. If you have information about legal actions related to Probate or the disposition of assets, include that on your application. Many people find it convenient to order copies in this way even if they have already made a search of the Probate indexes and located a record relating to the subject of their research, but if this is the case, please include the grant type, issuing Registry and grant issue date on your application, as well as the Folio number if applicable (see above) as this can speed up the supply of copies considerably. The fee should be payable to H.M.Paymaster General , and if it is paid from abroad, must be made by International Money Order or bank draft, payable through a United Kingdom bank and made out in £ sterling. If you are applying for a search as well, you can request a search of any length, and fees for this are outlined above.

The records referred to here relate only to estates in England and Wales. If the subject of your research lived elsewhere, you may still be able to trace their Will. Consult the relevant section of this book.

The list below shows what indexes the various Probate Registries hold. Most Registries will have had indexes dating back to 1858, but are not required to keep them for more than fifty years. Usually, the older indexes will have been donated to local authority archives. Contact your local public library or County/City Record Office to see what Probate records they have. If you know of any historical research institute in your area, find out if they have any Probate records. Please note that, since the York Probate Registry serves as a national centre for postal requests for searches and copies, it is not possible to inspect the Probate indexes in person there.

Probate Registries & Sub-Registries

REGISTRY	RECORDS	TELEPHONE
Bangor Probate Sub-Registry Council Offices, FFord, Bangor LL57 1DT	1946 to 1966 and 1973 to 1998	(01248) 362410
Birmingham District Probate Registry The Priory Courts, 33 Bull Street, Birmingham B4 6DU	1948 to date	(0121) 681 3400
Bodmin Probate Sub-Registry Market Street, Bodmin PL31 2JW	1858 to 1966 and 1973 to 1998	(01208) 72279
Brighton District Probate Registry William Street, Brighton BN2 2LG	1935 to date	(01273) 684071
Bristol District Probate Registry Ground Floor, The Crescent Centre, Temple Back, Bristol BS1 6EP	1901 to date	(0117) 927 3915
Carmarthen Probate Sub-Registry 14 King Street, Carmarthen SA31 1BL	1973 to 1998	(01267) 236238
Chester Probate Sub-Registry 5th Floor, Hamilton House, Hamilton Place, Chester CH1 2DA	1948 to 1966	(01244) 345082
Exeter Probate Sub-Registry Finance House, Barnfield Road, Exeter EX1 1QR	1858 to 1966 and 1973 to 1998	(01392) 274515
Gloucester Probate Sub-Registry 2nd Floor, Combined Court Building, Kimbrose Way, Gloucester GL1 2DG	1947 to 1966	(01452) 522585
Ipswich District Probate Registry Level 3, Haven House, 17 Lower Brook Street, Ipswich IP4 1DN	1936 to date	(01473) 253724
Leeds District Probate Registry 3rd Floor, Coronet House, Queen Street, Leeds LS1 2BA	1949 to date	(0113) 243 1505
Leicester Probate Sub-Registry 5th Floor, Leicester House, Lee Circle, Leicester LE1 3RE	1890 to 1966 and 1973 to date	(0116) 253 8558
Lincoln Probate Sub-Registry Mill House, Brayford Side North, Lincoln LN1 1YW	1936 to 1966 and 1973 to 1998	(01522) 523648
Liverpool District Probate Registry Queen Elizabeth II Law Courts, Derby Square, Liverpool L2 1XA	1946 to date	(0151) 236 8264
Manchester District Probate Registry 9th Floor, Astley House, 23 Quay Street, Manchester M3 4AT	1947 to date	(0161) 834 4319
Middlesbrough Probate Sub-Registry Teesside Combined Court Centre, Russell Street, Middlesbrough TS1 2AE	1973 to 1998	(01642) 340001
Newcastle-upon-Tyne District Probate Registry 2nd Floor, Plummer House, Croft Street, Newcastle-upon-Tyne NE1 6NP	1929 to date	(0191) 261 8383
Nottingham Probate Sub-Registry Butt Dyke House, Park Row, Nottingham NG1 6GR	1973 to 1998	(0115) 941 4288
Oxford District Probate Registry Combined Court Building, St.Aldates, Oxford OX1 1LY	1940 to date	(01865) 793050
Sheffield Probate Sub-Registry PO Box 832, The Law Courts, 50 West BarSheffield S3 8YR	1935 to 1966 and 1973 to 1998	(0114) 281 2596
Stoke-on-Trent Probate Sub-Registry Combined Court Centre, Bethesda Street, Hanley, Stoke-on-Trent ST1 3BP	1973 to 1998	(01782) 854065
Winchester District Probate Registry 4th Floor, Cromwell House, Andover Road, Winchester SO23 7EW	1944 to date	(01962) 863771
Probate Registry of Wales PO Box 474, 2 Park Street, Cardiff CF1 1ET	1951 to date	(029) 2037 6479
Principal Probate Registry First Avenue House, 42-49 High Holborn, London WC1	1858 to date	(020) 7947 6000

The Service has undergone a process of computerisation, but as yet this covers only recently-issued grants, which will be of limited interest to genealogists. However, anyone who is interested in checking up on grants since 1996 can search the Probate Service database themselves. To date, workstations for public use have been installed at the Principal Probate Registry and Manchester District Probate Registry. The Postal Searches and Copies Department at York is also completing a long period of computerisation, which should see a much-improved service to family history researchers, with clearer and more comprehensive information and quicker supply of documents.

This information is based on details supplied by the Probate Service. The details are liable to change without notice. Always telephone the Registry before visiting, to check opening times and the availability of records. While every effort is made to ensure the accuracy of these details, the Probate Service cannot be held responsible for any consequence of errors.

The Pavement
York

Probate Records in the Borthwick Institute
Professor D M Smith MA PhD FSA

The Borthwick Institute of the University of York houses the probate records of the Archbishop of York both as diocesan and as head of the northern province, so as such is a really valuable source for family history. The diocesan probate court was known as the Exchequer; that of the province as the Prerogative Court. Since the Church authorities were chiefly responsible for the administration of the probate jurisdiction before 1858 then it follows that the location of a particular will depends upon a familiarity with the jurisdictional structure of the Church - A from province through diocese, archdeaconry, rural deanery, to parish.

The Exchequer Court exercised probate jurisdiction in respect of the laity and (after the middle ages) unbeneficed clergy having goods solely in the diocese of York. The post Reformation diocese covered the whole of Yorkshire (except for the north western part of the county which formed part of the Richmond archdeaconry in Chester diocese) and Nottinghamshire and the Archbishop also possessed the liberties of Ripon and Hexhamshire (the latter being in Northumberland). The original wills are arranged chronologically by month of probate in rural deanery bundles. The series of original probate material begins in 1427 but before 1591 there are only one or two items for the years when wills survive. From 1591 there are some wills extant for most years but the series is not generally complete until the 1630s onwards. Between 1653 and 1660 when the Commonwealth authorities established their own central probate court system, probate records of Yorkshire and the north of England are at the Public Record Office, London. From about 1688 the bundles generally include inventories, probate and administration bonds, declarations, renunciations etc. The inventories do not survive much after the mid 18th century and are replaced by simple declarations of the value of the estate. The original probate records of the Exchequer Court from the Nottinghamshire rural deaneries of the diocese have been transferred to the Nottingham County Record Office. As well as the original records (which are contained in some 3,000 archive boxes, in itself an indication of the size of the collection), there is a more complete series of probate registers running from 1389 to January 1858, when the Church authorities ceased to exercise probate jurisdiction. These registers contain contemporary registered copies of wills proved in both the Exchequer and the Prerogative Courts. From 1502 grants of probate and administration of intestates were entered into act books arranged by individual rural deanery.

The Prerogative Court of the Archbishop has its origin in the late 16th century and exercised jurisdiction in respect of probate or administration of persons with bona notabilia that is, goods etc. to the value of £5 and over either in more than one jurisdiction within the diocesan boundaries of York, or in more than one diocese in the northern province (until the 19th century the dioceses of

York, Carlisle, Chester and Durham, covering the counties of Cheshire, Cumberland, Durham, Lancashire, Northumberland, Nottinghamshire, Westmorland and Yorkshire), or in both northern and southern provinces. In such as the last case, the Prerogative Court of Canterbury was also usually resorted to in the first instance (its records are at the Public Record Office, London). The original records of the Prerogative Court of York are also arranged chronologically by month of probate and are stored with the Exchequer material. The registered copies of wills proved in the Prerogative Court are entered in the same series of volumes as described above for the Exchequer Court. A separate series of act books for the Prerogative Court (containing probate acts and grants of administration) survive from 1587.

A third York probate court is found from the middle ages onwards the **Chancery Court of the Archbishop**. Originally used for wills proved before the Archbishop in person rather than before his probate officials in the Exchequer, the Chancery came to have jurisdiction over the probate and administration of the goods of beneficed clergy in the York diocese and probate by reason of the Archbishop s periodic visitations of an inferior ecclesiastical jurisdiction. The original records survive from 1535 onwards (although rather sparsely until the late 16th century) but copies of wills have been registered in the Archbishops registers from 1316 to 1857.

In addition to the diocesan and provincial probate jurisdictions there were a whole series of what were known as peculiar jurisdictions small ecclesiastical enclaves comprising several parishes or perhaps just one, linked to an ecclesiastical corporation such as a cathedral or monastery, or to a manor which exercised probate jurisdiction over laity h aving goods just in these enclaves. The Institute houses an extensive collection of the probate records of some 53 Yorkshire peculiars.

Most of the categories of probate jurisdictions described above have some kind of name index, whether printed, typescript, or manuscript. The indexes to the Exchequer and Prerogative Courts records have been published from 1359 to 1688 by the Yorkshire Archaeological Society Record Series (vols. 4, 6, 11, 14, 19, 22, 24, 26, 28, 32, 35, 49, 60, 68, 78, 89). Between 1688 and 1731 there are typescript indexes and from 1731 to 1858 there are 29 contemporaneous manuscript volumes of indexes arranged within short chronological probate periods by person. In respect of the Chancery Court there are two printed indexes published in the Yorkshire Archaeological Society Record Series under the erroneous title of Consistory Wills (vols. 73, 93). Details of these indexes are given in the *Guide to the Archive Collections in the Borthwick Institute of Historical Research* (1973), pp.155 - 180. A typescript Parish Index at the Borthwick Institute details which parishes were in which ecclesiastical jurisdiction.
(This article first appeared in the 1998 Edition)

Record Offices & Archives

NATIONAL ARCHIVES

British Film Institute
21 Steven Street, London W19 2LN
British Library Newspaper Library
Colindale Avenue, London NW9 5HE Tel: 020-7412-7353
Fax: 020-7412-7379 Email: newspaper@bl.uk
Web: www.bl.uk/collections/newspaper/
Commonwealth War Graves Commission - Enquiries
2 Marlow Road, Maidenhead, Berkshire, SL6 7DX
Tel: 01628-634221 Fax: 01628-771208
Email: general.enq@cwgc.org Web: www.cwgc.org
**Department of Special Collections & Western
Manuscripts - Bodleian Library**
Oxford, Oxfordshire, OX1 3BG Tel: 01865-277152
Fax: 01865-277187
Documentary Photography Archive - Manchester
7 Towncroft Lane, Bolton, Lancashire, BL1 5EW
Tel: 01204-840439 Fax: 01204-840439
Family Records Centre
1 Myddleton Street, London EC1R 1UW
Tel: 020-8392-5300 Fax: 020-8392-5307
Email: http://www.open.gov.uk/pro/prohome.htm
Images of England Project
National Monuments Records Centre, Kemble Drive,
Swindon, Wiltshire, SN2 2GZ Tel: 01793-414779
Web: www.imagesofengland.org.uk
National Maritime Museum
Romney Road, Greenwich, London SE1O 9NF
Tel: 020-8858-4422 Fax: 020-8312-6632
Web: www.nmm.ac.uk
National Monuments Record
National Monuments Record Centre, Great Western Village,
Kemble Drive, Swindon, Wiltshire, SN2 2GZ
Tel: 01793-414600 Fax: 01793-414606
Email: info@rchme.co.uk
Web: www.english-heritage.org.uk
National Register of Archives
Quality House, Quality Court, Chancery Lane, London
WC2A 1HP Tel: 020-7242-1198 Fax: 020-7831-3550
Email: nra@hmc.gov.uk Web: www.hmc.gov.uk
Office for National Statistics - 1901 Census Records
Room 4300E, Segensworth Road, Titchfield, Fareham,
Hampshire, PO15 5RR Tel: 01329-813429
Fax: 01329-813189 Email: rosemary.byatt@ons.gv.uk
Office of Population Censuses & Surveys
General Register House,, St Catherine s House, 10
Kingsway, London
Probate Service
Probate Sub Registry, Duncombe Place, York, YO1 7EA
Tel: 01904-624210
Public Record Office
Ruskin Avenue, Kew, Richmond, Surrey, TW9 4DU
Tel: 020-8876-3444 Web: www.pro.gov.uk
Royal Commission on Historical Manuscripts
Quality House, Quality Court, Chancery Lane, London
WC2A 1HP Tel: 020-7242-1198 Fax: 020-7831-3550
Email: nra@hmc.gov.uk Web: www.hmc.gov.uk
Society of Genealogists - Library
14 Charterhouse Buildings, Goswell Road, London EC1M
7BA Tel: 020-7251-8799, 020-7250-0291
Fax: 020-7250-1800 Email: librarg@sog.org.uk - Sales at
sales@sog.org.uk Web: www.sog.org.uk
Traceline - NHSCR - Office for National Statistics
To be put in touch with lost relatives and acquaintances. The
ONS must be satisfied that contact would be in the best
interests of the person being sought. Traceline uses the NHS
Central Register. NHSCR does not officially operate under
the name Traceline, Smedley Hydro, Trafalgar Road,
Birkdale, Southport, Lancashire, PR8 2HH
Tel: 0151-471-4811 Email: traceline@ons.gov.uk

SPECIALIST SUBJECTS

Archives of Worshipful Company of Brewers
Brewers Hall, Aldermanbury Square, London EC2V 7HR
Bank of England Archive
Archive Section HO-SV, The Bank of England,
Threadneedle Street, London EC2R 8AH
Tel: 020-7601-5096 Fax: 020-7601-4356
Email: archive@bankofengland.co.uk
Barnardo s Film & Photographic Archive
Aftercare Section, Barnardo s, Tanner Lane, Barkingside,
Essex, IG6 1QC Tel: 020-8550-8822 Fax: 020-8550-6870
Email: collette.bradford@barnados.org.uk
Bass Museum and Archive
Horninglow St, Burton on Trent, Staffordshire, DE14 1JZ
Berkshire Aviation Trust - Film & Video Archives
6 Richmond Road, Caversham Heights, Reading, Berkshire,
RG4 7PP Tel: 0118-947-3924
British Coal Corporation Records & Archive
Provincial House, Solly Street, Sheffield, South Yorkshire,
S1 4BA Tel: 0114-279-9643 Fax: 0114-279-9641
British Library Oriental & India Collections
197 Blackfriars Road, London SE1 8NG
Tel: 020-7412-7873 Fax: 020-7412-7641
Email: oioc-enquiries@bl.uk
Web: www.bl.uk/collections/oriental
British Library Western Manuscripts Collections
Note: The Department can only respond to enquiries related
to its own collections, 96 Euston Road, London NW1 2DB
Tel: 020-7412-7513 Fax: 020-7412-7745 Email: mss@bl.uk
Web: www.bl.uk/
British Red Cross Museum & Archives
9 Grosvenor Crescent, London SW1X 7EJ
Tel: 020-7201-5153 Fax: 020-7235-0876
Email: enquiry@redcross.org.uk Web: www.redcross.org.uk
BT Archives
3rd Floor, Holborn Telephone Exchange, 268 - 270 High
Holborn, London WC1V 7EE Tel: 020-7492-8792
Fax: 020-7242-1967 Email: archives@bt.com
Web: www.bt.com/archives
Cable & Wireless Archive & Museum of Submarine Telegraphy
Eastern House,, Porthcurno, St. Levan, Penzance, Cornwall,
TR19 6 Tel: 01736-810478/810811 Fax: 01736-810640
Email: mary.godwin@plc.cwplc.com
Web: www.porthcurno.org.uk
College of Arms
Queen Victoria Street, London EC4V 4BT
Tel: 020-7248-2762 Fax: 020-7248-6448
Email: enquiries@college-of-arms.gov.uk Web: www.col-
lege-of-arms.gov.uk
Co-operative Union Archive
Holyoake House, Hanover Street, Manchester, M60 0AS
Tel: 0161-246-2987 Fax: 0161-831-7684
Email: info@co-opunion.org.uk
Deed Poll Records Section
Room E15, Royal Courts of Justice, Strand, London WC2A
2LL Tel: 020-7947-6528 Fax: 020-7947-6807
Distington Oral Archive
10 Mill Cottages, Distington, Workington, Cumbria
CA14 5SR Tel: 01946-833060 Fax: 01946-833060
Email: davidfoster@cumberland.idps.co.uk
Dr Williams s Library
14 Gordon Square, London WC1H 0AG Tel: 020-7387-3727
Fax: 020-7388-1142 Email: 101340.2541@compuserve.com
Galton Institute
19 Northfields Prospect, London SW18 1PE
Guiness Archive
Park Royal Brewery, London NW10 7RR
House of Lords Record Office (The Parliamentary Archive)
House of Lords, London SW1A 0PW Tel: 020-7219-3074
Fax: 020-7219-2570 Email: hlro@parliament.uk
Web: www.parliament.uk

Huguenot Library
University College, Gower Street, London WC1E 6BT
Tel: 020-7380-7094 Email: s.massil@ucl.ac.uk
Web: www.ucl.ac.uk/ucl-info/divisions/library/hugenot.htm
Institution of Civil Engineers
Limited staffing have to charge £20 per name search. Visits
by appointment, Great George Street, London SW1P 3AA
Tel: 020-7665-2043 Fax: 020-7976-7610
Email: morgan_c@ice.org.uk Web: www.ice.org.uk
Institution of Electrical Engineers
Savoy Place, London WC2R 0BL Tel: 020-7240-1871
Fax: 020-7240-7735 Web: www.iee.org.uk
Institution of Mechanical Engineers
1 Birdcage Walk, London SW1H 9JJ Tel: 020-7222-7899
Fax: 020-7222-8762 Email: ils@imeche.org.uk
Web: www.imeche.org.uk
Institution of Mining & Metallurgy
Hallam Court, 77 Hallam Street, London W1N 5LR
**International Committee of the Red Cross Archives
Division**
19 Avenue de la Paix, 1202 Geneve, Switzerland,
Tel: +41-(0)22-734-6001 Fax: +41-(0)22-733-2057
Email: archives.gva@irrc.org Web: www.icrc.org
John Rylands University Library
150 Deansgate, Manchester, M3 3EH Tel: 0161-834-5343
Fax: 0161-834-5343 Email: j.r.hodgson@man.ac.uk
Web: www.rylibweb.man.ac.uk
Lambeth Palace Library
Lambeth Palace Road, London SE1 7JU Tel: 020-7898-1400
Fax: 020-7928-7932
Library of the Religious Society of Friends (Quakers)
Friends House, 173 - 177 Euston Road, London NW1 2BJ
Tel: 020-7663-1135 Fax: 020-7663-1001
Email: library@quakcr.org.uk Web: www.quaker.org.uk
Library of the Royal College of Surgeons of England
35-43 Lincoln s Inn Fields, London WC2A 3PN
Tel: 020-7869-6520 Fax: 020-7405-4438
Email: library@rseng.ac.uk
Liverpool University - Special Collections & Archives
University of Liverpool Library, PO Box 123, Liverpool,
L69 3DA Tel: 0151-794-2696 Fax: 0151-794-2081
Web: www.SCA.lib.liv.ac.uk
Manorial Documents Register
Quality House, Quality Court, Chancery Lane, London
WC2A 1HP Tel: 020-7242-1198 Fax: 020-7831-3550
Email: nra@hmc.gov.uk
Merseyside Maritime Museum
Maritime Archives and Library, Albert Dock, Liverpool,
Merseyside, L3 4AQ Tel: 0151-478-4418/4424
Fax: 0151-478-4590
Email: archives@nmgmarchives.demon.co.uk
Methodist Church Archives
No records held centrally - deposited at local record offices,
34 Spiceland Road, Northfield, Birmingham, West Midlands,
B31 1NJ, England Email: 106364.3456@compuserve.com
Metropolitan Police Archives
Wellington House, 67-73 Buckingham Gate
London SW1E 6BE
Museum of the Order of St John
St John s Gate, St John s Lane, Clerkenwell, London EC1M
4DA Tel: 020-7253-6644 Fax: 020-7336-0587
Web: www.sja.org.uk/history
Museum of the Royal Pharmaceutical Society
1 Lambeth High Street, London SE1 7JN
Tel: 020-7735-9141-ext-354 Fax: 020-7793-0232
Email: museum@rpsgb.org.uk Web: www.rpsgb.org.uk
Lloyds Register of Shipping
Personal callers only. Research cannot be undertaken.
71 Fenchurch Street, London EC3M 4BS
Tel: 020-7423-2077 Fax: 020-7423-2039 Web: www.Lr.org
National Gas Archive
Common Lane, Partington, Nr Manchester, M31 4BR
National Museum of Labour History
Labour History Archive and Study Centre, 103 Princess
Street, Manchester, M1 6DD Tel: 0161-228-7212
Fax: 0161-237-5965 Email: archives@nmlhweb.org
Web: www.nmlhweb.org

National Railway Museum
Leeman Road, York, YO26 4XJ Tel: 01904-621261
Fax: 01904-611112 Email: nrm@nmsi.ac.uk
Web: www.nrm.org.uk
National Sound Archive
British Library, 96 Euston Road, London NW1 2DB
Tel: 020-7412-7440 Fax: 020-7412-7441
Email: http://www.portico.bl.uk Reader/admissions@bl.uk
North West Sound Archive
Old Steward s Office, Clitheroe Castle, Clitheroe,
Lancashire, BB7 1AZ Tel: 01200-427897
Fax: 01200-427897 Web: www.nw-soundarchive.co.uk
Northern Region Film & Television Archive
Blandford House, Blandford Square, Newcastle upon Tyne,
Tyne and Wear, NE1 4JA Tel: 0191-232-6789-ext-456
Fax: 0191-230-2614 Email: chris.galloway@dial.pipex.com
Nottingham R.C. Diocese Nottingham Diocesan Archives
Willson House, Derby Streeet, Nottingham, NG1 5AW
Tel: 0115-953-9803
**Nottingham University Department of Manuscripts &
Special Collections**
Nottingham University Hallward Library, University Park,
Nottingham, NG7 2RD Tel: 0115-951-4565
Fax: 0115-951-4558 Email: mss-library@nottingham.ac.uk
Web: mss.library.nottingham.ac.uk
Port Sunlight Village Trust
95 Greendale Road, Port Sunlight, CH62 4XE
Tel: 0151-644-6466 Fax: 0151-645-8973
Portsmouth Roman Catholic Diocesan Archives
Private archives - arrangements to visit have to be agreed
beforehand, St Edmund House, Edinburgh Road,
Portsmouth, Hampshire, PO1 3QA Tel: 023-9282-2166
Post Office Heritage
Freeling House, Farringdon Road (Phoenix Place entrance),
London WC1X 0DL Tel: 020-7239-2570
Fax: 020-7239   2576
Email: catherine.orton@postoffice.co.uk
**Principal Registry of the Family Division - Probate
Department**
First Avenue House, 42 - 49 High Holborn, London WC1V
6NP Tel: 020-7947-7000 Fax: 020-947-6946
Registry of Shipping & Seamen
Anchor House, 12 Cheviot Close, Parc-Ty-Glas, Llanishen,
Cardiff, Glamorgan, CF14 5JA, Wales, Tel: 02920-768227
Fax: 02920-747877
**Royal Air Force Museum - Dept of Research &
Information Services**
Grahame Park Way, Hendon, London NW9 5LL
Tel: 020-8205-2266 Fax: 020-8200-1751
Email: info@rafmuseum.org.uk
Web: www.rafmuseum.org.uk
Royal College of Physicians
11 St Andrews Place, London NW1 4LE Tel: 020-7935-1174
Ext 312 Fax: 020-7486-3729 Email: info@rcplondon.ac.uk
Web: www.rcplondon.ac.uk
Royal College of Physicians
11 St Andrews Place, London NW1 4LE Tel: 020-7935-1174
Ext 312 Fax: 020-7486-3729 Email: info@rcplondon.ac.uk
Web: www.rcplondon.ac.uk
Royal Commission on Historical Manuscripts
Quality House, Quality Court, Chancery Lane, London
WC2A 1HP Tel: 020-7242-1198 Fax: 020-7831-3550
Email: nra@hmc.gov.uk Web: www.hmc.gov.uk
Royal London Hospital Archives & Museum
Royal London Hospital, Whitechapel, London E1 1BB
Tel: 020-7377-7608 Fax: 020-7377-7413
Email: r.j.evans@mds.qmw.ac.uk
Rugby School Archives
Temple Reading Room, Rugby School, Barby Road, Rugby,
Warwickshire, CV22 5DW Tel: 01788-556227
Fax: 01788-556228
Email: dnrm@rugby-school.warwks.sch.uk
Southern Courage Archives
Southern Accounting Centre, PO Box 85, Countership,
Bristol, BS99 7BT

St Bartholomew s Hospital Archives & Museum
West Smithfield, London EC1A 7BE Tel: 020-7601-8152
Fax: 020-7606-4790
Tennyson Research Centre
Central Library, Free School Lane, Lincoln, Lincolnshire,
LN2 1EZ Tel: 01522-552862 Fax: 01522-552858
Email: sue.gates@lincolnshire.gov.uk
Thackray Medical Museum
Beckett Street, Leeds, West Yorkshire, LS9 7LN
Tel: 0113-244-4343 Fax: 0113-247-0219
Email: info@thrackraymuseum.org
Web: www.thackraymuseum.org
The Documents Register
Quality House, Quality Court, Chancery Lane, London
WC2A 1HP Tel: 020-7242-1198 Fax: 020-7831-3550
Email: nra@hmc.gov.uk
United Reformed Church History Society
Westminster College, Madingley Road, Cambridge,
Cambridgeshire, CB3 0AA Tel: 01223-741300
Waterways Trust
Services are to be substantially reorganised - contact prior to
requesting information, Llanthony Warehouse, Gloucester
Docks, Gloucester GL1 2EJ Tel: 0151-356-4247
Fax: 01452-318076 Email: archivist@dial.pipex.com
Web: www.britishwaterways.org.uk
Wellcome Library for the History & Understanding of Medicine
183 Euston Road, London NW1 2BE Tel: 020-7611-8582
Fax: 020-7611-8369 Email: library@wellcome.ac.uk
Web: www.wellcome.ac.uk/library
Wesley Historical Society
No records held - advice only given, 34 Spiceland Road,
Northfield, Birmingham, West Midlands, B31 1NJ, England
Email: 106364.3456@compuserve.com
Westminster Diocesan Archives
Does not deal with genealogical enquiries these are referred
to the Catholic Family History Society, 16a Abingdon Road,
Kensington, London W8 6AF Tel: 020-7938-3580
Whitbread Archives
The Brewery, Chiswell Street, London EC1Y 4SD
Yorkshire Film Archive
University College of Ripon and York St John, College
Road, Ripon, North Yorkshire, HG4 2QX Tel: 01765-602691
Fax: 01765-600516
Young s & Co Brewery Archives
Ram Brewery, High Street, Wandsworth, London SW18 4JD

SPECIALIST SUBJECTS - MILITARY
(See also MILITARY MUSEUMS)

Worcestershire Regiment Museum and Archives
Office address: Worcester Regiment Museum Trust, RHQ
WFR, Norton Barracks, Worcester. WR5 2PA, Worcester
City Museum & Art Gallery, Foregate Street, Worcester,
Worcestershire, WR1 1DT Tel: 01905-353871
Email: rhq_wfr@lineone.net
Sherwood Foresters Museum & Archives
RHQ WFR, Foresters House, Chetwynd Barracks, Chilwell,
Nottingham, Nottinghamshire, NG9 5HA
Tel: 0115-946-5415 Fax: 0115-946-5712
Royal Marines Museum Archives & Library
Eastney, Southsea, Hampshire, PO4 9PX
Tel: 02392-819385 Ext 224 Fax: 02392-838420
Email: mathewlittle@royalmarinesmuseum.co.uk
Web: www.royalmarinesmuseum.co.uk
**Royal Dragoon Guards & Prince of Wales Own
Regiment of Yorkshire Military Museum**
3A Tower Street, York, North Yorkshire, YO1 9SB
Tel: 01904-662790, 01904-658051
Royal Air Force Museum
Grahame Park Way, Hendon, London NW9 5LL
Tel: 020-8205-2266 Fax: 020-8200-1751
Email: info@rafmuseum.org.uk
Web: www.rafmuseum.org.uk
National Inventory of War Memorials
Imperial War Museum, Lambeth Road, London SE1 6HZ
Tel: 020-7416-5353, 020-7416-5281 Fax: 020-7416-5379
Email: memorials@iwm.org.uk Web: www.iwm.org.uk

National Army Museum & Archives
Royal Hospital Road, London SW3 4HT Tel: 020-7730-0717
Fax: 020-7823-6573
Email: info@national-army-museum.ac.uk
Web: www.national-army-museum.ac.uk
**National Army Museum Department of Archives
(Photographs, Film & Sound)**
Royal Hospital Road, Chelsea, London SW3 4HT
Tel: 020-7730-0717 Fax: 020-7823-6573
Email: info@national-army-museum.ac.uk
Web: www.national-army-museum.ac.uk
Imperial War Museum - Department of Documents
Department of Documents, Lambeth Road, London SE1
6HZ Tel: 020-7416-5221/2/3/6 Fax: 020-7416-5374
Email: docs@iwm.org.uk Web: www.iwm.org.uk
Gallipoli Campaign 1915-16 Biographical Index
3966 Robin Avenue, Eugene, Oregon, 97402
United States of America Email: patrickg@efn.org
**Devonshire and The Devonshire and Dorset Regimental
Archives**
Wyvern Barracks, Barrack Road, Exeter, Devon, EX2 6AE
Tel: 01392-492436 Fax: 01392-492469
Cheshire Military Museum (Cheshire Regiment)
The Castle, Chester, Cheshire, CH1 2DN Tel: 01244-327617

LONDON and GREATER LONDON

Bethlem Royal Hospital Archives & Museum
Monks Orchard Road, Beckenham, Kent, BR3 3BX
Fax: 020-8776-4045 Email: museum@bethlem.co.uk
Centre for Metropolitan History
Institute of Historical Research, Senate House, Malet Street,
London WC1E 7HU Tel: 020-7862-8790
Fax: 020-7862-8793 Email: o-myhill@sas.ac.uk
Web: www.history.ac.uk/cmh/cmh.main.html
Chelsea Public Library
Old Town Hall, King s Road, London SW3 5EZ
Tel: 020-8352-6056, 020-8361-4158 Fax: 020-8351-1294
City of Westminster Archives Centre
10 St Ann s Street, London SW1P 2DE Tel: 020-7641-5180
Fax: 020-7641-5179 Web: www.westminster.gov.uk
Corporation of London Records Office
PO Box 270, Guildhall, London EC2P 2EJ Tel: 020-7332-1251
Fax: 020-7710-8682 Email: clro@corpoflondon.gov.uk
Web: www.cityoflondon.gov.uk/archives/clro
Ealing Local History Centre
Central Library, 103 Ealing Broadway Centre, Ealing, London
W5 5JY Tel: 020-8567-3656-ext-37 Fax: 020-8840-2351
Email: localhistory@hotmail.com
Guildhall Library - Manuscripts Section
Aldermanbury, London EC2P 2EJ Tel: 020-7332-1863
Fax: 020-7600-3384
Email: manuscripts.guildhall@corpoflondon.gov.uk
Web: www.ihr.sas.ac.uk/gh/
Hackney Archives Department (covers: Shoreditch &Stoke Newington)
43 De Beauvoir Road, London Borough of Hackney, London
N1 5SQ Tel: 020-7241-2886 Fax: 020-7241-6688
Email: archives@hackney.gov.uk
Web: www.hackney.gov.uk/history/data/ha_fr.htm
Hertfordshire Archives & Local Studies
County Hall, Pegs Lane, Hertford, Hertfordshire, SG13 8EJ
Tel: 01438-737333 Fax: 01992-555113
Email: hals@hertscc.gov.uk Web: www.hertsdirect.org
Hillingdon Heritage Service
Central Library, High Street, Uxbridge, London UB8 1HD
Tel: 01895-250702 Fax: 01895-811164
Email: ccotton@lbhill.gov.uk Web: www.,hillingdon.gov.uk
Kingston Museum & Heritage Service
North Kingston Centre, Richmond Road, Kingston upon
Thames, Surrey, KT2 5PE Tel: 020-8547-6738
Fax: 020-8547-6747 Email: local.history@rbk.kingston.gov.uk
Web: www.kingston.gov.uk/museum/
L B of Barking & Dagenham Local History Studies - Barking
This local studies department is being absorbed into a cen-
tralised department at Valence Library, Becontree Avenue,
Dagenham, Essex RM8 3HT Tel, etc as follows, Central
Library, Barking, Essex, IG11 7NB Tel: 020-8227-5297
Fax: 020-8227-5297 Email: valencelibrary@hotmail.com

L B of Barking & Dagenham Local History Studies -
Dagenham Valence Library & Museum, Becontree Avenue,
Dagenham, Essex, RM8 3HT Tel: 020-8592-6537
Fax: 020-8227-5297 Email: fm019@viscount.org.uk
Web: www.earl.org.uk/partners/barking/index.html

L B of Barnet Archives & Local Studies Department
Hendon Library, The Burroughs, Hendon, London NW4 4BQ
Tel: 020-8359-2876 Fax: 020-8359-2885
Email: hendon.library@barnet.gov.uk

L B of Brent Community History Library and Archive
152 Olive Road, London NW2 6UY Tel: 020-8937-3540
Fax: 020-8450-5211

L B of Bromley Local Studies Library
Central Library, High Street, Bromley, Kent, BR1 1EX
Tel: 020-8460-9955 Fax: 020-8313-9975

L B of Camden Local Studies & Archive Centre
Holborn Library, 32 - 38 Theobalds Road, London WC1X
8PA Tel: 020-7974-6342 Fax: 020-7974-6284
Web: www.camden.gov.uk

L B of Croydon Local Studies Library & Archives
Service
Central Library, Katharine Street, Croydon, CR9 1ET
Tel: 020-8760-5400-ext-1112 Fax: 020-8253-1004
Email: localstudies@library.croydon.gov.uk
Web: www.croydon.gov.uk/cr-libls.htm

L B of Enfield Archives & Local History Unit
Southgate Town Hall, Green Lanes, Palmers Green, London
N13 4XD Tel: 020-8379-2724

L B of Greenwich Local History Library
Library moving at end of 2001 to a new Heritage Centre - con-
tact library for details
Woodlands, 90 Mycenae Road, Blackheath, London SE3 7SE
Tel: 020-8858-4631 Fax: 020-8293-4721
Email: local.history@greenwich.gov.uk
Web: www.greenwich.gov.uk

L B of Hammersmith & Fulham Archives & Local
History Centre
The Lilla Huset, 191 Talgarth Road, London W6 8BJ
Tel: 020-8741-5159 Fax: 020-8741-4882
Web: www.lbhf.gov.uk

L B of Haringey Archives
Bruce Castle Museum, Lordship Lane, Tottenham, London
N17 8NU Tel: 020-8808-8772 Fax: 020-8808-4118

L B of Hounslow Local Studies Collection
Chiswick Public Library, Dukes Avenue, Chiswick, London
W4 2AB Tel: 020-8994-5295, 020-8994-1008
Fax: 020-8995-0016 & 020-8742-7411

L B of Islington Finsbury Library
245 St John Street, London EC1V 4NB Tel: 020-7527-7994
Fax: 020-7227-8821 Web: www.islington.gov.uk/htm

L B of Lambeth Archives Department
Minet Library, 52 Knatchbull Road, Lambeth, London SE5
9QY Tel: 020-79266076 Fax: 020-79266080

L B of Lewisham Local Studies Centre & Archives
Lewisham Library, 199 - 201 Lewisham High Street,
Lewisham, London SE13 6LG Tel: 020-8297-0682
Fax: 020-8297-1169 Email: local.studies@lewisham.gov.uk
Web: www.lewisham.gov.uk

L B of Merton Local Studies Centre
Merton Civic Centre, London Road, Morden, Surrey, SM4
5DX Tel: 020-8545-3239 Fax: 020-8545-4037
Email: mertonlibs@compuserve.com

L B of Newham Archives & Local Studies Library
Stratford Library, Water Lane, Stratford, London E15 4NJ
Tel: 020-8557-8856 Fax: 020-8503-1525

L B of Sutton Archives
Central Library, St Nicholas Way, Sutton, Surrey, SM1 1EA
Tel: 020-8770-4747 Fax: 020-8770-4777
Email: local.studies@sutton.gov.uk Web: www.sutton.gov.uk

L B of Waltham Forest Local Studies - Archives
Vestry House Museum, Vestry Road, Walthamstow, London
E17 9NH Tel: 020-8509-1917
Email: vestry.house@al.lbwf.gov.uk
Web: www.lbwf.gov.uk/vestry/vestry.htm

L B of Wandsworth Local History Collection
Battersea Library, 265 Lavender Hill, London SW11 1JB
Tel: 020-8871-7753 Fax: 020-7978-4376
Email: wandsworthmuseum@wandsworth.gov.uk
Web: www.wandsworth.gov.uk

London Metropolitan Archives
40 Northampton Road, London EC1R 0HB Tel: 020-7332-3520,
020-7278-8703 Fax: 020-7833-9136 Email: ask.lma@ms.cor-
poflondon.gov.uk Web: www.cityoflondon.gov.uk/archives/lma

National Army Museum & Archives
Royal Hospital Road, London SW3 4HT Tel: 020-7730-0717
Fax: 020-7823-6573
Email: info@national-army-museum.ac.uk
Web: www.national-army-museum.ac.uk

Royal Borough of Kensington & Chelsea Central Library
Phillimore Walk, Kensington, London W8 7RX
Tel: 020-7361-3036, 020-7361-3007
Email: information.services@rbkc.gov.uk
Web: www.rbkc.gov.uk

Southwark Local Studies Library
211 Borough High Street, Southwark, London SE1 1JA
Tel: 0207-403-3507 Fax: 0207-403-8633
Email: local.studies.library@southwark.gov.uk
Web: www.southwark.gov.uk

Tower Hamlets Local History Library & Archives
Bancroft Library, 277 Bancroft Road, London E1 4DQ
Tel: 020-8980-4366 ext 129 Fax: 020-8983-4510

Twickenham Local Studies Library
Note: the Twickenham Collection is to be moved to
Richmond Library - contact for information, Twickenham
Library, Garfield Road, Twickenham, Middlesex, TW1 3JS
Tel: 020-8891-7271 Fax: 020-8891-5934
Email: twicklib@richmond.gov.uk
Web: www.richmond.gov.uk

Westminster Abbey Library & Muniment Room
Westminster Abbey, East Cloister, London SW1P 3PA
Tel: 020-7222-5152-Ext-4830 Fax: 020-7654-4827
Email: library@westminster-abbey.org
Web: www.westminster-abbey.org

ENGLAND BY COUNTIES

Bath

Bath & North East Somerset Record Office
Guildhall, High Street, Bath, Somerset, BA1 5AW
Tel: 01225-477421 Fax: 01225-477439

Bedfordshire

Bedfordshire & Luton Archives & Record Service
County Hall, Cauldwell Street, Bedford, Bedfordshire,
MK42 9AP Tel: 01234-228833, 01234-228777
Fax: 01234-228854 Email: archive@csd.bedfordshire.gov.uk
Web: www.bedfordshire.gov.uk

Berkshire

Berkshire Aviation Trust - Film & Video Archives
6 Richmond Road, Caversham Heights, Reading, Berkshire,
RG4 7PP Tel: 0118-947-3924

Berkshire Record Office
9 Coley Avenue, Reading RG1 6AF Tel: 0118-901-5132
Fax: 0118-901-5131 Email: arch@reading.gov.uk

Portsmouth Roman Catholic Diocesan Archives
Private archives - arrangements to visit have to be agreed beforehand
St Edmund House, Edinburgh Road, Portsmouth, Hampshire,
PO1 3QA Tel: 023-9282-2166

Rural History Centre
University of Reading, Whiteknights PO Box 229, Reading,
RG6 6AG Tel: 0118-931-8664 Fax: 0118-975-1264
Email: jis.creasey@reading.ac.uk
Web: www.reading.ac.uk/instits/im/

Birmingham

Birmingham City Archives
Floor 7, Central Library, Chamberlain Square, Birmingham,
West Midlands, B3 3HQ Tel: 0121-303-4217
Fax: 0121-464-1176 Email: archives@birmingham.gov.uk
Web: www.birmingham.gov.uk/libraries/archives/home.htm

Bristol

Bristol Record Office
B Bond Warehouse, Smeaton Road, Bristol, BS1 6XN
Tel: 0117-922-4224 Fax: 0117-922-4236
Email: bro@bristol-city.gov.uk

Buckinghamshire

Buckinghamshire Record Office
County Offices, Walton Street, Aylesbury, Buckinghamshire,
HP20 1UU Tel: 01296-382587 Fax: 01296-382274
Email: archives@buckscc.gov.uk
Web: www.buckscc.gov.uk/leisure/libraries/archives

Cambridgeshire

Cambridgeshire Archive Service (Huntingdon)
County Record Office Huntingdon, Grammar School Walk,
Huntingdon, Cambridgeshire, PE18 6LF Tel: 01480-375842
Fax: 01480-375842
Email: county.records.hunts@camcnty.gov.uk
Web: www.camcnty.gov.uk/sub/archive/huntoff.htm
Cambridgeshire Archives Service County Record Office
Shire Hall, Castle Hill, Cambridge, Cambridgeshire
CB3 0AP Tel: 01223-717281 Fax: 01223-717201
Email: County.Records.Cambridge@camcnty.gov.uk
Web: www.cambridgeshire.gov.uk/sub/archive
Centre for Regional Studies
Anglia Polytechnic University, East Road, Cambridge,
Cambridgeshire, CB1 1PT Tel: 01223-363271 ext 2030
Fax: 01223-352973 Email: T.Kirby@bridge.anglia.ac.uk

Cheshire

Cheshire and Chester Archives & Local Studies Service
Cheshire Record Office, Duke Street, Chester, CH1 1RL
Tel: 01244-602574 Fax: 01244-603812
Email: recordoffice@cheshire.gov.uk
Web: www.cheshire.gov.uk/recoff/home.htm
Chester Community History and Heritage
All original archives transferred to Cheshire & Chester Archives
Secondary sources only such as census, cemetery registers, parish records,
etc and the Local History
St Michaels Church, Bridge Street Row, Chester CH1 1NG
Tel: 01244-317948 Email: s.oswald@chestercc.gov.uk
Web: www.chestercc.gov.uk/chestercc/htmls/heritage.htm
Ellesmere Port Boat Museum
South Pier Rd, Ellesmere Port CH65 4FW Tel: 0151-355-5017
Fax: 0151-355-4079 Email: boatmuseum@easynet.co.uk
John Rylands University Library
150 Deansgate, Manchester, M3 3EH Tel: 0161-834-5343
Fax: 0161-834-5343 Email: j.r.hodgson@man.ac.uk
Web: www.rylibweb.man.ac.uk
Stockport Archive Service
Central Library, Wellington Road South, Stockport,
Cheshire, SK1 3RS Tel: 0161-474-4530 Fax: 0161-474-7750
Email: localheritage.library@stockport.gov.uk
Tameside Local Studies Library
Stalybridge Library, Trinity Street, Stalybridge SK15 2BN
Tel: 0161-338-2708, 0161-338-3831 Fax: 0161-303-8289
Email: tamelocal@dial.pipex.com Web: www.tameside.gov.uk
Trafford Public Library & Local Studies Centre
Public Library, Tatton Road, Sale, M33 1YH
Tel: 0161-912-3013 Fax: 0161-912-3019
Email: trafford.local.studies@free4all.co.uk

Waterways Trust
Services to be substantially reorganised - contact prior to requesting information
Llanthony Warehouse, Gloucester Docks, Gloucester,
Gloucestershire, GL1 2EJ Tel: 0151-356-4247
Fax: 01452-318076 Email: archivist@dial.pipex.com
Web: www.britishwaterways.org.uk
Wirral Archives Service and Museum
Birkenhead Town Hall, Hamilton Street, Birkenhead,
Merseyside, CH41 5BR Tel: 0151-666-4010
Fax: 0151-666-3965 Email: archives@wirral-libraries.net
Cheshire and Chester Archives & Local Studies Service
Cheshire Record Office, Duke Street, Chester, CH1 1RL
Tel: 01244-602574 Fax: 01244-60381
 Email: recordoffice@cheshire.gov.uk
Web: www.cheshire.gov.uk/recoff/home.htm

Cleveland

Teesside Archives
Exchange House, 6 Marton Road, Middlesbrough,
Cleveland, TS1 1DB Tel: 01642-248321 Fax: 01642-248391

Cornwall

Cable & Wireless Archive & Museum of Submarine Telegraphy
Eastern House,, Porthcurno, St. Levan, Penzance, Cornwall,
TR19 6 Tel: 01736-810478/810811 Fax: 01736-810640
Email: mary.godwin@plc.cwplc.com
Web: www.porthcurno.org.uk
Cornwall Library Services - Cornish Studies Library
Clinton Road, Redruth TR15 2QE Tel: 01209-216760
Fax: 01209-210283 Email: cornishstudies@library.cornwall.gov.uk
Cornwall Record Office
County Hall, Truro, Cornwall, TRI 3AY Tel: 01872-323127
Fax: 01872-270340 Email: cro@ceo.cornwall.gov.uk
Web: www.cornwall.gov.uk

County Durham

Brandon & Byshottles Parish Archive
11 Commercial Square, Brandon, County Durham, DH7 8QJ
Tel: 0191-378-0241 Email: Ronald_Kitching@yahoo.co
Web: victorian.fortunecity.com/rushdie/172index.html
County Durham County Record Office
County Hall, Durham, County Durham, DH1 5UL
Tel: 0191-383-3474, 0191-383-3253 Fax: 0191-383-4500
Email: record.office@durham.gov.uk
Web: www.durham.gov.uk/recordoffice
Darlington Library Centre For Local Studies
The Library, Crown Street, Darlington, County Durham,
DL1 1ND Tel: 01325-349630 Fax: 01325-381556
Email: crown.street.library@darlington.gov.uk
Durham University Library Archives & Special Collections
Palace Green Section, Palace Green, Durham, DH1 3RN
Tel: 0191-374-3032 Email: pg.library@durham.ac.uk
Northern Region Film & Television Archive
Blandford House, Blandford Square, Newcastle upon Tyne,
Tyne and Wear, NE1 4JA Tel: 0191-232-6789-ext-456
Fax: 0191-230-2614 Email: chris.galloway@dial.pipex.com

Cumbria

Cumbria Record Office - Barrow in Furness
140 Duke Street, Barrow in Furness, Cumbria, LA14 1XW
Tel: 01229-894363 Fax: 01229-894371
Cumbria Record Office - Carlisle
The Castle, Carlisle, Cumbria, CA3 8UR Tel: 01228-607285,
01228-607284 Fax: 01228-607274
Email: carlisle.recordoffice@cumbriacc.gov.uk
Web: www.cumbria.gov.uk/archives/
Cumbria Record Office - Kendal
County Offices, Stricklandgate, Kendal, Cumbria, LA9 4RQ
Tel: 01539-773540 Fax: 01539-773439
Cumbria Record Office & Local Studies Library - Whitehaven
Scotch Street, Whitehaven, Cumbria, CA28 7BJ
Tel: 01946-852920 Fax: 01946-852919
Email: whitehaven.record.office@cumbriacc.gov.uk
Web: www.cumbria.gov.uk/archives

Distington Oral Archive
10 Mill Cottages, Distington, Workington, Cumbria, CA14
5SR Tel: 01946-833060 Fax: 01946-833060
Email: davidfoster@cumberland.idps.co.uk

Derbyshire

Chesterfield Local Studies Department
Chesterfield Library, New Beetwell Street, Chesterfield,
Derbyshire, S40 1QN Tel: 01246-209292
Fax: 01246-209304
Derby Local Studies Library
25b Irongate, Derby, Derbyshire, DE1 3GL
Tel: 01332-255393 Fax: 01332-255381
Derby Museum & Art Gallery
The Strand, Derby, Derbyshire, DE1 1BS Tel: 01332-716659
Fax: 01332-716670 Web: www.derby.gov.uk/museums
Derbyshire Record Office (See Note)
Postal Address: County Hall, Matlock DE4 3AG
Tel: 01629-580000-ext-35207 Fax: 01629-57611
Erewash Museum
The Museum, High Street, Ilkeston, Derbyshire, DE7 5JA
Tel: 0115-907-1141 Fax: 0115-907-1121
Email: erewashmuseum@free4all.co.uk
Web: www.erewash.gov.uk
Lichfield Record Office
Lichfield Library, The Friary, Lichfield, Staffordshire, WS13
6QG Tel: 01543-510720 Fax: 01543-510715
Email: lichfield.record.office@staffordshire.gov.uk
Nottingham R.C. Diocese Nottingham Diocesan Archives
Willson House, Derby Streeet, Nottingham, NG1 5AW
Tel: 0115-953-9803
Staffordshire and Stoke on Trent Archive Service
Staffordshire Record Office, Eastgate Street, Stafford,
Staffordshire, ST16 2LZ Tel: 01785-278379 (Enquiries),
01785-278373 (Bookings) Fax: 01785-278384
Email: staffordshire.record.office@staffordshire.gov.uk
Web: www.staffordshire.gov.uk

Devon

Beaford Photograph Archive
Barnstaple, Devon, EX32 7EJ Tel: 01271-288611
Devon Record Office
Castle Street, Exeter, Devon, EX4 3PU Tel: 01392-384253
Fax: 01392-384256 Email: devrec@devon-cc.gov.uk
Web: www.devon-cc.gov.uk/dro/homepage.html
Devonshire & The Devonshire & Dorset Regimental Archives
Wyvern Barracks, Barrack Road, Exeter, Devon, EX2 6AE
Tel: 01392-492436 Fax: 01392-492469
North Devon Record Office
Tuly Street, Barnstaple, Devon, EX31 1EL
Tel: 01271-388607, 01271-388608
Email: ndevrec@devon-cc.gov.uk
Web: www.devon-cc.gov.uk/dro/homepage
Plymouth & West Devon Record Office
3 Clare Place, Coxside, Plymouth, Devon, PL4 0JW
Tel: 01752-305940 Email: pwdro@plymouth.gov.uk

Dorset

Dorset Archives Service
Also covers: Bournemouth Borough & Borough of Poole, 9
Bridport Road, Dorchester, Dorset, DT1 1RP
Tel: 01305-250550 Fax: 01305-257184
Email: dcc_archives@dorset-cc.gov.uk
Web: www.dorset-cc.gov.uk/records.htm
Poole Local Studies Collection
The local studies collection relocated to The Waterfront
Museum, Poole. Some records moved to Dorset Record
Office, Dolphin Centre, Poole, Dorset, BH15 1QE
Tel: 01202-262424 Fax: 01202-262442
Email: poolereflib@hotmail.com Web: www.poole.gov.uk
Waterfront Museum & Local Studies Centre
4 High Street, Poole, Dorset, BH15 1BW Tel: 01202-683138
Fax: 01202-660896 Email: museums@poole.gov.uk
Web: www.poole.gov.uk

Essex

Essex Record Office
Wharf Road, Chelmsford CM2 6YT Tel: 01245-244644
Fax: 01245-244655 Email: ero.search@essexcc.gov.uk
(search service) ero.enquiry@essexcc.gov.uk (general
enquiries) Web: www.essexcc.gov.uk
Essex Record Office - Southend Branch
Central Library, Victoria Avenue, Southend on Sea SS2 6EX
Tel: 01702-464278 Fax: 01702-464253
Essex Record Office
Colchester & NE Essex Branch
Stanwell House, Stanwell Street, Colchester CO2 7DL
Tel: 01206-572099 Fax: 01206-574541
Web: www.essexcc.gov.uk/ero
L B of Barking & Dagenham Local History Studies - Barking
Local studies department is being absorbed into a centralised
department at Valence Library, Becontree Avenue,
Dagenham, Essex RM8 3HT Central Library, Barking,
Essex, IG11 7NB Tel: 020-8227-5297 Fax: 020-8227-5297
Email: valencelibrary@hotmail.com
L B of Barking & Dagenham Local History Studies -
Dagenham
Valence Library & Museum, Becontree Avenue, Dagenham,
Essex, RM8 3HT Tel: 020-8592-6537 Fax: 020-8227-5297
Email: fm019@viscount.org.uk Web: www.earl.org.uk
/partners/barking/index.html

Gloucestershire

Gloucestershire Record Office
Clarence Row, Alvin Street, Gloucester, GL1 3DW
Tel: 01452-425295 Fax: 01452-426378
Email: records@gloscc.gov.uk
Web: www.gloscc.gov.uk/pubserv/gcc/corpserv/archives
Waterways Trust
Services to be substantially reorganised contact prior to request-
ing information, Llanthony Warehouse, Gloucester Docks,
Gloucester, Gloucestershire, GL1 2EJ Tel: 0151-356-4247
Fax: 01452-318076 Email: archivist@dial.pipex.com
Web: www.britishwaterways.org.uk

Hampshire

Hampshire Record Office
Sussex Street, Winchester, Hampshire, SO23 8TH
Tel: 01962-846154 Fax: 01962-878681
Email: sadeax@hants.gov.uk
Web: www.hants.gov.uk/record-office
Portsmouth City Museum & Record Office
Museum Road, Portsmouth, Hampshire, PO1 2LJ
Tel: 023-9282-7261 Fax: 023-9287-5276
Email: portmus@compuserve.com
Web: ourworld.compuserve.com/homepages/portmus/
Portsmouth Roman Catholic Diocesan Archives
Private archives - arrangemets to visit have to be agreed
beforehand, St Edmund House, Edinburgh Road,
Portsmouth, Hampshire, PO1 3QA Tel: 023-9282-2166
Royal Marines Museum
Archives & Library
Eastney, Southsea, Hampshire, PO4 9PX Tel: 02392-819385
Ext 224 Fax: 02392-838420
Email: mathewlittle@royalmarinesmuseum.co.uk
Web: www.royalmarinesmuseum.co.uk
Southampton City Record Office
Civic Centre, Southampton, Hampshire, SO14 7LY
Tel: 023-8083-2251 Fax: 023-8083-2156
Email: city.archives@southampton.gov.uk

Herefordshire

Hereford Cathedral Archives & Library
Hereford Cathedral, 5 College Cloisters, Cathedral Close,
Hereford, Herefordshire, HR1 2NG Tel: 01432-359880
Fax: 01432-355929
Email: archives@herefordcathedral.co.uk
or
library@herefordcathedral.co.uk

Herefordshire Record Office
The Old Barracks, Harold Street, Hereford HR1 2QX
Tel: 01432-260750 Fax: 01432-260066
Email: shubbard@herefordshire.gov.uk
Web: www.herefordshire.gov.uk

Ashwell Education Services
Merchant Taylors Centre, Ashwell, Baldock, Hertfordshire,
SG7 5LY Tel: 01462-742385 Fax: 01462-743024
Email: aes@ashwell-education-services.co.uk
Web: www.ashwell-education-services.co.uk

Hertfordshire

Hertfordshire Archives & Local Studies
County Hall, Pegs Lane, Hertford, Hertfordshire, SG13 8EJ
Tel: 01438-737333 Fax: 01992-555113
Email: hals@hertscc.gov.uk Web: www.hertsdirect.org

Hull

Hull City Archives
79 Lowgate, Kingston upon Hull, HU1 1HN
Tel: 01482-615102, 01482-615110 Fax: 01482-613051
Web: www.hullcc.gov.uk

Hull Family History Unit
Central Library, Albion Street, Kingston upon Hull, HU1
3TF Tel: 01482-616828, 01482-616827 Fax: 01482-616827
Email: gareth.watkins@hullcc.gov.uk
Web: www.hullcc.gov.uk/genealogy

Hull Local History Unit
Hull College, Park Street Centre, Hull, HU2 8RR
Tel: 01482-598952

Huntingdonshire

Cambridgeshire Archive Service (Huntingdon)
County Record Office Huntingdon, Grammar School Walk,
Huntingdon, Cambridgeshire, PE18 6LF Tel: 01480-375842
Fax: 01480-375842 Email: county.records.hunts@camcnty.gov.uk
Web: www.camcnty.gov.uk/sub/archive/huntoff.htm

Kent

Bexley Local Studies Centre
Central Library, Townley Road, Bexleyheath, Kent, DA6
7HJ Tel: 020-8301-1545 Fax: 020-8301-7872
Email: archives.els@bexley.gov.uk

Canterbury City & Cathedral Archives
The Precincts, Canterbury CT1 2EH Tel: 01227-865330
Fax: 01227-865222 Email: archives@canterbury-cathedral.org
Web: www.canterbury-cathedral.org

Centre for Kentish Studies/Kent County Archives Service
Sessions House, County Hall, Maidstone, Kent, ME4 1XQ
Tel: 01622-694363 Fax: 01622-694379
Email: archives@kent.gov.uk

East Kent Archive Centre
Enterprise Zone, Honeywood Road, Whitfield, Dover
CT16 3EH Tel: 01304-829306 Fax: 01304-820783

London Borough of Bromley Local Studies Library
Central Library, High Street, Bromley, Kent, BR1 1EX
Tel: 020-8460-9955 Fax: 020-8313-9975

Margate Library Local History Collection
Cecil Square, Margate, Kent, CT9 IRE Tel: 01843-223626
Fax: 01843-293015

Medway Archives & Local Studies Centre
Civic Centre, Strood, Rochester, Kent, ME2 4AU
Tel: 01634-332714 Fax: 01634-297060
Email: local.studies@medway.gov.uk & archives@medway.gov.uk

Pembroke Lodge Museum & Family History Centre
4 Station Approach, Birchington on Sea, Kent, CT7 9RD
Tel: 01843-841649

Sevenoaks Archives Office
Central Library, Buckhurst Lane, Sevenoaks, Kent, TN13
1LQ Tel: 01732-453118, 01732-452384 Fax: 01732-742682

Thanet Branch Archives
The Archives moved to East Kent Archives Centre in late
1999. A local studies collection remains East Kent Archives
Centre, Enterprise Zone, Honeywood Road, Whitfield,
Dover CT16 3EH Tel: 01304-829306 Fax: 01304-820783

Lancashire

Blackburn Central Library Local Studies Department
Town Hall Street, Blackburn, Lancashire, BB2 1AG
Tel: 01254-587920 Fax: 01254-690539
Email: reference.library@blackburn.gov.uk

Bolton Archive & Local Studies Service
Central Library, Civic Centre, Le Mans Crescent, Bolton,
Lancashire, BL1 1SE Tel: 01204-332225
Email: archives.library@bolton.gov.uk

Bury Archive Service
1st Floor, Derby Hall Annexe, Edwin Street off Crompton
Street, Bury, Greater Manchester, BL9 0AS
Tel: 0161-797-6697 Email: information@bury.gov.uk
Web: www.bury.gov.uk/culture.htm

Crosby Library (South Sefton Local History Unit)
Crosby Road North, Waterloo, Liverpool, Merseyside, L22
0LQ Tel: 0151-257-6401 Fax: 0151-934-5770
Email: lochist.south.seflib@merseymail.com

Documentary Photography Archive - Manchester
c/o Towncroft Lane, Bolton, Lancashire, BL1 5EW
Tel: 01204-840439 Fax: 01204-840439

**Lancashire Record Office & the Lancashire Local
Studies Collection** Public searchroom closed for the first
full week (Mon to Fri) each month. For further details, Bow
Lane, Preston, Lancashire, PR1 2RE Tel: 01772-263039
Fax: 01772-263050 Email: record.office@lancscc.gov.uk
Web: www.lancashire.gov.uk/education/lifelong/ro/index.htm

North West Sound Archive
Old Steward s Office, Clitheroe Castle, Clitheroe,
Lancashire, BB7 1AZ Tel: 01200-427897
Fax: 01200-427897 Web: www.nw-soundarchive.co.uk

Oldham Local Studies & Archives
Local Studies Library, 84 Union Street, Oldham, Lancashire,
OL1 1DN Tel: 0161-911-4654 Fax: 0161-911-4654
Email: localstudies@oldham.gov.uk or archives@oldham.gov.uk
Web: www.oldham.gov.uk/local-studies
or http://www.oldham.gov.uk/archives

Rochdale Local Studies Library
Arts & Heritage Centre, The Esplanade, Rochdale,
Lancashire, OL16 4TY Tel: 01706-864915 Moving to temp
location contact Wheatsheaf Library for info Tel: 01706-864920

Salford City Archives
Salford Archives Centre, 658/662 Liverpool Road, Irlam,
Manchester, M44 5AD Tel: 0161-775-5643

Salford Local History Library
Peel Park, Salford M5 4WU Tel: 0161-736-2649

Southport Library (North Sefton Local History Unit)
Lord Street, Southport, Merseyside, PR8 1DJ
Tel: 0151-934-2119 Fax: 0151-934-2115

St Helen s Local History & Archives Library
Central Library, Gamble Institute, Victoria Square, St
Helens, Merseyside, WA10 1DY Tel: 01744-456952

Tameside Local Studies Library
Stalybridge Library, Trinity Street, Stalybridge, Cheshire,
SK15 2BN Tel: 0161-338-2708, 0161-338-3831
Fax: 0161-303-8289 Email: tamelocal@dial.pipex.com
Web: www.tameside.gov.uk

Trafford Public Library & Local Studies Centre
Public Library, Tatton Road, Sale, M33 1YH
Tel: 0161-912-3013 Fax: 0161-912-3019
Email: trafford.local.studies@free4all.co.uk

Wigan Heritage Service - Archives
Town Hall, Leigh, Lancashire, WN7 2DY
Tel: 01942-404430 Fax: 01942-404425
Email: heritage@wiganmbc.gov.uk
Web: www.wiganmbc.gov.uk

Wigan Heritage Service - History Shop
Library Street, Wigan, Greater Manchester, WN1 1NU
Tel: 01942-828020 Fax: 01942-827645
Email: heritage@wiganmbc.gov.uk

Leicestershire

Record Office Leicestershire - Leicester & Rutland
Long Street, Wigston Magna, Leicestershire, LE18 2AH
Tel: 0116-257-1080 Fax: 0116-257-1120
Email: recordoffice@leics.gov.uk
Nottingham R.C. Diocese Nottingham Diocesan Archives
Willson House, Derby Streeet, Nottingham, NG1 5AW
Tel: 0115-953-9803

Lincolnshire

Lincolnshire Archives
St Rumbold Street, Lincoln, Lincolnshire, LN2 5AB
Tel: 01522-526204 Fax: 01522-530047
Email: archives@lincolnshire.gov.uk
Web: www.lincs-archives.com
Lincolnshire County Library
Local Studies Section, Central Library, Free School Lane,
Lincoln LN2 1EZ Tel: 01522-510800 Fax: 01522-575011
Email: lincoln.library@lincolnshire.gov.uk
Web: www.lincolnshire.gov.uk/library/services/family.htm
North East Lincolnshire Archives
Town Hall, Town Hall Square, Grimsby, North East
Lincolnshire, DN31 1HX Tel: 01472-323585
Fax: 01472-323582 Email: john.wilson@nelincs.gov.uk

Liverpool

Liverpool Record Office & Local History Department
Annual closure 3rd & 4th weeks in June., Central Library,
William Brown Street, Liverpool, L3 8EW
Tel: 0151-233-5817 Fax: 0151-233-5886
Email: recoffice.central.library@liverpool.gov.uk
Web: www.liverpool.gov.uk

London - See at start of Section

Manchester

John Rylands University Library
150 Deansgate, Manchester, M3 3EH Tel: 0161-834-5343
Fax: 0161-834-5343 Email: j.r.hodgson@man.ac.uk
Web: www.rylibweb.man.ac.uk

Manchester - Greater Manchester

Bury Archive Service
1st Floor, Derby Hall Annexe, Edwin Street off Crompton
Street, Bury, Greater Manchester, BL9 0AS
Tel: 0161-797-6697 Email: information@bury.gov.uk
Web: www.bury.gov.uk/culture.htm
Greater Manchester County Record Office
56 Marshall Street, New Cross, Manchester M4 5FU
Tel: 0161-832-5284 Fax: 0161-839-3808
Email: archives@gmcro.co.uk Web: www.gmcro.co.uk
Oldham Local Studies & Archives
Local Studies Library, 84 Union Street, Oldham, Lancashire,
OL1 1DN Tel: 0161-911-4654 Fax: 0161-911-4654
Email: localstudies@oldham.gov.uk or archives@oldham.gov.uk
Web: www.oldham.gov.uk/local-studies
or
http://www.oldham.gov.uk/archives
Salford City Archives
Salford Archives Centre, 658/662 Liverpool Road, Irlam,
Manchester, M44 5AD Tel: 0161-775-5643
Wigan Heritage Service - Archives
Town Hall, Leigh, Lancashire, WN7 2DY
Tel: 01942-404430 Fax: 01942-404425
Email: heritage@wiganmbc.gov.uk
Web: www.wiganmbc.gov.uk
Wigan Heritage Service - History Shop
Library Street, Wigan, Greater Manchester, WN1 1NU
Tel: 01942-828020 Fax: 01942-827645
Email: heritage@wiganmbc.gov.uk

Medway

Medway Archives & Local Studies Centre
Civic Centre, Strood, Rochester, Kent, ME2 4AU
Tel: 01634-332714 Fax: 01634-297060
Email: local.studies@medway.gov.uk
also Email: archives@medway.gov.uk

Merseyside

Crosby Library (South Sefton Local History Unit)
Crosby Road North, Waterloo, Liverpool, Merseyside, L22
0LQ Tel: 0151-257-6401 Fax: 0151-934-5770
Email: lochist.south.seflib@merseymail.com
Huyton Central Library - Local Studies & Archives
Civic Way, Huyton, Knowsley, Merseyside, L36 9GD
Tel: 0151-443-3738 Fax: 0151-443-3739
Email: eileen.hume.dlcs@knowsley.gov.uk
Web: www.knowsley.gov.uk/leisure/libraries/huyton/index.html
Port Sunlight Village Trust
95 Greendale Road, Port Sunlight, CH62 4XE
Tel: 0151-644-6466 Fax: 0151-645-8973
Southport Library (North Sefton Local History Unit)
Lord Street, Southport, Merseyside, PR8 1DJ
Tel: 0151-934-2119 Fax: 0151-934-2115
Wirral Archives Service & Museum
Birkenhead Town Hall, Hamilton Street, Birkenhead,
Merseyside, CH41 5BR Tel: 0151-666-4010
Fax: 0151-666-3965 Email: archives@wirral-libraries.net

Middlesex

British Deaf History Society
288 Bedfont Lane, Feltham, Middlesex, TW14 9NU
Hertfordshire Archives & Local Studies
County Hall, Pegs Lane, Hertford, Hertfordshire, SG13 8EJ
Tel: 01438-737333 Fax: 01992-555113
Email: hals@hertscc.gov.uk Web: www.hertsdirect.org
London Borough of Harrow Local History Collection
PO Box 4, Civic Centre Library, Station Road, Harrow,
Middlesex, HA1 2UU Tel: 0208-424-1055, 0208-424-1056
Fax: 020-8424-1971

MIDLANDS

Midlands - West Midlands

Birmingham City Archives
Floor 7, Central Library, Chamberlain Square, Birmingham,
West Midlands, B3 3HQ Tel: 0121-303-4217
Fax: 0121-464-1176 Email: archives@birmingham.gov.uk
Web: www.birmingham.gov.uk/libraries/archives/home.htm
Birmingham Roman Catholic Archdiocesan Archives
Cathedral House, St Chad s Queensway, Birmingham, West
Midlands, B4 6EU Tel: 0121-236-2251 Fax: 0121-233-9299
Email: archives@rc-birmingham.org
Coventry City Archives
Mandela House, Bayley Lane, Coventry, West Midlands,
CV1 5RG Tel: 02476-832418 Fax: 02476-832421
Email: coventryarchives@discover.co.uk
Dudley Archives & Local History Service
Mount Pleasant Street, Coseley, Dudley, West Midlands,
WV14 9JR Tel: 01384-812770 Fax: 01384-812770
Email: archives.pls@mbc.dudley.gov.uk
Web: dudley.gov.uk/council/library/archives/archives1.htm
Sandwell Community History & Archive Service
Town Hall, High Street, West Bromwich, West Midlands,
B70 8DX Tel: 0121-569-4909 Fax: 0121-569-4907
Email: dm025@viscount.org.uk
Sandwell Community History & Archives Service
Smethwick Library, High Street, Smethwick, West Midlands,
B66 1AB Tel: 0121-558-2561 Fax: 0121-555-6064
Sutton Coldfield Library & Local Studies Centre
45 Lower Parade, Sutton Coldfield, Warwickshire, B72 1XX
Tel: 0121-354-2274, 0121-446-0164 Fax: 0121-464-0173
Walsall Local History Centre
Essex Street, Walsall WS2 7AS Tel: 01922-721305
Fax: 01922-634594 Email: localhistorycentre@walsall.gov.uk
Web: www.walsall.gov.uk/culturalservices/library/welcome.htm

Wolverhampton Archives & Local Studies
42 - 50 Snow Hill, Wolverhampton WV2 4AG
Tel: 01902-552480 Fax: 01902-552481
Email: wolvarch.and.ls@dial.pipex.com
Web: www.wolverhampton.gov.uk/library/archives.htm

Norfolk

Kings Lynn Borough Archives
The Old Gaol House, Saturday Market Place, Kings Lynn,
Norfolk, PE30 5DQ Tel: 01553-774297
Norfolk Record Office
Gildengate House, Anglia Square, Upper Green Lane,
Norwich, Norfolk, NR3 1AX Tel: 01603-761349
Fax: 01603-761885 Email: norfrec.nro@norfolk.gov.uk
Web: www.archives.norfolk.gov.uk

Northamptonshire

Northamptonshire Central Library
Abington Street, Northampton, NN1 2BA Tel: 01604-462040
Fax: 01604-462055 Web: www.northamptonshire.gov.uk
Northamptonshire Record Office
Also Peterborough Diocesan Record Office, Wootton Hall
Park, Northampton, Northamptonshire, NN4 8BQ
Tel: 01604-762129 Fax: 01604-767562
Email: archivist@nro.northamtonshire.gov.uk
Web: www.nro.northamptonshire.gov.uk

Northumberland

Berwick upon Tweed Record Office
Council Offices, Wallace Green, Berwick-Upon-Tweed, TD15 1ED
Tel: 01289-330044-Ext-265, 01289-301865 Fax: 01289-330540
Email: lb@berwick-upon-tweed.gov.uk
Web: www.swinhope.demon.co.uk/genuki/NBL/Northumberland
RO/Berwick.html
North Shields Local Studies Centre
Central Library, Northumberland Square, North Shields,
NE3O 1QU Tel: 0191-200-5424 Fax: 0191-200-6118
Email: local@ntlib.demon.co.uk
Northern Region Film & Television Archive
Blandford House, Blandford Square, Newcastle upon Tyne,
Tyne & Wear, NE1 4JA Tel: 0191-232-6789-ext-456
Fax: 0191-230-2614 Email: chris.galloway@dial.pipex.com
Northumberland Archive Service
Morpeth Records Centre, The Kylins, Loansdean, Morpeth,
Northumberland, NE6l 2EQ Tel: 01670-504084 Fax: 01670-514815
Web: www.swinhope.demon.co.uk/NRO/
Northumberland County Record Office
Melton Park, North Gosforth, Newcastle upon Tyne, NE3
5QX Tel: 0191-236-2680 Fax: 0191-217-0905
Web: www.swinhope.demon.co.uk/genuki/NBL

Nottinghamshire

Nottingham R.C. Diocese Nottingham Diocesan Archives
Willson House, Derby Streeet, Nottingham, NG1 5AW
Tel: 0115-953-9803
Nottinghamshire Archives
Castle Meadow Road, Nottingham, Nottinghamshire, NG2
1AG Tel: 0115-950-4524, 0115-9581634 Enquiries
Fax: 0115-941-3997 Email: archives@nottscc.gov.uk
Web: www.nottscc.gov.uk/libraries/archives/index.htm
Southwell Minster Library
Trebeck Hall, Bishop s Drive, Southwell, Nottinghamshire,
NG25 0JP Tel: 01636-812649 Fax: 01636-815904
Email: pat@southwellminster.prestel.co.uk

Oxfordshire

Centre for Oxfordshire Studies
Central Library, Westgate, Oxford, Oxfordshire, OX1 1DJ
Tel: 01865-815749 Fax: 01865-810187 Email: cos@oxford-
shire.gov.uk Web: www.oxfordshire.gov.uk/culture
Oxfordshire Archives
County Hall, New Road, Oxford, Oxfordshire, OX1 1ND
Tel: 01865-815203, 01865-810801 Fax: 01865-815429
Email: archives.occdla@dial.pipex.com
Web: www.oxfordshire.gov.uk

Plymouth

Plymouth & West Devon Record Office
3 Clare Place, Coxside, Plymouth, Devon, PL4 0JW
Tel: 01752-305940 Email: pwdro@plymouth.gov.uk

Rutland

Nottingham R.C. Diocese Nottingham Diocesan Archives
Willson House, Derby Streeet, Nottingham, NG1 5AW
Tel: 0115-953-9803
Record Office Leicestershire - Leicester & Rutland
Long Street, Wigston Magna, Leicestershire, LE18 2AH
Tel: 0116-257-1080 Fax: 0116-257-1120
Email: recordoffice@leics.gov.uk

Shropshire

Ironbridge Gorge Museum, Library & Archives
The Wharfage, Ironbridge, Telford, TF8 7AW
Tel: 01952-432141 Fax: 01952-432237 Email: library@iron-
bridge.org.uk Web: www.ironbridge.org.uk
Shropshire Records & Research Centre
Castle Gates, Shrewsbury, Shropshire, SY1 2AQ
Tel: 01743-255350 Fax: 01743-255355
Email: research@shropshire-cc.gov.uk
Web: www.shropshire-cc.gov.uk/research.nsf
Wrekin Local Studies Forum
Madeley Library, Russell Square, Telford, Shropshire, TF7
5BB Email: library@madeley.uk
Web: www.madeley.org.uk

Shropshire (north)

Lichfield Record Office
Lichfield Library, The Friary, Lichfield, Staffordshire, WS13
6QG Tel: 01543-510720 Fax: 01543-510715
Email: lichfield.record.office@staffordshire.gov.uk
Staffordshire & Stoke on Trent Archive Service
Staffordshire Record Office, Eastgate Street, Stafford,
Staffordshire, ST16 2LZ Tel: 01785-278379 (Enquiries),
01785-278373 (Bookings) Fax: 01785-278384
Email: staffordshire.record.office@staffordshire.gov.uk
Web: www.staffordshire.gov.uk

Somerset

Bath & North East Somerset Record Office
Guildhall, High Street, Bath, Somerset, BA1 5AW
Tel: 01225-477421 Fax: 01225-477439
Somerset Record Office
Obridge Road, Taunton, Somerset, TA2 7PU
Tel: 01823-337600 (appointment, 01823-278805 (enquiries)
Fax: 01823-325402
Email: Somerset_Archives@compuserve.com
Web: www.somerset.gov.uk

Staffordshire

Burton Archives
Burton Library, Riverside, High Street, Burton on Trent,
DE14 1AH Tel: 01283-239556 Fax: 01283-239571
Email: burton.library@staffordshire.gov.uk
Coal Miners Records
Cannock Record Centre, Old Mid-Cannock (Closed)
Colliery Site, Rumer Hill Road, Cannock, Staffordshire,
WS11 3EX Tel: 01543-570666 Fax: 01543-578168
Dudley Archives & Local History Service
Mount Pleasant Street, Coseley, Dudley, West Midlands,
WV14 9JR Tel: 01384-812770 Fax: 01384-812770
Email: archives.pls@mbc.dudley.gov.uk
Web: dudley.gov.uk/council/library/archives/archives1.htm
Lichfield Record Office
Lichfield Library, The Friary, Lichfield, Staffordshire, WS13
6QG Tel: 01543-510720 Fax: 01543-510715
Email: lichfield.record.office@staffordshire.gov.uk

Staffordshire & Stoke on Trent Archive Service
Eastgate Street, Stafford, Staffordshire, ST16 2LZ
Tel: 01785-278379 (Enquiries), 01785-278373 (Bookings)
Fax: 01785-278384 Email: staffordshire.record.office@
staffordshire.gov.uk Web: www.staffordshire.gov.uk
Stoke on Trent City Archives
Hanley Library, Bethesda Street, Hanley, Stoke on Trent,
Staffordshire, ST1 3RS Tel: 01782-238420
Fax: 01782-288499 Email: stoke.archives@stoke.gov.uk
William Salt Library
Eastgate Street, Stafford, Staffordshire, ST16 2LZ Tel: 01785-278372
Fax: 01785-278414 Email: william.salt.library@staffordshire.gov.uk
Web: www.staffordshire.gov.uk/archives/salt.htm

Suffolk

Suffolk Record Office - Bury St Edmunds Branch
77 Raingate Street, Bury St Edmunds, Suffolk, IP33 2AR
Tel: 01284-352352 Fax: 01284-352355 Email: bury.ro@lib-
her.suffolkcc.gov.uk
Web: www.suffolkcc.gov.uk/libraries_and_heritage/sro/
Suffolk Record Office - Ipswich Branch
Gatacre Road, Ipswich, Suffolk, IP1 2LQ Tel: 01473-584542
Fax: 01473-584533
Email: ipswich.ro.@libher.suffolkcc.gov.uk
Web: www.suffolkcc.gov.uk/libraries_and_heritage/sro/
Suffolk Record Office - Lowestoft Branch
Central Library, Clapham Road, Lowestoft, Suffolk, NR32
1DR Tel: 01502-405357 Fax: 01502-405350
Email: lowestoft.ro@libher.suffolkcc.gov.uk.
Web: www.suffolkcc.gov.uk/Libraries_and_heritage/sro/
Suffolk Regiment Archives
Suffolk Record Office, 77 Raingate Street, Bury St
Edmunds, Suffolk, IP33 2AR Tel: 01284-352352
Fax: 01284-352355 Email: bury.ro@libher.suffolkcc.gov.uk
Web: www.suffolkcc.gov.uk/libraries_and_heritage/

Surrey

Kingston Museum & Heritage Service
North Kingston Centre, Richmond Road, Kingston upon
Thames KT2 5PE Tel: 020-8547-6738 Fax: 020-8547-6747
Email: local.history@rbk.kingston.gov.uk
Web: www.kingston.gov.uk/museum/
London Borough of Merton Local Studies Centre
Merton Civic Centre, London Road, Morden, Surrey, SM4
5DX Tel: 020-8545-3239 Fax: 020-8545-4037
Email: mertonlibs@compuserve.com
London Borough of Sutton Archives
Central Library, St Nicholas Way, Sutton, Surrey, SM1 1EA
Tel: 020-8770-4747 Fax: 020-8770-4777
Email: local.studies@sutton.gov.uk Web: www.sutton.gov.uk
Public Record Office
Ruskin Avenue, Kew, Richmond, Surrey, TW9 4DU
Tel: 020-8876-3444 Web: www.pro.gov.uk
Surrey History Centre
130 Goldsworth Road, Woking, Surrey, GU21 1ND
Tel: 01483-594594 Fax: 01483-594595
Email: shs@surreycc.gov.uk Web: http://shs.surreycc.gov.uk

Sussex

East Sussex Record Office
The Maltings, Castle Precincts, Lewes, Sussex, BN7 1YT
Tel: 01273-482349 Fax: 01273-482341
West Sussex Record Office
County Hall, Chichester, West Sussex, PO19 1RN
Tel: 01243-753600, 01243-533911 Fax: 01243-533959
Email: records.office@westsussex.gov.uk
Web: www.westsussex.gov.uk/cs/ro/rohome.htm

Tyneside/Tyne & Wear

Gateshead Central Library & Local Studies Department
Prince Consort Road, Gateshead, NE8 4LN
Tel: 0191-477-3478 Fax: 0191-477-7454
Email: Local@gateslib.demon.co.uk Web: ris.niaa.org.uk

North Shields Local Studies Centre
Central Library, Northumberland Square, North Shields,
NE3O 1QU Tel: 0191-200-5424 Fax: 0191-200-6118
Email: local@ntlib.demon.co.uk
Northumberland County Record Office
Melton Park, North Gosforth, Newcastle upon Tyne, NE3
5QX Tel: 0191-236-2680 Fax: 0191-217-0905
Web: www.swinhope.demon.co.uk/genuki/NBL
Newcastle City Library Local Studies Section
Princess Square, Newcastle upon Tyne, NE99 1DX
Tel: 0191-261-0691
Northern Region Film & Television Archive
Blandford House, Blandford Square, Newcastle upon Tyne,
Tyne & Wear, NE1 4JA Tel: 0191-232-6789-ext-456
Fax: 0191-230-2614 Email: chris.galloway@dial.pipex.com
South Tyneside Central Library
Prince George Square, South Shields, Tyne & Wear, NE33
2PE Tel: 0191-427-1818-Ext-7860 Fax: 0191-455-8085
Email: reference.library@s-tyneside-mbc.gov.uk
Web: www.s.tyneside-mbc.gov.uk
Tyne & Wear Archives Service
Blandford House, Blandford Square, Newcastle upon Tyne,
Tyne & Wear, NE1 4JA Tel: 0191-232-6789
Fax: 0191-230-2614 Email: twas@dial.pipex.com
Web: www.thenortheast.com/archives/
North Shields Local Studies Centre
Central Library, Northumberland Square, North Shields,
NE3O 1QU Tel: 0191-200-5424 Fax: 0191-200-6118
Email: local@ntlib.demon.co.uk

Warwickshire

Coventry City Archives
Mandela House, Bayley Lane, Coventry, West Midlands,
CV1 5RG Tel: 02476-832418 Fax: 02476-832421
Email: coventryarchives@discover.co.uk
Modern Records Centre
University of Warwick Library, Coventry, Warwickshire,
CV4 7AL Tel: 024-7652-4219 Fax: 024-7652-4211
Email: archives@warwick.ac.uk
Web: warwick.ac.uk/services/library/mrc/mrc.html
Sutton Coldfield Library & Local Studies Centre
45 Lower Parade, Sutton Coldfield, Warwickshire, B72 1XX
Tel: 0121-354-2274, 0121-446-0164 Fax: 0121-464-0173
Warwick County Record Office
Priory Park, Cape Road, Warwick, Warwickshire, CV34 4JS
Tel: 01926-412735 Fax: 01926-412509
Email: recordoffice@warwickshire.gov.uk
Web: www.warwickshire.gov.uk

Warwickshire (North-East)

Lichfield Record Office
Lichfield Library, The Friary, Lichfield, Staffordshire, WS13
6QG Tel: 01543-510720 Fax: 01543-510715
Email: lichfield.record.office@staffordshire.gov.uk
Staffordshire & Stoke on Trent Archive Service
Staffordshire Record Office, Eastgate Street, Stafford,
Staffordshire, ST16 2LZ Tel: 01785-278379 (Enquiries),
01785-278373 (Bookings) Fax: 01785-278384
Email: staffordshire.record.office@staffordshire.gov.uk
Web: www.staffordshire.gov.uk

Wiltshire

Wiltshire & Swindon Record Office
Libraries HQ, Bythesea Road, Trowbridge, Wiltshire, BA14
8BS Tel: 01225-713709 Fax: 01225-713515
Wiltshire Studies Library
Trowbridge Reference Library, Bythesea Road, Trowbridge,
Wiltshire, BA14 8BS Tel: 01225-713732, 01225-713727
Fax: 01225-713715 Email: trowref@compuserve.uk or
trowreflib@compuserve.uk Web: www.wiltshire.gov.uk

Worcestershire

St Helen s Record Office
Fish Street, Worcester, Worcestershire, WR1 2HN
Tel: 01905-765922 Fax: 01905-765925
Email: recordoffice@worcester.gov.uk
Web: www.worcestershire.gov.uk/records
Worcestershire Regimental Archives
RHQ The Worcestershire & Sherwood Foresters Regiment,
Norton Barracks, Worcester, WR5 2PA Tel: 01905-354359
Fax: 01905-353871 Web: www.rhq_wfr@lineone.net
Worcesteshire Record Office
County Hall, Spetchley Road, Worcester, Worcestershire,
WR5 2NP Tel: 01905-766351 Fax: 01905-766363
Email: record.office@worcestershire.gov.uk

Worcestershire (Part)

Dudley Archives & Local History Service
Mount Pleasant Street, Coseley, Dudley, West Midlands,
WV14 9JR Tel: 01384-812770 Fax: 01384-812770
Email: archives.pls@mbc.dudley.gov.uk
Web: dudley.gov.uk/council/library/archives/archives1.htm

YORKSHIRE

Yorkshire Archaeological Society
Claremont, 23 Clarendon Road, Leeds, West Yorkshire, LS2
9NZ Tel: 0113-245-6342, 0113-245-7910
Fax: 0113-244-1979 Email: j.heron@sheffield.ac.uk
Web: www.yas.org.uk
Yorkshire Film Archive
University College of Ripon & York St John, College Road,
Ripon, North Yorkshire, HG4 2QX Tel: 01765-602691
Fax: 01765-600516
Borthwick Institute of Historical Research
Appointment necessary to use the archive., St Anthony s Hall,
Peasholme Green, York, YO1 7PW Tel: 01904-642315
Web: www.york.ac.uk/inst/bhir
York Minster Library Databank
Library & Archives, Dean s Park, York, YO1 7JQ Tel: 01904-611118
Fax: 01904-611119 Email: archives@yorkminster.org
Web: www.yorkminster.org

Yorkshire - East Yorkshire

East Riding of Yorkshire Archives Service
Site location for callers : The Chapel, Lord roberts Road,
Beverley, County Hall, Champney Road, Beverley HU17
9BA Tel: 01482-885007 Fax: 01482-885463
Email: archives.service@eastriding.gov.uk
Hull Family History Unit
Central Library, Albion Street, Kingston upon Hull, HU1
3TF Tel: 01482-616828, 01482-616827 Fax: 01482-616827
Email: gareth.watkins@hullcc.gov.uk
Web: www.hullcc.gov.uk/genealogy

Yorkshire - North Yorkshire

North Yorkshire County Record Office
County Hall, Northallerton, North Yorkshire, DL7 8AF
Tel: 01609-777585
Whitby Pictorial Archives Trust
Whitby Archives & Heritage Centre, 17/18 Grape Lane,
Whitby YO22 4BA Tel: 01947-600170 Fax: 01947-821833
Email: info@whitbyarchives.freeserve.co.uk
York City Archives
Exhibition Square, Bootham, York, YO1 7EW Tel: 01904-551878/9
Fax: 01904-551877 Email: archives@york.gov.uk
Web: www.york.gov.uk/heritage/museums/index

Yorkshire - South Yorkshire

Barnsley Archives & Local Studies Department
Central Library, Shambles Street, Barnsley, South Yorkshire,
S70 2JF Tel: 01226-773950, 01226-773938
Fax: 01226-773955 Email: Archives@Barnsley.ac.uk
also Email: librarian@barnsley.ac.uk
Web: www.barnsley.ac.uk/sites/library

Doncaster Archives Department
King Edward Road, Balby, Doncaster, DN4 0NA
Tel: 01302-859811
Rotherham Archives & Local Studies
Central Library, Walker Place, Rotherham S65 1JH
Tel: 01709-823616 Fax: 01709-823650
Email: archives@rotherham.gov.uk
Web: www.rotherham.gov.uk/pages/living/learning/islib/
callib.htm
Sheffield Archives
52 Shoreham Street, Sheffield, South Yorkshire, S1 4SP
Tel: 0114-203-9395 Fax: 0114-203-9398
Email: sheffield.archives@dial.pipex.com
Web: www.earl.org.uk/earl/members/sheffield/arch.htm

Yorkshire - West Yorkshire

Bradford District Archives
West Yorkshire Archive Service, 15 Canal Street, Bradford,
West Yorkshire, BD1 4AT Tel: 01724-731931
Fax: 01274-734013
John Goodchild Collection Local History Study Centre
Central Library, Drury Lane, Wakefield, West Yorkshire,
WF1 2DT Tel: 01924-298929
Local Studies Library - Leeds
Leeds Central Library, Calverley Street, Leeds, West
Yorkshire, LS1 3AB Tel: 0113-247-8290
Fax: 0113-247-8290 Email: local.studies@leeds.gov.uk
Web: www.leeds.gov.uk/library/services/loc_reso.html
Wakefield Library - Local Studies Department
Balne Lane, Wakefield, West Yorkshire, WF2 0DQ
Tel: 01924-302224 Fax: 01924-30224
 Email: localstudies@talk21.com
Web: www.wakefield.gov.uk

West Yorks Archive Service - Kirklees
Central Library, Princess Alexandra Walk, Huddersfield,
West Yorkshire, HD1 2SU Tel: 01484-221966
Fax: 01484-518361 Email: kirklees@wyjs.org.uk
Web: www.archives.wyjs.org.uk
West Yorkshire Archive Service Leeds
Chapeltown Road, Sheepscar, Leeds, West Yorkshire, LS7
3AP Tel: 0113-214-5814 Fax: 0113-214-5815
Email: leeds@wyashq.demon.co.uk
Web: www.archives.wyjs.org.uk
West Yorkshire Archive Service
Registry of Deeds, Newstead Road, Wakefield, West
Yorkshire, WF1 2DE Tel: 01924-305980 Fax: 01924-305983
Email: hq@wyashq.demon.co.uk
Web: www.archives.wyjs.org.uk
West Yorkshire Archive Service - Bradford
15 Canal Road, Bradford, West Yorkshire, BDI 4AT
Tel: 01274-731931 Fax: 01274-734013
Email: bradford@nyjs.org.uk
Web: www.archives.wyjs.org.uk
**West Yorkshire Archive Service
Calderdale**
Central Library, Northgate House, Northgate, Halifax, West
Yorkshire, HX1 1UN Tel: 01422-392636 Fax: 01422-341083
Email: calderdale@wyashq.demon.co.uk
Web: www.archives.wyjs.org.uk
**West Yorkshire Archive Service
Wakefield Headquarters**
Registry of Deeds, Newstead Road, Wakefield, West
Yorkshire, WF1 2DE Tel: 01924-305980 Fax: 01924-305983
Email: wakefield@wyjs.org.uk
Web: www.archives.wyjs.org.uk

Isle of Wight

Portsmouth Roman Catholic Diocesan Archives
Private archives - appointments required for visits
 St Edmund House, Edinburgh Road, Portsmouth,
Hampshire, PO1 3QA Tel: 023-9282-2166

Isle of Wight Record Office
26 Hillside, Newport, Isle of Wight, PO30 2EB
Tel: 01983-823820/1 Fax: 01983-823820

Isle of Man

General Registry Registries
Civil Registry, Registries Building, Bucks Road, Douglas,
Isle of Man, IM1 3ARTel: 01624-687039
Fax: 01624-687039 Email: civil@registry.gov.im
Manx National Heritage Library
Douglas, Isle of Man, IM1 3LY Tel: 01624-648000
Fax: 01624-648001 Email: enquiries@mnh.gov.im

Channel Isles

Judicial Greffe
Morier House, Halkett Place, St Helier, Jersey, JE1 1DD,
Tel: 01534-502300 Fax: 01534-502399/502390
Email: jgreffe@super.net.uk Web: www.jersey.gov.uk
Jersey Archives Service
Jersey Museum, The Weybridge, St Helier, Jersey, JE2 3NF,
Channel Islands, Tel: 01534-633303 Fax: 01534-633301
Guernsey Island Archives Service
29 Victoria Road, St Peter Port, Guernsey, GYI 1HU,
Channel Islands, Tel: 01481-724512

Scilly Isles

Islands of Scilly Museum
Church Street, St Mary s, Isles of Scilly, TR21 0JT
Tel: 01720-422337 Fax: 01720-422337

WALES

NATIONAL ARCHIVES

Department of Manuscripts - University of Wales
Main Library, University of Wales, College Road, Bangor,
Gwynedd, LL57 2DG, Wales, Tel: 01248-382966
Fax: 01248-382979 Email: iss177@bangor.ac.uk
National Library of Wales
Penglais, Aberystwyth, Ceredigion, SY23 3BU, Wales,
Tel: 01970-632800 Fax: 01970-615709
Email: holi@llgc.org.uk Web: www.llgc.org.uk
**National Monuments Record of Wales : Royal Commission on
the Ancient & Historical Monuments of Wales**
Crown Building, Plas Crug, Aberystwyth, Ceredigion, SY23
1NJ, Wales, Tel: 01970-621200 Fax: 01970-627701
Email: nmr.wales@rcahmw.org.uk
Web: www.rcahmw.org.uk
Office for National Statistics - 1901 Census Records
Room 4300E, Segensworth Road, Titchfield, Fareham,
Hampshire, PO15 5RR Tel: 01329-813429
Fax: 01329-813189 Email: rosemary.byatt@ons.gv.uk

Anglesey County Archives Service
Shirehall, Glanhwfa Road, Llangefni, Anglesey, LL77 7TW,
Tel: 01248-752080 Web: www.anglesey.gov.uk
Archifdy Meiron Archives
Swyddfeydd y Cyngor, Cae Penarlag, Dolgellau, Gwynedd,
LL40 2YB Tel: 01341-424444 Fax: 01341-424505
Email: EinionWynThomas@gwynedd.gov.uk
Web: www.llgc.org.uk
Carmarthenshire Archive Service
Parc Myrddin, Richmond Terrace, Carmarthen,
Carmarthenshire, SA31 1DS Tel: 01267-228232
Fax: 01267-228237 Email: archives@carmarthenshire.gov.uk
Web: www.carmarthenshire.gov.uk
Ceredigion Archives - Archifdy Ceredigion
Swyddfa r Sir, County Offices, Glan y Mor, Marine Terrace,
Aberystwyth, Ceredigion, SY23 2DE Tel: 01970-633697
Fax: 01970-633663 Email: archives@ceredigion.gov.uk
Denbighshire Record Office
46 Clwyd Street, Ruthin, Denbighshire, LL15 1HP
Tel: 01824-708250 Fax: 01824-708258
Email: archives@denbighshire.go.uk
Web: www.denbighshire.gov.uk

Flintshire Record Office
The Old Rectory, Rectory Lane, Hawarden, Flintshire, CH5 3NR
Tel: 01244-532364 Fax: 01244-538344
Email: archives@flintshire.gov.uk Web: www.flintshire.gov.uk
Glamorgan Record Office
King Edward VII Avenue, Cathays Park, Cardiff, CF1 3NE
Tel: 029-207-80282 Fax: 029-207-80284
Email: glamro@cardiff.ac.uk Web: www.llgc.org.uk/cac/
Gwent Record Office
County Hall, Croesyceiliog, Cwmbran, Gwent, NP44 2XH,
Tel: 01633-644886 Fax: 01633-648382
Email: 113057.2173@compuserve.com
Gwynedd Archives
Caernarfon Area Record Office, Victoria Dock, Caernarfon,
Gwynedd, LL55 1SH Tel: 01286-679095
Fax: 01286-679637 Email: archifau@gwynedd.gov.uk
Web: www.gwynedd.gov.uk/adrannau/addysg/archifau
Nelson Museum & Local History Centre
Priory Street, Monmouth, NP5 3XA Tel: 01600-713519
Fax: 01600-775001 Email: nelsonmuseum@monmouthshire.gov.uk
Pembrokeshire Record Office
The Castle, Haverfordwest, Pembrokeshire, SA61 2EF,
Wales, Tel: 01437-763707 Fax: 01437-768539
Powys County Archives Office
County Hall, Llandrindod Wells, Powys, LD1 5LG
Tel: 01597-826087/8 Fax: 01597-827162
Email: archives@powys.gov.uk Web: http://powys.gov.uk
Tenby Museum
Tenby Museum & Art Gallery, Castle Hill, Tenby,
Pembrokeshire, SA70 7BP Tel: 01834-842809
Fax: 01834-842809 Email: tenbymuseum@hotmail.com
Web: www.tenbymuseum.free-online.co.uk
West Glamorgan Archive Service
County Hall, Oystermouth Road, Swansea, West Glamorgan,
SA1 3SN, Wales, Tel: 01792-636589 Fax: 01792-637130
Email: archives@swansea.gov.uk
Web: www.swansea.gov.uk/archives
West Glamorgan Archive Service - Neath Archives Access Point
Neath Library, Victoria Gardens, Neath, Glamorgan, SA11
3BA, Wales, Tel: 01639-620139
West Glamorgan Archive Service - Port Talbot Access Point
Port Talbot Library, Aberfan Centre, Port Talbot, West
Glamorgan, SA13 1PJ, Wales, Tel: 01639-763430
Web: www.swansea.gov.uk/archives
Wrexham Archive Service
Wrexham Museum, County Buildings, Regent Street,
Wrexham, LL11 1RB, Wales, Tel: 01978-317976
Fax: 01978-317982 Email: helen.gwerfyl@wrexham.gov.uk

SCOTLAND

NATIONAL ARCHIVES
General Register Office for Scotland
Certificate orders: 0131-314-4411, New Register House,
Edinburgh EH1 3YT Tel: 0131-334-0380
Fax: 0131-314-4400 Email: records@gro-scotland.gov.uk
Web: www.gro-scotland.gov.uk pay-per-view search site
www.origins.net
National Archives of Scotland
HM General Register House, 2 Princes Street, Edinburgh
EH1 3YY Tel: 0131-535-1334 Fax: 0131-535-1328
Email: research@nas.gov.uk Web: www.nas.gov.uk
National Library of Scotland - Manuscripts Division
National Library of Scotland, George IV Bridge, Edinburgh
EH1 1EW Tel: 0131-466-2812 Fax: 0131-466-2811
Email: mss@nls.uk Web: www.nls.uk
National Register of Archives - Scotland
H M General Register House, 2 Princes Street, Edinburgh
EH1 3YY Tel: 0131-535-1405/1428 Fax: 0131-535-1430
Email: nra@nas.gov.uk Web: www.nas.gov.uk
Scottish Archive Network
Thomas Thompson House, 99 Bankhead Crossway North,
Edinburgh EH11 4DX Tel: 0131-242-5800
Fax: 0131-242-5801 Email: enquiries@scan.org.uk

Scottish Genealogy Society
15 Victoria Terrace, Edinburgh EH1 2JL Tel: 0131-220-3677
Fax: 0131-220-3677 Email: scotgensoc@sol.co.uk
Web: www.scotsgenealogy.com

Aberdeen City Archives
Aberdeen City Council, Town House, Broad Street,
Aberdeen AB10 1AQ Tel: 01224-522513
Fax: 01224-638556 Email: archives@legal.aberdeen.net.uk

Alloa Registration Office
Marshill House, Marshill, Alloa, Clackmannanshire FK10
1AB Tel: 01259-723850 Fax: 01259-723850
Email: clack.lib@mail.easynet.co.uk

Angus Archives
Montrose Library, 214 High Street, Montrose, Angus DD10
8PH Tel: 01674-671415 Fax: 01674-671810
Email: angus.archives@angus.gov.uk
Web: www.angus.gov.uk/history/history.htm

Argyll & Bute District Archives
Kilmory, Lochgilphead, Argyll, PA31 8RT Tel: 1546604120

Ayrshire Archives
Ayrshire Archives Centre, Craigie Estate, Ayr, Ayrshire KA8
0SS Tel: 01292-287584 Fax: 01292-284918
Email: archives@south-ayrshire.gov.uk
Web: www.south-ayrshire.gov.uk/archives/index.htm

Clackmannanshire Archivist
Alloa Library, 26/28 Drysdale Street, Alloa,
Clackmannanshire FK10 1JL Tel: 01259-722262
Fax: 01259-219469 Email: clack.lib@mail.easynet.co.uk

Dumfries & Galloway Archives
Archive Centre, 33 Burns Street, Dumfries DG1 2PS
Tel: 01387-269254 Fax: 01387-264126
Email: libsxi@dumgal.gov.uk Web: www.dumgal.gov.uk

Dundee City Archives
(callers use 1 Shore Terrace), 21 City Square, Dundee DD1
3BY Tel: 01382-434494 Fax: 01382-434666
Email: archives@dundeecity.gov.uk
Web: www.dundeecity.gov.uk/dcchtml/sservices/archives.html

Dundee University Archives
Tower Building, University of Dundee, Dundee DD1 4HN
Tel: 01382-344095 Fax: 01382-345523
Email: p.e.whatley@dundee.ac.uk
Web: www.dundee.ac.uk/archives/

East Ayrshire Council District History Centre & Museum
Baird Institute, 3 Lugar Street, Cumnock, Ayrshire KA18
1AD Tel: 01290-421701 Fax: 01290-421701
Email: Baird.institute@east-ayrshire.gov.uk
Web: www.east-ayrshire.gov.uk

East Dunbartonshire Local Record Offices & Ref Libraries
William Patrick Library, 2 West High Street, Kirkintilloch,
East Dunbartonshire G66 1AD Tel: 0141-776-8090
Fax: 0141-776-0408 Email: ref@edlib.freeserve.co.uk

Edinburgh City Archives
City Chambers, High St, Edinburgh EH1 1YJ
Tel: 0131-529-4616 Fax: 0131-529-4957

Ewart Library
Catherine Street, Dumfries DG1 1JB Tel: 01387-260285
Fax: 01387-260294 Email: libsxi@dumgal.gov.uk
Web: www.dumgal.gov.uk

Falkirk History Research Centre
Callendar House, Callendar Park, Falkirk FK1 1YR
Tel: 01324-503778 Fax: 01324-503771
Email: ereid@falkirkmuseums.demon.co.uk
Web: www.falkirkmuseums.demon.co.uk

Falkirk Library
Hope Street, Falkirk, FK1 5AU, Scotland

Glasgow City Archives
Mitchell Library, North Street, Glasgow G3 7DN
Tel: 0141-287-2913 Fax: 0141-226-8452
Email: archives@cls.glasgow.gov.uk

Highland Council Genealogy Centre
Inverness Public Library, Farraline Park, Inverness IV1 1NH
Tel: 01463-236463, 01463-220330 ext 9 Fax: 01463-711128

Lenziemill Archives
10 Kelvin Road, Cumbernauld, North Lanarkshire G67 2BA
Tel: 01236-737114 Fax: 01236-781762

Midlothian Archives
2 Clerk Street, Loanhead, Midlothian EH20 9DR
Tel: 0131-440-2210 Fax: 0131-440-4635
Email: mc_libhq_blossoming@compuserve.com

Moray Local Heritage Centre
Local Heritage Centre, Grant Lodge, Cooper Park, Elgin,
Moray IV30 1HS Tel: 01343-563413 Fax: 01343-549050
Email: graeme.wilson@techleis.moray.gov.uk

North Ayrshire Libraries
39 - 41 Princes Street, Ardrossan KA22 8BT Tel: 01294-469137
Fax: 01924-604236 Email: reference@naclibhq.prestel.co.uk

Orkney Archives
The Orkney Library, Laing Street, Kirkwall, Orkney KWI5
1NW Tel: 01856-873166 Fax: 01856-875260
Email: alison.fraser@orkney.gov.uk

Perth & Kinross Council Archive
A K Bell Library, 2 - 8 York Place, Perth, Perthshire PH2
8EP Tel: 01738-477012, 01738-477022 Fax: 01738-477010
Email: archives@pkc.gov.uk Web: :www.pkc.gov.uk

East Renfrewshire Record Offices
East Renfrewshire District Council, Rouken Glen Road
Road, Glasgow, East Renfrewshire G46 6JF
Tel: 0141-577-4976

Regimental Museum & Archives of the Black Watch
Balhousie Castle, Hay Street, Perth, Perthshire, PH1 5HS
Tel: 01738 621281 Fax: 01738-643245
Email: bwarchivist@btelick.com

Renfrewshire Archives
Central Library & Museum Complex, High Street, Paisley,
Renfrewshire PA1 2BB Tel: 0141-889-2350
Fax: 0141-887-6468

Scottish Borders Archive & Local History Centre
Library Headquarters, St Mary s Mill, Selkirk, Scottish
Borders TD7 5EW Tel: 01750-20842 Fax: 01750-22875
Email: archives@scotborders.gov.uk

Scottish Catholic Archives
No genealogical material held.Columba House, 16
Drummond Place, Edinburgh EH3 6PL Tel: 0131-5563661

Scottish Jewish Archive
The Synagogue, 125 Niddrie Road, Garnet Hill, Glasgow G42 8QA

Shetland Archives
44 King Harald Street, Lerwick, Shetland ZE1 0EQ
Tel: 01595-696247 Fax: 01595-696533
Email: shetland.archives@zetnet.co.uk

Stirling Council Archives
Unit 6, Burghmuir Industrial Estate, Stirling FK7 7PY
Tel: 01786-450745 Fax: 01786-473713
Email: archives@stirling-council.demon.co.uk

Stornoway Record Office
Town Hall, 2 Cromwell Street, Stornoway, Isle of Lewis
HS1 2BD Tel: 01851-709438, 01851-709217
Fax: 01851-709438 Email: emacdonald@cne-stor.gov.uk

Unst Heritage Centre
Haraldswick, Unst, Shetland ZE2 9EQ Tel: 01957-711528,
01957-711387 (Custodian home)

West Lothian Archives & Records Management
4 Rutherford Square, Brucefield Industrial Estate,
Livingston, West Lothian EH54 9BU Tel: 01506-460020
Fax: 01506-416167

NORTHERN IRELAND

Public Record Office of Northern Ireland
66 Balmoral Avenue, Belfast, BT9 6NY Tel: 028-9025-5905
Fax: 028-9025-5999 Email: proni@nics.gov.uk
Web: www.proni.nics.gov.uk

General Register Office of Northern Ireland -
Oxford House, 49 - 55 Chichester Street, Belfast BT1 4HL
Tel: 028-90-252000 Fax: 028-90-252120
Email: gro.nisra@dfpni.gov.uk Web: www.nisra.gov.uk/gro

Derry City Council Heritage & Museum Service
Harbour Museum, Harbour Square, Derry, Co Londonderry,
BT48 6AF Tel: 01504-377331 Fax: 01504-377633

Centre for Migration Studies at Ulster American Folk Park
Mellon Road, Castletown, Omagh BT78 8QY
Tel: 028-8225-6315 Fax: 028-8224-2241 Email: uafp@iol.ie
Web: www.folkpark.com also www.qub.ac.uk/cms

Belfast Family History & Cultural Heritage Centre
64 Wellington Place, Belfast, BT1 6GE Tel: 028-9023-5392
Fax: 028-9023-9885
Belfast Central Library
Irish & Local Studies Dept, Royal Avenue, Belfast, BT1
1EA Tel: 02890-243233 Fax: 02890-332819

REPUBLIC OF IRELAND

Waterford Archives & Local Records
St Joseph s Hospital, Dungarvan, Co Waterford, Ireland
Tel: 058-42199
Registrar General for Ireland
Joyce House, 8 - 11 Lombard Street East, Dublin 2, Ireland
Tel: Dublin-711000
Presbyterian Historical Society of Ireland
Church House, Fisherwick Place, Belfast, BT1 6DW,
Northern Ireland Tel: (028)-9032-2284
National Archives of Ireland
Bishop Street, Dublin 8, Ireland Tel: 01-407-2300
Fax: 01-407-2333 Email: mail@nationalarchives.ie
Web: www.nationalarchives.ie
Limerick City Library Local History Collection
The Granary, Michael Street, Limerick, Ireland
Tel: +353(0)61-314668 Fax: +353(0)61-411506
Email: noneill@citylib.limerickcorp.ie Web: www.limerick-
corp.ie/librarymain.htm
Limerick Archives & Limerick Ancestry
The Granary, Michael Street, Limerick, Ireland
Tel: 353-(0)61-415125 or 31298 Fax: 353-(0)61-312985
Web: www.mayo-ireland.ie
Leitrim Genealogy Centre
County Library, Ballinamore, County Leitrim, Ireland
Tel: 00-353-78-44012 Fax: 078-44425
Email: leitrimgenealogy@tinet.ie
Web: www.irishroots.net/leitrim.htm
Genealogical Office / Office Of The Chief Herald
Kildare Street, Dublin 2, Co Dublin, Ireland
Tel: +351-1-6030-200 Fax: +351-1-6621-06
 Email: herald@nli.ie Web: www.nli.ie
Dublin Heritage Group
Ballyfermot Library, Ballyfermot Road, Ballyfermot, Dublin,
10, Ireland Tel: 6269324 Email: dhgeneal@iol.ie
Dublin City Archives
City Assembly House, 58 South William Street, Dublin, 2,
Ireland Tel: (01)-677-5877 Fax: (01)-677-5954
Donegal County Council Archive Centre
Donegal County Concil, 3 Rivers Centre, Lifford, County
Donegal, Ireland Tel: +353-74-72490 Fax: +353-74-41367
Email: nbrennan@donegalcoco.ie Web: www.donegal.ie
Donegal Ancestry
The Old Meeting House, Back Lane, Ramleton, Letterkenny,
County Donegal, Ireland Tel: 00353-74-51266
Fax: 00353-74-51702 Email: donances@indigo.ie
Web: www.indigo.ie/~donances
Clare County Archives
New Road, Ennis, County Clare, Ireland Tel: 065-28525
Web: www.clare.ie
Church of Ireland Archives
Representative Church Body Library, Braemor Park,
Churchtown, Dublin 14, Ireland Tel: 01-492-3979
Fax: 01-492-4770 Email: library@ireland.anglican.org
Web: www.ireland.anglican.org/
Castlebar Local Record Offices
The Registration Office, New Antrim Street, Castlebar, Co
Mayo, Ireland Tel: 094-23249 Fax: 094-23249

AUSTRALASIA
AUSTRALIA

National Archives of Australia - Canberra
PO Box 7425, Canberra Mail Centre, Canberra, ACT, 2610
Tel: 02-6212-3600 Fax: 02-6212-3699
Email: archives@naa.gov.au Web: www.naa.gov.au

National Archives of Australia - Hobart
4 Rosny Hill Road, Rosny Park, Tasmania, 7018
Tel: 03-62-440101 Fax: 03-62-446834 Email: reftas@naa.gov.au
Web: www.naa.gov.au
National Archives of Australia - Northern Territories
Kelsey Crescent, Nightcliffe, NT, 810 Tel: 08-8948-4577
Fax: 08-8948-0276,
National Archives of Australia - Queensland
996 Wynnum Road, Cannon Hill, Queensland, 4170
Tel: 07-3249-4226 Fax: 07-3399-6589, Web: www.naa.gov.au
National Archives of Australia - South Australia
11 Derlanger Avenue, Collingwood, South Australia, 5081
Tel: 08-269-0100 Fax: 08-269-3234,
National Archives of Australia - Sydney
120 Miller Road, Chester Hill, Sydney, New South Wales, 2162
Tel: 02-96450-100 Fax: 02-96450-108
Email: refnsw@naa.gov.au Web: www.naa.gov.uk
National Archives of Australia - Victoria
PO Box 8005, Burwood Heights, Victoria, 3151 Tel: 03-9285-7900
Fax: 03-9285-7979,
National Archives of Australia - Western Australia
384 Berwick Street East, Victoria Park, Western Australia, 6101
Tel: 09-470-7500 Fax: 09-470-2787,
New South Wales - State Archives Office
2 Globe Street, Sydney, New South Wales, 2000
Tel: 02-9237-0254 Fax: 02-9237-0142,
Queensland State Archives
PO Box 1397, Sunnybanks Hills, Brisbane, Queensland, 4109
Tel: 61-7-3875-8755 Fax: 61-7-3875-8764
Email: qsa@ipd.pwh.qld.gov.au Web: www.archives.qld.gov.au
South Australia State Archives
PO Box 1056, Blair Athol West, South Australia, 5084
Tel: 08-8226-8000 Fax: 08-8226-8002,
Tasmania State Archives
Archives Office of Tasmania, 77 Murray Street, Hobart, Tasmania,
7000 Tel: (03)-6233-7488 Fax: (03)-6233-7471
Email: archives.tasmania@central.tased.edu.au
Web: www.tased.edu.au/archives
Victoria State Archives - Ballerat
State Offices, Corner of Mair & Doveton Streets, Ballarat, Victoria,
3350 Tel: 03-5333-6611 Fax: 03-5333-6609,
Victoria State Archives - Laverton North
57 Cherry Lane, Laverton North, Victoria, 3028 Tel: 03-9360-9665
Fax: 03-9360-9685,
Victoria State Archives - Melbourne
Level 2 Casselden Place, 2 Lonsdale Street, Melbourne, Victoria,
3000 Tel: 03-9285-7999 Fax: 03-9285-7953,
Western Australia - State Archives & Public Records Office
Alexander Library, Perth Cultural Centre, Perth, Western Australia,
6000 Tel: 09-427-3360 Fax: 09-427-3256,

NEW ZEALAND

National Archives of New Zealand
PO Box 10-050, 10 Mulgrave Street, Thorndon, Wellington, New
Zealand Tel: 04-499-5595 Fax: 04-495-6210
Email: national.archives@dia.govt.nz
Web: www.archives.dia.govt.nz

AFRICA
SOUTH AFRICA

Cape Town Archives Repository
Private Bag X9025, Cape Town, 8000, South Africa
Tel: 021-462-4050 Fax: 021-465-2960,
Dutch Reformed Church Archive
PO Box 398, Bloemfontein, 9301, South Africa Tel: 051-448-9546,
Dutch Reformed Church Archive of O.F.S
P O Box 398, Bloemfontein, 9301, RSA Tel: 051 448 9546,
Dutch Reformed Church Records Office
PO Box 649, Pietermaritzburg, 3200, South Africa
Tel: 0331-452279 Fax: 0331-452279,
**Dutch Reformed Church Synod Records Office of Kwa
Zulu-Natal**
P O Box 649, Pietermaritzburg , 3200, RSA Tel: 0331 452279
Fax: 0331 452279 Email: ngntlargrief@alpha.futurenet.co.za,

Free State Archives
Private Bag X20504, Bloemfontein, Free State, 9300, South Africa
Tel: 051-522-6762 Fax: 051-522-6765,
Free State Archives Repository
Private Bag X20504, Bloemfontein, 9300, South Africa
Tel: 051 522 6762 Fax: 051 522 6765,
National Archives - Pretoria
Private Bag X236, Pretoria, 1, South Africa Tel: 323 5300
Fax: 323 5287,
South Africa National Archives
Private Bag X236, Pretoria, 1, South Africa
South African Library - National Reference & Preservation
P O Box 496, Cape Town, 8000, South Africa Tel: 021 246320
Fax: 021 244848 Email: postmaster@salib.ac.za

NAMIBIA

National Archives of Namibia
Private Bag, Windhoek, 13250, Namibia Tel: 061 293 4386
Fax: 061 239042 Email: Renate@natarch.mec.gov.na
Web: www.witbooi.natarch.mec.gov.na

ZIMBABWE

National Archives of Zimbabwe
 Hiller Road, off Borrowdale Road , Gunhill, Harare, Zimbabwe
Tel: 792741/3 Fax: 792398

EUROPE
BELGIUM
Archives de l Etat a Liege
79 rue du Chera, Liege, B-4000, Belgium Tel: 04-252-0393
Fax: 04-229-3350 Email: archives.liege@skynet.be
De Kerk van Jezus Christus van den Heiligen
Der Laaste Dagen, Kortrijkse Steenweg 1060, Sint-Deniss-Westrem, B-9051, Belgium Tel: 09-220-4316
Provinciebestuur Limburg
Universititslaan 1, Afdeling 623 Archief, Hasselt, B-3500, Belgium
Rijks Archief te Brugge
Academiestraat 14, Brugge, 8000, Belgium Tel: 050-33-7288
Fax: 050-33-7288 Email: rijksarchief.brugge@skynet.be
Rijksarchief
Kruibekesteenweg 39/1, Beveren, B-9210, Belgium Tel: 03-775-3839
Service de Centralisation des Etudes Genealogique et Demographiques Belgique
Chaussee de Haecht 147, Brussels, B-1030, Belgium
Tel: 02-374-1492
Staatsarchiv in Eupen
Kaperberg 2-4, Eupen, B-4700, Belgium Tel: 087-55-4377
Stadsarchief te Veurne
Grote Markt 29, Veurne, B-8630, Belgium Tel: 058-31-4115
Fax: 058-31-4554

CYPRUS
Cyprus Center of Medievalism & Heraldry
P O Box 80711, Piraeus, 185 10, Greece Tel: 42-26-356

DENMARK
Association of Local History Archives
P O Box 235, Enghavevej 2, Vejle, DK-7100, Denmark
Fax: 45-7583-1801, Web: www.lokalarkiver.dk
Cadastral Archives
Rentemestervej 8, Copenhagen NV, DK-2400, Denmark
Fax: 45-3587-5064, Web: www.kms.min.dk
Danish Data Archive
Islandsgade 10, Odense C, DK-5000, Denmark
Fax: 45-6611-3060, Web: www.dda.dk
Danish Emigration Archives
P O Box 1731, Arkivstraede 1, Aalborg, DK-9100, Denmark
Tel: 45 9931 4221 Fax: 45 9810 2248 Email: bfl-kultur@aalbkom.dk, Web: www.cybercity.dk/users/ccc13656
Danish National Archives
Rigsdagsgaarden 9, Copenhagen, DK-1218 Tel: 45-3392-3310 Fax: 45-3315-3239, Web: www.sa.dk/ra/uk/uk.htm

Det Kongelige Bibliotek
POB 2149, Copenhagen K, DK-1016 Tel: 045-3393-0111
Fax: 045-3393-2218
Frederiksberg Municipal Libraries
Solbjergvej 21-25, Frederiksberg, DK-2000, Denmark
Fax: 45-3833-3677, Web: www.fkb.dk
Kobenshavns Stadsarkiv
Kobenhavns Radhus, Kobenhavn, DK01599, Denmark
Tel: 3366-2374 Fax: 3366-7039
National Business Archives
Vester Alle 12, Aarhus C, DK-8000, Denmark Tel: 45-8612-8533 Fax: 45-8612-8560 Email: mailbox@ea.sa.dk
Web: www.sa.dk/ea/engelsk.htm
Provincial Archives for Funen
Jernbanegade 36, Odense C, DK-5000, Denmark Tel: 6612-5885 Fax: 45-6614-7071, Web: www.sa.dk/lao/default.htm
Provincial Archives for Nth Jutland
Lille Sct. Hansgade 5, Viborg, DK-8800, Denmar
 Tel: 45-8662-1788 Fax: 45-8660-1006
Web:www.sa.dk/lav/default.htm
Provincial Archives for Southern Jutland
Haderslevvej 45, Aabenraa, DK-6200, Denmark
Tel: 45-7462-5858 Fax: 45-7462-3288
Web: www.sa.dk/laa/default.htm
Provincial Archives for Zealand etc
Jagtvej 10, Copenhagen, DK-2200, Denmark
Fax: 45-3539-0535, Web: www.sa.dk/lak.htm
Royal Library
Christains Brygge 8, Copenhagen K, DK-1219, Denmark
Fax: 45-3393-2219, Web: www.kb.dk
State Library
Universitetsparken, Aarhus C, DK-8000, Denmark
Tel: 45-8946-2022 Fax: 45-8946-2130
Web: www.sb.aau.dk/english

FINLAND
Institute of Migration
Piispankatu 3, Turku, 20500Tel: 2-231-7536
Fax: 2-233-3460 Email: jouni.kurkiasaaz@utu.fi
Web: www.utu.fi/erill/instmigr/

FRANCE
Centre d Accueil et de Recherche des Archives Nationales
60 rue des Francs Bourgeois, Paris Cedex, 75141, France
Tel: 1-40-27-6000 Fax: 1-40-27-6628
Centre des Archives d Outre-Mer
29 Chemin du Moulin de Testas, Aix-en-Provence, 13090,
Service Historique de la Marine
Chateau de Vincennes, Vincennes Cedex, 94304, France
Service Historique de l Armee de l Air
Chateau de Vincennes, Vincennes Cedex, 94304, France
Service Historique de l Armee de Terre
BP 107, Armees, 481, France

GERMANY
German Emigration Museum
Inselstrasse 6, Bremerhaven, D-2850 Tel: 0471-49096
Historic Emigration Office
Steinstr. 7, Hamburg, (D) 20095, Germany Tel: 4940-30- 51-282 Fax: 4940-300-51-220 Email: ESROKAHEA@aol.com
Web: users.cybercity.dk/gccc13652/addr/ger_heo.htm
Research Centre Lower Saxons in the USA
Postfach 2503, Oldenburg, D-2900, Germany Tel: 0441 798 2614 Fax: 0441-970-6180
Email: holtmann@hrzl.uni-oldenburg.de
Web: www.uni-oldenburg.de/nausa
Zentralstelle fur Personen und Familiengeschichte
Birkenweg 13, Friedrichsdorf, D-61381 Tel: 06172-78263,
Web: www.genealogy.com/gene/genealogy.html

GREECE
Cyprus Center of Medievalism & Heraldry
P O Box 80711, Piraeus, 185 10, Greece Tel: 42-26-356

LIECHENSTEIN
Major Archives Record Offices & Libraries Liechtenstein, Web:
www.genealogy.com/gene/reg/CH/lichts.html

NETHERLANDS
Amsterdam Municipal Archives
P O 51140, Amsterdam, 1007 EC, Netherlands
Brabant-Collectie
Tilburg University Library, P O Box 90153, Warandelaan,
Tilburg, NL-5000 LE, Netherlands Tel: 0031-134-662127
Gemeentelijke Archiefdienst Amersfoort
P O Box 4000, Amersfoort, 3800 EA, Netherlands Tel: 033-
4695017 Fax: 033-4695451
Het Utrechts Archief
Alexander Numankade 199/201, Utrecht, 3572 KW,
Tel: 030-286-6611 Fax: 030-286-6600
Email: Utrecht@acl.archivel.nl
Rijksarchief in Drenthe
P O Box 595, Assen, 9400 AN, Netherlands Tel: 0031-592-
313523 Fax: 0031-592-314697 Email: RADR@noord.bart.nl
Web: obd-server.obd.nl/instel/enderarch/radz.htm
Rijksarchief in Overijssel
Eikenstraat 20, Zwolle, 8021 WX, Netherlands Tel: 038-
454-0722 Fax: 038-454-4506 Email: RAO@euronet.nl,
Web: www.obd.nl/instel/arch/rkarch.htm
Zealand Documentation CTR
P O Box 8004, Middelburg, 4330 EA, Netherlands

NORWAY
Norwegian Emigration Centre
Strandkaien 31, Stavanger, 4005, Norway
Tel: 47-51-53-88-63 Email: detnu@telepost.no
Web: www.emigrationcenter.com

POLAND
Head Office Polish State Archives
Ul Dluga6 Skr, Poczt, Warsaw, 1005-00-950 Fax: 0-22-831-9222

SPAIN
Archivo Historico National
Serrano 115, Madrid, 28006, Espagne Tel: 261-8003-
2618004
Instituucion Fernando el Catolico
Plaza de Espagna 2, Zaragoza, 50071, Espagn
Tel: 09-7628-8878 Fax: 09-7628-8869
Email: ifc@isendanet.es.mail

SWEDEN
Harnosand Provincial Archive
Box 161, Harnosand, S-871 24, Sweden Tel: 611-835-00 Email:
landsarkivet@landsarkivet-harnosand.ra.se
Web: www.ra.se/hla
Goteborg Provincial Archive
Box 19035, Goteborg, S-400 12, Sweden Tel: 31-778-6800
House of Emigrants
Box 201, Vaxjo, S-351 04, Sweden Tel: 470-201-20
Email: info@svenskaemigrantinstitulet.g.se
Kinship Centre
Box 331, Karlstad, S-651 08, Sweden Tel: 54-107720
Lund Provincial Archive
Box 2016, Lund, S-220 02 Tel: 046-197000 Fax: 046-197070
Email: landsarkivet@landsarkivet-lund.ra.se
Orebro Stadsarkiv
Box 300, Orebro, S-701 35 Tel: 19-21-10-75 Fax: 19-21-10-50
Ostersund Provincial Archive
Arkivvagen 1, Ostersund, S-831 31, Sweden Tel: 63-10-84-85
Email: landsarkivet@landsarkivet-ostersund.ra.se
Web: www.ra.se/ola/
Stockholm City & Provincial Archives
Box 22063, Stockholm, S-104 22 Tel: 8-508-283-00
Fax: 8-508-283-01
Swedish Military Archives
Banergatan 64, Stockholm, S-115 88 Tel: 8-782-41-00
Swedish National Archives
Box 12541, Stockholm, S-102 29, Sweden Tel: 8-737-63-50
Uppsala Provincial Archive
Box 135, Uppsala, SE-751 04, Sweden Tel: 18-65-21-00
Vadstena Provincial Archive
Box 126, Vadstena, S-592 23, Sweden Tel: 143-130-30
Visby Provincial Archive
Visborgsgatan 1, Visby, 621 57, Sweden Tel: 498-2129-55

SWITZERLAND
Achives de la Ville de Geneve
Palais Eynard, 4 rue de la Croix-Rouge, Geneve 3, 1211,
Tel: 22-418-2990 Email: didier.grange@seg.ville-ge.ch
Archives Canonales Vaudoises
rue de la Mouline 32, Chavannes-pres-Renens, CH 1022,
Switzerland Tel: 021-316-37-11 Fax: 021-316-37-55
Archives de l Ancien Eveche de Bale
10 rue des Annonciades, Porrentruy, CH-2900, Suisse
Archives d Etat de Geneve
Casa Postale 3964, Geneve 3, 1211, Suiss
Tel: 022-319-3395 Fax: 319-3365
Staatsarchiv Appenzell Ausserhoden
Obstmarkt, Regierungsgebaede, Herisau, CH-9100,
Tel: 071-353-6111 Email: Peter.Witschi@kk.ar.ch
Staatsarchiv des Kantons Basel-Landschaft
Wiedenhubstrasse 35, Liestal, 4410 Tel: 061-921-44-40
Email: baselland@lka.bl.ch Web: www.baselland.ch
Staatsarchiv des Kantons Solothurn
Bielstrasse 41, Solothurn, CH-4509, Switzerland
Tel: 032-627-08-21 Fax: 032-622-34-87
Staatsarchiv Luzern
Postfach 7853, Luzern, 6000 Tel: 41-41-2285365
Email: archiv@staluzern.c Web: www.staluzern.ch

NORTH AMERICA - CANADA
Archives & Special Collections
PO Box 7500, Fredericton, New Brunswick, E3B 5H5
Tel: 506-453-4748 Fax: 506-453-4595,
Archives Nationales
PO Box 10450, Sainte Foy, Quebec, G1V 4N1 Tel: 418-643-8904
Fax: 418-646-0868,
Glenbow Library & Archives
130-9th Avenue SE, Calgary, Alberta, T2G 0P3 Tel: 403-268-4197
Fax: 403-232-6569,
Hudson s Bay Company Archives
200 Vaughan Street, Winnipeg, Manitoba, R3C 1T5
Tel: 204-945-4949 Email: hbca@chc.gov.mb.ca
Web: www.gov.mb.ca/chc/archives/hbca/index.html
Loyalist Collection & Reference Department
PO Box 7500, Fredericton, New Brunswick, E3B 5H5
Tel: 506-453-4749 Fax: 506-453-4596,
Manitoba Provincial Archives
200 Vaughan Street, Winnepeg, Manitoba, R3C 1T5
Tel: 204-945-4949 Fax: 204-948-3236,
National Archives of Canada
395 Wellington Street, Ottawa, Ontario, K1A 0N3
Tel: 613-996-7458 Email: http://www.archives.ca,
New Brunswick Provincial Archives
PO Box 6000, Fredericton, New Brunswick, E3B 5H1
Tel: 506-453-2122 Email: provarch@gov.nb.ca
Web: www.gov.nb.ca/supply/archives
Newfoundland & Labrador Archives
Colonial Building, Military Road, St Johns, Newfoundland, A1C
2C9 Tel: 709-729-0475 Fax: 709-729-0578,
Nova Scotia State Archives
6016 University Avenue, Halifax, Nova Scotia, B3H 1W4
Tel: 902-424-6060,
Ontario Archives
Unit 300, 77 Grenville Street, Toronto, Ontario, M5S 1B3
Tel: 416-327-1582 Email: reference@archives.gov.on.ca
Web: www.gov.on.ca/MCZCR/archives
Public Archives & Record Office
PO Box 1000, Charlottetown, Prince Edward Island, C1A 7M4
Tel: 902-368-4290 Fax: 902-368-6327 Email: archives@gov.pe.ca
Web: www.gov.pe.ca/educ/
Saskatchewan Archives Board - Regina
3303 Hillsdale Street, Regina, Saskatchewan, S4S 0A2
Tel: 306-787-4068 Email: sabreg@sk.sympatico.ca
Web: www.gov.sk.ca/govt/archives
Saskatchewan Archives Board - Saskatchewan
Room 91, Murray Building, University of Saskatchewan, 3
Campus Drive, Saskatoon, Saskatchewan, S7N 5A4
Tel: 306-933-5832 Email: sabsktn@sk.sympatico.ca
Web: www.gov.sk.ca/govt/archives

Yarmouth County Museums & Archives
22 Collins Street, Yarmouth, Nova Scotia, B5A 3C8
Tel: (902)-742-5539 Email: ycn0056@ycn.library.ns.ca
Web: www.ycn.library.ns.ca/museum/yarcomus.htm

UNITED STATES OF AMERICA

Alaska State Archives
141 Willoughby Avenue, Juneau, Alaska, 99801-1720,
United States of America, Tel: 907-465-2270
Email: sou@bham.lib.al.usarchives@educ.state.ak.us,
Arizona Department of Library
Archives & Public Records
State Capitol, 1700 West Washington, Phoenix, Arizona,
85007, United States of America, Tel: 602-542-3942
Arizona Historical Foundation Library
Hayden Library, Arizona State Univeristy, Tempe, Arizona,
85287, United States of America, Tel: 602-966-8331
Arkansas History Commission
OneCapitol Mall, Little Rock, Arkansas, 72201
Tel: 501-682-6900,
California State Archives
Office of the Secretary of State, 1020 O Street, Sacramento,
95814 Tel: (916)-653-7715 Email: archivesweb@ss.ca.gov
Web: www.ss.ca.gov/archives/archives.htm
Colorado State Archives
Room 1b-20, 1313 Sherman Street, Denver, Colorado, 80203-2236,
United States of America, Tel: 303-866-2390,
Connecticut State Archives
231 Capitol Ave, Hartford, Connecticut, 6106, Tel: 203-566-5650,
Daughters of the American Revolution Library
1776 D Street N W, Washington, District of Columbia, 20006-5392,
United States of America, Tel: 202-879-3229,
District of Columbia Archives
1300 Naylor Court North West, Washington, District of Columbia,
20001-4225 Tel: 203-566-3690,
Family History Library of the Church of Jesus Christ of LDS
35 N West Temple Street, Salt Lake City, Utah, 84150, USA,
Georgia State Archives
330 Capital Avenue SE, Atlanta, Georgia, 30334-9002
Tel: 404-656-2350 Email: http://www.state.ga.us/SOS/Archives/,
Hawaii State Library
478 South King Street, Honolulu, Hawaii, 96813
Indiana Archives
Room117, 140 N Senate Avenue, Indianapolis, Indiana, 46204-2296
Tel: 317-232-3660 Fax: 317-233-1085,
Kansas State Historical Society - Archives
6425 SW Sixth Street, Topeka, Kansas, 66615-1099
Tel: 913-272-8681 Fax: 913-272-8682
Email: reference@hspo.wpo.state.ks.us Web: www.kshs.org
Maryland State Archives
Hall of Records Building, 350 Rowe Boulevard, Annapolis,
Maryland, 21401 Tel: 410-974-3914,
Missouri State Archives
PO Box 778, Jefferson City, Missouri, 65102 Tel: 314-751-3280,
National Archives - California
100 Commodore Drive, San Bruno, California, 94066-2350
National Archives - Colorado
PO Box 25307, Denver, Colorado, 80225-0307 Tel: 303-866-2390,
National Archives - Georgia
1557 St Joseph Avenue, East Point, Georgia, 30344,
Tel: 404-763-7477 Fax: 404-763-7059 Web: www.nara.gov
National Archives - Illinois
7358 South Pulaski Road, Chicago, Illinois, 60629
National Archives - Massachusetts
380 Trapelo Road, Waltham, Massachusetts, 2154,
National Archives - Massachusetts
100 Dan Fox Drive, Pittsfield, Massachusetts, 01201-8230
National Archives - Missouri
2306 East Bannister Road, Kansas City, Missouri, 64131
National Archives - New York
201 Varick Street, New York, New York, 10014 - 4811
National Archives - Northwest Pacific Region
6125 Sand Point Way NE, Seattle, Washington, 98115
Tel: 206-524-6501 Email: archives@scattlc.nara.gov,
National Archives - Pennsylvania
Rom 1350, 900 Market Street, Philadelphia, PA 19144,

National Archives - Texas
Box 6216, 4900 Hemphill Road, Fort Worth, Texas, 76115
National Archives - Washington
Pennsylvania Avenue, Washington, District of Colombia, 20408,
National Archives - Pacific Alaska Region
654 West 3rd Avenue, Anchorage, Alaska, 99501 - 2145
Tel: 011-1-907-271-2443 Fax: 011-1-907-271-2442
Email: archives@alaska.nara.gov
Web: www.nara.gov/regional/anchorage.html
National Archives (Pacific Region)
1st Floor East, 24000 Avila Road, Orange County, Laguna Niguel,
California, 92677 Tel: (949)-360-2641 Fax: (949)-360-2624
Email: archives@laguna.nara.gov
Web: www.nara.gov/regional/laguna.html
Nevada State Archives
Division of Archives & Records, 100 Stewart Street, Carson City,
Nevada, 89710 Tel: 702-687-5210,
New Jersey State Archives
PO Box 307, 185 West State Street, Trenton, New Jersey,
08625-0307 Tel: 609-292-6260,
New Mexico State Archives
1205 Camino carlos Rey, Sante Fe, New Mexico, 87501
Tel: (505)-827-7332 Fax: (505)-476-7909
Email: cmartine@rain.state.nm.us Web: www.state.nmus/cpr
Ohio State Archives
1982 Velma Avenue, Columbus, Ohio, 43211-2497
Tel: 614-297-2510,
Pennsylvania State Archives
PO Box 1026, 3rd & Forster Streets, Harrisburg, Pennsylvania,
17108-1026 Tel: 717-783-3281,
South Carolina Department Archives & History
8301 Parklane Road, Columbia, South Carolina, 292223
Tel: 803-896-6100,
South Carolina State Archives
PO Box 11669, 1430 Senate Street, Columbia, South Carolina,
29211-1669 Tel: 803-734-8577,
South Dakota Archives
Cultural Heritage Center, 900 Governors Drive, Pierre, South
Dakota, 57501-2217 Tel: 605-773-3804,
Tennessee State Library & Archives
403 7th Avenue North, Nashville, Tennessee, 37243-0312
Tel: 615-741-2764 Email: reference@mail.state.tn.us
Web: www.state.tn.us/sos/statelib
Texas State Archives
PO Box 12927, Austin, Texas, 78711-2927 Tel: 512-463-5463,
Vermont Public Records Division
PO Drawer 33, U S Route 2, Middlesex, Montpelier,
Vermont, 05633-7601 Tel: 802-828-3700, 802-828-3286
Fax: 802-828-3710,
Vermont State Archives
Redstone Building, 26 Terrace Street, Montpelier, Vermont,
05609-1103 Tel: 802-828-2308,
Virginia State Archives
11th Street at Capitol Square, Richmond, Virginia,
23219-3491 Tel: 804-786-8929,
West Virginia State Archives
The Cultural Center, 1900 Kanawha Boulevard East,
Charleston, West Virginia, 25305-0300 Tel: 304-558-0230,
Wisconsin State Archives
816 State Street, Madison, Wisconsin, 53706 Tel: 608-264-6460
Fax: 608-264-6742
Email: archives.reference@ccmail.adp.wisc.edu
Web: www.wisc.edu/shs-archives
Wyoming State Archives
Barrett State Office Building, 2301 Central Avenue,
Cheyenne, Wyoming, 82002 Tel: 307-777-7826,

In order to provide additional useful listings the next pages contain a list of Cemeteries and Crematoria. The list is not exhaustive and we would be pleased to receive details of other cemeteries & crematoria to add to our future lists.

Cemeteries & Crematoria

England

Avon
Bristol General Cemetery Co
East Lodge, Bath Rd, Arnos Vale, Bristol BS4 3EW Tel:0117 971 3294
Canford Crematorium & Cemetery
Canford Lane, Westbury On Trym, Bristol BS9 3PQ
Tel:0117 950 3535
Cemetery of Holy Souls
Bath Rd, Bristol, Avon, BS4 3EW Tel:0117 977 2386
Haycombe Crematorium & Cemetery
Whiteway Rd, Bath, Avon, BA2 2RQ Tel:01225 423682
South Bristol Crematorium & Cemetery
Bridgwater Rd, Bristol, Avon, BS13 7AS Tel:0117 963 4141
Westerleigh Crematorium
Westerleigh Rd, Westerleigh, Bristol BS37 8QP Tel:0117 937 4619
Weston Super Mare Crematorium
Ebdon Rd, Worle, Weston-Super-Mare BS22 9NY Tel:01934 511717

Bedfordshire
Norse Rd Crematorium
104 Norse Rd, Bedford MK41 0RL Tel:01234 353701
Church Burial Ground
26 Crawley Green Rd, Luton LU2 0QX Tel:01582 722874
Dunstable Cemetery
West St, Dunstable, Bedfordshire, LU6 1PB Tel:01582 662772
Kempston Cemetery
2 Green End Rd, Kempston, Bedford MK43 8RJ Tel:01234 851823
Luton Crematorium
The Vale, Butterfield Green, Stopsley, Luton LU2 8DD
Tel:01582 723700
Luton General Cemetery
Rothesay Rd, Luton, Bedfordshire, LU1 1QX Tel:01582 727480

Berkshire
Easthampstead Park Cemetry & Crematorium
Nine Mile Ride, Wokingham RG40 3DW Tel:01344 420314
Henley Road Cemetery & Reading Crematorium
All Hallows Rd, Henley Rd, Caversham, Reading, RG4 5LP Tel:0118 947 2433
Larges Lane Cemetery
Larges Lane, Bracknell, Berkshire, RG12 9AL Tel:01344 450665
Newbury Cemetery
Shaw Hill Shaw, Newbury RG14 2EQ Tel:01635 40096
Slough Cemetery & Crematorium
Stoke Rd, Slough, Berkshire, SL2 5AX Tel:01753 523127 (Cemetery) Tel:01753 520702 (Crematorium)

Buckinghamshire
Chilterns Crematorium
Whielden Lane, Winchmore Hill, Amersham HP7 0ND Tel:01494 724263

Cambridgeshire
American Military Cemetery
Madingley Rd, Coton, Cambridge, CB3 7PH Tel:01954 210350
Cambridge City Crematorium
Huntingdon Rd, Girton, Cambridge, CB3 0JJ Tel:01954 780681
Ely Cemetary
Beech Lane, Ely, CB7 4QZ Tel:01353 669659
Marholm Crematorium
Mowbray Rd, Peterborough, PE6 7JE Tel:01733 262639

Cheshire
Altrincham Cemetery
Hale Rd, Altrincham, Cheshire, WA14 2EW Tel:0161 980 4441
Altrincham Crematorium
White House Lane, Dunham Massey, Altrincham WA14 5RH
Tel:0161 928 7771
Cemetery Management Ltd
Church Walk, Nantwich, Cheshire, CW5 5RG Tel:01270 626037

Chester Cemetries & Crematorium
Blacon Avenue, Blacon, Chester CH1 5BB Tel:01244 372428
Dukinfield Crematorium
Hall Green Rd, Dukinfield SK16 4EP Tel:0161 330 1901
Macclesfield Cemetery
87 Prestbury Rd, Macclesfield SK10 3BU Tel:01625 422330
Middlewich Cemetery
12 Chester Rd, Middlewich CW10 9ET Tel:01606 737101
Overleigh Rd Cemetery
The Lodge, Overleigh Rd, Chester CH4 7HW Tel:01244 682529
Walton Lea Crematorium
Higher Walton, Warrington WA4 6TB Tel:01925 267731
Widnes Cemetery & Crematorium
Birchfield Rd, Widnes WA8 9EE Tel:0151 471 7332

Cleveland
Teesside Crematorium
Acklam Rd, Middlesbrough TS5 7HD Tel:01642 817725

Cornwall
Glynn Valley Crematorium
Fletchers Bridge, Bodmin PL30 4AU Tel:01208 73858
Penmount Crematorium
Penmount, Truro, Cornwall, TR4 9AA Tel:01872 272871

County Durham
Birtley Cemetery & Crematorium
Birtley, Chester Le Street DH3 1PQ Tel:0191 4102381
Chester Le Street Cemetery
Chester Le Street District Council Civic Centre, Newcastle Rd, Chester Le Street, County Durham, DH3 3UT Tel:0191 3872117
Horden Cemetery
Lodge, Thorpe Rd, Horden, Peterlee SR8 4TP Tel:0191 5863870
Mountsett Crematorium
Ewehurst Rd, Dipton, Stanley DH9 0HN Tel:01207 570255
Murton Cemetery
Church Lane, Murton, Seaham SR7 9RD Tel:0191 5263973
Newton Aycliffe Cemetery
Stephenson Way, Newton Aycliffe DL5 7DF Tel:01325 312861
Princess Road Cemetery
Princess Rd, Seaham SR7 7TD Tel:0191 5812943
Trimdon Foundry Cemetary
Thornley Rd, Trimdon Station TS29 6NX Tel:01429 880592
Trimdon Parish Council Cemetery
Trimdon Grange, Trimdon Station TS29 6HN Tel:01429 880538
Wear Valley Cemetery
South Church Rd, Bishop Auckland DL14 7NA Tel:01388 603396

Cumbria
Carlisle Cemetery
Richardson St, Carlisle CA2 6AL Tel:01228 625310
Penrith Cemetery
Beacon Edge, Penrith CA11 7RZ Tel:01768 862152
Wigton Burial Joint Committee
Cemetery, Station Hill, Wigton CA7 9BN Tel:016973 42442

Derbyshire
Castle Donington Parish Council
Cemetery House, The Barroon, Castle Donington, Derby, Derbyshire, DE74 2PF Tel:01332 810202
Chesterfield & District Joint Crematorium
Chesterfield Rd, Brimington S43 1AU Tel:01246 345888
Clay Cross Cemetery
Cemetery Rd, Danesmoor S45 9RL Tel:01246 863225
Glossop Cemetery
Arundel House, Cemetery Rd, Glossop, Derbyshire, SK13 7QG
Tel:01457 852269
Markeaton Crematorium
Markeaton Lane, Derby DE22 4NH Tel:01332 341012
Melbourne Cemetery
Pack Horse Rd, Melbourne, Derby DE73 1BZ Tel:01332 863369

Devon
Drake Memorial Park Ltd
Haye Rd, Plympton, Plymouth, Devon, PL7 1UQ Tel:01752 337937
Exeter & Devon Crematorium
Topsham Rd, Exeter, Devon, EX2 6EU Tel:01392 496333
Littleham Church Yard
Littleham Village, Littleham, Exmouth, Devon, EX8 2RQ Tel:01395 225579
Mole Valley Green Burial Ground
Woodhouse Farm, Queens Nympton, South Molton, Devon, EX36 4JH Tel:01769 574512
North Devon Crematorium
Old Torrington Rd, Barnstaple, Devon, EX31 3NW Tel:01271 345431
Plymouth Devonport & Stonehouse Cemetery Co
Ford Park Rd, Plymouth, Devon, PL4 6NT Tel:01752 665442
Tavistock Cemetery
Cemetery Lodge, Plymouth Rd, Tavistock, Devon, PL19 8BY Tel:01822 612799
Torquay Crematorium & Cemetery
Hele Rd, Torquay, Devon, TQ2 7QG Tel:01803 327768

Dorset
Dorchester Cemetery Office
31a Weymouth Avenue, Dorchester, Dorset, DT1 2EN Tel:01305 263900
Parkstone Cemetery
134 Pottery Rd, Parkstone, Poole, Dorset, BH14 8RD Tel:01202 741104
Poole Cemetery
Dorchester Rd, Oakdale, Poole, Dorset, BH15 3RZ Tel:01202 741106
Poole Crematorium
Gravel Hill, Poole, Dorset, BH17 9BQ Tel:01202 602582
Sherborne Cemetery
Lenthey Rd, Sherborne, Dorset, DT9 3 Tel:01935 812909
Weymouth Crematorium
Quibo Lane, Weymouth, Dorset, DT4 0RR Tel:01305 786984
East Sussex
Brighton Borough Mortuary
Lewes Rd, Brighton, East Sussex, BN2 3QB Tel:01273 602345
Downs Crematorium
Bear Rd, Brighton, East Sussex, BN2 3PL Tel:01273 601601
Eastbourne Cemeteries & Crematorium
Hide Hollow, Langney, Eastbourne, East Sussex, BN23 8AE Tel:01323 766536(Cemetery)Tel:01323 761093(Crematorium)
Woodvale Crematorium
Lewes Rd, Brighton, BN2 3QB Tel:01273 604020

Essex
Basildon & District Crematorium
Church Rd, Bowers Gifford, Basildon, Essex, SS13 2HG Tel:01268 584411
Chadwell Heath Cemetery
Whalebone Lane, North Chadwell Heath, Romford, Essex, RM6 5QX Tel:0181 590 3280
Chelmsford Crematorium
Writtle Rd, Chelmsford, Essex, CM1 3BL Tel:01245 256946
Chigwell Cemetery
Frog Hall Lane, Manor Rd, Chigwell, Essex, IG7 4JX Tel:0181 501 0419
Colchester Cemetery & Crematorium
Mersea Rd, Colchester, Essex, CO2 8RU Tel:01206 282950
Eastbrookend Cemetery
Dagenham Rd, Dagenham, Essex, RM10 7DR Tel:01708 447451
Federation of Synagogues Burial Society
416 Upminster Rd North, Rainham RM13 9SB Tel:01708 552825
Great Burstead Cemetery
Church St, Great Burstead, Billericay CM11 2TR Tel:01277 654334
Harlow Crematorium
Parndon Wood Rd, Harlow CM19 4SF Tel:01279 423800
Pitsea Cemetery
Church Rd, Pitsea, Basildon, Essex, SS13 2EZ Tel:01268 552132
Romford Cemetery
Crow Lane, Romford, Essex, RM7 0EP Tel:01708 740791

Sewardstone Road Cemetery
Sewardstone Rd, Waltham Abbey, Essex, EN9 1NX Tel:01992 712525
South Essex Crematorium
Ockendon Rd, Corbets Tey, Upminster RM14 2UY Tel:01708 222188
Sutton Road Cemetary
The Lodge, Sutton Rd, Southend-On-Sea SS2 5PX Tel:01702 355015
Weeley Crematorium
Colchester Rd, Weeley, Clacton-On-Sea CO16 9JP Tel:01255 831108
Wickford Cemetery
Park Drive, Wickford, Essex, SS12 9DH Tel:01268 733335

Gloucestershire
Cheltenham Cemetery & Crematorium
Bouncers Lane, Cheltenham GL52 5JT Tel:01242 244245
Coney Hill Crematorium
Coney Hill Rd, Gloucester GL4 4PA Tel:01452 523902
Forest of Dean Crematorium
Yew Tree Brake, Speech House Rd, Cinderford GL14 3HU Tel:01594 826624
Mile End Cemetery
Mile End, Coleford GL16 7DB Tel:01594 832848

Hampshire
Aldershot Crematorium
48 Guildford Rd, Aldershot GU12 4BP Tel:01252 321653
Anns Hill Rd Cemetery
Anns Hill Rd, Gosport, Hampshire, PO12 3JX Tel:01705 580181
Basingstoke Crematorium
Manor Farm, Stockbridge Rd, North Waltham, Basingstoke, Hampshire, RG25 2BA Tel:01256 398784
Magdalen Hill Cemetery
Magdalen Hill, Arlesesford Rd, Winchester SO21 1HE Tel:01962 854135
Portchester Crematorium
Upper Cornaway Lane, Portchester, Fareham PO16 8NE Tel:01329 822533
Portsmouth Cemeteries Office
Milton Rd, Southsea, Hampshire, PO4 8 Tel:01705 732559
Southampton City Council
6 Bugle St, Southampton, Hampshire, SO14 2AJ Tel:01703 228609
Warblington Cemetery
Church Lane, Warblington, Havant, Hampshire, PO9 2TU Tel:01705 452540
Worting Rd Cemetery
105 Worting Rd, Basingstoke, Hampshire, RG21 8YZ Tel:01256 321737

Herefordshire
Hereford Cemetery & Crematorium
Westfaling St, Hereford, Herefordshire, HR4 0JE Tel:01432 272024

Hertfordshire
Almonds Lane Cemetery
Almonds Lane, Stevenage, Hertfordshire, SG1 3RR Tel:01438 350902
Bushey Jewish Cemetery
Little Bushey Lane, Bushey, Watford, Hertfordshire, WD2 3TP Tel:0181 950 6299
Chorleywood Road Cemetery
Chorleywood Rd, Rickmansworth WD3 4EH Tel:01923 772646
Woodwells Cemetery
Buncefield Lane, Hemel Hempstead HP2 7HY Tel:01442 252856
Harwood Park Crematorium Ltd,
Watton Rd, Stevenage, Hertfordshire, SG2 8XT Tel:01438 815555

Hatfield Road Cemetery
Hatfield Rd, St. Albans, Hertfordshire, AL1 3LA Tel:01727 819362
North Watford Cemetery
North Western Avenue, Watford, WD2 6AW Tel:01923 672157
Tring Cemetery
Aylesbury Rd, Aylesbury, Tring HP23 4DH Tel:01442 822248
Vicarage Road Cemetery
Vicarage Rd, Watford, Hertfordshire, WD1 8EJ Tel:01923 225147
Watton Rd Cemetery
Watton Rd, Ware, Hertfordshire, SG12 0AX Tel:01920 463261

West Herts Crematorium
High Elms Lane, Watford, Hertfordshire, WD2 7JS Tel:01923 673285
Western Synagogue Cemetery
Cheshunt Cemetery
Bulls Cross Ride, Waltham Cross EN7 5HT Tel:01992 717820
Weston Road Cemetery
Weston Rd, Stevenage, Hertfordshire, SG1 4DE Tel:01438 367109
Woodcock Hill Cemetery
Lodge, Woodcock Hill, Harefield Rd, Rickmansworth, Hertfordshire, WD3 1PT Tel:01923 775188

Isle Of Wight
Shanklin Cemetery
1 Cemetery Rd, Lake Sandown, Sandown PO36 9NN
Tel:01983 403743

Kent
Barham Crematorium
Canterbury Rd, Barham, Canterbury CT4 6QU Tel:01227 831351
Beckenham Crematorium & Cemetery
Elmers End Rd, Beckenham, Kent, BR3 4TD Tel:0208650 0322
Chartham Cemetery Lodge
Ashford Rd, Chartham, Canterbury CT4 7NY Tel:01227 738211
Gravesham Borough Council,
Old Rd West, Gravesend, Kent, DA11 0LS Tel:01474 337491
Hawkinge Cemetery & Crematorium
Aerodrome Rd, Hawkinge, Folkestone CT18 7AG Tel:01303 892215
Kent & Sussex Crematorium
Benhall Mill Rd., Tunbridge Wells, Kent, TN2 5JH Tel:01892 523894
Kent County Crematorium plc
Newcourt Wood, Charing, Ashford TN27 0EB Tel:01233 712443
Medway Crematorium
Robin Hood Lane, Blue Bell Hill, Chatham, Kent, ME5 9QU
Tel:01634 861639
Northfleet Cemetery
Springhead Rd, Northfleet, Gravesend, DA11 8HW Tel:01474 533260
Snodland Cemetery
Cemetery Cottage, Cemetery Rd, Snodland, Kent, ME6 5DN
Tel:01634 240764
Thanet Crematorium
Manston Rd, Margate, Kent, CT9 4LY Tel:01843 224492
The Cremation Society
Brecon House, 16 Albion Place, Maidstone, Kent, ME14 5DZ
Tel:01622 688292
Vinters Park Crematorium
Bearstead Rd, Weavering, Maidstone ME14 5LG Tel:01622 738172

Lancashire, Greater Manchester & Manchester
Accrington Cemetry & Crematorium
Burnley Rd, Accrington, Lancashire, BB5 6HA Tel:01254 232933
Audenshaw Cemetery
Cemetery Rd, Audenshaw, Manchester, Lancashire, M34 5AH
Tel:0161 336 2675
Blackley Cemetery & Crematorium
Victoria Avenue, Manchester, Lancashire, M9 8 Tel:0161 740 5359
Burnley Cemetery
Rossendale Rd, Burnley BB11 5DD Tel:01282 435411
Carleton Crematorium
Stocks Lane, Carleton, Poulton-Le-Fylde, Lancashire, FY6 7QS
Tel:01253 882541
Central & North Manchester Synagoguc Jcwish Ccmetery
Rainsough Brow, Prestwich, Manchester M25 9XW
Tel:0161 773 2641
Central & North Manchester Synagogue Jewish Cemetery
Rochdale Rd, Manchester M9 6FQ Tel:0161 740 2317
Chadderton Cemetery
Cemetery Lodge, Middleton Rd, Oldham OL9 Tel:0161 624 2301
Gidlow Cemetery
Gidlow Lane, Standish, Wigan WN6 8RT Tel:01257 424127
Greenacres Cemetery
Greenacres Rd, Oldham, Lancashire, OL4 3HT Tel:0161 624 2294
Hollinwood Cemetery
Roman Rd, Hollinwood, Oldham OL8 3LU Tel:0161 681 1312

Howe Bridge Crematorium
Lovers Lane, Atherton, Manchester M46 0PZ Tel:01942 870811
Leigh Cemetery
Manchester Rd, Leigh WN7 2 Tel:01942 671560
Lower Ince Crematorium
Warrington Rd, Lower Ince, Wigan WN3 4NH Tel:01942 866455
Lytham Park Cemetery & Cremarotium
Regent Avenue, Lytham St. Annes FY8 4AB Tel:01253 735429
Manchester Crematorium Ltd
Barlow Moor Rd, Manchester M21 7GZ Tel:0161 881 5269
Middleton New Cemetery
Boarshaw Rd, Middleton, Manchester M24 6 Tel:0161 655 3765
New Manchester Woodland Cemetery
City Rd, Ellenbrook, Worsley, Manchester M28 1BD
Tel:0161 790 1300
Overdale Crematorium
Overdale Drive, Chorley New Rd, Heaton, Bolton BL1 5BU
Tel:01204 840214
Padiham Public Cemetery
St. Johns Rd, Padiham, Burnley BB12 7BN Tel:01282 778139
Preston Cemetery
New Hall Lane, Preston, Lancashire, PR1 4SY Tel:01772 794585
Preston Crematorium
Longridge Rd, Ribbleton, Preston PR2 6RL Tel:01772 792391
Rochdale Cemetery
Bury Rd, Rochdale, Lancashire, OL11 4DG Tel:01706 645219
Southern Cemetery
Barlow Moor Rd, Manchester M21 7GL Tel:0161 881 2208
St. Mary s Catholic Cemetery
Manchester Rd, Wardley, Manchester M28 2UJ Tel:0161 794 2194
St.Joseph s Cemetery
Moston Lane, Mancheste M40 9QL Tel:0161 681 1582
United Synagogue Burial Ground
Worsley Hill Farm Whitefield, Manchester, M45 7ED
Tel:0161 766 2065
Whitworth Cemetery
Edward St, Whitworth, Rochdale OL16 2EJ Tel:01706 852352

Leicestershire
Melton Mowbray Cemetery
Cemetery Lodge, Thorpe Rd, Melton Mowbray LE13 1SH
Tel:01664 562223
Loughborough Crematorium
Leicester Rd, Loughborough LE11 2AF Tel:01743 353046
Saffron Hill Cemetery
Stonesby Avenue, Leicester LE2 6TY Tel:0116 222 1049

Lincolnshire
Boston Crematorium
Marian Rd, Boston, Lincolnshire, PE21 9HA Tel:01205 364612
Bourne Town Cemetery
South Rd, Bourne, Lincolnshire, PE10 9JB Tel:01778 422796
Grantham Cemetery & Crematorium
Harrowby Rd, Grantham, Lincolnshire, NG31 9DT Tel:01476 563083
Horncastle Cemetery
Boston Rd, Horncastle, Lincolnshire, LN9 6NF Tel:01507 527118
Stamford Cemetery
Wichendom, Little Casterton Rd, Stamford, Lincolnshire, PE9 1BB
Tel:01780 762316
Tyler Landscapes, Newport Cemetery
Manor Rd, Newport, Lincoln LN4 1RT Tel:01522 525195

London & Greater London
Brockley Ladywell Hithergreen & Grove Park Cemeteries
Verdant Lane, Catford, London , SE6 1TP Tel:0181 697 2555
Brompton Cemetery
Fulham Rd, London, SW10 9UG Tel:0171 352 1201
Cemetery Management Ltd
38 Uxbridge Rd, London, W7 3PP Tel:0181 567 0913
Charlton Cemetery
Cemetery Lane, London, SE7 8DZ Tel:0181 854 0235
City of London Cemetery & Crematorium
Aldersbrook Rd, London, E12 5DQ Tel:0181 530 2151

Coroners Court
8 Ladywell Rd, Lewisham, London, SE13 7UW Tel:0208690 5138
East London Cemetery Co.Ltd
Grange Rd, London, E13 0HB Tel:0171 476 5109
Edmonton Cemetery
Church St, Edmonton, London, N9 9HP Tel:0208360 2157
Eltham Cemetery & Crematorium
Crown Woods Way, Eltham, London, SE9 2RF
Tel:0181 850 2921 (Cemetery) Tel:0181 850 7046 (Crematorium)
Gap Road Cemetery
Gap Rd, London, SW19 8JF Tel:0208879 0701
Golders Green Crematorium
62 Hoop Lane, London, NW11 7NL Tel:0208455 2374
Greenwich Cemetery
Well Hall Rd, London, SE9 6TZ Tel:0181 856 8666
London Borough of Hackney Mortuary
Lower Clapton Rd, London, E5 8EQ Tel:0181 985 2808
Abney Park Cemetery
High St, Stoke Newington, London, N16 0LH Tel:0171 275 7557
Hendon Cemetery & Crematorium
Holders Hill Rd, London, NW7 1NB Tel:0181 346 0657
Highgate Cemetery
Swains Lane, London, N6 6PJ Tel:0181 340 1834
Honor Oak Crematorium
Brenchley Gardens, London, SE23 3RB Tel:0171 639 7499
Islington Cemetery & Crematorium
High Rd, East Finchley, London, N2 9AG Tel:0208883 1230
Kensal Green Cemetery
Harrow Rd, London, W10 4RA Tel:0181 969 0152
L.B.S Cemeteries
Brenchley Gardens, London, SE23 3RD Tel:0171 639 3121
Lambeth Cemetery and Crematorium
Cemetary Lodge, Blackshaw Rd, Tooting, London, SW17 0BY
Tel:0181 672 1390
Lewisham Crematorium
Verdant Lane, London, SE6 1TP Tel:0208698 4955
Liberal Jewish Cemetery
The Lodge, Pound Lane, London, NW10 2HG Tel:0181 459 1635
Manor Park Cemetery Co.Ltd
Sebert Rd, Forest Gate, London, E7 0NP Tel:0181 534 1486
New Southgate Cemetery & Crematorium Ltd
98 Brunswick Park Rd, London, N11 1JJ Tel:0181 361 1713
London Borough of Newham Cemeteries
High St South, London, E6 6ET Tel:0181 472 9111
Plumstead Cemetery
Wickham Lane, London, SE2 0NS Tel:0181 854 0785
Putney Vale Cemetery & Crematorium
Kingston Rd, London, SW15 3SB Tel:0181 788 2113
South London Crematorium & Streatham Park Cemetery
Rowan Rd, London, SW16 5JG Tel:0181 764 2255
St. Marylebone Crematorium
East End Rd, Finchley, London, N2 0RZ Tel:0208343 2233
St. Pancras Cemetery (London Borough Of Camden)
High Rd, East Finchley, London, N2 9AG Tel:0181 883 1231
St. Patrick s Catholic Cemetery
Langthorne Rd, London, E11 4HL Tel:0181 539 2451
St.Mary s Catholic Cemetery
Harrow Rd, London, NW10 5NU Tel:0181 969 1145
Tottenham Park Cemetery
Montagu Rd, Edmonton, London, N18 2NF Tel:0181 807 1617
United Synagogue
Beaconsfield Rd, Willesden, London, NW10 2JE Tel:0208459 0394
Chingford Mount Cemetery
Old Church Rd, London, E4 6ST Tel:0181 524 5030
West End Chesed V Ameth Burial Society
3 Rowan Rd, London, SW16 5JF Tel:0181 764 1566
West Ham Cemetery
Cemetery Rd, London, E7 9DG Tel:0208534 1566
West London Synagogue
Hoop Lane, London, NW11 7NJ Tel:0208455 2569
West Norwood Cemetery & Crematorium
Norwood Rd, London, SE27 9AJ Tel:0207926 7900

Woodgrange Park Cemetery
Romford Rd, London, E7 8AF Tel:0181 472 3433
Woolwich Cemetery
Kings Highway, London, SE18 2BJ Tel:0181 854 0740

Merseyside
Anfield Crematorium
Priory Rd, Anfield, Liverpool, Merseyside, L4 2SL Tel:0151 263 3267
Southport Cemeteries & Crematoria
Southport Rd, Scarisbrick, Southport PR8 5JQ Tel:01704 533443
St.Helens Cemetery & Crematorium
Rainford Rd, Windle, St. Helens WA10 6DF Tel:01744 26567
Thornton Garden Of Rest
Lydiate Lane, Thornton, Liverpool L23 1TP Tel:0151 924 5143

Middlesex
Adath Yisroel Synagogue & Burial Society
Carterhatch Lane, Enfield, Middlesex, EN1 4BG Tel:0181 363 3384
Breakspear Crematorium
Breakspear Rd, Ruislip, Middlesex, HA4 7SJ Tel:01895 632843
Enfield Crematorium
Great Cambridge Rd, Enfield EN1 4DS Tel:0181 363 8324
Heston & Isleworth Borough Cemetry
190 Powder Mill Lane, Twickenham, TW2 6EJ Tel:0181 894 3830
South West Middlesex Crematorium
Hounslow Rd, Hanworth, Feltham TW13 5JH Tel:0208894 9001
Spelthorne Borough Council
Green Way, Sunbury-On-Thames TW16 6NW Tel:01932 780244

Norfolk
Colney Wood Memorial Park
Colney Hall, Watton Rd, Norwich NR4 7TY Tel:01603 811556
Mintlyn Crematorium
Lynn Rd, Bawsey, King s Lynn PE32 1HB Tel:01553 630533
Norwich & Norfolk Crematoria - St. Faiths & Earlham
75 Manor Rd, Horsham St. Faith, Norwich, Norfolk, NR10 3LF
Tel:01603 898264
Sprowston Cemetery
Church Lane, Sprowston, Norwich NR7 8AU Tel:01603 425354

East Yorkshire
East Riding Crematorium Ltd
Octon Cross Rd, Langtoft, Driffield, East Yorkshire YO25 3BL
Tel:01377 267604
East Yorkshire Council
Cemetery Lodge, Sewerby Rd, Bridlington, East Yorkshire YO16 7DS
Tel:01262 672138
Goole Cemetery
Hook Rd, Goole DN14 5LU Tel:01405 762725

North Yorkshire
Fulford New Cemetery
Cemetery Lodge, Fordlands Rd, Fulford, York YO19 4QG
Tel:01904 633151
Mowthorpe Garden of Rest
Southwood Farm, Terrington, York YO60 6QB Tel:01653 648459
Stonefall Cemetery & Crematoria
Wetherby Rd, Harrogate HG3 1DE Tel:01423 883523
Waltonwrays Cemetery
The Gatehouse, Carlton Rd, Skipton BD23 3BT Tel:01756 793168
York Cemetery
Gate House, Cemetery Rd, York YO10 5AF Tel:01904 610578
Northamptonshire
Counties Crematorium
Towcester Rd, Milton Malsor, Northampton NN4 9RN
Tel:01604 858280
Dallington Cemetery
Harlstone Rd, Dallington, Northampton NN5 Tel:01604 751589

Northumberland
Alnwick Cemetary
Cemetary Lodge, South Rd, Alnwick NE66 2PH Tel:01665 602598
Blyth Cemetery
Links Rd, Blyth NE24 3PJ Tel:01670 369623

Cowpen Cemetery
Cowpen Rd, Blyth NE24 5SZ Tel:01670 352107
Embleton Joint Burial Committee
Spitalford, Embleton, Alnwick NE66 3DW Tel:01665 576632
Haltwhistle & District Joint Burial Committee
Cemetery Lodge, Haltwhistle NE49 0LF Tel:01434 320266
Rothbury Cemetery
Cemetery Lodge, Whitton Rd , Rothbury, Morpeth, Northumberland,
NE65 7RX Tel:01669 620451

Nottinghamshire
Bramcote Crematorium
Coventry Lane, Beeston, Nottingham NG9 3GJ Tel:0115 922 1837
Mansfield & District Crematorium
Derby Rd, Mansfield NG18 5BJ Tel:01623 621811
Northern Cemetery
Hempshill Lane, Bulwell NG6 8PF Tel:0115 915 3245
Shirebrook Town Council
Common Lane, Shirebrook, Mansfield,NG20 8PA Tel:01623 742509
Southern Cemetery & Crematoria
Wilford Hill, West Bridgford, Nottingham, Nottinghamshire, NG2 7FE
Tel:0115 915 2340
Tithe Green Woodland Burial Ground
Salterford Lane, Calverton, Nottingham NG14 6NZ Tel:01623 882210

Oxfordshire
Oxford Crematorium Ltd
Bayswater Rd, Headington OX3 9RZ Tel:01865 351255

Shropshire
Bridgnorth Cemetery
Mill St, Bridgnorth WV15 5NG Tel:01746 762386
Emstrey Crematorium
London Rd, Shrewsbury SY2 6PS Tel:01743 359883
Hadley Cemetery
85 Hadley Park Rd, Hadley, Telford TF1 4PY Tel:01952 223418
Longden Road Cemetery
Longden Rd, Shrewsbury SY3 7HS Tel:01743 353046
Market Drayton Burial Committee
Cemetery Lodge, Cemetery Rd, Market Drayton, TF9 3BD
Tel:01630 652833
Oswestry Cemetery
Cemetery Lodge, Victoria Rd, Oswestry SY11 2HU Tel:01691 652013
Whitchurch Joint Cemetery Board
The Cemetery Lodge, Mile Bank Rd, Whitchurch SY13 4JY
Tel:01948 665477

Somerset
Burnham Area Burial Board
The Old Courthouse, Jaycroft Rd, Burnham-On-Sea TA8 1LE
Tel:01278 795111
Chard Burial Joint Committee
The Chapel, Combe St, Chard TA20 1JH Tel:01460 62170
Minehead Cemetery
Porlock Rd, Woodcombe, Minehead TA24 8RY Tel:01643 705243
Sedgemoor District Council Cemetery
Quantock Rd, Bridgwater, Somerset, TA6 7EJ Tel:01278 423993
Taunton Deane Cemeteries & Crematorium
Wellington New Rd, Taunton TA1 5NE Tel:01823 284811
Wells Burial Joint Committee
127 Portway, Wells, Somerset, BA5 1LY Tel:01749 672049

Yeovil Cemetery
Preston Rd, Yeovil, Somerset, BA21 3AG Tel:01935 423742
Yeovil Crematorium
Bunford Lane, Yeovil BA20 2EJ Tel:01935 476718

Lincolnshire
Cleethorpes Cemetery
Trinity Rd, Cleethorpes DN35 8 Tel:01472 691685
Grimsby Crematorium
Weelsby Avenue, Grimsby DN32 0BB Tel:01472 324869
Woodlands Crematorium
Brumby Wood Lane, Scunthorpe DN17 1SP Tel:01724 280289

South Yorkshire
Barnsley Crematorium & Cemetery
Doncaster Rd, Ardsley, Barnsley S71 5EH Tel:01226 206053
City Road Cemetery
City Rd, Sheffield, South Yorkshire, S2 1GD Tel:0114 239 6068
Dronfield Cemetery
42 Cemetery Rd, Dronfield S18 1XY Tel:01246 412373
Ecclesfield Cemetery
Priory Lane, Ecclesfield, Sheffield, S35 9XZ Tel:0114 256 0583
Eckington Cemetery
Sheffield Rd, Eckington, Sheffield S21 4FP Tel:01246 432197
Grenoside Crematorium
5 Skew Hill Lane, Grenoside, Sheffield S35 8RZ Tel:0114 245 3999
Handsworth Cemetery
51 Orgreave Lane, Handsworth, Sheffield S13 9NE Tel:0114 254 0832
Hatfield Cemetery
Cemetery Rd, Hatfield, Doncaster DN7 6LX Tel:01302 840242
Mexborough Cemetery
Cemetery Rd, Mexborough S64 9PN Tel:01709 585184
Rose Hill Crematorium
Cantley Lane, Doncaster DN4 6NE Tel:01302 535191
Rotherham Cemeteries & Crematorium
Ridgeway East, Herringthorpe, Rotherham S65 3NN Tel:01709 850344
Sheffield Cemeteries
City Rd, Sheffield, South Yorkshire, S2 1GD Tel:0114 253 0614
Stainforth Town Council Cemetery
Office, Church Rd, Stainforth, Doncaster DN7 5AA Tel:01302 845158

Staffordshire
Bretby Crematorium
Geary Lane, Bretby, Burton-On-Trent, Staffordshire, DE15 0QE
Tel:01283 221505
Cannock Cemetery
160 Pye Green Rd, Cannock WS11 2SJ Tel:01543 503176
Carmountside Crematorium
Leek Rd, Milton, Stoke-On-Trent ST2 7AB Tel:01782 235050
Leek Cemetery
Condlyffe Rd, Leek ST13 5PP Tel:01538 382616
Newcastle Cemetery
Lymewood Grove, Newcastle ST5 2EH Tel:01782 616379
Newcastle Crematorium
Chatterley Close, Bradwell, NewcastleST5 8LE Tel:01782 635498
Stafford Crematorium
Tixall Rd, Stafford ST18 0XZ Tel:01785 242594
Stapenhill Cemetery
38 Stapenhill Rd, Burton-On-Trent DE15 9AE Tel:01283 508572
Stilecop Cematary
Stilecop Rd, Rugeley WS15 1ND Tel:01889 577739
Uttoxeter Town Council, Cemetery
Lodge, Stafford Rd, Uttoxeter ST14 8DS Tel:01889 563374

Suffolk
Brinkley Woodland Cemetery
147 All Saints Rd, Newmarket CB8 8HH Tel:01638 600693
Bury St. Edmunds Cemetery
91 Kings Rd, Bury St. Edmunds IP33 3DT Tel:01284 754447
Hadleigh Town Council
Friars Rd, Hadleigh, Ipswich IP7 6DF Tel:01473 822034
Haverhill Cemetery
Withersfield Rd, Haverhill CB9 9HF Tel:01440 703810

Ipswich Cemetery & Crematorium
Cemetery Rd, Ipswich, Suffolk, IP4 2HN Tel:01473 252931
Leiston Cemetery
Waterloo Avenue, Leiston IP16 4EH Tel:01728 831043
West Suffolk Crematorium
Risby, Bury St. Edmunds IP28 6RR Tel:01284 755118

Surrey
American Cemetery
Cemetery Pales, Brookwood, Woking GU24 0BL Tel:01483 473237
Bandon Hill Cemetery
Plough Lane, Wallington SM6 8JQ Tel:0181 647 1024

Brookwood Cemetery
Cemetery Pales, Brookwood, Woking GU24 0BL Tel:01483 472222
Confederation of Burial Authorities
The Gate House, Kew Meadow Path, Richmond TW9 4EN Tel:0181 392 9487
Guildford Crematorium & Cemetaries
Broadwater, New Pond Rd, Goldaming GU7 3DB Tel:01483 444711
Kingston Cemetary & Crematorium
Bonner Hill Rd, Kingston Upon Thames, Surrey, KT1 3EZ
Tel:0208546 4462
London Road Cemetery
Figs Marsh, London Rd, Mitcham CR4 3 Tel:0208648 4115
Merton & Sutton Joint Cemetery
Garth Rd, Morden, Surrey, SM4 4LL Tel:0208337 4420
Mortlake Crematorium Board
Kew Meadow Path, Town Mead Rd, Richmond TW9 4EN Tel:0181 876 8056
Mount Cemetery
Weyside Rd, Guildford GU1 1HZ Tel:01483 561927
North East Surrey Crematorium
Lower Morden Lane, Morden, Surrey, SM4 4NU Tel:0181 337 4835
Randalls Park Crematorium
Randalls Rd, Leatherhead KT22 0AG Tel:01372 373813
Red Stone Cemetery
Philanthropic Rd, Redhill RH1 4DN Tel:01737 761592
Reigate Road Cemetery
Reigate Rd, Dorking, Surrey, RH4 1QF Tel:01306 883769
London Borough of Richmond Cemeteries
 Sheen Rd, Richmond, Surrey, TW10 5BJ Tel:0208876 4511
Surbiton Cemetery
Lower Marsh Lane, Kingston Upon Thames, Surrey, KT1 3BN
Tel:0208546 4463
Sutton & Cuddington Cemetery
Alcorn Close, Sutton Common Rd, Sutton SM3 9PX Tel:0181 644 9437
The Godalming Joint Burial Committee
New Cemetery Lodge, Ockford Ridge, Godalming GU7 2NP
Tel:01483 421559
Woking Crematorium
Hermitage Rd, Woking, Surrey, GU21 1TJ Tel:01483 472197

Tyne And Wear
Byker & Heaton Cemetery
18 Benton Rd, Heaton, Newcastle Upon Tyne NE7 7DS
Tel:0191 2662017
Gateshead East Cemetery
Cemetery Rd, Gateshead NE8 4HJ Tel:0191 4771819
Heworth Cemetery
Sunderland Rd, Felling, Gateshead NE10 0NT Tel:0191 4697851
Longbenton Cemetery
Longbenton, Newcastle Upon Tyne NE12 8EY Tel:0191 2661261
Whitley Bay Cemetery
Blyth Rd, Whitley Bay NE26 4NH Tel:0191 2533664
Earsdon Cemetery
Earsdon, Whitley Bay NE25 9LR Tel:0191 2529455
Preston Cemetery & Tynemouth Crematorium
Walton Avenue, North Shields NE29 9NJ Tel:0191 2005861
Saltwell Crematorium
Saltwell Rd South, Gateshead NE8 4TQ Tel:0191 4910553
St. Andrews Cemetery
1-2, Great North Rd, Jesmond, Newcastl -Upon Tyne ,NE2 3BU
Tel:0191 2810953
St. Johns & Elswick Cemetery
Elswick Rd, Newcastle Upon Tyne NE4 8DL Tel:0191 2734127
St. Nicholas Cemetery
Wingrove Avenue Back, Newcastle Upon Tyne, NE4 9AP
Tel:0191 2735112
Union Hall Cemetery
Union Hall Rd, Newcastle Upon Tyne NE15 7JS Tel:0191 2674398
West Road Cemetery
West Rd, Newcastle Upon Tyne NE5 2JL Tel:0191 2744737

Warwickshire
Mid-Warwickshire Crematorium & Cemeteries
Oakley Wood, Bishops Tachbrook, Leamington Spa CV33 9QP
Tel:01926 651418

Nuneaton Cemetery & Crematorium
Oaston Rd, Nuneaton, Warwickshire, CV11 6JZ Tel:01203 376120
Stratford-on-Avon Cemetery
Evesham Rd, Stratford-Upon-Avon CV37 9AA Tel:01789 292676

West Midlands
Birmingham Crematorium
389 Walsall Rd, Perry Barr, Birmingham B42 2LR Tel:0121 356 9476
Birmingham Hebrew Congregation Cemetery
The Ridgeway, Erdington, Birmingham B23 7TD Tel:0121 356 4615
Brandwood End Cemetery
Woodthorpe Rd, Kings Heath, Birmingham B14 6EQ Tel:0121 444 1328
Coventry Bereavement Services
The Cemeteries & Crematorium Office, Cannon Hill Rd, Canley,
Coventry, West Midlands, CV4 7DF Tel:01203 418055
Grave Care
5 Ennersdale Close, Coleshill, Birmingham B46 1HA Tel:01675 463385
Handsworth Cemetery
Oxhill Rd, Birmingham, West Midlands, B21 8JT Tel:0121 554 0096
Lodge Hill Cemetery & Cremetorium
Weoley Park Rd, Birmingham, B29 5AA Tel:0121 472 1575
Quinton Cemetery
Halesowen Rd, Halesowen B62 9AF Tel:0121 422 2023
Stourbridge Cemetry & Crematorium
South Rd, Stourbridge, West Midlands, DY8 3RQ Tel:01384 813985
Streetly Cemetery & Crematorium
Little Hardwick Rd, Aldridge, Walsall, West Midlands, WS9 0SG
Tel:0121 353 7228
Sutton Coldfield Cemetery
Rectory Rd, Sutton Coldfield B75 7RP Tel:0121 378 0224
Sutton Coldfield Cremetorium
Tamworth Rd, Four Oaks, Sutton Coldfield B75 6LG Tel:0121 308 3812
West Bromwich Crematorium
Forge Lane, West Bromwich B71 3SX Tel:0121 588 2160
Willenhall Lawn Cemetery
Bentley Lane, Willenhall WV12 4AE Tel:01902 368621
Witton Cemetery
Moor Lane Witton, Birmingham, B6 7AE Tel:0121 356 4363
Woodlands Cemetery
Birmingham Rd, Coleshill, Birmingham, B46 2ET Tel:01675 464835

West Sussex
Chichester Crematorium
Westhampnett Rd, Chichester PO19 4UH Tel:01243 787755
Midhurst Burial Authority
Carron Lane, Midhurst GU29 9LF Tel:01730 812758
Surrey & Sussex Crematorium
Balcombe Rd, Crawley, West Sussex, RH10 3NQ Tel:01293 888930
Worthing Crematorium & Cemeteries
Horsham Rd, Findon, Worthing BN14 0RG Tel:01903 872678

West Yorkshire
Brighouse Cemetery
132 Lightcliffe Rd, Brighouse HD6 2HY Tel:01484 715183
Cottingly Hall
Elland Rd, Leeds, West Yorkshire, LS11 0 Tel:0113 271 6101
Dewsbury Moor Crematorium
Heckmondwike Rd, Dewsbury WF13 3PL Tel:01924 325180
Exley Lane Cemetery
Exley Lane, Elland, West Yorkshire, HX5 0SW Tel:01422 372449
Killingbeck Cemetery
York Rd, Killingbeck, Leeds LS14 6AB Tel:0113 264 5247
Lawnswood Cemetery & Crematorium
Otley Rd, Adel, Leeds, West Yorkshire, LS16 6AH Tel:0113 267
3188
Leeds Jewish Workers Co-Op Society
717 Whitehall Rd, New Farnley, Leeds LS12 6JL Tel:0113 285 2521
Moorthorpe Cemetery
Barnsley Rd, Moorthorpe, Pontefract WF9 2BP Tel:01977 642433
Nab Wood Crematorium
Bingley Rd, Shipley BD18 4DB Tel:01274 584109
Oakworth Crematorium
Wide Lane, Oakworth, Keighley BD22 0RJ Tel:01535 603162

Park Wood Crematorium
Park Rd, Elland HX5 9HZ Tel:01422 372293
Pontefract Crematorium
Wakefield Rd, Pontefract WF8 4HA Tel:01977 723455
Rawdon Crematorium
Leeds Rd, Rawdon, Leeds LS19 6JP Tel:0113 250 2904
Scholemoor Cemetery & Crematorium
Necropolis Rd, Bradford, West Yorkshire, BD7 2PS Tel:01274 571313
Sowerby Bridge Cemetery
Sowerby New Rd, Sowerby Bridge HX6 1LQ Tel:01422 831193
United Hebrew Congregation Leeds, Jewish Cemetery
Gelderd Rd, Leeds, West Yorkshire, LS7 4BU Tel:0113 263 8684
Wakefield Crematorium
Standbridge Lane, Crigglestone, Wakefield WF4 3JA Tel:01924 303380
Wetherby Cemetery
Sexton House, Hallfield Lane, Wetherby LS22 6JQ Tel:01937 582451

Wiltshire
Box Cemetery
Bath Rd, Box, Corsham, Wiltshire, SN13 8AA Tel:01225 742476
Devizes & Roundway Joint Burial Committee
Cemetry Lodge, Rotherstone, Devizes SN10 2DE Tel:01380 722821
Salisbury Crematorium
Barrington Rd, Salisbury, Wiltshire, SP1 3JB Tel:01722 333632
Chippenham Cemetery
London Road, Chippenham, Wiltshire, SN15 3RD Tel:01249 652728
West Wiltshire Crematorium
Devizes Rd, Semington, Trowbridge BA14 7QH Tel:01380 871101

Wirral
Landican Cemetery
Arrowe Park Rd, Birkenhead, Wirral, CH49 5LW Tel:0151 677 2361

Worcestershire
Pershore Cemetery
Defford Rd, Pershore, Worcestershire, WR10 3BX Tel:01386 552043
Redith Crematorium & Abbey Cemetary
Bordesley Lane, Redditch, Worcestershire, B97 6RR Tel:01527 62174
Westall Park Woodland Burial
Holberrow Green, Redditch B96 6JY Tel:01386 792806
Worcester Crematorium
Astwood Rd, Tintern Avenue, Worcester WR3 8HA Tel:01905 22633

Wales

Aberystwyth Crematorium
Clarach Rd, Aberystwyth SY23 3DG Tel:01970 626942

Carmarthenshire
Carmarthen Cemetery
Elim Rd, Carmarthen SA31 1TX Tel:01267 234134

Conwy
Bron-y-Nant Crematorium
Dinerth Rd, Colwyn Bay, LL28 4YN Tel:01492 544677

Gwent
Ebbw Vale Cemetery
Waun-y-Pound Rd, Ebbw Vale, Gwent, NP23 6LE Tel:01495 302187
Llanelli District Cemetery
Swansea Rd, Llanelli SA15 3EX Tel:01554 77371
Grave Tending Service
14 Kelly Rd, Newport, Gwent, NP19 7RF Tel:01633 667510
Christchurch Cemetry
Christchurch, Newport, Gwent, NP18 1JJ Tel:01633 277566
Gwent Crematorium
Treherbert Rd, Croesyceliog, Cwmbran NP44 2BZ Tel:01633 482784

Flintshire
Mold Town Cemetery
Cemetery Lodge, Alexandra Rd, Mold CH7 1HJ Tel:01352 753820
Gwynedd
Bangor Crematorium
Llandygai Rd, Bangor, Gwynedd, LL57 4HP Tel:01248 370500

Mid Glamorgan
Mid Glamorgan Cemetery Section, Monks St, Aberdare, Mid
Glamorgan, CF44 7PA Tel:01685 885345
Coychurch Crematorium
Coychurch, Bridgend, Mid Glamorgan, CF35 6AB Tel:01656 656605
Ferndale Cemetery
Cemetery Lodge, Highfield, Ferndale CF43 4TD Tel:01443 730321
Llwydcoed Crematorium
Llwydcoed, Aberdare CF44 0DJ Tel:01685 874115
Maesteg Cemetery
Cemetery Rd, Maesteg CF34 0DN Tel:01656 735485
Penrhys Cemetery
Cemetery Lodge, Penrhys Rd, Tylorstown, Ferndale CF43 3PN
Tel:01443 730465
Trane Cemetery
Gilfach Rd, Tonyrefail, Porth CF39 8HL Tel:01443 670280
Treorchy Cemetery
The Lodge, Cemetery Rd, Treorchy CF42 6TB Tel:01443 772336
Ynysybwl Cemetery
Heol Y Plwyf, Ynysybwl, Pontypridd, CF37 3HU Tel:01443 790159

Pembrokeshire
Milford Haven Cemetery
The Cemetery, Milford Haven SA73 2RP Tel:01646 693324

South Glamorgan
Bereavement Services, Thornhill Rd, Cardiff CF14 9UA Tel:01222
623294
Cathays Cemetery
Fairoak Rd, Cathays, Cardiff CF24 4PY Tel:01222 750433
Western Cemetery
Cowbridge Rd West, Cardiff CF5 5TF Tel:01222 593231

West Glamorgan
Goytre Cemetery
Goytre Rd, Port Talbot SA13 2YN Tel:01639 883378
Margam Crematorium
Longland Lane, Margam, Port Talbot SA13 2NR Tel:01639 883570
Oystermouth Cemetery
Oystermouth Rd, Swansea SA1 3SW Tel:01792 366302

Wrexham
Coedpoeth Cemetery
Cemetery Rd, Coedpoeth, Wrexham, LL11 3SP Tel:01978 755617
Wrexham Cemeteries & Crematorium
Pentre Bychan, Wrexham, Clwyd, LL14 4EP Tel:01978 840068
Wrexham Cemetery
Ruabon Rd, Wrexham LL13 7NY Tel:01978 263159

Scotland

Aberdeenshire
Springbank Cemetery
Countesswells Rd, Springbank, Aberdeen AB15 7YH
Tel:01224 317323
St. Peter s Cemetery
King St, Aberdeen AB24 3BX Tel:01224 638490
Trinity Cemetery
Erroll St, Aberdeen AB24 5PP Tel:01224 633747

Angus
Barnhill Cemetery
27 Strathmore St, Broughty Ferry, Dundee DD5 2NY Tel:01382 477139
Dundee Crematorium
Macalpine Rd, Dundee, Angus, DD3 8 Tel:01382 825601
Park Grove Crematorium
Douglasmuir, Friocheim, Arbroath DD11 4UN Tel:01241 828959

Ayrshire
Ardrossan Cemetery
Sorbie Rd, Ardrossan KA22 8AQ Tel:01294 463133
Dreghorn Cemetery
Station Rd, Dreghorn, Irvine KA11 4AJ Tel:01294 211101
Hawkhill Cemetery
Kilwinning Rd, Saltcoats, Stevenston KA20 3DE Tel:01294 465241

Holmsford Bridge Crematorium
Dreghorn, Irvine, Ayrshire, KA11 4EF Tel:01294 214720
Kilwinning Cemetery
Bridgend, Kilwinning KA13 7LY Tel:01294 552102
Largs Cemetery
Greenock Rd, Largs KA30 8NG Tel:01475 673149
Maybole Cemetery
Crosshill Rd, Maybole, Ayrshire, KA19 7BN Tel:01655 882217
Newmilns Cemetery
Dalwhatswood Rd, Newmilns, Ayrshire, KA16 9LT Tel:01560 320191
Prestwick Cemetery
Shaw Rd, Prestwick, Ayrshire, KA9 2LP Tel:01292 477759
Stewarton Cemetery
Dalry Rd, Stewarton, Kilmarnock KA3 3DY Tel:01560 482888
West Kilbride Cemetery
Hunterston Rd, West Kilbride, Ayrshire, KA23 9EX Tel:01294 822818

Banffshire
Moray Crematorium
Clochan, Buckie, Banffshire, AB56 5HQ Tel:01542 850488

Clackmannanshire
Alva Cemetery
The Glebe, Alva, Clackmannanshire, FK12 5HR Tel:01259 760354
Sunnyside Cemetery
Sunnyside Rd, Alloa FK10 2AP Tel:01259 723575
Tillicoultry Cemetery
Dollar Rd, Tillicoultry FK13 6PF Tel:01259 750216

Dunbartonshire
Cardross Crematorium
Main Rd, Cardross, Dumbarton G82 5HD Tel:01389 841313
Dumbarton Cemetery
Stirling Rd, Dumbarton, Dunbartonshire, G82 2PF Tel:01389 762033
Vale Of Leven Cemetery
Overton Rd, Alexandria , Dunbartonshire, G83 0LJ Tel:01389 752266
West Dumbartonshire Crematorium
North Dalnottar, Clydebank G81 4SL Tel:01389 874318
West Dunbartonshire Crematorium
Roseberry Place, Clydebank G81 1TG Tel:01389 738709

Fife
Dunfermline Cemetery
Halbeath Rd, Dunfermline KY12 7RA Tel:01383 724899
Dunfermline Crematorium
Masterton Rd, Dunfermline KY11 8QR Tel:01383 724653
Kirkcaldy Crematorium
Dunnikier Way, Kirkcaldy, Fife, KY1 3PL Tel:01592 260277

Inverness-Shire
Inverness Crematorium
Kilvean Rd, Kilvean, Inverness IV3 8JN Tel:01463 717849

Isle Of Cumbrae
Millport Cemetery
Golf Rd, Millport, Isle Of Cumbrae, KA28 0HB Tel:01475 530442

Lanarkshire
Airbles Cemetery
Airbles Rd, Motherwell, Lanarkshire, ML1 3AW Tel:01698 263986
Bedlay Cemetery
Bedlay Walk, Moodiesburn, Glasgow G69 0QG Tel:01236 872446
Bothwellpark Cemetery
New Edinburgh Rd, Bellshill ML4 3HH Tel:01698 748146
Cadder Cemetery
Kirkintilloch Rd, Bishopbriggs, Glasgow G64 2QG
Tel:0141 772 1977
Cambusnethan Cemetery
Kirk Rd, Wishaw, Lanarkshire, ML2 8NP Tel:01698 384481
Campsie Cemetery
High Church of Scotland, Main St, Lennoxtown, Glasgow, Lanarkshire, G66 7DA Tel:01360 311127
Cardonald Cemetery
547 Mosspark Boulevard, Glasgow G52 1SB Tel:0141 882 1059

Daldowie Crematorium
Daldowie Estate, Uddingston, Glasgow G71 7RU Tel:0141 771 1004
Glasgow Crematorium
Western Necropolis, Tresta Rd, Glasgow G23 5AA Tel:0141 946 2895
Glebe Cemetery
Vicars Rd, Stonehouse, Larkhall ML9 3EB Tel:01698 793674
Glenduffhill Cemetery
278 Hallhill Rd, Glasgow, Lanarkshire, G33 4RU Tel:0141 771 2446
Kilsyth Parish Cemetery
Howe Rd, Kirklands, Glasgow G65 0LA Tel:01236 822144
Larkhall Cemetery
The Cemetery Lodge, Duke St, Larkhall ML9 2AL Tel:01698 883049
Old Aisle Cemetery
Old Aisle Rd, Kirkintilloch, Glasgow G66 3HH Tel:0141 776 2330
St. Conval s Cemetery
Glasgow Rd, Barrhead, Glasgow G78 1TH Tel:0141 881 1058
St. Patrick s Cemetery
Kings Drive, New Stevenston, Motherwell ML1 4HY Tel:01698 732938
St. Peters Cemetery
1900 London Rd, Glasgow G32 8RD Tel:0141 778 1183
The Necropolis
50 Cathedral Square, Glasgow G4 0UZ Tel:0141 552 3145

Midlothian
Dean Cemetery
Dean Path, Edinburgh EH4 3AT Tel:0131 332 1496
Edinburgh Crematorium Ltd
3 Walker St, Edinburgh EH3 7JY Tel:0131 225 7227
Seafield Cemetery & Crematorium
Seafield Rd, Edinburgh EH6 7LQ Tel:0131 554 3496
Warriston Crematorium
36 Warriston Rd, Edinburgh EH7 4HW Tel:0131 552 3020

Perthshire
Perth Crematorium
Crieff Rd, Perth, Perthshire, PH1 2PE Tel:01738 625068
Hawkhead Cemetery
133 Hawkhead Rd, Paisley PA2 7BE Tel:0141 889 3472

Renfrewshire
Paisley Cemetery Co.Ltd
46 Broomlands St, Paisley PA1 2NP Tel:0141 889 2260

Stirlingshire
Larbert Cemetery
25 Muirhead Rd, Larbert, Stirlingshire, FK5 4HZ Tel:01324 557867

Northern Ireland

County Antrim
Ballymena Cemetery
Cushendall Rd, Ballymena BT43 6QE Tel:028 256656026
Ballymoney Cemetery
44 Knock Rd, Ballymoney BT53 6LX Tel:028 27666364
Blaris New Cemetery
25 Blaris Rd, Lisburn, County Antrim, BT27 5RA Tel:028 92607143
Carnmoney Cemetery
10 Prince Charles Way, Newtownabbey BT36 7LG Tel:029 90832428
City Cemetery
511 Falls Rd, Belfast BT12 6DE Tel:028 90323112
City of Belfast Crematorium
Roselawn Cemetery
Ballygowan Rd, Crossnacreevy, Belfast BT5 7TZ Tel:028 90448342
Greenland Cemetery
Upper Cairncastle Rd, Larne BT40 2EG Tel:01574 272543
Milltown Cemetery Office
546 Falls Rd, Belfast, County Antrim, BT12 6EQ Tel:028 90613972
Roselawn Cemetery
127 Ballygowan Rd, Crossnacreevy, Belfast BT5 7TZ Tel:028 90448288

County Armagh
Kernan Cemetery
Kernan Hill Rd, Portadown, Craigavon BT63 5YB Tel:028 38339059
Lurgan Cemetery
57 Tandragee Rd, Lurgan, Craigavon BT66 8TL Tel:028 38342853

County Down
Ballyvestry Cemetery
6 Edgewater Millisle, Newtownards BT23 5 Tel:028 91882657
Banbridge Public Cemetery
Newry Rd, Banbridge, County Down, BT32 3NB Tel:028 406 62623
Bangor Cemetery
62 Newtownards Rd, Bangor BT20 4DN Tel:028 91271909
Clandeboye Cemetery
300 Old Belfast Rd, Bangor BT19 1RH Tel:028 91853246
Comber Cemetery
31 Newtownards Rd, Comber, Newtownards BT23 5AZ Tel:028 91872529
Struell Cemetery
Old Course Rd, Downpatrick BT30 8AQ Tel:028 446613086
Lough Inch Cemetery
Riverside Rd, Ballynahinch BT24 8JB Tel:028 97562987
Kirkistown Cemetary
Main Rd, Portavogie, Newtownards, County Down, BT22 1EL Tel:028 4271773

Movilla Cemetary
Movilla Rd, Newtownards BT23 8EY Tel:028 91812276
Redburn Cemetery
Old Holywood Rd, Holywood BT18 9QH Tel:028 90425547
Whitechurch Cemetary
19 Dunover Rd, Newtownards, County Down, BT22 2LE Tel:028 9158659

County Londonderry
Altnagelvin Cemetery
Church Brae, Altnagelvin, Londonderry BT47 3QG Tel:028 713 343351
City Cemetery
Lone Moor Rd, Londonderry BT48 9LA Tel:028 71362615

County Tyrone
Greenhill Cemetery
Mountjoy Rd, Omagh, County Tyrone, BT79 7BL Tel: 028 82244918
Westland Road Cemetery
Westland Rd, Cookstown, BT80 8BX Tel:028 86766087

English Heritage ~ *Services to Genealogists*

Keynon Peel Hall, Little Sutton, 1881
' Crown Copyright. National Monuments Record
From the National Monuments Record,
the public archive of English Heritage

What does English Heritage do?

Our work falls into three main categories: identifying buildings of historical interest and ancient monuments for protection; assisting their owners and other bodies with conservation responsibilities to secure the future of England s historic environment; and helping the public to appreciate, understand and enjoy their heritage.

In addition, we are responsible for the management and presentation of over 400 historic properties, monuments and war memorials in the nation s care including Stonehenge, Dover Castle, Tintagel Castle, Cornwall and Osborne House on the Isle of Wight.

We are constantly expanding our knowledge of the past through excavations and other research projects. But perhaps the most significant service we have for the genealogist is our extraordinary public archive, the National Monuments Record.

The National Monuments Record includes information on just about every town and village in the country. This includes historic photography, detailed records of individual buildings including descriptions of 360,000 listed buildings, and aerial photographs covering all of England. Between them you can use our archives to build up a picture of the places your ancestors come from: if you know the name or details of an individual building related to a family member, ask us if we hold photographs or other records about that building. Alternatively ask us what aerial photographs we hold of a place of interest in the 1940s, 1950s, or 1960s.

You can search this treasure trove of information for free: simply write to us at the address below or fill in an enquiry form on our web site at:

http://www.english-heritage.org.uk/knowledge/National Monuments Record/services
E-mail:
National Monuments Recordinfo@english-heritage.org.uk
and ask for an information pack on our services. If you already have an enquiry in mind give as much detail as possible about the address and location of your building or place of interest. Our web site gives you more detailed information on our enquiry services and collections. If we find old photographs, drawings or records for you charges are made for photocopying and photographic prints, but the initial search is free subject to limitations on the complexity of your query.

If you are in London visiting the Family Records Centre or other archives why not make some time to pop into our small London Search Room at 55 Blandford Street W1H 3AF. The Search Room holds an exciting collection of photographic images of the buildings of London. Or arrange to visit the National Monuments Record Centre, our Swindon headquarters. The National Monuments Record also runs a programme of workshops and seminars aimed at showing groups how to use its materials for local history.

With all that we have to offer, a lover of the past may want to find out more about membership of English Heritage and enjoy free entry to its magnificent collection of properties, many of them containing priceless collections of paintings and other objects. Who knows, one of your forebears may have lived or worked in one.

Contact numbers

National Monuments Record Enquiry & Research Service
National Monuments Record Centre
Kemble Drive, Swindon SN2 2GZ
Telephone: 01793 414600
Fax: 01793 414606
e-mail: National Monuments Recordinfo@ english-heritage.org.uk National Monuments Recordinfo@english-heritage.org.uk
Open Tuesday to Friday, 9.30am to 5pm.

Our London Search Room in Blandford Street is open Tuesday to Friday 10am to 5pm.

Enquiries about English Heritage s other work:
English Heritage Customer Services Tel: 01793 414910 or visit

http://www.english-heritage.org.uk

Aldborough Roman Town
Main Street, Boroughbridge, North Yorks. YO5 9EF
Ashby De La Zouch Castle
South Street, Ashby De La Zouch, Leics. LE6 5PR
Audley End House
Saffron Walden, Essex, CB11 4JF
Aydon Castle
Northumberland, NE45 5PJ
Barnard Castle
Castle House, Barnard Castle, Durham, DL12 9AT
Battle Abbey
Battle, East Sussex, TN33 0AD
Bayham Abbey
Bayham, Lamberhurst, Kent, TN8 8DE
Beeston Castle
Beeston, Tarporley, Cheshire, CW6 9TX
Belsay Hall
Belsay, Near Ponteland, Northumberland, NE20 0DX
Berney Arms Mill
8 Manor Road, Southtown, Great Yarmouth, Norfolk, NR31 0QA
Berry Pomeroy Castle
Totnes, Devon, TQ9 6NJ
Berwick Barracks
Berwick-upon-Tweed, Northumberland, TD15 1DF
Bishop Waltham Abbey
Bishop Waltham, Hampshire, SO32 1DH
Bolsover Castle
Castle Street, Bolsover, Derbyshire, S44 6PR
Boscobel House
Brewood, Bishops Wood, Shropshire, ST19 9AR
Brinkburn Priory
Long Framlington, Morpeth, Northumberland, NE65 8AR
Brodsworth Hall
Brodsworth, Near Doncaster, South Yorks. DN5 7XJ
Brougham Castle
Brougham, Penrith, Cumbria, CA10 2AA
Buildwas Abbey
Iron Bridge, Telford, Shropshire, TF8 7BW
Busmead Priory
Colmworth, Bedfordshire, MK44 2LD
Byland Abbey
Coxwold, North Yorks, YO6 4BD
Calshot Castle
Cashot, Hants, SO4 1BR
Carisbrooke Castles
Newport, Isle Of Wight, O32 6JY
Carlisle Castle
Carlisle, Cumbria, CA3 8UR
Castle Acre Priory
Stocks Green, Castle Acre, Kings Lynn, Norfolk, E32 2XD
Castle Rising Castle
Castle Rising, Kings Lynn, Norfolk, E31 6AH
Chapter House
East Cloisters, Westminster Abbey, London, SW1P 3PE
Chester Roman Fort
Chollerford, Hexham, Northumberland, NE46 4EP
Chiswick House
Burlington Lane, Chiswick, London, W4 2RP
Chysauster Ancient Village
Newmill, Penzance, Cornwall, TR20 8XA
Cleeve Abbey
Washford, Watchet, Somerset, TA23 0PS
Clifford Tower
Cliffords Street, York, North Yorkshire, YO1 1SA
Conisburgh Castle
The Ivanhoe Trust, The Priory, High St, Conisburgh, Doncaster
Corbridge Roman Site
Corbridge, Northumberland, NE45 5NT
Dartmouth Castle
Castle Road, Dartmouth, Devon, TQ6 0JN
Deal Castle
Victoria Road, Deal, Kent, CT14 7BA
Denny Abbey
Ely Road, Chittering, Cambridgeshire, CB5 9TQ
Dorchester Castle
Dorchester, Hants, O16 9QW
Dover Castle
Dover, Kent, CT16 1HU

Byland Abbey, N Yorks, 1994
' Crown Copyright. National Monuments RecordFrom the
National Monuments Record, the public archive of English Heritage

Down House
Luxted Road, Downe, Kent, BR6 7JT
Dunstanburgh Castle
14 Queen St., Alnwick, Northumberland, NE66 1RD
Dymchurch Martello Tower
High Street, Dymchurch, Kent, CT16 1HU
Eltham Palace
Courtyard, Eltham, London, SE9 5QE
Endennis Castle
Falmouth, Cornwall, TR11 4LP
Etal Castle
Etal Village, Berwick-upon-Tweed, Northumberland, TD12 4TN
Evensey Castle
Evensey, East Sussex, BN24 5LE
Everil Castle
Market Place, Castleton, Derbyshire, S33 8WQ
Everil Castle
Castleton, Hope Valley, Sheffield, SW33 5LE
Farleigh Hungerford Castle
Farleigh Hungerford, Near Bath, Somerset, BA3 6RS
Farnham Castle
Castle Hill, Farnham, Surrey, GU6 0AG
Finchale Priory
Brasside, Newton Hall, Co Durham, DH1 5SH
Fort Brockhurst
Gunners Way, Elson, Gosport, Hants, PO12 4DS
Fort Cumberland
Fort Cumberland Rd., Eastney, Portsmouth, PO4 9LD
Framlingham Castle
Framlingham, Suffolk, IP8 9BT
Furness Abbey
Barrow In Furness, Cumbria, LH13 0TJ
Gainsborough Hall
Arnell Road, Gainsborough, Lincolnshire, DN12 2RN
Goodrich Castle
Goodrich, Ross on Wye, Worcestershire, HR9 6HY
Grimes Graves
Lynford, Thetford, Norfolk, IP26 5DE
Hailes Abbey
Near Winchcombe, Cheltenham, Glos., GL54 5PB
Halesowen Abbey
Halesowen, Huntington, West Midlands
Hardwick Old Hall
Doe Lea, Near Chesterfield, Derbyshire, S44 5QJ
Haughmond Abbey
Upton Magna, Uffington, Shrewsbury, SY4 4RW
Helmsley Castle
Helmsley, North Yorkshire, YO6 5AB
Housesteads Roman Fort
Haydon Bridge, Hexham, Northumberland, NE46 6NN
Jewel Tower
Abingdon Street, London, SW1P 3JY

Servants, 1890
© Crown Copyright. National Monuments Record
From the National Monuments Record, the public
archive of English Heritage

Kenilworth Castle
Kenilworth, Warwickshire, CV8 INE
Kenwood House
Hampstead Lane, London, NW3 7JR
Kirby Hall
Deene, Corby, Northants, NN17 3EN
Kirby Muxloe Castle
South Quay, Great Yarmouth, Norfolk, NR30 2RQ
Kirkham Priory
Whitwell-on-the-Hill, North Yorks, YO6 7JS
Lanercost Priory
Brampton, Cumbria, CA8 2HQ
Launceston Castle
Castle Lodge, Launceston, Cornwall, L15 7DR
Lincoln Bishops Palace
Minster Yard, Lincoln, Lincs, LN2 1PU
Lindisfarne Priory
Holy Island, Northumberland, TD15 2RX
Longthorpe Tower
Thorpe Road, Longthorpe, Peterborough, PE1 1HA
Lullingstone Roman Villa
Lullingstone Lane, Eynsford, Kent, DA4 0JA
Lyddington Bede House
Blue Coat Lane, Liecestershire, LE15 9LZ
Maison Deu
Water Lane, Ospring, Kent, NE13 0DW
Marble Hill House
Richmond Road, Twickenham, Middlesex, TW1 2NL
Medieval Merchants House
58 French Street, Southampton, Hants, SO1 0AT
Middleham Castle
Middleham, Leyburn, North Yorkshire, DL8 4QG
Milton Chantry
Gravesend, Kent
Mortimers Cross Water
Leominster, Herefordshire, HR6 9PE
Mount Grace Priory
Saddle Bridge, Northallerton, North Yorks. DL6 3JG
Muchelney Abbey
Muchelney, Langport, Somerset, TA10 0DQ
Norham Castle
Berwick-upon-Tweed, Northumberland, TD15 2JY
Okehampton Castle
Castle Lodge, Okehampton, Devon, EX20 1JB
Old Merchants House
South Quay, Great Yarmouth, Norfolk, IP13 2RQ
Old Sarum Castle
Castle Roads, Salisbury, Wilts, SP1 3SD

Old Wardour Castle
Tisbury, Salisbury, Wilts, SP3 6RR
Orford Castle
Woodbridge, Suffolk, IP12 2ND
Osborne House
Royal Apartments, East Cowes, Isle of Wight, PO32 6JY
Pickering Castle
Pickering, North Yorkshire, YO18 7AX
Portland Castle
Castleton, Portland, Dorset, DT5 1AZ
Prudhoe Castle
Prudhoe, Northumberland, NE42 6NA
Rangers House
Chesterfield Walk, Blackheath, London, SE10 8QX
Restormel Castle
Lostwithiel, Cornwall, PL22 0BD
Richborough Castle
Richborough, Sandwich, Kent, CT13 9JW
Richmond Castle
Richmond, North Yorkshire, DL10 4QW
Rievaulx Abbey
Rievaulx, Near Helmsley, North Yorkshire, DL10 5LB
Roche Abbey
Maltby, Rotherham, South Yorkshire, S66 8NW
Rochester Castle
The Keep, Rochester-upon-Medway, Kent, ME1 1SW
Rushton Triangular Lodge
Rushton, Kettering, Northants, NN14 1RP
Saxtead Green Post Mill
The Mill House, Saxtead Green, Suffolk, IP13 9QQ
Scarborough Castle
Castle Road, Scarborough, North Yorks. YO11 1HY
Sherborne Old Castle
Castleton, Dorset, DT19 0SY
Sibsey Trader Mill
Sibsey, Boston, Lincolnshire, PE22 0SY
St. Augustines Abbey
Canterbury, Kent, CT1 1TF
St. Mawes Castle
St. Mawes, Cornwall, TR2 3AA
Stokesay Castle
Craven Arms, Shropshire, SY7 9AH
Stonehenge
Stone Circle, Wiltshire, SP4 7DE
Stott Park Bobbin Mill
Low Stott Park, Ulverston, Cumbria, LA12 8AR
Tilbury Fort
Fort Road, Tilbury, Sussex, RN18 7NR
Tintagel Castle
Tintagel, Cornwall, DL34 0AA
Totnes Castle
Castle Street, Totnes, Devon, TQ9 5NU
Tynemouth Castle
North Shields, Tyne and Wear, NE30 4BZ
Upnor Castle
High Street, Upnor, Rochester, Kent, ME2 4XG
Wall Roman site
Watling Street, Near Litchfield, Staffs. WS14 0AW
Walmer Castle
Kingsdown Road, Deal, Kent, CT14 7LJ
Warkworth Castle
Morpeth, Northumberland, NE66 0UJ
Wenlock Priory
Much Wenlock, Shropshire, TF13 6HS
Whitby Abbey
Whitby, North Yorkshire, YO22 4JT
Wingfield Manor
South Wingfield, Alfreton, Derbyshire, DE2 7NH
Witley Court
Grest Witley, Worcestershire, WR6 6JT
Wolvesey Castle
College Street, Winchester, Hants, SO23 8NB
Wrest Park
Silsoe, Luton, Bedfordshire, MK45 4HS
Wroxeter Roman Site
Wroxeter, Shropshire, SY5 6PH
Yarmouth Castle
Quay Street, Yarmouth, Isle Of Wight, PO41 0P

Barclodiad y Gawres Burial Chamber, Anglesey
Basingwerk Abbey Flintshire
Beaumaris Castle
Beaumaris, Anglesey, LL58 8AP Tel: 01248-810361
Beaupre Castle, near Cowbridge, Vale of Glamorgan
Blaenavon Ironworks
North St, Blaenavon, Blaenau Gwent, NP4 9RN Tel: 01495-792615
Bodowyr Burial Chamber, Anglesey
Brecon Gaer Roman Fort Powys
Bronllys Castle, Bronllys, Powys
Bryn Celli Ddu Burial Chamber, Anglesey
Bryntail Lead Mine Buildings, Llanidloes, Powys
Caer Gybi Roman Fortlet, Anglesey
Caer L b, Anglesey
Caer y T¶r Hillfort, Anglesey
Caerleon Roman Baths & Amphitheatre
High Street, Caerleon, Newport, NP18 1AE Tel: 01633-422518
Caernarfon Castle
Castle Ditch, Caernarfon LL55 2AY Tel: 01286-677617
Caerphilly Castle
Caerphilly, CF83 1JD, 029 20 883143
Caerwent Roman Town, Monmouthshire
Capel Garmon Burial Chamber
near Betws-y-Coed, Conwy
Capel Lligwy, Anglesey
Carew Cross, Carew, Pembrokeshire
Carreg Cennen Castle
Tir y Castell Farm, Trapp, near Llandeilo SA19 6TS Tel: 01558-822291
Carreg Coetan Arthur Burial Chamber
Newport, Pembrokeshire
Carswell Old House, near Tenby, Pembrokeshire
Castell Bryn Gwyn, Anglesey
Castell Coch
Tongwynlais, Cardiff, CF15 7JS Tel: 029-20-810101
Castell y Bere, near Tywyn, Gwynedd
Chepstow Bulwarks Camp, Monmouthshire
Chepstow Castle
Bridge Street, Chepstow NP16 5EZ Tel: 01291-624065
Cilgerran Castle
Castle Hse, Cilgerran, Cardigan SA43 2SF Tel: 01239-615007
Coity Castle, near Bridgend
Conwy Castle
Conwy, LL32 8AY Tel: 01492-592358
Criccieth Castle
Castle Street, Criccieth LL55 0DP Tel: 01766-522227
Cymer Abbey
c/o Vanner Farm, Llanelltyd, Dolgellau LL40 2HE Tel: 01341-422854
Denbigh Castle, Denbigh, Denbighshire
Denbigh Friary
Leicester s Church and St Hilary s Chapel, Denbighshire
Derwen Churchyard Cross, near Corwen, Denbighshire
Din Dryfol Burial Chamber, Anglesey
Din Lligwy Hut Group, Anglesey
Dinefwr Castle, Llandeilo, Carmarthenshire
Dolbadarn Castle, Llanberis, Gwynedd
Dolforwyn Castle, near Newtown, Powys
Dolwyddelan Castle
Bryn Tirion Farm, Dolwyddelan LL25 OEJ Tel: 01690 750366
Dryslwyn Castle, near Llandeilo, Carmarthenshire
Dyffryn Arddudwy Burial Chamber, Gwynedd
Dyfi Furnace, near Machynlleth, Ceredigion
Eliseg s Pillar, near Llangollen, Denbighshire
Ewenny Priory, near Bridgend
Ewloe Castle, Flintshire
Flint Castle, Flintshire
Grosmont Castle, Monmouthshire
Gwydir Uchaf Chapel, near Llanrwst, Conwy
Harlech Castle
Castle Square, Harlech LL46 2YH Tel: 01766-780552
Haverfordwest Priory, Pembrokeshire
Hen Gwrt Moated Site
Llantilio Crossenny, Monmouthshire
Holyhead Mountain Hut Group, Anglesey
Kidwelly Castle
5 Castle Road, Kidwelly SA17 5BQ Tel: 01554-890104
Lamphey Bishops Palace
Lamphey, Pembroke, SA71 5NT Tel: 01646-672224
Laugharne Castle
King Street, Laugharne SA33 4SA Tel: 01994-427906
Llanmelin Wood Hillfort, Monmouthshire

Llansteffan Castle, Carmarthenshire
Llanthony Priory, Monmouthshire
Llawhaden Castle, Pembrokeshire
Lligwy Burial Chamber, Anglesey
Loughor Castle,near Swansea
Maen Achwyfan Cross, near Whitford, Flintshire
Margam Stones Museum, Port Talbot
Monmouth Castle, Monmouthshire
Montgomery Castle, Powys
Neath Abbey, Neath Port Talbot
Newcastle Castle, Bridgend
Newport Castle, Newport city centre
Ogmore Castle and Stepping Stones, near Bridgend
Oxwich Castle
c/o Oxwich Castle Farm, Oxwich, Swansea, SA3 1NG
Tel: 01792-390359
Parc le Breos Burial Chamber, Gower Peninsula
Penarth Fawr Medieval House
near Criccieth, Ll?n Peninsula
Penmon Cross & Dovecote, Anglesey
Penmon Priory, Anglesey
Penrhos Feilw Standing Stones, Anglesey
Pentre Ifan Burial Chamber,
near Newport, Pembrokeshire
Plas Mawr Elizabethan Town House
High Street, Conwy, LL32 8DE Tel: 01492-580167
Pont Minllyn, near Dinas Mawddwy, Gwynedd
Presaddfed Burial Chamber, Anglesey
Raglan Castle
Raglan, Monmouthshire, NP15 2BT Tel: 01291-690228
Rhuddlan Castle
Castle Gate, Castle Street, Rhuddlan, Rhyl LL18 5AD
Rug Chapel/Llangar Old Church
c/o Coronation Cottage, Rug, nr Corwen, Denbighshire, LL21
9BT Tel: 01490-412025
Runston Chapel, near Chepstow, Monmouthshire
Segontium Roman Fort & Museum
Llanbeblig Rd, Caernarfon LL55 2LN Tel: 01286-675625
Skenfrith Castle, Monmouthshire
St Cybi s Well, Llangybi, Ll?n Peninsula
St Davids Bishops Palace
St Davids, Pembrokeshire, SA62 6PE Tel: 01437-720517
St Dogmaels Abbey, Ceredigion
St Lythan s Burial Chamber
near St Nicholas, Vale of Glamorgan
St Non s Chapel, St Davids, Pembrokeshire
St Quentin s Castle
Llanblethian, Cowbridge, Vale of Glamorgan
St Seiriol s Well, Penmon, Anglesey
St Winifrid s Chapel and Holy Well
Holywell, Flintshire
Strata Florida Abbey
Ystrad Meurig, Ceredigion, SY25 6BT Tel: 01974-831261
Swansea Castle, Swansea City Centre
Talley Abbey, Llandeilo, Carmarthenshire
Tinkinswood Burial Chamber
near St Nicholas, Vale of Glamorgan
Tintern Abbey
Tintern, Monmouthshire, NP16 6SE Tel: 01291 689251
Trefignath Burial Chamber, Anglesey
Tregwehelydd Standing Stone, Anglesey
Tretower Court & Castle
Tretower, Crickhowell, Powys, NP8 1RD Tel: 01874-730279
Ty Mawr Standing Stone, Anglesey
Ty Newydd Burial Chamber, Anglesey
Valle Crucis Abbey
Llangollen, Denbighshire, LL20 8DD Tel: 01978-860326
Weobley Castle
Weobley Castle Farm, Llanrhidian, Swansea, SA3 1HB
Tel: 01792-390012
White Castle
Llantilio Crossenny, nr Abergavenny NP7 8UD
Tel: 01600-780380
Wiston Castle, Pembrokeshire

About Historic Scotland *Judith Sandeman*

Historic Scotland is a government agency set up to care for the country s rich built heritage, which spans a period of over 5000 years. It is responsible for protecting ancient monuments, listing buildings and maintaining over 330 properties open to the public. The agency also gives grants to private owners for conservation and repair, and a team of experts carries out technical conservation and is at the forefront of research in this field. There are currently about 8000 scheduled monuments in Scotland, and each year about 380 new sites are added. Most of these lie on private land and Historic Scotland works with owners to help preserve these. Over 47,000 buildings are listed as being of special architectural or historic interest. These comprise dwelling houses (large and small), churches, city terraces, coalmines, factories, shipyards and the Forth Rail Bridge. Gardens and designed landscapes are also included. A few of the well-known properties open to the public are Edinburgh Castle, Stirling Castle, Fort George, Skara Brae and Iona Abbey. About 260 smaller sites, such as standing stones and cairns, are free to visitors. A diverse programme of events takes place at a number of properties throughout the year and free visits for schools offer an important educational opportunity.

For further information check out
www.historic-scotland.gov.uk or phone **0131 668 8600**.
You can also find out about becoming a Friend of Historic Scotland which allows you free entry to all properties as well as other benefits.

Aberdour Castle
Aberdour, Fife, KY3 0SL Tel: 01383-860519
Arbroath Abbey
Arbroath, Angus, DD11 1EG   Tel: 01241-878756
Argylls Lodging
Castle Wynd, Stirling, FK8 1EJ Tel: 01786-431319
Balvenie Castle
Dufftown, Keith, Bannfshire, AB55 4GH Tel: 01340-820121
Bishop s and Earl s Palaces
Palace Road, Kirkwall, Orkney, KW15 1PD Tel: 01856-871918
Blackhouse
42 Arnol, Barvas, Isle of Lewis, HS2 9DB Tel: 01851-710395
Blackness Castle
Linlithgow, Lothian, EH8 8ED Tel: 01506 834807
Bonawe Iron Furnace
Taynuilt, Argyll, PA35 1JQ Tel: 01866-822432
Bothwell Castle
Uddingston, Glasgow, G4 0QZ Tel: 01698-816894
Broch of Gurness
Evie, Orkney, KW17 2NH Tel: 01856-751414
Caerlaverock Castle
Glencaple, Dumfries, DG1 4RU Tel: 01387-770244
Cairnpapple Hill
c0Linlithgow Palace, Linlithgow EH49 7AL Tel: 01506-634622
Calanais Vistors Centre
Callanish, Isle of Lewis, HS2 9DY, 01851-621422
Cardoness Castle
Gatehouse of Fleet, DG7 2EH Tel: 01557-814427
Castle Campbell
Dollar, Clackmannanshire, FK14 7PP Tel: 01259-742408
Corgarff Castle
White House, Strathdon AB36 8YL Tel: 01975-651460
Craigmillar Castle
Craigmillar Castle Road, Edinburgh, EH16 4SY Tel: 0131-661-4445
Craignethan Castle
Castle Cottage, Lesmahagow ML11 9PL Tel: 01555-860364
Crichton Castle
Crichton, Pathhead, Midlothian Tel: 01875-320017
Crossraguel Abbey
by Maybole, Ayrshire, KA19 8HQ Tel: 01655-883113
Dallas Dhu Distillery
Mannachie Road, Forres IV36 2RR Tel: 01309-676548
Dirleton Castle
Dirleton, East Lothian, EH39 5ER Tel: 01620-850330
Doune Castle
Castle Road, Doune, FK16 6EA Tel: 01786-841742
Dryburgh Abbey
Dryburgh, St Boswells, Melrose TD6 0RQ Tel: 01835-822381
Duff House
Banff, AB45 3SX Tel: 01261-818181
Dumbarton Castle
Castle Road, Dumbarton, Dunbartonshire, G82 1JJ Tel: 01389 732167
Dundonald Castle
Dundonald, nr Kilmarnock, Ayrshire, KA2 Tel: 01563-851489
Dundrennan Abbey

Dundrennan, Kirkcudbrightshire DG6 4QH Tel: 01557-500262
Dunfermline Palace and Abbey
St Margaret Street, Dunfermline KY12 7PE Tel: 01383-739026
Dunstaffnage Castle
Dunbeg, By Oban, Argyll, PA37 1PZ Tel: 01631-562465
Edinburgh Castle
Castle Hill, Edinburgh, EH1 2NG Tel: 0131 225 9846
Edzell Castle
Edzell, By Brechin, Angus, DD9 7DA Tel: 01356-648631
Elcho Castle
Rhynd, by Perth, PH2 8QQ Tel: 01738-639998
Elgin Cathedral
Elgin, Morayshire, IV30 1HU Tel: 01343-547171
Fort George
By Ardersier, Inverness, IV1 2TD Tel: 01667-462777
Glasgow Cathedral
Cathedral Square, Glasgow, G4 0QZ Tel: 0141-552-6891
Glenluce Abbey
Glenluce, Newton Stewart DG8 0AF Tel: 01581-300541
Hermitage Castle
Newcastleton, Hawick, TD9 0LU Tel: 01387-376222
Huntingtower Castle
Huntingtower, Perth, PH1 3JR Tel: 01738 627231
Huntly Castle
Huntly, Aberdeenshire, AB54 4SH Tel: 01466 793191
Incholm Abbey
Incholm Island, Firth of Forth, (c/o GPO Aberdour), Fife, KY3 0UA Tel: 01383-823332
Inchmahome Priory
Port of Menteith, by Kippen, Stirlingshire, FK8 3RA Tel: 01877-385294
Jarlshof Prehistoric and Norse Settlement
Sumburgh, Shetland, ZE3 9JN Tel: 01950-460112
Jedburgh Abbey
4/5 Abbey Bridgend, Jedburgh TD8 6JQ Tel: 01835-863925
Kildrummy Castle
Kildrummy by Alford, Aberdeenshire Tel: 01975-571331
Kinnaird Head Castle Lighthouse
Stevenson Road, Fraserburgh, AB43 9DU Tel: 01346-511022
Linlithgow Palace
Linlithgow, Lothian, EH49 7AL Tel: 01506-842896
Lochleven Castle
Kinross, Tayside, KY13 7AR Tel: 07778-040483
MacLellans Castle
24 High Street, Kirkcudbright, DG6 4JD Tel: 01557-331856
Maes Howe
Stenness, near Stromness, Orkney, KW16 3HA Tel: 01856-761606
Meigle Museum
Dundee Road, Meigle, Perthshire, PH12 8SB Tel: 01828-640612
Melrose Abbey
Abbey Street, Melrose, TD6 9LG Tel: 01896-822562
New Abbey Cornmill
New Abbey, Dumfries, DG2 8BX Tel: 01387-850260
Newark Castle
Castle Road, Port Glasgow, PA14 5NH Tel: 01475-741858
Rothesay Castle
Rothesay, Isle of Bute, PA20 0DA Tel: 01700-502691
Seton Collegiate Church
Longniddry, East Lothian, EH32 0BG Tel: 01875-813334
Skara Brae
Sandwick, Orkney, KW16 3LR Tel: 01856-841815
Smailholm Tower
Smailholm, Kelso, TD5 7PQ   Tel: 01573-460365
Spynie Palace
near Elgin, Morayshire, IV30 5QG Tel: 01343-546358
St Andrews Castle
The Scores, St Andrews, Fife, KY16 9AR Tel: 01334-477196
St Andrews Cathedral
The Pends, St Andrews, Fife, KY16 9QL Tel: 01334-472563
Stirling Castle
Castle Wynd, Stirling, FK8 1EJ Tel: 01786-431316
Sweetheart Abbey
New Abbey, by Dumfries, DG2 8BU Tel: 01387-850397
Tantallon Castle
North Berwick, East Lothian, EH39 5PN Tel: 01620-892727
Threave Castle
Castle Douglas, Kirkcudbrightshire, DG7 1RX Tel: 0411-223101
Tolquhon Castle
Tarves, Aberdeenshire, AB4 0LP Tel: 01650-851286
Urquhart Castle
by Drumnadrochit, Inverness-shire, IV3 2XJ Tel: 01456-450551
Whithorn Priory
6 Bruce Street, Whithorn, Wigtownshire, DG8 8PY
Tel: 01988-500508

ROYAL ARMOURIES

Royal Armouries
Nicholas Boole

The Royal Armouries is Britain s oldest museum, and one of the oldest museums in the world.

It began life as the main royal and national arsenal in the Tower of London. Indeed the Royal Armouries has occupied buildings within the Tower for making and storing arms, armour and military equipment for as long as the Tower itself has been in existence.

Although distinguished foreign visitors had been allowed to visit the Tower to inspect the Armouries from the 15th century at least, at first they did so in a way a visiting statesman today might be taken to a inspect a guard of honour, to impress him with the country s military prowess. In the reign of Queen Elizabeth I less exalted foreign and domestic visitors were allowed to view the collections which then consisted almost entirely of the relatively recent arms and armour from the arsenal of King Henry VIII. To make room for the modern equipment required by a great Renaissance monarch Henry had cleared the Tower s stores of the collections of his medieval predecessors.

The Tower and its Armouries were not regularly opened to the paying public until King Charles II returned from exile in 1660. Visitors then came to see not only the Crown Jewels but also the Line of Kings , an exhibition of some of the museums grander armours mounted on horses made by sculptors as Grinling Gibbons and representing the good monarchs of England. They would also have seen the Spanish Armoury , containing weapons and interments of torture said to have been taken from the Invincible Armada of 1588. The Royal Armouries had become, in effect what it has remained ever since , the national museum of arms and armour and museum of the Tower of London.

During the great age of Empire-building that followed, the collections grew steadily. Until its abolition in 1855 in the wake of various disasters in the Crimean campaign, the Board of Ordnance, with its headquarters in the Tower, designed and tested prototypes and organised the production of huge quantities of regulation arms of many sorts for the British armed forces. Considerable quantities of this material remain in the museum s collections today, some being seen on the walls of the Hall of Steel in the Royal Armouries Museum in Leeds. Also, throughout this period captured weapons were sent to the Tower and displayed as proof of Britain s continuing military successes and these too were added to the museums collections.

Early in the 19th century the nature and purpose of the museum began to change radically. Displays were gradually altered from exhibitions of curiosities to historically accurate and logically organised presentations designed to improve the visitor by illuminating the past. As part of this change items began to be added to the collection in new ways, by gift and purchase and this increased rate of acquisition continues to this day.

In this way the collection has developed enormously, the old Tower material having been joined in the last 150 years by the world-wide comparative material which now makes the Royal Armouries one of the greatest collections of its type in the world.

From 1977 onward, under the direction of the then Master of the Armouries, the late Nick Norman, the Royal Armouries began to consider developing its displays both inside and outside of the Tower in order to increase public access to its growing and increasingly diverse collections. Ten years later the Royal Armouries signed a lease with Hampshire County Council and took possession of Fort Nelson, near Portsmouth, which it now runs as a museum for its large collection of artillery. This wonderful collection includes many astonishing pieces including the great Turkish bombard of 1464 presented by Turkey to Queen Victoria in 1868 and two sections of the infamous Iraqi supergun.

However the museum recognised that if it was to fulfil its desire of widening public access to its collections still further more had to be done. This particularly applied to those elements of the collection that had no direct bearing on the story of the development of the Tower of London.

In 1990, after two years of preliminary research and deliberation, the decision was taken to establish a third Royal Armouries museum in the north of England in which the bulk of its collection of world-wide arms and armour was to be housed. In turn this enabled the museum to redisplay those parts of its Tower focused collections within the tower itself to tell visitors of its own rich and varied history. The extensive research phase that followed resulted in Leeds being selected as the site for the new museum in the north.

The project in Leeds began with a basic question How does the museum want to display its collections, and what stories does the museum want to tell through it? The answer came in two

The Hall of Steel
Royal Armouries, Leeds
© The Royal Armouries

tors. The use of violence by humankind for supremacy or survival, or its sublimation into sport or play always has been, and probably always will be one of the main forces for historical change. This is the underlying theme of the Royal Armouries through its museum in Leeds.

So in a period of just a few years the Royal Armouries has evolved from a one site national museum into a three site museum serving a broad community. Fort Nelson opened fully to the public in 1995, Leeds was opened by HM the Queen in 1996 and her Majesty returned to reopen the refurbished galleries in the Tower of London completed in 1998. The Royal Armouries collection has increased enormously in the period now numbering more than 50,000 objects. Its library has also developed with over 95,00 items now fully accessible to the public.

parts. First it was agreed that the museum wanted to tell the story of the development and use of arms and armour around the world for war, sport, hunting, self-defence and fashion. Second it was decided that to do this successfully it needed to employ the best available communication and exhibition techniques — including film and audio visual aids, tableaux, hands-on opportunities using computers and real objects, and live demonstrations of craft and weapon handling skills.

These decisions were used to develop a brief for the architectural and design teams that led to the development of the museum that best suited the needs of the museum and its visitors.

The aim was to tell a series of linked but different stories each of which could be enjoyed on its own, or in any order. The result has been the creation of a free flow museum designed for the 21st century that uses the best of traditional and modern design techniques. Its displays are intended to entertain and stimulate a desire to learn, with the museum striving to create a multi-layered experience to cater for the many different interests and interest levels of its visi-

But has this expansion been beneficial? With around 2.7m visitors to its collections each year, a 500% increase in academic publications since 1996, a film making programme that has seen two series broadcast in the United States and UK, and a near doubling of the number of objects on public display the Royal Armouries is in a better position than it has ever been.

However, in recognising its responsibilities as a national museum with an international public the Royal Armouries is now concerned with improving the quality and extent of its work yet further. This means that it will focus on increasing its exposure to as broad a public as possible reaching beyond its physical boundaries to connect with those who are unable to visit its collections in person. To find out more about the work of the Royal Armouries whether in HM Tower of London, Leeds or Fort Nelson please contact Nicholas Boole on 0113 220 1948 or visit the museum s web site at www.armouries.org.uk

Museums

National Collections

British Red Cross Museum & Archives
9 Grosvenor Crescent, London, SW1X 7EJ
Tel: 020-7201-5153 Fax: 020-7235-0876
Email: enquiry@redcross.org.uk
Web: www.redcross.org.uk
**Commonwealth War Graves Commission -
Information Services**
2 Marlow Road, Maidenhead, Berkshire, SL6 7DX
Tel: 01628-634221 Fax: 01628-771208
Imperial War Museum
Lambeth Road, London, SE1 6HZ Tel: 020-7416-5348
Fax: 020-7416-5246 Email: books@iwm.org.uk
Web: www.iwm.org.uk
Isles of Scilly Museum
Church Street, St Mary s, Isles of Scilly, TR21 0JT
Tel: 01720-422337
Museums Association
42 Clerkenwell Close, London, EC1R 0PA
Tel: 020-7250-1789 Fax: 020-7250-1929
The National Coal Mining Museum for England
Caphouse Colliery, New Road, Overton, Wakefield, West
Yorkshire, WF4 4RH Tel: 01924-848806
Fax: 01924-840694 Email: info@ncm.org.uk
Web: www.ncm.org.uk
National Dragonfly Museum
Ashton Mill, Ashton, Peterborough, PE8 5LB
Tel: 01832-272427 Email: ndmashton@aol.com
Web: www.natdragonflymuseum.org.uk
National Gallery
St. Vincent House, 30 Orange Street, London, WC2H
7HH Tel: 020-7747-5950
National Maritime Museum
Romney Road, Greenwich, London, SE1O 9NF
Tel: 020-8858-4422 Fax: 020-8312-6632
Web: www.nmm.ac.uk
National Maritime Museum Memorial Index
National Maritime Museum, Greenwich, London, SE10
9NF Tel: 020-8858-4422 Fax: 020-8312-4422
Email: manuscripts@nmm.ac.uk Web: www.nmm.ac.uk
National Museum of Photography, Film & Television
Bradford, West Yorkshire, BD1 1NQ Tel: 01274-202030
Fax: 01274-723155 Web: http:www.nmpft.org.uk
National Portrait Gallery
2 St. Martins Place, London, WC2H 0HE
Tel: 020-7306-0055 Fax: 020-7206-0058
Web: www.npg.org.uk
National Railway Museum
Leeman Road, York, YO26 4XJ Tel: 01904-621261
Fax: 01904-611112 Email: nrm@nmsi.ac.uk
Web: www.nrm.org.uk
National Waterways Museum
Llanthony Warehouse, Gloucester Docks, Gloucester,
GL1 2EH Tel: 01452-318054 Fax: 01452-318066
Email: curatorial1@nwm.demon.co.uk
Web: www.nwm.demon.uk
North West Sound Archive
Old Steward s Office, Clitheroc Castle, Clitheroe,
Lancashire, BB7 1AZ Tel: 01200-427897
Fax: 01200-427897 Web: www.nw-soundarchive.co.uk
Royal Armouries (Leeds)
Armouries Drive, Leeds, West Yorkshire, LS10 1LT
Tel: 0990-106666
Royal Armouries (Tower of London)
HM Tower Of London, Tower Hill, London, EC3N 4AB
Tel: (020) 7480 -6358 Ext 30 Fax: (020) 7481 2922
The Science Museum
Exhibition Road, London, SW7 2DD
Tel: 0870-870-4868 Email: sciencemuseum@nms.ac.uk
Victoria & Albert Museum
Cromwell Road, South Kensington, London, SW7 2RL
Tel: 020-7942-2164 Fax: 020-7942-2162

Regional Museums Organisations

The South West Museums Council
Hestercombe House, Cheddon Fitzpaine, Taunton,
Somerset, TA2 8LQ Tel: 01823-259696
Fax: 01823-413114
Email: robinbourne@swmuseums.co.uk
West Midlands Regional Museums Council
Hanbury Road, Stoke Prior, Bromsgrove, Worcestershire,
B60 4AD Tel: 01527-872258 Fax: 01527-576960
Email: wmrmc@btinternet.com
Yorkshire & Humberside Museums Council
Farnley Hall Hall Lane, Leeds, West Yorkshire
LS12 5HA Tel: 0113-263-8909

London & Greater London

Alexander Fleming Laboratory Museum
St Mary s NHS Trust Archives, St Mary s Hospital, Praed
Street, Paddington, London, W2 1NY Tel: 020-7886-6528
Fax: 020-7886-6739
Bethlem Royal Hospital Archives & Museum
Monks Orchard Road, Beckenham, Kent, BR3 3BX
Fax: 020-8776-4045 Email: museum@bethlem.co.uk
Bethnal Green Museum of Childhood
Cambridge Heath Road, London, E2 9PA
Tel: 020-8980-2415 Fax: 020-8983-5225
Email: k.bones@vam.ac.uk
Black Cultural Archives
378 Coldharbour Lane, London, SW9 8LF
Tel: 020-7738-4591
The British Museum
Great Russell Street, London, WC1B 3DG
Tel: 020-7323-8768, 020-7323-8224 Fax: 020-7323-8118
Email: jwallace@thebritishmuseum.ac.uk
British Red Cross Museum & Archives
9 Grosvenor Crescent, London, SW1X 7EJ
Tel: 020-7201-5153 Fax: 020-7235-0876
Email: enquiry@redcross.org.uk Web: www.redcross.org.uk
Cabaret Mechanical Theatre
Unit 33 , The Market, Covent Garden, London, WC2E 8RE
Tel: 020-7379-7961
Cabinet War Rooms
Clive Steps, King Charles Street, London, SW1A 2AQ
Tel: 020-7930-6961 Fax: 020-7839-5897
Email: cwr@iwm.org.uk Web: www.iwm.org.uk
Church Farmhouse Museum
Greyhound Hill, Hendon, London, NW4 4JR
Tel: 0208-359-2666
Web: www.earl.org.uk/partners/barnet/churchf.htm
Clink Prison Museum
1 Clink Street, London, SE1 9DG Tel: 020-7403-6515
Cutty Sark
Site address: King William Walk, London SE10 9HT, Cutty
Sark Offices (Enquiries address), 2 Greenwich Church
Street, London, SE10 9EG Tel: 020-8858-2698
Fax: 020-8858-6976 Email: info@cuttysark.org.uk
Web: www.cuttysark.org.uk
The Design Museum
Butlers Wharf 28, Shad Thames, London, SE1 2YD
Tel: 020-7403-6933, 020-7940-8791 Fax: 020-7378-6540
Email: enquiries@designmuseum.org.uk
Web: www.designmuseum.org.uk
Dickens House Museum - London
48 Doughty Street, London, WC1N 2LF
Tel: 020-7405-2127 Email: Dhmuseum@rmplc.co.uk
Web: www.dickensmuseum.com
Doctor Johnson s House
17 Gough Square, London, EC4A 3DE Tel: 020-7353-3745
The Fan Museum
12 Crooms Hill, London, SE10 8ER Tel: 020-8293-18889
Email: admin@fan-museum.org
Web: www.fan-museum.org

Florence Nightingale Museum
2 Lambeth Palace Road, London, SE1 7EW
Tel: 020-7620-0374 Fax: 020-7928-1760
Email: curator@florence-nightingale.co.uk
Web: www.florence-nightingale.co.uk

Freud Museum
20 Maresfield Gardens, London, NW3 5SX
Tel: 0207-435-2002, 0207-435-5167 Fax: 0207-431-5452
Email: freud@gn.apc.org Web: www.freud.org.uk

Geffrye Museum
Kingsland Road, London, E2 8EA Tel: 020-7739-9893

Geological Museum
Cromwell Road, London, SW7 5BD Tel: 020-7938-8765

Golden Hinde
St. Mary Overie Dock, Cathedral St, London, SE1 9DE
Tel: 08700-118700

Grange Museum of Community History
The Grange, Neasden Lane, Neasden, London, NW10 1QB
Tel: 020-8452-8311

Guards Museum
Wellington Barracks, Birdcage Walk, London, SW1E 6HQ
Tel: 020-7414-3271/3428 Fax: 020-7414-3429

Gunnersbury Park Museum
Gunnersbury Park, Popes Lane, London, W3 8LQ
Tel: 020-8992-1612

Hackney Museum Service
Parkside Library, Victoria Park Road, London, E9 7JL
Tel: 020-8986-6914 Fax: 020-8985-7600
Email: hmuseum@hackney.gov.uk
Web: www.hackney.gov.uk/hackneymuseum

Handel House Trust Ltd
10 Stratford Place, London, W1N 9AE Tel: 020-7495-1685

Hogarth s House
Hogarth Lane, Chiswick, London, W4 2QN
Tel: 020-8994-6757

Horniman Museum
100 London Road, Forest Hill, London, SE23 3PQ
Tel: 020-8699-1872 Fax: 020-8291-5506
Email: enquiries@horniman.co.uk
Web: www.horniman.co.uk

Imperial War Museum
Lambeth Road, London, SE1 6HZ Tel: 020-7416-5348
Fax: 020-7416-5246 Email: books@iwm.org.uk
Web: www.iwm.org.uk

Island History Trust
St. Matthias Old Church, Woodstock Terrace, Poplar High
St, London, E14 0AE Tel: 020-7987-6041

Islington Museum
Foyer Gallery, Town Hall, Upper St, London, N1 2UD
Tel: 020-7354-9442

Iveagh Bequest
Kenwood House, Hampstead Lane, London, NW3 7JR
Tel: 020-8348-1286

Jewish Museum
80 East End Road, Finchley, London, N3 2SY
Tel: 020-8349-1143 Fax: 020-343-2162
Email: jml.finchley@lineone.net

Keats House Museum
Wentworth Place, Keats Grove, London, NW3 2RR
Tel: 020-7435-2062

Kensington Palace State Apartments
Kensington Palace, London, W8 4PX Tel: 020-7937-9561

Kingston Museum & Heritage Service
North Kingston Centre, Richmond Road, Kingston upon
Thames, Surrey, KT2 5PE Tel: 020-8547-6738
Fax: 020-8547-6747
Email: local.history@rbk.kingston.gov.uk
Web: www.kingston.gov.uk/museum/

Leighton House Museum & Art Gallery
12 Holland Park Road, London, W14 8LZ
Tel: 0207602-3316

Library of the Royal College of Surgeons of England
35-43 Lincoln s Inn Fields, London, WC2A 3PN
Tel: 020-7869-6520 Fax: 020-7405-4438
Email: library@rseng.ac.uk

Livesey Museumfor Children
682 Old Kent Road, London, SE15 1JF Tel: 020-7639-5604
Fax: 020-7277-5384 Email: livesey.museum@southwark.gov.uk

**L B of Barking & Dagenham Local History Studies -
Dagenham** Valence Library & Museum, Becontree Avenue,
Dagenham, Essex, RM8 3HT Tel: 020-8592-6537
Fax: 020-8227-5297 Email: fm019@viscount.org.uk
Web: www.earl.org.uk/partners/barking/index.html

L B of Newham Museum Service
Old Town Hall, 29 The Broadway, Stratford, London, E15
4BQ Tel: 020-8534-2274

L B of Waltham Forest - Vestry House Museum
Vestry Road, Walthamstow, London, E17 9NH
Tel: 020-8509-1917 Email: vestry.house@al.lbwf.gov.uk
Web: www.lbwf.gov.uk/vestry/vestry.htm

London Canal Museum
12-13 New Wharf Road, London, N1 9RT
Tel: 020-7713-0836 Fax: 020-7713-0836
Web: www.canalmuseum.org.uk

London Fire Brigade Museum
94a Southwark Bridge Road, London, SE1 0EG
Tel: 020-7587-2894 Fax: 020-7587-2878
Email: esther.mann@london-fire.gov.uk

London Gas Museum
Museum Closed - Exhibits in Storage, Twelvetrees Crescent,
London, E3 3JH Tel: 020-7538-4982

London Toy & Model Museum
21-23 Craven Hill, London, W2 3EN Tel: 020-7706-8000

London Transport Museum
Covent Garden Piazza, London, WC2E 7BB
Tel: 020-7379-6344 Fax: 020-7565-7250
Email: contact@ltmmuseum.co.uk Web: www.ltmuseum.co.uk

Mander & Mitchenson Theatre Collection
c/o Salvation Army Headquarters, PO Box 249, 101 Queen
Victoria Street, London, EC4P 4EP Tel: 020-7236-0182
Fax: 020-7236-0184

Markfield Beam Engine & Museum
Markfield Road, London, N15 4RB Tel: 020-8800-7061

Metropolitan Police Museum
c/o Room 1317, New Scotland Yard, Broadway, London,
SW1H 0BG Tel: 020-8305-2824, 020-8305-1676
Fax: 020-8293-6692

Museum of London
London Wall, London, EC2Y 5HN Fax: 020-7600-1058
Email: kstarling@museumoflondon.org.uk

Museum of the Order of St John
St John s Gate, St John s Lane, Clerkenwell, London, EC1M
4DA Tel: 020-7253-6644 Fax: 020-7336-0587
Web: www.sja.org.uk/history

Museum of the Royal Pharmaceutical Society
1 Lambeth High Street, London, SE1 7JN
Tel: 020-7735-9141-ext-354 Fax: 020-7793-0232
Email: museum@rpsgb.org.uk Web: www.rpsgb.org.uk

Museum of Women s Art
3rd Floor, 11 Northburgh Street, London, EC1V 0AN
Tel: 020-7251-4881

National Army Museum & Archives
Royal Hospital Road, London, SW3 4HT
Tel: 020-7730-0717 Fax: 020-7823-6573
Email: info@national-army-museum.ac.uk
Web: www.national-army-museum.ac.uk

National Gallery
St. Vincent House, 30 Orange Street, London, WC2H 7HH
Tel: 020-7747-5950

National Maritime Museum
Romney Road, Greenwich, London, SE1O 9NF
Tel: 020-8858-4422 Fax: 020-8312-6632
Web: www.nmm.ac.uk

National Maritime Museum Memorial Index
National Maritime Museum, Greenwich, London, SE10 9NF
Tel: 020-8858-4422 Fax: 020-8312-4422 Email: manu-
scripts@nmm.ac.uk Web: www.nmm.ac.uk

National Portrait Gallery
2 St. Martins Place, London, WC2H 0HE
Tel: 020-7306-0055 Fax: 020-7206-0058
Web: www.npg.org.uk

North Woolwich Old Station Musuem
Pier Road, North Woolwich, London, E16 2JJ
Tel: 020-7474-7244

The Old Operating Theatre Museum & Herb Garret
9a Street. Thomas s Street, London, SE1 9RY
Tel: 020-7955-4791 Fax: 020-7378-8383
Email: curator@thegarret.org.uk Web: www.thegarret.org.uk

Percival David Foundation of Chinese Art
University of London, School of Oriental & African Studies,
53 Gordon Square, London, WC1H 0PD
Tel: 020-7387-3909 Fax: 020-7383-5163

Petrie Museum of Egyptian Archaeology
University College London, Gower Street, London, WC1E
6BT Tel: 020-7679-2884 Fax: 020-7679-2886
Email: petrie.museum@ucl.ac.uk

Pitshanger Manor & Gallery
Walpole Park, Mattock Lane, Ealing, London, W5 5EQ
Tel: 020-8567-1227 Fax: 020-8567-0595
 Email: pitshanger@ealing.gov.uk

Polish Institute & Sikorski Museum
20 Princes Gate, London, SW7 1PT Tel: 020-7589-9249

Pollock s Toy Museum
1 Scala Street, London, W1P 1LT Tel: 020-7636-3452

Pump House Educational Museum
Lavender Pond & Nature Park, Lavender Road, Rotherhithe,
London, SE16 1DZ Tel: 020-7231-2976

Ragged School Museum Trust
46-50 Copperfield Road, London, E3 4RR
Tel: 020-8980-6405 Fax: 020-8983-3481
Web: www.ics-london.co.uk/rsm

Royal Armouries (Tower of London)
HM Tower Of London, Tower Hill, London, EC3N 4AB
Tel: 020-7480-6358

Royal Artillery Regimental Museum
Old Royal Military Academy, Red Lion Lane, Woolwich,
London, SE18 4DN Tel: 0181 781 5628 ext 3128

Royal London Hospital Archives & Museum
Royal London Hospital, Whitechapel, London, E1 1BB
Tel: 020-7377-7608 Fax: 020-7377-7413
Email: r.j.evans@mds.qmw.ac.uk

Royal Regiment of Fusiliers Museum
H M Tower of London, London, EC3N 4AB
Tel: 0171 488 5610

Sam Uriah Morris Society
136a Lower Clapton Rd, London E5 0QJ Tel: 020-8985-6449

The Science Museum
Exhibition Road, London, SW7 2DD Tel: 0870-870-4868
Email: sciencemuseum@nms.ac.uk

The Sherlock Holmes Museum
221b Baker Street, London, NW1 6XE Tel: 020-7935-8866
Fax: 020-738-1269 Email: sherlock@easynet.co.uk
Web: www.sherlock-holmes.co.uk

Sir John Soane s Museum
13 Lincolns Inn Fields, London, WC2A 3BP
Tel: 020-7405-2107 Fax: 020-7831-3957
Web: www.soane.org

St Bartholomew s Hospital Archives & Museum
West Smithfield, London, EC1A 7BE Tel: 020-7601-8152
Fax: 020-7606-4790

Valence House Museum
Becontree Avenue, Dagenham, Essex, RM8 3HS
Tel: 020-8227-5293 Fax: 020-8227-5293
Email: valencehousemuseum@hotmail.com

Veterinary Museum
Royal Vetinerary College, Royal College Street, London,
NW1 0TU Tel: 020-7468-5165/6 Fax: 020-7468-5162
Email: fhouston@rvc.ac.uk Web: www.rvc.ac.uk

Victoria & Albert Museum
Cromwell Road, South Kensington, London, SW7 2RL
Tel: 020-7942-2164 Fax: 020-7942-2162

Wallace Collection
Hertford House, Manchester Square, London, W1M 6BN
Tel: 020-7935-0687

Wellcome Trust Centre for the History of Medecine
183 Euston Road, London, NW1 2BE Tel: 020-7611-8888
Fax: 020-7611-8545 Email: infoserv@wellcome.ac.uk
Web: www.wellcome.ac.uk

Wellington Museum
Apsley House, 149 Piccadilly Hyde Park Corner, London,
W1V 9FA Tel: 020-7499-5676

Westminster Abbey Museum
Westminster Abbey, Deans Yard, London, SW1P 3PA
Tel: 020-7233-0019

Wimbledon Lawn Tennis Museum
Church Road, Wimbledon, London, SW19 5AE
Tel: 020-8946-6131

Wimbledon Museum of Local History
22 Ridgeway, London, SW19 4QN Tel: 020-8296-9914

England by Locality

Bath & North East Somerset

Roman Baths Museum
Abbey Churchyard, Bath, BA1 1LZ Tel: 01225-477773
Fax: 01225-477243

Bedfordshire

Bedford Museum
Castle Lane, Bedford MK40 3XD Tel: 01234-353323

Bedford Museum Bedfordshire Yeomanry
Castle Lane, Bedford, Bedfordshire, MK40 3XD
 Tel: 01234 353323 Fax: 01234 273401

Bedfordshire and Hertfordshire Regimental Museum
Luton Museum, Wardown Park, Luton
 LU2 7HA Tel: 01582 546719

Cecil Higgins Art Gallery
Castle Close, Castle Lane, Bedford MK40 3RP
Tel: 01234-211222 Fax: 01234-327149

Elstow Moot Hall
Elstow, Bedford, Bedfordshire, MK42 9XT
Tel: 01234-266889, 01234-228330 Fax: 01234-228531
Email: wilemans@deed.bedfordshire.gov.uk
Web: www.bcdfordshire.gov.uk

Luton Museum & Art Gallery
Wardown Park, Old Bedford Road, Luton LU2 7HA
Tel: 01582-546725 Fax: 01582-546763
Email: adeye@luton.gov.uk

Shuttleworth (Flying) Collection
Old Warden Aerodrome, Old Warden, Biggleswade, SG18
9ER Tel: 01767-627288 Fax: 01767-626229
Email: collcction@shuttleworth.org Web: www.shuttleworth.org

John Dony Field Centre
Hancock Drive, Bushmead, Luton, Bedfordshire , LU2 7SF
Tel: 01582-486983

Berkshire

Blake s Lock Museum
Gasworks Road, Reading RG1 3DS Tel: 0118-939-0918

Duke of Edinburgh s Royal Regiment (Berks & Wilts) Museum
The Wardrobe, 58 The Close, Salisbury, SP1 2EX
Tel: 01722-414536

Household Cavalry Museum
Combermere Barracks, Windsor, Berkshire
Tel: 01753-755112 Fax: 01753-755112

Museum of Reading
Town Hall, Blagave Street, Reading, Berkshire, RG1 1OH
Tel: 0118-939-9800 Web: www.readingmuseum.org.uk

R.E.M.E. Museum of Technology
Isaac Newton Road, Arborfield, Reading, Berkshire, RG2
9NJ Tel: 0118-976-3567 Fax: 0118-976-3563
Email: reme-museum@gtnet.gov.uk
Web: www.eldred.demon.co.uk/reme-museum/index.htm

Royal Berkshire Yeomanry Cavalry Museum
T A Centre, Bolton Road, Windsor, Berkshire, SL4 3JG
Tel: 01753-860600

Slough Museum
278-286 High Street, Slough SL1 1NB Tel: 01753-526422

West Berkshire Museum
The Wharf, Newbury, Berkshire, RG14 5AS
Tel: 01635-30511

Bristol

Ashton Court Visitor Centre
Ashton Court, Long Ashton, Bristol, BS41 8JN
Tel: 0117-963-9174

Blaise Castle House Museum
Henbury, Bristol, BS10 7QS Tel:)117-950-6789

Bristol City Museum & Art Gallery
Queens Road, Bristol, BS8 1RL Tel: 0117-922-3571
Fax: 0117-922-2047
Email: general_museums@bristol-city.gov.uk
Web: www.bristol-city.gov.uk/museums

Bristol Industrial Museum
Princes Wharf, Wapping Road, Bristol, BS1 4RN
Tel: 0117-925-1470

Bristol Maritime Heritage Centre
Wapping Wharf, Gasferry Road, Bristol, BS1 6TY
Tel: 0117-926-0680

Clevedon Story Heritage Centre
Waterloo House, 4 The Beach, Clevedon, Bristol, BS21 7QU
Tel: 01275-341196

Clifton Suspension Bridge Visitor Centre
Bridge House, Sion Place, Bristol, BS8 4AP
Tel: 0117-974-4664 Fax: 0117-974-5255
Email: visitinfo@clifton-suspension-bridge.org.uk
Web: www.clifton-suspension-bridge.org.uk

Exploratory Hands on Science Centre
Bristol Old Station, Temple Meads, Bristol, BS1 6QU
Tel: 0117-907-9000

Georgian House, Bristol
7 Great George Street, Bristol, BS1 5RR
Tel: 0117-921-1362

Harveys Wine Museum
12 Denmark Street, Bristol, BS1 5DQ Tel: 0117-927-5036
Fax: 0117-927-5001 Email: alun.cox@adweu.com
Web: www.j-harvey.co.uk

Red Lodge
Park Row, Bristol, BS1 5LJ Tel: 0117-921-1360
Web: www.bristol-city.gov.uk/museums

Buckinghamshire

Amersham Local History Museum
49 High Street, Amersham, Buckinghamshire, HP7 0DP
Tel: 01494-725754 Fax: 01494-725754

Bletchley Park Trust
The Mansion, Bletchley Park, Bletchley, Milton Keynes,
MK3 6EB Tel: 01908-640404 Fax: 01908-274381
Email: jcgallehawk@bletchleypark.org.uk
Web: www.bletchleypark.org.uk

The Blue Max
Wycombe Air Park, Booker, Marlow
SL7 3DP Tel: 01494-449810

Buckinghamshire County Museum
Church Street, Aylesbury, Buckinghamshire, HP20 2QP
Tel: 01296-331441 Fax: 01296-334884
Email: museums@buckscc.gov.uk

Chesham Town Museum Project
Chesham Library, Elgiva Lane, Chesham HP5 2JD
Tel: 01494-783183

Chiltern Open Air Museum
Newland Park, Gorelands Lane, Chalfont St. Giles
HP8 4AB Tel: 01494-871117 Fax: 01494-872774

Milton Keynes Museum
Stacey Hill Farm, Southern Way, Wolverton, Milton Keynes,
MK12 5EJ Tel: 01908-316222

Royal Army Education Corps Museum
HQ Beaconsfield Station, Wilton Park, Beaconsfield,
Buckinghamshire, HP9 2RP Tel: 01494 683232

Wycombe Museum
Priory Avenue, High Wycombe HP13 6PX
Tel: 01494-421895 Fax: 01494-421897
Email: enquiries@wycombemuseum.demon.co.uk
Web: www.wycombe.gov.uk/museum

Cambridgeshire

Cambridge Brass Rubbing
The Round Church, Bridge St, Cambridge, Cambridgeshire,
CB2 1UB Tel: 01223-871621

Cambridge Museum of Technology
Old Pumping Station, Cheddars Lane, Cambridge,
Cambridgeshire, CB5 8LD Tel: 01223-368650

Cambridgeshire Regimental Collection
Ely Museum, The Old Goal, Market Street, Ely,
Cambridgeshire, CB7 4LS Tel: 01353-666655

The Denny Farmland Museum
Denny Abbey, Ely Road, Waterbeach, Cambridge,
Cambridgeshire, CB5 9PQ Tel: 01223-860988
Fax: 01223-860988 Email: f.h.denny@tesco.net
Web: www.dennyfarmlandmuseum.org.uk

Duxford Displays Ltd
Duxford Airfield, Duxford, Cambridge, Cambridgeshire,
CB2 4QR Tel: 01223-836593

Ely Museum
The Old Gaol, Market Street, Ely CB7 4LS
Tel: 01353-666655

Fenland & West Norfolk Aviation Museum
Lynn Road, West Walton, Wisbech PE14 7
Tel: 01945-584440

Folk Museum
2 Castle Street, Cambridge CB3 0AQ Tel: 01223-355159

Imperial War Museum

Fighter Collection
Duxford Airfield, Duxford, Cambridge, CB2 4QR
Tel: 01223-834973, 01223-835000 Fax: 01223-836956

March & District Museum
March & District Museum Society, High Street, March,
Cambridgeshire, PE15 9JJ Tel: 01354-655300

Norris Library & Museum
The Broadway, St Ives, Cambridgeshire, PE27 5BX
Tel: 01480-497314 Email: norris.st-ives-tc@co-net.com

Octavia Hill Birthplace Museum Trust
1 South Brink Place, WisbechPE13 1JE Tel: 01945-476358

Peterborough Museum & Art Gallery
Priestgate, Peterborough, Cambridgeshire, PE1 1LF
Tel: 01733-343329 Fax: 01733-341928
Email: museums@peterborough.gov.uk

Prickwillow Drainage Engine Museum
Main Street, Prickwillow, Ely CB7 4UN Tel: 01353-688360

Ramsey Rural Museum
The Woodyard, Wood Lane, Ramsey, Huntingdon,
Cambridgeshire, PE17 1XD Tel: 01487-815715

Sedgwick Museum
University of Cambridge, Downing Street, Cambridge,
CB2 3EQ Tel: 01223-333456 Email: mgd2@esc.cam.ac.uk

Wisbech & Fenland Museum
Museum Square, Wisbech PE13 1ES Tel: 01945-583817
Fax: 01945-589050 Email: wisbechmuseum.@beeb.net

Duxford Aviation Society
Duxford Airfield, Duxford CB2 4QR Tel: 01223-835594

Cheshire

Catalyst
Gossage Building, Mersey Road, Widnes, Cheshire, WA8
0DF Tel: 0151-420-1121

Cheshire Military Museum (Cheshire Regiment)
The Castle, Chester, Cheshire, CH1 2DN
Tel: 01244-327617

Chester Heritage Centre - Closed August 2000
St. Michaels Church, Bridge Street, Chester CH1 1NQ

Ellesmere Port Boat Museum
South Pier Road, Ellesmere Port, Cheshire, CH65 4FW
Tel: 0151-355-5017 Fax: 0151-355-4079
Email: boatmuseum@easynet.co.uk

Grosvenor Museum
27 Grosvenor Street, Chester CH1 2DD Tel: 01244-402008
Fax: 01244-347587 Email: s.rogers@chestercc.gov.uk
Web: www.chestercc.gov.uk/heritage/museum

Lion Salt Works Trust
Ollershaw Lane, Marston, Northwich CW9 6ES
Tel: 01606-41823 Fax: 01606-41823
Email: afielding@lionsalt.demon.co.uk
Web: www.lionsaltworkstrust.co.uk

Macclesfield Museums
Heritage Centre, Roe Street, Macclesfield, Cheshire, SK11
6UT Tel: 01625-613210 Fax: 01625-617880
Email: postmaster@silk-macc.u-net.com

Nantwich Museum
Pillory Street, Nantwich, CW5 5BQ Tel: 01270-627104

Norton Priory Museum Trust Ltd
Tudor Road, Manor Park, Runcorn WA7 1SX
Tel: 01928-569895

On The Air
42 Bridge St Row, Chester CH1 1NN Tel: 01244-348468

Paradise Mill
Park Lane, Macclesfield SK11 6TJ Tel: 01625-618228

Warrington Museum & Art Gallery
Bold Street, Warrington WA1 1JG Tel: 01925-442392

West Park Museum
Prestbury Road, Macclesfield SK10 3BJ Tel: 01625-619831

Wirral Archives Service and Museum
Birkenhead Town Hall, Hamilton Street, Birkenhead, CH41
5BR Tel: 0151-666-4010 Fax: 0151-666-3965
Email: archives@wirral-libraries.net

Cleveland

Captain Cook & Staithes Heritage Centre
High Street, Staithes, Saltburn-by-the-Sea TS13 5BQ
Tel: 01947-841454

Captain Cook Birthplace Museum
Stewart Park, Marton, Middlesbrough TS7 8AT
Tel: 01642-311211

Dorman Musuem
Linthorpe Road, Middlesbrough TS5 6LA Tel: 01642-813781

Green Dragon Museum
Theatre Yard, High St, Stockton-on-Tees, Cleveland, TS18
1AT Tel: 01642-393938

Margrove Heritage Centre
Margrove Park, Boosbeck, Saltburn-by-the-Sea TS12 3BZ
Tel: 01287-610368 Fax: 01287-610368

North East Mills Group
Research into wind and water mills in NE England
Blackfriars, Monk Street, Newcastle upon Tyne, NE1 4XN
Tel: 0191-232-9279 Fax: 0191-230-1474
WWW: www.welcome.to/North.East.Mill.Group

Preston Hall Museum
Yarm Road, Stockton-On-Tees TS18 3RH
Tel: 01642-781184

Stockton on Tees Museums & Gallery Service
Gloucester House, Church Road Cleveland, TS18 1YB
Tel: 01642-393983 Fax: 01642-393983

Cornwall

Automobilia
The Old Mill, Terras Rd, St. Austell PL26 7RX
Tel: 01726-823092

Bodmin Museum
Mount Folly, Bodmin PL31 2DB Tel: 01208-77067
Fax: 01208-79268

Cable & Wireless Archive & Museum of Submarine Telegraphy
Eastern House,, Porthcurno, St. Levan, Penzance, Cornwall,
TR19 6 Tel: 01736-810478/810811 Fax: 01736-810640
Email: mary.godwin@plc.cwplc.com
WWW: www.porthcurno.org.uk

Charlestown Shipwreck & Heritage Centre
Quay Road, Charlestown, St. Austell, Cornwall, PL25 3NX
Tel: 01726-69897 Fax: 01726-68025

Duke of Cornwall s Light Infantry Museum
The Keep, Bodmin, Cornwall, PL31 1EG Tel: 01208-72810

Helston Folk Museum
Market Place, Helston, Cornwall, TR13 8TH
Tel: 01326-564027 Fax: 01326-569714
Email: enquiries@helstonmuseum.org.uk
WWW: www.helstonmuseum.org.uk

John Betjeman Centre
Southern Way, Wadebridge PL27 7BX Tel: 01208-812392

Lanreath Folk & Farm Museum
Lanreath, Nr Looe PL13 2NX Tel: 01503-220321

Lawrence House Museum
c/o Lawrence House, 9 Castle Street, Launceston, Cornwall,
PL15 8BA Tel: 01566-773277

Maritime Museum Penzance
19 Chapel Street, Penzance TR18 4AW Tel: 01736-368890

Merlin s Cave Crystal Mineral & Fossil Museum & Shop
Molesworth Street, Tintagel PL34 0BZ Tel: 01840-770023

Mevagissey Museum Society
Frazier Ho, The Quay, Mevagissey, St. Austell, Cornwall
PL26 6QU Tel: 01726-843568

National Maritime Museum (Falmouth Cornwall)
48 Arwenack Street, Falmouth TR11 3SA
Tel: 01326-313388

National Maritime Museum (Saltash Cornwall)
Cotehele Quay, Cotehele, Saltash PL12 6TA
Tel: 01579-350830

Penryn Museum
Town Hall, Higher Market Street, Penryn TR10 8LT
Tel: 01326-372158 Fax: 01326-373004

Potter s Museum of Curiosity
Jamaica Inn Courtyard, Bolventor, Launceston, Cornwall,
PL15 7TS Tel: 01566-86838 Fax: 01566-86838

Royal Cornwall Museum
River Street, Truro, Cornwall, TR1 2SJ Tel: 01872-272205

County Durham

Bowes Museum
Newgate, Barnard Castle DL12 8NP Tel: 01833-690606

Darlington Museum & Art Gallery - Closed
Collection dispersed throughout other agencies in
Darlington, Tubwell Row, Darlington DL1 1PD
Tel: 01325-463795

Darlington Railway Centre & Museum
North Road Station , Station Road, Darlington, DL3 6ST
Tel: 01325-460532

Darlington Railway Preservation Society
Station Road, Hopetown, Darlington DL3 6ST
Tel: 01325-483606

Discovery Centre
Grosvenor House, 29 Market Place, Bishop Auckland
DL14 7NP Tel: 01388-662666 Fax: 01388-661941
Email: west.durham@groundwork.org.uk

Durham Arts
Library and Museums Department, County Hall, Durham,
County Durham, DH1 STY Tel: 0191-383-3595

Durham Heritage Centre
St Mary le Bow, North Bailey, Durham DH1 5ET

Durham Light Infantry Museum
Aykley Heads, Durham, DH1 5TU Tel: 0191-384-2214
Fax: 0191-386-1770 Email: dli@durham.gov.uk

Durham University Library Archives & Special Collections
Palace Green Section, Palace Green, Durham, DH1 3RN
Tel: 0191-374-3032 Email: pg.library@durham.ac.uk

Fulling Mill Museum of Archaeology
The Banks, Durham, County Durham

Killhope Lead Mining Centre
Cowshill, Weardale, County Durham, DL13 1AR
Tel: 01388-537505 Fax: 01388-537617
Email: killhope@durham.gov.uk
WWW: www.durham.gov.uk/killhope/index.htm

North East Mills Group
Blackfriars, Monk Street, Newcastle upon Tyne, NE1 4XN
Tel: 0191-232-9279 Fax: 0191-230-1474
WWW: www.welcome.to/North.East.Mill.Group

Timothy Hackworth Victorian & Railway Museum
Shildon DL4 1PQ Tel: 01388-777999 Fax: 01388-777999

Weardale Museum
South View, 2 Front Street, Ireshopeburn, County Durham,
DL13 1EY Tel: 01388-537417

Cumbria

Aspects of Motoring Western Lakes Motor Museum
The Maltings, The Maltings, Brewery Lane, Cockermouth, Cumbria, CA13 9ND Tel: 01900-824448
Border Regiment & Kings Own Royal Border Regt Museum
Queen Mary s Tower, The Castle, Carlisle, Cumbria, CA3 8UR Tel: 01228-532774 Fax: 01228-521275
Email: rhq@kingsownborder.demon.co.uk
The Dock Museum
North Road, Barrow-In-Furness, Cumbria, LA14 2PW
Tel: 01229-894444 WWW: www.barrowbc.gov.uk
Dove Cottage & The Wordsworth Museum
Town End, Grasmere, Ambleside LA22 9SH
Tel: 015394-35544
The Guildhall Museum
Green Market, Carlisle CA3 8JE Tel: 01228-819925
Haig Colliery Mining Museum
Solway Road, Kells, Whitehaven CA28 9BG
Tel: 01946-599949 Fax: 01946-61896
WWW: www.haigpit.com
Keswick Museum & Art Gallery
Station Road, Keswick, Cumbria, CA12 4NF
Tel: 017687-73263 Fax: 017687-80390
Email: hazel.davison@allerdale.gov.uk
Lakeland Motor Museum
Holker Hall, Cark In Cartmel, Grange-Over-Sands
LA11 7PL Tel: 015395-58509
Laurel & Hardy Museum
4c Upper Brook Street, Ulverston, Cumbria, LA12 7BH
Tel: 01229-582292
Maryport Steamship Museum
Elizabeth Dock South Quay, Maryport CA15 8AB
Tel: 01900-815954
Penrith Museum
Middlegate, Penrith CA11 7PT Tel: 01768-212228
Fax: 01768-867466 Email: museum@eden.gov.uk
Roman Army Museum
Carvoran House, Greenhead, Carlisle CA6 7JB
Tel: 016977-47485
Ruskin Museum
Coniston Institute, Yewdale Road, Coniston LA21 8DU
Tel: 015394-41164 Fax: 015394-41132
WWW: www.coniston.org.uk
Senhouse Roman Museum
The Battery, Sea Brows, Maryport CA15 6JD
Tel: 01900-816168
Solway Aviation Museum
Carlisle Airport, Carlisle CA6 4NW Tel: 01228-573823
Tullie House Museum & Art Gallery
Castle Street, Carlisle CA3 8TP Tel: 01228-534781
Fax: 01228-810249
Ulverston Heritage Centre
Lower Brook Street, Ulverston LA12 7EE
Tel: 01229-580820 Fax: 01229-580820
Email: heritage@tower-house.demon.co.uk
WWW: www.rootsweb.com/~ukuhc/
William Creighton Mineral Museum & Gallery
2 Crown Street, Cockermouth CA13 0EJ
Tel: 01900-828301 Fax: 01900-828001
Windermere Steamboat Museum
Rayrigg Road, Windermere LA23 1BN Tel: 015394-45565
Fax: 015394-48769 WWW: www.steamboat.co.uk

Derbyshire

Chesterfield Museum & Art Gallery
No archive or library material held., St Mary s Gate,
Chesterfield S41 7TY Tel: 01246-345727
Fax: 01246-345720
Derby Industrial Museum
Silk Mill Lane, Derby DE1 3AR Tel: 01332-255308
Derby Museum & Art Gallery
The Strand, Derby DE1 1BS Tel: 01332-716659
Fax: 01332-716670 WWW: www.derby.gov.uk/museums
Derwent Valley Visitor Centre
Belper North Mill, Bridge Foot, Belper DE56 1YD
Tel: 01773-880474

Donington Grandprix Collection
Donington Park, Castle Donington DE74 2RP
Tel: 01332-811027
Donington Park Racing Ltd
Donington Park, Castle Donnington DE74 2RP
Tel: 01332-814697
Elvaston Castle Estate Museum
Elvaston Castle Country Park, Borrowash Road, Elvaston,
Derby DE72 3EP Tel: 01332-573799
Erewash Museum
The Museum, High Street, Ilkeston, DE7 5JA
Tel: 0115-907-1141 Fax: 0115-907-1121 Email: erewash-museum@free4all.co.uk WWW: www.erewash.gov.uk
Eyam Museum
Eyam Museum Ltd, Hawkhill Road, Hope Valley, Eyam,
S32 5QP Tel: 01433-631371 Fax: 01433-630777
WWW: www.cressbrook.co.uk/eyam/museum
Glossop Heritage Centre
Bank House, Henry Street, Glossop SK13 8BW
Tel: 01457-869176
High Peak Junction Workshop
High Peak Junction, Cronford, Matlock DE4 5HN
Tel: 01629-822831
High Peak Trail
Middleton Top,, Rise End, Middleton, Matlock, Derbyshire,
DE4 4LS Tel: 01629-823204
Midland Railway Centre
Butterley Station, Ripley DE5 3QZ Tel: 01773-570140
Peak District Mining Museum
Pavilion, South Parade, Matlock DE4 3NR
Tel: 01629-583834
Pickford s House Museum
41 Friar Gate, Derby DE1 1DA Tel: 01332-255363
Fax: 01332-255277
Regimental Museum of the 9th/12th Royal Lancers
Derby City Museum and Art Gallery, The Strand, Derby,
DE1 1BS Tel: 01332-716656 Fax: 01332-716670
Email: akelsall@derbymuseum.co.uk
WWW: www.derby.gov.uk/museums
National Stone Centre
Porter Lane, Wirksworth, Matlock DE4 4LS
Tel: 01629-824833

Devon

Century of Playtime
30 Winner Street, Paignton TQ3 3BJ Tel: 01803-553850
The Dartmouth Museum
The Butterwalk, Dartmouth TQ6 9PZ Tel: 01803-832923
Devon & Cornwall Constabulary Museum
Middlemoor, Exeter, Devon, EX2 7HQ Tel: 01392-203025
Devonshire & The Devonshire and Dorset Regimental Archives
Wyvern Barracks, Barrack Road, Exeter, Devon, EX2 6AE
Tel: 01392-492436 Fax: 01392-492469
Dunkeswell Memorial Museum
Dunkeswell Airfield, Dunkeswell Ind Est, Dunkeswell,
Honiton, Devon, EX14 0RA Tel: 01404-891943
Fairlynch Art Centre & Museum
27 Fore Street, Budleigh Salterton EX9 6NP
Tel: 01395-442666
Finch Foundary Museum of Rural Industry
Sticklepath, Okehampton EX20 2NW Tel: 01837-840046
Ilfracombe Museum
Wilder Road, Ilfracombe EX34 8AF Tel: 01271-863541
The Keep Military Museum
Bridport Road, Dorchester, Dorset, DT1 1RN
Tel: 01305-264066 Fax: 01305-250373
Email: keep.museum@talk21.com
WWW: www.keepmilitarymuseum.org
Museum of Barnstaple & Devon incorporating Royal Devon Yeomanry Museum
The Square, Barnstaple, Devon, EX32 8LN
Tel: 01271-346747 Fax: 01271-346407
Newton Abbot Town & Great Western Railway Museum
2A St. Pauls Road, Newton Abbot TQ12 2HP
Tel: 01626-201121

North Devon Maritime Museum
Odun House, Odun Road, Appledore, Bideford, Devon,
EX39 1PT Tel: 01237-422064 Fax: 01237-422064
WWW: www.devonmuseums.net/appledore
North Devon Museum Service
St.Anne s Chapel, Paternoster Row, Barnstaple, Devon,
EX32 8LN Tel: 01271-378709
Otterton Mill Centre
Otterton, Budleigh Salterton, Devon, EX9 7HG
Tel: 01395-568521
Plymouth City Museum
Drake Circus, Plymouth, Devon, PL4 8AJ
Tel: 01752-304774
Royal Albert Memorial Museum
Queen Street, Exeter, Devon, EX4 3RX Tel: 01392-265858
Sidmouth Museum
Hope Cottage, Church St, Sidmouth EX10 8LY
Tel: 01395-516139
Teignmouth Museum
29 French Street, Teignmouth, Devon, TQ14 8ST
Tel: 01626-777041
Allhallows Museum of Lace & Antiquities
High Street, Honiton EX14 1PG Tel: 01404-44966
Fax: 01404-46591 Email: dyateshoniton@msn.com
WWW: www.honitonlace.com
Newhall Visitor & Equestrian Centre
Newhall, Budlake, Exeter EX5 3LW Tel: 01392-462453
Park Pharmacy Trust
Thorn Park Lodge, Thorn Park , Mannamead, Plymouth,
Devon , PL3 4TF Tel: 01752-263501

Dorset

Bournemouth Aviation Museum
Hanger 600 South East Sector, Bournemouth International
Airport Hurn, Christchurch, Dorset, BH23 6SE
Tel: 01202-580858 Fax: 01202-580858
Bridport Harbour Museum
West Bay, Bridport, Dorset, DT6 4SA Tel: 01308-420997
Cavalcade of Costume
Lime Tree House, The Plocks, Blandford Forum, Dorset,
DT11 7AA Tel: 01258-453006
Christchurch Motor Museum
Matchams Lane, Hurn, Christchurch BH23 6AW
Tel: 01202-488100
Dinosaur Land
Coombe Street, Lyme Regis DT7 3PY Tel: 01297-443541
The Dinosaur Museum
Icen Way, Dorchester DT1 1EW Tel: 01305-269880
Fax: 01305-268885
Dorset County Museum and Library
66 High West Street, Dorchester DT1 1XA
Tel: 01305-262735 Fax: 01305-257180
Email: dorsetcountymuseum@dor-mus.demon.co.uk
The Keep Military Museum
Bridport Road, Dorchester DT1 1RN Tel: 01305-264066
Fax: 01305-250373 Email: keep.museum@talk21.com
WWW: www.keepmilitarymuseum.org
Lyme Regis Philpot Museum
Bridge Street, Lyme Regis DT7 3QA Tel: 01297-443370
Email: info@lymeregismuseum.co.uk
Nothe Fort
Barrack Road, Weymouth DT4 8UF Tel: 01305-787243
Portland Museum
Wakeham, Portland, Dorset, DT5 1HS Tel: 01305-821804
Priest s House Museum
23-27 High St. Wimborne BH21 1HR Tel: 01202-882533
Red House Museum & Gardens
Quay Rd, Christchurch BH23 1BU Tel: 01202-482860
Russell-Cotes Art Gallery & Museum
East Cliff, Bournemouth BH1 3AA Tel: 01202-451800
Shelley Rooms
Museum at: Shelley Park, Beechwood Ave, Bournemouth
BH5 1NE, Russell Cotes Art Gallery & Museum
(Correspondence address), (Reference Shelley Rooms), East Cliff,
Bournemouth, BH1 3AA Tel: 01202-451800 Fax: 01202-451851
Email: dedge@russell-cotes.demon.co.uk
WWW: www.russell-cotes.bournemouth.gov.uk

Sherborne Museum Association
Abbey Gate House, Church Avenue, Sherborne, Dorset, DT9
3BP Tel: 01935-812252
The Tank Museum
Bovington, Dorset, BH20 6JG Tel: 01929-405096
Fax: 01929-405360 Email: david@tankmuseum.co.uk
WWW: www.tankmuseum.co.uk
Wareham Town Museum
5 East Street, Wareham BH20 4NN Tel: 01929-553448
Waterfront Museum and Local Studies Centre
4 High Street, Poole BH15 1BW Tel: 01202-683138
Fax: 01202-660896 Email: museums@poole.gov.uk
WWW: www.poole.gov.uk
Weymouth & Portland Museum Service
The Esplanade, Weymouth DT4 8ED Tel: 01305-765206
Shaftesbury Abbey Museum & Garden
Park Walk, Shaftesbury SP7 8JR Tel: 01747-852910
Shaftesbury Town Museum
Gold Hill, Shaftesbury SP7 8JW Tel: 01747-852157

Dorset — West Dorset

West Dorset Museums Service
The Coach House, Grundy Lane, Bridport DT6 3RJ
Tel: 01308-458703 Fax: 01308-458704
Email: j.burrell@westdorset-dc.gov.uk

Essex

Barleylands Farm Museum & Visitors Centre
Barleylands Farm, Billericay CM11 2UD
Tel: 01268-282090
Battlesbridge Motorcycle Museum The
Muggeridge Farm, Maltings Road, Battlesbridge, Wickford,
SS11 7RF Tel: 01268-560866
Castle Point Transport Museum Society
105 Point Road, Canvey Island SS8 7TJ Tel: 01268-684272
East England Tank Museum
Oak Business Park, Wix Road, Beaumont, Clacton-On-Sea,
CO16 0AT Tel: 01255-871119
Englands Secret Nuclear Bunker
Visitor access via the A128. Correspondence, Kelvedon
Hall Lane, Kelvedon Common, Kelvedon Hatch, Nr
Brentwood CM15 0LB, 01277-364883, 01277-372562
Epping Forest District Museum
39-41 Sun Street, Waltham Abbey EN9 1EL
Tel: 01992-716882
Essex Police Museum
Police Headquarters, PO Box 2, Springfield, Chelmsford,
Essex, CM2 6DA Tel: 01245-491491 x50771
Fax: 01245-452456
Essex Regiment Museum
Oaklands Park, Moulsham Street, Chelmsford CM2 9AQ
Tel: 01245-615101 Fax: 01245-611250
Email: pompadour@chelmsfordbc.gov.uk
WWW: www.chelmsfordbc.gov.uk
Essex Secret Bunker
Crown Building, Shrublands Road, Mistley, Essex, CO11
1HS Tel: 01206-392271 (24hr info)
Harlow Museum
Passmores House, Third Avenue, Harlow CM18 6YL
Tel: 01279-454959
Hollytrees Museum
High Street, Colchester CO1 1DN Tel: 01206-282940
Leigh Heritage Centre & Museum
c/o 13a High Street, Leigh-On-Sea, Essex, SS9 2EN
Tel: 01702-470834 Email: palmtree@northdell.demon.co.uk
**LB of Barking & Dagenham Local History Studies -
Dagenham** Valence Library & Museum, Becontree Avenue,
Dagenham, Essex, RM8 3HT Tel: 020-8592-6537
Fax: 020-8227-5297 Email: fm019@viscount.org.uk
WWW: www.earl.org.uk/partners/barking/index.html
Maldon District Museum
47 Mill Road, Maldon CM9 5HX Tel: 01621-842688
Mark Hall Cycle Museum
Muskham Road, Harlow CM20 2LF Tel: 01279-439680
National Motorboat Museum
Wattyler Country Park, Pitsea Hall Lane, Pitsea, Basildon,
Essex, SS16 4UH Tel: 01268-550077 Fax: 01268-581903

Saffron Walden Museum
Museum Street, Saffron Walden CB10 1JL
Tel: 01799-510333 Fax: 01799-510333
Email: museum@uttlesford.gov.uk

Southend Central Museum
Victoria Avenue, Southend-On-Sea, Essex, SS2 6EW
Tel: 01702-434449 Fax: 01702-34980

The Cater Museum
74 High Street, Billericay, Essex, CM12 9BS
Tel: 01277-622023

Valence House Museum
Becontree Avenue, Dagenham RM8 3HS
Tel: 020-8227-5293 Fax: 020-8227-5293
Email: valencehousemuseum@hotmail.com

Chelmsford & Essex Museum
Oaklands Park, Moulsham St, Chelmsford CM2 9AQ
Tel: 01245-615100 Fax: 01245-611250
Email: oaklands@chelmsford.gov.uk

Gloucestershire

Chepstow Museum
Bridge Street, Chepstow, Monmouthshire, NP16 5EZ
Tel: 01291-625981 Fax: 01291-635005
Email: chepstowmuseum@monmouthshire.gov.uk

Dean Heritage Centre
Soudley, Cinderford, Forest of Dean GL14 2UB
Tel: 01594-822170 Fax: 01594-823711
Email: deanmus@btinternet.com

Gloucester City Museum & Art Gallery
Brunswick Road, Gloucester GL1 1HP Tel: 01452-524131

Gloucester Folk Museum
99-103 Westgate Street, Gloucester GL1 2PG
Tel: 01452-526467 Fax: 01452-330495
Email: ChristopherM@glos.city.gov.uk

Guild of Handicraft Trust The
Silk Mill, Sheep St, Chipping Campden GL55 6DS
Tel: 01386-841417

Holst Birthplace Museum
4 Clarence Road, Cheltenham GL52 2AY
Tel: 01242-524846 Fax: 01242-580182

The Jenner Museum
Church Lane, Berkeley GL13 9BN Tel: 01453-810631
Fax: 01453-811690

John Moore Countryside Museum
42 Church Street, Tewkesbury GL20 5SN Tel: 01684-297174

National Waterways Museum
Llanthony Warehouse, Gloucester Docks, Gloucester, GL1
2EH Tel: 01452-318054 Fax: 01452-318066
Email: curatorial1@nwm.demon.co.uk
WWW: www.nwm.demon.uk

Nature In Art
Wallsworth Hall, Tewkesbury Road, Twigworth, Gloucester,
Gloucestershire, GL2 9PG Tel: 01452-731422
Fax: 01452-730937 Email: ninart@globalnet.co.uk
WWW: www.nature-in-art.org.uk

Regiments Of Gloucestershire Museum
Gloucester Docks, Gloucester GL1 2HE Tel: 01452-522682

Robert Opie Collection
Albert Warehouse, The Docks, Gloucester, Gloucestershire,
GL1 2EH Tel: 01452-302309

Shambles Museum
20 Church Street, Newent GL18 1PP Tel: 01531-822144

Soldiers of Gloucester Museum
Gloucester Docks, Commercial Road, Gloucester, GL1 2EH
Tel: 01452-522682

The Great Western Railway Museum (Coleford)
The Old Railway Station, Railway Drive, Coleford,
Gloucestershire, GL16 8RH Tel: 01594-833569,
01954-832032 Fax: 01594-832032

Gloucestershire — South Gloucestershire

Frenchay Tuckett Society & Local History Museum
247 Frenchay Park Road, Frenchay, South Gloucestershire,
BS16 1LG Tel: 0117-9569324
Email: raybulmer@compuserve.com
WWW: www.ourworld.compuserve.com/homepages/raybulmer

Hampshire

Airborne Forces Museum
Browning Barracks, Aldershot, Hampshire, GU11 2BU
Tel: 01252-349619 Fax: 01252-349203

Aldershot Military Historical Trust
Evelyn Woods Road, Aldershot, Hampshire, GU11 2LG
Tel: 01252-314598 Fax: 01252-342942

Aldershot Military Museum
Queens Avenue, Aldershot GU11 2LG Tel: 01252-314598
Fax: 01252-34294 Email: musim@hants.gov.uk

Andover Museum & Iron Age Museum
6 Church Close, Andover SP10 1DP Tel: 01264-366283
Fax: 01264-339152 Email: andover.museum@virgin.net
or musmda@hants.gov.uk WWW: www.hants.gov.uk/andoverm

Army Medical Services Museum
Keogh Barracks, Ash Vale, nr Aldershot, Hampshire, GU12
5RQ Tel: 01252-340212 Fax: 01252-340332
Email: museum@keogh72.freeserve.co.uk

Army Physical Training Corps Museum
ASPT, Fox Line, Queen s Avenue, Aldershot, Hampshire,
GU11 2LB Tel: 01252 347168 Fax: 01252 340785

The Bear Museum
38 Dragon Street, Petersfield GU31 4JJ Tel: 01730-265108
Email: judy@bearmuseum.freeserve.co.uk
WWW: www.bearmuseum.co.uk

Bishops Waltham Museum Trust
8 Folly Field, Bishop s Waltham, Southampton, SO32 1EB
Tel: 01489-894970

Eastleigh Museum
25 High Street, Eastleigh SO50 5LF Tel: 02380-643026
Email: musmst@hants.gov.uk
WWW: www.hants.gov.uk/museum/eastlmus/index.html

Eling Tide Mill Trust Ltd
The Tollbridge, Eling Hill, Totton, Southampton, Hampshire,
SO40 9HF Tel: 023-8086-9575

Gosport Museum
Walpole Road, Gosport PO12 1NS Tel: 023-9258-8035
Fax: 023-9250-1951 Email: musmie@hants.gov.uk

Gurkha Museum
Peninsula Barracks, Romsey Road, Winchester SO23 8TS
Tel: 01962 842832 Fax: 01962 877597

Gurkha Museum The
Peninsula Barracks, Romsey Road, Winchester SO23 8TP
Tel: 01962-842832

Hampshire County Museums Service
Chilcomb House, Chilcomb Lane, Winchester SO23 8RD
Tel: 01962-846304

Havant Museum
also Friends of Havant Museum Local History Section, 56
East Street, Havant P09 1BS Tel: 023-9245-1155
Fax: 023-9249-8707 Email: musmcp@hants.gov.uk
WWW: www.hants.gov.uk/museums

HMS Warrior (1860)
Victory Gate, HM Naval Base, Portsmouth PO1 3
Tel: 02392-778600 Fax: 02392-778601
Email: info@hmswarrior.org WWW: www.hmswarrior.org

Hollycombe Steam Collection
Iron Hill, Midhurst Rd, Liphook GU30 7LP Tel: 01428-724900

**King s Royal Hussars Museum (10th Royal Hussars
PWO 11th Hussars PAO and Royal Hussars PWO)**
Peninsula Barracks, Winchester SO23 8TS
Tel: 01962 828540 Fax: 01962 828538
Email: beresford@krhmuseum.freeserve.co.uk
WWW: www.hants.gov.uk/leisure/museums/royalhus/index.html

Light Infantry Museum
Peninsula Barracks, Romsey Road, Winchester, Hampshire,
SO23 8TS Tel: 01962 868550

Maritime Museum Southampton
Bugle Street, Southampton SO14 2AJ Tel: 023-8022-3941

The Mary Rose Trust
1-10 College Road, HM Naval Base, Portsmouth,
Hampshire, PO1 3LX Tel: 023-9275-0521

Museum of Army Flying
Middle Wallop, Stockbridge SO20 8DY Tel: 01980-674421
Fax: 01264-781694 Email: daa@flyingmuseum.org.uk
WWW: www.flying-museum.org.uk

New Forest Museum & Visitor Centre
High Street, Lyndhurst SO43 7NY Tel: (023)-8028-3194
Fax: (023)-8028-4236 Email: nfmuseum@lineone.net
Portsmouth City Museum & Record Office
Museum Road, Portsmouth PO1 2LJ Tel: 023-9282-7261
Fax: 023-9287-5276 Email: portmus@compuserve.com
WWW: ourworld.compuserve.com/homepages/portmus/
Priddy s Hard Armament Museum
Priory Road, Gosport PO12 4LE Tel: 023-9250-2490
Queen Alexandra s Royal Army Nursing Corps Museum
Regimental Headquarters Army Medica, Keogh Barracks,
Ash Vale, Aldershot, Hampshire, GU12 5RQ
Rockbourne Roman Villa
Rockbourne, Fordingbridge SP6 3PG Tel: 01725-518541
Royal Armouries
Fort Nelson Down End Road, Fareham PO17 6AN
Tel: 01329-233734 Fax: 01329-822092
WWW: www.armouries.org.uk
Royal Green Jackets Museum
Peninsula Barracks, Romsey Road, Winchester SO23 8TS
Tel: 01962-828549 Fax: 01962-828500
Royal Hampshire Regimental Museum
Serle s House, Southgate Street, Winchester SO23 9EG
Tel: 01962 863658
Royal Marines Museum Archives & Library
Eastney, Southsea PO4 9PX Tel: 02392-819385 Ext 224
Fax: 02392-838420
Email: mathewlittle@royalmarinesmuseum.co.uk
WWW: www.royalmarinesmuseum.co.uk
Royal Naval Museum
H M Naval Base (PP66), Main Road, Portsmouth, PO1
3NH Tel: 023-9272-3795 Fax: 023-9272-7575
Royal Navy Submarine Museum
Haslar Jetty Road, Gosport PO12 2AS Tel: 023-9251-0354
Sammy Miller Motor Cycle Museum
Bashley Manor Farm, Bashley Cross Road, New Milton,
BH25 5SZ Tel: 01425-620777
Search
50 Clarence Road, Gosport PO12 1BU Tel: 023-9250-1957
Westbury Manor Museum
West Street, Fareham PO16 0JJ Tel: 01329-824895
Fax: 01329-825917 Email: www.hants.gov.uk/museum/westbury
Whitchurch Silk Mill
28 Winchester Street, Whitchurch RG28 7AL
Tel: 01256-892065
The Willis Museum Of Basingstoke Town & Country Life
Old Town Hall, Market Place, Basingstoke, Hampshire,
RG21 7QD Tel: 01256-465902 Fax: 01256-471455
Email: willismuseum@hotmail.com
WWW: www.hants.gov.uk/leisure/museums/willis/index.html
Winchester Museums Service
75 Hyde Street, Winchester SO23 7DW Tel: 01962-848269
Fax: 01962-848299 Email: museums@winchester.gov.uk
WWW: www.winchester.gov.uk/heritage/home.htm

Herefordshire

Churchill House Museum
Venns Lane, Aylestone Hill, Hereford HR1 1DE
Tel: 01432-260693 Fax: 01432-267409
Cider Museum & King Offa Distillery
21 Ryelands Street, Hereford, HR4 0LW Tel: 01432-354007
Fax: 01432-341641 Email: thompson@cidermuseum.co.uk
WWW: www.cidermuseum.co.uk
Leominster Museum
Etnam Street, Leominster HR6 8 Tel: 01568-615186
Teddy Bears of Bromyard
12 The Square, Bromyard HR7 4BP Tel: 01885-488329
Waterworks Museum
86 Park Street, Hereford, HR1 2RE Tel: 01432-356653
Weobley & District Local History Society
Weobley Museum, Back Lane, Weobley, Herefordshire, HR4
8SG Tel: 01544-340292

Hertfordshire

First Garden City Heritage Museum
296 Norton Way South, Letchworth Garden City, SG6 1SU
Tel: 01462-482710 Fax: 01462-486056
Email: egchm@letchworth.com
Hertford Museum (Hertford Regiment)
18 Bull Plain, Hertford SG14 1DT Tel: 01992-582686
Fax: 01992-534797
Hitchin British Schools
41-42 Queen Street, Hitchin SG4 9TS Tel: 01462-452697
Hitchin Museum
Paynes Park, Hitchin SG5 1EG Tel: 01462-434476
Fax: 01462-431316 Email: nhdc.gov.uk
Kingsbury Water Mill Museum
St. Michaels Street, St. Albans AL3 4SJ Tel: 01727-853502
Letchworth Museum & Art Gallery
Broadway, Letchworth SG6 3PF Tel: 01462-685647
Mill Green Museum & Mill
Mill Green, Hatfield AL9 5PD Tel: 01707-271362
Fax: 01707-272511
Rhodes Memorial Museum & Commonwealth Centre
South Road, Bishop s Stortford CM23 3JG
Tel: 01279-651746 Fax: 01279-467171
Email: rhodesmuseum@freeuk.com
WWW: www.hertsmuseums.org.uk
Royston & District Museum
5 Lower King Street, Royston SG8 5AL Tel: 01763-242587
The De Havilland Aircraft Museum Trust
P.O Box 107, Salisbury Hall, London Colney, St. Albans,
AL2 1EX Tel: 01727-822051
The Environmental Awareness Trust
23 High Street, Wheathampstead, St. Albans AL4 8BB
Tel: 01582-834580
The Forge Museum
High Street, Much Hadham SG10 6BS Tel: 01279-843301
Verulamium Museum
St. Michaels Street, St. Albans AL3 4SW
Tel: 01727-751824 Fax: 01727-836282
Email: d.thorold@stalbans.gov.uk
The Walter Rothschild Zoological Museum
Akeman Street, Tring HP23 6AP Tel: 0207-942-6156
Fax: 0207-942-6150 Email: ornlib@nhm.ac.uk
WWW: www.nhm.ac.uk
Ware Museum
Priory Lodge, 89 High Street, Ware SG12 9AD
Tel: 01920-487848
Watford Museum
194 High Street, Watford WD1 2DT Tel: 01923-232297
Welwyn Hatfield Museum Service
Welwyn Roman Baths, By-Pass-Road, Welwyn, AL6 0
Tel: 01438-716096

Huntingdonshire

Peterborough Museum & Art Gallery
Priestgate, Peterborough PE1 1LF Tel: 01733-343329
Fax: 01733-341928 Email: museums@peterborough.gov.uk

Isle of Wight

Bembridge Maritime Museum & Shipwreck Centre
Providence House, Sherborne Street, Bembridge
Isle Of Wight, PO35 5SB Tel: 01983-872223
Calbourne Water Mill
Calbourne Mill, Newport, PO30 4JN Tel: 01983-531227
Carisbrooke Castle Museum
Carisbrooke Castle, Newport PO30 1XY Tel: 01983-523112
Fax: 01983-532126 Email: carismus@lineone.net
East Cowes Heritage Centre
8 Clarence Road, East Cowes PO32 6EP Tel: 01983-280310
Front Line Britain at War Experience
Sandown Airport, Scotchells Brook Lane, Sandown, Isle Of
Wight, PO36 0JP Tel: 01983-404448
Guildhall Museum — Newport, Isle of Wight
High Street, Newport PO30 1TY Tel: 01983-823366

The Lilliput Museum of Antique Dolls & Toy
High Street, Brading, Sandown PO36 0DJ
Tel: 01983-407231 Email: lilliput.museum@btconnect.com
WWW: www.lilliputmuseum.co.uk
Natural History Centre
High Street, Godshill, Ventnor PO38 3HZ Tel: 01983-840333
The Classic Boat Museum
Seaclose Wharf, Town Quay, Newport PO30 2EF
Tel: 01983-533493
Ventnor Heritage Museum
11 Spring Hill, Ventnor PO38 1PE Tel: 01983-855407

Kent

Bethlem Royal Hospital Archives & Museum
Monks Orchard Road, Beckenham, Kent, BR3 3BX
Fax: 020-8776-4045 Email: museum@bethlem.co.uk
Buffs Regimental Museum
Royal Museum & Art Gallery, 18 High Street, Canterbury
CT1 2RA Tel: 01227-452747 Fax: 01227-455047
Canterbury Roman Museum
Butchery Lane, Canterbury CT1 2JR Tel: 01227-785575
Chatham Dockyard Historical Society Museum
Likley to move 1/2/2001 to World Naval Base, Chatham,
Cottage Row, Barrack Road, Chatham Dockyard, Chatham,
Kent, ME4 4TZ Tel: 01634-844897, 01634-250647
Cobham Hall
Cobham DA12 3BL Tel: 01474-823371 Fax: 01474-822995
Dickens House Museum - Broadstairs
2 Victoria Parade, Broadstairs CT10 1QS
Tel: 01843-861232 Fax: 01843-862853
Dolphin Sailing Barge Museum
Crown Quay Lane, Sittingbourne ME10 3SN Tel: 01795-423215
Dover Castle
Dover, Kent, CT16 1HU Tel: 01304-211067

Dover Museum
Market Square, Dover, Kent, CT16 1PB Tel: 01304-201066
Dover Transport Museum
Old Park Barracks, Whitfield, Dover CT16 2HQ
Tel: 01304-822409
Drapers Museum of Bygones
4 High Street, Rochester ME1 1PT Tel: 01634-830647
Fleur de Lis Heritage Centre &Museum
13 Preston Street, Faversham ME13 8NS
Tel: 01795-534542 Fax: 01795-533261
Email: faversham@btinternet.com
WWW: www.faversham.org
Guildhall Museum — Rochester, Kent
High Street, Rochester, Kent, ME1 1PY Tel: 01634-848717
Herne Bay Museum Centre
12 William Street, Herne Bay CT6 5EJ Tel: 01227-367368
Hever Castle
Hever, Nr Edenbridge TN8 7NG Tel: 01732-865224
Email: mail@hevercastle.co.uk
WWW: www.hevercastle.co.uk
Kent Battle of Britain Museum
Aerodrome Road, Hawkinge, Folkestone CT18 7AG
Tel: 01303-893140
Leeds Castle
Maidstone, Kent, ME17 1PL Tel: 0870-600-8880 (Info line)
WWW: www.leeds-castle.co.uk
Maidstone Museum & Art Gallery
St. Faith Street, Maidstone ME14 1LH Tel: 01622-754497
Margate Old Town Hall Museum
Old Town Hall, Market Place, Margate CT9 1ER
Tel: 01843-231213
Minster Abbey Gatehouse Museum
Union Road, Minster On Sea, Sheerness, Kent, ME12 2HW
Tel: 01795-872303
Minster Museum Craft & Animal Centre
Bedlam Court Lane, Minster, Ramsgate CT12 4HQ
Tel: 01843-822312
Museum of Kent Life
Cobtree, Lock Lane, Sandling, Maidstone ME14 3AU
Tel: 01622-763936 Fax: 01622-662024
Email: enquiries@museum-kentlife.co.uk
WWW: www.museum-kentlife.co.uk

Pembroke Lodge Museum & Family History Centre
4 Station Approach, Birchington on Sea, Kent, CT7 9RD
Tel: 01843-841649
Penshurst Place and Gardens
Penshurst, Tonbridge, Knt, TN11 8DG Tel: 01892-870307
Fax: 01892-870866 Email: enquiries@penshurstplace.com
WWW: www.penshursrtplace.com
Powell-Cotton Museum
Quex Park, Birchington, Kent, CT7 0 Tel: 01843-842168
Queen s Own Royal West Kent Regiment Museum
Maidstone Museum and Art Gallery, St. Faith s Street,
Maidstone, Kent , ME14 1LH Tel: 01622 754497
Fax: 01622 602193
Royal Engineers Library
Brompton Barracks, Chatham, Kent, ME4 4UG
Tel: 01634-822416 Fax: 01634-822419
Royal Engineers Museum
Prince Arthur Road, Gillingham, Kent, ME4 4UG
Tel: 01634-406397 Fax: 01634-822371
Email: remuseum.rhgre@gtnet.gov.uk WWW:
www.army.mod.uk/army/museums
Royal Museum & Art Gallery
18 High Street, Canterbury, Kent, CT1 2RA
Tel: 01227-452747
Sheerness Heritage Centre
10 Rose Street, Sheerness, Kent, ME12 1AJ
Tel: 01795-663317
Squerryes Court
Westerham, Kent, TN16 1SJ Tel: 01959-562345/563118
Fax: 01959-565949
Tenterden Museum
Station Road, Tenterden, Kent, TN30 6HN
Tel: 01580-764310 Fax: 01580-766648
The C.M Booth Collection Of Historic Vehicles
63-67 High Street, Rolvenden, Cranbrook, Kent, TN17 4LP
Tel: 01580-241234
The Charles Dickens Centre
Eastgate House, High Street, Rochester, Kent, ME1 1EW
Tel: 01634-844176
Victoriana Museum The
Deal Town Hall, High Street, Deal, Kent, CT14 6BB
Tel: 01304-380546
Watts Charity Poor Travellers House,
97 High Street, Rochester ME1 1LX Tel: 01634-845609
West Kent Regimental Museum
Maidstone, Kent
Whitstable Museum & Gallery
5a Oxford Street, Whitstable CT5 1DB Tel: 01227-276998
Maritime Museum Ramsgate
Clock House, Pier Yard, Royal Harbour, Ramsgate, Kent
CT11 8LS Tel: 01843-587765 Fax: 01843-582359
Email: museum@ekmt.fsnet.co.uk
WWW: www.ekmt.fsnet.co.uk
Masonic Library & Museum
St. Peters Place, Canterbury CT1 2DA Tel: 01227-785625

Lancashire

Blackburn Museum & Art Gallery
Museum Street, Blackburn BB1 7AJ Tel: 01254-661730
Bolton Museum & Art Gallery
Le Mans Crescent, Bolton BL1 1SE Tel: 01204-332190
Fax: 01204-332241 Email: bolmg@gn.apc.org
Duke of Lancaster s Own Yeomanry
Stanley Street, Preston PR1 4AT Tel: 01772-264074
Ellenroad Trust Ltd
Ellenroad Engine House, Elizabethan Way, Milnrow,
Rochdale OL16 4LG Tel: 01706-881952
Email: ellenroad@aol.com
WWW: http:\\ellenroad.homepage.com
Fleetwood Museum
Queens Terrace, Fleetwood FY7 6BT Tel: 01253-876621
Fusiliers Museum Lancashire
Wellington Barracks, Bury BL8 2PL Tel: 0161 764 2208
Gawthorpe Hall
Habergham Drive, Padiham, Burnley BB12 8UA
Tel: 01282-771004

Greater Manchester Police Museum
Newton Street, Manchester, M1 1ES Tel: 0161-856-3287,
0161-856-3288 Fax: 0161-856-3286
Hall I Th Wood Museum
Hall I Th Wood, Tonge Moor, Bolton BL1 8UA
Tel: 01204-301159
Heaton Park Tramway (Transport Museum)
Tram Depot, Heaton Park, Prestwich, Manchester, M25
2SW Tel: 0161-740-1919
Helmshore Textile Museums
Holcombe Road, Helmshore, Rossendal BB4 4NP
Tel: 01706-226459 Fax: 01706-218554
Heritage Trust for the North West
Pendle Heritage Centre, Colne Road, Barrowford, Nelson,
Lancashire, BB9 6JQ Tel: 01282-661704
Judge s Lodgings Museum
Church Street, Lancaster LA1 1LP Tel: 01524-32808
Keighley Bus Museum Trust
47 Brantfell Drive, Burnley BB12 8AW Tel: 01282-413179
Fax: 01282-413179 WWW: www.kbmt.freeuk.com
King s Own Royal Regimental Museum
The City Museum, Market Square, Lancaster, LA1 1HT
Tel: 01524 64637 Fax: 01524 841692
Email: kingsownmuseum@iname.com
Kippers Cats
51 Bridge Street, Ramsbottom, Bury BL0 9AD
Tel: 01706-822133
Lancashire Mining Museum - Closed wef 30/6/2000
Buile Hill Park, Eccles Old Road, Salford M6 8GL
Lancaster City Museum
Market Square, Lancaster LA1 1HT Tel: 01524-64637
Fax: 01524-841692 Email: awhite@lancaster.gov.uk
Lytham Heritage Group
2 Henry St. Lytham St. Annes FY8 5LE Tel: 01253-730767
Manchester Museum
University of Manchester, Oxford Road, Manchester
M13 9PL Tel: 0161-275-2634
Manchester Museum Education Service
University of Manchester, Oxford Rd, Manchester
M13 9PL Tel: 0161-275-2630 Fax: 0161-275-2676
Email: education@man.ac.uk
WWW: www.museum.man.ac.uk
Museum of Lancashire
Stanley Street, Preston PR1 4YP Tel: 01772-264075
Fax: 01772-264079 Email: museum@lancs.co.uk
**Museum of Lancashire (Queen s Lancashire Regiment
Duke of Lancaster s Own Yeomanry Lancashire Hussar**
Stanley Street, Preston PR1 4YP Tel: 01772 264075
The Museum of Science and Industry In Manchester
Liverpool Road, Castlefield, Manchester, M3 4JP
Tel: 0161-832-2244, 0161-832-1830 24hr Info line
Fax: 0161-833-2184 WWW: www.msim.org.uk
Museum of the Manchesters
Ashton Town Hall, Market Place, Ashton-u-Lyne, OL6 6DL
Tel: Tel:0161 342 3078/3710 or
**Museum of the Queen s Lancashire Regiment (East
South and Loyal North LancashireRegiments)**
Fulwood Barracks, Preston PR2 8AA Tel: 01772 260362
Fax: 01772 260583 Email: rhqqlr@aol.com
North West Sound Archive
Old Steward s Office, Clitheroe Castle, Clitheroe, BB7 1AZ
Tel: 01200-427897 Fax: 01200-427897 WWW:
www.nw-soundarchive.co.uk
Oldham Museum
Greaves Street, Oldham OL1 1 Tel: 0161-911-4657
Ordsall Hall Museum
Taylorson Street, Salford M5 3HT Tel: 0161-872-0251
Pendle Heritage Centre
Park Hill, Colne Road, Barrowford, Nelson BB9 6JQ
Tel: 01282-661702 Fax: 01282-611718
Portland Basin Museum
Portland Place, Ashton-Under-Lyne OL7 0QA
Tel: 0161-343-2878
Queen St Mill
Harle Syke, Queen Street, Briercliffe, Burnley BB10 2HX
Tel: 01282-459996

Ribchester Roman Museum
Riverside, Preston PR3 3XS Tel: 01254-878261
Rochdale Museum Service
The Arts & Heritage Centre, The Esplanade, Rochdale,
Lancashire, OL16 1AQ Tel: 01706-641085
Rochdale Pioneers Museum
Toad Lane, Rochdale OL12 0NU Tel: 01706-524920
Rochdale Pioneers Museum
31 Toad Lane, Rochdale, Lancashire Tel: 01706-524920
Saddleworth Museum & Art Gallery
High Street, Uppermill, Oldham, Lancashire, OL3 6HS
Tel: 01457-874093 Fax: 01457-870336
Salford Museum & Art Gallery
Peel Park, The Crescent, Salford M5 4WU
Tel: 0161-736-2649 Email: info@lifetimes.org.uk
WWW: www.lifetimes.org.uk
Slaidburn Heritage Centre
25 Church Street, Slaidburn, Clitheroe, BB7 3ER
Tel: 01200-446161 Fax: 01200-446161
Email: slaidburn.heritage@htnw.co.uk
WWW: www.htnw.co.uk and also www.slaidburn.org.uk
Smithills Hall Museum
Smithills, Dean Rd, Bolton BL1 7NP Tel: 01204-841265
Weavers Cottage Heritage Centre
Weavers Cottage, Bacup Road, Rawtenstall, Rossendale,
BB4 7NW Tel: 01706-229828 Fax: 01706-210915
Wigan Heritage Service - History Shop
Library Street, Wigan, Greater Manchester, WN1 1NU
Tel: 01942-828020 Fax: 01942-827645
Email: hcritagc@wiganmbc.gov.uk

Leeds

Leeds City Art Gallery
The Headrow, Leeds, LS1 3AA Tel: 0113-247-8248
Leeds Museums Resource Centre
Moorfield Road, Moorfield Industrial Estate, Yeadon, Leeds,
LS19 7BN Tel: 0113-214-6526
Lotherton Hall
Lotherton Lane, Aberford, Leeds, LS25 3EB
Tel: 0113-281-3259
Temple Newsham House
Temple Newsham Road, off Selby Road, Leeds, LS15 0AE
Tel: 0113-264-7321
Thwaite Mills Watermill
Thwaite Lane, Stourton, Leeds, LS10 1RP
Tel: 0113-249-6453

Leicestershire

Abbey Pumping Station
Corporation Road, Abbey Lane, Leicester LE4 5PX
Tel: 0116-299-5111 Fax: 0116-299-5125
WWW: www.leicestermuseums.ac.uk
Ashby De La Zouch Museum
North Street, Ashby-De-La-Zouch LE65 1HU
Tel: 01530-560090
Belgrave Hall & Gardens
Church Road, Belgrave, Leicester LE4 5PE
Tel: 0116-2666590 Fax: 0116-2613063
Email: marte001@leicester.gov.uk
WWW: www.leicestermuseums.gov.uk
Bellfoundry Museum
Freehold Street, Loughborough LE11 1AR Tel: 01509-233414
Charnwood Museum
Granby Street, Loughborough, Leicestershire, LE11 3DU
Tel: 01509-233754 Fax: 01509-268140
WWW: www.leics.gov.uk/museums/musinleics.htm#charnwood
Foxton Canal Museum
Middle Lock, Gumley Road, Foxton, Market Harborough,
Leicestershire, LE16 7RA Tel: 0116-279-2657
Harborough Museum
Council Offices, Adam and Eve Street, Market Harborough,
Leicestershire, LE16 7AG Tel: 01858-821085
Fax: 01509-268140 Email: museums@leics.gov.uk
WWW: www.leics.gov.uk/museums/musinleics.htm#harborough

Hinckley & District Museum
Framework Knitters Cottages, Lower Bond Street, Hinckley, Leicestershire, LE10 1QX Tel: 01455-251218
Jewry Wall Museum
St. Nicholas Circle, Leicester LE1 4LB Tel: 0116-247-3021
Leicester City Museum & Art Gallery
53 New Walk, Leicester LE1 7EA Tel: 0116-255-4100
Leicester Gas Museum
To close by mid 2001. No genealogical records. Archive material transferred to National Gas Archive, Aylestone Road, Leicester LE2 7LF Tel: 0116-250-3190
Leicestershire Environmental Resources Centre
Holly Hayes, 216 Birstall Road, Birstall, Leicester, LE4 4DG Tel: 0116-267-1950 Email: museums@leics.gov.uk
WWW: www.leics.gov.uk
The Manor House
Manor Road, Donington Le Heath, Coalville LE67 2FW
Tel: 01530-831259 Fax: 01530-831259
Email: museums@leics.gov.uk
WWW: www.leics.gov.uk/museums/musinleics.htm#manor
Melton Carnegie Museum
Thorpe End, Melton Mowbray LE13 1RB
Tel: 01664-569946 Fax: 01664-569946
Email: museums@leics.gov.uk
WWW: www.leics.gov.uk/museums/musinleics.htm#melton
Royal Leicestershire Regiment Museum
Enquiries to: Newarke Houses Museum, The Newarke, Leicester. LE2 7BY - New Walk Museum, 53 New Walk, Leicester, LE1 7AE Fax: 0116-2470403
Rutland Railway Museum
Iron Ore Mine Sidings, Ashwell Road, Cottesmore, Oakham, Leicestershire, LE15 7BX Tel: 01572-813203
Snibston Discovery Park
Ashby Road, Coalville LE67 3LN Tel: 01530-510851
Fax: 01530-813301 Email: museums@leics.gov.uk
WWW: www.leics.gov.uk/museums/musinleics.htm#snibston
The Guildhall
Guildhall Lane, Leicester LE1 5FQ Tel: 0116-253-2569

Lincolnshire

Alford Civic Trust/Manor House Museum, Alford
Manor House Museum, West Street, Alford, LN13 9DJ
Tel: 01507-463073
Ayscoughfee Hall, Museum and Gardens
Churchgate, Spalding, Lincolnshire, PE11 2RA
Tel: 01775-725468 Fax: 01775-762715
Battle of Britain Memorial Flight Visits
R.A.F Coningsby, Coningsby, Lincoln LN4 4SY
Tel: 01526-344041
Boston Guildhall Museum
South Street, Boston PE21 6HT Tel: 01205-365954
Email: heritage@originalboston.freeserve.co.uk
Church Farm Museum, Skegness
Church Road South, Skegness PE25 2HF
Tel: 01754-766658 Fax: 01754-898243
Email: willf@lincolnshire.gov.uk
Gainsborough Old Hall
Parnell Street, Gainsborough DN21 2NB Tel: 01427-612669
Gordon Boswell Romany Museum
Hawthorns Clay Lake, Spalding PE12 6BL
Tel: 01775-710599
Grantham Museum
St. Peters Hill, Grantham NG31 6PY Tel: 01476-568783
Fax: 01476-592457 Email: grantham_museum@lineone.net
The Incredibly Fantastic Old Toy Show
26 Westgate, Lincoln LN1 3BD Tel: 01522-520534
Lincolnshire Aviation Heritage Centre
East Kirkby Airfield, East Kirkby, Spilsb PE23 4DE
Tel: 01790-763207
Lincs Vintage Vehicle Society
Whisby Rd, North Hykeham, Lincoln, LN6 3QT
Tel: 01522-500566
Louth Naturalists Antiquarian & Literary Society
4 Broadbank, Louth, LN11 0EQ Tel: 01507-601211

Museum of Lincolnshire Life & Museum of the Royal Lincolnshire Regiment Lincolnshire Yeomanry
Old Barracks, Burton Road, Lincoln LN1 3LY
Tel: 01522-528448 Fax: 01522-521264
Email: Finch@lincolnshire.gov.uk
National Fishing Heritage Centre
Alexandra Dock, Great Grimsby DN31 1UZ
Tel: 01472-323345 WWW: www.nelincs.gov.uk
also www.nelincsevents.co.uk
Queen s Royal Lancers Regimental Museum (16th/5th & 17th/21st Lancers)
Belvoir Castle, nr Grantham NG32 1PD
Tel: 01159-573295 Fax: 01159-573195
Wisbech & Fenland Museum
Museum Square, Wisbech PE13 1ES Tel: 01945-583817
Fax: 01945-589050 Email: wisbechmuseum.@beeb.net

Lincolnshire—North Lincolnshire

North Lincolnshire Museum
Oswald Road, Scunthorpe, DN15 7BD Tel: 01724-843533
Fax: 01724-270474 Email: davidwilliams@northlincs.gov.uk
WWW: www.northlincs.gov.uk/museums
Baysgarth House Museum
Caistor Road, Barton-Upon-Humber DN18 6AH
Tel: 01652-632318
Immingham Museum
Margaret St. Immingham, DN40 1LE Tel: 01469-577066

Liverpool

King s Regiment Collection
Museum of Liverpool Life, Pier Head, Liverpool, L3 1PZ
Tel: 0151-478-4062 Fax: 0151-478-4090
Maritime Museum, Liverpool
William Brown St. Liverpool, L3 8EN Tel: 0151-2070001

Manchester & Greater Manchester

Greater Manchester Police Museum
Newton Street, Manchester, M1 1ES Tel: 0161-856-3287, 0161-856-3288 Fax: 0161-856-3286
Manchester Jewish Museum
190 Cheetham Hill Road, Manchester, M8 8LW
Tel: 0161-834-9879, 0161-832-7353 Fax: 0161-834-9801
Email: info@manchesterjewishmuseum.com
WWW: www.manchesterjewishmuseum.com
Manchester Museum Education Service
University of Manchester, Oxford Road, Manchester, M13 9PL Tel: 0161-275-2630 Fax: 0161-275-2676
Email: education@man.ac.uk
WWW: www.museum.man.ac.uk
The Museum of Science and Industry In Manchester
Liverpool Road, Castlefield, Manchester, M3 4JP
Tel: 0161-832-2244, 0161-832-1830 24hr Info line
Fax: 0161-833-2184 WWW: www.msim.org.uk
National Museum of Labour History
Labour History Archive, 103 Princess Street, Manchester, M1 6DD Tel: 0161-228-7212 Fax: 0161-237-5965
Email: archives@nmlhweb.org WWW: www.nmlhweb.org
Wigan Heritage Service - History Shop
Library Street, Wigan, Greater Manchester, WN1 1NU
Tel: 01942-828020 Fax: 01942-827645
Email: heritage@wiganmbc.gov.uk

Merseyside

The Beatle Story Ltd
Britannia Vaults, Albert Dock, Liverpool L3 4AA
Tel: 0151-709-1963 Fax: 0151-708-0039
Ellesmere Port Boat Museum
South Pier Road, Ellesmere Port CH65 4FW
Tel: 0151-355-5017 Fax: 0151-355-4079
Email: boatmuseum@easynet.co.uk
King s Regiment Collection
Museum of Liverpool Life, Pier Head, Liverpool, L3 1PZ
Tel: 0151-478-4062 Fax: 0151-478-4090

Merseyside Maritime Museum
Maritime Archives and Library, Albert Dock, Liverpool, L3
4AQ Tel: 0151-478-4418/4424 Fax: 0151-478-4590
Email: archives@nmgmarchives.demon.co.uk
National Museums & Galleries on Merseyside
127 Dale Street, Liverpool L2 2JH Tel: 0151-207-0001
Port Sunlight Village Trust
95 Greendale Road, Port Sunlight, CH62 4XE
Tel: 0151-644-6466 Fax: 0151-645-8973
Prescot Museum
34 Church Street, Prescot L34 3LA Tel: 0151-430-7787
Shore Road Pumping Station
Shore Road, Birkenhead, CH41 1AG Tel: 0151-650-1182
Western Approaches
1 Rumford Street, Liverpool L2 8SZ Tel: 0151-227-2008
Fax: 0151-236-6913
Wirral Archives Service and Museum
Birkenhead Town Hall, Hamilton Street, Birkenhead, CH41
5BR Tel: 0151-666-4010 Fax: 0151-666-3965
Email: archives@wirral-libraries.net
Botanic Gardens Museum
Churchtown, Southport PR9 7NB Tel: 01704-227547
Fax: 01704-224112

Middlesex

Forty Hall Museum
Forty Hill, Enfield EN2 9HA Tel: 020-8363-8196
Hackney Museum Service
Parkside Library, Victoria Park Road, London, E9 7JL
Tel: 020-8986-6914 Fax: 020-8985-7600
Email: hmuseum@hackney.gov.uk
WWW: www.hackney.gov.uk/hackneymuseum
Harrow Museum & Heritage Centre
Headstone Manor, Pinner View, Harrow HA2 6PX
Tel: 020-8861-2626
Kew Bridge Steam Museum
Green Dragon Lane, Brentford TW8 0EN Tel: 020-8568-4757
Musical Museum
368 High Street, Brentford TW8 0BD Tel: 020-8560-8108

Midlands — West Midlands

Aston Manor-Road Transport Museum Ltd
208-216 Witton Lane, Birmingham B6 6QE
Tel: 0121-322-2298
Bantock House & Park
Bantock Park,, Finchfield Rd, Wolverhampton WV3 9LQ
Tel: 01902-552195 Fax: 01902-552196
Birmingham & Midland Museum Of Transport
Chapel Lane, Wythall, Birmingham, B47 6JX
Tel: 01564-826471 Email: enquiries@bammot.org.uk
WWW: www.bammot.org.uk
Birmingham Museum & Art Gallery
Chamberlain Square, Birmingham B3 3DH
Tel: 0121-303-2834 Fax: 0121-303-1394
WWW: www.birmingham.gov.uk/bmag
Birmingham Railway Museum Ltd
670 Warwick Road, Tyseley, Birmingham B11 2HL
Tel: 0121-707-4696
Black Country Living Museum
Tipton Road, Dudley DY1 4SQ Tel: 0121-557-9643
Fax: 0121-557-4242 Email: info@bcim.co.uk
WWW: www.bcim.co.uk
Blakesley Hall
Blakesley Road, Yardley, Birmingham B25 8RN
Tel: 0121-783-2193
Dudley Museum & Art Gallerey
St James s Road, Dudley, West Midlands, DY1
Haden Hall
Haden Hill Park, Barrs Road, Cradley Heath, West
Midlands, B64 7JX Tel: 01384-635846
Herbert Art Gallery & Museum
Jordan Well, Coventry CV1 5QP Tel: 024-76832381
Lock Museum
54 New Road, Willenhall WV13 2DA Tel: 01902-634542
Fax: 01902-634542
Email: http://members.tripod.co.uk/lock_museum/

Midland Air Museum
Coventry Airport, Coventry Road, Baginton, Coventry
CV8 3AZ Tel: 024-7630-1033
Museum of the Jewellery Quarter
75-79 Vyse Street, Hockley, Birmingham, B6 6JD
Tel: 0121-554-3598 Fax: 0121-554-9700
Oak House Museum
Oak Road, West Bromwich B70 8HJ Tel: 0121-553-0759
Selly Manor Museum
Maple Road, Birmingham, B30 2AE Tel: 0121-472-0199
Walsall Leather Museum
Littleton Street West, Walsall, West Midlands, WS2 8EQ
Tel: 01922-721153 Fax: 01922-725827
Email: leathermuseum@walsall.gov.uk
West Midlands Police Museum
Sparkhill Police Station, Stratford Road, Sparkhill,
Birmingham, West Midlands, B11 4EA Tel: 0121-626-7181
Whitefriars Gallery
London Road, Coventry CV3 4AR Tel: 024-7683-2432
Whitlocks End Farm
Bills Lane, Shirley, Solihull B90 2PL Tel: 0121-745-4891

Norfolk

Air Defence Battle Command & Control Museum The
Neatishead, Norwich, NR12 8YB Tel: 01692-633309
Castle Museum
Castle Hill, Norwich, Norfolk, NR1 3JU Tel: 01603-493624
City of Norwich Aviation Museum Ltd
Old Norwich Road, Horsham St Faith, Norwich, NR10 3JF
Tel: 01603-893080
Diss Museum
The Market Place, Diss IP22 3JT Tel: 01379-650618
Elizabethan House Museum
4 South Quay, Great Yarmouth NR30 2QH
Tel: 01493-855746
Feltwell (Historical & Archaeological) Society
Village Museum at The Beck, Feltwell - limited opening, 16
High Street, Feltwell, Thetford, Norfolk, IP26
Tel: 01842 828448 Email: petefeltwell@tinyworld.co.uk
Glandford Shell Museum
Church House, Glandford, Holt, NR25 7JR
Tel: 01263-740081
Iceni Village & Museums
Cockley Cley, Swaffham PE37 8AG Tel: 01760-721339
Lynn Museum
Old Market Street, King s Lynn, Norfolk, PE30 1NL
Tel: 01553-775001 Fax: 01553-775001
WWW: www.norfolk.gov.uk/tourism/museums
Maritime Museum for East Anglia
25 Marine Parade, Great Yarmouth NR30 2EN
Tel: 01493-842267
The Muckleburgh Collection
Weybourne, Holt NR25 7EG Tel: 01263-588210
Fax: 01263-588425 Email: jenny@muckleburgh.demon.co.uk
Norfolk Motorcycle Museum
Station Yard, Norwich Road, North Walsham, Norfolk,
NR28 0DS Tel: 01692-406266
Norfolk Rural Life Museum & Union Farm
Beech House, Gressenhall, East Dereham, Norfolk, NR20
4DR Tel: 01362-860563 Fax: 01362-860385
Email: frances.collinson.mus@norfolk.gov.uk
Royal Norfolk Regimental Museum
Shirehall, Market Avenue, Norwich, Norfolk, NR1 3JQ
Tel: 01603-493649 Fax: 01603-765651
Sheringham Museum
Station Road, Sheringham NR26 8RE Tel: 01263-821871
Shirehall Museum
Common Place, Walsingham, NR22 6BP
Tel: 01328-820510 Fax: 01328-820098
Email: walsingham.museum@farmline.com
Wisbech & Fenland Museum
Museum Square, Wisbech PE13 1ES Tel: 01945-583817
Fax: 01945-589050 Email: wisbechmuseum.@beeb.net
100 Bomb Group
Memorial Museum, Common Road, Dickleburgh, Diss,
Norfolk , IP21 4PH Tel: 01379-740708

327

Inspire Hands On Science Centre
Coslany Street, Norwich, Norfolk , NR3 3DJ
Tel: 01603-612612

Northamptonshire

Canal Museum
Stoke Bruerne, Towcester NN12 7SE Tel: 01604-862229
Museum of The Northamptonshire Regiment
Abington Park Museum, Abington NN1 5LW
Tel: 01604 635412
National Dragonfly Museum
Ashton Mill, Ashton, Peterborough, PE8 5LB
Tel: 01832-272427 Email: ndmashton@aol.com
WWW: www.natdragonflymuseum.org.uk
Northampton Iron Stone Railway Trust
Hunsbury Hill Country Park, Hunsbury Hill Road, West
Hunsbury, Northampton NN4 9UW
Tel: 01604-702031/757481, 01908-376821
Email: raf9687@aol.com also bnile98131@aol.com
Peterborough Museum & Art Gallery
Priestgate, Peterborough PE1 1LF Tel: 01733-343329
Fax: 01733-341928 Email: museums@peterborough.gov.uk
Rushden Historical Transport Society
The Station, Station Approach, Rushden, Northamptonshire,
NN10 0AW Tel: 01933-318988
Wellingborough Heritage Centre
Croyland Hall, Burystead Place, Wellingborough,
Northamptonshire, NN8 1AH Tel: 01933-276838

Northumberland

Bellingham Heritage Centre
Front Street, Bellingham, Hexham, NE48 2DF
Tel: 01434-220050
Berwick Borough Museum
The Barracks, The Parade, Berwick-Upon-Tweed,
Northumberland, TD15 1DG Tel: 01289-330933
Bewick Studios The
Mickley Square, Mickley, Stocksfield NE43 7BL
Tel: 01661-844055
Border History Museum & Library
Moothall, Hallgate, Hexham, Northumberland, NE46 3NH
Tel: 01434-652349 Fax: 01434-652425
Email: museum@tynedale.gov.uk
Chesterholm Museum (Vindolanda Museum)
The Vindolanda Trust, Bardon Mill, Hexham, NE47 7JN
Tel: 01434-344277 Fax: 01434-344060
Email: info@vindolanda.com
WWW: www.vindolanda.com
Fusiliers Museum of Northumberland
The Abbot s Tower, Alnwick Castle, Alnwick, NE66 1NG
Tel: 01665-602152 Fax: 01665-603320
Email: fusmusnorthld@btinternet.com
King s Own Scottish Borderers Museum
The Barracks, Berwick upon Tweed, TD15 1DG
Tel: 01289-307426
Marine Life Centre & Fishing Museum
8 Main Street, Seahouses NE68 7RG Tel: 01665-721257
North East Mills Group
Blackfriars, Monk St. Newcastle upon Tyne, NE1 4XN
Tel: 0191-232-9279 Fax: 0191-230-1474
WWW: www.welcome.to/North.East.Mill.Group
Tynedale Council Museums
Department of Leisure & Tourism, Prospect House,
Hexham, Northumberland, NE46 3NH Tel: 01461-652351

Nottinghamshire

D.H Lawrence Heritage
Durban House Heritage Centre, Mansfield Road, Eastwood,
Nottingham, NG16 3DZ Tel: 01773-717353
Galleries of Justice
Shire Hall, High Pavement, Lace Market, Nottingham, NG1
1HN Tel: 0115-952-0555 Fax: 0115-993-9828
Email: info@galleriesofjustice.org.uk
WWW: www.galleriesofjustice.org.uk

Great Central Railway
Nottingham Heritage Centre, Mere Way, Ruddington,
Nottingham, NG11 6JS Tel: 0115-940-5705
Greens Mill & Science Musuem
Windmill Lane, Sneinton, Nottingham, Nottinghamshire,
NG2 4QB Tel: 0115-915-6878
Harley Gallery
Welbeck, Worksop S80 3LW Tel: 01909-501700
Mansfield Museum & Art Gallery
Leeming Street, Mansfield, Nottinghamshire, NG18 1NG
Tel: 01623-463088 Fax: 01623-412922
Millgate Museum of Folk Life
48 Millgate, Newark NG24 4TS Tel: 01636-655730
Fax: 01636-655735
Email: museums@newark-sherwooddc.gov.uk
WWW: www.newark-sherwooddc.go.uk
The Museum of Nottingham Lace
3-5 High Pavement, The Lace Market, Nottingham
NG1 1HF Tel: 0115-989-7365 Fax: 0115-989-7301
Email: info@nottinghamlace.org
WWW: www.nottinghamlace.org
Natural History and Industrial Museum
The Courtyard, Wollaton Park, Nottingham, NG8 2AE
Tel: 0115-9153942 Fax: 0115-9153941
Newark (Notts & Lincs) Air Museum
The Airfield, Lincoln Road, Winthorpe, Newark,
Nottinghamshire, NG24 2NY Tel: 01636-707170
Fax: 01636-707170 Email: newarkair@lineone.net
Newark Museum
Appleton Gate, Newark NG24 1JY Tel: 01636-702358
Newstead Abbey Museum
Newstead Abbey Park, Nottingham NG15 8GE
Tel: 01623-455900
Nottingham Castle Museum & Art Gallery
Castle Road, Nottingham NG1 6EL Tel: 0115-915-3700
Fax: 0115-915-3653
Nottingham Musuem Shops
Canal Street, Nottingham NG1 7HG Tel: 0115-915-6871
Ruddington Frame Work Knitter s Museum
Chapel Street, Ruddington, Nottingham NG11 6HE
Tel: 0115-984-6914
Ruddington Village Museum
St. Peters Rooms, Church Street, Ruddington, Nottingham,
NG11 6HD Tel: 0115-914-6645
Sherwood Foresters (Notts & Derbyshire Regt) Museum
The Castle, Nottingham. NG1 6EL, RHQ WFR
Sherwood Foresters Museum & Archives
RHQ WFR, Foresters House, Chetwynd Barracks, Chilwell,
Nottingham, NG9 5HA Tel: 0115-946-5415
Fax: 0115-946-5712
Whaley Thorn Heritage & Environment Centre
Portland Terrace, Langwith, Mansfield NG20 9HA
Tel: 01623-742525

Oxfordshire

Abingdon Museum
County Hall, Market Place, Abingdon, Oxfordshire, OX14
3HG Tel: 01235-523703 Fax: 01235-536814
Ashmolean Museum
University of Oxford, University of Oxford, Beaumont St,
Oxford, Oxfordshire, OX1 2PH Tel: 01865-278000
Great Western Society Ltd
Didcot Railway Centre, Station Road, Didcot OX11 7NJ
Tel: 01235-817200
Oxfordshire & Buckinghamshire Light Infantry Regt Museum
Slade Park, Headington, Oxford OX3 7JL Tel: 01865 780128
The Oxfordshire Museum
Fletchers House, Park Street, Woodstock OX20 1SN
Tel: 01993-811456, 01993-814104 Fax: 01993-813239
Email: oxonmuseum@oxfordshire.gov.uk
Pitt Rivers Museum
University Of Oxford, South Parks Road, Oxford, OX1 3PP
Tel: 01865-270927 Fax: 01865-270943
Email: prm@prm.ox.ac.uk WWW: www.prm.ox.ac.uk

River & Rowing Museum
Mill Meadows, Henley on Thames RG9 1BF
Tel: 01491-415625 Fax: 01491-415601
Email: museum@rrm.co.uk also alicia.gurney@rrm.co.uk
WWW: www.rrm.co.uk

The Vale & Downland Museum
19 Church Street, Wantage, Oxfordshire, OX12 8BL
Tel: 01235-771447 Email: museum@wantage.com

Wallingford Museum
Flint House, High Street, Wallingford, Oxfordshire, OX10
0DB Tel: 01491-835065

Witney & District Museum
Gloucester Court Mews, High Street, Witney, Oxfordshire,
OX8 6LX Tel: 01993-775915 Email: janecavell@aol.com

Rutland

Rutland County Museum
Catmose Street, Oakham, Rutland, LE15 6HW
Tel: 01572-723654 Fax: 01572-757576
WWW: www.rutnet.co.uk

Shropshire

Acton Scott Historic Working Farm
Wenlock Lodge, Acton Scott, Church Stretton, Shropshire,
SY6 6QN Tel: 01694-781306

Blists Hill Open Air Museum
Ironbridge Gorge Museum Trust Ltd, Legges Way, Madeley,
Telford, Shropshire, TF7 5DU Tel: 01952-588016

Coalport China Museum
Ironbridge Gorge Museum Trust Ltd, High Street, Coalport,
Telford, Shropshire, TF8 7AW Tel: 01952-580650

Ironbridge Gorge Museum, Library & Archives
The Wharfage, Ironbridge, Telford, TF8 7AW
Tel: 01952-432141 Fax: 01952-432237
Email: library@ironbridge.org.uk
WWW: www.ironbridge.org.uk

Ironbridge Gorge Museums
Ironbridge Gorge Museum Trust Ltd, Ironbridge, Telford,
TF8 7AW Tel: 01952-432141 Fax: 01952-432237

Jackfield Tile Museum
Ironbridge Gorge Museum Trust Ltd, Jackfield, Telford,
Shropshire, TF8 7AW Tel: 01952-882030

Ludlow Museum
Castle Street, Ludlow, Shropshire, SY8 1AS
Tel: 01584-875384

Midland Motor Museum
Stanmore Hall, Stourbridge Road, Stanmore, Bridgnorth,
Shropshire, WV15 6DT Tel: 01746-762992

Museum Of Iron
Ironbridge Gorge Museum Trust Ltd, Coach Road,
Coalbrookdale, Telford TF8 7EZ Tel: 01952-433418

Museum Of The River Visitor Centre
Ironbridge Gorge Museum Trust Ltd, The Wharfage,
Ironbridge, Telford TF8 7AW Tel: 01952-432405

Oswestry Transport Museum
Oswald Road, Oswestry SY11 1RE Tel: 01691-671749

Rowley s House Museum
Shrewsbury Museums Service, Barker Street, Shrewsbury,
SY1 1QH Tel: 01743-361196 Fax: 01743-358411

Royal Air Force Museum
Cosford, Shifnal, Shropshire, TF11 8UP Tel: 01902-376200

Shropshire Regimental Museum
The Castle, Shrewsbury SY1 2AT Tel: 01743-358516

Somerset

Abbey Barn - Somerset Rural Life Museum
Abbey Barn, Chilkwell Street, Glastonbury, Somerset, BA6
8DB Tel: 01458-831197 Fax: 01458-834684 WWW:
www.somerset.gov.uk/museums

Admiral Blake Museum
Blake Street, Bridgwater, Somerset, TA6 3NB
Tel: 01278-435399 Fax: 01278-444076
Email: Museums@sedgemoor.gov.uk

American Museum
Claverton Manor, Bath, Somerset, BA2 7BD
Tel: 01225-460503, 01225-463538 Fax: 01225-480726

Bakelite Museum
Orchard Mill, Bridge St Williton, Taunton, Somerset, TA4
4NS Tel: 01984-632133

Bath Industrial Heritage Centre
Camden Works, Julian Road, Bath, Somerset, BA1 2RH
Tel: 01225-318348 Fax: 01225-318348
Email: bathindheritage@camdenworks.swinternet.com.uk

Bath Postal Museum
8 Broad Street, Bath, Somerset, BA1 5LJ
Tel: 01225-460333 WWW: www.bathpostalmuseum.org

Bath Royal Literary & Scientific Institution
16-18 Queen Square, Bath, Somerset, BA1 2HN
Tel: 01225-312084

Blazes Fire Museum
Sandhill Park, Bishops Lydeard, Taunton, Somerset, TA4
3DE Tel: 01823-433964

Building of Bath Museum
Countess of Huntingdon s Chapel, The Vineyards, Bath,
Somerset, BA1 5NA Tel: 01225-333-895
Fax: 01225-445-473 Email: admin@bobm.freeserve.co.uk
WWW: www.bath-preservations-trust.org.uk

Chard & District Museum
Godworthy House, High Street, Chard, Somerset, TA20 1QB
Tel: 01460-65091

Fleet Air Arm Museum
R.N.A.S Yeovilton, Yeovil, Somerset, BA22 8HT
Tel: 01935-840565

Fleet Air Arm Museum Records & Research Centre
Box D61, RNAS Yeovilton, Nr Ilchester, Somerset, BA22
8HT Tel: 01935-840565 Fax: 01935-840181

Glastonbury Lake Village Museum
The Tribunal, 9 High Street, Glastonbury, Somerset, BA6
9DP Tel: 01458-832949

The Haynes Motor Museum
Castle Cary Road, Sparkford, Yeovil, Somerset, BA22 7LH
Tel: 01963-440804 Fax: 01963-441004
Email: mike@gmpwin.demon.co.uk
WWW: www.haynesmotormuseum.co.uk

Holburne Museum & Crafts Study Centre
Great Pulteney Street, Bath, BA2 4DB Tel: 01225-466669

John Judkyn Memorial
Garden Thorpe, Freshford, Bath, BA3 6BX
Tel: 01225-723312

Lambretta Scooter Museum
77 Alfred Street, Weston-Super-Mare, North Somerset, BS23
1PP Tel: 01934-614614 Fax: 01934-620120
Email: lambretta@wsparts.force9.net

Museum Of East Asian Art
12 Bennett Street, Bath, BA1 2QL Tel: 01225-464640
Fax: 01225-461718
Email: museum@east-asian-art.freeserve.co.uk
WWW: www.east-asian-art.co.uk

No.1 Royal Crescent
1 Royal Crescent, Bath, BA1 2LR Tel: 01225-428126

Radstock, Midsomer Norton & District Museum
Waterloo Road, Radstock, Bath, Somerset, BA3 3ER
Tel: 01761-437722
Email: radstockmuseum@ukonline.co.uk
WWW: www.radstockmuseum.co.uk

Somerset & Dorset Railway Trust
Washford Station, Washford, Watchet, Somerset, TA23 0PP
Tel: 01984-640869, 01308-424630 Email: info@sdrt.org
WWW: www.sdrt.org

Somerset County Museum Service
Taunton Castle, Taunton, Somerset, TA1 4AA
Tel: 01823-320200

**Somerset Military Museum (Somerset Light Infantry
Yeomanry**
LI Office, 14 Mount Street, Taunton, Somerset, TA1 3QE
Tel: 01823-333434 Fax: 01832-351639

Wells Museum
8 Cathedral Green, Wells, Somerset, BA5 2UE
Tel: 01749-673477

West Somerset Museum
The Old School, Allerford, Minehead, Somerset, TA24 8HN
Tel: 01643-862529

William Herschel Museum
19 New King Street, Bath, BA1 2BL Tel: 01225-311342

Somerset — North East Somerset

Roman Baths Museum
Abbey Churchyard, Bath, BA1 1LZ Tel: 01225-477773
Fax: 01225-477243
Helicopter Museum
Locking Moor Road, Weston-Super-Mare, BS22 8PL
Tel: 01934-635227
North Somerset Museum Service
Burlington Street, Weston-Super-Mare, BS23 1PR
Tel: 01934-621028

Staffordshire

Bass Museum and Archive
Horninglow Street, Burton on Trent DE14 1JZ
Borough Museum & Art Gallery
Brampton Park, Newcastle ST5 0QP Tel: 01782-619705
Clay Mills Pumping Engines Trust Ltd
Sewage Treatment Works, Meadow Lane, Stretton,
Burton-On-Trent DE13 0DB Tel: 01283-509929
Etruria Industrial Museum
Lower Bedford St, Etruria, Stoke-On-Trent, Staffordshire,
ST4 7AF Tel: 01782-233144
Gladstone Pottery Museum
Uttoxeter Road, Longton, Stoke-On-Trent, Staffordshire,
ST3 1PQ Tel: 01782-319232
Hanley Museum & Art Gallery
Bethesda Street, Hanley, Stoke-On-Trent, Staffordshire, ST1
3DW Tel: 01782-232323
Museum of The Staffordshire Regiment
Whittington Barracks, Lichfield, Staffordshire, WS14 9PY
Tel: 0121-311-3229/3240 Fax: 0121-311-3205
Museum of the Staffordshire Yeomanry
The Ancient High House, Greengate Street, Stafford,
Staffordshire, ST16 2HS Tel: 01785 40204 (Tourist Info
Potteries Museum & Art Gallery
Bethesda Street, Hanley, Stoke-On-Trent, ST1 3DE
Tel: 01782-232323 Fax: 01782-232500
Email: museums@stoke.gov.uk
WWW: www.stoke,gov.uk/museums
Samuel Johnson Birthplace Museum
Breadmarket Street, Lichfield, Staffordshire, WS13 6LG
Tel: 01543-264972 WWW: www.lichfield.gov.uk
Uttoxeter Heritage Centre
34-36 Carter Street, Uttoxeter ST14 8EU Tel: 01889-567176

Suffolk

Christchurch Mansion & Wolsey Art Gallery
Christchurch Park, Soane Street, Ipswich, Suffolk, IP4 2BE
Tel: 01473-253246
East Anglia Transport Museum
Chapel Road, Carlton Colville, Lowestoft, Suffolk, NR33
8BL Tel: 01502-518459
Felixstowe Museum
Landguards Fort, Felixstowe IP11 8TW Tel: 01394-674355
Gainsborough House Society
Gainsborough Street, Sudbury CO10 2EU
Tel: 01787-372958 Fax: 01787-376991
Email: mail@gainsborough.org
WWW: www.gainsborough.org
International Sailing Craft Assoc Maritime Museum
Caldecott Road, Oulton Broad, Lowestoft, Suffolk, NR32
3PH Tel: 01502-585606 Fax: 01502-589014
Email: admin@isca-maritimemuseum.org
Ipswich Museum & Exhibition Gallery
High Street, Ipswich, Suffolk, IP1 3QH Tel: 01473-213761
Ipswich Transport Museum Ltd
Old Trolley Bus Depot, Cobham Rd, Ipswich, Suffolk, IP3
9JD Tel: 01473-715666
Long Shop Steam Museum
Main Street, Leiston, Suffolk, IP16 4ES Tel: 01728-832189
Fax: 01728-832189
WWW: www.suffolkcc.gov.uk/libraries_and_heritage/sro/garrett/index.html

Lowestoft Museum
Broad House, Nicholas Everitt Park, Oulton Broad,
Lowestoft, Suffolk, NR33 9JR Tel: 01502-511457,
01502-513795 Fax: 01502-513795
Maritime Museum Sparrows Nest
The Museum, Whapload Road, Lowestoft, Suffolk, NR32
1XG Tel: 01502-561963
Mid Suffolk Light Railway
Brockford Station, Wetheringsett, Stowmarket, Suffolk, IP14
5PW Tel: 01449-766899
Mildenhall & District Museum
6 King Street, Mildenhall, Bury St. Edmunds, Suffolk, IP28
7EX Tel: 01638-716970
The National Horseracing Museum & Tours
99 High Street, Newmarket CB8 8JH Tel: 01638-667333
Rougham Tower Association
Rougham Estate Office, Rougham, Bury St. Edmunds,
Suffolk, IP30 9LZ Tel: 01359-271471 Fax: 01359-271555
Email: bplsto@aol.com
Suffolk Regiment Museum
Suffolk Record Office, 77 Raingate Street, Bury St
Edmunds, Suffolk, IP33 2AR Tel: 01284-352352
Fax: 01284-352355 Email: bury.ro@libhev.suffolkcc.gov.uk
Dunwich Museum
St. James s Street, Dunwich, Saxmundham, Suffolk , IP17
3DT Tel: 01728-648796
Norfolk & Suffolk Aviation Museum
Buckaroo Way, The Street, Flixton, Bungay, Suffolk , NR35
1NZ Tel: 01986-896644 WWW: www.aviationmuseum.net

Surrey

Bourne Hall Museum
Bourne Hall, Spring Street, Ewell, Epsom, Surrey, KT17
1UF Tel: 020-8394-1734
 WWW: www.epsom.townpage.co.uk
Chertsey Museum
The Cedars, 33 Windsor Street, Chertsey, Surrey, KT16 8AT
Tel: 01932-565764 Fax: 01932-571118
Email: enquiries@chertseymuseum.org.uk
Dorking & District Museum
The Old Foundry, 62a West St, Dorking, Surrey, RH4 1BS
Tel: 01306-876591, 01306-743821
Elmbridge Museum
Church Street, Weybridge, Surrey, KT13 8DE
Tel: 01932-843573 Fax: 01932-846552
Email: info@elm-mus.datanet.co.uk
WWW: www.surrey-online.co.uk/elm-mus
Godalming Museum
109a High Street, Godalming, Surrey, GU7 1AQ
Tel: 01483-426510 Fax: 01483-869-495
Email: museum@godalming.ndo.co.uk
Guildford Museum
Castle Arch, Quarry St, Guildford, Surrey, GU1 3SX
Tel: 01483-444750 Fax: 01483-532391
Email: museum@remote.guildford.gov.uk
Haslemere Educational Museum
78 High Street, Haslemere, Surrey, GU27 2LA
Tel: 01428-642112 Fax: 01428-645234
Email: haslemere_museums@compuserve.com
Kingston Museum & Heritage Service
North Kingston Centre, Richmond Road, Kingston upon
Thames, Surrey, KT2 5PE Tel: 020-8547-6738
Fax: 020-8547-6747
Email: local.history@rbk.kingston.gov.uk
WWW: www.kingston.gov.uk/museum/
Merton Heritage Centre
The Cannons, Madeira Road, Mitcham, Surrey, CR4 4HD
Tel: 020-8640-9387
**Queen s Royal Surrey Regt Museum (Queen s Royal
Surrey East Surrey & Queen s Royal Surrey Regiments)**
Clandon Park, West Clandon, Guildford, Surrey , GU4 7RQ
Tel: 01483-223419 Fax: 01483-224636
Email: queenssurreys@care4free.net
WWW: www.surrey-online.co.uk/queenssurreys

Regimental Museum Royal Logistical Corps
Deepcut, Camberley, Surrey, GU16 6RW
Tel: 01252-340871, 01252-340984
Reigate Priory Museum
Reigate Priory, Bell Street, Reigate, Surrey, RH2 7RL
Tel: 01737-222550
Rural Life Centre
Old Kiln Museum, The Reeds, Tilford, Farnham, Surrey,
GU10 2DL Tel: 01252-795571 Fax: 01252-795571
Email: rural.life@argonet.co.uk
Wandle Industrial Museum
Vestry Hall Annex, London Road, Mitcham, Surrey, CR4
3UD Tel: 020-8648-0127
Woking Museum & Arts & Craft Centre
The Galleries, Chobham Road, Woking , Surrey, GU21 1JF
Tel: 01483-725517 Fax: 01483-725501
Email: the.galleries@dial.pipex.com
East Surrey Museum
1 Stafford Road, Caterham, Surrey , CR3 6JG
Tel: 01883-340275

Sussex

Brighton Fishing Museum
Research Officer & Administrator, 201 Kings Road, Arches,
Brighton, Sussex, BN1 1NB Tel: 01273-723064
Fax: 01273-723064
Royal Military Police Museum
Roussillon Barracks, Chichester, Sussex, PO19 4BN
Tel: 01243 534225 Fax: 01243 534288
Email: museum@rhqrmp.freeserve.co.uk
WWW: www.rhqrmp.freeserve.co.uk
**Sussex Combined Services Museum (Royal Sussex
Regiment and Queen s Royal Irish Hussars)**
Redoubt Fortress, Royal Parade, Eastbourne, Sussex, BN22
7AQ Tel: 01323 410300

Sussex — East Sussex

Anne of Cleves House Museum
52 Southover, High St, Lewes, East Sussex, BN7 1JA
Tel: 01273-474610
Battle Museum
Langton Memorial Hall, High Street, Battle, East Sussex,
TN33 0AQ Tel: 01424-775955
Bexhill Museum
Egerton Road, Bexhill-On-Sea, East Sussex, TN39 3HL
Tel: 01424-787950 Email: museum@rother.gov.uk
WWW: www.1066country.com
Bexhill Museum of Costume & Social History Association
Manor Gardens, Upper Sea Road, Bexhill-On-Sea, East
Sussex, TN40 1RL Tel: 01424-210045
BN1 Visual Arts Project
Brighton Media Centre, 9-12 Middle Street, Brighton, East
Sussex, BN1 1AL Tel: 01273-384242
Booth Museum
194 Dyke Road, Brighton, East Sussex, BN1 5AA
Tel: 01273-292777 Fax: 01273-292778
Email: boothmus@pavilion.co.uk
Dave Clarke Prop Shop
Long Barn, Cross In Hand, Heathfield, East Sussex, TN21
0TP Tel: 01435-863800
Eastbourne Heritage Centre
2 Carlisle Road, Eastbourne, East Sussex, BN21 4BT
Tel: 01323-411189, 01323-721825
The Engineerium
The Droveway, Nevill Road, Hove, East Sussex, BN3 7QA
Tel: 01273-554070 Fax: 01273-566403
Email: info@britishengineering.com
Filching Manor Motor Museum
Filching Manor, Jevington Rd, Polegate, East Sussex, BN26
5QA Tel: 01323-487838
Fishermans Museum
Rock A Nore Road, Hastings, East Sussex, TN34 3DW
Tel: 01424-461446
Hastings Museum & Art Gallery
Johns Place, Bohemia Rd, Hastings TN34 1ET
Tel: 01424-781155

Hove Musuem & Art Gallery
19 New Church Road, Hove, East Sussex, BN3 4AB
Tel: 01273-290200 Fax: 01273-292827
Email: abigail.thomas@brighton-hove.gov.uk
WWW: www.brighton-hove.gov.uk
How We Lived Then Museum of Shops
20 Cornfield Terrace, Eastbourne, East Sussex, BN21 4NS
Tel: 01323-737143
Michelham Priory
Upper Dicker, Hailsham, East Sussex, BN27 3QS
Newhaven Local & Maritime Museum
Garden Paradise, Avis Way, Newhaven, East Sussex
BN9 0DH Tel: 01273-612530
Preston Manor Museum
Preston Drove, Brighton, East Sussex, BN1 6SD
Tel: 01273-292770 Fax: 01273-292771
Rye Castle Museum
East Street, Rye, East Sussex, TN31 7JY Tel: 01797-226728
Seaford Museum of Local History
Martello Tower, The Esplanade, Seaford, East Sussex, BN25
1JH Tel: 01323-898222
Wish Tower Puppet Museum
Tower 73, King Edwards Parade, Eastbourne, East Sussex,
BN21 4BY Tel: 01323-411620

Sussex — West Sussex

Amberley Museum
Station Road, Amberley, Arundel, West Sussex, BN18 9LT
Tel: 01798-831370 Fax: 01798-831831
Email: office@amberleymuseum.co.uk
Chichester District Museum
29 Little London, Chichester, West Sussex, PO19 1PB
Tel: 01243-784683 Fax: 01243-776766
Email: chicmus@breathemail.net
Ditchling Museum
Church Lane, Ditchling, Hassocks, West Sussex, BN6 8TB
Tel: 01273-844744 Fax: 01273-844744
Email: info@ditchling-museum.com
Fishbourne Roman Palace
Roman Way, Salthill Road, Fishbourne, Chichester, West
Sussex, PO19 3QR Tel: 01243-785859
Horsham Museum
9 The Causeway, Horsham, West Sussex, RH12 1HE
Tel: 01403-254959 Fax: 01403-217581
Marlipins Museum
High Street, Shoreham-By-Sea, West Sussex, BN43 5DA
Tel: 01273-462994, 01323-441279 Fax: 01323-844030
Email: smomich@sussexpast.co.uk
The Mechanical Music & Doll Collection
Church Road, Portfield, Chichester, West Sussex, PO19 4HN
Tel: 01243-372646
Petworth Cottage Museum
346 High Street, Petworth, West Sussex, GU28 0AU
Tel: 01798-342100 Fax: 01798-343467
WWW: www.sussexlive.co.uk
The Doll House Museum
Station Road, Petworth, West Sussex, GU28 0BF
Tel: 01798-344044
Weald & Downland Open Air Museum
Singleton, Chichester, West Sussex, PO18 0EU
Tel: 01243-811363 Fax: 01243-811475
Email: wealddown@mistral.co.uk
WWW: www.wealddown.co.uk

Tyne and Wear

**A Soldier s Life 15th/19thThe King s Royal Hussars
Northumberland Hussars and Light Dragoons**
Discovery Museum, Blandford Square,
Newcastle-upon-Tyne, Tyne & Wear, NE1 4JA
Tel: 0191-232-6789 Fax: 0191-230-2614
Email: ralph.thompson@tyne-wear-museums.org.uk
Arbeia Roman Fort
Baring Street, South Shields, Tyne And Wear, NE33 2BB
Tel: 0191-4561369 Fax: 0191-4276862
Email: lizelliott@tyne-wear-museums.org.uk

Bede s World Museum
Church Bank, Jarrow NE32 3DY Tel: 0191-4892106
The Bowes Railway Co Ltd
Springwell Road, Springwell Village, Gateshead NE9 7QJ
Tel: 0191-4161847, 0191-4193349
Email: alison_gibson77@hotmail.com
WWW: www.bowesrailway.co.uk
Castle Keep
Castle Garth, St. Nicholas Street, Newcastle Upon Tyne,
Tyne and Wear, NE1 1RE Tel: 0191-2327938
Hancock Museum
Barras Bridge, Newcastle Upon Tyne NE2 4PT
Tel: 0191-2227418 Fax: 0191-2226753
Military Vehicles Museum
Exhibition Park Pavilion, Newcastle Upon Tyne NE2 4PZ
Tel: 0191-281-7222 Email: miltmuseum@aol.com
Newburn Motor Museum
Townfield Gardens, Newburn, Newcastle Upon Tyne NE15
8PY Tel: 0191-2642977
North East Aircraft Museum
Old Washington Road, Sunderland, SR5 3HZ
Tel: 0191-519-0662
North East Mills Group
Research into wind and water mills in NE England - promot-
ing public access and restoration of mills., Blackfriars,
Monk Street, Newcastle upon Tyne, NE1 4XN
Tel: 0191-232-9279 Fax: 0191-230-1474
WWW: www.welcome.to/North.East.Mill.Group
North East Museums
House of Recovery, Bath Lane, Newcastle Upon Tyne, Tyne
And Wear, NE4 5SQ Tel: 0191-2221661
Ryhope Engines Trust
Pumping Station, Stockton Road, Ryhope, Sunderland SR2
0ND Tel: 0191-5210235 WWW: www.g3wte.demon.co.uk/
South Shields Museum & Art Gallery
Ocean Road, South Shields, Tyne and Wear, NE33 2JA
Tel: 0191-456-8740 Fax: 0191-456-7850
Stephenson Railway Museum
Middle Engine Lane, North Shields NE29 8DX
Tel: 0191-200-7146 Fax: 0191-200-7146
Sunderland Museum & Art Gallery
Borough Road, Sunderland, Tyne and Wear, SR1 1PP
Tel: 0191-565-0723 Fax: 0191-565-0713
Email: martin.routledge@tyne-wear-museums.org.uk
Washington F Pit - Now Permanently Closed
Enquiries to Sunderland Museum & Art Gallery 0191 565 0723

Warwickshire

Leamington Spa Art Gallery & Museum
Royal Pump Rooms, The Parade, Royal Leamington Spa,
Warwickshire, CV32 4AA Tel: 01926-742700
Fax: 01926-742705 Email: prooms@warwickdc.gov.uk
WWW: www.royal-pump-rooms.co.uk
Nuneaton Museum & Art Gallery
Riversley Park, Nuneaton, Warwickshire, CV11 5TU
Tel: 024-7637-6473
**Regimental Museum of The Queen s Own Hussars (3rd
King s Own and 7th Queen s Own Hussars)**
The Lord Leycester Hospital, High Street, Warwick,
Warwickshire, CV34 4EW Tel: Tel:01926 492035
Royal Warwickshire Regimental Museum
St. John s House, Warwick CV34 4NF Tel:01926 491653
Shakespeare Birthplace Trust - Museum
Henley Street, Stratford upon Avon CV37 6QW
Tel: 01789-296083 Email: museums@shakespeare.org.uk
Warwick Castle
Warwick Tel: 01926-406600 Fax: 01926-401692
WWW: www.warwick-castle.co.uk
Warwick Doll Museum
Okens House, Castle Street, Warwick, Warwickshire, CV34
4BP Tel: 01926-495546
Warwickshire Market Hall Museum
Market Place, WarwickCV34 4SA Tel: 01926-412500
Warwickshire Yeomanry Museum
The Court House, Jury Street, Warwick, Warwickshire,
CV34 4EW Tel: 01926 492212 Fax: 01926 494837

Wiltshire

Alexander Keiller Museum
High Street, Avebury, Marlborough, Wiltshire, SN8 1RF
Tel: 01672-539250
Atwell-Wilson Motor Museum Trust
Stockley Lane, Calne, Wiltshire, SN11 0 Tel: 01249-813119
**Duke of Edinburgh s Royal Regiment (Berks & Wilts)
Museum**
The Wardrobe, 58 The Close, Salisbury, SP1 2EX
Tel: 01722-414536
Lydiard House
Lydiard Park, Lydiard Tregoze, Swindon, Wiltshire, SN5
9PA Tel: 01793-770401
Royal Army Chaplains Department Museum
Netheravon House, Salisbury Road, Netheravon, Wiltshire,
SP4 9SY Tel: 01980-604911 Fax: 01980-604908
Salisbury & South Wiltshire Museum
The King s House, 65 The Close, Salisbury, Wiltshire, SP1
2EN Tel: 01722-332151 Fax: 01722-325611
Email: museum@salisburymuseum.freeserve.co.uk
Sevington Victorian School
Sevington, Grittleton, Chippenham, Wiltshire , SN14 7LD
Tel: 01249-783070 Fax: 01249-783070
Steam: Museum of the Great Western Railway
Kemble Drive, Swindon, Wiltshire, SN2 2TA
Tel: 01793-466646 Fax: 01793-466614
Email: tbryan@swindon.gov.uk
Yelde Hall Museum
Market Place, Chippenham , Wiltshire, SN15 3HL
Tel: 01249-651488

Worcestershire

Almonry Museum
Abbey Gate, Worcestershire, WR11 4BG
Tel: 01386-446944
Avoncroft Museum of Historic Buildings
Stoke Heath, Bromsgrove B60 4JR Tel: 01527-831363
Fax: 01527-876934 Email: avoncroft1@compuserve.com
WWW: www.avoncroft.org.uk
Bewdley Museum and Research Library
Load Street, Bewdley DY12 2AE Tel: 01229-403573
The Elgar Birthplace Museum
Crown East Lane, Lower Broadheath, Worcester, WR2 6RH
Tel: 01905-333224 Fax: 01905-333224
Kidderminster Railway Museum
Station Drive, Kidderminster DY10 1QX Tel: 01562-825316
Malvern Museum
Abbey Gateway, Abbey Rd, Malvern, Worcestershire, WR14
3ES Tel: 01684-567811
The Commandery Civil War Museum
Sidbury, Worcester WR1 2HU Tel: 01905-361821
Worcester City Museum & Art Gallery
Foregate Street, Worcester WR1 1DT Tel: 01905-25371
Worcestershire City Museum
Queen Elizabeth House, Trinity Street, Worcester WR1 2PW
Worcestershire County Museum
Hartlebury Castle, Hartlebury, Worcestershire, DY11 7XZ
Tel: 01229-250416 Fax: 01299-251890
Email: museum@worcestershire.gov.uk
WWW: www.worcestershire.gov.uk/museum
Worcestershire Regiment Museum and Archives
Office address: Worcester Regiment Museum Trust, RHQ
WFR, Norton Barracks, Worcester. WR5 2PA, Worcester
City Museum & Art Gallery, Foregate Street, Worcester,
Worcestershire, WR1 1DT Tel: 01905-353871
Email: rhq_wfr@lineone.net

Yorkshire

Yorkshire — East Yorkshire

East Riding Heritage Library & Museum
East Riding Museum Service, Sewerby Hall, Bridlington,
East Yorkshire, YO15 1EA Tel: 01262-677874
Fax: 01262-674265 Email: museum@pop3.poptel.org.uk
WWW: www.bridlington.net/sew

The Hornsea Museum
Burns Farm, 11 Newbegin, Hornsea, North Humberside,
HU18 1AB Tel: 01964-533443 WWW: www.hornsea.com
Museum of Army Transport
Flemingate, Beverley, HU17 0NG Tel: 01482-860445
Withernsea Lighthouse Museum
Hull Road, Withernsea East Yorkshire HU19 2DY
Tel: 01964-614834

Yorkshire—North Yorkshire

Aysgarth Falls Carriage Museum
Yore Mill , Asgarth Falls, Leyburn DL8 3SR
Tel: 01969-663399
Beck Isle Museum of Rural Life
Bridge Street, Pickering YO18 8DU Tel: 01751-473653
Captain Cook Memorial Museum
Grape Lane, Whitby, North Yorkshire, YO22 4BA
Tel: 01947-601900 Fax: 01947-601900
Email: captcookmuseumwhitby@ukgateway.net
WWW: cookmuseumwhitby.co.uk/
Captain Cook Schoolroom Museum
Great Ayton, North Yorkshire Tel: 01642-723358
Dales Countryside Museum
Station Yard, Burtersett Road, Hawes DL8 3NT
Tel: 01969-667494 Fax: 01969-667165
Email: dcm@yorkshiredales.org.uk
Eden Camp Museum
Malton, North Yorkshire, YO17 6RT Tel: 01653-697777
Fax: 01653-698243 Email: admin@edencamp.co.uk
WWW: www.edencamp.co.uk
Embsay Steam Railway
Embsay Railway Station, Embsay, Skipton, North Yorkshire,
BD23 6QX Tel: 01756-794727
Green Howards Regimental Museum
Trinity Church Square, Richmond, North Yorkshire, DL10
4QN Tel: 01748-822133 Fax: 01748-826561
Life In Miniature
8 Sandgate, Whitby YO22 4DB Tel: 01947-601478
Malton Museum
The Old Town Hall, Market Place, Malton, North Yorkshire,
YO17 7LP Tel: 01653-695136
Nidderdale Museum
Council Offices, King Street, Pateley Bridge HG3 5LE
Tel: 01423-711225
Old Courthouse Museum
Castle Yard, Knaresborough Tel: 01423-556188
Fax: 01423-556130
Richmondshire Museum
Research enquiries must be by letter, Ryder s Wynd,
Richmond, North Yorkshire, DL10 4JA Tel: 01748-825611
Ripon Prison & Police Museum
Ripon Museum Trust, St Marygate, Ripon, North Yorkshire,
HG4 1LX Tel: 01765-690799 24hr answeri, 01765-690799
Email: ralph.lindley@which.net
Ripon Workhouse - Museum of Poor Law
Allhallowgate, Ripon, North Yorkshire, HG4 1LE
Tel: 01765-690799
Rotunda Museum
Vernon Road, Scarborough YO11 2NN Tel: 01723-374839
**Royal Dragoon Guards & Prince of Wales Own
Regiment of Yorkshire Military Museum**
3A Tower Street, York, North Yorkshire, YO1 9SB
Tel: 01904-662790 Tel: 01904-658051
Royal Pump Room Museum
Crown Place, Harrogate Tel: 01423-556188
Fax: 01423-556130 Email: lg12@harrogate.gov.uk
WWW: www.harrogate.gov.uk
Ryedale Folk Museum
Hutton le Hole YO62 6UA Tel: 01751-417367
Email: library@dbc-lib.demon.co.uk
Ryedale Folk Museum
Hutton le Hole, North Yorkshire, YO62 6UA
Tel: 01751-417367 Email: library@dbc-lib.demon.co.uk

The World of James Herriott
23 Kirkgate, Thirsk YO7 1PL Tel: 01845-524234
Fax: 01845-525333 Email: anne.keville@hambleton.gov.uk
WWW: www.hambleton.gov.uk
Upper Wharfdale Museum Society & Folk Museum
The Square, Grassington, North Yorkshire, BD23 5AU
Whitby Lifeboat Museum
Pier Road, Whitby YO21 3PU Tel: 01947-602001
Whitby Museum
Pannett Park, Whitby YO21 1RE Tel: 01947-602908
Fax: 01947-897638 Email: graham@durain.demon.co.uk
WWW: www.durain.demon.co.uk
Yorkshire Air Museum
Halifax Way, Elvington, York YO41 5AU Tel: 01904-608595

Yorkshire — South Yorkshire

Abbeydale Industrial Hamlet
Abbeydale Road South, Sheffield, South Yorkshire, S7 2
Tel: 0114-236-7731
Bishops House Museum
Meersbrook Park, Nortin Lees Lane, Sheffield, South
Yorkshire, S8 9BE Tel: 0114-255-7701
Cannon Hall Museum
Cannon Hall, Cawthorne, Barnsley S75 4AT
Tel: 01226-790270
Clifton Park Museum
Clifton Lane, Rotherham S65 2AA Tel: 01709-823635
Email: guy.kilminster@rotherham.gov.uk
WWW: www.rotherham.gov.uk
Fire Museum (Sheffield)
Peter House, 101-109 West Bar, Sheffield S3 8PT
Tel: 0114-249-1999 Fax: 0114-249-1999
WWW: www.hedgepig.freeserve.co.uk
Kelham Island Museum
Alma Street, Kelham Island, Sheffield S3 8RY
Tel: 0114-272-2106
**King s Own Yorkshire Light Infantry Regimental
Museum**
Museum & Art Gallery, Chequer Road, Doncaster, DN1
2AE Tel: 01302-734293 Fax: 01302-735409 Email: muse-
um@doncaster.gov.uk WWW: www.doncaster.gov,uk
**Regimental Museum 13th/18th Royal Hussars and The
Light Dragoons**
Cannon Hall, Cawthorne, Barnsley, South Yorkshire, S75
4AT Tel: 01226 790270
Sandtoft Transport Centre Ltd
Belton Road, Sandtoft, Doncaster, South Yorkshire, DN8
5SX Tel: 01724-711391
Sheffield City Museum
Weston Park, Sheffield, S10 2TP Tel: 0114-278-2600
York and Lancaster Regimental Museum
Library and Arts Centre, Walker Place, Rotherham, South
Yorkshire, S65 1JH Tel: 01709-823635 Fax: 01709-823631
Email: guy.kilminster@rotherham.gov.uk
WWW: www.rotherham.co.uk

Yorkshire—West Yorkshire

Armley Mills
Canal Road, Leeds, West Yorkshire, LS12 2QF
Tel: 0113-263-7861 Fax: 0113-263-7861
Bankfield Museum
Boothtown Road, Halifax HX3 6HG Tel: 01422-354823
Bolling Hall Museum
Bowling Hall Road, Bradford, West Yorkshire, BD4 7
Tel: 01274-723057 Fax: 01274-726220
Bracken Hall Countryside Centre
Glen Road, Baildon, Shipley, BD17 5ED
Tel: 01274-584140
Bradford Industrial Museum & Horses at Work
Moorside Road, Eccleshill, Bradford, West Yorkshire, BD2
3HP Tel: 01274-631756
Calderdale Museums & Arts
Piece Hall, Halifax HX1 1RE Tel: 01422-358087
Castleford Museum Room
Carlton Street, Castleford WF10 1BB Tel: 01977-722085

Cliffe Castle Museum
Spring Gardens Lane, Keighley, West Yorkshire, BD20 6LH
Tel: 01535-618231 Fax: 01535-610536
The Colour Museum
1 Providence Street, Bradford, West Yorkshire, BD1 2PW
Tel: 01274-390955 Fax: 01274-392888
Email: museum@sdc.org.uk WWW: www.sdc.org.uk
Duke of Wellington s Regimental Museum
Bankfield Museum, Akroyd Park, Boothtown Road, Halifax,
HX3 6HG Tel: 01422 354823 Email: Fax: 01422 249020
Eureka The Museum For Children
Discovery Road, Halifax HX1 2NE Tel: 01422-330069
Keighley Bus Museum Trust
47 Brantfell Drive, Burnley, Lancashire, BB12 8AW
Tel: 01282-413179 Fax: 01282-413179
WWW: www.kbmt.freeuk.com
Kirkstall Abbey
Kirkstall Road, Leeds, LS5 3EH Tel: 0113-275-5821
Leeds City Art Gallery
The Headrow, Leeds, LS1 3AA Tel: 0113-247-8248
Leeds Museums Resource Centre
Moorfield Road, Moorfield Industrial Estate, Yeadon, Leeds,
LS19 7BN Tel: 0113-214-6526
Lotherton Hall
Lotherton Lane, Aberford, Leeds, LS25 3EB
Tel: 0113-281-3259
Manor House Art Gallery & Museum
Castle Yard, Castle Hill, Ilkley LS29 9D Tel: 01943-600066
The National Coal Mining Museum for England
Caphouse Colliery, New Road, Overton, Wakefield, West
Yorkshire, WF4 4RH Tel: 01924-848806
Fax: 01924-840694 Email: info@ncm.org.uk
WWW: www.ncm.org.uk
National Museum of Photography, Film &Television
Bradford, West Yorkshire, BD1 1NQ Tel: 01274-202030
Fax: 01274-723155 WWW: http:www.nmpft.org.uk
Royal Armouries (Leeds)
Armouries Drive, Leeds LS10 1LT Tel: 0990-106666
Saddleworth Museum & Art Gallery
High Street, Uppermill, Oldham, Lancashire, OL3 6HS
Tel: 01457-874093 Fax: 01457-870336
Shibden Hall
Lister Road, Shibden, Halifax HX3 6AG
Tel: 01422-352246
Skopos Motor Museum
Alexandra Mills, Alexandra Road, Batley WF17 6JA
Tel: 01924-444423
Temple Newsham House
Temple Newsham Road, off Selby Road, Leeds, LS15 0AE
Tel: 0113-264-7321
Thackray Medical Museum
Beckett Street, Leeds LS9 7LN Tel: 0113-244-4343
Fax: 0113-247-0219 Email: info@thrackraymuseum.org
WWW: www.thackraymuseum.org
Thwaite Mills Watermill
Thwaite Lane, Stourton, Leeds, LS10 1RP
Tel: 0113-249-6453
Vintage Carriages Trust
Station Yard, South Street, Ingrow, Keighley, West
Yorkshire, BD21 1DB Tel: 01535-680425
Wakefield Museum
Wood Street, Wakefield, West Yorkshire, WF1 2EW
Tel: 01924-305351 Fax: 01924-305353

Yorkshire - York

Bar Convent Museum
17 Blossom Street, York, YO24 1AQ Tel: 01904-643238
Fax: 01904-631792 Email: info@bar-convent.org.uk
WWW: www.bar-convent.org.uk
Micklegate Bar Museum
Micklegate, York YO1 6JX Tel: 01904-634436
Richard III Museum
Monk Bar, York YO1 2LH Tel: 01904-634191
WWW: www.richardiiimuseum.co.uk

York Castle Museum
The Eye of York, York, YO1 9RW Tel: 01904-653611
Fax: 01904-671078 WWW: www.york.gov.uk
Yorkshire Museum
Museum Gardens, York, YO1 7FR Tel: 01904-629745
Fax: 01904-651221
Email: yorkshire.museum@yorks.gov.uk
WWW: www.york.gov.uk or also www.yorkgateway.co.uk

WALES

Museum of Welsh Life
St Fagans, Cardiff, CF5 6XB Tel: 029-205-73437
Fax: 029-205-73490

Anglesey

Beaumaris Gaol Museum
Bunkers Hill, Beaumaris, Anglesey, LL58 8EP
Tel: 01248-810921, 01248-724444 Fax: 01248-750282
Email: BeaumarisCourtandGaol@anglesey.gov.uk
Maritime Museum
Beach Road, Newry Beach, Holyhead, Anglesey, LL65 1YD
Tel: 01407-769745 Fax: 01407-769745
Email: cave@holyhead85.freeserve.co.uk

Caerphilly

Drenewydd Museum
26-27 Lower Row, Bute Town, Nr Rhyllney, Caerphilly
County Borough, NP22 5QH Tel: 01685-843039
Email: morgacl@caerphilly.gov.uk

Cardiff

1st The Queen s Dragoon Guards Regimental Museum
Cardiff Castle, Cardiff, Cardiff, CF1 2RB
Tel: 02920-222253, 02920-781232 Fax: 02920-781384
Email: morris602.hhq@netscapeonline
WWW: www.qdg.org.uk
Cardiff Castle
Castle Street, Cardiff, CF10 3RB Tel: 029-2087-8100
Fax: 029-2023-1417 Email: cardiffcastle@cardiff.gov.uk
Techniquest
Stuart Street, Cardiff, CF10 5BW Tel: 02920-475475

Carmarthenshire

Kidwelly Industrial Museum
Broadford, Kidwelly, Carmarthenshire, SA17 4UF
Tel: 01554-891078
Parc Howard Museum & Art Gallery
Mansion House, Parc Howard, Llanelli, Carmarthenshire,
SA15 3LJ Tel: 01554-772029

Ceredigion

Cardigan Heritage Centre
Bridge Warehouse, Castle St, Ceredigion, Dyfed, SA43 3AA
Tel: 01239-614404
Ceredigion Museum
Coliseum, Terrace Road, Aberystwyth, Ceredigion, SY23
2AQ Tel: 01970-633088 Fax: 01970-633084
Email: museum@ceredigion.gov.uk
Llywernog Silver Mine (Mid-Wales Mining Museum Ltd)
Ponterwyd, Aberystwyth, Ceredigion, SY23 3AB
Tel: 01970-890620
Mid-Wales Mining Museum Ltd
15 Market Street, Aberaeron, Ceredigion, SA46 0AU
Tel: 01545-570823

Conwy

Betws-y-Coed Motor Museum
Museum Cottage, Betws-Y-Coed, Conwy, LL24 0AH
Tel: 01690-710760
Teapot Museum
25 Castle Street, Conwy, Gwynedd, LL32 8AY
Tel: 01492-596533

Denbigh/Denbighshire

Cae Dai Trust
Cae Dai Trust/Cae Dai Lawnt, Denbigh, LL16 4SU
Tel: 01745-817004/812107
Llangollen Motor Museum
Pentrefelin, Llangollen, Denbighshire, LL20 8EE
Tel: 01978-860324

Glamorgan
Glamorgan — Mid Glamorgan

Cyfarthfa Castle Museum
Cyfarthfa Park, Brecon Road, Merthyr Tydfil, CF47 8RE
Tel: 01685-723112, 01685-383704 Fax: 01685-723112
Joseph Parrys Cottage
4 Chapel Row, Merthyr Tydfil, Mid Glamorgan, CF48 1BN
Tel: 01685-383704
Pontypridd Historical & Cultural Centre
Bridge Street, Pontypridd, Mid Glamorgan, CF37 4PE
Tel: 01443-409512 Fax: 01443-485565
Ynysfach Iron Heritage Centre
Merthyr Tydfil Heritage Trust, Ynysfach Road, Merthyr
Tydfil, Mid Glamorgan, CF48 1AG Tel: 01685-721858

Glamorgan — South Glamorgan

National Museum & Galleries of Wales
Cathays Park, Cardiff, South Glamorgan, CF10 3NP
Tel: 029-2039-7951
**Welch Regiment Museum of the Royal Regiment of
Wales**
The Black & Barbican Towers, Cardiff Castle, Cardiff, CF10
3RB Tel: 029-20229367 Email: welch@rrw.org.uk
WWW: www.rrw.org.uk

Glamorgan — West Glamorgan

Cefn Coed Colliery Museum
Blaenant Colliery, Crynant, Neath, West Glamorgan, SA10
8SE Tel: 01639-750556
Glynn Vivian Art Gallery
Alexandra Road, Swansea, West Glamorgan, SA1 5DZ
Tel: 01792-655006 Fax: 01792-651713
Email: glynn.vivian.gallery@business.ntl.com
WWW: www.swansea.gov.uk
Maritime & Industrial Museum
Museum Square, Maritime Quarter, Victoria Rd, Swansea,
West Glamorgan, SA1 1SN Tel: 01792-650351
Fax: 01792-652585
Email: swansea.museum@business.ntl.com
Neath Museum
4 Church Place, Neath, West Glamorgan, SA11 3LL
Tel: 01639-645741

Gwynedd

Gwynedd Museums Service
Victoria Dock, Caernarvon, Gwynedd, LL55 1SH
Tel: 01286-679098 Fax: 01286-679637
Email: amgueddfeydd-museums@gwynedd.gov.uk
Porthmadog Maritime Museum
Oakley Wharf 1, The Harbour, Porthmadog, Gwynedd,
LL49 9LU Tel: 01766-513736
Royal Welch Fusiliers Regimental Museum
Caernarfon Castle, Caernarfon, Gwynedd, LL55 2AY
Tel: 01286-673362
Segontium Roman Museum
Beddgelert Road, Caernarfon, Gwynedd, LL55 2LN
Tel: 01286-675625
Welsh Slate Museum
Padarn Country Park, Llanberis, Gwynedd, Gwynedd LL55
4TY Tel: 01286-870630 Fax: 01286-871906
Email: wsmpost@btconnect.com WWW: www.nmgw.ac.uk

Merthyr Tydfil

Cyfarthfa Castle Museum
Cyfarthfa Park, Brecon Road, Merthyr Tydfil, CF47 8RE
Tel: 01685-723112, 01685-383704 Fax: 01685-723112

Joseph Parrys Cottage
4 Chapel Row, Merthyr Tydfil, Mid Glamorgan, CF48 1BN
Tel: 01685-383704
Ynysfach Iron Heritage Centre
Merthyr Tydfil Heritage Trust, Ynysfach Road, Merthyr
Tydfil, Mid Glamorgan, CF48 1AG Tel: 01685-721858

Monmouthshire

Abergavenny Museum
The Castle, Castle Street, Abergavenny, Monmouthshire,
NP7 5EE Tel: 01873-854282
Castle & Regimental Museum
Monmouth Castle, Monmouth NP25 3BS Tel: 01600-772175
Chepstow Museum
Bridge Street, Chepstow, Monmouthshire, NP16 5EZ
Tel: 01291-625981 Fax: 01291-635005
Email: chepstowmuseum@monmouthshire.gov.uk
Monmouthshire Royal Engineers (Militia)
Castle and Regimental Museum, The Castle, Monmouth,
NP5 3BS Tel: 01600-712935
Nelson Museum & Local History Centre
Priory Street, Monmouth, NP5 3XA Tel: 01600-713519
Fax: 01600-775001
Email: nelsonmuseum@monmouthshire.gov.uk
Usk Rural Life Museum
The Malt Barn, New Market Street, Usk, Monmouthshire,
NP15 1AU Tel: 01291-673777

Pembrokeshire

Haverfordwest Town Museum
Castle Street, Haverfordwest, SA61 2EF Tel: 01437-763087
Milford Haven Museum
Old Customs House, The Docks, Milford Haven,
Pembrokeshire, SA73 3AF Tel: 01646-694496
Newport Museum & Art Gallery
John Frost Square, Newport NP20 1PA Tel: 01633-840064
Fax: 01633-222615 Email: museum@newport.gov.uk
Pembrokeshire Motor Museum
Keeston Hill, Haverfordwest, SA62 6EH Tel: 01437-710950
Pembrokeshire Museum Service
The County Library, Dew Street, Haverfordwest, SA61 1SU
Tel: 01437-775246 Fax: 01437-769218
Pillgwenlly Heritage Community Project
within Baptist Chapel, Alexandra Road, Newport,
Pembrokeshire, NP20 2JE Tel: 01633-244893
Roman Legionary Museum
High Street, Caerleon, Newport NP18 1AE
Tel: 01633-423134
Tenby Museum
Tenby Museum & Art Gallery, Castle Hill, Tenby,
Pembrokeshire, SA70 7BP Tel: 01834-842809
Fax: 01834-842809 Email: tenbymuseum@hotmail.com
WWW: www.tenbymuseum.free-online.co.uk
Wilson Museum of Narberth
Market Square, Narberth SA67 7AX Tel: 01834-861719

Powys

The Judge s Lodging
Broad Street, Presteigne, Powys, LD8 2AD
Tel: 01544-260650 Fax: 01544-260652
WWW: www.judgeslodging.org.uk
Llanidloes Museum
Great Oak Street, Llanidloes SY18 6BN Tel: 01686-412375
Powysland Museum & Montgomery Canal Centre
Canal Yard, Welshpool, Powys, SY21 7AQ
Tel: 01938-554656 Fax: 01938-554656
Radnorshire Museum
Temple Street, Llandrindod Wells, Powys, LD1 5DL
Tel: 01597-824513 Fax: 01597-825781
Email: radnorshire.museum@powys.gov.uk
**South Wales Borderers & Monmouthshire Regimental
Museum of the Royal Regt of Wales (24th/41st Foot)**
The Barracks, Brecon, Powys, LD3 7EB Tel: 01874-613310
Fax: 01874-613275 Email: rrw@ukonline.co.uk
WWW: www.ukonline.co.uk/rrw/index.htm

Water Folk Canal Centre
Old Store House, Llanfrynach, Brecon, Powys, LD3 7LJ
Tel: 01874-665382

Torfaen

Big Pit Mining Museum
Blaenavon, Torfaen, NP4 9XP Tel: 01495-790311
Valley Inheritance
Park Buildings, Pontypool, NP4 6JH Tel: 01495-752036
Fax: 01495-752043

Wrexham

Wrexham Museum
County Buildings, Regent Street, Wrexham, LL11 1RB
Tel: 01978-317970 Fax: 01978-317982
Email: museum@wrexham.gov.uk

SCOTLAND

Scottish United Services Museum
The Castle, Museum Square, Edinburgh, EH1 2NG
Tel: 0131-225-7534 Fax: 0131-225-3848
Scottish Museums Council
County House, 20/22 Torphichen Street, Edinburgh, EH3
8JB Tel: 0131-229-7465 Fax: 0131-229-2728
Email: inform@scottishmuseums.org.uk
WWW: www.scottishmuseums.org.uk

Aberdeenshire

Aberdeen Maritime Museum
Shiprow, Aberdeen, AB11 5BY Tel: 01224-337700
Fax: 01224-213066 Email: johne@arts-recreation.net.uk
WWW: www.aagm.co.uk
Alford & Donside Heritage Association
Mart Road, Alford, AB33 8AA Tel: 019755-62906
Arbuthnot Museum
St. Peter Street, Peterhead, Aberdeenshire, AB42 1LA
Tel: 01779-477778 Fax: 01771-622884

Fraserburgh Heritage Society
Heritage Centre, Quarry Road, Fraserburgh, AB43 9DT
Tel: 01346-512888
Gordon Highlanders Museum
St Lukes, Viewfield Road, Aberdeen AB15 7XH
Tel: 01224-311200 Fax: 01224-319323
Email: museum@gordonhighlanders.com
WWW: www.gordonhighlanders.com
Grampian Transport Museum
Alford, AB33 8AE Tel: 019755-62292
Hamilton T.B
Northfield Farm, New Pitsligo, Fraserburgh AB43 6PX
Tel: 01771-653504
Museum of Scottish Lighthouses
Kinnaird Head, Fraserburgh, Aberdeenshire, AB43 9DU
Tel: 01346-511022 Fax: 01346-511033
Email: enquiries@lighthousescom.co.uk
Provost Skene s House
Guestrow, Aberdeen AB10 1AS Tel: 01224-641086
Satrosphere
Moved in 2000 - new address contact, 19 Justice Mill Lane,
Aberdeen, AB11 6EQ Tel: 01224-213232
Fax: 01224-211685 Email: satrosphere@ssphere.ifb.co.uk

Angus

Arbroath Museum
Signal Tower, Ladyloan, Arbroath DD11 1PY Tel: 01241-875598
Fax: 01241-439263 Email: signal.tower@angus.gov.uk
WWW: www.angus.gov.uk/history
Glenesk Folk Museum
The Retreat, Glenesk, Brechin, Angus, DD9 7YT
Tel: 01356-670254 Email: retreat@angusglens.co.uk
WWW: www.angusglens.co.uk

The Meffan Institute
20 High Street West, Forfar, Angus, DD8 1BB
Tel: 01307-464123 Fax: 01307-468451
Email: the.meffan@angus.gov.uk

Argyll

Campbeltown Heritage Centre
Big Kiln, Witchburn Road, Campbeltown, Argyll, PA28 6JU
Tel: 01586-551400
Campbeltown Library and Museum
Hall Street, Campbeltown, Argyll, PA28 6BU
Tel: 01586-552366
Castle House Museum
Castle Gardens, Argyll Street, Dunoon, Argyll, PA23 7HH
Tel: 01369-701422
Kilmartin House Trust
Kilmartin House, Kilmartin, Lochgilphead, Argyll, PA31
8RQ Tel: 01546-510278 Fax: 01546-510330
Email: museum@kilmartin.org WWW: www.kilmartin.org
Regimental Museum Argyll and Sutherland Highlanders
Stirling Castle, Stirling, Stirlingshire, FK8 1EH
Tel: 01786 475165 Fax: 01786 446038

Ayrshire

Ayrshire Yeomanry Museum
Rozelle House, Monument Road, Alloway by Ayr, Ayrshire,
KA7 4NQ Tel: 01292-445400, 01292-264091
**Dalgarven Mill, Museum of Ayrshire Country Life &
Costume**
Dalry Road, Dalgarven, Kilwinning, Ayrshire, KA13 6PL
Tel: 01294-552448
East Ayrshire Council District History Centre & Museum
Baird Institute, 3 Lugar Street, Cumnock, Ayrshire, KA18
1AD Tel: 01290-421701 Fax: 01290-421701
Email: Baird.institute@east-ayrshire.gov.uk
WWW: www.east-ayrshire.gov.uk
Glasgow Vennel Museum
10 Glasgow, Vennel, Irvine KA12 0BD Tel: 01294-275059
Irvine Burns Club & Burgh Museum
28 Eglinton Street, Irvine KA12 8AS Tel: 01294-274511
Largs Museum
Kirkgate House, Manse Court, Largs, Ayrshire, KA30 8AW
Tel: 01475-687081
McKechnie Institute
Dalrymple Street, Girvan, Ayrshire, KA26 9AE
Tel: 01465-713643 Email: mkigia@ukgateway.net
North Ayrshire Museum
Manse Street, Saltcoats, Ayrshire, KA21 5AA
Tel: 01294-464174 Fax: 01294-464174
Email: namuseum@globalnet.co.uk
Rozelle House
Rozelle Park, Ayr, Ayrshire, KA7 4NQ Tel: 01292-445447

Banffshire

The Buckie Drifter Maritime Heritage Centre
Freuchny Road, Buckie AB56 1TT Tel: 01542-834646

Berwickshire

The Jim Clark Room
44 Newtown Street, Duns TD11 3DT Tel: 01361-883960
Museum of Coldstream Guards
Coldstream, Berwickshire

Caithness

Clangunn Heritage Centre & Museum
Old Parish Kirk, Latheron, Caithness, KW5 6DL
Tel: 01593-741700
Dunbeath Preservation Trust
Old School, Dunbeath KW6 6EG Tel: 01593-731233
Fax: 01593-731233 Email: DunTrust@aol.com
The Last House
John O Groats, Wick KW1 4YR Tel: 01955-611250
Wick Hertiage Centre
18 Bank Row, Wick KW1 5EY Tel: 01955-605393

Dumfries & Galloway/ Dumfriesshire

Dumfries Museum
The Observatory, Dumfries, DG2 7SW Tel: 01387-253374
Fax: 01387-265081 Email: info@dumgal.gov.uk
WWW: www.dumfriesmuseum.demon.co.uk

Ellisland Trust
Ellisland Farm, Dumfries DG2 0RP Tel: 01387-740426

Gretna Museum & Tourist Services
Headless Cross, Gretna Green DG16 5EA Tel: 01461-338441
Fax: 01461-338442 Email: info@gretnagreen.com
WWW: www.gretnagreen.com

John Paul Jones Birthplace Museum
Arbigland, Kirkbean, Dumfries DG2 8BQ Tel: 01387-880613

Old Bridge House Museum
Mill Road, Dumfries DG2 7BE Tel: 01387-256904
WWW: www.dumfriesmuseum.demon.co.uk

Robert Burns Centre
Mill Road, Dumfries DG2 7BE Tel: 01387-264808

Sanquhar Tolbooth Museum
High Street, Sanquhar DG4 6BL Tel: 01659-50186

Savings Banks Museum
Ruthwell, Dumfries DG1 4NN Tel: 01387-870640

Shambellie House Museum of Costume
New Abbey, Dumfries DG2 8HQ Tel: 01387-850375

Stranraer Museum
55 George Street, Stranraer, DG9 7JP Tel: 01776-705088
Fax: 01776-705835 Email: JohnPic@dumgal.gov.uk

Dunbartonshire

Scottish Maritime Museum
Gottries Road, Irvine, Ayrshire, KA12 8QE
Tel: 01294-278283 Fax: 01294-313211
Email: jgrant5313@aol.com

Dundee

Dundee Heritage Trust
Verdant Works, West Henderson s Wynd, Dundee, DD1 5BT
Tel: 01382-225282 Fax: 01382-221612
Email: info@dundeeheritage.sol.co.uk
WWW: www.verdant.works.co.uk

Royal Research Ship Discovery
Discovery Point, Discovery Quay, Dundee, DD1 4XA
Tel: 01382-201245 Fax: 01382-225891
Email: info@dundeeheritage.sol.co.uk
WWW: www.rrs-discovery.co.uk

Verdant Works - A Working Jute mill
West Henderson s Wynd, Dundee, DD1 5BT
Tel: 01382-225282 Fax: 01382-221612
Email: dundeeheritage@sol.co.uk
WWW: www.verdant-works.co.uk

Edinburgh

Heritage Projects (Edinburgh) Ltd
Castlehill, Royal Mile, Edinburgh, Midlothian EH1 2NE
Tel: 0131-225-7575

Huntly House Museum
142 Canongate, Edinburgh, EH8 8DD Tel: 0131-529-4143
Fax: 0131-557-3346

National Museums of Scotland - Library
Royal Museum, Chambers Street, Edinburgh, EH1 1JF
Tel: 0131-247-4137 Fax: 0131-247-4311
Email: library@nms.ac.uk WWW: www.nms.ac.uk

Royal Museum and Museum of Scotland
Chambers Street, Edinburgh, EH1 1JF Tel: 0131-225-7534,
0131-247-4027 (Text) WWW: www.nms.ac.uk

Royal Scots Regimental Museum
The Castle, Edinburgh, EH1 2YT Tel: 0131-310-5014
Fax: 0131-310-5019

Royal Yacht Britannia and Visitor Centre
Ocean Drive, Leith, Edinburgh, EH6 6JJ
Tel: 0131-555-5566, Group bookings 0131-555-8800
WWW: www.royalyachtbritannia.co.uk

Scottish United Services Museum
The Castle, Museum Square, Edinburgh, EH1 2NG
Tel: 0131-225-7534 Fax: 0131-225-3848

Scottish United Services Museum Library
The Castle, Museum Square, Edinburgh, EH1 1 2NG
Tel: 0131-225-7534-Ext-2O4 Fax: 0131-225-3848
Email: library@nms.ac.uk WWW: www.nms.ac.uk

Falkirk

Falkirk History Research Centre
Callendar House, Callendar Park, Falkirk, FK1 1YR
Tel: 01324-503778 Fax: 01324-503771
Email: ereid@falkirkmuseums.demon.co.uk
WWW: www.falkirkmuseums.demon.co.uk

Fife

Andrew Carnegie Birthplace Museum
Moodie Street, Dunfermline, Fife, KY12 7PL
Tel: 01383-724302

Dunfermline Museum
Enquiries can be made at this address for: Inverkeithing
Museum, Pittencrief House Museum and St Margaret s
Cave, Viewfield, Viewfield Terrace, Dunfermline, Fife,
KY12 7HY Tel: 01383-313838 Fax: 01383-313837

Inverkeithing Museum
Museum located at: The Friary, Queen Street, Inverkeithing,
Fife. Tel: 01383-313595, Enquiries to: Dunfermline
Museum, Viewfield, Viewfield Terrace, Dunfermline, Fife,
KY12 7HY Tel: 01383-313838 Fax: 01383-313837

John McDouall Stuart Museum
Rectory Lane, Dysart, Kirkcaldy, Fife, KY1 2TP
Tel: 01592-653118

Kirkcaldy Museum & Art Gallery
War Memorial Gardens, Abbotshall Road, Kirkcaldy, Fife,
KY1 1YG Tel: 01592-412860 Fax: 01592-412870

Methil Heritage Centre
272 High Street, Methil, Leven, Fife, KY8 3EQ
Tel: 01333-422100

Pittencrieff House Museum
Museum located at: Pittencrieff Park, Dunfermline, Fife
KY12 8QH Tel: 01383-722935, Enquiries to: Dunfermline
Museum, Viewfield, Viewfield Terrace, Dunfermline, Fife,
KY12 7HY Tel: 01383-313838 Fax: 01383-313837

Scotland s Secret Bunker
Underground Nuclear Command Centre, Crown Buildings
(Near St Andrews), Fife, KY16 8QH Tel: 01333-310301

Scottish Fisheries Museum
Scottish Fisheries Museum Trust Ltd, St. Ayles,
Harbourhead, Anstruther, Fife, KY10 3AB
Tel: 01333-310628 Fax: 01333-310628
Email: andrew@scottish-fisheries-museum.org
WWW: www.scottish-fisheries-museum.org

The Fife Folk Museum
High Street, Ceres, Cupar, Fife, KY15 5NF
Tel: 01334-828180

Glasgow

Glasgow Vennel Museum
10 Glasgow, Vennel, Irvine, Ayrshire, KA12 0BD
Tel: 01294-275059

Heatherbank Museum
Glasgow Caledonian University, Cowcaddens Road,
Glasgow, G4 0BA Tel: 0141-331-8637 Fax: 0141-331-3005
Email: a.ramage@gcal.ac.uk
WWW: www.lib.gcal.ac.uk/heatherbank

**Museum of The Royal Highland Fusiliers (Royal Scots
Fusiliers and Highland Light Infantry)**
518 Sauchiehall Street, Glasgow, G2 3LW
Tel: 0141-332-0961 Fax: 0141-332-5439

Scotland Street School Museum & Museum of Education
225 Scotland Street, Glasgow, Lanarkshire, G5 8QB
Tel: 0141-287-0500

Inverness-Shire

Highland Folk Museum
Duke Street, Kingussie, Inverness-Shire, PH21 1JG
Tel: 01540-661307 Fax: 01540-661631
Email: rachel.chisholm@highland.gov.uk

Highland Folk Park
Aultlarie Croft, Kingussie Road, Newtonmore,
Inverness-Shire, PH20 1AY Tel: 01540-673551
Highland Railway Museum
5 Druimlon, Drumnadrochit, Inverness, Inverness-Shire,
IV63 6TY Tel: 01456-450527
Inverness Museum & Art Gallery
Castle Wynd, Inverness V2 3ED Tel: 01463-237114
Mallaig Heritage Centre
Station Road, Mallaig PH41 4PY Tel: 01687-462085
Queen s Own Highlanders Regimental Museum
Fort George, Ardersier, Inverness, IV1 2TD
Tel: 01463-224380
The Clansman Centre
Canalside, Fort Augustus PH32 4AU Tel: 01320-366444
West Highland Museum
Cameron Square, Fort William, Inverness-Shire, PH33 6AJ
Tel: 01397-702169 Fax: 01397-701927

Isle Of Arran

Arran Heritage Museum
Rosaburn House, Brodick, Isle Of Arran, KA27 8DP
Tel: 01770-302636

Isle Of Islay

Finlaggan Trust The
The Cottage, Ballygrant, Isle Of Islay, PA45 7QL
Tel: 01496-840644

Isle Of Mull

The Columba Centre
Fionnphort, Isle Of Mull, Isle Of Mull, PA66 6BN
Tel: 01681-700660

Isle Of North Uist

Taigh Chearsabhagh Trust
Taigh Chearsabhagh, Lochmaddy, Isle Of North Uist, HS6
5AE Tel: 01876-500293
Email: taighchearsabhagh@zetnet.co.uk
WWW: www.taighchearsabhagh.org.uk

Isle Of South Uist

Kildonan Museum
Kildonan, Lochboisdale, Isle Of South Uist, HS8 5RZ
Tel: 01878-710343

Kinross

Perth Museum & Art Gallery
George Street, Perth, Tayside, PHI 5LB Tel: 01738-632488
Fax: 01738-443505 Email: scpayne@pkc.gov.uk

Lanarkshire

Auyld Kirk Museum
The Cross Kirkintilloch, Glasgow G66 1 Tel: 0141 578 0144
Barrhead Museum - Closed permanently wef 31/3/00
Main Street, Barrhead, Glasgow, Lanarkshire, G78 1SW
Tel: 0141-876-1994
Biggar Museum Trust
Moat Park Kirkstyle, Biggar ML12 6DT Tel: 01899-221050
Cameronians (Scottish Rifles) Museum
c/o Low Parks Museum, 129 Muir Street, Hamilton,
Lanarkshire, ML3 6BJ Tel: 01698-455714, 01698-328232
Discover Carmichael Visitors Centre
Warrenhill Farm, Warrenhill Road, Thankerton, Biggar,
Lanarkshire, ML12 6PF Tel: 01899-308169
Fossil Grove Museum
Victoria Park, Glasgow G65 9AH Tel: 0141-950-1448
Greenhill Covenanters House Museum
Kirkstyle, Biggar ML12 6DT Tel: 01899-221572
Heritage Engineering
22 Carmyle Avenue, Glasgow G32 8HJ Tel: 0141-763-0007
Hunter House
Maxwellton Road, East Kilbride, Glasgow, Lanarkshire, G74
3LW Tel: 01355-261261

John Hastie Museum
Threestanes Road, Strathaven, Lanarkshire, ML10 6EB
Tel: 01357-521257
Lanark Museum
7 Westport, Lanark, Lanarkshirc, ML11 9HD
Tel: 01555-666680 Email: paularchibald@hotmail.com
WWW: www.biggar-net.co.uk/lanarkmuseum
Low Parks Museum
129 Muir Street, Hamilton, Lanarkshire, ML3 6BJ
Tel: 01698-283981, 01698-328232
New Lanark Conservation Trust
Visitors Centre Mill No 3, New Lanark Mills, Lanark,
Lanarkshire, ML11 9DB Tel: 01555-661345
Fax: 01555-665378 Email: visit@newlanark.org
WWW: www.newlanark.org
The People s Palace
Glasgow Green, Glasgow, Lanarkshire, G40 1AT
Tel: 0141-554-0223
Scotland Street School Museum & Museum of Education
225 Scotland Street, Glasgow, Lanarkshire, G5 8QB
Tel: 0141-287-0500
The Lighthouse
11 Mitchell Lane, Glasgow, Lanarkshire, G1 3NU
Tel: 0141-221-6362
Weavers Cottages Museum
23-25 Wellwynd, Airdrie, Lanarkshire, ML6 0BN
Tel: 01236-747712
Auld Kirk Musuem
The Cross, Kirkintilloch, Glasgow, Lanarkshire , G66 1
Tel: 0141-578-0144

Lanarkshire - North Lanarkshire

Motherwell Heritage Centre
High Road, Motherwell, North Lanarkshire, ML1 3HU
Tel: 01698-251000 Fax: 01698-253433
Email: heritage@mhc158.freeserve.co.uk

Lothian

Lothian — East Lothian

Dunbar Museum
High Street, Dunbar, East Lothian, EH42 1ER
Tel: 01368-863734
John Muir House Museum
126-128 High Street, Dunbar, East Lothian, EH42 1JJ
Tel: 01368-862585
North Berwick Museum
School Road, North Berwick, East Lothian, EH39 4JU
Tel: 01620-895457

Lothian — West Lothian

Almond Valley Heritage Trust
Livingston Mill Farm, Millfield, Livingston, West Lothian,
EH54 7AR Tel: 01506-414957
Bennie Museum
Mansefield Street, Bathgate, West Lothian, EH48 4HU
Tel: 01506-634944
Kinneil Museum
Kinneil Estate, Bo Ness, West Lothian, EH51 0AY
Tel: 01506-778530
Linlithgow s Story
Annet House, 143 High Street, Linlithgow, West Lothian,
EH49 7EJ Tel: 01506-670677
Queensferry Museum
53 High Street, South Queensferry, West Lothian, EH30
9HP Tel: 0131-331-5545

Midlothian

History of Education Centre
East London Street, Edinburgh, Midlothian, EH7 4BW
Tel: 0131-556-4224
Lauriston Castle
2a Cramond Rd South, Edinburgh, Midlothian, EH4 5QD
Tel: 0131-336-2060
Nelson Monument
Calton Hill, Edinburgh, Midlothian, EH7 5AA
Tel: 0131-556-2716

Newhaven Heritage Museum
Pier Place, Edinburgh, Midlothian, EH6 4LP
Tel: 0131-551-4165
Scots Dragoon Guards Museum Shop
The Castle, Edinburgh, Midlothian, EH1 2YT
Tel: 0131-220-4387
Scottish Mining Museum Trust
Lady Victoria Colliery, Newtongrange, Dalkeith, Midlothian,
EH22 4QN Tel: 0131-663-7519 Fax: 0131-654-1618
WWW: www.scottishminingmuseum.com

Morayshire

Elgin Museum
1 High Street, Elgin, Morayshire, IV30 1EQ
Tel: 01343-543675 Fax: 01343-543675
Email: curator@elginmuseum.demon.co.uk
Falconer Museum
Tolbooth Street, Forres, Morayshire, IV36 1PH
Tel: 01309-673701 Fax: 01309-675863
Email: alisdair.joyce@techleis.moray.gov.uk
WWW: www.moray.gov.uk
Grantown Museum & Heritage Trust
Burnfield House, Burnfield Avenue, Grantown-On-Spey,
Morayshire, PH26 3HH Tel: 01479-872478
Fax: 01479-872478 Email: molly.duckett@btinternet.com
WWW: www.grantown-on-spey.co.uk
Lossiemouth Fisheries Museum
Pitgaveny Street, Lossiemouth, Morayshire, IV31 6TW
Tel: 01343-813772
Nairn Museum
Viewfield House, King Street, Nairn, Morayshire, IV12 4EE
Tel: 01667-456791

Orkney

Orkney Farm & Folk Museum - Birsay
Kirbister Farm, Birsay, Orkney, KW17 2LR
Tel: 01856-771268
Orkney Farm & Folk Museum - Harray
Corrigall Farm Museum, Harray, Orkney, KW17 2LQ
Tel: 01856-771411
Orkney Fossil & Vintage Centre
Viewforth Burray, Orkney, KW17 2SY Tel: 01856-731255
Orkney Muscum
Tankerness House, Broad Street, Kirkwall, Orkney, KW15
1DH Tel: 01856-873191 Fax: 01856-871560
Orkney Wireless Museum
Kiln Corner, Kirkwall, Orkney, KW15 1LB
Tel: 01856-871400
Scapa Flow Visitor Centre
Lyness, Stromness, Orkney, KW16 3NT Tel: 01856-791300
Stromness Museum
52 Alfred Street, Stromness, Orkney Tel: 01856-850025

Perthshire

Atholl Country Collection
The Old School, Blair Atholl, Perthshire, PH18 5SP
Tel: 01796-481232 Email: r.cam@virgin.net
Clan Donnachaidh (Robertson) Museum
Clan Donnachaidh Centre, Bruar, Pitlochry PH18 5TW
Tel: 01796-483338
Email: clandonnachaidh@compuserve.com
WWW: donkey3@freenetname.co.uk
Clan Menzies Museum
Castle Menzies, Weem, by Aberfeldy, Perthshire, PH15 2JD
Tel: 01887-820982
Dunkeld Cathedral Chapter House Museum
Dunkeld, Perthshire, PH8 0AW Tel: 01350-727601/727249
The Hamilton Toy Collection
111 Main Street, Callander, Perthshire, FK17 8BQ
Tel: 01877-330004
Meigle Museum
Dundee Road, Meigle, Blairgowrie, Perthshire, PH12 8SB
Tel: 01828-640612
Perth Museum & Art Gallery
George Street, Perth, Tayside, PHI 5LB Tel: 01738-632488
Fax: 01738-443505 Email: scpayne@pkc.gov.uk

Regimental Museum and Archives of the Black Watch
Balhousie Castle, Hay Street, Perth, Perthshire, PH1 5HS
Tel: 01738 621281 Fax: 01738-643245
Email: bwarchivist@btelick.com
Scottish Horse Regimental Museum
The Cross, Dunkeld, Perthshire, PH8 0AN

Renfrewshire

Mclean Museum & Art Gallery
15 Kelly Street, Greenock, Renfrewshire, PA16 8JX
Tel: 01475-715624
Old Paisley Society
George Place, Paisley PA1 2HZ Tel: 0141-889-1708
Paisley Museum
Paisley Museum and Art Galleries, High Street, Paisley,
Renfrewshire, PA1 2BA Tel: 0141-889-3151
Renfrewshire Council Library & Museum
Central Library & Museum Complex, High Street, Paisley,
Renfrewshire, PA1 2BB Tel: 0141-889-2350
Fax: 0141-887-6468
Email: local_studies.library@renfrewshire.gov.uk

Ross-Shire

Dingwall Museum Trust
Town Hall, High Street, Dingwall, Ross-Shire, IV15 9RY
Tel: 01349-865366
The Groam House Museum
High Street, Rosemarkie, Fortrose, Ross-Shire, IV10 8UF
Tel: 01381-620961 Fax: 01381-621730
Highland Museum of Childhood
The Old Station, Strathpeffer, Ross-Shire, IV14 9DH
Tel: 01997-421031 Email: info@hmoc.freeserve.co.uk
WWW: www.hmoc.freeserve.co.uk
Tain & District Museum
Tain Through Time, Tower Street, Tain, Ross-Shire, IV19
1DY Tel: 01862-893054
Email: info@tainmuseum.demon.co.uk
Ullapool Museum & Visitor Centre
7 & 8 West Argyle Street, Ullapool, Ross-Shire, IV26 2TY
Tel: 01854-612987 Fax: 01854-612987
Email: ulmuseum@wavereider.co.uk

Roxburghshire

Hawick Museum & Scott Gallery
Wilton Lodge Park, Hawick, Roxburghshire, TD9 7JL
Tel: 01450-373457 Fax: 01450-378506
Email: hawickmuseum@hotmail.com
also fionacolton@hotmail.com
Jedburgh Castle Jail Museum
Castlegate, Jedburgh, Roxburghshire, TD8 6BD
Tel: 01835-863254 Fax: 01835-864750
Mary Queen of Scots House and Visitor Centre
Queens Street, Jedburgh, Roxburghshire, TD8 6EN
Tel: 01835-863331 Fax: 01835-863331
Email: hawickmuseum@hotmail.com
also fionacotton@hotmail.com

Scottish Borders

Hawick Museum & Scott Gallery
Wilton Lodge Park, Hawick, Roxburghshire, TD9 7JL
Tel: 01450-373457 Fax: 01450-378506
Email: hawickmuseum@hotmail.com
also fionacolton@hotmail.com
Mary Queen of Scots House and Visitor Centre
Queens Street, Jedburgh, Roxburghshire, TD8 6EN
Tel: 01835-863331 Fax: 01835-863331
Email: hawickmuseum@hotmail.com
also fionacotton@hotmail.com

Selkirkshire

Halliwells House Museum
Halliwells Close, Market Place, Selkirk, Selkirkshire, TD7
4BL Tel: 01750-20096 Fax: 01750-23282
Email: museums@scotsborders.gov.uk

Shetland

Fetlar Interpretive Centre
Beach Of Houbie, Fetlar, Shetland, ZE2 9DJ
Tel: 01957-733206 Email: fic@zetnet.co.uk
WWW: www.zetnet.co.uk/sigs/centre
Old Haa Museum
Burravoe Yell, Shetland, Shetland Islands, ZE2 9AY
Tel: 01957-722339
Shetland Museum
Lower Hillhead, Lerwick, Shetland Islands, ZE1 0EL
Tel: 01595-695057 Email: shetland.museum@zetnet.co.uk
WWW: www.shetland-museum.org.uk
Shetland Textile Working Museum The
Weisdale Mill, Weisdale, Shetland, Shetland Islands, ZE2
9LW Tel: 01595-830419
Tangwick HAA Museum
Tangwick, Eshaness, Shetland, ZE2 9RS Tel: 01806-503389
Unst Heritage Centre
Haraldswick, Unst, Shetland, ZE2 9EQ Tel: 01957-711528
Fax: 01957-711387 (Custodian home)

Stirlingshire and Sutherland

Regimental Museum Argyll and Sutherland Highlanders
Stirling Castle, Stirling, Stirlingshire, FK8 1EH Tel: 01786
475165 Fax: 01786 446038
Strathnaver Museum
Bettyhill, Sutherland, KW14 7SS Tel: 01641-521418,
Fax: 01641-521315

Wigtownshire

Taylor s Farm Tradition
Barraer, Newton Stewart, Wigtownshire, DG8 6QQ
Tel: 01671-402184 Fax: 01671-404890
Email: j.taylor@bosinternet.com

Northern Ireland
Armagh County Museum
The Mall East, Armagh, County Armagh, BT61 9BE
Tel: (028) 37523070
Ballymoney Museum & Heritage Centre
33 Charlotte Street, Ballymoney, County Antrim, BT53 6AY
Tel: (028) 27662280
Centre for Migration Studies-Ulster American Folk Park
Mellon Road, Castletown, Omagh, County Tyrone, BT78
8QY Tel: 028-8225-6315 Fax: 028-8224-2241
Email: uafp@iol.ie WWW: www.folkpark.com
also www.qub.ac.uk/cms
Down County Museum
The Mall, Downpatrick, County Down, BT30 6AH
Tel: (028) 446615218
Downpatrick Railway Museum
Railway Station, Market St, Downpatrick, County Down,
BT30 6LZ Tel: (028) 446615779
Fermanagh County Museum
Enniskillen Castle Castle Barracks, Enniskillen, County
Fermanagh, BT74 7HL Tel: 028-6632-5000
Fax: 028-6632-7342 Email: castle@fermanagh.gov.uk
Foyle Valley Railway Museum
Foyle Road, Londonderry, County Londonderry, BT48 6SQ
Tel: (028) 712265234
Friends of the Ulster Museum Botanic Gardens
Botanic Gardens, Stranmillas Road, Belfast, County Antrim,
BT9 5AB Tel: (028) 9068-1606
Garvagh Museum
142 Main Street, Garvagh, County Londonderry, BT51 5AE
Tel: 028-295-58216/58188 Fax: 028-295-58993
Email: jclyde@garvaghhigh.garvagh.ni.sch.uk
Northen Ireland Museums Council
66 Donegall Pass, Belfast, County Antrim, BT7 1BU
Tel: (028) 90550215 Fax: (028) 90550216
Email: info@nimc.co.uk WWW: www.nimc.co.uk
Odyssey Science Centre Project Office
Project Office NMGNI, Botanic Gardens, Belfast, County
Antrim, BT9 5AB Tel: (028) 90682100
Roslea Heritage Centre

Church Street, Roslea, Enniskillen, County Fermanagh,
BT74 7DW Tel: (028) 67751750
Route 66
American Car Museum, 94 Dundrum Road, Newcastle,
County Down, BT33 0LN Tel: (028) 43725223
Royal Inniskillin Fusiliers Regimental Museum
The Castle, Enniskillen, Co Fermanagh, BT74 7BB
Tel: 028-6632-3142 Fax: (028) 6632-0359
Royal Irish Fusilers Museum
Sovereign s House, Mall East, Armagh, BT61 9DL
Tel: (028) 3752-2911 Fax: (028) 3752-2911
The Royal Irish Regiment Museum
St. Patricks Barracks, Demesne Avenue, Ballymena, County
Antrim, BT43 7BH Tel: (028) 256661355
Royal Ulster Rifles Regimental Museum
5 Waring Street, Belfast, BT1 2EW Tel: (028) 9023-2086
The Somme Heritage Centre
233 Bangor Road, Newtownards, County Down, BT23 7PH
Tel: (028) 91823202 Fax: (028) 91823214
WWW: www.irishsoldier.org
Ulster American Folk Park Project Team Belfast
4 The Mount Albert Bridge Road, Belfast, County Antrim,
BT5 4NA Tel: (028) 9045 2250
Ulster Aviation Society
Langford Lodge Airfield 97, Largy Road, Crumlin, County
Antrim, BT29 4RT Tel: (028) 94454444
Email: ernie@airni.freeserve.co.uk
WWW: www.d-n-a.net/users/dnetrazq/
Ulster Folk & Transport Museum
Cultra, Holywood, Co Down, BT18 0EU
Tel: (028) 90 428428 Fax: (028) 90 428728
The Ulster History Park
Cullion, Lislap, Omagh, County Tyrone, BT79 7SU
Tel: (028) 8164 8188 Fax: (028) 8164 8011
Email: uhp@omagh.gov.uk
WWW: www.omagh.gov.uk/historypark.htm
Ulster Museum
Botanic Gardens, Stranmillis Road, Belfast, BT9 5AB
Tel: (028) 9038 1000 Fax: (028) 9038 3003
Londonderry Harbour Museum
Harbour Square, Londonderry, County Londonderry, BT48
6AF Tel: (028) 713 377331

Ireland
Dublin Civic Museum
58 South William Street, Dublin, 2 Tel: 679-4260
Fax: 677-5954
Irish Jewish Museum
3 - 4 Walworth Road, South Circular Road, Dublin, 8
Tel: 453-1797

Belgium
In Flanders Fields Museum
Lakenhallen, Grote Markt 34, Leper, B-8900
Tel: 00-32-(0)-57-22-85-84 Fax: 00-32-(0)-57-22-85-89
WWW: www.inflandersfields.be

South Africa
Albany Museum
Somerset Street, Grahamstown, 6139 Tel: 046-622-2312
Fax: 046-622-2398 Email: w.jervois@ru.ac.za
Huguenot Memorial Museum
PO Box 37, Franschoek, Western Cape, 7690
Tel: 021-876-2532
Kafframan Museum
PO Box 1434, King William s Town, 5600 Tel: 0430-24506
Fax: 0433-21569 Email: stephani@hubertd.ry.ac.2a

Germany
German Emigration Museum
Inselstrasse 6, Bremerhaven, D-2850 Tel: 0471 49096

United States of America

Arizona

Phoenix Museum of History
PO Box 926, 002 West Van Buren Street, Phoenix, 85001
Tel: 602-253-2734
Historical Society Pioneer Museum
PO Box 1968, 2340 North Fort Valley Road , Flagstaff
86002 Tel: 602-774-6272

Nevada
Nevada State Museum
Division of Museums & History 600 North Carson Street,
Carson City 89710 Tel: 702-687-4810
Nevada State Museum
700 Twin Lakes Drive, Las Vegas 89107 Tel: 702-486-5205

Libraries &
Genealogical Research

Stuart A. Raymond

Where would we be without libraries? They are store-houses of information - not just books and journals, but also microfiche, microfilm, and, increasingly these days, CD-roms. Public libraries are there for everyone, and although the perception in some quarters may be that they merely offer light reading, in fact they provide information on every subject under the sun -- and beyond! Whether your interests are astronomy or cake making, the law or motoring, the public library is there to provide whatever information you need.

Libraries are one of the first places that genealogists should visit in their research. A vast amount of genealogical information has been published, and is available in print. Genealogists should check whether the information they require is in printed form before they consult the archives. Archives are unique and irreplaceable; any use may damage them, and they should be consulted as little as possible. If the information contained in them has been published, then you should go to the printed book first - although you may need to check its accuracy later against the original manuscript.

Virtually all of the information contained in published sources may be accessed via the public library network. Very few published books fail to find their way onto public library shelves. And the network of libraries is worldwide: I was able to write a book on Cornish genealogy by using the resources of the State Library of Victoria in Melbourne. In addition to public libraries, the genealogist will also find the libraries of family history societies - and especially of the Society of Genealogists - to be invaluable for research purposes. The libraries of county institutions such as the Yorkshire Archaeological Society or the Somerset Archaeological and Natural History Society hold many useful works, not just for the counties in which they are situated. Relevant material may also be found in University libraries - especially runs of the major county record society publications and local history society transactions. Institutions such as the British Library, the Library of Congress, and the National Library of Australia may also be worth visiting to locate elusive titles; these national libraries should have copies of every book published in their respective countries. The best guide to libraries for genealogists in England is probably Susannah Guy's English Local Studies Handbook (University of Exeter Press, 1992 - new edition in preparation).

Libraries can appear to be intimidating places to enter. They should not be. You, the taxpayer, fund them in order to meet your informational needs, and you should make sure that they do so. If you have a question you need

Libraries are one of the first places that genealogists should visit ...

answered, ask it! The librarian sitting at the information desk is there to provide an answer, and if you do not ask, you are preventing the librarian from doing his job. Be sure, however, that you ask the right person; it is no good asking the junior assistant about indexes to probate records; she may be able to direct you to the 929s, but is unlikely to be able to help you further. Horses for courses! Make sure that you ask the professional librarian, who should have a good knowledge of the collection, and ought to be able to point you to the reference work you need, to find addresses for you, to identify books on specific subjects, to direct you to other more appropriate libraries, or to explain the use of the catalogue. Do not, however, expect the reference librarian to do your research for you. He/she is expert in finding published information, but is not necessarily an experienced genealogist.

The catalogue provides you (usually) with a full list of the books in a library. Nowadays it is likely to be computerised, although it is always worth checking whether parts of the collection are still listed on cards. As I write this, the Society of Genealogists old card catalogue is in the process of being replaced by a computerised system, but you must still check the card catalogue for some items. You can usually search catalogues by author, title, or subject. Many computerised catalogues also permit you to search by a combination of author and title, or by keywords found in either. The catalogue record will tell you where the book is shelved, and may also indicate whether it is on loan. Most libraries shelve their books in accordance with the Dewey decimal classification (genealogy is at 929), although a number of other classification schemes are also in use. In larger library systems, the catalogue may include details of books in many library; if you do not understand what it is telling you, ask a librarian! An increasing number of library catalogues are available via the internet. At present, these are mainly university library catalogues, which should not be neglected; however, the most useful catalogue on the internet for genealogists is probably the British Library. Amongst much, much else, the library holds thousands of family histories -- so type in your surname, and see what comes up! If you cannot actually get to London, take a copy of the citation - you need author, title, and date as a minimum - and check it against the catalogues of libraries you are able to visit. Or ask your local librarian if you can obtain the book you need via Inter library loan.

Identifying the particular item you need generally involves more than just using the library catalogue - especially if it is an article in a journal, which is unlikely to be separately listed in most catalogues. How do you identify useful guides to sources? Which parish registers have been published? What monumental inscriptions are available on microfiche? Too often, genealogists rely on serendipity for answers to questions like these. If you are attempting a systematic search, however, and wish to check all available sources, then you need to consult bibliographies. Don't let the word put you off. Bibliographies simply list the books and journal articles etc that are available, and enable you to make a systematic study of the works listed.

A number of current genealogical bibliographies are available; these list works currently available for purchase (of course they may also be found in libraries). My own British Genealogical Books in Print (F.F.H.S., 1999) and British Genealogical Microfiche (F.F.H.S., 1999) list the publications of hundreds of commercial publishers, libraries, record offices, historical societies, and private publishers. The publications of family history societies are listed in John Perkins Current Publications on Microfiche by Member Societies (4th ed., F.F.H.S., 1997), and in the forthcoming 10th edition of Current Publications by Member Societies (F.F.H.S.) All of these titles should be checked for information on the many thousand works currently available. Of course, each month sees many more titles published; to keep up to date, the book reviews in Family History Monthly, Family Tree Magazine, Family History News & Digest, and the Genealogists magazine should all be checked.

These titles cover the whole country; however, most genealogists are likely to be researching in specific areas, and need information on all the publications relating to that area. The county volumes of my British Genealogical Library guides series (formerly British Genealogical Bibliographies) provide the information needed to conduct systematic searches of the genealogical lterature for specific counties. Counties covered to date include Buckinghamshire, Cheshire, Cornwall*, Cumberland & Westmorland*, Devon*, Dorset, Essex, Gloucestershire*, Hampshire, Kent, Lancashire, Lincolnshire, London & Middlesex, Norfolk, Oxfordshire, Somerset*, Suffolk* and Wiltshire* (* indicates out of print). These volumes complement my English Genealogy: a Bibliography (3rd ed. F.F.H.S., 1996), which lists publications of national importance. English Genealogy identifies innumerable handbooks on the whole range of genealogical topics, as well as numerous biographical dictionaries, pedigree collections, surname dictionaries, archival guides, handwriting manuals, etc., etc ., also many indexes to sources which are national in scope, e.g. Prerogative Court of Canterbury records,

The range of genealogical material revealed by these bibliographies is enormous; to try to dip into it without consulting them may be likened to searching for a needle in a haystack. And to try to describe that literature in an article of this length taxes the brain somewhat! The authoritative guide to our hobby is now Mark Heber's Ancestral Trails (Sutton, 1997). This is relatively expensive, and runs to 674 pages. There are many briefer, less expensive guides for beginners, for example, George Pelling's Beginning your Family History (7th ed., F.F.H.S. 1998), or Colin Chapman's Tracing your British Ancestors (2nd ed. Lochin, 1996). Encyclopaedias are also useful; Terrick Fitzhugh's Dictionary of Genealogy, and Pauline Saul's Family Historians Enquire Within (5th ed., F.F.H.S., 1995) may both be recommended.

Much invaluable information is to be found in genealogical journals. Reference has already been made to the major current journals; these are complemented by the journals or newsletters of family history societies. These generally provide lists of their members interests, together

with details of society activities, and brief articles on topics of interest - including many notes on the histories of particular families. Articles in these journals are regularly indexed in the digest section of Family History News and Digest. A number of genealogical journals published in the late 19th and early 20th centuries are also worth consulting. The most important of these were The Genealogist (1877-1921) and Miscellanea genealogica et heraldica (1868-1938). These include numerous extracts from original sources such as parish registers and monumental inscriptions, as well as many pedigrees and articles on particular families. I have indexed them, together with a number of other titles, in my British Genealogical Periodicals: a bibliography of their contents (3 vols. in 5; F.F.H.S., 1991-3), and also in my county bibliographies.

Historical journals also have much to offer the genealogist. In particular, the transactions of county historical and archaeological societies frequently contain many works of relevance. For example, between 1882 and 1908, the Yorkshire Archaeological Journal published many abstracts from the marriage allegations of York diocese. County record society series are also of considerable importance. These societies publish edited transcripts of important records, such as deed collections, probate records, diaries, ecclesiastical records, etc., etc. A full list of their publications may be found in E. L. C. Mullins' Texts and Calendars: an analytical guide to serial publications (Royal Historical Society, 1958). A supplement to Mullins was published in 1982, and an online update is available on the internet. Relevant items are also listed in my county bibliographies.

The majority of genealogical publications relate to specific sources, and the remainder of this essay will be devoted to discussing these. Parish registers are of major importance to the genealogist, and especially to those researching prior to the 19th century. Many record offices have produced listings of their own holdings; however, the most comprehensive guides are the county volumes of the National Index of Parish Registers, published by the Society of Genealogists. Phillimore's Atlas and Index of Parish Registers is also valuable, especially for its parish maps. Many registers have been published; these are listed in detail in my county bibliographies. In the early years of this century, many registers were printed by the Parish Register Society, and in Phillimore's Parish Register series. There are or have been a number of county parish register societies; those for Lancashire and Yorkshire have each produced over 100 volumes. Registers have also been published by bodies such as the Devon and Cornwall Record Society and, for London & Middlesex, the Harleian Society (see Mullins for details), by record offices (Bedfordshire is the best example), and by private individuals such as F. Crisp for East Anglia, E. Dwelly for Somerset and S.H.A. Hervey for Suffolk. Today, family history societies are increasingly publishing registers on microfiche, as a glance at Perkins work mentioned above will reveal.

Family history societies are also leading the way in transcribing and microfiching monumental inscriptions (see Perkins again) - although it is regrettable that most transcripts of inscriptions remain unpublished. Prior to the 1980s, although a small number of collections of inscriptions were published privately, most published inscriptions appeared either as appendices to parish registers, as chapters of local histories, or as individual inscriptions in journals such as Miscellanea genealogica et heraldica. Full lists of published inscriptions are provided in my county bibliographies

Probate records are much better documented. The standard guide to them is Jeremy Gibson's Probate Jurisdictions: where to look for wills (4th ed. F.F.H.S. 1997). Numerous published indexes to wills and probate inventories are available: the British Record Society's Index library, which now runs to over 100 volumes, is almost entirely devoted to probate indexes; these are listed in Mullins, as are a number of similar works published by county record societies. The latter have also published many edited transcripts of wills and probate inventories, as have a few university history departments and commercial publishers. Many individual wills etc., appear in journals such as Miscellanea genealogica et heraldica. Detailed listings of what is available are given in my county bibliographies. Probate records provide one of the best examples of genealogical sources that are also of great interest to historians in general; many studies of particular communities have been based upon them, and numerous aspiring Ph.Ds have mined them for information.

Official lists of names, such as tax lists, protestation returns, muster rolls, census returns, etc., have also been the subjects of much publishing effort. Jeremy Gibson has been responsible for a number of guides in this area, for example, The Hearth Tax, other late Stuart tax lists, and the association oath rolls (2nd ed. F.F.H.S., 1996); The Protestation Returns 1641--2, and other contemporary listings (with Alan Dell; F.F.H.S., 1995). Record societies have issued numerous editions of subsidy rolls, hearth tax returns, muster rolls, etc., these are listed by Mullins.

The major guide to census records is Susan Lumas's Making Use of the Census (PRO Publications 1997). In the last decade, the indexing of census records has been a major growth industry amongst genealogists. The 1881 census indexing project was one of the biggest projects of its kind, but it was not alone; numerous census indexes are now available from family history societies and other publishers; these are listed in the current bibliographies men-

tioned above, and in my county bibliographies.

Trade directories of the 19th and early 20th centuries provide unofficial lists of names which can be very useful. These are rarely found outside of the libraries for the areas they cover; however, a number of commercial publishers now have extensive lists of directories reprinted on microfiche; my British genealogical microfiche provides the relevant details. There are probably over 1,000 directories currently available; it is worth noting that one of the major publishers in this field, Nick Vine Hall, is based in Australia.

This article inevitably skims the surface of the material available; no mention has been made, for example, of ecclesiastical records other than parish registers, of school registers, of estate archives, or of guides to particular record offices. Many other bibliographies could have been mentioned; e.g., my Occupational Sources for Genealogists, or Michael Gandy s Catholic Family History: a Bibliography of General Sources (Michael Gandy, 1996).

Using bibliographies, libraries, and the published literature of genealogy effectively could considerably reduce the time you spend searching for information in the archives; that time, however, is likely to be more than used up checking the sources you identify. At least you should be able to do much of the work at home, and in local libraries. If you need more information, just check as many bibliographies as you can find!

Stuart Raymond
P.O.Box 35, Exeter, EX4 5EF.
Email: stuart@samjraymond.softnet.co.uk
Phone (01392) 252193.

This article previously appeared in the 2000 edition

Libraries
National

British Library
British Library Building, 96 Euston Road London
NW1 2DB Tel: (020) 712 7677
WWW: http://www.portico.bl.uk
Reader/admissions@bl.uk
British Library Early Printed Collections
96 Euston Road London, NW1 2DB
Tel: (020) 7412 7673 Fax: (020) 7412 7577
Email: rare books@bl.uk WWW: http://www.bl.uk
British Library Oriental and India Office Collections
96 Euston Road London, NW1 2DB Tel: (020) 7412
7873 Fax: (020) 7412 7641 Email: oioc enquiries@bl.uk
WWW: http://www.bl.uk/collections/oriental
British Library Newspaper Library
Colindale Avenue London, NW9 5HE Tel: 020 7412
7353 Fax: 020 7412 7379 Email: newspaper@bl.uk
WWW: http://www.bl.uk/collections/newspaper/
Catholic Central Library
Lancing Street London, NW1 1ND Tel: (020) 7383 4333
Fax: (020) 7388 6675
Email: librarian@catholic library.demon.co.uk
WWW: www.catholic library.demon.co.uk
Fawcett Library
London Guildhall University, Old Castle Street London,
E1 7NT Tel: (020) 7320 1189 Fax: (020) 7320 1188
Email: fawcett@lgu.ac.uk
WWW: http://www.lgu.ac.uk./fawcett
Jewish Museum
The Sternberg Centre for Judaism, 80 East End Road,
Finchley, London, N3 2SY Tel: (020) 8349 1143
Email: jml.finchley@lineone.net
WWW: www.jewmusm.ort.org
Huguenot Library
University College, Gower Street, London, WC1E 6BT
Tel: (020) 7380 7094 Email: s.massilk@ucl.ac.uk
WWW: http://www.ucl.ac.uk/ucl
info/divisions/library/hugenot.htm
House of Commons Library
House of Commons, 1 Derby Gate London, SW1A 2DG
Tel: (020) 7219 5545 Fax: (020) 7219 3921
Lambeth Palace Library
Lambeth Palace Road London, SE1 7JU
Tel: (020) 7898 1400 Fax: (020) 7928 7932
Museum of the Order of St John
St John's Gate, St John's Lane, Clerkenwell, London,
EC1M 4DA Tel: (020) 7253 6644 Fax: (020) 7336 0587
WWW: www.sja.org.uk/history
Library of the Royal College of Surgeons of England
35 43 Lincoln's Inn Fields London, WC2A 3PN
Tel: (020) 7869 6520 Fax: (020) 7405 4438
Email: library@rseng.ac.uk
The Royal Armouries
The Library, HM Tower of London, London
Tel: (020) 7480 6358 ext 30
Fax: (020) 7481 2922
Email: Bridget.Clifford@armouries.org.uk
WWW: www.armouries.org.uk
Royal Society of Chemistry Library
& Information Centre
Burlington House, Piccadilly London, W1V 0BN
Tel: (020) 7437 8656 Fax: (020) 7287 9798
Email: library@rsc.org, www.rsc.org
Library of the Religious Society of Friends (Quakers),
Friends House, 173   177 Euston Rd London, NW1 2BJ
Tel: 0207 663 1135 Tel: 0207 663 1001
Email: library@quaker.org.uk
WWW: http://www.quaker.org.uk

Society of Genealogists - Library
14 Charterhouse Buildings, Goswell Road, London,
EC1M 7BA Tel: 020 7251 8799 Tel: 020 7250 0291
Fax: (020) 7250 1800
Email: library@sog.org.uk
Email: sales@sog.org.uk
WWW: http://www.sog.org.uk
Trades Union Congress Library Collections
236 - 250 Holloway Road London, N7 6PP
Fax: 0171 753 3191 Email: tuclib@unl.ac.uk
WWW: http://www.unl.ac.uk/library/tuc
United Reformed Church History Society
Westminster College, Madingley Road Cambridge
CB3 0AA Tel: 01223 741300 (NOT Wednesdays)
**Wellcome Library for the History and Understanding
of Medicine**
183 Euston Road London, NW1 2BE
Tel: (020) 7611 8582 Fax: (020) 7611 8369
Email: library@wellcome.ac.uk
WWW: www.wellcome.ac.uk/library Library catalogue
is available through the internet: telnet://wihm.ucl.ac.uk
Westminster Abbey Library & Muniment Room
Westminster Abbey , London, SW1P 3PA
Tel: (020) 7222 5152 Ext 4830 Fax: (020) 7226 4827
Email: library@westminster abbey.org
WWW: www.westminster abbey.org
Dr Williams's Library
14 Gordon Square London, WC1H 0AG
Tel: (020) 7387 3727 Fax: (020) 7388 1142
Email: 101340.2541@compuserve.com

London
Bishopsgate Institute
Reference Librarian, 230 Bishopsgate London, ECM
4QH Tel: (020) 7247 6198 Fax: (020) 7247 6318
Brent Community History Library & Archive
152 Olive Road, London, NW2 6YT
Tel: (020) 8937 3540 Fax: (020) 8450 5211
London Borough of Bromley Local Studies Library
Central Library, High Street Bromley, BR1 1EX
Tel: 020 8460 9955 Fax: (020) 8313 9975
LB of Camden Local Studies & Archive Centre,
Holborn Library, 32-38 Theobalds Road London, WC1X
8PA Tel: (020) 7974 6342 Fax: (020) 7974 6284
WWW: www.camden.gov.uk
Chelsea Public Library
Old Town Hall, King's Road, London, SW3 5EZ
Tel: (020) 8352 6056 Tel: (020) 8361 4158
Fax: (020) 8351 1294 Local Studies Collection on Royal
Borough of Kensington & Chelsea south of Fulham Road
Local Studies Collection for Chiswick & Brentford
Chiswick Public Library
Dukes Avenue, Chiswick, London, W4 2AB
Tel: (020) 8994 5295 Fax: (020) 8995 0016
Fax: (020) 8742 7411 , Restricted opening hours for
local history room: please telephone before visiting
LB of Croydon Library and Archives Service
Central Library, Katharine Street Croydon, CR9 1ET
Tel: (020) 8760 5400 ext 1112 Fax: (020) 8253 1004
Email: localstudies@library.croydon.gov.uk
WWW: http://www.croydon.gov.uk/cr libls..htm
Ealing Local History Centre, Central Library
103 Broadway Centre, Ealing, London, W5 5JY
Tel: (020) 8567 3656 ext 37 Fax: (020) 8840 2351
Email: localhistory@hotmail.com
LB of Islington Finsbury Library
245 St John Street London, EC1V 4NB
Tel: (020) 7527 7994 Fax: (020) 7527 8821
WWW: www.islington.gov.uk/htm

LB of Barking & Dagenham Local History Studies
Central Library, Barking Dagenham, IG11 7NB
Tel: (020) 8517 8666 Local History studies from this Library
have been centralised at Valence Linbrary, Becontree Avenue,
Dagenham, Essex RM8 3HT Tel & Fax: (020) 8227 5297
Email: valencelibrary@hotmail.com
LB of Barking & Dagenham Local History Studies
Valence Library & Museum, Becontree Avenue
Dagenham, RM8 3HT Tel: 020 8592 6537
Tel: 020 822 75294 Fax: 020 822 75297
Email: fm019@viscount.org.uk
WWW: http://www.earl.org.uk/partners/barking/index.html
LB of Greenwich Local History Library
Woodlands, 90 Mycenae Road, Blackheath, London, SE3
7SE Tel: (020) 8858 4631 Fax: (020) 8293 4721
Email: local.history@greenwich.gov.uk
WWW: www.greenwich.gov.uk The Library
will be moving to a new Heritage Centre at the end of 2001.
Please contact the Library for more details
Guildhall Library, Manuscripts Section
Aldermanbury, London, EC2P 2EJ Tel: (020) 732 1863
Fax: (020) 7600 3384
Email: manuscripts.guildhall@ms.corpoflondon.gov.uk
WWW: http://www.ihr.sas.ac.uk/ihr/ghmnu.html
LB of Enfield Libraries
Southgate Town Hall, Green Lanes, Palmers Green,
London, N13 4XD Tel: (020) 8379 2724
Fax: (020) 8379 2761
LB of Barnet, Archives & Local Studies Department
Hendon Library, The Burroughs, Hendon NW4 3BQ
Tel: (020) 8359 2876 Fax: (020) 8359 2885
Email: hendon.library@barnet.gov.uk
Lewisham Local Studies & Archives
Lewisham Library, 199 201 Lewisham High Street,
Lewisham, London, SE13 6LG Tel: (020) 8297 0682
Fax: (020) 8297 1169
Email: local.studies@lewisham.gov.uk
WWW: http://www.lewisham.gov.uk
LB of Harrow Local History Collection
PO Box 4, Civic Centre Library, Station Road Harrow,
HA1 2UU Tel: 0208 424 1055 Tel: 0208 424 1056
Fax: 0181 424 1971
Hounslow Library & Local Studies
24 Treaty Centre, High Street Hounslow, TW3 1ES
Tel: (020) 8570 0622
LB of Islington Central Reference Library
Central Reference Library, 2 Fieldway Crescent London,
N5 1PF Tel: (020) 7619 6931 Fax: (020) 7619 6939
Email: local.history@islington.gov.uk
WWW: http://www.islington.gov.uk Reorganisation is immi-
nent planned move to Finsbury Library, 245 St John Street, London
EC1V 4NB Tel: (020) 7527 6931 Fax: (020) 7527 6937
LB of Lambeth Archives Department
Minet Library, 52 Knatchbull Road, Lambeth, London,
SE5 9QY Tel: (020) 7926 6076 Fax: (020) 7936 6080
Museum in Docklands Project Library & Archives
Unit C14, Poplar Business Park, 10 Prestons Road,
London, E14 9RL Tel: (020) 7515 1162
Fax: (020) 7538 0209
Email: docklands@Museum london.org.uk
LB of Newham Archives & Local Studies Library
Stratford Library, Water Lane London, E15 4NJ
Tel: (020) 8557 8856 Fax: (020) 8503 1525
Romford Reference Library LB of Havering
Reference Library, St Edward's Way, Romford, RM1
3AR Tel: 01708 772393 Tel: 01708 772394
Fax: 01708 772391 Email: romfordlib2@rmplc.co.uk
Southwark Local Studies Library
211 Borough High Street, Southwark, London, SE1 1JA
Tel: (020) 7403 3507 Tel: 0207 403 8633
Email: local.studies.library@southwark.gov.uk
WWW: www.southwark.gov.uk

Tower Hamlets Local History Library & Archives
Bancroft Library, 277 Bancroft Road London, El 4DQ
Tel: (020) 8980 4366 Ext 129 Fax: (020) 8983 4510
Twickenham Local Studies Library
Twickenham Library, Garfield Road Twickenham
TW1 3JS Tel: (020) 8891 7271 Fax: (020) 8891 5934
Email: twicklib@richmond.gov.uk
WWW: http://www.richmond.gov.uk The Twickenham
collection is moving to Richmond Local Studies Library
London Hillingdon Borough Libraries Uxbridge
Central Library, High Street, Uxbridge, UB8 1HD
Tel: 01895 250702 Fax: 01895 811164
Email: clib@hillingdon.gov.uk
WWW: www. hillingdon.gov.uk
LB of Waltham Forest Local Studies Library
Vestry House Museum, Vestry Road Walthamstow
E17 9NH Tel: (020) 8509 1917
Email: Vestry.House@al.lbwf.gov.uk
WWW: http://www.lbwf.gov.uk/vestry/vestry.htm
LB of Wandsworth
Local History Collection, Battersea Library, 265
Lavender Hill London, SW11 1JB Tel: (020) 8871 7753
Fax: (020) 7978 437
Email: wandsworthMuseum @wandsworth.gov.uk
WWW: www.wandsworth.gov.uk

England

Bedfordshire
Local Studies Library
Luton Central Library, St George's Square Luton, LU1
2NG Tel: 01582 547420 Tel: 01582 547421
Fax: 01582 547450 Email:
Bedford Central Library
Harpur Street Bedford, MK40 1PG Tel: 01234 350931
Fax: 01234 342163
Email: stephensonB@bedfordshire.gov.uk

Berkshire
Reading Local Studies Library
3rd Floor, Central Library
Abbey Square Reading, RG1 3BQ Tel: 0118 901 5965
Fax: 0118 901 5954 Email: info@readinglibraries.org.uk
Crowthorne Library
Lower Broadmoor Road Crowthorne, RG45 7LA
Tel: 01344 776431 Fax: 01344 776431
Sandhurst Library
The Broadway Sandhurst, GU47 9BL Tel: 01252 870161
Fax: 01252 878285
Whitegrove Library
5 County Lane Warfield, RG42 3JP Tel: 01344 424211
Fax: 01344 861233
Ascot Heath Library
Fernbank Road North Ascot, SL5 8LA
Tel: 01344 884030 Fax: 01344 884030
Bracknell Library
(Headquarters), Town Square Bracknell, RG12 1BH
Tel: 01344 423149 Fax: 01344 411392
Binfield Library
Benetfeld Road Binfield, RG42 4HD Tel: 01344 306663
Fax: 01344 486467

Birmingham
Birmingham Central Library
Local Studies & History Service, Floor 6, Central Library
Chamberlain Square Birmingham, B3 3HQ Tel: 0121 303
4549 Fax: 0121 464 0993,
Email: local.studies.library@birmingham.gov.uk,
Web: www.birmingham.gov.uk

Bolton
Central Library
Civic Centre, Le Mans Crescent, Bolton, BL1 1SE
Tel: 01204 333185

Bristol,
Bristol Central Library
Reference Section College Green, Bristol, BS1 5TL
Tel: 0117 929 9147 Tel: 0117 903 7259

Buckinghamshire
Milton Keynes Reference Library
555 Silbury Boulevard Milton Keynes, MK9 3HL
Tel: 01908 254160 Fax: 01908 254088
High Wycombe Reference Library
Queen Victoria Road High Wycombe, HP11 1BD
Tel: 01494 510241 Fax: 01494 533086
Email: hwrlib@hotmail.com
County Reference Library
Walton Street Aylesbury, HP20 1UU Tel: 01296 382250
Fax: 01296 382405

Cambridgeshire
Norris Library and Museum
The Broadway, St Ives PE27 5BX Tel: 01480 465101
Fax: 01480 497314 Email: norris.st ives tc@co net.com
Peterborough Library
Broadway Peterborough, PE1 1RX Tel: 01733348343
Fax: 01733 555377
Email: libraries@peterborough.gov.uk

Cheshire
Chester Library
Northgate Street Chester, CH1 2EF Tel: 01244 312935
Fax: 01244 315534
Crewe Library
Prince Albert Street Crewe, CW1 2DH
Tel: 01270 211123 Fax: 01270 256952
Email: ipcrewe@cheshire.gov.uk
Ellesmere Port Library
Civic Way Ellesmere Port, South Wirral, L65 0BG
Tel: 0151 355 8101 Fax: 0151 355 6849
Local Heritage Library
Central Library, Wellington Road South Stockport
SK1 3RS Tel: 0161 474 4530 Fax: 0161 474 7750
Email: localherirtage.library@stockport.gov.uk
Halton Lea Library
Halton Lea, Runcorn, WA7 2PF Tel: 01928 715351
Fax: 01928 790221
Macclesfield Library
Jordongate Macclesfield, SK10 1EE Tel: 01625 422512
Fax: 01625 612818
Tameside Local Studies Library
Stalybridge Library, Trinity Street Stalybridge
SK15 2BN Tel: 0161 338 2708 Tel: 0161 338 3831 and
0191 303 7937 Fax: 0161 303 8289
Email: tamelocal@dial.pipex.com
WWW: http://www.tameside.gov.uk
Warrington Library& Local Studies Centre
Museum, Street Warrington, WA1 1JB
Tel: 01925 442892 Fax: 01925 411395 Email:
library@warrington.gov.uk, www.warrington.gov.uk

Cleveland
Middlesbrough Libraries & Local Studies Centre
Central Library, Victoria Square Middlesbrough
TS1 2AY Tel: 01642 263358 Fax: 01642 648077
Stockton Reference Library
Church Road Stockton on Tees, TS18 1TU Tel: 01642
393994 Fax: 01642 393929
Email: reference.library@stockton.bc.gov.uk

Cornwall
Cornish Studies Library
2 4 Clinton Road Redruth, TR15 2QE
Tel: 01209 216760 Fax: 01209 210283
Email: cornishstudies@library.cornwall.gov.uk
Royal Institution of Cornwall & Courtney Library
Royal Cornwall Museum, River Street Truro, TR1 2SJ
Tel: 01872 272205 Fax: 01872 240514
Email: RIC@royal cornwall Museum.freeserve.co.uk
WWW: www.cornwall.online.co.uk/ric

Darlington
Centre For Local Studies
The Library, Crown Street Darlington, DL1 1ND
Tel: 01325 349630 Fax: 01325 381556
Email: crown.street.library@darlington.gov.uk

County Durham
Centre For Local Studies
The Library, Crown Street Darlington, DL1 1ND
Tel: 01325 349630 Fax: 01325 381556
Email: crown.street.library@darlington.gov.uk
Durham Arts Library and Museums Department
County Hall, Durham, DH1 STY Tel: 0191 383 3595
**Durham University Library Archives and Special
Collections**
Palace Green Section, Palace Green, Durham, DH1 3RN
Tel: 0191 374 3032 Email: pg.library@durham.ac.uk
Durham City Library
Reference & Local Studies Department, South Street
Durham, DH1 4QS Tel: 0191 386 4003 Fax: 0191 386
0379 Email: durhamcityref.lib@durham.gov.uk
WWW: www.durham.gov.uk

Cumbria
Carlisle Library
11 Globe Lane Carlisle, CA3 8NX Tel: 01228 607310
Fax: 01228 607333
Email: carlisle.library@cumbriacc.gov.uk
WWW: http://dspace.dial.pipex.com/cumherit/index.htm
**Cumbria Record Office and Local Studies Library
(Whitehaven)**
Scotch Street Whitehaven, CA28 7BJ Tel: 01946 852920
Fax: 01946 852919
Email: whitehaven.record.office@cumbriacc.gov.uk
WWW: http://www.cumbria.gov.uk/archives
Kendal Library
Stricklandgate Kendal, LA9 4PY Tel: 01539 773520
Fax: 01539 773530, kendal.library@cumbriacc.gov.uk
Penrith Library
St Andrews Churchyard Penrith, CA11 7Y Tel: 01768
242100 Fax: 01768 242101
Email: penrith.library@dial.pipexcom
Workington Library
Vulcans Lane Workington, CA14 2N
Tel: 01900 325170 Fax: 01900 325181
Email: workington.library@cumbriacc.gov.uk

Derbyshire
Chesterfield Local Studies Department
Chesterfield Library
New Beetwell Street Chesterfield, S40 1QN
Tel: 01246 209292 Fax: 01246 209304
Chesterfield Family History Research
Old Houses, Piccadilly Road Chesterfield, S41 0EH
Tel: 01246 557033 Email: 1maskell@compuserve.com
Derby Local Studies Library
25b Irongate Derby, DE1 3GL Tel: 01332 255393
Fax: 01332 255381
Local Studies Library Matlock
County Hall, Smedley Street Matlock, DE4 3AG Tel:
01629 585579 Fax: 01629 585049

Devon

Devon & Exeter Institution Library
7 The Close Exeter, EX1 1EZ Tel: 01392 251017
Fax: 01392 263871 Email: m.midgley@exeter.ac.uk
WWW: http://www.ex.ac.uk/library/devonex.html
Westcountry Studies Library
Exeter Central Library, Castle Street Exeter, EX4 3PQ
Tel: 01392 384216 Fax: 01392 384228
Email: dlaw@devon cc.gov.uk
WWW: http://www.devon cc.gov.uk/library/locstudy

Dorset

Poole Central Reference Library
Dolphin Centre , Poole, BH15 1QE Tel: 01202 262424
Fax: 01202 262442 Email: poolereflib@hotmail.com
WWW: www.poole.gov.uk
Dorset County Museum
High West Street Dorchester, DT1 1XA Tel: 01305
262735 Fax: 01305 257180
Email: dorsetcountyMuseum
@dor mus.demon.co.uk
Dorchester Reference Library
Colliton Park Dorchester, DT1 1XJ Tel: 01305 224448
Fax: 01305 266120

East Sussex

Brighton Local Studies Library
Church Street Brighton, BN1 1 UD Tel: 01273 296971
Fax: 01273 296962
Email: brightonlibrary@pavilion.co.uk
Hove Reference Library
182 - 186 Church Road Hove, BN3 2EG
Tel: 01273 296942 Fax: 01273 296947

Essex

LB of Barking & Dagenham Local History Studies
Valence Library & Museum, Becontree Avenue
Dagenham, RM8 3HT Tel: 020 8592 6537
Tel: 020 822 75294 Fax: 020 822 75297
Email: fm019@viscount.org.uk
WWW: http://www.earl.org.uk/partners/barking/index.html
Romford Reference Library
LB of Havering
Reference Library, St Edward's Way, Romford, RM1
3AR Tel: 01708 772393 Tel: 01708 772394
Fax: 01708 772391 Email: romfordlib2@rmplc.co.uk
Redbridge Library
Central Library, Clements Road, Ilford, Essex, IG1 1EA
Tel: (020) 8708 2417 Fax: (020) 8553 3299
Email: Local.Studies@redbridge.gov.uk
WWW: www.redbridge.gov.uk
Southend Library
Central Library, Victoria Avenue Southend on Sea, SS2
6EX Tel: 01702 612621 Fax: 01792 612652 and
Tel: 01702 469241 Minicom 01702 600579
Email: library@southend.gov.uk
WWW: www.southend.gov.uk/libraries/
LB of Barking & Dagenham Local History Studies
Central Library, Barking Dagenham, IG11 7NB
Tel: (020) 8517 8666 Local History studies from this Library
have been centralised at Valence Linbrary, Becontree Avenue,
Dagenham, Essex RM8 3HT Tel & Fax: (020) 8227 5297
Email: valencelibrary@hotmail.com
Chelmsford Library
PO Box 882, Market Road Chelmsford, CM1 1LH
Tel: 01245 492758 Fax: 01245 492536
Email: answers.direct@essexcc.gov.uk
WWW: www.essexcc.gov.uk
Colchester Central Library
Trinity Square Colchester, CO1 1JB Tel: 01206 245917
Fax: 01206 245901 Email: jane.stanway@essexcc.gov.uk
WWW: www.essexcc.gov.uk

Thomas Plume Library
Market Hill Maldon, CM9 4PZ
No facilities for incoming telephone or fax messages

Gloucestershire

Cheltenham Local Studies Centre
Cheltenham Library, Clarence Street Cheltenham, GL50
3JT Tel: 01242 532678 Fax: 01242 532673
Gloucestershire Family History Society
14 Alexandra Road Gloucester, GL1 3DR
Tel: 01452 52344 (RESOURCE CENTRE)
Email: cjack@gloster.demon.co.uk
WWW: http://www.cix.co.uk/~rd/genuki/gfhs.htm
Gloucestershire County Library
Brunswick Road Gloucester, GL1 1HT Tel: 01452
426979 Fax: 01452 521468
Email: clams@gloscc.gov.uk
WWW: http://www.gloscc.gov.uk
Gloucester Library, Arts & Museums
County Library, Quayside, Shire Hall, Gloucester
GL1 1HY Tel: 01452 425037 Fax: 01452 425042
Email: clams@gloscc.gov.uk
WWW: http://www.gloscc.gov.uk

South Gloucestershire

Yate Library
44 West Walk Yate, BS37 4AX Tel: 01454 865661
Fax: 01454 319178

Hampshire

Aldershot Library
109 High Street Aldershot, GU11 1DQ Tel: 01252 322456
Andover Library
Chantry Centre , Andover, SP10 1LT Tel: 01264 352807
Email: clceand@hants.gov.uk
Basingstoke Library
North Division Headquarters, 19 20 Westminster
House, Potters Walk, Basingstoke, RG21 7LS
Tel: 01256 473901 Fax: 01256 470666
Eastleigh Library
The Swan Centre , Eastleigh, SO50 5SF Tel: 01703
612513 Email: clweeas@hants.gov.uk
Fareham Library
South Division Headquarters, Osborn Road Fareham,
PO16 7EN Tel: 01329 282715 Fax: 01329 221551
Email: clsoref@hants.gov.uk
Farnborough Library
Pinehurst Farnborough, GU14 7JZ Tel: 01252 513838
Email: clnoref@hants.gov.uk
WWW: http://www.brit a r.demon.co.uk
Fleet Library
236 Fleet Road Fleet, GU13 8BX Tel: 01252 614213
Email: clnofle@hants.gov.uk
Gosport Library
High Street Gosport, PO12 1BT Tel: (023) 9252 3431
clsos@hants.gov.uk
Lymington Library
Cannon Street Lymington, SO41 9BR Tel: 01590 673050
Email: clwelym@hants.gov.uk
Hampshire Local Studies Library
Winchester Library
Jewry Street Winchester, SO23 8RX Tel: 01962 841408
Email: clceloc@hants.gov.uk
Hampshire County Library
West Division Headquarters, The Old School, Cannon
Street, Lymington, SO41 9BR Tel: 01590 675767
Fax: 01590 672561 Email: clwedhq@hants.gov.uk
WWW: http://www.hants.gov.uk

Royal Marines Museum
Eastney Southsea, PO4 9PX Tel: (023) 92 819385 Exts 224 Fax: (023) 92 838420
Email: matthewlittle@royalmarinesmuseum.co.uk
WWW: www.royalmarinesMuseum.co.uk
Portsmouth City Libraries
Central Library, Guildhall Square Portsmouth, PO1 2DX
Tel: (023) 9281 9311 X232 (Bookings)
Tel: (023) 9281 9311 X234 (Enquiries)
Fax: (023) 9283 9855
Email: reference.library@portsmouthcc.gov.uk
Southampton City Archives
Civic Centre Southampton, SO14 7L
Tel: 023 8083 2205 Fax: 023 8033 6305
Email: localstudies@southampton.gov.uk
WWW: www.southampton.gov.uk
Waterlooville Library
The Precinct , Waterlooville, PO7 7DT
Tel: (023) 9225 4626 Email: clsowvl@hants.gov.uk
Winchester Reference Library
81 North Walls Winchester, SO23 8BY Tel: 01962 846059 Fax: 01962 856615 Email: clceref@hants.gov.uk

Herefordshire
Bromyard Library
34 Church Street Bromyard, HR7 4DP
Tel: 01885 482657 No Genealogical information held
Colwall Library
Humphrey Walwyn Library
Colwall, Malvern, WR13 6QT Tel: 01684 540642
Ledbury Library
The Homend , Ledbury, HR8 1BT Tel: 01531 632133
Hereford Cathedral Archives & Library
5 College Cloisters, Cathedral Close Hereford, HR1 2NG
Tel: 01432 359880 Fax: 01432 355929
Email: archives@herefordcathedral.co.uk
Email: library@herefordcathedral.co.uk
Hereford Library
Broad Street Hereford, HR4 9AU Tel: 01432 272456
Fax: 01432 359668
Leominster Library
8 Buttercross Leominster, HR6 8BN Tel: 01568 612384
Fax: 01568 616025
Ross Library
Cantilupe Road Ross on Wye, HR9 7AN
Tel: 01989 567937

Hertfordshire
Hertfordshire Archives and Local Studies
County Hall, Pegs Lane Hertford, SG13 8EJ Tel: 01992 555105 Fax: 01992 555113 Email: hals@hertscc.gov.uk
WWW: http://hertsldirect.org
Hertfordshire Archives and Local Studies is comprised of the former Herts County Record Office and Herts Local Studies Library
Welwyn Garden City Central Library
Local Studies Section Campus West, Welwyn Garden City, AL8 6AJ Tel: 01438 737333 Fax: 01707 897 595

Hull
Hull Family History Unit, Central Library
Albion Street Kingston upon Hull, HU1 3TF
Tel: 01482 616828 Fax: 01482 6168274
Email: gareth.watkins@hullcc.gov.uk
WWW: http://www.hullcc.gov.uk/genealogy
Huntingdonshire
Peterborough Library
Broadway Peterborough, PE1 1RX Tel: 01733348343
Fax: 01733 555377
Email: libraries@peterborough.gov.uk

Isle of Wight
Isle of Wight County Library
Lord Louis Library, Orchard Street Newport, PO30 1LL
Tel: 01983 823800 Fax: 01983 825972
Email: rcflib@llouis.demon.co.uk

Kent
Institute of Heraldic and Genealogical Studies
79 82 Northgate Canterbury, CT1 1BA
Fax: 01227 765617, ihgs@ihgs.ac.uk, www.ihgs.ac.uk
Broadstairs Library
The Broadway Broadstairs, CT10 2BS
Tel: 01843 862994 Fax: 01843 861938
LB of Bromley Local Studies Library
Central Library, High Street Bromley, BR1 1EX
Tel: 020 8460 9955 Fax: (020) 8313 9975
Canterbury Cathedral Library
The Precincts , Canterbury, CT1 2EH Tel: 01227 865287
Fax: 01227 865222 Email: catlib@ukc.ac.uk
WWW: www.canterbury cathedral.org
Canterbury Library & local Studies Collection
18 High Street Canterbury, CT1 2JF Tel: 01227 463608
Fax: 01227 768338
Dartford Central Library Reference Department
Market Street Dartford, DA1 1EU Tel: 01322 221133
Fax: 01322 278271
Dover Library
Maison Dieu House, Biggin Street Dover CT16 1DW
Tel: 01304 204241 Fax: 01304 225914
Faversham Library
Newton Road Faversham, ME13 8DY
Tel: 01759 532448 Fax: 01795 591229
Folkestone Library & Local Heritage Studies
2 Grace Hill Folkestone, CT20 1HD Tel: 01303 256710
Fax: 01303 256710 Email: janet.adamson@kent.gov.uk
Gillingham Library
High Street Gillingham, ME7 1BG Tel: 01634 281066
Fax: 01634 855814
Email: Gillingham.Library@medway.gov.uk
Gravesend Library
Windmill Street Gravesend, DA12 1BE
Tel: 01474 352758 Fax: 01474 320284
Greenhill Library
Greenhill Road Herne Bay, CT6 7PN Tel: 01227 374288
Herne Bay Library
124 High Street Herne Bay, CT6 5JY Tel: 01227 374896
Fax: 01227 741582
Margate Library Local History Collection
Cecil Square Margate, CT9 1RE Tel: 01843 223626
Fax: 01843 293015
Medway Archives and Local Studies Centre
Civic Centre, Strood, Rochester, ME2 4AU
Tel: 01634 332714 Fax: 01634 297060
Email: archives@medway.gov.uk
Email: local.studies@medway.gov.uk
Ramsgate Library Local Strudies Collection & Thanet Branch Archives
Ramsgate Library, Guildford Lawn Ramsgate CT11 9AY Tel: 01843 593532
Archives at this Library, moved to East Kent Archives CentreEnterprise Zone, Honeywood Road, Whitfield, Dover, Kent CT16 3EH. A Local Studies Collection will remain
Ramsgate Library and Museum
Guildford Lawn Ramsgate, CT11 9QY
Tel: 01843 593532 Fax: 01843 852692
Sevenoaks Library
Buckhurst Lane Sevenoaks, TN13 1LQ
Tel: 01732 453118 Fax: 01732 742682
Sheerness Library
Russell Street Sheerness, ME12 1PL Tel: 01795 662618
Fax: 01795 583035 WWW: www.kent.gov.uk

Sittingbourne Library
Central Avenue Sittingbourne, ME10 4AH
Tel: 01795 476545 Fax: 01795 428376
WWW: www.kent.gov.uk
Sturry Library
Chafy Crescent, Sturry, Canterbury, CT2 0BA
Tel: 01227 711479 Fax: 01227 710768
Tunbridge Wells Library
Mount Pleasant Tunbridge Wells, TN1 1NS
Tel: 01892 522352 Fax: 01892 514657
Whitstable Library
31 33 Oxford Street Whitstable, CT5 1DB
Tel: 01227 273309 Fax: 01227 771812

Lancashire
Barnoldswick Library
Fernlea Avenue Barnoldswick, BB18 5DW
Tel: 01282 812147 Fax: 01282 850791
Colne Library
Market Street Colne, BB8 0AP Tel: 01282 871155
Fax: 01282 865227
Hyndburn Central Library
St James Street, Accrington, Lancs, BB5 1NQ
Tel: 01254 872385 Fax: 01254 301066
Email: accrington.localstudies@lcl.lancscc.gov.uk
Lancashire Record Office and Local Studies Library
Bow Lane Preston, PR1 2RE Tel: 01772 263029
Fax: 01772 23050
Email: record.office@ed.lancscc.gov.uk,
www.lancashire.gov.uk/education/lifelong/ro/index.htm,
The Lancashire Local Studies Collection is now housed here
Oldham Local Studies and Archives
Local Studies Library, 84 Union Street Oldham OL1 1DN
Tel: 0161 911 4654 Fax: 0161 911 4654
Email: archives@oldham.gov.uk
Email:localstudies@oldham.gov.uk
WWW: http://www.oldham.gov.uk/archives
WWW: http://www.oldham.gov.uk/local studies
Rochdale Local Studies Library
Arts & Heritage Centre, The Esplanade, Rochdale
OL16 4TY Tel: 1706 864915 Moving to temporary loca-
tion. Contact Wheatsheaf Library for information
Tel: 01706 864920
Salford Local History Library
Peel Park Salford, M5 4WU Tel: 0161 736 2649
References and Information Services
Bury Central Library, Manchester Road Bury, BL9 0DG
Tel: 0161 253 5871 Fax: 0161 253 5857
Email: information@bury.gov.uk
WWW: www.bury.gov.uk/culture.htm
Working Class Movement Library
51 The Crescent Salford, M5 4WX Tel: 0161 736 2649
Fax: 0161 745 9490
Burnley Central & Local Studies Library
Grimshaw Street Burnley, BB11 2BD Tel: 01282 437115
Fax: 01282 831682
Email: burnley.reference@lcl.lancscc.gov.uk
Leigh Library
Turnpike Centre, Civic Centre Leigh, WN7 1EB
Tel: 01942 404559 Fax: 01942 404567
Email: heritage@wiganmbc.gov.uk
Heywood Local Studies Library
Heywood Library, Church Street Heywood, OL10 1LL
Tel: 01706 360947 Fax: 01706 368683
Middleton Local Studies Library
Middleton Library, Long Street Middleton, M24 6DU
Tel: 0161 643 5228 Fax: 0161 654 0745
Blackburn Central Library
Town Hall Street Blackburn, BB2 1AG
Tel: 01254 587920 Fax: 01254 690539
Email:reference.library@blackburn.gov.uk

Salford Museum & Art Gallery
Peel Park Salford, M5 4WU Tel: 0161 736 2649
Email: info@lifetimes.org.uk
WWW: www.lifetimes.org.uk
Wigan Metropolitan Borough Council
Information Unit, Station Road Wigan, WN1 1WN

Leicestershire
Leicestershire Libraries & Information Service
929-931 Loughborough Road Rothley, LE7 7NH
Tel: 0116 267 8023 Fax: 0116 267 8039
Melton Mowbray Library
Wilton Road Melton Mowbray, LE13 0UJ
Tel: 01664 560161 Fax: 01664 410199 www.leics.gov.uk
Loughborough Library
Local Studies Collection Granby Street Loughborough,
LE11 3DZ Tel: 01509 238466 Fax: 01509 212985
Email: slaterjohn@hotmail.com
**Market Harborough Library and Local Studies
Collection**
Pen Lloyd Library, Adam and Eve Street Market
Harborough, LE16 7LT Tel: 01858 821272
Fax: 01858 821265
Hinckley Library Local Studies Collection
Hinckley Library, Lancaster Road Hinckley, LE10 0AT
Tel: 01455 635106 Fax: 01455 251385
Lincolnshire, Gainsborough Library
Cobden Street Gainsborough, DN21 2NG
Tel: 01427 614780 Fax: 01427 810318
Lincolnshire County Library
Local Studies Section, Lincoln Central Library
Free School Lane, Lincoln, LN1 1EZ Tel: 01522 510800
Fax: 01522 575011
Email: lincoln.library@lincolnshire.gov.uk
WWW: www.lincolnshire.gov.uk/library/services/family.htm
Boston Library
County Hall , Boston, PE21 6LX Tel: 01205 310010 ext
2874 Fax: 01205 357760
Lincoln Cathedral Library
Lincoln Cathedral Library, The Cathedral, Lincoln
LN2 1PZ England Tel: 01522 544544 Fax: 01522 511307
Grantham Library
Issac Newton Centre , Grantham, NG1 9LD
Tel: 01476 591411 Fax: 01476 592458
Peterborough Library
Broadway Peterborough, PE1 1RX Tel: 01733348343
Fax: 01733 555377
Email: libraries@peterborough.gov.uk
Stamford Library
High Street Stamford, PE9 2BB Tel: 01780 763442
Fax: 01780 482518

London & Greater London
See beginning of this Section

Manchester
Manchester Central Library
St Peter's Square Manchester, M2 5PD
Tel: 0161 234 1979 Fax: 0161 234 1927
Email: mclib@libraries.manchester.gov.uk
WWW: http://www..manchester.gov.uk/mccdlt/index.htm
John Rylands University Library
Special Collections Division, 150 Deansgate Manchester,
M3 3EH Tel: 0161 834 5343 Fax: 0161 834 5343
Email: j.r.hodgson@man.ac.uk
WWW: http://rylibweb.man.ac.uk

Merseyside

Crosby Library (South Sefton Local History Unit)
Crosby Road North, Waterloo, Liverpool, L22 0LQ
Tel: 0151 928 6401 Fax: 0151 934 5770
Email: lochist.south.seflib@merseymail.com
The Local History Units serve Sefton Borough Council area. The
South Sefton Unit covers Bootle, Crosby, Maghull and other commu-
nities south of the River Alt. The North Sefton Unit covers Southport,
Formby.

Huyton Central Library
Huyton Library, Civic Way, Huyton, Knowsley,
L36 9GD Tel: 0151 443 3738 Fax: 0151 443 3739
Email: eileen.hume.dlcs@knowsley.gov.uk
WWW: http://www.knowsley.gov.uk/leisure/libraries/huyton/index.html

Liverpool Record Office & Local History Department
Central Library, William Brown Street Liverpool
L3 8EW Tel: 0151 233 5817 Fax: 0151 233 5886
Email: recoffice.central,library@liverpool.gov.uk
WWW: http://www.liverpool.gov.uk

Liverpool University Special Collections & Archives
University of Liverpool Library, PO Box 123 Liverpool,
L69 3DA Tel: 0151 794 2696 Fax: 0151 794 2081
Email: archives@liv.ac.uk
WWW: http://www.lsca.lib.liv.ac.uk

Southport Library (North Sefton Local History Unit)
Lord Street Southport, PR8 1DJ Tel: 0151 934 2119
Fax: 0151 934 2115   The Local History Units serve Sefton
Borough Council area. The North Sefton Unit covers Southport,
Formby. The South Sefton Unit covers Bootle, Crosby, Maghull and
other communities south of the River Alt

St Helen's Local History & Archives Library
Central Library, Gamble Institute, Victoria Square St
Helens, WA10 1DY Tel: 01744 456952

Wirral Central Library
Borough Road Birkenhead, CH41 2XB
Tel: 0151 652 6106 Fax: 0151 653 7320
Email: birkenhead.library@merseymail.com

Middlesex

LB of Harrow Local History Collection
PO Box 4, Civic Centre Library, Station Road Harrow,
HA1 2UU Tel: 0208 424 1055 Tel: 0208 424 1056
Fax: 0181 424 1971

Twickenham Local Studies Library
Twickenham Library, Garfield Road Twickenham, TW1
3JS Tel: (020) 8891 7271 Fax: (020) 8891 5934
Email: twicklib@richmond.gov.uk
WWW: http://www.richmond.gov.uk
The Twickenham collection is moving to Richmond Local Studies Library

Norfolk

Family History Shop & Library
The Family History Shop, 24d Magdalen Street Norwich,
NR3 1HU Tel: 01603 621152
Email: jenlibrary@aol.com
WWW: http://www.jenlibrary.u net.com

Great Yarmouth Central Library
Tolhouse Street Great Yarmouth, NR30 2SH
Tel: 01493 844551 Tel: 01493 842279
Fax: 01493 857628

Kings Lynn Library
London Road King's Lynn, PE30 5EZ
Tel: 01553 772568 Tel: 01553 761393 Fax: 01553
769832Email: kings.lynn.lib@norfolk.gov.uk
WWW: http://www.norfolk.gov.uk/council/departments/lis/nslynn.htm

Thetford Public Library
Raymond Street Thetford, IP24 2EA Tel: 01842 752048
Fax: 01842 750125 Email: thetford.lib@norfolk.gov.uk
WWW: www.culture.norfolk.gov.uk

Norfolk Library & Information Service
Gildengate House, Anglia Square Norwich, NR3 1AX
Tel: 01603 215254 Fax: 01603 215258
Email: norfolk.studies.lib@norfolk.gov.uk

North East Lincolnshire

Grimsby Central Library Reference Department
Central Library, Town Hall Square Great Grimsby
DN31 1HG Tel: 01472 323635 Fax: 01472 323634

North Lincolnshire

Scunthorpe Central Library
Carlton Street Scunthorpe, DN15 6TX Tel: 01724
860161 Fax: 01724 859737
Email: scunthorpe.ref@central library.demon.co.uk
WWW: www.nothlincs.gov.uk/Library

Northamptonshire

Peterborough Library
Broadway Peterborough, PE1 1RX Tel: 01733348343
Fax: 01733 555377
Email: libraries@peterborough.gov.uk

Northumberland

Border History Museum and Library
Moothall, Hallgate Hexham, NE46 3NH
Tel: 01434 652349 Fax: 01434 652425
Email: Museum
@tynedale.gov.uk

Alnwick Library
Green Batt Alnwick, NE66 1TU Tel: 01665 602689
Fax: 01665 604740

Blyth Library
Bridge Street Blyth, NE24 2DJ Tel: 01670 361352

Hexham Library
Queens Hall, Beaumont Street Hexham, NE46 3LS
Tel: 01434 652474 01434 606043
Email: cheane@northumberland.gov.uk

Berwick upon Tweed Library
Church Street Berwick upon Tweed, TD15 1EE
Tel: 01289 307320 Fax: 01289 308299

Nottinghamshire

University of Nottingham Hallward Library
University Park Nottingham, NG7 2RD
Tel: 0115 951 4514 Fax: 0115 951 4558
WWW: http://www.nottingham.ac.uk/library/

Department of Manuscripts and Special Collections
Hallward Library, Nottingham University , University
Park, Nottingham, NG7 2RD Tel: 0115 951 4565
Fax: 0115 951 4558
Email: mss library@nottingham.ac.uk
WWW: www.library.nottingham.ac.uk

Southwell Minster Library
Trebeck Hall, Bishop's Drive Southwell, NG25 0JP
Tel: 01636 812649 Fax: 01636 815904
Email: pat@southwellminster.prestell.co.uk

Nottingham Central Library : Local Studies Centre
Angel Row Nottingham, NG1 6HP Tel: 0115 915 2873
Fax: 0115 915 2850
Email: nottingham_local_studies@hotmail.com
WWW: www.notlib.demon.co.uk

Sutton in Ashfield Library
Devonshire Mall Sutton in Ashfield, NG17 1BP
Tel: 01623 556296 Fax: 01623 551962

Retford Library
Denman Library, Churchgate Retford, DN22 6PETel:
01777 708724 Fax: 01777 710020

Beeston Library
Foster Avenue Beeston, NG9 1AE Tel: 0115 925 5168
Fax: 0115 922 0841

Arnold Library
Front Street Arnold, NG5 7EE Tel: 0115 920 2247
Fax: 0115 967 3378

Mansfield Library
Four Seasons Centre, Westgate Mansfield, NG18 1NH
Tel: 01623 627591 Fax: 01623 629276
Email: mansfield.library@nottscc.gov.uk

Newark Library
Beaumont Gardens , Newark, NG24 1UW
Tel: 01636 703966 Fax: 01636 610045
West Bridgford Library
Bridgford Road West Bridgford, NG2 6AT
Tel: 0115 981 6506 Fax: 0115 981 3199
Eastwood Library
Wellington Place Eastwood, NG16 3GB
Tel: 01773 712209

Oxfordshire
Wantage Library
Stirlings Road Wantage, OX12 7BB Tel: 01235 762291
Fax: 01235 7700951
Centre for Oxfordshire Studies
Central Library, Westgate Oxford, OX1 1DJ
Tel: 01865 815749 Fax: 01865 810187
Email: cos@oxfordshire.gov.uk
WWW: www.oxfordshire.gov.uk/culture
River & Rowing Museum
Rowing & River Museum, Mill Meadows Henley on
Thames, RG9 1BF Tel: 01491 415625
Fax: 01491 415601 Email: Museum@rrm.co.uk
WWW: www..rrm.co.uk
Thames linked families especially lock keepers , boat builders
Abingdon Library
The Charter Abingdon, OX14 3LY Tel: 01235 520374
Fax: 01235 532643
Email: abingdonlibrary@hotmail.com
Banbury Library
Marlborough Road Banbury, OX16 8DF
Tel: 01295 262282 Fax: 01295 264331
Henley Library
Ravenscroft Road Henley on Thames, RG9 2DH
Tel: 01491 575278 Fax: 01491 576187
Witney Library
Welch Way Witney, OX8 7HH Tel: 01993 703659
Fax: 01993 775993
The Bodelian Library
Broad Street Oxford, OX1 3BG Tel: 01865 277000
Fax: 01865 277182 WWW: www.bodley.ox.ac.uk
Peterborough, Peterborough Library
Broadway Peterborough, PE1 1RX Tel: 01733348343
Fax: 01733 555377
Email: libraries@peterborough.gov.uk

Shropshire
Wrekin Local Studies Forum
Madeley Library
Russell Square Telford, TF7 5BB Tel: 01952 586575
Email: library@madeley.uk
WWW: www.madeley.org.uk

Somerset
Bath Central Library
19 The Podium, Northgate Street Bath, BA1 5AN
Tel: 01225 428144 Fax: 01225 331839
Somerset Studies Library
Paul Street Taunton, TA1 3XZ Tel: 01823 340300
Fax: 01823 340301
Yeovil Library
King George Street Yeovil, BA20 1PY
Tel: 01935 421910 Fax: 01935 431847
Email: ransell@somerset.gov.uk
Bridgewater Reference Library
Binford Place Bridgewater, TA6 3LF Tel: 01278 450082
Fax: 01278 451027 Email: pcstoyle@somerset.gov.uk
WWW: www.somerset.gov.uk
Frome Reference Library
Justice Lane Frome, BA11 1BA Tel: 01373 462215
Fax: 01373 472003

Weston Library
The Boulevard Weston Super Mare, BS23 1PL
Tel: 01934 636638 Fax: 01934 413046
Email: weston.library@n somerset.gov.uk
Nailsea Library
Somerset Square Nailsea, BS19 2EX Tel: 01275 854583
Fax: 01275 858373

South Gloucestershire
Thornbury Library
St Mary Street Thornbury, BS35 2AA Tel: 01454 865655

Staffordshire
Lichfield Library (Local Studies Section)
Lichfield Library, The Friary Lichfield, WS13 6QG
Tel: 01543 510720 Fax: 01543 411138
William Salt Library
Eastgate Street Stafford, ST16 2LZ Tel: 01785 278372
Fax: 01785 278414
Email: william.salt.library@staffordshire.gov.uk
WWW: http://www.staffordshire.gov.uk/archives/salt.htm
**Staffordshire & Stoke on Trent Archive Service Stoke
on Trent City Archives**
Hanley Library, Bethesda Street, Hanley, Stoke on Trent,
ST1 3RS Tel: 01782 238420 Fax: 01782 238499
Email: stoke.archives@stoke.gov.uk
Burton Library
Burton Library, Riverside, High Street, Burton on Trent,
DE14 1AH Tel: 01283 239556 Fax: 01283 239571
Email: burton.library@staffordshire.gov.uk
Barton Library
Dunstall Road Barton under Needwood, DE13 8AX
Tel: 01283 713753
Biddulph Library
Tunstall Road, Biddulph, Stoke on Trent, ST8 6HH
Tel: 01782 512103
Brewood Library
Newport Street Brewood, ST19 9DT Tel: 01902 850087
Cannock Library
Manor Avenue Cannock, WS11 1AA Tel: 01543 502019
Fax: 01543 278509
Email: cannock.library@staffordshire.gov.uk
Cheslyn Hay Library
Cheslyn Hay, Walsall, WS56 7AE Tel: 01922 413956
Codsall Library
Histons Hill Codsall, WV8 1AA Tel: 01902 842764
Great Wyrley Library
John's Lane, Great Wyrley, Walsall, WS6 6BY
Tel: 01922 414632
Kinver Library
Vicarage Drive, Kinver, Stourbridge, DY7 6HJ
Tel: 01384 872348
Leek Library
Nicholson Institute, Stockwell Street Leek, ST13 6DW
Tel: 01538 483210 Fax: 01538 483216
Email: leek.library@staffordshire.gov.uk
Newcastle Library
Ironmarket Newcastle under Lyme, ST5 1AT
Tel: 01782 297310 Fax: 01782 297322
Email: newcastle.library@staffordshire.gov.uk
Perton Library
Severn Drive Perton, WV6 7QU Tel: 01902 755794
Fax: 01902 756123
Email: perton.library@staffordshire.gov.uk
Penkridge Library
Bellbrock Penkridge, ST19 9DL Tel: 01785 712916
Rugeley Library
Anson Street Rugeley, WS16 2BB Tel: 01889 583237
Tamworth Library
Corporation Street Tamworth, B79 7DN
Tel: 01827 475645 Fax: 01827 475658
Email: tamworth.library@staffordshire.gov.uk
WWW: www.staffordshire.gov.uk/locgov/county/cars/tamlib.htm

Uttoxeter Library
High Street Uttoxeter, ST14 7JQ Tel: 01889 256371
Fax: 01889 256374
Wombourne Library
Windmill Bank Wombourne, WV5 9JD
Tel: 01902 892032

Surrey
LB of Richmond upon Thames Local Studies Library
Old Town Hall, Whittaker Avenue Richmond upon
Thames, TW9 1TP Tel: (020) 8332 6820
Fax: (020) 8940 6899
Email: localstudies@richmond.gov.uk
WWW: http://www.richmond.gov.uk
Surrey History Service Library
Surrey History Centre, 130 Goldsworth Road Woking,
GU21 1ND Tel: 01483 594594 Fax: 01483 594595
Email: shs@surreycc.gov.uk
WWW: http://.shs.surreycc.gov.uk
Sutton Central Library
St Nicholas Way Sutton, SM1 1EA Tel: (020) 8770 4745
Fax: (020) 8770 4777
Email: sutton.information@sutton.gov.uk
WWW: www.sutton.gov.uk
LB of Merton Local Studies Centre, Merton Civic
Centre, London Road Morden, SM4 5DX
Tel: (020) 8545 3239 Fax: (020) 8545 4037
Email: mertonlibs@compuserve.com

Tyne and Wear
South Tyneside Central Library
Prince Georg Square South Shields, NE33 2PE
Tel: 0191 427 1818 Ext 7860 Fax: 0191 455 8085
Email: reference.library@s tyneside mbc.gov.uk
WWW: www.s tyneside mbc.gov.uk
City Library & Arts Centre
28 30 Fawcett Street Sunderland, BR1 1RE
Tel: 0191 514235 Fax: 0191 514 8444
Central Library
Northumberland Square North Shields, NE3O 1QU
Tel: 0191 200 5424 Fax: 0191 200 6118,
cen@ntlib.demon.co.uk
**Gateshead Central Library & Local Studies
Department**
Prince Consort Road Gateshead, NE8 4LN Tel: 0191 477
3478 Fax: 0191 477 7454 Email:
Local@gateslib.demon.co.uk WWW:
http://ris.niaa.org.uk
Newcastle City Library Local Studies Section
Princess Square Newcastle upon Tyne, NE99 1DX
Tel: 0191 261 0691 Fax: 0191 232 6885
Email: heritage@dial.pipex.com

Warwickshire
Shakespeare Birthplace Trust Library
Shakespeare Centre Library, Henley Street Stratford
upon Avon, CV37 6QW Tel: 01789 204016
Tel: 01789 201813 Fax: 01789 296083
Email: library@shakespeare.org.uk
WWW: http://www.shakespeare.org.uk
Sutton Coldfield Library & Local Studies Centre
43 Lower Parade Sutton Coldfield, B72 1XX
Tel: 0121 354 2274 Tel: 0121 464 0164
Fax: 0121 464 0173
University of Warwick Library
Coventry, CV4 7AL Tel: (024) 76524219
Warwick Library
Barrack Street Warwick, CV34 4TH Tel: 01926 412189
Tel: 01926 412194 Fax: 01926 412784
Email: warwicklibrary@warwickshire.gov.uk

Warwickshire County Library
Leamington Library, Royal Pump Rooms, The Parade,
Leamington Spa, CV32 4AA Tel: 01926 425873
Fax: 01926 330285
Email: leamingtonlibrary@warwickshire.gov.uk

West Midlands
Sandwell Community Libraries
Town Hall, High Street West Bromwich, B70 8DX
Tel: 0121 569 4909 Fax: 0121 569 4907
Email: dm025@viscount.org.uk
Dudley Archives & Local History Service
Mount Pleasant Street, Coseley, Dudley, WV14 9JR
Tel: 01384 812770 Fax: 01384 812770
Email: archives.pls@mbc.dudley.gov.uk
WWW: http://dudleygov.uk/council/library/archives/archive1.htm
Sandwell Community History & Archives Service
Smethwick Library, High Street Smethwick, B66 1AB
Tel: 0121 558 2561 Fax: 0121 555 6064
Walsall Local History Centre
Essex Street Walsall, WS2 7AS Tel: 01922 721305
Fax: 01922 634594
Email: localhistorycentre@walsall.gov.uk
WWW: http://www.walsall.gov.uk/culturalservices/library/welcome.htm
Wolverhampton Archives & Local Studies
42-50 Snow Hill Wolverhampton, WV2 4AG
Tel: 01902 552480 Fax: 01902 552481
Email: wolvarch.and.ls@dial.pipex.com
WWW: http://www.wolverhampton.gov.uk/library/archives.htm
Solihull Library
Homer Road Solihull, B91 3RG Tel: 0121 704 6977
Fax: 0121 704 6212 The Library is NOT an archive repos-
itory, sceondary sources only available for Solihull MBC
area only
Local Studies Library
Central Library, Smithford Way Coventry, CV1 1FY
Tel: 012476 832336 Fax: 02476 832440
Email: covinfo@discover.co.uk
WWW: www.coventry.gov.uk/accent.htm

West Sussex
Worthing Reference Library
Worthing Library, Richmond Road Worthing, BN11 1HD
Tel: 01903 212060 Fax: 01903 821902
Email: worthinglibrary@hotmail.com

Wigan
Wigan Metropolitan Borough Council
Information Unit, Station Road Wigan, WN1 1WN

Wiltshire
Wiltshire Studies Library
Trowbridge Reference Library, Bythesea Road
Trowbridge, BA14 8BS Tel: 01225 713732
Tel: 01225 713727 Fax: 01225 713715
Email: trowreflib@compuserve.uk
WWW: www.wiltshire.gov.uk
Swindon Local Studies Library
Swindon Central Library, Regent Circus Swindon,
SN11QG Tel: 01793 463240 Fax: 01793 541319
Email: swindonref@swindon.gov.uk
WWW: http://www.swindon.gov.uk
Salisbury Local Studies Library
Market Place Salisbury, SP1 1BL Tel: 01722 410073
Wiltshire Archaeological and Natural History Society
Wiltshire Heritage Library, 41 Long Street Devizes,
SN10 1NS Tel: 01380 727369 Fax: 01380 722150

Worcestershire

Redditch Library
15 Market Place Redditch, B98 8AR Tel: 01527 63291
Fax: 01527 68571
Email: redditchlibrary@worcestershire.gov.uk
Bewdley Museum Research Library
Load Street Bewdley, DY12 2AE Tel: 01229 403573
Bromsgrove Library
Stratford Road Bromsgrove, B60 1AP
Tel: 01527 575855 Fax: 01527 575855
Evesham Library
Oat Street Evesham, WR11 4PJ Tel: 01386 442291
Fax: 01386 765855
Email: eveshamlib@worcestershire.gov.uk
WWW: www.worcestershire.gov.uk
Kidderminster Library
Market Street Kidderminster, DY10 1AD
Tel: 01562 824500 Fax: 01562 827303
Email: kidderminster@worcestershire.gov.uk
WWW: www.worcestershire.gov.uk
Malvern Library
Graham Road Malvern, WR14 2HU Tel: 01684 561223
Fax: 01684 892999 Email:
Worcester Library
Foregate Street Worcester, WR1 1DT Tel: 01905 765312
Fax: 01905 726664
Email: worcesterlib@worcestershire.gov.uk
WWW: www.worcestershire.gov.uk/libraries

Yorkshire

City of York Libraries Local History & Reference Collection
York Central Library, Library, Square, Museum Street,
York, YO1 7DS Tel: 01904 655631 Fax: 01904 611025
Email: reference.library@york.gov.uk
WWW: http://www.york.gov.uk
York Minster Library'
York Minster Library & Archives, Dean's Park York,
YO1 2JD Tel: 01904 625308 Tel: 01904 611118
Fax: 01904 611119

East Yorkshire

East Riding Heritage Library & Museum
Sewerby Hall, Church Lane, Sewerby, Bridlington,
YO15 1EA Tel: 01262 677874 Tel: 01262 674265
Email: Museum@pop3.poptel.org.uk
WWW: www.bridlington.net/sew
Beverley Local Studies Library
Beverley Library, Champney Road Beverley, HU17 9BG
Tel: 01482 885358 Fax: 01482 881861
Email: user@bevlib.karoo.co.uk
Bridlington Local Studies Library
Bridlington Library, King Street Bridlington, YO15 2DF
Tel: 01262 672917 Fax: 01262 670208
Goole Local Studie Library
Goole Library, Carlisle Street Goole, DN14 5DS
Tel: 01405 762187 Fax: 01405 768329
Email: user@goolelib.karoo.co.uk

North Yorkshire

North Yorkshire County Libraries
21 Grammar School Lane Northallerton, DL6 1DF
Tel: 01609 776271 Fax: 01609 780793
Email: elizabeth.melrose@northyorks.gov.uk
WWW: http://www.northyorks.gov.uk
Northallerton Reference Library
1 Thirsk Road Northallerton, DL6 1PT Tel: 01609
776202 Fax: 01609 780793
Email: northallerton.libraryhq@northyorks.gov.uk
Harrogate Reference Library
Victoria Avenue Harrogate, HG1 1EG Tel: 01423 502744
Fax: 01423 523158

Pickering Reference Library
The Ropery Pickering, YO18 8DY Tel: 01751 472185
Scarborough Reference Library
Vernon Road Scarborough, YO11 2NN Tel: 01723
364285 Fax: 01723 353893
Email: scarborough.library@northyorks.gov.uk
Selby Reference Library
52 Micklegate Selby, YO8 4EQ Tel: 01757 702020
Fax: 01757 705396
Skipton Reference Library
High Street Skipton, BD23 1JX Tel: 01756 794726
Fax: 01756 798056
Whitby Library
Windsor Terrace Whitby, YO21 1ET Tel: 01947 602554
Fax: 01947 820288

South Yorkshire

Barnsley Archives and Local Studies Department,
Central Library
Shambles Street Barnsley, S70 2JF Tel: 01226 773950
Tel: 01226 773938 Fax: 01226 773955
Email: Archives@Barnsley.ac.uk &
librarian@barnsley.ac.uk
WWW: http://www.barnsley.ac.uk/sites/Library
Archives & Local Studies
Central Library, Walker Place Rotherham, S65 1JH
Tel: 01709 823616 Fax: 01709 823650
Email: archives@rotherham.gov.uk
WWW: www.rotherha.gov.uk/pages/living/learning/islib/callib.htm
Central Library
Surrey Street Sheffield, S1 1XZ Tel: 0114 273 4711
Fax: 0114 273 5009 Email:
sheffield.libraries@dial.pipex.com
Doncaster Libraries Local Studies Section
Central Library, Waterdale Doncaster, DN1 3JE
Tel: 01302 734307 Fax: 01302 369749
Email: reference.library@doncaster.gov.uk

West Yorkshire

Local Studies Library
Leeds Central Library, Calverley Street Leeds, LS1 3AB
Tel: 0113 247 8290 Fax: 0113 247 8290
Email: local.studies@leeds.gov.uk
WWW: www.leeds.gov.uk/library/services/loc_reso.html
British Library
Boston Spa, Wetherby, LS23 7BY
Calderdale Central Library
Northgate House, Northgate Halifax, HX11 1UN
Tel: 01422392631 Fax: 01422 349458 WWW:
www.calderdale.gov.uk
Huddersfield Local History Library
Huddersfield Library, & Art Gallery, Princess Alexandra
Walk Huddersfield, HD1 2SU Tel: 01484 221965
Fax: 01484 221952
Email: ref library@geo2.poptel.org.uk
WWW: http://www.kirkleesmc.gov.uk
Wakefield Library Headquarters Local Studies Department
Balne Lane Wakefield, WF2 0DQ Tel: 01924 302224
Fax: 01924 302245 Email: localstudies@talk21.com
WWW: www.wakefield.gov.uk
Yorkshire Archaeological Society
Claremont, 23 Clarendon Rd Leeds, LS2 9NZ
Tel: 0113 245 6342 Tel: 0113 245 7910 Fax: 0113 244
1979 Email: j.heron@sheffield.ac.uk
WWW: www.yas.org.uk
Local Studies Reference Library
Central Library, Prince's Way Bradford, BD1 1NN
Tel: 01274 753661 Fax: 01274 753660

Keighley Reference Library
North Street Keighley, BD21 3SX Tel: 01535 618215
Fax: 01535 618214
Email: keighleylibrary@bradford.gov.uk
WWW: www.bradford.gov.uk
Wakefield Metropolitan District Libraries
Castleford Library, & Local Studies Dept, Carlton Street
Castleford, WF10 1BB Tel: 01977 722085
Pontefract Library & Local Studies Centre
Pontefract Library, Shoemarket Pontefract, WF8 1BD
Tel: 01977 727692
Olicana Historical Society
54 Kings Road Ilkley, LS29 9AT Tel: 01943 609206

Wales
National Library of Wales
Penglais Aberystwyth, SY23 3BU Tel: 01970 632800
Fax: 01970 615709 Email: holi@llgc.org.uk
WWW: http://www.llgc.org.uk

Caerphilly
Bargoed Library
The Square Bargoed, CF8 8QQ Tel: 01443 875548
Fax: 01443 836057 Email: 9e465@dial.pipex.com
Caerphilly Library
Unit 7 Woodfieldside Business Park, Penmaen Road,
Pontllanfraith, Blackwood, NP12 2DG
Tel: 01495 235584 Fax: 01495 235567
Email: cael.libs@dial.pipex.com

Cardiff
Cardiff Central Library (Local Studies Department)
St Davids Link, Frederick Street Cardiff, CF1 4DT
Tel: (029) 2038 2116 Fax: (029) 2087 1599
Email: p.sawyer@cardlib.gov.uk
WWW: www.cardiff.gov.uk

Carmarthenshire
Carmarthen Library
St Peters Street Carmarthen, SA31 1LN
Tel: 01267 224822
Llanelli Public Library
Vaughan Street Lanelli, SA15 3AS Tel: 01554 773538
Fax: 01554 750125

Ceredigion
Aberystwyth Reference Library
Corporation Street Aberystwyth, SY23 2BU
Tel: 01970 617464 Fax: 01970 625059
Email: llyfrygell.library@ceredigion.gov.uk
WWW: www.ceredigion.gov.uk/libraries

Flintshire
Flintshire Reference Library
Headquarters, County Hall , Mold, CH7 6NW Tel:
01352 704411 Fax: 01352 753662
Email: libraries@flintshire.gov.uk
WWW: www.flintshire.gov.uk

Glamorgan
Bridgend Library & Information Service
Coed Parc, Park Street Bridgend, CF31 4BA Tel: 01656
767451 Fax: 01656 64571
 Email: blis@bridgendlib.gov.uk
Dowlais Library
Church Street, Dowlais, Merthyr Tydfil, CF48 3HS
Tel: 01985 723051

Merthyr Tydfil Central Library (Local Studies Department)
High Street Merthyr Tydfil, CF47 8AF
Tel: 01685 723057 Fax: 01685 722146
Email: library@merthyr.gov.btinternet.com
Pontypridd Library
Library, Road Pontypridd, CF37 2DY Tel: 01443 486850
Fax: 01443 493258 Email:
Treorchy Library
Station Road Treorchy, CF42 6NN Tel: 01443 773204
Fax: 01443 777407

Gwent
Abertillery Liberary Station Hill Abertillery, NP13 1TE
Tel: 01495 212332 Fax: 01495 320995
Ebbw Vale Library
Ebbw Vale Library, 21 Bethcar Street Ebbw Vale
NP23 6HH Tel: 01495 303069 Fax: 01495 350547
Tredegar Library
The Circle , Tredegar, NP2 3PS Tel: 01495 722687
Fax: 01495 717018

Gwynedd
Llyfrgell Caernarfon
Lon Pafiliwn , Caernafon, LL55 1AS Tel: 01286 679465
Fax: 01286 671137 Email: library@gwynedd.gov.uk
Canolfan Llyfrgell Dolgellau Library
FforddBala , Dolgellau, LL40 2YF Tel: 01341 422771
Fax: 01341 423560 WWW: http://www.gwynedd.gov.uk
Treharris Library
Perrott Street, Treharris, Merthyr Tydfil, CF46 5ET
Tel: 01443 410517 Fax: 01443 410517

Monmoputhshire
Chepstow Library & Information Centre
Manor Way Chepstow, NP16 5HZ Tel: 01291 635730
Tel: 01291 635731 Fax: 01291 635736
Email: chepstowlibrary@monmouthshire.gov.uk
WWW: www.monmouthshire.gov.uk/leisure/libraries

Pembrokeshire
Pembrokeshire Libraries
The County Library, Dew Street Haverfordwest, SA61
1SU Tel: 01437 762070 Fax: 01437 769218
Email: anita.thomas@pembrokeshire.gov.uk The Local
Studies Library covers people, places and events relating to The
County of Pembrokeshire past and present. The Library also
houses The Francis Green Genealogical Collection consisting of
over 800 pedigree sheets and 35 volumes of information

Powys
Brecon Area Library
Ship Street Brecon, LD3 9AE Tel: 01874 623346
Fax: 01874 622818 Email: breclib@mail.powys.gov.uk
Newtown Area Library
Park Lane Newtown, SY16 1EJ Tel: 01686 626934
Fax: 01686 624935 Email: nlibrary@powys.gov.uk
Llandrindod Wells Library
Cefnllys Lane Llandrindod Wells, LD1 5LD
Tel: 01597 826870
Email: llandod.library@powys.gov.uk

Rhondda Cynon Taff
Aberdare Library
Green Street Aberdare, CF44 7AG Tel: 01685 885318
Fax: 01685 881181

Newport
Newport Library & Information Service
Newport Central Library, John Frost Square Newport,
NP20 1PA Tel: 01633 211376 Fax: 01633 222615
Email: reference.library@newport.gov.uk
WWW: http://www.earl.org.uk/partners/newport/index.html

South Glamorgan
Barry Library
King Square, Holton Road Barry, CF63 4RW
Tel: 01446 735722 Fax: 01446 734427

West Glamorgan
Lifelong Learning Service
Theodore Road Port Talbot, SA13 1SP
Tel: 01639 898581 Fax: 01639 899914
Email: lls@neath porttalbot.gov.uk
Neath Central Library (Local Studies Department)
29 Victoria Gardens Neath, SA11 3BA
Tel: 01639 620139
W. Glamorgan Archive Service   Port Talbot Access Point
Port Talbot Library, Aberafan Centre Port Talbot, SA13
1PJ Tel: 01639 763430
WWW: http://www.swansea.gov.uk/archives
Port Talbot Library
1st Floor Aberafan Shopping Centre , Port Talbot
SA13 1PB Tel: 01639 763490
South Wales Miners' Library
University of Wales, Swansea, Hendrefoelan House,
Gower Road Swansea, SA2 7NB Tel: 01792 518603
Fax: 01792 518694 Email: miners@swansea.ac.uk
WWW: http://www.swan.ac.uk/lis/swml
Swansea Reference Library
Alexandra Road Swansea, SA1 5DX Tel: 01792 516753
Fax: 01792 516759 Email: swanlib@demon.co.uk
Extensive holdings of trade directories, local census returns,
newspapers (partially indexed)

Wrexham
Wrexham Library and Arts Centre
Rhosddu Road Wrexham, LL11 1AU Tel: 01978 292622
Fax: 01978 292611 Email: joy.thomas@wrexham.gov.uk
WWW: www.wrexham.gov.uk

Scotland
National Library of Scotland
George IV Bridge Edinburgh, EH1 1EW
Tel: 0131 226 4531 Fax: 0131 622 4803
 Email: enquiries@nls.uk WWW: http://www.nls.uk
Scottish United Services Museum Library
The Castle, Museum Square Edinburgh, EH1 1 2NG
Tel: 0131 225 7534 Ext 2O4 Fax: 0131 225 3848
Email: library@nms.ac.uk WWW: www.nms.ac.uk
National Museums of Scotland Library
Royal Museum, Chambers Street Edinburgh, EH1 1JF
Tel: 0131 247 4137 Fax: 0131 247 4311 Email:
library@nms.ac.uk WWW: www.nms.ac.uk, Holds large
collection of family histories, esp Scottish
Scottish Genealogy Society   Library
15 Victoria Terrace Edinburgh, EH1 2JL
Tel: 0131 220 3677 Fax: 0131 220 3677
Email: scotgensoc@sol.co.uk
WWW: www.scotsgenealogy.com

Aberdeenshire
Aberdeenshire Library & Information Service
The Meadows Industrial Estate, Meldrum Meg Way,
Oldmeldrum, AB51 0GN Tel: 01651 872707
Tel: 01651 871219/871220 Fax: 01651 872142
Email: ALIS@aberdeenshire.gov.uk
WWW :www.aberdeenshire.gov.uk
Aberdeen Central Library Reference & Local Studies
Rosemount Viaduct Aberdeen, AB25 1GW
Tel: 01224 652511 Tel: 01224 252512
Fax: 01224 624118
Email: refloc@arts rec.aberdeen.net.uk

University of Aberdeen DISS: Heritage Division
Special Collections & Archives
Kings College , Aberdeen, AB24 3SW
Tel: 01224 272598 Fax: 01224 273891
Email: speclib@abdn.ac.uk
WWW: http://www.abdn.ac.uk/diss/heritage

Angus
Angus Archives & Library
Montrose Library
214 High Street Montrose, DD10 8PH
Tel: 01674 671415 Fax: 01674 671810
Email: angu.archives@angus.govuk
WWW: www.angus.gov.uk/history/history.htm

Argyll
Argyll & Bute Council Archives
Highland Avenue, Sandbank, Dunoon, PA23 8PB
Tel: 01369 703214
Campbeltown Library and Museum
Hall St Campbeltown, PA28 6BU Tel: 01586 552366
Argyll & Bute Library Service
Library, Headquarters, Highland Avenue, Sandbank,
Dunoon, PA23 8PB Tel: 01369 703214
Fax: 01369705797
Email: andyewan@abc libraries.demon.co.uk

Ayrshire
East Ayrshire Council District History Centre &
Museum
Baird Institute, 3 Lugar Street Cumnock, KA18 1AD Tel:
01290 421701 Fax: 01290 421701
Email: Baird.institute@east ayrshire.gov.uk
WWW: www.east ayrshire.gov.uk
Leadhills Miners's Library
Main Street Leadhills Tel: 01659 74326
North Ayrshire Libraries
Library Headquarters, 39 41 Princes Street Ardrossan,
KA22 8BT Tel: 01294 469137 Fax: 01924 604236
Email: reference@naclibhq.prestel.co.uk
East Ayrshire Libraries   Cumnock
25 27 Ayr Road Cumnock, KA18 1EB
Tel: 01290 422804
South Ayrshire Library
Carnegie Library
12 Main Street Ayr, KA8 8ED Tel: 01292 286385
Fax: 01292 611593
Email: carnegie@south ayrshire.gov.uk
WWW: www.south ayrshire.gov.uk

Clackmannanshire
Clackmannanshire Libraries
Alloa Library, 26/28 Drysdale Street Alloa, FK10 1JL
Tel: 01259 722262 Fax: 01259 219469
Email: clack.lib@mail.easynet.co.uk
Ewart Library
Ewart Library, Catherine Street Dumfries, DG1 1JB
Tel: 01387 260285 Tel: 01387 252070 Fax: 01387
260294 Email: ruth_airley@dumgal.gov.uk
libsxi@dumgal.gov.uk WWW: www.dumgal.gov.ukf

Dunbartonshire
Dumbarton Public Library
Strathleven Place Dumbarton, G82 1BD Tel: 01389
733273 Fax: 01389 738324 Email: wdlibs@hotmail.com

Dundee
Central Library
The Wellgate , Dundee, DD1 1DB Tel: 01382 434377
Fax: 01382 434036
Email: local.studies@dundeecity.gov.uk
WWW: http://www.dundeecity.gov.uk/dchtml/nrd/loc_stud.htm
Material held mainly Angus and Dundee

357

Tay Valley Family History Society & Family History Research Centre
Family History Research Centre, 179–181 Princes Street Dundee, DD4 6DQ Tel: 01382 461845
Fax: 01382 455532
Email: tayvalleyfhs@sol.co.uk
WWW: http://www.sol.co.uk/t/tayvalleyfhs/

East Ayrshire
Auchinleck Library
Community Centre, Well Road Auchinleck, KA18 2LA
Tel: 01290 422829
Bellfield Library
79 Whatriggs Road , Kilmarnock, KA1 3RB
Tel: 01563 534266
Bellsbank Library
Primary School, Craiglea Crescent Bellsbank, KA6 7UA
Tel: 01292 551057
Catrine Library
A M Brown Institute , Catrine, KA5 6RT
Tel: 01290 551717
Crosshouse Library
11 13 Gatehead Road Crosshouse, KA2 0HN
Tel: 01563 573640
Dalmellington Library
Townhead Dalmellington, KA6 7QZ Tel: 01292 550159
Dalrymple Library
Barbieston Road Dalrymple, KA6 6DZ
Darvel Library
Town Hall, West Main Street Darvel, KA17 0AQ
Tel: 01560 322754
Drongan Library
Mill O'Shield Road Drongan, KA6 7AY
Tel: 01292 591718
East Ayrshire Libraries
Dick Institute, Elmbank Avenue Kilmarnock, KA1 3BU
Tel: 01563 554310 Tel: 01290 421701
Fax: 01563 554311
Email: baird.institute@east ayrshire.gov.uk
WWW: www.east ayrshire.gov.uk
Galston Library
Henrietta Street Galston, KA4 8HQTel: 01563 821994
Hurlford Library
Blair Road Hurlford, KA1 5BN Tel: 01563 539899
Kilmaurs Library
Irvine Road Kilmaurs, KA3 2RJ
Mauchline Library
2 The Cross Mauchline, Scotland
Muirkirk Library
Burns Avenue Muirkirk, KA18 3RH Fax: 01290 661505
Netherthird Library
Ryderston Drive Netherthird, KA18 3AR
Tel: 01290 423806
New Cumnock Library
Community Centre, The Castle New Cumnock
KA18 4AH Tel: 01290 338710
Newmilns Library
Craigview Road Newmilns, KA16 9DQ
Tel: 01560 322890
Ochiltree Library
Main Street Ochiltree, KA18 2PE
Tel: 01290 700425
Patna Library
Doonside Avenue Patna, KA6 7LX Tel: 01292 531538

East Dunbartonshire
East Dunbartonshire Local Record Offices and Reference Libraries
William Patrick Library 2 West High Street Kirkintilloch, G66 1AD Tel: 0141 776 8090 Fax: 0141 776 0408
Email: ref@edlib.freeserve.co.uk

East Renfrewshire
Giffnock Library
Station Road, Giffnock, Glasgow, G46 6J
Tel: 0141 577 4976 Fax: 0141 577 4978
Email: devinem@eastrenfrewshire.co.uk

Edinburgh
Edinburgh Central Library
Edinburgh Room, George IV Bridge Edinburgh
EH1 1EG Tel: 0131 242 8030 Fax: 0131 242 8009
Email: eclis@edinburgh.gov.uk
WWW: www.edinburgh.gov.uk

Falkirk
Falkirk Museum History Research Centre
Callendar House, Callendar Park Falkirk, FK1 1Y
Tel: 01324 503778 Fax: 01324 503771
Email: ereid@falkirkMuseums.demon.co.uk & callandar-house@falkirkMuseums.demon.co.uk
WWW: www.falkirkMuseums.demon.co.uk,
Records held: Local Authority, business, personal and estate records, local organmisations, trade unions, over 28,000 photographs Falkirk District
Falkirk Library
Hope Street Falkirk, FK1 5AU
Holds Local Studies Collection

Fife
Fife Council Central Area Libraries, Central Library
War Memorial Grounds Kirkcaldy, KY1 1YG
Tel: 01592 412878 Fax: 01592 412750
Email: info@kirkcaldy.fifelib.net
Dunfermline Library Local History Department
Abbot Street Dunfermline, KY12 7NL
Tel: 01383 312994 Fax: 01383 312608
Email: info@dunfermline.fifelib.net
St Andrews Library
Church Square St Andrews, KY16 9NN
Tel: 01334 412685 Fax: 01334 413029 Email:
info@standres.fiflib.net
St Andrews University Library
North Street St Andrews, KY16 9TR Tel: 01334 462281
Fax: 01334 462282
WWW: http://www.library.st and.ac.uk

Glasgow
Brookwood Library
166 Drymen Road, Bearsden, Glasgow, G61 3RJ Tel:
0141 942 6811 Fax: 0141 943 1119
Social Sciences Department History & Glasgow Room
The Mitchell Library, North Street Glasgow, G3 7DN
Tel: 0141 227 2935 Tel: 0141 227 2937 & 0141 227 2938 Fax: 0141 227 293
Email: history and glasgow@cls.glasgow.gov.uk
WWW: www.libarch.glasgow
Glasgow City Libraries & Archives Mitchell Library
North Street Glasgow, G3 7DN Tel: 0141 287 2937
Fax: 0141 287 2912
Email: history_and_glasgow @gcl.glasgow.gov.uk
WWW: www.glasgow.gov.uk/html/council/cindex.htm

Lanarkshire
Airdrie Library
Wellwynd Airdrie, ML6 0AG Tel: 01236 763221
Tel: 01236 760937 Fax: 01236 766027
Cumbernauld Central Library
8 Allander Walk Cumbernauld, G67 1EE
Tel: 01236 735964 Fax: 01236 458350
WWW: www.northlan.org.uk

Midlothian
Midlothian Libraries Local History Centre
Midlothian Council Libraries Headquarters, 2 Clerk
Street Loanhead, EH20 9DR Tel: 0131 440 2210
Fax: 0131 440 4635
Email: local.studies@midlothian.gov.uk
WWW: http://www.earl.org.uk.partners/midlothian/index.html

Morayshire
Buckie Library
Clunu Place Buckie, AB56 1HB Tel: 01542 832121
Fax: 01542 835237
Email: buckie.lib@techleis.moray.gov.uk
Forres Library
Forres House, High Street Forres, IV36 0BJ
Tel: 01309 672834 Fax: 01309 675084
Keith Library
Union Street Keith, AB55 5DP Tel: 01542 882223
Fax: 01542 882177
Email: keithlibrary@techleis.moray.gov.uk
Moray Local Heritage Centre
Grant Lodge, Cooper Park Elgin, IV30 1HS
Tel: 01343 544475 Tel: 01343 563413 Fax: 01343
549050, graeme.wilson@techleis.moray.gov.uk

North Lanarkshire
Motherwell Heritage Centre
High Road Motherwell, ML1 3HU Tel: 01698 251000
Fax: 01698 253433
Email: heritage@mhc158.freeserve.co.uk
Kilsyth Library
Burngreen Kilsyth, G65 0HT Tel: 01236 823147
Fax: 01236 823147
Shotts Library
Benhar Road Shotts, ML7 5EN Tel: 01501 821556

Perthshire
Perth & Kinross Libraries
A K Bell Library, 2 8 York Place Perth, PH2 8EP Tel:
01738 477062 Tel: Fax: 01738 477010
Email: jaduncan@pkc.gov.uk

Renfrewshire
Renfrewshire Council Library & Museum Services
Central Library & Museum, Complex, High Street
Paisley, PA1 2BB Tel: 0141 889 2350
Fax: 0141 887 6468
Email: local_studies.library@renfrewshire.gov.uk
Watt Library
9 Union Street Greenock, PA16 8JH Tel: 01475 715628

Scottish Borders
Scottish Borders Archive & Local History Centre
Library, Headquarters, St Mary's Mill Selkirk, TD7 5EW
Tel: 01750 20842 Tel: Fax: 01750 22875
Email: archives@scotborders.gov.uk

West Lothian
West Lothian Council Libraries, Connolly House,
Hopefield Road Blackburn, EH47 7HZ
Tel: 01506 776331 Tel: Fax: 01506 776345
Email: localhistory@westlothian.org.uk
WWW: http://www.wlonline.org

Orkney
Orkney Library
The Orkney Library, Laing Street, Kirkwall, KWI5 1NW
Tel: 01856 873166 Fax: 01856 875260 Email:
karen.walker@orkney.gov.uk

Shetland
Shetland Library
Lower Hillhead Lerwick, ZE1 0EL Tel: 01595 693868
Tel: Fax: 01595 694430
Email: info@shetland library.gov.uk
WWW: www.shetland library.gov.uk

Isle of Barra
Castlebay Community Library
Community School , Castlebay, HS95XD
Tel: 01871 810471 Fax: 01871 810650

Isle of Benbecula
Community Library
Sgoil Lionacleit Liniclate, HS7 5PJ Tel: 01870 602211
Fax: 01870 602817

Isle of Lewis
Stornoway Library
19 Cromwell Street Stornoway, HS1 2DA
Tel: 01851 703064 Fax: 01851 708676/708677
Email: stornoway library1@cne siar.gov.uk.gov.uk

Northern Ireland
North Eastern Library Board & Local Studies
Area Reference Library
Demesne Avenue Ballymena, BT43 7BG
Tel: (028) 25 6641212 Tel: Fax: (028) 256 46680,
Email: yvonne_hirt@hotmail.com, www.neelb.org.uk
Belfast Central Library
Irish & Local Studies Dept, Royal Avenue Belfast
BT1 1EA Tel: (028) 9024 3233 Fax: (028) 9033 2819,
EM: info@libraries.belfast elb.gov.uk, www.belb.org.uk
Belfast Linen Hall Library
17 Donegall Square North Belfast, BT1 5GD
Tel: (028) 90321707

County Antrim
Local Studies Service
Area Library, HQ, Demesne Avenue Ballymena, BT43
7BG Tel: (028) 25 664121 Fax: (028) 256 46680
Email: yvonne_hirst@hotmail.com
WWW: www.neelb.org.uk

County Fermanagh
Enniskillen Library
Halls Lane Enniskillen, BT1 3HP Tel: (028) 66322886
Fax: (028) 66324685
Email: librarian@eknlib.demon.co.uk

County Londonderry
Central and Reference Library
35 Foyle Street Londonderry, BT24 6AL
Tel: (028) 71272300 Fax: (028) 7122 69084
Email: trishaw@online.rednet.co.uk
Irish Room
Coleraine County Hall, Castlerock Road Ballymena, BT1
3HP Tel: (028) 705 1026 Fax: (028) 705 1247 WWW:
www.neelb.org.uk

Co Tyrone
Omagh Library
1 Spillars Place Omagh, BT78 1HL Tel: (028) 82244821
Fax: (028) 82246772 Email:
librarian@omahlib.demon.co.uk

County Down
South Eastern Library Board & Local Studies
Library HQ, Windmill Hill Ballynahinch, BT24 8DH Tel:
(028) 9756 6400 Fax: (028) 9756 5072 Email:
ref@bhinchlibhq.demon.co.uk

Isle of Man
Manx National Heritage Library
Douglas, IM1 3LY Tel: 01624 648000
Fax: 01624 648001 Email: enquiries@mnh.gov.im

Ireland
Dublin Public Libraries
Gilbert Library, Dublin & Irish Collections, 138-142
Pearse Street Dublin, 2 Tel: 353 1 677 7662
Fax: 353 1 671 4354 Email: dubcoll@iol.ie
WWW: http:/www.iol.ie/ dubcilib/index.html, The
Library will be closed during 2001 for refurbishment. The
stock is in storage and the Library will not be in a position
to answer enquiries
National Library of Ireland
Kildare Street Dublin, 2 Tel: 661 8811 Fax: 676 6690
Email: coflaherty@nli.ie
Society of Friends (Quakers) Historical Library
Swanbrook House, Bloomfield Avenue Dublin, 4
Tel: (01) 668 7157 By 2001 will have completed computer-
isation of card index

Co Clare
Clare County Library
The Manse, Harmony Row Ennis Tel: 065 6821616
Fax: 065 6842462 Email: clarelib@iol.ie
WWW: www.iol.ie/~clarelib

Co Cork
Cork City Library
Grand Parade Cork Tel: 021 277110
Fax: 021 275684 Email: cork.city.library@indigo.ie
Mallow Heritage Centre
27/28 Bank Place Mallow Tel: 022 50302

Co Dublin
Dun Laoghaire Library
Lower George's Street Dun Laoghaire Tel: 2801147
Fax: 2846141 Email: eprout@dlrcoco.ie
WWW: www.dlrcoco.ie/library/lhistory.htm

Co Kerry
Kerry County Library Genealogical Centre
Cathedral Walk Killarney Tel: 353 0 64 359946

Co Kildare
Kildare Hertiage & Genealogy
Kildare County Library
Newbridge Tel: 045 433602 Fax: 045 432490
Email: capinfo@iol.ie WWW: www.kildare.ie
Kildare County Library
Newbridge Tel: 045 431109 Fax: 045 432490

Co Mayo
Central Library
Castlebar Tel: 094 24444 Fax: 094 24774
Email: cbarlib@iol.ie

Co Sligo
Sligo County Library
Westward Town Centre, Bridge Street Sligo Tel: 00 353
71 47190 Fax: 00 353 71 46798 Email: sligolib@iol.ie

Co Tipperary
Tipperary County Libary Local Studies Department
Castle Avenue Thurles Tel: 0504 21555 Fax: 0504 23442
Email: studies@tipplibs.iol.ie
WWW: www.iol.ie/~TIPPLIBS

Co Waterford
Waterford County Library
Central Library Davitt's Quay Dungarvan Tel: 058 41231
Fax: 058 54877

Co Wexford
Wexford Branch Library
Teach Shionoid, Abbey Street Wexford Tel: 053 42211
Fax: 053 21097
Enniscorthy Branch Library
Lymington Road Enniscorthy Tel: 054 36055
New Ross Branch Library
Barrack Lane New Ross Tel: 051 21877

County Donegal
Donegal Local Studies Centre, Central Library
& Arts Centre, Oliver Plunkett Road Letterkenny
Tel: 00353 74 24950 Fax: 00353 74 24950
Email: dgcolib@iol.ie WWW: donegal.ie
Ballyfermot Public Library
Ballyfermot, Dublin, 10

County Limerick
Limerick City Library
The Granary, Michael Street Limerick Tel: 061 314668
Fax: 061 411506 Email: doyledolores@hotmail.com

Australia
ACT
National Library of Australia
Canberra, 2600 Tel: 02 6262 1111
WWW: http://www.nla.gov.au

New South Wales
Mitchell Library
Macquarie Street Sydney, 2000 Tel: 02 9230 1693
Fax: 02 9235 1687 Email: slinfo@slsw.gov.au
State Library of New South Wales
Macquarie Street Sydney, 2000 Tel: 02 9230 1414
Fax: 02 9223 3369 Email: slinfo@slsw.gov.au

Queensland
State Library of Queensland
PO Box 3488, Cnr Peel and Stanley Streets, South
Brisbane, Brisbane, 4101 Tel: 07 3840 7775
Fax: 07 3840 7840 Email: genie@slq.qld.gov.au
WWW: http://www.slq.qld.gov.au/subgenie/htm

South Australia
South Australia State Library
PO Box 419 Adelaide, 5001 Tel: (08) 8207 7235 Fax:
(08) 8207 7247 Email: famhist@slsa.sa.gov.au WWW:
http://www.slsa.sa.gov.au/library/collres/famhist/

Victoria
State Library of Victoria
328 Swanston Street Walk Melbourne, 3000 Tel: 03 9669
9080 Email: granth@newvenus.slv.vic.gov.au WWW:
http://www.slv.vic.gov.au/slv/genealogy/index

Western Australia
State Library
Alexander Library, Perth Cultural Centre Perth, 6000 Tel:
09 427 3111 Fax: 09 427 3256

New Zealand
Auckland Research Centre Auckland City Libraries
PO Box 4138, 44 46 Lorne Street Auckland
Tel: 64 9 377 0209 Fax: 64 9 307 7741
Email: heritage@auckland library.govt.nz

National Library of New Zealand
PO Box 1467 Thorndon, Wellington Tel: (0064)4 474
3030 Fax: (0064)4 474 3063
WWW: http://www.natlib.govt.nz
Alexander Turnbull Library
PO Box 12 349 , Wellington, 6038 Tel: 04 474 3050
Fax: 04 474 3063
Canterbury Public Library
PO Box 1466 , Christchurch Tel: 03 379 6914
Fax: 03 365 1751
Dunedin Public Libraries
PO Box 5542, Moray Place Dunedin Tel: 03 474 3651
Fax: 03 474 3660 Email: library@dcc.govt.nz
Fielding Public Library
PO Box 264 , Fielding, 5600 Tel: 06 323 5373
Hamilton Public Library
PO Box 933, Garden Place Hamilton, 2015
Tel: 07 838 6827 Fax: 07 838 6858
Hocken Library
PO Box 56 , Dunedin Tel: 03 479 8873
Fax: 03 479 5078
Porirua Public Library
PO Box 50218 , Porirua, 6215 Tel: 04 237 1541
Fax: 04 237 7320
Takapuna Public Library
Private Bag 93508 , Takapuna, 1309
Tel: 09 486 8466 Fax: 09 486 8519
Wanganui District Library
Private Bag 3005, Alexander Building, Queens Park,
Wanganui, 5001 Tel: 06 345 8195 Fax: 06 345 5516
Email: wap@wdl.govt.nz

South Africa
South African Library
PO Box 496 , Cape Town, 8000 Tel: 021 246320
Fax: 021 244848

Canada
Alberta
Calgary Public Library
616 MacLeod Tr SE Calgary, T2G 2M2 Tel: 260 2785
Glenbow Library & Archives
130 9th Avenue SE Calgary, T2G 0P3 Tel: 403 268 4197
Fax: 403 232 6569

British Columbia
British Columbia Archives
865 Yates Street Victoria, V8V 1X4 Tel: 604 387 1952
Fax: 604 387 2072 Email:
rfrogner@maynard.bcars.gs.gov.bc.ca
Cloverdale Library
5642   176a Street Surrey, V3S 4G9 Tel: 604 576 1384
Fax: 604 576 0120
Email: GenealogyResearch@city.surrey.bc.ca
WWW: http://www.city.surrey.bc.ca/spl/

New Brunswick
Harriet Irving Library
PO Box 7500 Fredericton, E3B 5H5 Tel: 506 453 4748
Fax: 506 453 4595
Loyalist Collection & Reference Library
PO Box 7500 Fredericton, E3B 5H5 Tel: 506 453 4749
Fax: 506 453 4596

Newfoundland
Newfoundland Provincial Resource Library
Arts and Cultural Centre, Allandale Road St Johns, A1B
3A3 Tel: 709 737 3955 Fax: 709 737 2660
Email: genealog@publib.nf.ca
WWW: http://www.publib.nf.ca

Ontario
National Library
395 Wellington Street Ottawa, K1A 0N4
Tel: 613 995 9481 Fax: 613 943 1112
Email:reference@nlc bnc.ca WWW: http://www.nlc bnc.ca
Toronto Reference Library
789 Yonge Street Toronto, M4W 2G8 Tel: 416 393 7155
Fax: 416 393 7229
James Gibson Reference Library
500 Glenridge Avenue St Catherines, L2S 3A1
Tel: 905 688 5550 Fax: 905 988 5490
Public Library
PO Box 2700, Station LCD 1 Hamilton, L8N 4E4
Tel: 546 3408 Fax: 546 3202
Email: speccol@hpl.hamilton.on.ca
Public Library
85 Queen Street North Kitchener, N2H 2H1
Tel: 519 743 0271 Fax: 519 570 1360
Public Library
305 Queens Avenue London, N6B 3L7
Tel: 519 661 4600 Fax: 519 663 5396
Public Library
301 Burnhamthorpe Road West Mississauga, L5B 3Y3
Tel: 905 615 3500 Fax: 905 615 3696
Email: library.info@city.mississauga.on.ca
WWW: http://www.city.mississauga.on.ca/Library
Toronto Public Library
North York (Entral Library) Canadiana Department,
5120 Yonge Street North York, M2N 5N9
Tel: 416 395 5623 WWW: http://www.tpl.tor.on.ca
Public Library
74 Mackenzie Street Sudbury, P3C 4X8
Tel: 01673 1155 Fax: 01673 9603
St Catharines Public Library
54 Church Street St Catharines, L2R 7K2
Tel: 905 688 6103 Fax: 905 688 2811
Email: scpublib@stcatharines.library.on.ca
WWW: http://www.stcatharines.library.on.ca

Quebec
Bibliotheque De Montreal
1210, Rue Sherbrooke East Street , Montreal, H2L 1L9
Tel: 514 872 1616 Fax: 514 872 4654
Email: daniel_olivier@ville.montreal.qc.ca
WWW: http://www.ville.montreal.qc.ca/biblio/pageacc.htm

Saskatchewan
Public Library
PO Box 2311 Regina, S4P 3Z5 Tel: 306 777 6011
Fax: 306 352 5550 Email: kaitken@rpl.sk.ca
Public Library
311   23rd Street East Saskatoon, S7K 0J6 Tel: 306 975
7555 Fax: 306 975 7542

United States of America

Alabama
Public Library
2100 Park Place Birmingham, 325203 2794
Tel: 205 226 3665 Email: sou@bham.lib.al.us

Arizona
Phoenix Public Library
12 East McDowell Phoenix, 85004 Tel: 602 262 4636

Flagstaff Public Library
300 West Aspen Flagstaff, 86001 Tel: 602 779 7670
Arizona Historical Foundation Library
Hayden Library, Arizona State Univeristy Tempe 85287
Tel: 602 966 8331

California
State Library
PO Box 942837, 914 Capitol Mall Sacramento 94237 0001 Tel: 916 654 0176
State Library
480 Winston Drive San Francisco, 94132
Tel: 415 557 0421
State Library
630 West Fifth Street Los Angeles, 90071 2002
Tel: 213 228 7400 Fax: 213 228 7409

Connecticut
Connecticut State Library
231 Capitol Avenue Hartford, 6106 Tel: 203 566 3690

District of Colombia
The Library of Congress
Local History & Genealogy Reading Room, 101 Independence Avenue SE Washington, 20540 4660
Tel: 202 707 5537 Fax: 202 707 1957
Email: lcinfo@loc.gov
WWW: http://www.lcweb.loc.gov//nn/genealogy
Daughters of the American Revolution Library
1776 D Street N W Washington, 20006 5392
Tel: 202 879 3229

Hawaii
Hawaii State Library
478 South King Street Honolulu, 96813,

Illinois
Newberry Library, The 60 West Walton Street Chicago 60610 3380 Tel: 312 943 9090
Indiana
Allen County Public Library
PO Box 2270 , Fort Wayne, 46801 2270
Tel: 219 424 7241 Fax: 219 4229688

Iowa
Iowa State Library
402 Iowa Avenue Iowa City, 52240 1806
Tel: 319 335 3916

Kansas
Kansas State Historical Society   Library
6425 SW Sixth Street Topeka, 66615 1099 Tel: 913 272 8681 Fax: 913 272 8682
Email: reference@hspo.wpo.state.ks.us
WWW: http://www.kshs.org

Kentucky
Alice Lloyd College Library
Appalachian Oral History Project , Pippa Passes, 414844
Tel: 606 368 2101

Louisiana
Louisiana State Archives, PO Box 94125 , Baton Rouge, 70804 9125 Tel: 504 922 1209

Vernon Parish Library
1401 Nolan Trace Leesville, 71446 Tel: 318 239 2027
Tel: 1 800 737 2231 Fax: 318 238 0666
Email: vernon@alpha.nsula.edu

Maryland
Maryland State Law Library
Courts of Appeal Building, 361 Rowe Boulevard Annapolis, 21401 1697 Tel: (410) 260 1430
Fax: (410) 974 2063
Email: mike.miller@courts.state.md.us
WWW: http://www.lawlib.state.md.us

Michigan
Detroit Public Library
5201 Woodward Avenue Detroit, 48202 Tel: 313 833 1480
Dickinson County Public Library
401 Iron Mountain Street Iron Mountain, 49801
Tel: 313 833 1480
Farmington Community Public Library
23500 Liberty Street Farmington, 48335
Tel: 313 474 7770
Herrick District Public Library
300 River Avenue Holland, 49423 Tel: 616 355 1427
Email: holrh@lakeland.lib.mi.us
Mitchell Public Library
22 North Manning Street Hillsdale, 49242
Tel: 517 437 2581
Jackson Public Library
244 West Michigan Avenue Jackson, 49201
Marguerite DeAngeli Branch Library
921 West Nepessing Street Lapeer, 48446
Tel: 313 664 6971

Missouri
Missouri State Library
PO Box 387, 301 West High Street Jefferson City, 65102
Tel: 314 751 3615
Public Library
15616 East Highway 24 Independence, 64050
Tel: 816 252 0950

Montana
Mansfield Library
University of Montana , Missoula, 59812 1195
Tel: 406 243 6860

Nebraska
Nebraska State Historical Society   Library/Archives,
PO Box 82554, 1500 R Street Lincoln, 68501 2554
Tel: 402 471 4751 Fax: 402 471 8922
WWW: http://www.nebraskahistory.org
Beatrice Public Library
100 North 16th Street Beatrice, 68310

Nevada
Nevada State Library
Division of Archives & Records, 100 Stewart Street Carson City, 89710 Tel: 702 687 5210

New Hampshire
New Hampshire State Library
20 Park Street Concord, 3301 Tel: 603 271 6823 Fax: 603 271 2205

New Jersey
New Jersey State Library
185 West State Street Trenton, 08625 0520
Tel: 609 292 6274
Morris County Library
30 East Hanover Avenue Whippany, 07981 1825
Tel: 973 285 6974 Email: heagney@main.morris.org

New Mexico
New Mexico State Library
325 Don Gaspar Avenue Sante Fe, 87503
Tel: 505 827 3805
Public Library
423 Central Avenue NE Alberquerque, 87102 3517

New York
New York Public Library
Center for Humanities, US Local History & Genealogy
Division, Fifth Avenue & 42nd Street New York 10018
Tel: 212 930 0828

Ohio
Ohio State Library
65 South Front Street Columbus, 43266 0334
Tel: 614 644 6966

Pennsylvania
Pennsylvania State Library
Forum Building, Walnut Street & Commonwealth
Avenue Harrisburg, 17105 Tel: 717 787 4440

South Carolina
South Carolina State Library
PO Box 11469, 1500 Senate Street Columbia, 29211
Tel: 803 734 8666

South Dakota
South Dakota State Library
Memorial Building Branch, 800 Governors Drive Pierre,
57501 2294 Tel: 605 773 3131

Tennessee
Tennessee State Library
403 7th Avenue North Nashville, 37243 0312
Tel: 615 741 2764

Texas
Texas State Library
PO Box 12927 Austin, 78711 2927 Tel: 512 463 5463
Dallas Public Library
1515 Young Street Dallas, 75201 5417
Tel: 214 670 1433
Houston Public Library
5300 Caroline Houston, 77004 6896 Tel: 713 524 0101
Midland County Public Library
310 West Missouri Midland, 79701 Tel: 915 688 8991

Amarillo Public Library
413 East Fourth Street Amarillo, 79189 2171
Tel: 806 378 3054

Utah
Church of Jesus Christ of Latter Day Saints
Family History Library 35 North West Temple Street
Salt Lake City, 84150 Tel: 801 240 2331 Fax: 801 240
5551 Email: fhl@ldschurch.org

Vermont
Vermont Department of Libraries, Pavilion Office
Building, 109 State Street Montpelier, 05609 0601
Tel: 802 828 3268

Virginia
Virginia State Library
11th Street at Capitol Square Richmond, 23219 3491
Tel: 804 786 8929

Library of Virginia
800 East Broad Street Richmond, 23219 3491
Tel: 804 692 3777

Public Library
220 North Washington Avenue Alexandria, 23219
Tel: 703 838 4577 Fax: 703 706 3912
Public Library,
1201 Caroline Street Fredericksburg, 22401
Tel: 540 372 1144

West Virginia
West Virginia State Library
The Cultural Center, 1900 Kanawha Boulevard East
Charleston, 25305 0300 Tel: 304 558 0230

Wisconsin
Wisconsin State Library
816 State Street Madison, 53706 Tel: 608 264 6535

Wyoming
Wyoming State Library
Supreme Court Building, 2301 Capitol Avenue
Cheyenne, 82002 Tel: 307 777 7281
Laramie County Library Service
2800 Central Avenue Cheyenne, 82001 2799
Tel: 307 634 3561

To All Librarians

Does Your Library hold Special Collections or other information of interest to

Family & Local Historians?

A feature Article in the *next edition* of the United Kingdom's bestselling
Family & Local History Handbook
would ensure that your facilites become better known.

If you wish to be featured then please contact:
The Editor
The Genealogical Services Directory
33 Nursery Road, Nether Poppleton, York YO26 6NN UK
Email: editor@genealogical.co.uk

FEDERATION OF FAMILY HISTORY SOCIETIES (PUBLICATIONS) LIMITED

Publishers and Suppliers of a wide range of books on Family History (and related subjects) to Family History Societies, individual Family Historians, and Booksellers

- *Well over 100 titles commissioned by the Federation of Family Historians and produced at attractive prices, plus a fine selection of titles from other publishers.*

- *A wide range of* **'Basic Series'** *and* **'Introduction to'** *books with detailed guidance on most aspects of family history research.*

- **Gibson Guides** *giving explicit advice on the precise extent and whereabouts of major record sources*

- **Stuart Raymond's** *extensive listings of published family history reference material at national and local level*

Most titles available from your local Family History Society and by post from:-

FFHS (Publications) Limited, Units 15 and 16 Chesham Industrial Centre, Oram Street, Bury, Lancashire, BL9 6EN

Visit our 'On-line bookshop' and Catalogue at

www.familyhistorybooks.co.uk

Tel: 0161 797 3843 Fax: 0161 797 3846

Email enquiries to: orders@ffhs.org.uk

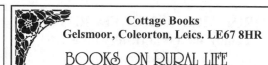

Ancestral Research

NATIONAL ORGANISATIONS FOR RESEARCHERS

Association of Genealogists & Record Agents
29 Badgers Close, Horsham, West Sussex, RH12 5RU
Email: agra@agra.org.uk Web: www.agra.org.uk
See Advert on Page: 50

COMPREHENSIVE RESEARCH AND ALL COUNTIES

Achievements Ltd
Centre for Heraldic & Genealogical Research and
Artwork, 79 - 82 Northgate, Canterbury, Kent, CT1
1BA (GSD) Tel: 01227-462618 Fax: 01227-765617
Email: achievements@achievements.co.uk
Web: www.achievements.co.uk
See Advert on Page: 47

Ancestral Locations
Elmhurst, Church Bank, Ruyton XI Towns,
Shrewsbury SY4 1LQ Tel: 01939-261722
Fax: 01939-261722 Email: lesleyt@ancestorsuk.com
Web: www.ancestorsuk.com
See Advert on Page: 367

Back to Roots Family History Service
16 Arrowsmith Drive, Stonehouse, Gloucestershire,
GL10 2QR Tel: 01453-821300, 0374-446128
Fax: 01453-821300 Email: mike@backtoroots.co.uk
Web: www.backtoroots.co.uk
See Advert on Page: Inside Back Cover & 160

Brewster International
12 Avery Gardens, Ilford, Essex, IG2 6UJ
Tel: 0208-550-0333 Fax: 0208-550-7766
Email: brewsterint@cs.com
Web: www.missing-people-found.com
See Advert : Inside Front Cover

Debrett Ancestry Research Limited
Dept GSD, PO Box 7, New Alresford, Hampshire,
SO24 9EN Tel: 01962-732676 Fax: 01962-734040
Email: enquiry@debrettancestry.demon.co.uk
Web: www.debrettancestry.demon.co.uk
See Advert on Page: 369

Patrick Yarnold Research
93 The Street, Puttenham, Guildford, Surrey, GU3
1AT Tel: 01483-810564 See Advert on Page: 372

People Search Tracing Services
30A Bedford Place, Southampton, SO15 2DG
Tel: 023-8056-2243 Fax: 023-8056-2243
Email: info@people-search.co.uk
Web: www.people-search.co.uk
See Advert on Page: 369

Seaham Super Index
53 Longlands Court, Westbourne Grove, London,
W11 2QF, 020-7792-2922, kch66@dial.pipex.com,
http://dspace@dial.pipex.com/town/street/kch66/
See Advert on Page: 377

Southern Counties Ancestry
St Michaels, 2 Church Road, Polegate, East Sussex,
BN26 5BX Tel: 01323-486769 Fax: 01323-488885
Email: drb@southern-counties-ancestry.co.uk
Web: www.southern-counties-ancestry.co.uk
See Advert on Page: 126

UK SEARCHES
Helouan, Merchant Street, Bognor Regis, West
Sussex, PO21 1QH Tel: 01243-842444,
01243-868999 Fax: 01243-841418
Email: hac@abel.co.uk Web: www.uksearches.com
See Advert on Page: 137

LONDON & GREATER LONDON

See also Researchers 'Comprehensive and All
Counties' Sub-section.

Ancestral Research by Michael Copsey
42 Moore Walk, Forest Gate, London, E7 0HY
Tel: 020-8519-1799 Fax: 020-8519-1799
Email: michael.copsey@btinternet.com
See Advert on Page: 373

Ancestral Research by Paul Lister
4 Sergison Road, Haywards Heath , RH16 1HS
Tel: 01444-453880 Email: piggleston@aol.com
Web:
members.aol.com/piggleston/ancestralresearch/index/html
See Advert on Page: 373

Brewster International
12 Avery Gardens, Ilford, Essex, IG2 6UJ
Tel: 0208-550-0333 Fax: 0208-550-7766
Email: brewsterint@cs.com
Web: www.missing-people-found.com
See Advert on Page: Inside Front Cover

Carolynn Boucher
1 Ivinghoe Close, Chiltern Park, St Albans,
Hertfordshire, AL4 9JR Tel: 01727-833664
Email: carolynn.boucher@tesco.net
See Advert on Page: 12

Grandpa Staten's Family History Services
37 Widgery Road, Exeter, Devon, EX4 8AX
Tel: 01392-207259, 07771-902104
Email: staten@one-name.org
Web: www.genealogy-cad.com
See Advert on Page: 368

Hertfordshire Archives & Local Studies
County Hall, Pegs Lane, Hertford, Hertfordshire,
SG13 8EJ Tel: 01438-737333 Fax: 01992-555113
Email: hals@hertscc.gov.uk
Web: www.hertsdirect.org See Advert on Page: 269

Lark Research
15 Park Avenue, St Albans, Hertfordshire, AL1 4PB
Tel: 01727-865631 Fax: 01727-865631
Email: Lark@harveyco.demon.co.uk
See Advert on Page: 372

Link Line Ancestral Research
16 Collingtree, Luton, Bedfordshire, LU2 8HN
Tel: 01582-614280 Fax: 01582-614280
Email: iwaller@ntlworld.com
Web: www.familyhistoryresearch.co.uk
See Advert on Page: 125

Michael Gandy, BA, FSG, Historical Research
3 Church Crescent, Whetstone, London, N20 0JR
Tel: 020-8368-1146 Email: mgandy@clara.co.uk
See Advert on Page: 18

Patrick Yarnold Research
93 The Street, Puttenham, Guildford, Surrey, GU3
1AT Tel: 01483-810564   See Advert on Page: 372

Relatively Speaking
10 Sussex Drive, Walderslade, Chatham, Kent, ME5
0NJ Tel: 01634-300964
Email: sjeeves@tinyworld.co.uk
See Advert on Page: 372

Rosie Taylor
103A Pemberton Road, London, N4 1AY
Tel: 020-8347-5107 Email: rosietay@supanet.com
See Advert on Page: 372

Seaham Super Index
53 Longlands Court, Westbourne Grove, London,
W11 2QF Tel: 020-7792-2922
Email: kch66@dial.pipex.com
Web: http://dspace@dial.pipex.com/town/street/kch66/
See Advert on Page: 377

Southern Searches
22 Portobello Grove, Fareham, Hampshire, PO16
8HU Tel: 023-92-373925 Email: dolina@research-
genealogy.com Web: www.researchgenealogy.com
See Advert on Page: 366

Sydney G Smith
59 Friar Road, Orpington, Kent, BR5 2BW
Tel: 01689-832800 Email: ss.famhist@virgin.net
See Advert on Page: 365

Timothy P Saxon
229 New Bedford Road, Luton, Bedfordshire, LU3
1LN Tel: 01582-727790 Fax: 01582-727790
Email: timothy@saxonlu31ln.freeserve.co.uk
See Advert on Page: 77

Victor Longhorn
53 Theydon Avenue, Woburn Sands, Milton Keynes,
MK17 8PN Tel: 01908-582660
Email: victor.longhorn@btinternet.com
See Advert on Page: 367

ENGLAND BY COUNTIES

BEDFORDSHIRE

See also Researchers 'Comprehensive and All
Counties' Sub-section.

Victor Longhorn
53 Theydon Avenue, Woburn Sands, Milton Keynes,
MK17 8PN Tel: 01908-582660
Email: victor.longhorn@btinternet.com
See Advert on Page: 367

Colin Davison Family History Research
66 Sudeley Walk, Putnoe, Bedford, Bedfordshire,
MK41 8JH Tel: 01234-364956
Email: C.Davison@ukgateway.net
Web: www.cbcs.co.uk/colindavison
See Advert on Page: 59

Timothy P Saxon
229 New Bedford Road, Luton, Bedfordshire, LU3
1LN Tel: 01582-727790 Fax: 01582-727790
Email: timothy@saxonlu31ln.freeserve.co.uk
See Advert on Page: 77

BERKSHIRE

See also Researchers 'Comprehensive and All
Counties' Sub-section.

Patrick Yarnold Research
93 The Street, Puttenham, Guildford, Surrey, GU3
1AT Tel: 01483-810564   See Advert on Page: 372

Southern Counties Ancestry
St Michaels, 2 Church Road, Polegate, East Sussex,
BN26 5BX Tel: 01323-486769 Fax: 01323-488885
Email: drb@southern-counties-ancestry.co.uk
Web: www.southern-counties-ancestry.co.uk
See Advert on Page: 126

BIRMINGHAM

See also Researchers 'Comprehensive and All
Counties' Sub-section.

Roots 'n' Branches
74 Lodge Hill Road, Selly Oak, Birmingham, B29
6NG, 01212-433180, www.rootsnbranches.co.uk
See Advert on Page: 373

Vanessa Morgan
33 Plymouth Road, Redditch, Worcestershire, B97
4PX Tel: 01527-62472 Fax: 01527-457176
Email: Vanessa@snackbox.freeserve.co.uk
Web: www.familysearch.uk.com/morgan.html
See Advert on Page: 367

BRISTOL

See also Researchers 'Comprehensive and All Counties' Sub-section.

Robert J Haines, BSc
25 Lynch Road, Berkeley, Gloucestershire, GL13 9TA
Tel: 01453-810052   See Advert on Page: 371
Abbey Genealogical Research
7 Cantilupe Road, Ross-on-Wye, Herefordshire, HR9
7AN Email: sean@seanparry.free-online.co.uk
See Advert on Page: 377

BUCKINGHAMSHIRE

See also Researchers 'Comprehensive and All Counties' Sub-section.

Colin Davison Family History Research
66 Sudeley Walk, Putnoe, Bedford, Bedfordshire,
MK41 8JH Tel: 01234-364956
Email: C.Davison@ukgateway.net
Web: www.cbcs.co.uk/colindavison
See Advert on Page: 59
Timothy P Saxon
229 New Bedford Road, Luton, Bedfordshire, LU3
1LN Tel: 01582-727790 Fax: 01582-727790
Email: timothy@saxonlu31ln.freeserve.co.uk
See Advert on Page: 77
Victor Longhorn
53 Theydon Avenue, Woburn Sands, Milton Keynes,
MK17 8PN Tel: 01908-582660
Email: victor.longhorn@btinternet.com
See Advert on Page: 367

CHESHIRE

See also Researchers 'Comprehensive and All Counties' Sub-section.

Paperchase Genealogical & Research Services
5 Glebe Close, Blythe Bridge, Stoke on Trent,
Staffordshire, ST11 9JN Tel: 01782-394147
Fax: 01782-394147 Email: elderton@one-name.org
Web: www.ukancestors.com
See Advert on Page: 365
Ancestral Locations
Elmhurst, Church Bank, Ruyton XI Towns,
Shrewsbury, Shropshire, SY4 1LQ
Tel: 01939-261722 Fax: 01939-261722
Email: lesleyt@ancestorsuk.com
Web: www.ancestorsuk.com
See Advert on Page: 367

CORNWALL

See also Researchers 'Comprehensive and All Counties' Sub-section.

Southern Counties Ancestry
St Michaels, 2 Church Road, Polegate, East Sussex,
BN26 5BX Tel: 01323-486769 Fax: 01323-488885
Email: drb@southern-counties-ancestry.co.uk
Web: www.southern-counties-ancestry.co.uk
See Advert on Page: 126

COUNTY DURHAM

See also Researchers 'Comprehensive and All Counties' Sub-section.

Geoff Nicholson
57 Manor Park, Concord, Washington, Tyne and
Wear, NE37 2BU Tel: 0191-417-9546
Email: geoff@genic.demon.co.uk
Web: www.genic.demon.co.uk/index.html
See Advert on Page: 117
Neil W Richardson
12 Banbury Way, South Beach Estate, Blyth,
Northumberland, NE24 3TY Tel: 01670-353605
Email: k.richardson@ukonline.co.uk
Web: www.ukonline.co.uk/northumweb/index.htm
See Advert on Page: 373
Turnstone Ventures
37 Hallgarth Street, Durham, DH1 3AT
Tel: 0191-386-4098 Fax: 0191-386-4098
See Advert on Page: 223

COUNTY DURHAM - EAST DURHAM
Seaham Super Index
53 Longlands Court, Westbourne Grove, London,
W11 2QF Tel:020-7792-2922
Email: kch66@dial.pipex.com
Web: http://dspace@dial.pipex.com/town/street/kch66/
See Advert on Page: 377

CUMBRIA

See also Researchers 'Comprehensive and All Counties' Sub-section.

Jane E Hamby, LHG
22 St Michaels Road, Preston, Lancashire, PR1 6LY
Tel: 01772-881873   See Advert on Page: 371
Sydney G Smith
59 Friar Road, Orpington, Kent, BR5 2BW
Tel: 01689-832800 Email: ss.famhist@virgin.net
See Advert on Page: 365

DERBYSHIRE

See also Researchers 'Comprehensive and All Counties' Sub-section.

Looking Back
5 Bishop's Close, Keyworth, Nottingham,
Nottinghamshire, NG12 5LS Tel: 0115-846-5211
See Advert on Page: 371

DEVON

See also Researchers 'Comprehensive and All Counties' Sub-section.

Caroline Belam, MA
The Strole, West Buckfastleigh, Devon, TQ11 0JH
Tel: 01364-644149 Fax: 01364-643215
See Advert on Page: 372
Southern Counties Ancestry
St Michaels, 2 Church Road, Polegate, East Sussex,
BN26 5BX Tel: 01323-486769 Fax: 01323-488885
Email: drb@southern-counties-ancestry.co.uk
Web: www.southern-counties-ancestry.co.uk
See Advert on Page: 126
Grandpa Staten's Family History Services
37 Widgery Road, Exeter, Devon, EX4 8AX
Tel: 01392-207259, 07771-902104
Email: staten@one-name.org
Web: www.genealogy-cad.com
See Advert on Page: 368

DORSET

See also Researchers 'Comprehensive and All Counties' Sub-section.

Southern Counties Ancestry
St Michaels, 2 Church Road, Polegate, East Sussex,
BN26 5BX Tel: 01323-486769 Fax: 01323-488885
Email: drb@southern-counties-ancestry.co.uk
Web: www.southern-counties-ancestry.co.uk
See Advert on Page: 126

ESSEX

See also Researchers 'Comprehensive and All Counties' Sub-section.

Family Trails
Old Forge Bungalow, Mill Lane, Boyton,
Woodbridge, Suffolk, IP12 3LN Tel: 01394-411806
Email: awaugh@familytrails.co.uk Web:
www.familytrails.co.uk See Advert on Page: 117
Ancestral Research by Michael Copsey
42 Moore Walk, Forest Gate, London, E7 0HY
Tel: 020-8519-1799 Fax: 020-8519-1799
Email: michael.copsey@btinternet.com
See Advert on Page: 373
Essex Record Office
Wharf Road, Chelmsford, Essex, CM2 6YT
Tel: 01245-244644 Fax: 01245-244655
Email: ero.search@essexcc.gov.uk (search service)
ero.enquiry@essexcc.gov.uk (general enquiries)
Web: www.essexcc.gov.uk See Advert on Page: 125

GLOUCESTERSHIRE

See also Researchers 'Comprehensive and All Counties' Sub-section.

Herefordshire Family History Research
17 Whitefriars Road, Hereford, HR2 7XE
Email: eleanor.harris@which.net
Web: www.herefordshireresearch.co.uk
See Advert on Page: 77
Jennifer Day
Lantern Cottage, Rhodyate, Blagdon, North Somerset,
BS40 7TP Tel: 01761-462426
Email: j.m.day@talk21.com See Advert on Page: 373
Robert J Haines, BSc
25 Lynch Road, Berkeley, Gloucestershire, GL13
9TA Tel: 01453-810052 See Advert on Page: 371
Miss J Edwards, MA, LL.B(Hons)
104 Earlsdon Avenue South, Coventry, CV5 6DQ
See Advert on Page: 371
Southern Counties Ancestry
St Michaels, 2 Church Road, Polegate, East Sussex,
BN26 5BX Tel: 01323-486769 Fax: 01323-488885
Email: drb@southern-counties-ancestry.co.uk
Web: www.southern-counties-ancestry.co.uk
See Advert on Page: 126
Abbey Genealogical Research
7 Cantilupe Road, Ross-on-Wye, Herefordshire, HR9
7AN Email: sean@seanparry.free-online.co.uk
See Advert on Page: 377
Vanessa Morgan
33 Plymouth Road, Redditch, Worcestershire, B97
4PX Tel: 01527-62472 Fax: 01527-457176
Email: Vanessa@snackbox.freeserve.co.uk
Web: www.familysearch.uk.com/morgan.html
See Advert on Page: 367

HAMPSHIRE

See also Researchers 'Comprehensive and All Counties' Sub-section.

People Search Tracing Services
30A Bedford Place, Southampton, SO15 2DG
Tel: 023-8056-2243 Fax: 023-8056-2243
Email: info@people-search.co.uk
Web: www.people-search.co.uk
See Advert on Page: 369
Ancestral Research by Paul Lister
4 Sergison Road, Haywards Heath, West Sussex,
RH16 1HS Tel: 01444-453880
Email: piggleston@aol.com
Web: members.aol.com/piggleston/ancestralresearch/i
ndex/html See Advert on Page: 373
Patrick Yarnold Research
93 The Street, Puttenham, Guildford, Surrey, GU3
1AT Tel: 01483-810564 See Advert on Page: 372

Southern Searches
22 Portobello Grove, Fareham, Hampshire, PO16
8HU Tel: 023-92-373925
Email: dolina@researchgenealogy.com
Web: www.researchgenealogy.com
See Advert on Page: 366

HAMPSHIRE & Isle of Wight

See also Researchers 'Comprehensive and All
Counties' Sub-section.

Southern Counties Ancestry
St Michaels, 2 Church Road, Polegate, East Sussex,
BN26 5BX Tel: 01323-486769 Fax: 01323-488885
Email: drb@southern-counties-ancestry.co.uk
Web: www.southern-counties-ancestry.co.uk
See Advert on Page: 126

HEREFORDSHIRE

See also Researchers 'Comprehensive and All
Counties' Sub-section.

Herefordshire Family History Research
17 Whitefriars Road, Hereford, HR2 7XE
Email: eleanor.harris@which.net
Web: www.herefordshireresearch.co.uk
See Advert on Page: 77

Abbey Genealogical Research
7 Cantilupe Road, Ross-on-Wye, Herefordshire, HR9
7AN Email: sean@seanparry.free-online.co.uk
See Advert on Page: 377

HERTFORDSHIRE

See also Researchers 'Comprehensive and All
Counties' Sub-section.

Victor Longhorn
53 Theydon Avenue, Woburn Sands, Milton Keynes,
MK17 8PN Tel: 01908-582660
Email: victor.longhorn@btinternet.com
See Advert on Page: 367

Timothy P Saxon
229 New Bedford Road, Luton, Bedfordshire, LU3
1LN Tel: 01582-727790 Fax: 01582-727790
Email: timothy@saxonlu31ln.freeserve.co.uk
See Advert on Page: 77

Hertfordshire Archives & Local Studies
County Hall, Pegs Lane, Hertford, Hertfordshire,
SG13 8EJ Tel: 01438-737333 Fax: 01992-555113
Email: hals@hertscc.gov.uk
Web: www.hertsdirect.org See Advert on Page: 269

Colin Davison Family History Research
66 Sudeley Walk, Putnoe, Bedford MK41 8JH
Tel: 01234-364956 Email: C.Davison@ukgateway.net
Web: www.cbcs.co.uk/colindavison
See Advert on Page: 59

Carolynn Boucher
1 Ivinghoe Close, Chiltern Park, St Albans,
Hertfordshire, AL4 9JR Tel: 01727-833664
Email: carolynn.boucher@tesco.net
See Advert on Page: 12

HULL

See also Researchers 'Comprehensive and All
Counties' Sub-section.

Hull Family History Unit
Central Library, Albion Street, Kingston upon Hull,
HU1 3TF Tel: 01482-616828, 01482-616827
Fax: 01482-616827
Email: gareth.watkins@hullcc.gov.uk
Web: www.hullcc.gov.uk/genealogy
See Advert on Page: 12

HUNTINGDONSHIRE

See also Researchers 'Comprehensive and All
Counties' Sub-section.

Southern Counties Ancestry
St Michaels, 2 Church Road, Polegate, East Sussex,
BN26 5BX Tel: 01323-486769 Fax: 01323-488885
Email: drb@southern-counties-ancestry.co.uk
Web: www.southern-counties-ancestry.co.uk
See Advert on Page: 126

Colin Davison Family History Research
66 Sudeley Walk, Putnoe, Bedford, Bedfordshire,
MK41 8JH Tel: 01234-364956
Email: C.Davison@ukgateway.net
Web: www.cbcs.co.uk/colindavison
See Advert on Page: 59

KENT

See also Researchers 'Comprehensive and All
Counties' Sub-section.

Relatively Speaking
10 Sussex Drive, Walderslade, Chatham, Kent, ME5
0NJ Tel: 01634-300964
Email: sjeeves@tinyworld.co.uk
See Advert on Page: 372

Ancestral Research by Paul Lister
4 Sergison Road, Haywards Heath, West Sussex,
RH16 1HS Tel: 01444-453880
Email: piggleston@aol.com
Web:
members.aol.com/piggleston/ancestralresearch/index/html
See Advert on Page: 373

Kin in Kent
Boundary House, Stodmarsh Road, Canterbury, Kent,
CT3 4AH Tel: 01227-455267 Fax: 01227-455267
Email: kentkin@lineone.net
See Advert on Page: 373

Southern Counties Ancestry
St Michaels, 2 Church Road, Polegate, East Sussex,
BN26 5BX Tel: 01323-486769 Fax: 01323-488885
Email: drb@southern-counties-ancestry.co.uk
Web: www.southern-counties-ancestry.co.uk
See Advert on Page: 126

Sydney G Smith
59 Friar Road, Orpington, Kent, BR5 2BW
Tel: 01689-832800 Email: ss.famhist@virgin.net
See Advert on Page: 365

Centre for Kentish Studies/Kent County Archives Service
Sessions House, County Hall, Maidstone, Kent, ME4 1XQ Tel: 01622-694363 Fax: 01622-694379
Email: archives@kent.gov.uk
See Advert on Page: 277

Maggi Young
Park View, Ninn Lane, Great Chart, Kent, TN23 3DB
Tel: 01233-626455, 07979-232828
Email: enquiries@maggiyoung.co.uk
Web: www.maggiyoung.co.uk
See Advert on Page: 370

LANCASHIRE

See also Researchers 'Comprehensive and All Counties' Sub-section.

Gene-genie
Castle Villa, 22 James Avenue, Marton, Blackpool, Lancashire, FY4 4LB Tel: 01253-694228
Email: pat@gene-genie.com
Web: www.gene.genie.com   See Advert on Page: 17

Sydney G Smith
59 Friar Road, Orpington, Kent, BR5 2BW
Tel: 01689-832800 Email: ss.famhist@virgin.net
See Advert on Page: 365

Jane E Hamby, LHG
22 St Michaels Road, Preston, Lancashire, PR1 6LY
Tel: 01772-881873   See Advert on Page: 371

Chris E Makepeace Local History Consultancy
5 Hilton Road, Disley, Cheshire, SK12 2JU
Tel: 01663-763346 Fax: 01663-764910
Email: chris.makepeace@talk21.com
See Advert on Page: 99

Lancashire Record Office and the Lancashire Local Studies Collection
Public searchroom closed for the first full week (Mon to Fri) each month. For further details, Bow Lane, Preston, Lancashire, PR1 2RE Tel: 01772-263039
Fax: 01772-263050
Email: record.office@lancscc.gov.uk
Web:
www.lancashire.gov.uk/education/lifelong/ro/index.htm
See Advert on Page: 269

LEICESTERSHIRE

See also Researchers in 'Comprehensive & All Counties' Sub-section at start of Ancestral Research pages.

Looking Back
5 Bishop's Close, Keyworth, Nottingham, Nottinghamshire, NG12 5LS Tel: 0115-846-5211
See Advert on Page: 371

LINCOLNSHIRE

See also Researchers 'Comprehensive and All Counties' Sub-section.

Links to Lincolnshire Genealogical Services
The Vicarage Cottage, 34 Church Lane, Reepham, Lincoln, LN3 4DO Tel: 01522-595700
Email: david@linkstolincs.co.uk
 Web: www.lincstolincs.co.uk
See Advert on Page: 370

Looking Back
5 Bishop's Close, Keyworth, Nottingham, Nottinghamshire, NG12 5LS Tel: 0115-846-5211
See Advert on Page: 371

MANCHESTER

See also Researchers 'Comprehensive and All Counties' Sub-section.

Chris E Makepeace Local History Consultancy
5 Hilton Road, Disley, Cheshire, SK12 2JU
Tel: 01663-763346 Fax: 01663-764910
Email: chris.makepeace@talk21.com
See Advert on Page: 99

MIDDLESEX

See also Researchers 'Comprehensive and All Counties' Sub-section.

Ancestral Research by Michael Copsey
42 Moore Walk, Forest Gate, London, E7 0HY
Tel: 020-8519-1799 Fax: 020-8519-1799
Email: michael.copsey@btinternet.com
See Advert on Page: 373

Hertfordshire Archives & Local Studies
County Hall, Pegs Lane, Hertford, Hertfordshire, SG13 8EJ Tel: 01438-737333 Fax: 01992-555113
Email: hals@hertscc.gov.uk
Web: www.hertsdirect.org   See Advert on Page: 269

NORFOLK

See also Researchers 'Comprehensive and All Counties' Sub-section.

Southern Counties Ancestry
St Michaels, 2 Church Road, Polegate, East Sussex, BN26 5BX Tel: 01323-486769 Fax: 01323-488885
Email: drb@southern-counties-ancestry.co.uk
Web: www.southern-counties-ancestry.co.uk
See Advert on Page: 126

Family Trails
Old Forge Bungalow, Mill Lane, Boyton, Woodbridge, Suffolk, IP12 3LN Tel: 01394-411806
Email: awaugh@familytrails.co.uk
Web: www.familytrails.co.uk
See Advert on Page: 117

Gill Blanchard, BA, MA, PGCE (PCE)
1 Whitwell Street, Reepham, Norwich, NR10 4RA
Tel: 01603-872367
Email: gblanchard@whitwellresearch.demon.co.uk
Web: www.whitwellresearch.demon.co.uk
See Advert on Page: 371

NORTHAMPTONSHIRE

See also Researchers 'Comprehensive and All Counties' Sub-section.

Victor Longhorn
53 Theydon Avenue, Woburn Sands, Milton Keynes, MK17 8PN Tel: 01908-582660
Email: victor.longhorn@btinternet.com
See Advert on Page: 367

NORTHUMBERLAND

See also Researchers 'Comprehensive and All Counties' Sub-section.

Neil W Richardson
12 Banbury Way, South Beach Estate, Blyth, Northumberland, NE24 3TY Tel: 01670-353605
Email: k.richardson@ukonline.co.uk
Web: www.ukonline.co.uk/northumweb/index.htm
See Advert on Page: 373

Geoff Nicholson
57 Manor Park, Concord, Washington, Tyne and Wear, NE37 2BU Tel: 0191-417-9546
Email: geoff@genic.demon.co.uk
Web: www.genic.demon.co.uk/index.html
See Advert on Page: 117

Southern Counties Ancestry
St Michaels, 2 Church Road, Polegate, East Sussex, BN26 5BX Tel: 01323-486769 Fax: 01323-488885
Email: drb@southern-counties-ancestry.co.uk
Web: www.southern-counties-ancestry.co.uk
See Advert on Page: 126

NOTTINGHAMSHIRE

See also Researchers 'Comprehensive and All Counties' Sub-section.

Looking Back
5 Bishop's Close, Keyworth, Nottingham, Nottinghamshire, NG12 5LS Tel: 0115-846-5211
See Advert on Page: 371

SHROPSHIRE

See also Researchers 'Comprehensive and All Counties' Sub-section.

Paperchase Genealogical & Research Services
5 Glebe Close, Blythe Bridge, Stoke on Trent, Staffordshire, ST11 9JN Tel: 01782-394147
Fax: 01782-394147 Email: elderton@one-name.org
Web: www.ukancestors.com
See Advert on Page: 365

Sue Cleaves, BSc, ALA
3 Gilbert Close, Newport, Shropshire, TF10 7UU
Tel: 01952-812060 Fax: 01952-812060
Email: suecleaves@breathemail.net
See Advert on Page: 371

Abbey Genealogical Research
7 Cantilupe Road, Ross-on-Wye, Herefordshire, HR9 7AN Email: sean@seanparry.free-online.co.uk
See Advert on Page: 377

Herefordshire Family History Research
17 Whitefriars Road, Hereford, HR2 7XE
Email: eleanor.harris@which.net
 Web: www.herefordshireresearch.co.uk
See Advert on Page: 77

Ancestral Locations
Elmhurst, Church Bank, Ruyton XI Towns, Shrewsbury, Shropshire, SY4 1LQ
Tel: 01939-261722 Fax: 01939-261722
Email: lesleyt@ancestorsuk.com
Web: www.ancestorsuk.com
See Advert on Page: 367

SOMERSET

See also Researchers 'Comprehensive and All Counties' Sub-section.

Bernard Welchman
The Cottage, Manor Terrace, Paignton, Devon, TQ3 3RQ Tel: 01803-401371 Email: B@bdwfh.com
Web: www.bdwfh.com   See Advert on Page: 376

Jennifer Day
Lantern Cottage, Rhodyate, Blagdon, North Somerset, BS40 7TP Tel: 01761-462426
Email: j.m.day@talk21.com
See Advert on Page: 373

Southern Counties Ancestry
St Michaels, 2 Church Road, Polegate, East Sussex,
BN26 5BX Tel: 01323-486769 Fax: 01323-488885
Email: drb@southern-counties-ancestry.co.uk
Web: www.southern-counties-ancestry.co.uk
See Advert on Page: 126

STAFFORDSHIRE

See also Researchers 'Comprehensive and All
Counties' Sub-section.

Paperchase Genealogical & Research Services
5 Glebe Close, Blythe Bridge, Stoke on Trent,
Staffordshire, ST11 9JN Tel: 01782-394147
Fax: 01782-394147 Email: elderton@one-name.org
Web: www.ukancestors.com
See Advert on Page: 365

Ancestral Locations
Elmhurst, Church Bank, Ruyton XI Towns,
Shrewsbury, Shropshire, SY4 1LQ
Tel: 01939-261722 Fax: 01939-261722
Email: lesleyt@ancestorsuk.com
Web: www.ancestorsuk.com   See Advert on Page: 367

Staffordshire and Stoke on Trent Archive Service
Staffordshire Record Office, Eastgate Street, Stafford,
ST16 2LZ Tel: 01785-278379 (Enquiries),
01785-278373 (Bookings) Fax: 01785-278384
Email:
staffordshire.record.office@staffordshire.gov.uk
Web: www.staffordshire.gov.uk
See Advert on Page: 272

Sue Cleaves, BSc, ALA
3 Gilbert Close, Newport, Shropshire, TF10 7UU
Tel: 01952-812060 Fax: 01952-812060
Email: suecleaves@breathemail.net
See Advert on Page: 371

STAFFORDSHIRE (PART)

Vanessa Morgan
33 Plymouth Road, Redditch, Worcestershire, B97
4PX Tel: 01527-62472 Fax: 01527-457176
Email: Vanessa@snackbox.freeserve.co.uk
Web: www.familysearch.uk.com/morgan.html
See Advert on Page: 367

SUFFOLK

See also Researchers 'Comprehensive and All
Counties' Sub-section.

Family Trails
Old Forge Bungalow, Mill Lane, Boyton,
Woodbridge, Suffolk, IP12 3LN Tel: 01394-411806
Email: awaugh@familytrails.co.uk
Web: www.familytrails.co.uk
See Advert on Page: 117

Southern Counties Ancestry
St Michaels, 2 Church Road, Polegate, East Sussex,
BN26 5BX Tel: 01323-486769 Fax: 01323-488885
Email: drb@southern-counties-ancestry.co.uk
Web: www.southern-counties-ancestry.co.uk
See Advert on Page: 126

SURREY

See also Researchers 'Comprehensive and All
Counties' Sub-section.

Patrick Yarnold Research
93 The Street, Puttenham, Guildford, Surrey, GU3
1AT Tel: 01483-810564   See Advert on Page: 372

Ancestral Research by Paul Lister
4 Sergison Road, Haywards Heath, West Sussex,
RH16 1HS Tel: 01444-453880
Email: piggleston@aol.com
Web:
members.aol.com/piggleston/ancestralresearch/index/html
See Advert on Page: 373

Southern Counties Ancestry
St Michaels, 2 Church Road, Polegate, East Sussex,
BN26 5BX Tel: 01323-486769 Fax: 01323-488885
Email: drb@southern-counties-ancestry.co.uk
Web: www.southern-counties-ancestry.co.uk
See Advert on Page: 126

SUSSEX

See also Researchers 'Comprehensive and All
Counties' Sub-section.

Southern Counties Ancestry
St Michaels, 2 Church Road, Polegate, East Sussex,
BN26 5BX Tel: 01323-486769 Fax: 01323-488885
Email: drb@southern-counties-ancestry.co.uk
Web: www.southern-counties-ancestry.co.uk
See Advert on Page: 126

Ancestral Research by Paul Lister
4 Sergison Road, Haywards Heath, West Sussex,
RH16 1HS Tel: 01444-453880
Email: piggleston@aol.com
Web:
members.aol.com/piggleston/ancestralresearch/index/html
See Advert on Page: 373

SUSSEX – WEST SUSSEX

West Sussex Record Office
County Hall, Chichester, West Sussex, PO19 1RN
Tel: 01243-753600, 01243-533911
Fax: 01243-533959
Email: records.office@westsussex.gov.uk
Web: www.westsussex.gov.uk/cs/ro/rohome.htm
See Advert on Page: 277

TYNE & WEAR

See also Researchers 'Comprehensive and All Counties' Sub-section.

Geoff Nicholson
57 Manor Park, Concord, Washington, Tyne and Wear, NE37 2BU Tel: 0191-417-9546
Email: geoff@genic.demon.co.uk
Web: www.genic.demon.co.uk/index.html
See Advert on Page: 117

WARWICKSHIRE

See also Researchers 'Comprehensive and All Counties' Sub-section.

Miss J Edwards, MA, LL.B(Hons)
104 Earlsdon Avenue South, Coventry, CV5 6DQ
See Advert on Page: 371

Vanessa Morgan
33 Plymouth Road, Redditch, Worcestershire, B97 4PX Tel: 01527-62472 Fax: 01527-457176
Email: Vanessa@snackbox.freeserve.co.uk
Web: www.familysearch.uk.com/morgan.html
See Advert on Page: 367

WEST MIDLANDS

See also Researchers 'Comprehensive and All Counties' Sub-section.

Roots 'n' Branches
74 Lodge Hill Road, Selly Oak, Birmingham, B29 6NG, 01212-433180, www.rootsnbranches.co.uk
See Advert on Page: 373

WESTMORLAND

See also Researchers 'Comprehensive and All Counties' Sub-section.

Sydney G Smith
59 Friar Road, Orpington, Kent, BR5 2BW
Tel: 01689-832800 Email: ss.famhist@virgin.net
See Advert on Page: 365

WILTSHIRE

See also Researchers in 'Comprehensive & All Counties' Sub-section at start of Ancestral Research pages.

Miss J Edwards, MA, LL.B(Hons)
104 Earlsdon Avenue South, Coventry, CV5 6DQ
See Advert on Page: 371

Southern Counties Ancestry
St Michaels, 2 Church Road, Polegate, East Sussex, BN26 5BX Tel: 01323-486769 Fax: 01323-488885
Email: drb@southern-counties-ancestry.co.uk
Web: www.southern-counties-ancestry.co.uk
See Advert on Page: 126

WORCESTERSHIRE

See also Researchers 'Comprehensive and All Counties' Sub-section.

Vanessa Morgan
33 Plymouth Road, Redditch, Worcestershire, B97 4PX Tel: 01527-62472 Fax: 01527-457176
Email: Vanessa@snackbox.freeserve.co.uk
Web: www.familysearch.uk.com/morgan.html
See Advert on Page: 367

Herefordshire Family History Research
17 Whitefriars Road, Hereford, HR2 7XE
Email: eleanor.harris@which.net
Web: www.herefordshireresearch.co.uk
See Advert on Page: 77

Abbey Genealogical Research
7 Cantilupe Road, Ross-on-Wye, Herefordshire, HR9 7AN Email: sean@seanparry.free-online.co.uk
See Advert on Page: 377

Miss J Edwards, MA, LL.B(Hons)
104 Earlsdon Avenue South, Coventry, CV5 6DQ
See Advert on Page: 371

YORKSHIRE

See also Researchers 'Comprehensive and All Counties' Sub-section.

Michael Ronald Pickard
Tel: 0113-2791037 Fax: 0113-2636198
See Advert on Page: 373

York Minster Library Databank
York Minster Library & Archives, Dean's Park, York, YO1 7JQ Tel: 01904-611118 Fax: 01904-611119
Email: archives@yorkminster.org
Web: www.yorkminster.org See Advert on Page: 12

Linklines Genealogy
5 Byron Road, Maltby, Rotherham, South Yorkshire, S66 7LR Tel: 07050-695482 Fax: 07050-695483
Email: help@linklines.co.uk
Web: www.linklines.co.uk See Advert on Page: 125

WALES

Achievements Ltd
Centre for Heraldic & Genealogical Research and Artwork, 79 - 82 Northgate, Canterbury, Kent, CT1 1BA (GSD) Tel: 01227-462618 Fax: 01227-765617
Email: achievements@achievements.co.uk
Web: www.achievements.co.uk
See Advert on Page: 47

Ancestral Locations
Elmhurst, Church Bank, Ruyton XI Towns, Shrewsbury SY4 1LQ Tel: 01939-261722
Fax: 01939-261722 Email: lesleyt@ancestorsuk.com
Web: www.ancestorsuk.com See Advert on Page: 367

CARW
4 Rhodfa Anwyl, Rhuddlan, Denbighshire, LL18
2SQ, Wales Tel: 01745-591372
Email: DThomas715@aol.com
See Advert on Page: 374

Southern Counties Ancestry
St Michaels, 2 Church Road, Polegate, East Sussex,
BN26 5BX Tel: 01323-486769 Fax: 01323-488885
Email: drb@southern-counties-ancestry.co.uk
Web: www.southern-counties-ancestry.co.uk
See Advert on Page: 126

UK SEARCHES
Helouan, Merchant Street, Bognor Regis, West
Sussex, PO21 1QH Tel: 01243-842444,
01243-868999 Fax: 01243-841418
Email: hac@abel.co.uk Web: www.uksearches.com
See Advert on Page: 137

SCOTLAND

Achievements Ltd
Centre for Heraldic & Genealogical Research and
Artwork, 79 - 82 Northgate, Canterbury, Kent, CT1
1BA (GSD) Tel: 01227-462618 Fax: 01227-765617
Email: achievements@achievements.co.uk
Web: www.achievements.co.uk
See Advert on Page: 47

Ancestral Locations
Elmhurst, Church Bank, Ruyton XI Towns,
Shrewsbury, Shropshire, SY4 1LQ
Tel: 01939-261722 Fax: 01939-261722
Email: lesleyt@ancestorsuk.com
Web: www.ancestorsuk.com
See Advert on Page: 367

Elizabeth Mortimer, MA, ASGRA
Kilcombe, St Thomas's Well, Stirling, FK7 9PR,
Scotland Tel: 01786-463470 Fax: 01786-463470
Email: elizabeth.mortimer@lineone.net
See Advert on Page: 133

John Adams Genealogical Research
8 North Gardner Street, Partickhill, Glasgow, G11
5BT, Scotland Tel: 0141-334-1021
Email: jadams@primex.co.uk
See Advert on Page: 131

Leslie Hodgson
5 St Stephen Place, Edinburgh, EH3 5AJ, Scotland
Tel: 0131-225-2723 See Advert on Page: 126

Root-Finder
10 Garden Terrace, Falkirk, FK1 1RL, Scotland
Email: jean.gibb@clara.co.uk
See Advert on Page: 131

Rosemary Philip, BA(Hons), CSFHS (Stirling)
15 Beresford Gardens, Edinburgh, EH5 3ER,
Scotland Tel: 0131-552-8021
Email: rsmry@philip63.freeserve.co.uk
See Advert on Page: 373

Scots Ancestry Research Society
8 York Road, Edinburgh, EH5 3EH, Scotland
Tel: 0131-552-2028 Fax: 0131-552-2028
Email: scotsanc@aol.com
Web: www.royalmile.com/scotsancestry
See Advert on Page: 133

Scots Heritage of Auchterarder
31 Beechtree Place, Auchterarder, Perthshire, PH3
1JQ, Scotland Tel: 01764-664998
Fax: 01764-664998
Email: norman@scots-heritage.co.uk
Web: www.scots-heritage.co.uk
See Advert on Page: 128

Scottish Roots
16 Forth Street, Edinburgh, EH1 3LH, Scotland
Tel: 0131-477-8214 Fax: 0131-550-3701
Email: stuart@scottish.roots.co.uk
Web: www.scottish-roots.co.uk
See Advert on Page: 133

Southern Counties Ancestry
St Michaels, 2 Church Road, Polegate, East Sussex,
BN26 5BX Tel: 01323-486769 Fax: 01323-488885
Email: drb@southern-counties-ancestry.co.uk
Web: www.southern-counties-ancestry.co.uk
See Advert on Page: 126

UK SEARCHES
Helouan, Merchant Street, Bognor Regis, West
Sussex, PO21 1QH Tel: 01243-842444,
01243-868999 Fax: 01243-841418
Email: hac@abel.co.uk Web: www.uksearches.com
See Advert on Page: 137

NORTHERN IRELAND

Achievements Ltd
Centre for Heraldic & Genealogical Research and
Artwork, 79 - 82 Northgate, Canterbury, Kent, CT1
1BA (GSD) Tel: 01227-462618 Fax: 01227-765617
Email: achievements@achievements.co.uk
Web: www.achievements.co.uk
See Advert on Page: 47

Debrett Ancestry Research Limited
Dept GSD, PO Box 7, New Alresford, Hampshire,
SO24 9EN Tel: 01962-732676 Fax: 01962-734040
Email: enquiry@debrettancestry.demon.co.uk
Web: www.debrettancestry.demon.co.uk
See Advert on Page: 369

Historical Research Associates
Glen Cottage, Glenmachan Road, Belfast, BT4 2NP,
Northern Ireland Tel: 028-9076-1490,
028-9336-8502 Web: www.blp-ni.com/hra
See Advert on Page: 147

IRELAND

Achievements Ltd
Centre for Heraldic & Genealogical Research and
Artwork, 79 - 82 Northgate, Canterbury, Kent, CT1
1BA (GSD) Tel: 01227-462618 Fax: 01227-765617
Email: achievements@achievements.co.uk
Web: www.achievements.co.uk
See Advert on Page: 47

Debrett Ancestry Research Limited
Dept GSD, PO Box 7, New Alresford, Hampshire,
SO24 9EN Tel: 01962-732676 Fax: 01962-734040
Email: enquiry@debrettancestry.demon.co.uk
Web: www.debrettancestry.demon.co.uk
See Advert on Page: 369

MC Research Service
Seabank, Castlebellingham, Dundalk, County Louth,
Ireland Tel: 042-9372046 Fax: 042-9372046
Email: mcres@iol.ie Web: www.mc-research.com
See Advert on Page: 147

Leitrim Genealogy Centre
c/o The County Library, Ballinamore, County Leitrim,
Ireland Tel: 078-44012 Fax: 078-44425
Email: letrimgenealogy@tinet.ie
See Advert on Page: 147

Mayo North Family Heritage Centre Limited
Enniscoe, Castlehill, Ballina, County Mayo, Ireland
Tel: 00-44-96-31809 Fax: 00-44-96-31885
Email: normayo@iol.ie
Web: http://mayo.irish-roots.net/
See Advert on Page: 147

Historical Research Associates
Glen Cottage, Glenmachan Road, Belfast, BT4 2NP,
Northern Ireland Tel: 028-9076-1490, 028-9336-8502
Web: www.blp-ni.com/hra See Advert on Page: 147

UK SEARCHES
Helouan, Merchant Street, Bognor Regis, West
Sussex, PO21 1QH Tel: 01243-842444,
01243-868999 Fax: 01243-841418
Email: hac@abel.co.uk Web: www.uksearches.com
See Advert on Page: 137

Flyleaf Press
4 Spencer Villas, Glenagarry, County Dublin, Ireland
Tel: 353-1-2806228 Fax: 353-1-8370176
Email: RyanJ@biores-irl.ie or flyleaf@indigo.ie
Web: www.flyleaf.ie See Advert on Page: 147

AUSTRALASIA

Debrett Ancestry Research Limited
Dept GSD, PO Box 7, New Alresford, Hampshire,
SO24 9EN Tel: 01962-732676 Fax: 01962-734040
Email: enquiry@debrettancestry.demon.co.uk
Web: www.debrettancestry.demon.co.uk
See Advert on Page: 369

AUSTRALIA

Genealogical Society of Victoria
Ancestor House, 179 Queen Street, Melbourne,
Victoria, 3000, Australia Tel: 3-9670-7033
Fax: 3-9670-4490, gsv@gsv.org.au, www.gsv.org.au
See Advert on Page: 233

NEW ZEALAND

New Zealand Genealogical Research
211 Vanguard Street, Nelson, 7001, New Zealand
Tel: 3-548-9243 Fax: 3-548-9243
Email: eparkes@ts.co.nz
Web: http://genealogynz.co.nz
See Advert on Page: 374

NORTH AMERICA

Debrett Ancestry Research Limited
Dept GSD, PO Box 7, New Alresford, Hampshire,
SO24 9EN Tel: 01962-732676 Fax: 01962-734040
Email: enquiry@debrettancestry.demon.co.uk
Web: www.debrettancestry.demon.co.uk
See Advert on Page: 369

Specialist Subjects

ADOPTION

Brewster International
12 Avery Gardens, Ilford, Essex, IG2 6UJ
Tel: 0208-550-0333 Fax: 0208-550-7766
Email: brewsterint@cs.com
Web: www.missing-people-found.com
See Advert on Page: Inside Front Cover

BRITISH COLONIAL FAMILIES

Abbey Genealogical Research
7 Cantilupe Road, Ross-on-Wye, Herefordshire
HR9 7AN Email: sean@seanparry.free-online.co.uk
See Advert on Page: 377

BRITISH INDIA

Link Line Ancestral Research
16 Collingtree, Luton, Bedfordshire, LU2 8HN
Tel: 01582 614280 Fax: 01582-614280
Email: iwaller@ntlworld.com
Web: www.familyhistoryresearch.co.uk
See Advert on Page: 125

CLOTHING

Jayne Shrimpton
100 Chester Terrace, Brighton, East Sussex, BN1 6GD
Tel: 01273-386176
Email: JayneShrimpton@photographdating.freeserve.co.uk
Web: www.photographdating.freeserve.co.uk
See Advert on Page: 61

CRIMINALS & CONVICTS

Black Sheep Search (Machine Breakers Rioters & Convict Research)
4 Quills, Letchworth Garden City, Hertfordshire, SG6 2RJ Tel: 01462-483706
Email: J_M_Chambers@compuserve.com
See Advert on Page: 369

Family History Indexes by Stuart Tamblin
14 Copper Leaf Close, Moulton, Northampton, NN3 7HS Tel: 01604-495106 Email: fhindexes@genfair.com
Web: www.genfair.com/fhindexes/
See Advert on Page: 50 & 156

Lightage Computing Ltd
40 Buttermere Road, Liverpool, L16 2NN
Tel: 0151-489-5702
Email: dwilcox@lightage.demon.co.uk
See Advert on Page: 366

Link Line Ancestral Research
16 Collingtree, Luton, Bedfordshire, LU2 8HN
Tel: 01582-614280 Fax: 01582-614280
Email: iwaller@ntlworld.com
Web: www.familyhistoryresearch.co.uk
See Advert on Page: 125

Napoleonic Wars, 1st or Grenadier Foot Guards & Other Regiments

39 Chatterton, Letchworth Garden City, Hertfordshire, SG6 2JY Tel: 01426-670918
Email: bcham2809@aol.com
Web: http://members.aol.com/bjcham2809/homepage.html
See Advert on Page: 209

DURHAM COALFIELD

Seaham Super Index
53 Longlands Court, Westbourne Grove, London, W11 2QF, 020-7792-2922 Email: kch66@dial.pipex.com,
Web: http://dspace@dial.pipex.com/town/street/kch66/
See Advert on Page: 377

EMIGRATION & IMMIGRATION

Kinship Genealogical Research
23 Friar Road, Brighton, East Sussex, BN1 6NG
Email: kinship2@hotmail.com See Advert on Page: 367
Link Line Ancestral Research
16 Collingtree, Luton, Bedfordshire, LU2 8HN
Tel: 01582-614280 Fax: 01582-614280
Email: iwaller@ntlworld.com
Web: www.familyhistoryresearch.co.uk
See Advert on Page: 125

FINE ART PICTURES

Timothy P Saxon
229 New Bedford Road, Luton, Bedfordshire, LU3 1LN
Tel: 01582-727790 Fax: 01582-727790
Email: timothy@saxonlu31ln.freeserve.co.uk
See Advert on Page: 77

GAMEKEEPERS

Southern Searches
22 Portobello Grove, Fareham, Hampshire, PO16 8HU
Tel: 023-92-373925
Email: dolina@researchgenealogy.com
Web: www.researchgenealogy.com
See Advert on Page: 366

MACHINE BREAKERS & RIOTERS

Black Sheep Search (Machine Breakers Rioters & Convict Research)
4 Quills, Letchworth Garden City, Hertfordshire, SG6 2RJ Tel: 01462-483706
Email: J_M_Chambers@compuserve.com
See Advert on Page: 369

MARINERS/SEAMEN

CARW
4 Rhodfa Anwyl, Rhuddlan, Denbighshire, LL18 2SQ,
Wales Tel: 01745-591372
Email: DThomas715@aol.com
See Advert on Page: 374

MILITARY

Abbey Genealogical Research
7 Cantilupe Road, Ross-on-Wye, Herefordshire, HR9
7AN Email: sean@seanparry.free-online.co.uk
See Advert on Page: 377
Battlefield Tours with The War Research Society
27 Courtway Avenue, Maypole, Birmingham, West
Midlands, B14 4PP Tel: 0121-430-5348
Fax: 0121-436-7401 Email: battletour@aol.com
Web: www.battlefieldtours.co.uk
See Advert on Page: 210
David J Barnes (Military & Aviation Research)
148 Parkinson Street, Burnley, Lancashire, BB11 3LL
Web: www.rfc-rnas-raf-register.org.uk
See Advert on Page: 198
Family History Indexes by Stuart Tamblin
14 Copper Leaf Close, Moulton, Northampton
NN3 7HS Tel: 01604-495106
Email: fhindexes@genfair.com
Web: www.genfair.com/fhindexes/
See Advert on Page: 50 & 156
Link Line Ancestral Research
16 Collingtree, Luton, Bedfordshire, LU2 8HN
Tel: 01582-614280 Fax: 01582-614280
Email: iwaller@ntlworld.com
Web: www.familyhistoryresearch.co.uk
See Advert on Page: 125
**Napoleonic Wars, 1st or Grenadier Foot Guards &
Other Regiments**
39 Chatterton, Letchworth Garden City, Hertfordshire,
SG6 2JY Tel: 01426-670918 Email: bcham2809@aol.com
Web: http://members.aol.com/bjcham2809/homepage.html
See Advert on Page: 209
Southern Searches
22 Portobello Grove, Fareham, Hampshire, PO16 8HU
Tel: 023-92-373925
Email: dolina@researchgenealogy.com
Web: www.researchgenealogy.com See Advert on Page: 366

MURDER FILES

Lightage Computing Ltd
40 Buttermere Road, Liverpool, L16 2NN
Tel: 0151-489-5702
Email: dwilcox@lightage.demon.co.uk
See Advert on Page: 366
Murder Files
81 Churchfields Drive, Bovey Tracy, Devon, TQ13 9QU
Tel: 01626-833487 Fax: 01626-835797
Email: enquiry@murderfiles.com
Web: www.murderfiles.com See Advert on Page: 59

NAPOLEONIC WARS

**Napoleonic Wars, 1st or Grenadier Foot Guards &
Other Regiments**
39 Chatterton, Letchworth Garden City, Hertfordshire,
SG6 2JY Tel: 01426-670918
Email: bcham2809@aol.com
Web: http://members.aol.com/bjcham2809/homepage.html
See Advert on Page: 209

NEWSPAPER LIBRARY

Colin Dale Researches (GSD)
1 Furham Field, Pinner, Middlesex, HA5 4DX
See Advert on Page: 371
Rosie Taylor
103A Pemberton Road, London, N4 1AY
Tel: 020-8347-5107 Email: rosietay@supanet.com
See Advert on Page: 372

GEOGHEGAN/MCGEOGHEGAN ONE NAME STUDY

Geoghegan/McGeoghegan One Name Study
330 Dereham Road, Norwich, Norfolk, NR2 4DL
Email: josi@geoghegan18.fsnet.co.uk
Web: www.jgeoghegan.org.uk See Advert on Page: 231

POLICE

Lightage Computing Ltd
40 Buttermere Road, Liverpool, L16 2NN
Tel: 0151-489-5702
Email: dwilcox@lightage.demon.co.uk
See Advert on Page: 366
Link Line Ancestral Research
16 Collingtree, Luton, Bedfordshire, LU2 8HN
Tel: 01582-614280 Fax: 01582-614280
Email: iwaller@ntlworld.com
Web: www.familyhistoryresearch.co.uk
See Advert on Page: 125

PROBATE

Abbey Genealogical Research
7 Cantilupe Road, Ross-on-Wye, Herefordshire
HR9 7AN, sean@seanparry.free-online.co.uk
See Advert on Page: 377

RAILWAY EMPLOYEES

CARW
4 Rhodfa Anwyl, Rhuddlan, Denbighshire, LL18 2SQ,
Wales Tel: 01745-591372
Email: DThomas715@aol.com
See Advert on Page: 374
Link Line Ancestral Research
16 Collingtree, Luton, Bedfordshire, LU2 8HN
Tel: 01582-614280 Fax: 01582-614280
Email: iwaller@ntlworld.com
Web: www.familyhistoryresearch.co.uk
See Advert on Page: 125

Support Services

ACCOMMODATION

ACCOMMODATION - LONDON

Ashley Hotel
15 Norfolk Square, Hyde Park, London, W2 1RU
Tel: 020-7723-3375 Fax: 020-7723-0173
Email: ashot@btinternet.com See Advert on Page: 371

ACCOMMODATION - NORTH YORKSHIRE

Mrs R M Norris
Downe, Baldersby, Thirsk, North Yorkshire, YO7 4PP
Tel: 01765-640283 Fax: 01765-640556
Email: doronical@cs.com See Advert on Page: 372
Upper Carr Chalet & Touring Park
Upper Carr Lane, Malton Road, Pickering, North
Yorkshire, YO18 7JP Tel: 01751-473115
Fax: 01751-475325
Email: green@uppercarr.demon.co.uk
Web: www.uppercarr.demon.co.uk
See Advert on Page: 409

ARMORIAL & HERALDRY

Achievements Ltd
Centre for Heraldic & Genealogical Research and
Artwork, 79 - 82 Northgate, Canterbury, Kent, CT1 1BA
(GSD) Tel: 01227-462618 Fax: 01227-765617
Email: achievements@achievements.co.uk
Web: www.achievements.co.uk See Advert on Page: 47
Institute of Heraldic & Genealogical Studies
79 - 82 Northgate, Canterbury, Kent, CT1 1BAGSD
Tel: 01227-768664 Fax: 01227-765617
Email: ihgs@ihgs.ac.uk Web: www.ihgs.ac.uk
See Advert on Page: 13
Marie Lynskey
109 Nutcroft Grove, Fetcham, Surrey, KT22 9LD
Tel: 01372-372334 Fax: 01372-372334
Email: ml@clara.net Web: www.ml.clara.net
See Advert on Page: 52

BATTLEFIELD TOURS

Bartletts Battlefield Journeys
Chart House, 9 Tudor Park, Horncastle, Lincolnshire,
LN9 5EZ Tel: 01507-523128 Fax: 01507-523130
Email: info@battlefields.co.uk
Web: www.battlefields.co.uk See Advert on Page: 200
Battlefield Tours with The War Research Society
27 Courtway Avenue, Maypole, Birmingham, West
Midlands, B14 4PP Tel: 0121-430-5348
Fax: 0121-436-7401 Email: battletour@aol.com
Web: www.battlefieldtours.co.uk
See Advert on Page: 210

BOOKSALES & SUPPLY

**Aberdeen & North East Scotland Family History
Society**
164 King Street, Aberdeen, AB24 5BD, Scotland
Tel: 01224-646323 Fax: 01224-639096
Email: enquiries@anesfhs.org.uk
Web: www.anesfhs.org.uk/ See Advert on Page: 222
ABM Publishing Ltd
61 Great Whyte, Ramsey, Huntingdon, Cambridgeshire,
PE17 1HL Tel: 01487-814050 Fax: 01487-711361
Email: family-tree-magazine@mcmail.com
Web: www.family-tree.co.uk
See Advert on Page: 65 & 89
Back to Roots Family History Service
16 Arrowsmith Drive, Stonehouse, Gloucestershire,
GL10 2QR Tel: 01453-821300, 0374-446128
Fax: 01453-821300 Email: mike@backtoroots.co.uk
Web: www.backtoroots.co.uk
See Advert on Page: Inside Back Cover & 160
Bob Dobson Books
Acorns, 3 Staining Rise, Staining, Blackpool,
Lancashire, FY3 0BU Tel: 01253-895678
Fax: 01253-895678 See Advert on Page: 43
British Association for Local History
PO Box 1576, Salisbury, SP2 8SY Tel: 01722-332158
Fax: 01722-413242 Web: www.balh.co.uk
See Advert on Page: 161, 164, & 173
Chapel Books
Chapel Cottage, Llanishen, Chepstow, NP16 6QT, Wales
Tel: 01600-860055 Fax: 01600-860100,
chapelbooks@btinternet.com See Advert on Page: 99
Chris E Makepeace Local History Consultancy
5 Hilton Road, Disley, Cheshire, SK12 2JU
Tel: 01663-763346 Fax: 01663-764910
Email: chris.makepeace@talk21.com
See Advert on Page: 99
Federation of Family History Societies
PO Box 8684, Shirley, Solihull, B90 4JU
Tel: 07041-492032 Fax: 07041-492032
Email: info@ffhs.org.uk Web: www.ffhs.org.uk
See Advert on Page: 6
Federation of Family History Societies (Publications) Ltd
Units 15 & 16 Chesham Industrial Estate, Oram Street,
Bury, Lancashire, BL9 6EN Tel: 0161-797-3843
Fax: 0161-797-3846 Email: orders@ffhs.org.uk
Web: www.familyhistorybooks.co.uk
See Advert on Page: 364
Genealogical Society of Victoria
Ancestor House, 179 Queen Street, Melbourne, Victoria,
3000, Australia Tel: +61-3-9670-7033
Fax: +61-3-9670-4490, gsv@gsv.org.au, www.gsv.org.au
See Advert on Page: 233
GENfair
9 Fairstone Hill, Oadby, Leicester, LE2 5RL
Tel: 0116-271-3494 Email: info@genfair.com
Web: www.genfair.com See Advert on Page: 18

Gould Books
PO Box 126, Gumeracha, South Australia, 5233,
Australia Tel: 08-8389-1611, +61-8-8389-1611
Fax: 08-8389-1599 Email: gould@adelaide.on.net
Web: www.gould.com.au See Advert on Page: 376

Harold Bayley, Bookseller
28 Ferndale Road, Hereford, HR4 0RW
See Advert on Page: 372

Interlink Bookshop & Genealogical Services
Mailing address: 4687 Falaise Drive, Victoria, BC, V8Y
1B4, Canada, Interlink Bookshop, 3840A Cadboro Bay
Road, Victoria, British Columbia, V8N 4G2, Canada
Tel: (250)-477-2708 Fax: (250)-658-3947
Email: ibgs@pacificcoast.net
Email: sales@interlinkbookshop.com
Web: www.InterlinkBookshop.com
See Advert on Page: 376

National Library of Scotland
George IV Bridge, Edinburgh, EH1 1EW, Scotland
Tel: 0131-226-4531 Fax: 0131-622-4803
Email: enquiries@nls.uk Web: www.nls.uk
See Advert on Page: 133

S A & M J Raymond
PO Box 35, Exeter, Devon, EX1 3YZ
Tel: 01392-252193 Email: stuart@samjraymond.soft-
net.co.uk See Advert on Page: 345

Society of Genealogists - Bookstore
14 Charterhouse Buildings, Goswell Road, London,
EC1M 7BA Tel: 020-7251-8799
See Advert on Page: 415

Sutton Publishing
Phoenix Mill, Thrupp, Stroud, Gloucestershire, GL5
2BU Tel: 01453-731114 Fax: 01453-731117
Email: sales@sutton-publishing.co.uk
See Advert on Page: 416

BOOKSEARCH

Harold Bayley, Bookseller
28 Ferndale Road, Hereford, HR4 0RW
See Advert on Page: 372

Kingfisher Free International Booksearch (GSD)
6 Ash Grove, Skegby, Sutton in Ashfield,
Nottinghamshire, NG17 3FH Tel: 01623-552530
Fax: 01623-552530 Email: malc.kbs@argonet.co.uk
Web: www.argonet.co.uk/users/malc.kbs
See Advert on Page: 367

COMPUTING & WEB SERVICES

Ancestry.com
360 W. 4800 N., Provo, Utah, UT 84604, United States
of America, 01-801-705-7036, 01-801-705-7120
Email: info@ancestry.com
Web: www.ancestry.com or www.ancestry.co.uk
See Advert on Page: 118 & 119

Back to Roots Family History Service
16 Arrowsmith Drive, Stonehouse, Gloucestershire,
GL10 2QR Tel: 01453-821300, 0374-446128
Fax: 01453-821300 Email: mike@backtoroots.co.uk
Web: www.backtoroots.co.uk
See Advert on Page: Inside Back Cover & 160

**Church of Jesus Christ of Latter Day Saints - North
America Distribution Centre**
1999 West 1700 South, Salt Lake City, Utah, 84104,
United States of America See Feature on Page: 405

**Church of Jesus Christ of Latter Day Saints - UK
Distribution Centre**
399 Garretts Green Lane, Birmingham, West Midlands,
B33 0HU Tel: 0870-010-2051 See Feature on Page: 405

GENfair
9 Fairstone Hill, Oadby, Leicester, LE2 5RL
Tel: 0116-271-3494 Email: info@genfair.com
Web: www.genfair.com See Advert on Page: 18

Gould Books
PO Box 126, Gumeracha, South Australia, 5233,
Australia Tel: 08-8389-1611, +61-8-8389-1611
Fax: 08-8389-1599 Email: gould@adelaide.on.net
Web: www.gould.com.au See Advert on Page: 376

Grandpa Staten's Family History Services
37 Widgery Road, Exeter, Devon, EX4 8AX
Tel: 01392-207259, 07771-902104
Email: staten@one-name.org
Web: www.genealogy-cad.com See Advert on Page: 368

Havas Interactive
2 Beacontree Plaza, Gillette Way, Reading, Berkshire,
RG2 0BS Tel: 0118-920-9100
Email: sierrahome@knowledgeadventure.co.uk
See Advert on Page: 104

Internet Bookmarks
39 Barnfield Crescent, Wellington, Telford, Shropshire,
TF1 2EU Tel: 01952-404349
Email: orders@internet-bookmarks.co.uk
Web: www.internet-bookmarks.co.uk
See Advert on Page: 77

Marathon Microfilming Ltd
27/29 St Mary's Place, Kingsway, Southampton, SO14
3HY Tel: 023-8022-0481 Fax: 023-8023-0452
Email: sales@marathon-microfilm-cdrom.co.uk
Web: www.marathon-microfilm-cdrom.co.uk
See Advert on Page: 365

P A & S Smith (Custodian)
PO Box 180, 2 Church Cottages, Bishopstone, Hereford,
HR4 7YP Tel: 01981-590309, 07801-503144 (mobile)
Email: PandSSmith@aol.com
Web: www.members.aol.com/pandssmith/custodian.htm
See Advert on Page: 368

People Search Tracing Services
30A Bedford Place, Southampton, SO15 2DG
Tel: 023-8056-2243 Fax: 023-8056-2243
Email: info@people-search.co.uk
Web: www.people-search.co.uk
See Advert on Page: 369

S & N Genealogy Supplies
Greenacres, Salisbury Road, Chilmark, Salisbury,
Wiltshire, SP3 5AH Tel: 01722-716121
Fax: 01722-716160
Email: 100064.737@compuserve.com
Web: www.genealogy.demon.co.uk
See Advert on Page: 4

DATE BY CLOTHING SERVICE

Jayne Shrimpton
Identify Your Ancestors Through Their Clothing, 100
Chester Terrace, Brighton, East Sussex, BN1 6GD
Tel: 01273-386176
Email: JayneShrimpton@photographdating.freeserve.co.uk
Web: www.photographdating.freeserve.co.uk
See Advert on Page: 61

EDUCATION & COURSES

Battlefield Tours with The War Research Society
27 Courtway Avenue, Maypole, Birmingham, West
Midlands, B14 4PP Tel: 0121-430-5348
Fax: 0121-436-7401 Email: battletour@aol.com
Web: www.battlefieldtours.co.uk
See Advert on Page: 210
Chris E Makepeace Local History Consultancy
5 Hilton Road, Disley, Cheshire, SK12 2JU
Tel: 01663-763346 Fax: 01663-764910
Email: chris.makepeace@talk21.com
See Advert on Page: 99
Elizabeth Mortimer, MA, ASGRA
ASGRA, Kilcombe, St Thomas's Well, Stirling, FK7
9PR, Scotland Tel: 01786-463470 Fax: 01786-463470
Email: elizabeth.mortimer@lineone.net
See Advert on Page: 133
Gill Blanchard, BA, MA, PGCE (PCE)
1 Whitwell Street, Reepham, Norwich, NR10 4RA
Tel: 01603-872367 Email: gblanchard@
whitwellresearch.demon.co.uk
Web: www.whitwellresearch.demon.co.uk
See Advert on Page: 371
Institute of Heraldic & Genealogical Studies
79 - 82 Northgate, Canterbury, Kent, CT1 1BAGSD
Tel: 01227-768664 Fax: 01227-765617
Email: ihgs@ihgs.ac.uk Web: www.ihgs.ac.uk
See Advert on Page: 13
Turnstone Ventures
37 Hallgarth Street, Durham, DH1 3AT
Tel: 0191-386-4098 Fax: 0191-386-4098
See Advert on Page: 223

FAMILY HISTORY FAIRS

Essex Society for Family History
Research Centre, c/o Essex Record Office, Wharf Road,
Chelmsford, Essex, CM2 6YT Tel: 01245-244670
Web: www.genuki.org.uk/big/eng/ESS/efhs
See Advert on Page: 231 & 410
Keithley & District Family History Society
Mrs Sue Daynes, 2 The Hallows, Shann Park, Keighley
BD20 6HY See Advert Page: 400
North West Group of FHS Family History Fairs
North West Group of Family History Societies, 4
Lawrence Avenue, Simonstone, Burnley, Lancashire,
BB12 7HX Tel: 01282-771999
Email: ed@gull66.freeserve.co.uk
See Advert on Page: 400

Northern Family History Fairs
206 Moseley Wood Gardens, Leeds, LS16 7JE
Tel: 0113-267-6499 (Mr S Merridew)
Tel: 01642-486615 (Mr A Sampson), 01642-486615
See Advert on Page: 410
South West Group of Family History Societies
55 Osborne Road, Weston Super Mare BS23 3EJ
Tel: 01934-627053 See Advert on Page: 231 & 410
West Yorkshire Archive Service
Local & family History Day Autumn 2001
Email: lbirch@wyjs.org.uk
See Advert on Page 342
Yorkshire Family History Fair
1 Oxgang Close, Redcar, Cleveland, TS10 4ND
Tel: 01642-486615 Fax: 01642-486615
See Advert on Page: 411

GRAVE MAINTENANCE
& PHOTOGRAPHS

Grave Concern
45 Caledon Road, Nottingham, NG5 2NF
Tel: 0115-985-6827 Fax: 0115-847-5681
Email: mgp@grave-concern.com
Web: www.grave-concern.com See Advert on Page: 368
Lightage Computing Ltd
40 Buttermere Road, Liverpool, L16 2NN
Tel: 0151-489-5702
Email: dwilcox@lightage.demon.co.uk
See Advert on Page: 366

HOUSE HISTORIES
Achievements Ltd
Centre for Heraldic & Genealogical Research and
Artwork, 79 - 82 Northgate, Canterbury, Kent, CT1 1BA
(GSD) Tel: 01227-462618 Fax: 01227-765617
Email: achievements@achievements.co.uk
Web: www.achievements.co.uk See Advert on Page: 47
Debrett Ancestry Research Limited
Dept GSD, PO Box 7, New Alresford, Hampshire, SO24
9EN Tel: 01962-732676 Fax: 01962-734040
Email: enquiry@debrettancestry.demon.co.uk
Web: www.debrettancestry.demon.co.uk
See Advert on Page: 369

INSURANCE

British Association for Local History
PO Box 1576, Salisbury, SP2 8SY Tel: 01722-332158
Fax: 01722-413242 Web: www.balh.co.uk
See Advert on Page: 161, 164, & 173

LOCATION PHOTOGRAPHY

Southern Counties Ancestry
St Michaels, 2 Church Road, Polegate, East Sussex,
BN26 5BX Tel: 01323-486769 Fax: 01323-488885
Email: drb@southern-counties-ancestry.co.uk
Web: www.southern-counties-ancestry.co.uk
See Advert on Page: 126

MAGAZINES, PERIODICALS & NEWSPAPERS

Able Publishing
13 Station Road, Knebworth, Hertfordshire, SG3 6AP
Tel: 01438-814316/812320 Fax: 01438-815232
Email: fp@ablepublishing.co.uk
Web: www.ablepublishing.co.uk
See Advert on Page: 117

ABM Publishing Ltd
61 Great Whyte, Ramsey, Huntingdon, Cambridgeshire,
PE17 1HL Tel: 01487-814050 Fax: 01487-711361
Email: family-tree-magazine@mcmail.com
Web: www.family-tree.co.uk
See Advert on Page: 65 & 89

British Association for Local History
PO Box 1576, Salisbury, SP2 8SY Tel: 01722-332158
Fax: 01722-413242 Web: www.balh.co.uk
See Advert on Page: 161, 164, & 173

Colin Dale Researches (GSD)
1 Furham Field, Pinner, Middlesex, HA5 4DX
See Advert on Page: 371

Family Chronicle Magazine
Suite 500, 505 Consumers Road, Toronto, Ontario, M2J
4V8, Canada Tel: 416-491-3699, 1-888-326-2476
Fax: 416-491-3996
Email: magazine@familychronicle.com
Web: www.familychronicle.com
See Advert on Page: 375

Family History Monthly
45 St Mary's Road, Ealing, London, W5 5RQ
Tel: 020-8579-1082 Fax: 020-8566-0529
See Advert on Page: 32

Institute of Heraldic & Genealogical Studies
79 - 82 Northgate, Canterbury, Kent, CT1 1BAGSD
Tel: 01227-768664 Fax: 01227-765617
Email: ihgs@ihgs.ac.uk Web: www.ihgs.ac.uk
See Advert on Page: 13

Old Yorkshire Publications
111 Wrenbeck Drive, Otley, West Yorkshire, LS21 2BP,
01943-461211, 01943-464702
Email: brian@oldyorkshire.co.uk
Web: www.oldyorkshire.co.uk See Advert on Page: 366

MICROFICHE & MICROFILM

Marathon Microfilming Ltd
27/29 St Mary's Place, Kingsway, Southampton, SO14
3HY Tel: 023-8022-0481 Fax: 023-8023-0452
Email: sales@marathon-microfilm-cdrom.co.uk
Web: www.marathon-microfilm-cdrom.co.uk
See Advert on Page: 365

Microfilm Shop
15 Hammond Close, Attleborough Fields Industrial
Estate, Nuneaton, Warwickshire, CV11 6RY
Tel: 024-7638-3998/1196 Fax: 024-7638-2319
Email: sales@microfilm.com Web: www.microfilm.com
See Advert on Page: 137

MM Publications
The White Cottage, The Street, Lidgate, Near
Newmarket, Suffolk, CB8 9PP
Email: michael@mmpublications.softnet.co.uk
Web: mmpublications.co.uk See Advert on Page: 377

MILITARY UNIFORM IDENTIFICATION

David J Barnes (Military & Aviation Research)
148 Parkinson Street, Burnley, Lancashire, BB11 3LL
Web: www.rfc-rnas-raf-register.org.uk
See Advert on Page: 198

MISSING PERSONS SEARCH

Brewster International
12 Avery Gardens, Ilford, Essex, IG2 6UJ
Tel: 0208-550-0333 Fax: 0208-550-7766
Email: brewsterint@cs.com
Web: www.missing-people-found.com
See Advert on Page: Inside Front Cover

People Search Tracing Services
30A Bedford Place, Southampton, SO15 2DG
Tel: 023-8056-2243 Fax: 023-8056-2243
Email: info@people-search.co.uk
Web: www.people-search.co.uk
See Advert on Page: 369

PHOTOGRAPHIC & REPRODUCTIVE

Ancestral Locations
Elmhurst, Church Bank, Ruyton XI Towns, Shrewsbury,
Shropshire, SY4 1LQ Tel: 01939-261722
Fax: 01939-261722 Email: lesleyt@ancestorsuk.com
Web: www.ancestorsuk.com See Advert on Page: 367

Audrey Linkman Consultant Photohistorian
7 Towncroft Lane, Bolton, Lancashire, BL1 5EW
Tel: 01204-840439 Fax: 01204-840439
See Advert on Page: 117

Battlefield Tours with The War Research Society
27 Courtway Avenue, Maypole, Birmingham, West
Midlands, B14 4PP Tel: 0121-430-5348
Fax: 0121-436-7401 Email: battletour@aol.com
Web: www.battlefieldtours.co.uk
See Advert on Page: 210

Caroline Belam, MA
The Strole, West Buckfastleigh, Devon, TQ11 0JH
Tel: 01364-644149 Fax: 01364-643215
See Advert on Page: 372

Creative Digital Imaging
3 Post Office Row, Station Road, Legbourne, Louth,
Lincolnshire, LN11 8LL Tel: 01507-608700
Fax: 01507-600059 Email: cdilouth@cs.com
Web: http://ourworld.cs.com/cdilouth/
See Advert on Page: 368

CW & S Parkinson (GSD)
16 Foxhills Close, Ashurst, Southampton, SO40 7ER
Tel: 023-8029-3608 Email: CwS@sirdar.demon.co.uk
Web: www.sirdar.demon.co.uk See Advert on Page: 57

Grandpa Staten's Family History Services
37 Widgery Road, Exeter, Devon, EX4 8AX
Tel: 01392-207259, 07771-902104
Email: staten@one-name.org
Web: www.genealogy-cad.com See Advert on Page: 368

Marathon Microfilming Ltd
27/29 St Mary's Place, Kingsway, Southampton, SO14
3HY Tel: 023-8022-0481 Fax: 023-8023-0452
Email: sales@marathon-microfilm-cdrom.co.uk
Web: www.marathon-microfilm-cdrom.co.uk
See Advert on Page: 365

Parchment Oxford Limited
Printworks, Crescent Road, Cowley, Oxford,
Oxfordshire, OX4 2PB Tel: 01865-747547
Fax: 01865-747551 Email: parch2000@cs.com
Web: www.PrintUK.com See Advert on Page: 159

Timeless Images
Sunnyvale, Kemnay, Inverurie, Aberdeenshire, AB51
5PE, Scotland Tel: 01467-642777
Email: simpson@mannofield.freeserve.co.uk
See Advert on Page: 131

Vanessa Morgan
33 Plymouth Road, Redditch, Worcestershire, B97 4PX
Tel: 01527-62472 Fax: 01527-457176
Email: Vanessa@snackbox.freeserve.co.uk
Web: www.familysearch.uk.com/morgan.html
See Advert on Page: 367

PLANS & MAPS

Chris E Makepeace Local History Consultancy
5 Hilton Road, Disley, Cheshire, SK12 2JU
Tel: 01663-763346 Fax: 01663-764910
Email: chris.makepeace@talk21.com
See Advert on Page: 99

Gould Books
PO Box 126, Gumeracha, South Australia, 5233,
Australia Tel: 08-8389-1611, +61-8-8389-1611
Fax: 08-8389-1599 Email: gould@adelaide.on.net
Web: www.gould.com.au See Advert on Page: 376

MM Publications
The White Cottage, The Street, Lidgate, Near
Newmarket, Suffolk, CB8 9PP
Email: michael@mmpublications.softnet.co.uk
Web: mmpublications.co.uk See Advert on Page: 377

POSTCARDS

Picture Past
47 Manor House Park, Codsall, Staffordshire, WV8 1ES
See Advert on Page: 374

PRESENTATION SERVICES

APC Clothing
Unit 6A Guardian Park, Station Road Industrial Estate,
Tadcaster, North Yorkshire, LS24 9SG
Tel: 01937-833449 Fax: 01937-832649
Email: sales@apc-clothing.co.uk
See Advert on Page: 370

Debrett Ancestry Research Limited
Dept GSD, PO Box 7, New Alresford, Hampshire, SO24
9EN Tel: 01962-732676 Fax: 01962-734040
Email: enquiry@debrettancestry.demon.co.uk
Web: www.debrettancestry.demon.co.uk
See Advert on Page: 369

Grandpa Staten's Family History Services
37 Widgery Road, Exeter, Devon, EX4 8AX
Tel: 01392-207259, 07771-902104
Email: staten@one-name.org
Web: www.genealogy-cad.com See Advert on Page: 368

Marie Lynskey
109 Nutcroft Grove, Fetcham, Surrey, KT22 9LD
Tel: 01372-372334 Fax: 01372-372334
Email: ml@clara.net Web: www.ml.clara.net
See Advert on Page: 52

**RE: GENERATION Family History & Booklovers
Supplies**
162 Devonshire Street, Sheffield, South Yorkshire, S3
7SG Tel: 0114-275-9049 See Advert on Page: 59

PRINTING SERVICES

AWP
718 Ripponden Road, Oldham, OL4 2LP
Tel: 07041 428220 (BT Lo Call)
Web: www.awpdigital.co.uk
See Advert Page 342

Grandpa Staten's Family History Services
37 Widgery Road, Exeter, Devon, EX4 8AX
Tel: 01392-207259, 07771-902104
Email: staten@one-name.org
Web: www.genealogy-cad.com See Advert on Page: 368

Parchment Oxford Limited
Printworks, Crescent Road, Cowley, Oxford,
Oxfordshire, OX4 2PB Tel: 01865-747547
Fax: 01865-747551 Email: parch2000@cs.com
Web: www.PrintUK.com See Advert on Page: 159

PRIVATE INVESTIGATIONS

Ancestral Research by Michael Copsey
42 Moore Walk, Forest Gate, London, E7 0HY
Tel: 020-8519-1799 Fax: 020-8519-1799
Email: michael.copsey@btinternet.com
See Advert on Page: 373

Brewster International
12 Avery Gardens, Ilford, Essex, IG2 6UJ
Tel: 0208-550-0333 Fax: 0208-550-7766
Email: brewsterint@cs.com
Web: www.missing-people-found.com
See Advert on Page: Inside Front Cover

PROMOTIONAL CLOTHING

APC Clothing
Unit 6A Guardian Park, Station Road Industrial Estate,
Tadcaster, North Yorkshire, LS24 9SG
Tel: 01937-833449 Fax: 01937-832649
Email: sales@apc-clothing.co.uk
See Advert on Page: 370

PUBLICATIONS

PUBLICATIONS - GENERAL APPEAL

Marie Lynskey
109 Nutcroft Grove, Fetcham, Surrey, KT22 9LD
Tel: 01372-372334 Fax: 01372-372334
Email: ml@clara.net Web: www.ml.clara.net
See Advert on Page: 52

S & N Genealogy Supplies
Greenacres, Salisbury Road, Chilmark, Salisbury,
Wiltshire, SP3 5AH Tel: 01722-716121
Fax: 01722-716160
Email: 100064.737@compuserve.com
Web: www.genealogy.demon.co.uk
See Advert on Page: 4

S A & M J Raymond
PO Box 35, Exeter, Devon, EX1 3YZ
Tel: 01392-252193 Email: stuart@samjraymond.soft-
net.co.uk See Advert on Page: 345

Sutton Publishing
Phoenix Mill, Thrupp, Stroud, Gloucestershire, GL5
2BU Tel: 01453-731114 Fax: 01453-731117
Email: sales@sutton-publishing.co.uk
See Advert on Page: 416

PUBLICATIONS - ENGLAND

Chapel Books
Chapel Cottage, Llanishen, Chepstow, NP16 6QT, Wales
Tel: 01600-860055 Fax: 01600-860100,
chapelbooks@btinternet.com See Advert on Page: 99

PUBLICATIONS - BIRMINGHAM

**Birmingham & Midland Society for Genealogy &
Heraldry**
2 Castle Croft, Oldbury, West Midlands, B68 9BQ
Tel: 0121-429-9712
Email: birmingham@terrymorter.fsnet.co.uk
Web: www.bmsgh.org See Advert on Page: 227

PUBLICATIONS - BUCKINGHAMSHIRE

Buckinghamshire Family History Society
PO Box 403, Aylesbury, Buckinghamshire, HP21 7GU
Tel: 01494-712258 Fax: 01296-484783
Email: society@bucksfhs.org.uk
Web: www.bucksfhs.org.uk See Advert on Page: 229

Hillingdon Family History Society
20 Moreland Drive, Gerrards Cross, Buckinghamshire,
SL9 8BB Tel: 01753-885602
Email: gillmay@dial.pipex.com
Web: http//www.dspace.dial.pipex.com/town/terrace/xmq42/
See Advert on Page: 228

PUBLICATIONS - CHESHIRE

Bob Dobson Books
Acorns, 3 Staining Rise, Staining, Blackpool,
Lancashire, FY3 0BU Tel: 01253-895678
Fax: 01253-895678 See Advert on Page: 43

North Cheshire Family History Society
2 Denham Drive, Bramhall, Stockport, Cheshire, SK7
2AT Tel: 0161-439-9270
Web: www.genuki.org.uk/big/eng/chs/NorthChsFHS
See Advert on Page: 226

Northern Writers Advisory Services
77 Marford Crescent, Sale, Cheshire, M33 4DN
Tel: 0161-969-1573 Email: grovesjill@aol.com
See Advert on Page: 369

PUBLICATIONS - CLEVELAND

**Cleveland, North Yorkshire & South Durham Family
History Society**
1 Oxgang Close, Redcar, Cleveland, TS10 4ND
Tel: 01642-486615 See Advert on Page: 224

PUBLICATIONS - CORNWALL

Cornwall Family History Society
5 Victoria Square, Truro, Cornwall, TR1 2RS
Tel: 01872-264044 Email: secretary@cornwallfhs.com
Web: www.cornwallfhs.com See Advert on Page: 228

PUBLICATIONS - COUNTY DURHAM

**Cleveland, North Yorkshire & South Durham Family
History Society**
1 Oxgang Close, Redcar, Cleveland, TS10 4ND
Tel: 01642-486615 See Advert on Page: 224

Neil W Richardson
12 Banbury Way, South Beach Estate, Blyth,
Northumberland, NE24 3TY Tel: 01670-353605
Email: k.richardson@ukonline.co.uk
Web: www.ukonline.co.uk/northumweb/index.htm
See Advert on Page: 373

PUBLICATIONS - CUMBRIA

Cumbria Family History Society
Ulpha, 32 Granada Road, Denton, Manchester, M34 2LJ
Web: www.genuki.org.uk/big/eng/CUL/cumbfhs
/membership.html See Advert on Page: 229

Northern Writers Advisory Services
77 Marford Crescent, Sale, Cheshire, M33 4DN
Tel: 0161-969-1573 Email: grovesjill@aol.com
See Advert on Page: 369

PUBLICATIONS - HEREFORDSHIRE

Herefordshire Family History Society
6 Birch Meadow, Gosmore Road, Clehonger, Hereford,
HR2 9RH Tel: 01981-250974
Email: prosser_brian@hotmail.com
Web: www.freespace.virgin.net/bruce.donaldson
See Advert on Page: 227

PUBLICATIONS - HERTFORDSHIRE

Hertfordshire Family & Population History Society
2 Mayfair Close, St Albans, Hertfordshire, AL4 9TN
Email: hfphs@btinternet.com
Web: www.btinternet.com/~hfphs/index.htm
See Advert on Page: 229

PUBLICATIONS - LANCASHIRE

Bob Dobson Books
Acorns, 3 Staining Rise, Staining, Blackpool,
Lancashire, FY3 0BU Tel: 01253-895678
Fax: 01253-895678 See Advert on Page: 43
Northern Writers Advisory Services
77 Marford Crescent, Sale, Cheshire, M33 4DN
Tel: 0161-969-1573 Email: grovesjill@aol.com
See Advert on Page: 369

PUBLICATIONS - LANCASHIRE NORTH

Cumbria Family History Society
Ulpha, 32 Granada Road, Denton, Manchester, M34 2LJ
Web:
www.genuki.org.uk/big/eng/CUL/cumbfhs/membership.html
See Advert on Page: 229

PUBLICATIONS - LINCOLNSHIRE

Lincolnshire Family History Society
135 Balderton Gate, Newark, Nottinghamshire, NG24
1RY Tel: 01636-671192
Web: www.genuki.org.uk/big/eng/LIN/ifhs
See Advert on Page: 230

PUBLICATIONS - LONDON (HILLINGDON)

Hillingdon Family History Society
20 Moreland Drive, Gerrards Cross, Buckinghamshire,
SL9 8BB Tel: 01753-885602
Email: gillmay@dial.pipex.com
Web: http//www.dspace.dial.pipex.com/town/terrace/xmq42/
See Advert on Page: 228

PUBLICATIONS - MANCHESTER AREA

Chris E Makepeace Local History Consultancy
5 Hilton Road, Disley, Cheshire, SK12 2JU
Tel: 01663-763346 Fax: 01663-764910
Email: chris.makepeace@talk21.com
See Advert on Page: 99

PUBLICATIONS - MERSEYSIDE

Northern Writers Advisory Services
77 Marford Crescent, Sale, Cheshire, M33 4DN
Tel: 0161-969-1573 Email: grovesjill@aol.com
See Advert on Page: 369

PUBLICATIONS - MIDDLESEX

Hillingdon Family History Society
20 Moreland Drive, Gerrards Cross, Buckinghamshire,
SL9 8BB Tel: 01753-885602
Email: gillmay@dial.pipex.com
Web: http//www.dspace.dial.pipex.com/town/terrace/xmq
42/ See Advert on Page: 228

PUBLICATIONS - NORTHUMBERLAND

Neil W Richardson
12 Banbury Way, South Beach Estate, Blyth,
Northumberland, NE24 3TY Tel: 01670-353605
Email: k.richardson@ukonline.co.uk
Web: www.ukonline.co.uk/northumweb/index.htm
See Advert on Page: 373

PUBLICATIONS - STAFFORDSHIRE

**Birmingham & Midland Society for Genealogy &
Heraldry**
2 Castle Croft, Oldbury, West Midlands, B68 9BQ
Tel: 0121-429-9712
Email: birmingham@terrymorter.fsnet.co.uk
Web: www.bmsgh.org See Advert on Page: 227

PUBLICATIONS - SUSSEX

PBN Publications
22 Abbey Road, Eastbourne, East Sussex, BN20 8TE
Tel: 01323-731206 See Advert on Page: 43
Sussex Family History Group
54 Shirley Drive, Hove, Sussex, BN3 6UF
Tel: 01273-556382 Email: tonyh@sfhg.org.uk
Web: www.sfhg.org.uk See Advert on Page: 230

PUBLICATIONS - WARWICKSHIRE

**Birmingham & Midland Society for Genealogy &
Heraldry**
2 Castle Croft, Oldbury, West Midlands, B68 9BQ
Tel: 0121-429-9712
Email: birmingham@terrymorter.fsnet.co.uk
Web: www.bmsgh.org See Advert on Page: 227

PUBLICATIONS - WESTMORLAND

Cumbria Family History Society
Ulpha, 32 Granada Road, Denton, Manchester, M34 2LJ
Web:
www.genuki.org.uk/big/eng/CUL/cumbfhs/membership.html
See Advert on Page: 229

PUBLICATIONS - WORCESTERSHIRE

**Birmingham & Midland Society for Genealogy &
Heraldry**
2 Castle Croft, Oldbury, West Midlands, B68 9BQ
Tel: 0121-429-9712
Email: birmingham@terrymorter.fsnet.co.uk
Web: www.bmsgh.org See Advert on Page: 227

PUBLICATIONS - YORKSHIRE

Bob Dobson Books
Acorns, 3 Staining Rise, Staining, Blackpool,
Lancashire, FY3 0BU Tel: 01253-895678
Fax: 01253-895678 See Advert on Page: 43

PUBLICATIONS - YORKSHIRE
- North Yorkshire

City of York & District Family History Society
4 Orchard Close, Dringhouses, York, YO24 2NX
Email: secretary@yorkfamilyhistory.org.uk
Web: www.yorkfamilyhistory.org.uk
See Advert on Page: 226

Cleveland, North Yorkshire & South Durham Family History Society
1 Oxgang Close, Redcar, Cleveland, TS10 4ND
Tel: 01642-486615 See Advert on Page: 224
Ripon Historical Society & Ripon Harrogate & District Family History Group
18 Aspin Drive, Knaresborough, North Yorkshire, HG5 8HH Tel: 01423-863728 Email: gdl@globalnet.co.uk
Web: www.users.globalnet.co.uk/~gdl/index.htm
See Advert on Page: 230

PUBLICATIONS - YORKSHIRE
- South Yorkshire

Doncaster & District Family History Society
Marton House, 125 The Grove, Wheatley Hills, Doncaster, DN2 5SN Tel: 01302-367257
Email: tonyjunes@aol.com
Web: www.doncasterfhs.freeserve.co.uk
See Advert on Page: 225

PUBLICATIONS - Yorkshire
- West Yorkshire

Bradford Family History Society
2 Leaventhorpe Grove, Thornton, Bradford, West Yorkshire, BD13 3BN Email: Dflax@aol.com
Web: www.genuki.org.uk/big/eng/YKS/bfhs/
See Advert on Page: 224
Keighley & District Family History Society
2 The Hallows, Shann Park, Keighley, West Yorkshire, BD20 6HY Tel: 01535-672144
See Advert on Page: 230
Wakefield Family History Society
11 Waterton Close, Walton, Wakefield, WF2 6JT
Tel: 01924-258163
Email: howgate@close66.freeserve.co.uk
Web: www.homepage.virgin.net/wakefield.fhs
See Advert on Page: 223

PUBLICATIONS - WALES

Chapel Books
Chapel Cottage, Llanishen, Chepstow, NP16 6QT, Wales
Tel: 01600-860055 Fax: 01600-860100,
chapelbooks@btinternet.com See Advert on Page: 99
Montgomeryshire Genealogical Society
1Moreton Road, South Croydon, Surrey, CR2 7DN
Email: montgensoc@freeuk.com
Web: http://home.freeuk.net/montgensoc
See Advert on Page: 220
Pennar Publications
37 Owen Street, Pennar, Pembroke Dock, Pembrokeshire, SA72 6SL, Wales Tel: 01646-681391
Email: bashughes@aol.com See Advert on Page: 179
Powys Family History Society
Oaker's Lodge, The Vineyards, Winforton, Herefordshire, HR3 6EA Tel: 01544-327103 Fax: 01544-327103
Email: 114241.2276@compuserve.com
Web:ourworld.compuserve.com/homepages/michael macsorley/powys1.htm and also via Genuki
See Advert on Page: 232

PUBLICATIONS - SCOTLAND

Aberdeen & North East Scotland Family History Society
164 King Street, Aberdeen, AB24 5BD, Scotland
Tel: 01224-646323 Fax: 01224-639096
Email: enquiries@anesfhs.org.uk
Web: www.anesfhs.org.uk/ See Advert on Page: 222
Glasgow & West of Scotland Family History Society
Unit 5, 22 Mansfield Street, Glasgow, G11 5QP, Scotland
Tel: 0141-339-8303 Fax: 0141-339-8303
Web: www.gwsfhs.org.uk See Advert on Page: 231
National Library of Scotland
George IV Bridge, Edinburgh, EH1 1EW, Scotland
Tel: 0131-226-4531 Fax: 0131-622-4803
Email: enquiries@nls.uk Web: www.nls.uk
See Advert on Page: 133
Scottish Genealogy Society
15 Victoria Terrace, Edinburgh, EH1 2JL, Scotland
Tel: 0131-220-3677 Fax: 0131-220-3677
Email: scotgensoc@sol.co.uk
Web: www.scotsgenealogy.com
See Advert on Page: 232

PUBLICATIONS - IRELAND

Flyleaf Press
4 Spencer Villas, Glenagarry, County Dublin, Ireland
Tel: 353-1-2806228 Fax: 353-1-8370176
Email: RyanJ@biores-irl.ie or flyleaf@indigo.ie
Web: www.flyleaf.ie See Advert on Page: 147

PUBLISHERS

Able Publishing
13 Station Road, Knebworth, Hertfordshire, SG3 6AP
Tel: 01438-814316/812320 Fax: 01438-815232
Email: fp@ablepublishing.co.uk
Web: www.ablepublishing.co.uk
See Advert on Page: 117
GR Specialist Information Services
33 Nursery Road, Nether Poppleton, York, North Yorkshire, YO26 6NN Tel: 01904-799301
See Advert on Page: 262 & 307
Lochin Publishing
6 Holywell Road, Dursley, Gloucestershire, GL11 5RS
Tel: 01453-547531 See Advert on Page: 27
The Memoir Club
Whitworth Hall, Spennymoor, County Durham, DL16 7QX Tel: 01388-811747 Fax: 01388-811363
Email: memoirclub@email.msn.com
See Advert on Page: 370

SECRETARIAL SERVICES

Christine Foley Secretarial & Transcription Services
Glyndedwydd, Login, Whitland, Carmarthenshire, SA34 0TN, Wales Tel: 01994-448414 Fax: 01994-448414
See Advert on Page: 367

SPECIALIST RECORDS & INDEXES

CONVICTS & CRIMINALS

Family History Indexes by Stuart Tamblin
14 Copper Leaf Close, Moulton, Northampton, NN3
7HS Tel: 01604-495106 Email: fhindexes@genfair.com
Web: www.genfair.com/fhindexes/
See Advert on Page: 50 & 156

DIRECTORIES

MM Publications
The White Cottage, The Street, Lidgate, Near
Newmarket, Suffolk, CB8 9PP
Email: michael@mmpublications.softnet.co.uk
Web: mmpublications.co.uk See Advert on Page: 377

GYPSIES

Cottage Books
The Cottage, Gelsmoor, Coleorton, Leicester, LE67 8HR
See Advert on Page: 372

INTERNATIONAL GENEALOGICAL INDEX

**Church of Jesus Christ of Latter Day Saints - North
America Distribution Centre**
1999 West 1700 South, Salt Lake City, Utah, 84104,
United States of America See Feature on Page: 405
**Church of Jesus Christ of Latter Day Saints - UK
Distribution Centre**
399 Garretts Green Lane, Birmingham, West Midlands,
B33 0HU Tel: 0870-010-2051
See Feature on Page: 405

MARINERS/SEAMEN

Neil W Richardson
12 Banbury Way, South Beach Estate, Blyth,
Northumberland, NE24 3TY Tel: 01670-353605
Email: k.richardson@ukonline.co.uk
Web: www.ukonline.co.uk/northumweb/index.htm
See Advert on Page: 373

MILITARY

Family History Indexes by Stuart Tamblin
14 Copper Leaf Close, Moulton, Northampton, NN3
7HS Tel: 01604-495106 Email: fhindexes@genfair.com
Web: www.genfair.com/fhindexes/
See Advert on Page: 50 & 156
MM Publications
The White Cottage, The Street, Lidgate, Near
Newmarket, Suffolk, CB8 9PP
Email: michael@mmpublications.softnet.co.uk
Web: mmpublications.co.uk See Advert on Page: 377
South African War 1899 - 1902
14a Pembroke Crescent, Glendowie, Auckland, 1005,
New Zealand Tel: (09)-575-8572
Email: smgray@ihug.co.nz See Advert on Page: 198

MURDER FILES

Murder Files
81 Churchfields Drive, Bovey Tracy, Devon, TQ13 9QU
Tel: 01626-833487 Fax: 01626-835797
Email: enquiry@murderfiles.com
Web: www.murderfiles.com See Advert on Page: 59

POLICE AND COURT SUBJECTS

Lightage Computing Ltd
40 Buttermere Road, Liverpool, L16 2NN
Tel: 0151-489-5702
Email: dwilcox@lightage.demon.co.uk
See Advert on Page: 366

POSTCARDS OF CHURCHES

Picture Past
47 Manor House Park, Codsall, Staffordshire, WV8 1ES
See Advert on Page: 374

RESEARCH LISTINGS

ABM Publishing Ltd
61 Great Whyte, Ramsey, Huntingdon, Cambridgeshire,
PE17 1HL Tel: 01487-814050 Fax: 01487-711361
Email: family-tree-magazine@mcmail.com
Web: www.family-tree.co.uk
See Advert on Page: 65 & 89

RURAL LIFE

Cottage Books
The Cottage, Gelsmoor, Coleorton, Leicester, LE67 8HR
See Advert on Page: 372

SOUTH AFRICAN WAR

South African War 1899 - 1902
14a Pembroke Crescent, Glendowie, Auckland, 1005,
New Zealand Tel: (09)-575-8572
Email: smgray@ihug.co.nz See Advert on Page: 198

STATIONERY & STORAGE

Back to Roots Family History Service
16 Arrowsmith Drive, Stonehouse, Gloucestershire,
GL10 2QR Tel: 01453-821300, 0374-446128
Fax: 01453-821300 Email: mike@backtoroots.co.uk
Web: www.backtoroots.co.uk
See Advert on Page: Inside Back Cover & 160
**Church of Jesus Christ of Latter Day Saints - North
America Distribution Centre**
1999 West 1700 South, Salt Lake City, Utah, 84104,
United States of America See Feature on Page: 405
**Church of Jesus Christ of Latter Day Saints - UK
Distribution Centre**
399 Garretts Green Lane, Birmingham, West Midlands,
B33 0HU Tel: 0870-010-2051 See Page: 405
CW & S Parkinson (GSD)
16 Foxhills Close, Ashurst, Southampton, SO40 7ER
Tel: 023-8029-3608 Email: CwS@sirdar.demon.co.uk
Web: www.sirdar.demon.co.uk See Advert on Page: 57

P A & S Smith (Custodian)
PO Box 180, 2 Church Cottages, Bishopstone, Hereford,
HR4 7YP Tel: 01981-590309, 07801-503144 (mobile)
Email: PandSSmith@aol.com
Web: www.members.aol.com/pandssmith/custodian.htm
See Advert on Page: 368

TRANSCRIPTION
& TRANSLATION

Abbey Genealogical Research
7 Cantilupe Road, Ross-on-Wye, Herefordshire
 HR9 7ANEmail: sean@seanparry.free-online.co.uk
See Advert on Page: 377

Christine Foley Secretarial & Transcription Services
Glyndedwydd, Login, Whitland, Carmarthenshire
SA34 0TN, Wales Tel: 01994-448414
Fax: 01994-448414 See Advert on Page: 367

Kin in Kent
Boundary House, Stodmarsh Road, Canterbury, Kent,
CT3 4AH Tel: 01227-455267 Fax: 01227-455267
Email: kentkin@lineone.net See Advert on Page: 373

Michael Gandy, BA, FSG, Historical Research
3 Church Crescent, Whetstone, London, N20 0JR
Tel: 020-8368-1146 Email: mgandy@clara.co.uk
See Advert on Page: 18

PBN Publications
22 Abbey Road, Eastbourne, East Sussex, BN20 8TE
Tel: 01323-731206 See Advert on Page: 43

Family History Resources –
State Library of
New South Wales, Australia
Kathi Spinks (Librarian, State Reference Library)&
Mark Hildebrand (Dixson Librarian)

The State Library of New South Wales consists of
two major research collections : the
State Reference Library and the Mitchell and
Dixson Libraries which make up the Australian
Research Collections.

Address:
State Library of New South Wales, Macquarie
Street, Sydney 2000 Australia Phone: 61 2 9273
1414 Fax: 61 2 9 273 1255

Opening hours:
The State Reference Library is open on weekdays
between 9am and 9pm, weekends 11am to 5pm.
The Mitchell Library is open on weekdays between
9am to 9pm and on Saturday between 11am to
5pm. It is closed on Sundays.

Services
The Family History Service in the State Reference
Library is where people should begin their family
history research in the State Library. It is staffed by
librarians and holds a large collection of useful
material, both Australian and International.

The Mitchell Library is based on the collection of
David Scott Mitchell (1836-1907) Australia's first
and greatest collector of Australian historical materials. The Dixson Library was the private collection of Sir William Dixson (1870-1952) Both collections are useful for fleshing out family history
and include the largest collection of Australiana in
the world as well as coins, manuscripts, medals,
stamps and pictures.

Clients can place an information request via the
State Library of New South Wale's web page at
http://www.slnsw.gov.au/request/yrreq.htm.
Should clients need more time-consuming research
done for them then they should be advised to
employ a researcher. The Library has developed a
list of researchers available on our web site at
.http://www.slnsw.gov.au/request/profres.htm

Catalogues
Material in the pictures and manuscripts collections of the Mitchell Library and Dixson Library
catalogued since 1992 is now available on the PIC-
MAN database which is available on our web site
at http://www.slnsw.gov.au/picman/welcome.htm
 The computer catalogue can be searched through
the State Library's web site at
http://www.slnsw.gov.au/cat/welcome.htm

Major Australian resources:
Births, Deaths and Marriages
The Family History Service holds indexes to
births, deaths and marriages for NSW and the
other Australian states on CD ROM and on microfiche. These are indexes only, you need to write to
the appropriate registry in each state to order the
full certificate.

We hold pre 1856 church records for New South
Wales on microfilm, which are part of the Archives
Office Kit of New South Wales. Civil registration
commenced in NSW in 1856 and before 1856
there are no official certificates, only church
records or parish registers which cover baptisms,
burials and marriages.

Electoral rolls
We hold NSW electoral rolls from 1859 to the
present day. We hold some early electoral rolls for
other Australian states and all electoral rolls for
other states from 1990 onwards. Before 1990
names in electoral rolls are arranged by electorate
and subdivision, so it is necessary to know the suburb where a person lived. From 1990 onwards
names are listed in alphabetical order by state. To
check for the electorate before 1900 the Family
History Service has a card index for New South
Wales divisions and for post 1900 electorates for
the whole of Australia, you need to check the
Commonwealth of Australia electoral redistribu-
tion maps.

Archives Office of NSW
Genealogical Research Kit
In 1988 the Archives Office of New South Wales
(now known as the State Records New South
Wales) made available their most popular records -
the Archives Office of NSW Genealogical
Research Kit. This Kit includes passenger lists
and indexes for New South Wales between 1826-
1900, which include Victoria and Brisbane until
1851 and 1859 respectively before they became
separate colonies and also convict indents, which
list convicts who arrived on transports to New
South Wales and Van Diemens Land (Tasmania)
between 1788-1842. The State Library of New
South Wales also holds passenger arrivals and
indexes for other states.

Sands Directories for New South Wales
The Library holds a number of postal directories,

mainly for New South Wales, and some for other states, which list people alphabetically, and by street, suburb and by trade. The most popular postal directory is Sands directory for NSW, which we hold on microfiche from 1858-1932

Telephone directories
The Family History Service holds Sydney telephone directories between 1889 - 1985 and New South Wales country directories between 1915 - 1985 on microfiche. Later years for New South Wales are held in book form in the Mitchell Library. Incomplete series are held for other Australian states.

Newspapers
The State Library of New South Wales collects and keeps an extensive collection of local newspapers published in New South Wales. Various indexes to newspapers such as to the Sydney Gazette, 1803-1829 and the Australian, 1824-1842 are held.

Major international genealogical resources available include: International Genealogical Index (IGI): St. Catherine's House Index (England & Wales) : Tithe Applotment Books (Ireland)

The Irish Transportation Records on CD ROM was a bicentennial gift from the Government and people of Ireland to the Government and people of Australia. It contains an index to the names of over 20,000 men and women who were sentenced to transportation or death between 1788-1868. We have the full records on microfilm. These contain information such as name, age, place, date of trial, crime and may include the name of ship and sentence, and petitions of prisoners pleading for clemency.

Internet
Internet access is available in both the State Reference Library and Mitchell Library. We have bookmarked some popular and useful sites.

Mitchell Library:
Maps
The Mitchell Library holds an extensive collection of Australian maps: sheet maps (including parish maps and subdivision plans), charts, series sheets, aerial photographs and atlases. The emphasis is on Australia but overseas maps are also included.
Manuscripts
The manuscripts collections of the Mitchell and Dixson Libraries include unpublished personal papers, diaries and journals eg. some describe the experiences of settlement in the colonies or voyages by ship, company records, records of organisations, family trees, family bibles, transcriptions of governors despatches. Some of these records are frequently used for family history such as the records of the Benevolent Society.
Pictures
The Mitchell and Dixson Libaries also hold very large collections of documentary pictures in all

media such as oils, watercolour, prints, drawings and photographs. You can search under the name of a ship, residence, locality/place, person or topic.

The Australian Joint Copying Project (AJCP)
The AJCP is a very useful research tool and historical records relating to Australia, New Zealand and the Pacific held in the Public Record Office, London, and other British libraries and archives. The bulk of the records copied are from the Public Record Office, London and comprise the archives of the departments of central government (eg. Colonial Office, Home Office, War Office, Admiralty etc).

Other Resources:
Mitchell Library holds copies of convict trials in London's Central Criminal Court (the Old Bailey) between 1776-1870.

The Mitchell Library is recognised as one of the worlds largest repositories of information by, for and about Aboriginal people. A pathfinder is available called "Black routes through the library: a guide to aboriginal family and local history resources relating to NSW" which identify the main resources for aboriginal family history in one easy to read guide.

NSW Colonial secretary 1788 to 1825
Index to papers
Historical Records of Australia
& the Havard Index to these
Church Registers on microfilm

The United States of America Library of Congress
Reference Services & Facilities of
The Local History & Genealogy Reading Room

The Local History and Genealogy (LH&G) Reading Room is on the ground floor of the Thomas Jefferson Building, Room LJ G42 and is open 8:30 A.M. to 9:30 P.M.- Monday, Wednesday & Thursday; 8:30 A.M. to 5 P.M., Tuesday, Friday & Saturday. It is closed on all federal holidays.

Volumes from the Library's general collections may used in the Reading Room. In addition to these works, there are some 10,000 indexes, guides, and other reference works available in the Reading Room. Most special catalogues and indexes are arranged by family name.

The reference collection and catalogues are intended primarily to facilitate research in U.S. rather than foreign local history and genealogy. Research in foreign genealogy or local history should begin in the Thomas Jefferson Building, at the Computer Catalogue Centre and the Main Card Catalogue. Check appropriate subject headings, e.g., Germany-Genealogy; Heraldry-Poland; Registers of Births, etc, Dublin, to learn what material is available at the Library.

Reference staff are available to assist readers identify publications that relate to the subjects of their research, chiefly by explaining how to use the indexes and catalogues in the room. A Reader Registration Card is required to use the Library's reading rooms. Readers must present identification which includes a photograph and current address, such as a driver's licence, or passport. This card may be obtained at the Reader Registration Station, Room LJ 640.

The staff of the Library of Congress cannot undertake research in family history or heraldry. Some assistance may be obtained from the Board for Certification of Genealogists, P. O. Box 14291, Washington, DC 20044 (http://www .genealogy .org/-bcg/). Another source is the The Genealogical Helper, a periodical published bimonthly by the Everton Publishers, Inc. P.O. Box 368, Logan, Utah 84321, which generally carries as annual features a "Directory of Genealogical Societies, Libraries, Periodicals and Professionals" in the United States and abroad, and a "Directory of Genealogists" in the United States, including amateurs as well as professionals. Names of professional genealogists can also be obtained from the advertisements of their services carried in many genealogical periodicals. A convenient list of these periodicals appears in Ulrich's International Periodicals Directory, a standard reference work available in many libraries.

A complete transcript of the Family Name Index in the LH&G Reading Room, as of December 1971, was published in two volumes in 1972 by the Magna Carta Book Company. Entitled Genealogies in the Library of Congress, a Bibliography, and edited by Marion J. Kaminkow, it lists over 20,000 genealogies, including many in foreign languages. One volume supplements, issued in 1977 and 1987 list works added to the Library's collections from January; 1972 to June 1986. An additional supplement entitled Genealogies Catalogued by the Library of Congress since 1986 was issued by the

Library in 1992. These works are available in many public libraries.

United States Local Histories in the Library of Congress, a Bibliography, also edited by Marion J. Kaminkow and published by the Magna Carta Book Company in 1975, lists in five volumes some 90,000 works, arranged according to the Library's classification for U.S. local history, which is primarily geographical (regional, subdivided by state and further subdivided by period, county, and city). Many of the works listed in the bibliography provide information on early settlers, the establishment of government, churches, schools, industry and trade, and biographical sketches of community leaders. This compendium also may be available in large libraries.

Inquiries for information on ship passenger lists and on census, land, naturalisation, and military service records should be directed to the National Archives, Washington, D.C. 20408 (http ://www.nara.gov/).

The Library does not permit its books on genealogy, heraldry, and U.S. local and state history to circulate on interlibrary loan. However, material in microform for which the Library holds the master negative is available for loan (or purchase). Since the Library has microfilmed most of its books relating to United States genealogy published from 1876-1900, a significant part of the genealogical collection is available for loan. Consult a local reference library about borrowing microfilmed material.

The Library; does not have copies of genealogies for sale. Dealers in books, including out-of-print materials, may be able to assist in securing copies of publications. It also may be possible to purchase photocopies of out of print items. Detailed suggestions are given in a circular entitled "Out-of-Print Materials and Reprinted Publications," available free from Library of Congress, National Reference Service, Washington, D.C. 20540-4720.

The Library's Photoduplication Service routinely supplies photocopies of items located in the Library collections if there are no copyright restrictions. The Library of Congress, Photoduplication Service, Washington, D.C. 2054-4570.

The Library of Congress provides many resources and services via the Internet, all are described or available from the Library's homepage at http ://lcweb.loc,gov. The Home page (http ://lcweb.loc.gov/rr/genealogy) provides general information about the reading room (hours; location; requirements for reader registration; information about tours; descriptions of the collections; details for presenting gift books to the Library; the full-text of the reading room's bibliographies and guides; and links to other Internet sources on local history and genealogy.) Both the Library's and the Local History and Genealogy Reading Room's homepages provide access to the Library's online catalogue. While the Library is beginning to offer some digital versions of books in the collections, no genealogies are included and only a few local histories have been digitised. To search for genealogies on the Library's online catalogue, use the search term "Family" after the name of the family, e.g. Hill Family.

The Regional Archives System of the National Archives United States of America

You don't have to go to Washington, D.C., to visit the National Archives. The National Archives has regional archives in or near Boston, New York, Philadelphia, Atlanta, Chicago, Kansas City, Fort Worth, Denver, Los Angeles, San Francisco, Seattle, and Anchorage. They are national resources in local settings.

In 1969 the Archivist of the United States established a regional archives system to make regionally-created, historically valuable Federal records more accessible to the public. Each regional archives in the system has historical records from Federal courts and from regional offices of Federal agencies in the geographic areas each serves.

Records
Records preserved at regional archives (except Pittsfield) document Federal Government policies and programs at the local and regional level. They are kept because of their permanent historical, fiscal, and legal value, and their importance to the continuing work of the U.S. Government.

Record content varies from region to region. As a rule, each regional archives accessions records from field offices of Federal agencies located in the area it serves. Records unique to a single region include:
> Government of American Samoa, 1899-1965, at the Pacific Sierra Region;
> Tennessee Valley Authority, at the Southeast Region;
> Alaska Railroad, 1894-1969, at the Alaska Region;
> U.S. Commission for the U.S. Science Exhibit at the Seattle World's Fair, 1956-1963,at the Pacific Northwest Region.

Because certain Federal field activities are normally performed in all regions, many records accessioned by several regional archives arc similar. Records common to several regions are from the District Courts of the United States, the Bureau of Indian Affairs, Bureau of Customs, and Office of the Chief of Engineers.

Before using original records, every researcher must obtain a researcher identification card. An applicant must show identification that includes a photograph, such as a driver's licence, school or business identification, or passport, and complete a short form giving name, address, telephone number, and brief description of the proposed research topic. A researcher ID card, valid for two years and renewable, is then issued. It must be presented during each research visit.

Microfilm Publications
The regional archives have extensive holdings of National Archives microfilm publications, which reproduce with introductions and annotations some of the most frequently requested records in National Archives custody. They contain basic documentation for the study of pre-Federal and early Federal history, U.S. diplomacy, immigration, Indian affairs, the land and other natural resources, and war and military service. Of special interest are Federal population censuses for all states, 1790 to 1920.

Guides to Regional Holdings
Guides to regional archive' records and microfilm publications are available free of charge. Requests for these two separate publications should be addressed to individual regional archives. Titles Titles by region, for example, Guide to Records in the National Archives - New England Region or Microfilm Publications in the National Archive-Great Lakes Region.

Public Programs
Public programs supplement regional archives research and archival services. Each regional archives gives tours of its facility; presents workshops on archival research, genealogy, or related subjects; hosts exhibits; and plans other special programs to commemorate historical events. Such programs are often coordinated with colleges and universities, historical societies, genealogical groups, museums, and other archives.

Volunteers & Gift Fund
Each regional archives has a volunteer program and a gift fund. Volunteers have opportunities to learn about archives by assisting staff in various aspects of archival work. The gift fund permits purchases, not otherwise possible, of microfilm and reference materials which facilitate research.

Agency Services
The regional archives provide access to the historical records that an agency previously transferred to a regional archives, and assist agencies with historical programs, exhibits, and commemorations. In cooperation with other offices of the National Archives and Records Administration, the regional archives assist field offices of Federal agencies in identifying valuable historical records for transfer to NARA.

Hours
The regional archives are open for research weekdays, except Federal holidays, from 8.00. A.M. to 4.00 P.M. Contact individual regional archives for information on additional research hours.

The Church of Jesus Christ of Latter Day Saints and Genealogical Resources

The International Genealogical Index (IGI)

Arising from its religious beliefs The Church of Jesus Christ of Latter Day Saints has produced the marvellous International Genealogical Index (known as the I.G.I.). The Index is unique source of information on family histories gathered world-wide. For many researchers it is the first location they check for leads in their quest for information on ancestors being as it is an index to millions of records of births, deaths and marriages recorded in church records in many countries from medieval times prior to civil registration.

Currently the I.G.I. is available on microfiche and CD-ROM viewable at the Family History Centres of the Church (UK Centres listed later in the GSD) and also at many public locations such as libraries, record centres, etc. It is also available on-line on the internet via Church

Stationery and Recording Aids

The Church also produces a very useful range of forms for recording family history details which may be purchased by non-Church members at very reasonable charges from the Family History Centres usually located at the local Church premises referred to above.

Support for computer storage of information

The Church also caters for those who use computers as tools in their family history researches in producing the very fine 'Personal Ancestral File' (PAF) computer program for organising and managing genealogical information plus supplementary programs which enhance the basic program. Copies of the PAF program can obtained via the Web Site: www.lds.org and the other items are obtainable from the Distribution Centres now detailed:

Church of Jesus Christ of Latter Day Saints - North America Distribution Centre

1999 West 1700 South, Salt Lake City, Utah, 84104, United States of America

Church of Jesus Christ of Latter Day Saints - UK Distribution Centre

399 Garretts Green Lane, Birmingham, West Midlands, B33 0HU Tel: 0870-010-2051

Family History Centres ~ *The Church of Jesus Christ of The Latter Day Saints*

England

Bedfordshire
St Albans Family History Centre
London Road/Cutenhoe Road, Luton LU1 3NQ Tel: 01582-482234

Berkshire
Reading Family History Centre
280 The Meadway, Tilehurst, Reading RG3 4PF
Tel: 0118-941 0211

Bristol
Family History Centre
721 Wells Road, Whitchurch, Bristol, BS14 9HU
Tel: 01275-838326

Cambridgeshire
Cambridgeshire Family History Centre
670 Cherry Hinton Road, Cambridge CB1 4DR
Tel: 01223-247010,
Peterborough Family History Centre
Cottesmore Close off Atherstone Av, Netherton Estate,
Peterborough, PE3 9TP Tel: 01733-263374

Cheshire
Chester Family History Centre
Clifton Drive, Blacon, Chester CH1 5LT Tel: 01244-390796

Cleveland
Billingham Family History Centre
The Linkway, Billingham TS23 3HG Tel: 01642-563162

Cornwall
Helston Family History Centre
Clodgey Lane, Helston Tel: 01326-564503

Cumbria
Carlisle Family History Centre
Langrigg Road, Morton Park, Carlisle CA2 5HT Tel: 01228-26767

Devon
Exeter Family History Centre
Wonford Road, Exeter Tel: 01392-250723
Plymouth Family History Centre
Mannamead Road, Plymouth PL3 5QJ Tel: 01752-668666

Dorset
Poole Family History Centre
8 Mount Road, Parkstone, Poole BH14 0QW Tel: 01202-730646

East Sussex
Crawley Family History Centre
Old Horsham Road, Crawley RH11 8PD Tel: 01293-516151

East Yorkshire
Hull Family History Centre
725 Holderness Road, Kingston upon Hull HU4 7RT
Tel: 01482-701439

Essex
Romford Family History Centre
64 Butts Green Road, Hornsuch RM11 2JJ Tel: 01708-620727

Gloucestershire
Cheltenham Family History Centre
Thirlestaine Road, Cheltenham GL53 7AS Tel: 01242-523433
Forest of Dean Family History Centre
Wynol's Hill, Queensway, Coleford, Tel: 01594-542480

Greater Manchester
Manchester Family History Centre
Altrincham Road, Wythenshawe Road, Manchester, M22 4BJ
Tel: 0161-902-9279

Hampshire
Portsmouth Family History Centre
82 Kingston Crescent, Portsmouth PO2 8AQ Tel: (023) 92696243

Isle of Wight
Newport Family History Centre
Chestnut Close, Shide Road, Newport PO30 1YE
Tel: 01983-529643

Kent
Maidstone Family History Centre
76b London Road, Maidstone ME16 0DR Tel: 01622-757811

Lancashire
Ashton Family History Centre
Patterdale Road, Ashton-under-Lyne OL7 Tel: 0161-330-1270
Blackpool Family History Centre
Warren Drive, Cleveleys, Blackpool, FY5 3TG Tel: 01253-858218
Chorley Family History Centre
33 - 41 Water Street, Chorley, PR7 1EE Tel: 01257-233687
Lancaster Family History Centre
Ovangle Road, Lancaster, LA1 5HZ Tel: 01254-33571
Rawtenstall Family History Centre
Haslingden Road, Rawtenstall, Rossendale, BB4 0QX
Tel: 01706-213460

Leicestershire
Leicestershire Family History Centre
Wakerley Road, Leicester LE5 4WD Tel: 0116-233-5544

Lincolnshire
Lincoln Family History Centre
Skellingthorpe Road, Lincoln LN6 0PB Tel: 01522-680117
Email: dann.family@diamond.co.uk

London
Hyde Park Family History Centre
64 - 68 Exhibition Road, South Kensington, London, SW7 2PA
Tel: (020) 789-8561
Wandsworth Family History Centre
149 Nightingale Lane, Balham, London, SW12
Tel: (020) 8673-6741

Merseyside
Liverpool Family History Centre
4 Mill Bank, Liverpool L13 0BW Tel: 0151-228-0433
Fax: 0151-252-0164

Middlesex
Staines Family History Centre
41 Kingston Road, Staines TW14 0ND Tel: 01784-462627

Norfolk
Kings Lynn Family History Centre
Reffley Lane, Kings Lynn PE30 3EQ Tel: 01553-67000
Norwich Family History Centre
19 Greenways, Eaton, Norwich NR4 6PA Tel: 01603-452440

North East Lincolnshire
Grimsby Family History Centre
Linwood Avenue (NO LETTER BOX), Scartho, Grimsby DN33 2NL
Tel: 01472-828876

North Yorkshire
Scarborough Family History Centre
Stepney Drive/Whitby Road, Scarborough

Northamptonshire
Northampton Family History Centre
137 Harlestone Road, Duston, Northampton NN5 6AA
Tel: 01604-587630

Nottinghamshire
Mansfield Family History Centre
Southridge Drive, Mansfield NG18 4RJ Tel: 01623-26729,
Nottingham Family History Centre
Hempshill Lane, Bulwell, Nottingham, NG6 8PA Tel: 0115-927-4194

Shropshire
Telford Family History Centre
72 Glebe Street, Wellington Shropshire,

Somerset
Yate Family History Centre
Wellington Road, Yate BS37 5UY Tel: 01454-323004
Yeovil Family History Centre
Forest Hill, Yeovil, BA20 2PH Tel: 01935-26817

South Yorkshire
Sheffield Family History Centre
Wheel Lane, Grenoside, Sheffield S30 3RL Tel: 0114-245-3124

Staffordshire
Lichfield Family History Centre
Purcell Avenue, Lichfield WS14 9XA Tel: 01543-414843,
Newcastle under Lyme Family History Centre
PO Box 457, Newcastle under Lyme, ST5 0TD Tel: 01782-620653
Fax: 01782-630178

Suffolk
Ipswich Family History Centre
42 Sidegate Lane West, Ipswich IP4 3DB Tel: 01473-723182
Lowestoft Family History Centre
165 Yarmouth Road, Lowestoft, Tel: 01502-573851

Tyne and Wear
Sunderland Family History Centre
Linden Road off Queen Alexandra Road, Sunderland SR2 9BT
Tel: 0191-528-5787

West Midlands
Coventry Family History Centre
Riverside Close,Whitley, Coventry Tel: (024) 76301420
Harborne Family History Centre
38 Lordswood Road, Harborne, Birmingham, B17 9QS
Tel: 0121-427-9291,
Sutton Coldfield Family History Centre
185 Penns Lane, Sutton Coldfield, Birmingham, B76 1JU
Tel: 0121-386-1690,
Wednesfield Family History Centre
Linthouse Lane, Wednesfield, Wolverhampton, Tel: 01902 724097

West Sussex
Worthing Family History Centre
Goring Street, Worthing,West Sussex, BN12 5AR

West Yorkshire
Huddersfield Family History Centre
12 Halifax Road, Birchencliffe, Huddersfield HD3 3BS
Tel: 01484-454573
Leeds Family History Centre
Vesper Road, Leeds, LS5 3QT Tel: 0113-258-5297

Worcestershire
Redditch Family History Centre
321 Evesham Road, Crabbs Cross, Redditch B97 5JA
Tel: 01527-550657

York
Family History Centre
West Bank, Acomb, York, Tel: 01904-785128

Wales
Denbighshire
Rhyl Family History Centre
Rhuddlan Road, Rhyl, Denbighshire

Glamorgan
Merthyr Tydfil Family History Centre
Swansea Road, Merthyr Tydfil CF 48 1NR Tel: 01685-722455
Swansea Family History Centre
Cockett Road, Swansea, SA2 0FH Tel: 01792-419520

South Glamorgan
Cardiff Family History Centre
Heol y Deri, Rhiwbina, Cardiff CF4 6UH Tel: (029) 20620205

Scotland
Edinburgh Family History Centre
30a Colinton Road, Edinburgh, EH4 3SN Tel: 0130-337-3049,
Glasgow Family History Centre
35 Julian Avenue, Glasgow, G12 0RB Tel: 0141-357-1024

Ayrshire
Kilmarnock Family History Centre
Wahtriggs Road, Kilmarnock KA1 3QY Tel: 01563-26560

Dumfrieshire
Dumfries Family History Centre
36 Edinburgh Road, Albanybank, Dumfries DG1 1JQ Tel: 01387-254865

Fife
Kirkcaldy Family History Centre
Winifred Crescent, Forth Park, Kirkcaldy KY2 5SX Tel: 01592-640041

Grampian
Aberdeen Family History Centre
North Anderson Dr, Aberdeen AB2 6DD Tel: 01224-692206

Highlands
Inverness Family History Centre
13 Ness Walk, Inverness IV3 5SQ Tel: 01463-231220

Johnstone
Paisley Family History Centre
Campbell street, Paisley PA5 8LD Tel: 01505-20886

Shetland
Lerwick Family History Centre
Baila Croft, Lerwick, Shetland, ZE1 0EY Tel: 01595-695732 Tel: 01950-431469

Tayside
Dundee Family History Centre
22 - 26 Bingham Terrace, DundeeDD4 7HH Tel: 01382-451247

Isle of Man
Douglas Family History Centre
Woodbourne Road, Douglas IM2 3AP Tel: 01624-675834

Channel Islands
Jersey
St Helier Family History Centre
La Rue de la Vallee, St Mary, Jersey, JE3 3DL Tel: 01534-82171

Northern Ireland
Belfast Family History Centre
401 Holywood Road, Belfast, BT4 2GU Tel: (028) 90768250,
Londonderry Family History Centre
Racecourse Road, Belmont Estate, Londonderry, Tel: Sun-only-
(028) 71350179

Republic of Ireland
Co Dublin
Dublin Family History Centre
The Willows, Finglas, Dublin, Co Dublin, 11 Tel: ++-353-4625609

East Anglian Group
of
Family History Societies

Day Conference
2001
A FAMILY HISTORY ODYSSEY

hosted by
Essex Society for Family History
at the
Latton Bush Centre,
Southern Way, Harlow, Essex
on
Saturday May 19th 2001
(from- 9.30am)

Visit our website: www.esfh.org.uk

e-mail enquiries: 106551.535@compuserve.com

Tickets from:
E.S.F.H.
53, Finchmore, Harlow Essex CM18 6UB

South West Area Group
of
Family History Societies

Family History Fair

Saturday 7th July 2001
10.00.a.m. until 4.00.p.m.

At
The Winter Gardens
Royal Parade
Weston Super Mare

Further Details from:
Kerry James
55 Osborne Road
Weston Super Mare
North Somerset
BS23 3EJ

Please include a
Stamped Self Addressed Envelope

NORTHERN
FAMILY HISTORY FAIRS
Family History Fairs in the North throughout 2001

Saturday 3rd February 2001   *Pudsey Civic Hall*
Sunday 25th March 2001   *Bedale*
Saturday 5th May 2001   *Bishop Auckland*

10.00.a.m. to 4.30.p.m. Admission £1.00
Free Car Parking, Refreshments

Further Details and for other dates and venues contact:

Northern Family History Fairs
206 Moseley Wood Gardens
Leeds LS16 7JE
Tel: 0113 267 6499 or 01642 486615

YORKSHIRE
FAMILY HISTORY FAIR
KNAVESMIRE EXHIBITION CENTRE
YORK RACECOURSE

SATURDAY 23RD JUNE 2001
10.00.a.m. to 4.30.p.m.

Many Stalls including:
Society of Genealogists, Federation Publications
The Genealogical Services Directory
Family Tree Magazine, Local Archives,
Family History Societies from all over Great Britain
Maps, Postcards, Printouts,
New & Second-hand Microfiche Readers
Genealogy Computer Programs
Advice Table

FREE CAR PARKING
ADMISSION £2.00

Further Details from:
Mr A Sampson
1 Oxgang Close
Redcar TS10 4ND
Tel: 01642 486615

NOTE FOR YOUR DIARY:

*YEAR 2002 - YORKSHIRE FAMILY HISTORY FAIR
SATURDAY 22ND JUNE 2002*

About the Editor

Robert Blatchford

has been involved in genealogy for several
years. He is a member of Cleveland, Devon,
Dyfed, Glamorgan and Gwent Family History
Societies. A former Chairman of The City of
York & District Family History Society and
former Vice Chairman of the North East
Group of Family History Societies. He has
undertaken research in the United Kingdom
& Australia.

Disclaimer

The Editor and Publishers of The Genealogical Services Directory make every effort to verify all
information published. Nearly every organisation in this handbook has been contacted and asked to confirm
that our information is correct. We provided reply paid envelopes and are grateful to those organisations who
took the time to reply. We must express our disappointment that there were some organisations who did not
reply. We cannot accept responsibilty for any errors or omissions or for any losses that may arise.

Advertisers are expected to provide a high standard of service to our readers. If there is a failure to provide
such a service the Editor and Publishers reserve the right to refuse to accept advertising in future editions.

The Editor and Publishers cannot be held responsible for the errors, omissions or non performance by
advertisers. Where an advertiser's performance falls below an acceptable level readers are asked to notify
The Genealogical Services Directory in writing.

The views and opinions expressed in each of the articles are those of the author and do not necessarily
reflect the opinions of the Editor.

Email and Internet or Web Addresses

Email and Web addresses shown in this book have been notified to us by the
Organisation or advertiser. Unlike a normal postal address these addresses are
subject to change, sometimes fairly frequently, especially since the introduction
of Free Internet Service Providers (e.g. Freeserve).

In the case of businesses Email forwarding and Website transfer are usually provided by links to the original address. This does not always happen and the only
solution is to use the various search engines available on the internet.

Many of the Browsers and Search engines will accept an address beginning
with either http:// or www

The Family & Local Historian's Events Diary

2001

Sun, Jan 28, 2001	Family History Fair Bracknell	Sports Centre, Bagshot Road Bracknell Details: Tel 01344 451479 and 0793 239 1891
Sat, Feb 3, 2001	Family History Fair, Pudsey Civic Centre, Leeds, West Yorkshire	10.00.a.m. to 4.30.p.m. Admission £1.00 Details:Northern Family History Fairs, 206 Moseley Wood Gardens, Leeds LS16 7JE Tel: 0113 267 6499 or 01642 486615
Sun, Feb 11, 2001	Family History Fair Crawley	Leisure Centre, Crawley Tel 01344 451479 and 0793 239 1891
Sun, Feb 18, 2001	Family History Fair Kidlington	Exeter Hall, Oxford Road, Kidlington Tel 01344 451479 & 0793 239 1891
Sun, Feb 25, 2001	Family History Fair Thurrock	Civic Hall, Grays Essex Tel 01344 451479 and 0793 239 1891
Sun, Mar 4, 2001	Family History Fair Royal Leamington Spa	Royal Spa Centre, Royal Leamington Spa, Warwickshire Tel 01344 451479& 0793 239 1891
Sun, Mar 11, 2001	Family History Fair Watford	Watford Leisure Centre, Horseshoe Lane, Garston, Watford Tel 01344 451479 & 0793 239 1891
Sun, Mar 18, 2001	Family History Fair Port Sunlight	Hulme Hall, Port Sunlight Village, Wirral Tel 01344 451479 and 0793 239 1891
Sun, Mar 18, 2001	Family History Fair Oadby, Leicester	Parklands Leisure Centre, Oadby, Leicester
Sat, Mar 24, 2001	A Family History Day	Alsager Campus, Hassal Road, Alsager, Cheshire SAE to: Bob Wright, 9 Lough Green, Wirral CH63 9NH
Sat, Mar 24, 2001	City of York & District F H S Open Day	The Priory Centre, Priory Street, York Tel: 01904 792945
Sun, Mar 25, 2001	Family History Fair, Bedale, North Yorkshire	10.00.a.m. to 4.30.p.m. Admission £1.00 Details:Northern Family History Fairs, 206 Moseley Wood Gardens, Leeds LS16 7JE Tel: 0113 267 6499 or 01642 486615
Sat, Apr 7, 2001	**Yesterday Belongs to You 5 Family & Local History Day**	County Hall, Durham DH1 5UL Tel: 0191 383 3575 10.00.a.m. to 4.00.p.m.
Fri, Apr 20, 2001 to Sun, Apr 22, 2001	From the Cup of Love Federation of Family History Societies Conference	Leicester University, Oadby Details: Mrs Y J Bunting, Firgrove, Horseshoe Lane, Ash Vale, Aldershot, Hants GU12 5LL
Sun, Apr 29, 2001	Family History Fair Worthing	Worthing Pavilion, Marine Parade, Worthing Tel 01344 451479 & 0793 239 1891
Sat, May 5, 2001	Family History Fair, Bishop Auckland	10.00.a.m. to 4.30.p.m. Admission £1.00 Details:Northern Family History Fairs, 206 Moseley Wood Gardens, Leeds LS16 7JE Tel: 0113 267 6499 or 01642 486615
Sat, May 5, 2001 & Sun, May 6, 2001	**Society of Genealogists Family History Fair**	RHS, New Hall & Conference Centre,Greycoat Street, Westminster, London SW1 10.00.a.m. - 5.00.p.m.
Sat, May 19, 2001	E ast Anglian Group FH Fair Essex Society for Family History	Latton Bush Centre, Harlow, Essex Details: ESFH, 53 Finchmore, Harlow CM18 6UB
Sat, May 26, 2001	Family History Fair Maidstone	Market Hall Lockmeadow, Barker Road, Maidstone Tel 01344 451479 & 0793 239 1891
Sat, Jun 9, 2001	Hartlepool 800 Family History Fair	Borough Hall, Hartlepool
Sat, Jun 16, 2001	"How do I do That?" The Blue Mountains F H S Inc Seminar	Faulconbridge Community Hall, Home Street, Faulconbridge, New South Wales, Australia Details: Suzanne Voytas Tel: 4751 2746
Sat, Jun 16, 2001	Devon Family History Society Family History Day	Shebbear, Devon Details from The Secretary, Devon FHS
Sat, Jun 23, 2001	**Yorkshire Family History Fair**	The Racecourse, Knavesmire, York Details from: Mr A Sampson, 1 Oxgang Close, Redcar TS10 4ND Tel: 01642 486615
Sun, Jul 1, 2001	Hillingdon Family History Society Family History Fair	The Great Barn, Bury Street, Ruislip Details from Kerry James, 55
Sat, Jul 7, 2001	Family History Fair, Winter Gardens, Weston Super Mare, South West Area Group of Family History Societies	Osborne Road, Weston Super Mare BS23 3EJ
Sat, Aug 11, 2001	The Heartland Family History Fair Nuneaton & N Warwickshire FHS	Atherstone Memorial Hall. Details: Norman , Raisen, 79 Edward Street, Nuneaton CV11 5RF Tel (024) 7673 6233 EMail:normraisen@aol.com
Sat, 8th Sept, 2001	**The North Wales Family History Fair**	Gwynedd & Clwyd Family History Societies Conference Centre, Llandudno 10.00.a.m. to 4.30.p.m. Details: secretary@wales-international.org
Sat, Oct 27, 2001	Doncaster Family History Day	School & College for the Deaf, Ledger Way Doncaster Details from Mrs June Staniforth, 125 The Grove,Wheatley Hills, Doncaster DN2 5SN
Autumn	**North West Family History Fair**	Details: Mr E W Gullick, 4 Lawrence Avenue, Simonstone, Burnley, Lancs BB12 7HX (SSAE reqd)

2002

Sat, Jun 22, 2002	Yorkshire Family History Fair	The Racecourse, Knavesmire, York Details from: Mr A Sampson, 1 Oxgang Close, Redcar, TS10 4ND Tel: 01642 486615
Thu, Jul 25, 2002 to Sat, Aug 4, 2002	Manchester - A Common Heritage	Details from Manchester & Lancashire FHS Clayton House, 59 Piccadilly, Manchester M1 2AQ

2003

Sat, Jun 21, 2003	Yorkshire Family History Fair	The Racecourse, Knavesmire, York Details from: Mr A Sampson, 1 Oxgang Close, Redcar, TS10 4ND Tel: 01642 486615

Published by
The Genealogical Services Directory
33 Nursery Road, Nether Poppleton
YORK, YO26 6NN
England

E Mail: publishers@genealogical.co.uk

WWW: http://www.genealogical.co.uk

The Genealogical Services Directory
First Edition Published 1997

Second Edition Published January 1998
(Revised & Reprinted April 1998)
Third Edition Published January 1999

Fourth Edition Published January 2000

© Robert Blatchford and Geoffrey Heslop

Family & Local History Handbook
5th Edition
Published January 2001

©
2001
Robert Blatchford

ISSN 1368-9150

ISBN 0 9530297 4 3

Printed by
AWP
718 Ripponden Road
Oldham
OL4 2LP

Index to Advertisers & Related Features

Abbey Genealogical Research	377
Aberdeen & North East Scotland FHS	222
Able Publishing	117
Achievements Ltd	47
Adams, John, Genealogical Research	131
Ancestral Locations	367
Ancestry.com	118 & 119
APC Clothing	370
Ashley Hotel	371
Association of Genealogists & Record Agents	50
Back to Roots Family History Service	
Inside Back Cover & 160	
Barnes, David J, (Military & Aviation Research)	198
Bartletts Battlefield Journeys	200
Battlefield Tours with The War Research Society	210
Bayley, Harold, Bookseller	372
Belam, Caroline, MA	372
Birmingham & Midland Society	
for Genealogy & Heraldry	227
Black Sheep Search	
(Machine Breakers, Rioters & Convict Research)	369
Blanchard,Gill, BA, MA, PGCE (PCE)	371
Blue Mountains Family History Society	404
Border Regiment & Kings Own Royal	
Border Regiment Museum	215
Boucher, Carolynn	12
Bradford Family History Society	224
Brewster International	Inside Front Cover
British Association for Local History	161, 164, & 173
Buckinghamshire Family History Society	229
CARW	374
Centre for Kentish Studies(Kent County Archives Service)	277
Chapel Books	99
Church of Jesus Christ of Latter Day Saints	
- North America Distribution Centre	405
Church of Jesus Christ of Latter Day Saints	
- UK Distribution Centre	405
City of York & District Family History Society	226
Cleaves, Sue, BSc, ALA	371
Cleveland, North Yorkshire &	
South Durham Family History Society	224
Clwyd Family History Society	231
Colin Dale Researches	371
Copsey, Michael, Ancestral Research by	373
Cornwall Family History Society	228
Cottage Books	372
Creative Digital Imaging	368
Cumbria Family History Society	229
Davison, Colin, Family History Research	59
Day, Jennifer	373
Debrett Ancestry Research Limited	369
Dobson, Bob, Books	43
Doncaster & District Family History Society	225
Edwards, Miss J, MA, LL.B(Hons)	371
Elvet Local & Family History Groups	223
Essex Record Office	125
Essex Society for Family History	231 & 409
Family Chronicle Magazine	375
Family History Indexes by Stuart Tamblin	50 & 156
Family History Monthly	32
Family Trails	117
Family Tree Magazine/Practical Family History	65 & 89
Federation of Family History Societies	6
Federation of Family History Societies (Publications) Ltd	364
Flyleaf Press	147
Foley, Christine, Secretarial & Transcription Services	367
Gandy, Michael, BA, FSG, Historical Research	18
Genealogical Services Directory	262, 307 & 341
Genealogical Society of Victoria	233
Gene-genie	17
General Register Office for Scotland	128
GENfair 18	
Geoghegan/McGeoghegan One Name Study	231
Glasgow & West of Scotland Family History Society	231
Gould Books	376
Grandpa Staten's Family History Services	368
Grave Concern	368
Haines, Robert J , BSc	371
Hamby, Jane E , LHG	371
Hamley, Hambly & Hamlyn	
Family History Society (International)	230
Havas Interactive	104
Herefordshire Family History Research	77
Herefordshire Family History Society	227
Hertfordshire Archives & Local Studies	269
Hertfordshire Family & Population History Society	229
Hillingdon Family History Society	228
Historical Research Associates	147
Hodgson, Leslie	126
Huddersfield & District Family History Society	222
Hull Family History Unit	12
Institute of Heraldic & Genealogical Studies	13
Interlink Bookshop & Genealogical Services	376
Internet Bookmarks	77
Jewish Genealogical Society of Great Britain	84
Keighley & District Family History Society	230 & 400
Kin in Kent	373
Kingfisher Free International Booksearch (GSD)	367
Kinship Genealogical Research	367
Lancashire Record Office and the	
Lancashire Local Studies Collection	269
Lark Research	372
Leicestershire, Leicester & Rutland - Record Office	21
Leitrim Genealogy Centre	147
Lightage Computing Ltd	366
Lincolnshire Family History Society	230
Link Line Ancestral Research	125
Linklines Genealogy	125
Linkman, Audrey, Consultant Photohistorian	117
Links to Lincolnshire Genealogical Services	370
Lister, Paul, Ancestral Research	373
Lochin Publishing	27
Longhorn, Victor	367
Looking Back	371
Lynskey, Marie	52
Makepeace, Chris E, Local History Consultancy	99
Marathon Microfilming Ltd	365
Mayo North Family Heritage Centre Limited	147
MC Research Service	147
Memoir Club, The	370
Microfilm Shop	137
MM Publications	377
Montgomeryshire Genealogical Society	220
Morgan, Vanessa	367
Mortimer, Elizabeth, MA, ASGRA	133
Murder Files	59

Napoleonic Wars, 1st or	
Grenadier Foot Guards & Other Regiments	209
National Library of Scotland	133
National Library of Wales	121
New Zealand Genealogical Research	374
Nicholson, Geoff	117
North Cheshire Family History Society	226
North West Group of FHS Family History Fairs	400
Northern Family History Fairs	409
Northern Writers Advisory Services	369
Old Yorkshire Publications	366
Paperchase Genealogical & Research Services	365
Parchment Oxford Limited	159
Parkinson, CW & S	57
PBN Publications	43
Pennar Publications	179
People Search Tracing Services	369
Philip, Rosemary, BA(Hons), CSFHS (Stirling)	373
Pickard, Michael Ronald	373
Picture Past	374
Pontefract & District Family History Society	223
Powys Family History Society	232
Raymond, S A & M J	345
RE: GENERATION Family History& Booklovers Supplies	59
Relatively Speaking	372
Richardson, Neil W	373
Ripon Accomodation - Mrs R M Norris	372
Ripon Historical Society & Ripon,	
Harrogate & District Family History Group	230
Romany & Traveller Family History Society	231
Root-Finder	131
Roots 'n' Branches	373
S & N Genealogy Supplics	4
Saxon, Timothy P	77
Scots Ancestry Research Society	133
Scots Heritage of Auchterarder	128

Scottish Genealogy Society	232
Scottish Records Association	140
Scottish Roots	133
Seaham Super Index	377
Sheffield & District Family History Society	223
Shrimpton, Jayne	61
Smith, P A & S, (Custodian)	368
Smith, Sydney G	365
Society of Genealogists	415
South African War 1899 - 1902	198
South West Group of Family History Societies	231 & 409
Southern Counties Ancestry	126
Southern Scarches	366
Staffordshire and Stoke on Trent Archive Service	272
Suffolk Record Office - Bury St Edmunds Branch	277
Suffolk Record Office - Ipswich Branch	277
Suffolk Record Office - Lowestoft Branch	277
Sussex Family History Group	230
Sutton Publishing	416
Taylor, Rosie	372
Timeless Images	131
Turnstone Ventures	223
UK SEARCHES	137
Upper Carr Chalet & Touring Park	408
Wakefield Family History Society	223
Welchman, Bernard	376
West Sussex Record Office	277
West Yorkshire Archive Service	342
Yarnold, Patrick, Research	372
York Minster Library Databank	12
Yorkshire Family History Fair	410
Young, Maggi	370

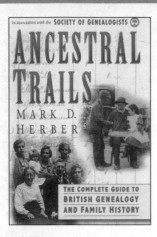